HISTORY OF PSYCHOTHERAPY

A CENTURY OF CHANGE

EDITED BY

DONALD K. FREEDHEIM

ASSOCIATE EDITORS:

HERBERT J. FREUDENBERGER

JANE W. KESSLER

STANLEY B. MESSER

DONALD R. PETERSON

HANS H. STRUPP

PAUL L. WACHTEL

AMERICAN PSYCHOLOGICAL ASSOCIATION

WASHINGTON, DC

Third printing July 1995

Published by the
American Psychological Association
750 First Street, NE
Washington, DC 20002

Copies may be ordered from
APA Order Department
P.O. Box 2710
Hyattsville, MD 20784

In the United Kingdom and Europe, copies may be ordered from
American Psychological Association
3 Henrietta Street
Covent Garden
London WC2E 8LU
England

Typeset in Goudy by Easton Publishing Services, Inc., Easton, MD

Printer: Braun-Brumfield, Inc., Ann Arbor, MI
Cover, jacket, and photo section designer: GrafikCommunications Ltd., Alexandria, VA
Text designer: Richard Steele, Petree Graphics, McLean, VA
Production coordinator: Valerie Montenegro
Copyeditors: Donna Stewart and Valerie Montenegro

Library of Congress Cataloging-in-Publication Data

History of psychotherapy: a century of change/edited by Donald K. Freedheim; associate
    editors, Herbert J. Freudenberger . . . [et al.].
        p.   cm.
    Includes bibliographical references and index.
    ISBN 1-55798-149-3 (cb: acid-free paper)
    1. Psychotherapy—United States—History.   2. Psychotherapy—History.
    I. Freedheim, Donald K.
    RC443.H57   1992
    616.89′14′0973—dc20   91-43409
                                                                              CIP

Printed in the United States of America

HISTORY OF PSYCHOTHERAPY

This book was prepared in honor of the Centennial of the American Psychological Association and is dedicated to all of the men, women, and children who have had the courage to share their innermost self with a psychotherapist.

CONTENTS

CONTRIBUTORS

George W. Albee, PhD, is professor of psychology at the University of Vermont. He has served two Presidential Commissions on Mental Health (Eisenhower, 1957 – 1960; Carter, 1977 – 1978), is a past president of the American Psychological Association (APA), and is a founder of the Vermont Conference on Primary Prevention.

Hal Arkowitz, PhD, associate professor of psychology at the University of Arizona, is coeditor of *Psychoanalytic Therapy and Behavior Therapy: Is Integration Possible?* (Plenum Press, 1984). Currently, he is editor of the *Journal of Psychotherapy Integration.*

Diane B. Arnkoff, PhD, associate professor of psychology at The Catholic University of America, is an associate editor of *Cognitive Therapy and Research.*

David H. Barlow, PhD, is Distinguished Professor in the Department of Psychology at the State University of New York at Albany and Director of the Center for Stress and Anxiety Disorders at that institution. He is past president of the Association for the Advancement of Behavior Therapy and former editor of both the *Journal of Applied Behavior Analysis* and *Behavior Therapy.* His latest book is *Anxiety and Its Disorders* (Guilford Press, 1988).

Allen E. Bergin, PhD, professor and director of clinical psychology at Brigham Young University, is well known for his coedited *Handbook of Psychotherapy and Behavior Change* (Wiley, 1986).

David R. Chabot, PhD, is director of clinical psychology at Fordham University and director of the Child–Adolescent–Young Adult Project at the Center for Family Learning.

Louis D. Cohen, PhD, founder and first chair of the Department of Clinical Psychology at the University of Florida, is now professor emeritus. Previously he was professor of psychology and medical psychology and founding director of the Division of Medical Psychology at Duke University and its Medical School.

Nicholas A. Cummings, PhD, is chairman and chief executive of American Biodyne, Inc. He is a former president of the American Psychological Association and founder of the California School of Professional Psychology.

Philip Cushman, PhD, is in private practice in Oakland and is on the adjunct faculty of the California School of Professional Psychology. He recently published "Why the Self Is Empty: Toward a Historically Situated Psychology" in *American Psychologist*.

Eugene J. D'Angelo, PhD, instructor in psychology at Harvard Medical School, is codirector of training in psychology at Children's Hospital and the Judge Baker Children's Center in Boston.

Patrick H. DeLeon, PhD, JD, MPH, is the Administrative Assistant to U.S. Senator Daniel Inouye. He is past president of the APA Divisions of Clinical Psychology, Psychotherapy, and Psychology and the Law. He is recipient of several APA Distinguished Contributions awards.

Morris N. Eagle, PhD, is professor of psychology at the Ontario Institute for Studies in Education. He is the author of *Recent Developments in Psychoanalysis: A Critical Evaluation* (Harvard University Press, 1987).

Irene Elkin, PhD, is a professor of psychology in the School of Social Service Administration at the University of Chicago. Previously, she served in various positions with the National Institute of Mental Health (NIMH), including coordinator of the NIMH Treatment of Depression Collaborative Research Program.

Daniel B. Fishman, PhD, is professor of clinical psychology in the Graduate School of Applied and Professional Psychology of Rutgers University. He is past president of the Society for Studying Unity Issues in Psychology and is coauthor of *Paradigms in Behavior Therapy: Present and Promise* (Springer, 1988).

Jerome D. Frank, PhD, MD, is professor emeritus of psychiatry at The Johns Hopkins University School of Medicine. He has written widely on major issues facing all schools of psychotherapy. His latest book is *Persuasion and Healing* (Johns Hopkins University Press, 1991).

Cyril M. Franks, PhD, Distinguished Professor at Rutgers University, is cofounder and was first president of the Association for Advancement of Behavior Therapy. He is also the founding editor of the journal *Behavior Therapy* and founding and current editor of *Child and Family Behavior Therapy*.

Donald K. Freedheim, PhD, is associate professor at Case Western Reserve University. He is past president of the APA Division of Psychotherapy, is the founding editor of *Professional Psychology*, and currently edits the journal *Psychotherapy*.

Herbert J. Freudenberger, PhD, is an independent practitioner in New York City. He is past president of the APA Division of Psychotherapy. He was the first to use the term *burnout* and has published *Burnout: The High Cost of High Achievement* (Anchor, 1980) and *Women's Burnout* (Doubleday, 1985).

Sol L. Garfield, PhD, is professor emeritus of psychology at Washington University. He is a former president of the Society for Psychotherapy Research and coeditor of the *Handbook of Psychotherapy and Behavior Change* (Wiley, 1986).

Ann M. Garner, PhD, is professor emeritus of medical psychology and former training director at the Child Development and Rehabilitation Center of the Oregon Health Sciences University. Her recent publications are in clinical child psychology.

Margaret Gatz, PhD, professor of psychology at the University of Southern California, has published chapters on psychological interventions and family caregiving in the *Handbook of the Psychology of Aging* (Von Nostrand Reinhold, 1985).

Carol R. Glass, PhD, is associate professor of psychology at The Catholic University of America and has published widely in areas of cognitive assessment, cognitive–behavioral therapy, and social anxiety.

Leslie S. Greenberg, PhD, is professor at York University. He is a past president of the Society for Psychotherapy Research and coauthor of *Emotion in Psychotherapy* (Guilford Press, 1987).

Philip J. Guerin, Jr., MD, is director of the Center for Family Learning and adjunct professor of psychology at Fordham University. He edited *Family Therapy: Theory and Practice* (Gardner, 1976) and authored *The Evaluation and Treatment of Marital Conflict* (Basic Books, 1987).

William P. Henry, PhD, is assistant professor of psychology and associate clinical training director at Vanderbilt University. His research has focused on measurement of psychotherapy process and outcome.

Mardi J. Horowitz, MD, is professor of psychiatry at the Langley Porter Psychiatric Institute of the University of California, San Francisco. He founded the Center for the Study of Neurosis at the university, and his many books include *Personality Styles and Brief Psychotherapy* (Basic Books, 1984).

Kenneth I. Howard, PhD, professor of psychology at Northwestern University, is the founding president of the Society for Psychotherapy Research.

Miriam Kelly is a doctoral student majoring in clinical psychology and aging at the University of Southern California.

Jane W. Kessler, PhD, is Distinguished Professor of Psychology Emerita and founder of the Mental Development Center at Case Western Reserve University. She is the author of *Psychopathology of Childhood* (Prentice-Hall, 1988).

Bob G. Knight, PhD, is the Merle H. Bensinger Associate Professor of Gerontology and Psychology and director of the Andrus Older Adult Center of the University of Southern California. His writings on the elderly include *Psychotherapy With the Older Adult* (Sage, 1986).

Gerald P. Koocher, PhD, associate professor of psychology at Harvard

Medical School, is also chief of psychology at Boston's Children's Hospital and Judge Baker Children's Center. His writings include *Children, Ethics, and the Law* (University of Nebraska Press, 1990).

Martin Lakin, PhD, is professor of psychology at Duke University. He is the author of *Interpersonal Encounter* (McGraw-Hill, 1972), *The Helping Group* (Addison-Wesley, 1985), *Ethical Issues in the Psychotherapies* (Oxford University Press, 1980), and *Coping With Ethical Dilemmas in Psychotherapy* (Pergamon Press, 1991).

Michael J. Lambert, PhD, is professor of psychology at Brigham Young University and author of numerous reviews on the effects of psychotherapy on patient outcome.

Peter M. Lewinsohn, PhD, is research scientist at the Oregon Research Institute. He has developed the Coping With Depression course and schedules for evaluating depression.

Zanvel A. Liff, PhD, is a training analyst and senior supervisor at the Psychoanalytic Institute, Postgraduate Center for Mental Health in New York City. He is a past president of the APA Division of Psychoanalysis.

Lester Luborsky, PhD, is professor of psychology in psychiatry at the University of Pennsylvania School of Medicine. He is the author of *Principles of Psychoanalytic Psychotherapy* (Basic Books, 1984).

Ruth G. Matarazzo, PhD, is professor of medical psychology at the Oregon Health Sciences University, where she is director of the Inpatient Consultation Service. She has published on the process of learning to practice therapy and is the author of a chapter in *The Handbook of Psychotherapy and Behavior Change* (Wiley, 1986).

Rollo May, PhD, is one of the deans of American psychotherapy. He is perhaps best known for the book *Love and Will* (Norton, 1969). His most recent work is *The Cry for Myth* (Norton, 1991). He is affiliated with the Saybrook Institute.

Vickie M. Mays, PhD, is associate professor of psychology at the University of California, Los Angeles. She has written widely on ethnic and gender issues in the design, delivery, and accessibility of services to the underserved.

Stanley B. Messer, PhD, is professor of clinical psychology in the Graduate School of Applied and Professional Psychology at Rutgers University. He is coeditor and contributor to *Psychoanalytic Therapy and Behavior Therapy: Is Integration Possible?* (Plenum Press, 1984).

Dana L. Moore, PhD, is the executive director of the Department of Veterans Affairs' (VA) Leadership VA program. She is formerly the director of the VA's Psychology Training program.

John C. Norcross, PhD, is professor and chair of the Department of Psychology at the University of Scranton. He is the former editor of the *Journal of Eclectic and Integrative Psychotherapy*, coeditor of *Therapy Wars* (Jossey-Bass, 1990), and he guest edited a special issue of *Psychotherapy* (1992) on the Future of Psychotherapy.

Agnes N. O'Connell, PhD, is professor of psychology and director of the Community Psychology Program at Montclair State College. Her publications include *Models of Achievement: Reflections of Eminent Women in Psychology* (Columbia University Press, 1983).

David E. Orlinsky, PhD, professor of psychology at the University of Chicago, is a founder and past president of the Society for Psychotherapy Research.

Morris B. Parloff, PhD, is clinical professor of psychiatry at Georgetown University. Formerly he was chief of the Psychosocial Treatments Research Branch, Division of Extramural Research Programs at the National Institute of Mental Health.

Donald R. Peterson, PhD, professor emeritus at Rutgers University, was the founder of the Doctor of Psychology program at the University of Illinois and first dean of the Graduate School of Applied and Professional Psychology at Rutgers University. He is a recipient of American Psychological Association awards for both Distinguished Contributions to Professional Psychology as a Practice and for Distinguished Career Contributions to Education and Training in Psychology.

Nathaniel J. Raskin, PhD, is professor of psychiatry and behavioral sciences at Northwestern University Medical School. He is past president of the American Academy of Psychotherapists and coauthored with Carl

Rogers a chapter on person-centered therapy in *Current Psychotherapies* (Peacock, 1989).

Laura N. Rice, PhD, professor emeritus in psychology at York University, is coeditor of *Patterns of Change: Intensive Analysis of Psychotherapy Process* (Guilford Press, 1984).

Bernard F. Riess, PhD, is a training analyst and senior supervisor at the Postgraduate Center for Mental Health in New York. He is a past president of the New York State Psychological Association.

Howard B. Roback, PhD, is professor of psychiatry and psychology at Vanderbilt University. He is editor of *Helping Patients and Their Families Cope With Medical Problems: A Guide to Therapeutic Group Work in Clinical Settings* (Jossey-Bass, 1984) and is coeditor (with S. Abramowitz and D. Strassberg) of *Group Psychotherapy Research* (Krieger, 1979).

Max Rosenbaum, PhD, is adjunct professor at Nova University, following more than 40 years of independent practice in New York City. He is a pioneer in the field of group psychotherapy and editor of *Ethics and Values in Psychotherapy* (Free Press, 1982).

Nancy Felipe Russo, PhD, is professor of psychology and director of Women's Studies at Arizona State University. She is the coeditor of *Women in Psychology: A Bio-Bibliographical Sourcebook* (Greenwood Press, 1990).

Harold Sampson, PhD, is clinical professor of psychiatry at the University of California, San Francisco, codirector of the Mt. Zion Psychotherapy Research Group, and coauthor of *The Psychoanalytic Process: Theory, Clinical Observation and Empirical Research* (Guilford Press, 1986).

R. Bruce Sloane, MD, is professor and chairman of the Department of Psychiatry and the Behavioral Sciences at the University of Southern California School of Medicine. He has been an eminent researcher in the study of outcome of psychotherapy, with particular emphasis in the behavioral therapy field.

Fred R. Staples, PhD, is chief of psychological services at the Kingston Psychiatric Hospital in Ontario, Canada. His work at Temple University is reported in *Psychotherapy versus Behavior Therapy* (Harvard University Press, 1975).

George Stricker, PhD, is professor and dean of The Derner Institute, Adelphi University. He is a past president of the National Council of Schools of Professional Psychology. He has published *Self-Disclosure in the Therapeutic Relationship* (Plenum Press, 1990) and is a recipient of the APA Award for Distinguished Contributions to Applied Psychology.

Hans H. Strupp, PhD, is Distinguished Professor of Psychology at Vanderbilt University. He has authored or coauthored more than 250 published works in the area of psychotherapy research.

Gary R. VandenBos, PhD, is Executive Director of Publications and Communications for the American Psychological Association. Formerly, he was the research coordinator for the Michigan State Psychotherapy Research Project with Schizophrenics. He coauthored *Psychotherapy With Schizophrenics: The Treatment of Choice* (Aronson, 1981) and edited *Psychotherapy: Research, Practice, Policy* (Sage, 1980).

Paul L. Wachtel, PhD, is Distinguished Professor of Psychology at City University of New York and author of *Psychoanalysis and Behavior Therapy* (Basic Books, 1977) and *Action and Insight* (Guilford Press, 1987).

Robert S. Wallerstein, MD, is professor of psychiatry and former chairman of the Department of Psychiatry at the University of California, San Francisco School of Medicine. He is past president of both the American Psychoanalytic Association and the International Psychoanalytical Association. He was principal investigator of the Psychotherapy Research Project of the Menninger Foundation and author of *Forty-Two Lives in Treatment: A Study of Psychoanalysis and Psychotherapy* (Guilford Press, 1986).

Joseph Weiss, MD, codirector of the San Francisco Psychotherapy Research Group, is a training analyst and faculty member at the San Francisco Psychoanalytic Institute. He is also a clinical professor in the Department of Psychiatry, School of Medicine at the University of California, San Francisco.

David L. Wolitzky, PhD, associate professor of psychology at New York University (NYU), is also director of the NYU Psychology Clinic.

He is coauthor of a forthcoming book, *Psychoanalysis and Psychology* (American Psychological Association, in press).

Fred M. Zimring, PhD, is professor of psychology at Case Western Reserve University. Formerly, he worked with Carl Rogers at the counseling center at the University of Chicago. He is coauthor of a chapter in *Five Therapists and One Client* (Peacock, 1991).

FOREWORD

In each transitional period in cultural history, some accepted ways of life are destroyed and new ones are formed. When such periods of radical change occur, old customs are discarded and new forms of life are then accompanied by greater or lesser sense of upheaval. Ours is such a time of upheaval, war, and destruction while new ways of life are being discovered.

In order to understand our period, we need to look back to past centuries when people endured similar kinds of upheaval. For example, we find the following statement from 22 centuries ago describing life with "psychological" pangs at that time:

> Epicurus saw that all that was wanted to meet men's vital needs was already at their disposal . . . He saw men in full enjoyment of riches and reputation . . . happy in the fair fame of their children. Yet for all that, he found aching hearts in every home, racked incessantly by pangs the mind was powerless to assuage and forced to vent themselves in recalcitrant repining.

This "aching hearts in every home, racked incessantly" is an expression of the need for psychotherapy, although it is in Roman times, more than 20 centuries ago.

As we go down through history, we see other transitional periods that are like our own.[1] We find other examples in the past that are remarkably relevant to our age. We need only turn to Shakespeare at the end of the 16th century. In one of his dramas, Macbeth is hiding with his doctor

---

[1] Barbara Tuchman's *A Distant Mirror: The Calamitous Fourteenth Century* (Knopf, 1978) is a description of such a time of painful destruction of a culture. Ms. Tuchman describes the 14th century, which she believes was parallel to our own time of transition. That was a time of war and destruction while new ways of life were discovered and accepted.

behind the curtains while they watch Lady Macbeth in her psychotic sleep-walking. She is trying to rub off the imagined blood from her hands.

As she moans in her hysterical guilt, Macbeth begs the physician, Is there psychotherapy for his wife? He cries in an amazingly modern phrase,

> Canst thou not minister to a mind diseased,
> Pluck from the memory a rooted sorrow,
> Raze out the written troubles of the brain,
> And with some sweet oblivious antidote
> Cleanse the stuffed bosom of that perilous stuff
> Which weighs upon the heart?

> William Shakespeare
> *Macbeth*, Act V, Scene 3

He is indicating that his wife needs some other mixture of professions—indeed, a psychological form. The physician answers, in what seems in our age a platitude, "Therein the patient/Must minister to himself." Macbeth rightly retorts, "Throw physic to the dogs, I'll none of it." For physic—no matter how many forms of Valium or Librium we invent—will not basically confront the rooted sorrow or raze out the written troubles of the brain. This requires some form of psychotherapy.

From the past century, we find other references to the great need for psychotherapy. Friedrich Nietzsche proclaimed that science in the late 19th century was becoming a factory, and he feared that the advances in technology and techniques without a parallel advance in ethics would lead to annihilation. Nietzsche then uttered his prophetic warnings about what would happen in the 20th century in a parable called "The Death of God." It is a haunting story of a madman who ran into the village square shouting, "Where is God?" The people in the village square did not believe in God. They laughed and said, "Perhaps God has gone on a vacation" or "Perhaps God has emigrated."

But the madman continued to shout, "Where is God?" Then he proclaimed:

> "I shall tell you. We have killed him, you and I. Yet how have we done this? Who gave us the sponge to wipe away the whole horizon? What did we do when we unchained this earth from its sun? Whither do we move now? Away from our suns? Do we not fall backwards, incessantly sidewards, forwards in all directions? Is there yet any up or down? Do we not err as though in an infinite naught? Do we not feel the breath of empty space? Has it yet not become colder? Is not night and more night coming on all the while?

"God is dead!" continued the madman. "God remains dead and we have killed him."[2]

Here the madman became silent and looked around at his listeners. They too remained silent and looked at him. Then he said, "I come too early. This tremendous event is still on its way." Fifty years later, it certainly arrived in the present century.

This parable was written more than 100 years ago. People now ponder for hours on the question, Has our great progress in technology led us to a development without ethical parallel, which has caused the death of God? Nietzsche was surely not calling for a return to the old belief in God. He was, rather, pointing out what happens when any society loses its structure of values. That the tremendous event did become true was only too obvious to us in the phenomena of World War I, Hitler, World War II, and almost continuous wars ever since. What Nietzsche is describing is that we live in a world where there are no directions, no north or south, no up or down. The event was "too early" when he wrote it, as he said, but there is a real probability that this is what we are experiencing in our own day. The question is one that psychotherapy tries to answer.

Just 100 years ago, and 15 years after Nietzsche, the playwright Henrik Ibsen produced *Peer Gynt*. In this drama, Peer Gynt pretends he is a great blustering hero who actually turns out to be a lost human being, raping and stealing. Halfway through the drama, the doctor points out to him his failings and loss of humanness. He then starts back to search for the one person whom he really loves, Solveig. This is the drama of a man who represents a form of neurosis very common in our own day, the person who is filled with braggadocio, who finally finds that his way of life is no longer bearable. Sadder but wiser, Peer is at last on a ship bound back to Solveig.

As he stands at the railing of the ship in a storm, another ship is sinking nearby. A character on the ship whom Ibsen has called the "Strange Passenger" stands beside Peer. He proceeds to draw out Peer Gynt's neurosis and remarks, "When a man stands with one foot in the grave, he sometimes tends to be generous." Peer becomes disgusted with the Strange Passenger and expostulates to him, "Go away!" The Strange Passenger answers, "But, my dear sir, consider: I'll open you up and let in the light. I want to discover the source of your dreams. I want to find out how you are put together." Peer Gynt bursts out in anger, "Go away from me!" And he backs away from the railing, calling back to the Strange Passenger, "Blasphemous man!"

The Strange Passenger is a description of psychotherapy 10 years before Freud; it was put in place by Ibsen's poetic imagination. The story illustrates

---

[2]From *Nietzsche* (p. 75) by W. Kaufmann, 1950, Princeton, NJ: Princeton University Press.

the social endeavor which Freud so profoundly occupied and which he called psychoanalysis.

When we think of humankind all the way down from the time of the cavemen, we realize that we have needed people who played the role of the psychotherapist. This occurred every 400–500 years, at times of crisis. We can find in the history of different centuries this cry for help, this begging for an understanding of the inner person. We seek an understanding of the consciousness and the unconsciousness where we think our most serious thoughts and where we experience our deepest joy.

When we endeavor to clarify our methods of "ministering to a mind diseased" as Shakespeare puts it, there comes to mind the heroic days in the infancy of our own profession. My memory goes back to the years of 1955 and 1956, when there were only a handful of us in the whole state of New York practicing psychotherapy.

We thought of those as the "dangerous years." We few psychologists were continually under the threat of being declared outlaws in our conflict with the narrow wing of the American Medical Association (AMA). I recall those days when the legislature for New York state was in session. We knew the legislators had before them a bill introduced by the conservative wing of the AMA that would make all psychotherapy a branch of medicine. If this passed, we would be explicitly outlawed and possibly arrested for practicing medicine.

My own office was on the 25th floor of the Master Hotel overlooking the Hudson River and the skyline of New York. Whenever a depressed client would tell me that he or she was contemplating suicide, I secretly glanced to see that my windows were tightly locked, for I had fantasies of the patient jumping out and being squashed on the sidewalk far below.

For 6 or 8 years, intense anxiety visited me and my colleagues almost continually when the legislature was in session. We employed a part-time psychologist, Arthur Combs, as our representative on the floor of the state legislature. I recall a special day, when we were to have a crucial meeting that evening in the ballroom of the Hotel New Yorker, on which I did not dare answer the phone for fear it would be Art Combs in Albany to announce that the "outlawing" legislation had gone through and we psychologists were all about to be arrested. When I did finally answer the phone, it was Art simply wanting to tell us that he had gained promises from the leaders of the legislature that the medical bill would not be passed, at least in that session.

Several months later, I concluded, along with a psychiatrist who sympathized with our cause, that the best step for us as psychologists would be to clarify all the different branches of psychotherapy. The plan we then developed was to bring together selected members of the five professions that practice psychotherapy as part of their work: psychiatrists, psychologists, social workers, ministers, and educators. The five professions would appoint commissions and prepare for an inclusive conference on psychotherapy in one year's time. Preparatory to this major conference, the five groups would study what kind of training was necessary for its members, and the aims each group sought. Each commission met bimonthly. The members of each group undertook to find out what persons in the other fields did in the form of training and practice, what safeguards they honored, and so on.

The psychology group consisted of Nevitt Sanford, Harry Bone, Peter Blos, George Klein, and myself. The psychiatry group consisted of Frederich Allen, William Cooper, Louis Fraud, Florence Powdermaker, Robert Sooley, and Exie Welsch.

The results were available in the regular *Annals of the New York Academy of Sciences*.[3] I do not know how many states made concrete use of the published results of the conference; I can only say that from that moment on, the fact that psychotherapy was conducted by psychologists and by each of the above groups was then accepted in the various legislatures around the country.

In my task as head of the Joint Council, I telephoned Carl Rogers to get his ideas on licensing. I had never met Carl, who was then in Chicago. Expecting his enthusiastic help, I was taken aback by his stating that he was not sure whether it would be good or not to have psychologists licensed. Although I could not understand then why he had this hesitation, I think I do understand it now.

During the following years, I kept thinking of Carl Rogers' doubts about our campaign for licensing. I think he foresaw that we psychologists could be as rigid as any other group, and this certainly has been demonstrated. We have discovered that we also tend to lose our sensitivity and that we also face dangers similar to those faced by the AMA before us.

There is a serious dilemma occurring in our vocation and in our practice of helping people with their personal problems. The question is, Are we training technicians or professionals?

The leaders and seminal thinkers in psychoanalysis and psychotherapy—Freud, Jung, Adler, Rank, and others—treated psychological problems as opportunities for the therapist and patient to discover the deeper

---

[3]The proceedings of this conference were published in *Annals of the New York Academy of Sciences*, 63, 319–432, as *Psychotherapy and Counseling*, edited by Roy Waldo Miner and Rollo May. I do not know whether any more copies of this valuable booklet are attainable beyond my copy and several other copies that are privately owned.

levels of human experience.[4] These leaders used crises as ways to find the unexpressed possibilities in the client's behavior. It means uncovering the buried talents in the mysterious depths of the human mind and personality. In his famous statement, Freud called dreams the "royal road to the unconscious." He and those who followed found free associations and myths not only in dreams or as goals in themselves but also as ways of revealing the mental and emotional difficulties of their clients.

In our day, however, the goals of therapy have often been radically changed. I have taught a student seminar for seniors who are about to graduate from the California School of Professional Psychology. This school graduates each year a substantial number of therapists who will work with individuals and groups in this country. These students are excellent in intelligence and experience. In the seminar, each student presents one case for discussion. Last year, not one student mentioned a dream or a free association of the client, and this year there was only one. Never was a free association brought up; indeed, I often had to explain what is meant by the term *free association*. These students are learning to be very good technicians; my fear is that they will join the great flood of professionals whose task is to help counselees who are to be adjusted only, and they will never get to the deeper level our original explorers described.

Although I would be the last person in the world to recommend withholding information from anyone who would be helped by it, the problem here is different. It is, rather, that we in America have become a society devoted to the individual self. The danger is that psychotherapy becomes a self-concern, fitting what has recently been called a new kind of client, the narcissistic personality. Robert Bellah has rightly stated in his book *Habits of the Heart* (University of California Press, 1985) that we have made of therapy a new cult, a method in which we hire someone to act as a guide to our success and happiness. Rarely does one speak of duty to one's society—almost everyone undergoing therapy is concerned with individual gain, and the psychotherapist is hired to assist in this endeavor.

Some therapists recognize this problem chiefly through the fact that therapy gets boring. There are only so many practical problems in our day—sex, family, financial support; soon therapists begin to feel that they are

---

[4]My own background in the field began in 1930 when I went to Europe to teach in a boys' school in Greece. In my second year there, I had what is now called "nervous exhaustion," with which I coped as best I could with rest and some sessions at a summer seminar in the mountains near Vienna at the school of Alfred Adler. When I came back to this country, I got a job called Advisor to Men Students at Michigan State College. In those days there were no books on therapy in any card catalogue I could find. In the middle of the 1930s, I found myself giving seminars around the country chiefly based on my work with Alfred Adler. A publisher wished to publish these talks, and the volume *The Art of Counseling* appeared. This book was reprinted 50 years later in 1989 by Gardner Press.

hearing the same story again and again. One of the graduates with whom I dealt spoke dolefully of his work as "the McDonald's of therapy." No wonder one of them writes, "Some of the fire that used to make therapy creative and fun seems to have diminished."[5]

I well remember 5 decades ago, when I was getting my training in psychoanalysis, that we were chiefly open to *surprise*. We were never certain what interesting data were going to come out in work with this or that client. We were so filled with *wonder* that we could scarcely wait to get to our home-formed little discussion group of therapists one night a week to share what we had discovered that day.

The blocking of one's capacity for wonder and the loss of the capacity to appreciate mystery can have serious effects on our psychological health, not to mention the health of our whole planet. Psychologically, this "psychic numbing," to borrow Robert Lifton's phrase, the dulling or absence of sensitivity, leads to a loss of a sense of the grandeur of life and death. The personality type called compulsive–obsessional in some quarters and narcissistic personality in others comes to mind when we consider psychological numbing. Frighteningly, this type is increasing in our time. Caused generally by an inability to reach out and relate more than superficially to other people, it is the type of the mechanical man or woman, the "man in the gray suit," atrophied of emotions, inwardly lonely and outwardly detached. All of this appears externally as the boredom in the loss of the capacity to wonder. One therapist writes,

> . . . the passion is gone. A lot of the therapists I have talked with have a deep sadness about the erosion of this creative edge. A number referred to an earlier day when they felt more adventurous. Others noted that they have matured and have found quieter ways to be more effective. Still others acknowledge they have moved to a more cognitive level and are less willing to live on the edge.[6]

Psychotherapy and the problems that lead people to come for psychological help emerge when the values held by the culture break down and disintegrate, as I have said earlier. And as these values are mediated by myths, it is in the breakdown of the myths that we can most clearly discern the conflicts that lead people to come to psychotherapists. A dream is a private myth; a myth is a public dream.

These thoughts are offered with the hope of restoring, so far as we can, the richness, the mystery, the fascination that the original leaders of

---

[5]From "Life in the Glass House" by G. Criswell, 1987, *Pilgrimage, Psychotherapy and Personal Exploration, 13*, 17.
[6]From "Life in the Glass House" by G. Criswell, 1987, *Pilgrimage, Psychotherapy and Personal Exploration, 13*, 17.

the movement gave us. Although everyone must endure some boredom, which indeed is part of experience, I am proposing that we examine the deeper levels of the human adventure where this sense of awe and wonder is present.

The danger is that we lose our sensitivity in the presence of our work. We take refuge in definitions, putting aside our awareness that every moment in psychotherapy is distinctive and needs to be seen as new. Carl Rogers meant this, I propose, in his emphasis on empathy, the need to experience each client as unique. The differences between each client in this regard are more important than their similarities. To my mind, these constitute the essence of human nature in each individual. It is especially important to clarify the fact that each client is not "just like the others." The need to assert one's uniqueness is why the client is in therapy in the first place, and it is also why he or she is interesting to others and worth working with for us.

Saybrook Institute   ROLLO MAY
San Francisco

PREFACE

Four centuries ago a great psychologist, William Shakespeare, wrote, "What's past is prologue. . . ." (*The Tempest*, Act II, Scene 1). In the hope of not repeating our prologue, and perhaps even moving forward, the Division of Psychotherapy of the American Psychological Association (APA) has supported our endeavor to capture in this volume a portion of the history of psychotherapy. The 100th anniversary of the association appears to be an appropriate time to record such a history. Although the use of psychological treatment for human problems is as old as humanity, our current understanding of psychotherapy has its roots in the latter part of the 19th century.

In 1909, Hugo Münsterberg (one of the founders of APA) referred to psychotherapy as "This new movement . . . probably only in its beginning . . . ."[1] His modest prediction has been realized beyond all expectations. In fact, the burgeoning nature of the field may suggest that it is too early to write its history. Some of the areas covered in this volume, such as family therapy, are less than 50 years old, and many of the authors are among the originators of the systems and programs about which they are writing. The perspective of time, which can be helpful in assessing historical influences, is nonexistent for many of the topics covered in this volume. Indeed, much of the book is a living history, presented firsthand.

One might ask whether it is appropriate to write a history of *psychotherapy*, as we still have little unanimity in defining what we mean by the term. How much have we really learned in the past 100 years? Following two major conferences on the evolution of psychotherapy,[2] we are still seeking definitions of our subject.

[1]From *Psychotherapy* (p. 2) by H. Münsterberg, 1909, New York: Moffatt, Yard and Co.
[2]From *The Evolution of Psychotherapy* edited by J. K. Zeig, 1987, New York: Brunner/Mazel.

During a recent meeting (Berkeley, California, 1989) of the Society for the Exploration of Psychotherapy Integration (SEPI), members were asked to provide metaphors for the process of psychotherapy. Nothing struck me as very imaginative. Some time later, however, as I was working with my new home computer, I discovered a function that seemed to have ramifications for the question posed at the SEPI meeting. The command was "Reveal Codes," by which the screen reveals the hidden codes that determine the format of the manifest text. It occurred to me that this insight is what we strive for in psychotherapy. Imagine all the years of therapy (not to mention dollars) that would be saved if we could simply reveal the codes of our feelings and behavior.

Another issue that has persisted throughout the past century is whether psychotherapy really works. Research findings have usually indicated 50–75% success rates, which would not be deemed a very high probability according to any scientific standard. As the chapters on research will attest, measuring the multitude of dimensions in the process of psychotherapy is a challenging, if not an impossible, endeavor. The very identification of variables is a formidable task in itself.

In recent years, the field of psychotherapy has expanded so rapidly that it is difficult to know when and what to measure. Persons[3] has suggested that our usual methods of studying outcome may be off base. She claims that we should be evaluating outcomes using a case formulation model and not the traditional standardized treatment approach. By its nature, psychotherapy is field-oriented, not a laboratory science. Finding the crucial techniques of research has always been one of the major obstacles to breakthroughs in the study of the process.

In addition to the difficulties in studying the process of psychotherapy, establishing standards among those who carry out the work is increasingly complex. Practitioners have entered the field from a variety of backgrounds, educational tracks, and degrees of experience. For example, some drug rehabilitation programs require that the therapist recover from an addiction before being qualified to treat it. Münsterberg's words, "The chaotic character of psychotherapy in this first decade of the 20th century . . ."[4] might well apply to this *last* decade of the 20th century!

The current confusing state of the field presented difficult options and decisions in developing any historical picture of psychotherapy. We knew from the onset that only a partial view of the history could be recorded within the limitations of a single volume. However, we desired to present

---

[3]From "Psychotherapy Outcome Studies Do Not Accurately Represent Current Models of Psychotherapy" by J. B. Persons, 1991, *American Psychologist*, 46, 99–106.
[4]From *Psychotherapy* (p. 2) by H. Münsterberg, 1909, New York: Moffatt, Yard and Co.

as comprehensive a view as possible. The present volume does not follow any single line of inquiry or model in its perspective of the field. The recent interesting commentary on the history of psychology[5] might criticize the work for being rather inconsistent, as what follows is a collection of personal experiences, scholarly views, and critical commentary.

The volume evolved out of a series of meetings with the associate editors in a psychotherapist's office in New York City. We developed the concept of organizing the text somewhat differently than might be expected for a historical treatment of the subject. Instead of following systems of psychotherapy and their implications for research, training, and so on, we divided the text into four major areas: theory, research, practice, and training. Within each of these areas, we attempted to consider the critical links and turning points that have shaped the field from both internal and external sources. Internal influences arise from research, theories, and other expansions of knowledge, whereas external forces are created by cultural, political, and socioeconomic dimensions in the environment.

The *History* begins with an introductory section of three chapters. The first is a snapshot of psychotherapy in 1892. Jane Kessler has recreated the period both in story and in style as she describes the available psychotherapeutic techniques of the era. The next chapter traces psychotherapy in a sociological context from 1892 to the present, describing how cultural and social changes have influenced our views of psychotherapy and how, in turn, psychotherapy has influenced the culture. The third chapter tracks changes in settings and in patterns of reimbursement. In considering the evolution of psychotherapy in this context, we have an account of where and how it has been practiced through the century.

The section on theory that follows was overseen by Stanley Messer and Paul Wachtel. We attempted to select comprehensive theoretical frameworks in psychotherapy and encouraged the authors to provide thorough reviews of them. The authors of these chapters also consulted with authors of chapters in the section on practice in order to limit inevitable duplication.

Hans Strupp was responsible for the section on research, in which we attempted to cover the major issues and achievements as well as limitations of research in the field. In this section we have a unique chapter consisting of 12 reports from leading psychotherapy research centers throughout the United States. We asked the founders of the centers to write vignettes explaining how they became active in psychotherapy research, recalling

---

[5]From "The History of Psychology: A Survey and Critical Assessment" by E. R. Hilgard, D. E. Leary, and G. R. McGuire, 1991, *Annual Review of Psychology, 42,* 79–107.

who their important collaborators were and identifying their most significant contributions. It is of interest to note the interrelationships among the centers, with ideas and themes interwoven throughout. We hope this chapter will give the reader a somewhat more personal look into both the researchers and the centers in which they worked.

Herbert Freudenberger and I took responsibility for the section on practice, and in that portion we had to exercise the most selectivity in the book. Out of the many hundreds of psychotherapeutic techniques that might have been described, we could choose only a handful. Within those constraints, we wanted to include historic contributions of women and ethnic minority practitioners. We also singled out work with children and the elderly as populations with distinct histories in our field.

The section on training was edited by Donald Peterson, who balanced personal influences on training programs with documentation of the landmarks of the educational movements. Much of this history is very recent, with stories in the text that have never been told before.

To end the volume, we thought it would be appropriate to speculate on the future of psychotherapy, because the knowledge of all that precedes should give us some guidelines for directions of the field. If we can be as prophetic as Münsterberg in predicting the future of psychotherapy over the next 100 years, we certainly will have achieved some success. However, we would feel an even greater sense of accomplishment if the offerings in this *History* could help clarify the past and allow us to better understand a century of change.

Case Western Reserve University   DONALD K. FREEDHEIM
Cleveland, Ohio
September 1991

ACKNOWLEDGMENTS

An endeavor of this scope and magnitude requires the cooperation of many individuals. When the idea for the project was first presented to the Publications Board of the Division of Psychotherapy of the American Psychological Association (APA), Arthur Kovacs, the then chair of the Board, responded immediately. He carried the idea to the Executive Committee, who added enthusiastic support and provided the initial funding for the project. The presidents of the division during the preparation of the volume, Aaron Canter, Norman Abeles, and Ellen McGrath, were supportive throughout. In addition, the staff from the division office, especially Anne Mello and Pauline Wampler, were always helpful in smoothing administrative matters.

In the Publications Office of APA I had the privilege of working with accomplished professionals. The director of the office, Gary R. VandenBos, not only was a supporter of the project at its inception but also is a key contributor to the final product. I would also like to thank Theodore J. Baroody, W. Ralph Eubanks, Julia Frank-McNeil, Valerie Montenegro, and Donna Stewart for their fine work in the development and production processes.

At Case Western Reserve University I have the good fortune of a most cooperative and skillful staff in the Department of Psychology. My assistants with the journal *Psychotherapy*, Hilary E. Katz and Donna T. Zloba, spent extra time with that publication to allow me the opportunity to work on the volume. I also want to thank Open P. Weaver, Janet L. Reid, Tami Holcomb, and Cathleen M. Uveges for patiently transcribing endless manuscript drafts.

Among many who read chapters and offered suggestions, I would like to thank Erving Betts, Robert Dies, Lon Gieser, Morris Goodman, Howard

Hall, Evelyn Hill, John Kennedy, Joe Matarazzo, James Overholser, Reuben Silver, Arthur Teicher, Judy Turner, and the late Jules Barron.

Special thanks to John A. Popplestone, director of the Archives of the History of American Psychology, for help with historical facts and photographs.

A major debt of gratitude must go to my associate editors, who spent many hours conceptualizing the project, working with authors, and coordinating the sections of the publication. Of course, the volume would not have been possible without the contributions of the chapter authors, who drafted and redrafted their manuscripts with care and grace. Working with all of them has been a real pleasure in addition to a wonderful learning experience.

Last of all, I would like to thank my wife, Gerda, who provided encouragement and critical commentary throughout the project.

DONALD K. FREEDHEIM

I

ONE HUNDRED YEARS OF PSYCHOTHERAPY: AN INTRODUCTION

1

1892: AN EPISTOLARY RECONSTRUCTION

JANE W. KESSLER

What follows is largely a product of the author's imagination, but every effort has been made to check historical details for plausibility. Before launching into fantasy, however, I will present the reality concerning the putative authoress of the letters.

THE BACKGROUND

Christine Ladd-Franklin (1847–1930) was born in New York City, the eldest of three children. After her mother's death when she was 12 years of age, Christine was separated from her father and siblings and lived with various relatives. With much vigor and persistence over a 3-year period, she prevailed upon her reluctant father to borrow the money to send her to Vassar College, described in her diary as the "Land of my Longing!" In the fall of 1866, she enrolled in the second class to enter Vassar College. For some 10 years after graduation, she taught science and mathematics with an ever-increasing dislike for the vocation of teaching, perhaps because it was virtually the only option for the women of her time.

The difficulties that Christine Ladd-Franklin encountered because of gender discrimination are well chronicled by Scarborough and Furumoto (1987). Soon after The Johns Hopkins University opened, she applied for advanced study in mathematics. By special intervention only, she was allowed to attend lectures, and she completed the requirements for a doctoral degree in 1882. Because of her sex she was ineligible for a "real" degree. On the occasion of its 50th anniversary in 1926, Johns Hopkins presented her with the long-delayed degree!

When she was about 35 years of age, Christine Ladd married Fabian Franklin, a member of the mathematics faculty at Johns Hopkins, and had two children, a son who died in infancy and a daughter born in 1884. Her career interests changed to the experimental study of vision, which she pursued both at Johns Hopkins and later at Columbia University as well as throughout her life. She never achieved faculty rank either at Johns Hopkins or at Columbia, because her male colleagues in psychology followed the discrimination policies of the time. Despite her repeated efforts, she was unable to persuade E. B. Titchener to admit women into the "club" of experimental psychologists that he organized in 1904. Nonetheless, Christine Ladd-Franklin was one of three women included in a list of 50 top psychologists chosen by peer ranking in 1903.

Christine Ladd-Franklin was outspoken, persistent, and held definite opinions on many subjects. She was a frequent contributor to *The Nation* and held forth on women's rights. At the least, she was an assertive personality and at most, an ascerbic one. In 1914, Titchener wrote that he was "pestered by abuse" from Mrs. Ladd-Franklin and that she had threatened to make various scenes in person and in print for not having women at the meetings. Her efforts at the time seemed to have had little payoff for her; the women who followed were the real beneficiaries.

To set the stage for the time of our letters, Christine Ladd-Franklin accompanied her husband on his sabbatical leave in Germany in 1891–1892. Again she managed to circumvent university policies in order to study with G. E. Muller and von Helmholtz. During this year, she developed her theory of color vision, which she presented at the International Congress of Psychology in London in 1892.

I am presuming that, living abroad, Christine Ladd-Franklin might well have pursued an active correspondence with a mythical friend living in Baltimore named Pamela. The focus of this correspondence is Sophia, Pamela's younger sister, who is living with her parents as a chronic invalid. In my imagination, Christine Ladd-Franklin is very well read and *au courant* with the contemporary theories of causation and techniques of treatment for the neuroses, in France and Germany as well as the United States.

THE LETTERS

September 5, 1891

My dear Pamela,

Now that we are settled with Margaret in school and Fabian at the university, my thoughts have returned to our conversation before I left Baltimore. I well understand your great distress and concern about Sophia's nervous weakness which has persisted for so long! I was flattered that you asked for my help as a psychologist. However, psychology training in our modern laboratories does not include abnormal psychology. We are well versed in measurements of apperception, cognition, discrimination, association, and will, but the goal has been to tie these events with physiology rather than the operations in real life. But one cannot help but be drawn to the mystery and tragedy of those who suffer from nervous maladies, which include, amongst other things, a failure of will.

It is an unfortunate fact that these nervous illnesses are more incapacitating to the female sex. Possibly it is because of a more delicate constitution—that is certainly what they say. But for whatever reason, the story of your sister is typical in many ways. The chlorotic condition diagnosed when she was 14 is almost epidemic for well-bred girls in puberty. It is unfortunate that the usual treatment of iron salts, increased meat, and regular rests did not help her. I have read that marriage is the best cure for chlorosis with the caveat that it should not be resorted to except on the recommendation of a responsible physician! I do not quite understand how marriage corrects a disorder of the blood, but even more to the point, arranging marriage with a willing partner for this purpose seems rather difficult.

In regard to this subject, much has been written about the importance of personal habits in causing a morbid condition of the organs of generation. At Johns Hopkins, Professor Hall expounded on the causes and effects of the practice of self-abuse and plans to include a full discussion in his upcoming work on adolescence. He feels that a prominent cause is precocious mental development with mental overwork and straining of the memory, but he allows for external causes such as springtime, a "peculiarly dangerous season." He is of no doubt about the devastating results, such as youthful melancholia and a weak heart.

To me there seemed to be some inconsistency in his logic. Although he cites countless studies showing the long history and universality of this sexual practice, he asserts that the sins of the parents are visited on their children, which will ultimately lead to exterminating the race. I can see no direct evidence for this dire prediction, but such ominous words are enough to put a scare into any thoughtful adolescent!

Did you by chance come upon a reprint of the letter written last year by Robert Louis Stevenson defending the reputation of Father Damien? A Reverend Hyde claimed that Damien acquired leprosy as a direct consequence of his vices and improper relations with women. Sex always seems to be the hidden culprit when bad things happen to good people. No doubt it was the injustice of this and the impassioned defense made by Stevenson that made me write about sex so much in this epistle.

I am sure that this has no bearing on the nervous plight of your sister and I hope that my digressions have not offended you. Here in Germany many scientific publications are available on this subject and there is always a new edition of Krafft-Ebing's work! But there is still much concern that this reading material stay out of the hands of the public, so the explicit parts are written in Latin—as if the educated public could not read it. How foolish in this day and age when women as well as men are well versed in this language.

I shall await further news about your sister; perhaps we need say nothing more about psychological matters, which would be good news indeed. With fond hopes, I remain,

Yours very truly,
Christine

October 18, 1891

My dear Pamela,

Your letter with continued unhappy tidings arrived, and I hasten to reasseverate how little psychology has to offer in the way of practical help. You write that your mother believes that Sophia's invalidism is "an elevating, ennobling experience eradicating pride and self-sufficiency." That may help your mother resign herself to the role of constant caretaker, but it may not be so helpful for Sophia. I was reminded of a discussion on Hysteria which recently appeared in Villaret's encyclopedia of general medicine. Although the author's name was not given, it is generally ascribed to a Dr. Freud of Vienna.

You may find the exposition interesting, so here is my feeble attempt to abstract it from the German. The author contends that "as a rule, an hysterical man or woman is not the only neurotic member of the family circle." Family members expect recurrence of the problems and their obvious concern ensures that it will happen. He says it is important to guard against excessive interest in slight hysterical symptoms lest one unwittingly encourage them. Paradoxically, education in the better classes of society may increase nervous problems because of the importance assigned to delicate refinement of feeling and sensibility.

Ideally, relatives should be persuaded to look on hysterical spells calmly and with apparent indifference, but Dr. Freud writes that this is almost impossible. Therefore, the first step in treatment is removal of the patient from regular life conditions and strict isolation from the social circle in which the nervous outbreak occurred. In the sanitorium, the physician conveys a cheerful conviction that the neurosis is not dangerous and can be rapidly cured.

Dr. Freud endorses the rest cure proposed by Weir Mitchell, identified as a highly original nerve specialist in Philadelphia. This procedure combines rest in bed, isolation, feeding-up, massage, and electricity in a strictly regulated manner. Allegedly, this treatment is of extraordinary value for hysteria, but in the case of neurasthenia, the success is far less certain and depends merely on the value of excessive feeding.

There is agreement on the importance of good nutrition to build up the blood, but increase in fat is also a consequence. I would think that following the popular practice of "Fletcherism" would rule out the fat gain! Fletcher's prescription to "chew each mouthful of food 300 times and you will be on the road to health and happiness" sounds like a difficult road to travel. I believe William James remarked that he tried this, but it nearly killed him, to say nothing of the effect on one's dining companion!

Returning to our person of mutual concern, I am somewhat at a loss as to the medical diagnosis. If indeed it is neurasthenia, there seems little to do except build up one's constitution. Although George Beard has somewhat modified his ideas since first identifying this condition, he still believes that it is a question of the balance between the demands of the nervous system and the available nervous energy. "What matters, therefore, is not to expend more force than one can afford to." On the other hand, he asserts that neurasthenia is a disease proper to men because of social factors that spare the weaker sex from undue exertion! Although Sophia's symptoms—such as the extreme lassitude—fit the picture, it seems that the condition developed under minimal demands for exertion, if I recall correctly. What is your opinion on this matter, as it does seem to make a difference with respect to treatment?

I recently reread Henry James's *The Bostonians* and was struck anew by his disparaging portrayal of female characters. His special target seems to be those involved in the women's suffrage movement. Still I am confident that someday the nation will follow the course of little Wyoming. Strange that such a newcomer in the family of states would be the first to give women equal civil rights! Perhaps Wyoming is trying to persuade women to follow Horace Greeley's advice to "Go West."

Although it is indeed stimulating to work in the laboratory of von Helmholtz, I confess I will be glad "to go West" when our year is finished here. With my fondest hopes for your sister's welfare and humblest apologies for knowing so little, I remain,

Your friend,
Christine

November 20, 1891

My dear friend,

I am not waiting for your reply, in view of the uncertain sailing dates in winter. In my last letter I discussed all manner of "body-based" treatments, none of which has a stellar record of success. But I feel that I should inform you of an alternative method of healing, namely, the mind-cure movement, or what is popularly called "New Thought." The sources for this movement are religious–mystical rather than medical, and there is a great deal of controversy and splits in the various schools.

Mary Baker Eddy's book, *Science and Health*, has just this year appeared in its fiftieth edition. She has certainly accomplished a great deal since she was "made well" by Phineas Quimby some thirty years ago! The Christian Science approach to healing rests on faith that the Lord would never make one ill, so illness is a delusion that can be evaporated by spiritual regeneration. This gives the mind tremendous power over the body, a hopeful thought when the body is giving pain. However, there are many occasions that test this pious hope. For Mary Baker Eddy, the death of her husband was one such. Her remarks in the *Boston Globe* about his "mental murder" through "mesmeric poison" have been much cited. In a way she is consistent—if thoughts can cure, thoughts can kill.

I have not followed all the arguments presented by the defectors or faithful zealots that swirl around this complicated person. She has railed against imposters and false prophets and tried to protect the public by issuing annual certificates for accredited healers. But there is no way that she could check the spread of the New Thought movement. This movement stresses positive thinking and uses any religious or belief system to support a very eclectic spirituality. The healing power comes from healthy-minded atti-tudes—courage, hope, and trust as opposed to doubt, fear, and worry. This doctrine of optimism is not restricted to the ailing. One hears of the "Gospel of Relaxation," the "Don't Worry Movement," of people who repeat to themselves, "Youth, health, vigor!" as their motto for the day. New Thought offers systematic exercise in relaxation, concentration, and meditation, all towards the end of attaining self-control. There is quite a good bit more to it than positive affirmations.

An important aspect of this treatment is the exercise of will. Professor William James, a true believer in individual will and choice, has spoken movingly of a deep depression that he suffered soon after receiving his medical degree. He chanced to read Renouvier's essay on free will and felt much improved by the belief that he could be what he believed himself to be. Although this self-help approach (one might call it bibliotherapy) worked well for him at that time, I know he continued to have low spells and periods of prolonged fatigue. More recently he sought help from a mind-cure doctress, a Mrs. Lydia Pinkham. In the spirit of scientific research, he has been investigating the extraordinary phenomena of a famous me-dium, Mrs. Pipes; I do not know his conclusions. It is a curious fact that most of the healers are women, perhaps because it is a self-selected occu-pation without formal educational requirements to limit access for women. I believe that Dr. James has gone on record against the bill to be proposed in the Massachusetts legislature limiting the practice of mental therapy to licensed physicians.

There is more to say on this topic, but I will let it rest until I hear further. I continue to hope that these issues will become irrelevant to your family.

With fond hopes,
Christine

December 14, 1891

My dearest Pamela,

Our last letters must have crossed in mid-ocean, but our thoughts were as close as peas in a pod. It is not surprising that we were both thinking of the mind cures in view of the well-publicized accounts of success and failure. Your questions about the respectability of mind healing are well put.

And now I must come to a personal confession. A few years back I consulted a mind-cure healer with very satisfactory results. I hesitated to bring this to your attention because one experience does not prove the case—perhaps my malaise would have lightened as a natural course. Hoping that a scientific study could be undertaken, I wrote Professor James because of his close ties with the American branch of the Society for Psychical Research. I have included a copy of his reply (with some deletion), which shows how difficult it is to obtain proof in these matters. Apparently some respond well to mind-cure treatments and some do not, and the reasons for success—or failure—are still obscure.

I cannot close this letter without some words about William James, with whom you may not be so familiar. Last year he published a two-volume tome on *Principles of Psychology* after some twelve years of work! Except for its monumental size, it provides interesting reading for anyone. He takes on the big subjects like the Self, consciousness, habits, cognition, and will, which have absorbed philosophers for eons. He is definitely giving a new cast to American psychology by looking at these broad vistas of human experience rather than those discrete elements that lend themselves to brass instrument measurement. It is something of a problem as to where these new directions will take us. In his position as the first professor of psychology at Harvard, he is establishing a psychology laboratory, but he has written to me that he plans to ask Hugo Münsterberg to accept the position as director. Experimentation is not his first, or second love!

I apologize for this digression. The future of American psychology is of little interest compared with Sophia's invalidism. I would not hesitate to bring in a healer with a good record, best judged by what people say. Above all, you must communicate your optimism to Sophia so she can draw strength from your faith. Remember, Professor James found it helpful, perhaps coupled with his determination to move ahead.

> With my best wishes to all,
> *Christine*

Cambridge
April 12 [1888]

Dear Mrs. Franklin,

Your letter interests me very much, because the account you give is similar to accounts which I have heard from others of the influence upon them of the hand of a certain Mrs. Wetherbee who is a "magnetic healer" here, and who, on members of my wife's family, has certainly "charmed away pain" in a most surprising manner. I know Dr. Crockett also, and like him. I have had hitherto only his own accounts of his performances, not knowing any of his patients but one, on whom he failed.

But I am very dubious of the poor little Soc. for Psych. Re. accomplishing much by seeking to "investigate" these things. Of all earthly things, therapeutic effects are the hardest to run to ground, and convince a skeptic of. There will always be a dozen loopholes of escape from any conclusion about therapeutics, and the mind will take which ever one it prefers. I think the history of opinion about homeopathy (or about the single drug alcohol) is enough to make anyone hopeless of making therapeutic evidence satisfactory to all. Money was offered to the Society for the purpose of investigating the "mind cure." It was (as I thought, rightly) refused. Practical physicians are the only ones who can say an influential word in these matters; and they must have already made themselves influential in other matters, or they will simply discredit themselves by speaking of such things as those of which you write. A Charcot can afford to risk his reputation in this way; a common practitioner cannot. Meanwhile such experiences as yours, mentioned by such a person as yourself, will accrete with others and little by little invite the attention of the competent.

Very sincerely yours,
Wm James

January 18, 1892

My dear friend,

I am much in admiration of your family devotion. It is indeed difficult to be truly helpful when you are a day's journey apart and cannot speak in person. The matter is further complicated by your reliance on me for information. There is not only the ocean to cross but also deep chasms of ignorance in my mind that need to be bridged for me to reply with any confidence.

I have given much thought to your question about the usefulness of hypnosis. Indeed, in many hands it has been a parlor trick, or a stage show with prearranged help from the subjects. It bears a superficial resemblance to the thoroughly discredited animal magnetism claims of Mesmer a hundred years ago and so has been an object of suspicion. However, there is no longer any doubt as to the reality of hypnotic phenomena. Particularly on the Continent one hears and reads much serious discussion.

Persons of excellent repute are drawn to France to study with the masters at Salpetriere and Nancy. The lists of those attending the international congresses and writing on this subject shows it to be a masculine arena—in contrast to the feminine representation in mind cures! Also, William James is one of the very few who come from America, but, of course, he is always taking long trips for his health!

In addition to the clinical demonstrations, people are drawn to discuss the conflicting theories. Briefly, the central issue is whether the hypnotic state represents a physiological alteration, a species of abnormality characteristic of hysterical individuals. Charcot at Salpetriere feels that the physiological changes are evident in the fixed sequence of different manifestations of the hypnotic trance. Bernheim of the Nancy school denies that hypnosis is a physiologically abnormal susceptibility limited to hysterics. He describes hypnosis as a state of enforced suggestibility which can be created in persons of any age, normal and neurotic. Bernheim's optimistic view of the value of hypnosis is expressed in his promises that "Stupid children are made gifted by this discovery of hypnotism with mere verbal suggestion and instruction. The confirmed bad habits of years' standing are now also cured by hypnotism. It is claimed that in fifty years more such a thing as a chronic drunkard will be unknown."

I cannot weigh the merits of the Bernheim/Charcot dispute, but it appears that Charcot's work is coming under increasing criticism. There is a possibility that some of his long-term patients have been coached or at least have "learned" how to be classical hypnotic cases.

But again I digress from the point of therapeutic utility. What might be the risks? Much attention is given to the possibility of crime under hypnosis. Instead of the plea "not guilty, by reason of insanity," some are pleading not guilty by reason of undue influence, or hypnosis. In trial testimony, the psychology experts have been divided about the possibility of post-hypnotic suggestion causing a person to commit a violent crime. Although public opinion has been much aroused, there has been no incontrovertible evidence to substantiate this defense. I cannot imagine this to be a risk for your sister as it also presupposes some malignant intention on the part of the hypnotist.

On a less "real" basis, there is some resistance to hypnotism because one subrogates one's will to another. On this I turn to Freud's comments in the preface of his translation of Bernheim's work on suggestion and in his review of Forel's article on hypnotism.

Freud admits that suggestion plays a major part in hypnosis. Suggestion differs from commands or exhortations in that an idea is aroused in another person's brain that is not examined as to origin but is accepted just as though it had arisen spontaneously. This notion that you do not know where your ideas come from is repugnant to many. Freud counters by asking if massive doses of bromide, morphine, and chloral are more effective in retaining one's independence. He further states that the entire social up-bringing of human beings is based on a suppression of unserviceable ideas and motives and their replacement by better ones. He emphasizes that the suppression of a patient's independence by hypnotic suggestion is always a partial one aimed at the symptoms of an illness. He concludes with the firm statement that there is nothing dangerous in hypnotic therapy but its misuse and that a physician who does not trust the purity of his intention should eschew the practice.

I found this very reassuring and hasten to commend it to your atten-tion. Hypnosis seems a more powerful therapeutic tool than the various mind cures, which require an act of will on the part of the patient. If indeed this is the very function that is most impaired, it seems unlikely that it can be mobilized to fight the illness. Now I can close with high hopes in spirit as well as words.

Your faithful friend,
Christine

March 14, 1892

My patient friend,

Because I have been so much in Leipzig, I only now received your last two letters. They gave me much to ponder. There seems to be both good news and bad news. As I read it, Sophia's general lassitude and melancholy ameliorated in late fall, but shortly thereafter she became en-tirely mute. I assume that neurological disease was ruled out because it was so sudden and total with no evidence of organic pathology.

It was very wise to bring Sophia to your home so that these studies could be done at the new Johns Hopkins Hospital. Dr. Osler has chosen a progressive, if very young, medical staff. They will soon be opening a medical school, but it is rumored that much more money is needed. There are some possible benefactresses who are insisting that women be admitted to the new school. If that happens, it will be the first in the country to offer women the opportunity for a medical education.

One would hope that Sophia would see these changes as portents for her personal future, but your second letter described further developments that are indeed daunting to such hopes. With the diagnosis of hysteria firmly established, you were quite justified to proceed with the treatment of hypnosis. You wrote that it only took a few sessions to restore her voice, or I should say, two voices. At times she uses a voice as deep as a man's voice, but even more disturbing is that her speech is then garbled and unintelligible. Sophia's reaction seems to be one of puzzlement and surprise as if someone else were speaking with her tongue.

Reading your description, I thought of Pierre Janet's work on *Psychological Automatism*, which he defended at the time of the Universal Exposition of 1889 in Paris—a very impressive showing for a 30-year-old man! (That work is based on observation of patients, but he abstained from discussing therapeutic implications because he had not started his medical training.) His thesis ranges widely over the field of consciousness in an attempt to explain all degrees and forms of automatisms (that is, behaviors of which one is *not* conscious) from hypnosis and multiple personalities to automatic writing. Sophia might be said to exhibit automatic talking but for the fact that voice and articulation are so entirely altered. This seems to approach the idea of another personality. It would be interesting to know if she also behaves strangely during these periods of garbled speech.

Janet suggests that in cases of hysteria there is a psychological weakness (hence the diagnosis psychasthenia) that causes narrowing of the field of consciousness. And here is the important part. With this narrowed consciousness, certain parts are split off, and these subconscious fixed ideas have a separate autonomy. As I interpret this, one can have the situation of autosuggestion where one part of the person is directing the other with no integration between the two parts.

Janet has gone further to explain these phenomena. He suggests that memories of certain dramatic circumstances present themselves to the mind in the form of unsolved problems, reproduce the original emotions, and give rise to hysterical symptoms. He termed this the traumatic memory of an unassimilated event. Therapeutically, he feels that it is important to recapture the memory and the accompanying emotion. By evoking the original trauma (usually by hypnosis), the subject can assimilate the experience, albeit belatedly, and restore the integration of the personality.

This sounds like a new beginning for treating the mind and its disorders. You have of course noted how central the concept of consciousness is and will not be at all surprised to know that philosophers, psychologists, and physicians are of different opinions. Is consciousness simply a matter of attending? What causes the apparent boundaries of accessibility to consciousness? Alfred Binet and William James are amongst the many who have wrestled with these questions. It is not an entirely foreign subject even to the experimental psychologists. In my work on visual perception I am familiar with Helmholtz's term "unconscious inference."

The phenomena of memory are very much related to consciousness. I recall reading Nietzsche on the subject of inhibition where he emphasizes the very active forces that can militate against remembering. He describes the conflict thusly, "I have done it, says my memory. I cannot have done it, says my pride and remains inexorable. Finally the memory gives way." I can understand this even though so much of his writing is entirely abstruse. He certainly enjoyed great cachet with our young students, but I suppose that is all lost since his mental breakdown and confinement to asylum.

Nothing we have now will help the Nieztsche-type illness, since it was the final outcome of a syphilis. But the outlook for the psychical illnesses continues to look promising. I particularly look forward to hearing Dr. Janet, as we are both presenting this summer at the International Congress of Experimental Psychology in London.

Incidentally, with regard to Sophia's "other voice," does it remind you of anyone or anything? Perhaps it is a replay of some experience, and you, as the older sister, might recognize the event.

With warmest wishes,
Christine

April 21, 1892

Dearest Pamela,

What glad tidings! And how very clever of you! Apparently the observation that during the queer talking spells, Sophia moved as if she were "tethered like a horse" gave you the key. Of course you would remember the events differently than she did because she was only five years of age. However, I can picture it clearly. An active little girl, bored with the quiet isolation of her grandmother's farm, finds a nearby playmate. The fact that he is a young man with a severe speech impediment does not deter her because he is always happy to see her and play her games.

It was your impression at that time that there was something improper with their play, at least suggestively sexual, and that was why an abrupt halt was called to their friendship. Sophia was restricted to her yard. And since the young man was not mentally responsible, he was loosely tied to a tree in his front yard. It must have been a very great puzzle to her as to what was so bad about whatever they had done—so bad that he was tied like a horse. I am sure that it was a great help that you could reconstruct the summer of 1876 for the therapist to bring back in hypnosis. It was also helpful for Sophia to be informed about the young man's mental condition and be relieved of any sense of sin surrounding their innocent play. It is unfortunate that the people of Dover were too isolated to know that the young man's idiocy could have been cured if he had been taught by Seguin's physiological training method in one of the new schools established in many states.

I am not surprised that Sophia, although now of sound mind, is not content with her life. Some five years have been spent in the shadows of the sickroom and now that she is out in the open, where should she go? It is probably unwise for her to return to her parents' home, but remaining with you also has difficulties. As I recall, she took quite a sick spell when you married and she could not attend the wedding. Since she cannot fully participate in your family life, the role of governess to your young children cannot be entirely satisfactory. Even now there is much truth in Alice James's statement that matrimony is the only successful occupation a woman can undertake.

I have heard through her brother that Alice James is dying of cancer. She is a brilliant woman who has been bedridden for most of her 42 years! William says that she welcomed the diagnosis of a palpable disease because for so many years, her pains were said to be in her mind. Alice was about Sophia's age when she had her first nervous breakdown. She described it as violent inclinations invading her muscles, pushing her to throw herself out the window or knock her father's head off. Some ten years later, Alice talked with her father about suicide and he urged her only to "do it in a perfectly gentle way in order not to distress her friends!" He deserved to have his head knocked off way back when!

Alice James had the loving support of her brothers, William and Henry, but that was not always so salutary. It was that circumstance that prompted my remarks on her wasted life. You cannot take over your mother's place in caring for Sophia; she will have to find her own fulfillment, and perhaps indeed outside of marriage. I wrote a book review on the The Evolution of Marriage, which was published in The Nation last July; bear with my repetition of some of those words.

Nothing is more hazardous to the happiness and permanence of marriage, or more destructive of the feeling of equality that ought to pervade the married state, than for young girls to feel, to even a slight degree, that they are expected to marry as the only natural mode of providing for themselves. Friends of women will do well to concern themselves with opening the more lucrative professions to them and with seeing to it that they obtain equal wages with men for equal work. And there is another moral concerning the retention of personal property rights. It is the duty of a woman, no matter how much confidence she may feel in the honor and integrity of the coming husband, to preserve her property rights intact, as a not inessential element of a wider than personal morality.

I am not sure how the reading public responded to that editorial. It was as usual unsigned, so no one spoke to me in person. I sent a copy to William James, who said only that he had suspected the authorship! This sermonizing about women's rights is designed not only to change laws and the attitudes of the male sex but also to change the expectations of young women like Sophia so that they can comfortably consider other life options than marriage.

I have one last question, namely, do you have any thought as to why this event of Sophia's childhood came forward with such force at this particular time?

Your ever-curious friend,
Christine

May 26, 1892

My dear Pamela,

This communication will be brief, as we are packing steamer trunks for imminent departure and wending our way homeward with stops in Paris and London. I am glad your missive arrived and provided the final piece to complete the picture. It is ironic that Sophia's improved mental health in a way initiated the second round of difficulties. Her parents were more sympathetic with her languor than with her liveliness! Her father's tirade about her expenditure of money for new outfits and stepping out was indeed unkind. Hurling the epithet "virago" was the culmination—did she know the meaning of the word? In any case, being out of favor, restricted in her activities, and confused as to the reason clearly reawakened the memories of that long-ago summer. I doubt that this would have been made clear if she had remained at home.

I am relieved to hear, however, that your role is coming to an end *vis-a-vis* Sophia's care. Her trip to Cuba will no doubt continue her recovery, especially with exciting plans on her return. I have heard many good things about the work of Jane Addams at Hull House, even though her activities on behalf of labor laws and slum clearance have aroused hostility in some quarters. It is surprising that the Daughters of the American Revolution described her as a factor in a movement to destroy civilization and Christianity. This is pure intolerance and narrow-mindedness; her work represents Christianity at its finest, and Sophia will be uplifted by the association.

Chicago will be the hub of national excitement soon with the upcoming Columbian Exposition. I understand that it is scheduled for the summer of 1893. It is strange that it is a year late, considering how long they have known the proper date—1892!

But one event that is occurring on time, that is, in 1892, is a meeting to organize an association for American psychology. Professor Hall has invited some six professors to join him at Clark University in July to develop a plan of organization and future scientific programs. It is a step in developing an identity apart from philosophy—or physiology, for that matter. I shall watch closely to see when, or if, they nominate their first women members!

The fight for recognition of women seems never-ending. There are so many restrictions having to do with what is considered "ladylike" in behavior that a well-brought-up female must watch constantly if she wants to keep in society's mold. I, for one, am becoming increasingly restive with these social mores; in fact, I do not hesitate to smoke a cigarette when I am with fashionable society. I do not know how I will fit in when I return to Baltimore—but I will very soon have the opportunity to find out!

In anticipation of our reunion, I am

Your friend,
Christine

EPILOGUE

Mrs. C. Ladd-Franklin of Baltimore, Maryland was one of 13 new members elected to the American Psychological Association at the second annual meeting held at Columbia College in 1893, attended by 33 psychologists. At the meeting, the treasurer reported expenditures for the past year totaling $10.80, with a balance on hand of $69.50. Unlike her contemporary, Miss M. W. Calkins of Wellesley College, Mrs. Franklin never held office in the Association.

With respect to the status of psychotherapy, Ellenberger commented that in 1892 there was a choice of psychotherapies ranging from hypnotic suggestion and catharsis to the combination of supportive, expressive, and directive therapy. One might add that there were suggestions of family therapy, drug therapy (including the unrestricted use of cocaine), therapies based on diet, and milieu therapy. The wide range of approaches parallels the variety of options available a century later.

The reader may be curious about the veracity of the details in the preceding letters. With the obvious exception of Pamela and her unhappy sister, Sophia, the characters existed in fact and their statements are quoted from usually reliable sources. The letters from William James to Christine Ladd-Franklin from 1888–1892 are published (1986), including the one in which he stated that "therapeutic effects are the hardest to run to ground."

Some liberties were taken with historical dates, in that material was used from Hall's work on adolescence, which did not appear until 1902, and from James's book on varieties of religious experience, published in 1904. The author took the liberty of assuming that these gentlemen might well have expressed the same views at an earlier time.

REFERENCES

James, W. (1986). Selected unpublished correspondence 1885–1910. (P. J. D. Scott, Ed.). Columbus, OH: Ohio State University Press.

Scarborough, E., & Furumoto, L. (1987). *Untold lives: The first generation of American women psychologists.* New York: Columbia University Press.

BIBLIOGRAPHY

The author drew on the following sources for authenticity in the chapter:

Alexander, F. G., & Selesnick, S. T. (1966). *The history of psychiatry.* New York: Harper & Row.

Bernheim, H. (1889). *Suggestive therapeutics: A treatise on the nature and uses of hypnotism* (2nd rev. ed.; C. A. Herter, Trans.). New York: G. P. Putnam Sons.

Bjork, D. W. (1988). *William James: The center of his vision.* New York: Columbia University Press.

Brumberg, J. J. (1988). Chlorotic girls, 1870–1920: A historical perspective on female adolescence. *Child Development, 53,* 1468–1477.

Ellenberger, H. F. (1970). *The discovery of the unconscious.* New York: Basic Books.

Feinstein, H. M. (1984). *Becoming William James.* Ithaca, NY: Cornell University Press.

Freud, S. (1966). Hysteria. Pre-psychoanalytic publications and unpublished drafts. In J. Strachey (Ed. and Trans.), *The standard edition of the complete psychological works of Sigmund Freud* (Vol. 1; pp. 39–58). London: Hogarth Press. (Original work published in 1888)

Furumoto, L. (1988). Shared knowledge: The experimentalists, 1904–1929. In J. G. Morawski (Ed.), *The rise of experimentation in American psychology.* New Haven, CT: Yale University Press.

Furumoto, L., & Scarborough, E. Placing women in the history of psychology. *American Psychologist, 41*(1), 35–42.

Hall, G. Stanley (1904). *Adolescence. Its psychology and its relations to physiology, anthropology, sociology, sex, crime, religion and education* (Vol. I.). New York: Appleton & Co.

James, A. (1934/1987). *The diary of Alice James*. (L. Edel, Ed.). New York: Penguin Books.

James, W. (1902). *The varieties of religious experience*. London: Longmans, Green & Co.

Janet, P. (1930). L'analyse psychologique [Psychological analysis]. In C. Murchison (Ed.), *Psychologies of 1930*. Worcester, MA: Clark University Press.

Murphy, G., & Ballou, R. O. (1960). *William James on psychical research*. New York: Viking Press.

Peel, R. (1971). *Mary Baker Eddy. The years of trial*. New York: Holt, Rinehart & Winston.

Reisman, J. M. (1966). *The development of clinical psychology*. New York: Appleton-Century Crofts.

Schuster, M. L. (Ed.). (1940). *The world's great letters*. New York: Simon & Schuster.

Strouse, J. (1980). *Alice James, A biography*. Boston: Houghton Mifflin Co.

2

PSYCHOTHERAPY TO 1992: A HISTORICALLY SITUATED INTERPRETATION

PHILIP CUSHMAN

Psychotherapy is one of the most complex, colorful, and significant artifacts of our modern American cultural terrain, reflecting and shaping the central themes of the past 100 years. The history of psychotherapy is intertwined with the history of the United States: its promise, optimism, and vitality; its corruptions, collusions, and dangers. America's history is a grand history, filled with new beginnings and unlimited opportunities; yet it is also a history of oppression, exploitation, and profound betrayal. Most of all, it is a history of a mixture of people who attempt to live together without a common tradition of shared meanings in a rapidly changing world of powerful social and economic forces such as industrialization, urbanization, immigration, and secularization. It is the story of religious institutions and moral discourse that, confronted with economic and political pressures to conform and collude, have had difficulty maintaining authority and developing viable alternatives to sociopolitical trends. As a result, America's history has become a history of the modern ills of uncertainty and doubt. It was into this world that psychotherapy was born.

This chapter is based on the belief that, in order to understand American psychotherapy, we must study that world. We must study the historical contexts in which psychotherapy is embedded: its European antecedents, Victorian growth, modern confusion, and postmodern emptiness. Of course, one chapter cannot examine psychotherapy's entire history; it can, however, highlight important trends and explore their relation to the larger body politic. A historically situated approach might seem to most therapists unusual and perhaps even hostile. We are not used to thinking about our field in historical and political terms. This is an understandable response, since early theorists and historians of psychology portrayed psychology as an apolitical, transhistorical science in order to justify psychology's inclusion in American academia (Ash, 1983; Danziger, 1979). Also, therapists have not until recently been exposed to a historiographically rigorous treatment of psychology's history, nor have we been trained in critical textual analysis. However, although a wary response is understandable, it should not impede the pursuit of a more contextualized approach. Therefore, I will discuss in this chapter issues such as the match between the state's need to control the populace and Freud's early theory; mesmerism as the first secular American psychotherapy; some possible political reasons for the difference between Europe's emphasis on hysteria and American's emphasis on neurasthenia; the waning of Victorian *character* and the ascendance of the concept of *personality* and *the therapeutic*; the economic uses of the combination of the Mental Hygiene movement and the Freudian concept of the unconscious in the United States; Sullivan's interpersonal vision; the increasing interiorization of interactional processes by object relations theory; and the therapeutic uses of the *life-style solution* (the filling up of the empty self) by advertising and psychotherapy in the post–World War II era.

Above all, the common thread uniting all these historical eras and their psychological theories is the concept of the psychotherapist as the doctor of the *interior*. This is true not only for psychodynamic theories but also for post–World War II era modalities as theoretically diverse as humanistic psychology, self psychology, and cognitive psychology. Psychotherapists shape, maintain, and heal the realm of the private that the modern era has located within each self-contained individual. Psychological discourse has described the shape of the private and provided a rationale for gaining entrance *into* it through psychotherapy techniques, advertising images, and commercial commodities. Psychological practices have refined the technologies that psychotherapists, advertising executives, and political tacticians use to gain entrance into the private. These activities, of course, have far-ranging political implications both for the field of psychotherapy and for society as a whole.

HISTORICAL CONTEXT

This chapter reflects a different, more critical perspective than is typical in accounts of the development of psychotherapy. Rather than restricting an analysis to the influence of one psychotherapist upon another, by using the hermeneutic approach I seek to place the entire enterprise of therapy within a social and historical context. It is an attempt to guard against developing a celebration, a panegyric rather than a critical history. Celebrations in the guise of history are inaccurate and sometimes politically dangerous. In the case of psychotherapy, a celebratory history would be disastrous, because psychotherapy is central to our culture and important to the functioning of our late 20th-century social institutions (Prilleltensky, 1989). The most common way historians of psychotherapy celebrate rather than critically interpret their subject is by decontextualizing it. In other words, by failing to situate the various theories and practices of psychotherapy within the larger history and culture of their respective eras, some historians treat psychotherapy as though it were a transhistorical science that treats universal illnesses. These historians imply that because psychotherapy is a science, its findings are akin to facts and that because it is a transhistorical technology, its practices are apolitical.

Therefore, if we are to undertake a contextual history of psychotherapy, we would do well to consider its historical antecedents, economic constitutents, and political consequences. If we do not situate psychotherapy in its historical context, I am concerned that we will not do justice to the brave and creative effort that it is, nor will we be able to see our way to new constructions of theory and practice that will extend our capacity to help others.

In this chapter, I will touch upon theories as diverse as medieval Christian theology, Anton Mesmer's "animal magnetism", and practices as far removed from what we normally think of as psychotherapy as Christian Science and advertising. Without these examples we would be unable to interpret psychotherapy because we would not know in what historical constellation a particular therapy was embedded, how it was socially constructed, or what political and economic roles it played.

Considering that modern medical psychotherapy had not been officially invented until the second half of the 19th century, psychotherapy's rise to power has been rapid and pervasive. Especially in the last 100 years in the United States, there has been an amazing advance in its prevalence, status, and influence. In the early 1890s, Sigmund Freud set out to psychoanalyze himself and by so doing became the first analyst. In 1990 in California alone there are approximately 10,000 psychologists, 6,500 psychiatrists, 11,000 clinical social workers, and 19,000 marriage, family, and child therapists! What does this tremendous growth mean?

I do not think it means that psychotherapy has perfected its science. It means that psychotherapy somehow is so accurately attuned to the 20th-century cultural frame of reference that it has come to provide human services that are crucial, perhaps indispensable, to our current way of life. Psychotherapy has become emblematic of the postmodern era, a new age with a new sociopolitical configuration. It is the historian's job to interpret psychotherapy in such a way as to illuminate this new configuration, to describe the functions and influences of psychotherapy so that we can better understand and repair the world in which we live. If the role of the psychotherapist is constructor and caretaker of the realm of the interior, then we can ask a host of questions regarding the nature and function of personal interiority, how it is constructed, and what political and economic role it plays in our society. I understand that an exploration of this type may be unsettling to those of us actively involved in the practice of psychotherapy. But we must be able to tolerate our discomfort in order to better understand our work and bring it into an ever closer alignment with our goals and ideals. This chapter is an attempt to struggle with these issues.

SOCIAL CONSTRUCTIONISM

The ideas developed herein have grown out of the social constructionist argument articulated by writers such as Buss (1975, 1979), Gergen (1973, 1985), Harre (1984), Morawski (1984), and Sampson (1977, 1983, 1985). In earlier articles (Cushman, 1987, 1990, 1991) I have attempted to extend these ideas in order to discuss the current configuration of the self and its relationship to psychological discourse and practice. In this chapter I will argue that by tracing the changing configurations of the self at various times in Western society, we will be able to situate modern psychotherapy historically. Each society or era could be studied according to historical judgments pertaining to (a) the predominant configuration of self, (b) the illnesses with which that self was characteristically afflicted, (c) the institutions or officials most responsible for healing those illnesses, and (d) the technologies that particular institutions or practitioners have used in order to heal the self's characteristic illnesses.

Space does not permit a discussion of premodern eras in the West, their particular configurations of self, their illnesses, and their cures. It is crucially important to remember, however, that the predominant configuration of self of our current era, the self that Baumeister (1987), Bellah,

Madsen, Sullivan, Swidler, and Tipton (1985), Logan (1987), Sampson (1977, 1988), and Taylor (1989) have characterized as the bounded, masterful, hypertrophied self, is not universal and transhistorical. It is a self that has been configured in order to conform to the requirements of a particular era. Just as the Athenian playwright healed the communal self of classical Greece, and just as the hand-to-hand combat of a holy crusade healed by solidifying the Christian knight's relationship with his feudal lord and with God, so in our world it is psychotherapy that is one of the institutions responsible for healing the illnesses of the masterful, bounded 20th-century self.

IMPLICATIONS OF THE HISTORY OF THE SELF IN THE MODERN ERA

A few prominent writers such as Foucault (1979, 1980), Heiddeger (1977), Poster (1984), Taylor (1989), and Wachtel (1989) have developed an interpretation of the configuration of the modern self and its function within Western society. This interpretation suggests that the flowering of individualism begun by the Renaissance was both an expression and a cause of changing socioeconomic structures. The beginning of modern individualism both undermined the foundational underpinnings of the feudal system and brought financial growth and change by joining forces with mercantile capitalism. As the restrictiveness of the feudal world loosened, individuals were in theory free to move around geographically and become involved in the more fluid market economy. However, this also meant that they were in danger of being cut off from the communities, traditions, and families that gave meaning, stability, and continuity to their lives. Predictably, with increased mobility came a lessening of the power of religious authority. Equally predictable, given the growth of industrial power, was a horrific exploitation of the ex-peasants, who, stripped of their ties to land, family, community, and local religion, were transformed into "the working class."

Increased industrialization, urbanization, and secularization caused renewed interest in the physical world, the humanities, science, commerce, and rationality. However, the evolving self, ever more individual, presented new problems for the emerging modern state. The state had to develop ways to control a new kind of subject: more mobile, less constrained by tradition and religion, less confined by role, and less predictable. Feudal restrictions and roles had been broken; the emerging monarchy used the concept of the king's absolute control over the subject's body to control the populace (Foucault, 1979). But that idea had limited success.

Foucault in particular has suggested how the state solved this dilemma. By tracing the changing nature of criminal punishment from the ancient regime into the Enlightenment, Foucault (1979, 1988) showed how the configuration of the self changed from a self under the absolute control of the monarchy to a self that was isolated, less communal and more individual, a self more confused about right and wrong, the ethical and unethical. This new self was a self that needed guidance; tradition and its moral guidelines were just not as available as before. A sense of certainty and truth was lost.

Foucault argued that in this new atmosphere, the state needed to develop new ways of controlling an isolated, more confused and yet more independent subject. It began by using a new kind of expert: the modern philosopher and soon to be social scientist, who began developing techniques to observe, count, predict, and control the behavior of these new subjects (see Darnton, 1984, pp. 145–189). An important aspect of this new self was its sense of self-consciousness. Intellectual discourse, from Montaigne and Descartes to Bentham and Locke, helped construct a self that was forever observing itself, wondering about its true nature, agonizing about what it was hiding and what it was revealing, and speculating about its true nature and its true identity (Sass, 1987; Taylor, 1989). This discourse described a world in which subject is split off from object, soul from body, and reason from feeling. Bentham, in a move Foucault thought emblematic of the modern age, developed an idea for a new prison: one in which the prisoner was not physically dismembered and burned in public (as in the *ancien regime*) but continuously observed. The prison, the Panopticon, was designed so that the guards could always see the prisoner but the prisoner could never see the guards. Prisoners never knew when they were being observed; they were potentially exposed to public scrutiny at any time (Poster, 1984).

Foucault argued that this created or was designed to create in prisoners (a) an increasing tolerance for being observed, (b) an increasing propensity to and a capacity for observing themselves, (c) an increasing pressure to be "normal", and (d) increasing attempts to practice self-observation and conscious behavioral change. Foucault suggested that the Panopticon was the perfect symbol for the new order: A private, yet observable realm had to be socially constructed *inside* the self. The private had contributed to the overthrow of the feudal regime by being the seat of independent thinking and resistance to authority. But then the modern state was faced with a dilemma; it had to develop a means by which to control the new, less obedient populace and its more skeptical, independent interior. The realm of the private was potentially far too subversive because by definition it was not available to public control or manipulation. Thus, according to the Foucaultian analysis, evolving social institutions helped the state solve its dilemma by developing practices that gained entrance to the private (Rose, 1990). The new social philosophy and social sciences were in the process of developing a justification for entering, the means by which to enter, and a self that looked for, expected, and in the postmodern era, yearned to be entered.

Slowly, over time, the self was constructed to accept as a given that the realm of the private was to be scrutinized, entered, and ultimately controlled. This is why Foucault disagreed with what he called Freud's "repressive hypothesis" (1980). Foucault argued that Freud's belief that society by nature had to control sexuality and aggression was a history-bound concept that held a great deal of utility for the modern state. Freud's concept, in this view, was intellectual discourse that unknowingly justified the control of the state by describing a self that had to be controlled by "civilization." According to Foucault, Freud's theory thus became supportive data for Hobbes's (1651/1958) earlier contention that the state is needed to protect citizens from one another.

I am not arguing that the concept of individual aggression was Freud's creation, nor am I suggesting that Freud consciously colluded with the state in order to justify repressive regimes. Freud's genius in part lay in his ability to articulate—and, in certain ways, oppose—the frame of reference of the modern era in general and the Victorian age in particular. Foucault's analysis of Freud cannot be reduced to a conspiracy theory. His idea is not that a few powerful individuals conspired to manipulate the populace, but that culture and the practices of daily living, art, politics, and intellectual discourse mutually influence one another in complex ways that forcefully discredit unidimensional causative theories. Freud did not manipulate an era, he described it. By describing and interpreting it, however, he also reproduced it and affected it. This is, of course, true for any social artifact.

Over time the Western world had witnessed an unprecedented event: the rise of self-contained individualism. The modern age featured an overarching valorization of the unique individual who was politically free, unencumbered by community, religion, and tradition and who contained within himself or herself all hope for transcendence and meaning. As we shall see, however, the underside of the modern individualist agenda has also resulted in moral illiteracy, confusion, isolation, loneliness, and self-preoccupation, leading to the need for the social practice of psychotherapy.

THE VICTORIAN ERA IN EUROPE

In certain respects the Victorian age was the culmination of the modern agenda. The bourgeois self was a secular, rational, subjective, divided, sexually conflicted, linear self that viewed the world as objectifiable and quantitative (Lowe, 1982). With the ascendance of the bourgeoisie, everything was thought to be reducible, knowable, understandable, and figured into the calculations of everyday living. The force of religion became increasingly circumscribed, and hard work assumed an almost transcendent value. As the workplace changed from the rural farm or medieval guild to the urbanized, industrialized factory or business office, workers and management alike suffered from an increasing alienation. Especially in the middle classes, this seriously affected family life; women were increasingly restricted, desexualized, and removed from the seats of power. Their primary responsibility was thought to be the protection of the family as a "haven in a heartless world" (Lasch, 1977). Thus the gulf between genders widened and became more distinct. Before the 19th century, the unknown was thought to reside in the external world. Slowly, however, with the increased belief in rationality, science, and calculation, the unknown became removed from or calculated out of the external physical world, and relocated. Freud "found" it in the interior of the self, hidden and secret: the unconscious.

We could describe the Victorian self, then, as interiorized, rational, secular, hardworking, self-disciplined, frugal, split along gender, and secretly sexual and aggressive. Four predominant psychological illnesses of the Victorian European self were hysteria, neurasthenia, sexual perversion, and violent criminal behavior such as murder and rape (Drinka, 1984). The causes of these illnesses were thought to be located in the private unconscious in the form of uncontrollable, uncivilized impulses. Interestingly, hysteria was understood to be primarily a female disease, whereas sexual perversion and criminal violence primarily afflicted males.

Physicians developed competing theories regarding the etiology and treatment of these diseases. Freud, however, eventually carried the day. He was first a student of Charcot and Breuer, but their formulations were not sufficient for him. He also shared information and ideas with Wilhelm Fliess, a physician who thought that hysteria was an expression of sexual distress caused by the malformation of certain bones in the nose. His solution was to operate and rearrange the patient's facial structure. After several years, Freud broke with Fliess and proclaimed his own sexual theories of hysteria, which he then elaborated over the course of his life into a complex theory of the mind.

It is important to note that Victorian illnesses were thought to be caused by the eruption of primitive, intrapsychic sexual and aggressive impulses or *drives* that the individual could not effectively control. This was especially true for hysteria. Drawing on 19th-century physics, Freud conceived of the mind as a kind of hydraulic machine. It was fueled by energy (libido) that had to be released in one form or another. If it was repressed, the energy would take up another form; it might be projected, displaced, or sublimated, but eventually it had to be expressed. Since many of these sexual or aggressive impulses were potentially dangerous to others and destructive of the social order, the goal was to effectively control the machine so that libido was expressed in socially appropriate or productive activity. Freud, in tune with the cultural frame of his time, believed that, by nature, women were passive and their wish to be active and powerful was simply an expression of penis envy; with proper treatment their "phallic" behavior would subside and they would be able to return to their natural feminine passivity. Recently some feminist and Foucaultian historians (e.g., Bernheimer & Kahane, 1985) have argued that a scientific justification for the control of the populace in general and women in particular was implicitly embedded in Freud's theory.

There were two primary institutions responsible for curing the European Victorian illnesses of hysteria, neurasthenia, sexual perversion, and criminal violence: medicine and the state. Medicine used several technologies to combat Victorian illnesses. Escape, travel, rest, and moral exhortation were prescribed for the neurasthenic; lifting the repression through hypnosis or free association were prescribed for the hysteric; masturbation, thought by some to be the primary cause of hysteria, was combated through proscription (and occasionally clitoridectomy or castration; see Englehardt, 1985). The state used incarceration (either jail or the asylum) for sexual "perverts" and the criminally violent (Scull, 1989).

THE VICTORIAN ERA IN THE UNITED STATES

The Victorian self in the United States presented the basic Victorian qualities such as rationality, dividedness, sexual conflictedness, and linearity, but it was somewhat more optimistic and naive than its European counterpart. There were general indications that the predominant middle-class self was tense, repressed, overworked, somewhat humorless, effete, and overintellectualized (Drinka, 1984; Lowe, 1982; Marcus, 1984; Slotkin, 1985). The illnesses characteristic of this American self, like its European counterpart, were described by the medical profession as hysteria and neurasthenia. Unlike its European counterpart, however, the suffering of the American bourgeois self was more often described and conceptualized as neurasthenia than hysteria, even though the symptoms were often quite similar.

There were nonmedical descriptions of the problems of this self as well. For instance, from the literature and popular culture of the era it could be implied that many middle-class American males suffered from tension and overwork (Drinka, 1984; Fuller, 1982); middle-class American females were tense, exhausted, and cut off from the world of commerce and politics. They were prisoners of the "sanctuary" of the home, frustrated and underutilized (Lasch, 1977). Both men and women complained of or were accused of being too citified and cut off from the land, "honest" physical labor, and their own bodies.

MESMERISM: THE BEGINNING OF AMERICAN PSYCHOTHERAPY

A number of observers have suggested that one of the prominent characteristics of the Victorian cultural landscape in the United States was spiritual emptiness, moral confusion, and a yearning for religious sensibility and intense experience (Fuller, 1982; Lears, 1983; Susman, 1973). This set of problems in living was the province of a new type of religious or spiritual practice that emerged in the middle of the century. Variously referred to as mesmerism, mind-cure philosophy, positive thinking, abundance theory, or spiritualism, the institution of popular, unchurched religious psychology emerged and became quite popular in the mid- and late 19th century (Fuller, 1982, p. 167). These ideologies could be interpreted, in part, as a response to an urge of middle-class Victorians to break out of the rigid strictures of the bourgeois world of secularism, quantification, and linear thinking. Some of these practices, most notably mesmerism, were thought by Meyer (1980) and Fuller (1982) to be the first secular psychotherapies. These movements featured practices such as hypnosis, telekinesis, telepathy, spiritual advice, instruction in religious texts, psychological counseling, and group experiences.

Charles Poyen brought mesmerism to the United States in 1836. It found a constituency suffering from strange psychiatric symptoms such as listlessness, convulsions, physical weakness, and moral confusion. In retrospect, some American historians have attributed these symptoms to the social ills caused by the vast upheavals of industrialization, urbanization, European immigration, and secularization. Middle-class America, Fuller (1982, p. 108) and Wiebe (1967) have noted, was at this time a "society without a core." Although at first Poyen faithfully followed Mesmer, his practices soon took on a characteristic American cast, emphasizing optimism and pragmatism. As the years passed, mesmerism evolved and gave birth to ever new and more American offshoots, anticipating the immense cultural changes that would come into being at the turn of the century. These changes caused what Rieff (1966) has called the "triumph of the therapeutic," the ascendance of a new cultural frame of reference that featured a secular, scientific psychology. Today the psychological therapeutic stands unchallenged as the healer of the American soul.

The major underlying tenet in all these theories was a belief in the accessibility and availability of the realm of the spirit in a nontraditional and experiential setting. They featured a secular universalism and a valorization of self-expression that was rooted in the larger Romantic and Counter-Enlightenment movements in Europe. Characteristic of this universal vision was Anton Mesmer's statement: "There is only one illness, and one cure." Poyen used hypnotic trance to help patients get in touch with a generalized, nondenominational spirituality (i.e., animal magnetism) that dwells within every individual. After contact with this source of spiritual energy, patients felt invigorated, renewed, transformed. Mesmerism and its heirs emphasized alternative states of consciousness, exotica, American naivete and optimism, and a secular, anti-intellectual spiritualism.

However, mesmerism also claimed to be a scientific technology. By solving a spiritual problem through science, it revealed itself to be quintessentially Victorian. Mesmerism, and especially its heirs, also foreshadowed many 20th-century forms of psychotherapy and contemporary restrictive groups such as religious cults, mass marathon psychology trainings, and New Age experiential programs. Seen in this light, mesmerism was simply the first in a long line of attempts to heal the psychological problems, spiritual hunger, and moral confusion of the American unchurched.

Through their exposure to American life, mesmerists and mind curists recognized the existence of new problems and saw new possibilities. Americans craved ethical guidance, a renewed sense of purpose and authority, and intense spiritual experiences. The new popular religious psychologies delivered all of this, complete with a claim that this spiritual experience was not sectarian but scientific (a perspective that was clearly on the ascent).

Even William James, one of the most important psychologists of the era, was interested in mind cure (Meyer, 1980).

Historians have found several aspects of mesmerism and its offshoots that set the stage for 20th-century psychotherapy. It promoted ideas that are quintessentially American and have become permanent theoretical features of our 20th-century psychological landscape. One, mesmerism valorized apolitical interiority. In other words, the doctrine stated that individuals suffered from inner emotional or spiritual ills that were caused by personal inadequacies and spiritual deprivation, not by the political and economic conditions of their lives. Two, it relied on an early type of cognitivism—that is, emotional illness was thought to be caused by improper thoughts, usually negative in nature. Health, in this theory, was the direct product of thinking the right thoughts. Thinking properly, according to certain Positive Thinkers such as Mary Baker Eddy, could *directly* affect the material world (Meyer, 1980). Three, its healing technology emphasized a mystical transformation of identity from an everyday, "false" self to an extraordinary, "true" self. Identity was thought to be a function of one's personal psychology rather than the stipulations of communal norms and roles. Four, it argued that there was a direct progression from psychological cure to economic abundance. According to this way of thinking, personal wealth was limited only by individual psychological development, not by the socioeconomic arrangements of power and class. Obviously, mesmerism and its heirs developed ideologies that fit beautifully with sociohistorical trends, supported the political status quo, and protected the privileges of the economic elite.

MEDICAL APPROACHES TO EMOTIONAL ILLS

The American emphasis on economic productivity as a justifier for the state is also present in the discourse of medical psychotherapy. Medical psychotherapy in America started slowly in the 19th century. It was only in 1870, when George Beard developed his technique of electrical "tonics," that medicine began to explicitly diagnose and then effectively treat neurasthenia, thus joining the other institutions in their efforts to heal the Victorian psychological self. It is important to notice that common Victorian ills were seen by Beard in a manner quite different from that of European physicians. Whereas Europeans such as Richard von Kraft-Ebing, Max Nordau, Cesare Lombruso, and Freud saw symptoms as eruptions of dangerous instincts or degenerate traits, Beard theorized that Victorian symptoms were the result of exhaustion and a lack of natural bodily electricity. Starting with the optimistic (and very American) assumption that individuals were naturally energetic and sought to work and achieve, Beard decided that the stress of "brain work" in bourgeois life caused patients, especially "sensitive" souls, to be depleted of energy, much like an electric light bulb "browns out" when deprived of its required energy. The cure that Beard devised was directly in line with his theory: rest cure, electrical stimulation, and, finally, friendly moral exhortation. Beard's aim was to remove patients from their everyday environments in order to reduce the level of stress, and to recharge their natural emotional energy by direct doses of electricity. Thomas Edison, the inventor of the electric light, was a close friend of and a strong influence on Beard. S. Weir Mitchell (1878), another renowned American physician, also relied heavily on a rigid regime of rest and dietary restriction. The American cure, with its emphasis on restoring energy, was something of a departure from Freud's stress on dangerous, secret impulses that threatened to overwhelm the safeguards of civilization. Beard sought to revitalize the individual's energy and free it for work, while Freud sought to control and rechannel it.

It appears that the European self was often conceptualized in psychological discourse as a dangerous self, sexual and aggressive. The self became ill when its instincts overwhelmed or conflicted with the ego and the safeguards installed by culture and spilled out in overt behavior (e.g., violent crime) or symbolic behavior (e.g., hysterical seizures, compulsive rituals, aggressive jokes). Psychoanalysis, as the technology that treated the European Victorian self, uncovered hidden instincts by interpreting symbolic language, carefully observing actual behavior, and courageously speaking the undisguised truth about sex and aggression.

The American self, on the other hand, was configured somewhat differently. The early 19th-century American self was an eager, achievement-oriented self that, although base in its animal nature, could transcend that impediment through religious devotion and hard work. Later in the century, as the country became more secularized, work took on an increasing role in the sanctification of the individual. Its most serious illness was a lack of economic productivity, which was treated by psychiatry through the technology of the rest cure and the administration of electricity directly into spent muscles. The aim of Beard's treatment was the housewife returned to the management of the bourgeois home, and the bourgeois male returned with renewed enthusiasm to the world of commerce and brain work.

Nonpsychiatric treatment strategies in the United States during the second half of the 19th century usually centered around moral exhortation and encouragement of one form or another. For instance, one type of exhortive genre was the advice manual. The manuals were published by small presses and written by the philosopher-preacher-teacher, a common type in this era. They were popular and numerous within the middle classes. Susman (1973) and Lears (1983) have both reported on the prevalence of theories of restriction and discipline before the 1890s.

Why were these Victorian symptoms interpreted in such different ways, depending on the geographical location of the psychiatrist? Could we not infer that the European and American diagnoses were different because the concerns of the two societies were somewhat different? The Europeans, with a relatively concentrated, industrialized, urbanized population, were primarily concerned with how to control their populations. The modern era in Europe had been convulsed first by centuries of monarchical and religious wars and then by great revolutionary uprisings. Also, multigenerational bourgeois families were often living in close quarters. Young middle-class men were sometimes trapped in boring and depersonalizing jobs (Drinka, 1984). Young women were forced into idleness and restricted to the home at the same time that communications about the world and its possibilites were flooding into Europe. The conflicts between forced idleness, sexual restrictiveness, and the increased possibilities of real world adventures were somewhat overwhelming to young Victorians, especially women who comprised the vast majority of hysterical patients (Van den Berg, 1961). At the same time, religion was beginning to lose its power to persuade and threaten (Drinka, 1984). Is there any wonder that the forces of social and political conservatism were so concerned with controlling the sexual behavior and gender roles of the youth, especially women?

In America the social picture was different. One of the main preoccupations of the state was how to increase economic productivity. There was a continent to settle and an economy to manage and industrialize. The worst illness imaginable must have been a lack of ambition, energy, and will. American physicians, faced with symptoms that debilitated white-collar workers, viewed these symptoms through the concerns of their time and place. They looked at the suffering and saw not dangerous impulses but a lack of resolve and energy.

I am not implying that the state in either Europe or America conspired to force physicians to falsify their diagnoses and treatment goals. I am instead suggesting that psychotherapy theory and practice are social artifacts and as such both reflect and shape the configuration of the self and the illnesses of their era. Artifacts such as political institutions, psychotherapy theories, and common psychiatric illnesses fit together. They are not direct, conscious conspiracies; they are interactive forces that mutually influence one another.

With this disclaimer in mind, I think it is possible to sum up this section on the Victorian bourgeois era. In Europe the configuration of the self as container for dangerous, universal human instincts fit with the state's attempt to justify its role as the official controller of selves. In the United States the configuration of the self as an ambitious, energetic seeker of spiritual and practical improvement fit well with the view that the state was the guarantor of independent, economically productive selves.

AMERICA AT THE TURN OF THE CENTURY

In this section we will begin to see the growing hegemony of the therapeutic in 20th-century America, the complex and multilayered relationship between politics and "personal growth" that has come to dominate our time. Historians have described how an important change in the concept of the self came about in the 1890s. They described this as a change from the dominance of the ingredient character to the ingredient personality as the most important quality of the self.

Susman (1973) and Lears (1983) studied advice manuals, a genre quite popular with the middle classes during the second half of the 19th century. Before the 1890s, the most important ingredient of the self was thought to be moral character. Character, preached the advice manuals, was the only safeguard against a life of sloth, waste, or degeneracy. Fortunately, as befits a young and ambitious nation, the manuals taught that character and moral integrity could be built through self-discipline, thrift, hard work, cleanliness, and religious instruction.

Personality, on the other hand, was conceived of as the sum of personal qualities that caused one to be liked by others. Unlike character, which stressed moral integrity and stability, personality was expressed by one's ability to stand out in a crowd. Personal charisma, getting others to be attracted to you, became more important than performing the morally correct act. The United States was becoming an increasingly urbanized nation of faceless masses, peopled by markedly secular citizens, and fueled by an economy run by white-collar managers. Several writers such as Fuller (1982), Lears (1983), Levin (1987), and Zaretsky (1976) have speculated that the lack of community feeling, spiritual experience, and meaningful work was causing personal problems, ethical confusion, and psychiatric symptoms in the middle classes. Correspondingly, the search for personal recognition, spiritual meaning, and unalienated, bodily connectedness became major concerns. The development of personality as an answer to each of these three concerns was pushed by advice manuals, mind-cure preachers, psychiatrists, and advertising campaigns.

Psychologists like William James were drawn to mind-cure philosophy at the turn of the century. By that time, what had started out as mesmerism's attempt to help patients get in touch with the ever-present divine within each person had combined with the concern for developing personality and evolved into a kind of think-properly-and-grow-rich program (Meyer, 1980). Lears (1983) has explained how the stresses of modern living, especially the alienating, less down-to-earth managerial jobs, contributed to an epidemic of derealization and a lack of expressiveness and spontaneity in the middle classes. Advertising became increasingly influential at this time. It addressed itself directly to the worries of confused and frightened individuals who were searching for a way to reintegrate their sense of selfhood.

We could describe this turn-of-the-century self as confused and faceless. It was beset by feelings of derealization, moral confusion, and a lack of a sense of meaning and a place in society. The professions ministering to this self were mind cure and advertising. The technology of the mind-cure practitioner was positive thinking and abundance theory. Advertising attempted to cure by implying that products would magically transform the customer's life. Ads associated the product with happy, clean, vigorous (and increasingly "popular") models and "imaginary state[s] of being" (Lears, 1983, p. 19). They also gave so-called scientific guidance to its readership, instructing them on how to make their way through the bewildering maze of modern living in a world bereft of religious and moral certainty.

EUROPEAN PSYCHOANALYSIS AT THE TURN OF THE CENTURY

Into this particularly American setting in 1909 stepped the quintessentially European Victorian, Freud. In the decade after the turn of the century, Freud had begun what would become an intellectual revolution in Europe. Slowly his ideas regarding infantile sexuality, the Oedipus complex, and the unconscious began to be regarded with more interest. The small band of loyal followers that had initially gathered around him had grown and were becoming more confident. Once each week the group would meet to discuss cases and argue theory. Out of this mix would come Freud's increasingly sophisticated theoretical formulations. During the 39 years Freud was alive in the 20th century, his theory would go through changes of emphasis and his practices, structural shifts. What was originally a highly didactic and rationalistic theory became over time a sophisticated explication of the unconscious and an emotional *working through* of transference. What was once a kind of day-long walking psychoanalysis with

Gustav Mahler around the town of Leiden (Grunfeld, 1979, p. 37) became over time a 50-minute hour. It was a most remarkable and creative effort.

But there was conflict and anger in the inner circle (Roazen, 1984). Many historians have reported that Freud was an authoritarian leader who was completely committed to his theory and could tolerate little disagreement. Also, it began to appear that the social forces at work in the early 20th century could sometime in the near future make psychological technologies a powerful road to power and fame. The battle over who held the truth of psychoanalysis, and thus who would lead the movement in the future, was soon joined. As a result, several members of the inner circle, most notably Adler, Jung, Rank, and Reich, would resign or were cast out. Much has been written regarding these defections. Some writers have suggested that theoretical differences masked personality clashes. Kurzweil (1989) has recently suggested that differences between disciples were often due as much to culture and politics as to theory. Unfortunately, space does not allow an in-depth discussion of this fascinating chapter in psychoanalytic history. It is important to note Reiff's suggestion that Freud's rejection of Jung (Reiff, 1966) was based on Freud's disagreement with Jung's basic program: Jung's attempt to forge a holistic theory of religious transformation. Could it be that the cultural differences between Freud's vibrant, passionate, conflicted, dangerous, diverse Vienna and Jung's more stable, homogeneous Zurich were reflected in their two theories? However, for many observers the events surrounding World War II justified Freud's rejection of Jung's future leadership role. Jung collaborated with the Nazis when they took control of Europe, and he accepted control of a new psychoanalytic establishment tolerated and used by the Nazis. He denounced Freudian psychoanalysis as "the Jewish science" and claimed that it was unfit to minister to the Aryan soul (Karier, 1976). After the war Jung at least was able to publicly disagree with Nazi ideology, unlike several intellectuals such as literary figures T. S. Eliot, Ezra Pound, and philosopher Martin Heidegger.

FREUD IN AMERICA

When Freud was asked to speak at Clark College in Massachusetts in 1909, Jung and Ferenczi, still in the early years of their friendship with Freud, accompanied him. Much to everyone's surprise, they were warmly and enthusiastically received. William James, perhaps the most famous and well-respected psychologist in America, greeted Freud by exclaiming, "Yours is the psychology of the future." Hale (1971) reported that, incredibly, "within six years of the Clark conference psychoanalysis had eclipsed all other psychotherapies in the nation's magazines" (p. 397).

Indeed, Freud's theories have taken over the United States, both in psychotherapy practice and in popular culture. Yet the spirit of America also infused psychoanalysis with an optimistic and pragmatic spirit that, in many ways, has transformed it and used it in ways never dreamed of by Freud. Demos (1981) explored the irony that the United States, which Freud so much despised, granted him a great deal of respect and success. Demos suggested that "the main line of historical change in the 19th century . . . [created] a situation in which Oedipal issues became highly charged for many people. And among all the Western counries, this situation was most fully elaborated in the U.S." (p. 304).

Demos cited several historical reasons for this irony, emphasizing especially the American concern for instilling in male children the conflicting qualities of independence and self-control, guilt, and a kind of internal sense of self-government. All of these combined to imply "a massive intensification of the parent–child bond" (p. 299). Yet Demos pointed out that the combination of geographical immigration and American economic ideology defined male success as the surpassing of the father. Thus a unique type of competition was injected into the father–son relationship that fit very well with Freudian theory.

American psychiatry in the first decade of the 20th century was still grounded in the physiological model of illness and cure, whereas psychoanalysis presented an approach that was psychological as well as scientific. Psychoanalysis appeared to be more proper and civilized than mind cure, more scientific than Christian science and positive thinking, and more medical than advertising. But most important, psychoanalysis took American ideology into a new realm of cultural experience. It provided a new terrain for enhancement and productivity: the realm of the private, unconscious interior. Psychoanalysis provided something that was beyond the grasp of positive thinking: a new, virgin territory, an *interior frontier*.

The concept of the unconscious provided several unintended productive economic possibilities. It provided a new territory for psychological exploration and excavation, and by definition, it assigned the new terrain to professional psychologists and psychoanalysts. It also gave expanded meanings and possibilities to the concept of the therapeutic. The transformations that modern life in the United States demanded of its citizens (e.g., the continuing self-development of personality, the economic successes, the geographical mobility, the creative use of leisure activities, the independence from others, and the adaptability to new places and new roles) now took on a more explicit, medicalized, mysterious form with the "discovery" of the unconscious (Kovel, 1980). Therapeutic transformation became at once more explicit and more mysterious; it became the province of a highly trained group of medical experts using a new, complex, highly scientific technology. At the same time it unintentionally opened up countless opportunities for other industries, such as advertising, entertainment, and politics, because the concept of the unconscious provided potential resources that could be exploited for profit. For example, unconscious sexual desire could be used to sell products unrelated to sex, such as cars or cigarettes. Jealousy and envy could be used to manipulate consumers into buying what they don't actually need or even desire. Competitiveness or rage against the oedipal rival or siblings could be exploited in order to sway voters toward one candidate or against another. The possibilities were endless.

Thus, psychoanalysis inadvertently brought to America a crucial piece of the capitalist puzzle: a description of the unconscious. Just as the American wilderness had to be settled and conquered, so too did the internal wilderness. Through Freud, the therapeutic in the United States took on a "deeper," more interior meaning. Therapeutic improvement became an infinitely more complex and psychological phenomenon, one less natural and automatic than the advocates of mind cure could ever have imagined.

There were powerful forces at work in America that influenced and diluted psychoanalysis' message. The Mental Hygiene movement began as a reform movement in the spirit of the general Progressivism of the era and was greatly influenced by the philosophy of Pragmatism. It was started by a former psychiatric hospital inmate, Clifford Beers, but by 1912 famous psychologists and physicians such as Adolf Meyer, William James, and Thomas Salmon (of the U.S. Public Health Service) had joined and taken control of the movement. Once it received federal funding, it became an influential force in psychiatric hospital reform and especially preventive education.

The movement applied the bourgeois values of quantification, objectification, and cleanliness (see Lowe, 1982) to the realm of emotional and psychological complaints. Kovel (1980) argued that it neutralized and co-opted Freud's more radical posture by conceptualizing the unconscious as a container for psychological uncleanliness. The proper middle-class solution, then, was to periodically sanitize the unconscious. This led, in Kovel's view, to a diluted, banalized psychoanalysis. A few other writers, notably Adler (1988), Jacoby (1975), and Lichtman (1982) have argued that Freud's theories carry within them aspects of a politically radical and historically situated theory that remain mostly unrecognized by many historians of psychotherapy. In line with Kovel's argument, it is true that the more radical combination of psychoanalysis and Marxism that in Europe produced the *rundbriefe* within Freud's inner circle (Jacoby, 1983) and the critical theory of the Frankfurt school (Held, 1980) were never influential in the United States.

The Mental Hygiene movement also contributed to and profited by the modern historical trend in the West that delegitimized religious judgments about social deviance and replaced them with scientific "facts." Deviants were no longer judged as "undesirable, bad, mad, or possessed: they . . . [were] *sick*, and need[ed] the ministrations of a mental hygienist . . ." (Kovel, 1980, p. 82; italics in original). The unseating of religion as the dominant arbiter of deviance, Kovel thought, was indispensable to capitalism's growing hegemony, because the moral codes of traditional religion were hostile to the obsessive consumption of modern commodities. The Mental Hygiene movement furthered that historical process by substituting psychological science, a discourse that claimed to be detached from all moral codes, in place of religion.

Finally, Kovel noted that by conceiving of emotional problems as analogous to physical illness (i.e., in need of hygienic practices), the movement led to their medicalization and objectification. It was then possible, in a more banalized and objectified atmosphere, for psychotherapy to be calculated according to quantifiable measures such as the amount of time and money expended during treatment. This, in time, allowed psychotherapy to take "its place in the general framework of capitalist relations" (Kovel, 1980, p. 81). Psychotherapy was on its way to becoming a profession within the medical establishment.

Politically, it was after Salmon joined the hygienist movement in 1912 that a connection was made between the state and the psychiatric profession that continues to this day (Reisman, 1976). The advent of World War I brought a host of 20th-century problems and opportunities that attracted psychologists to the war effort. The state needed to be able to evaluate soldiers on a scale never before attempted (Samelson, 1979), and the technology of modern warfare created a new kind of casualty, the psychiatric casualty. The Veterans Administration had an immediate postwar need for psychiatrists and psychologists. The government responded by funding large projects under the auspices of the newly created National Committee for Mental Hygiene and expanding training programs in universities and campaigns of public education (Reisman, 1976, p. 135).

BEHAVIORISM AND BIG BUSINESS

Another important trend in psychological theory that appeared before World War I and grew in strength in the postwar era was the successful attempt by experimental psychologists such as John Watson to define psychology as "a purely objective experimental branch of natural science. Its theoretical goal is the prediction and control of *behavior*" (Watson, 1913). Foucault could not have said it any better. However, again we see the peculiarly American way in which control is exercised: Through optimism and pragmatism in the realm of business. Watson urged psychologists to focus on "problems of living . . . and . . . to deal with matters of practical consequence, e.g., the psychology of advertising and of testing. . . ." (Reisman, 1976, p. 134). Two years later, in 1915, Watson was elected president of the American Psychological Association (APA). Five years after his presidency, he began working in an advertising agency (Marchand, 1985), and by 1924 he had achieved the position of vice president of a prominent firm. In this pursuit he had the company of A. A. Brill, who used his psychological expertise to develop advertising that encouraged women to smoke, and of many amateur psychologists and public relations men such as Edward Bernays, Freud's nephew. Psychology was used by business to ensure that consumption kept pace with production. Bernays advised advertising executives to use psychology in order to "make customers" by understanding "the personality . . . of a potentially universal public" (Bernays, 1928, pp. 50–52, 63). Walter Scott, an industrial psychologist, was president of APA in 1919; he argued that psychology could determine what type of worker would fit with a particular job. Scott thought that the task and worker were "a unity, a biological kind of relationship . . . . [in which] the man [would profit] from his labor, not only materially, but intellectually and emotionally" (Reisman, 1976, p. 135). Psychology had become the scientific adviser for two prominent 20th-century middle-class forms of the therapeutic: advertising and personnel management.

One way in which behaviorism was able to develop applications more relevant to everyday life in the office and factory was to moderate the theories of radical behaviorism (e.g., Skinner, 1931, 1972). It did this by hypothesizing mechanisms within the organism that mediated between the environmental stimulus and the organism's behavioral response. Hull and Tolman first suggested such mediating mechanisms (Leahey, 1987, pp. 389–393). Through the hypothetical mediations, mental processes such as memory and intention could then be hypothesized and discussed, which in turn helped explain symbolic processes and important considerations such as motivations, values, and attitudes. Eventually this line of behaviorist theorizing contributed to the development of cognitive psychology, a growing force in psychotherapy practice. It is important to notice that, even as the least interior of all psychotherapies, behaviorism has to some degree succumbed to the cultural trend of situating important psychological events within the self-contained individual.

To summarize this interpretation of the early 20th-century self, we could say that this self was a container for various ingredients of personality that could be developed and presented socially in order for the individual to become noticed, popular, and economically successful in the emerging world of consumerism and mass electronic media. Included in the container was a hidden unconscious that was conceptualized as somewhat dirty and in need of what the new Mental Hygiene movement conceived of as a periodic cleaning (Kovel, 1980). Psychotherapists, industrial psychologists, and advertising executives were early 20th-century practitioners of therapeutic instruction and transformation. These healers used various techniques: Advertising executives used techniques that linked products with imaginary states of being (Lears, 1983, p. 19), industrial psychologists used fledgling assessment tools and personal exhortation, and psychotherapists used talking cures.

THE ERA OF THE 1920s AND 1930s

The 1920s brought an increasing elaboration of the more prominent theories of psychotherapy, particularly psychoanalysis and behaviorism. Although in this decade psychoanalysis had to contend with the continuing popularity and productivity of the outcasts Adler, Jung, Rank, and Reich, for the most part the 1930s has been characterized as one of "consolidation and dissemination" (Reisman, 1976, p. 177). Freud, despite his ongoing struggle with cancer, continued his creative and prolific writing. Chief among his works in the 1920s was his elaboration of the tripartite organization of the mind (id, ego, and superego), and his origination of the concept of the death instinct. Rank hypothesized that anxiety was in part caused by the birth trauma and the overall process of psychological separation. This was an idea that would have greater salience in the second half of the century, when relationship issues appeared in the forefront of popular thought. Adler elaborated on his more socially oriented therapy, including his idea that the perception of inferiority (the major cause of neurosis) was itself caused by damaging interactions within the family, such as the emotional rejection of the child. In the 1920s, American psychologists, in a direction similar to Adler's, were struggling to integrate the influences of the social environment with what was conceived of as the individual's inherited capacities and intrapsychic mechanisms. Psychologists were also attempting to delineate and justify their place within the university

(Ash, 1983; Danziger, 1979) and medical practice (Reisman, 1976; Samelson, 1979). Early clinical psychologists thought that treatment should be educational in nature and stressed early behavior modification techniques (Reisman, 1976, pp. 70–90). An interest in juvenile delinquency moved child guidance clinics, which usually employed social workers, to become more interested in patterns of family interaction.

Freud (1961a, 1961b), Jung (1923), Kretschmer (1925), and Berman (1921) published or extended broad typologies during these years. Although unacknowledged at the time, the increased interest in typologies was probably motivated by an attempt to address the challenge presented by broad, nonneurotic patterns of emotional suffering not adequately dealt with by Freud's early intrapsychic conflict model or Jung's earlier formulations. World War I had given psychological testing an enormous boost in the United States (Samelson, 1979). The increasing bureaucratic needs of the state and the growing need of industry and advertising to develop more effective influence and personnel management techniques contributed to the demand for more elaborate typologies and more accurate psychological testing, including market research techniques.

Kovel (1980) has suggested that in analyzing psychotherapy's place within 20th-century life, we must take into account the major problem of 20th-century capitalism: economic stagnation. He argued that capitalism responded to this problem by emphasizing the consumption of commodities and by increasing technical control of labor. These two agendas were accomplished, Kovel suggested, by using psychological techniques "to penetrate and control everyday life, including [especially] subjectivity" (1980, p. 75).

The American emphasis on the analyzability of the unconscious and the possibility of sublimating the id infused psychoanalysis with a characteristic American optimism and economic preoccupation. The unconscious was conceived of as a partly hidden terrain that could be made known, understood, and thus eventually used for "civilized" (especially economic) purposes. Kovel argued that most psychotherapy theories—by the 1920s subsumed under the rubric of mental hygiene—took as a given the ultimate value of psychological "health." In order for individuals to be healthy, psychotherapy had to enter psychologically into the individual's private interior. Thus, the 20th-century self was constructed so as to *want* to be psychologically entered.

The losses of community and of tradition were prime elements in the construction of a self available and even seeking inner cleaning and guidance. In the past, social norms and understandings were thought to possess certainty and divine authority; the "truth" was passed down from parents to children. By the first three decades of the 20th century, however, parents appeared openly confused as to what to impart, and children were less secure about the value of what their parents could offer. The world had become increasingly complicated, and sources of communal and religious guidance were losing their authority. As a result, scientific findings and professional expertise began to take on a new importance. Research (Susman, 1973) on the growing popularity of child-rearing advice manuals in the early years of the 20th century has demonstrated a willingness on the part of the middle classes to turn to and rely upon "scientific" guidance. Individuals were experiencing a lack of emotional resources and personal conviction that was caused by a loss of community. It was into this absence, increasingly conceptualized as an interior void, that the processes of advertising and psychotherapy inserted themselves; they were welcomed by the middle classes.

I would like to argue that the individual's feelings and thoughts, because they were located by psychotherapy as being *inside* the bounded, masterful self, were considered by psychotherapists to be products of intrapsychic processes (see Greenberg & Mitchell, 1983), and not the products of culture, history, or interpersonal interactions. Although Freud taught that the superego was given its content in part by culture, the cultural content was thought to be mediated and distorted by the instincts and inadequacies of childhood and influenced from its inception by unavoidable oedipal conflicts. Some theorticians such as Adler (1988), Jacoby (1975), and Lacan (1977) have more recently interpreted the oedipal conflict as Freud's attempt to articulate the constructivist nature of social processes and the politically subversive practices of culture critique and deconstruction. In this interpretation there is no autonomous, conflict-free ego or unquestioned reality principle. Instead, the ego is understood as other. However, this complex, historically situated interpretation was not the one usually developed by psychoanalytic institutes. Institutes preferred a more normative, politically adaptive view. The superego was conceived of as a kind of imposition from the external world that could be resisted and modulated. The greatest reality, and the ultimate seat of legitimate initiative and authority, was the interior, ego-led self. By denying the central influence of history and culture, early psychotherapy in the United States mystified the social influence and control exercised by the state and by social institutions of all kinds. This caused symptoms characteristic of the modern Western world such as alienation, a desire for commodities, and extreme competitiveness to be considered natural and unavoidable and thereby outside the realm of politics and history.

During the historic 500-year development of the modern self, the seat of initiative, control, and transcendence progressively moved from outside to inside the self. This development aided in the neutralization and eventual overthrow of the legitimacy of external authority such as the feudal state, the monarchy, and the Church. Especially in the 20th century, when the final vestiges of religious morality were loosened and no longer stood in the way of conspicuous consumption, the self came to be considered the only legitimate seat of opinion and desire. From that time on, it became expedient for corporate capitalism and the state to control by devising strategies that made their influence invisible; that is, by making it appear as though the various feelings and opinions of individuals originated solely from within the individual.

Invisible control, Kovel argued, was accelerated through the ideology of mental hygiene. Psychological science was presented as the objective truth rather than just another external or superstitious authority. It was then embraced by the state as the "paramount criterion of what is socially desirable or deviant" (Kovel, 1980, p. 82). Disease was conceptualized as residing within the person and caused by intrapsychic conflicts or malfunctions and not as products of the social world. "The medical model," Kovel argued, "exist[s] to gobble . . . [up social problems] and medicalize them" (1980, p. 86). By conceiving of mental ills in this way, deviant behavior such as alienation, depression, and narcissism were depoliticized, and psychological control of the population was hidden from view unintentionally by an unknowing psychology.

SULLIVAN AND INTERPERSONAL THEORY

At this time, there was a psychotherapist who stood out as someone able to think in a more socially contextualized, historical manner: Harry Stack Sullivan. Throughout his working life, he struggled to include the social within his therapeutic formulations and to integrate what he had learned from his contacts with anthropologists and social scientists, especially those of the Chicago school. His childhood experience as a victim of ethnic group prejudice and discrimination also appeared to have sensitized him to the effects of the political. Not surprisingly, because his theory emphasized interpersonal interaction rather than intrapsychic structures, Sullivan is one of the least understood and least credited theoreticians in the history of psychotherapy. Although his thinking appears to have influenced or anticipated many current psychotherapies, he is rarely given the credit he deserves (Havens & Frank, 1971).

Sullivan is usually identified with the New York–Washington, DC group that began in the 1930s, comprised of Erich Fromm, Karen Horney, Frieda Fromm-Reichmann, Clara Thompson, and William Alanson White. However, Sullivan actually began his unusual career in the early 1920s, surprising the psychiatric world with an 80% success rate on a schizophrenic ward at Sheppard and Enoch Pratt Hospital in Towson, Maryland during the years 1923–1931 (Perry, 1982). Because he wrote so seldom (and so poorly), we have little information about those early years of his work. In his later years he wrote about the self and what he called the *self system* long before the self was fashionable in psychoanalytic circles. He was convinced that children develop a pattern of behavior, a personality, in order to prevent, avoid, or assuage the anxiety of their parents. The self system, therefore, is more of a response to the interpersonal environment and less an inevitable product of conflicting internal psychic structures. His therapeutic technique focused on the interaction between the therapist (conceptualized as a *participant-observer*) and the patient within the therapy setting. At the end of his life, appalled by World War II and the atom bomb, he devoted himself to an expanded interpersonal realm: political activity related to world peace and nuclear disarmament.

As Perry (1982) has stressed, Sullivan appears to embody many American cultural traits and traditions, especially his emphasis on pragmatism. But to the usual list of Sullivan's American attributes, I would like to add one more: an awareness of the politics of ethnicity and discrimination. Sullivan was personally acquainted with the grinding destructiveness of ethnic group hatred, racism, and economic injustice. The loneliness, confusion, and crushing sense of inadequacy from which he suffered when he first migrated to an urban setting at 19 years of age undoubtedly would have been psychologized and, he thought, thereby misunderstood by the psychiatric establishment had he sought professional help.

Sullivan became convinced that his personal experiences with what he sarcastically called the "industrial revolution" played a crucial role in his therapeutic practices and his success rate at Sheppard. At the same time, Sullivan was a psychiatrist, not a community organizer; he was dedicated to helping individual patients, and his professional standing was determined by his acceptance of this orientation. Thus he was caught between his wish to help individuals and his understanding that many of the emotional ills of his time were caused not by intrapsychic structures or inherent drives, but by sociohistorical structures (Sullivan, 1964). This is a bind psychotherapists are still caught in today. We are maneuvered by training and an absence of alternative practices into conveying, in Kovel's words, "the myth of individual psychology and cure in the midst of a diseased society" (1980, p. 100). This is, I believe, what Sullivan was trying to articulate when he wrote "The Illusion of Personal Individuality," a paper so upsetting and potentially apolitic that it was published only after his death.

Sullivan was profoundly troubled by the inadequacies and implications of an over-psychologized, ahistorical psychiatry. Yet in the early years of his career, he did not have the intellectual tools or the supportive colleagues that would eventually help him develop the words to name the fundamental problem and oppose it. When he did begin to understand psychotherapy's collusion with racism and economic injustice through its ahistoricism, he devoted the rest of his life to researching and developing an alternative.

In the 1930s, Sullivan even found compatriots within the field of psychotherapy. Joining him and his longtime friend Clara Thompson were Karen Horney and Erich Fromm, two former Europeans who had studied Freud and eventually developed their differences with him. Horney presented the most direct challenge to Freud's view of female sexuality. Unlike Sabina Spielrein, who seemed to allow Freud and Jung either to co-opt or silence her ideas (Carotenuto, 1984), Horney assertively put forth her disagreements with Freud in a way that caused her great disfavor within psychoanalytic circles. Among the most creative ideas of Horney's prolific career were her insights on relatedness, culture, and epidemiology. She believed that neurosis was caused by disturbances in interhuman relationships as well as intrapsychic conflict. Included within the interhuman realm were history and culture. Horney developed one of the first straightforward cultural critiques of the United States by a psychoanalyst. Although Horney's cultural critique was a target of extreme psychoanalytic derision in the 1930s, her ideas appear surprisingly contemporary.

Fromm also began to develop his own ideas that took him away from Freud; he was more interested than Freud in political and cultural issues and how they impact on individual personality. He developed a psychoanalytic–Marxist–interpersonal–existential synthesis that inspired a productive literary career. He also accomplished something few psychoanalysts have done: He wrote openly and knowledgeably about his Jewishness and how it significantly informed and shaped his psychological theory (Fromm, 1966). In his emphasis on the effects of culture he was joined by Horney, and they both found Sullivan in the rich confluence of New York intellectual life in the 1930s.

Sullivan's major disagreement with Freud stemmed from their different concepts of the self. Freud's drive theory, described earlier, presupposed a Victorian self that contained interior, instinctual drives. Sullivan's concept was that the self is located in and derived from the interpersonal field, which includes interpersonal interactions and the larger sociohistorical sphere of cultural values and beliefs.

Sullivan's theory was one attempt to change psychoanalytic drive theory and bring it more in line with the intellectual spirit of the 1920s and 1930s, which was more focused on social interaction than was the Victorian era. Drive theory was too mechanistic for some analysts; they tried to shift its emphasis and alter Freud's views without appearing to criticize or challenge him. Sullivan's directness was something of an exception to this pattern; Melanie Klein and the growing school of object relations theory was not.

KLEIN AND THE BEGINNING OF OBJECT RELATIONS THEORY

Rank discussed separation anxiety in the context of the birth process, and Wilhelm Reich began developing the concept of character style and its effect on the body. However, neither of these two Freudian disciples could effect a wide-ranging restructuring of psychoanalysis while still managing to stay within the friendly confines of Freud's accepted circle. Melanie Klein did. Although in some ways her formulations directed psychoanalysis onto a path that was radically different and infinitely more characteristic of the 20th century, she remained loyal to Freud and convinced that her ideas were faithful to him.

Klein's greatest contribution was her reorientation of psychoanalysis away from Victorian notions of Newtonian energy machines and toward the 20th-century emphasis on relating. In this respect she was similar to Sullivan, but she managed to develop a theory of human relatedness that maintained Freud's emphasis on the dangerous interiority of the bounded self. Sullivan's critique, so much influenced by the Chicago school, could not maintain allegiance to Freud's mechanistic, interior Victorian configuration of the self, the predetermined developmental unfolding of universal aspects of the self, and an ahistorical, decontextualized vision of interaction. Klein's critique added a relational quality to the self and yet maintained its bounded, interior configuration.

Hers was an ingenious strategy that depended on geography. Whereas Sullivan situated relational life in the space *between* individuals, Klein maintained her tie to Freud by placing the struggles and dramas of relationship *within* each individual. To do otherwise—to leave human relating where it is usually located, in the public realm—would have necessitated a break with Freud. Klein's interior, then, takes on all the rough and tumble of the public: love and hate, envy and goodwill, hope and despair. Although many find it difficult to impute all these feelings to the infant (as Klein insisted upon), by doing so she made the interactive accessible to psychoanalysis in the only way it seemed possible: within the interior of the self-contained individual. In this way Klein helped psychoanlysis join the predominant cultural trend of the 20th century while remaining loyal to Freud.

Although some of her formulations about infant emotion appear difficult for some to believe, she has also provided psychotherapy with many concepts that object relations theory would be hard-pressed to do without. By situating object relatedness within the interior of the individual, she rescued self-contained individualism from the early fate of interpersonal theory. By elaborating on the concept of splitting, she developed a way of explaining the distortions and rages (seen in personality disorders, especially the Borderline Disorder) that have become increasingly common in descriptions of post–World War II Western pathology. By devising the concept of projective identification, she was able to explain to therapists the most puzzling of all therapeutic phenomena: why therapists find themselves unconsciously demonstrating the worst aspects of the behavior of their patient's parents. Finally, by conceptualizing the psychological ills of our era and culture (such as splitting, personal isolation, voracious hunger, paranoia, and envy toward loved ones) as being predetermined, universal, natural human traits, Klein diverted responsibility for them away from socioeconomic arrangements and onto the self-contained individual. This move inadvertently constructed a self that has insatiable, dangerous impulses and desires that must be controlled and diverted into the economy of competition and consumerism in order to save civilization. Of course, at the time, few people beyond the small group of analysts knew anything about Klein's theory. I am not suggesting that Klein had even the slightest immediate political influence. But her theory has had a growing effect on psychoanalytic theory in the post–World War II years and has most recently been drawn upon by some of the more recent and influential object relations theorists such as Greenberg and Mitchell (1983), Mitchell (1988), Ogden (1986), and Goldberg (1990).

Klein's great struggle in life was with Anna Freud, Freud's daughter, who also focused on the observation and treatment of children. Anna, in contrast with Klein, took a more normative, drive-defense position. Their intellectual conflict drove a wedge between analysts in England, where they both lived and worked. Although many felt obligated to choose one side or the other, one group refused to cut itself off from either side. D. W. Winnicott (1964, 1965) and Harry Guntrip came out of that tradition, and from them we have some of the least mechanical and most relational theory of the second half of our century.

THE POST–WORLD WAR II SELF EMERGES: WINNICOTT AND KOHUT

Winnicott's debts to Freud (especially the concepts of the unconscious, early childhood development, and transference) and Klein (the concept of internal objects, primitive infant feelings, and the value of fantasy) are obvious, but what is most striking about Winnicott is his divergence from them both. Although always playing a careful political strategy, Winnicott developed several new and creative concepts that fit with the new post–World War II era in a way that Freud and Klein could never accomplish. Winnicott brought psychoanalytic thought into the mobile, isolated, acommunal, antitraditional, monadic–dyadic world of the late 20th century.

Winnicott's major contribution was in his description of the post–World War II self and how it was developed. Just as Klein "updated" Freud's Victorian self with a (slightly) more interactive post–World War I self, Winnicott updated Klein with a much more relational, interactive self. Winnicott injected into psychoanalysis a sophisticated relational, interactive theory while remaining within an intrapsychic model. He continued and elaborated on the Kleinian strategy: Interactional theory can still be considered acceptable analytic theory if it can be located within instead of outside of the bounded self.

With an ever-increasing emphasis on the self-contained individual, unencumbered by community ties, ideological allegiances, moral traditions, and geographical boundaries, the post–World War II era had important questions to answer. Yet it was unclear which institutions, if any, had the status and credibility to step forward and offer guidance. People had to know the shape of this new self, how was it developed, what were its illnesses, and how were they healed. Winnicott helped psychotherapy fill the cultural void and thereby take a leadership role in the postwar era.

Winnicott (1964, 1965) argued that the self was developed through the relationship between parent and child. Although he described a conflict between the need for intimacy and the urge for separation, Winnicott defined the struggle as one that could be resolved so that inevitable separations make for a different, more independent form of union. The mother is responsible for enabling the self of the infant to unfold; she accomplishes this by providing a "holding environment," which psychologically contains and protects the child. The mother's job is to anticipate the child's needs and provide for them. Chief among these needs is the function of mirroring, wherein the mother's anticipation is so accurate that the infant actually thinks it creates the objects it needs because the mother produces them in such a timely fashion.

Winnicott defined mental health as the integrity and spontaneity of the self, psychopathology as the restriction of the activity and expressiveness of the self. When the growing self of the child is impinged upon or attacked, a split occurs between the true self (which withdraws into "hiding") and the false self (which is based on compliance and inauthenticity). Interestingly, this true self–false self dichotomy echoes a mesmerist concept discussed earlier. The true self withdraws in order to avoid "annihilation," and the false self protects the true self by complying with the parents' wishes and by diverting the parents' attention from the vulnerable true self. Winnicott believed that the healing quality of psychoanalysis came not from the interpretations delivered by the analyst but from corrective experiences derived from the analyst's ability to compensate for parental failures. When this is achieved, the natural growth pattern within the self takes over, reinvigorating the true self and thus filling up the emptiness (Greenberg & Mitchell, 1983, p. 201).

Winnicott described a self that is at the center of human social life. In the post–World War II world, the overriding issues relate to how to live independently without feeling lonely; how to cooperate and give without being used; and how to live with others, receive from them, and rely on them, without being engulfed or stunted. Many of these issues were either introduced or researched by developmental psychologists such as Mahler, Pine, and Bergman (1975). By elaborating on the concept of separation-individuation, by regarding it as the centerpiece of human development, and by situating it within the individual's interior, Winnicott answered pressing post–World War II questions and kept the answers acceptable to analytic theory.

For Freud the basic unit of the self was the Victorian self, with a driven and conflicted interior; for Klein the basic unit was the individual self with a populated, interactive interior; for Winnicott the basic unit of the self was the caretaker–infant unity, the "nursing couple," torn between intimacy and isolation. Winnicott's interactive, relational vision, however, stopped with the parent–child dyad. The dyadic struggle over engulfment and intimacy was not situated in history or culture; Winnicott implied that it was a transhistorical, inherent, unavoidable aspect of human life. Therefore, Winnicott not only described or reflected our currently configured self, he also prescribed it.

Another prominent psychodynamic theory in the post–World War II United States is Heinz Kohut's self psychology. Kohut's concerns were similar to Winnicott's. He became curious about the self and began to place its development at the heart of theory and practice (Kohut, 1977). Kohut also attempted for many years to stay within the boundaries of psychoanalytic approval. Unlike Winnicott, however, he finally embraced the obvious and publicly admitted that he had developed a new and somewhat competitive theory (1984).

Many aspects of Winnicott's theory and Kohut's theory are similar. They were both attempts to describe the post–World War II self in "experience-near" terms, explain it by using developmental theory, and heal it through the use of corrective emotional experience as well as intellectual interpretations. Both theorists, although developing new theories, tried to stay within the boundaries of psychoanalytic thought. Both theorists made drives secondary to the interactional parent–child relationship. Both theorists thought that a period of infantile grandiosity was a prerequisite for healthy adult functioning. Both theorists held an individual caretaker to be responsible for the development of the self. Both theorists situated the self inside the individual and described the growth of the self as an organicistic, expressional, and universal process (Sass, 1988). Although they both credited interpersonal, pre-oedipal interactions with significantly influencing the formation of the self, they both located the significant transformative events that create the self within the individual. Kohut exhibited a fondness for history and applied his theory to historical issues; also, at the end of his life he stated that selfobject relationships continue throughout life and should not necessarily be evaluated as regressive or pathological. Even so, Kohut's concept of self is obviously still masterful and interior.

THE POST–WORLD WAR II EMPTY SELF

Both Winnicott's and Kohut's theories describe a self that is bounded, masterful, subjective—a continuation of the late modern and post–World War II self in the West. However, both theories also have added something new and extremely germane to the description of post–World War II life: The interior of their concept of self is *empty*. It is true that the interior of the self in both theories has something in it (i.e., objects), but what seems most prominent in each interior is an absence. I have discussed this at length in an earlier article (Cushman, 1990). The post–World War II self does not possess an interior that is stuffed to overflowing with urges, desires, feelings, conflicts, instincts, drives, fantasies, character, morals, values, and opinions. It is an interior that is graced by the momentary presence of a selfobject, or sparsely populated by internalized part-objects or the true, hidden self.

There are many indications in our society that our configuration of self in middle-class America is the empty self. Chief among these is one of our patients' major complaints: emptiness. Both self psychology and object relations theory conceptualize psychotherapy treatment as a type of "filling up" of the self, through the "taking in" of the selfobject or the growth of the true self. Several prominent psychiatric symptoms today feature an empty self that yearns to be filled up: overeating, addictions, interpersonal loneliness, compulsive shopping. Previously (Cushman, 1990), I argued that advertising sells commodities primarily by implying that by purchasing and "consuming" the product, the consumer's identity will become magically transformed through ingesting the life-style of the model or celebrity featured in the ad (see also Ewen, 1989). Commodities, then, have become the transformational object of our time, and consuming has become the ultimate transformative process (see also Wachtel, 1989). By using an interpretive approach to popular culture, I believe a strong case can be made for describing the current self as empty and desperately hungry for food, consumer products, drugs, celebrities, and charismatic leaders.

Addiction theory (e.g., Donovan & Marlett, 1988; Norwood, 1985; Schaef, 1987), one of the fastest growing of psychotherapy theories, takes this empty self dynamic to its furthest extreme. Drugs (the consumer item) are conceptualized as the most powerful force in the addict's (the consumer's) life. When consumers are addicted, the commodity has complete control over them. It is the irresistible object. The consumer item, used in order to fill the consumer up, takes on a life of its own. In addiction theory, the commodity has become the ultimate transformative device: It can completely remake identity, recasting consumers into "drug fiends." The only hope the addict has, most addiction theories teach, is to completely abstain from consuming the dangerous, all-powerful commodity.

For instance, a recent television ad portrayed a scenario in which a senior citizens center and a college fraternity both threw parties on the same day. However, the respective soft drink orders were mistakenly switched and subsequently delivered to the wrong parties. As a result, the senior citizens "boogied down" and the fraternity brothers found themselves snoozing through their newly instituted bingo game. This story line is representative of many ad campaigns in which, through the act of purchasing and consuming, the very nature or identity of the individual is transformed. The commodity is conceived of as the ultimate transformative object. In a second type of ad, commodities are actually portrayed as possessing human traits and personalities. In ads of this type, there is little that distinguishes humans from commodities; a qualitative difference no longer seems to exist. Examples of this type of ad are commercials that feature (a) the 7 UP dot, who sings and dances; (b) a loving "couple" composed of a human and a car; and (c) walking, talking, football-playing beer cans. "The Bud Bowl" is a serial commercial composed of an imaginary football game played by two kinds of beer, the Bud team and the Bud Light team. For 3 years this game has been "played" during the real Super Bowl, America's most significant football game of the year. The beer cans have identities and personalities, and the games revolve around human-like dramas. If commodities are like humans, then consuming is like relating: It is satisfying, soothing, energizing, it drives away loneliness, and it makes life rich and rewarding. Indeed consuming is often portrayed in this way in contemporary advertising. Individuals who have been addicted to a drug often describe their relationship with the drug in a similar way. For instance, taking heroin is sometimes referred to as riding the white lady, and a crack pipe has been likened to a lover.

In a previous article (Cushman, 1990) I have speculated that there are two broad causes for the emptiness of the current configuration of self. First, the absence of ongoing communal experiences, meaningful traditions, and religious or philosophical certainty is experienced interiorly. Second, in order to avoid economic stagnation or depression, contemporary capitalism had to devise a way to ensure the continual purchase of nonessential and quickly obsolete consumer products. It accomplished this through the economic development of easy credit and the construction of a gnawing emotional hunger within the self that could not be satisfied.

To the aforementioned reasons for the empty self I would now like to add a third. An intellectual bind confronted psychoanalytic thinkers throughout this century. They had to adjust psychoanalytic theory to the broad historical trend of personal relatedness while staying within the limitations of the masterful, bounded self. Because the individual infant obviously is not a completely self-contained entity, interactional activity, nourishment, guidance, and a cultural frame of reference had to be brought from the outside to the inside. Therefore, the inside had to be vacated in order to make room for the important supplies from outside: The interior had to be constructed as empty.

The major implication of the empty self analysis is that the empty self dovetails strikingly with the needs of the current economic and political system. Psychotherapy theory not only reflects but also adds to the construction of the empty self. The empty self has both been "given" to us and is reproduced by us through our discourse and practices. Psychotherapy is thus in the position of contributing to the very ills it is attempting to heal.

HUMANISTIC PSYCHOLOGY, COGNITIVE PSYCHOLOGY, AND FAMILY THERAPY

Three other late 20th-century schools of psychotherapy—humanistic psychology, cognitive psychology, and family therapy—also attempt to address the needs of the empty self. All three have developed theory that has expanded psychology's subject and initiated alternative therapeutic practices. However, by not situating the post–World War II self historically, most theorists from these schools have failed to offer a healing that does not also reproduce the illness.

Humanistic psychology (e.g., Bugental, 1967; Maslow, 1968; May, 1972; Rogers, 1951) started as a rebellion against what it characterized as the mechanistic, impersonal, formalized, hierarchical, elitist psychoanalytic establishment and against an overly scientistic, cold, removed behaviorism. With its roots in the values of existentialism, humanism, and the liberation movements of the 1960s, humanistic psychology developed a four-point philosophical platform (Buhler & Allen, 1972) that focused on the experiencing person and emphasized choice, valuation, self-realization, and the development of individual human potential and uniqueness. However, at the same time, it also exhibited a blindness to the problems inherent in vague categories like "experience" and a lack of historical perspective on the ethnocentrism and classism inherent in the values of hypertrophied individualism. It unquestioningly embraced the post–World War II configuration of the self: completely subjective, isolated, and antitraditional (see also Buss, 1979a; Sass, 1988; Wachtel, 1989, chapter 6).

Cognitive psychology (e.g., Baars, 1986; Kruglanski, 1979; Weisz & Zigler, 1979), because it evolved in part from behaviorism, at first appears to offer a type of psychotherapy immune from the charge of aiding in the construction of the interior self. However, upon closer inspection it becomes obvious that the information processing models of cognitive psychology are also built upon a foundation of interiorization. Cognitive psychology has not grown as directly out of radical behaviorism (e.g., Skinner, 1931, 1972) as it has out of the more normative tradition of Hull and Tolman (see Leahey, 1987, pp. 389–393). It was Hull and Tolman who began the process of locating mediating mechanisms within the individual, *between* the classic behaviorist stimulus–response dyad. Information processing models challenged psychology to study a new subject: cognitive processes, the putative universal building blocks of the mind. It presented itself to the field as the height of scientific precision, holding out the hope for a pure scientific psychology.

However, as Sampson (1981) has pointed out, cognitivism's aspiration to a value-free science has failed: It is guilty of the very same subjectivist and individualistic reductions to which other schools of psychology have fallen prey. Behavior, in cognitive psychology, "is a function of the subjective world as transformed and represented internally" (Sampson, 1981, p. 731). Cognitive psychology's mediational mechanism, symbolic representation, is located within the individual. It thus reproduces (again) an interior self, populated not with part objects, as in object relations theory, but with symbolic representations of external events.

Sampson argued that cognitive psychology describes a self that is "free to engage in internal mental activity and yet . . . remain[s] relatively impotent or unconcerned about the objective social world" (1981, p. 735). In therapy, individuals are encouraged to change their subjective experience of reality rather than work to change their objective reality (1981, p. 735). Cognitive therapy strategies privilege the internal, subjective experience of the client and place responsibility for the behavior with the way the client thinks about the world (see also Prilleltensky, 1990). The overall effect, Sampson explained, is that the current concept of self and the political arrrangements of power and privilege are accepted as givens and remain unchallenenged by cognitive therapies.

Family therapy (e.g., Haley, 1976; Hoffman, 1981; Minuchin, 1974), with its roots in sociology, interpersonal theory, and the child guidance movement, is an attempt to bring interactive processes to bear on an expanded subject. The shift, operative in some family therapies, is from the isolated, deeper, individual self to a wider group self (i.e., the family). However, there is a reification present in some family therapy theories such as systems theory that treats groups such as families or businesses as if they were removed from the larger social context. I believe that this is true even in one of the most ontologically advanced systems theories, organizational culture theory (e.g., Ott, 1989). In this respect, systems theory is limited in ways similar to the advances made by object relations theory. It reforms by applying the interactive, relational perspective to a slightly expanded subject; but it does not take its analysis into the realm of history and culture. By limiting its analysis, family therapy has fallen short of a thorough social critique, thereby protecting the status quo (Jacoby, 1975).

Most recently, a social constructionist perspective has been applied to family therapy (e.g., Efran, Luckens, & Luckens, 1990). Usually this is done in a relatively ahistorical manner, with emphasis placed primarily on the interactional, dialogic construction of meaning within the therapy setting. Although these family therapists express a concern for nonhierarchical, coauthoring practices, they do not fully take into account the impact of larger sociohistorical forces on the family or analyze psychotherapy's political functions within the larger society. However, in an important new development, feminist constructionists such as Hare-Mustin (1991), L. Hoffman (1988), and Luepnitz (1988) have begun to utilize the issues of gender construction, power, and class to interpret psychotherapy as a cultural artifact and to develop new treatment practices. These authors represent the most promising possibility to date of developing a historically situated psychotherapy. Their work should be watched with great interest.

Although very different from one another, humanistic psychology, cognitive psychology, and family therapy have one element in common: None have been able to develop a complex historical perspective on its work or a robust historical critique of its culture. As a result, they are not excluded from the pull to conformist practices and corporate clients that continues to seduce and therefore plague all schools of psychotherapy.

CONCLUSION

There are three aspects of the history of psychotherapy that immediately stand out above all others. One, the sociopolitical developments of the two world wars and the particular shape of contemporary capitalism (especially the hegemony of advertising in the service of a rampant consumerism) have been a tremendous stimulus to psychotherapy's growth and popular acceptance. Two, the modernist agenda of the construction and healing of personal interiority within each self-contained individual has been embraced by psychotherapy as its primary task and is, in fact, its reason for being. Psychotherapists have become, first and foremost, doctors of the psychological interior. Three, the justification for entering the deep, modernist interior, and the technological means by which to do so, have been developed in large part by psychology's and psychotherapy's discourse and practices.

The task of managing the population during times of societal crisis or for the purposes of economic restructuring has often fallen to the social sciences. The state's attempt to control a population of self-contained individuals has provided psychology with a rationale for existing as an independent discipline: The private interior needs to be protected, understood, cared for, healed, and made to thrive. In turn, psychotherapy discourse has provided an increasingly articulate description and explanation of the interior, and a set of practices that gain entrance into the interior in order to effect a putative healing and, parenthetically, to influence. Seen in this light, psychotherapy can be interpreted as a set of practices that inadvertently has been creating, adapting, and accommodating psychological theories of the self in order to construct and refine the concept of the interior and develop the means by which to enter it. It is a herculean task, and one indispensible to contemporary capitalism and the postmodern age.

The empty self of the post–World War II era is simply the latest in a long line of constructions that feature the modern project of the masterful, bounded self with a deep and financially profitable interior. As doctors of the interior, psychotherapists have been assigned the role of caring for and also, unavoidably, constructing ever anew our era's current configuration of self. In doing so we try to help, we hope we help, we look for new ways of helping. What we can't do within our current professional structures, or what we haven't yet been able to do, is to develop a way of constructing a different, more cooperative, peaceful self.

If we could reverse the trend of the last 150 years, that is, if we could situate psychotherapy historically and stop constructing and protecting the private interior, we could perhaps contribute to a fuller, more productive cultural critique. Recently, theorists Sampson (1988) and Dreyfus and Wakefield (1989), psychoanalysts I. Hoffman (1991), Mitchell (1991), and Stern (1991), and feminists Hare-Mustin (1991), L. Hoffman (1988), and Luepnitz (1988) have suggested developing new sets of practices that would describe and reproduce a slightly different configuration of self. By doing so we might be able to collude less with contemporary capitalism and actually devise ways of treating the primary causes of psychological ills, the political and economic structures of our particular social world. In the long run this might bring about a much greater healing.

REFERENCES

Adler, N. (1988, November). *Changing concepts of the ego in historical and cultural perspective.* Paper presented at the meeting of the Northern California Society for Psychoanalytic Psychotherapy, San Francisco, CA.

Ash, M. (1983). The self presentation of a discipline: History of psychology in the United States between pedagogy and scholarship. In L. Graham, W. Lepinies, & P. Weingart (Eds.), *Functions and uses of disciplinary histories* (pp. 143–189). Boston: D. Reidel.

Baars, B. (1986). *The cognitive revolution in psychology.* New York: Guilford.

Baumeister, R. (1987). How the self became a problem: A psychological review of historical research. *Journal of Personality and Social Psychology, 52,* 163–176.

Bellah, R., Madsen, R., Sullivan, W., Swidler, A., & Tipton, S. (1985). *Habits of the heart: Individualism and commitment in American life.* Berkeley: University of California Press.

Berman, L. (1921). *The glands regulating the personality*. New York: Macmillan.

Bernays, E. (1928). *Propaganda*. New York: Liveright.

Bernheimer, C., & Kahane, C. (Eds.). (1985). *In Dora's case: Freud-hysteria-feminism*. New York: Columbia University Press.

Bugental, J. (Ed.). (1967). *Challenges of humanistic psychology*. New York: McGraw-Hill.

Buhler, C., & Allen, M. (1972). *Introduction to humanistic psychology*. Monterey, CA: Brooks/Cole.

Buss, A. (1975). The emerging field of the sociology of psychological knowledge. *American Psychologist, 30*, 988–1002.

Buss, A. (1979). Humanistic psychology as liberal ideology. *Journal of Humanistic Psychology, 19*, 43–55.

Carotenuto, A. (1984). *A secret symmetry: Sabina Spielrein between Jung and Freud*. (Trans. by A. Pomeras, J. Shipley, & K. Winston). New York: Random House.

Cushman, P. (1986). The self besieged: Recruitment-indoctrination processes in restrictive groups. *Journal for the Theory of Social Behavior, 16*, 1–32.

Cushman, P. (1987). History, psychology, and the abyss: A constructionist-Kohutian proposal. *Psychohistory Review, 15*, 29–45.

Cushman, P. (1990). Why the self is empty: Toward a historically situated psychology. *American Psychologist, 45*, 599–611.

Cushman, P. (1991). Ideology obscured: Political uses of the self in Daniel Stern's infant. *American Psychologist, 46*, 206–219.

Danziger, K. (1979). The social origins of modern psychology. In A. Buss (Ed.), *Psychology in social context* (pp. 27–44). New York: Irvington.

Darnton, R. (1984). *The great cat massacre and other episodes in French cultural history*. New York: Basic Books.

Demos, J. (1981). Oedipus and America: Historical perspectives on the reception of psychoanalysis in the United States. In R. Brugger (Ed.), *Our selves/our past: Psychological approaches to American history* (pp. 292–306). Baltimore: The Johns Hopkins University Press.

Donovan, D., & Marlett, G. (Eds.). (1988). *Assessment of addictive behaviors*. New York: Guilford Press.

Dreyfus, H., & Wakefield, J. (1988). From depth psychology to breadth psychology: A phenomenological approach to psychopathology. In S. Messer, L. Sass, & R. Woolfolk (Eds.), *Hermeneutics and psychological theory: Interpretive perspectives on personality, psychotherapy, and psychopathology* (pp. 272–288). New Brunswick, NJ: Rutgers University Press.

Drinka, G. (1984). *The birth of neurosis: Myth, malady, and the Victorians*. New York: Simon & Schuster.

Efran, J., Luckens, M., & Luckens, R. (1990). *Language structure and change: Frameworks of meaning in psychotherapy*. New York: Norton.

Englehardt, H. (1985). The disease of masturbation: Values and the concept of disease. In J. Leavitt & R. Numbers (Eds.), *Sickness and health in America: Readings in the history of medicine and public health* (pp. 13–21). Madison, WI: University of Wisconsin Press.

Ewen, S. (1989). Advertising and the development of consumer society. In I. Angus & S. Jhally (Eds.), *Cultural politics in contemporary America* (pp. 82–95). New York: Routledge.

Foucault, M. (1979). *Discipline and punishment: The birth of the prison*. New York: Vintage/Random House.

Foucault, M. (1980). *The history of sexuality: Vol. I. An introduction*. New York: Random House.

Foucault, M. (1988). The political technologies of individuals. In L. Martin, H. Gutman, & P. Hutton (Eds.), *Technologies of the self: A seminar with Michel Foucault* (pp. 145–161). Amherst: University of Massachusetts Press.

Freud, S. (1961a). Some character-types met with in psychoanalytic work. In J. Strachey (Ed. and Trans.), *The standard edition of the complete psychological works of Sigmund Freud* (Vol. 14; pp. 309–333). London: Hogarth Press. (Original work published in 1916)

Freud, S. (1961b). Inhibitions, symptoms and anxiety. In J. Strachey (Ed. and Trans.), *The standard works of Sigmund Freud* (Vol. 20; pp. 77–175). London: Hogarth Press. (Original work published in 1926)

Fromm, E. (1966). *You shall be as gods: A radical interpretation of the Old Testament and its traditions*. New York: Holt, Rinehart and Winston.

Fuller, R. (1982). *Mesmerism and the American cure of souls*. Philadelphia: University of Pennsylvania Press.

Gergen, K. (1973). Social psychology as history. *Journal of Personality and Social Psychology, 26,* 309–320.

Gergen, K. (1985). The social constructionist movement in modern psychology. *American Psychologist, 40,* 266–275.

Goldberg, A. (1990). *The prisoners of psychoanalysis*. Hillsdale, NJ: Analytic Press.

Greenberg, J., & Mitchell, S. (1983). *Object relations in psychoanalytic theory*. Cambridge, MA: Harvard University Press.

Grunfeld, R. (1979). *Prophets without honor: A background to Freud, Kafka, Einstein and their world*. New York: McGraw-Hill.

Hale, J. (1971). *Freud and the Americans*. New York: Oxford University Press.

Haley, J. (1976). *Problem solving therapy: New strategies for effective family therapy*. San Francisco: Jossey-Bass.

Hare-Mustin, R. (1991). Sex, lies, and headaches: The problem is power. In T. Goodrich (Ed.), *Women and power: Perspectives for therapy* (pp. 63–85). New York: Norton.

Harre, R. (1984). *Personal being: A theory for individual psychology*. Cambridge, MA: Harvard University Press.

Havens, L., & Frank, J. (1971). Review of psychoanalysis and interpersonal psychiatry. *American Journal of Psychiatry, 127,* 1704–1705.

Heelas, P., & Lock, A. (Eds.). (1981). *Indigenous psychologies: The anthropology of the self*. London:Academic Press.

Heidegger, M. (1977). *The question concerning technology and other essays*. New York: Harper & Row.

Held, D. (1980). *Introduction to critical theory: Horkheimer to Habermas*. Berkeley: University of California Press.

Hobbes, T. (1958). *Leviathan, or the matter, form and power of a commonwealth, ecclesiastical and civil*. New York: Macmillan. (Original work published in 1651)

Hoffman, I. (1991). Discussion: Toward a social constructivist view of the psychoanalytic situation. *Psychoanalytic Dialogues, 1*, 121–147.

Hoffman, L. (1981). *Foundations of family therapy: A conceptual framework for systems change*. New York: Basic Books.

Hoffman, L. (1988). A constructivist position for family therapy. *The Irish Journal of psychology, 9*.

Jacoby, R. (1975). *Social amnesia: A critique of conformist psychology from Adler to Laing*. Boston: Beacon Press.

Jacoby, R. (1983). *The repression of psychoanalysis: Otto Fenichel and the political Freudians*. New York: Basic Books.

Jung, C. (1923). *Psychological types* (Trans. by H. Baynes). New York: Harcourt Brace.

Karier, C. (1976). The ethics of a therapeutic man. In G. Kren & L. Rappoport (Eds.), *Varieties of psychohistory* (pp. 333–363). New York: Springer.

Kohut, H. (1977). *The restoration of the self*. New York: International Universities Press.

Kohut, H. (1984). *How does analysis cure?* Chicago: University of Chicago Press.

Kovel, J. (1980). The American mental health industry. In D. Inglesby (Ed.), *Critical psychiatry: The politics of mental health* (pp. 72–101). New York: Random House.

Kruglanski, A. (1979). Causal explanation, teleological explanation: On radical particularism in attribution theory. *Journal of Personality and Social Psychology, 37*, 1447–1457.

Kretschmer, E. (1925). *Physique and character*. New York: Harcourt Brace.

Kurzweil, E. (1989). *The Freudians: A comparative perspective*. New Haven, CT: Yale University Press.

Lacan, J. (1977). *Ecrits: A selection*. (Trans. by A. Sheridan). New York: Norton. (Original work published in 1966)

Lasch, C. (1977). *Haven in a heartless world: The family besieged*. New York: Basic Books.

Leahey, T. (1987). *A history of psychology: Main currents in psychological thought*. Englewood Cliffs, NJ: Prentice-Hall.

Lears, T. (1983). From salvation to self-realization: Advertising and the therapeutic roots of the consumer culture, 1880–1930. In R. Fox & T. Lears (Eds.), *The culture of consumption: Critical essays in American history, 1880–1980* (pp. 1–38). New York: Pantheon Books.

Levin, D. (1987). Psychopathology in the epoch of nihilism. In D. Levin (Ed.), *Pathologies of the modern self: Postmodern studies on narcissism, schizophrenia, and depression* (pp. 21–83). New York: New York University Press.

Lichtman, R. (1982). *The production of desire: The integration of psychoanalysis into Marxist theory.* New York: The Free Press.

Logan, R. (1987). Historical change in prevailing sense of self. In K. Yardley & T. Honess (Eds.), *Self and identity: Psychosocial perspectives* (pp. 13–26). Chichester, England: John Wiley and Sons.

Lowe, D. (1982). *History of bourgeois perception.* Chicago: University of Chicago Press.

Luepnitz, D. (1988). *The family interpreted: Feminist theory in clinical practice.* New York: Basic Books.

Mahler, M., Pine, F., & Bergman, A. (1975). *Psychological birth of the infant.* New York: Knopf.

Marchand, R. (1985). *Advertising the American dream: Making way for modernity, 1920–1940.* Berkeley: University of California Press.

Marcus, S. (1984). *Freud and the culture of psychoanalysis: Studies in the transition from Victorian humanism to modernity.* New York: Norton.

Maslow, A. (1968). *Toward a psychology of being.* New York: Van Nostrand Reinhold.

May, R. (1972). *Love and will.* New York: Norton.

Meyer, D. (1980). *Positive thinkers: Religion as pop psychology from Mary Baker Eddy to Oral Roberts* (2nd ed.). New York: Pantheon Books.

Minuchin, S. (1974). *Families and family therapy.* Cambridge, MA: Harvard University Press.

Mitchell, S. (1988). *Relational concepts in psychoanalysis: An integration.* Cambridge, MA: Harvard University Press.

Mitchell, S. (1991). Contemporary perspectives on self: Toward an integration. *Psychoanalytic Dialogues, 1,* 121–147.

Mitchell, S. W. (1878). *Fat and blood: And how to make them.* Philadelphia: Lippincott.

Morawski, J. (1984). Historiography as a metatheoretical text for social psychology. In K. Gergen & M. Gergen (Eds.), *Historical social psychology* (pp. 37–59). Hillsdale, NJ: Erlbaum Press.

Norwood, R. (1985). *Women who love too much: When you keep wishing and hoping he'll change.* New York: St. Martin's Press.

Ogden, T. (1986). *The matrix of the mind: Object relations and the psychoanalytic dialogue.* Northvale, NJ: Jason Aronson.

Ott, J. (1989). *The organizational culture perspective.* Pacific Grove, CA: Brooks/Cole.

Perry, H. (1982). *Psychiatrist of America: The life of Harry Stack Sullivan.* Cambridge, MA: Harvard University Press.

Poster, M. (1984). *Foucault, Marxism and history: Modes of production versus mode of information.* Cambridge, England: Polity Press.

Prilleltensky, I. (1989). Psychology and the status quo. *American Psychologist, 44,* 795–802.

Prilleltensky, I. (1990). On the social and political implications of cognitive psychology. *Journal of Mind and Behavior, 11,* 127–136.

Reiff, P. (1966). *The triumph of the therapeutic: Uses of faith after Freud.* Chicago: University of Chicago Press.

Reisman, J. (1976). *A history of clinical psychology.* New York: Irvington.

Roazen, P. (1984). *Freud and his followers.* New York: New York University Press.

Rogers, C. (1951). *Client-centered therapy: Its current practice, implications, and theory.* Boston: Houghton Mifflin.

Rose, N. (1990). *Governing the soul: The shaping of the private self.* New York: Routledge.

Samelson, F. (1979). Putting psychology on the map: Ideology and intelligence testing. In A. Buss (Ed.), *Psychology in social context* (pp. 103–168). New York: Irvington.

Sampson, E. E. (1977). Psychology and the American ideal. *Journal of Personality and Social Psychology, 32,* 309–320.

Sampson, E. E. (1981). Cognitive psychology as ideology. *American Psychologist, 36,* 730–743.

Sampson, E. E. (1983). *Justice and the critique of pure psychology.* New York: Plenum.

Sampson, E. E. (1985). The decentralization of identity: Towards a revised concept of personal and social order. *American Psychologist, 40,* 1203–1211.

Sampson, E. E. (1988). The debate on individualism: Indigenous psychologies of the individual and their role in personal and societal functioning. *American Psychologist, 43,* 15–22.

Sass, L. (1987). Schreber's panopticism: Psychosis and the modern soul. *Social Research, 54,* 101–145.

Sass, L. (1988). The self and its vicissitudes: An "archeological" study of the psychoanalytic avant-garde. *Social Research, 55,* 551–607.

Schaef, A. (1987). *When society becomes an addict.* San Francisco: Harper & Row.

Scull, A. (1989). *Social order/mental disorders: Anglo-American psychiatry in historical perspective.* Berkeley: University of California Press.

Skinner, B. (1931). The concept of reflex in the description of behavior. *Journal of General Psychology, 5,* 427–458.

Skinner, B. (1972). *Beyond freedom and dignity.* New York: Knopf.

Slotkin, R. (1985). *The fatal environment: The myth of the frontier in the age of industrialization, 1800–1890.* Middletown, CT: Wesleyan University Press.

Stern, D. (1991). A philosophy for the embedded analyst. *Contemporary Psycho-analysis, 27,* 51–80.

Sullivan, H. (1964). The illusion of personal individuality. In H. Perry (Ed.), *The fusion of psychiatry and social science* (pp. 198–226). New York: Norton.

Susman, W. (1973). *Culture as history: The transformation of American society in the twentieth century.* New York: Pantheon Books.

Taylor, C. (1989). *Sources of the self.* Cambridge, MA: Harvard University Press.

Van den Berg, J. (1961). *The changing nature of man: Introduction to a historical psychology.* New York: W. W. Norton.

Wachtel, P. (1989). *The poverty of affluence: A psychological portrait of the American way of life.* Philadelphia: New Society.

Watson, J. (1913). Psychology as the behaviorist views it. *Psychological Review, 20,* 158–179.

Weisz, J., & Zigler, E. (1979). Cognitive development on retarded and nonretarded persons: Piagetian tests of the similar sequence hypothesis. *Psychological Bulletin, 86,* 831–885.

Wiebe, R. (1967). *The search for order.* New York: Hill & Wang.

Winnicott, D. (1964). *The child, the family, and the outside world.* New York: Penguin.

Winnicott, D. (1965). *The maturational process and the facilitating environment.* New York: International Universities Press.

Zaretsky, E. (1976). *Capitalism, the family, and personal life.* New York: Harper & Row.

3

A CENTURY OF PSYCHOTHERAPY: ECONOMIC AND ENVIRONMENTAL INFLUENCES

GARY R. VANDENBOS, NICHOLAS A. CUMMINGS, AND
PATRICK H. DELEON

Today, in 1992, when most psychotherapists are asked to identify the "creator" of modern psychotherapy, they think of Sigmund Freud. The setting of his work was private practice in Vienna, Austria. In the United States, the first psychology *clinic* was established at the University of Pennsylvania by Lightner Witmer in 1896 (Cattell, 1954). The employment setting was an academic one. Witmer's first case involved a child with an apparent academic problem (Brotemarkle, 1947), although one would infer from the initial report that the child may actually have been retarded.

Over the course of the past 100 years, there have been many contributors to the development, evolution, and today's practice of psychotherapy, and they have been employed within a host of settings: private practice, universities, public psychiatric hospitals, child and family guidance centers, private psychotherapeutic centers, independent offices, schools, prisons, and the military. The sites themselves have influence over practice because the settings have provided differing patient populations.

The setting in which psychotherapy has been practiced has influenced both the public's access to psychotherapy and its image of psychotherapy. When it was conducted primarily in private practice and exclusive clinics, it was neither accessible to nor affordable by the general public. To the extent that psychotherapy was provided within psychiatric hospitals, it was viewed as a treatment for individuals who were grossly impaired and often dysfunctional, or else as stigmatized intervention provided only to "crazy people." Broad availability of psychotherapeutic services through child guidance centers, university counseling centers, and community social service programs was essential to achieving general public acceptance of the value of psychotherapy as well as to creating psychotherapeutic interventions for the full range of psychological and behavioral problems. Public funding, whether through governmental programs or health insurance plans, has played a major role in the development of various psychotherapy approaches, the availability of fully trained practitioners, and the current acceptance of psychotherapy by the general public.

This chapter will examine the impact of settings and of economic and reimbursement mechanisms on the nature and practice of psychotherapy. First, discussion of developments in the period 1920–1939 will focus primarily on the establishment of psychoanalytic clinics, the development of university counseling centers, and the establishment of community-based child guidance clinics. Second, we will examine events occurring in the period 1940–1959 in terms of their influence on the growth and nature of psychotherapy by examining the impact of World War II, the contribution of postwar Veterans Administration (VA) programs, the establishment of the National Institute of Mental Health (NIMH), the expansion of health insurance, and the evolution of an array of federal, social, and health programs. Third, we will explore emerging events during the last 30 years.

SETTINGS FOR THE BIRTH OF MODERN PSYCHOTHERAPY: 1920–1939

Historically, the setting in which the psychotherapist was employed greatly determined the types of patients and the kind of clinical problems with which the psychotherapist would work. In turn, the development of psychotherapy was influenced by patient populations. Theoretical and clinical developments in three highly different practice settings contributed to the evolution of modern psychotherapy. These three primary settings in which psychotherapeutic advancements occurred between 1920 and 1939 were psychoanalytic clinics, university counseling centers, and community-based child guidance clinics. The first was dominated by physicians, the second by psychologists, and the third by social workers. There was, of course, a fair amount of overlap and cross-fermentation.

Psychoanalytic Clinics: 1920–1939

It was Freud who, from the assortment of 19th-century neurological and psychiatric currents, synthesized psychoanalysis—a method of treatment that became the precursor for scientifically oriented psychotherapy. Freud began private practice in Vienna in 1886, receiving referrals from some of the leading Viennese physicians. Freud worked relatively alone, although he attracted a small core of followers by the late 1890s. The group was first known as the Vienna Psychological Society (Burnham, 1977; Haynie, 1984) and later evolved into the Vienna Psychoanalytic Society. In 1912, an informal "committee" of six individuals was established to maintain and oversee the psychoanalytic movement (Burnham, 1977; Haynie, 1984). The Internationaler Psychoanalytischer Verlag, a publishing house, was established in 1918. Finally, in 1922, the Vienna Psychoanalytic Society established the psychoanalytic ambulatorium, which served as a diagnostic and referral center for its members. In 1925, the training institute of the Vienna Psychoanalytic Society officially opened (Sterba, 1982).

Freud was invited to the United States for the first time in 1909 by psychologist G. Stanley Hall and delivered a series of lectures at Clark University, where he received an honorary degree. Psychoanalytic training institutes in the United States began to form in the 1930s, with foundings in the cities of Chicago (1932), Baltimore–Washington (1933), Boston (1933), New York (1940), and San Francisco (1942) (American Psychoanalytic Association, 1990). Freud was still alive during most of this period, and nonphysician analysts (called *lay analysts*) were still accepted.

Along with the formation of psychoanalytic institutes, a parallel phenomenon was making its appearance—the psychoanalytic clinic. A few of these were residential programs (often in remote rural settings), and such care has always been more expensive. The staffs of these psychoanalytic clinics published extensively and provided a steady flow of influential and widely read papers that made dynamically oriented psychotherapy the dominant mode for decades to come. These early mainstays of psychoanalysis were said to be specializing in the "neuroses of the rich," and several were to become world-renowned, such as Austen Riggs, Chestnut Lodge, and the Menninger Clinic.

The Austen Riggs Center in Stockbridge, Massachusetts developed out of the private practice of Austen Fox Riggs. While recuperating from tuberculosis, he studied psychiatry and psychology and gradually began practicing "psychotherapy of the nerves." His patients moved to rural Stockbridge for an extended period while in treatment, living in local boarding houses and hotels. In 1919, the Stockbridge Institute was formed, although the name was soon changed to Austen Riggs Foundation and later to Austen Riggs Center (Kubie, 1960).

Between 1920 and 1939, Riggs treated mostly middle-aged patients. They were individuals who seemed unable to adapt to the rigors and routines of everyday living. Riggs was ambivalent about Freud and psychoanalysis. His treatment consisted of helping patients gain insight into the causes of their disability, together with balanced periods of exercise, work, play, and rest. He also emphasized the value of manual skills and built a craft shop for patients. By 1924, five doctors were in training with Riggs at his treatment center ("Austen Riggs Center," n.d.). Riggs died in 1940, and the Austen Riggs Center lacked clear direction until after World War II.

Robert Knight was appointed medical director in 1947. The most significant impact on the evolution of psychotherapy would occur over the next 10 years. Under Knight's leadership, the patient population in the Austen Riggs Center changed to those who were mostly in their twenties, sicker, and required longer hospital stays (1 to 2 years). Knight also recruited such eminent professionals as David Rapaport, Merton Gill, Margaret Brenman, Joseph Chassell, and Erik Erikson. The Austen Riggs Center initially served as a teaching institute for psychiatric residents; a program for the education of postdoctoral trainees in clinical psychology was instituted in 1954. Later directors of the Austen Riggs Center included Otto Will and Daniel Schwartz.

Chestnut Lodge Hospital (originally called the Chestnut Lodge Sanatorium) was founded by Ernest Luther Bullard in 1910 to care for patients suffering from serious mental illness ("Chestnut Lodge Hospital," n.d.). It was located outside of Washington, DC, on the way to Baltimore. Upon the founder's death in 1931, his son, Dexter Means Bullard, Sr., gradually established the sanatorium as a "psychoanalytic hospital" operating on Freudian treatment principles.

Bullard believed that there were psychotic persons, but not "psychotics," and he believed that psychotic people could be treated by psychotherapy. He engaged Marjorie Jarvis as the first psychoanalytically trained staff psychiatrist in 1933. Bullard and Jarvis soon evolved the "Lodge belief" of providing an administrator and a therapist for each patient, in order to minimize the patient's tendency to manipulate the therapist into decision-making and judgmental modes. Chestnut Lodge was one of the first hospitals in the United States to utilize a psychodynamic approach and emphasize interpersonal relationships in treatment. The hospital initially specialized in the long-term residential treatment of severely ill (and usually chronic) psychotic and borderline patients.

Bullard subsequently recruited some of the most brilliant and innovative therapists of the time, such as Frieda Fromm-Reichmann, Harry Stack Sullivan, and David Rioch. This remarkable group of individuals were interested in extending the frontiers of psychoanalysis (Artiss, 1978). Because they considered orthodoxy to be anathema, they were dubbed Neo-Freudians. The writings of this group (Fromm-Reichmann, 1950; Sullivan, 1958; 1962) were extensive, and they were probably the most influential in what was to be the dominant theme in psychotherapy: a *dynamic* orientation.

The Menninger Clinic in Topeka, Kansas was founded in 1919 by Charles Menninger and his sons, Karl and William. The clinic started as a modest provincial health center and later expanded into a psychiatric hospital and educational institution. The 19th-century version of "moral therapy" was the treatment initially advocated by the clinic. The idea was to provide humane treatment with dignity to mentally ill patients (as opposed to the traditional "warehouse" treatment of patients with violence and mechanical restraints) and to provide individually designed occupational therapy, religious programs, and recreation in order to reeducate patients into a new life (Friedman, 1990).

The Menninger Clinic would achieve its widest recognition and have its greatest impact between 1940 and 1960. William Menninger played a central role during World War II in shaping the future role of mental health professionals and psychotherapy. Karl Menninger was a conceptualizer and prolific writer. His book, *Man Against Himself* (1938), became a national bestseller, and it earned for the Menninger Clinic the title "The Mayo Clinic of Psychiatry" within the media. The Menninger Clinic was later reshaped in many ways by emigre psychotherapists from Europe, who introduced their European training and insights. One of these emigres was a Hungarian psychologist, David Rapaport, who was hired by Menninger in 1940 to institute a new program in psychological testing.

The early psychoanalytic clinics, with a number of smaller and less renowned centers, became settings through which psychotherapy was initially popularized in the United States. Initially considered a European import, psychoanalytic psychotherapy gradually became synonymous in the public's mind with psychotherapy itself, and that image remained largely unchanged as a general public image until well into the 1960s.

University Counseling Centers: 1920–1939

The development of intelligence testing prior to and during World War I, together with the widespread application of intelligence testing in schools and colleges after the war, greatly influenced the development of university counseling centers. Following the war and as the result of the impetus provided by the personnel work in the army, there were a variety of developments. The Division of Anthropology and Psychology of the National Research Council held a series of meetings to discuss the possibilities of initiating a scientific vocational guidance program at the college level. As a result of these conferences, the American Council on Education sponsored a cooperative intelligence test program and in 1923, organized its Committee on Cooperative Experiments in Student Personnel. The activities of the committee stimulated tremendous nationwide interest in undertaking student guidance programs in high schools and colleges. The committee provided instruments for making guidance work effective through the development of the cumulative record card (the simplified rating scale for students), aided and encouraged E. K. Strong, Jr. in his work of measuring vocational interests, and encouraged experimentation in constructing adequate vocational information monographs. The committee also developed adequate achievement tests at the secondary school and at the junior college levels, from which evolved the batteries of objective achievement tests constructed by the Cooperative Test Service, directed by Ben D. Wood (Williamson & Darley, 1937, p. ix).

The growth in counseling centers paralleled the rapid expansion of psychology departments in colleges and universities in America. The University of Minnesota established the University Testing Bureau in 1932, organizing counseling functions in a separate operating unit within the university (Hedahl, 1978). Before the end of the 1930s, similar services were provided at other institutions, such as the University of Chicago, University of Illinois, Ohio State University, University of Missouri, and University of Pennsylvania.

The role of counseling in college and university settings was broadly defined as helping students remove or overcome a variety of obstacles or problems (e.g., personality, educational, financial, and health) so that students could maximally benefit from course instruction (Williamson, 1939). The terms *counseling*, *vocational guidance*, and *student personnel* were often used interchangeably, resulting in conceptual uncertainties as well as confusion about what student services were provided by whom (Hedahl, 1978; Super, 1955). It was not fully clear what kind of students utilized the early counseling centers—or why. Williamson and Bordin (1941) found that vocational problems were the most commonly presented concerns, followed by educational issues and personal problems. Some studies suggested that the users of counseling center services were not atypical students when compared to the entire student population (Raphael, 1936; Schneidler & Berdie, 1942).

As student services and formalized counseling grew in the late 1930s, professional books began to appear with titles such as *Student Personnel Work* (Williamson & Darley, 1937), *The Art of Counseling* (May, 1939), *How to Counsel Students* (Williamson, 1939), *Guidance for College Students* (McCaul, 1939), and *Student Personnel Work: An Outline of Clinical Procedures and Techniques* (Schneidler, Paterson, & Williamson, 1935).

World War II would later have a considerable impact on the development of counseling centers. There was a need after the war for universities to assist returning World War II veterans to adjust to the campus environment (Pepinsky, Hill-Frederick, & Epperson, 1978). The VA guidance program was a major factor in the expansion of college counseling services (Embree, 1959; Long, 1952; see chapter 2).

Both conscious self-reflection and behavioral models were more comfortable to the American academic community than was European psychoanalysis. There were early attempts at behavior therapy that often reflected both the early stimulus—response simplicity of behavior theory at the time, as well as the then current naivete toward clinical procedures. The latter brought derision from dynamically oriented psychotherapists off campus, who were also smarting from the ridicule to which psychoanalysis was being subjected in psychology classrooms. Given the context of the time, it was understandable that *client-centered therapy* as conceptualized by Carl Rogers (Rogers, 1942; 1951) became the dominant force in the university counseling centers (see chapter 19). First, it was compatible with American behaviorism. Second, it was not pathology-oriented and was suited to the intelligent, relatively normal problems of the college student. The basic concept was that an individual possesses a self-actualizing tendency that promotes health and growth. The psychotherapist facilitated the removal of emotional blocks or impediments to growth and promoted maturation, self-cure, and the assimilation of new experiences (Rogers, 1951; see chapter 19).

The child guidance clinic movement grew out of efforts in the early 1900s to change the way the legal system handled youthful offenders. The first clinic devoted to working with juvenile delinquents was established in Chicago in 1909 by psychiatrist William Healy and psychologist Augusta Bronner (Ridenour, 1961, p. 36). Healy and Bronner would later move to Boston in 1917, when the Judge Baker Guidance Center was established.

The National Committee on Mental Hygiene, established by Clifford Beers (also in 1909), provided considerable leadership during the child guidance movement, particularly under the medical directorship of George Stevenson. Many of the National Committee's activities were supported by the Commonwealth Fund in New York. [In September 1950, the National Committee merged with two other organizations, the National Mental Health Foundation and the Psychiatric Foundation, to form what is now the National Mental Health Association.] Under the auspices of the National Committee for Mental Hygiene and the Commonwealth Fund, a series of demonstration child guidance clinics were established during the 1920s: the first, a court-affiliated program in St. Louis; the second (which failed) in Norfolk; the third, a school and social agency-linked program in Dallas; and the fourth, a university-related program in Minnesota/St. Paul. Three other programs were also quickly established in Los Angeles, Cleveland, and Philadelphia (Ridenour, 1961, p. 37).

As implied above, until 1916 there had been only one clinic in the United States (the Healy/Bronner Chicago Clinic) using what has come to be called the child guidance clinic model. There were 72 by 1926, and the total further increased to 102 in 1927 (Lowrey & Smith, 1933, p. 3). Twenty-seven of these clinics were full-time programs with full-time staffs, and the rest provided part-time services (Ridenour, 1961, p. 38).

Although these new child guidance clinics often initially specialized in work with delinquents, they generally served a broad spectrum of the younger population and their families. Working in child guidance clinics provided mental health professionals experience with the broadest array of clinical problems, development issues, and family conflict. The child guidance clinics could serve a large segment of the nation's population, from the middle class to the poor, by regarding the child as the identified patient or the focal point for treating individually all of the family members. The orientation of most child guidance clinics was psychodynamic, resulting in a prohibition against one therapist's seeing more than one member of the family. Family therapy (see chapter 8) had not yet been conceptualized, and different therapists saw each of the family members. The team approach was interdisciplinary (Ridenour, 1961, p. 36) and was regarded as radical and the cutting edge for the time. With the psychiatrist firmly in charge, the social worker conducted initial clinical intakes (and later worked with the parents), the psychologist did the psychological testing, and the psychiatrist made the diagnosis and carried out the treatment.

Although social work was the dominant profession in this movement, child guidance clinics were, nonetheless, a significant practice setting for psychologists. Thus, the early child guidance centers, along with schools and the military, gave testing-oriented psychologists important access to a broad spectrum of children—as well as to childhood psychological, educational, and behavioral problems with which to work and to develop assessment instrumentations and normative data. Child guidance centers also provided psychologists with experience in counseling and psychotherapy. For example, Carl Rogers began his career at the Institute for Child Guidance in New York City in 1927 (see chapter 19). In 1928, he accepted a position at the Child Study Department of the Society for the Prevention of Cruelty to Children in Rochester, New York. In 1939, he accepted the directorship of the program, which had evolved into the Rochester Guidance Center (Corsini, 1984, p. 248).

In general, child guidance centers played an important role in the evolution of modern psychotherapy. They provided the "laboratory" for extending techniques developed with adults to younger populations and also provided a setting within which techniques specific to clinical work with children (and families) could be developed and refined. They provided a setting in which the so-called core mental health professions could interact and collaborate, learning about and from the skills and expertise of each other. In addition, they provided psychotherapists with exposure to an expanding range of psychological and behavioral problems, including "normal" life struggles, so that theories of psychological development and conceptions of approaches for change could broaden and deepen.

A Trickle Into Private Practice

A small number of psychologists began to venture into independent practice during these decades. Most private psychotherapists were trained psychoanalysts, and only a small number were psychologists. Most notable was Theodore Reik, who was charged with practicing medicine without a license by virtue of his practicing psychoanalysis. Freud supported the rights of lay analysts and trained a number of them, including Reik. Illness prevented Freud from appearing in court as an expert witness. Rather, what was to be published later as *The Question of Lay Analysis* (Freud, 1926) was

Exhibit A for the defense at Reik's trial. Reik was exonerated and not one nonphysician has been subsequently and similarly prosecuted!

Those few psychologists who were trained as analysts practiced at the more liberal psychoanalytic institutes and received referrals from them into their independent practices. Prominent among these was Sigfried Bernfeldt, who possessed a European doctorate in psychology and was trained by Freud in Vienna. Bernfeldt founded the San Francisco Psychoanalytic Institute, practiced privately in that city, and soon found himself deposed when the psychoanalytic movement, following Freud's death, retrenched as solely a medical profession. Subsequently, the San Francisco Psychoanalytic Institute developed the reputation of being the most orthodox and restrictive of the American psychoanalytic institutes. In Detroit, Richard and Edith Sterba started the Detroit Psychoanalytic Institute but soon lost their hold on the organization, which subsequently assumed a new name and leadership.

Following the freezing-out of nonphysicians by the psychoanalytic institutes, some psychologists, mostly on a master's degree level, scattered across the nation, continued their personal analyses, and accepted overflow referrals from their analysts. These were lean times; a combination of the Great Depression and the relative nonacceptance of psychotherapy by the American public brought limited prospective patients.

EXPANSION OF TRAINING AND PRACTICE IN MENTAL HEALTH DISCIPLINES (AND IN PSYCHOTHERAPY): 1940–1959

In 1939, the American Psychological Association (APA) had 2,527 members. The vast majority of psychologists in the 1930s were in academic settings, and they did not identify themselves as psychotherapists or clinical psychologists. The American Psychiatric Association had 2,235 members. The majority of psychiatrists had psychiatric hospital affiliations (or university affiliations), perhaps with part-time private practice on the side. Even within psychiatry, there were only a few psychotherapists, because about 80% of psychiatrists were organically and biologically oriented. The majority of social workers worked in the department of social welfare and other public employment settings. Almost none identified themselves primarily as psychotherapists.

To the general public, psychotherapy was still a little-known clinical activity in 1940. To the extent that it was known, psychotherapy was synonymous with psychoanalysis in the public mind. Between 1940 and 1959, the American public would begin to learn about (and use) psychotherapy—primarily because of a major expansion of training opportunities for mental health professionals after World War II. The availability of providers led to greater public knowledge about and use of psychotherapy.

It is not known with certainty the percentage of the U.S. population who had used any type of mental health services at any point in their lives as of 1940, but it is highly unlikely that that number exceeded 3 or 4%. By 1957, approximately 14% of the U.S. public had, at one point or another in their lifetime, received some type of psychological care, education, or intervention from a physician, nurse, pastor, psychologist, social worker, or other professional (Gurin, Veroff, & Feld, 1960); and the majority of this psychotherapeutic contact was occurring on an outpatient basis.

Five major events or initiatives fueled the recognition of mental health and illness during the period from 1940 through 1959. These events contributed to the expansion of training opportunities in psychotherapy, and they stimulated greater availability and use of psychotherapy by the general public. These events and initiatives were World War II, the VA programs after World War II, the establishment of the National Institute of Mental Health (NIMH) in the late 1940s, the expansion of health insurance programs as basic employment benefits, and increased efforts by the federal government in developing social and health programs to benefit the well-being of all Americans.

World War II

World War II saw the majority of major industrialized nations fully recognizing the role that psychological factors, chronic stress, and terrifying circumstances played in behavior and functioning. Rowntree, McGill, and Edwards (1943) listed mental disease, neurologic disorders, and mental deficiency as among the 10 leading causes for rejection among 18- and 19-year-old Selective Service registrants during World War II. In addition, the army reported that almost 45% of its first 1.5 million medical discharges were due to neuropsychiatric disabilities, and the army estimated that at least 2 million veterans would need psychiatric or psychological treatment by the end of the war (Grinker & Spiegel, 1945; Kirsch & Winter, 1983). The myth that only "weaklings" develop psychiatric disturbances was finally dismissed because of reports coming from combat. The incidence of psychiatric cases was uniformly higher among veteran combat troops than among fresh, green troops. It became evident that anybody could manifest psychological and behavioral problems under certain circumstances (Farrell & Appel, 1944).

Due to limitation of professional personnel and urgency of the military situation, priority was given to those individuals expected to return to duty. Attempts were made to keep psychiatric patients out of hospitals. Thus, patients were treated on an outpatient basis. World War II forced a broadening in the conceptualization of mental health ideology and treatment from the exclusive reliance on personal pathology to an expansion in the thinking and activities of mental health professionals, particularly among those with interests in psychotherapy.

World War II also saw the greatest use ever of psychiatrists, psychologists, and psychiatric social workers (Hutt, Menninger, & O'Keefe, 1947). At the war's end, over 2,400 medical officers, 400 commissioned clinical psychologists, and 600 enlisted social workers were assigned to military psychiatric facilities—generally working in interdisciplinary neuropsychiatric teams (Menninger, 1947). However, the military had trained the majority of these individuals in intensive training programs during the war.

Psychiatrist William Menninger was commissioned in the U.S. Army in November of 1942, and he became the director of the Neuropsychiatric Consultants Division of the Office of the Surgeon General in December of 1943. Under the War Powers Act, Menninger took over a large portion of Pilgrim State Hospital in Long Island, New York, renamed it Mason General Hospital, and created the School of Military Neuropsychiatry, through which psychiatrists were trained. Clinical psychologists were given direct commissions and received additional training at the Adjutant General's School and in the neuropsychiatric sections of general hospitals (Hutt, Menninger, & O'Keefe, 1947). Among the psychologists who came into the army program was a master's level individual named Max Hutt. He was initially drafted, promoted to sergeant, and soon after became the first psychologist to be commissioned as an officer—a second lieutenant. Hutt was centrally involved in shepherding a large number of individuals with some training in psychology through the army program and into assignments as clinical psychologists both in the field and in military hospitals worldwide.

Although psychiatrists were clearly defined as the head of the military neuropsychiatric teams (and psychologists and social workers were clearly expected to work under the supervision of a psychiatrist), the magnitude of the World War II psychiatric service needs forced the military to allow psychologists and social workers increased responsibilities beyond their usual activities. Through the efforts of William Menninger, psychologists became included in the official table of organizations of the larger army hospitals by March of 1944 (Friedman, 1990, p. 225). Menninger's efforts provided the opportunity for psychologists as well as nurses to become actively involved in the treatment process of military personnel experiencing psychological and behavioral difficulties. In addition to advocating for a strong clinical psychology presence on military psychiatric treatment teams, psychologists were allowed to assist in the treatment process in the Menninger Clinic in Kansas.

Thus, the military health care system during World War II played a key role as a setting in providing the opportunity for nonphysician practitioners (primarily psychologists) to receive clinical training in psychotherapy as well as actual supervised experience in the conduct of psychotherapy (Napoli, 1981). In addition, both the "battlefield setting" and the "military hospital setting" provided nonphysicians with experience in treating different levels and types of psychological problems through psychotherapy, and laid the experiential base for community psychology/psychiatry. Shortly after World War II, it was clear that psychologists viewed psychotherapy as a legitimate part of their professional role, second only to assessment (Hutt & Milton, 1947).

Veterans Administration Programs

A large number of veterans were experiencing psychological and behavioral problems after the conclusion of World War II. The VA had to deal with the rehabilitation and vocational training of those less severely impaired, as well as the long-term care of those veterans who were permanently disabled. In April of 1946, VA hospitals had 74,000 patients, of whom 59.5% (or 44,000) were "neuropsychiatric" patients (Miller, 1946, p. 182). The VA learned, just as the military had during the war, that there was a major shortage of mental health personnel to provide psychotherapy and other mental health services to these World War II veterans.

It was clear to the federal government, as military forces were demobilized, that the traditional private medical care model would probably result in either inadequate or nontreatment of most veterans. The VA would have to provide such care at VA hospitals and clinics across the United States. Almost overnight, the VA became the single largest employer of clinical psychologists (and psychiatrists and psychiatric social workers).

For two decades, clinical psychologists had been moving toward formally incorporating psychotherapy training into their profession (and pressing for the establishment of higher standards of training). The VA was the force that transformed that ambition into reality. The VA did so by providing paid traineeships for clinical graduate students and jobs for the graduates, by establishing the PhD as the minimum educational requirement for clinical psychologists, and by defining the psychologist's role to include the practice of individual and group psychotherapy.

The VA put in place a major training program for clinical psychologists, a program that was created in consultation with organized psychology (Ash, 1968a, 1968b; Miller, 1946; chapter 24, this volume). Similar collaborative initiatives were developed between the VA and psychiatry and social work. George A. Kelly was the first psychological consultant to the VA clinical psychology program and James G. Miller was the first chief of VA Psychology (Ash, 1968b). The VA's 4-year training program included actual supervised clinical experience. Although the primary focus of such clinical experience was on psychological testing and interviewing skills, the principles of psychotherapy were explicit components of training and fell within the expected activities of third- and fourth-year VA trainees (Miller, 1946, p. 187).

The VA clinical psychology training program, combined with the efforts of the NIMH, were designed explicitly to increase the numbers of trained mental health professionals qualified to provide psychotherapy. By the fall of 1946, 22 universities had undertaken doctoral level training programs for clinical psychologists in collaboration with the VA (Ash, 1968a). These programs grew rapidly, from 200 trainees in 1946 to 650 by 1950. There would be more than 700 graduate student trainees and interns in psychology each year in the VA system for several decades to follow. Moreover, the number of university-based psychology programs collaborating with the VA would grow to over 100. And, important to the VA mission, many of the VA trainees went on to employment within the VA. In a report on the first 10 years of the VA psychology program, Wolford (1956) noted that as of January 1, 1956, there were 585 clinical psychologists employed by the VA, with as many as five additional slots being created each month. Wolford also noted that the VA expected that when the psychology program was fully implemented, approximately 1,500 clinical psychologists would be in their employ. Wolford also commented on the contribution of VA psychologists to research, noting that at that time there were over 336 federally funded research projects being conducted by VA psychologists, not only in the area of psychotherapy research but also in physiological psychology, psychopharmacology, basic experimental psychology, social and personality psychology, and other areas.

National Institute of Mental Health Programs

NIMH was established in 1948. It represented a postwar effort of the federal government to expand basic and applied research and increase the number of mental health professionals available to serve the nation's psychological needs. The establishment of NIMH served as a symbol and as a means of concretizing the idea that psychological problems were real problems for which treatment and interventions, such as psychotherapy, were appropriate and needed. NIMH's role was to serve as the funding institution for meeting the federal government's objectives.

In August 1949, the Boulder Conference on Graduate Training and Clinical Psychology (Raimy, 1950) was held, with funding from NIMH. The Boulder Conference was psychology's first attempt to look at the social value of applied psychology. It represented an encouraging development for those within the APA whose interests were in the applied use of psychology, but it was not appealing to those more satisfied with the traditional pursuit of scientific psychology, wherein applications were only incidental to research itself.

The outcome of the Boulder Conference was the establishment of a scientist-practitioner model for professional training (see chapters 25 and 26). The model was a strongly academic one, and both didactic preparation and practical internship training became the responsibility of university-based departments of psychology. Clinical psychologists were to be simultaneously trained as scientists and as service providers and were expected to combine both roles in their postgraduate professional activities. It was agreed that all clinical doctoral students should be trained in psychotherapy, but independent private practice was opposed by most of those present (Cummings & VandenBos, 1983; Kirsch & Winter, 1983). The dual-training model adopted was to provide clinical psychology with unique skills and perspectives among mental health professionals. The Boulder Conference recognized the doctoral degree as the minimal standard for the practicing professional psychologist and recommended that the APA and the state associations act to further legislate for the licensing and/or certification of psychologists (Pottharst, 1976). Despite the persistence of negative attitudes toward private practice on the part of academic psychologists, by the mid-1970s, nearly one in four clinicians were primarily private practitioners, and almost half were engaged in part-time private practice (Garfield & Kurtz, 1976).

Following up on the initiative of the VA, NIMH provided the support for the core academic-based mental health training programs, and supported students in the first 2 years of academic training. Thus, in the late 1940s, universities across the United States became, for the first time, heavily involved in the clinical training of psychologists through encouragement by and support of the federal government—especially the VA and NIMH. In 1948, the NIMH appropriation for clinical training was $1,107,000, or 17.6% of the NIMH budget for fiscal year (FY) 1948. The 1948 NIMH research training budget was $277,000. By FY 1950, the total had increased to $3,182,000 for clinical training (and an additional $796,000 for research training). The combined 1950 research/clinical training budget represented 35% of the total NIMH budget. This support would grow to $4.6 million by 1955 and $22.9 million by 1960. The funds were used to support university-based clinical faculty as well as to provide traineeships for individuals (Cummings & VandenBos, 1983). The funds supported the core training of individuals in their *given* disciplines, and whether or not an individual received training in psychotherapy depended on the discipline, the particular university-based program attended, and the specific clinical setting for placement, internship, or residency.

NIMH clinical training support far exceeded research training support for the first 30 years in the existence of NIMH. Out of the first-year total of $1.1 million, the distribution among professions was approximately 40:20:20:20 among psychiatry, psychology, psychiatric social work, and psychiatric nursing. The initial pattern of the distribution of clinical training funds was not to last long. For most of the years between 1950 and 1975, psychiatry was to receive between 47% and 48% of the NIMH clinical training dollars. Psychology departments received $750,000 of such NIMH support in 1955 (16.3%) and $3.3 million by 1960 (14.4%). At its highest point, in 1974, NIMH clinical training support reached $111,813,000 (NIMH, 1990).

For the young psychiatrist, this meant university training (including practical experience in a training hospital) and advanced clinical experience in a hospital setting. For psychologists, the situation could be highly varied. Perhaps the most common pattern was university-based training, university-based practica (often either in a clinic run by the psychology department [see chapter 22] or in a university counseling center) and internships—a very large percentage of which were initially in the VA system. In the late 1940s, only a small percentage of psychiatric social workers and psychiatric nurses were receiving training and supervision in psychotherapy as part of their core training.

For more than 20 years, the positive experience of the benefits derived from mental health personnel during World War II served as the underlying basis of national policy. The postwar goal was to increase the supply of mental health personnel. The mechanism for achieving this was federally funded university-based clinical training programs that were reviewed, approved, selected, and funded through the NIMH.

NIMH, likewise, formalized and legitimized the area of mental health as a topic of research. One of the early research foci of NIMH was on both the process and outcome of psychotherapy. NIMH was interested in knowing if psychotherapy worked, how it worked, and what helped or hindered the effectiveness of the process.

A series of three NIMH-assisted Research in Psychotherapy Conferences followed in 1958, 1961, and 1966. Each conference had the general purpose of developing a comprehensive picture of current research in psychotherapy and of bringing together active researchers in psychotherapy to promote collaboration and weighing of the evidence. The first conference was designed to provide a comprehensive picture of ongoing research in psychotherapy (see chapter 12) and to foster dialogue between psychologists and psychiatrists (Rubinstein & Parloff, 1959). The agenda of the second conference was to deal more intensively with a few selected research issues relevant to individual psychotherapy with adult neurotic patients, to assess new research developments, to ensure continuity of exchange of information among investigators, and to place research in psychotherapy more squarely within psychological research concerned with understanding interpersonal processes (Strupp & Luborsky, 1962, p. vi). The third conference had a broad range, reflecting the diversity and intensity in the field, and included international participants. The 1966 conference resulted in plans for increased collaborative research efforts and in the creation of a continuing committee to develop the guidelines for collaborative endeavor (Shlien, 1968).

Thus, throughout the 1950s, NIMH provided significant financial resources for university-based programs to provide the basic or core training for the mental health professions—as well as support for research training, investigator-initiated research projects on psychotherapy, and other basic and applied psychological issues.

Private Health Insurance Initiatives

There were few health insurance plans prior to 1920. An individual either fully paid for health care as a routine personal expense or else received "charity" health care if viewed as truly in need. The massive growth in voluntary health insurance began in response to urgent needs precipitated by the catastrophic economic depression of the early 1930s (Falk, 1964). Similar to the Social Security system installed in 1935 under the Social Security Act (Public Law [PL] 74-271), health insurance was looked upon by many as "creeping socialism", and it was opposed for philosophical and political reasons.

The World War II experience had shown how personally paid health care coverage (backed up by so-called charity medical coverage and limited governmental support) had left the nation without an adequate health care system to mobilize for the war effort. It was also clear that health status (and health care) previously had not been a national priority, although labor unions in the 1930s were beginning efforts to make health care a national priority and a benefit of employment. During World War II, individuals serving in the military became exposed to the ready availability of medical care, and the civilian population was beginning to receive health insurance as an employment benefit (with the latter occurring, in large part, because there were anti-inflationary governmental restrictions on wage increases but not on fringe benefit increases such as pensions and health insurance). After the war, those who had some claim on VA health services also continued to have readier access to routine health care, often at little or no cost to them.

Just prior to World War II, only 12 million Americans were covered by some type of health insurance plans, but this expanded during the war such that 37 million persons had some form of health insurance by the end of the war (Falk, 1964). Unions began after the war to systematically negotiate to make health insurance a basic employee benefit. Corporations began to find that the availability of health insurance was increasingly important for the recruitment and retention of skilled employees. Approximately 125 million Americans (69.2% of the U.S. population) had some level of health insurance by 1960 (United States Department of Health, Education, and Welfare [DHEW], 1962).

However, as of 1960, the amount of annual health care expenditures actually reimbursed or reimbursable under then existing health insurance plans was only in the 24–27% range (Mott & Hudenberg, 1959). Thus, in the 1960s, union efforts, as well as the efforts of other groups, would focus on expanding the scope of benefits and increasing the percentage of health care expenditures that were actually reimbursed by health insurance plans.

Psychotherapy, and particularly outpatient psychotherapy, was rarely a benefit in health insurance plans in 1959–1960. However, the expansion of third party health insurance reimbursement and the expansion of the supply of providers were setting the stage for the further recognition and use of psychotherapy in the 1960s and the 1970s.

Paralleling the insurance-related events above was expansion of state legislation statutorily recognizing nonphysician mental health providers, legally giving them authority to be providers of psychotherapy. Medicine and hence, psychiatry had long had state licensure, but psychology, social work, and the specialty area of psychiatric nursing did not.

In 1945 Connecticut had become the first state to certify psychologists, and in 1946 Virginia passed the first state law that licensed individuals to practice psychology (Dörken, 1976). There was a distinction between licensing and certification. A licensing law defines the practice of a profession and restricts its functions to qualified individuals; a certification law permits the use of a specific professional title to qualified individuals, and it may or may not include the definition of practice (Cummings & VandenBos, 1983). By 1960, 15 states enacted either psychology licensing or certification laws, although this number would increase to 42 states by 1970; in 1977, the last state, Missouri, would pass a psychology licensing law.

In the case of social work, the first licensing law for social workers was enacted in Puerto Rico in 1934. California passed a social work license law in 1945, and no other states developed such legislation until the 1960s. Rhode Island adopted a registration law in 1961, and six additional states would pass licensing laws by 1970. A total of 24 states and U.S. territories had social work licensing or registration laws by 1980. By 1990, 50 states and territories required licensing or registration of social workers. Twenty states plus the District of Columbia issue specific licenses for clinical social workers (National Association of Social Workers, 1990).

The position of organized psychiatry toward certification or licensing of nonphysician mental health providers has always been a difficult one, both within organized psychiatry and between the American Psychiatric Association and the other mental health disciplines. For example, the American Psychological Association established the Committee on Clinical Psychology in 1945, whose purpose was to clarify the relationship between clinical psychology and psychiatry, and the American Psychiatric Association had appointed a parallel committee (APA, 1945). Interprofessional collaboration was stressed; not explicitly stated, however, was what kinds of collaboration were being proposed. For psychologists, it was consultation with psychiatric colleagues; for psychiatrists, it was supervision of lesser qualified health care technicians (Hildreth, 1967). Psychiatrists sought to refer for psychological testing in the same manner they would order an X-ray or a laboratory test, and they resented any attempt by the reporting psychologist to go beyond merely describing a patient's test performance to diagnosis or even personality description. Needless to say, this resistance was met with fierce hostility from practicing psychologists (Cummings & VandenBos, 1983, p. 1307). As psychologists strove to achieve legal recognition for their profession, psychology and psychiatry were soon enmeshed in considerable conflict. By the mid-1950s, organized psychiatry began opposing the licensure of psychologists (Sanford, 1955, pp. 93–96) and their ability and authority to provide psychotherapy independent of a psychiatrist. In the 1960s, however, third party health insurance carriers would prove to be open to nonphysician mental health providers.

Federal Involvement in Health Care

After World War II, the federal government began to play an in-creasing role in its support of health care, education, social services, basic research, transportation, and many other areas. Much of this expanded involvement between 1946 and 1959 hinged upon the rationale that such involvement was essential for national defense reasons (cf. DeLeon & VandenBos, 1985, p. 411). In the late 1950s, the rationale for the need for and benefit of social programs began to change as basic concern about social, economic, educational, and health needs emerged.

Even before World War II ended, Congress became concerned about the health, educational, vocational, and readjustment needs after the war of those individuals serving in the military. On June 22, 1944, President Roosevelt signed into law the Servicemen's Readjustment Act of 1944 (PL 78-346). This became known as the GI Bill, and it had three main provisions for individual veterans: (a) up to 1 year of readjustment for unemployment benefits to veterans after their discharge until they could find jobs; (b) guaranteed loans for the purchase of a home, farm, or business; and (c) college or technical school tuition and monthly subsistence for former veterans seeking additional vocational or educational training. In addition, the legislation authorized up to $500 million for construction of additional VA facilities.

As increasing numbers of veterans and their dependents were residing at distances far from military bases and VA facilities, the Congress developed in 1956 the Civilian Health and Medical Program of the Uniformed Ser-vices, or CHAMPUS (PL 84-567). This particular federal program is cur-rently responsible for providing health care to approximately 7 million dependents of active duty personnel, retirees, and the dependents of retirees and deceased military personnel, as well as certain veterans. For FY 1992, the Bush Administration requested $3.5 billion for CHAMPUS, of which approximately 25% would be for mental health care, and 77% of the mental health care allocation would be for inpatient mental health services. The CHAMPUS program provides important sources of reimbursement for psy-chotherapy (such as in Norfolk, San Diego, and Honolulu) and stimulated the delivery of psychotherapy in private practice settings in the 1960s and 1970s.

The federal government also took the initiative in the late 1950s to develop a comprehensive model for health insurance when the Congress developed and passed the Federal Employees' Health Benefit Program Act of 1959 (FEHBPA, PL 86-382), which established the largest voluntary health insurance plan in the United States. The plan covered all federal employees, annuitants, and their dependents. In 1960, 5.5 million individuals were covered by the program at a cost of $120 million to the federal government. By 1990, 9 million individuals were covered by the plan. In 1992, the estimated federal government contribution for the FEHBPA insurance plan is $10.5 billion.

Mental health services per se were not legislatively mandated benefits in the FEHBPA program, but the U.S. Office of Personnel Management increasingly negotiated such benefits into the FEHBPA plans. There would be no limits on outpatient psychotherapy under the two largest plans, Blue Cross/Blue Shield and Aetna, until 1974. The FEHBPA plan was an early model for other insurance carriers. Because of the high concentration of federal employees in such cities as Washington, DC, New York, Chicago, and Los Angeles, the outpatient reimbursement possibilities offered under FEHBPA coverage would facilitate the expansion of private practice psychotherapy by psychologists and psychiatrists in the 1960s.

President Eisenhower appointed the Joint Commission on Mental Illness and Health in 1955 (Joint Commission on Mental Illness and Health, 1961). The Joint Commission conducted a national survey of public attitudes toward and use of mental health care in 1956. One in four respondents indicated he or she had experienced some type of psychological or behavioral problem during his or her lifetime for which professional help would have been useful. One out of seven had actually sought some type of help for past psychological problems. This "went for help" group tended to be women, younger persons, and better educated individuals. They had a tendency to define their problems in psychological terms and to seek some form of psychological help. Among those who sought help, 42% consulted clergymen, 29% consulted general physicians, 18% consulted psychiatrists or psychologists, and 13% went to social agencies or marriage clinics. Thus, only 31% of those who sought help obtained those services from a professional trained in a mental health discipline (Gurin, Veroff, & Feld, 1960).[1] Using the latter definition, one could argue that, in the mid-1950s, the genuine rate of use of professional mental health services at any point in a person's life was 3.99% (although the public defined their lifetime probability of use as 14.3%).

As the period 1940–1959 was coming to an end, America was enjoying expanded economic opportunities. Employment, gross national product (GNP), and incomes were increasing. The federal government's role in American society was also expanding. Many social and political forces were coming together in the late 1950s that would contribute to major expansion

---

[1] Percentages total more than 100 because of multiple responses.

in federal social programs as well as in public and private health insurance during the 1960s and 1970s.

INFLUENCES ON THE EXPANSION OF PSYCHOTHERAPY PRACTICE: 1960–1992

When President Kennedy instituted his community mental health efforts in the early 1960s, it appeared that only 14% of our nation's population (then 180 million) had ever used psychiatric services from any type of provider (Gurin, Veroff, & Feld, 1960). By 1976, data suggested that over 26% had used mental health services at some point in their lives, and 33% could have used or might need help (Kulka, Veroff, & Douvan, 1979). In 1990, the population of the United States totaled over 250 million, and it is probable that at least 33% of the population have received mental health services at some point in their lives—or, over 65 million Americans.

In 1960, APA had 18,215 members. This increased to 30,839 by 1970; 50,933 in 1980; and 70,266 by 1990. By 1983, the majority of all psychologists were employed in service settings (VandenBos, Stapp, & Kilberg, 1981; Stapp, Tucker, & VandenBos, 1985), and the majority of psychologists identified themselves as psychotherapists. In 1960, the American Psychiatric Association had 11,037 members. This grew to 18,407 in 1970; 25,345 in 1980; and 37,077 in 1990. Similar growth was noted within psychiatric social work. The psychiatric nurse psychotherapist emerged during the latter half of this period in sufficient numbers to be recognized. Also, marriage and family therapists emerged during the 1980s as licensable providers of family and couples work, and mental health counselors began to be viewed as acceptable providers of counseling. Thus, by the mid-1980s, some social observers estimated that there were about 159,000 psychotherapists in the United States, an increase of over 100% since the 1975 estimate of 72,000 psychotherapists (Goleman, 1985).

Four major initiatives stimulated the use of psychotherapy during the period between 1960 and 1992. The events built on the earlier expansion of training opportunities in psychotherapy, and they were stimulated by governmental policy, insurance/corporate recognition of mental health care, and consumer demand. The initiatives were the federal community mental health legislation, the passage of Medicare/Medicaid, further development of private health insurance plans, and the federal health maintenance organization (HMO) legislation. The latter initiative evolved into a broader managed health care movement, which served about 15% of the U.S. population by 1990 (DeLeon, VandenBos, & Bulatao, 1991).

Community Mental Health Centers

The Congress, in 1962–1963, enacted far-reaching legislation intended to establish a comprehensive, nationwide system of community mental health centers (CMHCs). The Mental Retardation Facilities and Community Mental Health Center Construction Act of 1963 (PL 88-164) mandated a major shift in program emphasis, from large mental hospitals to smaller local facilities. CMHCs were to become a major setting for the delivery of outpatient psychotherapy, perhaps second only to private practice. These local CMHCs were required to provide outpatient services, emergency mental health care, partial hospitalization, inpatient care, and consultation and education. Hence, they needed to employ a broad array of service providers and treatment techniques.

This law had significant ramifications for the nature of mental health service delivery; the locus of delivery changed, the overall level of services increased, and differing client/patient needs had to be addressed. The community mental health legislation would serve to entice local communities to become involved more extensively in the provision of psychotherapy and other mental health services. The original plan of a CMHC in every community over 30,000 was never completely realized, but thousands of psychologists practiced in the CMHCs and the CMHC Construction Act was the greatest single contributor to the dispersal of psychotherapists (including psychologists) to rural America. Prior to the CMHC Construction Act, the majority of psychotherapists were concentrated in seven or eight metropolitan areas.

Tension among federal, state, and local governments ensued, because the federal program bypassed the state authorities. Historically, the state government, in collaboration with local authorities, had been responsible for long-term psychiatric hospitalization. Ultimately, the federal funding would return to the "state to local" mechanism in the early 1980s, but not before 20 years of direct funding to local entities established a fairly extensive system of community mental health centers. These community-based mental health programs had significant impact on the training of psychotherapists as well as the provision of psychotherapy in the late 1960s and through most of the 1970s. Within 20 years following the establishment of the CMHCs, the movement began to lose its federal funding support. Most states were either unable or unwilling to pick up the costs, and the CMHCs began a trend toward privatization.

Medicare/Medicaid

In 1965, Congress enacted Title XVIII and Title XIX (Medicare/Medicaid) of the Social Security Act. Medicare is a nationwide health

insurance program of an entitlement nature in which the primary beneficiaries are those eligible for Social Security disability benefits; various rail-
road retirees; and most important, nearly every senior citizen 65 years or
older. Benefits under the program are uniform across the nation, and one's
eligibility does not depend upon income or financial assets. Medicare is
100% federally financed. Medicaid, on the other hand, is a medical assistance program (rather than health insurance program) targeted for certain
needy and low-income persons. It is a state-operated and state-administered
program, and each state has the authority to create its own range of programmatic benefits within broad federal guidelines. Medicaid is funded at
ratios that can vary according to a number of factors. At the minimum,
the federal government will pay 50% of the medical assistance costs incurred
by a state (DeLeon & VandenBos, 1980).

Mental health care (and psychotherapy) were included in the original
legislation. However, mental health care was not a high priority, as shown
by a 50% patient copayment rate (as compared to only a 20% patient
copayment rate for physical health care); $500 per year maximum benefit
for outpatient care; and the exclusion of nonphysician providers, such as
psychologists and social workers. From the inception, the congressional
committees with jurisdiction over these two programs have stressed their
intention that these be health, not social welfare, programs. As such, both
have always had an express and deliberate medical orientation, and both
have included the requirement that only services that are "medically necessary" should be reimbursed.

Of considerable historical importance to psychology is the fact that
the Senate report accompanying the original bill (the Social Security
Amendments of 1965, PL 89-97) expressly stated that "the committee's
bill provides that the physician is to be the key figure in determining
utilization of health services" (United States Senate Committee on Finance,
1965, p. 46). In response to subsequent efforts by various nonphysician
health care providers to broaden the basic orientation of the programs, the
Congress directed the Department of Health, Education, and Welfare to
conduct a formal study of the possibility of expanding the availability of
various types of health services (PL 90-248). In December 1968, the department submitted its *Independent Practitioners Report* (Cohen, 1968) to
the Congress. The report specifically stated that the services of clinical
psychologists should be reimbursed when they are provided in an organized
setting and when there has been physician referral. Furthermore, it was
recommended that a physician should establish a plan for the patient's total
care and also retain overall responsibility for patient management (DeLeon,
VandenBos, & Kraut, 1986).

Later Medicare/Medicaid amendments expanded access to mental health services. Based on a 1972 amendment (PL 92-603), the Colorado Medicare Study was conducted (Bent, Willens, & Lassen, 1983; McCall & Rice, 1983). In 1980, psychological services and psychotherapy were expressly enumerated under several Medicare provisions (PL 96-499) authorizing payment for rehabilitation services. In 1984, the first significant Medicare success directly benefiting psychologists was the inclusion of language in the Deficit Reduction Act of 1984 (PL 98-369), which authorized coverage for psychologists as autonomous providers under the risk-sharing HMO provisions of the Act. PL 98-369 also allowed nonphysicians to head a Medicaid clinic. The Mental Health Organizational Amendments of 1986 (PL 99-660) explicitly listed psychologists among the authorized HMO professions, whereas prior to this modification, psychologists' services were actually only recognized under the broad heading of "other health care providers." This 1986 Medicare recognition of psychologists represented the first official recognition of psychologists in any Medicare-related legislation. A year later, the Omnibus Budget Reconciliation Act of 1987 (PL 100-203) amended the Social Security Act to include coverage of clinical social worker services provided by HMOs to their enrollees. During the 101st Congress, professional psychology obtained autonomous recognition under Part B of Medicare, as a provision of the Omnibus Budget Reconciliation Act of 1989 (PL 101-239).

The Medicare legislation contributed little to the evolution of psychotherapy during the 1970s and 1980s. Although it provided an important policy issue for debate, for the resolution of issues related to patient access to outpatient mental health care, and for the recognition of nonphysician psychotherapists, it had little impact on the practice of psychotherapy and on the training of psychotherapists. However, the Medicare restrictions virtually eliminated nursing homes and other settings primarily servicing elderly patients from contributing to (a) the conceptualization of the evolving goals for psychotherapy (see chapter 23), (b) technical developments in psychotherapy, and (c) the welfare of patients of primary concern to psychotherapists.

Private Health Insurance Plans

It was clear in the 1960s that the long-term economic viability of psychotherapy rested on third party recognition of psychotherapy as a reimbursable "medical" expense and mental health professionals as reimbursable providers of health care services. In 1964, Leonard Small and Rogers Wright were instrumental in establishing the APA Ad Hoc Committee on Insurance and Related Social Development (AHCIRSD) with Milton Theaman (chair), George Copple, Nicholas Cummings, Melvin Gravitz, William Schofield, and Wright, which undertook an aggressive educational campaign to persuade the health insurance industry to include psychotherapy as a benefit (Cummings, 1979). In 1967, Eugene Shapiro and Morris Goodman succeeded in getting a state "freedom of choice" (foc) law in New Jersey whereby a psychologist would be reimbursed for services on an equal basis with a physician. In 1968, a new APA standing Committee on Health Insurance (COHI) was formed, with Cummings (chair), Theaman, Schofield, Cooper Clements, and Jack Wiggins, which disseminated information on foc legislation to other states. By 1990, 42 states, covering 92.4% of the U.S. population, had passed foc statutes.

In 1972, the Council for the Advancement of the Psychological Professions in the Sciences (CAPPS) was created as an independent lobbying organization in Washington, DC. CAPPS brought a historic class action suit against the fiscal intermediaries of the FEHBPA program. In 1974, the National Register of Health Service Providers in Psychology was initiated, enabling psychologists in states without licensure to be identified for insurance reimbursement. Armed with the earlier COHI success and aided by gradual additional initiatives, COHI (Wiggins [chair] with Shapiro, Herbert Dörken, Russel Bent, and David Rodgers, and John McMillan as staff) led the struggle for gaining recognition of outpatient psychotherapy and psychologist providers in Medicare, CHAMPUS, FEHBPA, and the Vocational Rehabilitation Act of 1973 (with the latter creating parity between mental and physical services). The public gained increased access to psychotherapy in the late 1960s and early 1970s, largely because of the championing by psychology. However, in 1975 the Employee Retirement Income Security Act (ERISA) deregulated health insurance, and the new self-funded health benefit plans were exempted from state laws, including psychotherapy mandates and the supervision of state insurance commissioners. Thus, "managed care" of mental health care, as well as of physical health care, was born, controlled by corporate benefit departments and insurance brokers.

Health Maintenance Organizations

Despite their commitment to comprehensive care, the prototype HMOs of the 1940s and 1950s, with few exceptions, did not include benefits or treatment for mental illness. Mental health or psychological care is a relatively new addition in health maintenance organization coverage. Cummings wrote the first prepaid, comprehensive psychotherapy benefit for

Kaiser-Permanente beginning in 1959. Except for Kaiser-Permanente, the initial inclusion of psychotherapy in HMO health coverage was limited to treatment by psychiatrists.

It was President Nixon's 1971 Health Message to Congress that institutionalized the concept of managed mental health care into modern health policy (DeLeon, VandenBos, & Bulatao, 1991). Nixon's idea of a health care system emphasizing health maintenance, disease prevention, and wellness was adopted—along with the concept of the health maintenance organization—by his administration and all subsequent Republican administrations. These concepts were subsequently expressed in the Health Maintenance Organization Act (HMO Act) of 1973 (PL 93-222).

The HMO Act provided federal funding for the development of new health maintenance organizations. To qualify for federal subsidies, HMOs were required by law to provide a comprehensive set of eight basic services, including 20 visits per year for emergency and outpatient crisis intervention services. Alcohol and substance abuse services were also required. The initial legislation was somewhat imprecise concerning the nature and extent of mandated mental health coverage, and administrative interpretation of this legislation has allowed considerable latitude in services provided. This vagueness emerged as a larger and larger problem over time in relation to the provision of psychotherapy.

Nonetheless, HMOs provided a setting in which both health promotion and disease prevention initiatives and behavioral interventions with physical health problems were developed; and, for a time, HMOs provided a setting for experimenting with planned and focused short-term psychotherapy.

Managed Health Care

Modern managed health care as reflected by HMOs, independent practice associations (IPAs), and preferred provider organizations (PPOs) were clearly viable forces in health care by 1980. However, it should be noted that even traditional fee-for-service indemnity insurance had never been "unmanaged," because copayments, limits on number of sessions, and deductibles characterized most psychotherapy benefits long before the advent of what is now called managed health care (Duhl & Cummings, 1987). Also, because both employers and the federal government believed that the inflationary spiral in health costs had to be controlled, a number of proprietary managed health care organizations emerged. These HMOs contracted with large health plans to cover health services on a fixed fee basis.

Managed health care did slow down, but did not eliminate, the inflationary cost increases of medicine and surgery. However, inpatient psychiatric costs began to accelerate at three times the inflation rate of general medical and surgical costs. The period of 1985–1990 became the era in which cost containment was vigorously directed toward inpatient *and* outpatient mental health, alcohol, and drug abuse services.

Initially, managed mental health care relied on two mechanisms of cost control: benefit limitations and utilization review. This can be viewed as the first-generation model of managed mental health care. The second-generation model added was unmanaged provider networks, administered through the traditional fee-for-service model but permitting the providers to deliver services to plan members at a discounted rate (paid by the centralized management system). Third-generation managed care models are currently using a defined continuum of care, clinical case management of outpatient services, on-site hospitalization utilization review, more open benefits, life-style management programs, and networks of providers trained in managed care. In the first- and second-generation models, practitioners were simply subjected to the sentinel effect as a means of ensuring efficiency. In third-generation models, the responsibility of efficiency and effectiveness shifts fully to the provider.

These trends impact psychotherapy in a number of ways. First, as is characteristic of all managed health care, the locus of control of service provision shifted from the provider to the system manager. The strength of the so-called consumer voice, whether in managed care or fee-for-service care, remains unclear. Second, managed mental health care is impacting psychotherapy in its demand for efficiency. Thus, effective brief psychotherapy, targeted psychoeducational interventions, and problem-focused behavioral strategies are favored over longer term psychotherapy. Third, managed care systems hold psychotherapists accountable for their treatment and for demonstrable results.

Physician Payment Review Commission

With nonphysician inclusion in Part B (professional services) of Medicare, the Health Care Financing Administration (HCFA) began, in the late 1980s, to seriously consider the various policy issues relevant to such reimbursement. As we have already indicated, psychology's original inclusion under the program was within organized systems of health care, such as HMOs, rural health clinics, and community mental health centers. Individual providers do not set their hourly salary in such settings. However, with the enactment of PL 101-239, the Omnibus Budget Reconciliation Act of 1989 (OBRA '89), it became evident that the locus of treatment was no longer to be considered a controlling factor for reimbursement of psychology or of clinical social work.

Earlier legislation directed the Secretary to establish a national fee schedule for psychology, and OBRA '89 directed the Physician Payment Review Commission (PPRC) to study the implications of payment reform on the various classes of *nonphysician providers* (NPPs), the proper level of payment, and whether NPP payments should be included in the Volume Performance Standards (VPS) process. This latter initiative establishes an annual acceptable rate of increase in Medicare health care costs, including volume of services to be provided. The Physician Payment Review Commission was established in 1986 by the Congress to provide advice on reforming the methods of paying physicians under Medicare and addressed the various policy options regarding the nonphysician issue in its 1991 Annual Report to the Congress.

During the initial 1990 deliberations of the Commission, it appeared that clinical psychology would be deemed a *limited licensed practitioner* (LLP) in the same manner that optometry and podiatry are currently treated. The Commission's 1990 report (Physician Payment Review Commission, 1990) noted that psychologists were not actually defined as *physicians* by the Medicare statute; however, it gave every indication that psychology would receive the LLP designation. The 1990 report also began the process of addressing the fundamental issue of whether the LLPs were providing the same or equivalent services (e.g., psychotherapy) as physicians, when they used the same procedure codes.

Incorporated in the various staff recommendations, as well as the Commission's deliberations throughout 1990, was the notion that psychologists would be deemed LLPs. In fact, the draft 1991 report contained language to the effect that "Clinical psychologists should be paid under the Medicare Fee Schedule, using the same relative values and conversion factors as applied to psychiatrists." Commission staff documents further reported that "There appears to be growing consensus among the Commissioners that clinical psychologists should be paid the same as physicians for services that they both provide. This issue, however, has not yet been brought before the Commission for a decision." During its January 1991 meeting, the Commission did address this issue and initially agreed with staff recommendations. However, at its subsequent meeting, the Commission modified its earlier decision and decided instead to consider psychologists as nonphysician providers rather than limited licensed practitioners.

As a practical matter, the different designation does not represent a significant policy difference. From a public policy frame of reference, the main advantage of being designated a physician or limited licensed practitioner is the possibility of being automatically included in relevant policy determinations without having to seek separate administrative or legislative decisions. For example, when the Health Omnibus Programs Extension Act of 1988 (PL 100-607) included psychology in the Title VII definition section of the "health professions schools" (i.e., the Medicines of Osteopathy, Dentistry, Veterinary, Optometry, Podiatry, Psychology, and Public Health, or MODVOPPP), the profession's educational institutions automatically became eligible for various programs under the Act due solely to the manner in which the underlying statute referenced the definition provision.

Prior to the enactment of the OBRA '89, Medicare paid for professional services on the basis of "reasonable charges." Under this approach, the individual practitioner determined his or her own "usual and customary" charges. OBRA '89 established a new payment system for Part B of Medicare, with the transition period from a traditional fee-for-service program to a national Medicare Model Fee Schedule for all professional services (based upon "human capital" expenditures) beginning in 1992. The policy importance for nonphysician mental health providers of obtaining independent recognition under Medicare is that such recognition is the basis of the federal government's health reimbursement decisions. Some viewed the fact that OBRA '89 eliminated the long-standing limit on Part B reimbursement for mental health care as paramount; however, in our judgment, independent recognition of psychologists and social workers as psychotherapists, regardless of the locus of treatment, is more important.

Prescription Privileges

The role of psychoactive drugs in mental health treatment has been a recurring topic of professional debate since such drugs were introduced in the late 1950s. Biologically oriented psychiatrists have heralded such drugs as psychiatry's one effective tool. Psychodynamic psychotherapists from all disciplines have expressed doubts about the real long-term value of such psychoactive pharmacological agents, and some have argued that such drugs actually interfere with the process of psychotherapy.

Psychiatrists have generally been thought of as the mental health professionals who handle prescriptions for "psychiatric" patients. However, professional nurses (and a wide range of other nonphysician health care providers) have been seeking prescription authority. At present, 28 states provide this privilege to psychiatric nurses, in some states without physician involvement or review. However, organized psychology did not express interest in using this clinical modality until the late 1980s (DeLeon, Folen, Jennings, Willis, & Wright, 1991; DeLeon, Fox, & Graham, 1991).

In November 1984, U.S. Senator Daniel K. Inouye urged the Hawaii Psychological Association to pursue prescription privileges as part of their legislative agenda. During its 1989–1990 session, after extensive public hearings, the Hawaii State House of Representatives called for a series of meetings on the topic. This was the first time in the history of psychology that a state legislature had addressed this prescription privilege issue. There is every indication that the issue will continue to advance in Hawaii, and the state's psychologists are currently negotiating with both the local school of nursing and the State Department of Health to establish credible training experiences during the coming year. Efforts are also being made to encourage similar efforts within other states, and task forces have now been established in Missouri and the state of Washington.

The prescription privilege issue is fundamentally a training issue (Burns, DeLeon, Chemtob, Welch, & Samuels, 1988). However, most psychology training institutions appeared unprepared to provide the needed training. At the federal level, psychologists began to report publicly that they were, in fact, legally prescribing—for example, within the Indian Health Service and the Veterans Administration. During its deliberations on the Fiscal Year 1989 Department of Defense (DoD) Appropriations bill (PL 100-463), the Congress directed the DoD to initiate a pilot psychology prescription demonstration project. DoD agreed to proceed; however, organized psychiatry attempted to block the program, essentially claiming that provision of such services by psychologists would represent a public health hazard. However, during the closing days of Fiscal Year 1990, DoD instituted a "fast-track" program in which two active-duty psychologists participated in the relevant didactic portion of its physician assistant training program. Also, in the fall of 1991, pursuant to additional congressional direction, DoD will enroll four psychologists in a comprehensive 2-year training program. For psychology, the DoD experience represents the first formal systematic prescription training program in its history, although a significant number of psychology training programs provide an introduction to psychopharmacology.

There is growing support for obtaining prescription privileges throughout the psychological community. As psychology has advanced its proposals in this arena, similar interest is beginning to emerge within the social work community. The eventual impact on psychotherapy of limited prescription privileges for all nonphysician health providers is unclear.

Policy Involvement and Advocacy

Prior to the 1970s, few psychotherapists, regardless of discipline, were actively involved in the political process in a regular and systematic fashion.

Because of the continually expanding federal support of mental health training, research, and services from the end of World War II through the end of the 1960s, most psychotherapists felt that advocacy was unnecessary for the field.

However, as the economic growth slowed down in the 1970s, and the costs of mandated social programs expanded, psychotherapists began to realize that they had to organize themselves into effective advocacy groups in order to attempt to influence the Congress in specific ways concerning specific legislative bills that would benefit consumers of needed mental health care. Debates ensued regarding the appropriate role of professional associations in national politics. The exclusion of psychologists and social workers as providers under Medicare and Medicaid prompted splits and fights within the mental health community.

President Carter signed Executive Order No. 11973 on February 19, 1977. By so doing, he established the President's Commission on Mental Health (PCMH) "to review the mental health needs of the Nation and to make recommendations to the President as to how the Nation might best meet these needs" (*Report to the President*, 1978, p. i). From the beginning of his administration, President Carter was interested in mental health care, and Mrs. Carter, having been involved with the National Mental Health Association (NMHA), became actively associated with the President's Commission. The Commission held public hearings across the country, and several fact-finding task panels were created consisting of the nation's foremost mental health authorities. There were 50 psychologists who were appointed to the 30 task panels; many of them had been recommended by name by APA (Pallak & VandenBos, 1984).

The President's Commission provided the mental health field with a vehicle for getting involved in national health policy. Each mental health discipline's national professional association got involved, organized internal task forces, expanded Washington, DC-based professional staff and examined policy issues. Expansion of examination led to expanded involvement in legislative advocacy and policy formation. Psychotherapists of all disciplines began providing their expertise to the Congress, federal agencies, and state governments. Many of the events described in the preceding pages are the direct result of such involvement. Most psychotherapists today understand that it is vital to the future of the mental health field for psychotherapists to be active or well represented in public policy debates at the national and state levels (DeLeon, 1988). Psychotherapists will be assured that the future mental health needs of the nation are met by staying involved in today's public policy initiatives.

SOME CLOSING REMARKS

Psychotherapy, as it is practiced in 1992, is far different and much more developed than that which was practiced in the 1890s. Economic factors, such as government support and insurance reimbursement, have played a major role in making psychotherapy a viable social enterprise and profession. The setting in which psychotherapy has been delivered has influenced the evolution of therapeutic models and training.

In the 1890s, only a very small number of individuals could reasonably have been called psychotherapists, and it is probably the case that only a fraction of a percent of the population ever received services that could reasonably be referred to as psychotherapy. By 1990, a minimum of one third of the U.S. population had used psychotherapy at some point in their lives as an appropriate means for treating a broad array of physical, psychological, and behavioral problems and disorders. Today, many accredited master's, doctoral, postdoctoral, and continuing education training programs related to psychotherapy exist. By even the most stringent criteria related to level of training and licensure, a minimum of 100,000 fully qualified, highly trained psychotherapists are available to serve the mental health needs of the United States today. Using the broadest definition, there may be as many as 250,000 psychotherapists and counselors available.

The need for psychological services continues. In fact, the demand for psychological services has steadily increased over the last 40 years as the public has grown to understand psychological and behavioral problems and to accept the provision of psychotherapeutic care. The stigma attached to receiving psychotherapy has progressively lessened as more and more individuals have experience with it and understand the broad range of conditions under which it is helpful and needed.

Essential to the continuing acceptance of the role, value, and contribution of psychotherapy and psychotherapists is public awareness and political advocacy. It is vital that high school and college students learn about personality development, psychological growth, behavioral change, and so forth, so that they are informed about what is possible and can avail themselves of appropriate services when needed. Likewise, it is important that an educated public let its public officials, corporate and union leaders, and health policy officials know of their interest in and support of psychotherapy services. Finally, it is essential that psychotherapists remain involved in public policy formation through participation in social advocacy and the political process.

REFERENCES

Alexander, F., & French, T. (1946). *Psychoanalytic therapy: Principles and applications.* New York: Ronald Press.

American Psychoanalytic Association. (1990). *Roster, 1988–1990.* New York: Author.

American Psychological Association. (1945). Report of the Committee on Clinical Psychology. *Psychological Bulletin, 42,* 724–725.

Artiss, K. L. (1978, June). Profile: Dexter Bullard and the idea. *Newsletter* of the American Academy of Psychoanalysis, pp. 14–15.

Ash, E. (1968a). The Veterans Administration psychology training program. *The Clinical Psychologist, 21,* 67–69.

Ash, E. (1968b). Issues faced by the VA psychology training program in its early development. *The Clinical Psychologist, 21,* 121–123.

"Austen Riggs Center." (n.d.). Unpublished document. (Available from Austen Riggs Center library)

Bent, R. J., Willens, J. G., & Lassen, C. L. (1983). The Colorado Clinical Psychology/Expanded Mental Health Benefits Experiment: An introductory commentary. *American Psychologist, 38,* 1274–1278.

Brotemarkle, R. A. (1947). Fifty years of clinical psychology: Clinical psychology 1896–1946. *Journal of Consulting Psychology, 11,* 1–4.

Burnham, J. C. (1977). Freud, Sigmund (1856–1939). In B. B. Wolman (Ed.), *International encyclopedia of psychiatry, psychology, psychoanalysis, & neurology: Vol. 5* (pp. 94–99). New York: Aesculapius Publishers.

Burns, S. M., DeLeon, P. H., Chemtob, C. M., Welch, B. L., & Samuels, R. M. (1988). Psychotropic medication: A new technique for psychology? *Psychotherapy: Theory, Research, Practice, and Training, 25,* 508–515.

Cattell, R. B. (1954). The meaning of clinical psychology. In L. A. Pennington & I. A. Berg (Eds.), *An introduction to clinical psychology* (2nd ed.; pp. 3–25). New York: Ronald Press.

"Chestnut Lodge Hospital." (n.d.). [Brochure]. Rockville, MD: Chestnut Lodge Hospital.

Cohen, W. J. (1968). *Independent practitioners under Medicare: A report to the Congress.* Washington, DC: Department of Health, Education, and Welfare.

Corsini, R. J. (Ed.). (1984). *Encyclopedia of psychology.* New York: John Wiley & Sons.

Cummings, N. A. (1979). Mental health and national health insurance: A case study of the struggle for professional autonomy. In C. A. Kiesler, N. A. Cummings, & G. R. VandenBos (Eds.), *Psychology and national health insurance: A sourcebook* (pp. 5–16). Washington, DC: American Psychological Association.

Cummings, N. A., & VandenBos, G. R. (1983). Relations with other professions.

In C. E. Walker (Ed.), *The handbook of clinical psychology: Theory, research, and practice: Vol. II* (pp. 1301–1327). Homewood, Illinois: Dow Jones-Irwin.

DeLeon, P. H. (1988). Public policy and public service: Our professional duty. *American Psychologist, 43,* 309–315.

DeLeon, P. H., Folen, R. A., Jennings, F. L., Willis, D. J., & Wright, R. H. (1991). The case for prescription privileges: A logical evolution of professional practice. *Journal of Clinical Child Psychology, 20,* 254–267.

DeLeon, P. H., Fox, R. E., & Graham, S. R. (1991). Prescription privileges: Psychology's next frontier? *American Psychologist, 46,* 384–393.

DeLeon, P. H., & VandenBos, G. R. (1980). Psychotherapy reimbursement in federal programs: Political factors. In G. R. VandenBos, (Ed.), *Psychotherapy: Practice, research, policy* (pp. 247–285). Beverly Hills, CA: Sage Publications.

DeLeon, P. H., & VandenBos, G. R. (1985). Public policy and advocacy on behalf of the gifted and talented. In F. D. Horowitz & M. O'brien (Eds.), *The gifted and talented: Developmental perspectives* (pp. 409–435). Washington, DC: American Psychological Association.

DeLeon, P. H., VandenBos, G. R., & Bulatao, E. Q. (1991). Managed mental health care: A history of the federal policy initiative. *Professional Psychology: Research and Practice, 22,* 15–25.

DeLeon, P. H., VandenBos, G. R., & Kraut, A. G. (1986). Federal recognition of psychology as a profession. In H. Dorken & Associates, *Professional psychology in transition: Meeting today's challenges* (pp. 99–117). San Francisco, CA: Jossey-Bass.

Dörken, H. (1976). Laws, regulations, and psychological practice. In H. Dörken & Associates, *The professional psychologist today: New developments in law, health insurance, and health practice* (pp. 33–58). San Francisco, CA: Jossey-Bass.

Duhl, L. J., & Cummings, N. A. (1987). The emergence of the mental health complex. In L. J. Duhl & N. A. Cummings (Eds.), *The future of mental health services: Coping with crisis* (pp. 1–13). New York: Springer.

Embree, R. B. (1959). Developments in counseling bureaus and clinics. *Educational and Psychological Measurement, 10,* 465–475.

Falk, I. S. (1964). Medical care: Its social and organizational aspects. Labor unions and medical care. *New England Journal of Medicine, 270,* 22–28.

Farrell, M. J., & Appel, J. W. (1944). Current trends in military neuropsychiatry. *American Journal of Psychiatry, 101,* 12–19.

Freud, S. (1926). *Die frage der laienanalyse* [The question of lay analysis]. Leipzig, Germany: Internationaler Psychoanalytischer Verlag.

Friedman, L. J. (1990). *Menninger: The family and the clinic.* New York: Alfred A. Knopf.

Fromm-Reichmann, F. (1950). *Principles of intensive psychotherapy.* Chicago: University of Chicago Press.

Garfield, S. L., & Kurtz, R. (1976). Clinical psychologists in the 1970s. *American Psychologist, 31,* 1–9.

Goleman, D. (1985, April 30). Social workers vault into a leading role in psychotherapy. *The New York Times*, pp. C1, C9.

Grinker, R. R., & Spiegel, J. P. (1945). *Men under stress*. Philadelphia, PA: Blakiston.

Gurin, G., Veroff, J., & Feld, S. (1960). Americans view their mental health: A nationwide interview survey. *Joint Commission on Mental Illness and Health Monograph Series No. 4*. New York: Basic Books.

Haynie, N. A. (1984). Freud, Sigmund (1856–1939). In R. J. Corsini (Ed.), *Encyclopedia of psychology: Vol. 2* (pp. 37–38). New York: John Wiley & Sons.

Hedahl, B. M. (1978). The professionalization of change agents: Growth and development of counseling centers at institutions. In B. M. Schoenberg (Ed.), *A handbook and guide for the college and university counseling center* (pp. 24–39). Westport, CT: Greenwood Press.

Hildreth, J. D. (1967). Psychology's relations with psychiatry: A summary report. In B. Lubin & E. E. Levitt (Eds.), *The clinical psychologist: Background, roles, and functions*. New York: Aldine Publishing.

Hutt, M. L., Menninger, W. C., & O'Keefe, D. E. (1947). The neuropsychiatric team in the United States Army. *Mental Hygiene, 31*, 103–119.

Hutt, M. T., & Milton, E. O. (1947). An analysis of duties performed by clinical psychologists in the army. *American Psychologist, 2*, 52–56.

Joint Commission on Mental Illness and Health. (1961). *Action for mental health: Final report of the Joint Commission on Mental Illness and Health*. New York: Basic Books.

Kirsch, I., & Winter, C. (1983). A history of clinical psychology. In C. E. Walker (Ed.), *The handbook of clinical psychology: Theory, research, and practice: Vol. 1* (pp. 3–30). Homewood, IL: Dow Jones-Irwin.

Kubie, L. S. (1960). *The Riggs story: The development of the Austen Riggs Center for the Study and Treatment of the Neuroses*. New York: Paul B. Hoeber (Medical Division of Harper & Brothers).

Kulka, R. A., Veroff, J., & Douvan, E. (1979). Social class and the use of professional help for personal problems: 1957 and 1976. *Journal of Health and Social Behavior, 20*, 2–17.

Long, T. (1952). The V.A. guidance program. *Personnel and Guidance Journal, 31*, 104–107.

Lowrey, L. G., & Smith, G. (1933). *The Institute for Child Guidance: 1927–1933*. New York: The Commonwealth Fund.

May, R. (1939). *The art of counseling*. New York: Abingdon Press.

McCall, N., & Rice, T. (1983). A summary of the Colorado Clinical Psychology/Expanded Mental Health Benefits Experiment. *American Psychologist, 38*, 1279–1291.

McCaul, M. E. (1939). *Guidance for college students*. Scranton, PA: International Textbook.

Menninger, K. A. (1938). *Man against himself*. New York: Harcourt, Brace & Co.

Menninger, W. C. (1947). Psychiatric experience in the war, 1941–1946. *American Journal of Psychiatry, 103*, 577–586.

Miller, J. G. (1946). Clinical psychology in the Veterans Administration. *American Psychologist, 1*, 181–189.

Mott, F. D., & Hudenburg, R. (1959). Labor's influence on health care developments. *Hospital Management*, Part I, 88 (October), 42–44; 108; Part II, 88 (November), 39, 66; Part III, 88 (December), 52–53, 123–129.

Napoli, D. S. (1981). *Architects of adjustment: The history of the psychological profession in the United States.* National University Publications. Port Washington, NY: Kennikat Press.

National Association of Social Workers. (1990 May). *State comparison of laws regulating social work.* Unpublished manuscript.

National Institute of Mental Health. (1990, March). *Appropriation history table.* Unpublished document.

Pallak, M. S., & VandenBos, G. R. (1984). Employment of psychologists in the U.S.A.: Responses in the crisis of the 1970s. *Tidsskrift for Norsk Psykologforening* [Journal of the Norwegian Psychological Association], *21*, 65–73.

Pepinsky, H. B., Hill-Frederick, K., & Epperson, D. L. (1978). The *Journal of Counseling Psychology*, as a matter of policies. *Journal of Counseling Psychology, 25*, 483–498.

Physician Payment Review Commission: Annual Report to Congress 1989. (1990). Washington, DC.

Pottharst, K. E. (1976). A brief history of the professional model of training. In M. Korman (Ed.), *Levels and patterns of professional training in psychology* (pp. 33–40). Washington, DC: American Psychological Association.

Raimy, V. C. (Ed.). (1950). *Training in clinical psychology.* Englewood Cliffs, NJ: Prentice-Hall.

Raphael, T. (1936). Four years of student mental-hygiene work at the University of Michigan. *Mental Hygiene, 20*, 218–231.

Report to the President from the President's Commission on Mental Health: Vol. 1. (1978). Washington, DC: U.S. Government Printing Office.

Ridenour, N. (1961). *Mental health in the United States: A fifty-year history.* Cambridge, MA: Harvard University Press for the Commonwealth Fund.

Rogers, C. R. (1942). *Counseling and psychotherapy.* New York: Houghton Mifflin.

Rogers, C. R. (1951). *Client-centered therapy: Its current practice, implications, and theory.* Boston: Houghton Mifflin.

Rowntree, L. G., McGill, K. H., & Edwards, T. I. (1943). Causes of rejection and the incidence of defects among 18- and 19-year-old Selective Service registrants. *Journal of the American Medical Association, 123*, 181–185.

Rubinstein, E. A., & Parloff, M. B. (Eds.). (1959). *Research in psychotherapy: Vol. 1. Proceedings of a conference*, Washington, DC, April 9–12, 1958. Washington, DC: American Psychological Association.

Sanford, F. H. (1955). Across the secretary's desk: Relations with psychiatry. *American Psychologist, 10*, 93–96.

Schneidler, G. G., & Berdie, R. F. (1942). Representativeness of college students who receive counseling services. *Journal of Educational Psychology, 33*, 545–551.

Schneidler, G. G., Paterson, D. G., & Williamson, E. G. (1935). *Student personnel procedures and techniques.* Minneapolis, MN: University of Minnesota Press.

Shlien, J. M. (Ed.). (1968). *Research in psychotherapy: Vol. 3. Proceedings of the third conference,* Chicago, Illinois, May 31–June 4, 1966.

Stapp, J., Tucker, A. M., & VandenBos, G. R. (1985). Census of psychological personnel: 1983. *American Psychologist, 40*, 1317–1351.

Sterba, R. F. (1982). *Reminiscences of a Viennese psychoanalyst.* Detroit, MI: Wayne State University Press.

Strupp, H. H., & Luborsky, L. (Eds.). (1962). *Research in psychotherapy: Vol. 2. Proceedings of a conference,* Chapel Hill, North Carolina, May 17–20, 1961. Washington, DC: American Psychological Association.

Sullivan, H. S. (1958). *The interpersonal theory of psychiatry.* New York: W.W. Norton.

Sullivan, H. S. (1962). *Schizophrenia as a human process.* New York: W.W. Norton.

Super, D. E. (1955). Transition: From vocational guidance to counseling psychology. *Journal of Counseling Psychology, 2*, 3–9.

United States Department of Health, Education, and Welfare. Public Health Service. (1962). *Medical care financing and utilization.* (No. 947, *Health Economics Series,* No. 1.). Washington, DC: U.S. Government Printing Office.

United States Senate Committee on Finance. (1965). *Social Security Amendments of 1965: Part 1.* (Report No. 389-404 to accompany H.R. 6675). Washington, DC: U.S. Government Printing Office.

VandenBos, G. R., Stapp, J., & Kilberg, R. R. (1981). Health service providers in psychology: Results of the 1978 APA Human Resources Survey. *American Psychologist, 36*, 1395–1418.

Williamson, E. G. (1939). *How to counsel students.* New York: McGraw-Hill.

Williamson, E. G., & Bordin, E. S. (1941). An analytical description of student counseling. *Educational and Psychological Measurement, 1*, 341–354.

Williamson, E. G., & Darley, J. G. (1937). *Student personnel work.* New York & London: McGraw-Hill.

Wolford, R. A. (1956). A review of psychology in VA hospitals. *Journal of Counseling Psychology, 3*, 243–248.

II

THEORETICAL PERSPECTIVES IN PSYCHOTHERAPY

OVERVIEW

THEORETICAL PERSPECTIVES IN PSYCHOTHERAPY

STANLEY B. MESSER AND PAUL L. WACHTEL

The proper function of theory may be best captured by the tension between two conflicting visions of its role, offered by two noted authorities on the process of making sense of bewildering observations. On the one hand, Sherlock Holmes commented, in *A Scandal in Bohemia*, that "It is a capital mistake to theorize before one has data. Insensibly one begins to twist the facts to suit theories, instead of theories to suit facts." On the other, Albert Einstein remarked to Werner Heisenberg in Heisenberg's 1971 book *Physics and Beyond*, that "in principle it is quite wrong to try founding a theory on observable magnitude alone. In reality, the very opposite happens. It is the theory which decides what we can observe" (p. 63).

The chapters in this section start from the standpoint of theory. They convey the history of the conceptual approaches that have been most significant through this century in guiding psychotherapists to "decide what to observe." But as the authors of these chapters also show, these theories have not been impervious to the message conveyed by the observations they have spawned. In response to the observations that have accrued from both practice and research, the theories have continued to evolve. No doubt that process will continue, and perhaps even accelerate, as the walls dividing the various "schools" of therapy proceed with their discernible, if not necessarily intentional, emulation of the wall in Berlin.

Does this process reflect simply the accrual of empirical findings showing fewer differences in psychotherapy outcome than the proponents of competing approaches would have expected, or might it actually reflect more basic shifts in the larger social and political system within which the practice and theory of psychotherapy are embedded? As Cushman argues in the Introductory section of this volume, our theories derive quite considerably from the social and cultural forms and forces impinging on us, of which we are often unaware, much as we are oblivious of the air we breathe. Cushman demonstrates how such cultural forces—economic, political, and ideological—shaped the form that psychotherapy theories have taken over the past century. Others, such as Stolorow and Atwood (1979) have illustrated how theories of personality and therapy derive from the history, personality, and even psychopathology of their authors. Still others, such as Gergen and Gergen (1986), argue that theories are governed by conventions of discourse, linguistic practice, and literary devices, and that it is the narrative properties of a theory that determine its preeminence and staying power. Such properties include the way that a theory specifies developmental goals, organizes events leading toward or away from such goals, spells out the causal connection of such events, and provides a sense of drama.

In this section, the authors lay out the major ideas contained in several enduring theories of psychotherapy, often make mention of the authors who formulated and expanded them, and describe the evolution of these central concepts over time. We have deliberately kept the number of theories covered to a minimum, choosing those that are important historically and that continue to be central in guiding research and practice today. In addition, by not subdividing the major theoretical outlooks into their many variants, we have challenged the authors to describe historical branching of one variant or another from the major theoretical trunk out of which it grew. Thus, the chapter on psychoanalysis includes discussion of classical Freudian theory, ego psychology, interpersonal theory, object relations theory, and self psychology; that on behavioral and cognitive theories encompasses behavioral, neo-behavioral, cognitive, and cognitive-behavioral outlooks; the chapter on humanistic theories incorporates client-centered, Gestalt, and existential streams; the one on family theories covers strategic, systemic, and structural approaches; and the chapter on integrative theories embraces theoretical integration, common factors, and technical eclecticism as routes to rapprochement among the therapies. Read in their entirety,

these five chapters will give the reader an overview of the field of psychotherapy as it has evolved in the twentieth century, as well as a glimpse
of the shape it will take as we enter the 21st century.

REFERENCES

Gergen, K. J., & Gergen, M. M. (1986). Narrative form and the construction of
    psychological science. In T. R. Sarbin (Ed.), *Narrative psychology: The storied
    nature of human conduct* (pp. 22–44). New York: Praeger.

Heisenberg, W. (1971). *Physics and beyond: Encounters and conversations.* New York:
    Harper & Row.

Stolorow, R. D., & Atwood, G. E. (1979). *Faces in a cloud.* New York: Aronson.

4

PSYCHOANALYTIC THEORIES OF PSYCHOTHERAPY

MORRIS N. EAGLE AND DAVID L. WOLITZKY

To a significant extent, the history of theoretical developments in psychoanalysis can be understood as a series of successive reactions to Freudian drive theory, with its emphasis on libidinal and aggressive wishes as the primary motives for behavior. Thus, following Pine (1990), the main foci of theorizing in psychoanalysis subsequent to drive theory—ego, object, and self—can be meaningfully viewed as entailing modification or abandonment of that drive theory. These theoretical developments gave greater primacy to interpersonal and social determinants of personality development and psychopathology.

The extension of drive theory to include ego psychological considerations was begun quite early by Freud himself with the concept of defense (Freud, 1894/1962), continued with his paper, "On Narcissism" (1914/1957a) where consideration of self and object and of pre-oedipal periods of development came to the fore, and culminated with the exposition of the tripartite, structural theory of the mind (Freud, 1923/1961, 1926/1959). Generally speaking, the period from 1900 to 1914 can be considered the era of "id psychology" (partly initiated by Freud's [1897/1954] abandonment of the seduction theory) and the period from 1914 to 1939 can be regarded as the era in which "ego psychology" was developed (A. Freud, 1936; S. Freud, 1923/1961, 1926/1959; Hartmann, 1939). In the United States, the three decades from 1940 to 1970 were strongly dominated by psychoanalytic ego psychology. Although much of their work was roughly contemporaneous with the literature on ego psychology, it is mainly in the past 20 years that the contributions of the British object relations theorists (Balint, 1965, 1968; Fairbairn, 1941, 1952; Guntrip, 1969; Klein, 1921–1945; Winnicott, 1958) have heavily influenced American psychoanalysts. In the past two decades, Kohut's (1971, 1977, 1984) presentation of self psychology has also had a profound impact on the theory and practice of psychoanalysis. Many psychoanalysts (e.g., Pine, 1990; Silverman, 1986) believe that each of these perspectives is vital to a comprehensive and clinically useful account of human experience. In fact, at no time in the history of psychoanalysis have we seen as great a theoretical diversity and pluralism within what might be called the mainstream or common ground of psychoanalytic thought (Wallerstein, 1988a, 1990b). Given this current theoretical pluralism, it is not accurate to talk of *the* psychoanalytic theory of psychopathology or of treatment.

The topics and authors covered in this chapter will generally follow the historical sequence we have briefly outlined. First, we will discuss traditional Freudian drive theory, followed by a section on its ego psychological extensions. We will then present object relations theory, interpersonal theory (which, as Guntrip [1969] suggests, can be viewed as an American version of object relations theory), self psychology, and a sampling of other recent developments (by Mahler, Kernberg, and Weiss and Sampson). Roughly parallel with these theoretical changes, conceptions of therapeutic action have shifted from a primary and near-exclusive emphasis on insight into unconscious conflicts (primarily oedipal ones) to an increasing stress on relationship factors in treatment and their efficacy in ameliorating the maladaptive impact of early defects, deficits, and developmental arrests. This latter emphasis reflects a shift from the drive discharge model to the person point of view (Gill, 1983), or what Greenberg and Mitchell (1983) called the "drive/structure" versus the "relational/ structure" model. Others (e.g., Modell, 1984) have referred to the same distinction as being between a "one-person" versus a "two-person" psychology.

These models of therapeutic action focus mainly on psychoanalysis and, by extension and modification, to psychoanalytic psychotherapy. The issue of the similarities and differences between these two forms of treatment has been a topic of continuing discussion and lively debate (Gill, 1954,

1984; Wallerstein, 1983, 1986, 1990a). The distinction between them is generally drawn less sharply today than it has been in the past, and for the purposes of this chapter we will treat them as more overlapping than different.[1]

FREUDIAN DRIVE THEORY

Roots in Prepsychoanalytic "Dynamic Psychiatry"

One of the core set of ideas that Freud inherited from the prepsychoanalytic thinking of Charcot (1882) and Janet (1889, quoted in Ellenberger, 1970) was that certain mental contents (i.e., ideas, memories, thoughts) cannot be integrated into one's dominant self-organization and therefore exist outside normal consciousness; furthermore, by virtue of their "underground," unintegrated status, these contents exert powerful pathogenic influences upon one's behavior, thoughts, and feelings.

It is clear that Freud picked up the preceding set of ideas and soon gave them a special psychoanalytic cast. In his early work, however, his position was quite similar to Charcot's and Janet's. He identified the associative isolation of certain ideas and traumas as the proximate causes of hysteria. In *Studies on Hysteria* (Breuer & Freud, 1895), affect and the beginnings of a more distinctively psychoanalytic formulation enter the explanatory picture and are added to the associative isolation account. Every experience, according to Freud, is accompanied by a "quota of affect" which is normally discharged through conscious experience (including labelling and talking about the experience) and is worn away through associative connection with other mental contents. Freud also tells us that it is especially difficult for ideas accompanied by large amounts of affect to achieve associative connection with other ideas. Because traumas are, by definition, affectively intense experiences, they present a special challenge for the tasks of discharge and associative connection. In hysteria, neither of these tasks is carried out effectively, with the result that the affect remains in a "strangulated" state, and the memory of the experience is cut off from associative connection with other mental contents. The ultimate result of affect stran-

---

[1]Note that we will not include separate discussions of the theories of Adler, Jung, Horney, and Fromm. This will undoubtedly disappoint some readers, but any chapter must recognize realistic limitations. Our decision regarding which material to cover and which to omit is based on limitations on our knowledge and areas of competence and on our judgment of what appear to be the main areas of interest in a large part of the current psychological and psychoanalytic communities.

gulation and associative isolation is the development of hysterical symptoms.

It follows quite logically that perhaps the symptoms can be removed through *abreacting* (so to speak, unstrangulating) the affect by an adequate response including a verbal response and by bringing the memory of the trauma into associative connection with other ideas. As Breuer and Freud (1895, p. 17) put it, psychotherapy allows "strangulated affect [of the idea] to find a way out through speech; and also subjects the idea to associative correction by introducing it into normal consciousness."

Much of the early history of psychoanalytic theories of treatment can be understood as being organized around the question of how best to bring traumatic memories and their accompanying affect into conscious experience and how best to permit them to achieve expression and associative connection with the other ideas of normal consciousness. Of course, once free association became the standard technique for psychoanalytic treatment, the primary purposes for which it was being employed had changed; the earlier goals of abreaction of strangulated affect and "associative correction" had been replaced by later process goals such as making the unconscious conscious and insight. However, one can see the rather direct line from the earlier concepts of strangulated affect and associative isolation, embedded in prepsychoanalytic theory, to the more modern conception of psychoanalytic treatment.[2] Furthermore, these earlier ideas were never entirely relinquished, but were instead absorbed and integrated into later formulations.

In "The Neuro-Psychoses of Defense," Freud (1894) explicitly and specifically disputed Janet's claim that hysterical symptoms are a consequence of the hysteric's innate weakness in the capacity for psychic synthesis. Although he continued to employ such terms as "splitting of consciousness" and "the formation of separate psychical groups," he maintained that splitting of consciousness is not the result of innate weakness, but "*of an act of will on the part of the patient* [Freud's emphasis]; that is to say, it is initiated by an effort of will whose motive can be specified" (p. 46). In *defense hysteria*, which is caused by "an incompatibility . . . [in the patient's] ideational life," the ego is faced with an experience, idea, or feeling "which aroused such a distressing affect that the subject decided to forget about it because he had no confidence in his power to resolve the contradiction between that incompatible idea and his ego by means of thought activity" (1894/1962, p. 47). Freud observes that in females it is mainly sexual experiences and sensations that constitute the source of incompatible ideas.

One finds in this 1894 paper, then, the beginnings of a distinctively

---

[2]As Freud (Breuer & Freud, 1895) acknowledges, Breuer and his patient, Anna O., are due a great deal of credit for "discovering" free association and the "talking cure."

psychoanalytic formulation of hysteria. Hysterical symptoms are held to be, not a matter of constitutional weakness, but *motivated* expulsion (forgetting) of distressing material from consciousness. Here are the essential elements of the core idea of repression, which Freud later called "the cornerstone on which the whole structure of psycho-analysis rests" (Freud, 1914/1957b, p. 16).

What are the implications for treatment of this shift from a prepsychoanalytic to a distinctively psychoanalytic theory of psychopathology? To the extent that the expulsion of certain mental contents from consciousness (which, it will be recalled, was held to be fraught with pathogenic significance) is not a matter of a constitutionally based inability to integrate expelled ideas or to discharge large quotas of affect, but, rather, is motivated (by such motives as the desire to avoid pain or to protect one's picture of oneself), it follows that mere mechanical abreaction of affect or associative connection of ideas will not suffice as therapeutic goals. Rather, the therapist will have to deal with the motives for repression themselves, with such questions as why the patient is so intent on expelling a particular set of mental contents from consciousness and with the general issue of the relation between these mental contents and the rest of the personality.

This seemingly simple, but in fact critical, explanatory shift from constitutional weakness to motivated expulsion opens the door to a whole host of therapeutic implications. One must now deal not only with the patient's motives for expulsion as well as the expulsion itself, but also with what the patient is passionately trying to hide from himself or herself, with the self-image the patient is desperately trying to protect, and with the relation between the patient's neurotic symptoms and the expelled ideas. Also, it can be seen that simply bringing expelled memories and ideas to consciousness through hypnosis (or through suggestion or pressure techniques) is not likely to be therapeutically adequate. For if the patient is actively trying to hide certain memories, ideas, and desires from himself or herself, then it is necessary to come to terms with the act of hiding, with the reasons for hiding, and with the aspects of self that he or she is trying to hide and protect. In short, one must deal, above all, with the unconscious personal meanings of the patient's memories, ideas, and desires in their relation to unconscious conflicts.

PSYCHOANALYTIC EGO PSYCHOLOGY

The concept of unconscious conflict is central to the traditional Freudian model and to its ego-psychological extensions by Hartmann (1939, 1950, 1964); Hartmann, Kris, and Lowenstein (1946); Rapaport (in Gill,

1967); Arlow and Brenner (1964); and many others. The components of an intrapsychic, unconscious conflict are an unacceptable or threatening wish (or so-called drive derivative), an anticipation of danger or anxiety associated with awareness of and expression of the wish, defenses against the wish, and a compromise between the wish and the defense. The compromise may be more or less adaptive and more or less ego-alien. It may take the form of a symptom, a character trait or style, or an inhibition (Freud, 1926/1959).

Signals of anxiety trigger the activation of defense, currently understood to include not only the classic mechanisms of defense (such as projection, denial, repression, reaction formation, etc.), but any aspect of ego functioning that can be used for defensive purposes (Brenner, 1982). The primary anxieties or danger situations of childhood are loss of the object, loss of the object's love, castration anxiety, and super ego anxiety (guilt). The failure of signal anxiety to activate adequate defenses leads to traumatic anxiety and an extreme state of unpleasure in which the ego is totally overwhelmed and rendered helpless. It is this traumatic situation of overstimulation that some (e.g., A. Freud, 1936; Waelder, 1960) regard as the basic, bedrock anxiety (cf. Hurvich, 1985, on annihilation anxiety). Brenner (1982) has extended this formulation to include depressive affect as a trigger for defense.

As is well known, a core contribution of psychoanalytic ego psychology was an emphasis on the autonomy of certain ego functions such as memory, thinking, and intelligence. What Hartmann (1939) calls "primary autonomy" refers to the claim that certain ego functions have an inborn basis that, in an average expectable environment, will develop relatively independently of the vicissitudes of drives. "Secondary autonomy" refers to the fact that, although certain ego functions may have originally developed in the context of conflict and may have originally served defensive functions, they may subsequently develop a secondary autonomy in the sense of becoming relatively conflict-free and carried out for their own sake. For example, although intellectualization may have originally served mainly defensive purposes, intellectual activities and pursuits may achieve a relatively conflict-free and autonomous status. (Hartmann's concept of secondary autonomy is very similar to Allport's (1950) concept of "functional autonomy.")

In short, one of the main clinical and theoretical contributions of psychoanalytic ego psychology was to soften and modulate the sweeping claim of Freudian instinct theory that virtually all behavior was energized by, and directly or indirectly, overtly or covertly, in the service of, drive gratification. Following the theoretical emendations of ego psychology, there was now room in psychoanalytic theory for behavior and functions relatively autonomous of the vicissitudes of drive. At the same time, one of the main treatment implications of ego psychology is that, because patients can be unaware of both their wishes and their defenses against them, a central focus of interpretation is on the patient's defensive strategies.

For patients with neurotic personality organization, repressed conflicts involving libidinal and aggressive drive derivatives are understood in terms of Freud's structural, tripartite theory of id, ego, and superego and its ego-psychological extensions by A. Freud (1936), Hartmann (1939), Arlow and Brenner (1964), and others. The most common neurotic conflict is considered to be an unresolved oedipal struggle. Unconscious conflicts over the gratification of unacceptable oedipal longings are expressed not only in symptomatic behavior, but also in the maladaptive, self-punitive characterological patterns to which this conflict can give rise (e.g., those "wrecked by success," work inhibitions). For more detailed accounts of basic psychoanalytic theory, see Brenner (1982), Meissner (1980), and Waelder (1960).

The theoretical understanding and treatment of more severe forms of psychopathology (e.g., borderline conditions) is a matter of controversy. Some clinicians (Abend, Porder, & Willick, 1983; Arlow & Brenner, 1964) rely primarily on traditional psychoanalytic ego psychology in understanding these patients while other clinicians (see Greenberg & Mitchell, 1983) minimize the importance of oedipal and pre-oedipal conflicts and emphasize the role of ego defects and deficits. Opinions regarding the proper therapeutic approach to borderline patients range from support (Knight, 1953; Zetzel, 1971) to standard psychoanalysis (Segal, 1967), with some clinicians modifying their standard psychoanalytic technique at the start of treatment but allowing it to evolve into psychoanalysis in later stages (Kernberg, 1975, 1976).

We should note that, although the theory of psychoanalytic treatment was built on the model of the moderately neurotic, oedipally conflicted patient, analysts have always treated a wide range of psychopathology. Freud had distinguished among psychoneuroses, actual neuroses, and narcissistic neuroses, believing that only the first group was suitable for analytic treatment. Several of Freud's own cases, however, were clearly beyond the neurotic range, and other psychoanalytic pioneers (e.g., Abraham, 1927) treated very disturbed patients.

In the early 1950s one began to see more frequent, explicit discussions of the so-called "widening scope" (Stone, 1954) of psychoanalytic treatment, that is, the treatment of more severely disturbed patients. The adaptations of classical technique considered necessary to treat such patients have been a frequent topic of discussion for the past 40 years. Alterations in the basic analytic stance have been discussed under the heading of "parameters," a term introduced by Eissler (1953) to refer to a deviation from sole reliance on interpretation and strict adherence to the principle of abstinence. Such deviations were considered necessary for patients who could not tolerate the rigors of the standard psychoanalytic situation due to ego defects and deficits originating in traumas of early childhood.

Treatment Implications of Traditional Freudian Theory

The main features of the traditional psychoanalytic theory of treatment can be summarized as follows:

1. The patient is suffering from pathological compromise formations (e.g., symptoms and maladaptive character traits) based on repressed conflicts.

2. These conflicts are based on instinctual wishes originating in early childhood, especially oedipal wishes, and they are subject to fixation and regression. They become expressed in the context of the therapeutic relationship, particularly in the form of resistance and transference.

3. The emergence of the patient's readiness for transference reactions is facilitated when the treatment situation is unstructured and fosters free associations that will allow the unconscious, unresolved conflicts to be expressed via dreams, memories, reactions to the therapist, and so on.

4. The analyst listens with free-floating or evenly hovering attention and a neutral (i.e., nonbiased), nonjudgmental, empathic attitude, which facilitates the "therapeutic alliance"—that is, the patient's desire to cooperate despite conflicting attitudes about wanting to recover (Curtis, 1980; Greenson, 1965).

5. The analyst generally adheres to the principle of abstinence. That is, deliberate transference gratifications normally are withheld. The process proceeds on the principle of optimal frustration on the grounds that this approach will most efficaciously stimulate the patient's conflicts and fantasies and center them on the person of the analyst. It will help the patient to experience and to understand the intrapsychic basis of his or her interpersonal problems.

6. These conditions promote the development of an analyzable transference, defined and discussed later. However, deviations from these conditions (parameters, per Eissler,

1953) may be required in order to maintain the therapeutic alliance under various circumstances.

7. The analyst's interpretations of the patient's unconscious conflicts and resistances, as they are manifested in the transference, will yield insights into the origin and nature of these conflicts and into the anxieties associated with them.

8. Through the repetitive experience and interpretation of long-standing conflicts, in the context of affectively vivid "here-and-now" transference reactions, the patient gradually "works through" (Greenson, 1978a) his or her difficulties by shifting to more adaptive emotional and behavioral patterns inside and outside the treatment situation. Repeated insight into and increased tolerance and acceptance of disavowed, split-off, anxiety-laden wishes, conflicts, and fantasies (in Freud's terminology, the id or drive derivatives) allows them to become more integrated into the ego, particularly when the insights are accompanied by behavioral changes that convince patients that they will not be overwhelmed by their fears. This goal is expressed in Freud's (1933/1964b, p. 80) famous epigram, "Where id was, there shall ego be," an alteration of the earlier goal, based on the topographic model, of making the unconscious conscious (Freud, 1905/1953, p. 266).

There are other important, noninterpretive ingredients in the therapeutic relationship that are considered to facilitate change (Stone, 1981). Although these allegedly curative factors are considered important by many analysts who regard themselves as Freudians, these factors nonetheless take us beyond the traditional Freudian account with its overriding emphasis on insight as the primary curative agent (Blum, 1979). Freudian clinicians who also find aspects of an object relations or a self-psychology approach useful tend, relatively speaking, to deemphasize insight in favor of the other factors or conditions. We shall list these elements here and explicate them later in the chapter in our discussion of different authors who represent more recent trends in the history of psychoanalysis.

1. The actual experience and internalization (Loewald, 1960) of a new, benign relationship with a nonjudgmental parental figure helps reduce the harshness of the patient's superego. This element was discussed by Strachey as early as 1934.

2. The patient has an opportunity to form a new identification; the patient can form an identification with the analyst's approach (i.e., with the analytic attitude) and with

the analyst's conception of the patient's potential for growth (Loewald, 1960) and can introject and later identify with the analyst as a person.

3. The analyst and the analyst–patient relationship can provide a safe, supportive base, a "holding environment" (Modell, 1976; Winnicott, 1958) that can foster the patient's progressive urges toward greater autonomy and individuation (as against regressive longings to merge and to cling to infantile dependence).

4. In Kohut's view (1984), the analyst serves a critical function by allowing the patient to use him or her to aid in the patient's efforts to regulate his or her own tension states. The therapist's empathy, as experienced by the patient, is held to be a vital element in this process and in therapeutic change in general. This component is stressed particularly by Kohut (1984) and his followers, who regard feeling that one is understood (and its positive implications for the experience of affirmed selfhood) as the ultimately curative factor, the one that gives insight its impact.

Variations in the way analysts apply these principles are mainly a function of their theoretical persuasion and the type of patient they are treating. These differences allow three main generalizations: (a) Among sicker patients, especially those manifesting borderline and narcissistic pathology, the various ways in which the therapeutic relationship can help are considered relatively more important than insight. However, among healthier patients (i.e., those with neuroses), the relationship factors are seen as secondary, as primarily a background to insight which retains its earlier preeminence as the mutative therapeutic agent. (b) Regardless of levels and types of pathology, Freudian clinicians accord greater weight to insight into unconscious conflicts, while analysts espousing an object relations or self psychology view place relatively more stress on aspects of the therapeutic relationship that they claim have curative properties in their own right (e.g., by facilitating the belated acquisition of a more cohesive sense of self). (c) Those who stress insight tend to see oedipal conflicts as primary, whereas those who focus more on the relationship concentrate more on pre-oedipal developmental arrests and worry less about issues of transference gratification.

When such transference gratifications are mutative in their own right, when they facilitate interpretive work which the patient could not otherwise tolerate, and when they fail to facilitate the treatment in any manner or impede it are questions to which we do not have answers. These are also questions that go back at least as far as Ferenczi and Rank's (1956) controversial experiments with "active techniques." The generalizations just offered, of course, fail to do justice to important nuances discernible among those who share similar views, but they do seem to us accurate in their broad outlines. It should also be noted that, even within the Freudian tradition, the relative emphasis on insight versus relationship factors has varied over the years. (See Friedman, 1978, for an excellent account of trends in the psychoanalytic theory of treatment.)

A complete statement of the necessary and sufficient conditions for therapeutic personality change as a function of psychoanalytic treatment would have to include a specification of the patient and therapist variables (and their interaction) which facilitate or impede improvement. It would, of course, also have to address what is meant by change, particularly "structural" change (Wallerstein, 1988b; Weinshel, 1988). (For the most recent attempts to conceptualize the psychoanalytic process, see the special issue of *The Psychoanalytic Quarterly*, Erle, 1990.)

Having presented general principles and concepts of psychoanalytic psychotherapy, we will now elaborate on some of the key aspects of the traditional Freudian treatment model. An oft-quoted definition of classical psychoanalysis is that given by Gill (1954, p. 775), who stated, "Psychoanalysis is that technique which, employed by a *neutral* analyst, results in the development of a *regressive transference neurosis* and the ultimate resolution of this neurosis by techniques of *interpretation* alone" [emphasis added; original entirely in italics]. Let us consider each of these concepts in turn.

Neutrality, Empathy, Countertransference, and the Analytic Attitude

As indicated previously, *neutrality* means that the analyst takes a position equidistant from the various components of the patient's conflicts. Neutral also means nonjudgmental; it does not mean indifferent or uncaring. It requires that analysts' countertransference reactions not interfere with their understanding of the patients' conflicts nor with their interpretations and other interventions.

The concept of technical neutrality is closely linked to Freud's (1912/1958, 1937/1954) proscription that the analysis be conducted in a state of *abstinence*. This technical precept has been the subject of lengthy, often passionate debate in the history of psychoanalytic treatment. The rule of abstinence refers to the idea that the analyst should not deliberately provide the patient with any gratifications other than those intrinsic to the analytic process. Abstinence protects analysts from their proclivity to change the analytic relationship into an ordinary relationship, including sexual contact with patients; fosters analytic neutrality by avoidance of selective transference gratifications; facilitates the patient's motivation for analytic work; and highlights in the transference the ways that patients deal with past and current conflicts by centering them regressively on the person of the analyst. Abstinence avoids the partial solutions to be gained from direct gratification of unmet needs and wishes. Such gratification would be a temporary expedient; it would impede insight and the possibility of structural change. This is not to say that the patient experiences no gratification in the relationship. Rather, as already indicated, it is the inherent features of the relationship (i.e., the analyst's listening, nonjudgmental attitude, the regularity and dependability of the relationship, etc.) which provide significant and necessary support.

The so-called classical analytic attitude that we have been describing (Stone, 1981) also requires analysts to retain relative anonymity in an effort not to "contaminate" the transference. As has been noted, primarily by Stone (1961), there is a danger that this attitude could be overdone (e.g., a callous, aloof, arbitrary, withholding attitude). Such a stance clearly includes the risk of inducing an iatrogenic regression. This attitude is not inherent in Freud's theory of treatment, but is a caricature of it.

The notions of technical neutrality and the rule of abstinence are closely linked to the concepts of empathy, countertransference, and the analytic attitude. Analysts listen with an attitude of "evenly hovering attention" as a way of apprehending the unconscious fantasies and conflicts within the patient. They want to enter the patient's frame of reference in order to understand in a cognitive and affective manner, through partial, transient identifications, what it feels like to be the patient and how the patient deals with psychic conflicts. This is what is meant by *empathy* (Greenson, 1978b; Schafer, 1959; Schwaber, 1981).

Ideally, psychoanalysts are participant-observers (see Sullivan, 1953). By effecting an oscillating split in their ego between an experiential mode and an observational mode (observing their own experience, that of the patient, and their interaction), they engage in a "regression in the service of the ego" (Kris, 1952) similar to that which they hope to encourage in the patient. In order to accomplish this difficult task, analysts monitor the presence and potential intrusiveness of their own feelings, attitudes, and conflicts to keep them from interfering in their ability to understand the patient and to offer interventions. This is referred to as the detection and management of the *countertransference*. The training analysis is said to aid in this process, supplemented by the analyst's ongoing self-analysis. This is a constant challenge, and success is variable. Countertransference reactions are considered a vital source of information about the psychology of the patient. However, undetected, and therefore unmanaged, countertransference can seriously impede the treatment. In fact, Langs (1982) boldly asserts that this is the primary cause of treatment failure.

In summary, a neutral analyst, as defined in the preceding text, is one who listens with evenly hovering attention, recognizes and tries to control personal biases, applies the rule of abstinence with appropriate tact and dosage, is genuinely nonjudgmental, safeguards the "working alliance" (Greenson, 1965), recognizes his or her stimulus value to the patient (including behaviors which are a standard part of the technique, such as silence), and creates an atmosphere of safety for the patient. These are some of the main components of what is referred to as the analytic attitude (Schafer, 1983) or the basic analytic stance and are regarded as necessary conditions for a favorable therapeutic outcome.

Transference

Transference, according to Greenson's commonly cited definition, is the

> . . . experiencing of impulses, feelings, fantasies, attitudes, and defenses with respect to a person in the present which do not appropriately fit that person but are a repetition of responses originating in regard to significant persons of early childhood, unconsciously displaced onto persons in the present. The two outstanding characteristics of transference phenomena are (1) it is an indiscriminate, non-selective repetition of the past, and (2) it ignores or distorts reality. It is inappropriate. (Greenson & Wexler, 1978, p. 28)

There are problems with this definition. First, the patient may be aware, even before an interpretation, of certain displaced transference feelings and attitudes. Second, not all transference reactions are repetitions of the past in any simple, literal, or isomorphic sense. To take one obvious example, patients often engage in attempts at role reversal. In an effort to master an experience which they endured passively in childhood, they try to make the analyst the victim and seek the role of the active, dominant partner. For instance, a patient who was constantly kept waiting by his mother and who, in virtually every way, felt coerced by her, kept his analyst waiting by frequently showing up late for sessions.

With these qualifications, traditional Freudian analysts would accept Greenson's definition of transference. It should be noted, however, that in actual practice, what one regards as transference is a matter of judgment and theoretical preference. For example, a not particularly intense or inappropriate erotic wish directed toward the analyst is apt to be regarded as transference, although it does not meet the definitional criteria indicated above (Schimek, 1983).

The "regressive transference neurosis," now considered unnecessary by some (e.g., Gill, 1984) and a misleading term by others (e.g., Brenner, 1982), refers to the intense, emotional revival in the relationship with the analyst of important aspects of the infantile neurosis. As Macalpine (1950) observed, the transference neurosis is not simply due to the patient's readiness to develop transferences. It develops by virtue of the features of the psychoanalytic situation which encourage it—the freedom to free associate, the supine position, the absence of visual cues from the analyst, the analyst's relative silence, the frequency of visits, and the open-endedness of the treatment which give rise to a sense of timelessness. As Gill (1984) and others (Cooper, 1987, 1989; Modell, 1989) have noted, this formulation is based on a one-person, as opposed to a two-person, psychology and thereby fails to consider adequately the ways in which the analyst's personality shapes the patient's transference.

Although we cannot take the space to discuss in detail the various altered conceptions of Freud's views of transference, we will briefly present and comment on Gill's (1982) position because it has received considerable attention in the past decade and will cite Cooper's (1987) overview of the changing conception of transference.

Gill's Conception of Transference

In recent years, the traditional view of transference has been severely criticized by Gill (1982) who objects to the conceptualization of transference as a distortion because it implies an assumption of arbitrary power which places the analyst in the position of the final arbiter of reality. Gill argues for a relativistic position in which the analyst does not judge what is distorted or inappropriate, but adopts a perspectival view of reality and attempts to understand how the patient's behaviors constitute plausible reactions to aspects of the analyst's real behavior. Transference for Gill is very broadly conceived and seems to be virtually synonymous with the patient's experience of the relationship. His view is a welcome corrective to the tendency of some analysts to lose sight of the fact that what they regard as normative analytic behaviors (e.g., silence, offering interpretations) are not simply neutral, technical devices but have meanings to patients in light of their own experiences.

Related Conceptions of Transference

Cooper (1987) presents a useful overview of changes in the conceptualization of transference by contrasting what he calls the *historical* and the *modernist* views of transference, acknowledging that this distinction is oversimplified. The historical model which refers to Freud's view of the transference, expressed previously in Greenson's definition, is that it is the reproduction of essential elements of important, early relationships in the relationship with the analyst (as well as with others in the patient's current life). Insofar as the patient constructs his relationship to the analyst on the basis of these past prototypes, ". . . what he takes to be new in real life is a reflection of the past" (Freud, 1940/1964a, p. 177). From this perspective, the value of interpreting the transference neurosis is that it allows the patient to "reexperience and undo the partially encapsulated, one might say 'toxic', neurotogenic early history" (Cooper, 1987, p. 81). In this view, the "here-and-now" transference is the royal road to the infantile neurosis. The affective immediacy of the here-and-now transference is vital because, as Freud (1912/1958, p. 108) noted, one cannot slay anyone *in absentia* or *in effigie*.

The modernist view, according to Cooper (1987, p. 81), "regards the transference as a new experience rather than an enactment of an old one." In this view, the purpose of transference interpretation "is to help the patient to see, in the intensity of the transference, the aims, character, and mode of his current wishes and expectations as influenced by the past." Resolving the here-and-now transference is tantamount to dissipating the neurosis (see Gill, 1984).

Whether these are matters of emphasis or they constitute a new paradigm is a matter of debate. Our inclination, following Wallerstein (1984), is to regard these conceptions of transference not as basic theoretical differences but as differences of emphasis, with the so-called modernist view allowing clinicians more technical latitude in working with more disturbed patients.

Interpretation

We come now to the third main element in Gill's (1954, p. 775) definition, ". . . by techniques of interpretation alone." The emphasis on interpretation recognizes that there are many other verbal and nonverbal interventions employed by the analyst (cf. Bibring, 1954). These interventions (e.g., confrontations, clarifications, questions, etc.) are regarded as preparatory to interpretations and as not having any mutative effect of their own. Broadly speaking, the term, interpretation, is used to encompass not only the attribution of meanings to discrete aspects of the patient's experience and behavior but also constructions which entail a more comprehensive account of aspects of the patient's history, an evolving narrative of the patient's neurosis.

According to the theory, the most effective interpretations are those which offered, with suitable tact, dosage, and timing, focus on the transference and its links to the patient's current and past unconscious conflicts and fantasies. In other words, a focus on the dynamics of the here-and-now transference, coupled with reconstructions of the dynamic and genetic basis (the "then-and-there") of the current transference, facilitates mutative insights that lead to the resolution of the transference. Some clinicians (e.g., Limentani, 1975) assert that interpretations other than of the transference are, at best, a waste of time, if not actually deleterious, while others (e.g., Blum, 1983) claim that extra-transference interpretations have a definite place in treatment, not only as preparation for transference interpretations but in their own right.

An important point to be made here is that a primary feature of psychoanalysis (as opposed to psychoanalytic psychotherapy and, even more so, other therapies) is the minimization of suggestion through deliberate manipulation of the transference (as in the case of Alexander's [1948] corrective emotional experience) or by more subtle directives. In this context, it is worth noting Stein's (1981) concern that the so-called unobjectionable positive transference (Freud, 1912/1958) often is a tacit, tenacious form of resistance. The patient's contribution to the "working alliance" (Greenson, 1965a) has to be scrutinized for indications of excessive compliance in accepting the analyst's interpretations.

In fact, the major focus of psychoanalytic interpretation is on the patient's resistance. Resistance is a central concept in the theory of treatment. It can be defined, following Gill (1982), as defense expressed in the transference, both as resistance to the awareness of transference and to its resolution (Gill, 1982).

Resistance, though it often has had a pejorative connotation (Schafer, 1983), is a necessary and inevitable aspect of treatment. As Freud (1912/1958, p. 103) put it, "The resistance accompanies the treatment step by step. Every single association, every act of the person under treatment must reckon with the resistance and represents a compromise between the forces that are striving towards recovery and the opposing ones." Resistance thus includes opposition to free association, to the procedures of analysis, to recall, to insight, and to change. The sources and forms of resistance have been written about extensively, and resistances have been classified in various ways (A. Freud, 1936; S. Freud, 1926/1959, 1937/1954; Greenson, 1967; Reich, 1949; Wachtel, 1982). According to Freud (1937/1954), the causes and motives for resistance include the constitutional strength of the drives, particularly aggression, impaired ego plasticity, the "adhesiveness of the libido," the so-called negative therapeutic reaction and its connection to unconscious guilt, the repetition compulsion, castration anxiety and passive/homosexual wishes in men, and penis envy in women.

The therapist's task in a traditional analysis, and to a lesser extent in psychoanalytic psychotherapy, is to clarify and interpret that the patient is resisting, how and what the patient is resisting, and why. A detailed discussion of the typical clinical signs of resistance and the techniques for dealing with it can be found in Greenson (1967) and Wachtel (1982).

Psychoanalysis and Psychoanalytic Psychotherapy (Expressive and Supportive)

In the past we have seen passionate debates (Alexander, 1954; Bibring, 1954; Gill, 1954; Rangell, 1954; Stone, 1954) regarding whether we should or can make a clear distinction between psychoanalysis and psychoanalytic psychotherapy. As noted earlier, psychoanalysis and psychoanalytic psychotherapy, particularly of the expressive variety, currently are considered by most clinicians as overlapping rather than as sharply distinct from one another, as was the case 40 years ago when classical analysts were at great pains to distance their therapeutic approach from Alexander's (1948) corrective emotional experience. Nonetheless, there still is considerable controversy concerning the proper criteria for what is to be rightly regarded as psychoanalysis. Some clinicians stress the criteria of frequency of sessions, the use of the couch, and free association. We agree with Gill (1982, 1984) who, among others, emphasizes the centrality of a focus on the transference as the defining, intrinsic characteristic of psychoanalysis and psychoanalytic psychotherapy, as distinct from other forms of psychotherapy.

It has long been believed, if not always explicitly asserted, that, all things being equal, psychoanalysis is the treatment of choice. Expressive therapy and particularly supportive therapy have been regarded as less effective. Yet, Freud (1919/1955) had long ago recognized the necessity of combining the "pure gold" of psychoanalysis with the "copper" of direct suggestion in order to create a therapy of wider applicability. For many years the clinical rule of thumb has been to offer as much support as is needed but as little as necessary (Luborsky, 1984; Wallerstein, 1986). More recently, it has been recognized that different forms of psychoanalytically informed treatment appear suitable for different kinds of patients.

The basis for the alleged superiority of psychoanalysis is that it would more likely lead to so-called structural change by virtue of the insights it could offer into the patient's conflictual and defensive behavior. Structural change, a thorny concept which we cannot discuss here, implies greater stability, generalizability, and resistance to new stressors (Wallerstein, 1988b; Weinshel, 1988). However, if structural change can occur on grounds other than insight (e.g., the partial undoing of ego deficits as a result of a benign, new therapeutic relationship), the preeminence of insight as the curative agent is thrown into question, as is the alleged superiority of psychoanalysis compared with psychoanalytic psychotherapy. This is what Wallerstein (1986) had to conclude after a very detailed, long-term study of patients in the Menninger Foundation's Psychotherapy Research Project. (For the most recent, comprehensive account of the history of this issue see Wallerstein, 1990a.)

OBJECT RELATIONS THEORY

Just as ego psychology established relative autonomy for the domain of ego functions, so similarly did object relations theory attempt to establish autonomy for the domain of object relations. An assertion of the autonomy of object relations is most succinctly expressed in Fairbairn's (1952) claim that "libido is object-seeking, not pleasure-seeking." Just as Hartmann (1939) argued that certain ego functions are primary and not a secondary derivative of drive gratification, so Fairbairn claimed that our interest in and attachment to objects have a primary inborn basis and are not secondary derivatives of the libidinal (and aggressive) drive-gratifying functions that objects serve. This basic claim is most fully articulated and elaborated in Bowlby's (1969) attachment theory.

Although many of the writings of ego psychology and object relations theory were roughly contemporaneous, it is meaningful to think of object relations theory *following* ego psychology in at least two senses: First, as far as North American psychoanalysis is concerned, the popularity and influence of ideas taken from object relations theory (or the so-called English School) followed the assimilation of ego psychology into psychoanalytic theory. Second, compared with ego psychology, object relations theory represents a more radical break with and transformation of traditional psychoanalytic theory.

As noted earlier, virtually every theoretical development in psychoanalytic theory entails either a substantial modification or outright rejection of Freudian instinct theory. This is also the case for object relations theory, the subject of this section.

The historical and theoretical origins of object relations theory or the English School are clear. They began with Ferenczi and include Hermann, the Balints, and Melanie Klein (who, collectively, can be referred to as the "Budapest School"). Mainly through Klein's direct influence, these origins found expression in the work of Fairbairn, Winnicott, and Guntrip. Bowlby's attachment theory, although it has developed along somewhat independent lines and was strongly influenced by ethological theory, can also broadly be seen as an expression of object relations theory.

Although Klein's (1921–1945) work strongly influenced the English School, Kleinian theory and Kleinian adherents have retained a sufficiently separate identity to be distinguished from the English School. In addition, there are central aspects of Kleinian theory (primarily those having to do with Klein's instinct theory) that are rejected by the object relations theorists. Hence, while acknowledging the influence of Klein, object relations theory will be discussed separately from Kleinian theory. Finally, we want to note that we will be dealing mainly with the work of Fairbairn (1941, 1952) as representative of object relations theory because he presents the most systematic and comprehensive account of object relations theory.

Basic Tenets of Object Relations Theory

From a broad, theoretical perspective, what most clearly distinguishes object relations theory from Freudian theory is captured by Fairbairn's (1952) dictum that "libido is object seeking, not pleasure seeking" (p. 82) (and by Balint's [1965] concept of "primary object-love"). In this dictum Fairbairn is disputing Freud's interrelated claims that (a) behavior is primarily motivated by the push for sexual and aggressive instinctual gratification and discharge and (b) our interest in and relation to objects is based primarily on the object's role in serving instinctual discharge.

With regard to our relation to actual external objects, the issue seems quite clear. The evidence strongly suggests that we are inherently object-seeking creatures and that our interest in objects is not a secondary derivative of some presumably more basic drive (Eagle, 1987). However, a significant part of object relations theory deals with *internalized objects* and *internalized object relations*. In contrast to Freud's psychic world, which is populated by unconscious wishes and defenses against those wishes, Fairbairn's psychic world is populated by internalized objects and internalized object relations.

The essential idea that is conveyed by the concept of internalized object (as well as by the concept of introject) is that aspects of the other (prohibitions, evaluations, characteristics, etc.) are taken in *but are not fully metabolized and integrated* into one's self-organization, with the result that these aspects are experienced as felt "presences" (Schafer, 1968) rather than as natural and unquestioned parts of oneself. As Fairbairn informs us, the notion of internalized object can be traced to Freud's concept of the superego. According to that concept, punishments, prohibitions, evaluations, rules, and so on, whose original source was external objects, are eventually internalized as a psychic structure. However, frequently the internalization is not complete, as expressed in the common tendency to experience and describe the internalized prohibitions as a homunculus standing outside oneself and observing or directing what one does and in such locutions as "my conscience tells me . . ." (rather than "I believe . . ."). The incomplete internalization suggests that the superego often has the status of an introject rather than of a fully and smoothly assimilated identification.

As a rather clear example of what we believe is meant by the concept of internalized object, we cite a patient who, before each occasion of sexual intercourse, would experience the obsessive thought, "If they could see me now." The patient reported that the "they" were her parents and also that the feeling accompanying the thought was one of defiance. Thus, to each sexual occasion, this patient brought representations of her parents and played out her internal object relations with them. Further, the ego-alien, obsessive quality of the thought—it is there almost as a felt presence—bespeaks the unintegrated status of these internal representations. The thought is her thought, but it is unbidden, as if it had a life of its own.

According to Fairbairn, objects are internalized for two basic reasons: (a) Incorporation and internalization are natural psychological modes for the young infant; and (b) the infant assumes and takes in the badness of the environment in order to make the latter more benevolent and controllable. As Fairbairn (1952, p. 66) stated, "It is better to be a sinner in a world ruled by God than to live in a world ruled by the Devil." Implied in this latter point is the idea that it is mainly under the impact of negative depriving and frustrating experiences that objects are internalized.

Fairbairn's (1952) concepts of internalized objects and internalized object relations are embedded in a complex and somewhat arcane metapsychological structure of splits in the object correlated with splits in the ego. There is not sufficient space to cover this material (and we are far from certain that it repays the efforts necessary to understand it).

Implications of Object Relations Theory for Treatment

Before discussing the implications of object relations theory for psychotherapy, one general comment that also applies to other theoretical developments in psychoanalysis is in order. Because most of the writing in this area is highly theoretical, it is often difficult to determine what therapists of different theoretical persuasions actually do and to what extent and in what specific ways their therapeutic activities differ from each other (Sandler, 1983). Detailed clinical data (as would be available, for example, from tape recorded sessions) are simply not available. The result is that, although we know a great deal about Fairbairn's theory, we know very little about how and to what extent his theory was expressed and implemented in his treatment. What we can do, however, is note some implications of object relations theory for the practice of psychotherapy.

1. To the extent that interpretation continues to be a main activity of object relations therapists, one would certainly expect that the *content* of interpretations would tend to differ from those provided by traditional analysts.[3] One would expect, for example, much less emphasis on sexual and aggressive wishes and on oedipal issues and correspondingly greater attention to so-called pre-oedipal issues and to issues such as early infant–mother interaction, relationships with internalized objects, merging fantasies, fears of loss of an object world, and feelings of ego weakness and fragility.

   As a specific example of differences in the content of interpretations, contrast Fairbairn's (1952) understanding of agoraphobia with that of traditional theory. According to the latter, the *fear* of walking in the streets is related to the unconscious *wish* to street-walk. That is, unconscious prostitution wishes and fantasies are held to be a key element underlying the agoraphobic symptom (Freud, 1887–1902/1954a). One would expect that the content of interpretations given to patients in treatment by a traditional analyst would reflect this particular way of understanding the nature of the agoraphobic syndrome. Contrast this interpretation of agoraphobia with Fairbairn's (1952, p. 43) claim that it represents a conflict between "the regressive lure of identification" and "the progressive urge of separation." In short, Fairbairn understands agoraphobia, not in terms of conflict around sexual wishes, but in terms of what Mahler (1968) would refer to as a separation-individuation inner conflict. (See Eagle, 1979, for a comparison of traditional and object relational conceptions of phobias.)

---

[3]We are aware that interpretations offered by therapists of any theoretical persuasion should really be determined by the patient's productions rather than by theoretical predilection. However, it is clear that the therapist's theoretical orientation does influence his or her interpretations, particularly when patients' productions are susceptible to different interpretations, as they very often are. There is a critical issue of the degree to which the therapist's theoretical point of view is *imposed* upon the patient. (See Peterfreund, 1983, for a discussion of "stereotyped" versus "heuristic" therapists).

2. Along with other clinical and theoretical developments in psychoanalytic theory, object relations theory deemphasizes a number of therapeutic factors that are central to traditional theory—for example, insight, making the unconscious conscious, transforming id into ego, and analysis of the transference—and instead places primary emphasis on the therapeutic relationship which is understood as a therapeutic agent in its own right. This focus on the relationship is summed up by Fairbairn's statement that an overriding goal of treatment is to replace the "bad object" with a "good object."

Although he does not employ the same terminology, Fairbairn clearly suggests that, to use Alexander and French's (1946) term, "corrective emotional experiences" with the therapist are the vehicle for change. However, much remains unclear in this formulation. Although ideas such as replacing bad objects with good objects are evocative and one has a general sense of what they mean, they are far from precise. And Fairbairn does not attempt to make them more precise.

3. As noted above, the therapeutic goal of "dissolution," or what Fairbairn (1952) refers to as "exorcism," of internalized objects is quite consistent with his object relations theory. This goal, more than any other, highlights important theoretical differences between object relations theory and traditional theory. According to traditional theory, one central goal of treatment is to claim or own what was disclaimed and disowned, as expressed in Freud's (1933/1964) dictum, "Where id was, there ego should be" (p. 80). One way of putting this is to say that one makes personal and internal what was defensively expelled and made impersonal and external (see Eagle, 1987). A central therapeutic goal in object relations theory is precisely the opposite—to render impersonal and external (that is, to exorcise) that which, under the impact of trauma, was improperly and defensively *internalized*. One wants to reduce the degree to which one's psychic life is dominated by these internalized objects.

There is a parallel between the therapeutic goal in traditional theory of softening the harshness of the superego (Strachey, 1934) and the goal of exorcising internalized objects. The superego is the one psychic structure in traditional theory that is based entirely on internalizing that which was initially and inherently external. In a certain sense the idea of softening the harshness of the superego can be understood as generally synonymous with the notion of exorcising the internal saboteur. That is to say, in contrast to a mature conscience, a primitive and harsh superego can be understood as an internalized object (or archaic introject) that needs to be exorcised or, at least, tempered and modulated.

In certain respects, however, the idea of exorcising internalized objects goes further than softening the superego. What the former suggests on the clinical-behavioral level is that patients are driven by unconscious fantasies in which the exciting object will finally be available, loving, and accepting rather than elusive and rejecting. Thus, to say that these internalized objects need to be exorcised seems to us to be tantamount to the relinquishment of the above fantasy. As Fairbairn (1952, p. 73) stated, the difficult task in treatment is "the overcoming of the patient's devotion to his repressed [internalized] object." Evidence for this sort of change would be reflected in such areas as alterations in object choice (e.g., interest in actual caring and available objects), different patterns in intimate interpersonal relations (mainly a modulation of the tendency to induce and create interactions in which the object combines the lure of excitement with rejection) and, of course, changes in transference reactions. Indeed, the main vehicle for such changes would likely consist in a living out and a persistent examination of the ways in which the patient "transforms" the therapist and experiences him or her as an exciting and rejecting object.

Note that different theoretical language notwithstanding, the object relations approach does not seem very different from the traditional and familiar idea of analysis of the transference. Even the idea of experiencing the therapist as an exciting and rejecting object may not be too different, in practice, from the traditional conception of transferring one's instinctual wishes on to the therapist. Certainly, the idea of internalizing the other as an object with exciting and rejecting (read also, forbidden) features is consistent with an oedipal account in which enticement, excitement, rejection, and prohibition are all components of the object as well as of the oedipal triangle.

4. Object relations theorists place a great deal of emphasis on the role of *regression* in treatment. It is true that in classical Freudian treatment, partial and circumscribed regression is induced by the analytic setting. However, in object relations theory, particularly in the writings of Winnicott (1958) and Guntrip (1969), regression has a different and more directly therapeutic role. Both Winnicott and Guntrip refer to the importance of the patient returning to an earlier point at which psychological development went askew and

to that point at which development turned in the direction of a "false self" (Winnicott, 1958). The basic idea behind these various formulations seems to be that under the impact of trauma, certain defensive and defective structures (e.g., false self, a pseudo-adult self masking an underlying ego weakness) developed that are at the heart of the patient's pathology. According to this view, what needs to be accomplished in treatment is a regression to the point at which these structures developed and a resumption of developmental growth along new and better pathways.

The basic idea that successful treatment makes possible a return to some earlier point of trauma at which development began its pathological course and that one can resume development on a new basis characterizes not only object relations theory, but also, as we shall see, self psychology. As is true of other ideas in object relations theory, it is evocative and even compelling. It certainly feeds into fantasies of a rebirth and of starting all over again. However, it is also a very vague idea and does not tell us very much regarding the specific processes and the specific changes that are involved in successful treatment.

INTERPERSONAL PSYCHOANALYSIS

As noted earlier, Greenberg and Mitchell (1983) distinguish two main paradigms in psychoanalytic thinking. One is Freud's drive theory (which they refer to as the drive/structure model) in which "all facets of personality and psychopathology are understood essentially as a function, a derivative, of drives and their transformations" (p. 3). In this view, object relations are drive vicissitudes. The other model is one they term a "relational/ structure" model in which "relations with others constitute the fundamental building blocks of mental life. The creation, or re-creation, of specific modes of relatedness with others replaces drive discharge as the force motivating human behavior" (p. 3).

Interpersonal psychoanalysis refers to theories which subscribe to the relational/structure model. Historically, the main proponents of this model have been Sullivan (1953), Horney (1945, 1950), Fromm-Reichmann (1950), and Fromm (1941). More recent, research-oriented versions of interpersonal psychoanalytic psychotherapy have been presented by Strupp and his colleagues (Strupp & Binder, 1984) and by Klerman and his co-workers (Klerman, Rounsaville, Chevron, & Weissman, 1984). Space limitations preclude an account of all of these authors' theories of treatment. We shall restrict ourselves to the work of Sullivan because he was the originator of, and the most ardent, influential spokesperson for, this point of view. As noted earlier, Sullivan's (1953) theory can be seen as the first important American version of an object relations theory.

Sullivan's Theory

Central to Sullivan's conception of personality development and psychopathology is his overriding emphasis on the interpersonal field beginning with the infant–mother dyad. The organism has two main needs—biological satisfaction and psychological and interpersonal security—the latter playing a vital role in personality development and psychopathology. In Sullivan's (1953) theory, anxiety originates from a disturbance in the emotional connection ("empathic linkage") between mother and infant. Anxiety in the mother induces anxiety in the infant. The reduction of this anxiety generates a feeling of interpersonal security. The relative freedom from anxiety is crucially dependent on parental tenderness and empathy. Infants learn to regulate their conscious experience, their behavior, and their developing conceptions of themselves in accord with an anxiety gradient in order to avoid anxiety and thereby maximize their feelings of security. In this process, experiences linked with a reduction of anxiety and, therefore, a sense of "good mother" become internalized and represented as "good me." Experiences associated with "bad mother" (i.e., disapproving or anxious mother) lead to the conceptions of "bad me" and "not me," the latter referring to disowned, unintegrated realms of experience associated with truly intense anxiety.

Without being explicit about it, Sullivan appears to have a two-factor theory of anxiety induction (anxiety in the mother and maternal disapproval). The developing child constructs a "self-system" which assesses the probability of anxiety (similar to Freud's notion of signal anxiety) and tries to avoid it through the triggering of "security operations" (analogous to defenses in Freud's theory, although Levenson [1985, p. 50] points out what is defended against is a ". . . contagious terror set in motion *by the other person*" rather than by unconscious drive derivatives). It is in this sense that the self is said to be constructed from "reflected appraisals." A detailed account of these and other important aspects of the theory can be found in Sullivan (1953). See Zucker (1989) for a statement of the key premises of interpersonal theory.

Treatment Implications of Sullivan's Theory

As far as we can tell there has been no systematic development of Sullivan's theory and therefore no coherent, current core of interpersonal theory shared by analysts who trace their lineage to Sullivan. It is, therefore, not possible to present *the* interpersonal theory of treatment. Although they rely on Sullivan as their theoretical common ground, many contemporary interpersonal psychoanalysts depart from him in their clinical approach. We cannot hope to do justice to the considerable range of theory and technique within contemporary interpersonal psychoanalysis. As Levenson (1985, p. 53) points out, a wide variety of positions exist "under the loose rubric of 'interpersonal.'" He notes that "Interpersonalists range from extreme interactionalists through viewpoints largely indistinguishable from object-relations theorists, especially Winnicott and Fairbairn, and even on to some closet 1930s Freudians." We can, however, indicate the main orienting assumptions and treatment implications stemming from a Sullivanian perspective.

Perhaps the main bond that unites Sullivanians is their emphasis on the concept of the participant-observer (Witenberg, 1974). Recall that Sullivan (1953, pp. 110–111) defined personality as "the relatively enduring pattern of recurrent interpersonal situations which characterize a human life." According to Sullivan, it is misleading to talk about personality traits or states as though they were self-contained, intrapsychic entities. Nursing at the breast is first and foremost an interpersonal situation for both mother and infant. Applied to the analytic situation, the idea of a participant-observer has come to mean (Levenson, 1988) that the therapist is always as much a participant in the interaction as is the patient. For example, the therapist's restraint (e.g., in the form of silence or relative anonymity) is a communication which may be experienced by the patient in various ways. The therapist is not simply an observer focusing on the patient's predominant modes of interaction, but is an integral part of the interpersonal field as both subject and object.

Within this perspective, a central feature of Sullivan's theory of treatment is the elucidation of the patient's interpersonal interactions with significant others, including the therapist. Interactions fraught with overt and covert anxiety and misunderstanding obviously are the most important ones in need of attention and clarification. The "security operations" the patient uses to avoid anxiety are a major focus of exploration. Awareness of the archaic nature of the self-system, its selectively unattended "bad-me" and dissociated "not-me" aspects, and its detrimental impact on the patient's interpersonal relationships provide a major impetus for change. The therapist, through a "detailed inquiry" (Sullivan, 1954), helps the patient unpack current and past anxiety-laden experiences which were avoided through "selective inattention" at the time they occurred. Experiences of demystification have therapeutic power. Clarification through language leads to what Levenson (1982) calls "semiotic competence." He reminds us that Sullivan said that "no one has grave difficulties in living if he has a very good grasp of what is happening to him" (quoted in Levenson, 1985, p. 49).

The emphasis on participant-observation, with its stress on the overt and covert mutual influence of the two participants and the idea that the act of observation alters the phenomena observed, has been contrasted with the classical psychoanalytic position which is seen as static and as implying that the observer could somehow stand outside the interaction. Witenberg (1974, p. 852), for example, claims that in classical psychoanalysis the analyst is a detached observer and that the notion of the therapist as a participant-observer "puts at the disposal of the therapist more of the relevant clinical data, and it frees him from the inhibition imposed by classical theory of the use of his emotional reactions in treatment." We might point out here that revisions of the traditional psychoanalytic theory of treatment (e.g., Gill, 1982; Kernberg, 1975, 1980; Kohut, 1984; Muslin & Gill, 1978) by those who began in the Freudian tradition have brought the traditional Freudian view closer to the concept of participant-observation. This shift is evident, for example, in Cooper's (1987) depiction of the modernist view of transference, outlined earlier, and in the discussions of a one-person versus a two-person psychology (Gill, 1983; Modell, 1984). It has been prompted in part by the focus on the nonclassical analytic patient and by enlarged conceptions of the nature of countertransference (Racker, 1968). As Gill (1983) pointed out, there is no necessary connection between the analyst's subscribing to the drive discharge paradigm versus the interpersonal paradigm and the degree to which the analyst believes that he or she is participating in the analytic situation.

In any case, it is our impression that there is a considerable range of therapeutic approaches among those who regard themselves as Sullivanians, as well as significant deviations from Sullivan's own treatment methods. First, although inspired by Sullivan, many therapists depart from him in their stress on transference interpretations and vary among themselves regarding how vital they believe such interpretations to be. Second, interpersonalists seem to differ a great deal in the degree to which they emphasize relationship factors versus insight in their conceptualization of therapeutic action. Third, they differ in the degree to which they advocate revealing their countertransference feelings and reactions to their patients. With regard to the last point, Ehrenberg (1982), for example, in the course of asserting the value of active engagement and participation by the analyst, advocates the explicit acknowledgement to the patient of his or her emotional impact on the analyst, that is, disclosure of the countertransference, broadly defined. For example, in response to a patient's detached and disinterested attitude about everything, including the sessions, the analyst made it plain that she was concerned that the sessions be useful and that she "did not like to feel useless" (Ehrenberg, 1982, p. 551).

While interpersonalists vary in the extent to which they share their countertransference reactions with their patients, they repeatedly stress that they are very much in the interaction they are attempting to analyze and that this focus is itself an important aspect of the interaction. Thus, for Levenson (1988, p. 140), "the analysis of the relationship between what is being said and who is saying it to whom and how it is being said and heard—the classic linguistic formula of message and metamessage—is at the core of the psychoanalytic process." Levenson (1988, p. 101) believes that "*the power of psychoanalysis may well depend on what is said about what is done* [italics as in original] as a continuous, integral part of the therapy." As suggested above, this is a view increasingly shared by many traditional Freudians who also emphasize the importance of an oscillation between the enactment and experiencing of the here-and-now transference and countertransference configurations and their analysis.

While Levenson's (1988) conception of recursive patterning is consistent with a Freudian view, he does point to what he believes to be a sharp demarcation of Freudian and interpersonal approaches to dealing with this patterning. He sees the Freudian position as "*the search for the truth behind appearances*" and the interpersonal position as "*search for the truth inherent in appearances.* For the Freudian, the key question is, what does it truly mean? For the interpersonalist, the question is, what's going on around here?" (Levenson, 1985, p. 53).

Kohut's Self Psychology

Freud's (1914/1957a) "On Narcissism" represents an important point of departure for those theoretical orientations that give central consideration to the self, the object, and the relations between them. Nowhere is this clearer than in Kohut's self psychology. In his essay, "On Narcissism," Freud (1914/1957a) looked at psychological development, not so much from the point of view of drive, psychosexual stages, and growth of ego functions, but from the perspective of increasing differentiation between self and object. It is this perspective that Kohut (e.g., 1971, 1977, 1984) began with and developed into a psychoanalytic self psychology in which the narcissistic line of development is the central dimension of psychological growth and in which a unitary, cohesive self is the central developmental achievement.

As noted elsewhere (Eagle, 1987), in his earlier work, Kohut (e.g., 1971) presented self psychology as an outgrowth and supplement to traditional Freudian theory. In the earlier writings, traditional Freudian theory is held to be applicable to the "structural neuroses," which are characterized by conflict between intact structures, while self psychology is applicable to those conditions, such as narcissistic personality disorders, in which defects and disorders of the self are at the core of pathology. In the course of time, however, this two-factor apportionment of domains came to be increasingly replaced by an outright rejection of traditional Freudian theory and its thoroughgoing replacement by self psychology. Thus, in all pathology, intrapsychic conflict regarding sexual and aggressive wishes was always secondary to the issue of self-cohesiveness. In short, although self psychology emerged from traditional Freudian theory, its further development led to a splitting away from mainstream psychoanalytic theory. Further, there appears to be little interest or faith in the possibility of integrations of the two perspectives. Thus, Ornstein (1978, p. 98) wrote: "The essential advance made . . . is the development of a self psychology that is conceptually independent from and has moved beyond drive theory and ego psychology."

Finally, one sociological note: Largely because, for the most part, self psychologists did not break with existing psychoanalytic training institutes and did not go on to establish their own training institutes, in a political sense they have continued to be viewed as a perspective *within* mainstream psychoanalysis in contrast, say, to followers of Adler, Jung, and Horney who are viewed as *outside* mainstream psychoanalysis.

Kohut's self psychology diverges from traditional psychoanalytic theory in a number of ways. From a broad theoretical point of view, Kohut's main departure from traditional psychoanalytic theory is his positing of a separate line of development along the dimension of narcissism. According to Freud, normal development is characterized by a *decreasing* investment of libido in the ego and an *increasing* investment of libido in the object. In short, according to traditional theory, in normal development we move from self love to object love (although Freud noted that a certain minimal degree of self love is necessary for psychological health). Furthermore, given the limited supply of libido, there is a *reciprocal* relation between self interest and object interest. Too much absorption in the self is necessarily at the expense of interest in the other, and conversely, too much absorption in the other is at the expense of the interest of the self.

One of Kohut's main objections to the Freudian theoretical treatment of narcissism is that it is viewed as inherently pathological and regressive— a state or condition one grows away from in the normal course of development. Kohut rejects this view and argues instead that narcissism is a separate line of development that, as a function of the vicissitudes of early experiences, can proceed in either a healthy or a pathological direction. Healthy narcissism is marked, above all, by the development of a cohesive self and by the productive and joyful carrying out of one's "nuclear program," that is, by the exercise of one's talents and skills in the pursuit of one's basic ambitions and goals, and culminating in the development of a set of ideals and values. By contrast, narcissistic personality disorders, a primary expression of pathological narcissism, are characterized by self-defects, a proneness to "disintegration anxiety," archaic grandiosity and exhibitionism (a pathological expression of ambitions and goals), and marked failures in the carrying out of one's nuclear program.

According to Kohut, one can lead a productive, meaningful, and even joyful life without the pursuit of object love being at its center. As Kohut (1984, p. 7) puts it, "There are . . . good lives, including some of the greatest and most fulfilling lives recorded in history, that were not lived by individuals whose psychosexual organization was heterosexual-genital or whose major commitment organization was to unambivalent object love." In a recent book, *Solitude*, Storr (1988) makes a similar point, with an illustration from the life of the historian Gibbons, the author of *The Decline and Fall of the Roman Empire*. Storr (1988) writes:

> Modern insistence that true happiness can only be found in intimate attachments, more especially in sexual fulfillment, does not allow a place for a character like Gibbon. It is clear that, although his friendships were many, his chief source of self-esteem and of pleasure was his work. (p. xi)

Implied in Kohut's position on object love is his rejection of Freudian instinct theory. That is, contrary to Freud, Kohut does not believe that instinctual gratification and the need to find the object(s) through which such gratification can occur are superordinate motives governing behavior and mental life. In self psychology, the need for self-cohesiveness and self-esteem are the superordinate motives that replace instinctual gratification. For Kohut, being compelled or driven by sexual and aggressive drives is not a normal expression of our psychobiological nature, but is rather a "disintegration product," reflecting failures in self-cohesiveness.

Both as a developmental–etiological theory and in the context of treatment, Kohut's main emphasis is on the achievement of a cohesive self. According to Kohut, the development of a cohesive self requires the parental provision of empathic mirroring and the later availability of a parental figure permitting idealization. Such early mirroring and later idealization are held to facilitate the smooth development of the normal and necessary narcissistic phase of grandiosity and exhibitionism and the construction of an "idealized parent image." The experience of grandiosity and the availability of an idealized parental image enable the child to feel powerful and full rather than powerless and empty in the face of the unavoidable shortcomings and frustrations of reality.

The traumatic failure to provide empathic mirroring and adequate conditions for idealization are, according to Kohut, the primary etiological factors in the generation of pathological narcissism or, more specifically, in the development of a noncohesive self (or self defects). As noted earlier, clinically, the markers of pathological narcissism include archaic grandiosity and exhibitionism, proneness to disintegration anxiety, sensitivity to narcissistic injury, and narcissistic rages.

Pathological narcissism is also manifested in the individual's relations to others. And here Kohut introduces a term that plays a special role in self psychology, namely, *selfobject*. As the term suggests, the selfobject is neither fully self nor fully other. Broadly speaking, it is a response to the other, not as a separate other, but primarily in terms of the other's role in sustaining one's self-cohesiveness. In narcissistic personality disorders, the individual establishes primarily archaic self-selfobject bonds with others. The psychological importance of the other lies mainly in the others' role in providing self-aggrandizement, the regulation of self-esteem, and the maintenance of self-cohesiveness. That is, the other carries out functions that, in healthy development, one would eventually carry out oneself.

In Kohut's earlier writings, he gives the impression that, in normal development along the line of narcissism, one moves from a reliance on selfobjects to carry out self-regulation and self-sustaining functions to an increasing ability to execute these functions oneself. However, in his 1984 book, in rejecting the desirability or even possibility of autonomy as a developmental goal, Kohut argues that we continue to need selfobjects all our lives. (So vital is this need for selfobjects in Kohut's view that he compares it to a lifelong need for oxygen.) The issue, according to Kohut, is not presence or absence of selfobjects, but a move from an archaic selfobject (based, for example, on merging) to more mature self–selfobject bonds which are based on "empathic resonance."

To sum up, in contrast to traditional psychoanalytic theory, in which pathology (as well as a wide range of normal behavior) is viewed from the perspective of intrapsychic conflict, the primary emphasis in self psychology is on developmental *defects*, in particular, self defects. In this sense, self psychology is one expression of what might generally be referred to as a mini-paradigm shift (Kuhn, 1962) from a psychology of conflict to a psychology of developmental defects and arrests that has characterized recent developments in psychoanalysis.

Implications of Kohut's Theory for Treatment

It seems to us that more than other psychoanalytic developments, self psychology is primarily a theory of treatment, with an etiological theory of pathology and a theory of personality development grafted on. Indeed, Kohut (1979) himself tells us that an important impetus for the development of self psychology was his experience in the two analyses of the patient he called Mr. Z. Very briefly, the second analysis of Mr. Z was more successful than the first, according to Kohut, largely because Kohut shifted from understanding Mr. Z's sense of "entitlement" as an expression of a clinging to infantile wishes, to understanding this behavior as a response to lack of self-cohesiveness.

According to Kohut, a theory that interprets a patients' narcissistic attitudes and demands as resistances against relinquishing infantile wishes, as "clinging to outdated drive-pleasures that must be opposed by the reality principle and the strictures of adult morality" (1984, p. 89), will communicate a "censorious and disapproving" attitude to the patient. By contrast, the self psychology analyst, Kohut tells us, tends to be more accepting of such behaviors because he or she understands them, not as clinging to infantile gratification, but as reflecting "faulty structures responsible for [the] faulty functioning" (1984, p. 86). In short, from a self psychology perspective, much of the patient's behavior in and out of treatment is understood, not as the covert and conflicted pursuit of infantile wishes, but as the consequence of self-defects and lack of self-cohesiveness.

How are such self-defects dealt with in self psychology treatment? According to Kohut, narcissistic patients spontaneously form mirroring and idealizing transferences. Other kinds of transferences are also discussed in the self psychology literature, but it is the mirroring and idealizing transferences that are the primary innovative emphases of self psychology. The core expressions of these transferences are, respectively, a need to be perfectly mirrored and to merge with an idealized figure. Kohut views these transferences, not as clinging to infantile wishes, but as expressions of the patient's poignant attempt to resume developmental growth. In that sense, these transference expressions are not regressive but *progressive*. Or perhaps one can say that its aim for progressive growth is pursued through regressive means. Because the patient's basic fear is retraumatization at the hands of the therapist, for a period of time resistances against the full formation of mirroring and idealizing transferences are likely to operate. These resistances are dealt with by interpretations regarding the patient's motives and sources. No therapist, of course, can provide perfect empathic understanding or provide a perfect figure for idealization. In other words, the therapist will fail the patient's needs for perfect mirroring and idealization. Such failures will often be met with rage, despair, withdrawal, and regression, as if they did indeed retraumatize the patient. However, as long as the therapist's failures are not, in fact, of traumatic proportions and as long as the therapist acknowledges them, interprets the patient's regressive retreats, and continues to attempt to understand the patient, these failures will function as "optimal failures" or "optimal frustrations."

According to Kohut, after each optimal failure "new self structure will be acquired and existing ones will be firmed" (1984, p. 69). He also notes that following the working through of optimal failure the patient will become more resilient and, finally, "empathic resonance" will replace the bondage of archaic self–selfobject relationships. For Kohut, empathic understanding and the repeated working through of optimal failures in empathy constitute "the basic therapeutic unit" of treatment.

Why should feeling understood be such a potent therapeutic agent, ultimately playing the critical role in the repair of self-defects and the building up of psychic structure?[4] Clearly, understanding and feeling understood are general *desiderata* in virtually every context of human communication, including that of psychotherapy. But why the special role that it is given in the self psychology conception of treatment? In order to answer this question adequately, one must turn to Kohut's etiological theory of pathology. Very simply, and briefly, underlying the therapeutic role given to feeling understood are the implicit assumptions that (a) being understood (empathic mirroring) is a universal developmental need; (b) traumatic failures in this area lead to self-defects; (c) mirroring transferences bespeak the poignant efforts of a person with a defective self to complete his or her development and finally to have his or her need for empathic mirroring met; and, finally, (d) the meeting of this need by the therapist serves as a critical contribution to the repair of self-defects, the building up of psychic structures, and the resumption of developmental growth. In short, the provision of empathic understanding is so critical because it meets a traumatically unfulfilled developmental need and thereby facilitates the resumption of developmental growth. As Friedman (1986) characterized it, "being understood is a maturing environment."

---

[4]We are using Kohut's language in referring to "repair" of self-defects and building up of psychic structure. The precise meaning and referents of these terms are not at all clear to us.

OTHER CONTRIBUTIONS TO PSYCHOANALYTIC THEORY AND TREATMENT

We now turn to a brief summary of some of the more recent developments in psychoanalytic theories of psychopathology and treatment. We limit our discussion to the work of Mahler, Kernberg, and Weiss and Sampson. If space permitted, we would have included the work of other important contributors such as Jacobson, Winnicott, Loewald, Sandler, Modell, Gedo, Gill, Schafer, and Brenner, among others. We would also have discussed the development of brief psychoanalytic psychotherapy (Budman, 1981).

The last three approaches we cover in this chapter—the work of Mahler (1968), the work of Kernberg (1975, 1976, 1980, 1984), and the "unconscious-control" theory of Weiss and Sampson (1986) and their colleagues (the Mt. Zion Group)—are a representative sample of contemporary theoretical developments in psychoanalysis that do not as readily lend themselves as the previous approaches discussed to categorization in terms of Pine's (1990) four different foci of drive, ego, object, and self.

We begin with a few introductory comments concerning these three approaches. Mahler's theory represents a combination of a number of different psychoanalytic perspectives. Although many of her formulations are presented in the language of drive theory, her theory focuses on the differentiation between self and object, the development of concepts of self and of object, and the relation between the two. In an important sense, Mahler's work on separation-individuation is both an object relations theory and a self psychology.

Kernberg acknowledges the influence both of Mahler and of Jacobson (1964). His work represents an early psychoanalytic mainstream version of an object relations theory and self psychology. Kernberg's (1975, 1976, 1984) clinical and theoretical efforts have been explicitly directed toward an attempted integration of aspects of Freud's drive theory and object relations theory. Although much of Kernberg's theory has been directed toward an understanding of borderline conditions, his formulations have broader application. He presents a picture of psychological development in which self and object representations are initially organized in accord with the dominant affective tone (i.e., gratification versus frustration) of self and object interactions in which a major developmental challenge is the integration of opposite self-object-affect structural units.

Finally, from a certain perspective, Weiss and Sampson's (1990) unconscious-control theory can be seen as an extension and elaboration of ego psychology, in the sense that a major emphasis is placed on unconscious ego processes of belief, judgment, testing, and so on. However, unconscious-control theory is also interactional and object relational, in the sense that unconscious pathogenic beliefs are acquired through interactions with and communications from parental figures and are tested in treatment through interaction with the therapist. In addition, unconscious-control theory can also be understood as a psychoanalytic expression of a zeitgeist in which cognitive processes (including unconscious cognitive processes) and cognitive psychology have come to occupy center stage in the behavioral sciences.

Mahler

The first, recent contribution we consider is the work of Mahler and her colleagues. Unfortunately, we cannot cover Mahler's rich formulations with the detail they deserve. We will focus on the essentials of her theory and its implications for treatment.

Mahler places separation-individuation as a core and separate dimension of psychological development, which, while related to and even overlapping with the dimensions of psychosexual and ego development, is both sufficiently different and important to warrant a central place in a psychoanalytic theory of development. Further, severe psychopathology involves deformation in this dimension of development.

Mahler characterizes the infant's early extrauterine life as a state of *normal autism*. In this stage, which is concerned mainly with attempts to achieve homeostasis, the infant cannot differentiate between the mother's need-reducing ministrations and its own efforts at getting rid of unpleasurable tension (through defecating, urinating, regurgitating, etc.) mainly because there is no concept yet of an object or a self.

From the second month on, "dim awareness of the need-satisfying object marks the beginning of the phase of *normal symbiosis*, in which the infant behaves and functions as though he and his mother were an omnipotent system—a dual unity in their one common boundary" (Mahler 1968, p. 8; italics added). During this stage, the infant requires the help of the "auxiliary ego" of the mother in order to maintain homeostasis. In this state of fusion, the "I" is not differentiated from the "not I," and "inside and outside are only gradually coming to be sensed as different" (Mahler, 1968, p. 9). According to Mahler, in "symbiotic child psychosis," the ego regresses to this state of delusional omnipotent fusion. From the more traditional perspective, this is a stage of an undifferentiated id–ego matrix.

According to Mahler, the infant must experience "optimal human symbiosis" (1968, p. 14) in order to successfully negotiate the separation-individuation process and achieve both a clear sense of identity and libidinal object constancy. Stated in more metapsychological terms, in the course of normal development the child achieves differentiation between self-representations and object representations "from the hitherto fused symbiotic self-plus-object representations" (Mahler, 1968, p. 18). From another perspective, one can describe the separation-individuation process in terms of "the child's achievement of separate functioning in the presence and emotional availability of the mother" (Mahler, 1968, p. 20).

Finally, we note the distinction made between the two complementary processes of separation and individuation. "Separation consists of the child's emergence from a symbiotic fusion with the mother . . . and individuation consists of the achievements making the child's assumption of his own individual characteristics" (Mahler, Pine, & Bergman, 1975, p. 4).

We have attempted to provide a general description of Mahler's theory rather than a detailed account, which would include a description of the various subphases of separation-individuation (e.g., the differentiation, practicing, and rapprochement subphases). The detailed account is readily available elsewhere (e.g., Bergman & Ellman, 1985; Mahler 1968; Mahler, Pine, & Bergman, 1975).

Mahler distinguishes between autistic and symbiotic psychoses, with most of her attention given to the latter. Very briefly and crudely, in autistic psychosis the child is unable to experience and enter the symbiotic mother–infant dual unity. He or she is unable to respond to stimuli emanating from the mother and reacts with rage or panic when threatened with human intrusion. In symbiotic psychosis, the child is unable to *leave* the state of symbiotic unity or fusion and reacts with panic and disorganization at any hint of separateness. In both cases, there is a severe disturbance of identity, "not in a sense of *who* I am but *that* I am" (Mahler, Bergman, & Pine, 1975, p. 8). Also in both cases, the child is unable to use the mother as a basis for developing a sense of separate identity and of relatedness to the world. As Mahler (1968) states it, "In the psychotic child, . . . there seems to be a limitation to his inner capacity to utilize the mother, as a result of which he does not obtain the gratification and relief of tension that are preconditions for progressive development" (p. 231).

Implications of Mahler's Theory for Treatment

In considering the implications of Mahler's theory for treatment, one must distinguish between the direct implications for the treatment of severe childhood pathology (mainly, infantile autism and symbiotic psychosis) and the more indirect and implicit implications for the conceptualization and treatment of adult pathology (mainly, borderline conditions). We shall consider only the latter. One important implication of Mahler's work is that at the center of adult pathology, particularly severe pathology, are issues having to do with differentiation and separation-individuation. That is, many lives are made or broken as a function of one's ability or inability to achieve the differentiation between self and other needed to develop a clear sense of one's identity and a clear and stable sense of an object to whom one can relate libidinally and affectively.

It will be recognized that this emphasis on the development of a sense of self, of object representations, and of the relation between the two is also central to Kohut's self psychology and to object relations theory. For example, Fairbairn's (1952, p. 43) earlier noted characterization of agoraphobia in terms of a conflict between "the regressive lure of identification and the progressive urge for separation" is entirely consistent with Mahler's developmental theory of symbiosis and separation-individuation. Despite her frequent use of the language of Freudian drive theory and metapsychology, Mahler's theory, in many respects, is a version of object relations theory.

As we shall see, Mahler's influence on conceptions of adult pathology is especially evident in Kernberg's work, particularly his formulations of borderline personality organization. For example, Kernberg's developmental stages quite closely parallel Mahler's subphases of separation-individuation. As another example, in both Mahler's and Kernberg's work, excessive aggression, particularly failures in the neutralization of aggression, plays a central role in understanding pathology. And more generally, in both Mahler and Kernberg's formulations, at the heart of pathology lie failures in the achievement of both a stable and integrated sense of self and sense of the object. Mahler writes in regard to borderline patients, "In essence, in these adult patients, as with the children, it is the object and self-representation that seem particularly vulnerable to distortion and obliteration" (Mahler, 1968, pp. 235–236).

It is easier to write about the implications of Mahler's theory for *conceptualization* than for *treatment* of adult pathology. This is often the case in the psychoanalytic literature. For example, one can say a great deal more about the conception of pathology in object relations theory than its prescriptions for treatment. Nevertheless, Mahler's developmental theory does have certain implications for the treatment of adult pathology. It seems to us that there are two broad and related ways in which these implications are manifested. One is the emphasis on the therapeutic relationship, and the other is the emphasis on self and object representations in treatment.

A central idea in Mahler's description of treatment of psychotic children is that the therapist must provide the child with a set of experiences that were not available, indeed that were traumatically unavailable, in the course of development. This is summed up by Mahler in her concept of the "corrective symbiotic experience." It seems to us that this basic idea, that the treatment provides what was not available in the course of development, is also central to many current conceptions of treatment of adults. Thus, in self psychology the therapist provides the empathic mirroring that was traumatically unavailable in the patient's early life. And in object relations theory, the therapist attempts to replace a "bad object situation" with a "good object situation." All of these ideas show obvious links to Alexander and French's (1946) concept of the "corrective emotional experience," a concept which can also be traced back to the influence of Ferenczi and Rank (1925).

As for the emphasis on self and object representations, common to both Mahler's treatment of psychotic children and much current work with adult patients is the idea that central therapeutic tasks in treatment have to do with modifications in self representations, object representations, and relations between the self and objects. Although there are different nuances and somewhat different languages among the different theoretical approaches of, say, self psychology, object relations theory, and Kernberg's formulations, there is convergence on the common emphasis in treatment on the importance of self and object representations and the relations between them.

Kernberg

Kernberg has contributed in a number of different but related areas: (a) He has attempted to integrate object relations, ego psychology, and drive theories (e.g., Kernberg, 1976), along with the contributions of M. Klein and Mahler, in a psychoanalytic developmental theory of psychopathology. (b) He has developed a theory of "borderline personality organization" and has presented ways of diagnosing and assessing such organization (e.g., Kernberg, 1975, 1984). (c) He and his colleagues have offered guidelines for the psychoanalytic treatment of borderline patients (Kernberg, Selzer, Koenigsberg, Carr, & Applebaum, 1989). (d) He has attempted to apply his approach to hospital treatment and other group settings.

According to Kernberg, a central characteristic clearly observed in the transference patterns of borderline patients is the alternation or *splitting* of contradictory affective responses and object relations—from idealization and admiration (love) to devaluation and rage (hate). Furthermore, the borderline patient's reaction to being confronted with the existence of these contradictory ego states is characteristically one of anxiety. For Kernberg (1976, p. 25), these alternating and contradictory states are "the pathologically fixed remnants of the normal processes of early introjection."

In order to understand this quoted phrase, one must examine Kernberg's developmental theory. It is a complex and dense theory, and we do not have sufficient space to do it justice here. However, we can describe some of its key features. A central feature of Kernberg's developmental theory is an emphasis on internalization processes, the basic components being (a) self representations, (b) object representations, and (c) affective states associated with different self-object interactions. One can refer to the organization of the above components as S(self)-O(object)-A(affect) units. Early in development, S-O-A units of opposite affective valences are unintegrated, initially as a function of immaturity (i.e., normal age-appropriate limitations in integrative capacity), and then as a defensive process of splitting. Later in development, the more primitive defense of splitting is normally replaced by repression and other higher level defenses. For borderline patients, this maturational process does not occur, and splitting as well as other primitive defenses (e.g., projective identification) predominate. Introjections that take place under the positive valence of libidinal gratification are organized as the "good internal object" and introjections that take place under the negative valence of the aggressive drive are organized as the "bad internal object." In splitting, these two psychic organizations are kept apart, with the result that an integrated organization of the object and one's relation to the object, an organization that includes ambivalent and complex feelings and perceptions, is not achieved. Because intense anxiety is experienced when the person confronts the existence side-by-side of contradictory positive and negative affective organizations, splitting as a defense is instituted and maintained.

Why should the confrontation with contradictory ego states elicit intense anxiety? Kernberg's answer, clearly derived from the work of Klein and Fairbairn, appears to be that the patient fears that his or her aggression will destroy the good internal object and thus leave him or her living in an inner world with no benevolent objects and at the mercy of bad internal objects.[5] According to Kernberg (1975), the borderline patient is especially susceptible to this danger because of intense oral aggression which is the result of early extreme frustration or a constitutional predisposition. This "excessive pregenital and particularly oral aggression tends to be projected

---

[5]The specific defensive functions served by splitting or keeping apart "good" and "bad" object representations are not always entirely clear. According to Klein as well as Fairbairn, the main defensive function served by splitting is to preserve the good object, that is, to keep it from being infiltrated and destroyed by the bad object.

and causes a paranoid distortion of the early parental images, especially of the mother. Through the projection of predominantly oral-sadistic but also anal-sadistic impulses, the mother is seen as potentially dangerous." (p. 41).

Recently, Kernberg et al. (1989) have provided a handbook for the psychoanalytically oriented treatment of borderline patients. The treatment recommendations are based on Kernberg's conception of the nature of borderline personality organization, according to which the borderline patient attempts to avoid conflict by "unrealistically cleaving loving and hating aspects of both self and others into separate parts" (p. 9). The result of this "dissociative act that completely separates aggression from love" is that relations between self and others are "either totally idealized or totally persecutory" (p. 9). As we understand Kernberg, the aim of the treatment is to clarify, through interpretation, the dissociated or split-off components of the patient's self and object representations, as they are expressed in the transference; and, then help the patient integrate these components "into more realistic and stable [self and object] images" (Kernberg et al., 1989, p. 50). The emphasis in the treatment is on interpretation of here-and-now primitive defensive operations as they are expressed in the transference. Just as these primitive defensive operations weaken the ego, so will interpretation of them strengthen the ego.

Weiss, Sampson, and Their Colleagues (The Mt. Zion Group)

One of the noteworthy recent developments in psychoanalysis is a theory of treatment (and, to a certain extent, an accompanying theory of psychopathology) put forth by Weiss and Sampson at Mt. Zion Hospital in San Francisco. In the past, they have referred to their approach as "control-mastery theory," but more recently have labelled it "the unconscious-control hypothesis" (Weiss, 1990). The Mt. Zion group is unique in the psychoanalytic community in that they have attempted to evaluate their hypothesis (which is pitted against a more traditional Freudian hypothesis) through the relatively rigorous use of clinical data and through testing out specific predictions in systematic research.

What is the unconscious-control hypothesis? One can begin by contrasting it to what Weiss (1990) refers to as Freud's "dynamic hypothesis." According to the latter, whether or not material reaches consciousness is entirely an automatic consequence of the relative strengths of the (sexual and aggressive) impulses seeking gratification and the repressive forces opposing these impulses. By contrast, according to the unconscious-control hypothesis, people exert some control over unconscious functioning and make unconscious decisions regarding the conditions under which they will keep impulses and ideas repressed versus permitting them to reach consciousness. In general, mental contents are kept repressed when an unconscious assessment is made that expressing them would be dangerous; ideas and impulses are experienced or expressed when an assessment is made that conditions of safety obtain.

According to this view, patients come to treatment, not to gratify infantile wishes, but to find conditions in which it is safe to bring forth repressed material and to master the conflicts, anxieties, and traumas that are associated with them.

In contrast to the dynamic hypothesis, Weiss and Sampson maintain that pathology is rooted not in repressed impulses but in unconscious pathogenic beliefs. The essence of pathogenic beliefs is that developmentally normal, desirable goals are experienced as endangering oneself and are fraught with anxiety, guilt, and fear. These pathogenic beliefs can be understood as taking an if-then form: If I pursue such and such a goal, then I will be punished or I will endanger a vital relationship, or I will be hurting someone important to me. One person might have the pathogenic belief that "if I pursue the goal of leading an independent life, it can only be at the expense of my parent(s)," thus engendering intense separation guilt (versus separation anxiety). Another person may suffer from a pathogenic belief that "if I pursue my ambitions and desire to be successful, I will be severely punished for surpassing my parents or siblings," thus resulting in the experience of survivor guilt and the inhibition of ambitious strivings. (Note that this last example is essentially a restatement of the Freudian concept of castration anxiety in the context of Weiss and Sampson's theory.)

In order to determine whether it is safe to bring forth repressed material, patients unconsciously present tests to the therapist. If these tests are passed, the patient is more likely to bring forth repressed material. If tests are failed, the patient is less likely to lift repressions. Much of the clinical richness of Weiss and Sampson's model is expressed in the accounts of what constitutes test-passing and test-failing for particular patients. In general, test-passing can be understood to occur when the therapist's interventions are in accord with the patient's unconscious plan as to how to lift repressions and master anxieties, conflicts, and traumas. Test-failing can be understood to occur when the therapist's interventions are not in accord with or are contrary to the patient's unconscious plan.

An example of a patient presenting tests in treatment is taken from a recent paper by Weiss (1990, pp. 107–108). "A woman who feared she would hurt her parents and her male therapist by becoming independent might experiment with independent behavior in her sessions by disagreeing with the therapist's opinions and then unconsciously monitoring him to see if he feels hurt." Obviously, the therapist's tolerance and acceptance of disagreement would constitute test-passing, while his or her anger or attempts to direct or control the patient would constitute test-failing. Test-passing and the conditions of safety that this implies will, according to Weiss and Sampson, both facilitate the patient's insight into his or her pathogenic beliefs and serve to disconfirm them.

CONCLUSION

Historically, an important general trend in psychoanalytic theory and practice has been the clear and steady shift from Freud's emphasis on instinctual wishes and on conflicts and defenses in relation to these wishes, to the increasing centrality of issues having to do with the development of self representations, of object representations, and of the relationship between them. Although in traditional theory, lives were believed to founder around issues of instinctual gratification and conflict, particularly oedipal conflict, in the more contemporary view, relative success or failure in the achievement of separation-individuation, self-cohesiveness, and supportive object relations is the hallmark of pathology versus health. As Jones put it some time ago, in his Preface to Fairbairn's (1952) *Psychoanalytic Studies of the Personality*:

> If it were possible to condense Dr. Fairbairn's new ideas into one sentence, it might run somewhat as follows. Instead of starting, as Freud did, from stimulation of the nervous system proceeding from excitation of various erotogenous zones and internal tension arising from gonadic activity, Dr. Fairbairn starts at the center of the personality, the ego, and depicts its strivings and difficulties in its endeavor to reach an object where it may find support. (p. v)

Also characterizing contemporary psychoanalytic theory is a relative shift from a psychology of conflict to one of defects, deficits, and arrests, although some contemporary psychoanalytic theorists have broadened the traditional Freudian concept of conflict so that it also is applicable to object relational issues (e.g., see Eagle, 1987; Mitchell, 1988; Weiss & Sampson, 1986).

Finally, changes in concepts of psychological development and of psychopathology have also been accompanied by changes in conceptions of treatment. There has been a shift involving a relative deemphasis on the therapeutic role of interpretation and insight and an increasing emphasis on the importance of the therapeutic relationship as the effective therapeutic agent. In the course of this shift, certain key concepts such as transference and countertransference have been reconceptualized to reflect the more interactional, two-person view of treatment. Thus as noted earlier, in Gill's (1982) writings, transference is not understood as a patient distorting a "blank screen" therapist, but as a patient responding to the therapist's cues and giving them his or her personal meanings.

For a good part of its history, the mainstream psychoanalytic community reacted to opposing views as heresies that needed to be uprooted and condemned. What seems to be distinctive about the contemporary psychoanalytic scene is the tolerance for and assimilation of formulations that were once viewed as deviant and heretical. In short, more than at any other period of its history, contemporary psychoanalysis is characterized by pluralism and theoretical diversity, and it is clear that our current conceptualizations of the nature of therapeutic change are more complex and multifaceted than ever. But to what extent the theoretical perspectives and treatment models presented here (and others which were omitted) are actually associated with different therapist behaviors and attitudes (Gray, 1982) and to what extent the use of one or another or some combination of these models is in fact associated with variations in the effectiveness of treatment outcome are among the important questions we need to answer in the future.

REFERENCES

Abend, S. M., Porder, M. S., & Willick, M. S. (1983). *Borderline patients: Psychoanalytic perspectives*. New York: International Universities Press.

Abraham, K. (1927). *Selected papers on psychoanalysis*. London: Hogarth.

Alexander, F. (1948). *Fundamentals of psychoanalysis*. NewYork: Norton.

Alexander, F. (1954). Psychoanalysis and psychotherapy. *Journal of the American Psychoanalytic Association, 2,* 722–733.

Alexander, F., & French, T. M. (1946). *Psychoanalytic therapy: Principles and application*. New York: Ronald Press.

Allport, G. W. (1950). *The nature of personality: Selected Papers* (pp. 79–91). Cambridge, MA.: Addison-Wesley.

Arlow, J., & Brenner, C. (1964). *Psychoanalytic concepts and the structural theory*. New York: International Universities Press.

Balint, M. (1965). *Primary love and psychoanalytic techniques*. New York: Liveright.

Balint, M. (1968). *The basic fault*. New York: Brunner/Mazel.

Bergman, A., & Ellman, S. (1985). Margaret S. Mahler: Symbiosis and separation-individuation. In J. Reppen (Ed.), *Beyond Freud* (pp. 231–256). Hillsdale, NJ: Analytic Press.

Bibring, E. (1954). Psychoanalysis and the dynamic psychotherapies. *Journal of the American Psychoanalytic Association, 2,* 745–770.

Blum, H. P. (1979). The curative and creative aspects of insight. *Journal of the American Psychoanalytic Association, 27* (Supplement), 41–65.

Blum, H. P. (1983). The position and value of extratransference interpretation. *Journal of the American Psychoanalytic Association, 31*(3), 587–618.

Bowlby, J. (1969). *Attachmen and loss* (Vol. 1). New York: Basic Books.

Brenner, C. (1982). *The mind in conflict.* New York: International Universities Press.

Breuer, J., & Freud, S. (1955). Studies on hysteria. In *Standard edition of the complete psychological works of Sigmund Freud* (Vol. 2). London: Hogarth. (Original published in 1895)

Budman, S. H. (Ed.). (1981). *Forms of brief therapy.* New York: Guilford Press.

Charcot, J. M. (1882). Physiologie pathologique: Sur les divers etats nerveux determines par l'hypotization chez les hysteriques [Pathological physiology: On the different nervous states hypnotically induced in hysterics]. *CR Academy of Science Paris, 94,* 403–405.

Cooper, A. M. (1987). Changes in psychoanalytic ideas: Transference interpretation. *Journal of the American Psychoanalytic Association, 35,* 77–98.

Cooper, A. M. (1989). Concepts of therapeutic effectiveness in psychoanalysis: A historical review. *Psychoanalytic Inquiry, 9,* 4–25.

Curtis, H. C. (1980). The concept of therapeutic alliance: Implications for the "widening scope." In H. Blum (Ed.), *Psychoanalytic explorations of technique* (pp. 159–192). New York: International Universities Press.

Eagle, M. (1979). Psychoanalytic formulations of phobias. In L. Saretsky, G. D. Goldman, & D. S. Milman (Eds.), *Integrating ego psychology and object relations theory* (pp. 97–118). Dubuque, IA: Kendall/Hunt.

Eagle, M. (1987). *Recent developments in psychoanalysis: A critical evaluation.* Cambridge, MA: Harvard University Press.

Ehrenberg, D. (1982). Psychoanalytic engagement: The transaction as primary data. *Contemporary Psychoanalysis, 18,* 535–555.

Eissler, K. R. (1953). The effect of the structure of the ego on psychoanalytic technique. *Journal of the American Psychoanalytic Association, 1,* 104–143.

Ellenberger, H. (1970). *The discovery of the unconscious.* New York: Basic Books.

Erle, J. (1990). Studying the psychoanalytic process: An introduction. *Psychoanalytic Quarterly, 59*(4), 527–531.

Fairbairn, W. R. D. (1941). A revised psychopathology of the psychoses and psychoneuroses. *International Journal of Psychoanalysis, 22,* 250–279.

Fairbairn, W. R. D. (1952). *Psychoanalytic studies of the personality.* London: Tavistock Publications & Routledge & Kegan Paul.

Ferenczi, S., & Rank, O. (1956). *The development of psychoanalysis*. New York: Dover Publications. 1956. (Original work published 1925)

Freud, A. (1936). *The ego and the mechanisms of defense*. New York: International Universities Press.

Freud, S. (1953). On psychotherapy. *Standard edition* (Vol. 7; pp. 255–268). London: Hogarth. (Original work published in 1905)

Freud, S. (1954). Analysis terminable and interminable. *Standard edition* (Vol. 23, pp. 209–253). London: Hogarth. (Original work published in 1937)

Freud, S. (1954a). *The origins of psychoanalysis: Freud's letters to Wilhelm Fliess, 1887–1902*. New York: Basic Books.

Freud, S. (1954b). *The origins of psychoanalysis*, (Letter 69), New York: Basic Books. (Original work written in 1897)

Freud, S. (1955). Lines of advance in psycho-analytic therapy. *Standard edition* (Vol. 17, pp. 157–168). London: Hogarth. (Original work published in 1919)

Freud, S. (1957a). On narcissism. *Standard edition* (Vol. 14; pp. 67–102). London: Hogarth. (Original published in 1914)

Freud, S. (1957b). On the history of the psychoanalytic movement. *Standard edition* (Vol. 14; pp. 2–66). London: Hogarth. (Original work published in 1914)

Freud, S. (1958). The dynamics of transference. *Standard edition* (Vol. 12; pp. 97–108). London: Hogarth. (Original work published in 1912)

Freud, S. (1959). Inhibitions, symptoms, and anxiety. *Standard edition* (Vol. 20; pp. 77–174). London: Hogarth. (Original work published in 1926)

Freud, S. (1961). The ego and the id. *Standard edition* (Vol. 19; pp. 3–68). London: Hogarth. (Original work published in 1923)

Freud, S. (1962). The neuro-psychoses of defense. In J. Strachey (Ed. and Trans.), *Standard edition of the complete psychological works of Sigmund Freud* (Vol. 3; pp. 43–61). London: Hogarth. (Original work published 1894)

Freud, S. (1964a). An outline of psychoanalysis. *Standard edition* (Vol. 23, pp. 141–207). London: Hogarth. (Original published in 1940)

Freud, S. (1964b). New introductory lectures. *Standard edition* (Vol. 22, pp. 3–182). London: Hogarth. (Original work published in 1933)

Friedman, L. (1978). Trends in the psychoanalytic theory of treatment. *Psychoanalytic Quarterly*, XLVII(4), 524–567.

Friedman, L. (1986). Kohut's testament. *Psychoanalytic Inquiry*, 6, 321–347.

Fromm, E. (1941). *Escape from freedom*. New York: Holt, Rinehart & Winston.

Fromm-Reichmann, F. (1950). *Principles of intensive psychotherapy*. Chicago: University of Chicago Press.

Gill, M. M. (1954). Psychoanalysis and exploratory psychotherapy. *Journal of the American Psychoanalytic Association*, 2, 771–797.

Gill, M. M. (1967). *The collected papers of David Rapaport*. New York: Basic Books.

Gill, M. M. (1976). *Analysis of transference*. New York: International Universities Press.

Gill, M. M. (1982). Analysis of the transference. In H. J. Schlesinger (Ed.), *Psychological Issues Monograph Series* (No. 53). New York: International Universities Press.

Gill, M. M. (1983). The point of view of psychoanalysis: Energy discharge or person. *Psychoanalysis and Contemporary Thought, 6,* 523–551.

Gill, M. M. (1984). Psychoanalysis and psychotherapy: a revision. *International Review of Psycho-Analysis, 11,* 161–179.

Gray, P. (1982). "Developmental lag" in the evolution of technique for psychoanalysis of neurotic conflict. *Journal of the American Psychoanalytic Association, 30,* 621–655.

Greenberg, J. R., & Mitchell, S. A. (1983). *Object relations in psychoanalytic theory.* Cambridge, MA: Harvard University Press.

Greenson, R. R. (1965). The working alliance and the transference neurosis. *Psychoanalytic Quarterly, 34,* 155–181.

Greenson, R. R. (1967). *The technique and practice of psychoanalysis,* Vol. 1. New York: International Universities Press.

Greenson, R. R. (1978a). The problem of working through. In R. R. Greenson (Ed.), *Explorations in psychoanalysis* (pp. 255–267). New York: International Universities Press.

Greenson, R. R. (1978b). Empathy and its vicissitudes. In R. R. Greenson (Ed.), *Explorations in psychoanalysis* (pp. 147–161). New York: International Universities Press.

Greenson, R. R., & Wexler, M. (1978). The nontransference relationship in the psychoanalytic situation. In R. R. Greenson (Ed.), *Explorations in psychoanalysis* (pp. 359–386). New York, International Universities Press.

Guntrip, H. (1969). *Schizoid phenomena, object relations and the self.* New York: International Universities Press.

Harlow, H. F., & Harlow, M. K. (1962). Social deprivation in monkeys. *Scientific American, 207*(5), 136–146.

Hartmann, H. (1958). *Ego psychology and the problem of adaptation.* New York: International Universities Press.

Hartmann, H. (1964). *Essays on ego psychology: Selected problems in psychoanalytic theory.* New York: International Universities Press.

Hartmann, H., Kris, E., & Lowenstein, R. M. (1946). Comments on the formation of psychic structure. *Psychoanalytic Study of the Child, 2,* 11–38.

Horney, K. (1945). *Our inner conflicts.* New York: W. W. Norton.

Horney, K. (1950). *Neurosis and human growth.* New York: W. W. Norton.

Hurvich, M. (1985). *Traumatic moment, basic dangers, and annihilation anxiety.* Paper presented to the New York Freudian Society, New York, May.

Jacobson, E. (1964). *The self and the object world.* New York: International Universities Press.

Kernberg, O. F. (1975). *Borderline conditions and pathological narcissism.* New York: Jason Aronson.

Kernberg, O. F. (1976). *Object relations theory and clinical psychoanalysis*. New York: Jason Aronson.

Kernberg, O. F. (1980). *Internal world and external reality*. New York: Jason Aronson.

Kernberg, O. F. (1984). *Severe personality disorders*. New Haven: Yale University Press.

Kernberg, O. F., Selzer, M. A., Koenigsberg, H. W., Carr, A. C., & Applebaum, A. H. (1989). *Psychodynamic psychotherapy of borderline patients*. New York: Basic Books.

Klein, M. (1948). *Contributions to Psychoanalysis (1921–1945)*. London: Hogarth Press.

Klerman, G. L., Rounsaville, B., Chevron, E., & Weissman, M. (1984). *Interpersonal psychotherapy of depression*. New York: Basic Books.

Knight, R. P. (1953). Management and psychotherapy of the borderline schizophrenic patient. *Bulletin of the Menninger Clinic, 17*, 139–150.

Kohut, H. (1971). *The analysis of the self*. New York: International Universities Press.

Kohut, H. (1977). *The restoration of the self*. New York: International Universities Press.

Kohut, H. (1979). The two analyses of Mr. Z. *International Journal of Psychoanalysis, 60*, 3–27.

Kohut, H. (1984). *How does analysis cure?* Chicago: University of Chicago Press.

Kris, E. (1952). *Psychoanalytic explorations in art*. New York: International Universities Press.

Kuhn, T. (1962). *The structure of scientific revolutions* (2nd ed.). Chicago: University of Chicago Press.

Langs, R. (1982). *The psychotherapeutic conspiracy*. New York: Jason Aronson.

Levenson, E. (1982). Language and healing. In. S. Slipp (Ed.), *Curative factors in dynamic psychotherapy* (pp. 91–103). New York: McGraw-Hill.

Levenson, E. (1985). The interpersonal (Sullivanian) model. In A. Rothstein (Ed.), *Models of the mind* (pp. 49–67). New York: International Universities Press.

Levenson, E. (1988). Show and tell: The recursive order of the transference. In A. Rothstein (Ed.), *How does treatment help?—On the modes of therapeutic action in psychoanalytic psychotherapy*. Madison, CT: International Universities Press.

Limentani, A. (1975). Discussion. *Psychoanalytic Forum, 5*, 288–294.

Loewald, H. (1960). On the therapeutic action of psychoanalysis. *International Journal of Psycho-Analysis, 2*, 17–33.

Luborsky, L. (1984). *Principles of psychoanalytic psychotherapy: A manual for supportive-expressive treatment*. New York: Basic Books.

Macalpine, I. (1950). The development of the transference. *Psychoanalytic Quarterly, 19*, 501–539.

Mahler, M. (1968). *On human symbiosis and the vicissitudes of individuation. Vol. I: Infantile psychosis.* New York: International Universities Press.

Mahler, M., Pine, F., & Bergman, A. (1975). *The psychological birth of the human infant.* New York: Basic Books.

Meissner, W. W. (1980). Theories of personality and psychopathology: Classical psychoanalysis. In H. J. Kaplan, A. M. Freedman, & B. J. Sadock (Eds.), *Comprehensive textbook of Psychiatry: Vol. 1* (pp. 631–728). Baltimore: Williams and Wilkins.

Mitchell, S. A. (1988). *Relational concepts in psychoanalysis.* Cambridge, MA: Harvard University Press.

Modell, A. H. (1976). "The holding environment" and the therapeutic action of psychoanalysis. *Journal of the American Psychoanalytic Association, 24*, 285–307.

Modell, A. H. (1984). *Psychoanalysis in a new context.* New York: International Universities Press.

Modell, A. H. (1989). The psychoanalytic setting as a container of multiple levels of reality: A perspective on the theory of psychoanalytic treatment. *Psychoanalytic Inquiry, 9*(1), 67–87.

Muslin, H., & Gill, M. M. (1978). Transference in the Dora case. *Journal of the American Psychoanalytic Association, 26*, 311–328.

Ornstein, P. (Ed.). (1978). *The season for the self: Selected writings of Heinz Kohut: 1950–1978.* New York: International Universities Press.

Peterfreund, E. (1983). *The process of psychoanalytic therapy.* Hillsdale, NJ: Analytic Press.

Pine, F. (1990). *Drive, ego, object, and self.* New York: Basic Books.

Racker, H. (1968). *Transference and countertransference.* New York: International Universities Press.

Rangell, L. (1954). Similarities and differences between psychoanalysis and dynamic psychotherapy. *Journal of the American Psychoanalytic Association, 2*, 734–744.

Reich, W. (1949). *Character analysis* (3rd ed.; T. P. Wolfe, trans.). New York: Noonday Press.

Sandler, J. (1983). Reflections on some relations between psychoanalytic concept and psychoanalytic practice. *International Journal of Psychoanalysis, 64*, 1–11.

Schafer, R. (1959). Generative empathy in the treatment situation. *Psychoanalytic Quarterly, 28*, 342–373.

Schafer, R. (1968). *Aspects of internalization.* New York: International Universities Press.

Schafer, R. (1983). *The analytic attitude.* New York: Basic Books.

Schimek, J. G. (1983). The construction of the transference: The relativity of the "here and now" and the "there and then." *Psychoanalysis and Contemporary Thought, 6,* 435–456.

Schwaber, E. (1981). Empathy: A mode of analytic listening. *Psychoanalytic Inquiry, 1,* 357–392.

Segal, H. (1967). Melanie Klein's technique. In B. Wolman (Ed.), *Psychoanalytic techniques: A handbook for the practicing psychoanalyst* (pp. 168–190). New York: Basic Books.

Silverman, D. K. (1986). A multi-model approach: Looking at clinical data from three theoretical perspectives. *Psychoanalytic Psychology, 3,* 121–132.

Stein, M. H. (1981). The objectionable part of the transference. *Journal of the American Psychoanalytic Association, 29*(4), 869–892.

Stone, L. (1954). The widening scope of indications for psychoanalysis. *Journal of the American Psychoanalytic Association, 2,* 567–594.

Stone, L. (1961). *The psychoanalytic situation: An examination of its development and essential nature.* New York: International Universities Press.

Stone, L. (1981). Notes on the noninterpretive aspects of the psychoanalytic situation and process. *Journal of the American Psychoanalytic Association, 29,* 89–118.

Storr, A. (1988). *Solitude: A return to the self.* New York: Ballantine Books.

Strachey, J. (1934). The nature of the therapeutic action of psycho-analysis. *International Journal of Psychiatry, IV,* 127–159.

Strupp, H. H., & Binder, J. L. (1984). *Psychotherapy in a new key.* New York: Basic Books.

Sullivan, H. S. (1953). *The interpersonal theory of psychiatry.* New York: Norton.

Sullivan, H. S. (1954). *The psychiatric interview.* New York: W. W. Norton.

Wachtel, P. L. (Ed.). (1982). *Resistance.* New York: Plenum.

Waelder, R. (1960). *Basic theory of psychoanalysis.* New York: International Universities Press.

Wallerstein, R. S. (1983). *Psychoanalysis and psychotherapy: Relative roles reconsidered.* Presented as a plenary address at the Boston Psychoanalytic Society and Institute Symposium on "Psychoanalysis Today: The Interpretation of Theory and Practice." Boston, MA, October 29, 1983.

Wallerstein, R. S. (1984). The analysis of transference: A matter of emphasis or of theory reformulation. *Psychoanalytic Inquiry, 4*(3), 325–354.

Wallerstein, R. S. (1986). *Forty-Two lives in treatment. A study of psychoanalysis and psychotherapy.* New York/London: Guilford Press.

Wallerstein, R. S. (1988a). One psychoanalysis or many? *International Journal of Psychoanalysis, 69,* 5–21.

Wallerstein, R. S. (1988b). Assessment of structural change in psychoanalytic therapy and research. *Journal of the American Psychoanalytic Association, 36,* (Suppl.), 241–261.

Wallerstein, R. S. (1990a). Psychoanalysis and psychotherapy: An historical perspective. *International Journal of Psychoanalysis, 70*(4), 563–592.

Wallerstein, R. S. (1990b). Psychoanalysis: The common ground. *International Journal of Psychoanalysis, 71*, 3–20.

Weinshel, E. M. (1988). Structural changes in psychoanalysis. *Journal of the American Psychoanalytic Association* (Suppl. 36), 263–280.

Weiss, J. (1990). Unconscious mental functioning. *Scientific American, 262* (no. 3), 103–109.

Weiss, J., & Sampson, H. (1986). *The psychoanalytic process: Theory, clinical observations, and empirical research.* New York: Guilford Press.

Winnicott, D. W. (1958). *Through pediatrics to psychoanalysis.* London: Tavistock Publications.

Witenberg, E. G. (1974). American Neo-Freudian schools—A. The interpersonal and cultural approaches. In S. Arieti (Ed.), *American Handbook of Psychiatry* (2nd ed.). New York: Basic Books.

Zetzel, E. R. (1971). A developmental approach to the borderline patient. *American Journal of Psychiatry, 127*, 867–871.

Zucker, H. (1989). Premises of interpersonal theory. *Psychoanalytic Psychology, 6*(4), 401–419.

5

EVOLUTION AND DIFFERENTIATION WITHIN BEHAVIOR THERAPY: A THEORETICAL AND EPISTEMOLOGICAL REVIEW

DANIEL B. FISHMAN AND CYRIL M. FRANKS

All major conceptual approaches to psychotherapy — behavior therapy, psychoanalysis, family systems, humanistic therapy, and so forth—are embedded in some broad paradigm that involves a number of dimensions. These include (a) adherence to certain epistemological, philosophy-of-science assumptions; (b) a particular set of theoretical positions; (c) a body of scientific and other data; (d) particular collections of techniques and technologies; (e) specific values and ethical positions; and (f) a particular sociological, political, and historical context (Fishman, Rotgers, & Franks, 1988; Kuhn, 1962). This chapter focuses upon the evolution of behavior therapy in terms of epistemology and theory, in particular. Research, practice, and training in behavior therapy are dealt with in detail elsewhere in this volume. However, a full understanding of behavior therapy depends in part upon a consideration of the interrelationships among the various components of the overall paradigm, as just defined. Therefore, because we view the development of theory in behavior therapy as a reflection of the philosophical, social, cultural, political, and ethical contexts in which it is embedded rather than as an independent and isolated endeavor, considerable space is devoted to these relationships.

We view behavior therapy[1] as being closely linked with the patterns of thought and values developed during the 17th- and 18th-century Age of Enlightenment and later expanded in terms of 20th-century modernism. These include a focus on rationally and scientifically derived, "value-neutral" technology used in the service of promoting individual growth and freedom from irrational authority and arbitrary privilege (see also Fishman, Rotgers, & Franks, 1988, and Woolfolk & Richardson, 1984). In theoretical terms, we view behavior therapy as an approach to the understanding of behavior and therapeutic behavior change that relies upon the methodology of behavioral science, with important links to learning theory, cognitive psychology, and various other experimental psychology models. *Behavior* is defined broadly to include both overt actions and observable manifestations of more covert affective and cognitively mediated processes. These processes may occur at several levels: psychophysiological, individual, small group, organizational, and community.

In practical terms, we regard behavior therapy as the data-based application of this theoretical approach to generate a technology whose primary goal is cost-effective and constructive behavior change. By *constructive* we mean behavior change that is endorsed by all concerned and considered ethical. From either point of view, theory or practice, behavior therapy is viewed by its founders as a major conceptual advance rather than as simply another therapeutic innovation.

With the preceding prologue, this chapter begins with a brief historical review of the development of contemporary behavior therapy.[2] The epistemological assumptions and theoretical principles of contemporary behav-

---

[1]The reader will note that, up to this point, we are focussing upon the evolution of behavior therapy per se and not using the currently fashionable term, *cognitive behavior therapy*. We do this in order to communicate our conviction that cognitive behavior therapy is best considered within the overall context of behavior therapy, of which it is a part, rather than as a separate entity (see also Franks, 1987a). Although it is true that the evolution of cognitive behavior therapy involved changes in the metatheoretical foundations of behavior therapy (Baars, 1986; Mahoney, 1988), other developments in behavior therapy have also involved changes at this basic level. In fact, a major theme of this chapter is that such foundational changes have been typical of behavior therapy as it has evolved in response to new philosophical and theoretical models in psychology at large, such as general systems theory (Kanfer & Schefft, 1988) and "social constructionism" (Fishman, 1988), a philosophical alternative to the logical positivism underlying traditional science. It is our intent to describe both these types of foundational changes in behavior therapy and those continuities which justify the ongoing use of the term *behavior therapy*.

[2]A comprehensive history can be found in Kazdin (1978); and detailed commentaries documenting developments in behavior therapy on an ongoing, integrated basis in which the same writers pick up themes in the major subject areas from year to year are provided by Franks, Wilson, and associates in the 12 volumes to date of their *Review of Behavior Therapy: Theory and Practice*.

ior therapy will then be discussed, and the manner in which these relate both to other psychotherapies and to applied psychology in general will be examined.

HISTORY

Learning Theory Beginnings

It was not until the 1950s that behavior therapy as we know it today began to emerge. But in another sense, behavior therapy has many roots, many origins, and no single leader or starting point. It was during the intellectual and cultural climate of the Enlightenment, that period of European history emphasizing reason and scientific study of the natural world, that the foundations of behavior therapy emerged. For example, the British empiricists, who spanned the period from 1600 to 1900, emphasized four main principles: (a) that knowledge comes from experience with the world rather than introspective rumination or divine inspiration; (b) that scientific procedures have to be based upon observation rather than opinion, intuition, or authority; (c) that the mind of the child is a blank slate (tabula rasa) upon which experience writes, so that adult mental life is primarily a recording and unfolding of the previous history of the person concerned; and (d) that consciousness is best viewed in terms of "mental chemistry," in which all thoughts can be broken down into basic elements which have become connected into more complex ideas through various laws, such as continuity, similarity, contrast, vividness, frequency, and recency (Kimble, 1985).

It was similar thinking that led to the conceptualization of behavior therapy in the 1950s as the application of "modern learning theory" to clinical problems (Eysenck, 1959). Nowadays, with the dubious advantage of hindsight, there is a tendency to downplay these early beginnings as being simplistic and naive, an oversimplification which summarily dismissed all other points of view; indeed, this was the case. It was not until the mid-1980s that behavior therapists became sufficiently secure to accept the possibility that scientific methodology did not have to be confined to their definition of science and their notions about what constitute valid data. It took many years for behavior therapists to recognize that the methodology of science could legitimately mean different things to different people, that there is no single and invariant scientific methodology, and that the belief in any form of science itself is no more than a belief.

In any event, psychology emerged as a discipline distinct from philosophy when Wundt established the first formal experimental psychology laboratory at Leipzig in 1879. At that time, psychology was a minor subsection of philosophy and it was not until the close of the 19th century that independent university departments of psychology began to emerge. Soon thereafter, Titchener, one of Wundt's followers, established a similar laboratory at Cornell University and became a dominant figure in American psychology. In the tradition of the British associationists, Titchener developed a stream of psychology called "structuralism," designed to discover the so-called elements of mental chemistry and the principles of association that could be used to explain how such elements combined to form everyday experience. Titchener's methodology, the training of subjects to introspect and report in detail on their conscious experiences, is in direct contrast with the tradition of experimental animal psychology practiced by such individuals as Pavlov and Thorndike and their emphasis upon objectively observable behavior rather than subjective reports of intrapsychic experiences.

Watson brought this conflict into dramatic focus and used it to develop an alternative system of psychology called "behaviorism." His primary vehicle for launching behaviorism as a movement was a 1913 manifesto in the *Psychological Review*, entitled "Psychology as the Behaviorist Views It":

> Psychology as the behaviorist views it is a purely objective branch of natural science. Its theoretical goal is the prediction and control of behavior. Introspection forms no essential part of its methods, nor is the scientific value of its data dependent upon the readiness with which they lend themselves to interpretation in terms of consciousness. The behaviorist, in his efforts to get a unitary scheme of animal response, recognises no dividing line between man and brute. The behavior of man, with all of its refinement and complexity, forms only a part of the behaviorist's total scheme of investigation. (p. 158)

Thus, according to Watson, if psychology were to become a science— as he defined this word—it must become materialistic (as opposed to mentalistic), mechanistic (as opposed to anthropomorphic), deterministic (as opposed to accepting of free will), and objective (as opposed to subjective). For Watson, emotions are exclusively visceral bodily reactions, involving primarily the glands and smooth or "involuntary" muscles. Similarly, Watson viewed thinking as "laryngeal habits," that is, tiny movements of the vocal chords. These movements, argued Watson in a series of data-devoid speculations which ironically we would now regard as the antithesis of scientific methodology, are developed from random, unlearned vocalizations. Thus, language is at first overt and, by a process of conditioning, the child acquires words. Because words may be a substitute for things and concrete situations, this gives the child the power of liberation from the environment without making the actual overt movements.

It was around this period that Pavlov demonstrated that dogs could learn to salivate at the ringing of a bell through a process of temporally and spatially contiguous associations between the bell and the sight of and direct access to food. Distrusting absolutism in any form, he deliberately employed the term "conditional" in his writings rather than "conditioned." His intent was to convey the essentially temporary nature of the connections thus formed, connections which lacked the certainty and regularity of innate reflexes. For Pavlov, as for his precursor Sechenov, the conditional reflex was a creative, emergent, and highly responsive activity of the organism rather than (as is still the common misbelief) a stereotyped and unchanging process (Franks, 1969).

In Pavlov's first book to be translated into English, the correct English translation, *conditional reflex*, was employed. It was in later translations, probably from the German, that the misleading term *conditioned* was introduced. In translating Pavlov into English in what was to become the standard English language text, Gantt deliberately maintained this inaccuracy in the interests of consistency, a decision which he said he regretted ever since (Gantt, 1966).

Another closely related development was the establishment in 1913 of Thorndike's general principles of human and animal learning. Cats learned to escape from a "puzzle box" to obtain release and bits of food as rewards. Studies such as these led to the formulation of Thorndike's "law of effect":

> Of several responses made to the same situation, those which are accompanied or closely followed by satisfaction of the animal will, other things being equal, be more firmly connected with the situation, so that, when it recurs, they will be more likely to recur; those which are accompanied or closely followed by discomfort to the animal will, other things being equal, have their connections with that situation weakened, so that, when it recurs, they will be less likely to occur. . . . By a satisfying state of affairs is meant one which the animal does nothing to avoid, often doing such things as to attain and preserve it." (1911, pp. 244–245)

Pavlovian classical or respondent conditioning, based upon Aristotelian association by contiguity, and Thorndike's instrumental or operant conditioning, in which the subject is rewarded for making the desired response and punished whenever an undesired response is elicited, became the foundation upon which major developments in behavioristic learning theory were based for the next 50 years. It was this movement that dominated American psychology until the cognitive shift of the 1970s and 1980s, a shift that spilled over from psychology at large into the realm of behavior therapy.

Formation of Behavior Therapy as a Distinct Movement

In the first article devoted exclusively to "behavior therapy" in the *Annual Review of Psychology*, Krasner (1971) argued that 15 streams of development within the science of psychology came together during the 1950s and 1960s to form this new approach to behavior change. These streams may be briefly summarized as follows:

1. the concept of behaviorism in experimental psychology;

2. the operant conditioning of Thorndike and Skinner;

3. the development of Wolpe's (1958) systematic desensitization;

4. the emergence of behavior therapy as an experimental science at the University of London Institute of Psychiatry, Maudsley Hospital, under the direction of Eysenck;

5. the application of conditioning and learning concepts to human behavior problems in the United States, from the 1920s to the 1950s;

6. the interpretation of psychoanalysis in terms of learning theory (e.g., Dollard & Miller, 1950);

7. the application of Pavlovian principles in explaining and changing both normal and deviant behavior;

8. theoretical concepts and research studies of social role learning and interactionism in social psychology and sociology;

9. research in developmental and child psychology emphasizing vicarious learning and modeling;

10. social influence studies of demand characteristics, experimenter bias, hypnosis, and placebo;

11. an environmentally based social learning model as an alternative to the "disease" model of human behavior (Bandura, 1969; Ullmann & Krasner, 1965);

12. dissatisfaction with the prevailing psychoanalytically based psychotherapy model, particularly as articulated in Eysenck's (1952) critical empirical study of therapy outcome;

13. the development of the idea of the *clinical psychologist* within the scientist-practitioner model;

14. a movement within psychiatry away from the then-orthodox focus on internal dynamics and pathology, toward human interaction and environmental influence; and

15. a Utopian emphasis on the planning of social environments to elicit and maintain the best of human behavior (e.g., Skinner's [1948] *Walden Two*).

As Krasner (1982) pointed out, these streams of development are neither independent nor static, and, as we shall show, new streams of influence are continually emerging.

Behavior therapy in the United States was influenced both by the classical conditioning of Palov and by Thorndike and Skinner's instrumental or operant conditioning. The possibility of explaining behavioral abnormalities in Pavlovian and other conditioning terms was outlined in two independent and equally outstanding publications by Watson (1924) and Burnham (1924), respectively. In 1917, Mateer produced a monograph on the application of conditioning techniques to children. But perhaps the most prophetic publication was that of Dunlap (1932; currently reissued in paperback form: Dunlap, 1972). The techniques outlined by Dunlap, and even the theoretical formulations to a lesser extent, foreshadowed the armamentarium of the contemporary behavior therapist.

The 1930s saw many attempts to explore the nature of neurosis by inducing so-called neurotic behavior in various animals, such as the pig (Liddell, 1958) and the cat (Masserman, 1943); the pioneering work of Wolpe, to be discussed shortly, arose in large part out of his investigations of neurotic behavior in cats.

Within the universities and in closely related clinical settings, it was the integration of experimental research with clinical procedures, coupled with a general dissatisfaction with prevailing psychodynamic formulations, that led to the development of behavior therapy as a viable intervention strategy. A leader in this effort was Mowrer, who became disenchanted with his original orientation as a psychoanalyst and shifted from a focus on intrapsychic dynamics to the view that a disturbance in interpersonal relationships is often a cause rather than a symptom of neurosis. In conjunction with Mowrer's formulation of two distinct kinds of learning, he and his wife, Mary, developed a treatment for eneuresis based upon direct conditioning procedures, known as the bell-and-pad method (Mowrer & Mowrer, 1938).

Other writers of distinction in this context in the early postwar period include Shaw (1948), one of the first to apply principles of learning based on animal work, principally those of Mowrer, to the clinical process of psychotherapy in a systematic fashion; Shaffer (1947), who reviewed the implications of learning-theory based models of behavior for the therapist; and Shoben (1949), who attempted to integrate Mowrer's learning theory approach with the field of mainstream psychotherapy (Krasner, 1982).

Another important influence in the 1940s stemmed from the work of a group of investigators at Yale, notably Dollard and Miller (1950), who attempted to develop a learning theory basis for psychoanalytic formulations. For these individuals, it seemed probable that psychoanalytic theory formed the ultimate basis for understanding and predicting deviant behavior and that a learning theory formulation was viewed primarily as a hopefully acceptable translation of psychoanalytic terminology and concepts for those steeped in stimulus–response (S–R) learning theory. It was also hoped that this exercise in dictionary construction would facilitate the development and investigation of testable hypotheses in learning theory terms by scientists presumably wedded to the methodology of behavioral science. These could then be retranslated back into the psychoanalytic model where, according to Dollard and Miller, they really belonged.

The start of these developments was in the United Kingdom, notably at the Maudsley Hospital, the physical home of the University of London Institute of Psychiatry.[3] At that time, in the United Kingdom and elsewhere, the only available and acceptable form of psychotherapy was based upon psychoanalytic premises actualized under the leadership of a physician. Psychopharmacology had relatively little to contribute and the only nonmedical influence of positive significance stemmed from the ministrations of social workers. Psychologists, having little of practical value to offer, began to question the utility of spending three or four undergraduate years studying a body of knowledge which stressed the methodology of the behavioral scientist only to find that graduate training in clinical psychology and its eventual application rested upon the goodwill and psychodynamic tutelage of the physician.

Given this set of circumstances, it was understandable that it was a disease model of medical illness which prevailed. Disorders of behavior were regarded as diseases for which an "etiology" had to be found, leading to some form of "treatment." Hence the stress on "diagnosis," "patient," "therapy," and "cure." The treatment of psychiatric disturbance remained fundamentally a medical problem in which the nonmedical psychologist was, at best, a useful ancillary worker.

Unfortunately—or perhaps fortunately in the long run—their rigorous training as behavioral scientists soon led psychologists at the Maudsley

---

[3]One of the authors of this chapter, Cyril Franks, was in London, at the Maudsley Hospital, during this period.

to the realization that traditional psychiatric diagnoses were fraught with many problems of reliability, validity, and general utility. To compound matters yet further, when psychologists examined the limited role that was imposed upon them, that of diagnostic assistant to the psychiatrist, it became increasingly evident that the traditional psychometric test batteries they were expected to administer were themselves of questionable validity and that new assessment devices would need to be generated.

In any event, dissatisfaction with the role of the clinical psychologist, the lack of viable alternatives, and the perceived deficiencies of psychodynamic therapy served as an impetus for the search for new directions. Many models were considered and discarded and, eventually, it became apparent that stimulus–response learning theory, in particular the work of Pavlov, offered at that time the most promise for the testing of theoretically generated predictions and the eventual accumulation of a database for therapeutic intervention. Leaning heavily on empirical verification, the hope was that a rational model, based on theoretical formulations and hypothesis testing and rooted in the discipline of psychology, would lead eventually to the development of valid, learning-theory based assessment and intervention strategies. Thus, the concept of *behavior therapy* was born in the United Kingdom under the leadership of Eysenck and his associates at the Institute of Psychiatry (Franks, 1987b).

Over the years, Eysenck's many students established Maudsley enclaves and offshoots throughout the world. The first publication of a case based on these principles was Jones's (1956) application of conditioning and learning techniques for the treatment of a psychiatric patient. Those were exciting times, leading to the publication of probably the first behaviorally based textbook of abnormal psychology in the world (Eysenck, 1960) and one of the first collections of case studies in behavior therapy (Eysenck, 1964); the creation of the first journal devoted exclusively to behavior therapy, *Behaviour Research and Therapy*; and to the invention of a new name for this mode of treatment, behavior therapy. (See Eysenck's autobiography, 1990, for a more detailed account of these exciting events.)

At about the same time, a parallel development was proceeding in South Africa under the impetus of a Johannesburg psychiatrist dissatisfied with both the theory and clinical usefulness of prevailing psychodynamic concepts. At first in South Africa, and later in the United States, Wolpe (1958) used Pavlovian principles to develop his theory of psychotherapy by reciprocal inhibition, primarily on the basis of the technique to be known as "systematic desensitization."

Without doubt, systematic desensitization was the first viable "talk-therapy" alternative to traditional psychotherapy. Prior to the advent of systematic desensitization, conditioning was regarded as a strategy to be applied exclusively to animals, small children, seriously impaired individuals, or perhaps those suffering from some specific and highly focalized disorder. Now, at long last, an alternative to psychodynamic therapy became available, an alternative which could be meaningfully and efficiently applied to the sophisticated patients who came to the psychiatrist's private office for treatment of complex problems. The fact that Wolpe's laborious procedures have been modified many times as a result of subsequent study and the fact that his original theoretical explanation in terms of classical conditioning and Sherringtonian inhibition has long been rejected (e.g., Wilson & O'Leary, 1980) in no way detract from the practical significance of these remarkable accomplishments.

The 1950s and 1960s was a pioneering era, an era of ideology and polemics in which behavior therapists strove to present a united front against the common psychodynamic "foe." As behavior therapy became established as a respected and respectable method of treatment in the 1970s, behavior therapists gradually abandoned missionary zeal and began to search for new frontiers within which to extend their approach. These included general outpatient psychotherapy practice, biofeedback, health psychology, community psychology, and the worlds of business, administration, and government. It was an era of intellectual expansion into concepts, methods, and ways of viewing data over and beyond those of traditional learning theory. It was also the era of the rise of cognitive behavior therapy, in part a reflection of the "cognitive revolution" in psychology as a whole (Baars, 1986). This latter development is very much a part of the contemporary scene in behavior therapy and more needs to be said about its impact and significance.

One might expect that behavior therapy would have been particularly appreciated in the Soviet Union, with its monolithic emphasis (until the advent of Gorbachev and *glasnost*) upon Pavlovian psychology. Yet, with a few notable exceptions, such as the use of aversion conditioning for the treatment of alcoholism, behavior therapy as we know it in the West has been virtually nonexistent in the Soviet Union until very recently.

There appear to be several explanations to account for this state of affairs (Franks, 1969). First, until very recently, the profession of clinical psychology and the necessary training programs to back this discipline up did not exist in the USSR. Second, psychologists, in common with most Soviet citizens, were not privy to intellectual and professional developments in the West. Third, under the influence of a state-directed Marxism, Western associationism and, hence, behavior therapy were dismissed as "vulgar materialism," attempts to substitute an "inferior" mechanistic materialism for the dialectic alternative stemming from Marxist ideology. (We will not discuss here the intricacies of dialectic materialism and the doctrine of reflection, the belief that psychological processes are reflections of objective reality.) For most Soviet psychologists the process of mediation between the external world and the self was an active and dynamic one in which there was little place for what they viewed as the simplistic concepts of mechanistic behaviorism. For Pavlovian psychologists, consciousness and its concomitants—cognition, memory, and emotion—are unique to humans because they alone possess the second signal system, speech, and this is what distinguishes them from animals. And this consciousness can be interpreted only in terms of Marxist ideology, or so it was until very recently.

In 1967 the Association for Advancement of Behavior Therapy (AABT) was created in the United States as an organizational home for a growing number of psychologists and other mental health professionals practicing, researching, teaching, or otherwise interested in behavior therapy. Today the AABT, with over 3,500 members, is among the largest behavior therapy associations in the world. The other major behavioral organization in the United States is the Association for Behavior Analysis. With several thousand members, this latter group is primarily oriented to the application of Skinner's operant psychology, and it remains opposed in principle and practice to much of cognitive behavior therapy.

Since 1970, the European Association of Behaviour Therapy has organized annual conferences in various European countries. Their 10th annual meeting in Jerusalem evolved into the First World Congress in Behaviour Therapy. Since then, behavior therapy has prospered throughout the world, and there are now literally scores of behavior therapy societies in existence and at least 50 journals devoted primarily or exclusively to behavior therapy and its many offshoots.

Emergence of Theoretical Submovements

In the 1970s, behavior therapy began to cohere into more distinct streams, all sharing a common methodological and learning theory core. At least five are noteworthy (see Wilson and Franks, 1982, for a more extended discussion). *Applied behavior analysis*, the first submovement, is a term used to describe the application of principles derived from Skinnerian operant conditioning to a wide range of clinical and social problems. For the most part, applied behavior analysts assume that behavior is exclusively a function of its consequences. There are no intervening variables, mentalistic inferences are disavowed, and intervention procedures are evaluated primarily in terms of single-case experimental designs in which the subject serves as his or her own control. The emphasis is upon the manipulation of environmental variables to bring about behavioral change and upon the use of laboratory-based principles, such as reinforcement, punishment, extinction, and stimulus control.

The second approach, described by Wilson and Franks (1982) as the "neobehavioristic, mediational S–R model," invokes primarily the application of classical conditioning and the works of Pavlov, Mowrer, and Wolpe, among others. Intervening variables and hypothetical constructs are acceptable, and publicly unobservable processes, such as the imaginal representation of anxiety-eliciting stimuli in systematic desensitization, are accepted and even encouraged.

Next, "social learning theory" was developed primarily by Bandura and his colleagues, and now, together with cognitive behavior therapy, it constitutes the mainstream of contemporary behavior therapy. In its most advanced form (e.g. Bandura, 1982), social learning theory is interactional, interdisciplinary, and multimodal. Behavior is influenced by stimulus events (primarily through classical conditioning), by external reinforcement (through operant conditioning), and by cognitive mediational processes. Behavior change is brought about largely through observational learning, a process in which people are influenced by observing someone else's behavior. The term *model* is reserved for the exemplar, the person who demonstrates the behavior that the observer views. *Live modelling* occurs when the exemplar is directly seen, while *symbolic modelling* takes place when the model is observed indirectly, as in movies, on television, by reading, though an oral description of someone else's behavior, or even by imagining a model's behaviors. Social learning emphasizes reciprocal interactions between the individual behavior and the environment. The individual is considered capable of self-directed behavior change. Bandura's theory of perceived *self-efficacy* is one of the first major attempts to provide a unified theoretical explanation of how behavior therapy and other psychotherapy procedures work. *Self-efficacy* refers to an individual's belief or expectation that he or she can master a situation and bring about desired outcomes. Self-efficacy is viewed as a common cognitive mechanism which mediates the effects of all psychological change procedures, that is, these procedures are postulated to be effective because they create and strengthen a client's expectations of personal efficacy.

Staats' (1975) "social behaviorism," now updated as "paradigmatic behaviorism" (Eifert & Evans, 1990), developed more or less independently of social learning theory. Paradigmatic behaviorism emphasizes the integration of conditioning theory with traditional concepts in personality, clinical, and social psychology. Staats sees the foundational elements of personality as formed by conditioning. He views the principles of contiguity and reinforcement as always present and interacting, with operant conditioning affecting overt behavior patterns and classical conditioning affecting emotional and cognitive response patterns. Staats' concept of "cumulative–hierarchical learning and development" explains how complex combinations of simple behaviors learned by basic conditioning can, over time, evolve into three complex "personality repertoires" of responses: sensory–motor, emotional–motivational, and language–cognitive. Taken together, these ideas provide the conceptual tools for Staats to apply the principles of conditioning to all areas of traditional psychology, including such clinically relevant domains as personality assessment, psychopathology, and psychotherapy and behavior change.

Finally, "cognitive behavior therapy," a very popular theoretical submovement, derives its main impetus from the so-called cognitive revolution in general psychology. Cognitive behavior therapists emphasize cognitive processes and private events as mediators of behavior change. Kendall and Bemis (1983, pp. 565–566) summarized six basic assumptions within cognitive behavior therapy:

1. The human organism responds primarily to cognitive representations of its environments rather than to these environments per se.

2. Most human learning is cognitively mediated.

3. Thoughts, feelings, and behaviors are causally interrelated.

4. Attitudes, expectancies, attributions, and other cognitive activities are central to producing, predicting, and understanding psychopathological behavior and the effects of therapeutic interventions.

5. Cognitive processes can be cast into testable formulations that are easily integrated with behavioral paradigms, and it is possible and desirable to combine cognitive treatment strategies with enactive techniques and behavioral contingency management.

6. The task of the cognitive–behavioral therapist is to act as diagnostician, educator, and technical consultant, assessing maladaptive cognitive processes and working with the client to design learning experiences that may ameliorate these dysfunctional cognitions and the behavioral and affective patterns with which they correlate.

DEFINITION OF BEHAVIOR THERAPY

The term *behavior therapy* seems to have been introduced more or less independently by three widely separated groups of researchers: by Skinner, Solomon, and Lindsley (1953) in the United States in a status report, to refer to their application of operant conditioning of a plunger-pulling response to bring about social interactions in hospitalized psychotic patients; by Lazarus (1958) in South Africa, to refer to Wolpe's application of his "reciprocal inhibition" technique to neurotic patients; and by Eysenck's Maudsley group in England to describe their "new look" at clinical intervention, in which behavior therapy is defined simply as the application of modern learning theory to the understanding and treatment of behavioral and behaviorally related disorders (Eysenck, 1959).[4]

With the exception of applied behavior analysis, the prevailing submovements all embrace the use of cognitive mediational concepts and emphasize the integration of principles derived from traditional learning theory and conditioning with those stemming from cognitive and social psychology.

Many authors (e.g., Erwin, 1978; Franks, 1990; Wilson, 1982) point out that it is difficult to articulate a succinct definition of contemporary behavior therapy which does justice to the field. Erwin (1978) notes that most definitions of behavior therapy tend to fall into one of two categories: doctrinal or epistemological. Doctrinal definitions attempt to link behavior therapy to doctrines, theory, laws, or principles of learning. Epistemological definitions are more inclined to characterize behavior therapy in terms of the various ways of studying clinical phenomena. By and large, doctrinal definitions tend to be narrow and thereby fail to accommodate all of behavior therapy, whereas epistemological definitions tend to be excessively accommodating and, hence, potentially applicable to many nonbehavioral therapies.

Fishman (1988) suggested that this definitional dilemma results from the fact that behavior therapy, like many areas in the social sciences, consists of a series of overlapping domains, as represented in the five circles of Figure 1. These circles include: (a) therapeutic principles derived from learning theory; (b) therapeutic principles derived from experimental psychology generally; (c) specific therapeutic techniques originated by behaviorally oriented clinicians, such as contingency contracting and systematic desensitization; and (d) ideas and strategies adapted from the general psy-

---

[4]Cyril Franks, coauthor of this chapter and an active member of this third group, recalls the evolution of the term *behavior therapy* in England.

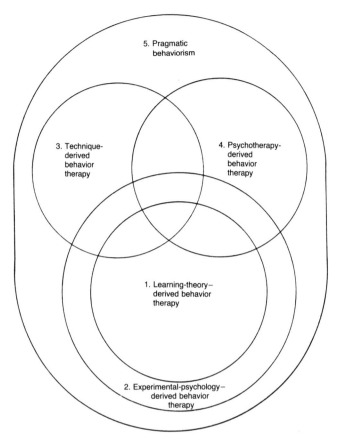

5. Pragmatic
behaviorism

3. Technique-
derived
behavior
therapy

4. Psychotherapy-
derived
behavior
therapy

1. Learning-theory—
derived behavior
therapy

2. Experimental-psychology—
derived behavior
therapy

Figure 1: The overlapping domains of the behavioral movement. From *Paradigms in Behavior Therapy: Present and Promise* (p. 268) edited by D. B. Fishman, F. Rotgers, and C. M. Franks, 1988, New York: Springer. Copyright 1988 by Springer Publishing Company. Reprinted by permission.

chotherapy literature, such as the relationship-enhancement methods of Rogerian therapy, therapy process models taken from systems theory (cf. Kanfer & Schefft, 1988), and short-term therapy (e.g., Wells & Gianetti, 1990).

In Figure 1, the partial overlap among the circles is noteworthy. For example, Circle 3 overlaps only parts of Circles 1 and 2. This reflects the fact that some of the accepted techniques in Circle 3, such as contingency contracting, are clearly deducible from the contemporary experimental principles associated with Circles 1 and 2, while other accepted techniques in Circle 3, such as systematic desensitization, are not (Wilson & O'Leary, 1980, pp. 162–164). As another example, Circle 4 overlaps only parts of Circles 1, 2, and 3. This reflects the fact that, whereas some of the approaches from the psychotherapy literature, such as goal setting and short-term therapy, are clearly deducible from traditional behavioral techniques and contemporary experimentally based principles, others, such as Rogerian relationship enhancement techniques, are not.

Circle 5, which embraces the other four, involves the methodological principles of behavioral science, such as empiricism, operational definition, quantification, value-neutrality of theoretical concepts, and experimental research design. As described next, these principles can be framed in epistemological terms, either within the positivist paradigm (traditional experimental science) or within the alternative epistemology of social constructionism (Fishman, 1988).

Recognizing the difficulty of succinctly defining behavior therapy, O'Leary & Wilson (1987, p. 12) provided a useful list of 9 "common core" assumptions that behavior therapists hold. In our view, these assumptions are beliefs held by the majority of contemporary behavior therapists:

1. Most abnormal behavior is acquired and maintained according to the same principles as normal behavior.

2. Most abnormal behavior can be modified through the application of social learning principles.

3. Assessment is continuous and focuses on the current determinants of behavior.

4. People are best described by what they think, feel, and do in specific life situations. . . .

5. Treatment methods are precisely specified, replicable, and objectively evaluated. . . .

6. Treatment outcome is evaluated in terms of the initial induction of behavior change, its generalization to the real life setting, and its maintenance over time.

7. Treatment strategies are individually tailored to different problems in different individuals. . . .

8. Behavior therapy is broadly applicable to a full range of clinical disorders and educational problems.

9. Behavior therapy is a humanistic approach in which treatment goals and methods are mutually contracted, rather than arbitrarily imposed.

A METATHEORETICAL FRAMEWORK FOR CHARACTERIZING CONTEMPORARY BEHAVIOR THERAPY

A theory in psychology is a conceptual framework that identifies important dimensions of human experience and behavior, and which describes relationships among these dimensions. A "metatheory" is a fundamental viewpoint which stands "behind," or logically prior to the theory. Thus,

TABLE 1
The Metatheoretical Location of Behavior Therapy Within
Applied Psychology

DOMINANT THEORETICAL WORLD VIEW	EPISTEMOLOGICAL PARADIGM		
	Logical Positivism	Social Constructionism	
	Experimental Paradigm	Pragmatic Paradigm[a]	Hermeneutic Paradigm
Trait	Cattell's psychometrically based theory of personality composed of 16 universal source traits (Cattell, 1966).[b]	Psychometric polling models for predicting voter behavior (e.g., Louis Harris polls).	Freud's theory of oral, anal, and phallic character types (e.g., Freud, 1924).
Interactional	Earlier and later behavior therapy theory.	Later behavior therapy theory only.	[c]
Organismic	General systems theory as applied to living systems (e.g., Miller, 1978).	Program evaluation theory (e.g., Morell, 1979).	Structural family therapy theory (e.g., Minuchin, 1974).
Transactional	[c]	[c]	Humanistic/existential therapy theory (e.g., Rogers, 1961).

[a]In previous writings, this has been called the "Technological Paradigm" (Fishman, 1988; Fishman & Neigher, 1987; Neigher & Fishman, 1985).
[b]Entries in the grid cells are illustrative, not exhaustive.
[c]These cells involve logically incompatible perspectives, and thus they cannot support viable theories (see text).

metatheory consists of those assumptions that are made before the creation, validation, and refinement of a theory.

Table 1 presents an overview of the metatheoretical location of earlier and later versions of behavior therapy relative to other systems of psychotherapy and applied psychology theory. The table is organized as a grid formed by two cross-cutting typologies of metatheoretical assumptions: Fishman's (1988) "epistemological paradigms" (divided into the "experimental," "pragmatic," and "hermeneutic"); and Altman and Rogoff's (1987) "world views" (divided into "trait," "interactional," "organismic," and "transactional"). A more detailed differentiation of the different branches within behavior therapy theory in terms of Altman and Rogoff's world views is presented in Table 2.

TABLE 2
Behavioral Therapy's Incorporation of Elements From Noninteractional World Views

World View	Examples
"Pure" Interactional	Watson's behaviorism (1913).
	Age of Grand Theory of Learning (1930–1960).
	Skinner, Solomon, & Lindsley's application of operant principles to changing the behavior of psychiatric hospital patients (1953).
	Behavior therapy techniques based on covert conditioning, e.g. Wolpe's (1958) systematic desensitization.
Interactional With Trait Components	Mischel's (1968) and Cantor's (1990) "cognitive social learning" approach to personality.
	Staats' (1981) notion of personality as composed of "basic personality repertoires."
	Turkat and Maisto's (1985) "behavioral case formulation" for cases with personality disorders.
	Persons' (1989) "underlying psychological mechanisms" in case formulation.
Interactional With Organismic Components	Peterson's (1968) application of behavioral functional analysis to changing family transactions and social systems.
	Bandura's (1978) "reciprocal determinism."
	Jacobson & Margolin's (1979) "behavior exchange" approach to marital therapy.
	Birchler and Spinks's (1980) behavioral-systems marital therapy.
	Behavioral community psychology (Glenwick & Jason, 1980).
	Organizational behavior management (Frederiksen, 1982).
	Paul's (1986) behavioral-systems analysis of clinical decision-making in residential settings.
	Schwartz's (1988) cognitive-behavioral "systems therapy."
	Robin & Foster's (1989) behavioral-family systems approach.
Interactional With Transactional Components	Fishman's (1988) "pragmatic behaviorism."
	Kanfer & Schefft's (1988) "process" model of cognitive behavior therapy.
	Mahoney's (1988) "structural/developmental" cognitive therapy.
	Linehan and Wagner's (1990) "dialectical" behavior therapy.

Epistemological Paradigms

Epistemology is the branch of philosophy that investigates the origins, nature, methods, and limits of human knowledge. An epistemological paradigm sets forth the criteria according to which the relevance and validity of a particular body of knowledge are judged. In other words, no knowledge is simply *given* in any absolute sense. Rather, there are a variety of possible, coherent epistemological systems that have been set forth, and the evaluation of a statement's truth or falsity will depend, in part, upon the epistemological criteria chosen for the evaluation, and not just the content of the statement per se (Fishman, 1988; Gergen, 1982).

Until recently, American psychology was dominated by the epistemology of conventional natural science, that of logical positivism. In broad terms, logical positivism contends that there is an external world independent of human experience and that objective, "scientific" knowledge about this world can be obtained through direct sense experience, as interpreted within the framework of the theory-embedded, hypothesis-testing laboratory experiment. The data upon which this knowledge is founded consist of discrete, molecular, sensorily based "facts," many of which can be quantified. Knowledge is in the form of a cumulative body of context-free, universal laws about the phenomenon studied. Psychologists who have adopted a positivist perspective generally assume that the universal laws which emerge from "scientific" study will have a form so that they can be applied to help solve significant psychological and social problems in a unique, rationally based manner.

For a variety of philosophical, scientific, cultural, and practical reasons, since about 1960, there has been a growing movement in psychology and the other social sciences that rejects positivism as the appropriate epistemology for the field and proposes in its stead, "social constructionism" (e.g., Fishman, 1988; Gergen, 1985; Krasner & Houts, 1984; Scarr, 1985).

In contrast to logical positivism, social constructionism takes the position that reality as an individual or group experiences it is, to a substantial degree, conceptually constructed rather than sensorily discovered by that group. Objective knowledge about the world is significantly limited because "facts" and "raw data" can only be known within a particular, pre-empirically established cultural, social, and linguistic context.

As reflected in Table 1, social constructionism has encouraged the growth of two types of nonpositivist epistemological paradigms. The more radical is a hermeneutic paradigm that emphasizes qualitative interpretation; experiential, phenomenological meaning; and a historically situated psychology. This model views the goals and proper methods of psychology as similar to those of history, literary criticism, and investigative reporting (Messer, Sass, & Woolfolk, 1988; Packer, 1985).

The alternative approach spawned by social constructionism is the technological or pragmatic paradigm (Fishman, 1988; Fishman & Neigher, 1987). This is a hybrid between the experimental and hermeneutic approaches. Like the hermeneutic paradigm, the pragmatic paradigm is based upon social constructionism and eschews the theory-based laboratory experiment and the search for general psychological laws, preferring case-based knowledge. However, like the experimental paradigm, the pragmatic paradigm values a quantitative, elementalistic, observational approach and adapts some of the research methods of the laboratory into quasi-experimental and single-subject research designs (Barlow & Hersen, 1984). Instead of scientific understanding per se, the pragmatic paradigm values humanistic relevance, adopting action-oriented approaches from engineering and the field of research and development (e.g. Azrin, 1977; Morell, 1979; Fishman, 1988; Fishman & Neigher, 1987; Neigher & Fishman, 1985).

In the pragmatic model, a conceptually coherent program is designed to address a significant social or psychological problem within a naturalistic, real-world setting, in a manner which is feasible, effective, and efficient. Quantification is used to develop performance indicators of a system's functioning. This paradigm focuses upon getting a project or program to work within a particular, real-world setting. The generalizability of the particular, substantive program principles is secondary, although there is an interest in the general utility of the conceptual framework as a whole.

As described above and reflected in Table 1, the origins of the behavior therapy movement are clearly and directly embedded in logical positivism. Watson's original model for behavioristic theory was experimental animal psychology, and this model was continued by Hull, Skinner, Tolman, Guthrie, and the other learning theory researchers in the so-called age of grand theory (Kimble, 1985). Applying the model of physics and chemistry, in which natural phenomena are assumed to be governed by a small number of foundational laws, these researchers assumed that there were a few basic, universal laws of learning that applied to both animals and humans. Because of their assumption of such universal laws, these researchers could pursue scientific psychology by focusing on the publicly observable, simple behaviors of food-seeking white mice or pigeons in controlled laboratory conditions. This model thus allowed them to capture the core features which characterized positivistic physical science: a focus on objective, elemental data in controlled experiments which tested hypotheses about very general laws relating to the phenomenon in question. Although these researchers did not deny the world of consciousness, complex human relationships, and cultural products like literature and politics, these domains were either overlooked or deliberately excluded because they were highly subjective and not clearly amenable to objective, scientific study in the tradition of logical positivism.

As also shown in Table 1, while some groups in later behavior therapy theory have remained within the experimental paradigm (see, e.g., Ross in Baars, 1986; Wilson & Franks, 1982), others have moved away from the experimental epistemological paradigm and into the pragmatic paradigm. In fact, in our recent review of various paradigms in behavior therapy (Fishman, Rotgers, & Franks, 1988), the ten views sampled were rather evenly distributed, ranging from "pure" positivism, to a "middle" point of view, to "pure," pragmatically oriented constructionism.

There are at least three reasons why many behavior theorists have moved from the experimental to the pragmatic paradigm. First, as behavior therapy was just beginning in the 1960s, the epitome of the experimental paradigm upon which behavior therapy was originally theoretically based, the age of grand theory of learning, was coming to an unsuccessful end. Its demise derived from the failure of animal-based learning theorists to agree upon a single theory and to apply the extant models in theoretically rigorous ways to complex human behavior (Baars, 1986; Kimble, 1985). Thus, after reviewing learning research through the mid-1970s, Erwin concluded that "There is no known theory or law of any kind that is of sufficient scope to serve as a foundation for [behavior therapy] and that has also been empirically confirmed" (1978, p. 128).

A second possible reason for the breakdown in behavior therapy's commitment to the experimental paradigm came from the experiences of behavioral practitioners. Like other clinicians, these professionals discovered that they could practice without having to show a tight link between their activities and the experimental literature (Barlow, Hayes, & Nelson, 1984; Marshall, 1982). The third reason for behavior therapy's movement away from the experimental paradigm was the loss of support generally for logical positivism in the philosophical community beginning in the 1960s (Campbell, 1984; Gergen, 1982; Putnam, 1984).

One of the clearest and most explicit statements of the move by behavior therapists toward the pragmatic paradigm was made by Azrin (1977). This applied researcher began his career solidly aligned with the experimental paradigm, but was led to an identification with the pragmatic paradigm after focusing upon the development of effective change programs for significant human problems in areas such as controlling aggression, toilet training, marital adjustment, alcoholism, tics, and job finding. In line with the pragmatic paradigm, Azrin took his measurement methods from the experimental tradition, but the substance of what he did was pragmatically focused, with an emphasis upon emergent clinical techniques and practical success with specific problems in specific situations, not upon the derivation of theory-based, general laws.

In a related vein, Agras, Kazdin, and Wilson (1979) set forth a pragmatically oriented model for validating behavior therapy treatments. Although new procedures can be generated from basic, experimental research, they also can be generated from clinical observation. In either case, the ultimate validation of the procedures comes from their utility in effecting desired psychological change, ideally as measured in rigorous outcome studies using the methods of quantitative, positivistic science.

Spiegler's (1983) *Contemporary Behavioral Therapy* is a good example of the pragmatic paradigm reflected in a basic behavior therapy textbook. The author described his approach as "operational," viewing behavior therapy "in terms of *how* it functions and *what* it accomplishes (rather than in terms of theoretical explanations of *why* it works)" (p. xvii).

Daniel Fishman, a coauthor of this chapter, recently stated the advantages of locating behavior therapy in the pragmatic paradigm (Fishman, 1988). This position begins with Erwin's critique of traditional "ideological" behaviorism, which claims that in principle only publicly observable behavior is worthy of scientific study. Erwin then introduces the concept of "pragmatic behaviorism," which he defines as

> the philosophical assumption that *clinical problems should generally be analyzed in behavioral terms.* . . . In treating a client, behavioral counterparts should generally be sought that correlate with (but are not equivalent to) any relevant problematic mental state. *The treatment should focus primarily on behavior, not because the mind is behavior, but for practical reasons.* . . . It may be of some use to learn, for example, that an obese patient has a *craving for food*, but it is even more useful to learn how many eating response are engaged in each day and under exactly what conditions. (1978, p. 80, emphasis added)

Building on this view and that of Mahoney (1974), Fishman has defined pragmatic behaviorism in terms of a commitment to ten methodological principles for the conduct of behavior therapy (Fishman, 1988, pp. 270–277). These include (a) an emphasis upon empiricism; (b) variables which are objective, specific, and concrete; (c) the analysis of problems into smaller parts to be dealt with one at a time; (d) quantification; (e) a view of behavior as a sample (rather than a sign) of personality; (f) functional analysis of the relation between behavior and the environment; and (g) a commitment to link any cognitive and affective variables which are employed to behavioral and environmental referents.

In Table 1, the nonbehavioral examples reflect differences among the three epistemological paradigms. Within the experimental paradigm can be found two examples of theories that search for general, objective, quantitative laws: Cattell's factor-analysis derived theory of personality composed of 16 universal source traits which transcend social and cultural context and second, Miller's living systems theory, which hypothesizes general principles that cut across seven different levels of living systems (from the cell to the individual organism to the supranational system) and that also transcend social and cultural context. Within the pragmatic paradigm are quantitative methodologies for predicting voter behavior and for evaluating the effectiveness of service programs. These methodologies do not search for general knowledge. Rather they are intended to collect information that can aid practical decision making in contextually specific situations—for example, how to revise a particular political campaign or whether to continue a particular service program.

Finally, within the hermeneutic paradigm, Freud's theory of oral, anal, and phallic character types, structural family therapy, and humanistic therapy all emerged from qualitative and clinical (as opposed to quantitative and scientific) contexts. Each emphasizes innovative ways to interpret psychological and social phenomena in a manner which focuses on symbolic, metaphorical meanings, high levels of inference, and a role for the interpreter which highlights subjectivity and intuition.

World Views

Altman and Rogoff posit four world views, termed "trait," "interactional," "organismic," and "transactional." They described these views as "philosophical approaches that presently and historically underlie research and theory in psychology." As such, each view is associated with

> different definitions of psychology and its units of study, different assumptions about the nature of person-environment relationships, varying conceptions about the philosophy and goals of science, and potentially different theories, methods, and strategies of research. (1987, p. 7)

The four world views parallel those proposed earlier by Pepper (1942, 1967). Pepper associated each view with a root metaphor: the trait view with the similarity and differences in the intrinsic qualities of entities, the interactional view with the machine, the organismic view with the living organism, and the transactional view with the historical event and the purposive act.

The trait view sees behavior as emerging from the individual. In other words, individuals act as they do primarily because of their inherent natures, without much attention to the temporal aspects of behavior or to the contexts within which the behaviors are embedded.

The interactional view treats the person and the environment as separate underlying entities that interact in a linear, causal, predictable manner, like the parts of a watch or dynamo. Psychological phenomena are analyzed in terms of the antecedent conditions which lead to certain behaviors, which in turn lead to various consequences, which in turn become antecedents for certain subsequent events. Within this framework, the goal of theory development is to enhance the ability to predict and control behavior. (Note that because of the mechanistic nature of the interactional view, in Table 1 this row is blank under the hermeneutic paradigm column, because (a) the hermeneutic paradigm emphasizes conscious, purposive acts which are inconsistent with a mechanistic perspective, and (b) the hermeneutic paradigm takes a phenomenological view which emphasizes holistic phenomena, not linearly interacting, discrete phenomena.)

The organismic view conceives of both person and environment as a system with complex, reciprocal, and dynamic relationships and influences among the parts. Change usually occurs in accord with underlying regulatory mechanisms (homeostasis) and long-range directional teleological mechanisms (such as psychological development from birth to adulthood). A system is seen as having an ideal end point toward which it optimally develops.

Finally, the transactional view concentrates on the changing relations among psychological and environmental aspects of holistic entities. As in an historical event generally, a psychological event is viewed as intrinsically embedded in its surrounding context and unfolding in time. Thus, the event is viewed as a complex and holistic phenomenon whose parts interpenetrate. The person and the environment are not separate parts or elements, but rather are mutually defining. Change occurs continuously. The directions of change are emergent rather than preestablished and quantification is rejected because it strips away contextual richness. (Note that the rejection of quantification in the transactional view is reflected in Table 1 by blank entries in the experimental and pragmatic paradigm columns.)

Table 1 reflects the fact that behavior therapy, from its origins to its present form, has been primarily embedded in the interactional world view. This is in contrast to Freud's theory of psychosexual character types, which has been associated primarily with the trait view; family systems therapy, which has been primarily embedded in the organismic view; and humanistic therapy, which has been primarily embedded in the transactional view.

Table 2 outlines how behavior therapy started with Watson and his followers and was embedded in a purely interactional perspective; then over time, it has branched out to add to this interactional view components from the other world views. Each of these developments is briefly illustrated next.[5]

"Pure" Interactional Theories

As just described and reflected in Table 1, the origins of the behavior therapy movement are clearly and directly embedded in both logical positivism and the interactional view. In Watson's behaviorism and in the animal-based conditioning research in the the age of grand theory, the metatheory involved a focused, mechanistic, "billiard ball," linear causal model which emphasized functional links between present environmental stimuli and an organism's responses. This "pure" interactional view was carried over into the early development of behavior therapy procedures by Skinner, Solomon, and Lindsley, who simply applied animal-based operant learning theory to the alleviation of socially unresponsive schizophrenic behavior.

Cognitive components were present early in the development of behavior therapy in the form of "covert conditioning." Mahoney (1974) described this model as follows:

> As its name implies, the covert conditioning model imposes the theory and language of conditioning on private experience. Thoughts, images, memories, and sensations are described as covert stimuli, covert responses, or covert consequences. The skull becomes a rather crowded Skinner box in which such conventional principles as reinforcement, punishment, and extinction are said to describe the function and patterning of private experience. . . . [There is an] assumption of continuity or identity between overt and covert learning principles. . . . [Since this is so,] we can make logical extrapolations from overt learning phenomena to covert processes. (pp. 61–62)

Thus, the covert conditioning model posits that the traditional logic of overt stimulus–response conditioning can be applied to that of covert stimulus–response conditioning. The covert conditioning model provides the theoretical rationale for such behavior therapy procedures as systematic desensitization (a type of "covert counterconditioning" [Wolpe, 1958]), thought stopping (Wolpe, 1958), covert sensitization (Cautela, 1967), and covert reinforcement (Cautela, 1970).

---

[5]Note that for the purposes of this chapter, it is sufficient simply to illustrate in Table 2 and the following discussion, instances of theory in which elements from the interactional view are combined with elements from one other point of view. In fact, the literature also includes examples of every possible combination of the interactional point of view with two or more of the other three world views.

Interactional Theories With Trait Components

In 1968, in independent efforts, Mischel and Peterson each published a book that linked the interactional thinking of behavior therapy with the emphasis on intrapersonal variables of the trait view. These two authors first criticized the prevalent approach at the time, employed by both psychometrically oriented trait theorists and psychoanalytically oriented, personality-dynamics theorists, who assumed that through the use of a limited number of behavioral signs yielded by personality tests (objective tests for trait theorists and projective tests for psychodynamic theorists), one could assign individuals to fixed positions on the assessor's favorite nomothetic trait dimensions. Mischel and Peterson argued that, empirically, such a "behavior sign" approach simply had not been shown to be useful or valid because personality studies found high levels of situational specificity in behavior rather than the cross-situational consistency predicted by the trait approach.

As an alternative to traditional trait and psychodynamic views of personality, Mischel proposed that personality and situation constructs be reconceptualized in terms of social learning theory and cognitive psychology. A recent statement of this approach by Cantor (1990) is illustrative. Cantor does not deny the existence of underlying personality dispositions that persons have, but focuses her attention on "how these dispositions are cognitively expressed and maintained in social interaction," what she calls the "doing" side of personality. Cantor takes a middle position between the trait and interaction views by positing the cognitively oriented personality constructs of "schema," "tasks," and "strategies" at the "middle" level of personality inference. Schemas are

> organized structures of knowledge about particular domains of life and the self which provide each person with unique cognitive filters that color the perception of events. . . . The shy schematic person, for example, is dishearteningly quick to see his or her social faux pas, to retrieve from memory numerous examples of prior mistakes, and to pit the self against an elaborate vision of the outgoing person that he or she is decidedly not like. (1990, pp. 736, 738)

Schemas are used to interpret life tasks, or personal goals for which to strive, which are distilled from the culturally prescribed and biologically based demands of social life, such as work, play, intimacy, power, and health. Finally, individuals develop various strategies for accomplishing their tasks. These strategies represent

> an intricate organization of feelings, thoughts, effort arousal and actions. . . . Constructive anticipation can, for example, create moti-

vation to pursue hard tasks, . . . and destructive thinking, . . . when individuals frame a task at too lofty a level of abstraction, can halt problem solving altogether. (Cantor, 1990, p. 743)

Interactional Theories With Organismic Components

Because of the importance of the environment in the interactional approach and because of the social context of much behavior, behavior therapy theorists became interested, early on, in social interaction, social relationships, and the social environment generally. In his 1968 book, Peterson illustrated how functional analysis could be applied using a similar perspective for solving dysfunction in an individual, a family, and a social system (a state psychiatric hospital). To show the link between individual and group behavior, Peterson pointed out that "social interaction" (as distinct from the "interactional" world view)

> refers to a class of social phenomena involving mutuality of stimulation and effect. . . . Explicit behavior by person 1 serves as a stimulus for person 2, who reacts in some way. This either terminates the interchange or leads to a further reaction on the part of person 1, perhaps to an action-reaction chain of indefinite length. . . . [Thus], in his motives and cognitive beliefs, each person takes the other, who has his own motives and beliefs, into account. When relatively stable patterns of [social] interaction develop between two individuals, a relationship has been formed. Concepts of [social] interaction and relationship are useful for the same reasons social psychology has been useful in general social science. Groups of people [socially] interacting can be studied as emergent units. A different class of phenomena can be examined, and with this a new order of comprehension may result. (pp. 82–84)

In short, Peterson was showing how an interactional view could incorporate organismic, systemic concepts, such as the notion of two-way causality between individuals' reactions to one another and the notion of a pattern of recurrent social interactions that become a network of social relationships, which creates an emergent entity at a "higher," more complex systems level than individual action (Miller, 1978). Many later behavior theorists have built upon this type of reasoning to integrate concepts from family systems therapy (e.g., Gurman & Kniskern, 1981) into cognitive behavior therapy with families. Robin and Foster's (1989) "behavioral–family systems" model for negotiating parent–adolescent conflict is an excellent recent example of this approach.

Robin and Foster (1989) view the detailed molecular analysis of contingency arrangements from the "pure" interactional, behavioral tradition as providing an excellent starting point for a functional analysis of a family's behavior with each other. However, they argue for the need to add orga-nismic elements to this approach, for the "pure" interactional approach

> has often failed to address the circular nature of [social] interaction patterns and the hierarchical structure of families, which overlay con-tingency arrangements. By contrast, the cybernetic, molar analysis of hierarchy inherent in the [family] systems tradition provides a rich conceptual basis for a structural analysis of families. Unfortunately, the molar concepts of a systems approach are often difficult to relate to an operational analysis of specific sequences of interactions within families. We have therefore found it useful to integrate concepts from both schools in building a comprehensive behavioral–family systems theory of family functioning, adding notions of contingency arrangements, social learning principles, and cognitive-behavioral theory to the anal-ysis of the family as a circular system with a definite structural config-uration. (pp. 7–8)

Interactional Theories With Transactional Elements

As discussed previously, Azrin (1977), Fishman (1988), Kanfer and Schefft (1988), and others have conceptualized behavior therapy within a social constructionist, pragmatic metatheory. A major aspect of this per-spective is the emphasis upon the contextual specificity of behavior. The focus is on developing practical strategies for solving particular problems in particular situations, not upon the derivation of empirically confirmed gen-eral laws. Fishman points out that this perspective leads to a focus on the individual case study, which in turn highlights the fact that each inter-vention program with a client—be it an individual, group, or organiza-tion—consists of a social interactional process over time between the client and the behavior change agent. This process consists of a series of sequential, interdependent steps or phases, which Kanfer and Schefft identify as "role structuring and creating a therapeutic alliance"; "developing a commitment for change"; "behavioral analysis"; "negotiating treatment objectives and methods"; "implementing treatment and maintaining motivation"; "mon-itoring and evaluating progress"; and "maintenance, generalization, and termination of treatment" (1988, pp. 94–95).

Fishman views phases as organized into a decisional flowchart with a variety of feedback loops. Because of the great variety of different patterns created by different choicepoint decisions, this perspective highlights the idiosyncratic particularities of each case. Kanfer and Schefft (1988) describe these particularities in terms consistent with many elements in the trans-actional world view:

> The dynamic qualities of all human experiences and the fluidity of social systems and environments suggest that neither therapy plans nor

programs for change should be rigid. . . . The everchanging opportunities and limitations that occur as a client progresses along a given path require constant adjustments and appraisal of therapeutic goals. For these reasons, clients are . . . helped to recognize that there may be many different paths to reach a goal and that it is unsound to give up the effort to change if one's specific plan fails. (p. 113)

CONCLUSIONS

Watsonian behaviorism, one of the major theoretical and epistemological sources of behavior therapy, was a radical departure from the mentalistic models of psychology predominant in his time. Behaviorism's power, in part, came from its contrast with commonsense psychology. In ordinary experience, as reflected in the vocabulary of our language, we typically think of ourselves as being conscious and intentional in our actions and as moving among a variety of subjective emotional states. We also see ourselves as being embedded in complex ways in the social institutions in our lives—family, neighborhood, work and school organizations, church, city, country, and so forth.

Watsonian behaviorists rejected subjective inner states, intentionality, and the importance of larger social and cultural forces. Rather, it was argued that people's behavior is determined by focused stimulus–response relationships, and the best models for studying the basic forces in our lives are dogs, cats, and rats. This narrow and exclusionary vision allowed post-Watsonian learning theorists to develop ways of viewing human behavior that maximized objectivity, quantification, operational definition, precision in describing relationships between variables, and the ability to frame psychological questions in clear, linearly causal ways which lend themselves to elegant experimental designs.

Thus, behaviorists deliberately took an exclusionary and focused approach, embracing logical positivism and a "pure" interactional world view, and this made for the exciting possibility of developing a true science of human behavior. This vision was pursued by Hull, Tolman, Skinner, Guthrie, and the other major figures in the era of grand theories of learning. As this age came to a close at the end of the first half of this century, the first behavior therapy practitioners began to apply seriously and systematically behavioristic or, more often, behavioral concepts and principles to solving human problems in the clinic and hospital rather than in the laboratory. The gradual disillusionment with learning theory as "the" answer in the field of scientific psychology as a whole perhaps allowed many of these early behavior therapists to be somewhat pragmatic rather than completely positivistic in their approach. And as behavior therapists gained more and more clinical experience, they realized the value of bringing back into their thinking those elements that behaviorism had originally rejected—consciousness, cognition, inner emotional states, the self, choice and freedom, and individual behavior as interdependently embedded in small groups and organizational and community systems—but always within some kind of explicit, data-oriented, broadly behaviorally based learning theory framework.

In sum (as illustrated in Table 2 and the related commentary), behavior theorists have rediscovered "personality" from the trait world view, "the family as a system" from the organismic world view, and "psychotherapy process" from the transactional world view. However, in these rediscoveries, behavior theorists have brought their unique, underlying perspective from the interactional world view and thereby created new ways to conceptualize, measure, and institute change in these traditional areas of psychotherapy.

Moreover, as pointed out by Pepper (1942), each of these world views is only "relatively adequate" from an epistemological perspective; that is, each does a pretty good job in deriving a conceptually coherent and empirically reasonable view of human experience. However, none of them is completely adequate. Rather, each involves a particular trade-off of adequate and inadequate characteristics, and these different patterns turn out to be mirror images of one another. For example, whereas pure interactional theory maximizes the maintenance of reliability, specifiability, observability, and manipulability, interactional theorists have a difficult time addressing such issues as the nature of human freedom, consciousness, and empathy. Transactional theory has just the opposite pattern of trade-offs. As another example, even though trait theory can easily create constructs that are subject to psychometrically rigorous measurement, it cannot easily account for dynamic interdependency among the systems levels of individual and social behavior. Organismic theory has just the opposite pattern of trade-offs. (For an extended discussion of these issues, see Chapter 13 in Fishman, Rotgers, and Franks, 1988.)

In the 1990s, the principles of behavior therapy are applicable to all types of disorders, individual situations, and settings. Biofeedback, behavioral medicine, community and environmental psychology are increasingly part of the behavior therapy scene. However, it has to be recognized that expansion is not necessarily synonymous with success. Thus, although behavior therapy may be regarded as the treatment of choice for autism, for example, in no way can it be regarded as a cure. The strength of behavior therapy lies not in its demonstration of therapeutic success, gratifying as this might be, but in the uniqueness of its approach. Appropriately investigated failure can be as valuable as success (see the following for more extended discussion of these matters: Barbrack, 1985; Foa & Emmelkamp, 1983; Mays & Franks, 1985).

As we see it, perhaps the major area which is currently of concern pertains to the predominance of professionalism in the field's major association, the Association for Advancement of Behavior Therapy (AABT), and the related lack of concern with those conceptual, scholarly, and scientific issues which triggered off the formation of this association in the first place. (It is surely no coincidence that there is a striking parallel with current events in the American Psychological Association.) Regrettably, at least to our way of thinking, it is clinical, methodological, and professional matters and a guild mentality which dominate contemporary behavior therapy today. It seems to us that, while methodology and clinical know-how have advanced significantly over the past four decades, accruing to the benefit of all concerned and in particular the client population, there has been no equivalent conceptual development of significance. Much has been written about the pros and cons of these two opposing perspectives (see Franks, 1990; 1987b). Future generations of behavior therapists are likely to be influenced both by the training they have received and the role models offered by their older peers. It is for these reasons that behavior therapy needs to "get its house in order" along some of the lines indicated.

On the positive side, although we fully recognize the need for professionalism, we see some evidence of a reversal of this exclusive emphasis in favor of a return to theoretical and conceptual concerns, in other words, a return to our founding mandate. In this respect, the formation of a Special Interest Group in the AABT geared toward the encouragement and support of philosophical and conceptual issues is particularly encouraging (Haas, Rosenfarb, & Hayes, 1987; Rosenfarb, 1987).

A second development, equally important and somewhat related to the first in terms of a return to conceptual thinking, is characterized by the shift from a simplistic stimulus–response model to a nonlinear, multicausal, but methodologically rigorous, perspective. In other words (as already discussed and reflected in Table 2), there is an incorporation into behavior therapy's traditional interactional world view of elements from the organismic and transactional perspectives. For example, while recognizing the need for both forms of intervention, Goldiamond (1984) used the term "linear" to refer to topical, focused interventions in which treatments are defined by the presenting problems and addressed directly towards these areas; and "nonlinear analysis" to refer to the use of both topical and broader, systemic interventions, initiated by the presenting problems but conceptualized and addressed in terms of behavior–contingency systems rather than more direct, one-to-one relationships. Similarly, Delprato (1989) offers a nonlinear approach which cuts across and yet interfaces with several closely related areas. Delprato defines his "developmental interactionism" as "a relatively recent outgrowth of several confluent movements, including heredity × environment interactionism, the integrated-field perspective, evolutional thinking, Schneirla's comparative–developmental psychology, behavioral embryology, life-span developmental psychology, retreat from reductionism, and the systems approach."

The recent revival of interest in Kantor's (1959) much neglected "interbehavioral" psychology is equally exciting. With the probable exception of behavior therapists in Mexico and certain other areas of Latin America, Kantor has been overlooked or misunderstood despite his lifelong contributions and numerous publications. Kantor was an outspoken critic of metaphysical dualism. He insisted, perhaps prematurely, that behavioral theory and therapy can be as scientific as the physical sciences. In the place of metaphysical dualism, Kantor offered a monistic behavioral field theory with an organismic focus upon mutual and simultaneous interactions between organism and environment. For Kantor, psychology's primary subject matter is the holistic and naturalistic coordination of the entire organism. Thus, there is no artificial and exclusively linear, one-to-one relationship between stimulus and response (see Ruben & Delprato, 1987).

What all this adds up to is that behavior therapy is building logically and even predictably upon its foundation and that there is, indeed, hope for the future. The original emphasis on accountability, rigorous but open-minded thinking, scientific methodology, and learning theory remains much the same but in an evolved form. What has changed is the complexity of the problems addressed, the increased sophistication of the methods with which they are investigated, and the abandonment of an exclusively one-to-one linear approach. The conceptual problem still remains: How can we adopt a multidimensional, interdisciplinary perspective that takes into account data, formulation, and methodologies from disciplines once considered to be largely outside the traditional behavior therapist's bailiwick, yet retain the essential unity of behavior therapy (Franks, 1981; 1987b)? How can we take these innovative developments into account and incorporate them into an overall model that still retains the spirit of scientific integrity which brought behavior therapy into being in the first place? In so doing, it must be recognized that behavior therapy is still an emerging and new science, rather akin in status and its knowledge base to physics and medicine in the 16th and 17th centuries. It is too early to expect either unity or resolution of the issues in the field, and certainly it would seem premature to think in terms of any paradigmatic or unifying conceptual integration of behavior therapy. It is our hope that the brief overview of behavior therapy presented in this chapter will serve to place these matters in context, to clarify issues, and to renew the process of constructive thinking which started it off less than four decades ago.

REFERENCES

Agras, W. S., Kazdin, A. E., & Wilson, G. T. (1979). *Behavior therapy: Towards an applied clinical science*. San Francisco: Freeman.

Altman, I., & Rogoff, B. (1987). World views in psychology: Trait, interactional, organismic, and transactional perspectives. In D. Stokols & I. Altman (Eds.), *Handbook of environmental psychology* (pp. 7–40). New York: John Wiley.

Azrin, N. H. (1977). A strategy for applied research: Learning based but outcome oriented. *American Psychologist, 30*, 469–485.

Baars, B. J. (1986). *The cognitive revolution in psychology*. New York: Guilford Press.

Bandura, A. (1969). *Principles of behavior modification*. New York: Holt, Rinehart, & Winston.

Bandura, A. (1978). The self-system in reciprocal determinism. *American Psychologist, 33*, 344–358.

Bandura, A. (1982). Self-efficacy mechanisms in human agency. *American Psychologist, 37*, 122–147.

Barbrack, C. R. (1985). Negative outcome in behavior therapy. In D. T. Mays & C. M. Franks (Eds.), *Negative outcome in psychotherapy and what to do about it* (pp. 76–105). New York: Springer.

Barlow, D. H., Hayes, S. C., & Nelson, R. O. (1984). *The scientist practitioner: Research and accountability in clinical and educational settings*. Elmsford, NY: Pergamon Press.

Barlow, D. H., & Hersen, M. (1984). *Single case experimental designs: Strategies for studying behavioral change (Second edition)*. New York: Pergamon Press.

Birchler, G. R., & Spinks, S. (1980). Behavioral-systems marital and family therapy: Integration and clinical application. *American Journal of Family Therapy, 8*, 6–28.

Burnham, W. H. (1924). *The normal mind*. New York: Appleton.

Campbell, D. T. (1984). Can we be scientific in applied social science? In R. F. Connor, D. G. Altman, & C. Jackson (Eds.), *Evaluation studies review annual (Vol. 9)* (pp. 26–48). Beverly Hills, CA: Sage.

Cantor, N. (1990). From thought to behavior: "Having" and "doing" in the study of personality and cognition. *American Psychologist, 45*, 735–750.

Cattell, R. B. (1966). *The scientific analysis of personality*. Chicago: Aldine.

Cautela, J. R. (1967). Covert sensitization. *Psychological Reports, 20*, 459–468.

Cautela, J. R. (1970). Covert reinforcement. *Behavior Therapy, 1*, 33–50.

Delprato, D. J. (1989). Developmental interactionism: An emerging integrative framework for behavior therapy. *Advances in Behavior Research and Therapy, 9,* 173–205.

Dollard, J., & Miller, N. E. (1950). *Personality and psychotherapy.* New York: McGraw-Hill.

Dunlap, K. (1932). *Habits: Their making and unmaking.* New York: Liveright.

Dunlap, K. (1972). *Habits: Their making and unmaking (introduction by Irwin Lublin).* New York: Liveright.

Eifert, G. H., & Evans, I. M. (Eds.). (1990). *Unifying behavior therapy: Contributions of paradigmatic behaviorism.* New York: Springer.

Erwin, E. (1978). *Behavior therapy: Scientific, philosophical, and moral foundations.* New York: Cambridge University Press.

Eysenck, H. J. (1952). The effects of psychotherapy: An evaluation. *Journal of Consulting Psychology, 16,* 319–324.

Eysenck, H. J. (1959). Learning theory and behaviour therapy. *Journal of Mental Science, 195,* 61–75.

Eysenck, H. J. (Ed.). (1960). *Handbook of abnormal psychology: An experimental approach.* London: Pitman.

Eysenck, H. J. (Ed.). (1964). *Experiments in behaviour therapy: Readings in modern methods of treating mental disorders derived from learning theory.* London: Pergamon Press.

Eysenck, H. J. (1990). *Rebel with a cause.* London: W. H. Allen.

Fishman, D. B. (1988). Pragmatic behaviorism: Saving and nurturing the baby. In D. B. Fishman, F. Rotgers, & C. M. Franks (Eds.), *Paradigms in behavior therapy: Present and promise* (pp. 254–293). New York: Springer.

Fishman, D. B., & Neigher, W. D. (1987). Technological assessment: Tapping a "third culture" for decison-focused psychological measurement. In D. R. Peterson & D. B. Fishman (Eds.), *Assessment for decisions* (pp. 44–76). New Brunswick, NJ: Rutgers University Press.

Fishman, D. B, Rotgers, F., & Franks, C. M. (Eds.). (1988). *Paradigms in behavior therapy: Present and promise.* New York: Springer.

Foa, E. B., & Emmelkamp, P. M. G. (1983). *Failures in behavior therapy.* New York: Wiley.

Franks, C. M. (1969). Behavior therapy and its Pavlovian origins. In C. M. Franks, *Behavior therapy: Appraisal and status* (pp. 1–26). New York: McGraw-Hill.

Franks, C. M. (1969). *Behavior therapy: Appraisal and status.* New York: McGraw-Hill.

Franks, C. M. (1981). 2081: Will we be many or one—or none? *Behavioural Psychotherapy, 9,* 287–290.

Franks, C. M. (1987a). Behavior therapy: An overview. In G. T. Wilson, C. M. Franks, P. C. Kendall, & J. P. Foreyt (Eds.), *Review of behavior therapy: Theory and practice* (Vol. 11; pp. 1–39). New York: Guilford Press.

Franks, C. M. (1987b). Behavior therapy and AABT: Personal recollections, conceptions, and misconceptions. *Behavior Therapist, 10,* 171–174.

Franks, C. M. (1990). Behavior therapy: An overview. In C. M. Franks, G. T. Wilson, P. C. Kendall, & J. P. Foreyt (Eds.), *Review of behavior therapy: Theory and practice* (Vol. 12; pp. 1–43). New York: Guilford Press.

Frederiksen, L. W. (Ed.). (1982). *Handbook of organizational behavior management.* New York: Wiley.

Freud, S. (1924). Character and anal eroticism. In S. Freud, *Collected papers: II.* London: Institute of Psychoanalysis and Hogarth Press.

Gantt, W. H. (1966). Conditional or conditioned, reflex or response? *Conditional Reflex, 1,* 69–73.

Gergen, K. J. (1982). *Towards transformation in social knowledge.* New York: Springer-Verlag.

Gergen, K. J. (1985). The social constructionist movement in modern psychology. *American Psychologist, 40,* 266–275.

Glenwick, D., & Jason, L. (Eds.). (1980). *Behavioral community psychology: Progress and prospects.* New York: Praeger.

Goldiamond, I. (1984). Training parent trainers and ethicists in nonlinear analysis of behavior. In R. F. Dangel & R. A. Polster (Eds.), *Parent training: Foundations of research and practice* (pp. 504–546). New York: Guilford Press.

Gurman, A. S., & Kniskern, D. P. (1981). *Handbook of family therapy.* New York: Brunner/Mazel.

Haas, J. R., Rosenfarb, I. S., & Hayes, S. C. (1987). Back to basics: The formation of a special interest group concerned with the contribution of philosophy, theory, and basic research to behavior therapy. *Behavior Therapist, 4,* 88.

Jacobson, N. S., & Margolin, G. (1979). *Marital therapy: Strategies based on social learning and behavior exchange principles.* New York: Brunner/Mazel.

Jones, H. S. (1956). The application of conditioning and learning techniques to the treatment of a psychiatric patient. *Journal of Abnormal and Social Psychology, 52,* 414–420.

Kanfer, F. H., & Schefft, B. K. (1988). *Guiding the process of therapeutic change.* Champaign, IL: Research Press.

Kantor, J. R. (1959). *Interbehavioral psychology.* Granville, OH: Principia Press.

Kazdin, A. E. (1978). *History of behavior modification: Experimental foundations of contemporary research.* Baltimore: University Park Press.

Kendall, P. C., & Bemis, K. M. (1983). Thought and action in psychotherapy: The cognitive behavioral approaches. In M. Hersen, A. E. Kazdin, & A. S. Bellak (Eds.), *The clinical psychology handbook* (pp. 565–592). Elmsford, NY: Pergamon Press.

Kimble, G. A. (1985). Conditioning and learning. In S. Koch & D. E. Leary (Eds.), *A century of psychological science* (pp. 284–321). New York: McGraw-Hill.

Krasner, L. (1971). Behavior therapy. In P. H. Mussen (Ed.), *Annual Review of Psychology (Vol. 22)* (pp. 483–532). Palo Alto, CA: Annual Reviews.

Krasner, L. (1982). Behavior therapy: On roots, contexts, and growth. In G. T. Wilson & C. M. Franks (Eds.), *Contemporary behavior therapy: Conceptual and empirical foundations* (pp. 11–62). New York: Guilford Press.

Krasner, L., & Houts, A. C. (1984). A study of the "value" systems of behavioral scientists. *American Psychologist, 39,* 840–850.

Kuhn, T. S. (1962). *The structure of scientific revolutions.* Chicago: University of Chicago Press.

Lazarus, A. A. (1958). New methods in psychotherapy: A case study. *South African Medical Journal, 32,* 600–664.

Liddell, H. S. (1958). A biological basis for psychopathology. In P. H. Hoch & J. Zubin (Eds.), *Problems of addiction and habituation* (pp. 183–196). New York: Grune & Stratton.

Linehan, M. M., & Wagner, A. W. (1990). Dialectical behavior therapy: A feminist-behavioral treatment of borderline personality disorder. *Behavior Therapist, 13,* 9–14.

Mahoney, M. J. (1974). *Cognition and behavior modification.* Cambridge, MA: Ballinger.

Mahoney, M. J. (1988). The cognitive sciences and psychotherapy: Patterns in a developing relationship. In K. S. Dobson (Ed.), *Handbook of cognitive-behavioral therapies* (pp. 357–386). New York: Guilford Press.

Marshall, W. L. (1982). A model of dysfunctional behavior. In A. S. Bellak, M. Hersen, & A. E. Kazdin (Eds.), *International handbook of behavior modification* (pp. 57–76). New York: Plenum.

Masserman, J. M. (1943). *Behavior and neurosis.* Chicago: University of Chicago Press.

Mateer, F. (1917). *Child behavior: A critical and experimental study of young children by the method of conditioned reflexes.* Boston: Badger.

Mays, D. T., & Franks, C. M. (Eds.). (1985). *Negative outcome in psychotherapy and what to do about it.* New York: Springer.

Messer, S. B., Sass, L. A., & Woolfolk, R. L. (Eds.). (1988). *Hermeneutics and psychological theory.* New Brunswick, NJ: Rutgers University Press.

Miller, J. G. (1978). *Living systems.* New York: McGraw-Hill.

Minuchin, S. (1974). *Families and family therapy.* Cambridge, MA: Harvard University Press.

Mischel, W. (1968). *Personality and assessment.* New York: Wiley.

Morell, J. A. (1979). *Program evaluation in social research.* Elmsford, NY: Pergamon Press.

Mowrer, O. H., & Mowrer, W. M. (1938). Enuresis: A method for its study and treatment. *American Journal of Orthopsychiatry, 8,* 436–459.

Neigher, W. D., & Fishman, D. B. (1985). From science to technology: Reducing problems in mental health evaluation by paradigm shift. In L. Burstein,

H. F. Freeman, & P. H. Rossi (Eds.), *Collecting evaluation data: Problems and solutions* (pp. 263–298). Beverly Hills, CA: Sage Publications.

O'Leary, K. D., & Wilson, G. T. (1987). *Behavior therapy: Application and outcome.* Englewood Cliffs, NJ: Prentice-Hall.

Packer, M. J. (1985). Hermeneutic inquiry in the study of human conduct. *American Psychologist, 40,* 1081–1093.

Paul, G. L. (Ed.). (1986). *Assessment in residential treatment settings: Principles and methods to support cost-effective quality operations.* Champaign, IL: Research Press.

Pepper, S. C. (1942). *World hypotheses: A study in evidence.* Los Angeles: University of California Press.

Pepper, S. C. (1967). *Concept and quality: A world hypothesis.* LaSalle, IL: Open Court.

Persons, J. B. (1989). *Cognitive therapy in practice: A case formulation approach.* New York: W. W. Norton.

Peterson, D. R. (1968). *The clinical study of social behavior.* New York: Appleton-Century-Crofts.

Putnam, H. (1984). After Ayer, after empiricism. *Partisan Review, 51,* 265–275.

Robin, A. L., & Foster, S. L. (1989). *Negotiating parent-adolescent conflict: A behavioral-family systems approach.* New York: Guilford Press.

Rogers, C. R. (1961). *On becoming a person.* Boston: Houghton-Mifflin.

Rosenfarb, I. S. (1987). A note from the chair. *The Issues: A Publication of the Theoretical and Philosophical Issues SIG of the AABT, 1,* 1.

Ruben, D. H., & Delprato, D. J. (Eds.). (1987). *New ideas in therapy: Introduction to an interdisciplinary approach.* Westport, CT: Greenwood Press.

Scarr, S. (1985). Construing psychology: Making facts and fables for our times. *American Psychologist, 40,* 499–512.

Schwartz, G. E. (1988). From behavior therapy to cognitive behavior therapy to system therapy: Toward an integrative health science. In D. B. Fishman, F. Rotgers, & C. M. Franks (Eds.), (pp. 294–320). *Paradigms in behavior therapy: Present and promise.* New York: Springer.

Shaffer, L. F. (1947). The problem of psychotherapy. *American Psychologist, 2,* 459–467.

Shaw, F. J. (1948). Some postulates concerning psychotherapy. *Journal of Consulting Psychology, 12,* 426–431.

Shoben, E. J., Jr. (1949). Psychotherapy as a problem in learning theory. *Psychological Bulletin, 46,* 366–392.

Skinner, B. F. (1948). *Walden two.* New York: Macmillan.

Skinner, B. F., Solomon, H. C., & Lindsley, O. R. (1953). *Studies in behavior therapy: Status report I, November 30, 1953.* Unpublished report, Metropolitan State Hospital, Waltham, MA.

Spiegler, M. D. (1983). *Contemporary behavioral therapy*. Palo Alto, CA: Mayfield Publishing.

Staats, A. W. (1975). *Social behaviorism*. Homewood, IL: Dorsey Press.

Staats, A. W. (1981). Paradigmatic behaviorism, unified theory, unified theory construction, and the zeitgeist of separatism. *American Psychologist, 36*, 240–256.

Thorndike, E. L. (1911). *Animal intelligence*. New York: Macmillan.

Turkat, D., & Maisto, S. A. (1985). Personality disorders: Application of the experimental method to the formulation and modification of personality disorders. In D. H. Barlow (Ed.), *Clinical handbook of psychological disorders* (pp. 502–570). New York: Guilford Press.

Ullmann, L. P., & Krasner, L. (Eds.) (1965). *Case studies in behavior modification*. New York: Holt, Rinehart, & Winston.

Watson, J. B. (1913). Psychology as the behaviorist views it. *Psychological Review, 20*, 158–177.

Watson, J. B. (1924). *Behaviorism*. Chicago: The People's Institute.

Wells, R. A., & Giannetti, V. J. (Eds.) (1990). *Handbook of the brief psychotherapies*. New York: Plenum Press.

Wilson, G. T. (1982). Psychotherapy process and procedure: The behavioral mandate. *Behavior Therapy, 13*, 291–312.

Wilson, G. T., & Franks, C. M. (Eds.) (1982). *Contemporary behavior therapy: Conceptual and empirical foundations*. New York: Guilford Press.

Wilson, G. T., & O'Leary, K. D. (1980). *Principles of behavior therapy*. Englewood Cliffs, NJ: Prentice-Hall.

Wolpe, J. (1958). *Psychotherapy by reciprocal inhibition*. Stanford: Stanford University Press.

Woolfolk, R. L., & Richardson, F. C. (1984). Behavior therapy and the ideology of modernity. *American Psychologist, 39*, 777–786.

6

HUMANISTIC APPROACHES TO PSYCHOTHERAPY

LAURA N. RICE AND LESLIE S. GREENBERG

The theories of psychotherapy designated as humanistic share beliefs and principles that differentiate them clearly from other major orientations such as cognitive–behavioral and psychodynamic. As we explain in this chapter, the ways in which these principles are implemented in the actual therapy sessions vary substantially in the different humanistic approaches. Nevertheless, all share an emphasis on subjectivity and awareness in understanding behavior, and a resistance against the view of the person as an object, to be seen objectively from an external vantage point that ignores the individual's existential reality. The position of Kierkegaard (1843/1954), as well as that of Sartre (1943/1956), was that both objective reality and one's uniquely human subjective reality must be respected in order to grasp the more complete reality underlying both the subjective and the objective. The European philosophers Husserl (1925/1977), Heidegger (1949/1962), Jaspers (1963), and Marcel (1951) were all influential in explicating and extending this position.

Humanistic theorists, often spoken of as the "third force" in psychology, have written extensively on the nature of human existence, on methods by which uniquely human modes of functioning can be studied and grasped, and on implications of humanistic assumptions for the goals and processes of psychotherapy (Bugental, 1967; Buhler, 1967; Jourard, 1968; Lewin, 1951; Maslow, 1968; May, 1961).

A number of authors have attempted to characterize the core beliefs of humanistic psychology (e.g., McWaters, 1977, and Sutich & Vich, 1969). The most recent comprehensive attempt (Tageson, 1982) has focused in detail on a number of major themes of humanistic psychology. We consider four of these to be of primary importance in all the humanistic psychotherapy approaches.

1. The first and most central characteristic of humanistic psychology and psychotherapy is the commitment to a phenomenological approach. This approach is grounded in the belief in the uniquely human capacity for reflective consciousness, and in the belief that it is this capacity that can lead to self-determination and freedom. Tageson (1982) states the core assumption in a way that is especially relevant to psychotherapy. "Whatever terminology is preferred, all seem agreed on the inescapable uniqueness of human consciousness and on the importance of understanding *this* person's perception of reality if we are ever completely to understand his or her behaviour" (p. 33).

2. The operation of some form of actualizing or growth tendency is a second highly significant issue for humanistic therapists, although it is one on which they take somewhat different positions. All would agree with the importance of the antihomeostatic view of human beings as striving toward growth and development rather than merely toward the maintenance of stability (Maslow, 1970). All would agree that one's choices are guided by awareness of the future and the immediate present rather than only by the past. Tageson (1982) emphasized the point that this *actualizing* tendency is more than a biological concept and makes the interesting comment, "It is my conviction that the attribute of consciousness transforms the actualizing tendency in the organism into a directional tendency that has more to do with the notion of the self as a centre of intentionality in a more or less constant search for meaning" (p. 40).

3. The belief in human capacity for self-determination is an important and sometimes controversial focus of humanistic theorists. The ways in which this capacity is developed, facilitated, or blocked are a key issue. Choice and will are central aspects of human functioning. Individuals are not

determined solely by their past or by their environments but are agents in the construction of their world.

4. The fourth shared basic principle is that of person-centeredness. This involves concern and real respect for each person, whether they are subjects of study in research or are engaged in the process of psychotherapy. Each person's subjective experience is of central importance to the humanist, and in the effort to grasp this experience, one is attempting to share the other person's world in a special way that goes beyond the subject–object dichotomy. Being allowed to share another person's world is viewed as a special privilege requiring a special kind of relationship.

The focus of this chapter will be on the emergence and development of the three humanistic approaches to psychotherapy that have been the most influential: the client-centered (person-centered) approach of Carl Rogers, the Gestalt approach of Fritz Perls, and the existential approach. Although there is great variability in the processes engaged in by existential therapists, we will concentrate primarily on the positions shared by Rollo May and Irvin Yalom and, to a lesser extent, on the European existentialists, Binswanger, Boss, and Frankl.

ORIGINS

In examining the historical, geographical and professional origins of humanistic therapists, it is apparent that, although they emerged from quite different environments, all were directly or indirectly influenced by humanistic philosophers. All were searching for understandings and approaches that would build on the uniquely human capacity for self-reflective consciousness and on the search for meanings, choices, and growth. All were attempting to move beyond what they regarded as the restricted views of human functioning represented in the other two major orientations— psychoanalysis and behavior therapy. Although all humanistic theories explicated views of pathological functioning, the humanistic therapists' primary focus was on understanding ways in which people could be helped to move toward healthy or even ideal functioning.

The Client-Centered Approach

Carl Rogers was born in Illinois in 1902. He began his doctoral studies at Union Theological Seminary in New York, but transferred to Columbia University Teachers College for graduate training in clinical psychology.

His thesis supervisor was Goodwin Watson, who was a well-known expert on group leadership training. Rogers was also indirectly influenced by the ideas of John Dewey through one of his teachers, W. H. Kilpatrick. He received intensive training in psychological assessment, and, through a year's internship at the Institute for Child Guidance, he received training in the psychoanalytic approach. His professional identity was clearly that of a psychologist, strongly imbued with the scientific methods that characterized American psychology. He was president of the American Psychological Association in 1946.

After finishing graduate school, Rogers joined the Child Study Department of a social agency in Rochester. During his 12 years in Rochester he was introduced by social workers to some of the ideas and methods of the psychoanalyst, Otto Rank. Rank's belief in the person's constructive forces, including a will to health, and a belief in the crucial importance of the spontaneous human relationship in psychotherapy influenced and confirmed the views that Rogers had already begun to develop.

During the period when he was on the faculty at Ohio State University (1940–1944), Rogers and his colleagues and students began the practice of studying complete transcripts of audio-recorded therapy interviews in an effort to achieve a fuller understanding of the processes involved. (The practice of recording therapy sessions was almost unheard of in other clinical settings.) Some of the ideas that emerged from this intensive, inductive effort to become aware of and understand some of the essential change processes in psychotherapy were described in his book, *Counseling and Psychotherapy* (Rogers, 1942), which also contained a complete transcript of an actual therapy. (See chapter 19 for further information on this topic.)

After Rogers moved to the University of Chicago in 1945, the intensive listening process continued. Through listening to and discussing their own or each others' therapy sessions, Rogers and his colleagues attempted to identify and reflect on some of the crucial change processes that took place, and how these changes were facilitated by the therapist (Rogers, 1957). The emphasis was usually not on specific content nor on particular insights arrived at, but on process changes in the client that seemed to take place in therapies with successful outcomes. The hypotheses emerging from this experiential understanding were then formulated and tested by means of verification studies conducted by usual scientific methods. Later on at Chicago, there was a strong emphasis on conducting empirical research at the Counseling Center (Rogers & Dymond, 1954). An entire issue of the *Journal of Consulting Psychology* was devoted to research conducted by Rogers' graduate students, including Haigh (1949), Raskin (1949), and Seeman (1949).

Rogers' book, *Client-Centered Therapy* (1951), built on the earlier formulations and laid some of the most important foundations for his later work.

There were two indirect but valuable influences on Rogers' thinking. First, he adopted Goldstein's concept of an actualizing tendency in human beings (Goldstein, 1939). Kurt Goldstein was an eminent neuropsychologist at the Institute for Brain Damaged Soldiers in Germany, who had become impressed by the capacity of soldiers with brain injuries to reorganize their own modes of functioning. Goldstein's observations that people reorganized in constructive ways confirmed Rogers' view of the basic human motivation toward growth and wholeness, the actualizing tendency, which became the one central motivational concept in his theoretical system.

A second indirect influence came from the writings of Martin Buber (1957), brought to Rogers' attention by graduate theology students at the University of Chicago. Rogers recognized that the I–Thou relationship, which was viewed by Buber as having a healing effect was exactly the experience that emerged in especially good therapy hours.

In listing the most important sources of his ideas, Rogers (1980) placed much value on what he had learned from graduate students and colleagues. For instance, Eugene Gendlin, a graduate student and later a colleague, formulated the concept of "experiencing" (Gendlin, 1962), based on the view that, within human beings, there is an ongoing flow of experiencing to which the person can turn, under the right conditions, in order to discover the "felt meanings" of experiences. Rogers felt that the concept of experiencing had influenced his view of therapist empathy as well as a number of other important issues.

In 1957 Rogers moved to the faculty at the University of Wisconsin and began an extensive research project on the processes and effects of client-centered therapy with hospitalized schizophrenic patients (Rogers, Gendlin, Kiesler & Truax, 1967). In 1964 he moved to California, first to the Western Behavioral Sciences Institute and then to the Center for Studies of the Person. During these years he became increasingly interested in working with groups and with a wide range of issues, including international relations and the prevention of nuclear war. It was also during this period that he decided that client-centered therapy should be renamed "person-centered therapy."

For those interested in a general overview of Rogers' life and ideas, we suggest the chapter by Raskin and Rogers (1989; see also chapter 19 in this volume). Rogers' book, *On Becoming a Person* (1961), is a useful source for getting an "inside feel" for client-centered therapy. Then, after getting a basic background in his thinking, his book *A Way of Being* (1980), in which he discussed a variety of ideas and turning-points as well as learnings from his own personal and professional life, would be especially meaningful and moving.

The Gestalt Approach

Frederick Perls was born in Germany in 1893. After acquiring medical training, he worked as an assistant to Kurt Goldstein and was strongly influenced by Goldstein's ideas about the organism and the self-actualizing tendency. It was in Germany that he met Laura Perls, who became his wife and collaborator in developing the Gestalt approach to psychotherapy. Laura Perls introduced him to the work of the Gestalt psychologists, Koffka (1935), Kohler (1959) and Wertheimer (1945). She herself had been influenced by the existential writings of Buber and Tillich.

Perls became a psychoanalyst and was especially influenced by his own analyst, Wilhelm Reich. He was also informed by the works of psychoanalysts Karen Horney and Otto Rank. Dissatisfied with psychoanalytic dogmatism, and working within a zeitgeist in Europe that was strongly influenced by phenomenological and existential viewpoints, he began to make revisions of psychoanalytic theory (Perls, 1947). Eventually, in 1951, Perls, Hefferline, and Goodman proposed a new integration among Gestalt, existential, and analytic approaches in the form of a Gestalt therapy, originally called "concentration therapy."

Two additional important influences on Perls's thinking were that of the philosopher Friedlander and the South African statesman and Prime Minister, Jan Smuts. Perls was impressed by Friedlander's (1918) work on the nature of polarities and the importance of a balance between them in human functioning. Perls integrated Smuts's (1926) work on holism with Kurt Lewin's (1951) field theory, leading him to view the person as part of an organism/environment field and to view the mind and body holistically. Zen also has had an important influence on the development of Gestalt therapy, especially in its later years, and it has been referred to as "western Zen," or as a form of existential therapy.

When Perls arrived in the United States after his stay in South Africa, where he had fled as war approached in Europe, he began the active promotion of Gestalt therapy. The New York Institute for Gestalt Therapy was formed in the 1950s, and workshops and study groups were established throughout the country. Perls moved to the west coast in the 1960s and settled for a while at the Esalen Institute in California to establish training workshops. Later he moved to Canada to establish a new institute. Throughout this period many people were trained in the Gestalt approach.

Perls developed many ideas that were subsequently incorporated into general humanistic and eclectic psychotherapy practice. The emphasis on body awareness, direct experience, the importance of encounter, the use of active experimentation and the use of awareness exercises all became incorporated into the humanistic therapies in the 1960s and 1970s.

As originally practiced by Perls, the Gestalt approach involved some abrasive techniques, including client frustration, when working with clients viewed as manipulative. Since Perls's death in 1970, the Gestalt movement has shifted toward a softer form of therapy, with less use of modes of frustrating clients and more emphasis on the I–Thou dialogue.

The best introduction to Gestalt therapy is the chapter by Yontef and Simkin (1989), followed by Perls's four lectures (Fagan & Shepherd, 1970; Perls, 1969), which can be followed by a reading of *Gestalt Therapy, Excitement and Growth in the Personality* (Perls, Hefferline, & Goodman, 1951). Perls's posthumous work, *The Gestalt Approach and Eyewitness to Therapy* (Perls, 1973), combines a description of the overall approach not provided elsewhere, with transcripts of Perls's practice. *Gestalt Therapy Integrated* (Polster & Polster, 1973) provides an innovative effort to expand the boundaries of the Gestalt approach and is required reading for the serious student who wishes to understand the Gestalt approach.

The Existential Approaches

The existential approaches emerged more or less independently in the 1940s and 1950s in different countries in Europe. There were a number of possible reasons for the spontaneous emergence of this movement. Most existential therapists were psychiatrists with a background in psychoanalysis who felt that the person, as he or she really existed, was being lost in the psychodynamic approaches. Also, European theorists were usually much more aware of the writings of the philosophers Kierkegaard, Nietzsche, Husserl, Sartre, Marcel, Jaspers, and Heidegger than were the North American psychologists and psychiatrists. Moreover, as May and Yalom (1984) have mentioned, this period in Europe was a period of alienation and anxiety, in which there was not only the threat of nuclear war, but awareness of major cultural changes that were taking place in society.

Two of the most influential Existential approaches were those of Binswanger (1963) and Boss (1963), who rejected the exclusively biological and mechanistic view of human functioning in Freud's position. Adopting Heidegger's concept of Dasein (existence), they developed an approach that was called *Daseinanalyse*, which emphasized the human capacity for giving meaning to existence. Victor Frankl was another influential European psychiatrist. His existential approach, which he called Logotherapy (1963), has a unique flavor, based to some extent on his own experience at the Nazi death camp at Auschwitz.

Rollo May was largely responsible for introducing existential therapy into the United States (May, Angel, & Ellenberger, 1958). May was trained as a psychoanalyst at the William Alanson White Institute in New York, a neo-Freudian setting in which the views of Sullivan, Fromm, and Horney were incorporated. He practiced as a psychoanalyst and during the period became dissatisfied with some of the methods and underlying assumptions of the psychoanalytic approaches. He began reading about the European existential theories in the early 1950s, and began to focus on what he saw as missing from the Freudian and neo-Freudian positions. As May suggests, the interpersonal world had been incorporated into the views of the neo-Freudians, but the relationship to oneself was still missing in the approaches.

Two other existential therapists in the United States who have written extensively on the theory and practice of existential therapy are Bugental (1967) and Yalom (1981), the latter having provided the first comprehensive volume entitled *Existential Psychotherapy*. Probably the most useful introduction to existential therapy is the chapter by May and Yalom (1989) and the books by May (1977), Yalom (1981), and Bugental (1967).

THE THERAPEUTIC PROCESSES

In this section we would like to convey some flavor of the centrality of the four humanistic principles described in the introduction that guide the actual processes engaged in by humanistic therapists. Although the different approaches implement the principles in different ways, the themes are of central importance in all the humanistic orientations.

1. The phenomenological approach—Discovery-oriented with the client viewed as the expert on his or her own experience. The phenomenological theme in humanistic psychology yields two related but distinctive features of humanistic therapy. First, the emphasis is on the client's process of discovery as opposed to an interpretive focus. In other words, clients are encouraged to identify and symbolize their inner experience for themselves, rather than having the therapist offer symbols to them to help them make sense of their experience. Second, clients are viewed as having privileged access to their unique, inner awareness and are therefore viewed as experts on their own experience; no attempts are made to contradict, oppose, or otherwise shape the content of experience.

Rogers believed that human beings have the "gift of awareness" (Rogers & Skinner, 1956), and if the therapist could provide the appropriate conditions, clients could become aware of their own perceptions of inner and outer reality and thus could increasingly guide their own life's choices in fulfilling directions. The emphasis is on trying to establish optimal conditions for inner exploration, rather than on providing insight, or trying to understand the choices that the client needs to make, or pushing for choice. Empathic reflection of the client's moment-by-moment inner awareness is viewed as the most effective way of enabling clients to discover for themselves the awareness that will motivate and guide their choices.

Viewing clients as experts on their own experience is a central aspect of the client-centered process. The therapist's reflections carry the message of empathic understanding and also the explicit or implicit expectation that the client will correct that reflected understanding and will carry it further. The assumption is that the personal *meaning* of the client's experience is in the experience itself, and under optimal conditions, clients can grasp these meanings for themselves. Thus, the therapist works consistently within the client's frame of reference, reflecting what it is like to *be* the person at that moment and making sure never to assume the position of being more expert than the client about the client's experience. The therapist conveys to clients that they are the best judges of their own reality. This is a very important active ingredient of client-centered therapy because the process provides an experience which is viewed as an antidote to one of the clients' major psychological problems—not trusting their own experience because of learned conditions of worth.

Gestalt therapy is also discovery oriented, with the belief that it is only client discoveries that lead to changes in their view of themselves or the world. In client-centered therapy, with its greater emphasis on following the client's inner track, discovery occurs in the context of self-directed search. In the Gestalt approach however, the therapist both leads and follows. The therapist is, therefore, more directive and influencing, creating experiments in order to help clients discover aspects of their experience, sharing hunches about what may be occurring, and teaching the client about specific interruptive and avoidance processes. Gestalt therapists train clients to become aware both of their experience and of how they interfere with their experience, and the therapists direct them to attend to sensations, nonverbal expressions, and interruptive processes.

In addition, many Gestalt therapists may, at times, confront, frustrate, or challenge blocks or interruptions of experience. Their primary emphasis, however, is on supporting clients in discovering for themselves what it is that they are experiencing and in getting in touch with what they feel and need. The ultimate belief in Gestalt therapy is that clients must discover the truth for themselves from their own internal experience and that truth or insight cannot be provided by the therapist. The therapist does, however, facilitate the process by setting experiments that enable clients to discover their own truths.

In Gestalt therapy, awareness is regarded as the royal road to cure, with awareness knowable only by the client. In this regard, clients are clearly viewed as experts on their own experience. However, a Gestalt therapist makes observations about clients' process, particularly on non-verbal aspects of client expression, and thus, to some degree, the Gestalt therapist views clients as not having full access to, and not being fully expert on, their experience. Although Gestalt therapists emphasize that awareness is curative in itself, they also believe that conflict between aspects of experience can interfere with functioning and that a confrontation between these different aspects of experience, if suitably facilitated, is important in the therapeutic process. In order to achieve conflict resolution, the Gestalt therapist does not always remain nondirective, but may directly encourage or instruct clients to actively express certain emotions or attitudes and may offer opinions or hunches about what the client is experiencing.

The existential position is less clear in its position regarding discovery in the process of therapy. The theoretical base of European existentialists such as Boss (1963) and Binswanger (1963) led them to emphasize that meaning lies in phenomena themselves and that even if the meaning is not seen at first, it can be discovered and brought to light. Thus, their view of the unconscious is that it is potentially accessible to awareness without having to be interpreted from an external agent or vantage point.

In the process of therapy, existentialists use a combination of discovery, interpretation, and confrontation. They challenge and interpret obstacles to choice and action, often confronting and challenging people to turn their wishes into willed action. They confront the blocks, but value clients' finding their own directions and setting their own goals. They clearly see individuals as aware, self-reflective beings and respect consciousness as being at the apex of humanness. Existential therapists do not probe for latent intents, but believe in the centrality of phenomenological understanding. They attempt to avoid making hypotheses or inferences and try to allow phenomena to present themselves on their own terms (Boss, 1963).

In the actual conduct of therapy, the situation is more complicated. On the one hand, existential therapists assume that each person's experience of self and the world is unique, and thus knowledge of any experience, with its own special flavor, must come from the client rather than being imposed by the therapist. It is the client's own goals and choices that are addressed. In another sense, however, existential therapists view the anxiety aroused by awareness of "ultimate concerns" such as death, freedom, isolation, and meaninglessness, as leading to defense mechanisms such as repression, distortion, or avoidance. It is these kinds of "avoidances" that are often directly challenged by the therapist.

The humanistic view of people being able to discover for themselves their own authentic inner experience, endorsed by the three approaches in the manner just described, is often strongly criticized from many perspectives. Critics view the idea that one can know one's own experience and be transparent to oneself as placing too strong a value on each person's inner uniqueness as well as placing too much faith in the validity of a person's self-awareness.

Dynamically oriented therapists believe that awareness reveals only the tip of the iceberg and that much behavior is unconsciously determined, and therefore awareness may need to be interpreted from a frame of reference external to the client. Hermeneuticists, on the other hand, hold that all meaning construction is an interpretive process and that there is, therefore, no essential truth for the client to discover (Sass, 1988).

In response to the unconscious motivation critique, the humanist position does not claim that there is no unconscious processing of information, but subscribes to a view of a cognitive rather than a dynamic unconscious. The key difference is that in a cognitive–affective schematic processing view, the unconscious does not directly motivate behavior, but rather influences perception and construal. Much of whatever is unconscious is simply not currently in awareness and can be made aware by attentional focusing.

With regard to the complex issue of the possibility of knowing oneself, although humanists would not deny the complexity and constructive nature of the creation of meaning, they believe that there *is* an experiential reality for each person and that awareness of this reality can be progressively approximated. Although there may be no single truth that can be attained, there will be many perspectives that would *not* fit the experiential data, and only a few, and perhaps only one, will provide a good fit. We know our world through our bodily felt experience (Gendlin, 1962; Lakoff, 1987; Johnson, 1987). Once one accurately symbolizes bodily experience (for example, that one feels tense or afraid or angry), one can construct a variety of meanings from this. But symbolizing one's tension as calmness, one's experience of fear as grief, or one's anger as joy would be inherently inaccurate. People are seen as being able to determine the right paths for themselves from an intensive process of discovery, leading to an inner sense of certitude. Thus, although the person is always constructing the meaning of the experience by a synthesizing process, the elements of the synthesis have an experiential validity, and can be more or less accurately symbolized.

2. The actualizing tendency involving growth, self-determination, and choice. Rogers' belief in a fundamental human motivation toward growth—toward developing autonomy, seeking new experience, and developing one's own potentialities—is central in understanding the process in Rogerian therapy. Rogers, like other humanistic theorists, took a teleological position, viewing human beings as influenced by a vision of the future rather than being directed wholly by the experiences of the past. There is assumed to be a strong motivation toward becoming what one truly can become, but it does not lead Rogerians to push the client to confront the future and make choices. Rather, the therapist's focus is on enabling clients to turn inward, to get in touch with their own *present* organismic experience, and to value it as a trustworthy guide, rather than having their perceptions and feelings screened by their learned criteria of worth. Under these conditions the person can and will make choices that will lead to growth. This conception gives the whole process of therapy a particular flavor. The emphasis is on process rather than on choosing goals, and it is not viewed primarily as a struggle against opposing forces, but as something that can be achieved under the right conditions. The therapeutic conditions of empathy, unconditional prizing, and genuineness are viewed as being sufficient to release and foster the actualizing tendency.

The client-centered therapist is almost never confrontative. The assumption is that the inherent strength of the actualizing tendency, if the person can learn to trust it, will lead in directions that will be growth producing and inherently satisfying for the person. The therapist is very active in fostering inward experiential search, but not in judging what is best for this person.

There is one further process issue related to growth that needs to be discussed, and that is the approach to dealing with conflict in therapy. In the formal statement of his theory of therapy, personality, and interpersonal relationships (1959), Rogers advanced a model in which there was an almost inevitable conflict between the person's inherent tendency to move toward growth, autonomy, and development of his or her full potential and the opposing need to maintain a concept of self, learned from early experience with parents and others. Feeling or behaving in ways inconsistent with one's learned self-concept was assumed to generate anxiety and, thus, to limit the extent to which the person could follow the authentic actualizing tendency. In practice, however, Rogers and other client-centered therapists do not focus on this conflict. The assumption is that in an atmosphere of true empathy and nonjudgmental prizing, clients will be able to let go of their learned conditions of worth and be guided by their own actualizing tendency toward growth and autonomy.

Perls also believed in an actualizing tendency, drawing on Goldstein's (1939) view that the individual's search for ways to maintain and enhance the self is never ending. To the Gestalt therapist, self-actualization becomes possible when people fully identify with themselves as growing, changing organisms and clearly discriminate their feelings and needs. Perls particularly emphasized self-regulation, which is seen as a natural or organismic tendency. Effective self-regulation depends on discriminating feelings and needs by means of sensory awareness. This leads to awareness of intuitive appraisals of either what is good for the person and should be assimilated, or of what is bad and should be rejected. The assumption is that the healthy organism "knows" what is good for it. This organismic wisdom works by a spontaneous emergence of needs to guide action.

Life is the process of a need arising and being satisfied and another need emerging and being satisfied. The figure–background Gestalt formation and destruction process is used to describe the process. A dominant need emerges as figure from a background that claims attention, is satisfied, and fades into the background again, and a compelling new need emerges into the foreground.

Pathology or dysfunction occurs when this need-satisfaction process is interrupted. The cycle is viewed as consisting of four major stages: awareness, excitement, action, and contact. In the cycle, *awareness* of inner or outer stimuli leads to the mobilization of *excitement* which provides an *action* tendency. Finally, action leads to *contact* and need satisfaction. Much of the focus in therapy is on becoming aware of different points at which the cycle is interrupted. Thus the emergence of a clear need can be blocked at the initial sensation stages by dulled sensation and poor awareness of inner or outer stimuli. Therapeutic work, then, involves helping people become more aware of sensation or experience. Blocking at the arousal or excitement stage results from dampening or disavowal of emotional experience. Therapeutic work at this stage focuses on increasing awareness of muscular constriction and clients' other methods of suppressing emotional experience.

At the action stage, need satisfaction is seen as being interrupted by introjected attitudes and values which create a split between wants and 'shoulds' in the personality. Two-chair dialogues are used at this point to resolve the split (Greenberg, 1979). Finally, interruption can occur at the completion stage by the person not experiencing the satisfaction of the need and completion of the cycle. At this stage, awareness is again implemented to help the person become aware of the experience of satisfaction and how one may be preventing it.

Thus, the Gestalt perspective focuses clients' attention on aspects of any situation in which they are involved for which they are responsible and ultimately, the therapists help them to recognize their choice in being involved in the situation. That is, awareness is seen as leading to choice, thus allowing the person to choose how to behave. The emphasis in Gestalt therapy on self-determination and independence led initially to an over-emphasis on self-sufficiency and to an underemphasis on interdependence. More recently, Gestalt therapists have proposed "self-support" as more desirable than "self-sufficiency." If one is self-supportive, one can ask for what one needs and thereby maintain a sense of both autonomy and connectedness.

Existential therapists, although viewing life as purposive and the organism as active in choosing its own destiny, do not explicitly posit a growth tendency. No essence precedes existence; rather, people determine themselves. However, some kind of growth principle can be discerned in the writings of existentialist therapists. Frankl (1963), for example, proposes a "will to meaning," and May and Yalom (1984) suggest that the therapist cannot create engagement or wishing but the desire to engage life is always there.

The existentialists tend to be more future oriented, seeing the person as striving toward and being motivated by goals and ideals. They believe in *possibility* in the sense of potentiality, ability, or capacity. The person exists as a bundle of possibilities for relating to the world, and, at any time, a particular possibility is carried out. In addition, human beings have the capacity for *understanding* that they have possibilities and, therefore, are also aware if they fail to carry them out. Each individual has to choose which possibilities will be carried out and which will not, and the person is viewed as responsible for this choice. In this way, therapy is focused on having people make the choice of which potentialities to carry out.

In understanding how people confront the choices in their lives, conflict is a primary concept for existential therapists. There is an inevitable conflict between the individual and the "givens" of existence, the ultimate concerns such as finiteness, freedom, isolation, and meaninglessness (May, 1977; Yalom, 1981). It is the anxiety generated by the person's awareness of these ultimate concerns that is considered to lead to defense mechanisms which block the person's capacity for making authentic choices. The crucial difference between this conflict model and that of Freud is that in the Freudian model it is repressed instinctual drives that lead to anxiety and thus to defense mechanisms; while for the existentialists, it is the *awareness* of the ultimate concerns that leads to anxiety and defenses (May & Yalom, 1989; Yalom, 1981). Therapy focuses predominantly on dealing with the ultimate concerns.

In the existential approach, freedom is the central issue, with will and choice being the major constituents of freedom. The goal of therapy is to increase persons' freedom to notice where and in what domains they are unfree and then to confront the obstacles to freedom. Therapists work to free people to be engaged, to open up, and be free to relate to whatever happens to them. Rather than asking "why," the existential therapist asks "why not," thus encouraging clients to confront their own blocks and enabling them to turn wishing into willing.

3. *Fostering the construction of new meaning.* Client-centered therapy, with its focus on the reflection of feelings and inner meanings, engages the client in a process of experiential search which involves attending to, differentiating, and integrating an inner referent in order to construct new meanings. Experiential symbolization, in which one moves from an inner felt referent to symbolizing the experience in words is a key process in client-centered and experiential therapy (Gendlin, 1962; 1984). The process, emphasized by both Rogers and Gendlin, involves the client's explicating the subtle nuances associated with tacit meanings. The clients engage thereby in an experiential search, a type of "inner tasting" process, in order to symbolize accurately their own reactions and feelings.

In the Gestalt process the emphasis is more on intensifying experience or heightening awareness so that a clear emotion and attendant need emerge. There is far less focus in therapy on the work of conceptually symbolizing for oneself the meaning of experience and more emphasis on having an intense experience of what one is talking about. In fact, the Polsters (1973) suggest that meaning is reflexive and that if one has a vivid experience, meaning automatically flows from the experience. Thus, in the Gestalt approach, construction of meaning is viewed as a perceptual awareness process rather than a conceptual process. The world is organized into particular figure–background configurations and the organization of figure in relation to ground provides meaning. Clients, after a vivid experience, are often asked to sit quietly by themselves rather than engage with others or talk about their experience. The solitude is suggested in order to allow clients to absorb the experience and create their own meaning from it, in order not to impose meaning on the client.

In existential therapy, meaning and its creation is a central goal of therapy. The type of meaning pursued is often about more ultimate, even philosophical, concerns about life. Ultimately, it is the meaningfulness of being human that is explored in therapy, and this leads to concerns with universals at the heart of existence, such as time, death, anxiety over mortality, awareness of the future, and guilt at not fulfilling one's possibilities. The human being is, as Sartre put it, condemned to freedom (Sartre, 1943/1956), and each individual has to confront one's own freedom and responsibility. In addition, individuals in therapy need to deal with isolation and the wish to belong and how to find meaning in a meaningless world (Yalom, 1981). In existential therapy, anxiety over ultimate concerns is thus at the center of personality and psychotherapy.

4. *Person-centeredness: The therapeutic relationship.* The process dimension in therapy that most clearly involves the humanistic principle of person-centeredness is the relationship established between the two participants. The humanistic approaches all dispute the claim that the relationship between the client and the therapist can be reduced to an unconscious repetition of previous attachments. Rather, they propose that a real relationship is developed between the participants and that this real relationship provides a new interpersonal experience for the client.

Rogers always viewed the relationship in therapy as the primary agent of change. Clients' experience of the therapist's genuine and unconditional empathic prizing is viewed as freeing them from the "conditions of worth" that have been assimilated from early experiences with parents and others (Rogers, 1959). Rogers assumed that, in an atmosphere of noncontingent caring, the client can get in touch with and acknowledge feelings and other inner experiences that are organismically experienced, even though they are inconsistent with the learned self-concept. Rogers' view of the therapist's participation in this relationship changed somewhat over the years, and he described therapists as being freer to express some of their own feelings in his later writings. Nevertheless, the emphasis has always been on the belief in the centrality of a relationship that is *real* as opposed to a transference relationship. And there is never an attempt to use confrontation as a therapeutic tool.

The relationship conditions of personal genuineness and empathic prizing enable clients to express and explore their moment-to-moment experience as they describe issues, events, and frustrations in their daily lives. The therapist's empathic reflections of the most poignant feelings and other inner experiences enable the client to explore these inner experiences more deeply and to get in contact with aspects that have never before been fully expressed to others or even to themselves. The therapist's clear, nonjudgmental caring reduces clients' interpersonal anxiety, enabling them to tolerate their own intrapersonal anxiety as they explore more and more deeply. Thus the relationship is not only a primary change agent in itself, but it establishes a climate allowing inner awareness in which clients can engage in the exploratory process of experiential search.

Perls himself did not emphasize the role of the relationship in therapy, although Buber's I–Thou relationship was offered as the model of relating for Gestalt therapy. In Buber's view, the therapist relates with immediacy and is fully present to the other, letting the other in on his or her own inner experience. The genuine dialogue is mutual and nonexploitive with both participants caring about each other's side of the dialogue. Buber (1957) sees the I–Thou relationship as a genuine meeting between two people in which both openly respect the essential humanity of the other. Healing is viewed as occurring in the meeting. Therefore, the relationship is an active change agent in Gestalt therapy. In practice, Perls was more involved in demonstrating the basic Gestalt principles through active interventions than in relating over time to his client's concerns. Thus his practice diverged somewhat from his theory. However, some branches of the Gestalt approach (Yontef, 1969), work predominantly with the I–Thou, here and now, contact between the client and therapist.

True contact is the major principle of relating in the Gestalt approach. Essentially, contact means that the client is fully present and engaged in a congruent fashion in whatever is occurring at the moment. When that contact with the self or therapist is interrupted by the client, the therapist attempts to bring this disengagement to the client's awareness by inquiring about what happened at the point of interruption. Gestalt therapists believe that ultimately it is only in the context of an authentic relationship that the uniqueness of the individual can be truly recognized. So the therapist strives for the genuine contact of a true encounter. How this is done technically is not fully prescribed other than to stress that the therapist needs to be authentic. Authenticity, however, does not mean belaboring clients with self-disclosure or honesty without consideration of their needs or personal readiness.

Existentialists consider that a *real* relationship between client and therapist is a crucial ingredient of therapy. The relationship is difficult to define because it is an essential kind of *being* in the therapy. May has emphasized "presence" on the part of the therapist, who must be fully present and strive for an authentic human encounter with the client.

Psychotherapy then, is first and foremost a unique form of being together, in which "being-with" the client is an essential ingredient (Craig, 1986; Moustakas, 1986). For May and Yalom it is a very direct, nonformal relationship of equals in which first names are used, and therapists are free to share their own feelings. They view this real, authentic encounter as a change agent in itself. The experience of the relationship is an example of a kind of intimacy from which the client can learn how fulfilling it is to be cared about (Yalom, 1981).

The nature of the authentic relationship is, however, very different from the client-centered relationship. The therapist is often confrontational and sometimes interpretive, but it is important to note that it is not the person's own basic goals that are confronted. These are recognized and respected. It is the blocks and avoidances and other client-perceived obstacles to these goals that are challenged and interpreted. The therapist's emphasis is on whatever stops the person from achieving these goals. Frankl (1963) and other existential therapists, however, sometimes challenge even the client's expressed goals from the position of the expert.

RECENT DECADES

The humanistic approaches have clearly had a substantial impact on the practice of psychotherapy and counseling, as well as related fields such as education and group work. Humanistic approaches have also been influential in less obvious ways, such as the assimilation of the Rogerian conditions of empathy, positive regard, and genuineness into other orientations.

During the last two decades, however, the humanistic psychotherapy approaches have become increasingly separated from mainstream theoretical psychology, especially in North America. The separation from theoretical psychology has been true for the whole humanistic psychology movement. In his article "The Crisis of Humanistic Psychology," Giorgi (1987) vividly described this split and discussed some dilemmas it presents.

There seem to be a number of interrelated causes for the decreasing contact between humanistic theories of therapy and mainstream psychology. One of the more obvious ones has been the overenthusiastic, uncritical adoption of some humanist approaches during the "counter-culture" era of the 1960s and early 1970s. Scholars have turned away from the "faddishness." In *Psychology and Humanism*, Smith (1982) mentioned that the Saybrook conference of 1964—at which the concept of a "third force" in psychology was seriously discussed—was attended by the influential personality psychologists Gordon Allport, Henry Murray, Gardner Murphy, and George Kelly, among others. These pioneers in the psychology of personality, who had been moving toward the third force, later dropped out of the movement, dissatisfied by the direction in which it seemed to be moving.

Humanistic ideals clearly fit well with many of the positive goals of the counterculture movement, such as freedom and individuality. Unfortunately, many of the techniques of the humanist therapies were used indiscriminately in a wide variety of "consciousness raising" contexts as "quick fixes" without firm grounding in humanistic therapy theory and practice. Thus the approaches came to be viewed as unprofessional and even potentially dangerous. Encounter groups, cathartic expression, body work, and the like were often viewed with suspicion.

Another factor that may have played a role in the separation of humanistic psychotherapy from mainstream psychology was the shortage of available academic positions in the 1970s. The few available positions were less likely to be offered to individuals perceived as espousing anti-intellectual or "intuitive" approaches or as less likely to conduct standard empirical research.

During Rogers' years at Ohio State, the University of Chicago, and the University of Wisconsin, courses and internships in client-centered therapy were popular options in graduate psychology programs, but this has not been true in recent years. The Gestalt approach customarily has been taught in freestanding training institutes in the United States and Canada. For instance, in 1982 there were more than 50 Gestalt training institutes in the United States and Canada, but the approach has been poorly represented in universities, with few academic psychologists trained in, or truly knowledgeable about, Gestalt theory. Although there have been a number of books written on different existentialist approaches, there are no established training centers, and, as May and Yalom have mentioned (1984), few existential therapists have received formal training in the approach.

The most striking and potentially serious trend has been the small amount of research in humanistic approaches in recent years. For many years research was an extremely important part of the client-centered tradition. Although Rogers has been viewed as the most "radical" (Tageson, 1982) of the humanistic therapists, he was the least radical in his continuing belief in the need for empirical research on psychotherapy. In fact, in 1956 he received the APA Distinguished Scientific Contribution Award, along with Wolfgang Kohler and Kenneth Spence.

Rogers viewed research as consisting of two very different stages. The first involved intensive listening to taped therapy sessions conducted by himself or by colleagues, trying to get a feel for the "process strands" (Rogers, 1958) that characterized positive change and its facilitation, and then letting hypotheses emerge from this experience. Then the second stage was testing of the hypotheses by the usual positivist methods (Rogers & Dymond, 1954; Rogers, Gendlin et al., 1967). However, he attributed the weak impact of humanistic theory on mainstream psychology to the lack of significant, humanistically oriented research (Rogers, 1985).

With the exception of the program of studies by Greenberg and his associates on the process of change and the effects of particular Gestalt interventions (Daldrup, Beutler, Engle, & Greenberg, 1988; Greenberg, 1984; Greenberg & Dompierre, 1981; Greenberg & Webster, 1982) and a few studies that showed improved self-actualization and self-concept following Gestalt group experiences (Foulds & Hannigan, 1976), there has been little research on Gestalt approaches.

Within the Existential therapy approach, there has been little empirical research. Although research from the Duquesne University group (Giorgi, 1970; Van Kaam, 1966) focused on topics relevant to humanistic psychology as method, there has been little specific application to therapy. One obstacle to research with existential therapy has been the tremendous variability among the different theorists in their manner of conducting therapy, as well as variability even within the different systems. Primary commitment is to "the person" rather than to technique or to research (May & Yalom, 1984).

Intellectual work relevant to the humanistic therapeutic approaches has taken place in Europe in recent years. At the first annual conference on client-centered and experiential therapy, held at Leuven, Belgium, in 1988, there was surprise and excitement among North Americans at the amount of theory development and research occurring in Belgium, Germany, and the Netherlands. Many of the papers presented at the conference have been published in English in a volume edited by Lietaer, Rombauts, and Van Balen (1990). And in his recommendations for the future, Lietaer (1990) stressed the need for more research.

New Developments

One interesting, recent theoretical development evident at this conference is the emergence of two strands within the client-centered approach. One is the more strongly person-centered perspective that considers the Rogerian relationship conditions of empathy, unconditional positive regard, and genuineness, experienced by the client, as the sole change agents (Brodley, 1990; Bozarth, 1990). In the other, more process-oriented view that has been emerging, the centrality of the relationship conditions is still respected, but process-directive components have been added. The therapist's participation is seen as guiding clients toward particular modes of processing in the session in order to facilitate the exploration of their own experience (Greenberg, Rice, Rennie, & Toukmanian, 1991; Rice & Greenberg, 1991). Within the more experiential framework, Gendlin's (1962, 1984) focusing interventions and Rice's (1974, 1984) systematic, evocative, unfolding procedure have each proposed a series of different steps in which the client can engage in the process of discovery and change.

Also, Mahrer (1986), in his version of experiential therapy, proposes certain key steps in which the client needs to engage. Greenberg and his colleagues have proposed and studied a number of process-experiential tasks derived from the gestalt approach, which can be implemented within the framework of a client-centered relationship.

Interestingly, Gestalt therapy is also undergoing a change, one in which the I–Thou relationship is being emphasized more than the use of technique. In addition, a growing interest in self psychology and in the importance of empathy in providing a healing environment has become manifest (Yontef, 1981). The development of a more process-directive aspect within the client-centered framework and a more relational perspective in Gestalt approaches represents an interesting expansion of each tradition and a possible trend toward integration by incorporation and adaptation of the strengths of different humanistic approaches.

May, Yalom, and Bugental remain the most prolific writers in North America on existential approaches. Although no specific new trends appear to be emerging in existential therapy, many of the insights of the existential theorists are being absorbed into integrative practice.

FUTURE DEVELOPMENTS

In looking toward the future of the humanistic therapies, it seems clear that some important developments are already taking place. The anti-intellectual trend seems to have decreased, and clearly with the aging of the academic population, we hope that many more academic openings will be available for younger psychologists interested in theory and research in psychotherapy.

Even more important have been some of the advances in theoretical psychology that seem to fit increasingly well with the basic assumptions and methods of humanistic therapies. The rigid constriction of strict behaviorism has been moderated or replaced by cognitive psychology with its focus on awareness and such human functions as perception, memory, and problem solving. Initially, information processing approaches in experimental psychology appeared equally constricting to the humanist. As Neisser (1976) and others have suggested, the underlying model for these functions was the computer metaphor, in which the person was ignored. Much research involved laboratory studies focusing on separate functions out of context. "Lacking in ecological validity, indifferent to culture, even missing some of the main features of perception and memory as they occur in ordinary life, psychology could become a narrow and uninteresting specialized field" (Neisser, 1976, p. 7). He recommended that we need to study cognitive functions as they occur in the real world, in the context of natural, purposeful activity, which sounds similar to Kierkegaard's lament that ignoring the person as "subject" and viewing him or her only as "object" resulted in losing the real, existing person. Modern constructivist approaches to cognition appear, however, to be far more compatible with the awareness-oriented, humanistic approaches to therapy.

During the last two decades, an approach to understanding human cognitive processes such as perception, memory, and problem solving, occurring in realistic contexts has evolved, resulting in human information-processing models that assign a central role to the constructive functions of mental activity (Craik & Lockhart, 1972; Johnson-Laird, 1988; Mahoney & Gabriel, 1987; Neisser, 1976). This development in psychology, stressing the concept of schema, holds promise for a reuniting of humanistic approaches with mainstream psychology.

A second recent development that is likely to help reintegrate humanistic approaches into mainstream psychology is the focus on emotion, which, until recently, had been sorely neglected in the study of human information processing. In the last decade, a number of schematic and network theories of emotion have been proposed (Bower, 1981; Lang, 1984; Leventhal, 1984), and various attempts at investigating and explaining emotional behavior have appeared (Leventhal & Tomarken, 1986). Drawing on these theoretical developments and on the practice of emotionally focused therapy, Greenberg and Safran (1987) have outlined an integrative model of emotional processing for use in therapy. Emotion is viewed as an action tendency which provides people with biologically adaptive feedback about their responses to situations. When emotion is understood as providing action potentials, it becomes a crucial source of information for therapy. The humanistic therapies focus on awareness of feeling but lack an adequate theory to explain its importance. Developments such as these in emotion theory provide a framework for understanding humanistic therapies and further provide for the possibility of an integration of humanistic approaches back into the mainstream of psychology.

One of the most important areas for both theory and research is the focus on intensive observation of the change processes in the session, followed by descriptive measurement and understanding of these processes. (Rice & Greenberg, 1984). These events could become the building blocks for understanding therapeutic change. The process analysis of change points would be one move toward understanding. Another extremely important approach to understanding is the use of "interpersonal process recall" (Elliott, 1986; Rennie, 1990) in order to have the client identify times in the therapy session when something interesting happened and to obtain from the clients' perspective a sense of what these incidents felt like and what seemed to be happening for them.

CONCLUSION

Since their emergence during the 1940s, the humanistic psychotherapies have had periods of striking growth and periods of relative neglect and separation from theory and research in psychology. The humanistic approaches all share the belief in several fundamental aspects of humanness. They all emphasize individuals' awareness of their own subjective experience. They all posit a healthy striving toward choice and potential growth, and all share a belief in the importance of a genuine human relationship as a healing agent in itself. These fundamental humanistic insights into psychotherapy and healthy functioning are too important to lose. In the expanding perspectives that are emerging in psychology, attempting to capture more fully the complexities of real human functioning in the world, we are optimistic that humanistic psychotherapy will both contribute to and be enriched by future developments in theory and research.

REFERENCES

Binswanger, L. (1963). *Being in the world* (J. Needleman, Trans.). New York: Basic Books. (Originally published 1951)

Boss, M. (1963). *Psychoanalysis and daseinanalysis* (L. B. Lefebre, Trans.). New York: Basic Books. (Originally published 1957)

Bower, G. H. (1981). Mood and memory. *American Psychologist, 31,* 129–148.

Bozarth, J. D. (1990). The essence of client-centered therapy. In G. Lietaer, J. Rombauts, & R. Van Balen (Eds.), *Client-centered and experiential psychotherapy in the nineties* (pp. 59–64). Leuven, Belgium: Leuven University Press.

Brodley, B. T. (1990). Client-centered therapy and experiential: Two different therapies. In G. Lietaer, J. Rombauts, & R. Van Balen (Eds.), *Client-centered and experiential psychotherapy in the nineties* (pp. 87–108). Leuven, Belgium: Leuven University Press.

Buber, M. (1957). *I and thou.* New York: Charles Scribners Sons.

Bugental, J. F. T. (Ed.). (1967). *Challenges of humanistic psychology.* New York: McGraw-Hill.

Buhler, C. (1967). Human life as a whole as a central subject of humanistic psychology. In J. F. T. Bugental (Ed.), *Challenges of humanistic psychology* (pp. 140–165). New York: McGraw-Hill.

Craig, E. (1986). Sanctuary and presence: An existential view of the therapist's contribution. *The Humanistic Psychologist, 1,* 22–28.

Craik, F. I. M., & Lockhart, R. S. (1972). Levels of processing: A framework for memory research. *Journal of Verbal Learning and Verbal Behavior, 11,* 671–684.

Daldrup, R., Beutler, L., Engle, D., & Greenberg, L. (1988). *Focused expressive psychotherapy.* New York: Guilford.

Elliott, R. (1986). Interpersonal process recall (IPR) as a process research method. In L. S. Greenberg & W. M. Pinsof (Eds.), *The psychotherapeutic process* (pp. 503–528). New York: Guilford.

Fagan, J., & Shepherd, I.L. (Eds.). (1970). *Gestalt therapy now.* Palo Alto, CA: Science and Behaviour Books.

Foulds, M., & Hannigan, M. (1976). Effects of a Gestalt Marathon workshop on measures of self actualization: A replication and follow-up study. *Journal of Consulting Psychology, 23,* 60–65.

Frankl, V. (1963). *Man's search for meaning: An introduction to logotherapy.* New York: Pocket Books.

Friedlander, S. (1918). *Schopferische indifferenz* [Creative indifference]. Munich, Germany: Georg Muller.

Gendlin, E. (1962). *Experiencing and the creation of meaning.* New York: Free Press.

Gendlin, E. (1984). *Focusing* (Rev. ed.). New York: Bantam Books.

Giorgi, A. (1970). *Psychology as a human science: A phenomenologically based approach.* New York: Harper & Row.

Giorgi, A. (1987). The crisis of humanistic psychology. *The Humanistic Psychologist, 15,* 5–20.

Goldstein, K. (1939). *The organism: A holistic approach derived from pathological data in man.* New York: American Book.

Greenberg, L. S. (1979). Resolving splits: Use of the two-chair technique. *Psychotherapy: Theory, Research & Practice, 16,* 316–324.

Greenberg, L. S. (1984). A task-analysis of intrapersonal conflict resolution. In L. N. Rice & L. S. Greenberg (Eds.), *Patterns of change* (pp. 67–123). New York: Guilford.

Greenberg, L. S., & Dompierre, L. (1981). Differential effects of the two-chair dialogue and empathic reflections at a conflict marker. *Journal of Counseling Psychology, 28,* 288–294.

Greenberg, L. S., Rice, L. N., Rennie, D. L., & Toukmanian, S. G. (1991). York University psychotherapy research program. In L. E. Beutler & M. Crago (Eds.), *Psychotherapy research: An international review of programmatic studies* (pp. 175–181). Washington, DC: American Psychological Association.

Greenberg, L. S., & Safran, J. D. (1987). *Emotion in psychotherapy.* New York: Guilford.

Greenberg, L. S., & Webster, M. (1982). Resolving decisional conflict by means of two-chair dialogue and empathic reflection at a split in counseling. *Journal of Counseling Psychology, 29,* 468–477.

Haigh, G. (1949). Defensive behavior in client-centered therapy. *Journal of Consulting Psychology*, 13, 181–189.

Heidegger, M. (1962). *Being and time* (J. Macquarrie & E. S. Robinson, Trans.). New York: Harper and Row. (Originally published 1949)

Husserl, E. (1977). *Phenomenological psychology* (J. Scanlon, Trans.). The Hague: Nijhoff. (Original work published 1925)

Jaspers, K. (1963). *General psychopathology*. Chicago: University of Chicago Press.

Johnson, M. (1987). *The body in the mind: The bodily basis of meanings, imagination, and reason*. Chicago: University of Chicago Press.

Johnson-Laird, P. N. (1988). *The computer and the mind: An introduction to cognitive science*. Cambridge: Harvard University.

Jourard, S. M. (1968) *Disclosing man to himself*. Princeton, NJ: Van Nostrand.

Kierkegaard, S. (1954). *Fear and trembling and the sickness unto death* (W. Lowrie, Trans.) Garden City, NY: Doubleday Anchor. (Originally published 1843)

Koffka, K. (1935). *Principles of Gestalt psychology*. New York: Harcourt, Brace.

Kohler, W. (1959). *Gestalt psychology*. New York: New American Library of World Literature.

Lang, P. J. (1984). The cognitive psychophysiology of emotion: Fear and anxiety. In A. J. Tuma & J. D. Maser (Eds.), *Anxiety and the anxiety disorders* (pp. 130–170). Hillsdale, NJ: Erlbaum.

Leventhal, H. (1984). A perceptual-motor theory of emotion. In L. Berkowitz (Ed.), *Advances in experimental social psychology* (pp. 117–182). New York: Academic.

Leventhal, H. & Tomarken, R. (1986). Emotion: Today's problems. *Annual Review of Psychology*, 37, 565–610.

Lewin, K. (1951). *Field theory in social science: Selected theoretical papers*. New York: Harper & Row.

Lietaer, G. (1990). The client-centered approach after the Wisconsin project: A personal view on its evolution. In G. Lietaer, J. Rombauts, & R. Van Balen (Eds.), *Client-centered and experiential psychotherapy in the nineties* (pp. 19–46). Leuven, Belgium: Leuven University Press.

Lietaer, G., Rombauts, J., & Van Balen, R. (Eds.). (1990). *Client-centered and experiential psychotherapy in the nineties*. Leuven, Belgium: Leuven University Press.

Mahoney, M., & Gabriel, T. (1987). Psychotherapy and the cognitive sciences. *Journal of Cognitive Psychotherapy: An International Quarterly*, 1, 39–59.

Mahrer, A. (1986). *Therapeutic experiencing: The process of change*. New York: Morton.

Marcel, S. (1951). *Homo Viator: Introduction to a metaphysic of hope*. Chicago: Henry Regnery.

Maslow, A. H. (1968). *Toward a psychology of being* (2nd ed.). Princeton, NJ: Van Nostrand.

Maslow, A. H. (1970). *Motivation and personality* (Rev. ed.). New York: Harper & Row.

May, R. (Ed.). (1961). *Existential psychology*. New York: Random House.

May, R. (1977). *The meaning of anxiety* (Rev. ed.). New York: Norton.

May, R., Angel, E., & Ellenberger, H. (Eds.). (1958). *Existence: A new dimension in psychiatry and psychology*. New York: Basic Books.

May, R., & Yalom, I. (1984). Existential therapy. In R. J. Corsini (Ed.), *Current psychotherapies* (3rd ed.; pp. 354–391). Itaska, IL: Peacock.

May, R., & Yalom, I. (1989). Existential therapy. In R. J. Corsini & D. Wedding (Eds.), *Current psychotherapies* (4th ed.; pp. 363–402). Itaska, IL: Peacock.

Moustakas, C. (1986). Being in, being for, and being with. *The Humanistic Psychologist, 14*, 100–104.

McWaters, B. (Ed.). (1977). *Humanistic perspective: Current trends in psychology*. Monterey, CA: Brooks/Cole.

Neisser, U. (1976). *Cognition and reality: Principles and implications of cognitive psychology*. New York: Freeman.

Perls, F. S. (1947). *Ego, hunger, and aggression*. London: Allen & Unwin.

Perls, F. S. (1969). *Gestalt therapy verbatim*. Moab, UT: Real People Press.

Perls, F. S. (1973). *The Gestalt approach and eyewitness to therapy*. New York: Science and Behavior Books.

Perls, F. S., Hefferline, R. F., & Goodman, P. (1951). *Gestalt therapy*. New York: Julian Press.

Polster, E., & Polster, M. (1973). *Gestalt therapy integrated*. New York: Bruner/Mazel.

Raskin, N. J. (1949). An analysis of six parallel studies of the therapeutic process. *Journal of Consulting Psychology, 13*, 206–220.

Raskin, N. J., & Rogers, C. R. (1989). Person-centered therapy. In R. J. Corsini & D. Wedding (Eds.), *Current psychotherapies* (4th ed.; pp. 155–194). Itaska, IL: Peacock.

Rennie, D. (1990). Toward a representation of the client's experience of the therapy hour. In G. Lietaer, J. Rombauts, & R. Van Balen (Eds.), *Client-centered and experiential psychotherapy in the nineties* (pp. 152–172). Leuven, Belgium: Leuven University Press.

Rice, L. N. (1974). The evocative function of the therapist. In D. A. Wexler & L. N. Rice (Eds.), *Innovations in client-centered therapy* (pp. 282–302). New York: Wiley.

Rice, L. N. (1984). Client tasks in client-centered therapy. In R. F. Levant & J. M. Shlein (Eds.), *Client-centered therapy and the person-centered approach* (pp. 182–202). New York: Praeger.

Rice, L. N., & Greenberg, L. S. (Eds.). (1984). *Patterns of change: Intensive analysis of psychotherapy process*. New York: Guilford.

Rice, L. N., & Greenberg, L. S. (1991). Two affective change events in client-centered therapy. In J. D. Safran & L. S. Greenberg (Eds.), *Emotion, psychotherapy and change* (pp. 197–226). New York: Guilford.

Rogers, C. R. (1942). *Counseling and psychotherapy* Boston: Houghton Mifflin.

Rogers, C. R. (1951). *Client-centered therapy*. Boston: Houghton Mifflin.

Rogers, C. R. (1957). The necessary and sufficient conditions for therapeutic personality change. *Journal of Consulting Psychology, 21*, 95–103.

Rogers, C. R. (1958). A process conception of psychotherapy. *American Psychologist, 13*, 142–149.

Rogers, C. R. (1959). A theory of therapy, personality, and interpersonal relationships, as developed in the client-centered framework. In S. Koch (Ed.), *Psychology: A study of science; formulations of the person and the social context* (pp. 184–256). New York: McGraw-Hill.

Rogers, C. R. (1961). *On becoming a person*. Boston: Houghton Mifflin.

Rogers, C. R. (1980). *A way of being*. Boston: Houghton Mifflin.

Rogers, C. R. (1985). Toward a more human science of the person. *Journal of Humanistic Psychology, 25*, 7–24.

Rogers, C. R., & Dymond, R. F. (Eds.). (1954). *Psychotherapy and personality change*. Chicago: University of Chicago Press.

Rogers, C. R., Gendlin, G. T., Kiesler, D. V., & Truax, C. (Eds.). (1967). *The therapeutic relationship and its impact: A study of schizophrenics*. Madison: University of Wisconsin Press.

Rogers, C. R., & Skinner, B. F. (1956). Some issues concerning the control of human behavior. *Science, 124*, 1057–1066.

Sartre, J. P. (1956). *Being and nothingness*. (H. Barnes, Trans.). New York: Philosophical Library. (Originally published 1943)

Sass, L. A. (1988). Humanism, hermeneutics, and the concept of the human subject. In S. B. Messer, L. A. Sass, & R. L. Wolfolk (Eds.), *Hermeneutics and psychological theory* (pp. 222–271). New Brunswick, NJ: Rutgers University Press.

Seeman, J. A. (1949). A study of the process of nondirective therapy. *Journal of Consulting Psychology, 13*, 157–169.

Smith, M. B. (1982). Psychology and humanism. *Journal of Humanistic Psychology, 22*, 44–55.

Smuts, J. (1926). *Holism and evolution*. New York: Macmillan.

Sutich, A. J., & Vich, M. (Eds.). (1969). *Readings in humanistic psychology*. New York: Free Press.

Tageson, W. C. (1982). *Humanistic psychology: A synthesis*. Homewood, IL.: Dorsey Press.

VanKaam, A. (1966). *Existential foundations of psychology*. Pittsburgh: Duquesne University Press.

Wertheimer, M. (1945). *Productive thinking*. New York: Harper & Brothers.

Yalom, I. (1981). *Existential psychotherapy*. New York: Basic Books.

Yontef, G. (1969). *A review of the practice of Gestalt therapy.* Los Angeles: Trident Books.

Yontef, G. (1981). The future of Gestalt therapy: A symposium with I. Perls, M. Polster, J. Zinker, & M. V. Miller. *The Gestalt Journal, 4,* 7–11.

Yontef, G. M., & Simkin, J. S. (1989). Gestalt therapy. In R. J. Corsini & D. Wedding (Eds.), *Current psychotherapies* (4th ed.; pp. 323–361). Itaska, IL.: Peacock.

7

DEVELOPMENT OF FAMILY SYSTEMS THEORY

PHILIP J. GUERIN, JR. AND DAVID R. CHABOT

The family has long been recognized as an important factor in the physical, spiritual, and emotional well-being of its individual members. Research and c' nical work on emotional dysfunction in families dates back at least as far as Freud. Thinking about the family in relation to the emotional well-being of its individual members appears to have gone through a series of evolving, yet somewhat repetitive, cycles. In the years when emotional problems were viewed as a by-product of neurological or moral failings within the individual, the family was seen as the victim of its dysfunctional member. As psychological theories moved toward explanations based on deficiencies in nurturing, families came to be viewed as the malignant victimizers.

Today an interesting dichotomy exists. On the one hand, advances in biological psychiatry and neuropsychology have focused on the family as a genetic source of schizophrenia and depression while the family is simultaneously viewed as being traumatized by the stress of living with the disorder in a family member. On the other hand, self-help movements such as the Adult Children of Alcoholics, in essence, have framed every conceivable malady as a by-product of the victimizing experience of having a parent with a dysfunction such as alcoholism.

From a clinical perspective, the family has long been included in dynamic formulations and treatment planning. Freud's published cases exhibited an interest in and appreciation of family factors. The phobic problems of Little Hans (Freud, 1909/1959) were treated by Freud's coaching of the father, a method not too discrepant from what a modern-day family therapist might use. Alfred Adler's investment in the Child Guidance Movement (1931), with its emphasis on the importance of family in the diagnosis and treatment of emotional problems in children, is another example of focus on the importance of the family. Nathan Ackerman (1937), one of the founders of the modern family therapy movement, demonstrated his interest in the emotional power within the family early in his career, when he studied the impact of the Great Depression on coal miners' families. Minuchin (1987) called attention to the work of child psychiatrist Fred Allen, who interviewed families as part of the clinical evaluations of children at the Philadelphia Child Guidance Clinic as early as 1924.

In the early 1950s, small groups of professionals in the mental health field, working separately and in disparate places, began a movement to make the "family unit" a primary focus of research and clinical intervention. From 1950 to 1990, family psychotherapy has evolved from the research studies of families with a schizophrenic member, and the child psychiatrists' attempts to incorporate family members into the treatment of troubled children and adolescents, to a full-fledged division of the mental health field.

There are many histories of family therapy already in existence. Among those most useful to the student and practitioner are Guerin (1976), Kaslow (1980), Goldenberg and Goldenberg (1985), and Nichols (1984). Each of these is a historical survey of those people whose interactions played a significant part in the development of the family therapy movement. This chapter, in contrast, attempts to focus more on the development of the theory of family psychotherapy than on the oral history of the family therapy movement.

In a paper on comparative approaches to family therapy, Guerin (1979) proposed the first theory-based classification of family therapy. He distinguished between those practitioners who based their clinical methodology on traditional psychoanalytic theory and those who attempted to formulate a systems-based conceptual framework. If this classification were reorganized using the metaphor of the family tree, there would be two major theoretical sources or trunks from which most of what we know as family psychotherapy

derived its concepts. One, the communication context trunk was represented in the early 1950s by the Bateson Project. Psychoanalysis, the other
major source, has multiple and diverse branches, ranging from technique-
oriented, minimal use of the family in support of individual therapy, through
group therapy, and on to multigenerational systems therapy. There is a
further division within the psychoanalytic trunk into those who became
interested in the family via studies of schizophrenia, those whose interest
stemmed from working with the families of less severely disturbed children
and adolescents, and those who went on to use humanistic psychology as
their primary framework. For purposes of using a family tree metaphor to
clarify the development of the concepts and clinical methodology of family
psychotherapy, the authors of this chapter have tracked the developmental
history of four key groups of theorists.

1. The communications trunk began with the Bateson Project, continued with the work of Jackson and Haley, and
extended to the brief therapy project of Watzlawick, Weakland, and Fisch. The Ackerman Brief Therapy Project and
the work of the Milan Associates also branched from this
trunk.

2. The psychoanalytic multigenerational systems trunk included the work of Bowen who developed his theory at
the Menninger Clinic, at the National Institute of Mental
Health (NIMH), and at Georgetown University; we will
describe also the contributions of his major professional
descendants. This section of the chapter will also include
a view of the work of Wynne, who succeeded Bowen at
NIMH, and Nagy and Framo, two other prominent mul-
tigenerationalists. All of these clinicians began by studying
schizophrenics and moved on to work with a less dysfunctional population.

3. The experiential systems trunk included the work of Whitaker and Satir, both of whom worked independently of
one another but shared common humanistic frameworks
overlaying primarily psychoanalytic beginnings.

4. The structural family therapy theorists began their work in
the child guidance movement. It included the significant
contributions of Nathan Ackerman, a child psychiatrist,
and continues to the present in the work of Salvadore
Minuchin, another child psychiatrist.

5. Behavioral family therapy, which is viewed by the authors
as outside family systems theory, is commented on briefly.

COMMUNICATION THEORISTS

Gregory Bateson

The Bateson Project began in California in the early 1950s. Its goal was to demonstrate how the communication patterns in families with a schizophrenic member made logical sense if one understood the rules of the relationship context or culture in which the symptoms were produced.

Gregory Bateson, an anthropologist and student of animal behavior, evolution, ecology, and cybernetics, brought a knowledge and understanding of context, culture, and the structure and function of communications to the work. He was far more interested in the science of communication and in theory building than in therapy. Bateson derived his model for studying communication from the theory of logical types (Whitehead & Russell, 1910). He began his work in psychiatry through a collaboration on the social matrix of psychiatry with Jurgen Ruesh (Ruesh & Bateson, 1951) at the Langley Porter Institute in California.

In 1952, he received a grant from the Rockefeller Foundation to study the nature of communications. The following year, Bateson was joined by Jay Haley, who had just received his MA in Communications from Stanford. Also joining the project at that time was John Weakland, a chemical engineer interested in cultural anthropology. In 1954, Bateson was awarded a grant from the Macy Foundation to study patterns of communication in schizophrenics. It was at this point that Don Jackson, a psychiatrist, joined the project as clinical consultant and supervisor of psychotherapy. Jackson had been supervised as a psychiatric resident by Harry Stack Sullivan and brought with him an understanding of the interpersonal dimension of psychopathology. Bateson, Haley, Weakland, and Jackson then undertook the study of communication in families with a schizophrenic member.

In the early phases of their work, staff members interviewed individual hospitalized patients at the Palo Alto Veterans Hospital. From these interviews and the staff collaboration that followed, the concept of the *double bind* began to emerge. It was based on several preliminary ideas having to do with notions of family homeostasis and multiple, often-contradictory levels of communication in relationships. In certain relationship situations, an overt and explicit meaning of a communication is contradicted by the implicit or "metamessage." Hoffman (1981) cites an excellent example of such a bind when one person in a relationship expresses to the other the command "dominate me." Clearly the person addressed can only dominate by obeying the command, thereby complying—which is the opposite of domination. Hoffman points out that the only way one can respond to such a request is to point out the impossibility, make a joke, or leave the field. However, families often block all attempts to make the implicit explicit, or attempts to clarify contradictory messages even in a joking way, and often, especially in the case of children, it is not possible to leave. When these conditions exist, a potentially malignant context has been established that can foster significant symptomatic behavior.

The six basic characteristics of the double bind may be summarized as follows: (Nichols, 1984)

1. Two or more persons are involved in an important relationship.

2. The relationship is a repeated experience.

3. A primary negative injunction is given, such as "do not do or I will punish you."

4. A second injunction is given that conflicts with the first, but at a more abstract level. This injunction is also enforced by a perceived threat. This second injunction is often nonverbal and frequently involves one parent's negating the injunction of the other.

5. A third-level negative injunction exists that prohibits escape from the field while also demanding a response.

6. Once the victim is conditioned to perceive the world in terms of a double bind, the necessity for every condition to be present disappears and almost any part is enough to precipitate panic or rage.

The concept of the double bind (Bateson, Jackson, Haley, & Weakland, 1956), like many ideas before and since, did little to alter the outcome of the treatment of schizophrenia. However, it did mark the beginning formulation of a series of interconnected ideas that form the basis for what is known today as strategic family therapy.

The Bateson group continued to refine the ideas underlying the double bind concept and to obtain a more expansive understanding of communication and the role it plays in family dysfunction. Each of the members of this group went on to make significant further contributions to the field.

Jackson's continued refinement of the double bind concept manifested itself in his work on creating a *therapeutic double bind*. The therapeutic double bind is an intervention wherein the therapist attempts to double bind the patient or family. Whereas the double bind is defined as containing the preceding six characteristics, the *therapeutic* double bind is more loosely constructed. This technique prescribes the symptom and is based on an attempt to turn the natural oppositional forces within the family system onto the pathological process under investigation, thereby neutralizing the pathological forces and eliminating the symptoms.

Nichols (1984) provided an example of Haley's early use of the therapeutic double bind to explain the idea. In this example, Haley recommended hearing voices to a schizophrenic patient. If the patient responds by hearing voices, he is being compliant with the therapist. If he fails to hear voices, he must give up the claim to being crazy. In reality then, the therapeutic double bind was the earliest beginning of what has come to be known as paradoxical injunction.

In the *Pragmatics of Human Communications* (Watzlawick, Beavin, & Jackson, 1967), Jackson and his coauthors provide an enriched version of this treatment strategy used with individuals and couples. Hoffman (1981) described two examples of Jackson's work. In one example, a woman with intractable headaches was told her headaches cannot be cured, but that the therapist will direct his attention toward helping her live with her disability. In another case, a couple with a chief complaint of constant arguing and bickering was informed by the therapist that their bickering is a sign of emotional involvement, and, therefore, this apparent continuous conflict only proves how much they love each other. From these two examples, we again see the genesis of the techniques of paradoxical intervention and reframing as practiced in the strategic model of family therapy today.

Jackson founded the Mental Research Institute (MRI) in 1959 and invited Virginia Satir to join him. Although MRI and the Bateson group occupied the same building for three years, there was no formal link between them. MRI had a clinical treatment bent, while the Bateson Project continued its interest in theory. Although the Bateson Project failed to produce a cohesive, comprehensive theory, it did produce a series of interconnected ideas and develop a diverse and multitalented group of clinicians and researchers, many of whom continue to contribute to the field.

At the time of Jackson's death in 1968, he had already published two outstanding books, *The Pragmatics of Human Communication*, with Watzlawick and Beavin (Watzlawick, Beavin, & Jackson, 1967) and *The Mirages of Marriage*, with William Lederer (Lederer & Jackson, 1968). As the psychiatrist in the Bateson group, Jackson perhaps felt the most pressure to convert the ideas and observations of the project into clinical methods useful in working with families. His early death in a field dominated by personalities has, to some degree, obscured his contributions.

Jackson shared Bateson's belief that behavior and communication are synonymous. Like Bowen, he borrowed some of his ideas from biology. Jackson's concept of family homeostasis described how families, like other organic systems, resist change, and how, when challenged, these relationship systems strive to maintain the status quo even at considerable emotional cost to one of their members. He was among the first to observe the organizing function that a child's behavioral symptoms provide for camouflaging covert parental conflict.

Thus far we have considered, in a very abbreviated way, some of the ideas of Bateson, the anthropologist, and Jackson, the psychiatrist. Their influence on generations of descendants was strong but often not fully acknowledged or documented. Of the persons who played a part in the Bateson Project, those most directly influential on the clinical behavior of succeeding generations of family therapists have been Haley and Satir. In the remainder of this section, we describe the contributions of Haley and John Weakland who, with his collaborator Richard Fisch, developed one of the first family-based systems of brief therapy. The work of the Ackerman Brief Therapy Group of Hoffman, Papp, and Silverstein and the work of the Milan Associates will also be considered. Satir's work is summarized in the section about the experiential group.

Jay Haley

Jay Haley emerged from his work on the Bateson project with a twofold conviction that clinical symptoms were a by-product of context and that a power struggle for control was the process behind the behavior patterns in a relationship. A logical consequence of this thinking is the view that a symptom in a person is a strategy for obtaining control within a relationship. The covert nature of the process, its being out of everyone's awareness, and the function it serves for the symptomatic individual and for the family homeostasis, make direct confrontation of the symptom and attempts to make the process explicit fruitless endeavors. Therefore, counterstrategies that bypass or confuse the homeostatic mechanism, creating chaos and allowing for spontaneous reorganization, represent the required clinical methodology. From the beginning of his work, Haley paid close attention to hierarchical structure as it relates to power distribution and advocated therapeutic strategies to defeat entrenched patterns of dysfunctional behavior.

Haley's work with Minuchin and Montalvo helped fashion *structural family therapy*, a method described in detail later in the chapter. Early training videotapes from the structural family therapy project at the Philadelphia Child Guidance Clinic demonstrate clearly Haley's penchant for creating strategies intended to bypass the naturally occurring power struggle between the family and the therapist. Haley believed in exerting influence from an "outsider" position. For example, he formulated intervention plans and supervised their clinical implementation by trainees but did not do clinical work himself.

In the 1970s, Haley left Philadelphia and established his own Family Institute in Washington, DC. From then on his focus shifted away from structural family therapy concepts to the pursuit of a more refined understanding of hierarchy, power, and strategic intervention.

At this time he revealed his affiliation with Milton Erickson, a psychiatrist with a penchant for the creative use of hypnotic techniques that, in some vaguely understood way, seemed to move his patients (mostly individuals) from dysfunction to function. Erickson too "encouraged resistance" as a technique to bypass direct confrontation with symptoms. Haley's derived methods of strategic problem-oriented therapy based on Erickson's methods were presented in his 1976 publication, *Problem-Solving Therapy*. The method came along at a time when long-term psychotherapy was beginning to be viewed by some as inefficient and even abusive to the patient's finances, as well as self-serving for the therapist. By the 1980s, strategic family therapy clearly began to dominate the field of family therapy.

Two predominant characteristics of Haley's methods are his firm belief in the uselessness of direct educational techniques and his corollary commitment never to explain himself but rather to operate covertly upon the processes of power within a relationship. This second concept is perhaps most easily demonstrated with Haley's approach to the concept of triangulation.

Often family therapists will try to deal with triangulation by educating families about how they are caught in the process. Haley rarely ever mentions the concept, but in his training tapes and publications, he frequently operates in a strategic fashion that relies strongly on the concept. For example, in his training tape, "The Boy with the Dog Phobia," he uses the task of the father's buying a dog to confront the father's and son's anxiety about dogs, while simultaneously closing the distance between them. An important side effect of this combined structural and strategic intervention (illustrating the notion of triangulation) is a surfacing of the mother's depression and the covert conflict between the parents.

Since the founding of the Washington Family Institute, Haley's major collaborator has been his wife, Cloé Madanes, who has become a respected clinician and author in her own right. Haley and Madanes have fashioned a clinical method for working strategically with severe marital dysfunction, called ordeal therapy (Haley, 1984). In this method a strategic ordeal is fashioned that provides, on the one hand, a ritual of penance and absolution, and on the other, a bond formed between two people who experience an ordeal together. A classic illustration of this method describes the formation of a strategic ordeal for a couple with a long-term sadomasochistic, physically abusive relationship. They were instructed to shave their heads completely, then to take the hair and bury it in a particular place several hours from their home. As a follow-up they were instructed to make repeated visits on a regular schedule to the burial ground. This strategic ritual represented not only a shared ordeal but also a symbolic burying of their old dysfunctional patterns of relating, thus freeing them to activate the potential of numerous unused, more-functional patterns in the relationship.

Haley has been critical of traditional psychiatric methods and family therapy methods that fail to take into consideration his basic premises about the importance of power and control. In our opinion, there is nothing incompatible in the structural–strategic approach of Haley and the multigenerational system approaches of Bowen and his descendants. One of the places this becomes evident is in the discussion of the systemic therapy of the Milan group which follows.

Milan Associates

The Milan Associates consisted in its early years of four principals (Selvini-Palazoli, Boscolo, Cecchin, and Prata). Maria Selvini-Palazoli, a psychoanalytically trained psychiatrist, began in the late 1960s to treat anorexic children and their families. She moved on to work with schizophrenic families from a systems perspective. The Milan Associates model is an interesting method, with fibers from the work of the Bateson Project, the strategic therapists, Minuchin, Jackson, and Bowen all woven together into a highly creative fabric. Their method stresses the importance of defining the family's rules—an approach similar to that of Jackson in his early work. In addition it pays specific attention to Haley's emphasis on power and control.

The frequency of the sessions—once a month—is often described as making this method "long brief" therapy. This same frequency has been used by Bowen in his work with individuals, families and multiple family groups since the early 1960s. Bowen, whose methods will be dealt with in detail later in the chapter, has long believed that less frequent sessions were more beneficial to the process of change than once-a-week meetings, which, he felt, fostered dependency between therapist and family and impeded change. Another similarity between the Milan method and Bowen's work has to do with what the Milan group calls "circular questioning." This technique is described as framing every question so as to address differences in perceptions about events and relationships. Any study of Bowen's clinical interviews on videotape demonstrates a very similar technique that Bowen and his descendants have termed the "process question."

Both the Milan model and the work of Bowen emphasize "therapist neutrality," although each approaches the problem from the opposite position. In the Milan model, the therapist tries to remain allied with all family members and thereby attempts to avoid getting caught up in family alliances and coalitions. If opposites are the same, then being allied with all family members is the same as being allied with none of them, which is Bowen's therapeutic stance.

The Milan Associates also include techniques of paradox and counterparadox closely related to the work of Bateson, Jackson, and Weakland on the therapeutic double bind. In this country, the Milan Associates' methods were built upon and modified by Papp, Silverstein, and Hoffman, who worked at the Ackerman Institute and fashioned an American version of the Milan method.

Watzlawick, Weakland, and Fisch

Weakland, one of the original principals in the Bateson Project, collaborated with Jackson on an article that centered on theory, technique, and outcome results of conjoint family therapy used with schizophrenic families (Jackson & Weakland, 1961). In 1967, Watzlawick wrote a book with Beavin and Jackson entitled the *Pragmatics of Human Communications*. In this text they explained what they developed—a "calculus" of human communications—that is, a series of principles about communication and metacommunication. They defined disturbed behavior as a communicative reaction to a particular family relationship situation rather than evidence of a disease of the individual mind.

After Jackson's death in 1968, Watzlawick and Weakland were joined by a psychiatrist, Richard Fisch, to form the Brief Therapy Project at the Mental Research Institute. The core of their work became an attempt to define clearly the clinical problem as presented and then carefully link this problem to the repetitive sequences of behavior observable in the relationships surrounding the problem. It was their assumption, derived from the concept of family homeostasis, that these repetitive cycles of relationship behavior, while intended as a solution, end up reinforcing the problem.

For example, in an adolescent-focused family, the problem might be defined as the son's underachieving in school for 10 years. The mother is involved in an intense effort to structure her son's activities and improve his study habits. The more she pressures, the less he does. The strategic therapist, after investigating the "problem" in great detail, suggests the following approach: The mother is told that her interest and caring for her son are admirable, and the only reason it isn't working is that she hasn't done it with quite enough intensity and should increase her efforts. The therapist explains that the reason this is needed is that her son, despite being a fine young man, is somewhat immature for his age and therefore, at present, is unable to assume responsibility for his school performance.

The mother and the son both develop oppositional responses to the intervention. The mother stops pressuring her son, reasoning that she already has too much responsibility and does not have any more time and that he has to grow up some day. The son is incensed that the therapist has labeled him as immature and proceeds to prove him wrong by accepting responsibility for structuring his time better and being less passive about his school performance. With this result, the strategic therapist has completed the work of therapy.

In their book, the three investigators emphasized both the pathological and potentially therapeutic aspects of paradox in human communications and the value of the therapeutic double bind. They demonstrated no interest in triangles or transmission of anxiety, in the son's developmental issues, or in the fact that the mother's father is seriously ill. These factors are not included in the problem definition or in the treatment plan unless presented as a problem by the family to the therapist.

In 1974, Watzlawick, Weakland, and Fisch collaborated on another text that concentrated on "how problems arise, are perpetuated in some instances and resolved in others." It was an outgrowth of the work of the three in MRI's Brief Therapy Center. Problem formation, problem resolution, first-order change, second-order change, and reframing are among the important issues addressed. A summary of the principles of first-order and second-order change reveals the importance of this text.

1. First-order change occurs within a given system which itself remains unchanged. It is a logical, commonsense solution to a problem. If Johnny is failing in school, mother must supervise his school work more closely.

2. Second-order change is applied when first-order change, the logical, commonsense solution, is clearly demonstrated to be at the center of an escalating problem. In other words, use second-order change when first-order change is making the problem worse. The mother's hovering in the previous clinical example is the escalating problem.

3. Second-order change based on reframing and paradox flies in the face of logic and common sense and usually is perceived as weird and unexpected. The second-order change

in our example is the defining of mother's escalating be-havior as desirable and as required in greater amounts to produce the desired result.

4. The use of second-order change lifts the situation out of the trap created by the self-reflexive, commonsense solu-tion and places it in a different frame. The entrapping, repetitive cycle of mother's pressure and son's responsive passivity is replaced by a new sequence of behaviors which eliminates the symptoms.

Over the first 40 years of the family therapy movement, what began as Bateson's interest in culture, communication, and the mysteries of schiz-ophrenia has become a clinical methodology for dealing with a wide spec-trum of psychological disturbances within the individual and in relation-ships. The clinical methodology rests on a loosely connected set of concepts about the nature and patterns of communication (i.e., the double bind), about family homeostasis as the natural tendency for the perpetuation of dysfunction in relationship systems, and about triangles as structural expres-sions of the relationship patterns that maintain a dysfunctional equilibrium. These concepts are then linked under two global assumptions that determine the form of the specific clinical methodology to be applied to a particular situation. The first assumption is that individuals or persons in relationships in dysfunction are emotionally caught in a reactive process in such a way that they are unable to free themselves. Increasing efforts to break free only increase friction, frustration, and anxiety; eventually symptoms appear. The second assumption is that in each individual and in each relationship system, there is a naturally occurring oppositional reaction, that is, resistance to attempts at change.

The clinical methodology that arises from these concepts and as-sumptions is at once simple and complex. The therapist must devise a strategy that neutralizes or bypasses the naturally occurring "resistance" mechanisms. If this task is accomplished, a corrective program may be introduced that has a better chance of being successful. The system will thereby lower friction and tension and alleviate symptoms. Once symptoms have been relieved, the system and its individual members are free to resume their individual and collective developmental pathways.

Interventions traditionally developed in this method are more of an art form than other more linear models. The therapy as an art form aspect of this model is reminiscent of the healing methods of the shaman, a particularly interesting twist when viewed in the light of Bateson's begin-nings as an anthropologist.

PSYCHOANALYTIC MULTIGENERATIONAL THEORISTS

The next group of theorists to be considered is implicitly defined by several common features in their work. Each of them maintained a multigenerational focus—that is, their definition of the family unit included a minimum of three generations. In addition, they all began to study family relationships through an interest in schizophrenia and started their work with psychoanalytic theory as their conceptual base. The group can be divided into four subcategories: object relations and multigenerational themes (Nagy and Framo), a group focus, (Bell and Wynne), the Bowen group, and the experientialists (Whitaker and Satir). In this section, we will deal with each of them in turn, particularly emphasizing the work of Bowen and his descendants.

Object Relations

As mentioned earlier, Freudian theory has long been influential in understanding the impact of family relationships on the psychological functioning of its individual members. In the early days of family therapy, attempts to formulate a separate theory for "family" were resisted by the core of the psychoanalytic community. Family therapy was viewed as a technique similar to group work which had successfully adapted traditional Freudian theory to its clinical methods. Clinical work with families, from the perspective of the analytic community, was indicated in two situations. One situation was when family members needed education about the ways in which they were potentially defeating the transferential therapy of an individual. The other family situation was one that needed opening up of communications around tension-filled issues within the family. Initially there was considerable skepticism about seeing families because of its possible effects upon the transference, but eventually, a group of therapists still committed to psychoanalytic theory began to experiment with such methods. Those in the analytic community who maintained both the allegiance to analytic theory and an interest in clinical interventions with families moved toward the model of object relations theory as their primary conceptual base.

The theoretical underpinnings of the object relations approach to family therapy rest on the work of Klein and Fairbairn. The Kleinian concept of *good breast/bad breast* refers to infantile ambivalence about the mother derived from the developmental experiences of nurturance and deprivation. Fairbairn developed the idea of the existence of internalized relationship structures. Contained within these proposed structures were partial objects, that is, a portion of the ego and the affect associated with the relationship. The external object was perceived as either all good, all bad, or both, in alternating cycles, which Fairbairn referred to as *splitting.* It was Fairbairn's belief that when the splitting process was not resolved, the individual's ability to objectify relationships was impaired. This concept of splitting has been developed further in the notion of *projective identification.*

Projective identification is defined as a process whereby an individual first projects onto another person certain denied behaviors or characteristics of his or her own personality. Then in the relationship interaction the person behaves in ways that either provoke such behaviors from the other or reacts as if the other possesses these characteristics, which thereby reinforces the projective perception. A simple example from a marital relationship would be when a wife with an internalized judgmental and negative image of herself projects the perception of a harsh, critical, unloving person onto her husband and then behaves in ways that predictably bring forth critical and withholding behaviors on his part.

Family therapists working with these concepts as a theoretical base can track this type of interactional process within the session and interpret the object relation forces that are driving the conflict. These methods closely resemble those used early on in psychoanalytically based family therapy, wherein the existence of naturally occurring "transferences" in the family was hypothesized and interpreted clinically to explain relationship conflict and dysfunction.

Nagy and Framo

Ivan Nagy, a psychiatrist, and James Framo, a psychologist, edited a volume titled *The Intensive Family Therapy of Schizophrenia* (Boszormenyi-Nagy & Framo, 1965) that brought together papers from most of the leading family researchers at that time. Framo adopted Fairbairn's object relations theory as the basis for his work. In his practice, this position led to his inviting significant extended family members into the sessions, especially when dealing with marital conflict. Framo also expended considerable effort in his attempts at integrating his work with that of others whose theoretical stance derived primarily from psychoanalytic theory.

Nagy also maintained his primarily psychoanalytic orientation when he changed from the study of schizophrenia to study the issue of loyalty in families, particularly as it influences coalitions and alliances over multiple generations. This work is described in his book *Invisible Loyalties* written with his colleague Geraldine Spark (Boszormenyi-Nagy & Spark, 1973).

In this text Nagy offers the concept of the "family ledger," an invisible ledger of multigenerational accounts of obligations, debts, and events perceived as relationship atrocities. These firmly entrenched emotional wounds require retribution of some kind over the generations. Hoffman (1981) designates forgiveness as the key to therapy. She also draws attention to the aspects of Nagy's method that resemble the reframing techniques of strategic therapy. Hoffman reasons that if a problem's genesis is reframed in terms of old wounds and loyalties, family members have a face-saving mechanism that allows them to give up their present-day conflict.

Group Focus

The family as a naturally occurring group was a logical unit of focus for those who had developed and refined methods of working with artificially formed therapeutic groups. One of the earliest pioneers in the family therapy movement, John Bell (1961) maintained his theoretical group orientation in his work with families (1975). Lyman Wynne, director of the Family Division at NIMH for many years, is another prominent family therapist who uses a group model.

John Bell

Bell began his clinical work with families in the early 1950s. His conceptual framework is based on the work of Bion and the Tavistock Group. His efforts to adapt group therapy principles and techniques to the family unit resulted in his formulation of seven stages in the work of family group therapy (1975).

These seven stages demonstrate clearly Bell's investment in traditional analytic and group theory. They include the "initiation," a feeling-out process between family and therapist in which the goals are defined and the therapeutic contract set. The initiation phase is followed by a period of "testing," in which the rules of the contract formed in the preceding stage are tested and, when necessary, are rewritten to fit more closely the reality of the clinical situation. The third stage is termed the "struggle for power." In this phase individuals and subgroup coalitions maneuver for power and influence within the process of the group. The next two phases consist of "settling on a common task" and working toward "completion of a common task." The working through of the first five stages culminates in the sixth stage, termed "achieving completion." In this stage, having dealt with the power struggles and coalitions, the group is ready to include all members in the task of developing a climate of mutual support as individual and relationship issues are discussed and worked out. This having been accomplished, the family group is ready to separate from the therapist and resume its "natural" developmental life. This seventh and final stage is logically termed "separation." Bell (1975) strongly believes in the importance of maintaining effective boundaries between the therapist and the family group.

Lyman Wynne

Lyman Wynne, who suceeded Murray Bowen as Director of the Family Division at NIMH in 1959, also came to the study of schizophrenia and the family with a psychoanalytic background. In addition, his approach to the family was primarily that of an analytically based group model developed at Tavistock Clinic. In his research on schizophrenic families, he developed two interlocking concepts that were mostly descriptive of the family as a group. These two concepts were "pseudomutuality" and the "rubber fence" phenomenon.

Pseudomutuality was the term used to describe a surface appearance of agreement and attachment among family members, while in reality, the family members were tightly locked into dysfunctional roles that did not permit individuation from the family or truly close relationships within it. Externally, however, particularly in public, the family was unpredictably impenetrable because of its seeming automatic ability to expand and contract in a reflexive fashion. An "outside" person, such as a therapist, seeking to engage family members, might feel a certain ease of entry into the family, only to be bounced out later, as if by a rubber fence, if certain unwritten rules were violated. These concepts describe phenomena present in varying degrees in families throughout the spectrum of dysfunction, but particularly in families with a schizophrenic member. Developed in a research program, the concepts have yet to be integrated into a more diverse and elaborate clinical model of family therapy.

The Bowen Group

Bowenian family systems therapy is a theoretical–clinical model that evolved directly from psychoanalytic principles and practice. It is the most comprehensive model of family systems theory in so far as it consists of a defined number of concepts with a corresponding clinical methodology closely linked with the theory. Murray Bowen, its originator and major contributor, began with an interest in studying the problem of schizophrenia, and brought to his study of the family extensive training in psychoanalysis, including 13 years of personal training analysis.

In the early years of the family therapy movement, many of the pioneers trod lightly in the area of theory. Bowen was the exception to this rule, both in his emphasis on the primary importance of theory and in his belief that his observations and ideas could form the beginning of a new theory of human emotional functioning. He hoped his theory would be viewed as evolving from Freudian theory but as being clearly and distinctly different from it in its systems orientation.

Bowen (1978) believed that the task of the theorist was to find the smallest numbers of congruent concepts that could fit together and serve as a working blueprint for understanding that part of the human experience under observation. He repeatedly warned of the pitfalls of lowest common denominator eclecticism. Bowen dates the beginning of his theory to his clinical work with schizophrenia at the Menninger Clinic from 1946 to 1954. During this time he studied mothers and their schizophrenic offspring who lived together in small cottages on the Menninger campus. From this clinical research he was hoping to gain a better understanding of mother–child symbiosis. Observations from these studies led to the formation of his concept of differentiation. From the Menninger Clinic, Bowen moved to NIMH, where he formed a project to hospitalize and study whole families with a schizophrenic member. It was this project that expanded the concept of mother–child symbiosis to involve fathers and inevitably led to the Bowen concept of triangulation, described later in this section.

In 1959, Bowen left NIMH and went to Georgetown Medical School where he was a professor of psychiatry until his death in the fall of 1990. In his 31 years at Georgetown, Bowen refined his theory by applying it to less dysfunctional populations and by developing a clinical methodology that he could pass on to the psychiatric residents in training at Georgetown. As he developed his method of family psychotherapy, he saw the need for a corresponding method that would assist the psychotherapist in the development of his or her own personal autonomy. For this purpose, Bowen began to research and experiment with the emotional process within his own personal family system. The developing concepts of his theory were presented in two key papers in 1966 and 1976. A documentation of his "research" on his own family of origin was first presented at a national family therapy conference in 1967 and published in 1972.

In these articles, Bowen designates eight concepts as central to his theory: differentiation of self; triangles; nuclear family emotional system; family projection process; emotional cutoff; multigenerational transmission process; sibling position; and societal regression. The concepts of *differentiation* and *triangulation* form the core of Bowen's theoretical contribution.

Differentiation

Bowen's concept of differentiation consists of two component parts: emotional fusion within the dyad and differentiation of the individual. In his observations on mother–child symbiosis, Bowen recorded alternating cycles of closeness and distance within the mother–child dyad. He hypothesized that sequential cycles of separation anxiety and incorporation anxiety were the primary emotional forces driving these seemingly automatic and reactive relationship patterns. The very interdependent nature of the relationship between mother and child limited the potential for autonomous functioning in both of them. Their behaviors were determined by their anxious attachment to each other rather than by their own internal choices. They may be said to be emotionally fused to one another. On a structural level, this fusion denotes a blurring of appropriate personal boundaries.

On a process level, there is a contagious anxiety that entraps both members of the dyad, determining their behavior in relation to one another as well as their individual levels of emotional functioning. Anxiety in either the mother or child produces an automatic reflexive response in the other. These automatic emotional responses and behaviors describe the *fusion* (or lower) level of Bowen's proposed spectrum of emotional functioning.

The opposite profile is of a high functioning individual capable of emotional connection without being determined by the anxiety in an important other person or in the relationship. This differentiated self is capable of behaving in response to his or her own instinct and judgment guided by principles and opinions, even in the presence of considerable anxiety. This profile of autonomy represents differentiation, which is the opposite of fusion and sits at the higher end of Bowen's spectrum of emotional functioning.

Bowen developed a scale of differentiation that ranged from extreme fusion to the opposite, high differentiation, within the person. Higher scores indicated an increasing ability to withstand high levels of anxiety while continuing to be autonomous in life choices, including relationship behavior.

Bowen believed that in dysfunctional families each individual was caught in a reactive emotional process that determined his or her behavior. He further believed that if one individual could, by conscious effort, lower his or her anxiety and reactivity to the surrounding emotional forces, that person could get free of this dysfunctional process. Once even partially free, other potential pathways of behavior would become clear to the individual. These new pathways would be more determined by principles of function than by feelings or by the reactive search for emotional comfort and refuge.

If one person in the family could do this, others in the family would be afforded the chance to follow, and the functioning level of the entire relationship system would improve.

Bowen thought that if one individual in a family could get free of the entrapment of the reactive emotional process and begin a potential chain reaction of lowering anxiety throughout the relationship system, this would lead to certain therapeutic consequences. The main one is that a therapist who can remain emotionally free of a family's reactive emotional process can begin the aforementioned desirable chain reaction. How, then, does one train therapists to be capable of such a procedure? In response to this question, Bowen developed his method for training therapists to differentiate a self in their own families of origin. He began by doing it himself in his own family, publishing the results, and then challenging those he trained to follow suit. In a 1972 paper, Bowen spelled out his method in detail. Included in this method were four important steps.

1. *Know the facts about your family relationship system.* Bowen encouraged his trainees to construct comprehensive family diagrams in order to document the structural relationships among members of their family and to gather facts about the timing of important events such as deaths, births, and so forth, which he termed *nodal events.* He also taught the importance of including in the family diagram evidence of physical and emotional dysfunction, relationship conflicts, and emotional cut-offs, which he viewed as indicators of a family's level of emotional functioning.

2. *Become a better observer of your family and learn to control your own emotional reactivity to these people.* Bowen charged therapists-in-training with this central task to be accomplished on planned visits with key members from their family of origin.

3. *Detriangling self from emotional situations.* This part of the method entails developing an ability to stay nonreactive during periods of intense anxiety within one's own family system. To foster this process of "detriangling," Bowen encouraged those in training to visit their families of origin at times of predictably high tension, such as serious illness or imminent death of a key family member. During these visits the goal was to make contact with family members around an anxiety-ridden issue, to remain less emotionally reactive than other family members, and to not choose sides when competing influences and differences of opinions led to relationship conflict.

4. *Develop person-to-person relationships with as many family*

members as possible. This double-barreled axiom was aimed at fostering detriangulation and encouraging the reestablishment of relationship connections where cut-offs or potential cut-offs had previously existed.

From this consideration of the concept of differentiation and its application to the training of therapists, the complexity of the idea becomes obvious. One of the major difficulties in operationalizing the concept is that, by definition, differentiation represents an inborn psychological state inherited at birth from the emotional struggles of previous generations and only changeable to some small measure during an individual's lifetime.

Triangles

Bowen began his working model of the relationship triangle during the NIMH project after including fathers in the study. The interdependence observed in the mother–child dyad also appeared to be present in the relationships involving fathers. Initially, Bowen expressed the idea of an interdependent triad and compared it to a three legged stool, where the removal of one leg destroyed the essence of the stool. Beginning with his observation of the reactive emotional instability of the fusion-laden dyad, Bowen proposed that the transmission of the anxiety in the dyad to involve the most vulnerable other in the relationship system formed a potentially stabilizing but dysfunctional structure called a *triangle.* Considered by many to be the originator of the concept of triangulation, Bowen placed heavy emphasis on the relationship-process part of triangulation and little or none on its structural aspects. He focused instead on the potentially everchanging configurations of relationship triangles. These automatic shifts were driven by the reactive emotional process within the relationship system.

Bowen's method of therapy closely followed his conceptual framework. As a therapist he placed himself in contact with both members of a conflictual dyad and worked to remain emotionally neutral while spelling out the emotional process within the conflictual relationship by using a series of "process questions," such as "What about your wife's criticism upsets you the most?" Theoretically this was meant to induce a corrective emotional experience for the family members in conflict, allowing them to lower their anxiety and seek more functional pathways of relating to each other.

It should be noted that there is a distinction to be made between "triangles" as a relationship *structure,* and "triangulation" as a relationship *process.* A triangle is an abstract way of thinking about a structure in human relationships, and triangulation is the reactive emotional process that goes on within that triangle. In any relationship system, there are any number of potential triangles, and the emotional process of triangulation within the triangle can be either dormant or active in varying degrees at any moment in time.

The clinical description of a triangle is the way the three-way relationship looks at a given moment or the pattern to which it regularly returns after temporary realignments. For example, at the time a couple presents for treatment, the triangle with their son may have become relatively fixed so that the mother and the son are overly close and the father is in the distant, outsider position. This alignment may occasionally shift, so that there are times when either the mother or the son is in the outside position and the father has some closeness with his son or his wife, but then it shifts back to its usual structure.

Triangulation is the emotional process that goes on among the three people who make up the triangle. For example, in the triangle just described, the father might desire a connection with his son and resent his wife's monopoly of the boy's affections; the mother may be angry at the father's distance from her and compensate by substituting closeness with her son. The child, in turn, may resent his father's inattention and criticism and may move toward his mother but, at the same time, be anxious about his overly close relationship with her. As the emotional process of triangulation moves around the triangle, it can produce changes in its structure. For example, the father may try to reduce his loneliness by moving toward his son or his wife, or the son may try to avoid fusion with his mother by distancing toward his peers, causing his parents to draw together in their concern for him.

Thus, triangles can shift their structure at any time for a variety of reasons, and the process of triangulation has the potential for motion at any time. As changes do occur, demands are placed on the individuals and on the system to realign in a way that ensures the emotional comfort of the most powerful person and preserves the stability of the system. As Bowen (1978) pointed out, the most uncomfortable person in the triangle may try to lower his or her anxiety or emotional tension by moving toward a person or thing. If that effort is successful, another person becomes the uncomfortable one and will work to become more comfortable. Bowen's concept of the relationship triangle most clearly differentiated his family systems theory from other theories of human emotional functioning.

Bowen's Descendants

During his 31 years at Georgetown University, Bowen worked on the refinement of his theory and its clinical application with nonpsychotic families. During this time he was instrumental in the training of many psychiatrists. Among the most prominent and influential of these are Philip Guerin and Thomas Fogarty. Both were trained by Bowen during the 1960s, left Georgetown, and joined the Einstein Family Studies Section in New York where Zwerling and Ferber were assembling a faculty representative of the diversity of thinking and practice in the field of family therapy. While at Einstein, they trained Betty Carter, Monica McGoldrick, Ed Gordon, Eileen Pendagast, and Katherine Guerin. All of them, along with Peggy Papp, joined Guerin and Fogarty in 1973 to form the Center for Family Learning in New Rochelle, New York, the other major research and training facility for Bowenian theory and methods.

The work of Philip Guerin and Fogarty, Carter, McGoldrick, and Michael Kerr (Bowen's closest long-term associate at Georgetown) has been the most extensive and influential in the field at large. Similar to the descendants of the Bateson Group, the interconnections of these individuals is of interest in studying the development of Bowenian theory. Fogarty, Guerin, and Kerr were all psychiatric residents in the Georgetown program. Kerr remained at Georgetown as Bowen's closest associate and his theoretical contributions have been reflective of that close collaboration. Fogarty, although influenced by Bowen, was less wedded to the multigenerational model and most of his contributions to the theory have been confined to the nuclear family and the individual. Guerin adhered more closely to Bowen's emphasis on the importance of family of origin work than Fogarty, but was also influenced by Fogarty and the Einstein faculty, particularly Andrew Ferber and Albert Scheflen. Guerin's most important contributions to family theory are clarifications and elaborations of the concepts of both Bowen and Fogarty, as well as the specific application of the theory to the building of clinical models for the treatment of marital conflict and child- and adolescent-centered families. Carter and McGoldrick were trained by Guerin during his tenure as director of training at Einstein. As third generation descendants, Carter and McGoldrick have contributed to family theory in the areas of the family life cycle, as well as around the issues of ethnicity and feminism.

Fogarty and Guerin

Thomas Fogarty, like Bowen, began his work with a focus on the individual. Unlike Bowen, he paid more attention to the development of structural concepts and their clinical usefulness in therapy. Fogarty's concept of the individual is a highly structural one, which he termed the four-dimensional self, including the lateral dimension, the vertical dimension, the depth dimension, and the dimension of time (Fogarty, 1976a). The lateral dimension represented the interactive part of the individual, where movement toward and away from others is formed and operationalized. It is within this dimension that Fogarty developed his most widely known contribution, the notion of repetitive patterns of pursuit and distance with the corresponding concept of the emotional pursuer and the emotional distancer in the marital relationship.

Closely connected to the lateral dimension was the depth dimension wherein, Fogarty (1984) hypothesized, was stored the residue of an individual's emotions accumulated over time as a by-product of relationship experiences. He proposed a link of significant influence between this depth dimension and the lateral dimension of the individual. Of additional importance in this depth dimension is Fogarty's later focus on the importance of the existential state of emptiness to the process of developing an autonomous self. This intense feeling-level experience is the ultimate experience of the depth dimension.

The vertical dimension contained the occupational and professional potential and actualization of productivity of an individual. The time dimension had to do with the individual's experience of time, the way in times of stress he or she tended to develop future anxiety or ruminate on the failures and misfortunes of the past. In addition, the time dimension contained a person's basic rhythm and was linked to the lateral dimension's pursuit and distance. For example, an emotional pursuer's rhythm was observed to be erratic, varying between high speeds and dead stop, while the emotional distancer was observed to have a much more constant or steady rhythm.

Fogarty's goal in working with this structural model of the individual was to produce a functional emotional balance. The individual should be "centered," that is, in touch with and regulating the appropriate balance among each of the four dimensions of self in his or her life. For example, he or she should not be preoccupied with productivity and irresponsible in personal relationships. Drawing on this concept, Fogarty was the first to describe the relationship dance of emotional pursuit and distance in the marital relationship. This concept, more than any other of Fogarty's, has been incorporated into the work of most practicing family therapists.

Fogarty (1976b) also contributed extensively to the development of the concept of triangulation. Again, unlike Bowen, Fogarty focused on the structural aspect of triangulation especially as it related to the treatment planning. He was perhaps the first to focus on the structural aspects of child-centered triangles with his strategies of altering these structures by moving overinvolved mothers away from, and distant fathers in toward, the symptomatic child. Minuchin, in his structural family therapy, brought together this same type of structural alteration of triangles and combined it with creative strategic movement around the organizing symptom of the child, such as having lunch served in a therapy session with a family in which one of the children has an eating disorder.

Philip Guerin's theoretical contributions also began with the individual. While director of training at Einstein, he formed the first formal training groups for therapists who wished to study themselves in their families of origin. In this work, he focused on the development of the concept of an individual's adaptive level of functioning in order to operationalize the more fixed, innate aspects of differentiation. He drew a distinction between the automatic emotional responses of individuals that emanate from their innate level of differentiation and those more functional responses that can be fashioned over time by conscious effort on the part of individuals within the context of their relationships. The changes brought about by these conscious efforts can be measured by improved functioning in face of significant stress, especially in the categories of productivity, more functional relationship connectedness, and personal well being. Over long periods of time, these conscious effort changes may become automatic, thereby marking an increase in differentiation. In this way the concept of adaptive level of functioning is consistent with Bowen's concept of differentiation.

Guerin has also contributed an elaboration and further development of Fogarty's emotional pursuer and distancer concept into a paradigm termed "the interactional sequence." This sequence of behavior is central to the clinical methods entailed in his model of marital therapy (Guerin, Fay, Burden, & Kautto, 1987). In that model, as well as in his model for child- and adolescent-centered families, Guerin has proposed a typology of triangles which describes and categorizes the numerous potential triangles in any case of marital discord or child-centered dysfunction. The purpose of the typology is to foster more accurate and teachable (reproducible) methods of intervention.

Carter and McGoldrick's contributions to Bowenian theory have included an expansion of the concept of the genogram and important nodal events into a more developmental perspective. They proposed a "family life cycle" (Carter & McGoldrick, 1980) as a backdrop for understanding development of stress and its role in the production of relationship conflict and symptoms in an individual. In addition, McGoldrick, working with Pearce and Giordano, added the consideration of culture and ethnicity to the view of the "family relationship system." Carter, working with Papp, Silverstein, and Walters, focused on the importance of women's issues in the study of and clinical intervention with families.

In conclusion, it is of interest that Bowen's model consists of the multigenerational family unit as the context in which to study individuals and their relationship conflicts under the seige of intense anxiety. Fogarty and Guerin each focus on the individual, the dyad, and triangles. Kerr focuses on anxiety, and Carter and McGoldrick-Orfanidis on the impact of the contextual aspects of developmental stress, ethnicity, and feminism on the family system.

The Experientialists

Experiential family therapy is characterized by its emphasis on intuition, feelings, unconscious processes, and an atheoretical stance. The two major figures in this branch of the family therapy movement are Carl Whitaker (Whitaker & Keith, 1981) and Virginia Satir (1967). Both of them draw upon quite different epistemologies for their therapies, but they share a common set of experiential assumptions and techniques in their clinical work.

Carl Whitaker

Whitaker's approach to family therapy is pragmatic and atheoretical (to the point of being antitheoretical). He considers theory to be useful only for the beginning therapist. He believes that the real role of theory for the novice therapist is to control his or her anxiety about managing the clinical situation. Whitaker prefers to use the support of a cotherapist and a helpful supervisor to deal with these stresses rather than relying on theory.

The basic goal of therapy for Whitaker is to facilitate individual autonomy and a sense of belonging within the family. The emphasis is on the emotional experience, not conceptual understanding. Above all, the process of therapy is a very personal experience for the therapist.

Existential encounter is believed to be the most important aspect of the psychotherapeutic process for both the therapist and the family. In his own clinical interviews Whitaker's highest stated priority is to "get something out of it for myself." What he does clinically, on a fairly consistent basis, is to seize on a perception of the family's "craziness" and attempt to escalate this state of affairs to the level of the absurd. Hoffman (1981) offers a classical example of this method in her report of an interview in which Whitaker turns to a young man who has recently made a suicide gesture and says to him, "Next time you try that, you should go first class, take someone with you like your therapist." Whitaker explains this maneuver as an attempt at augmenting the pathology of the family until the symptoms disappear. Although Whitaker's contributions to the family therapy movement have been considerable, his contribution to a theory of family psychotherapy has been minimal.

Virginia Satir

Virginia Satir, like Whitaker, represents a clinical method that is highly personalized, experiential, and immensely popular. Satir began her work with families in Chicago, and in 1959 came to California to join Don Jackson at MRI. There she organized what may be the first formal training program in family therapy. Although she left MRI to work at the Esalen Institute, where she further developed her humanistic experiential approach, much of her conceptual framework is based on the ideas of the Bateson Project, especially in the formulations of Jackson concerning the rules that govern relationships and the forces of family homeostasis. Satir speaks of the family as a "balanced" system and, in her assessment, seeks to determine the price individual family members pay to maintain this balance. She views symptoms as blockages to growth which help to maintain the family status quo. She is more important as a skilled clinician and teacher than as an original theorist. However, her impact on the practices of family therapists was far from minor. Indeed, she may be the most influential of all the people mentioned in this chapter.

Despite the fact that Satir did not primarily concern herself with theory, there are several basic theoretical premises that are contained in her work. First, there is a strong emphasis on individual growth stemming from positive self-esteem. Second, there is an emphasis on communication patterns among family members. Third, she addresses the rules by which the family members interact with one another, and, fourth, she emphasizes the family linkage to society.

These four aspects of family life are viewed as universal needs and forces operating in all families. In Satir's definition of healthy families, the individual member has positive self-esteem and communication is clear, emotionally honest, and direct. The family rules by which the system maintains itself are conducive to individual growth. Thus, family rules are human, flexible, and appropriate to the situation at hand. Fifth, the family does not function as a closed emotional system but is open to larger systems in society and hopeful in its outlook. As a counterpoint, Satir believes that troubled families do not foster positive self-worth; communication patterns are indirect and vague; rules are not flexible but absolute, and the family functions as a closed emotional system in a defensive and negative manner.

Satir stated her goals in family therapy: "We attempt to make three changes in the family system. First, each member of the family should be able to report congruently, completely, and obviously on what he sees and hears, feels and thinks, about himself and others, in the presence of others. Second, each person should be addressed and related to in terms of his uniqueness, so that decisions are made in terms of exploration and negotiation rather than in terms of power. Third, differentness must be openly acknowledged and used for growth." (Satir, 1972, p. 120). While conceptualizing the family by using the above theoretical premises, Satir's technique of therapy involved heavy use of herself in a direct, pragmatic, and supportive way. She described herself both as a "mirror" allowing the family to see how it was functioning and as a "teacher" suggesting ways to grow by offering specifics on how to improve self-esteem and communication patterns.

There is some suggestion that Satir may have overworked the theoretical concepts of self-esteem and communication in her attempts to account for both normal and pathological family functioning. Again, like Whitaker, her highly individual and powerful persona makes reproducibility a problem for descendant generations. On the other hand, the opportunistic view of the potential for growth in families and her dynamic teaching of many other family therapists make her a major personality in the family therapy field.

THE STRUCTURAL FAMILY THERAPY THEORISTS

As mentioned earlier in this chapter, the work of Adler (1931) and others demonstrated the influence of families on troubled children. In this section we will consider the contributions of Ackerman and Minuchin to the theory of family psychotherapy, which came from their work with dysfunctional children and adolescents.

Nathan Ackerman

A man of broad interests, Nathan Ackerman was a prolific writer on a variety of topics. Early in his medical career he published on the psychological aspects of hypertension and on the impact of the economic depression of the 1930s on coal miners' families. A psychoanalyst, he maintained his commitment to psychoanalytic thought and practice. Ackerman's belief in the primacy of analytic theory resulted in his not developing a conceptual model for the clinical work he did with families. His clinical artistry was tied to his ability to utilize psychodynamic concepts in clinical work with families.

A study of his clinical interviews on film suggests three themes in his work, consistent with his use of analytic theory: nurturance and dependency, control and anger, sexuality and aggression. These themes can be viewed as corresponding to the different stages of psychosexual development of the individual: oral, anal, and phallic. Operationalizing the oral theme, Ackerman would challenge family members on their excessive need to be fed, on their "sucking" behavior, and on their desire to be a baby. He would provoke them into expressing their anger and would openly discuss their unconscious oedipal strivings. As a clinician in a family session he quickly took charge and made contact with each family member after playfully teasing the children, flirting with the women and challenging the men in a fairly aggressive style. He was an activist, stirring up emotion by a process he called "tickling the defenses." He believed it was healthy to let emotions out, especially to express anger openly.

Today, Nathan Ackerman's contribution to family psychiatry is experienced by many as remote, in much the same way most people experience the process in their own extended families—interesting, but irrelevant to the present.

As remote as Ackerman's contribution may seem to some, it remains relevant to the major issues in family therapy. A disciplined clinical investigator with a broad perspective, he was sensitive to the impact of the social context on families far earlier than most. His study of the families of coal miners enduring the lingering depression of the late 1930s remains a model for studying the impact of social context on the internal dynamics of the family. It raises questions still pertinent today, such as what constitutes a functional adaptation versus a maladaptation? What are the premorbid or pre-event characteristics of those who adapt well as opposed to those families who are thrown into chaos and fragmentation?

A current issue in the field of family therapy to which Ackerman contributed is the need for a typology of families. The advent of the *Diagnostic and Statistical Manual III* and the federal government's push for evaluation of clinical results are two factors that have reawakened interest in this area. In Ackerman's 1958 book *The Psychodynamics of Family Life* he presented a preliminary typology of families. The categories included were: disturbance of marital pairs; disturbance of parental pairs; disturbance of childhood; disturbance of adolescence; and psychosomatic families. A clinical typology, even one that is symptom-focused as is this one, is essential to the development of corresponding clinical methodologies, which can then be evaluated.

Hoffman (1981) offers an interesting thesis concerning the connection between Ackerman and Minuchin. She sees Ackerman as basically a structuralist in his approach to dysfunctional families. In her analysis of a transcript of one of Ackerman's cases she draws some fascinating parallels between the clinical work of the two men. Indeed, it is interesting to note that Ackerman had been Minuchin's supervisor in the latter's psychiatric training.

Salvador Minuchin

Salvador Minuchin, a child psychiatrist and psychoanalyst, began to do family therapy at the Wiltwyck School for Boys in New York in the late 1950s, in which he included the parents and siblings of the identified patients in family sessions. The staff of the Wiltwyck Project, begun in 1962, included E. H. (Dick) Auerswald, Richard Rabkin, Bernice Rossman, and Braulio Montalvo. Auerswald, who was strongly influenced by Bateson's "ecological system" ideas, brought these ideas to the Wiltwyck project. Rabkin (1970), also a psychiatrist, brought a certain irreverence for traditional theories and methods, best documented in his text *Inner and Outer Space* and in an essay entitled "Is the Unconscious Necessary?"

The Wiltwyck Project was an important experience for Minuchin, greatly enriching his developing models of family therapy. The Wiltwyck experience was followed by his tenure as Director of the Philadelphia Child Guidance Clinic to which he brought along Montalvo and Rossman, and also attracted Jay Haley, Lynn Hoffman, Peggy Papp and Carl Whitaker. When all of the major early contributions to family therapy are considered, Minuchin stands out for his openness to the ideas and work of others. This is perhaps best demonstrated by his 1962 tour of family therapy centers throughout the country to observe and learn what others were doing with symptomatic families.

As a practicing clinician, Minuchin's training videotapes show him to be a flamboyant and skilled operator of relationship systems, and at times outrageous, in the tradition of Ackerman and Whitaker. Minuchin differs from Ackerman and Whitaker in his conceptual framework, however, just as they differ from each other. Ackerman remained wedded to psychoanalytic theory, while Whitaker maintained the anti-theoretical position that theory can be a rationalization for certain behaviors and a method for avoiding the emotional experience of the moment. Although analytically trained, Minuchin formed his model based on the family as a relationship system. This model rests heavily on the notion that most symptoms, whether they present as a dysfunction in an individual (such as anorexia) or as a conflict in a relationship, are a by-product of structural failings within the family organization.

The conceptual model begins with the notion that the family is normally determined by structure, function, boundaries between subsystems, and degrees of functional attachment among individuals. The family, as defined by Minuchin, is the nuclear family or household. Minuchin would include the grandparental generation into his observational lens only when the grandparent was a part of the household. His description of the family system as a whole relates to the degree to which a family structure demonstrates appropriate boundaries. Those families with dysfunctional structures are grouped into two categories. "Enmeshed" is the term used for those families characterized by overly permeable or absent boundaries, and the term "disengaged" is used for families with rigid boundaries between individuals that do not allow enough flexibility of response or sufficient relationship attachment. The "structure" of structural family therapy can be best understood by a consideration of the concept of boundaries and triangles or "conflict detouring triads" as triangles have at times been termed within this model.

Minuchin's concept of boundaries calls for clearly demonstrated "membranes" among the various subsystems within the family organization. The family monitor or gatekeeper, so designated by appropriate function and position of power, decides what member or members of the family may pass through these membranes and when they may do so. For example, the father might be designated as the gatekeeper of the membrane or boundary surrounding the marital relationship, and the oldest sibling might be viewed as the appropriate gatekeeper for the sibling subsystem. Developmental issues are also a part of these boundary decisions. This is most clearly evident in the theraputic importance given to establishing and maintaining the privacy of an adolescent's room.

The structural therapist maps out weaknesses in the boundaries of family organization and plans direct interventions as remedies to this problem. For example, in a child-centered family in which the parents expend most of their time and emotional energy on the kids, the structural therapist, very early in the therapy, might suggest that the parents retire to their room by 9:30 p.m. three evenings a week, keeping the door closed until at least ll:30 p.m. and that once a month they go away by themselves. In a similar way, an adolescent might be given permission to close the door of her bedroom for two hours every evening. These interventions make explicit therapist-perceived boundary problems and allow the relationship and individual process linked to them to surface.

In his classic text, *Families and Family Therapy* (1974), Minuchin relies heavily on the construct of relationship triangles both to track the pathological relationship process in the family and to provide the rationale for various structural interventions. In a later text, *Psychosomatic Families* (Minuchin, Rosman, & Baker, 1978), based on his work with the families of children suffering from either asthma, diabetes, or anorexia, Minuchin proposed a typology of triangles in these families. In this typology he has designated two types of what he terms "conflict detouring triads: detouring attacking or detouring supportive."

In the detouring attacking triads, the parents are joined together in agreement over what is wrong with their child's behavior. Both parents are angry with the child and they take turns in criticizing the behavior. However, the fact that each of them usually has a different idea of how to fix the problem may drive them into conflict with each other. In the "detouring supportive" structure both parents join together in mutual concern over a child with emotional or psychosomatic problems. Rather than attacking their child, they are almost overly concerned and supportive in their efforts to alleviate the situation for him.

It is evident in Minuchin's case reports that there is a consistent application of principles based on a theory of family structure and organization. These principles include

(a) the importance of the therapist relating to the power distribution within the family system and the hierarchical structure of that system. For example, his first move in a therapy session is often to connect with the father as the gatekeeper to the family system. At times he will even ask explicit permission of the father to talk to the other family members present in the room.

(b) An assessment of the generational boundaries and the dysfunctional structure of the intergenerational triangles. This is demonstrated by the way Minuchin fashions his interventions around boundary problems and around alterations in the structure of a central symptomatic triangle.

Minuchin's model was a major breakthrough in the history of family therapy. His video training tapes demonstrated the systemic aspects of clinical problems formerly thought of as residing within the individual. In addition, these same tapes demonstrated relief of the symptoms over time. The impact of Minuchin's model was to turn the attention of the mental health movement toward the developing field of family therapy. One of the most admirable aspects of Minuchin's work has been the ability to make his conceptual ideas and clinical methodologies effective with an underprivileged population.

COMMENT ON BEHAVIORAL FAMILY THERAPY

Behavioral therapists have a long history of applying their behavioral principles to a variety of problems that occur within the family. However, the major part of this work has occurred outside the mainstream of the family systems therapy movement. Family system therapists, for the most part, left the established theoretical groups with which they were originally associated to form their own informal, and later formal, organizations. These organizations were committed to the development of new theoretical formulations of family functioning. On the other hand, behavioral family therapists tended to maintain their identification with organizations wedded to established behavioral theory. This was mostly due to their commitment to established behavioral theory.

However, there have been some noteworthy efforts by behaviorists to deal more fully with the problems of the family system. Jacobson and Margolin (1979) in their marital therapy work have developed a view of reinforcement that is both circular and reciprocal. An example is the following: A wife asks her husband for more time together, the husband is not so inclined and does not respond. The wife begins to become angry and demanding, and the husband says, "There is no way I'm going to spend time with you when you act like such a shrew." This only serves to increase the wife's anger and behavioral tirade. Finally, in exhaustion the husband gives in, saying, "Okay—if you just stop we will go out somewhere to eat."

In this sequence the wife has been reinforced for throwing the tirade and the husband has been reinforced for giving in to the wife's negative behavior by her stopping her tirade after he agrees to go out. In their model each marital partner's behavior is both being affected by and influencing the other. Thus, this model maintains the centrality of behavior modification by intervening to alter the reinforcement contingencies, while at the same time attempting to deal with a relationship focus by focusing on how both spouses participate in the process of reinforcement.

Gordon and Davidson (1981) in their work with behavioral parent training acknowledge the importance of a broad-based model of assessment. This broad-based model includes factors in the family system which may potentially interfere with behavioral parent training such as marital conflict. They even go so far as to state, "In certain situations, successful treatment of these other family difficulties may obviate the need for any further treatment (of the child)" (p. 521). The "broad-based model" of assessment extends the potential focus of treatment to other areas of the family system. However, the theory used to conceptualize and treat the problems of the child remains embedded in individual behavioral psychology.

Stuart (1980) in his behavioral marital therapy makes a point of including some efforts to improve the general communication skills of the couple. The attempt to improve communication skill is over and beyond his attempts to modify specific behaviors in the relationship. Liberman (1972) acknowledges the importance of the therapeutic relationship over and above the specific behavioral techniques: "Without the positive therapeutic alliance between the therapist and those he is helping, there can be little or no successful intervention (p. 332)."

Thus, as behavior therapists attempt to deal with the complex problems of families, they are not only modifying their procedures but are attempting to incorporate systems principles. To date, however, a real difference continues to exist between the underlying theory of behavioral family therapy and family systems therapy.

CONCLUSION

Due to restrictions of length, the significant contributions of a number of prominent family therapists have not been included in this chapter. We have attempted to present the work of those investigators who have been most focused on the development of a conceptual framework for family psychotherapy. Forty years into its life-cycle, the family therapy movement has not yet developed a single comprehensive integrated theory. Three major models have been developed and emphasized in this chapter: the strategic, the multigenerational (Bowen), and the structural (Minuchin) approaches. Each of these models has its strengths as well as its weaknesses. The strategic model, although it clearly demonstrates the power of context and *the magic* of paradox and reframing, fails to offer a consideration of the internal developmental struggles of the individual. Therefore, it overvalues context in much the same way that a theory of the individual undervalues it.

The multigenerational models of Bowen and his descendants represent the most consistent effort at developing a broad-based theory of family psychotherapy, including their attention to the development of individual autonomy. However, Bowenian models become somewhat murky in attempts to define and describe differentiation and triangulation. In addition, their clinical techniques can become overly ritualized and constricted.

The structural model of Minuchin is the clearest and most easily understood among the three models. However, it is much more a model for doing therapy than an attempt at developing a comprehensive theory of family psychotherapy. In addition, although it is eminently teachable and reproducible, it is almost entirely a method for working with child-focused families. It offers little assistance for working with the problems of relationship conflict between adults and/or working with an individual.

One of the most important questions for the future of the family therapy movement is what will happen as the old guard of pioneers moves on and a new generation steps forward. How much of an attempt will be made to elaborate further some or all of the concepts developed in the first 40 years? If family theory is to continue to develop as the conceptual basis of a comprehensive model for understanding the individual's emotional functioning in relationship context, several eventualities must occur. There must be a sophistication and refinement of the characteristics of functional compared with dysfunctional relationship systems, a systemic model of the individual including a continuum linking his or her "inner and outer space," and a model for tracking dyadic interaction and triangle formation. The goal of these refined family concepts and models would be the development of an integrated system of interventions that would enhance the ability of a therapist to steer relationship process toward better functioning both for individuals and for the family systems as a whole. If this is not forthcoming, family psychotherapy may become more like group therapy—a clinical modality to be used at specific times in response to specific clinical indications in conjunction with, or in lieu of, traditional psychodynamically based individual therapy.

REFERENCES

Ackerman, N. (1937). The family as a social and emotional unit. *Bulletin of the Kansas Mental Hygiene Society.*

Ackerman, N. (1958). *The psychodynamics of family life.* New York: Basic Books.

Adler, A. (1931). *Guiding the child.* New York: Greenberg.

Bateson, G., Jackson, D., Haley, J., & Weakland, J. (1956). Toward a theory of schizophrenia. *Behavioral Science, 1,* 251–264.

Bell, J. E. (1961). *Family group therapy.* (Public Health Monograph No. 64). Washington, DC: U.S. Government Printing Office.

Bell, J. E. (1975). *Family therapy.* New York: Jason Aronson.

Boszormenyi-Nagy, I., & Framo, J. (Eds.). (1965). *Intensive family therapy: Theoretical and practical aspects.* New York: Harper & Row.

Boszormenyi-Nagy, I., & Spark, G. (1973). *Invisible loyalties: Reciprocity in intergenerational family therapy.* New York: Harper & Row.

Bowen, M. (1966). The use of family theory in clinical practice. *Comprehensive Psychiatry, 7,* 345–374.

Bowen, M. (1972). On the differentiation of self. In J. Framo, (Ed.), *Family interaction: A dialogue between family researchers and family therapists* (pp. 111–173). New York: Springer.

Bowen, M. (1976). Theory in the practice of psychotherapy. In P. Guerin (Ed.), *Family therapy: Theory and practice* (pp. 42–90). New York: Gardner Press.

Bowen, M. (1978). *Family therapy in clinical practice.* New York: Aronson.

Carter, E. A., & McGoldrick, M. (1980). *The family life cycle: A framework for family therapy.* New York: Gardner Press.

Fogarty, T. F. (1976a). Systems concepts and the dimensions of self. In P. J. Guerin (Ed.), *Family therapy: Theory and practice* (pp. 144–153). New York: Gardner Press.

Fogarty, T. F. (1976b). Marital crisis. In P. J. Guerin (Ed.), *Family therapy: Theory and practice.* New York: Gardner Press.

Fogarty, T. F. (1984). The individual and the family. In E. Pendagast (Ed.), *Compendium II: The best of the family (1978–1983)* (pp. 71–77). New Rochelle, NY: Center for Family Learning.

Freud, S. (1959). Analysis of a phobia in a five-year-old boy. *Collected papers, Vol. III.* New York: Basic Books. (Original published 1909)

Goldenberg, I., & Goldenberg, H. (1985). *Family therapy: An overview* (rev. ed.). Monterey, CA: Brooks/Cole.

Gordon, S., & Davidson, N. (1981). Behavioral parent training. In A. Gurman and D. Kniskern (Eds.), *Handbook of family therapy* (pp. 517–555). New York: Brunner/Mazel.

Guerin, P. (1976). Family therapy: The first twenty-five years. In P. Guerin (Ed.), *Family therapy: Theory and practice* (pp. 2–23). New York: Gardner Press.

Guerin, P. (1979). System, system, who's got the system? In E. Pendagast (Ed.), *Compendium I: The best of the family, 1973–1978,* (pp. 9–16). New Rochelle, NY: Center for Family Learning.

Guerin, P., Fay, L., Burden, S., & Kautto, J. (1987). *The evaluation and treatment of marital conflict: A four stage approach.* New York: Basic Books.

Haley, J. (1976). *Problem solving therapy.* San Francisco: Jossey Bass.

Haley, J. (1984). *Ordeal therapy.* San Francisco: Jossey Bass.

Hoffman, L. (1981). *Foundations of family therapy.* New York: Basic Books.

Jackson, D. D., & Weakland, J. H. (1961). Conjoint family therapy. *Psychiatry,* 24, 30–45.

Jacobson, N., & Margolin, G. (1979). *Marital therapy: Strategies based on social learning and behavioral exchange principles.* New York: Brunner/Mazel.

Kaslow, F. (1980). History of family therapy in the United States. *Marriage and Family Review,* 3, 77–111.

Lederer, W., & Jackson, D. (1968). *The mirages of marriage.* New York: Norton.

Liberman, R. P. (1972). Behavioral approaches to family and couple therapy. In

C. J. Sager and H. S. Kaplan (Eds.), *Progress in group and family therapy*, (pp. 329–345). New York: Brunner/Mazel.

Minuchin, S. (1974). *Families and family therapy*. Cambridge: Harvard University Press.

Minuchin, S. (1987). My Many Voices. In J. Zeig (Ed.), *The evolution of psychotherapy* (pp. 5–14). New York: Brunner/Mazel.

Minuchin, S., Rosman, B., & Baker, L. (1978). *Psychosomatic families: Anorexia nervosa in context*. Cambridge, MA: Harvard University Press.

Nichols, M. (1984). *Family therapy: Concepts and methods*. New York: Gardner Press.

Rabkin, R. (1970). *Inner and outer space*. New York: Norton.

Ruesh, J., and Bateson, G. (Eds.), (1951). *Communication: The social matrix of psychiatry*. New York: Norton.

Satir, V., (1967). *Conjoint family therapy*. Palo Alto: Science and Behavior Books.

Satir, V., (1972). *Peoplemaking*. Palo Alto: Science and Behavior Books.

Stuart, R., (1980). *Helping couples change*. New York: Guilford Press.

Watzlawick, P., Beavin, J., & Jackson, D., (1967). *Pragmatics of human communication*. New York: Norton.

Watzlawick, P., Weakland, J., & Fisch, R. (1974). *Change: Principles of problem formation and problem resolution*. New York: Norton.

Whitaker, C. (1976). The hindrance of theory in clinical work. In P. J. Guerin (Ed.), *Family therapy: Theory and practice*. New York: Gardner Press.

Whitaker, C., Felder, R., & Warkentin, J. (1965). Countertransference in the family treatment of schizophrenia. In I. Boszormenyi-Nagy and J. Framo (Eds.), *Intensive family therapy* (pp. 323–342). New York: Harper and Row.

Whitaker, C., & Keith, D. (1981). Symbolic experiential family therapy. In A. Gurman and D. Kniskern (Eds.), *Handbook of family therapy* (pp. 187–225). New York: Brunner/Mazel.

Whitehead, A. N., & Russell, B. (1910). *Principia Mathematica*. Cambridge, England: Cambridge University Press.

8

INTEGRATIVE THEORIES OF THERAPY

HAL ARKOWITZ

There are many contradictions in the field of psychotherapy. On the one hand, a large number of psychotherapists have a strong commitment to a particular psychotherapy approach. On the other hand, there is little evidence that any of the over 400 different psychotherapy approaches (Karasu, 1986) is more effective than another (e.g., Beckham, 1990; Elkin et al., 1989; Lambert, Shapiro, & Bergin, 1986; Sloane, Staples, Cristol, Yorkston, & Whipple, 1975; Smith, Glass, & Miller, 1980; Stiles, Shapiro, & Elliot, 1986).

Another contradiction exists as well. On the one hand, societies, institutes, centers, and journals devoted to particular therapy approaches dominate the field of psychotherapy. On the other hand, the majority of practicing therapists do not identify themselves as adhering to one particular approach, but instead refer to themselves as "eclectic" or "integrative" (Garfield & Kurtz, 1976; Norcross & Prochaska, 1983, 1988).

In part, the emergence of the field of *psychotherapy integration* has been a response to these contradictions. Psychotherapy integration has had a

I would like to express my appreciation to Stanley Messer and Paul Wachtel for their helpful comments on an earlier draft of this chapter.

long history, but it was not until the late 1970s that it crystallized into a strong and coherent force on the psychotherapy scene. It is characterized by a dissatisfaction with single-school approaches and a concomitant desire to look across and beyond school boundaries to see what can be learned from other ways of thinking about psychotherapy and change.

Other chapters in this book document the evolution of the major schools of psychotherapy. Proponents of each school share certain fundamental assumptions about human nature, psychopathology, psychotherapy, and change. Along with the growth of each of these approaches, another development was occurring, albeit more quietly and steadily. Over the past 60 years, a number of writers have attempted to examine various ways to cross school boundaries, integrate theories and techniques from two or more approaches, or suggest factors that the different therapies have in common. Often, they were not aware of the work of others who proposed somewhat different integrations nor aware that they were part of a growing movement in which integration was the defining theme.

Beginning around 1980, interest in psychotherapy integration grew dramatically. In this chapter, I will discuss what psychotherapy integration is, the historical context from which it emerged, and the factors that shaped its development. Further, I will consider what impact integrative thinking has already had on the field of psychotherapy, as well as some of the potentials it holds for the future.

WHAT IS PSYCHOTHERAPY INTEGRATION?

In some respects, it is easier to define what psychotherapy integration *is not* rather than what it *is*. Psychotherapy integration is not an adherence to one particular approach to psychotherapy. In the single-school approach, the therapist believes in the theory on which the approach is based, uses the techniques and strategies associated with it, and may conduct research on hypotheses derived from that theory.

Psychotherapy integration includes various attempts to look beyond the confines of single-school approaches in order to see what can be learned from other perspectives. It is characterized by an openness to various ways of integrating diverse theories and techniques.

This description may sound suspiciously like what has been called "eclecticism." The term eclecticism has been used to denote a largely pragmatic approach in which the therapist uses whatever techniques he or she believes are likely to be effective, with little or no underlying theory to guide these choices. By contrast, the integrative approaches of today all attempt to build some coherent framework for understanding or predicting change and for determining the choices of therapy procedures.

Presently, there are three main directions that characterize the field of psychotherapy integration (Arkowitz, 1989). They are (1) theoretical integration; (2) common factors; and (3) technical eclecticism. All are guided by the general assumption that we have much to learn by looking beyond the boundaries of single approaches. However, they do so in rather different ways. In *theoretical integration*, two or more therapies are integrated in the hope that the result will be better than the individual therapies on which they were based. As the name implies, there is an emphasis on integrating the underlying theories of psychotherapy (what London, 1986, has so eloquently labelled "theory smushing") along with the integration of therapy techniques from each (what London has called "technique melding"). The various proposals to integrate psychoanalytic and behavioral approaches best illustrate this direction, most notably the work of Paul Wachtel (1977; 1987). Other writers have focused on different integrations (e.g., Appelbaum, 1976; Feldman & Pinsof, 1982; Greenberg & Safran, 1987; Gurman, 1981; Lebow, 1984; Segraves, 1982; Thoresen, 1973; Wachtel & Wachtel, 1986; and Wandersman, Poppen, & Ricks, 1976).

The *common factors* approach attempts to look across different therapies to search for elements that they may share in common. This view is based on the belief that these factors may be at least as important in accounting for therapy outcome as the unique factors that differentiate among them. The common factors identified may then become the basis for more parsimonious theory and technique. Frank (1961, 1982) and Goldfried (1980, 1991) have been among the most important contributors to this approach.

Technical eclecticism is considerably less theoretical than either theoretical integration or the common factors approach. Technical eclectics seek to improve our ability to select the best treatment for the person and problem. This search is guided primarily by data on what has worked best for others in the past with similar problems and similar characteristics. In contrast to theoretical integration and common factors, technical eclecticism pays significantly less attention to why these techniques work and instead focuses on predicting for whom they will work. The foundation for technical eclecticism is primarily actuarial rather than theoretical. The work of Beutler (1983), Beutler and Clarkin (1990), and Lazarus (1976, 1981) are illustrations of this form of integration.

PSYCHOTHERAPY INTEGRATION: A HISTORY OF IDEAS

In this section, I will trace the history of each of these three trends in psychotherapy integration. The review focuses on selected proposals exemplifying each integrative direction. These are presented in sufficient detail to give the reader a sense of the ideas involved. More comprehensive histories of the entire field of psychotherapy integration can be found in Goldfried & Newman (1986) and of theoretical integration in Arkowitz (1984).

Theoretical Integration

Early History

The history of theoretical integration is largely the history of attempts to combine psychoanalytic and behavioral approaches to psychotherapy. Several early writers attempted to demonstrate that concepts from psychoanalysis could be translated into the language of learning theory (e.g., French, 1933; Kubie, 1934; Sears, 1944; Shoben, 1949). With these notable exceptions, the 1930s and 1940s were mainly characterized by growth and development within psychoanalytic and behavioral approaches respectively, with relatively few attempts to relate them.

A significant event in the history of theoretical integration occurred in 1950 with the publication of Dollard and Miller's book, *Personality and Psychotherapy: An Analysis in Terms of Learning, Thinking, and Culture*. This book went far beyond its usual description as a simple attempt to translate psychoanalytic concepts into behavioral language. In fact, it was far more than that. It was an attempt to synthesize and integrate ideas about neurosis and psychotherapy from these two perspectives in order to provide a unifying theory for the field. In the opening, Dollard and Miller wrote:

> The ultimate goal is to combine the vitality of psychoanalysis, the rigor of the natural science laboratory, and the facts of culture. We believe that a psychology of this kind should occupy a fundamental position in the social sciences and humanities—making it unnecessary for each of them to invent its own special assumptions about human nature and personality. (p. 3)

What they achieved was no less than an integrative theory of neurotic behavior based on anxiety and conflict and new suggestions for psychotherapy that grew out of their integration. It is true that some of their work is an attempt to translate the concepts of psychoanalysis into the language of learning theory (e.g., they attempted to explain the pleasure principle in terms of reinforcement and repression in terms of the inhibition of cue-producing responses that mediate thinking). However, they also presented a rather sophisticated formulation of the dynamics of conflict and anxiety in neurosis, drawing from concepts in both learning theory and psychoanalysis. They also suggested procedures for overcoming repression and proposed the use of modeling, self-control strategies, and homework assignments in therapy. Many of these techniques have since been "rediscovered" and are now a basic part of several modern-day therapies.

Although their theory of anxiety and conflict caught the attention of researchers in learning (see review by Heilizer, 1977), their integration did not have very much direct influence on the field of psychotherapy. Its influence has been more indirect, serving as a reminder of the possibility and potentials of integration during times when integrative thinking was not a part of the Zeitgeist. Now that psychotherapy integration is more established as a field, perhaps their work will be rediscovered as it deserves to be.

The work of Dollard and Miller still stands as one of the most comprehensive and ambitious attempts to integrate these two seemingly diverse approaches. However, the time was not right for this integration, in part because of the nature of the behavioral approach of the time. There was a considerable body of learning theory and learning research, but there was not yet much of a behavior *therapy* with which to integrate psychoanalytic therapy. Thus, Dollard and Miller were only able to attempt to integrate what was there—a learning *theory* with a psychoanalytic theory *and* therapy.

Behavior therapy emerged during the 20 years following the publication of Dollard and Miller's book. This period was one in which behavior therapists offered definitions of their approach that emphasized its differences from psychoanalytic theory and therapy (e.g., Eysenck, 1960; Wolpe & Rachman, 1960). The strident tone of many of these papers probably contributed to an antagonism between the two approaches that may have discouraged any further attempts at integration during this time. Of those who did raise the possibility of integration, most answered in the negative. The title of a paper by Levis (1970), a behavior therapist, illustrates this: "Integration of Behavior Therapy and Dynamic Psychiatry: A Marriage With a High Probability of Ending in Divorce."

Through much of the 1960s and early 1970s, behavior therapists were actively defining and expanding the scope of behavior theory and therapy. Again, the time was not right for behavior therapists to consider an integration with the very approach they sought to replace.

Another factor contributing to the relative lack of interest in integration during this period was that early behavior therapy was distinctly noncognitive, if not anticognitive (e.g., Wolpe, 1958). This made any potential links to the highly cognitive psychoanalytic approach even more difficult.

Despite these constraints, there remained a small but steady stream of writers from both sides who continued to explore a behavioral-psychodynamic integration. From the analytic side, Franz Alexander (1963) wrote that much of what happens in psychotherapy could best be understood in terms of learning theory, especially the principles of reward and punishment. Weitzman (1967) took an important step toward integration when he presented a cognitive and psychoanalytic interpretation of systematic desensitization, pointing the way not only to convergences but also to how psychoanalytic free association and imaginal desensitization might be integrated into a unified clinical approach. He argued that "dynamically rich material," typically ignored by behavior therapists, was produced and could be utilized during the course of systematic desensitization. Weitzman's proposal was one of the first that pointed to integration at the level of therapy techniques.

During this time, some behavior therapists also expressed interest in integration (e.g., London, 1964; Marks & Gelder, 1966), but others like Bandura (1969) remained highly critical of psychoanalytic approaches and showed no interest in integration. London (1964) characterized most existing therapies as oriented primarily toward either insight or action. He argued that action therapies were more successful in the treatment of symptoms but that they mostly ignored thinking as a means of controlling human behavior. He suggested that a system that attempts to integrate insight and action might be more effective for a wider variety of problems than one emphasizing only one of these approaches. London's book was widely cited and was one of the earliest and most eloquent statements calling for a broad integration between very different therapy approaches. The second edition of his book (London, 1986) also remains influential in the field.

The end of the 1960s was marked by the appearance of a unique paper reflecting the observations of several prominent psychoanalytically oriented therapists (Klein, Dittman, Parloff, & Gill, 1969), who reported their conclusions after a week of observing the clinical work of prominent behavior therapists. The authors suggested that the relationship in behavior therapy and the general clinical skills of the behavior therapist were important factors that were ignored in the writings on behavior therapy. Although they did not advocate an integration, they did argue against the development of behavior therapy as a "closed system of treatment" and thought that behavioral approaches did have a contribution to make in psychotherapy.

Increasing Interest in the 1970s

In the 1970s, interest in a behavioral-psychoanalytic integration showed signs of acceleration, increasing specificity, and greater comprehensiveness.

In 1972, Feather and Rhoads (1972a, 1972b; Rhoads & Feather, 1972) published a series of papers describing their "psychodynamic behavior therapy." In one illustration of their approach, systematic desensitization was applied to hypothesized underlying psychodynamic themes and fantasies. A summary of these and other related clinical integrations is available in Rhoads (1984). Birk (1970) and Birk and Brinkley-Birk (1974) also presented several clinical illustrations demonstrating how insight-oriented therapies might enhance behavior change and how behavior change could, in turn, facilitate cognitive changes. All of these papers were important in illustrating the clinical feasibility of the integration of behavioral and psychoanalytic techniques. The case illustrations and underlying rationales were also important in facilitating the later emergence of more specific proposals for a psychodynamic–behavioral integration. The appearance of this work and others (e.g., N. E. Murray, 1976; Silverman, 1974; Wachtel, 1975, 1977) pointed to a noticeable increase in the interest in psychodynamic-behavioral integration during this period.

Some important trends in both psychoanalytic and behavioral therapies during the 1970s may have contributed to the increased interest in integration. Messer (1986) pointed out that a number of changes in psychoanalytic theory and therapy were occurring during this time that made an integration with behavior therapy more feasible. These included a greater emphasis on goal-setting and treatment focus (e.g., Malan, 1976); greater attention to the actual effects of events on people's lives (Shengold, 1979); more attention to people's adaptive efforts to deal with those events (Blanck & Blanck, 1976; Langs, 1976); and greater emphasis on patient responsibility for their feelings and actions (e.g., Appelbaum, 1982; Schafer, 1983).

Important trends in behavior therapy during this time also allowed more room for the possibility of integration. By this time, behavior therapy had firmly established its identity and made a significant impact on the field of psychotherapy. There was now an expanded social learning theory (Bandura, 1969, 1977; Mischel, 1973) and a body of behavior therapy techniques to consider for integration with psychoanalytic approaches. During this time, behavior therapy was beginning to incorporate cognitive mediating constructs (e.g., Bandura, 1969) and even cognitively-oriented techniques (Mahoney, 1974; Meichenbaum, 1977). Thus, as behavior therapy became somewhat more cognitive, there was an even greater potential for exploring integration with psychoanalytic therapies that so strongly emphasized the exploration of mental content (Gill, 1984).

Wachtel's Proposal for Psychodynamic–Behavioral Integration

In 1977, Wachtel published his book *Psychoanalysis and Behavior Therapy: Toward an Integration.* It remains the most comprehensive and successful attempt to integrate behavioral and psychodynamic approaches and one of the most influential books in the entire field of psychotherapy integration. Wachtel did his graduate work at Yale when both Dollard and Miller were on the faculty. In fact, Dollard was one of his first therapy supervisors. Wachtel (1987) notes that he was quite impressed with their attempt to build a theoretical bridge between the concepts of psychoanalysis and learning theory.

Wachtel (1977) noted that any attempt to integrate behavioral and psychoanalytic approaches needs to appreciate the diversity within both and must be specific about the components of such an integration. Which behavior therapy and which psychoanalytic therapy shall be integrated? Some may be more compatible than others. For example, orthodox Freudian psychoanalysis and operant behavioral therapies are probably so incompatible that an integration between the two is unlikely. By contrast, Wachtel pursued an integration that incorporated a behavior therapy emphasizing anxiety reduction and changes in interpersonal behavior with interpersonal psychoanalytic approaches (e.g., those of Erikson, Horney, and Sullivan) that emphasized the current interpersonal context of the individual and encouraged greater therapist activity than many other psychoanalytic approaches.

Wachtel's goal was to build a framework that could incorporate selected elements of interpersonal psychodynamic approaches and behavioral approaches. It is important to note that his goal was not a fixed superordinate theory (or therapy) that would be a hybrid of two sub-approaches. Instead, Wachtel sought to include what he believed were some of the virtues of both in an evolving framework that could incorporate elements of each in a logical and internally consistent way, benefiting from what he saw as their complementary strengths (Wachtel, 1984). This framework, which might change with further developments in each field, could show how concepts from each of the therapies interacted with each other in ways that might suggest new theory for understanding the causes of psychopathology and new clinical strategies for change. From the psychodynamic perspective, he emphasized unconscious processes and conflict and the importance of meanings and fantasies that influenced our interactions with the world. From the behavioral side, the elements included the use of active-intervention techniques, a concern with the environmental context of behavior, a focus on the patient's goals in therapy, and a respect for empirical evidence (Wachtel, 1977, 1987).

In understanding the origins of psychopathology, Wachtel paid considerable attention to the importance of early experience. He adopted the psychoanalytic view that ways of feeling, acting, and behaving that reflect unresolved conflicts will persist into our later life, continuing to influence us even outside of our awareness. Had he stopped here, he would have remained a primarily psychodynamic theorist. However, based on learning and interpersonal orientations, he also saw the importance of present interpersonal influences. He wrote:

> Thus, from this perspective, the early pattern persists, not in spite of changing conditions but because the person's pattern of experiencing and interacting with others tends continually to recreate the old conditions again and again. (Wachtel, 1977, pp. 52–53)

In this view, our past experiences skew our present environment and often lead us to create the very conditions that perpetuate our problems in a kind of vicious circle. For example, the people we choose and the relationships we form may confirm the dysfunctional views that we carry forward from our past and that are at the heart of many of our problems. Wachtel later called this approach "cyclical psychodynamics" (1987). The view of causality in this theory is circular and reciprocal, rather than the linear causal views of behavioral and psychoanalytic theories.

Wachtel also explored the implications of this integration for the practice of psychotherapy. It follows from cyclical psychodynamic theory that intervening into the factors currently maintaining the problem will be an important aid to change. In addition, active behavioral interventions may also serve as a source of new insights (Wachtel, 1975), and insights can promote changes in behavior (Wachtel, 1982), with the two working synergistically. In some respects, the most important achievement of Wachtel's book for psychotherapy integration was his demonstration that an integrative framework was possible. The challenge of psychotherapy integration was now a comprehensive and concrete proposal. This allowed the debate about the merits of integration to move beyond broad polemics and to focus on substantive issues. In this sense, Wachtel's work served as a catalyst to the entire field of psychotherapy integration, as well as constituting a significant achievement in its own right.

The achievement and challenge of Wachtel's integration was acknowledged by the contributors to a book edited by Arkowitz and Messer (1984) entitled *Psychoanalytic Therapy and Behavior Therapy: Is Integration Possible?* In it, prominent representatives of behavioral, psychodynamic, and integrative points of view addressed the possibilities and problems of a psychodynamic-behavioral integration. While the contributors raised many provocative issues, the most basic ones that cut across the chapters concerned questions about the *units* and *forms* of an integration.

Schacht (1984) suggested that different writers have often referred to theoretical integration at different levels or units of analysis. For example, integrations have been addressed to theories, techniques, assumptions about human nature, methods of verification, or combinations of these. Schacht suggested that some of the conflict and confusion that characterized previous discussions may have resulted from ambiguity about the units and levels that were being discussed.

Gill (1984) distinguished among psychodynamic therapy, psychoanalytic therapy, and psychoanalysis, and he characterized them as having increasing emphases on examination of mental processes and analysis of the transference. He acknowledged "that psychodynamic and behavioral theories of intervention can be combined is no longer in question. They can be and are being combined" (1984, p. 180). However, he suggested that integration becomes less possible and less desirable as we move toward psychoanalytic therapy and psychoanalysis because the techniques and approaches necessary for exploration and analysis of the transference are antithetical to the active intervention techniques of behavior therapy. Thus, the issue of the form of psychoanalytic therapy or the units to be integrated was relevant for Gill as well.

Franks (1984) also believed that some kind of integration at the clinical level was possible, although he believed that it would not advance practice in any significant ways. His strongest conclusion was that an integration at the conceptual or theoretical level was neither possible nor desirable. He argued that the two approaches differed in basic ways involving what constitutes acceptable evidence, the methods of verification, the goals of change, and how outcome should be evaluated.

Other contributors also concluded that some form of integration between psychoanalytic and behavioral approaches was possible, but they questioned whether it was desirable (e.g., Kazdin, 1984; Mahoney, 1984). Still others presented further critiques or proposals for integration (Mahoney, 1974; Mendelsohn & Silverman, 1984; Rhoads, 1984).

Messer and Winokur (1984) discussed the underlying views of human nature in the two approaches. They characterized the behavioral approach as oriented toward the external world of reality, in which conflict resulted from situations in which people found themselves, and that conflict could be eliminated by action. By contrast, they characterized psychoanalytic views as incorporating the inevitability and centrality of internal conflict, the limits that an individual's early history places on the extent of possible change, and emphasis on contradiction and ambiguity in the process of therapy. They pointed to how these different visions are important not only at an abstract philosophical level but also at a more concrete clinical level where they may determine how we act at various choice points in therapy

(Messer, 1986). Nonetheless, Messer and Winokur did not entirely rule out the possibility of some form of integration. In later work by Messer (Lazarus & Messer, 1991), he seems to have moved cautiously toward what he has called assimilative integration in which "techniques and concepts from one therapy do indeed find their way into another and get incorporated within its slowly evolving theory and mode of practice" (p. 153).

Contributors also raised questions about the forms or models integration may take. Schacht (1984) saw the most elementary one as a simple *translation* of concepts. In a *complementary model*, each approach is seen as appropriate for dealing with different problems in the same patient (e.g., systematic desensitization for a phobia and psychoanalytic therapy for identity problems). A third model is a *synergistic* one in which the two therapies may be applied to the same problem and are expected to interact in the patient to produce clinical results superior to what might be obtained by either therapy alone. The techniques of each therapy remain unchanged, but the locus of their integration lies in their effects on the patient. In the *emergent* model, the different therapies merge to produce a novel hybrid approach with new characteristics not contained by either therapy alone. This is exemplified by Feather and Rhoads' (1972a, 1972b) psychodynamic behavior therapy involving the application of desensitization to inferred underlying fantasies and conflicts. Finally, according to Schacht, the most challenging level is *theoretical integration* in which there is an integration of theories and metapsychologies, with the hope for an emergent model of human behavior. Wachtel's work best illustrates this approach.

In his chapter, Wachtel (1984) addressed criticisms of integration. He made the point that many of the arguments have focused on how psychoanalytic and behavioral approaches are different. However, he argued that it is precisely because of these differences that integration was proposed in the first place. The goal of the integration was to incorporate some of the different strengths and contributions of each. By carefully selecting which elements of each theory to incorporate and by creating a new framework to fit them together, he argued, a coherent synthesis can be achieved even if, taken as a whole, the two separate theories are quite different.

Recent Developments

The debate about integration was now dealing with important and substantive issues in psychotherapy theory and practice. Interest in a psychodynamic-behavioral integration has continued to grow and remains a strong force in psychotherapy integration. Published in the 1980s were three books that reprinted classic papers relating to theoretical integration (Marmor & Woods, 1980; Goldfried, 1982a; Wachtel, 1987). It seemed that there was interest in reading and rereading earlier contributions, now that they could be understood in the context of a growing body of thought on psychotherapy integration. A number of books and papers appeared during the 1980s that continued to develop clinical strategies and debate issues relating to psychodynamic-behavioral integration (Arkowitz, 1985, 1989; Beutler, 1989; Fensterheim, 1983; Fitzpatrick & Weber, 1989; Lazarus & Messer, 1988, 1991; Papajohn, 1982; Rhoads, 1984; Segraves, 1982; Wachtel, 1977, 1987, 1991; Wachtel & Wachtel, 1986; Wolfe, 1989).

The spirit of lively debate has also continued with the appearance of several series of articles in different journals reflecting the controversy that theoretical integration had sparked, as well as psychotherapy integration more broadly. These appeared in clinical psychology, counseling, and psychiatry journals, both within and outside of the United States. The journals included *Behavior Therapy* (Garfield, 1982; Goldfried, 1982b; Kendall, 1982; Wachtel, 1982); the *British Journal of Clinical Psychology* (Davis, 1983; Messer, 1983; E. J. Murray, 1983; Wachtel, 1983; Yates, 1983); the *British Journal of Guidance and Counselling* (Beitman, 1989; Dryden & Norcross, 1989; Lazarus, 1989; Messer, 1989; Norcross & Grencavage, 1989); and *Psychiatric Annals* (Babcock, 1988; Birk, 1988; London & Palmer, 1988; Powell, 1988; Rhoads, 1988). In addition, a major article on psychotherapy integration appeared in the *American Journal of Psychiatry* (Beitman, Goldfried, & Norcross, 1989). The National Institute of Mental Health sponsored a workshop on research in psychotherapy integration (Wolfe & Goldfried, 1988) in which theoretical integration was extensively discussed. In addition, theoretical integration was reviewed prominently in the recent *Annual Review of Psychology* chapter on individual psychotherapy (Goldfried, Greenberg, & Marmor, 1990).

There has also been some interest in theoretical integration other than the psychodynamic–behavioral. Some papers have discussed the possibility of an integration between humanistic and behavioral therapies (e.g., Thoresen, 1973; Wandersman, Poppen, & Ricks, 1976). In addition, a number of writers from the family therapy area have been exploring various clinical and theoretical integrations between family/systems therapies and others (e.g., Feldman & Pinsof, 1982: Gurman, 1981; Lebow, 1984; Pinsof, 1983; Segraves, 1982; Wachtel & Wachtel, 1986). There has also been a small but growing literature on incorporating interpersonal factors into an integrative model (e.g., Andrews, 1991a, 1991b; Safran & Segal, 1990).

New Directions in Theoretical Integration

Clearly, theoretical integration is having an impact on thinking and practice in the field of psychotherapy. Yet, there is a potential contradiction to the integration of two or more approaches to psychotherapy: The integration of today may become the single-school approach of tomorrow. Such a scenario suggests visions of Institutes for Integrative Psychotherapy and certification of integrative therapists. Is this what theoretical integration is about? I believe not. Such a path takes us full circle back to where we started.

It is important to keep Wachtel's original vision in mind. He sought an "evolving framework" for integration rather than a fixed integration of one approach with another. What does the concept of an evolving framework imply? This question may hold the key to the one of the most important new directions for psychodynamic–behavioral integration and theoretical integration more broadly. I believe that we may be moving toward what Schwartz (1991) and others have described as an "open system" model that not only consists of the interaction of its existing components, but also allows for new elements to be introduced and old ones to exit. There is some internal cohesiveness to the system—not all elements can enter readily into it. Some elements fit more readily into the existing system than others. Other elements either are unable to enter into the system or must change in order to do so. In addition, a change in one element of the system potentially changes the entire system.

For example, a psychodynamic–behavioral integration may be an overall framework that encourages attempts to introduce a number of different elements from an evolving behavior therapy and to introduce them at different times, to see how they interact with elements that are also introduced from an evolving body of psychodynamic theory and therapy. Different elements can be introduced and different resulting systems can be explored. This view of integration is quite different from a fixed synthesis of two static entities. The open system framework is one which can generate different models at different times that may lead to new theories, new variations of clinical therapy, and new research.

There has been a trend in recent theory in psychotherapy toward a framework even broader than a psychodynamic–behavioral one which seeks to integrate cognitive, affective, behavioral, and interpersonal aspects of human functioning (e.g., Andrews, 1991b; Beckham, 1990; Goldfried & Safran, 1986; Greenberg & Safran, 1987, 1989; Horowitz, 1988, 1991; Safran & Segal, 1990; Schwartz, 1991). Some are even questioning a sharp distinction among these response systems, suggesting that such a distinction may be artificial (e.g., Schwartz, 1984, 1991). A recent paper by Beckham illustrates this trend. After reviewing the outcome research on depression, Beckham (1990) suggested that:

Depression may be viewed as a homeostatic system to the extent that it involves many different components of a patient's life and consists of feedback loops of reciprocal maintaining processes between those components. According to this model the effect of a psychotherapy in altering one element of the depressive homeostasis quickly spreads to other elements in the depressive system. (Beckham, 1990, p. 211)

He further suggested that the elements in this homeostasis are cognitive, affective, interpersonal, and biological. Further, Beckham argued that different therapies for depression may be equally effective because they all disturb this homeostatic balance by intervening through one part of the system (cognitive, affective, interpersonal or behavioral, or biological). Others have also presented integrative systems proposals as a basis for theoretical integration (e.g., Schwartz, 1984, 1991).

This broader systemic framework for psychotherapy integration parallels the interest in similar views in other areas of psychology (e.g., Izard, Kagan, & Zajonc, 1983; Schwartz, 1984). This type of theory holds a great deal of promise for a more comprehensive framework for theoretical integration.

Evaluation of Theoretical Integration

It is clear that a great deal of work in theoretical integration has already been done, but much work remains. Theoretical integration has led us to question and challenge the assumptions of the single-school approach. It has presented the field with new proposals for theory and practice. However, it has not yet led to any new research. Well-controlled outcome studies of integrative therapies have not yet been conducted so we do not yet know if their promise of greater effectiveness is real. Further, the new theory development has not been accompanied by experiments to test hypotheses about psychopathology and change derived from these theories. Part of the problem is that integrative theories have not yet led to clear hypotheses that are identifiably different from those derived from the separate theories that entered into the integration. More recent integrative proposals dealing with the interactions among cognition, affect, and behavior hold considerable promise for new hypotheses and new research because of the close connections that these views have to basic research, theory, and measurement in other areas of psychology.

At the level of practice, a large number of therapists identify themselves as practicing some type of theoretical integration (Norcross & Prochaska, 1982). However, this endorsement probably does not convey much specific information about their practice. The term *theoretical integration* suggests an overall framework rather than the endorsement of a specific integrative theory and specific therapy techniques.

Common Factors

The common factors approach has been a search for the basic ingredients that different therapies may share. Whereas theoretical integration emphasizes the integration of *differences*, the common factors approach seeks to abstract *similarities* across different therapies.[1] These similarities may be at the level of theory or clinical practice. Those persons interested in common factors believe that apparent differences in theoretical constructs or clinical techniques are more superficial than real and may mask some basic underlying similarities. Implicit in the common factors approach has been the promise that identification of common factors can help us build not only better theories of change but more effective therapies as well.

One of the guiding themes in the search for common factors is the view that all reasonable therapies are equally effective. Until around 1970, this was simply an unconfirmed belief. After this time, a large number of well-controlled comparative outcome studies appeared whose results were also consistent with this conclusion (see Beckham, 1990; Elkin et al., 1989; Lambert, 1986; Lambert, Shapiro, & Bergin, 1986, Sloane et al., 1975, Smith, Glass, & Miller, 1980; Stiles, Shapiro, & Elliot, 1986).

How can the identification of what is already there create something better than what we started with? The concept of bootstrapping may be useful here. The dictionary defines *bootstrapping* as a procedure that creates something better without external aid. In statistical terms, bootstrapping tries to improve our ability to predict by reducing the bias and measurement error that are associated with each of the individual predictors (see example by Dawes, 1971). In the case of psychotherapy integration, those individual predictors are the different therapies. The bias and measurement errors relate to those sources of error uniquely associated with each therapy which may obscure the "true" factors that may be the causal agents for change in all therapies.

Crucial to the bootstrapping process is the relation of the identified factors to some important criterion. One goal of the common factors approach is to discover the profile of factors *that are most strongly associated with positive therapeutic outcome*. Once identified, such factors may be used

---

[1] It should be noted that theoretical integration *does* seek commonalities among different approaches to some degree. Without such common ground, theoretical integration would be impossible. However, the strongest emphasis in theoretical integration is in integrating different components from different approaches into a unified framework.

as starting points for the development of improved theories and therapies. It is even conceivable that such bootstrapping can yield a weighting of different factors for different clinical problems.

Early History

In many ways, the history of the common factors approach parallels that of theoretical integration. Early proposals appeared as far back as the 1930s. During the next 40 years, occasional and isolated publications on the topic appeared. There was a rapid growth in the number of publications in the late 1970s and thereafter.

One of the earliest papers on common factors was by Rosenzweig (1936). In it, he pointed to several factors that he believed might account for the effectiveness of different therapies. These included the therapist's ability to inspire hope, the importance of providing the patient with alternative and more plausible ways of viewing the self and the world. Alexander and French (1946) coined the term "corrective emotional experience" for what they believed was a central process of change in psychotherapy. They wrote:

> In all forms of etiological psychotherapy, the basic therapeutic principle is the same: To re-expose the patient, under more favorable circumstances, to emotional situations which he could not handle in the past. The patient, in order to be helped, must undergo a corrective emotional experience suitable to repair the traumatic influence of previous experiences. (p. 66)

The corrective emotional experience involves a relationship different from ones expected or experienced in the past. This basic concept has remained a central one in more recent formulations (e.g., Arkowitz & Hannah, 1989; Brady et al., 1980, Frank, 1961, 1982; Strupp, 1973).

Results from a series of studies by Fiedler (1950a, 1950b) also focused on the relationship as a source of common factors in psychotherapy and provide a fascinating, although indirect, examination of some of these factors. Fiedler asked therapists of different experience levels and orientations to describe what they considered to be the components of the ideal therapeutic relationship. He found that expert therapists of different schools agreed more with each other than they did with novices from their own school. In a companion study using ratings of actual therapy sessions, Fiedler found a similar pattern of findings using actual ratings of the therapy sessions. The experts from different schools were more similar to each other than to novices within their own school in the characteristics of the relationship they actually developed with their clients. Although Fiedler did not examine the outcome of these therapies, his results provide some indirect support for the common factors notion by suggesting that experience may shape therapists to behave in some basically similar ways, at least with respect to the type of relationship they establish.

Certainly, one of the most influential early writings on common factors was a book by Jerome Frank (1961) titled *Persuasion and Healing*. Frank argued that psychotherapy was an influencing process and that we may learn about what accounts for change by looking at other influencing processes. He examined basic similarities among psychotherapy, placebo effects in medicine, brainwashing, and faith-healing in our own culture and in others. Based upon his review, he suggested that some of the basic ingredients in all psychotherapies include arousing hope, causing emotional arousal, encouraging changed activity outside of the session, and encouraging new ways of understanding oneself and one's problems through interpretations and corrective emotional experiences.

In a book with a title as provocative as its content, Schofield (1964) raised the issue as *Psychotherapy: The Purchase of Friendship*. He discussed a number of possible common factors in different psychotherapies but stressed the importance of relationship factors. He suggested that therapists, as representatives of their culture, provide to their patients "acceptance in our culture in this time" (1964, p. 109), and in this sense they provide a very special, perhaps ideal, form of friendship.

Carl Rogers (1951, 1957) indirectly contributed to the common factors theme by proposing that therapy was effective not because of specific techniques but because it provided a particular type of human relationship in which change could occur. Truax and his associates (e.g., Truax & Mitchell, 1971) elaborated on some of these ideas and pointed to the importance of warmth, empathy, and unconditional positive regard in the outcome of therapy.

In 1966, an unusual book by Goldstein, Heller, and Sechrest (1966) appeared. These authors conceptualized psychotherapy as a persuasion process and looked to the social psychological literature on attitude change and persuasion to see what can be learned of benefit to psychotherapy. They reviewed literature from social psychology on such topics as the attractiveness, credibility, and status of the persuader; the distance between the two positions; and expectancies. Their fascinating journey from psychotherapy to social psychology led them to make concrete suggestions about ways to increase the amount of attitude change in psychotherapy. Their book was one of the earliest attempts to conceptualize psychotherapy as an influence and persuasion process and to draw on social psychology for concepts and ideas for techniques. Perhaps because these authors, as well as Frank, saw psychotherapy as a process of persuasion, they clashed with the trends in psychotherapy of that time that were antithetical to the idea of direct influence and active intervention.

The 1960s and 1970s yielded several other discussions of common factors (e.g., Garfield, 1973; Goldstein, 1962; Hobbs, 1962), but overall, there was little published on the topic. Raimy (1975) suggested that all forms of psychotherapy were directed toward changing misconceptions about the self by presenting the person with evidence to challenge these misperceptions. He suggested that therapies differed only on the methods used to present this challenging evidence. Raimy pointed to the importance of changing beliefs and schemas in virtually all psychotherapies. This emphasis on changing schemas was at the heart of Beck's cognitive therapy and has also received attention in the later common factors literature (Arkowitz & Hannah, 1989; Goldfried & Robins, 1983).

Jerome Frank (1961, 1973, 1974, 1982) continued to modify and develop his common factors model and has more recently focused on the restoration of morale as a significant common factor. Frank hypothesized that all therapies address a common problem—a "demoralization," consisting of a loss of self-esteem and subjective feelings of incompetence, alienation, hopelessness, and helplessness. He suggested that all therapies may be equally effective in restoring morale, despite the different ways in which they do so. He has also further articulated his earlier work and suggested the following as therapeutic components shared by different psychotherapies: An emotionally charged confiding relationship with a helping person; a healing setting; a rational conceptual scheme or myth to explain symptoms; and a ritual to help resolve symptoms (Frank, 1982).

Some of the central themes of common factors thinking were already apparent during this time. There was a strong emphasis on the commonalities in the therapy *relationship* and various attempts to conceptualize these relationship factors. Many proposals also included corrective emotional experiences in therapy and the disconfirmation of dysfunctional expectancies, the arousal of hope and positive expectancies, changes in self-perceptions, persuasion and attitude change, and restoration of morale.

From the time of Rosenzweig's paper (1936) until about 1980, there was a slow but steady progression of thought regarding common factors. Nonetheless, this kind of thinking did not exert any significant impact on psychotherapy until the late 1970s. Many of the reasons for this paralleled those affecting theoretical integration, discussed earlier. For the most part, the therapies were too busy defining themselves and their differences to seek commonalities that might threaten their distinct identities.

Recent Developments

Since 1980, there has been a sharp increase in interest in a common factors approach, with more books and papers published during these years than perhaps all previous years combined (e.g., Arkowitz & Hannah, 1989; Beutler, 1983; Brady et al., 1980; Cornsweet, 1983; Garfield, 1980; Goldfried, 1980, 1982a; Grencavage & Norcross, 1990; Haaga, 1986; Jones, Cumming, & Horowitz, 1988; Karasu, 1986; Lambert, 1986; Orlinsky & Howard, 1987; Prochaska, 1984). The proposals became more specific and there was more discussion about the locus of the common factors (e.g., in patient, in therapist, in relationship, in techniques, etc.). During the 1980s, a considerable amount of therapy outcome research appeared consistent with a common factors argument; finally, and perhaps, most important, empirical studies growing out of a common factors perspective began to appear (e.g., Goldfried, 1991). Such studies attempted to measure common factors, test hypotheses about them, and determine the correlations of different possible common factors with therapy outcome.

The 1980s opened with two papers significant to the common factors approach. In a study by Brady et al. (1980), prominent therapists from a variety of orientations responded to a series of questions regarding the effective ingredients in psychotherapy. There was consensus that *providing the patient with new experiences*, both inside and outside of therapy, was a central ingredient of all psychotherapies. These new experiences were considered important because they lead to changes in the ways people think about themselves. While there were differences in how such experiences should be provided and their precise role in the change process, all agreed on the centrality of such experiences. This emphasis on new experiences was consistent with earlier proposals involving the corrective emotional experience. However, "new experiences" is only a very general description, and how these new experiences may be provided and how they facilitate change are themes that remained to be developed more precisely in common factors models.

In another significant paper, Goldfried (1980) raised the issue of the level of abstraction that might be most useful from which to derive common factors. He suggested that we search for commonalities at an intermediary level of abstraction, between broad theories and specific techniques. He called this the level of "clinical strategies" or change principles that guide our efforts during therapy. He suggested two strategies that are important in all psychotherapies. One is having the patient engage in new, corrective experiences. The second was providing feedback, a process in which the therapist's interventions help patients increase their awareness of thoughts, feelings, and actions.

Goldfried focused his subsequent efforts on feedback and has developed an extensive coding system for measuring different aspects of feedback. He has completed several preliminary but provocative studies using this coding system (Goldfried, 1991). His work points to the importance of *both* common and unique factors in different approaches to therapy.

In one study, Goldfried (1991) found that both cognitive–behavioral therapists and psychodynamic–interpersonal therapists tended to focus more on feedback about interpersonal themes than on feedback about intrapersonal themes, despite theoretical differences that might lead one to think otherwise. Some differences between the two did emerge. Cognitive–behavioral therapists focused more on patients' actions, whereas psychodynamic–interpersonal therapists focused more on emotions and expectations. One particularly provocative finding was that, although the two therapies did not differ in their emphasis on interpersonal feedback, this type of feedback was associated with outcome more strongly in the psychodynamic than in the cognitive–behavioral therapy. In addition, feedback relating to "transference" themes had a stronger relation to outcome for psychodynamic therapy than for cognitive therapy. Thus, the same strategy may have a different impact in the context of different patients, therapies, and therapy relationships. This suggests the possibility that our conceptualization of common factors may be too unitary and simplistic and that we may need to examine contextual factors as well (cf. Jones, Cumming, & Horowitz, 1988). Although many of Goldfried's results are still preliminary, his work stands as an excellent illustration of how psychotherapy integration can lead to new research directions on clinically interesting questions. His focus has been to search for common factors starting with what therapists actually do in therapy, rather than on what they say they do. Further, his findings point to the importance of both common and unique factors in therapy outcome.

In another proposal, Prochaska and his associates (Prochaska, 1984; Prochaska & DiClemente, 1986; Prochaska, Rossi, & Wilcox, 1991) focused on commonalities in the process of change across different problems and different methods of change. Prochaska pointed to stages of change (e.g., precontemplation, contemplation, action, and maintenance), levels of change (e.g., symptoms, maladaptive cognitions, current interpersonal conflicts, family/systems conflicts; intrapersonal conflicts), and change processes (e.g., consciousness raising, stimulus control, self-reevaluation, environmental reevaluation). Prochaska and his associates have demonstrated that it is possible to measure these stages, levels, and processes and have published several studies that have demonstrated interesting interactions among them in people trying to change (Prochaska, 1984; Prochaska & DiClemente, 1986; Prochaska, Rossi, & Wilcox, 1991).

A number of other interesting proposals and discussions of common factors have appeared in recent years (e.g., Arkowitz & Hannah, 1989; Beitman, 1987; Beutler, 1983; Kilbourne & Richardson, 1988; Orlinsky & Howard, 1987; Wills, 1982). In a recent paper, Grencavage and Norcross (1990) took the unique approach of looking for the commonalities among common factors suggested in the writings of different psychotherapists. They grouped the various suggestions into categories and presented the most frequent ones within each. Under *client characteristics*, they found that positive expectations, hope, or faith were by far the most frequent. For *therapist qualities*, they found a general category of positive descriptors, followed by cultivation of hope and positive expectancies, as well as factors relating to warmth, positive regard, and empathic understanding. The largest number of different factors related to *change processes*. These included catharsis, acquisition and practice of new behaviors, provision of rationale, fostering insight or awareness, and emotional and interpersonal learning. *Treatment structures* that were frequently suggested included use of techniques and rituals, focus on inner world and exploration of emotional issues, adherence to theory, and a healing setting. Under *relationship elements*, there was a general factor endorsed by a majority of the writers that they described as the development of the alliance or relationship. In addition to trying to extract what common wisdom there may be among those proposing common factors, this paper also draws our attention to possible loci of the various common factors. Clearly, they are all interrelated (e.g., the relationship and change processes), but there are still questions to be answered about the best places to look for the most potent common factors.

The accelerating interest in common factors in the 1980s was largely sparked by the well-controlled therapy outcome studies that began to appear which suggested a lack of differential outcome among different therapies. In addition, reviews by Beutler, Mohr, Grawe, Engle, and MacDonald (1991) and by Lambert (1989) suggested that techniques accounted for less than 15 percent of the outcome variance in psychotherapy. This conclusion provided a further impetus to look toward common factors and away from the technique factors uniquely associated with the different therapies.

Evaluation of the Common Factors Approach

The common factors approach has led to some fascinating speculations about factors that may cut across therapies, to promising beginnings of the measurement of common factors, to studies looking at the association of common factors with therapy outcome, and to formulations that have potential for new lines of research and hypothesis testing. However, the impact of the common factors approach on clinical practice has been relatively minor thus far. Because we have not yet been able to confidently identify what the potent factors really are, we are unable to modify our practice accordingly.

An important requirement for the common factors bootstrapping strategy is the demonstration that the factor is correlated with therapy outcome. Some beginnings have been made in this direction (e.g., Goldfried, 1991), but reviews of other studies in this area have yielded only low to moderate correlations of process and outcome variables (Orlinsky & Howard, 1986).

Even if we do demonstrate a strong correlation between a factor and therapy outcome, we are still left with many questions about causality. For example, the arousal of hope and positive expectancies has been frequently referred to as an important commonality across therapies. Several studies have demonstrated correlations between this variable and therapy outcome (see review by Orlinsky & Howard, 1986). Does this suggest that hope causes positive outcome? It is just as plausible that as positive outcomes begin to occur, hope is aroused. Further, a third factor such as a supportive relationship may increase both hope and positive outcome. Essentially, we are generating correlational data to try to answer questions about causal factors, and so our conclusions are limited at best. Perhaps correlational research relating process and outcome might benefit from statistical procedures involving causal modeling (e.g., James, Mulaick, & Brett, 1982). These procedures allow the investigator to rule out alternative explanations to a greater degree than do simple correlational techniques. In addition, as research on common factors moves toward true experimental designs and the manipulation of variables, problems of interpretation of causality will diminish.

Determining the *type* and *level* of common factors is another challenge facing this area. What common factors shall we examine? We can search for commonalities in therapist characteristics, patient characteristics and processes, setting characteristics, change processes, relationship processes, clinical techniques, and theories of change. Further, not every commonality is necessarily important. There are many similarities among the different therapies. For example, most psychotherapies involve two or more people in seated positions who make eye contact. Nonetheless, few would suggest that these are crucial change elements in psychotherapy. Thus, simply identifying a factor common across therapies is only a first step to finding out the contribution of that factor to the change process. In addition, as Goldfried (1980) has pointed out, we can seek commonalities at many levels. A strategy that can help us determine what the important factors might be is still lacking, as are methods to determine which are the most important factors. Perhaps part of the answer lies in better theories, along with true experimental designs or causal modeling procedures to test out hypotheses from these theories.

The *degree of specificity* of the proposed common factors has also been a problem in the past. I have serious questions about the merits of discussing the therapy relationship as a common factor without attempting to define what *specific aspects* of the relationship may be important in creating change. Greater specificity also permits measurement and research to examine the role of the identified relationship factors.

In addition to trying to specify and measure the factors that are important in the therapy relationship, it may also be helpful to look at *other* relationships that involve helping, influence, or change (Higginbotham, West, & Forsyth, 1988; Wills, 1982). In this regard, recent work on social support (e.g., Brown & Harris, 1978; Cohen & Syme, 1985) suggests that it may be a useful construct for thinking about common factors. The relative effectiveness of control conditions in psychotherapy research that consist mostly of support and positive expectancies (e.g., Elkin et al., 1989) point to the potential importance of social support as a common factor.

We may also need to look at interactions of particular common factors with particular forms of psychopathology. For example, it may not be a coincidence that the "control group" therapies involving social support have been shown to be almost equivalent to other therapies for treating depression, given the association of low social support and depression (e.g., Brown & Harris, 1978).

Another issue that needs to be considered in common factors is the unidimensional and linear view of causality inherent in most common factors proposals. Most of the proposals reviewed suggest that a certain number of specified factors are important. They do not suggest that the factors may relate to one another and to other contextual variables (e.g., Goldfried, 1991) or that the factors may change over the course of therapy. We need to think more in terms of multivariate and interactive relationships among common factors to explain changes in therapy as well as possible changes in the role of particular common factors over the course of therapy.

Finally, the reader of the common factors literature may come away from it with the impression that advocates of this position are arguing for common *versus* unique factors in determining therapy outcome. While most discussions of common factors either ignore or minimize factors that differentiate among different therapies, I believe that it is a mistake to do so. The issue can be more productively posed as common *and* unique factors and the contributions that both may make to the therapy process. Studies like those of Goldfried (1991) and of Jones, Cumming, and Horowitz (1988) provide support for both common and unique factors.

Finally, the main foundation for the search for common factors has been the lack of differential outcome in many studies comparing the effectiveness of different therapies. This type of finding is by no means uniform, and Stiles, Shapiro, and Elliot (1986) have discussed a number of possible interpretations, only one of which is compatible with a common factors point of view. One particularly plausible explanation of this finding is that the lack of group differences obscures the important *variability* in outcome for different people in the different therapies. This line of thinking suggests that we ought to try to identify individual differences in response to therapy and use these as the basis for building a conceptual framework. It is exactly this strategy that is adopted by those interested in the third main direction in psychotherapy integration—technical eclecticism.

Technical Eclecticism

Background and Early History

Eclecticism is a strategy of selecting whatever seems best from a variety of alternatives. Eclectic psychotherapists choose from among available therapy techniques on the basis of what they think will work best for the particular person and problem. Different techniques from different therapies may be applied to the same person, or a certain technique may be used with different patients and problems.

In eclecticism, the basis for treatment selection is more actuarial than theoretical. The main criterion used by eclectic therapists when selecting treatments is what has worked best for similar people with similar problems in the past. Theory is not viewed as a particularly important basis for treatment selection. This relative deemphasis on theory distinguishes eclecticism from both theoretical integration and the common factors approach.

An eclectic approach was not really feasible until the 1970s. Prior to that time, the field of psychotherapy was, to a large extent, dominated by monolithic psychoanalytic and client-centered approaches that were being applied to all people and all problems. In none of these therapies were there many specific or clearly described techniques from which therapists could choose to form an eclectic approach.

Prior to the 1980s, there was little interest in eclecticism in the published literature on psychotherapy. Nonetheless, various surveys since the early 1960s demonstrated that a large percentage of practicing therapists endorsed some form of eclecticism to describe their approach (e.g., Garfield

& Kurtz, 1976; Kelly, 1961; Norcross & Prochaska, 1983). This suggests that the realities of practice were leading practicing clinicians toward some form of eclecticism and that psychotherapy theories were not reflecting this fact. Nonetheless, prior to 1980, eclecticism was often little more than an idiosyncratic mixture of techniques selected on no clearly discernible conceptual basis. There was little information about how therapists practiced and how techniques were selected and combined. This chaotic situation led Eysenck (1970) to describe eclecticism as "a mish-mash of theories, a hugger-mugger of procedures, a gallimaufry of therapies (p. 145)." Eysenck strongly criticized eclectics for lacking an acceptable rationale and empirical evaluation of their approach.

Since 1980, a number of books and articles have appeared that presented more systematic bases for eclecticism and included debates on the merits of such an approach (e.g., Beutler, 1979, 1983; Beutler & Clarkin, 1990; Frances, Clarkin, & Perry, 1984; Garfield, 1980, 1986; Lazarus, 1986; Norcross, 1986). In this period we also saw the appearance of the *International Journal of Eclectic Psychotherapy*, which was later changed to the *Journal of Integrative and Eclectic Psychotherapy*. A *Handbook of Eclectic Psychotherapy* (Norcross, 1986) was also published. This book brought together the major contributors to eclecticism and included chapters on a wide variety of eclectic approaches. Why was there now so much interest in eclecticism in the literature? Part of the answer may have to do with developments in behavior therapy.

In 1969, Gordon Paul posed a question for behavior therapy that was to later guide psychotherapy research more generally. Paul asked: "What treatment, by whom, is most effective for this individual with that specific problem, under which set of circumstances, and how does it come about?" (Paul, 1969, p. 44). This question directed the attention of therapists and researchers to the many variables that could possibly influence the outcome of psychotherapy. It also pointed to the possibility of maximizing treatment outcome by an optimal selection and matching of particular therapies with particular people and problems. Paul's question became the cornerstone of later eclectic approaches to psychotherapy.

As noted earlier, in the 1960s and 1970s behavior therapy made its greatest impact on psychotherapy. In many respects, behavior therapy can be viewed as a form of limited eclecticism. It is characterized by a diversity of behavioral techniques from which to choose, with an emphasis on selecting the best techniques for the particular problem based on probable efficacy. It may be that the success of the eclecticism of behavior therapy stimulated interest in broader eclectic proposals that drew from a wider range of therapies. Consistent with this point of view, it is probably not purely coincidental that one of the earliest and most important eclectic proposals was developed by a leading figure in behavior therapy, Arnold Lazarus.

The Technical Eclecticism of Arnold Lazarus

The concept of *technical eclecticism* was introduced by Lazarus in 1967. In this and subsequent publications, Lazarus (1967, 1971, 1973, 1976, 1981, 1986; Lazarus & Messer, 1988, 1991) broadened the potential base of eclecticism from behavior therapy to techniques associated with other therapy systems. Lazarus (1971) argued that clinicians can use techniques from different therapy systems without necessarily accepting the theoretical bases associated with them.

Lazarus referred to his eclectic approach as "multimodal behavior therapy" (Lazarus, 1973, 1976) and later as "multimodal therapy" (Lazarus, 1981, 1986). He demonstrated the importance of assessment and intervention in the various modalities that characterize human functioning including behavior, affect, sensation, imagery, cognition, interpersonal relationships, and biology. Consistent with other modern eclectics, Lazarus emphasizes treatment specificity, the matching of techniques to persons and problems and the selecting of treatments based on empirical evidence of their effectiveness.

Despite his deemphasis on theory, Lazarus (1986) acknowledged that every practitioner uses at least some theory to guide their choices. Multimodal therapy, Lazarus (1986) asserted, rests primarily on the theoretical foundation of social learning theory, drawing also from general systems theory and communications theory. Indeed, the techniques that Lazarus (1986) lists as part of multimodal therapy draw most heavily from behavioral and cognitive therapies, and minimally, if at all, from psychodynamic and other therapies. This is surprising given Lazarus' criterion of empirical data for selecting therapies and the accumulating evidence of the effectiveness of such approaches (e.g., Sloane, Staples, Cristol, Yorkston, & Whipple, 1975; Smith, Glass, & Miller, 1980; Steuer et al., 1984). Lazarus' eclectic approach appears to fall somewhere between a broadened version of behavior therapy and an eclectic strategy that can choose from among *any* therapy system if there is empirical data to support that choice. Beutler's (1983, 1986) systematic eclecticism is closer to a comprehensive and empirical eclecticism, and it is to this approach that we turn next.

Beutler's Systematic Eclectic Psychotherapy

Beutler's systematic eclectic psychotherapy shares several features with Lazarus' technical eclecticism: an emphasis on treatment specificity and the matching of technique to person and problem; an emphasis on empirical data to determine choice of therapy; and a relative deemphasis on the role of theory to guide the choice of therapy (Beutler, 1983, 1986). Unlike Lazarus' technical eclecticism, Beutler's approach draws from the entire range of psychotherapy approaches.

Beutler, Mohr, Grawe, Engle, & MacDonald (1991) have argued that there are data to suggest that most of the variance in outcome in psychotherapy is due to variables other than specific techniques. Systematic eclecticism concentrates on the matching of a broad array of patient variables, treatment variables, and patient–treatment interactions that are most likely to maximize therapy outcome. Instead of focusing primarily on the match between problem and technique, Beutler also includes such variables as therapist characteristics (e.g., experience, attitudes, beliefs), patient characteristics (e.g., symptom complexity, coping style and resistance to influence), technique variables, and interactions among these variables. According to Beutler, it is only within this broad context that we should seek the best match between problems and techniques.

As Beutler et al. (1991) correctly point out, the number of potential variables to be considered in such a matrix are limitless. Further, there is little to guide us in the selection of variables that might be most productive or relevant. It is here that Beutler turns to theory to help guide these choices.

Beutler (1986) suggests that a *functional* theory must be developed that encourages and dictates the utilization of these approaches. Such a functional approach would be highly actuarial in nature, emphasizing what has worked best in the past in similar matches among variables. In addition, Beutler bases his work on social psychological theories of persuasion and influence to understand some of the possible interactions of patient and treatment characteristics.

In a recent extension of the systematic eclectic approach, Beutler and Clarkin (1990) tried to empirically identify the patient qualities that hold most promise for enhancing the fit between specific patients and treatments. These dimensions included level of motivating distress, problem severity, coping style, and the propensity to resist interpersonal influence. Beutler (1989) found that the mean amount of outcome variance accounted for by such variables was substantially higher than the amount of variance that could be accounted for by techniques alone. Beutler et al. (1991) reviewed research on patient coping style and reactance levels as predictors of different rates of response to different procedures and have presented some preliminary data from prospective studies in which some of these variables were used to predict therapy outcome. Thus, Beutler's systematic eclecticism continues to evolve and has begun to stimulate empirical research as well.

Evaluation and Current Status of Technical Eclecticism

Clearly, recent versions of eclecticism are less vulnerable to critics like Eysenck who see them as unsystematic approaches with little or no associated conceptual foundations or research. In fact, proposals like those of Lazarus and Beutler strive for coherent frameworks for organizing and selecting treatments. Each also looks to empirical research to help guide the choice of technique.

Beutler's systematic eclecticism comes closest to an actuarial approach that can sample the whole range of therapies based on evidence for the effectiveness of the techniques. In addition, Beutler includes the many variables that need to be taken into account beyond those associated with technique and problem.

At the very heart of modern eclecticism is an actuarial approach that uses data from past cases to predict what will work best for new cases. This actuarial approach requires a search for relations among variables, rather than for an overall theory to fit to these data. The hypothetical matrix that such an approach might generate shows promise for guiding clinicians in choosing the best therapy for the person and problem. This is the promise of eclecticism. However, the actuarial strategy is also the Achilles heel of eclecticism.

One problem is the enormous number of possible variables that may correlate with the enormous number of outcome measures. How can we organize such an incredible number of variables to permit the kinds of predictions that eclecticism seeks? Orlinsky and Howard (1986) reviewed over 1,100 studies over a 35-year period relating process variables to outcome measures. There were almost as many specific variables as there were different studies, and the magnitudes of many of the significant correlations were often disappointingly small. Without some theory to guide our search for relevant variables, we run the risk of generating another 1,100 correlational studies that tell us little. As Arkowitz (1989) has pointed out, eclecticism may need more theory to help select and order the variables and to generate hypotheses about what causes change.

The variables in this hypothetical matrix are also not independent of one another. Technical eclectics are not simply searching for correlations between two events, but for multivariate interactions among a wide array of intercorrelated variables. If the number of variables is limitless, the number of interactions among them is also limitless. In simple terms, the task seems overwhelming unless we have some coherent framework to guide the selection of relevant variables and to help in understanding the interactions among variables. It is here that theory is helpful, and perhaps even essential.

There is yet another problem. The actuarial matrix sought by eclectics is basically a correlation matrix of process variables and outcome variables with different types of people and problems. Even if we were able to meaningfully organize such a matrix of variables, our hypothetical actuarial table does not help us to identify those truly causal factors that, if employed, would influence the outcome of psychotherapy. Again, it appears that some greater theoretical structure is needed.

The empiricism of eclecticism and the theory of common factors and theoretical integration may be complementary rather than antagonistic approaches to the same goals. Eclecticism emphasizes the collection of data on relationships among variables with minimal theory to guide that undertaking. More theoretically oriented integration approaches emphasize theories but have been weak in data. The data of eclecticism should form the basis for the theories of psychotherapy integration, just as the theories of psychotherapy integration may serve to guide the search for data of the eclectics. All of the psychotherapy integration approaches share similar goals. They do differ, however, on the level and type of theory that are considered to be most helpful at this stage in the development of the field.

WHY INTEGRATION NOW?

To some extent, different factors have influenced the development of each of the three approaches to psychotherapy integration. However, there have also been some important influences that they have shared. For example, the temporal fluctuations in interest in each of the three approaches (as indexed by the number of publications) is rather similar. There was little interest in integration before 1970, a growing interest during the 1970s, and a rapidly accelerating interest from 1980 up to the present. What factors could have accounted for this pattern?

First, psychotherapy integration has, in part, been a response to *the improved quality of psychotherapy outcome research* during this period, and to the lack of strong evidence to support differential outcomes among existing therapies. Prior to the late 1970s, there were very few well-designed studies on the outcome of psychotherapy. Since then, the number of such studies has increased dramatically (e.g., see review by Lambert, Shapiro, & Bergin, 1986), and meta-analytic procedures (e.g., Smith, Glass, & Miller, 1980) have provided more objective ways to summarize and compare the results of different studies. These studies have revealed surprisingly few significant differences in outcome among different therapies. Although we do need to be cautious in accepting the null hypothesis and to remember that there are many possible interpretations of such findings (e.g., Stiles, Shapiro, & Elliot, 1986), they very likely served as a catalyst for many who began to consider integrative interpretations of these results.

Another likely contributing factor was *the increase in the number of specific therapies* that became available. Paralleling the growth of interest in psychotherapy integration has been a sharp increase in the number of different therapies (Karasu, 1986) and in the number of variations within each of the major psychotherapies. This increasing diversity had two effects. One was to make available a greater range of theories and techniques, from which an integration could be crafted. Another was to alert therapists to the almost infinite number of variations in technique. The latter may have discouraged the search for further variations and encouraged therapists to seek more creative ways to utilize existing therapies.

Along with the growing number of therapies was a trend toward *more specific and operational descriptions of psychotherapy techniques and strategies.* Prior to 1970, there were few specific, operational descriptions of techniques and strategies in psychotherapy. From the late 1970s on, a number of specific treatment manuals appeared (e.g., Beck, Rush, Shaw, & Emery, 1979; Luborsky, 1984; Strupp & Binder, 1984), often growing out of research on the different therapies. Luborsky and DeRubeis (1984) referred to this sharply increasing emphasis on manuals as a "small revolution." The availability of more clearly described therapy procedures permitted more accurate comparisons and contrasts among them, providing further impetus for various approaches to psychotherapy integration.

Increasing interest in short-term psychotherapies during the past 20 years (e.g., see Budman, 1981) also contributed to the growing interest in integration. An interest in short-term therapies was accompanied by the development of more problem-focused therapies. Emphasis on a problem focus in different therapies (although there were still differences in how to define "problem") may have created a greater awareness of commonalities among therapies.

The success and popularity of cognitive therapy, which emerged during the 1970s, may also have contributed to the interest in integration. Some have suggested that cognitive therapy can be thought of as an integrative therapy (e.g., Alford & Norcross, 1991; Beck, 1991) that combines behavioral techniques with cognitive techniques and theory. The popularity of this therapy, as well as the evidence for its effectiveness (see Freeman,

Simon, Beutler, & Arkowitz, 1989) may have served as an impetus to examine other types of integration.

London and Palmer (1988) have suggested that the trend toward *increasing interactions among professionals of different therapy orientations in specialized clinics for the treatment of specific disorders* may also have affected the development of psychotherapy integration. After the 1970s, there was a movement toward specialized clinics for a variety of problems including sexual dysfunctions, agoraphobia, obsessive-compulsive disorders, depression, and eating disorders, to name just a few. These clinics were often staffed by professionals of different therapy orientations, who placed greater emphasis on their expertise about the clinical problem than on their theoretical orientation per se. This diversity stood in contrast to the earlier emphasis on institutes devoted to specific therapies. At the very least, the exposure to other theories and therapies in such clinics may have stimulated some to consider other orientations more seriously.

The development of a professional network has been both a consequence and cause of the interest in psychotherapy integration. Earlier, I noted that most writers on psychotherapy integration before 1970 tended to be unaware of the work of others who had also published on integration. In fact, the term *psychotherapy integration* was not even used to describe these efforts until the 1980s. The strands for psychotherapy integration were there, but they did not yet form a connected and unified body of thought. In 1983, the Society for the Exploration of Psychotherapy Integration (SEPI) was formed (see description by Goldfried and Newman, 1986) to bring together those who were interested in various forms of rapprochement among the psychotherapies. Even at the outset, many professionals from a variety of orientations and backgrounds supported this group. The organization has brought together those interested in integration through a newsletter and annual conferences. In addition, the *Journal of Psychotherapy Integration* appeared in 1991, sponsored by SEPI.

The emphasis of SEPI has been on the *exploration* of integration, rather than on formalizing or promoting any particular forms of integration. The growth and success of this organization is a consequence of the growing interest in psychotherapy integration. It has also been a catalyst for this interest, because it helped to define the field and is providing avenues of communication for developing a coherent body of thought about psychotherapy and change.

PSYCHOTHERAPY INTEGRATION: CONTRIBUTIONS, PROBLEMS, AND PROMISES

After reviewing the history and current status of the three main directions in psychotherapy integration, I shall conclude this chapter with a broader look at the contributions that integrative thinking has made to the field of psychotherapy, as well as some of its problems and promises. At present, psychotherapy integration has probably had its strongest impact in desegregating the field of psychotherapy, rather than in truly integrating it. Integrative perspectives have been catalytic in the search for new ways of thinking about and doing psychotherapy that go beyond the confines of single-school approaches. Practitioners and researchers are examining what other theories and therapies have to offer. These perspectives have also encouraged new ways of thinking about psychotherapy and change. Further, this has been accomplished without institutionalizing any one way as "the" way. Integration is still an open field in which different ways of thinking and acting are being proposed, explored, and debated. This exploration has already been a healthy challenge to more established ways of thinking about psychotherapy.

Integrative perspectives have already opened up several new avenues for theory, research, and practice in psychotherapy. One type of theoretical integration suggests new ways of thinking about therapy by integrating existing theories. Another type of theoretical integration, based on systemic interactions among affect, behavior, cognition, and social factors has also begun to stimulate new thinking in the field. Both theoretical integration and common factors approaches have begun to suggest new research questions and strategies for therapy. Finally, technical eclecticism has been a stimulus for research in psychotherapy in its search for data on optimal matching strategies to improve therapy outcome. There have also been a number of integrative clinical proposals that suggested new therapy strategies. The achievements of integration have already been noteworthy.

There are a number of problems facing the field as well. In part, this may be due to its relatively early stage of development. At a clinical level, there have been several new suggestions for clinical strategies based on psychotherapy integration. However, these have been relatively few. I believe that we are not yet sure what integrative therapies look like. They are probably not fixed hybrids. They may grow out of general strategies or frameworks, but they remain elusive. Several promising starts have been made in clinical proposals for integrative therapies, but it is clear that much more work needs to be done in the area of integrative therapies, as well as in integrative theory and research.

There are also problems with theories of psychotherapy integration (both theoretical integration and common factors). Such theories are more like general perspectives than formal theories. It is often difficult to derive testable hypotheses from them that allow us to accept or reject their ideas. They may be good general ideas, but they are still far from good theory.

In addition, those proposals that call for an integration of two existing therapy theories have yet to demonstrate that they can lead to predictions other than those generated by each theory separately. The relative lack of good theory in psychotherapy integration may be one of the reasons that it has been so hard to generate very much new research as yet.

While psychotherapy integration has stimulated some research, the number of empirical studies that have derived directly from this way of thinking has been disappointingly low. Even technical eclecticism, with its empirical emphasis, has not yet generated new hypotheses. The data of technical eclecticism are largely the data of single-school approaches. Perhaps the problems with integration theories discussed earlier have limited research attempts or perhaps it is partially a matter of time until more people initiate research programs in the area.

I believe that the single biggest challenge facing the field of psychotherapy integration is to find ways to generate and test hypotheses from these new points of view. Without such data, integrative theories will either become extinct or become a part of a large body of unsubstantiated clinical lore. In this chapter, I have reviewed several promising research programs that have grown out of integrative thinking. However, we need more. The NIMH workshop on research on psychotherapy integration (Wolfe and Goldfried, 1988) generated specific suggestions for research in the area. It is time to take those recommendations seriously in order to create a stronger empirical foundation for psychotherapy integration.

If we can overcome some of the problems discussed above, psychotherapy integration can be a strong factor in encouraging the development of new ways to think about psychotherapy, new strategies for the conduct of therapy, and new theories and research to advance our knowledge about psychotherapy and change. Further, by expanding our scope beyond theories of psychotherapy and by looking toward areas of theory and research in other areas of psychology (e.g., cognitive sciences, social psychology, health psychology, psychobiology), psychotherapy integration promises to bring psychotherapy back to the field of psychology from which it has become somewhat isolated.

REFERENCES

Alexander, F. (1963). The dynamics of psychotherapy in light of learning theory. *American Journal of Psychiatry, 120,* 440–448.

Alexander, F., & French, T. M. (1946). *Psychoanalytic therapy: Principles and application.* New York: Ronald Press.

Alford, B., & Norcross, J. C. (1991). Cognitive therapy as an integrated therapy. *Journal of Psychotherapy Integration*, *1*, 175–190.

Andrews, J. (1991a). *The active self in psychotherapy: An integration of therapeutic styles*. Boston: Allyn & Bacon.

Andrews, J. (1991b). Interpersonal challenge: The second integrative relationship factor. *Journal of Psychotherapy Integration*, *1*, 267–288.

Appelbaum, S. A. (1976). A psychoanalyst looks at gestalt therapy. In C. Hatcher and P. Himmelstein (Eds.), *The handbook of gestalt therapy* (pp. 215–232). New York: Aronson.

Appelbaum, S. A. (1982). Challenges to traditional psychotherapy from the "new therapies." *American Psychologist*, *37*, 1002–1008.

Arkowitz, H. (1984). Historical perspective on the integration of psychoanalytic therapy and behavior therapy. In H. Arkowitz and S. B. Messer (Eds.), *Psychoanalytic therapy and behavior therapy: Is integration possible?* (pp. 1–30). New York: Plenum.

Arkowitz, H. (1985, May). *A behavioral-psychodynamic approach to depression*. Paper presented at the annual meeting of the Society for the Exploration of Psychotherapy Integration, Annapolis, MD.

Arkowitz, H. (1989). The role of theory in psychotherapy integration. *Journal of Integrative and Eclectic Psychotherapy*, *8*, 8–16.

Arkowitz, H., & Hannah, M. T. (1989). Cognitive, behavioral, and psychodynamic therapies: Converging or diverging pathways to change? In A. Freeman, K. Simon, L. Beutler, & H. Arkowitz (Eds.), *Comprehensive handbook of cognitive therapy* (pp. 144–167). New York: Plenum.

Arkowitz, H., & Messer, S. B. (Eds.). (1984). *Psychoanalytic therapy and behavior therapy: Is integration possible?* New York: Plenum.

Babcock, H. H. (1988). Integrative psychotherapy: Collaborative aspects of behavioral and psychodynamic therapies. *Psychiatric Annals*, *18*, 271–272.

Bandura, A. (1969). *Principles of behavior modification*. New York: Holt, Rinehart, & Winston.

Bandura, A. (1977). *Social learning theory*. Englewood Cliffs, NJ: Prentice-Hall.

Beck, A. T. (1991). Cognitive therapy as *the* integrative therapy. *Journal of Psychotherapy Integration*, *1*, 191–198.

Beck, A. T., Rush, A. J., Shaw, B. F., & Emery, G. E. (1979). *Cognitive therapy of depression*. New York: Guilford.

Beckham, E. E. (1990). Psychotherapy of depression at the crossroads: Directions for the 1990s. *Clinical Psychology Review*, *10*, 207–228.

Beitman, B. D. (1987). *The structure of individual psychotherapy*. New York: Guilford.

Beitman, B. D. (1989). Why I am an integrationist (not an eclectic). *British Journal of Guidance and Counselling*, *17*, 259–273.

Beitman, B. D., Goldfried, M. R., & Norcross, J. C. (1989). The movement toward integrating the psychotherapies: An overview. *American Journal of Psychiatry, 146,* 138–147.

Beutler, L. E. (1979). Toward specific psychological therapies for specific conditions. *Journal of Consulting and Clinical Psychology, 47,* 882–892.

Beutler, L. E. (1983). *Eclectic psychotherapy: A systematic approach.* New York: Pergamon.

Beutler, L. E. (1986). Systematic eclectic psychotherapy. In J.C. Norcross (Ed.), *Handbook of eclectic psychotherapy* (pp. 94–131). New York: Brunner/Mazel.

Beutler, L. E. (1989). Differential treatment selection: The role of diagnosis in psychotherapy. *Psychotherapy, 26,* 271–281.

Beutler, L. E., & Clarkin, J. (1990). *Differential treatment selection: Toward targeted therapeutic interventions.* New York: Brunner/Mazel.

Beutler, L. E., Mohr, D. C., Grawe, K., Engle, D., & MacDonald, R. (1991). Looking for differential treatment effects: Cross-cultural predictors of differential therapeutic efficacy. *Journal of Psychotherapy Integration, 1,* 121–141.

Birk, L. (1970). Behavior therapy: Integration with dynamic psychiatry. *Behavior Therapy, 1,* 522–526.

Birk, L. (1988). Behavioral/psychoanalytic psychotherapy with overlapping social systems: A natural matrix for diagnosis and therapeutic change. *Psychiatric Annals, 18,* 292–308.

Birk, L., & Brinkley-Birk, A. (1974). Psychoanalysis and behavior therapy. *American Journal of Psychiatry, 131,* 499–510.

Blanck, G., & Blanck, R. (1976). *Ego psychology* (Vol. 1). New York: Columbia University Press.

Brady, J. P., Davison, G. C., DeWald, P. A., Egan, G., Fadiman, J., Frank, J. D., Gill, M. M., Hoffman, I., Kempler, W., Lazarus, A. A., Raimy, V., Rotter, J. B., & Strupp, H. H. (1980). Some views on effective principles of psychotherapy. *Cognitive Therapy and Research, 4,* 269–306.

Brown, G. W., & Harris, T. (1978). *Social origins of depression: A study of psychiatric disorder in women.* New York: Free Press.

Budman, S. H. (Ed.). (1981). *Forms of brief therapy.* New York: Guilford.

Cohen, S., & Syme, S. L. (1985). *Social support and health.* New York: Academic Press.

Cornsweet, C. (1983). Nonspecific factors and theoretical choice. *Psychotherapy: Theory, Research, and Practice, 20,* 307–313.

Davis, J. D. (1983). Slaying the psychoanalytic dragon: An integrationist's commentary on Yates. *British Journal of Clinical Psychology, 22,* 133–144.

Dawes, R. M. (1971). A case study of graduate admissions: Application of three principles of human decision making. *American Psychologist, 26,* 180–188.

Dollard, J., & Miller, N. E. (1950). *Personality and psychotherapy: An analysis in terms of learning, thinking, and culture.* New York: McGraw-Hill.

Dryden, W., & Norcross, J. C. (1989). Eclecticism and integration in counselling and psychotherapy: Introduction. *British Journal of Guidance and Counselling, 17,* 225–226.

Elkin, I., Shea, M. T., Watkins, J. T., Imber, S. D., Sotsky, S. M., Collins, J. F., Glass, D. R., Pilkonis, P. A., Leber, W. R., Docherty, J. P., Fiester, S. J., & Parloff, M. B. (1989). National Institute of Mental Health Treatment of Depression Collaborative Research Program: General effectiveness of treatments. *Archives of General Psychiatry, 46,* 971–982.

Eysenck, H. J. (1960). Learning theory and behaviour therapy. In H. J. Eysenck (Ed.), *Behaviour therapy and the neuroses* (pp. 67–82). London: Pergamon.

Eysenck, H. J. (1970). A mish-mash of theories. *International Journal of Psychiatry, 9,* 140–146.

Feather, B. W., & Rhoads, J. M. (1972a). Psychodynamic behavior therapy: I. Theory and rationale. *Archives of General Psychiatry, 26,* 496–502.

Feather, B. W., & Rhoads, J. M. (1972b). Psychodynamic behavior therapy: II. Clinical aspects. *Archives of General Psychiatry, 26,* 503–511.

Feldman, L. B., & Pinsof, W. M. (1982). Problem maintenance in family systems: An integrative model. *Journal of Marriage and Family Therapy, 8,* 295–308.

Fensterheim, H. (1983). Introduction to behavioral psychotherapy. In H. Fensterheim and H. I. Glazer (Eds.), *Behavioral psychotherapy: Basic principles and case studies* (pp. 3–23). New York: Brunner/Mazel.

Fiedler, F. E. (1950a). The concept of the ideal therapeutic relationship. *Journal of Consulting Psychology, 14,* 239–245.

Fiedler, F. E. (1950b). Comparisons of therapeutic relationships in psychoanalytic, nondirective, and Adlerian therapy. *Journal of Consulting Psychology, 14,* 436–445.

Fitzpatrick, M. M., & Weber, C. C. (1989). Integrative approaches in psychotherapy: Combining psychodynamic and behavioral treatments. *Journal of Integrative and Eclectic Psychotherapy, 8,* 102–117.

Frances, A., Clarkin, J., & Perry, S. (1984). *Differential therapeutics in psychiatry.* New York: Brunner/Mazel.

Frank, J. D. (1961). *Persuasion and healing.* Baltimore: Johns Hopkins Press.

Frank, J. D. (1973). *Persuasion and healing* (2nd ed.). Baltimore: Johns Hopkins University Press.

Frank, J. D. (1974). Psychotherapy: The restoration of morale. *American Journal of Psychiatry, 131,* 271–274.

Frank, J. D. (1982). Therapeutic components shared by all psychotherapies. In J. H. Harvey and M. M. Parks (Eds.), *The Master Lecture Series. Vol. 1. Psychotherapy research and behavior change* (pp. 73–122). Washington, DC: American Psychological Association.

Franks, C. M. (1984). On conceptual and technical integrity in psychoanalysis and behavior therapy: Two fundamentally incompatible systems. In H. Arkowitz and S. B. Messer (Eds.), *Psychoanalytic therapy and behavior therapy: Is integration possible?* (pp. 223–248). New York: Plenum.

Freeman, A., Simon, K., Beutler, L., & Arkowitz, H. (Eds.). (1989). *Comprehensive handbook of cognitive therapy*. New York: Plenum.

French, T. M. (1933). Interrelations betwen psychoanalysis and the experimental work of Pavlov. *American Journal of Psychiatry, 89*, 1165–1203.

Garfield, S. L. (1973). Basic ingredients or common factors in psychotherapy? *Journal of Consulting and Clinical Psychology, 41*, 9–12.

Garfield, S. L. (1980). *Psychotherapy: An eclectic approach*. New York: Wiley.

Garfield, S. L. (1982). Eclecticism and integration in psychotherapy. *Behavior Therapy, 13*, 610–623.

Garfield, S. L. (1986). An eclectic psychotherapy. In J. C. Norcross (Ed.), *Handbook of eclectic psychotherapy* (pp. 132–162). New York: Brunner/Mazel.

Garfield, S. L., & Kurtz, R. (1976). Clinical psychologists in the 70s. *American Psychologist, 31*, 1–9.

Gill, M. M. (1984). Psychoanalytic, psychodynamic, cognitive behavior, and behavior therapies compared. In H. Arkowitz and S. B. Messer (Eds.), *Psychoanalytic therapy and behavior therapy: Is integration possible?* (pp. 179–188). New York: Plenum.

Goldfried, M. R. (1980). Toward the delineation of therapeutic change principles. *American Psychologist, 35*, 991–999.

Goldfried, M. R. (1982a). *Converging themes in psychotherapy: Trends in psychodynamic, humanistic, and behavioral practice*. New York: Springer.

Goldfried, M. R. (1982b). On the history of therapeutic integration. *Behavior Therapy, 13*, 572–593.

Goldfried, M. R. (1991). Research issues in psychotherapy integration. *Journal of Psychotherapy Integration, 1*, 5–25.

Goldfried, M. R., Greenberg, L. S., & Marmor, C. (1990). Individual psychotherapy: Process and outcome. *Annual Review of Psychology, 41*, 659–688.

Goldfried, M. R., & Newman, C. (1986). Psychotherapy integration: An historical perspective. In J. C. Norcross (Ed.), *Handbook of eclectic psychotherapy* (pp. 25–61). New York: Brunner/Mazel.

Goldfried, M. R., & Robins, C. J. (1983). Self-schema, cognitive bias, and the processing of therapeutic experiences. In P. C. Kendall (Ed.), *Advances in cognitive-behavioral research and therapy* (Vol. 2). New York: Academic Press.

Goldfried, M. R., & Safran, J. D. (1986). Future directions in psychotherapy integration. In J. C. Norcross (Ed.), *Handbook of eclectic psychotherapy* (pp. 463–483). New York: Brunner/Mazel.

Goldstein, A. P. (1962). *Therapist-patient expectancies in psychotherapy*. New York: MacMillan.

Goldstein, A. P., Heller, K. H., & Sechrest, L. B. (1966). *Psychotherapy and the psychology of behavior change*. New York: Wiley.

Greenberg, L. S., & Safran, J. D. (1987). *Emotion in psychotherapy: Affect, cognition, and the process of change*. New York: Guilford.

Greenberg, L. S., & Safran, J. D. (1989). Emotion in psychotherapy. *American Psychologist, 44*, 19–29.

Grencavage, L. M., & Norcross, J. C. (1990). Where are the commonalities among the therapeutic common factors? *Professional Psychology: Research and Practice, 21*, 372–378.

Gurman, A. S. (1981). Integrative marital therapy: Toward the development of an interpersonal approach. In S. Budman (Ed.), *Forms of brief therapy* (pp. 415–457). New York: Guilford.

Haaga, D. A. (1986). A review of the common principles approach to the integration of psychotherapies. *Cognitive Therapy and Research, 10*, 527–538.

Heilizer, F. (1977). A review of theory and research on Miller's response competition (conflict) models. *Journal of General Psychology, 97*, 227–280.

Higginbotham, H. N., West, S. G., & Forsyth, D. R. (1988). *Psychotherapy and behavior change: Social, cultural, and methodological perspectives.* New York: Pergamon.

Hobbs, N. (1962). Sources of gain in counseling and psychotherapy. *American Psychologist, 17*, 741–747.

Horowitz, M. J. (1988). *Introduction to psychodynamics: A new synthesis.* New York: Basic Books.

Horowitz, M. J. (1991). New theory for psychotherapy integration. *Journal of Psychotherapy Integration, 1*, 85–102.

Izard, C., Kagan, J. & Zajonc, R. (Eds.). (1983). *Emotion, cognition, and behaviour.* New York: Cambridge University Press.

James, J. R., Mulaick, S. A., & Brett, J. M. (1982). *Causal analysis: Assumptions, models, and data.* Beverly Hills, CA: Sage.

Jones, E. E., Cumming, J. D., & Horowitz, M. J. (1988). Another look at the nonspecific hypothesis of therapeutic effectiveness. *Journal of Clinical and Consulting Psychology, 56*, 48–55.

Karasu, T. B. (1986). The specificity versus nonspecificity dilemma: Toward identifying therapeutic change agents. *American Journal of Psychiatry, 143*, 687–695.

Kazdin, A. E. (1984). Integration of psychodynamic and behavioral psychotherapies: Conceptual versus empirical syntheses. In H. Arkowitz and S. B. Messer (Eds.), *Psychoanalytic therapy and behavior therapy: Is integration possible?* (pp. 139–170). New York: Plenum.

Kelly, E. L. (1961). Clinical psychology—1960. Report of survey findings. *Newsletter, Divison of Clinical Psychology, 14*, 1–11.

Kendall, P. C. (1982). Integration: Behavior therapy and other schools of thought. *Behavior Therapy, 13*, 559–571.

Kilbourne, B. K., & Richardson, J. T. (1988). A social psychological analysis of healing. *Journal of Integrative and Eclectic Psychotherapy, 7*, 20–34.

Klein, M., Dittman, A. T., Parloff, M. B., & Gill, M. M. (1969). Behavior therapy: Observations and reflections. *Journal of Consulting and Clinical Psychology, 33,* 259–266.

Kubie, L. S. (1934). Relation of the conditioned reflex to psychoanalytic technique. *Archives of Neurology and Psychiatry, 32,* 1137–1142.

Lambert, M. J. (1986). Implications of psychotherapy outcome research for eclectic psychotherapy. In J. C. Norcross (Ed.), *Handbook of eclectic psychotherapy* (pp. 436–462). New York: Brunner/Mazel.

Lambert, M. J. (1989, May). *Contributors to treatment outcome.* Paper presented at the annual meeting of the Society for the Exploration of Psychotherapy Integration, Berkeley, CA.

Lambert, M. J., Shapiro, D. A., & Bergin, A. E. (1986). The effectiveness of psychotherapy. In S. L. Garfield and A. E. Bergin (Eds.), *Handbook of psychotherapy and behavior change* (3rd ed.; pp. 157–211). New York: Wiley.

Langs, R. (1976). *The bipersonal field.* New York: Aronson.

Lazarus, A. A. (1967). In support of technical eclecticism. *Psychological Reports, 21,* 415–416.

Lazarus, A. A. (1971). *Behavior therapy and beyond.* New York: McGraw-Hill.

Lazarus, A. A. (1973). Multimodal behavior therapy: Treating the BASIC ID. *Journal of Nervous and Mental Disease, 156,* 404–411.

Lazarus, A. A. (1976). *Multimodal behavior therapy.* New York: Springer.

Lazarus, A. A. (1981). *The practice of multimodal therapy.* New York: McGraw-Hill.

Lazarus, A. A. (1986). Multimodal therapy. In J. C. Norcross (Ed.), *Handbook of eclectic psychotherapy* (pp. 65–93). New York: Brunner/Mazel.

Lazarus, A. A. (1989). Why I am an eclectic (not an integrationist). *British Journal of Guidance and Counselling, 19,* 248–258.

Lazarus, A. A., & Messer, S. B. (1988). Clinical choice points: Behavioral versus psychoanalytic interventions. *Psychotherapy, 25,* 59–70.

Lazarus, A. A., & Messer, S. B. (1991). Does chaos prevail? An exchange on technical eclecticism and assimilative integration. *Journal of Psychotherapy Integration, 1,* 143–158.

Lebow, J. L. (1984). On the value of integrating approaches to family therapy. *Journal of Marital and Family Therapy, 10,* 127–138.

Levis, D. (1970). Integration of behavior therapy with dynamic psychiatry: A marriage with a high probability of ending in divorce. *Behavior Therapy, 1,* 531–537.

London, P. (1964). *The modes and morals of psychotherapy.* New York: Holt, Rinehart, and Winston.

London, P. (1986). *The modes and morals of psychotherapy* (2nd ed.). New York: Hemisphere.

London, P., & Palmer, M. (1988). The integrative trend in psychotherapy in historical context. *Psychiatric Annals, 18,* 273–279.

Luborsky, L. (1984). *Principles of psychoanalytic psychotherapy: A manual for supportive-expressive treatment.* New York: Basic Books.

Luborsky, L., & DeRubeis, R. J. (1984). The use of psychotherapy treatment manuals: A small revolution in psychotherapy research style. *Clinical Psychology Review, 4,* 5–14.

Mahoney, M. J. (1974). *Cognition and behavior modification.* Cambridge, MA: Ballinger.

Mahoney, M. J. (1984). Psychoanalysis and behaviorism: The yin and yang of determinism. In H. Arkowitz and S. B. Messer (Eds.), *Psychoanalytic therapy and behavior therapy: Is integration possible?* (pp. 303–326). New York: Plenum.

Malan, D. H. (1976). *The frontier of brief psychotherapy.* New York: Plenum.

Marks, I. M., & Gelder, M. G. (1966). Common ground between behavior therapy and psychodynamic methods. *British Journal of Medical Psychology, 39,* 11–23.

Marmor, J., & Woods, S. E. (Eds.). (1980). *The interface between the psychodynamic and behavioral therapies.* New York: Plenum.

Meichenbaum, D. (1977). *Cognitive behavior modification.* New York: Plenum.

Mendelsohn, E., & Silverman, L. H. (1984). The activation of unconscious fantasies in behavioral treatments. In H. Arkowitz and S. B. Messer (Eds.), *Psychoanalytic therapy and behavior therapy: Is integration possible?* (pp. 255–294). New York: Plenum.

Messer, S. B. (1983). Integrating psychoanalytic and behavior therapy: Limitations, possibilities, and trade-offs. *British Journal of Clinical Psychology, 22,* 131–132.

Messer, S. B. (1986). Behavioral and psychoanalytic perspectives at therapeutic choice points. *American Psychologist, 41,* 1261–1272.

Messer, S. B. (1989). Integrationism and eclecticism in counselling and psychotherapy: Cautionary notes. *British Journal of Guidance and Counselling, 19,* 275–285.

Messer, S. B., & Winokur, M. (1984). Ways of knowing and visions of reality in psychoanalytic therapy and behavior therapy. In H. Arkowitz and S. B. Messer (Eds.), *Psychoanalytic therapy and behavior therapy: Is integration possible?* (pp. 63–100). New York: Plenum.

Mischel, W. (1973). Toward a cognitive social learning reconceptualizaton of personality. *Psychological Review, 80,* 252–283.

Murray, E. J. (1983). Beyond behavioral and dynamic therapy. *British Journal of Clinical Psychology, 22,* 127–128.

Murray, N. E. (1976). A dynamic synthesis of analytic and behavioral approaches to symptoms. *American Journal of Psychotherapy, 30,* 561–569.

Norcross, J. C. (Ed.). (1986). *Handbook of eclectic psychotherapy.* New York: Brunner/Mazel.

Norcross, J. C., & Grencavage, L. M. (1989). Eclecticism and integration in counselling and psychotherapy: Major themes and obstacles. *British Journal of Guidance and Counselling, 19,* 227–247.

Norcross, J. C., & Prochaska, J. O. (1982). A national survey of clinical psychologists: Affiliations and orientations. *The Clinical Psychologist, 35,* 1–2, 4–6.

Norcross, J. C., & Prochaska, J. O. (1983). Clinicians' theoretical orientations: Selections, utilization, and efficacy. *Professional Psychology: Research and Practice, 14,* 197–208.

Norcross, J. C., & Prochaska, J. O. (1988). A study of eclectic (and integrative) views revisited. *Professional Psychology: Research and Practice, 19,* 170–174.

Orlinsky, D. E., & Howard, K. I. (1986). Process and outcome in psychotherapy. In S. L. Garfield & A. E. Bergin (Eds.), *Handbook of psychotherapy and behavior change* (3rd ed.; pp. 311–381). New York: Wiley.

Orlinsky, D. E., & Howard, K. I. (1987). A generic model of psychotherapy. *Journal of Integrative and Eclectic Psychotherapy, 6,* 6–27.

Papajohn, J. C. (1982). *Intensive behavior therapy: The behavioral treatment of complex emotional disorders.* New York: Pergamon.

Paul, G. L. (1969). Behavior modification research: Design and tactics. In C. M. Franks (Ed.), *Behavior therapy: Appraisal and status* (pp. 29–62). New York: McGraw-Hill.

Pinsof, W. M. (1983). Integrative problem centered therapy (IPCT): Toward the synthesis of family and individual psychotherapies. *Journal of Marriage and Family Therapy, 9,* 19–35.

Powell, D. H. (1988). Spontaneous insights and the process of behavior therapy: Cases in support of integrative psychotherapy. *Annals of Psychiatry, 18,* 288–294.

Prochaska, J. O. (1984). *Systems of psychotherapy: A transtheoretical analysis* (2nd ed.). Homewood, IL: Dorsey.

Prochaska, J. O., & DiClemente, C. C. (1986). The transtheoretical approach. In J. C. Norcross (Ed.), *Handbook of eclectic psychotherapy* (pp. 163–200). New York: Brunner/Mazel.

Prochaska, J. O., Rossi, J. S., & Wilcox, N. S. (1991). Change processes and psychotherapy outcome in integrative case research. *Journal of Psychotherapy Integration, 1,* 103–120.

Raimy, V. (1975). *Misunderstandings of the self.* San Francisco: Jossey-Bass.

Rhoads, J. M. (1984). Relationships between psychodynamic and behavior therapies. In H. Arkowitz and S. B. Messer (Eds.), *Psychoanalytic therapy and behavior therapy: Is integration possible?* (pp. 195–212). New York: Plenum.

Rhoads, J. M. (1988). Combinations and synthesis of psychotherapies. *Annals of Psychiatry, 18,* 280–287.

Rhoads, J. M., & Feather, B. W. (1972). Transference and resistance observed in behavior therapy. *British Journal of Medical Psychology, 45,* 99–103.

Rogers, C. R. (1951). *Client-centered therapy.* Boston: Houghton-Mifflin.

Rogers, C. R. (1957). The necessary and sufficient conditions of therapeutic personality changes. *Journal of Consulting and Clinical Psychology, 21,* 95–103.

Rosenzweig, S. (1936). Some implicit common factors in diverse methods in psychotherapy. *American Journal of Orthopsychiatry*, 6, 412–415.

Safran, J. D., & Segal Z. V. (1990). *Interpersonal process in cognitive therapy*. New York: Basic Books.

Schacht, T. E. (1984). The varieties of integrative experience. In H. Arkowitz and S. B. Messer (Eds.), *Psychoanalytic therapy and behavior therapy: Is integration possible?* (pp. 107–132). New York: Plenum.

Schafer, R. (1983). *The analytic attitude*. New York: Basic Books.

Schofield, W. (1964). *Psychotherapy: The purchase of friendship*. Englewood Cliffs, NJ: Prentice-Hall.

Schwartz, G. E. (1984). Psychobiology of health: A new synthesis. In B. L. Hammonds and C. J. Scheirer (Eds.), *Psychology and health*. Washington, DC: American Psychological Association.

Schwartz, G. E. (1991). The data are always friendly: A systems approach to psychotherapy integration. *Journal of Psychotherapy Integration*, 1, 55–69.

Sears, R. R. (1944). Experimental analysis of psychoanalytic phenomena. In J. McV. Hunt (Ed.), *Personality and the behavior disorders* (pp. 297–323). New York: Ronald Press.

Segraves, R. T. (1982). *Marital therapy: A combined psychodynamic–behavioral approach*. New York: Plenum.

Shengold, L. L. (1979). Child abuse and deprivation: Soul murder. *Journal of the American Psychoanalytic Association*, 27, 533–539.

Shoben, E. J. (1949). Psychotherapy as a problem in learning theory. *Psychological Bulletin*, 46, 366–392.

Silverman, L. H. (1974). Some psychoanalytic considerations of non-psychoanalytic therapies: On approaches and related issues. *Psychotherapy: Theory, Research, and Practice*, 11, 298–305.

Sloane, R. B., Staples, F. R., Cristol, A. H., Yorkston, N. J., & Whipple, K. (1975). *Psychotherapy versus behavior therapy*. Cambridge, MA: Harvard University Press.

Smith, M. L., Glass, G. T., & Miller, T. I. (1980). *The benefits of psychotherapy*. Baltimore: Johns Hopkins University Press.

Steuer, J. L., Mintz, J., Hammen, C. L., Hill, M. A., Jarvik, L. F., McCarley, T., Motoike, P., & Rosen, R. (1984). Cognitive–behavioral and psychodynamic group psychotherapy in treatment of geriatric depression. *Journal of Consulting and Clinical Psychology*, 52, 180–189.

Stiles, W. G., Shapiro, D. A., & Elliot, R. (1986). "Are all psychotherapies equivalent?" *American Psychologist*, 41, 165–180.

Strupp, H. H. (1973). On the basic ingredients of psychotherapy. *Journal of Consulting and Clinical Psychology*, 41, 1–8.

Strupp, H. H., & Binder, J. L. (1984). *Psychotherapy in a new key: A guide to time-limited dynamic psychotherapy*. New York: Basic Books.

Thoresen, C. E. (1973). Behavioral humanism. In C. E. Thoresen (Ed.), *Behavior modification in education* (pp. 98–122). Chicago: University of Chicago Press.

Truax, C. B., & Mitchell, K. M. (1971). Research on certain therapist interpersonal skills in relation to process and outcome. In A. E. Bergin and S. L. Garfield (Eds.), *Handbook of psychotherapy and behavior change* (1st ed.; pp. 299–344). New York: Wiley.

Wachtel, P. L. (1975). Behavior therapy and the facilitation of psychoanalytic exploration. *Psychotherapy: Theory, Research, and Practice. 12*, 68–72.

Wachtel, P. L. (1977). *Psychoanalysis and behavior therapy: Toward an integration.* New York: Basic Books.

Wachtel, P. L. (1982). What can dynamic therapies contribute to behavior therapy? *Behavior Therapy, 13*, 594–609.

Wachtel, P. L. (1983). Integration misunderstood. *British Journal of Clinical Psychology, 22*, 129–130.

Wachtel, P. L. (1984). On theory, practice, and the nature of integration. In H. Arkowitz and S. B. Messer (Eds.), *Psychoanalytic therapy and behavior therapy: Is integration possible?* (pp. 31–52). New York: Plenum.

Wachtel, P. L. (1987). *Action and insight.* New York: Guilford.

Wachtel, P. L. (1991). From eclecticism to synthesis: Toward a more seamless psychotherapeutic integration. *Journal of Psychotherapy Integration, 1*, 43–54.

Wachtel, P. L., & Wachtel, E. F. (1986). *Family dynamics in individual psychotherapy.* New York: Guilford.

Wandersman, A., Poppen, P. J., & Ricks, D. F. (Eds.). (1976). *Humanism and behaviorism: Dialogue and growth.* Elmsford, NY: Pergamon.

Weitzman, B. (1967). Behavior therapy and psychotherapy. *Psychological Review, 74*, 300–317.

Wills, T. A. (1982). *Basic processes in helping relationships.* New York: Academic Press.

Wolfe, B. E. (1989). Phobias, panic, and psychotherapy integration. *Journal of Integrative and Eclectic Psychotherapy, 8*, 264–276.

Wolfe, B. E., & Goldfried, M. R. (1988). Research on psychotherapy integration: Recommendations and conclusions from an NIMH workshop. *Journal of Consulting and Clinical Psychology, 56*, 448–451.

Wolpe, J. (1958). *Psychotherapy by reciprocal inhibition.* Stanford, CA: Stanford University Press.

Wolpe, J., & Rachman, S. (1960). Psychoanalytic "evidence": A critique based on Freud's case of Little Hans. *Journal of Nervous and Mental Disease, 131*, 135–148.

Yates, A. J. (1983). Behavior therapy and psychodynamic therapy: Basic conflicts or reconciliation or integration. *British Journal of Clinical Psychology, 22*, 107–125.

III

PSYCHOTHERAPY RESEARCH

OVERVIEW

PSYCHOTHERAPY RESEARCH

HANS H. STRUPP

Modern psychotherapy is barely 100 years old, and, like the practice of medicine, it remains a clinical art. It owes its existence to the revolutionary discoveries of Sigmund Freud, whose influence on contemporary theory and practice remains profound and far-reaching. During the last half of the present century, psychotherapy has grown from a narrow medical specialty to a welter of activities to ameliorate, if not to resolve, a number of psychiatric disorders as well as the gamut of problems that are grouped under the heading of "problems in living."

Dozens of therapeutic modalities, some anchored in Freud's discoveries and others starting from very different theoretical assumptions, have appeared, and the modern psychotherapist in the Western world has become a kind of secular priest.

Science and the scientific method have long been held in high esteem in the Western world, and they have become trusted allies in solving difficult problems. In the same spirit, Freud aspired for his brainchild psychoanalysis to become a science and for the practice of psychoanalysis (and other forms of psychotherapy) to be "scientific." If that is the goal, then psychotherapy must be subjected to the scientific method, that is, "[the] method of research in which a problem is identified, relevant data are gathered, a hypothesis is formulated from these data, and the hypothesis is empirically tested" (*Random House Dictionary*, 1967, p. 1279). Although Freud, in contradistinction to scientific requirements, wished to exempt psychoanalytic practice from systematic study, he—and his followers—could not escape the basic question of whether psychotherapy (in a broad sense) is effective, and if so, with whom and under what conditions. As this part demonstrates, the scientific study of psychotherapy by empirical methods has emerged as an enterprise of considerable magnitude and sophistication.

In chapter 9, Hans Strupp and Kenneth Howard describe the evolution of research in psychotherapy. We hope that our chapter provides at least a glimpse of what the research enterprise is about, how it came into being, and the forces that have contributed to its current status.

In chapter 10, Sol Garfield, another prominent researcher and one of the field's most noted chroniclers, examines major issues in contemporary psychotherapy research, particularly with respect to the study of therapeutic outcomes. He also notes that for a full understanding of the psychotherapeutic process, researchers will have to devote sustained attention to the complex events transpiring in the patient–therapist relationship.

In chapter 11, Michael Lambert and Allen Bergin, both highly respected contributors to the research literature, direct the spotlight to substantive accomplishments of psychotherapy research. They conclude their assessment by noting the increments in technical and methodological sophistication that characterize research today.

Finally, in chapter 12, which may be seen as a supplement to the preceding ones, the authors provide accounts by some of the field's most productive exponents. This "look behind the scene" will demonstrate to the reader that psychotherapy research is a profoundly social enterprise, as is true of modern science in general. Progress in science can often not be measured in decades, especially in the case of a science that has barely outgrown its infancy. Not only has the psychotherapy research enterprise been advanced in recent years, but it has also begun to produce greater rapprochement between practitioners and researchers. The evolving dialogue may well result in an enrichment of both camps.

9

A BRIEF HISTORY OF PSYCHOTHERAPY RESEARCH

HANS H. STRUPP AND KENNETH I. HOWARD

Psychotherapy research today is an established branch of clinical research. The existence of this chapter attests to the importance of establishing a base of empirical research from which to understand, develop, and evaluate psychotherapeutic techniques. The current manifestations of the viability of this branch of inquiry are (a) the multidisciplinary international Society for Psychotherapy Research (SPR), which was founded in 1970 and now has more than 1,000 members from 27 countries; (b) the development of an international scientific journal, *Psychotherapy Research*, which has recently published its first issue; (c) the establishment of a special peer review committee by the National Institute of Mental Health (NIMH) to evaluate grant applications in the area of psychosocial treatments; and (d) the publication of three editions of the *Handbook of Psychotherapy and Behavior Change: An Empirical Analysis* (Bergin & Garfield, 1971; Garfield & Bergin, 1978, 1986).

The history of the field has been influenced by an interplay between several factors. First, there is a continuing development of psychotherapeutic interventions and the scientific requirement to demonstrate the relative efficacy of different approaches. Next, there is the continuing development of new social science methodologies and statistical techniques that lend themselves more readily to the kinds of questions psychotherapy researchers seek to answer. There is a growing use of psychotherapeutic services on the public's part and a growing political awareness of quality of life issues and provision of financial support for such services. Finally, there is a steady attraction of talented individual researchers to the subtle and complex issues in the empirical investigation of psychotherapeutic phenomena.

THE EMERGENCE OF PSYCHOTHERAPY RESEARCH

From its inception, modern psychotherapy has been considered a practical art much like the practice of medicine. However, as soon as Freud had advanced bold claims for a uniquely effective psychological treatment, he was forced to answer critics who demanded to be shown hard empirical evidence. Freud's (1916/1963) answer took two forms. On the one hand, he appealed to the clinical findings obtained by him and his collaborators, asserting that the case-study method, on which they had placed primary reliance, was fully adequate to satisfy the challenges. Thus, Freud contended that anyone who had been properly trained in the practice of psychoanalysis would obtain results comparable to his own; he believed that his case histories had adequately documented and replicated his assertions. The evidence, as far as he was concerned, was conclusive. His argument further implied that only trained psychoanalysts could be objective and impartial observers.

Second, Freud voiced a skeptical attitude toward "statistics," which he equated with the rudimentary procedures of behavioral research as it existed in the early 1900s. He asserted that the clinical material available to the investigator was so diverse and heterogeneous as to make meaningful comparisons all but impossible. In addition, he had some harsh words for critics who disparaged his treatment results (Freud, 1916/1963, pp. 457–463).

Despite Freud's rejoinders, the critics' basic question—"Does the treatment work?"—has not been withdrawn. Indeed, it has continued to occupy a position of central interest and, at least in the judgments of skeptics, has not yet received a satisfactory response despite the accumulation of a sizable body of empirical research. The birth of psychotherapy research might have occurred when the question of its effectiveness and efficacy was first broached. Also, treatment centers associated with psychoanalytic training institutes (first in Berlin, later in London, then in Chicago and Topeka) began to collect systematic data on treatment results at about 1920, disregarding Freud's strictures (Bergin & Lambert, 1978). These studies may be regarded as the precursors of modern psychotherapy research.

Does Psychotherapy Work?

As we have stated, Freud was convinced of the scientific and clinical value of his treatment method. Not only did he claim superior treatment outcomes, but he argued at length that the modus operandi of psychoanalytic therapy was well understood and that little remained to be learned (Freud, 1937/1964). Posterity has strongly disagreed with this assessment, and the voluminous literature on psychotherapy research provides eloquent testimony that the process and the outcome of therapeutic interventions embody important clinical and scientific questions that are not yet adequately answered. In this and the following chapters, we and our fellow authors more closely examine these questions. In this chapter, we begin by delineating the domains of inquiry that occupy the modern psychotherapy researcher (see Bergin & Garfield, 1971; Garfield & Bergin, 1978, 1986).

The period of 1920–1940 includes the first stirrings of scientific investigations in psychotherapy. Between 1940 and 1960, researchers initiated empirical investigations to illuminate the process of psychotherapy and its outcomes. From about 1960 to the present, the rapidly growing literature contains a host of studies that shed important light on the basic questions that set the agenda for the future. As we will show, methodology and research strategies have undergone developments, and the number and sophistication of researchers who typically are also skilled practitioners have significantly increased.

Following the early efforts of analytic institutes and clinics to document their treatment results, studies of psychotherapeutic outcomes based on eclectic (nonpsychoanalytic) treatments gradually made their appearance in the 1930s (Bergin & Lambert, 1978). The patient samples were typically small, the diagnoses were vague, and the treatments were not described in great detail. By contrast, the studies of psychoanalytic treatments, deficient as they were in many respects, adopted stringent criteria for evaluating outcomes (Fenichel, 1930).

As an interesting historical aside, the practice by analytic training centers of reporting treatment outcomes was effectively discontinued in the 1940s. Perhaps this policy changed because the outcomes were not as impressive as had been hoped and data were often used by critics as ammunition for wholesale attacks on psychoanalysis. A large-scale effort by collaborating analysts, the so-called "fact-gathering study" mounted in the 1940s, was notably slow in being published (Hamburg et al., 1967) and, in many respects, was judged disappointing. The analysts' most ambitious entry into process and outcome research was the ground-breaking Menninger Psychotherapy Project (to be discussed later), which spanned a 30-year period, beginning around 1950. It was one of the most carefully designed and well-executed investigations of its kind and is still impressive.

The modern era of outcome research is generally dated to Eysenck's (1952) broadside attack on all forms of psychotherapy. Ironically, his results supported the efficacy of psychotherapy, but his conclusion—to abandon the training of psychotherapists—was very damning. The field responded with a variety of attacks on the database, methodology, and motives of this piece and finally with an explosion of research activity. Bergin and Lambert (1978) reanalyzed Eysenck's data and showed that a variety of conclusions could have been reached on the basis of different codings of the original data. In fact, what Eysenck's data purported to show was that 67% of emotionally disturbed people who do not seek individual psychotherapy are improved in 2 years—the results of a myriad of therapeutic events (except formal psychotherapy). In contrast, 67% of those who do seek psychotherapy are improved in about 2 months (Howard, Kopta, Krause, & Orlinsky, 1986; McNeilly & Howard, 1991). This was a clear demonstration of the efficacy of psychotherapy, but Eysenck's conclusion that the effect of psychotherapy does not exceed the spontaneous remission rate is still widely quoted.

Some 30 years later, Smith, Glass, and Miller (1980) presented a meta-analysis of the psychotherapy outcome research literature and concluded that psychotherapy was highly effective. They reported a mean "effect size" for psychotherapy of .85 (p. 87), which they interpreted to mean that the average treated person would have an outcome equal to or better than 80% of the average of untreated people. Researchers in the field were elated by this statistical–scientific finding, and the efficacy of psychotherapy seemed firmly established. No psychotherapy researcher, to our knowledge, challenged their reasoning, although many challenged their study selection and methodology. To balance their conclusion, however, it seems fair to point out that 50% of the untreated group would have had an outcome equal to or better than the average untreated person (i.e., in a normal distribution, half of the subjects will fall at or above the mean). In other words, psychotherapy added 30% to this statistical criterion. Moreover, their findings indicate that 20% of the treated people presumably would have an outcome equal to or less than the average untreated person. On the whole, however, there seems little sense in attempting to answer such a global question as "Does psychotherapy work?" One might just as usefully ask physicians, "Does surgery work?" (Lambert, Shapiro, & Bergin, 1986).

How Does Psychotherapy Work? Common Versus Unique Factors

From the inception of psychoanalysis, Freud (1916/1963) was at pains to differentiate the nature of its therapeutic influence from "suggestion," which he regarded as the moving force in hypnotherapy. His reasoning was as follows: Claiming the modus operandi of psychoanalytic therapy to be unique, it was incumbent on him to demonstrate that it differed radically from other psychological therapies. If, on the other hand, this claim could not be sustained, then psychoanalysis, despite its supposedly unique technical features (especially analysis of the transference) was merely another variant of a psychological treatment, perhaps not very different from "hypnosis," for which Freud had developed considerable disdain. The crux of the difference was the purportedly differential use of suggestion in the two forms of therapy. To this day, a lively controversy persists concerning the therapeutic action in "psychoanalysis" and "psychotherapy." (The latter, of course, is no longer equated with the relatively crude techniques of direct suggestion practiced by 19th-century hypnotists.)

As other systems of psychotherapy were developed, beginning prominently with Rogers's (1951) nondirective (or client-centered) therapy in the 1940s, each claimed uniqueness, both in terms of advocated techniques and purported psychological mechanisms. Behavior therapy extolled "principles of learning" (Emmelkamp, 1986) and cognitive–behavioral therapy invoked reorganization of beliefs (Hollon & Beck, 1986).

The developing controversy had other far-reaching implications. If, as the growing research literature has strongly suggested, generic (or common) relationship factors in all forms of psychotherapy (e.g., empathic understanding, respect, caring, genuineness, warmth) carry most of the weight, other purportedly unique features of a system may be relatively inconsequential. The seeming uniqueness of each system might simply be semantic or stylistic or reflect prevailing fashions. The view that common factors may be of overriding importance in all forms of psychotherapy has been persuasively argued by Frank (1973, 1982) and has found widespread acceptance. If correct, it would cast serious doubt on the accuracy of Freud's (1916/1963) original assertion concerning the unique therapeutic action of psychoanalysis.

The controversy between "unique" and "common" factors in the therapeutic influence has had other implications. With respect to the training of therapists, it has been argued that if professionals essentially use "common factors" in their work, what is unique about their expertise? Furthermore, might not naturally talented and intuitive people, without prolonged and thorough training, be able to function as effectively in the therapist role? Thus, therapists have been challenged to demonstrate precisely the nature of their professional expertise. Practicing therapists, as well as researchers, have understandably taken a defensive position, pointing to such areas as professional commitment and responsibility, technical skill (e.g., in the therapeutic management of difficult patients, who tend to be the rule rather than the exception), and adherence to codes of ethics that protect clients from harm (Strupp, Butler, & Rosser, 1988). Nonetheless there remain considerable lacunae in the field's ability to define the nature of competence and professional expertise.

THE EMERGENCE OF TECHNIQUES FOR STUDYING PROCESS AND OUTCOME

The problem of how therapeutic change occurs in psychoanalysis and in all other forms of psychotherapy remains the central issue of concern to the scientist. What are the parameters? Why does change occur under some conditions but not under others? Who are the patients who will benefit? What causes a symptom or pattern of maladaptive behavior to yield to therapeutic intervention? Does prolonged and intensive therapy produce more pervasive changes (i.e., in the patient's personality makeup or character structure) than short-term or more "superficial" treatments? These and related questions occupied Freud and those following in his footsteps, and, in a somewhat different garb, are still around today. Freud and his followers used their observations in the consulting room and the resulting case histories as their sole database. They were not equipped to use experimental controls in the modern sense, nor has it been possible to reconstruct the precise transactions between the early patients and their therapists. Instead, case histories are typically sharply condensed accounts, summarizing many hours of therapy. Moreover, they tend to be heavily interlaced with the author's theoretical speculations, inferences, and appeals to received theory. Clearly, in this approach there is no way of checking the reliability of observations or the justification for particular inferences.

The scene gradually changed as psychiatrists, psychologists, and other behavioral scientists demanded studies based on "hard" data, that is, on records that progressed beyond uncontrolled clinical observations and the pronouncements of theorists and practitioners. These developments were greatly hastened by the advent of electronic recording techniques and the slowly growing willingness of patients and therapists to subject their transactions to rigorous scrutiny. Beginning in the 1940s, Carl Rogers and his students collected sound recordings of therapy sessions, using them as a basis for intensive studies of therapeutic technique and the patient–therapist relationship. Predictably, there were many objections to such "invasions" of the privacy of therapy, a possibility against which Freud had already inveighed, asserting flatly that psychoanalysis did not tolerate the presence of third parties. Objections to recordings, however, eventually diminished, with the result that sound recordings have become common, particularly in training and research. In recent years, the filming and videotaping of therapy have become widely accepted and are now tolerated well by most clients and therapists. We should note, however, that the new technology creates distortions of its own.[1]

Having thus gained access to the primary behavioral data of psychotherapy, it became possible for external observers to scrutinize the communications between patient and therapist. The search for the "basic ingredients" of psychotherapy in the verbal (as well as in the nonverbal) exchanges between the participants formed part of an emerging trend in the social sciences, particularly in the United States, founded in positivism and behaviorism. The belief that through studying the verbal and nonverbal processes one could discover the essential ingredients of the therapeutic interaction continues to support this research paradigm. Thus, *process analysis*, and to a lesser extent *content analysis*, of psychotherapy came into being.

Beginning in the 1930s, content analysis formed part of a set of investigations by political scientists and others, who systematically studied speeches, newspapers, books, and other communications for explicit and implicit meanings (e.g., propaganda). Communications analysts in psychology used and adapted the technical procedures created by the content analysts, eventually developing systems of their own.

In the late 1940s and early 1950s, psychotherapy researchers began

---

[1]Beginning in the 1950s, even conservative psychoanalysts foresaw the value of filming analytic interviews. Franz Alexander spearheaded an effort to create a film studio-consulting room in Chicago. The aim was to film an entire psychoanalysis. For some time the project languished because, despite the availability of a willing patient, no willing analyst could be found. Some years later, after David Shakow had built a similar facility at the National Institute of Mental Health in Bethesda, Maryland, Paul Bergman filmed an entire psychoanalysis. Hundreds of hours were stored in metal containers, under controlled climatic conditions. Subsequently, small samples of these interactions were studied intensively by such investigators as Dittmann (1972). Eventually, because of space and storage problems, the films were destroyed, with many hours remaining unstudied.

to devote increasing energy to analyses of the psychotherapeutic process. These research efforts were sustained by the belief that the *outcomes* of psychotherapy could be illuminated, perhaps even explained, by intensive study of the transactions between patients and therapists. Thus, it became essential to develop adequate methodological tools and to forge links between process and outcome. The dual thrust of process and outcome research has been the hallmark of psychotherapy research to this day, together with the realization that the two must necessarily complement each other.

RESEARCH GROUPS AND CENTERS

The history of any field of inquiry must not only take intellectual trends into account but must also credit the contributions of the individual scientists who have shaped these trends. In this section, we present some highlights of these contributions by prominent psychotherapy researchers.[2]

Menninger Foundation

In the mid-1940s, Karl Menninger, in the context of developing the Menninger Clinic as a preeminent treatment and training center, spearheaded psychoanalytic training for psychologists as well as psychiatrists. He was able to attract a critical mass of talent who supported curiosity about the nature of psychoanalysis, psychotherapy, and psychotherapeutic change. These investigators (with support from the Ford Foundation, the Foundations Fund for Research in Psychiatry, the New York Foundation, and NIMH) launched an ambitious project to "study the process and course of psychotherapy in order to increase our understanding of how psychotherapy contributes to changes in patients suffering from mental illness" (Robbins & Wallerstein, 1956, p. 223). This was primarily a naturalistic study in which psychiatric case summaries, psychological testing, and social history were used. One of its unique features was that neither therapists nor patients were aware that they were part of a study. Together with other innovations, the Menninger Project used the then-novel statistical technique of facet analysis to try to explicate the complex relationships among a host of variables (Kernberg et al., 1972). Studies of the original panel of 42 patients are still underway, the latest report being a book on the 40-year follow-up

---

[2]As in any such account, however, we have had to be selective (as well as brief) in order to provide a reasonably coherent discussion. We apologize in advance to the many colleagues whose important contributions we were unable to include (also see chapter 12, this volume).

results (Wallerstein, 1986). Most members of the original team have scattered, but the tradition of research at the Menninger Foundation continues.

Among the early researchers at Menninger were Lester Luborsky and Robert Holt, who engaged in an innovative exploration of who would make a good psychiatrist (Holt & Luborsky, 1958). One of the achievements of the Menninger group was the Health–Sickness Rating Scale (Luborsky, 1962), which is still widely used in clinical research.

University of Chicago Counseling Center

In 1940, Carl Rogers moved to Ohio State University and began a program of research on his evolving nondirective, later called client-centered, approach (Rogers, 1951). He attracted a number of talented graduate students and began to systematically wire-record and transcribe entire sessions of psychotherapy. In 1945, Rogers moved to the University of Chicago, where he established a counseling center that attracted a creative faculty and a core of graduate students who became a productive hub of psychotherapy research (receiving substantial support from the Rockefeller Foundation and to a lesser extent from NIMH). There the Q-sort was introduced as a measure of personality change, and factor analysis was used extensively as a means of reducing complexity. Although the main focus of the counseling center group was on psychotherapeutic processes, controlled studies were mounted to establish the efficacy of client-centered therapy. The book by Rogers and Dymond (1954) was one of the first devoted exclusively to psychotherapy research. The counseling center group treated primarily college students and other well-educated individuals. Eventually, Rogers became interested in exploring the potential of the client-centered approach with more severely disturbed hospitalized patients, many of whom were diagnosed as schizophrenics. With this aim in mind, in the late 1050s, Rogers and his group moved to the Department of Psychiatry of the University of Wisconsin, where they undertook an intensive study of schizophrenic patients (Rogers, Gendlin, Kiesler, & Truax, 1967). Several members of the Chicago group moved to other universities, where they pursued research in the Rogerian tradition. One of them, Laura Rice, moved to York University, where she continued to investigate critical change incidents in sessions and to train psychotherapy researchers.

Johns Hopkins University (Phipps Clinic)

Responding to the consistent lack of demonstrable differences in the efficacy of different treatment approaches, Jerome Frank and his colleagues

(Frank, 1974, 1982; Frank, Gliedman, Imber, Nash, & Stone, 1957) designed a series of studies (supported by the Veterans Administration and by NIMH) "to try to identify attributes of patients determining their responsiveness to . . . common features of psychotherapy" (Rubinstein & Parloff, 1959, p. 11). They studied 54 patients and conducted 20-year follow-up evaluations of many of these patients. The Phipps group, for a long time among the most productive, has been most notable for their general approach to understanding healing factors in contrast to a focus on a specific theory or technique.

University of Michigan

Edward Bordin joined the University of Michigan psychology department in 1948 and developed a team to explore psychotherapeutic processes such as depth of interpretation, warmth, and free association in relation to patient and therapist characteristics. Bordin (1979) was among the first to formulate the concept of the therapeutic (or working) alliance, which has become a major theme of contemporary psychotherapy research. The Michigan psychotherapy research group continues under the leadership of Robert Hatcher.

Pennsylvania State College

Around 1950, William U. Snyder organized a psychotherapy research group at Pennsylvania State College (now Pennsylvania State University). Working with a number of graduate students under his supervision, he established a "criterion" group of 43 clients (college students) who were treated, in client-centered therapy, for 353 sessions by clinical psychology graduate students. The research resulted in a number of dissertations dealing with various statistical relations among client, therapist, and outcome variables. Snyder and his group were among the first to devise client and counselor content categories. The studies were based on typescripts of therapy sessions, a limitation Snyder recognized. He also concluded that the results obtained by members of his group might apply primarily to client-centered therapy and that other approaches should be studied.

Snyder's group experienced difficulty in attracting external funding, in part perhaps because the client population consisted of college students and the research staff, apart from Snyder, was made up of graduate students. The latter did receive financial support through traineeships funded by the Veterans Administration and the U.S. Public Health Service. Subsequently, Snyder, in collaboration with June Snyder, studied the relationships between one therapist and 20 of his clients (Snyder, 1961). Snyder was among the first to assign primary importance to the client–therapist relationship.

Veterans Administration

In the late 1950s and early 1960s, Maurice Lorr, a prominent personality researcher and then-chief of the Neuropsychiatric Research Laboratory of the Veterans Administration, headed one of the first psychotherapy research programs. Among other objectives, Lorr and his collaborators tested the hypothesis that therapeutic gains resulting from individual psychotherapy increase with the number of treatment interviews received over fixed time intervals (marking the entrance of the field into services research). A total of 133 randomly assigned outpatients and 75 therapists participated. Most therapists were psychoanalytic in orientation, although Sullivanian and modified Rogerian approaches were represented (Lorr, 1962, pp. 134–141). The study was one of the few at the time to use follow-up interviews. Lorr and his collaborators (Lorr, McNair, Michaux, & Raskin, 1962) found that the duration of treatment was a more influential parameter than sheer number of sessions. They recommended that traditional treatment frequency schedules be examined more critically, with the view of spreading therapist time over more patients with fewer contacts and less cost to patients.

University of Pennsylvania

In 1959, Lester Luborsky, who had been a member of the Menninger research group, moved to the Department of Psychiatry of the University of Pennsylvania. There he developed and implemented the Penn Psychotherapy Research Project, a naturalistic study of 73 patients in individual dynamic psychotherapy. This group was not only interested in discovering predictors of successful treatment but also tape-recorded sessions in an attempt to discover critical change indicators in the psychotherapeutic process. The data from this project have served as the base for the development and evaluation of new measures (e.g., helping alliance, core conflictual relationship theme method). They also developed a treatment manual (Luborsky, 1984) and made other important contributions (Luborsky, Crits-Christoph, Mintz, & Auerbach, 1988). At this writing, the Penn group continues to be one of the most active and productive research centers. Morris Parloff (Luborsky et al., 1988), one of the elder statesmen of psychotherapy research and one of its keenest observers, characterized the achievements of the Penn group as follows:

> I dimly recall that at some point in my youth (a number of weeks ago) I brashly advised researchers that their continued efforts to mine old research in the hope of finding some overlooked nuggets of information would be nugatory. More specifically, I suggested that in view of flagrant flaws and limitations old psychotherapy research studies, unlike old wines, did not improve with age. In the light of what the Luborsky group has now presented (Luborsky, et al., 1988), however, I am willing to modify my statement. Clearly they have demonstrated that old research, like old wine, can add much to the flavor of the ragout. (p. xix)[3]

Vanderbilt University

Hans Strupp, who had been involved in psychotherapy process research since 1953, moved in 1966 to the Department of Psychology at Vanderbilt, where he began a series of research projects that focused on the effects of differences among psychotherapists on process and outcome. One large (NIMH-funded) project compared college teachers who had been selected for their warmth and popularity with experienced dynamically oriented psychotherapists in the treatment of anxious and depressed male college students. The major purpose of that study was to determine whether specific technical skills presumably used by highly experienced therapists might lead to outcomes strongly favoring the professional group. This did not prove to be the case,[4] which suggested that common (interpersonal) factors in all forms of psychotherapy were major determinants of outcome (Strupp & Hadley, 1979). Further analyses of selected patient–therapist dyads (Strupp, 1980) contributed to a better understanding of patient and therapist factors.

The Vanderbilt II Study, formally initiated in 1983, was designed to investigate the effects of specialized therapist training in a form of time-limited dynamic psychotherapy, based on a treatment manual (Strupp & Binder, 1984), on the therapeutic process. Two groups of adult outpatients, each comprising 32 members, were studied intensively before and after the therapists had received specialized training. The study, which is still in progress as of this writing, has shown clear-cut training effects on the process

---

[3]To this we might add that the Penn group has also produced a good deal of new wine.
[4]It is interesting to note, however, that experienced therapists who had seldom worked in a time-limited framework with these kinds of patients (shy male college students) did as well as college teachers who had years of experience with these students, were specially selected, and were not limited to 45-minute-a-week contacts.

but that therapeutic skill encompasses many other elements beyond "adhering" to a treatment manual. Sound and videotaped recordings of therapy sessions, together with psychological tests and questionnaires, were used in that research program. The group has also developed, tested, and applied several process measures and explored the problem of negative effects (Strupp, Hadley, & Gomes-Schwartz, 1977).

Temple University

The emergence of behavior therapy and its challenge to traditional psychotherapy, circa 1950, led Bruce Sloane, Arnold Lazarus, Joseph Wolpe, and their colleagues to design a study, supported by NIMH, directly comparing the processes and outcomes of these two approaches. This was probably the first controlled clinical trial comparing two psychotherapies and using "real" patients. They conducted a controlled experiment (random assignment to 16 sessions of behavior therapy or 16 sessions of traditional dynamic therapy or a wait-list control group) using experienced therapists and general outpatients. The results of this widely quoted study showed few differences between the two active treatment modalities, although both studies produced results superior to the control group (Sloane, Staples, Cristol, Yorkston, & Wipple, 1975).

University of Chicago/Northwestern University

In 1964, David Orlinsky and Kenneth Howard initiated a phenomenological naturalistic study—the Psychotherapy Session Project—at the Katherine Wright Clinic in Chicago. This was one of the first studies to make use of emerging computer technology for handling large data sets and to focus entirely on the subjective reports of patients and therapists about their experiences in therapy sessions. Their pilot study (Orlinsky & Howard, 1975) involved the reports of 60 patients on 890 sessions and 31 therapist-cases (17 therapists) on 470 sessions. Subsequent studies have yielded a large archive of therapy session reports (Orlinsky & Howard, 1966). Gradually, this team moved into outcome and service-delivery research (supported by NIMH), in addition to developing more refined instruments for measuring the experiences of patients and therapists.

University of California, San Francisco

One of the major research centers was created at the University of California Medical Center in San Francisco by Mardi J. Horowitz, whose team has made notable contributions to brief psychotherapy, primarily with patients suffering from stress response syndromes. (For a detailed description of the Center for the Study of Neuroses, see chapter 12.)

NIMH Treatment of Depression Collaborative Research Program

In 1977, the staff of the NIMH Psychotherapy and Behavioral Intervention Section (which later became the Psychosocial Treatments Research Branch) initiated the NIMH Treatment of Depression Collaborative Research Program. The decision was based, in part, on progress that had been made in the treatment of depressed outpatients, the fact that new methods had been developed for more systematic diagnosis and characterization of specific subgroups of depressed patients, and the emergence of promising new psychotherapeutic approaches. Under the direction of Morris Parloff and Irene Elkin, a multisite controlled clinical trial was initiated to study the relative efficacy of two forms of psychotherapy (cognitive–behavioral therapy [CBT] and interpersonal psychotherapy [IPT]) and one form of pharmacological intervention (imipramine; Elkin, Parloff, Hadley, & Autry, 1985). The study entailed random assignment of 250 patients to 16–20 sessions of CBT, IPT, imipramine, or placebo. The last two conditions were administered in the context of "clinical management," described as a "generally supportive atmosphere" (Elkin et al., 1985, p. 311). Therapists were trained according to standardized procedures, and all therapies were based on specially prepared treatment manuals. All therapy sessions were videotaped to allow for checks on the competence of the delivery of each therapy as well as to permit studies of the therapeutic process. Patients were assessed extensively at pretreatment, at several points during treatment, at termination, and at 6-, 12-, and 18-month follow-up periods.

Several articles describing the results have been published (Elkin et al., 1989; Imber et al., 1990), but additional analyses of the data have not been completed. It is impossible to provide a brief summary of the results emerging from such a large-scale, complex investigation. In general, though, patients in all treatment conditions showed significant improvement, but differences attributable to the different treatment modalities were relatively slight.

In addition to the research centers we have briefly discussed, the field has also been enriched by the work of several individual investigators who have either worked alone or in collaboration with graduate students.[5] As

---

[5]Their findings have been chronicled in the three editions of the *Handbook of Psychotherapy and Behavior Change: An Empirical Analysis* (Bergin & Garfield, 1971; Garfield & Bergin, 1978, 1986), as well as in other chapters of this book.

experimental rigor and sophistication have increased, so has the expense of intensive process and outcome analyses. By its very nature, psychotherapy research is labor intensive and costly. It also makes heavy demands on the commitment and perseverance of all participants. Therefore, there is an increasing need for collaboration among research centers, together with a need for archives that would be accessible to a larger number of researchers. The need for continued government support is clearly essential, but the most critical role is played by the individual investigator's creativity and dedication.

THE STRUCTURAL EMERGENCE OF PSYCHOTHERAPY RESEARCH AS A DISTINCT FIELD OF INQUIRY

Individual psychotherapy researchers constitute an "invisible college" (Price, 1963) through the sharing of preprints and informal exchanges through letters, telephone calls, and conversations at conventions. In the late 1950s, there emerged a need for a clearer identity for the field and for more formal means of exchanging, coordinating, and communicating ideas and findings.

American Psychological Association (APA) Conferences: 1958, 1961, and 1966

In response to this need for more formal means of exchanging ideas and findings, the first major conference on research in psychotherapy (Rubinstein & Parloff, 1959) was convened in Washington, DC in 1958. Planning and programming were carried out by an ad hoc committee of the Division of Clinical Psychology of the APA, with funding provided by NIMH. There were 37 invited conference participants (psychologists and psychiatrists) representing the major psychotherapy research groups in the United States. The conference provided a structure within which the invisible college of psychotherapy researchers could gather and exchange ideas. The major goal was to "afford an opportunity for taking stock of the present status of research in psychotherapy and thus provide information for and stimulus to further research" (Rubinstein & Parloff, 1959, p. v.). The conference was organized around three research themes: problems of controls, methods for assessment of change, and the therapist–patient relationship.

The second conference, paralleling the first in structure and format, was held in Chapel Hill, North Carolina in 1961 (Strupp & Luborsky,

1962). It was aimed at examining several large projects that had been completed since the 1958 meeting and at considering new research developments and problems in three areas: (a) measuring personality change in psychotherapy; (b) the psychotherapist's contribution to the treatment process; and, (c) the definition, measurement, and analysis of such variables as transference, resistance, and so forth.

A third (and final) conference was held in Chicago in 1966 (Shlien, Hunt, Matarazzo, & Savage, 1968). It examined psychotherapy research as a practical art and centered on behavior therapy, therapist–patient interaction, and, as an innovation, psychopharmacology in relation to psychotherapy.

The three conferences, besides facilitating exchanges of ideas, pointed up the need for investigators to pool their resources and to consider the design of research projects that might be executed on a collaborative basis. Precedents for such ventures were, of course, available in biomedical research but had been conspicuously absent in psychotherapy.

Exploring the Feasibility of Collaborative Research

Following the Chicago conference, a small group of investigators became articulate about the need for collaboration. Furthermore, the recently formed Clinical Research Branch of NIMH (see the next section) took an active interest in the possibilities of large-scale collaborative research in the area. To this end, an informal committee of researchers (chaired by Joseph D. Matarazzo) was formed, which in turn recruited Hans Strupp and Allen Bergin to take responsibility for a major feasibility study that was eventually supported by NIMH. Following a comprehensive and critical review of the literature (Strupp & Bergin, 1969), individual interviews with 36 experts (researchers, clinicians, methodologists, and other scientists representing a broad spectrum of interests and commitments) were held. A number of recommendations emerged from this exploration, the major one being that large-scale collaborative studies of psychotherapy did not appear feasible at the time (Bergin & Strupp, 1972). In 1977, however, NIMH reevaluated the situation, concluding that a collaborative study could and should be undertaken. Accordingly, the NIMH Treatment of Depression Collaborative Research Program was initiated. It became the largest psychotherapy study of its kind (see the previous discussion of this program).

The Role of NIMH

By 1966, the Clinical Research Branch (CRB) of the Division of Extramural Research Programs had taken shape. One of the major functions of the CRB was to serve as the central administrative unit for grants and fellowships dealing particularly with the psychosocial therapies. In 1969, NIMH created the Psychotherapy and Behavioral Intervention Section within the CRB. A. Hussain (Sein) Tuma was its first chief.

During Tuma's tenure as chief, some of his contributions to the field of psychotherapy research included (a) organizing the first NIMH conference on behavior therapy and behavioral modification, (b) supporting the feasibility study of possibilities for collaborative efforts (mentioned earlier), and (c) conducting workshops on critical theoretical and design issues in psychotherapy research (e.g., Fiske et al., 1970). In the course of representing the newly organized CRB, NIMH, Sein played an important facilitative role in the 1966 Psychotherapy Research Conference.

In 1980, the section was elevated to branch status and renamed the Psychosocial Treatments Research Branch (PTRB). Morris Parloff was its first chief. The PTRB existed for 5 years when, in accordance with a new reorganization plan, it was dismantled and integrated into the new Division of Clinical Research. Both in his official role and as a creative thinker in his own right, Parloff has been a major influence in psychotherapy research.

Society for Psychotherapy Research

The 1966 Psychotherapy Research Conference was held in Chicago and, as was true of the preceding conferences, was by invitation. David Orlinsky and Kenneth Howard concluded that the field had grown so much that a broader forum was needed (i.e., one that included new investigators such as themselves). It also appeared unlikely that NIMH would continue to support research conferences. Because they were in the process of reviewing the psychotherapy research literature, Howard and Orlinsky (1972), along with Nathaniel Raskin and Ferdinand van der Veen, decided to invite as many active investigators as possible to attend a preconference meeting prior to the 1968 annual convention of the APA. Enough interest was shown to plan a 1969 "interest group" meeting in Chicago, with the support of the Institute for Juvenile Research, the American Academy of Psychotherapists, and Psychologists Interested in the Advancement of Psychotherapy (the precursor of APA's Division 29). The first meeting of what became the international, multidisciplinary Society for Psychotherapy Research (SPR) was held in Chicago in 1970. A constitution and by-laws were enacted, Howard and Orlinsky were elected president and president-elect, respectively, and Curt Barrett, secretary-treasurer. As noted earlier, SPR has grown impressively in size (over 1,000 members) and has become the major voice for psychotherapy research throughout the world.

OUTLOOK

Psychotherapy has always been a very practical undertaking, emerging from the clinician's desire to help a suffering human being in the most effective, economical, efficient, and humane ways. Psychotherapeutic techniques, accordingly, have, in Einstein's phrase, been "free inventions of the human spirit" rather than blueprints created in the armchair or the laboratory. The clinician's first question has always been, "How can I help?" Almost simultaneously, practitioners have devised theories to explain why a treatment works. Of course, a treatment or a set of therapeutic procedures may work when the theory is wrong, or the theory may be reasonable but the techniques may be inefficient or ineffective. The point is that the individual practitioner has no sure way of answering these questions because one must necessarily rely on the clinical method (i.e., on the naturalistic observation of a few cases). Furthermore, the history of science amply demonstrates that humanity's capacity for self-deception is so great that misconceptions (e.g., the geocentric view of the universe) may persist for centuries.

As modern psychotherapy gained momentum around the turn of the century and as its practitioners grew in number, questions were raised about the quality of outcome, the nature of the problems to which psychotherapy might be applied, and the relative effectiveness of different techniques. From slow beginnings in the 1940s, research in psychotherapy has grown in size and quality. It plays a significant part in developments in contemporary behavioral and clinical science, and as such exemplifies the application of modern scientific methodology to the solution of important clinical and theoretical problems. There are numerous indications that research in this area is coming of age and that several developments warrant greater optimism about the future than was common among researchers only a decade or two ago (Bergin & Strupp, 1972).

The quality of research has markedly increased. The main requirements of good research—to describe with increasing precision the nature of the therapeutic interventions, the kinds of patients whom a particular form of therapy is designed to benefit, and the changes expected from these interventions—are being taken much more seriously. Journal editors and granting agencies, as well as researchers themselves, demand greater specificity that is rapidly becoming the hallmark of well-designed studies. Although definitive studies are still difficult to find, researchers have developed a better grasp of the design requirements of good research in the area, and they are better able to avoid studies leading predictably to dead ends. If progress in science means, in part, to become increasingly aware of the sources of one's ignorance, together with an ability to ask better questions, psychotherapy research has made significant advances. Persisting problems relate less to questions of what needs to be done than to the logistics of doing it (e.g., recruiting adequate samples of a patient population, obtaining the cooperation of clinic staffs, dealing with the enormously time-consuming and labor-intensive tasks faced by studies addressed to the process of therapy).

Research in psychotherapy is expensive, but the cost is far less than that for research in the physical and biomedical sciences. Although governmental support of research in psychotherapy has not kept pace with inflation and social needs, well-designed research continues to have a fair chance of being supported, with NIMH being by far the leading funding source.

The desideratum of specificity has enormous practical implications because it will lead to more focused therapeutic strategies and provide sharper answers to the question of what psychotherapy can do for particular patients, at what cost, and over what periods of time. Other important areas of growth that can only be briefly mentioned include the following: (a) greater rapprochement between researchers, therapists, and theoreticians reflecting a trend toward eclecticism; (b) clarification of what constitutes a good therapeutic outcome; (c) refinement of diagnostic categories to aid in treatment planning; (d) explorations of what briefer or time-limited forms of psychotherapy can contribute as well as specification of the limitations of such treatment; (e) development of more clearly defined techniques for the treatment of particular patient problems (e.g., biofeedback techniques for the treatment of tension headaches and insomnia, brief dynamic psychotherapy for the resolution of "focal" problems, the treatment of sexual dysfunctions by behavioral techniques); (f) improvements in the training of psychotherapists; and (g) a greater understanding of factors leading to negative effects.

In conclusion, we offer a comment on the future relationships between practicing therapists and researchers. In the past, therapists have tended to regard researchers as unwelcome intruders who disrupted the sanctity of the patient–therapist relationship, produced findings of peripheral or trivial interest to the practitioner, and robbed a living human relationship of its excitement and vitality. To be sure, every scientific effort seeks to order, simplify, condense, and control. It is also true that practitioners cannot directly apply statistical trends (such as averages) in their everyday dealings with patients; they must deal with the inevitable idiosyncrasies of every patient–therapist interaction. The greater contribution of psychotherapy research may ultimately lie on a different plane: Researchers of the future, who must also be well-trained clinicians, must learn to work more closely with practicing therapists on vital issues encountered in everyday clinical work, subject these issues to empirical analysis and testing, and provide clinicians with information they can use more readily. What is envisaged is a form of action research, originally proposed by Lewin (1947), in which research is brought to bear on a practical (clinical) problem; research findings are then applied in the clinical setting; and their utility is again tested by means of research. Thus, there results a continuous and productive feedback loop in which practice inspires research and research provides information that is relevant to practice. For example, researchers may recommend to a clinic, on the basis of available research data relating to optimal matches between therapists and patients, that particular patients be assigned to particular therapists. The outcome of these dyads may then be studied and compared with contrasting assignments; on the basis of these results, subsequent assignment procedures may then be modified in the light of new information, at which point the process is repeated. This approach might also have important implications for the selection and training of young therapists. Obviously, it would not replace more sustained research efforts along traditional lines, but it would be one means of bringing about a closer "working alliance" between therapists and researchers.

As responsible professionals, therapists must learn to think critically and scrutinize continually the quality of their professional activities and the "therapeutic product." This has always been the hallmark of a mature profession (Peterson, 1976). As steps are taken in this direction, it is predictable that psychotherapy will become a better and more mature profession, meriting society's confidence and respect. Last, but not least, psychotherapy will become a profession based on solid scientific knowledge.

FUTURE DIRECTIONS

Psychotherapy is a service offered by professionals drawn from a variety of disciplines (e.g., medicine, nursing, psychology, social work). It is a treatment system that is influenced by the values and norms of each discipline; the public (e.g., patients, families, schools, courts); and mental health policymakers (e.g., governmental agencies, insurers). Each of these constituencies has unique requirements regarding the kinds of psychotherapy research information that would be useful. Moreover, from the viewpoint of an investigator, clinical practitioners add yet another set of values and norms. How is psychotherapy research going to serve these varied constituencies in the future?

1. Psychologists' training leads them to an application of the experimental approach (the true experiment) in order to specify the causal mechanisms of change. In this context, psychologists must develop theoretical propositions and subject these to rigorous empirical tests. Psychology trains psychologists in this methodology, and their colleagues (personality, social, cognitive, physiological, etc.), reviewers, and review committees hold this methodology in the highest esteem. This has led to a focus on a clearer specification and monitoring of the main independent variable: the treatment conditions (e.g., the development of treatment manuals and integrity checks). The future should witness an even stronger trend in this direction, especially with the emergence of a more phenomenologically oriented cognitive psychology. However, one should not overlook the fact that psychotherapy proceeds in the context of a human relationship; therefore, patient qualities, therapist qualities, and their interactions in a given dyad play an important role that is perhaps greater than that of techniques per se.

2. The vast majority of people in need of psychotherapy do not come to the attention of any mental health professional. More research attention should be directed toward prevention and outreach programs, rehabilitation (e.g., relapse prevention), and the development of psychotherapeutic applications to a broader array of disorders (e.g., substance abuse). Psychologists also need to be more active in the development and evaluation of new therapeutic approaches. Moreover, more attention should be given to evaluations of training programs and to certification of competence if psychologists are to present a better image to the public and destigmatize the use of their services.

3. Psychotherapists operate in the public interest as a service. They must develop a fuller understanding of how this service is financed and distributed, how people are trained to deliver this service, how patients find their way into the system, and the impact of this service on the productive functioning of patients. The delivery of these services has been significantly influenced by the decisions of policymakers (e.g., session limits, fee limits, selection of providers). These policymakers must be provided with the best information on which to base their decisions. Here, psychologists must leave the "laboratory" for more real-world naturalistic investigations and must attend to the outcome criteria (e.g., work days lost, turnover, cost effectiveness, cost-efficiency) that concern these policymakers. Psychol-

ogists can no longer ignore this important constituency. Also, information must be provided regarding the ways in which psychological services may be of use, in a manner that can be communicated to the public, so that they can become effective advocates of the profession.

4. In order to make research more relevant to clinicians, results have to be disaggregated to focus on relevant patient parameters: either individual patients or groups of patients who are clinically (meaningfully) alike in some important way. No clinician will be convinced that a particular treatment is superior for all patients (main effects). Indeed, an important component of clinical work entails making decisions about the appropriateness of an intervention for a particular patient. (Although penicillin is more effective than aspirin in treating pneumonia, a doctor would not give penicillin to a patient who is allergic to the drug.) Statistical procedures need to be developed for identifying the joint characteristics of patients, therapists, techniques, and settings that provide acceptable outcomes and those that require the development of new therapeutic approaches. The advances of psychopharmacological interventions should be recognized and included, when suitable and feasible, in research designs.

The existence of these four constituencies creates a healthy tension between naturalistic (discovery) and experimental (confirmatory) research methodologies. The field of psychotherapy research is charged by this tension and is characterized by excitement and innovation. There is plenty of work to be done by a growing complement of highly trained, productive professionals. The fundamental short-term goal of psychotherapy research is to provide the necessary information for determining to which of a specified set of treatments future patients are to be assigned. The ultimate goal is to refine the best treatments available (i.e., to make them more nearly optimal for all patients) and, perhaps most important, to achieve a better scientific understanding of the variables contributing to psychotherapeutic change.

REFERENCES

Bergin, A. E., & Garfield, S. L. (Eds.). (1971). *Handbook of psychotherapy and behavior change: An empirical analysis.* New York: Wiley.

Bergin, A. E., & Lambert, M. J. (1978). The evaluation of therapeutic outcomes. In S. L. Garfield & A. E. Bergin (Eds.), *Handbook of psychotherapy and behavior change: An empirical analysis* (2nd ed., pp. 139–190). New York: Wiley.

Bergin, A. E., & Strupp, H. H. (1972). *Changing frontiers in the science of psychotherapy*. Chicago: Aldine-Atherton.

Bordin, E. S. (1979). The generalizability of the psychoanalytic concept of the working alliance. *Psychotherapy: Theory, Research and Practice, 16*, 252–260.

Dittmann, A. T. (1972). *Interpersonal messages of emotion*. New York: Springer.

Elkin, I., Parloff, M., Hadley, S., & Autry, J. (1985). NIMH Treatment of Depression Collaborative Research Program: Background and research plan. *Archives of General Psychiatry, 42*, 305–316.

Elkin, I., Shea, M. T., Watkins, J. T., Imber, S. D., Sotsky, S. M., Collins, J. F., Glass, D. R., Pilkonis, P. A., Leber, W. R., Docherty, J. P., Fiester, S. J., & Parloff, M. B. (1989). NIMH Treatment of Depression Collaborative Research Program: General effectiveness of treatments. *Archives of General Psychiatry, 46*, 971–983.

Emmelkamp, P. M. G. (1986). Behavior therapy with adults. In S. L. Garfield & A. E. Bergin (Eds.), *Handbook of psychotherapy and behavior change: An empirical analysis* (3rd ed., pp. 385–442). New York: Wiley.

Eysenck, H. J. (1952). The effects of psychotherapy: An evaluation. *Journal of Consulting Psychology, 16*, 319–324.

Fenichel, O. (1930). Statistischer Bericht über die therapeutische Tätigkeit, 1920–1930 [Statistical report on the therapeutic activities, 1920–1930]. In *Zehn Jahre Berliner Psychoanalytisches Institut* [Ten years of the Berlin Psychoanalytic Institute] (pp. 13–19). Vienna, Austria: Internationaler Psychoanalytischer Verlag.

Fiske, D. W., Hunt, H. F., Luborsky, L., Orne, M. T., Parloff, M. D., Reiser, M. F., & Tuma, A. H. (1970). Planning of research on effectiveness of psychotherapy. *Archives of General Psychiatry, 22*, 22–32.

Frank, J. D. (1973). *Persuasion and healing: A comparative study of psychotherapy* (2nd ed.). Baltimore: Johns Hopkins University Press.

Frank, J. D. (1974). Therapeutic components of psychotherapy: A 25-year progress report of research. *Journal of Nervous and Mental Disease, 159*, 325–342.

Frank, J. D. (1982). Therapeutic components shared by all psychotherapies. In J. H. Harvey & M. M. Parks (Eds.), *Psychotherapy research and behavior change: The Master Lecture Series* (Vol. 1, pp. 5–37). Washington, DC: American Psychological Association.

Frank, J. D., Gliedman, L. H., Imber, S. D., Nash, E. H., & Stone, A. R. (1957). Why patients leave psychotherapy. *Archives of Neurology and Psychiatry, 77*, 283–299.

Freud, S. (1963). Analytic therapy. In J. Strachey (Ed. and Trans.), *The standard edition of the complete psychological works of Sigmund Freud* (Vol. 16, pp. 448–463). London: Hogarth Press. (Original work published 1916)

Freud, S. (1964). Analysis terminable and interminable. In J. Strachey (Ed. and Trans.), *The standard edition of the complete psychological works of Sigmund Freud* (Vol. 23, pp. 216–253). London: Hogarth Press. (Original work published 1937)

Garfield, S. L., & Bergin, A. E. (Eds.). (1978). *Handbook of psychotherapy and behavior change: An empirical analysis* (2nd ed.). New York: Wiley.

Garfield, S. L., & Bergin, A. E. (Eds.). (1986). *Handbook of psychotherapy and behavior change: An empirical analysis* (3rd ed.). New York: Wiley.

Hamburg, D. A., Bibring, G. L., Fisher, C., Stanton, A. H., Wallerstein, R. S., Weinstock, H. I., & Haggard, E. (1967). Report of Ad Hoc Committee on Central Fact-Gathering Data of the American Psychoanalytic Association. *Journal of the American Psychoanalytic Association, 15,* 841–861.

Hollon, S. D., & Beck, A. T. (1986). Research on cognitive therapies. In S. L. Garfield & A. E. Bergin (Eds.), *Handbook of psychotherapy and behavior change: An empirical analysis* (3rd ed., pp. 443–482). New York: Wiley.

Holt, R. R., & Luborsky, L. (1958). *Personality patterns of psychiatrists.* New York: Basic Books.

Howard, K. I., Kopta, S. M., Krause, M. S., & Orlinsky, D. E. (1986). The dose-effect relationship in psychotherapy. *American Psychologist, 41,* 159–164.

Howard, K. I., & Orlinsky, D. E. (1972). Psychotherapeutic processes. *Annual Review of Psychology, 23,* 615–668.

Imber, S. D., Pilkonis, P. A., Sotsky, S. M., Watkins, J. T., Shea, M. T., Elkin, I., Collins, J. F., Leber, W. R., & Glass, D. R. (1990). Mode-specific effects among three treatments for depression. *Journal of Consulting and Clinical Psychology, 58,* 352–359.

Kernberg, O. F., Bernstein, C. S., Coyne, R., Appelbaum, D. A., Horwitz, H., & Voth, T. J. (1972). Psychotherapy and psychoanalysis: Final report of the Menninger Foundation's Psychotherapy Research Project. *Bulletin of the Menninger Clinic, 36,* 1–276.

Lambert, M. J., Shapiro, D. A., & Bergin, A. E. (1986). The effectiveness of psychotherapy. In S. L. Garfield & A. E. Bergin (Eds.), *Handbook of psychotherapy and behavior change: An empirical analysis* (3rd ed., pp. 157–211). New York: Wiley.

Lewin, K. (1947). Frontiers in group dynamics: II. Channels of group life: Social planning and action research. *Human Relations, 1,* 143–153.

Lorr, M. (1962). Relation of treatment frequency and duration to psychotherapeutic outcome. In H. H. Strupp & L. Luborsky (Eds.), *Research in psychotherapy* (Vol. 2, pp. 134–141). Washington, DC: American Psychological Association.

Lorr, M., McNair, D. M., Michaux, W., & Raskin, A. (1962). Frequency of treatment and change in psychotherapy. *Journal of Abnormal and Social Psychology, 64,* 281–292.

Luborsky, L. (1962). The patient's personality and psychotherapeutic change. In H. H. Strupp & L. Luborsky (Eds.), *Research in psychotherapy* (Vol. 2, pp. 115–133). Washington, DC: American Psychological Association.

Luborsky, L. (1984). *Principles of psychoanalytic psychotherapy.* New York: Basic Books.

Luborsky, L., Crits-Christoph, P., Mintz, J., & Auerbach, A. (1988). *Who will benefit from psychotherapy? Predicting therapeutic outcomes.* New York: Basic Books.

McNeilly, C. L., & Howard, K. I. (1991). The effects of psychotherapy: A reevaluation based on dosage. *Psychotherapy Research, 1,* 74–78.

Orlinsky, D. E., & Howard, K. I. (1966). Process and outcome in psychotherapy. In S. L. Garfield & A. E. Bergin (Eds.), *Handbook of psychotherapy and behavior change: An empirical analysis* (3rd ed., pp. 311–381). New York: Wiley.

Orlinsky, D. E., & Howard, K. I. (1975). *Varieties of psychotherapeutic experience.* New York: Teachers College Press.

Peterson, D. R. (1976). Is psychology a profession? *American Psychologist, 31,* 553–560.

Price, D. J. (1963). *Little science, big science.* New York: Columbia University Press.

Random House Dictionary of the English Language. (1967). New York: Random House.

Robbins, L. L., & Wallerstein, R. S. (1956). The psychotherapy research project of the Menninger Foundation: I. Orientation. *Bulletin of the Menninger Clinic, 20,* 223–225.

Rogers, C. R. (1951). *Client-centered therapy.* Boston: Houghton Mifflin.

Rogers, C. R., & Dymond, R. F. (Eds.). (1954). *Psychotherapy and personality change.* Chicago: University of Chicago Press.

Rogers, C. R., Gendlin, G. T., Kiesler, D. J., & Truax, C. B. (1967). *The therapeutic relationship and its impact: A study of psychotherapy with schizophrenics.* Madison: University of Wisconsin Press.

Rubinstein, E. A., & Parloff, M. B. (Eds.). (1959). *Research in psychotherapy* (Vol. 1). Washington, DC: American Psychological Association.

Shlien, J. M., Hunt, H. F., Matarazzo, J. D., & Savage, C. (Eds.). (1968). *Research in psychotherapy* (Vol. 3). Washington, DC: American Psychological Association.

Sloane, R. B., Staples, F. R., Cristol, A. H., Yorkston, N. J., & Wipple, K. (1975). *Psychotherapy versus behavior therapy.* Cambridge, MA: Harvard University Press.

Smith, M. L., Glass, G. V., & Miller, T. I. (1980). *The benefits of psychotherapy.* Baltimore: Johns Hopkins University Press.

Snyder, W. U. (1961). *The psychotherapy relationship.* New York: Macmillan.

Strupp, H. H. (1980). Success and failure in time-limited psychotherapy: Further evidence (Comparison 4). *Archives of General Psychiatry, 37,* 947–954.

Strupp, H. H., & Bergin, A. E. (1969). Some empirical and conceptual bases for coordinated research in psychotherapy. *International Journal of Psychiatry, 7,* 18–90.

Strupp, H. H., & Binder, J. L. (1984). *Psychotherapy in a new key: A guide to time-limited dynamic psychotherapy.* New York: Basic Books.

Strupp, H. H., Butler, S. F., & Rosser, C. L. (1988). Training in psychodynamic psychotherapy. *Journal of Consulting and Clinical Psychology, 56,* 689–695.

Strupp, H. H., & Hadley, S. W. (1979). Specific versus nonspecific factors in psychotherapy: A controlled study of outcome. *Archives of General Psychiatry, 36*, 1125–1136.

Strupp, H. H., Hadley, S. W., & Gomes-Schwartz, B. (1977). *Psychotherapy for better or worse: An analysis of the problem of negative effects.* New York: Jason Aronson.

Strupp, H. H., & Luborsky, L. (Eds.). (1962). *Research in psychotherapy* (Vol. 2). Washington, DC: American Psychological Association.

Wallerstein, R. S. (1986). *Forty-two lives in treatment: A study of psychoanalysis and psychotherapy.* New York: Guilford Press.

10

MAJOR ISSUES IN PSYCHOTHERAPY RESEARCH

SOL L. GARFIELD

A variety of issues have tended to accompany the development of psychotherapy research, and as our knowledge has increased, so has the number of important issues. A long list could be given of these issues, each of which has potential importance for psychotherapy research. Because of space considerations and because many issues are complex, I will discuss a limited number of them here.

One important issue can be mentioned at the outset. From time to time, the view has been voiced that psychotherapy is an art and not a science (Lehrer, 1981). Consequently, according to this view, research has no role to play in psychotherapy. Although some psychotherapists may agree with this view, I and other researchers obviously do not accept it. Fortunately, this issue has not seriously held back activity or progress in research on psychotherapy. Nevertheless, some related aspects do have implications that deserve discussion and appraisal, and I will explore those aspects.

THE INTEGRITY OF TREATMENT VERSUS ACTUAL CLINICAL PRACTICE

One of the issues raised by both researchers and practitioners, although from different vantage points, pertains to how accurately the psychotherapy studied by researchers actually mirrors the reality of clinical practice. The researcher's questions about the integrity of the therapy being evaluated center on whether a given type of therapy is actually being conducted according to its designated procedures and "rules." In other words, was the dynamic psychotherapy or the behavior therapy carried out in ways that experts of each orientation would accept as accurate representations of the designated therapies? If not, valid conclusions or generalizations cannot be drawn. Many of the early studies simply described the therapy by name, based on what the therapists stated, and did not examine any of the actual therapy performed.

As a means of handling this problem, recent research studies have used therapy manuals to ensure the integrity of a given form of therapy. Therapists then are trained, evaluated, and monitored in terms of the therapy manual and deviations can be noted and corrections made. In the National Institute of Mental Health (NIMH) Collaborative Study of the Treatment of Depression, for example, manuals were used in the training and monitoring of the two forms of psychotherapy as well as for the psychopharmacological treatment (Elkin, Parloff, Hadley, & Autry, 1985).

Although the "manualization" of psychotherapy may appear to have solved the issue of the integrity of the therapy investigated, it also raises other issues, particularly what appears to be the problem of external validity. In other words, do the research findings have relevance for the psychotherapy that is performed by most psychotherapists in most clinical settings? It can be said, with at least some degree of confidence, that most therapists perform in their own individual style with little conformity to some therapeutic manual. Thus, the results of research using therapy manuals may have little direct relevance for practice. This is an intriguing issue and illustrates the type of complex problems encountered in research on psychotherapy. Earlier issues pertaining to the use of analogue studies and inexperienced therapists seemingly were overcome by the use of manuals, but then a new and more complicated issue becomes evident.

A related issue concerns the potential variability of therapists in securing positive outcome. The focus in many past research studies as well as the more recent ones using manuals has been on the type of therapy, with little attention paid to therapist competence and differences. Is the therapeutic approach more important than the overall therapeutic skill of specific therapists? Are good therapists good, regardless of theoretical orientation, or is the approach the significant variable? Is competence the same thing as adherence to a given approach, or should a truly competent therapist vary his or her approach in terms of the problems of the client? Clearly, these are important issues that remain to be evaluated in terms of future research. The existing research is practically nonexistent and much too limited to provide a basis for drawing even rather tentative conclusions (Elkin, 1986; Luborsky, McLellan, Woody, O'Brien & Auerbach, 1985; Luborsky et al., 1986).

The broad issue here is how much can we generalize to the everyday clinical situation from the results secured by psychotherapy researchers? This is a research issue that transcends the field of psychotherapy but is certainly a critical issue for psychotherapists. The more experimental controls operationalized in research, the more highly trained and selected the therapists, the more voluntary options provided the research subjects in terms of research safeguards, the more extensive the appraisals of patients made both at pre- and posttherapy, and the more detailed the selection criteria for research subjects are made, the greater the divergence from clinical practice. How to ensure sufficient experimental rigor and at the same time to make the research investigation have clear relevance for clinical practice is a critical concern that confronts every researcher in the field of psychotherapy.

ETHICAL ISSUES IN RESEARCH ON PSYCHOTHERAPY

For about the past 20 years, increased concern has also been expressed about ethical issues pertaining to research with human subjects. This has been particularly the case where individuals with psychological problems are seeking or are offered psychotherapeutic treatment. In research of this type, it is apparent that the requirements of a specific research design may at times conflict with the treatment needs of a specific patient. Such potential conflicts highlight the kind of important ethical issues that may arise, and are particularly evident in cases where a no-treatment control group is a basic part of the research design. "The withholding of treatment from patients judged by research diagnostic criteria to be in need of such treatment clearly presents an ethical issue of some importance. . . . A similar case can be made in those instances in which a control group being given a placebo is used. Because the placebo, by definition, is a nontreatment that simply resembles a treatment, in essence the patient who receives a placebo is being denied treatment" (Garfield, 1987a, p. 116).

Some investigators have attempted to avoid this problem of a no-treatment control by using a wait-list control group, whereby research patients are promised treatment within a specified time, for example, 4 months (Sloane, Staples, Cristol, Yorkston, & Whipple, 1975). However, in such instances, as with the no-treatment and placebo control groups, actual treatment is both withheld and delayed. Furthermore, the delay can have significant consequences if the control patients are seriously disturbed and a truly effective treatment is withheld. There is little question that such a situation needs very careful and thoughtful appraisal by the psychotherapy researcher. At the same time that such clinical concerns for the welfare of the patient have to be considered, the requirements for conducting a well-designed and potentially clinically significant research study also require consideration. The issues involved in the use of such control groups have been stated succinctly by O'Leary and Borkovec (1978) as follows:

> Two ethical principles appear to be in conflict in discussions of the use of placebo conditions in psychotherapy research. On the one hand, we have an ethical responsibility to society and to our patients to evaluate the efficacy of our treatments by the best methodological means available. A design comparing treatment to placebo and no-treatment conditions is currently the most frequently advocated method of obtaining such evidence. On the other hand, the ethical nature of these methods can be questioned. (p. 824)

Although the problem is clear, the means of handling it are complicated. There is no question in my mind that meaningful research to evaluate psychotherapeutic procedures requires adequate controls. As I have stated elsewhere, "Therapeutic changes secured by means of uncontrolled investigations cannot be conclusively ascribed to the therapy used because other variables (e.g., maturation, the passage of time) conceivably may have been responsible for the changes secured. A moderate number of outcome studies in psychotherapy, both old and recent, unfortunately have been uncontrolled studies, and their findings cannot be taken as conclusive indications of the efficacy of psychotherapy" (Garfield, 1987a, pp. 117–118).

There is no unanimity among researchers and clinicians or even among researchers on this issue. However, before discussing this matter further, one additional related issue should be mentioned. In most research on psychotherapy currently, the therapy conducted is usually limited to a set number of sessions, specified in advance. Therapy is not supposed to continue beyond this point, and posttherapy evaluations are generally made thereafter. In addition, because the maintenance of whatever therapeutic gains have been made is also considered important, some attempts at follow-up evaluations at stated intervals after completion of treatment is usually included in the research protocol. The issue presented by this design pertains to the disposition of research patients who are still in need of treatment at the time of the last scheduled session. A specific example can be offered from the Sloane et al. study (1975). In that study, the two therapies evaluated had a time limit of 4 months and follow-up evaluations were conducted 1 year after treatment was begun. The agreement between patients and researchers allowed patients to continue in therapy after the 4-month period if they wished to do so, and just over half of them did so. Although this aspect of the study seriously limited the value of the follow-up evaluation, as slightly over half of the patients had secured additional therapy, it clearly would have been unethical to withhold the additional treatment. "Ideally, for research purposes, none of the patients would have received therapy between the four-month assessment and the one-year interview, but ethically we could not completely control treatment after the initial four-month period." (Sloane et al., 1975, p. 117). The conflict between research needs and patient welfare is clearly apparent in the preceding quotation.

As a result of the greater sensitivity to the ethical issues in psychotherapy research recently, some suggestions have been made to resolve these issues while attempting to keep the research standards high. (Again, the description of these suggested means of coping with the ethical issues will be brief.)

Although the use of no-treatment, wait-list, or placebo control groups all present potential ethical problems, the need for some type of control group or treatment appears necessary for securing valid and meaningful results. In medical research, one commonly used procedure is to compare a new drug or treatment with an established one that is viewed as the standard treatment. For example, chlorpromazine was the first pharmacological agent to be seen as an effective treatment for patients diagnosed as suffering from schizophrenia. Consequently, when newer compounds were prepared, they were compared with chlorpromazine and any improvements in success rate, side effects, speed of improvement, and the like could be appraised.

Unfortunately, there is no accepted standard form of psychotherapy to be used as a control therapy in psychotherapy research, although this approach has been recommended by some individuals (Parloff, 1986; Stricker, 1982). In the laissez-faire arena of contemporary psychotherapy, where more than 400 supposedly different forms of psychotherapy compete for recognition, it would appear difficult to get strong agreement on a specific psychotherapy to be designated as the standard for purposes of comparison. Another problem here, as well as for other aspects of psychotherapy research, is that a number of the psychotherapies purport to have different therapeutic goals. Consequently, it would be difficult to have just one standard that was appropriate for all. Furthermore, even where one form of psychotherapy such as behavior therapy might be viewed as most effective for phobic disorders, there are several different types of behavioral approaches or techniques that could be evaluated as equally effective: systematic desensitization, flooding, or exposure.

Parloff (1986) has also suggested comparing two "known" forms of psychotherapy instead of using a placebo control. However, this suggestion does not really control for such variables as the passage of time or spontaneous improvement, and not everyone will necessarily agree as to what treatments are known. New treatments could be compared with older treatments that have been evaluated, but again, in the absence of a truly acknowledged standard for comparison, this would not be fully satisfactory.

Similar limitations are evident in some other proposals. The dismantling procedure used by behavior therapists, where one or more therapeutic components are omitted and the therapy evaluated (Kazdin & Wilson, 1978), is also not a solution to this problem. Although one or more components may be shown to be more important than others, the total approach used would still have to be evaluated in terms of efficacy. A somewhat similar procedure was suggested by Stricker (1982), but it also falls short. He suggested varying the length of treatment, the frequency of sessions, and types of patients and therapists. This might be worthwhile for evaluating variables that conceivably might have an effect on outcome, but it would not be adequate for evaluating the effectiveness of a given form of therapy.

Before concluding this discussion of ethical issues, a brief reference can be made to the NIMH Collaborative Study of the Treatment of Depression (Elkin et al., 1985). One of the difficulties encountered was the choice of a suitable control group. There was no standard therapy or valid control group for the two psychotherapies being evaluated. However, since Imipramine, a pharmacotherapy, was also being evaluated, a pill-placebo group was added as a control for it. Even though the pill-placebo was not judged as a proper control for the two psychotherapies, the safeguards set up for subjects in this study were noteworthy. Patients judged to have severe pathology or to be suicidal were excluded. All patients were given thorough medical examinations and were screened prior to the start of the study. Patients were informed about the nature of the study, were told about random assignments to treatment conditions, were allowed to ask questions, were promised confidentiality, and were told they could withdraw from the study whenever they made this decision. In this manner, the rights of research patients were balanced with the requirements of the research study.

The deliberations in the NIMH study and the decisions reached illustrate the range and complexity of potential issues that face conscientious researchers in the area of psychotherapy. Even in this instance, some issues remained. For example, some prospective subjects preferred one of the treatments in the study, and when they were not assigned to the treatment of their choice, they withdrew from the study or were referred elsewhere. This did affect the procedure of random assignments. Also, in the so-called pill-placebo control group, patients were seen weekly by a psychiatrist. In this way, patients who theoretically were not receiving any active treatment were actually in weekly contact with a psychiatrist who showed interest in their welfare and who could handle any potential emergency such as a suicidal preoccupation or threat. However, this kind of essentially supportive treatment certainly removed any semblance of a no-treatment control condition, and this was openly recognized by the collaborating investigators. Thus, an ideally controlled study of psychotherapy is probably not attainable, and researchers must settle for investigations that approximate the ideal and do not have any fatal flaws.

EVALUATION OF OUTCOME

There is little question that appraising the outcome or effectiveness of psychotherapy is one of the basic goals of psychotherapy research. It is also a major concern to those who provide psychotherapeutic services and, of course, to those who are the consumers of these services. Consequently, it may appear surprising that there has been considerable controversy surrounding this area of research (Garfield, 1983). However, evaluating the outcome of psychotherapy is a complicated matter, and over the years, a number of important issues have been raised.

Measures and Criteria of Outcome

One such issue pertains to how outcome is measured or evaluated. In much of the early research, outcome was evaluated by judgments or rating scales completed by the therapists. Numerous criticisms were made of many of the rating scales used, such as global and undefined rating categories and the like. However, even with psychometrically improved scales, there remained the issue of the potential bias of the therapist in evaluating his or her own therapy.

In part, to improve this situation, the individuals receiving the therapy were also asked to provide their ratings of the outcome of therapy. Having both participants contribute to the evaluations of therapy conceivably would lessen the bias of relying on only one source of appraisal. Although this reasoning was sound, the lack of congruence between the two sets of raters raised an additional issue. For example, in a study by Garfield, Prager, and Bergin (1971), both sets of ratings indicated an improvement rate of approximately 70%, but the correlation between the ratings was .44. The correlations reported in other studies have been even lower. A correlation of only .21 was secured by Sloane et al. (1975) between ratings of patients and therapists, whereas a nonsignificant correlation of .10 was secured by Horenstein, Houston, and Holmes (1973). Such limited agreement among the two participants in psychotherapy thus raises some question about the significance or meaning of these evaluations.

As one means of improving the evaluation of outcome, additional ratings from supervisors, significant others, and independent judges also have been used. At present, it appears that most researchers use ratings from independent clinical judges in addition to those secured from therapists and patients. Thus, several different sources of data are secured to overcome potential limitations of any single source. Furthermore, because overall global judgments made at the end of therapy may be unduly influenced by the patient's general level of functioning rather than by the amount of change ostensibly due to therapy, a variety of variables can be evaluated before and after therapy. Also, a variety of psychological tests, questionnaires, rating scales, and behavioral measures can be used to provide a comprehensive appraisal. The type of evaluative measures used should be relevant for the kinds of problems for which the patient has sought therapy. This is not always easy to do, but researchers clearly need to keep this in mind.

The variety of evaluative measures potentially available and the potentially different results that may be secured as a result of this does constitute an issue of some importance. Strupp and Hadley (1977), in evaluating this problem concluded that each evaluation perspective is important and have suggested a tripartite system of evaluation. Three vantage points—society, patient, and mental health professional—are recommended. The societal viewpoint focuses on social roles and mores; the patient viewpoint involves subjective perceptions and feelings; and the professional view includes an appraisal based on observations of behavior, tests, and clinical judgment and professional knowledge. Although this schema has advantages over reliance on more limited measures, it does not present a complete solution to the problem of evaluating outcome. When different evaluations from the three viewpoints are secured, how do we integrate them or reach some overall judgment? Is some viewpoint more important than the others? Some research has indicated that therapists' ratings tend to give the most positive outcomes (Garfield, 1978) and that judges' ratings, based on interviews with the patients, tend to correlate more highly with patients' ratings than with therapists' ratings (Sloane et al., 1975). Thus, there is no easy solution to the issues related to measures of outcome. One must choose multiple measures that are clearly geared to the problems that have led the patient to seek therapy.

Factors Influencing Outcome

Apart from the kinds of measures to be used in evaluating outcome, investigators have to be sensitive to other factors that may influence both the process and outcome of psychotherapy. These include the patients being treated, the therapists providing the therapy, and external events and support systems that may influence the patients' response to therapy and their subsequent progress. A number of issues surrounding some of these factors were raised with reference to earlier research attempts. These involved the use of a variety of different patients as they presented themselves in the day-to-day clinical situation and in the use of subjects who were not perceived as "real" clinical patients. In the former instance, chance determined what the composition of the patient sample was, and generalization to other samples as well as future samples was difficult to make with any degree of accuracy. In the latter instance, volunteers and college students were frequently used as research subjects, and their appropriateness was questioned. This issue has largely been resolved because most recent studies have set up reasonably rigid criteria for selection of subjects, and many have been limited to the appraisal of therapies for specific problems such as depression, agoraphobia, and so on.

An issue remains, however, with respect to the kinds of patients who respond best to psychotherapy or to different kinds of psychotherapy. It has sometimes been said that the individuals in least need of help usually receive the most intensive psychotherapy, whereas the most seriously disturbed are viewed as poor bets for therapy. A critique of this kind was made in the past by a congressional commission authorized to evaluate resources and practices in mental health (Joint Commission on Mental Illness and Health, 1961). Strupp (1980a, 1980b) has also published analyses of cases in brief psychotherapy that indicate that certain patients are able to secure positive results in psychotherapy and others are not. Thus, not only must researchers be aware of the kinds of patients being selected and studied in research projects, but at some point, the results of research should indicate which patients can profit from psychotherapy or certain types of psychotherapy and which patients cannot.

A related factor in psychotherapy research is the therapist. Two issues in particular can be mentioned with reference to the therapist, although both refer to the competence of the therapist. Many of the previous studies relied on graduate students or those who were willing to participate. Because many of these therapists were not fully trained or experienced, the results obtained could be questioned. A second issue (already mentioned in the discussion of training manuals) is the variability in competence among psychotherapists. If we acknowledge that psychotherapy is a complex interpersonal process that requires both personal qualities and a high level of skill, then we should expect differential results from different therapists (Garfield, 1981a). Instead, as noted, most attention has been paid to the type of psychotherapy. It is surprising that so few studies have been conducted on the skill and competence of psychotherapists. In this area, we have certainly shown no questioning of the uniformity myth mentioned by Kiesler (1966, 1971) some years ago. The related issue of what kind of therapists functions best with what kind of patients has received some research, but as yet the answers are far from conclusive (Parloff, Waskow, & Wolfe, 1978; Beutler, Crago, & Arizmendi, 1986).

A final factor to be mentioned here is the potential influence on process and outcome of external factors in the life of the patient. In most research studies of psychotherapy, very little attention has been paid to the possible influence of events outside of therapy that conceivably could play a significant role in the patient's overall adjustment and thus have an impact on what goes on in therapy. Perhaps understandably, what occurs in the therapy hour each week is considered to be of prime importance, and what occurs on the outside during the remaining 167 hours is considered to be of lesser importance. Although not all patients seek therapy because of an acute crisis in their life, the resolution of a crisis can bring therapy to a positive termination very quickly in a number of cases (Garfield, 1989). In a similar fashion, serious life events or traumas that occur during therapy may negatively affect the therapeutic process. The psychotherapy project of the Menninger Foundation was one of the few projects to recognize explicitly the importance of situational variables, to provide for an appraisal of such variables (Sargent, Modlin, Faris, & Voth, 1958), and to acknowledge the difficulties in appraising the impact of such variables on outcome in psychotherapy (Voth, Modlin, & Orth, 1962). Very few other studies have made serious attempts to evaluate the importance of such variables on psychotherapy process and outcome. Consequently, it remains a significant issue.

Spontaneous Remission

One issue that has been raised repeatedly in research on outcome in psychotherapy is that of spontaneous remission, or the self-limiting nature of certain disorders. This issue was first brought to prominence by Eysenck (1952) in his controversial paper on the effects of psychotherapy, in which he argued that the outcome of psychotherapy was no better than that of spontaneous remission. This led to a long controversy concerning the "true" spontaneous remission rate (Bergin, 1971; Rachman, 1973; Subotnick, 1972). In a review of this issue, Lambert (1976) pointed out that various estimates of the spontaneous remission rate in neurotic disorders varied from 0–90% and that there are no adequate data from which to secure what might be viewed as a valid estimate.

There are thus no well-validated data to indicate the self-limiting duration of most psychological disorders. Although estimates of 2 years have sometimes been given (Lambert, 1976), these apparently were applied to general "neurotic" disorders, a rather gross category. Some situational disorders, some reactions to momentary crises, and some types of fears or depressions may improve or remit in a relatively short time, but many disorders do not. It does not appear prudent, therefore, to posit a generalized spontaneous remission effect that is meaningful as a basis for comparison for all so-called neurotic disorders. Furthermore, if the results secured with psychotherapy are significantly better than those secured from a suitable control group, then it seems to me that the issue of spontaneous remission is no longer an issue of great importance. Even if a specific psychological disturbance would remit "naturally" in a year or two, a course of brief psychotherapy could reduce the period of discomfort for the individual involved.

Follow-up Studies

One of the major issues in evaluating the efficacy of psychotherapy pertains to the duration of the improvement secured from psychotherapy. The matter of the maintenance of therapeutic gains is clearly of some importance. In order to evaluate the maintenance of treatment gains and the incidence of relapses, follow-up appraisals have been recommended as essential aspects of research studies evaluating psychotherapy. Although many researchers would agree on the importance of follow-up studies, there is no clear agreement as to how long the follow-up interval should be. Many doctoral dissertations on evaluating outcome in psychotherapy have used follow-up periods of 1 to 3 months, for obvious reasons. In studies carried out in clinical research settings by more experienced investigators, longer periods ranging from 6 to 24 months have been used, and some studies have used even longer follow-up periods.

Although adequate follow-up studies can provide us with potentially important information on the long-term effects of psychotherapy, there are some difficulties associated with them. An obvious one is that they take time. Researchers have to make a real commitment to such research, particularly if the follow-up interval is long and it has taken several years to accumulate an adequate group of subjects who have completed the required treatments. To give a concrete example, I refer to a small study that two colleagues and I conducted, in which we evaluated patient–therapist interactions during the first interview and related our appraisals to continuation in psychotherapy (Garfield, Affleck, & Muffly, 1963). We specifically selected patients applying for outpatient treatment who had had *no* previous psychotherapy treatment. At the end of 1 full year, we were able to secure just 24 patients, and at that time not all of them had completed therapy. In this study, we focused on the first interview and on continuation in therapy rather than on evaluating outcome or effectiveness. If we had been conducting an outcome study, it would have taken several years to get a moderately sized sample because half of the patients in the previous study terminated by the seventh interview. Thus, if something like a 2-year follow-up is added to the posttreatment evaluation, the study will usually take many years. There is also a related problem.

Unless one is particularly fortunate, has an unusual research sample, or is able to develop a unique relationship with the research subjects, securing the cooperation of all subjects at the required follow-up time is quite difficult. People die, move away, and for a number of reasons refuse to cooperate after treatment is completed. Not only does the number of research subjects shrink, but there is always the possibility that the remaining sample may not be representative of the group that began therapy. Any research project that extends over many years also has a greater probability of staff and personnel changes that also present difficulties for the research project.

Recently, however, a meta-analysis of 67 studies that included follow-up periods of varying lengths secured results that appeared to indicate that follow-up studies may not be required for most studies of outcome in psychotherapy (Nicholson & Berman, 1983). In this report of adult psychotherapy, the average period of follow-up was over 8 months, and almost half of the studies had follow-ups of at least 6 months. In general, the results showed relatively little change from posttreatment to follow-up. These authors suggested that follow-up designs may be required only where the disorders have been found to have high relapse rates or where the focus is on the maintenance of treatment gains.

Statistical and Methodological Issues

In addition to the issues already discussed with reference to evaluating outcome in psychotherapy, there are some statistical and related issues that also merit our attention. Obviously, appropriate statistical measures need to be used and basic research standards adhered to strictly. However, there are aspects that deserve special emphasis.

One general issue pertains to the interpretation of the significance of the results secured in any research study. This issue has sometimes been expressed as "clinical versus statistical significance." It has been traditional in psychological research to categorize results as significant when they reach or exceed the .05 level of probability. This measure, however, refers only to the probability that the finding is not due to chance and we can refer to this as statistical significance. However, clinicians are more concerned about the practical or clinical significance of the results secured. Many factors may lead to a statistically significant result that at the same time may have little practical utility. Large samples of subjects and limited variability of samples increase the chances of securing results that are statistically significant, but the results may be lacking in clinical significance. For example, if a therapy program for patients labeled as schizophrenic produced a statistically significant reduction on the MMPI Schizophrenia Scale from 82 to 75, we might not regard this as a clinically important change. Thus, apart from statistical significance, we are concerned with the extent of change and its normative significance.

Results of research investigations on psychotherapy have been reported in a variety of ways, and some do not provide adequate information concerning the extent of improvement or change. A report that states that 64% of the patients treated showed "some improvement" tells very little in this regard. Part of the problem has been due to the use of nonstandardized measures of outcome and to the reliance on the .05 level of significance. The use of standard measures such as the Beck Depression Inventory, the Hamilton Rating Scale of Depression, or the MMPI can help to rectify this deficiency. It is also important to report clearly the actual change in scores or ratings and not just the statistical analysis.

One possible issue regarding the effectiveness of psychotherapy is whether an individual is capable of normal functioning after the completion of therapy. Until fairly recently, this concern has received relatively little attention. However, it is an issue worth emphasizing. If a group at the start of treatment in a research study differs widely from the norm but at the end of treatment has reached a point that approximates the norm, the results would be viewed as clinically meaningful. On the other hand, if at the end of therapy the group shows some gain, significant at the .05 level but noticeably far from the norm, the gain would not be evaluated so positively. This type of analysis is being performed increasingly in studies of psychotherapy with children (Kazdin, Bass, Siegel, & Thomas, 1989;

Kendall & Norton-Ford, 1982), and such analyses have also been made in the NIMH Collaborative Study of the Treatment of Depression (Elkin, Parloff, Hadley, & Autry, 1985).

Reference can also be made to some recent attempts by Jacobson and his colleagues to develop statistical procedures for assessing the clinical significance of treatment effects in psychotherapy research (Jacobson, Follette, & Revenstorf, 1984, 1986; Jacobson & Revenstorf, 1988). The goal of these investigators was to help develop and foster the adoption of standardized methods for determining clinical significance. They felt that research would have a much greater impact on clinical practice if the results were reported in a more meaningful manner to practitioners. In their continuing work they also have been guided by a normative framework. The major problems they still face are: "how to deal with the use of multiple outcome measures within a single study; how to minimize the problem of measurement error in subject classification; and how to deal with measures that are not normally distributed" (Jacobson & Revenstorf, 1988, p. 133).

Two other somewhat related issues can also be mentioned briefly here. One pertains to the use of a standard battery of outcome procedures versus the use of individualized measures, selected for the specific patient. Each side of this issue has some merit. Standard measures allow more meaningful comparisons and syntheses of individual studies. At the same time, the complaints of patients seeking psychotherapeutic help are not identical, and differential outcomes may be meaningfully sought. However, in the latter instances, it is more difficult to secure an organized or integrated body of findings. My own recommendation is to use a standard battery for all investigations of specific problems and to supplement the battery in terms of the specific interests of the investigator or the requirements of a particular project.

A final issue (alluded to previously) concerns the use of solicited and unsolicited subjects in psychotherapy research. This issue has assumed importance in recent years as research has focused more specifically on clearly diagnosed cases of a specific disorder (e.g., unipolar depression or agoraphobia). In the usual clinical setting, it will usually take many years to accumulate a reasonably sized sample of patients who meet the desired diagnostic criteria. Consequently, investigators have turned to media advertisements and other channels to secure samples of adequate size, and the question has been raised concerning the comparability of such "patients" with "real patients" who have voluntarily sought psychotherapy. In other words, are the results obtained with such patients generalizable to the unsolicited patients? At present, the available data are too limited to draw conclusions, but they suggest that comparable samples of solicited and unsolicited patients can be secured with adequate screening (Krupnick, Shea, & Elkin, 1986).

WHAT ARE THE THERAPEUTIC VARIABLES THAT LEAD TO PATIENT CHANGE?

In this section we will examine some issues that really transcend the area of psychotherapy research—they involve the whole field of psycho-therapy. We can begin by noting the tremendous proliferation of psycho-therapeutic approaches or orientations. As I have noted elsewhere:

> This growth and proliferation of therapeutic approaches has been most marked in the past 20 to 30 years. In the mid-1960s, for example, I collected my own list of over 60 different approaches to psychotherapy and thought this was an amazing phenomenon. A few years later, a report of the Research Task Force of the National Institute of Mental Health (1975) mentioned that there were over 130 different types of psychotherapy. Just 5 years later, Herink (1980) published his account of over 200 different forms of psychotherapy, and more recently Kazdin (1986a) referred to a statement of over 400 different techniques. Need-less to say, if this rate of increase continues, at some point we will have a different form of psychotherapy for every person in the United States. (Garfield, 1989, p. 19)

When one is confronted with such a situation, it is natural to ask if all of the different therapies are equally effective or if some are "more equal" than others. What kind of recommendations can be made in this regard to prospective patients? These are issues that research conceivably might be able to illuminate, but definitive answers are few and far between. Most of the diverse psychotherapies have not been evaluated in any systematic manner. Of those that have received research investigation, some findings can be mentioned. In general, subjects treated by psychotherapy have shown significantly more improvement than control subjects (Bergin & Lambert, 1978; Lambert, Shapiro, & Bergin, 1986; Smith, Glass, & Miller, 1980). Also, with a few exceptions, the therapies evaluated have secured com-parable results. Although some have been critical of these findings (Eysenck, 1966; Rachman & Wilson, 1980), there has tended to be a general ac-ceptance of them. The preliminary results of the NIMH Collaborative Study of the Treatment of Depression also indicate no statistically significant differences between Beck's cognitive therapy and the interpersonal therapy developed by Klerman, Weissman, and their colleagues (Elkin, 1986).

These research results suggest that, despite very different theories and procedures, such different therapies as behavior therapy and psychodynamic therapies appear to secure comparable outcomes. This suggestion raises fundamental questions about what variables produce positive change by means of psychotherapy. With so many different forms of psychotherapy, the most parsimonious hypothesis is that factors common to most of the therapies produce the changes secured. Although still not a popularly accepted explanation, an increasing number of psychotherapy researchers have alluded to the existence of common factors in psychotherapy, including Strupp (1977), Luborsky, Crits-Christoph, Mintz, and Auerbach (1988), Kazdin (1986b), and Lambert, Shapiro, and Bergin (1986). This is an encouraging development even though some of us have been emphasizing this possibility for a number of years.

The implications of this hypothesis are important. For example, research on identifying and appraising possible common factors may lead more quickly to discovering the variables that are truly therapeutic in the practice of psychotherapy. Certainly, the findings of the Sloane et al. (1975) study and those of the Vanderbilt study (Strupp & Hadley, 1979) comparing analytically oriented therapists, experientially oriented therapists, and selected college professors that indicated no significant difference in outcome between the different groups of therapists lend support to this view. Such results raise significant questions about the real utility of the types of theory-oriented process and outcome research that have appeared in the past. Some results of the NIMH Collaborative Study of the Treatment of Depression also are supportive of this hypothesis (Elkin, 1986). Special scales of social adjustment and cognitive functioning used to evaluate expected differences between cognitive therapy and interpersonal therapy failed to reveal such differences (Elkin et al., 1989). In addition, a recent study by Glass and Arnkoff (1988) did evaluate common and specific factors across three structured group therapies and one unstructured group for shyness and social anxiety. "The frequency of explanations of change due to common factors were fairly similar across the structured groups. It is important to note that approximately half of the subjects in each of the structured conditions emphasized common group process factors as accounting for their improvement, citing these factors as often or more often than factors specific to the methods used in their treatment program." (Glass & Arnkoff, 1988, p. 435). It is also important to note that the structured therapies employed in this study may have emphasized the specific features of the therapies more than might be the case in actual clinical practice.

Another indication that existing formulations of psychotherapy may not be fully satisfactory is the apparent increase in eclecticism and the present interest in psychotherapy integration (Conway, 1988; Garfield, 1980, 1982; Goldfried, 1982a, 1982b; Norcross, 1986). Although eclecticism covers a variety of actual therapeutic procedures and approaches and thus is difficult to research, integration as exemplified in the Society for the Exploration of Psychotherapy Integration has a more systematic' rationale and may be a source of research in the future.

Closely related to issues about common factors in psychotherapy is the possibility of specific factors, or specific treatments for specific problems. Whereas in the past therapies were considered to be all-purpose or universal therapies, with the growth of behavioral and cognitive therapies in recent years, a whole host of specific therapies have appeared on the therapeutic scene. There are therapies for depression, various forms of anxiety, bulimia, aggressive behavior, marital problems, insomnia, obsessive-compulsive disorders, and so on. These problem-oriented therapeutic approaches are distinctly different in their theoretical assumptions and procedures from the more traditional psychodynamically oriented therapies and raise a significant issue concerning the most effective approach to treating specific psychological problems. In their review of the research literature on the effectiveness of psychotherapy, Lambert, Shapiro, and Bergin (1986) commented on this matter as follows:

> Although there is little evidence of clinically meaningful superiority of one form of psychotherapy over another with respect to moderate outpatient disorders, behavioral and cognitive methods appear to add a significant increment of efficacy with respect to a number of difficult problems (e.g., phobias and compulsions) and to provide useful methods with a number of nonneurotic problems with which traditional therapies have shown little effectiveness (e.g., childhood aggression, psychotic behavior, stuttering).
>
> Given the growing evidence that there are probably some specific technique effects, as well as large common effects across treatments, the vast majority of therapists have become eclectic in orientation. (pp. 201–202)

This area appears to be a very important one in need of systematic research. If there are basic therapeutic variables that are common to most of the psychotherapies, then we should strive to delineate them. Although a number have been suggested (Garfield, 1980), only a few have received serious research attention. The therapeutic relationship is one of the few obvious ones that has received some study. At the same time, equal attention should be paid to evaluating the issue of specific therapies for specific problems because this may lead to more efficient therapeutic results. Finally, the proper use of common *and* specific factors in therapy will probably be the most efficacious approach to psychotherapy.

ACCOUNTABILITY, NEGATIVE EFFECTS, AND THE IMPACT OF PSYCHOTHERAPY RESEARCH

A number of important research issues have been addressed in the preceding pages, but there are some additional ones that merit some mention before this chapter is concluded. Among these are the general issues of accountability and the possibility of negative effects in psychotherapy. Since these are related, I will discuss them together.

The issue of negative effects was raised in the early 1960s by Truax (1963) and Bergin (1963). It was pointed out that although the "average" results of psychotherapy may be positive, the good results for some patients may cancel out the negative results or deterioration of some others. Bergin (1971) indicated particularly the increased variability of outcome measures at posttreatment as compared with pretreatment. Psychotherapy was viewed as being a treatment of some power, but it could be for "better or for worse." This view was challenged in a paper by Braucht (1970). Truax's (1963) view that low levels of therapist-offered empathy, warmth, and genuineness led to negative effects in psychotherapy also has failed to receive adequate confirmation (Garfield & Bergin, 1971; Mitchell, Bozarth, & Krauft, 1977).

The issue of possible negative effects resulting from psychotherapy was clearly an important one and with stimulation and support from NIMH, Strupp, Hadley, and Gomes-Schwartz (1977) undertook a survey of a sample of distinguished clinicians and researchers and also performed a critical review of the existing research literature. Negative effects of psychotherapy were clearly viewed by the expert panel surveyed as a significant problem for both clinicians and researchers, and a list of potential factors to consider was suggested. The review of available empirical studies also revealed important limitations in the studies published. Among the problems noted were a lack of appropriate control groups, confounded treatments, partially trained therapists, and questionable outcome criteria. Thus, no truly valid conclusions could be drawn, and more adequate research designs using a variety of outcome measures (the tripartite model) were recommended.

Further controversies about the issue of negative effects of psychotherapy have continued but need not be detailed here. A comprehensive volume edited by Mays and Franks (1985b) on negative outcome in psychotherapy summarized many of the viewpoints and problems on this issue, and some reference to it is made here. These authors, although agreeing that negative outcome occurs in psychotherapy, emphasized that variables in addition to therapist factors contribute to negative outcome. Thus, they felt "the question was incorrectly posed from the start" (Mays & Franks, 1985a, p. 4), because other potential factors may influence negative outcome. Mentioned specifically as potential variables in this regard were patient characteristics and events that occur outside of therapy, events that have received little research attention because of the focus on therapist attributes. Research issues were also pointed out:

Additionally, negative outcome has lagged behind other areas of outcome research for reasons peculiar to the field. For example, since patients who decline in functioning during therapy are a small subgroup of the patient population, it is hard to accumulate a sample size sufficient to permit a meaningful examination of contributing factors. Furthermore, for obvious reasons, it is not ethical to manipulate negative outcome experimentally. Thus, the major direct avenues to exploration of contributing factors are blocked. (Mays & Franks, 1985a, p. 4)

It is clear that additional research is necessary to increase our understanding of the variables leading to possible negative effects and what can be done by psychotherapists to lessen the probability of such effects. This issue, however, is just one component of the overall issue concerning the efficacy of psychotherapy and the increased emphasis on "accountability" in recent years. Rather surprisingly, there was little demand in the past on the part of the public or federal agencies for evidence demonstrating the efficacy of psychotherapy. However, the situation has changed, and during the past decade, a number of reports in popular as well as in more scientific publications have indicated the recent interest in the efficacy of psychotherapy (Garfield, 1981b; Gross, 1978; Marshall, 1980; Meredith, 1986; Zilbergeld, 1983, 1986). In an article in *Science* a few years ago, Marshall (1980) offered the following appraisal:

> The field's most insistent critic at the moment is Congress, which has begun to demand hard clinical proof of psychotherapy's accomplishments before agreeing to finance it under Medicare. . . . This demand and other demands from within the field for standardization of research have put new stress on attempts to demonstrate that psychotherapy really works. (p. 506)

Although the stress on accountability may have diminished somewhat the past couple of years, the issues surrounding the evaluation of the efficacy of psychotherapy have not disappeared. The follow-up results and analysis of the large-scale NIMH Collaborative Study of the Treatment of Depression have not yet been published, but the preliminary results at posttreatment suggest that there may be varying interpretations of the results. Furthermore, this study appraised only two forms of therapy out of the hundreds that exist. Regardless of the final results that are secured, there is the obvious issue of how far such results can be generalized to other untested forms of psychotherapy. Also, as mentioned earlier, there are diverse views of the value of research on psychotherapy, ranging from those who believe research on psychotherapy is inappropriate to those at the other extreme who can find fault with all of the studies performed (Garfield, 1984; Prioleau, Murdock, & Brody, 1983). The reactions of practicing therapists to the research on psychotherapy undoubtedly also vary, although many are inclined to respond positively when research data lend support to the claims for efficacy.

In this era of accountability, third-party payments, and increased costs of health care services, the various services offered—including psychotherapy—will receive increasing scrutiny, despite the reservations that some may hold concerning the value of research on psychotherapy. There is little doubt that there will be continued emphasis on the need for evaluating the psychotherapy that is being performed. Although there has been no official requirement that psychotherapy or particular forms of psychotherapy be evaluated for efficacy, there is no assurance that such a requirement will not appear in the future. The Food and Drug Act in the United States was passed initially in 1908 and emphasized honesty in labeling. In 1938, new federal legislation emphasized the safety and nonnoxious elements of drugs. "However, in 1962 concerns had shifted from safety to matters of efficacy and 10 years later regulations were developed by the Food and Drug Administration to evaluate efficacy. Psychotherapy has been spared such regulatory concerns thus far but the situation may be changing" (Garfield, 1987b, p. 99).

CONCLUSION

It should be evident that carrying out research on psychotherapy is a complex, difficult, and even controversial activity. As our research knowledge and sophistication have increased during the past 25 years, so has our awareness of the issues and problems associated with psychotherapy research. The basic variables that influence such research—patient, therapist, type of intervention, outcome measures, and extratherapy events—are extremely difficult to control and evaluate. Unlike a controlled experiment in a research laboratory, clinical research cannot exert such a degree of control but can only strive for approximations.

It should also be mentioned that most of the discussion of issues in psychotherapy research presented here essentially has focused on the efficacy of psychotherapy, or outcome research. This is clearly warranted because issues pertaining to efficacy are basic issues and (as pointed out in the previous section) have received a great deal of attention and emphasis recently. However, there is also interest on the part of researchers in what has been called *process research*, which focuses more on what events in therapy actually facilitate or impede the positive process or movement in psychotherapy. Such research appears to be potentially even more complicated than the research devoted exclusively to the appraisal of outcome, and there are many difficult issues associated with it (Garfield, 1990). For the sake of clarity and brevity, these potential issues have not been discussed here, although some of them are similar to the issues discussed in relation to outcome. For a full understanding of the psychotherapeutic process, researchers will have to devote attention to both process and outcome. Although the task will be extremely demanding and the issues complex, such research is essential both to increase our knowledge of the variables that are therapeutic in psychotherapy and to provide society with the most efficient and effective psychotherapeutic procedures. We have made definite progress in the past. There is no reason that progress cannot be made in the future.

REFERENCES

Bergin, A. E. (1963). The effects of psychotherapy: Negative results revisited. *Journal of Counseling Psychology, 10,* 244–250.

Bergin, A. E. (1971). The evaluation of therapeutic outcomes. In A. E. Bergin & S. L. Garfield (Eds.), *Handbook of psychotherapy and behavior change: An empirical analysis* (pp. 217–279). New York: Wiley.

Bergin, A. E., & Lambert, M. J. (1978). The evaluation of therapeutic outcomes. In S. L. Garfield & A. E. Bergin (Eds.), *Handbook of psychotherapy and behavior change* (2nd ed.; 139–189). New York: Wiley.

Beutler, L. E., Crago, M., & Arizmendi, T. G. (1986). Research on therapist variables in psychotherapy. In S. L. Garfield & A. E. Bergin (Eds.), *Handbook of psychotherapy and behavior change* (3rd ed.; pp. 257–310). New York: Wiley.

Braucht, G. N. (1970). The deterioration effect: A reply to Bergin. *Journal of Abnormal Psychology, 75,* 293–299.

Conway, J. B. (1988). Differences among clinical psychologists: Scientists, practitioners, and scientist-practitioner. *Professional Psychology: Research and Practice, 19,* 642–655.

Elkin, I. (1986, June 19). *NIMH Treatment of Depression Collaborative Research Program.* Paper presented at the annual meeting of the Society for Psychotherapy Research, Wellesley, MA.

Elkin, I., Parloff, M. B., Hadley, S. W., & Autry, J. H. (1985). NIMH Treatment of Depression Collaborative Research Program. *Archives of General Psychiatry, 42,* 305–316.

Elkin, I., Shea, T., Watkins, J. T., Imber, S. D., Sotsky, S. M., Collins, J. F., Glass, D. R., Pilkonis, P. A., Leber, W. R., Docherty, J. P., Fiester, S. J., & Parloff, M. B. (1989). National Institute of Mental Health Treatment of Depression Collaborative Research Program. *Archives of General Psychiatry, 46,* 971–982.

Eysenck, H. J. (1952). The effects of psychotherapy: An evaluation. *Journal of Consulting Psychology, 16,* 319–324.

Eysenck, H. J. (1966). *The effects of psychotherapy.* New York: International Science Press.

Garfield, S. L. (1978). Research on client variables in psychotherapy. In S. L. Garfield & A. E. Bergin (Eds.), *Handbook of psychotherapy and behavior change* (2nd ed.; pp. 191–232). New York: Wiley.

Garfield, S. L. (1980). *Psychotherapy: An eclectic approach.* New York: Wiley.

Garfield, S. L. (1981a). Evaluating the psychotherapies. *Behavior Therapy, 12,* 295–307.

Garfield, S. L. (1981b). Psychotherapy: A 40-year appraisal. *American Psychologist, 36,* 174–183.

Garfield, S. L. (1982). Eclecticism and integration in psychotherapy. *Behavior Therapy, 13,* 610–623.

Garfield, S. L. (1983). The effectiveness of psychotherapy: The perennial controversy. *Professional Psychology, 14,* 35–43.

Garfield, S. L. (1984). Psychotherapy: Efficacy, generality, and specificity. In J. B. W. Williams & R. L. Spitzer (Eds.), *Psychotherapy research: Where are we and where should we go?* (pp. 295–305). New York: Guilford Press.

Garfield, S. L. (1987a). Ethical issues in research on psychotherapy. *Counseling and Values, 31,* 115–125.

Garfield, S. L. (1987b). Towards a scientifically oriented eclecticism. *Scandinavian Journal of Behaviour Therapy, 16,* 95–109.

Garfield, S. L. (1989). *The practice of brief psychotherapy.* New York: Pergamon.

Garfield, S. L. (1990). Issues and methods in psychotherapy process research. *Journal of Consulting and Clinical Psychology, 58,* 273–280.

Garfield, S. L., Affleck, D. C., & Muffly, R. A. (1963). A study of psychotherapy interaction and continuation in psychotherapy. *Journal of Clinical Psychology, 19,* 473–478.

Garfield, S. L., & Bergin, A. E. (1971). Therapeutic conditions and outcome. *Journal of Abnormal Psychology, 77,* 108–114.

Garfield, S. L., Prager, R. A., & Bergin, A. E. (1971). Evaluation of outcome in psychotherapy. *Journal of Consulting and Clinical Psychology, 37,* 307–313.

Glass, C. R., & Arnkoff, D. B. (1988). Common and specific factors in client descriptions of and explanations for change. *Journal of Integrative and Eclectic Psychotherapy, 7,* 427–440.

Goldfried, M. R. (1982a). *Converging themes in psychotherapy: Trends in psychodynamic, humanistic, and behavioral practice.* New York: Springer.

Goldfried, M. R. (1982b). On the history of therapeutic integration. *Behavior Therapy, 13,* 572–593.

Gross, M. L. (1978). *The psychological society: A critical analysis of psychiatry, psychotherapy, psychoanalysis, and the psychological revolution.* New York: Random House.

Herink, R. (Ed.) (1980). *The psychotherapy handbook: The A to Z guide to more than 250 different therapies in use today.* New York: New American Library.

Horenstein, D., Houston, B. K., & Holmes, D. S. (1973). Clients', therapists', and judges' evaluation of psychotherapy. *Counseling Psychology, 20,* 149–150.

Jacobson, N. S., Follette, W. C., & Revenstorf, D. (1984). Psychotherapy outcome research: Methods for reporting variability and evaluating clinical significance. *Behavior Therapy, 15,* 336–352.

Jacobson, N. S., Follette, W. C., & Revenstorf, D. (1986). Toward a standard definition of clinically significant change. *Behavior Therapy, 17,* 308–311.

Jacobson, N. S., & Revenstorf, D. (1988). Statistics for assessing the clinical significance of psychotherapy techniques: Issues, problems, and new developments. *Behavioral Assessment, 10,* 133–145.

Joint Commission on Mental Illness and Health. (1961). *Action for mental health.* New York: Basic Books.

Kazdin, A. E. (1986a). Comparative outcome studies of psychotherapy: Methodological issues and strategies. *Journal of Consulting and Clinical Psychology, 54,* 95–105.

Kazdin, A. E. (1986b). The evaluation of psychotherapy: Research design and methodology. In S. L. Garfield & A. E. Bergin (Eds.), *Handbook of psychotherapy and behavior change* (3rd ed.; pp. 23–68). New York: Wiley.

Kazdin, A. E., Bass, D., Siegel, T., & Thomas, C. (1989). Cognitive behavioral therapy and relationship therapy in the treatment of children referred for antisocial behavior. *Journal of Consulting and Clinical Psychology, 57,* 522–535.

Kazdin, A. E., & Wilson, G. T. (1978). *Evaluation of behavior therapy: Issues, evidence, and research strategies.* Cambridge, MA: Ballinger.

Kendall, P. C., & Norton-Ford, J. D. (1982). Therapy outcome research methods. In P. C. Kendall & J. N. Butcher (Eds.), *Handbook of research methods in clinical psychology* (pp. 429–460). New York: Wiley.

Kiesler, D. J. (1966). Some myths of psychotherapy research and the search for a paradigm. *Psychological Bulletin, 65,* 110–136.

Kiesler, D. J. (1971). Experimental designs in psychotherapy. In A. E. Bergin & S. L. Garfield (Eds.), *Handbook of psychotherapy and behavior change* (pp. 36–74). New York: Wiley.

Krupnick, J., Shea, T., & Elkin, I. (1986). Generalizability of treatment studies utilizing solicited patients. *Journal of Consulting and Clinical Psychology, 54,* 68–78.

Lambert, M. J. (1976). Spontaneous remission in adult neurotic disorders: A revision and summary. *Psychological Bulletin, 83,* 107–119.

Lambert, M. J., Shapiro, D. A., & Bergin, A. E. (1986). The effectiveness of psychotherapy. In S. L. Garfield & A. E. Bergin (Eds.), *Handbook of psychotherapy and behavior change* (3rd ed.; pp. 157–211). New York: Wiley.

Lehrer, A. (1981, February). Letter. *APA Monitor.* p. 42.

Luborsky, L., Crits-Christoph, P., McLellan, A. T., Woody, G., Piper, W., Liberman, B., Imber, S., & Pilkonis, P. (1986). Do therapists vary much in their success? Findings from four outcome studies. *American Journal of Orthopsychiatry*, 56, 501–512.

Luborsky, L., Crits-Christoph, P., Mintz, J., & Auerbach, A. (1988). *Who will benefit from psychotherapy?* New York: Basic Books.

Luborsky, L., McLellan, A. T., Woody, G. E., O'Brien, C. P., & Auerbach, A. (1985). Therapist success and its determinants. *Archives of General Psychiatry*, 42, 602–611.

Marshall, E. (1980). Psychotherapy works, but for whom? *Science*, 207, 506–508.

Mays, D. T., & Franks, C. M. (1985a). Negative outcome: Historical context and definitional issues. In D. T. Mays & C. M. Franks (Eds.), *Negative outcome in psychotherapy and what to do about it* (pp. 3–19). New York: Springer.

Mays, D. T., & Franks, C. M. (1985b). *Negative outcome in psychotherapy and what to do about it.* New York: Springer.

Meredith, N. (1986). Testing the talking cure. *Science 86*, 7, 30–37.

Mitchell, K. M., Bozarth, J. D., & Krauft, C. C. (1977). A reappraisal of the therapeutic effectiveness of accurate empathy, nonpossessive warmth, and genuineness. In A. S. Gurman & A. M. Razin (Eds.), *Effective psychotherapy: A handbook of research* (pp. 482–502). New York: Pergamon Press.

National Institute of Mental Health. (1975). *Research in the service of mental health.* (Report of the Research Task Force; DHEW Publication No. ADM 75-236). Rockville, MD: Author.

Nicholson, R. A., & Berman, J. S. (1983). Is follow-up necessary in evaluating psychotherapy? *Psychological Bulletin*, 93, 261–278.

Norcross, J. C. (Ed.) (1986). *Handbook of eclectic psychotherapy.* New York: Brunner/Mazel.

O'Leary, K. D., & Borkovec, T. D. (1978). Conceptual, methodological, and ethical problems of placebo groups in psychotherapy research. *American Psychologist*, 33, 821–830.

Parloff, M. B. (1986). Placebo controls in psychotherapy research: A "sine qua non" or a placebo for research problems? *Journal of Consulting and Clinical Psychology*, 54, 79–87.

Parloff, M. B., Waskow, I. E., & Wolfe, B. E. (1978). Research on therapist variables in relation to process and outcome. In S. L. Garfield & A. E. Bergin (Eds.), *Handbook of psychotherapy and behavior change* (2nd ed.; pp. 233–282). New York: Wiley.

Prioleau, L., Murdock, M., & Brody, N. (1983). An analysis of psychotherapy versus placebo studies. With commentary. *The Behavioral and Brain Sciences*, 6, 275–310.

Rachman, S. J. (1973). The effects of psychological treatment. In H. J. Eysenck (Ed.), *Handbook of abnormal psychology* (2nd ed.; pp. 805–861). New York: Basic Books.

Rachman, S. J., & Wilson, G. T. (1980). *The effects of psychotherapy: Second enlarged edition.* New York: Pergamon.

Sargent, H. D., Modlin, H. C., Faris, M. T., & Voth, H. M. (1958). The psychotherapy research project of the Menninger Foundation. Second report. III. Situational variables. *Bulletin of the Menninger Clinic, 22,* 148–166.

Sloane, R. B., Staples, F. R., Cristol, A. H., Yorkston, N. J., & Whipple, K. (1975). *Psychotherapy versus behavior therapy.* Cambridge, MA: Harvard University Press.

Smith, M. L., Glass, G. V., & Miller, T. I. (1980). *The benefits of psychotherapy.* Baltimore: The Johns Hopkins University Press.

Stricker, G. (1982). Ethical issues in psychotherapy research. In M. Rosenbaum (Ed.), *Ethics and values in psychotherapy: A guidebook* (pp. 402–424). New York: Free Press.

Strupp, H. H. (1977). A reformulation of the dynamics of the therapist's contribution. In A. S. Gurman & A. M. Razin (Eds.), *Effective psychotherapy: A handbook of research* (pp. 3–22). New York: Pergamon.

Strupp, H. H. (1980a). Success and failure in time-limited psychotherapy: A systematic comparison of two cases. (Comparison 1). *Archives of General Psychiatry, 37,* 595–603.

Strupp, H. H. (1980b). Success and failure in time-limited psychotherapy: A systematic comparison of two cases. (Comparison 2). *Archives of General Psychiatry, 37,* 708–716.

Strupp, H. H., & Hadley, S. W. (1977). A tripartite model of mental health and therapeutic outcomes: With special reference to negative effects in psychotherapy. *American Psychologist, 32,* 187–196.

Strupp, H. H., & Hadley, S. W. (1979). Specific versus nonspecific factors in psychotherapy. *Archives of General Psychiatry, 36,* 1125–1136.

Strupp, H. H., Hadley, S. W., & Gomes-Schwartz, B. (1977). *Psychotherapy for better or worse: The problem of negative effects.* New York: Jason Aronson.

Subotnik, L. (1972). Spontaneous remission: Fact or artifact? *Psychological Bulletin, 77,* 32–48.

Truax, C. B. (1963). Effective ingredients in psychotherapy. *Journal of Consulting Psychology, 10,* 256–263.

Voth, H. M., Modlin, H. C., & Orth, M. H. (1962). Situational variables in the assessment of psychotherapeutic results. *Bulletin of the Menninger Clinic, 26,* 73–81.

Zilbergeld, B. (1983). *The shrinking of America: Myths of psychological change.* Boston: Little, Brown and Co.

Zilbergeld, B. (1986). Psychabuse. *Science 86, 7,* 48–53.

11

ACHIEVEMENTS AND LIMITATIONS OF PSYCHOTHERAPY RESEARCH

MICHAEL J. LAMBERT AND ALLEN E. BERGIN

It is not possible to discuss all the achievements of the thousands of studies and decades of psychotherapy research that are now part of our history. As a consequence, we have chosen to focus on those achievements having the greatest relevance to practice and training. This focus is consistent with the major goals of psychotherapy research as an applied clinical science, namely, protecting and promoting the welfare of the client by identifying the principles and procedures that enhance positive outcomes.

We have divided achievements into two major categories: (a) those that have been attained directly in response to the goals of research and (b) those that are conceptual and methodological by-products of the research itself. Such a classification allows us to see how successful we have been in answering the questions we have asked and, at the same time, to examine the fortunate side effects of undertaking research.

We turn our attention first to the direct achievements of psychotherapy research. The discussion is organized around questions of historical and contemporary concern. We will address the following questions: Is psychotherapy effective? Is psychotherapy more effective than placebo controls?

Are the effects of therapy enduring? Is one type of psychotherapy more effective than another type? What causes therapeutic effects? Are all patients helped by psychotherapy? Do we know how to measure the effects of therapy?

ACHIEVEMENTS OF RESEARCH AS REFLECTED IN ANSWERS TO CENTRAL RESEARCH QUESTIONS

The General Effects Question

The first question to be addressed in psychotherapy research is the general question of its effects. Is psychotherapy effective? Does psychotherapy help the client solve problems, reduce symptoms, and improve interpersonal functioning? Of course, these general questions were not the specific issues addressed in any particular study. The specific questions addressed by researchers were connected to the specific therapy that they practiced. Is psychoanalysis effective? Is client-centered therapy effective? Literally hundreds of studies have been directed at variations of the general effects question. Beginning in the 1930s and continuing through the 1960s, this was the question of importance. It was dealt with first in quasiexperimental studies of patients who participated in any of a number of verbal psychotherapies.

Typical of this research was the Berlin Psychoanalytic Institute's report of their first 10 years of existence (Fenichel, 1930). The institute had 1,955 consultations (between 1920 and 1930), which led to the commencement of 721 analyses. At the time of the report, 363 patients had concluded treatment, while 241 terminated prematurely and 117 were still in analysis. Of those who had completed treatment, 47 were considered uncured, 116 improved, 89 very much improved, and 111 cured. There are various ways of calculating the percentage of cases improved, depending on whether dropouts are included (they could be excluded, as one is interested in the effects of treatment, and dropouts were more or less untreated) and whether one considers those classified as "improved" as essentially equivalent to "much improved" and "cured." Reasonable estimates of outcome vary between 59% and 91% (cf. Bergin, 1971, for an extensive discussion).

A serious problem in this study (and similar single group studies) is that although it allowed evaluation of the outcome of therapy as assessed by therapists and independent clinicians, it did not provide an estimate of change that might have occurred in patients with the passage of time. Many studies conducted in the ensuing years had the same problem, and those who were skeptical about the value of therapy were quick to point out that people who are disturbed and who do not undergo therapy also improve. In fact, Hans Eysenck (1952) wrote a challenging paper in which he purported to show that the "spontaneous remission rate" in untreated patients was about two thirds, which was identical if not higher than the improvement rate for treated cases quoted by Fenichel and others who had published reports on psychotherapy outcome at the time. Eysenck's critical view did not go unchallenged and was ultimately refuted; but it was difficult to demonstrate the effects of therapy because the usual research design did not include random assignment of patients to treatment and no-treatment comparison groups (a point we shall return to shortly). Following Eysenck's article, there was an increase in outcome studies that assigned patients to either the treatment group or to a wait-list or no-treatment control group, thus allowing for a reasonable comparison of treated with untreated clients of comparable pathology over time.

This research is typified by a study of client-centered therapy reported by Rogers and Dymond (1954). These authors conducted one of the more important early studies of therapy that incorporated assessments of outcome for a group of untreated clients with which the treated group could be compared. Unfortunately, this study and many others of the same period had a critical flaw. They divided clients into two groups, one receiving client-centered therapy, the other assigned to a wait-list. Clients in the treated groups were assessed on outcome measures at the beginning of therapy and after its completion. The wait-list group was assessed at the start of the waiting period (that lasted 60 days), after the wait-period, and again when they finished their (delayed) therapy experience, but the wait-period was not equivalent to the treatment time period. Clients were not assigned to groups randomly (or through some other method that assured their equivalence) but were assigned to wait lists only if it was felt that they could wait for counseling without serious harm or discomfort. Wait-list clients were also allowed to enter treatment early if they felt a pressing need to do so. Also, a separate control group consisted of *normal* subjects, so the controls were not equivalent in pathology to the experimental group.

Researchers of the day were very concerned about the ethical problems associated with withholding therapy from patients in need. The wait-list control group seemed to be a solution to this problem since, ordinarily, clients may well be delayed in entering treatment because of limited clinic resources. Early studies of therapy that employed a comparison group to answer the general effects question often drew their comparison group from clients who needed therapy but refused it, or dropped out of therapy early in the process but who would agree to undergo posttesting. Unfortunately, these groups of clients were often not equivalent to those who actually underwent treatment. Often they were less motivated, less insightful, more disturbed, and sometimes less disturbed, than the treated clients. Often, the differences were not assessed or reported. Also, the time periods between pre- and posttesting were often not equal across treated and untreated groups.

How can we conclude that the after-treatment status of clients is due to therapy and not to an independent process within the client if the clients, as a group, are different from the start? The usual method for overcoming this problem is to randomly assign clients to therapy and control groups or to match clients on important dimensions (like psychopathology) to ensure equivalence.

To a large extent, early psychotherapy research studies grappled with numerous methodological issues. The Rogers and Dymond (1954) study is but one example of the growing sophistication and effort of researchers to face and overcome the numerous obstacles in the empirical analysis of treatment. Progress was made in designing studies with adequate control groups that dealt with a variety of threats to internal validity such as maturation, instrumentation, statistical regression, selection bias, attrition, and combinations of these. Threats to external validity were also identified and overcome through the increased use of real patients and a large number of subjects, unobtrusive measures, assessment from a variety of sources, improved measurement instruments, and evaluation across varied time periods.

Psychotherapy research has been exemplary in facing nearly insurmountable methodological problems and finding ways of making the subjective more objective. Even in the form of literature summary and integration techniques, psychotherapy research has been a highly productive leader in this scientific domain (e.g., Smith, Glass, & Miller, 1980). The vast number of studies (Lambert & Lauper, 1980, cited more than 4,000 publications through 1978) using wide-ranging methodologies and designs have led to a variety of conclusions.

This research has been reviewed by numerous authors (e.g., Bergin & Lambert, 1978; Lambert, Shapiro, & Bergin, 1986; Smith, Glass, & Miller, 1980) with the same general conclusion: Psychotherapy is effective at helping people achieve their goals and overcome their psychopathology at a rate that is faster and more substantial than changes that result from the clients' natural healing processes and supportive elements in the environment. This conclusion is limited by the fact that not all therapies have been empirically tested and new therapies are being developed with staggering rapidity. Many clinicians appear to be amazingly eager to develop, apply, and advocate therapies without any formal evaluation.

Those therapies that have been formally evaluated include: analytic therapy and many of its dynamic variations, client-centered therapy, rational–emotive therapy, systematic desensitization, behavior therapies, cognitive therapies, and to a limited degree, various other intervention strategies. Every psychotherapy has not been studied with every patient disorder so that one must be careful not to generalize too far about the empirical support for therapy's effects. However, to the extent that traditional therapies have been tested, there has been enough evidence accumulated to suggest that positive effects have been clearly demonstrated.

The most simple expression of the impact of therapy in contrast to no-treatment controls is that produced by Smith, Glass, and Miller (1980), based on a statistical analysis (meta-analysis) of 475 controlled outcome studies. These authors suggest that at the end of treatment, the average psychotherapy patient is better off than 80% of the untreated sample. Similarly, Lambert, Shapiro, and Bergin (1986) have suggested at least a 70% improvement rate for treated patients (as have Howard, Kopta, Krause, & Orlinsky, 1986) and an improvement rate of about 40% in untreated patients, although these figures are abstractions in light of the variations due to diagnosis, severity, and so forth. In addition, the untreated group improvement rates are inflated for various reasons, including the fact that the patients in these groups often seek help elsewhere while serving as controls in treatment studies!

The importance of demonstrating the general effects of therapy cannot be underestimated. It is not reasonable to move on to more specific questions of causality (e.g., by undertaking a microscopic examination of therapy process or therapist characteristics) without first showing that therapy has a general effect. Specific causal relations are unimpressive unless the overall impact of therapy has been shown to be beneficial. The demonstration by researchers that many psychotherapies are effective opened the door to this next generation of questions—those concerned with the mechanisms of change. What is it in psychotherapy that facilitates patient improvement?

The Placebo Question

Some critics of psychotherapy (e.g., Prioleau, Murdock, & Brody, 1983; Rachman & Wilson, 1980) and many psychotherapy researchers themselves were interested in the possibility that psychotherapy embodied nothing more than a pseudotreatment that gave patients hope. Borrowing from medical research, largely in the area of psychopharmacology, outcome researchers started applying the concept of placebo controls. In medicine, the effects of an active chemical are contrasted with the effects of pharmacologically inert substances. This contrast allows researchers to rule out the effects of attention, belief by the patient that they are being treated or helped (because the patients don't know if they are actually receiving the active drug or the placebo drug), and belief in the treatment by the physician (who is also "blind" to which patients are actually getting the experimental drug) (Shapiro, 1971). In psychotherapy, the placebo construct has been variously conceptualized and studied as the effects of attention, expectation for change, emotional support, and so on. This type of research calls for a placebo comparison group that controls for nonspecific aspects of treatment that may be causing improvements, thereby helping to ascertain how much of the observed improvements can be attributed to such theory-based mechanisms as insight, working through, transference interpretation, systematic desensitization, biofeedback, and the like.

Currently there is considerable disillusionment over the meaning and importance of the placebo concept in outcome research (Critelli & Neumann, 1984; Kazdin, 1986; Wilkins, 1984). Much of the problem arises because of the difference between prescribing drugs and offering psychotherapy. Drugs achieve their results directly through chemical activity as well as psychological mechanisms called placebo effects. The point of drug efficacy research is to separate chemical from psychological effects. By this criteria, it does not make much sense to use placebo controls in psychotherapy research, because it amounts to trying to separate psychological effects from psychological effects!

Nevertheless, it is important to demonstrate that psychotherapy techniques accomplish more than nontechnical support, attention, belief in a procedure, or similar processes that are not unique to professional treatments. Psychotherapy research has produced a body of knowledge on this question. Clients in so-called placebo control groups typically show greater improvement than patients in wait-list or no-treatment control groups (Shapiro & Shapiro, 1982; Smith, Glass, & Miller, 1980). However, patients in these groups show less improvement than those who are receiving specific psychological interventions (cf. Blanchard, Andrasik, Ahler, Teders, & O'Keefe, 1980; Miller & Berman, 1983; Quality Assurance Project, 1983).

We might say that the second achievement of psychotherapy research is the demonstration that many therapies have components or active ingredients that are more powerful than the variety of placebo controls that have been tested. This and the controversial nature of the placebo construct itself suggest the importance of moving beyond the placebo question to similar questions that deal with the actual mechanism of change. What causes change?

The Comparative Effects Question

A great deal of energy and expense has been expended to test hypotheses about the comparative effects of different therapies. Because different theories give diverse accounts of the way that psychopathology develops and the interventions that are necessary to restore health, it is not surprising that the differential effect of therapies has been a focus of research for over three decades. The polemics surrounding the questions asked, the conduct of research, and the interpretation of the results of comparative outcome studies is still a matter of debate. As some people are still committed to a single theory-based approach to treatment with underlying assumptions about the nature of humanity, the nature of change, and other philosophical/value positions, comparative outcome studies will continue to occupy psychotherapy outcome research in the near future (even though some researchers have deserted this approach in favor of examining mechanisms of change that may cut across therapies). This emphasis is likely not only because of commitments to school-based approaches but also because the most suitable control group for many future studies will be the "best alternative treatment." Because of the ethical and methodological problems involved in no-treatment, wait-list, and placebo controls, contrasting a new therapy with an existing effective therapy has become more common. What has been achieved from conducting comparative studies?

Effects of Behavioral Therapy With Specific Symptoms

A variety of psychotherapy research strategies have confirmed the powerful and superior effects of some behavior therapies on certain specific problems. The clearest superiority for a particular treatment is that which deals with phobic disorders. Research has suggested the necessary procedures to facilitate rapid reduction of anxiety to phobic situations. These procedures involve selecting patients with clearly identified fears that are evoked by specific stimuli. In addition to identifying the evoking stimuli, the patient must be motivated to seek and complete treatment. Early reports indicated that as many as 25% of patients may refuse or drop out of treatment (Marks, 1978), although this is not a high figure for a research protocol. In order for the treatment to work, clients must be willing to "make contact" with the evoking stimuli until their discomfort subsides.

Numerous behavioral approaches are based on this "exposure" paradigm. Desensitization involves repeated brief exposure in fantasy or in vivo with a counteracting response, such as relaxation, during and between exposure. Flooding involves rapid prolonged approach into the phobic situation in fantasy or in vivo. Operant approaches have been used via systematic rewards for moving toward or staying in the feared situation. Modeling follows a similar paradigm in which the therapist models approach behaviors and then encourages the patient to do the same. Even in cognitive rehearsal and self-regulation approaches, the patient is encouraged to face feared situations and attain mastery of those situations through the use of effective coping strategies. Therapies for some other anxiety-based disorders such as sexual dysfunctions and compulsive rituals are conducted through the use of similar exposure techniques. These include gradual practice in sexual situations, and response prevention following exposure to the anxiety that precedes and accompanies rituals.

Although the exposure principle does not explain the reasons for improvement, it does suggest the necessary conditions for improvement and the therapeutic strategy that is to be used: Identify the provoking stimuli, encourage exposure, help the patient remain exposed until his or her anxiety subsides, and assist in mastering thoughts and feelings linked with the disordered responses. Given enough contact with the feared situation, patients cease to respond with avoidance, anxiety, or rituals. Contrary to the expectations of some professionals and the patients themselves, increased sensitization to the anxiety-provoking situation is rare. Marks (1978) suggests such sensitization occurred in only 3% of the cases who were expected to be successful (i.e., had adequate motivation, absence of serious depression, no attempts to escape exposure in fantasy or reality, and completed a reasonable amount of treatment).

Numerous studies have tried to sort out the specific procedures necessary for successful treatment. Is deep muscle relaxation necessary? Is gradual exposure through a hierarchy required? Is high arousal necessary (as in implosion)? Should exposure be in vivo or through mental images? Does modeling enhance other exposure methods? Should exposure be prolonged or brief? Will the addition of cognitive coping strategies enhance the effects of exposure treatments? The bulk of evidence on these and similar questions suggests that achieving lasting reductions in fears and rituals is a function of exposure. Time spent with deep muscle relaxation, the use of tranquilizers, and high levels of arousal, add little or nothing to treatments that focus on any effective means of encouraging exposure until anxiety reduction occurs (Emmelkamp, 1986; Marks, 1978). Likewise, interactional exposure without modeling produces fear reduction, but modeling without interactional exposure does not (Marks, 1978, p. 505).

Although the earliest studies on anxiety reduction were undertaken with simple phobias and nonclinical populations such as speech phobics, there is now an abundance of studies on clinical populations that substantiate the specific effects of exposure treatments when contrasted with other therapeutic modalities and specific techniques that do not include an exposure component. Still, research has identified boundaries to these effects. Exposure treatments, although effective with agoraphobia, simple phobias, and compulsions, are not as effective nor uniquely effective with social phobias, generalized anxiety disorders, or combinations of these. The exposure principle seems to have more limited specific applicability with sexual dysfunctions, where the short-term effects are not followed with the same long-term effects as exposure for agoraphobics (Emmelkamp, 1986). It is important to note that psychotherapy research is the only practical method for answering these questions and for discovering the boundaries or limits within which treatment effects operate. And certainly the research conducted by behavior therapists on phobias is a testimony to the importance of research and its powerful impact on theory, training and practice.

Cognitive Treatment With Depression

Another achievement of psychotherapy research is the demonstration of the efficacy of cognitive and interpersonal therapies with depressed patients. While the evidence of unique effects is not nearly as clear as it is for exposure procedures and phobias, it has now been demonstrated that these theories are at least equal to those of tricyclic pharmacotherapy (the current standard of treatment). Furthermore, Hollon and Beck (1986) have suggested that if early studies that showed relapse with cognitive therapy to be less than with pharmacotherapy hold up in future studies, then cognitive therapy may prove to be the treatment of choice for depression, either alone or in combination with pharmacotherapy.

Still, these approaches cannot be said to have proved their effects unique nor to have clearly explained the mechanisms of their effects. These therapies have rarely been compared with other therapies in the treatment of depression (other than pharmacotherapy), and the few comparisons that have been made have not shown a clear superiority for cognitive therapy (Hollon & Beck, 1986) or interpersonal therapy. The results of the NIMH collaborative study support this conclusion and suggest that the superiority of cognitive therapy is certainly questionable (Elkin et al., 1989).

The Equal Outcomes Phenomenon

At first, the achievements of research on comparative psychotherapy may appear to be surprisingly meager. It can be simply stated: Differences in outcome between various forms of therapy are not as pronounced as might have been expected. Behavior therapy, cognitive therapy, and eclectic mixtures of these sometimes show superior outcomes to traditional verbal therapies in studies of specific disorders, although this is by no means the general case. Although there is little evidence of clinically meaningful superiority of one form of psychotherapy over another with respect to moderate outpatient disorders, behavioral and cognitive methods appear to add a significant increment of efficacy with respect to a number of difficult problems. Reviews of comparative outcome studies have been undertaken and reported by numerous authors with the same general conclusion— relative equivalence (Bergin & Lambert, 1978; Dush, Hirt, & Schroeder, 1983; Lambert, Shapiro, & Bergin, 1986; Luborsky, Singer, & Luborsky, 1975; Meltzoff & Kornreich, 1970; Quality Assurance Project, 1983; Shapiro & Shapiro, 1982; Smith, Glass, & Miller, 1980). The finding of relative equivalence has had an impact on the practice of therapy and affected the future direction of theory, practice, and training.

In our view, some of the more important consequences of these findings are:

1. The decline of single orientations such as psychoanalytic and behavior therapies.

2. The growth of eclecticism or integrative therapies as a reflection of both the trend for equivalence and occasional superiority of certain techniques.

3. The increase in short-term, time-limited and group approaches that appear to be as effective as long-term approaches, and individual approaches with a large portion of the client population.

4. A renewed focus on the mechanisms of change via process research.

The general findings of no-difference in the outcome of therapy for clients who have participated in highly diverse therapies has a number of alternative explanations: (a) Different therapies can achieve similar goals through different processes; (b) different outcomes do occur but are not detected by past research strategies; and (c) different therapies embody common factors that are curative although not emphasized by the theory of change central to a particular school. At this time, any of the aforementioned interpretations can be advocated and defended because there is not enough evidence available to rule out alternative explanations. Clearly, different therapies require the client to undergo different experiences and engage in different behaviors. Diverse therapies could be effective for different reasons. However, we do not yet know enough about the boundaries of effectiveness for each therapy to discuss alternative (a) and its merits. Alternative (b), the inadequacy of past research, will not be fully discussed here, because our emphasis is on achievements. Suffice it to say that there are many methodological reasons for failing to reject the null hypothesis. Kazdin and Bass (1989) have questioned the value of the majority of past comparative studies on the basis of a "lack of statistical power." As they point out, these studies usually have subject populations that are too small to detect differences that may in fact exist. As researchers are well aware, one must be extremely careful in interpreting the failure to reject the null hypothesis, because the lack of differences between groups could be due not only to actual equivalence but to any one of a host of methodological shortcomings.

The third alternative, (c), emphasizing common factors in different therapies, is the possibility that has received the most research attention and the one that has the clearest implications for practice. It is not only an interpretation of the comparative outcome literature but is based on other research aimed at discovering the active ingredients of psychotherapy. Alternative (c) also has a relationship to the placebo literature previously discussed, as researchers have been interested in understanding placebo effects and making certain that the components of placebos are incorporated by therapies to maximize their effects.

The Common Factors Question

Interpersonal, social, and affective factors common across therapies loom large as stimulators of patient improvement. In fact, psychotherapy research suggests that these factors may be more important than "technique" factors in facilitating patient gains. This is true despite the fact that (a) most research has been aimed at identifying the potency of technique factors, (b) most theories emphasize the place of theoretically based interventions or techniques, and (c) training programs devote the majority of their resources to the development of theoretical and technical skills rather than relationship skills.

What common factors have been shown to be curative? A host of common factors have been identified under the microscope of good process studies: support, warmth, empathy, feedback, reassurance, suggestion, credibility, attention, expectations for improvement, exposure to feared situations and objects, encouragement to face fears, and altering expectations for personal effectiveness or power. Several of these common factors have received considerable empirical support.

Relationship Factors

Of the common factors investigated in psychotherapy, none has received more attention and confirmation than the importance of the therapeutic relationship. Among the variables that have received most attention are the core conditions of empathy, warmth, and positive regard. Although these variables have formed the core of therapy for client-centered theory, they are also central to other verbal therapies in which a similar therapeutic attitude is encouraged and described by terms much as acceptance, tolerance, therapeutic alliance, working alliance, and support (Lambert, 1983). They are also alluded to in cognitive and behavior therapies (although often minimized) as an essential means for establishing the rapport necessary to motivate clients to complete treatment.

Therapist Factors

Research support for the relationship dimensions come from a variety of research efforts. First, there is considerable consensus in studies that merely ask clients what was most helpful to them in their therapy. Clients tend to emphasize the importance of the therapist rather than specific technical interventions or interpretations (Strupp, Fox, & Lessler, 1969). For example, in an uncontrolled follow-up study of 112 patients whom he had seen in his behaviorally oriented practice, Lazarus (1971) asked patients to provide their perceptions of the effects and desirability of treatment, the therapeutic process, and therapist. With regard to therapist characteristics, those adjectives used to describe the therapist were *sensitive*, *honest*, and *gentle*. Patients clearly thought the personal qualities of the therapist were more important than specific technical factors, about which there was little agreement.

Along similar lines, Sloane, Staples, Cristol, Yorkston, and Whipple (1975), in their study of behavior and insight therapies, administered a 32-item questionnaire 4 months following treatment. The items included statements descriptive of both behavior therapy techniques (e.g., training in muscle relaxation) and dynamic therapy techniques (e.g., explaining the relationship of one's problem to early life events) as well as others thought to be present in both therapies. The successful patients in both therapies placed primary importance on more or less the same items. Seventy percent or more of the successful clients listed the following items as "extremely important" or "very important" in causing their improvement:

1. The personality of the therapist.

2. The therapist's helping them to understand problems.

3. Encouragement to gradually practice facing the things that bothered them.

4. Being able to talk to an understanding person.

5. The therapist's helping them to greater self-understanding.

None of the items regarded as "very important" by the majority of either patient group described techniques specific to one therapy (although item 3 is, in general, approached more systematically in behavior therapies). Marmor (1975), in his foreword to the Sloane et al. (1975) book, identified these factors as relationship, insight, practice—"working through," catharsis, and trust. He compared these to a previously published set of factors that he considered to be the primary common ingredients in all therapies: (a) release of tension, (b) cognitive learning, (c) operant conditioning, (d) identification with the therapist, and (e) reality testing. He suggested ways to construe both dynamic and behavioral intervention in these terms. Although all of these common factors have not been specifically scaled and monitored, as such, in research studies, they provide further ideas for such assessments.

The foregoing suggests that, at least from the patient's point of view, effective treatment was due to factors associated with relationship variables, self-understanding, and active involvement. Although this type of data is limited by methodological problems (e.g., patients may not actually know how they are being helped), its repeated occurrence with different questionnaires not aimed at maximizing the importance of relationship factors suggests that they are prominent ingredients of change, at least from the client's point of view.

Another research strategy that has been employed to investigate relationship factors is the rating of therapist attitudes from transcripts of video- or audiotape recordings of sessions, followed by assessments of outcome attained at the end of treatment. If a positive relationship is evident then these results would be consistent with the hypothesis that the relationship plays a causal role in psychotherapy outcome. Studies showing both positive and equivocal support for the hypothesized relationship have been reviewed in depth elsewhere (Gurman, 1977; Lambert, DeJulio, & Stein, 1978; Mitchell, Bozarth, & Krauft, 1977; Orlinsky & Howard, 1986; Patterson, 1984). Reviewers are virtually unanimous in their opinion that the therapist–patient relationship is central to therapeutic change; however, they point out that research support for this position is more ambiguous than might be expected. Studies using client-perceived ratings of the relationship factors, rather than those given by objective raters, obtain consistently more positive results, but the larger correlations with outcome are often between client process ratings and client self-reports of outcome.

Patient Factors

It is becoming increasingly clear that the attributes of the patient, as well as of the therapist, play an important part in creating the quality of the therapeutic relationship and in the outcome of psychotherapy. Strupp (1980a, 1980b, 1980c, 1980d) reported a series of four studies in which two patients were seen by one therapist in time-limited psychotherapy. In each instance, one of the therapist's patients was seen as having a successful outcome, whereas the other was considered to be a treatment failure. These individualized reports were part of a larger study that used extensive outcome measures and an analysis of patient–therapist interactions during the process of therapy. In each instance, the therapist was working with college males who were suffering from anxiety, depression, and social withdrawal. Although each therapist was seen as having good interpersonal skills, a different relationship developed with the two patients. In all reports (eight cases with four therapists), the patients who had successful outcomes appeared more willing and able to have a meaningful relationship with the therapist, whereas the patients who did not do well in therapy did not relate well to the therapist and had a tendency to keep the interaction on a more superficial level.

In Strupp's analysis, the contributions of the therapists remained relatively constant throughout therapy, and the difference in outcome were attributed to patient factors such as the nature of the patient's personality make-up, including ego organization, maturity, motivation, and ability to become productively involved in the verbal therapy being offered. On the other hand, the poorer outcomes with the less functional clients could be attributed just as well to the failure of the therapists to adapt their techniques to the more difficult problems!

Despite the many methodological issues that can be raised, one finding remains clear: Relationship factors predict, if not cause, outcome. If we want an early estimate of the likelihood of the patient's ultimate success, it can be obtained by patient reports of the client-centered dimensions. Nevertheless, ratings of therapist attitudes such as *empathy*, *regard*, *warmth*, and *genuineness* are far from perfectly correlated with outcome. Thus, research has identified a certain limit or boundary to the effects of therapist attitudes, casting doubt on the accuracy of Carl Rogers's bold attempt at specifying the *necessary* and *sufficient* conditions for positive personality change. Obviously, these conditions are much more relevant to Axis I and milder disorders than they are to Axis II and more severe disorders. Rogers's indifference to diagnosis precluded a clear demonstration of where these relationship factors did and did not make a major impact. Had research results clearly supported his hypothesis, there would be many more client-centered practitioners and the search for active ingredients would be over.

An important achievement of psychotherapy research is both the demonstration of the importance of the relationship for therapy outcome and a gross specification of the limits that the relationship variables have. Future research may eventually be able to specify the extent to which positive relationship factors enhance the effects of specific techniques that are known to be effective. Emmelkamp and Foa (1983) have suggested such a facilitative role by pointing out the importance of these variables in mediating the success of particular patients who undergo behavioral treatments. For example, despite the importance of effective techniques, the therapeutic factors have been shown to correlate with outcome in in vivo exposure (Emmelkamp & Van der Hout, 1983; Rabavilas, Boulougouris, & Perissaki, 1979). On the other hand, psychotherapy research suggests that when very specific techniques are applied to very specific problems (e.g., insomnia, Morin & Azrin, 1988) then the relationship factors may be less important.

Other Common Factors

Research has identified other common factors that could account for the general equivalence of therapeutic outcomes. Zeiss, Lewinsohn, and Munoz (1979), for example, compared interpersonal skills training (a reinforcement theory–based program to increase pleasant activities and the enjoyment of potentially pleasant activities) with a cognitive approach to the modification of depressive thoughts. Noting the improvements recorded by all the groups, they cite Frank's (1973) demoralization hypothesis as the most parsimonious explanation for the results. They suggest that the impact of treatment was due to the enhancement of self-efficacy via training in self-help skills, thus increasing expectations of mastery and perceptions of obtaining greater positive reinforcement as a function of the patient's greater skillfulness. Similar explanations for positive outcomes due to common factors were offered by Thompson, Gallagher, and Breckenridge (1987) in their comparison of cognitive, behavioral, and brief dynamic therapies.

Additional elements common across treatments are *exposure* and *skill development*. As already mentioned, behavior therapy techniques that have been aimed at systematic exposure to fear-evoking stimuli have specific unique effects. It is also true, however, that virtually all therapies require patients to discuss and look at anxiety-provoking memories, situations, and relationships. Although this is done in a structured programmatic fashion in behavior therapy, it is also required in dynamic, humanistic, and cognitive approaches (although more subtly or even haphazardly). All therapies attempt to help patients, or at least encourage patients to develop new skills for coping with emotional reactions.

The common factors explanation for the general equivalence of diverse therapeutic interventions has resulted in the following consequence: Psychotherapy research has been a central force in the current trend toward eclectic practice by implying that the dogmatic advocacy of a school's approach is not supported by research. Research also suggests core issues or "common factors" that can become the focal point for integration of seemingly diverse therapies.

The Negative Effects Question: Are All Patients Helped by Psychotherapy?

Another achievement of psychotherapy research is the documentation of both improvement and deterioration of psychotherapy patients. As a consequence of carefully studying the progress and outcome of patients undergoing therapy, it is clear that while the majority of patients improve, a minority remain unchanged, and still others actually deteriorate. It is a matter of some urgency to identify those patients who cannot benefit and those who may actually have a negative outcome in therapy. Therapy research has used various quasi-experimental procedures to discover the correlates of treatment failure and deterioration. Needless to say, negative effects are difficult to study in a scientifically controlled way. Still, research indicates that some patients are worse after therapy than they were before treatment. This does not mean that all worsening is therapy-produced. Some cases may be on a progressive decline that no therapeutic effort can stop. Other patients may undergo life traumas and untoward events extraneous to therapy that are not moderated by the therapeutic relationship. Research suggests that a variety of extratherapeutic events, patient characteristics, therapy interventions, and therapist attitudes are correlated with negative outcomes.

In a review of relevant literature, Bergin and Lambert (1978) and Lambert, Bergin, and Collins (1977) cited evidence from more than 50 studies on the incidence, prevalence, and magnitude of negative change. These reviews pieced together obscure sets of evidence, as there are few definitive studies on the topic and considerable hesitation even to address the issues directly. Many early outcome studies failed to include a "worse" category in ratings of change, and contemporary studies rarely analyze treatment failure data in their initial reports of outcome. It appears that rates for negative change (excluding no-change), when they are reported, vary from zero to 15%. They are widespread, occurring across a variety of treatment modalities, including group and family therapies, across theoretical orientations (e.g., behavioral, cognitive, dynamic, and client-centered), and across patient populations (e.g., phobics, encounter group participants, and schizophrenics). Although the evidence is widespread, it is also sketchy and incomplete. Despite this incompleteness, nearly all practitioners and researchers believe that negative effects occur (Strupp, Hadley, & Gomes-Schwartz, 1977).

Information on the negative consequences of therapist maladjustment, exploitiveness, and immaturity can be gathered with ease from client reports. Striano (1982), in a consumer report study, examined the personal experiences of 25 selected patients who had been to more than one therapist, one of whom was reported as being helpful and one of whom was said to be unhelpful or harmful. She documented through the reports of these clients a variety of "horror stories" of the type that are often shared privately among clients and professionals but are rarely published. A number of such reports are also recounted by Lambert et al. (1977). Grunebaum (1985) has added to this repertoire of reports via surveys of mental health professionals who described therapy they had undergone. Ten percent of these professionals reported being harmed by therapy. Such accounts lack documentation independent of client report, so they could be laden with subjective biases to an unknown degree; however, such complaints are of social and clinical importance, and they provide reasons to continue inquiries into the therapist's contribution to negative change.

Many other variables would seem to be of obvious importance in causing negative outcomes. Some of these are the subject of litigation, such as the sexual involvement of therapist with client, violations of the basic contract of therapy involving patients' rights to confidentiality, right to refuse treatment, and the like. Less obvious are issues related to treatment termination and abandonment of clients. One of the times at which patients are most vulnerable is around referral and termination from treatment. To the extent that this is a neglected issue in training and practice (especially in settings that employ trainees who rotate across service centers), negative effects will no doubt occur. Many of these issues couple the vulnerability and dependence of the patient with the naivete, incompetence, negligence, or exploitiveness of the therapist. Further study of these issues is needed. Past research (Bentley, DeJulio, Lambert, & Dinan, 1975; Lieberman, Yalom, & Miles, 1973) suggests that therapists often underreport, or are less sensitive to negative effects, than both clients and other group members.

Thus, the study of negative effects will be facilitated by both a more open attitude on the part of clinicians as well as data collection from sources other than the therapist (Strupp, Hadley & Gomes-Schwartz, 1977).

An important achievement of psychotherapy research is the documentation of subtle and obvious occurrences of negative effects, their association with various technique, therapist, and client variables and their implications for research, training, and practice.

The Dose Question

Of central theoretical and practical concern is the proper number of treatment sessions for positive therapy outcome. Will neurotic problems yield only to frequent sessions that occur over prolonged periods of time? Who is an appropriate candidate for short-term therapy? Investigation of short-term or time-limited therapy versus long-term or time-unlimited therapy have been conducted since the mid-1950s. Most recently, the focus of research has been on the efficacy of brief dynamic therapy and patient selection.

Although many conclusions have been drawn and reported (cf. Koss & Butcher, 1986; Luborsky, Chandler, Auerback, Cohen, & Bachrach, 1971), a major general finding represents an important practical conclusion. Moderate doses of psychotherapy have substantial impact on patient status. A recent meta-analytic review of 2,431 cases from published research covering a 30–year span (Howard, Kopta, Krause, & Orlinsky, 1986) showed a stable pattern across studies reflecting the relationship of amount of therapy and improvement.

These data indicate that by the eighth session, approximately 50% of patients are measurably improved and that 75% of patients have shown measurable improvement by the end of 6 months of weekly psychotherapy. From the 26th session on, the percentage of patients improving approaches an asymptote.

This finding certainly raises questions about the general necessity of long-term treatments for the majority of patients and has clear implications for the practice of psychotherapy. Long-term therapy cannot be easily justified on the basis of research in this area of investigation.

The Permanence Question

Although research has focused primarily upon the immediate post-treatment status of patients undergoing psychotherapy, there is considerable interest in the long-term effects of treatment. What kinds of change persist?

At what level? For whom? What factors increase the likelihood of maintenance and relapse? Research has demonstrated that many patients who undergo therapy achieve healthy adjustments for long periods of time even when they have a long history of recurrent problems. The most impressive review of this topic was published by Nicholson and Berman (1983), who summarized 67 follow-up studies of patients with a broad range of neurotic disorders. Their review is consistent with the conclusion that psychotherapy has relatively lasting effects. At the same time, a portion of patients who are improved relapse and continue to seek help or develop a different disorder that requires treatment. In fact, several problems such as addictions, alcohol abuse, smoking, obesity, and depression are so likely to recur that they are not considered properly studied without data collection 1 year after treatment.

ACHIEVEMENTS OF RESEARCH THAT HAVE RESULTED FROM THE PROCESS OF RESEARCH

As a result of subjecting psychotherapies to empirical analysis, a number of positive developments have accrued. Because empirical studies require operational definitions of both independent and dependent variables, the process of carrying out research has demanded clear specification of the most important theoretical constructs. Thus, the conduct of psychotherapy research has necessitated the specification of such theoretically diverse notions as transference interpretations, empathic understanding, reframing, positive personality change, and so forth. As a consequence of this specification, theoretical, clinical, and educational and training areas have all been affected. We now focus on some of the more important results of this specification or operationalization.

The Achievements of Treatment Operationalization

The earliest studies of psychotherapy made little attempt to specify treatment beyond general titles such as *dynamically oriented*, *client-centered*, *Gestalt*. Gradually, researchers became dissatisfied with this degree of vagueness, especially since these general terms gave the appearance of greater clarity and distinctness in the treatments offered than actually existed. Furthermore, within each school there was growing interest in exploring the specific effects of particular theoretically important aspects of the therapeutic endeavor. Efforts to operationalize and measure these theoretically important aspects of treatment often resulted in the development of both *treatment manuals* and *rating scales* that could be applied not only in the research protocol but later in training therapists. This development promises to move therapy from an art that is difficult to pass on to other artisans to a science-based technology that can be more easily taught, learned, and replicated. There are many examples of these developments that could be presented. We will limit ourselves to two that illustrate the general principle.

Therapy Manuals

Research on psychoanalytic psychotherapy has a long history. Many problems have been encountered in the empirical understanding of this treatment modality, especially in defining what this treatment entails and what its essential elements are thought to be. Recently, a number of different analytic therapists have developed treatment manuals to train therapists more explicitly in the use of key analytic techniques. These manuals differ from traditional books on psychoanalytic technique by clearly operationalizing interventions and providing rating scales for measuring compliance and competence in treatment (cf. Strupp & Binder, 1984).

Luborsky (1984), for example, developed a manual that rests on a long tradition of systematic research and practice. Luborsky's supportive–expressive psychotherapy manual is a prototype for the impact of research on practice and training. Foremost among the techniques made explicit in this manual is the identification of the patient's core relationship problem and the therapist's focus, interpretation, and role in helping the patient work through this problem. The manual provides a systematic reliable method for problem conceptualization that can be formulated and judged by the therapist as well as independent raters. The procedure calls for the identification of instances within the therapy narrative in which the patient speaks of his or her relationships with various people. These "relationship episodes" are then separately rated with regard to the patient's wishes, the responses that the wishes elicit (or are imagined to elicit) in others, and the patient's characteristic response. Once a conflict of central importance to the patient that appears across a number of relationships is identified, then the therapist and patient direct considerable energy towards its analysis. Transference interpretations are viewed in the context of this focal theme, which is expected to manifest itself within as well as outside the therapeutic relationship.

It is notable that such an explicit approach has been developed in psychoanalytic treatment. The manual enhances treatment efforts (that can now be offered in a brief rather than long-term format) and the training of therapists. The material assists not only in making the analysis more explicit but also in providing consensus among raters as well as feedback for the therapists' immediate consideration. Of course, competently offered manual-guided therapy can also be studied in relation to treatment outcomes.

Treatment manuals are becoming more numerous, and although they vary in quality, most facilitate not only the testing of therapy but the training of therapists. A number of these manuals have been reviewed elsewhere (Beutler, 1989; Lambert & Ogles, 1988) and include not only analytic therapies but a variety of dynamic, humanistic, cognitive, and behavioral treatments as well. It is interesting to note that although behavioral manuals began appearing in the 1960s, dynamic manuals did not appear until the 1980s, and then only in response to the needs of research protocols, not as a response to the needs of training programs.

Process Rating Scales

Another example of the important impact of researchers' attempts to operationalize treatment has come from the research program of Carl Rogers and his colleagues. Rogers, in the highest tradition of the scientist-practitioner model, made numerous attempts to phrase client-centered theory in terms that would lend itself to empirical investigation. He and his colleagues undertook serious and ambitious efforts to explore client-centered theory through research. Early in this program of research, considerable energy was devoted to defining explicitly such elusive therapist attitudes as empathy, warmth, unconditional positive regard, and genuineness; the depth of client self-exploration was defined in terms of the Experiencing Scale; and positive personality change was measured with the Q-sort technique.

Client-centered work on empathy is characteristic of the interaction between practice and research. The researchers developed a rating scale for quantifying the empathy observed in therapy sessions. The scale was explicit enough so that the ratings could be made by laypersons with no psychological training. Empathy was divided into a 9-point scale, with each point along the scale defined and exemplified. Raters were given transcripts or audiotape examples of the different levels of empathy in an attempt to help them use the scales in a reliable manner. The experimenters were successful in training raters to make reliable ratings. These rating scales proved to be of value in research studies examining the relationship between therapist attitudes and client improvement but had an even greater effect on training programs.

Many educators realized that the rating scales and teaching methods that had been used to train lay raters could be successfully employed to train novice therapists. Many training programs quickly adopted them for training graduate students. Clinical and counseling trainees used the rating scales first to distinguish high and low levels of empathy and later to practice empathic responding and obtain feedback about their own empathic efforts. The scales, in various new formats, came to be used as training outcome criteria and even as selection criteria (cf. Ivey, 1988; Truax & Carkhuff, 1967). In less formal activities, the explicit definitions of empathy—developed originally for psychotherapy outcome studies—were used broadly in education, business, industry and religion (Rogers, 1980). Even though the helping principles embodied in client-centered theory may have had this impact without a link to research, it is clear that the research made the theory more specific, concrete, and applicable.[1]

Achievements of Outcome Operationalization

A final area of consideration is the development of scales for rating patient change and their use in both research and clinical practice. In calling for reliable and accurate measures of treatment outcome, research has been a primary stimulus behind the development of numerous assessment tools that have important clinical uses. As a consequence of psychotherapy outcome research, certain scales and practices that are still widely used in clinical settings (such as the Rorschach, TAT, Human Figure Drawings and the MMPI) have been rejected as measures of change. These devices have not proved sensitive to change and to a large extent do not provide evidence for the effects of therapy. They are rarely used as outcome measures (Froyd & Lambert, 1989; Lambert, 1983). Instead, research has favored the use of behavioral measures, symptomatic scales, and other instruments specific to the disorder being modified or the theory being tested. Thus, psychotherapy research has resulted in redefining the assessment endeavor and the targets of treatment.

This focus has led to the development of many scales that have subsequently been applied more broadly in clinical practice. Several examples can be cited to illustrate this point. Most notable, perhaps, has been the use of diagnostic evaluations, often based on interviews. Research Diagnostic Criteria were originally developed for research protocols. Such cri-

---

[1]There are numerous other similar examples of the impact of research on practice that could be offered, but space limitations make this impossible. The reader may wish to examine literature on the training of group leaders (through the identification of research-based curative factors or the application of group process rating scales such as the Hill Interaction Matrix); training in cognitive therapy (through competence ratings); and marriage and family therapy training programs (use of family process scales), to name just a few.

teria as those for depression, anorexia nervosa, and schizophrenia became the model for revisions and improvements in the *Diagnostic and Statistical Manual* (*DSM–III–R*; American Psychiatric Association, 1987). This manual in its revisions from *DSM* to *DSM–III–R* has shown the increase in precision typical of that demanded in empirical research. These rather remarkable indirect effects of research are possibly the most important single achievement of research and already have had a significant effect on research, practice, and the advancement of knowledge about disorders generally.

Few other achievements in assessment rival changes in the *DSM* brought about by the activities of researchers. Nevertheless, other important achievements can be seen in a number of areas. Literally hundreds of new scales have been developed. The growing number of scales is most noticeable within both behavioral and cognitive theoretical orientations. The behavioral schools have contributed to general practice through such measures as the Fear Survey Schedule, Behavioral Avoidance Test, Subjective Units of Discomfort, Pleasant Events Schedule, Rathus Assertiveness Test, and a host of similar devices that often prove to be an integral part of treatment as well as a means of testing the effects of treatment.

The same can be said for new measures in the cognitive therapies. Here such devices as the Irrational Beliefs Test, the Autonomic Thoughts Questionnaire, and similar scales have gained widespread use in clinical practice. Similar developments are apparent in social learning theory (Locus of Control Scale; Lambert, Christensen, & DeJulio, 1983).

More broadly, one can see that the advances in assessment measures necessitated by therapy research also affected clinical practice through the development of marital satisfaction inventories; measures of sexual satisfaction and performance; and measures of addictive behaviors, eating disorders, depression, and anxiety. Obviously a significant contribution of outcome research is clearer specification of treatment goals, more precise measurement of change, and well-defined links between these and the specific nature of interventions.

CONCLUSION

Achievements in Methodology

Much of psychotherapy research, like research in other sciences, has been devoted to making the subjective more objective. To a large extent, these efforts have been successful. Studies such as those by the staff of the Berlin Institute, Rogers and his associates, and Strupp and his colleagues already mentioned; the research reported on cognitive and behavioral techniques; and many other studies reviewed by Lambert, Shapiro, and Bergin (1986) clearly demonstrate some of the notable early achievements of psychotherapy research. Over time, more and more studies have been conducted. The huge list of problems facing researchers who have applied experimental methods to the amorphous, organic, fluid process of therapy have been gradually overcome.

Among the most important methodological accomplishments of psychotherapy research are the following:

1. Experimental and control groups were equated and contrasted.

2. The problems of withholding treatment were overcome.

3. Defining, describing, and offering treatment in precise terms and actions was accomplished.

4. Therapist cooperation for evaluation and recording of sessions was obtained, allowing for the systematic analysis of the therapy process.

5. Ethical problems in research were addressed and guidelines for practice were developed.

6. Suitable, reliable, and valid measures of change were developed and applied, resulting in higher standards for evaluating the effects of therapy.

7. The development or creative application of a variety of research designs (e.g., Single Subject Designs, Small Sample Designs, Intensive Designs) contributed to the sense that therapy process and outcome could be adequately studied.

8. The development of a variety of methods of estimating prepost changes that are clear of bias from pretest scores, regression, and similar factors resulted in findings that were more acceptable to even the harshest critics.

Achievements in Research Findings

As a partial consequence to the aforementioned achievements in methodology, psychotherapy research gradually moved from the most general questions about the efficacy of therapy to specific questions that address more precisely the boundary conditions for therapeutic effects. Psychotherapy research has resulted in a host of important findings. Some of these findings have been embraced by the profession, whereas others remain an enigma that can only lead to further studies that attempt to clarify the picture we have of therapeutic effects.

Some of the more important achievements of therapy research include:

1. Demonstrating that the general effects of therapy exceeded spontaneous remission.

2. Demonstrating that therapy effects were generally positive.

3. Providing evidence that therapy effects exceeded the effect of placebo controls.

4. Helping to change the definition of placebo controls in psychological studies so that we have a precise and appropriate definition.

5. Demonstrating that outcomes varied even in homogeneous samples, due to therapist factors rather than technique factors.

6. Demonstrating the relative equivalence in outcome for a large number of therapies, therapeutic modalities, and temporal arrangements.

7. Demonstrating the unique effectiveness of a few therapies with specific disorders.

8. Demonstrating the interactive and synergistic role of medication and psychotherapy.

9. Demonstrating the central importance of the therapist/patient relationship in predicting and possibly causing positive personality change.

10. Documenting negative effects in treatment and studying processes that lead to patient deterioration.

Achievements in Empirical Analysis

As a consequence of the achievements of psychotherapy research, a number of accomplishments can be linked to the empirical analysis of psychotherapy. Chief among these accomplishments are those that affect theory and practice. A description of these achievements follows.

First, the impact of research on the various theories of psychotherapy has been similar across theories. The failure of highly touted methods to demonstrate dramatic results when put to the test has repeatedly resulted in questions about the actual mechanisms that cause change. For example, the importance of transference interpretations, the need for an exposure hierarchy, and the importance of self-talk have all been questioned by research, and other mechanisms that explain change have been offered as it becomes clear that a particular theory of change is not supported by empirical evidence.

Unfortunately, our present review is far from complete. Numerous achievements are not discussed because of space limitations. Some of these include the fact that psychotherapy research often sets an empirical standard for innovations and provides a restraining effect (over time) on bizarre or unworthy techniques. This same restraining force is exerted by research on the claims and beliefs of traditional practice as well. This has had an important impact on the credibility of therapy in the eyes of other scientists, insurance companies, government agencies, and possibly, even the public. A manifestation of this impact is evident in the frequent request for research studies to help make public policy decisions.

Further achievements of psychotherapy research are manifest in the identification of the salient role of patients and contextual factors in change and the resistance to change. Much of this research has been summarized by Garfield (1986) and Lorion and Felner (1986) who have reviewed the role of cultural values, social norms, family status, gender issues, and educational and economic status, along with a host of related variables. Surely we know now much about those patients who are most likely to drop out of therapy prematurely. We also understand methods of socializing these patients and their therapists so as to maximize the likelihood of success.

Psychotherapy research has also made clear that few differences in outcome are evident as a function of field of professional training (whether psychiatry, social work, or psychology). In addition, research has suggested the similarity of behaviors across therapists with diverse orientations as well as the occasional marked behavioral differences between those who subscribe to the same theoretical orientations (Sundland, 1977).

We are gradually closing in on those variables that are most important in maximizing our treatment efforts. These variables are often not those that are touted as important prior to empirical scrutiny.

It is our belief that future research has a strong foundation provided by past achievements. Upon this foundation, scientifically based, efficient therapies may continue to be built—to the benefit of all.

A second achievement is the development of process scales, resulting in major modifications in clinical training.

Third, the development of scales and behavioral rating procedures has certainly had an irreversible impact on the testing and assessment enterprise. Many new symptom-oriented scales have been created and are used widely.

Although psychotherapy research between 1930 and 1960 might have been considered primitive by comparison with other fields, the past three decades mark a period of enormous growth in the sophistication and in results. Clearly, the evaluation of therapeutic processes and outcomes has come of age, and the future is rich with potential for new insights concerning how people change.

REFERENCES

American Psychiatric Association. (1987). *Diagnostic and Statistical Manual of Mental Disorders (DSM–III–R)* (3rd ed., rev.) Washington, DC: Author.

Bentley, J. C., DeJulio, S. S., Lambert, M. J., & Dinan, W. (1975). *The effects of traditional versus confrontative leadership styles in producing causalities in encounter group participants.* Unpublished manuscript, Brigham Young University, Provo, UT.

Bergin, A. E. (1971). The evaluation of therapeutic outcomes. In A. E. Bergin and S. L. Garfield (Eds.), *Handbook of psychotherapy and behavior change* (pp. 217–270). New York: Wiley.

Bergin, A. E. & Lambert, M. J. (1978). The evaluation of therapeutic outcomes. In S. L. Garfield & A. E. Bergin (Eds.), *Handbook of psychotherapy and behavior change* (2nd ed.; pp. 139–190). New York: Wiley.

Beutler, L. E. (1989). Differential treatment selection: The role of diagnosis in psychotherapy. *Psychotherapy, 26,* 271–281.

Blanchard, E. B., Andrasik, F., Ahler, T. A., Teders, S. J., & O'Keefe, D. O. (1980). Migraine and tension headache: A meta-analytic review. *Behavior Therapy, 11,* 613–631.

Critelli, J. W., & Neumann, K. F. (1984). The placebo: Conceptual analysis of a construct in transition. *American Psychologist, 39,* 32–39.

Dush, D. M., Hirt, M. L., & Schroeder, H. (1983). Self-statement modification with adults: A meta-analysis. *Journal of Consulting and Clinical Psychology, 94,* 408–422.

Elkin, I., Shea, T., Watkins, J. T., Imber, S. D., Sotsky, S. M., Collins, J. F., Glass, D. R., Pilkonis, P. A., Leber, W. R., Docherty, J. P., Fiester, S. J., & Parloff, M. B. (1989). National Institute of Mental Health treatment of depression collaborative research program: General effectiveness of treatment. *Archives of General Psychiatry, 46,* 971–982.

Emmelkamp, P. M. G. (1986). Behavior therapy with adults. In S. L. Garfield & A. E. Bergin (Eds.), *Handbook of psychotherapy and behavior change* (3rd ed., pp. 385–442). New York: Wiley.

Emmelkamp, P. M. G., & Foa, E. B. (1983). The study of failures. In E. B. Foa & P. M. G. Emmelkamp (Eds.), *Failures in behavior therapy* (pp. 1–9). New York: Wiley.

Emmelkamp, P. M. G. & Van der Hout, A. (1983). Failure in treating agoraphobia. In E. B. Foa & P. M. G. Emmelkamp (Eds.), *Failures in behavior therapy.* New York: Wiley.

Eysenck, H. J. (1952). The effects of psychotherapy: An evaluation. *Journal of Consulting Psychology, 16*, 319–324.

Fenichel, O. (1930). Ten years of the Berlin Psychoanalytic Institute, 1920–1930. Berlin: Berlin Psychoanalytic Institute.

Frank, J. D. (1973). *Persuasion and healing* (2nd ed.). Baltimore: John Hopkins University Press.

Froyd, J. E., & Lambert, M. J. (1989, May). *A 5-year survey of outcome measures in psychotherapy research.* Poster presented at the meeting of the Western Psychological Association, Reno, Nevada.

Garfield, S. L. (1986). Research on client variables in psychotherapy. In S. L. Garfield & A. E. Bergin (Eds.), *Handbook of psychotherapy and behavior change* (3rd ed.; pp. 213–256). New York: Wiley.

Grunebaum, H. (1985). Helpful and harmful psychotherapy. *The Harvard Medical School Mental Health Newsletter, 1*, 5–6.

Gurman, A. S. (1977). The patient's perception of the therapeutic relationship. In A. S. Gurman & A. M. Razin (Eds.), *Effective psychotherapy: A handbook of research* (pp. 503–543). New York: Pergamon.

Hollon, S. D. & Beck, A. T. (1986). Cognitive and cognitive–behavioral therapies. In S. L. Garfield & A. E. Bergin (Eds.), *Handbook of psychotherapy and behavior change* (3rd ed.; pp. 443–482). New York: Wiley.

Howard, K. I., Kopta, S. M., Krause, M. S., & Orlinsky, D. E. (1986). The dose-effect relationship in psychotherapy. *American Psychologist, 41*, 159–164.

Ivey, A. (1988). *Intentional interviewing and counseling: Facilitating client development.* Pacific Grove, CA: Brooks/Cole.

Kazdin, A. E. (1986). Research designs and methodology. In S. L. Garfield & A. E. Bergin (Eds.), *Handbook of psychotherapy and behavior change* (3rd ed.; pp. 23–68). New York: Wiley.

Kazdin, A. E., & Bass, D. (1989). Power to detect differences between alternative treatments in comparative psychotherapy outcome research. *Journal of Consulting and Clinical Psychology, 57*, 138–147.

Koss, M. P., & Butcher, J. N. (1986). Research on brief psychotherapy. In S. L. Garfield & A. E. Bergin (Eds.), *Handbook of psychotherapy and behavior change* (3rd ed.; pp. 627–670). New York: Wiley.

Lambert, M. J. (1983). Introduction to assessment of psychotherapy outcome: Historical perspective and current issues. In M. J. Lambert, E. R. Christensen, & S. S. DeJulio (Eds.), *The assessment of psychotherapy outcome* (pp. 3–32). New York: Wiley.

Lambert, M. J., Bergin, A. E., & Collins, J. L. (1977). Therapist-induced deterioration in psychotherapy. In A. S. Gurman & A. M. Razin (Eds.), *Effective psychotherapy: A handbook of research* (pp. 452–481). New York: Pergamon.

Lambert, M. J., Christensen, E. R., & DeJulio, S. S. (1983). *The assessment of psychotherapy outcome.* New York: Wiley.

Lambert, M. J., DeJulio, S. S., & Stein, D. M. (1978). Therapist interpersonal skills: Process, outcome, methodological considerations and recommendations for future research. *Psychological Bulletin, 85,* 467–489.

Lambert, M. J., & Lauper, L. (1980). *Behavior change research: A bibliography.* Jonesboro, TN: Pilgrimacy, Inc.

Lambert, M. J., & Ogles, B. M. (1988). Psychotherapy treatment manuals: Problems and promise. *Journal of Integrative and Eclectic Psychotherapy, 7,* 187–204.

Lambert, M. J., Shapiro, D. A., & Bergin, A. E. (1986). The effectiveness of psychotherapy. In S. L. Garfield & A. E. Bergin (Eds.), *Handbook of psychotherapy and behavior change* (3rd ed.; pp. 157–212). New York: Wiley.

Lazarus, A. A. (1971). *Behavior therapy and beyond.* New York: McGraw-Hill.

Lieberman, M. A., Yalom, I. D., & Miles, M. B. (1973). *Encounter groups: First facts.* New York: Basic Books.

Lorion, R. P., & Felner, R. D. (1986). Research on mental health interventions with the disadvantaged. In S. L. Garfield & A. E. Bergin (Eds.), *Handbook of psychotherapy and behavior change* (3rd ed.; pp. 739–775). New York: Wiley.

Luborsky, L. (1984). *Principles of psychoanalytic psychotherapy: A manual for supportive–expressive treatment.* New York: Basic Books.

Luborsky, L., Chandler, M., Auerback, A. H., Cohen, J., & Backrach, H. M. (1971). Factors influencing the outcome of psychotherapy: A review of quantitative research. *Psychological Bulletin, 75,* 145–185.

Luborsky, L., Singer, B., & Luborsky, L. (1975). Comparative studies of psychotherapy. *Archives of General Psychiatry, 32,* 995–1008.

Marks, I. (1978). Behavioral psychotherapy of adult neurosis. In S. L. Garfield & A. E. Bergin (Eds.), *Handbook of psychotherapy and behavior change* (2nd ed.; pp. 493–547). New York: Wiley.

Marmor, J. (1975). Foreword. In B. Sloane, F. Staples, A. Cristol, N. Yorkston, & K. Whipple (Eds.), *Psychotherapy versus behavior therapy* (pp. xv–xviii). Cambridge, MA: Harvard University Press.

Meltzoff, J., & Kornreich, M. (1970). *Research in psychotherapy.* New York: Atherton Press.

Miller, R. C., & Berman, J. S. (1983). The efficacy of cognitive behavior therapies: A quantitative review of the research evidence. *Psychological Bulletin, 94,* 39–53.

Mitchell, K. M., Bozarth, J. D., & Krauft, C. C. (1977). A re-appraisal of the therapeutic effectiveness of accurate empathy, nonpossessive warmth, and genuineness. In A. S. Gurman & A. M. Razin (Eds.), *Effective psychotherapy: A handbook of research* (pp. 482–502). New York: Pergamon.

Morin, C. M., & Azrin, N. H. (1988). Behavioral and cognitive treatments of geriatric insomnia. *Journal of Consulting and Clinical Psychology, 56,* 748–753.

Nicholson, R. A., & Berman, J. S. (1983). Is follow-up necessary in evaluating psychotherapy? *Psychological Bulletin, 93,* 261–278.

Orlinsky, D. E., & Howard, K. I. (1986). Process and outcome in psychotherapy.

In S. L. Garfield & A. E. Bergin (Eds.), *Handbook of psychotherapy and behavior change* (pp. 311–384). New York: Wiley.

Patterson, C. H. (1984). Empathy, warmth, and genuineness in psychotherapy: A review of reviews. *Psychotherapy, 21,* 431–438.

Prioleau, L., Murdock, M., & Brody, N. (1983). An analysis of psychotherapy versus placebo studies. *The Behavioral and Brain Sciences, 6,* 275–310.

Quality Assurance Project (1983). A treatment outline for depressive disorders. *Australian and New Zealand Journal of Psychiatry, 17,* 129–146.

Rabavilas, A. D., Boulougouris, J. C., & Perissaki, C. (1979). Therapist qualities related to outcome with exposure in vivo in neurotic patients. *Journal of Behavior Therapy and Experimental Psychiatry, 10,* 293–294.

Rachman, S. J., & Wilson, G. T. (1980). *The effects of psychological therapy: Second enlarged edition.* New York: Pergamon.

Rogers, C. R. (1980). *A way of being.* Boston: Houghton Mifflin Co.

Rogers, C. R., & Dymond, R. (1954). *Psychotherapy and personality change.* Chicago: University of Chicago Press.

Shapiro, A. K. (1971). Placebo effects in medicine, psychotherapy and psychoanalysis. In A. E. Bergin & S. L. Garfield (Eds.), *Handbook of psychotherapy and behavior change* (pp. 439–473). New York: Wiley.

Shapiro, D. A., & Shapiro, K. (1982). Meta-analysis of comparative outcome studies: A replication and refinement. *Psychological Bulletin, 92,* 581–604.

Sloane, R. B., Staples, F. R., Cristol, A. H., Yorkston, N. J., & Whipple, K. (1975). *Psychotherapy versus behavior therapy.* Cambridge, MA: Harvard University Press.

Smith, M. L., Glass, G. V., & Miller, T. I. (1980). *The benefits of psychotherapy.* Baltimore: Johns Hopkins University Press.

Striano, J. (1982). Client perception of "helpful" and "not helpful" psychotherapeutic experience. *Dissertation Abstracts International, 43,* 4303B. (University Microfilms No. 80–17, 382)

Strupp, H. H. (1980a). Success and failure in time-limited psychotherapy: A systematic comparison of two cases—comparison 1. *Archives of General Psychiatry, 37,* 595–603.

Strupp, H. H. (1980b). Success and failure in time-limited psychotherapy: A systematic comparison of two cases—comparison 2. *Archives of General Psychiatry, 37,* 708–716.

Strupp, H. H. (1980c). Success and failure in time-limited psychotherapy: With special reference to the performance of a lay counselor. *Archives of General Psychiatry, 37,* 831–841.

Strupp, H. H. (1980d). Success and failure in time-limited psychotherapy: A systematic comparison of two cases—comparison 4. *Archives of General Psychiatry, 37,* 947–954.

Strupp, H. H., & Binder, J. L. (1984). *Psychotherapy in a new key: A guide to time-limited dynamic psychotherapy.* New York: Basic Books.

Strupp, H. H., Fox, R. E., & Lessler, K. J. (1969). *Patients view their psychotherapy.* Baltimore: Johns Hopkins University Press.

Strupp, H. H., Hadley, S. W., & Gomes-Schwartz, B. (1977). *Psychotherapy for better or worse.* New York: Jason Aronson.

Sundland, D. M. (1977). Theoretical orientations of psychotherapists. In A. S. Gurman & A. M. Razin (Eds.), *Effective psychotherapy: A handbook of research* (pp. 189–219). New York: Pergamon Press.

Thompson, L. W., Gallagher, D., & Breckenridge, J. S. (1987). Comparative effectiveness of psychotherapies for depressed elders. *Journal of Consulting and Clinical Psychology, 55,* 385–390.

Truax, C. B., & Carkhuff, R. R. (1967). *Toward effective counseling and psychotherapy.* Chicago: Aldine Publishing Co.

Wilkins, W. (1984). Psychotherapy: The powerful placebo. *Journal of Consulting and Clinical Psychology, 52,* 570–573.

Zeiss, A. M., Lewinsohn, P. M., & Munoz, R. F. (1979). Nonspecific improvement effects in depression using interpersonal skills training, pleasant activity schedules, and cognitive training. *Journal of Consulting and Clinical Psychology, 47,* 427–439.

Sigmund Freud's only visit to the
United States, at Clark University's
20th anniversary conference,
Worcester, MA, September 1909.
*(Courtesy of the Clark University
Archives; key, courtesy of the Archives
of the History of American Psychology,
University of Akron)*

1. Franz Boas	11. C. E. Seashore	22. B. T. Baldwin	32. S. P. Hayes
2. E. B. Titchener	12. Joseph Jastrow	23. F. L. Wells	33. E. B. Holt
3. William James	13. J. M. Cattell	24. G. M. Forbes	34. C. S. Berry
4. William Stern	14. E. F. Buchner	25. E. A. Kirkpatrick	35. G. M. Whipple
5. Leo Burgerstein	15. E. Katzenellenbogen	26. Sandor Ferenczi	36. Frank Drew
6. G. S. Hall	16. Ernest Jones	27. E. C. Sanford	37. J. W. A. Young
7. Sigmund Freud	17. A. A. Brill	28. J. P. Porter	38. L. N. Wilson
8. C. G. Jung	18. W. H. Burnham	29. Sakyo Kanda	39. K. J. Karlson
9. Adolf Meyer	19. A. F. Chamberlain	30. Kikoso Kakise	40. H. H. Goddard
10. H. S. Jennings	20. Albert Schinz	31. G. E. Dawson	41. H. I. Klopp
	21. J. A. Magni		42. S. C. Fuller

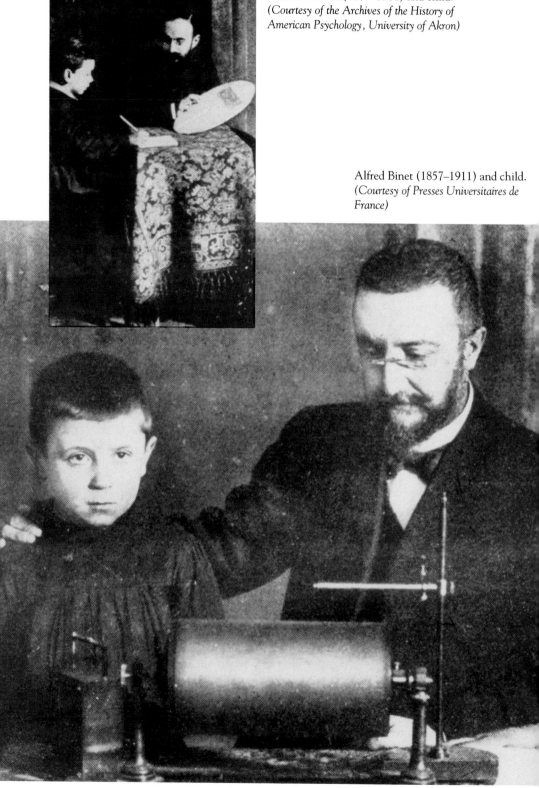

Theodor Simon(1873–1961) and child.
(*Courtesy of the Archives of the History of American Psychology, University of Akron*)

Alfred Binet (1857–1911) and child.
(*Courtesy of Presses Universitaires de France*)

William James (1842–1910) founded the first psychological laboratory in America, at Harvard University in 1875. (*Courtesy of the Archives of the History of American Psychology, University of Akron*)

Hugo Münsterberg (1863–1916) wrote the first book entitled *Psychotherapy*, in 1909. (*Courtesy of the Archives of the History of American Psychology, University of Akron*)

Christine Ladd-Franklin (1847–1930), the first woman elected to membership in the American Psychological Association (APA). (*Courtesy of the Archives of the History of American Psychology, University of Akron*)

Lightner Witmer (1867–1956) founded The Psychological Clinic at the University of Pennsylvania in 1896. (*Courtesy of the Archives of the History of American Psychology, University of Akron*)

Trigant Burrow (*right*; 1875–1950),
Kurt Lewin (*below*; 1890–1947),
and J. L. Moreno (*below, right*; 1889–
1974), three pioneers in the develop-
ment of group therapy techniques.
(*Photograph of Burrow courtesy of the
Lifwynn Foundation; photograph of Lewin
courtesy of the Archives of the History of
American Psychology, University of
Akron; photograph of Moreno courtesy of
Zerka Moreno*)

John B. Watson (1878–1958) pioneered behaviorism. *(Courtesy of the Archives of the History of American Psychology, University of Akron)*

Francis C. Sumner (1895–1954), the first Black American to be awarded a PhD in psychology, from Clark University in 1920. *(Courtesy of the Clark University Archives)*

Thomas Parran (1892–1968), U.S. surgeon general when the National Mental Health Act was passed in 1946. *(Courtesy of Theodore V. Parran)*

Carl Rogers (1902–1987), founder of client-centered therapy.

Anna Freud (1895–1982) and Melanie Klein (1882–1960), two early pioneers in psychoanalytic therapy. (*Courtesy of the Archives of the History of American Psychology, University of Akron and Klein Trust/Wellcome Institute Library, London*)

Helen Sargent (1904–1959),
noted for early research work in
psychotherapy at the Menninger
Clinic.

Abraham Maslow (1908–
1987) laid the foundations
for humanistic therapy.
(*Courtesy of the Archives of
the History of American
Psychology, University of
Akron*)

Gordon Derner (1915–1983), pioneer of
professional training in psychology, pictured
with child psychologist Hiam Ginott
(*center*) and Adelphi University President
Robert Olmsted (*right*). (*Courtesy of Adelphi
University*)

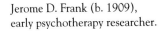

Jerome D. Frank (b. 1909),
early psychotherapy researcher.

Colorado Conference on Graduate Education in Clinical Psychology, Boulder, CO, August 1949. The conference produced the well-known Boulder scientist-practitioner model of clinical education. (*Courtesy of the Archives of the History of American Psychology, University of Akron; key, courtesy of Eliot H. Rodnick*)

1. Isabelle V. Kendig (St. Elizabeth's Hospital, Washington, DC)
2. R. A. Brotemarkle (University of Pennsylvania)
3. Robert G. Bernreuter (Pennsylvania State College)
4. Nicholas Hobbs (Columbia University)
5. Edward S. Bordin (University of Michigan)
6. C. Roger Myers (University of Toronto)
7. Joseph E. Brewer (Wichita Guidance Center, Kansas)
8. Arthur L. Benton (State University of Iowa)
9. Graham B. Dimmick (Univeristy of Kentucky)
10. E. J. Asher (Purdue University)
11. Delton C. Beier (Indiana University)
12. Robert E. Harris (University of California Medical School)

13. Earl E. Swarzlander (Veterans Administration Hospital, Long Island, NY)
14. George F. J. Lehner (University of California)
15. H. M. Hildreth (Veterans Administration, Washington, DC)
16. J. Hildreth (APA staff, guest)
17. Robert R. Blake (University of Texas)
18. Cecil W. Mann (Tulane University)
19. Lyle H. Lanier (University of Illinois)
20. Albert I. Rabin (Michigan State College)
21. John Gray Peatman (APA Policy and Planning Board)
22. Ruth Tolman (Los Angeles VA Hospital)
23. Jerry W. Carter (National Institute of Mental Health)
24. Donald K. Adams (Duke University)

25. George E. Levinrew (American Association of Psychiatric Social Workers)
26. Robert C. Challman (Menninger Foundation)
27. Julian B. Rotter (Ohio State University)
28. Chester C. Bennett (Boston University)
29. John W. Stafford (The Catholic University of America)
30. Bertha M. Luckey (Cleveland Public Schools)
31. William R. Grove (Phoenix Elementary Schools)
32. Carrol A. Whitmer (University of Pittsburgh)
33. Howard F. Hunt (University of Chicago)
34. T. Ernest Newland (University of Tennessee)
35. M. E. Bunch (Washington University)

36. Starke R. Hathaway (University of Minnesota)
37. H. P. Longstaff (University of Minnesota)
38. Brian E. Tomlinson (New York University)
39. Paul Henry Mussen (University of Wisconsin)
40. Carlyle Jacobsen (State University of Iowa)
41. Marshall R. Jones (University of Nebraska)
42. C. L. Winder (Stanford University)
43. Helen M. Wolfle (Managing Editor, American Psychologist)
44. Rex M. Collier (University of Illinois)
45. Dael Wolfle (Executive Secretary, APA)
46. Randall (no further identification)
47. James W. Layman (University of North Carolina)
48. D. B. Klein (University of Southern California)
49. Lawrence F. Shaffer (Columbia University)

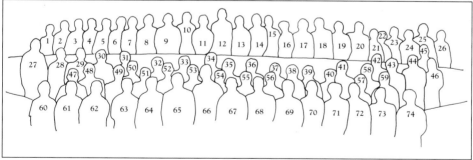

50. Paul E. Huston
(State University of Iowa)
51. Mary Schmitt
(National League of
Nursing Education)
52. Virginia T. Graham
(University of
Cincinnati)
53. O. H. Mowrer
(University of Illinois)
54. Eliot H. Rodnick
(Worcester State
Hospital)
55. Max L. Hutt
(University of Michigan)

56. Martin Sheerer
(University of Kansas)
57. David Shakow
(University of Illinois)
58. Jean W. MacFarlane
(University of California)
59. Bert Kaplan
(Harvard University)
60. Thelma G. Alper
(Clark University)
61. Lt. Col. Charles Gersoni
(U.S. Army)
62. Joseph M. Bobbit
(National Institute of
Mental Health)

63. C. R. Strother
(University of
Washington)
64. James G. Miller
(University of Chicago)
65. Wayne Dennis
(University of
Pittsburgh)
66. John C. Eberhart
(National Institute of
Mental Health)
67. E. Lowell Kelly
(University of Michigan)
68. Karl F. Heiser
(Associate Executive
Secretary, APA)

69. William H. Hunt
(Northwestern University)
70. V. C. Raimy
(University of Colorado)
71. Dorothea McCarthy
(Fordham University)
72. Seymour B. Sarason
(Yale University)
73. Robert H. Felix
(National Institute of
Mental Health)
74. G. R. Wendt
(University of Rochester)
Not pictured: Dwight Miles
(Western Reserve University)

University of Vienna
Psychological Institute

July 12 — August 7, 1937

Sixth Annual Summer School in Psychology

Eight courses for English-speaking students

(1) HUMAN PERSONALITY (Karl Bühler)

A survey of different means of determining personality and character. — **(6 hours lectures.)**

(2) SPEECH AND LANGUAGE (Karl Bühler)

An analysis of the structure of language; speech in its three aspects: expression, representation, appeal. — **(6 hours lectures.)**

(3) CHILDHOOD AND ADOLESCENCE (Charlotte Bühler)

A survey of the most important recent experimental and observational studies on children and adolescents, tracing the entire development of the individual from birth to maturity through its five principal phases. — **(10 hours lectures, 4 hours demonstrations.)**

(4) BIOGRAPHICAL METHODS (Charlotte Bühler, Else Frenkel)

An analysis of those attitudes towards life that are common to and typical of all individuals in certain periods of life. A new methodology, based on a detailed psychological examination of biographies and case histories. — **(10 hours lectures.)**

(5) EXPERIMENTAL PSYCHOLOGY (Egon Brunswik)

Demonstration and theoretical discussion of outstanding recent European investigations in experimental psychology, including: object-constancy in perception, Gestalt, eidetic imagery, perception-types, psychology of thinking. — **(12 hours lectures with demonstrations.)**

(6) VIENNESE TESTS FOR CHILDREN (Lotte Danzinger, Liselotte Frankl)

A discussion, with demonstrations, of the Viennese Developmental Tests and of the technique of testing young children. — **(6 hours lectures, 10 hours demonstrations.)**

(7) CASES OF PROBLEM CHILDREN (Charlotte Bühler)

Discussion of the application of the Viennese Tests in cases of different developmental and character problems. Profiles of normal children and of borderline cases. — **(10 hours lectures.)**

(8) PSYCHOLOGY OF EXPRESSION (Käthe Wolf)

A historical survey of the theories of expression; the expressive values of the human voice, face and hands; an inventory of the expressions of the motion picture actor; modes of expression in the film, novel and drama; the film contrasted with speech; indirect interpretation of expression by means of the environmental situation; expression in insanity. — **(10 hours lectures.)**

All Courses taught in English.

Further Information

regarding courses, tuition fees, registration, certificates, examinations, credit, living arrangements in Vienna

may be obtained from:	or from:
Psychological Institute	Dr. Henry Beaumont
University of Vienna	Dep. of Psychology
I. Liebiggasse 5, Vienna, Austria	University of Kentucky
(Phone A-21-0-74)	Lexington, Ky.

Printed in Austria — ARTUR SCHROFFZIK & SÖHNE, WIEN, VII., BREITE GASSE 1A

Please post

Notice of early professional training in psychology at the University of Vienna. (*Courtesy of the Archives of the History of American Psychology, University of Akron*)

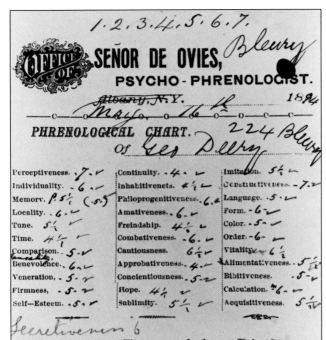

Three original psychological
assessment forms.
*(Courtesy of the Archives
of the History of American
Psychology, University
of Akron)*

SEÑOR DE OVIES,
PSYCHO-PHRENOLOGIST.

Albany, N.Y. _____ 1894

PHRENOLOGICAL CHART.

Perceptiveness. 7	Continuity. 4	Imitation. 5½
Individuality. 6	Inhabitivenets. 4½	Constructiveness. 7
Memory. P. 5½ (.5.)	Philoprogenitiveness. 6	Language. 5
Locality. 6	Amativeness. 6	Form. 6
Tune. 5½	Freindship. 4½	Color. 5
Time. 4½	Combativeness. 6	Order. 6
Comparison. 5	Cautiousness. 6½	Vitality. 6½
Benevolence. 6	Approbativeness. 4	Alimentativeness. 5½
Veneration, 5	Concientiousness. 5	Bibitiveness. 5
Firmness, 5	Hope. 4½	Calculation. 6
Self—Esteem. 5	Sublimity. 5½	Acquisitiveness. 5½

Secretiveness 6

☞ Explanatory Charts worked out. Price $4. extra.

FAMILIES & CLUBS at Reduced Rates.
ADDRESS-

Señor de Ovies,
SPANISH HOTEL,
W. 14 th. St. NEW YORK CITY.

PSYCHODIAGNOSTIK

METHODIK UND ERGEBNISSE EINES WAHR-
NEHMUNGSDIAGNOSTISCHEN EXPERIMENTS
(DEUTENLASSEN VON ZUFALLSFORMEN)

VON
Dr. med. HERMANN RORSCHACH

Mit dem zugehörigen Test
bestehend aus zehn teils farbigen Tafeln

1921

ST BIRCHER VERLAG IN BERN UND LEIPZIG

MINNESOTA MULTIPHASIC
PERSONALITY INVENTORY

S. R. HATHAWAY, PHD.
J. C. McKINLEY, M. D.

SPECIAL INSTRUCTIONS FOR
MAYO CLINIC
PATIENTS

READ AND CAREFULLY FOLLOW
INSTRUCTIONS ON THE BACK SIDE
OF THIS CARD

NAME_____

NUMBER_____

DATE_____

AGE_____SEX_____

SECTION AND DESK_____

MMPI. COPYRIGHT 1943
UNIV. OF MINN. PRESS.
PUBLISHED BY THE
PSYCHOLOGICAL CORP.

Psychotherapy interview being measured
by Matarazzo's interaction recorder.
(*Courtesy of the University of Oregon*)

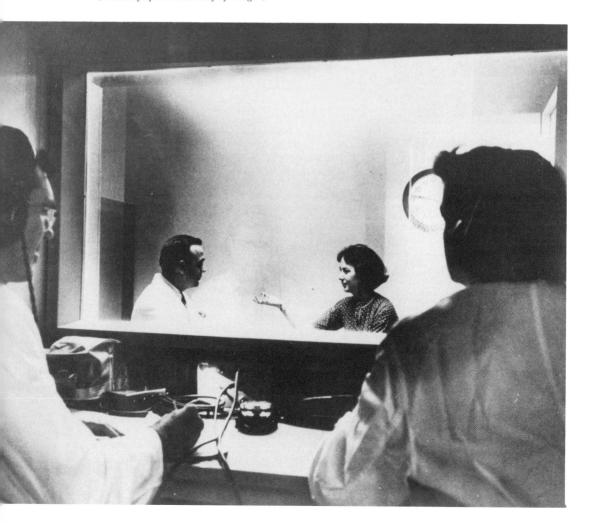

First APA Committee on
Graduate and Professional
Training, 1947.

Robert R. Sears
Chairman; State University of Iowa

John G. Darley
University of Minnesota

E. Lowell Kelly
University of Michigan

Elaine Kinder
Rockland State Hospital

Jean Walker MacFarlane
University of California

Donald G. Marquis
University of Michigan

Bruce V. Moore
Pennsylvania State College

Marion W. Richardson
*Richardson, Bellows, Henry,
and Company*

Carroll L. Shartle
Ohio State University

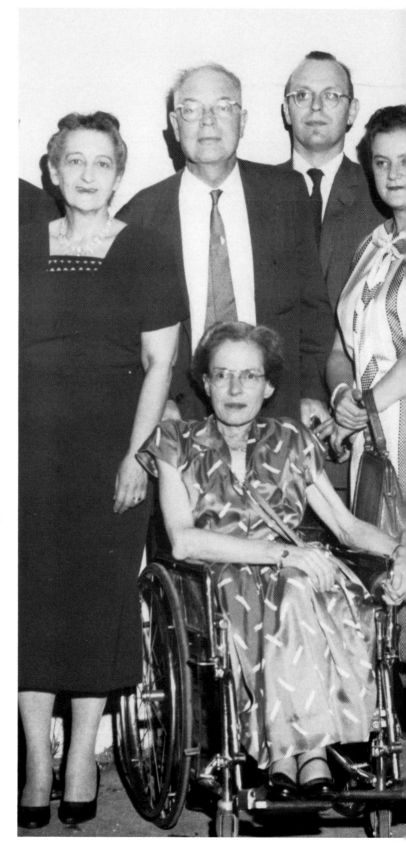

Menninger Foundation research group, May 1959 (detail). Pictured left to right are Michalina Fabian, Gardner Murphy, Helen Sargent (*seated*), Robert Wallerstein, and Gertrude Ticho.

Second Psychotherapy Research
Conference, Chapel Hill, NC,
May 1961.

1. Maury Lorr
2. Hans Strupp
3. Dave Shakow
4. Leon Bernstein
5. Irwin Rosen
6. Morris Parloff
7. Richard Siegal
8. George Mahl
9. Ed Bordin
10. George Saslow
11. Barbara Betz
12. Mabel Cohen
13. Hedda Bolgar

14. Dan Levinson
15. Stan Imber
16. Donald Glad
17. John Schlein
18. Henry Lennard
19. Nevitt Sanford
20. Jerry Frank
21. Will Snyder
22. Len Krasner
23. Don Bloch
24. Ken Colby
25. Donald Gorham

26. Martin Lakin
27. Dave Hamburg
28. Martin Wallach
29. Jack Butler
30. Lester Luborsky
31. J. McV. Hunt
32. Otto Will
33. Ian Stevenson
34. Ernest Haggard
35. Jack Block

Evolution of Psychotherapy Conference,
Phoenix, AZ, December 1985.(*Courtesy
of the Milton H. Erickson Foundation, Inc.*)
FRONT ROW (*left to right*): Albert Ellis,
Mary Goulding, Robert Goulding, Zerka
Moreno, Cloé Madanes, Virginia Satir,
Miriam Polster, and Carl Rogers.
SECOND ROW: Rollo May, Arnold Lazarus,
Judd Marmor, Aaron Beck, Carl Whitaker,
Murray Bowen, Thomas Szasz, Paul
Watzlawick, Jay Haley, and Joseph Wolpe.
BACK ROW: Bruno Bettelheim, James
Masterson, Jeffrey Zeig, Ronald D. Laing,
Ernest Rossi, Erving Polster, Salvador
Minuchin, and Lewis Wolberg.

12

HISTORICAL DEVELOPMENTS IN RESEARCH CENTERS

In scientific communications, the emphasis is properly on conceptualization, design, methods, results, and conclusions. One rarely gets a glimpse of the scientist as a person; and yet research is always closely intertwined with the personality of the investigator. Research in psychotherapy is no exception; indeed, the person of the author may be even more important than in most branches of scientific investigation. As in practice, psychotherapy research reflects the aspirations, hopes, and highly personal agenda of the author. The personal contribution of the investigator is typically hidden from readers, who may form their own impressions about the motives of the author.

In this chapter, we introduce readers to the persons who have shaped and are shaping the psychotherapy research enterprise. We invited a number of authors who have contributed significantly to our storehouse of knowledge. We asked them to provide a personalized account of their research careers—what they did, why they did it, what they found, and, perhaps most important, who they are. Our selection of authors is obviously somewhat arbitrary, and undoubtedly there are other researchers whose work may have equal claim to be cited. However, there can be no doubt that the individuals represented in this chapter have been prominent contributors to the body of psychotherapy research; and their careers over the decades have been closely related to progress of the field.

We have reports from twelve research centers. We hope the reader will enjoy reading the vignettes as much as we enjoyed collecting them. They do reveal, to a greater extent than is usually possible, the person behind the work. Although we know all the contributors personally and are familiar with their work, there are a number of surprises and new insights. In particular, we hope that the new generation of investigators will find the accounts of their senior colleagues interesting and appealing. — *The Editors*

THE JOHNS HOPKINS PSYCHOTHERAPY RESEARCH PROJECT

Jerome D. Frank

After discharge from the armed services in 1947, I took a job with the Veterans Administration (VA) in Washington, DC and considered how best to continue my interrupted civilian academic career. Fortunately, I was soon spotted by Florence B. Powdermaker, a gifted research-oriented psychoanalyst interested in group therapy. She was organizing an interdisciplinary study of group psychotherapy with inpatient and outpatient veterans and recruited me as the project's Principal Assistant, a title no longer in use. Other project staff consisted of psychiatrists, psychologists, and social workers.

In those far-off days, the division of labor by disciplines was unquestioned: Psychologists did intelligence testing and assessment of personality, usually by the Rorschach test; social workers did interviewing; and psychiatrists conducted therapy. Because the psychologists and social workers on the project had some previous research background, we all participated in creating the research design as well as the tests and interview schedules. The project was primarily descriptive, and we succeeded in delineating various recurrent themes and patterns of behavior in therapeutic groups (Powdermaker & Frank, 1953). At least one of these patterns, the "help-rejecting complainer," has received considerable subsequent attention (Berger & Rosenbaum, 1975).

In 1951, I was invited to Johns Hopkins and soon was placed in charge of the psychiatric outpatient department. Despite the change of venue, I was able to continue with the project with just enough holdovers to provide a thread of continuity. The new research population differed from that of the earlier project by including women and a considerably larger proportion of Black people. Also, we confined our interest solely to outpatients. While getting established in the new setting, we continued to pursue qualitative studies of therapeutic groups. We hoped to move to quantitative studies, but the complexities of group interaction defeated our efforts.

Accordingly, we decided to switch to individual therapy and continued with this focus until the dissolution of the project in 1974, some 2½ decades later. With the shift toward measurement and quantification, the psychologists assumed the primary role in research design, collection, and analysis of data.

At the time of the project's inception, the obvious research challenge was to determine the relative effectiveness of different therapies. We soon realized that the minimal essential knowledge for approaching this question was lacking. In other words, there were no satisfactory ways of describing patients, characterizing therapies, or determining degrees of improvement. After much agonizing, we concluded that if we waited to devise measures that satisfied us, we might never get started, so we decided to plunge in with the tools at hand. We would not attempt to characterize patients other than by exclusion of alcoholics (and other addicted persons), psychotics, and those with brain disease. We would offer 6 months of group therapy, 1½ hours a week; individual therapy, 1 hour a week; and, to control for amount of therapeutic contact, minimal therapy of ½ hour every 2 weeks, the smallest amount we could reconcile with our professional consciences. As measures of improvement, we would use a simple global rating made by patients after the first interview, at the end of 6 months (or whenever therapy terminated), and a scale of social ineffectiveness, completed by a research social worker on the basis of a structured interview.

To our astonishment and chagrin, despite the obvious differences in therapies, the only significant difference between them was the degree of social ineffectiveness, which improved less with minimal contact therapy than with either group or individual therapy, both of which produced the same effect. The most striking finding was that all three therapies were followed by the same considerable average degree of symptomatic relief; and this relief occurred before any differences in the components of the three therapies had time to operate. While recognizing that the many inadequacies of the research design could well have obscured actual differences in effectiveness of the three therapies, we were nevertheless forced to conclude that features shared by all three must have been responsible for much of patients' improvement. This serendipitous, if hardly welcome finding, which has stood the test of time, set the goal of the project for the remainder of its existence: to identify and explore the common therapeutic features of psychotherapies. Those we identified were arousal of hope as manifested by the placebo effect, emotional arousal, and enhancement of the sense of mastery.

The long duration of the project enabled us to follow two cohorts of patients at 5- and 10-year intervals, and one of these also twenty years after initial treatment. All the follow-up interviews were conducted by the same research social worker, thereby eliminating one common source of variance in such studies (Frank, Hoehn-Saric, Imber, Liberman, & Stone, 1978).

With respect to the conceptualization of psychotherapy in the 1950s, psychoanalysis (modified in the United States by more emphasis on interpersonal as compared with intrapersonal determinants of psychological distress) dominated the field. Behavioral and cognitive therapies, not to mention existential ones, were either still below or just emerging above the horizon. Hence, the decision to study only psychodynamically oriented psychotherapy was essentially foreordained.

The literature consisted mainly of polemics by advocates of various psychodynamic schools, each stressing its alleged advantages, buttressed by arguments and case examples, but including little else. The resulting unresolvable cacophony of competing claims encouraged research efforts to compare the relative outcomes of different therapies—the so-called horse race design—which has continued to yield disappointing findings. As a result, emphasis has shifted over the years toward integrating the various approaches or toward elucidating attributes of patients, therapists, and features of therapy that might determine the success of a particular approach, rather than comparing it with its rivals.

The location of the project within a department of psychiatry in a prestigious teaching hospital enhanced the staff's morale on the one hand; but on the other, it generated some tension, especially on the part of the psychologists. In those days, nonmedical professionals in hospitals were distinctly second-class citizens compared to physicians. This source of dissatisfaction may have contributed to the decision of several of our psychologists to seek more welcoming surroundings. As both a psychologist and psychiatrist, I could empathize with their resentment.

A major cultural change that occurred during the project's life, although too late to affect us directly, was the gradual disappearance of public financing for psychotherapy research conducted by psychiatrists. When our project started, the number of military casualties, coupled with exaggerated expectations of what psychotherapy could accomplish, led governmental and private funding agencies to encourage and amply fund research by psychiatrists. Although today a few psychiatrists are members of research projects conducted by psychologists, public financial support for research in psychotherapy conducted under medical auspices has largely evaporated.

At least two developments have contributed to its demise. One was a growing shift in the providers of psychotherapy. Initially almost exclusively the province of psychiatrists, psychotherapeutic practice is now mainly in the hands of psychologists, social workers, mental health counselors, and pastoral counselors. Furthermore, advances in psychopharmacology, neurophysiology, and micromolecular genetics have increasingly lured psychiatrists away from psychotherapy into these fields, for which their medical knowledge especially qualifies them. It will be interesting to see whether eventually any research project in psychotherapy must include neurochemical, genetic, or pharmacological components to be financed by a public agency or private foundation.

A particularly troublesome impact of societal values on psychotherapeutic research has been the insistent demand that all patients be fully informed about every feature of a research project as the basis for their participation. One cannot quarrel with the ethical purpose of such a requirement, but the limits it imposes on the ability of research to generate knowledge should also be recognized. Although the classic Milgram study on obedience (Milgram, 1974) may have exceeded the bounds of ethical acceptability, it produced highly significant findings that could not have been obtained without deception. Our study, not of such import, involved minor deceptions to investigate how patients' beliefs might affect therapeutic outcome (Liberman, 1978). All patients were given tests to determine the extent to which their locus of control was external or internal. At the start of each of a series of therapy sessions, half the patients were given a pill which they believed to be active but which actually was pharmacologically inert (a so-called placebo). The other half received nothing. After each session, all patients were given therapeutically related tests and *all* were informed that the test results indicated improvement. Those who received the placebo were told that it was responsible for their improvement. The others were told that their improvement resulted from their own efforts. Their *actual* degree of improvement (as determined by other tests) could then be related to their locus of control. This experiment could not be carried out under today's research guidelines.

More subtly, but equally problematical from a research standpoint, is the systematic but indeterminate bias introduced into double-blind research studies by having to inform potential subjects of the conditions of the study, thereby automatically excluding those who refuse to accept it. The issues of full disclosure and informed consent as they affect psychotherapy research warrant more study.

In conclusion, while recognizing that the director of a research project is probably the person least able to evaluate its influence, I submit that our findings and conclusions contributed considerably to the shift in emphasis, in both teaching and research, from differences in psychotherapeutic methods to features common to all forms, with concomitant greater emphasis on elucidating personal features of patient and therapist contributing to outcome.

REFERENCES

Berger, M. M., & Rosenbaum, M. (1975). Notes on help-rejecting complainers. In M. Rosenbaum & M. M. Berger (Eds.), *Group psychotherapy and group function, Revised Edition* (pp. 629–641). New York: Basic Books.

Frank, J. D., Hoehn-Saric, R., Imber, S. D., Liberman, B. L., & Stone, A. R. (1978). *Effective ingredients of successful psychotherapy.* New York: Brunner/Mazel.

Liberman, B. L. (1978). The role of mastery in psychotherapy: Maintenance of improvement and prescriptive change. In Frank et al., *Effective ingredients of successful psychotherapy* (pp. 35–72). New York: Brunner/Mazel.

Milgram, S. (1974). *Obedience to authority.* New York: Harper and Row.

Powdermaker, F. B., & Frank, J. D. (1953). *Group psychotherapy: Studies in methodology of research and practice.* Cambridge, MA: Harvard University Press.

THE PENN RESEARCH PROJECT

Lester Luborsky

My earliest thought of doing psychotherapy research goes back 53 years, to the beginning of my college years. I had chosen Penn State from the options open to a student with no money because of the excellent reputation of its botany department. Botany was chosen because I wanted to understand the origins of life processes, and botany had always seemed to me a likely entry point to begin the search. But a transformation occurred in my freshman year. I happened upon a Modern Library edition of Freud in my landlady's library. The interest it aroused shifted my earlier preoccupation toward psychological life processes. Then, at the end of college (at Temple, to which I had transferred) while reading *The Clinical Treatment of the Problem Child* (Rogers, 1930), I began thinking of someday applying Rogers' methods to testing Freud's theories of therapy.

In 1945, I received a PhD in experimental psychology from Duke University. An old back injury kept me from World War II service, but I did my thesis on principles of brief exposure perception that was relevant to the Navy's training system in aircraft recognition. In order to continue with studies that I had begun at Duke with Raymond Cattell, I started teaching at the University of Illinois (Urbana), where he had moved. He had been developing his P-technique method of intra-individual correlations over time. To advance this method, we decided to study repeated daily measures during a patient's psychotherapy and to relate the content of the patient's free associations to the main dimensions within the daily measurements of personality (Cattell & Luborsky, 1950; Luborsky, 1953). Because the patient selected happened to have a stomach ulcer, we were also able to include some measurements of the ups and downs in the ulcer-related symptoms. It was through this work that the idea for my symptom-context method gradually took shape (Luborsky, 1967).

Ever since graduate school, I had intended to undergo training in psychoanalysis. I wanted to practice it, but even more, I hoped that it would help me do better research (Luborsky, 1969, 1987). Obtaining such training was not easy to arrange in that era for someone without an MD. Cattell suggested that I contact his old mentor in England, J. C. Flugel, who accepted me. However, when he requested permission from the British Psychoanalytic Institute, they informed me that they had decided on a new "cricket principle"—in all fairness, they would no longer give training to people from countries where nonmedical analysts were not recognized. I then visited the Menninger Foundation and worked out an arrangement with David Rapaport—I would work in his research department on a study of the selection of physicians for training in psychiatry with Robert R. Holt; Rapaport, in turn, would support my application for training in the Topeka Psychoanalytic Institute. So, I moved with my family to Topeka in 1947.

In addition to the work on the selection project, I joined the Psychotherapy Research Committee (1949–1953). The lasting contribution of that committee was the initiation of the Health–Sickness Rating Scale (Luborsky, 1962). It was a team product, which I continued to develop over the years (Luborsky, 1975; Luborsky & Bachrach, 1974). More recently, the scale was simplified and renamed the Global Assessment Scale (Endicott, Spitzer, Fliess, & Cohen, 1976). It is now part of *DSM-III-R* as Axis 5.

My first involvement in large-scale psychotherapy research came in 1953 with the launching of the Menninger Foundation Psychotherapy Research Project by Robert Wallerstein and Lewis Robbins (see Wallerstein, The Menninger Project, in the following section).

In 1959, after completing psychoanalytic training, I moved to the Department of Psychiatry at the University of Pennsylvania, and in 1968 I was awarded a 5-year grant to study factors influencing the outcomes of psychotherapy of depressed and anxious patients. The Menninger project served as an impetus and a foil for this later research, the Penn Psycho-therapy Research Project.

In the later Menninger period, and continuing with accelerating intensity in the Penn period, the agenda was the testing of propositions about theories of curative factors in dynamic psychotherapy. This research was a continuation of my early interest in basic psychological life processes. One of the earliest of the tests was for the proposition that patients who possess greater psychiatric severity will show lesser gains from psychotherapy. This factor was demonstrated by use of the Health–Sickness Rating Scale (Luborsky, 1962). The highly generative research collaboration with colleagues in our department who were affiliated with the Philadelphia VA Hospital showed the same factor in the psychotherapy of substance abuse patients (McLellan, Luborsky, Woody, O'Brien, & Druley, 1983). These findings were the first instances of a generally supported trend in treatment studies (Luborsky, Crits-Christoph, Mintz, & Auerbach, 1988).

One major resource in the Penn Project was the inclusion of tape recordings of the psychotherapies for all 73 patients. These recordings have been a golden egg, repeatedly used for testing theories of psychotherapeutic change. Each time we wish to work on another proposition about a curative factor, we first retest it in the original sample before trying it in more recently acquired samples.

A proposition that has received much attention in my research is that the alliance with the therapist will predict the outcomes of psychotherapy. I reported on the first measure of the alliance with psychotherapy sessions (Luborsky, 1976) for a Society for Psychotherapy Research panel organized by Ed Bordin in 1975. When measured in the early sessions, the positive alliance showed a positive correlation with outcomes of treatment. A review of eight studies all showed significant positive correlations (Luborsky et al., 1988).

Another proposition is that a method of assessment of transference will be important for explaining the outcomes of psychotherapy. After a long series of false starts, I fashioned a reliable operational measure of the Core Conflictual Relationship Theme (Luborsky, 1977). Over the years, this measure has gradually been shown to fit with the main observations that Freud made about his transference concept (Luborsky and Crits-Christoph, 1990).

Alongside, and within my preoccupation with testing propositions about curative processes, two of my lifelong research styles became more and more apparent. One was a powerful predilection for predictive designs that are applied to naturalistic data (Holt & Luborsky, 1958); and the other was a zest for creation of new assessment methods, of which there are now 27!

Among the 27 are a manual and associated adherence scales for conducting dynamic psychotherapy. I started it for the teaching of residents at Penn in 1976 (Luborsky, 1984). It was for supportive–expressive psychotherapy, the therapy I began to learn at the Menninger Foundation.

My research career was advanced by my good fortune in realizing two necessities: funding and collaborators. Since my Menninger days, I have not received a salary that was independent of grants that I generated. As I consumed the expanse of time to write proposals, I remember thinking of Martin Orne's somberly wry and similar reflection about himself, "When I die they will publish my Collected Research Proposals."

In the post-1984 Penn period, the most productive collaborators in psychotherapy studies were Paul Crits-Christoph and, joining us in the last several years, Jacques P. Barber. During the earlier Penn period, the leading collaborative member had been Jim Mintz, with significant contributions by Thomas Todd and Arthur Auerbach. Fifteen years of continuous generative collaboration in psychotherapy studies for the therapy of addictive disorders has been maintained with Thomas McLellan, George Woody, and Charles O'Brien. Over the past 10 years, a stimulating collaboration in studies of psychotherapy with explanatory style methods has been carried out with Martin E. P. Seligman.

A new larger phase has just begun for research in psychotherapy with the beginning of the Penn Clinical Research Center for Psychotherapy in 1990. The Center for Psychotherapy Research (CPR) under Principal Investigator (PI) Paul Crits-Christoph (with co-PIs, Lester Luborsky, Aaron Beck, and Martin E. P. Seligman) is devoted to large-scale testing of the efficacy of two short-term psychotherapies, dynamic and cognitive–behavioral, for specific diagnostic groups. With each study, attention will be devoted to further understanding of the curative factors that are responsible within each of the pilot studies. Eventually, a large clinical trial will compare each form of treatment for each diagnostic group. The CPR is likely to fulfill many of the needs in the field, yet it is a safe prediction that its journey will be strenuous.

REFERENCES

Cattell, R. B., & Luborsky, L. B. (1950). P-Technique demonstrated as a new clinical method for determining personality structure. *Journal of General Psychology, 42,* 3–24.

Endicott, J., Spitzer, R., Fliess, J., & Cohen, J. (1976). The Global Assessment Scale. *Archives of General Psychiatry, 33,* 766–771.

Holt, R. R., & Luborsky, L. B. (1958). *Personality patterns of psychiatrists: A study in selection techniques* (Vol. 1). New York: Basic Books.

Luborsky, L. (1953). Intraindividual repetitive measurements (P-technique) in understanding symptom structure and psychotherapeutic change. In O. H. Mowrer (Ed.), *Psychotherapy: Theory and research* (pp. 389–413). New York: The Ronald Press.

Luborsky, L. (1962). Clinicians' judgments of mental health: A proposed scale. *Archives of General Psychiatry, 7,* 407–417.

Luborsky, L. (1967). Momentary forgetting during psychotherapy and psychoanalysis: A theory and research method. In R. R. Holt (Ed.), *Motives and thought: Psychoanalytic essays in honor of David Rapaport* (pp. 177–217). New York: International Universities Press. (*Psychological Issues, 5,* No. 2–3, Monograph 18/19.)

Luborsky, L. (1969). Research cannot yet influence clinical practice. (An evaluation of Strupp and Bergin's "Some empirical and conceptual bases for coordinated research in psychotherapy: Critical review of issues, trends and evidence.") *International Journal of Psychiatry, 7,* 135–140.

Luborsky, L. (1975). Clinicians' judgments of mental health: Specimen case descriptions and forms for the Health–Sickness Rating Scale. *Bulletin of the Menninger Clinic, 35,* 448–480.

Luborsky, L. (1976). Helping alliances in psychotherapy: The groundwork for a study of their relationship to its outcome. In J. L. Claghorn (Ed.), *Successful psychotherapy* (pp. 92–116). New York: Brunner/Mazel.

Luborsky, L. (1977). Measuring a pervasive psychic structure in psychotherapy: The core conflictual relationship theme. In N. Freedman & S. Grand (Eds.), *Communicative structures and psychic structures* (pp. 367–395). New York: Plenum Press.

Luborsky, L. (1984). *The principles of psychoanalytic psychotherapy: A manual for supportive–expressive treatment.* New York: Basic Books.

Luborsky, L. (1987). Research can now affect clinical practice—a happy turnaround. *The Clinical Psychologist* (The APA award presentation), *40,* 56–60.

Luborsky, L., & Bachrach, H. (1974). Factors influencing clinicians' judgments of mental health: Eighteen experiences with the Health–Sickness Rating Scale. *Archives of General Psychiatry, 31,* 292–299.

Luborsky, L., & Crits-Christoph, P. (1990). Understanding transference—the CCRT Method (The Core Conflictual Relationship Theme). New York: Basic Books.

Luborsky, L., Crits-Christoph, P., Mintz, J., & Auerbach, A. (1988). *Who will benefit from psychotherapy? Predicting therapeutic outcomes.* New York: Basic Books.

McLellan, A. T., Luborsky, L., Woody, G. E., O'Brien, C. P., & Druley, K. A.

(1983). Predicting response to alcohol and drug abuse treatments: Role of psychiatric severity. *Archives of General Psychiatry, 40,* 620–625.

Rogers, C. (1930). *The clinical treatment of the problem child.* Boston: Houghton Mifflin.

THE MENNINGER PROJECT

Robert S. Wallerstein

My career in psychotherapy research is centrally identified with the Psychotherapy Research Project (PRP) of The Menninger Foundation, of which I was a main architect and the principal investigator. The 30-year longitudinal study was conceived in 1954 and brought to definitive closure in my 1986 book, *Forty-Two Lives in Treatment: A Study of Psychoanalysis and Psychotherapy* (Wallerstein, 1986, p. 784), a final clinical accounting of the treatment and the subsequent life careers of 42 patients, half in psychoanalysis and half in varyingly expressive and supportive psychoanalytic psychotherapies. The importance of this project both to clinical research into the nature of psychoanalytic treatment courses and outcomes, and also to the wider field of psychotherapy research is, of course, for others to assess. The following account is rather a personalized statement of the creation of my own career as a researcher.

As with most of the small number of us in my generation in psychiatry and psychoanalysis who came into research careers, the evolving research course was serendipitous and the research training happenstance. I entered medical school just before World War II with the intention of becoming a general physician, with romantic notions of a career in tropical medicine, and a vaguely idealistic commitment to research as a good thing. After returning from military service to complete residency training in internal medicine, I switched for somewhat fuzzily articulated reasons into a further 3-year residency in psychiatry with the then crystallized intention to become a psychoanalyst. At the time, I was not explicitly aware of Freud's dictum that in psychoanalysis the road to (research) understanding and the road to (clinical) cure were one and the same.

During my residency years at the Topeka VA Hospital, psychologist colleague John Chotlos and I created a comparative treatment study of hospitalized alcoholic patients. The study consisted of three specific intervention modalities: antabuse, conditioned-reflex aversion therapy, and group hypnotherapy, with a fourth control group that had only the same general hospital management and psychotherapeutic help that was common to all. The project was actually born out of despair at the treatment courses and outcomes in the then routine hospital and psychotherapeutic management regimen. We evolved a methodology that allowed us to determine which treatment modality was more successful with which kinds of alcoholic patients. The results were published in my first book, *Hospital Treatment of Alcoholism: A Comparative Experimental Study* (Wallerstein, 1957, p. 212).

It was on the basis of this study of alcoholism, that George Klein, an experimentally minded psychologist-psychoanalyst, called me to the attention of Gardner Murphy, the recently arrived Director of Research at the Menninger Foundation. He was seeking a research-minded psychiatrist and offered me a split position in the research department and in outpatient clinical services. It was 1953 and I was a staff psychiatrist on the Psychosomatic Service at the Topeka VA Hospital, a position I had obtained on the basis of my combined residency training in internal medicine and psychiatry, and barely 2 years beyond my psychiatric residency training. I had realistic misgivings and considerable trepidations about accepting a position as a designated researcher with no formal research training or knowledge, but Gardner felt that my work on the alcoholism project had established my research credentials to his satisfaction.

When I started my new job at The Menninger Foundation in January 1954, I discovered that Gardner had given me a title, assistant director of research, and a charge to foster and carry out research on and within the clinical enterprise, which was, after all, the chief *raison d'être* of the entire institution. As assistant director, I had regular meetings with Gardner, during which he solicited my views on a great range of research issues, both scientific and political, and which to my surprise he most often acted on very directly. I learned rapidly to temper my off-the-top-of-my-head responses into more carefully reasoned and modulated statements.

Together with Lewis Robbins, the director of clinical services, we forged a partnership to build a research study of the enterprise that was the heart of the clinical activity of the Menninger Foundation—long-term psychoanalytic therapy. We started with the intent to investigate two questions: (a) What changes take place in therapy? and (b) How do those changes come about—through the interaction of what factors in the patients, in the therapy, in the therapist, and in the patient's evolving life situation? To assist in the study of these questions, we engaged Lester Luborsky, the principal architect of the Health–Sickness Rating Scale (see Luborsky, The Penn Research Project, in the preceding section). We also had the good fortune to recruit Helen Sargent from the Topeka VA Hospital as the fourth member of our planning group.

Helen Sargent deserves special mention in this saga. An academic psychologist trained by Rogers, she had a fine feel for the psychodynamic clinical enterprise, although she was not psychoanalytically trained. She also had an extraordinary sense for philosophy of science issues involved in providing the conceptual framework and the operational conditions that would allow a fruitful melding of the rigors of research method and the suppleness of clinical problems. The union is difficult. The clinicians bring their firm conviction that there should be no tampering with the treatment situation and the therapeutic responsibility that data should not be forced into groupings that destroy their individual uniqueness. Whatever research design evolves must be consistent with the spirit and the theory of clinical practice. The researchers bring equally time-honored convictions about the spirit, if not the precise particulars, of formal rules of proof, of evidence, and of the concepts of reliability and validity and objectivity. Sargent knew that both groups were right in their stipulations and that proper clinical research must meet the conditions of each without doing violence to the other.

Within that framework, she wrote the methodological papers of the project, which elaborated and documented our viewpoint that the essential data of the clinical research enterprise are clinical judgments about the patient's intrapsychic organization. These data could be subjected to systematic research inquiry (Sargent, 1961), to confirmation by rigorous and carefully specified prediction (Sargent, Horwitz, Wallerstein, & Appelbaum, 1968), and even to some varieties of quantitative manipulation (Sargent, Coyne, Wallerstein, & Holtzman, 1967), without ever distorting the data or the spirit of the clinical situation. My own final summary book on the 30-year-long project (Wallerstein, 1986) is a direct application of these clinical research tenets originally elaborated for us by Sargent.

From that beginning, and guided by our two orienting questions, PRP grew like Topsy. The framework was a naturalistic study of therapy as it took place within that clinical setting, not impinged upon in any way by the research activity. In fact, it was carried out without the patient or therapist even knowing that the therapeutic process was the subject of research scrutiny. How the research program was constructed within these constraints has been described at length elsewhere (including my book). The overall design did involve at least three major cross-sectional perspectives, an Initial Study (pretherapy) based on the material of the clinical evaluation process; a Termination Study whenever the therapy ended; and a planned Follow-Up Study 2 or 3 years later (extending to 30 years for half the patients), when the patient returned for a follow-up evaluation ("Psychotherapy Research Project," 1958, 1960; Wallerstein, Robbins, Sargent, & Luborsky, 1956).

In addition to these sequential cross-sectional assessments, we tracked three sets of major variables: (a) in the patient's personality organization and illness structure, (b) in the therapeutic process with the therapist, and (c) in the concomitantly interacting life situation of the patient. We also built in a specific prediction study, elaborating in each of the 42 cases, a set of specific predictions to the therapeutic course and outcome (averaging about 50 predictions per patient). An additional set of predictions to the subsequent follow-up course and outcome included the further enhancement, maintenance, or erosion of the changes achieved by the termination point (averaging another 10 predictions per patient). All these predictions were set up in such a way that the evidence required to confirm or refute them would be specified in advance, and that independent judges at the termination and follow-up points would certify the presence or absence of the necessary evidence without knowing the original predictions in regard to the expected therapeutic course or outcome.

Because our predictions were built on the prevailing theory of therapeutic change in psychoanalytic treatment processes, the outcome of some 2,000-plus individual predictions (42 patients times about 50 predictions per patient) could lead to an altered set of the theoretical assumptions underlying the specific predictions. Some predictions would be strengthened and some weakened in their correctness and their importance, creating a hierarchically altered assumptive tree, that is, a refined and better (research) supported theory of analytic therapy (Horwitz, 1974, p. 372; Sargent et al., 1968; Wallerstein, 1964).

Finally, we rank-ordered the strength and saliency of our arrays of patient, therapy and therapist, and situational variables as they varied over the three points in time of the formal study. Proceeding from the rank orderings (which had been obtained via a modification of the Fechnerian Method of Paired Comparisons), we created profiles for each patient of the three sets of variables at each of the three points in time, making group aggregation and comparison possible. We also developed intercorrelational matrices that were based on the quasicardinal qualities that our rankings exhibited. Factor analytic studies were then conducted. Under the guidance of Louis Gutmann at the Institute of Applied Social Research in Jerusalem, we applied the mathematical methods of facet theory and Multidimensional Scalogram Analysis. These programs were created by James Lingoes at Michigan (Kernberg et al., 1972; Sargent et al., 1967).

All of the preceding gradually evolved in the stepwise pyramiding of research objective and specific method appropriate to it. It required the wholehearted cooperation and participation of a major clinical institution where all the therapists of the project's patients were on the institutional payroll. It required the participation of a large variety of clinical and formal researchers (between 15 and 20 giving time from 6 hours per week to full-time); a psychological testing team able to administer blindly the identical psychological projective test battery at the three cross-sectional points in time; a prediction study team to translate the informal clinical discursive predictions into discrete formal predictive statements (each built on an if-then-because logical model, with the specification in advance of the evidence, in fact or judgment, necessary at the end to confirm or refute the prediction); and a quantitative studies team to take the rank orderings derived from the paired comparisons and evolve the statistical factor-analytic studies and the mathematical facet mapping and Multidimensional Scalogram Analyses.

Building this overall research group with its interlocking teams and holding it all together over time while people's interests and commitments shifted was itself a major project task and object lesson in the sociology of large-scale collaborative research. As principal investigator of PRP, I had intensive on-the-job training in the travails of project management; it took up the largest single part of the half-time that I devoted to the research enterprise.

All this work, of course, took substantial funding. The Menninger Foundation through Gardner Murphy's and my positions in the Research Department committed significant ongoing support. We also obtained a grant from the Foundations' Fund for Research in Psychiatry. The Ford Foundation awarded us a $350,000 grant, one of about a dozen that they made in support of mental health research at that time. Finally, we obtained substantial National Institute of Mental Health (NIMH) support to bring our data gathering and analysis to completion. In all, we garnered about $1 million in research support, and this carried the project throughout the decade of its major data gathering and data organizing.

We were also fortunate in our project consultants. Louis Gutmann, with whom I first consulted on a visit to Israel, helped us master the concepts of facet theory mapping and techniques of Multidimensional Scalogram analysis. When I presented our data initially to his group in Jerusalem, he was enthused that we had magnificent data in search of proper (mathematical) methods and that he had a magnificent method in search of appropriate and worthy data. It was a fortuitous marriage. Over the whole span of the project, we also had the regular consulting services of Wayne Holtzman of the Hogg Foundation in Austin, Texas, originally brought to us by Helen Sargent. As an essentially statistical and quantitative methodological consultant, he could creatively and flexibly adapt his statistical and experimental rigor to the subtlety and complexity of our nuanced clinical data.

An equally regular consultant visitor to the project was John Benjamin of the University of Colorado, who brought his psychoanalytic and developmental methodological expertise to the problems of an ongoing research study of long-term psychotherapeutic processes. He drew novel and useful comparisons concerning the common longitudinal issues in developmental and psychotherapy research. David Malan came from England and returned to work out a scaled-down creative adaptation of our project methods and design for his pioneering studies of brief dynamic therapy (Malan, 1963, p. 312), and Arnold Pfeffer, another consultant, from New York, was also publishing psychoanalytic follow-up data during those same years (Pfeffer, 1959, 1961, 1963).

When my own career development led me to San Francisco in 1966 as chief of psychiatry at Mount Zion Hospital, PRP had been in operation for a dozen years and its major data gathering was completed. The various data analytic tasks that were to lead to a variety of books and monographs were all still in the future: Horwitz on the prediction study (1974), Appelbaum on the psychological testing (1977, p. 308), Voth and Orth on the role of life situational variables in psychotherapy process and outcome (1973, p. 354), Kernberg et al. on the quantitative factor–analytic studies and the mathematical Multidimensional Scalogram Analysis studies (1972), and my own final overall clinical accounting based on the full 30-year span (Wallerstein, 1986).

When I left Topeka, I continued as senior collaborator involved in all major policy decisions and responsible for my own ultimate book of clinical accounting. After my departure, the role of principal investigator was taken over by Otto Kernberg, whom I had originally invited from Chile. He coordinated the completion of the project before he left for New York. It was in the study of the PRP patients that he arrived at his first formulations about the borderline personality organization.

For my part, this is the abbreviated chronicle of my own serendipitous evolution into a psychotherapy researcher, absorbing by on-the-job contact and the good fortune of the talents of the group and the clinical/research wisdom of our consultants, a reasonable state-of-the-art grasp of the then (in the 1950s) nascent field of psychodynamic psychotherapy research.

On the basis of the work in PRP, I was personally invited to participate in a succession of research-related activities, each a significant experience in learning from and with my peers. These included the Group for the Advancement of Psychiatry (GAP) Committee on Research, which I chaired during the production of the GAP Report on Psychiatric Research and the Assessment of Change (Group for the Advancement of Psychiatry, 1966); the NIMH Research Scientist Career Development Award Committee (1966–

1970), which I chaired; two fellowship years at the Center for Advanced Study in the Behavioral Sciences at Stanford, California, in 1964–1965 and again in 1981–1982, where my book, *Forty-Two Lives in Treatment*, was written. Also, we participated in the three major Conferences of Research in Psychotherapy sponsored by the American Psychological Association, in Washington, DC in 1958 (Rubinstein & Parloff, 1959, p. 293), in Chapel Hill in 1961 (Strupp & Luborsky, 1962, p. 342), and in Chicago in 1966 (Shlien, 1968, p. 618), conferences that significantly shaped the parameters of this crystallizing field of research activity.

All of this narrative adds up to an essentially unschooled, "self-made," or, better, "on-the-job-made," research career, possible in the heady days of the 1950s, when the field of systematic psychotherapy research was being born and when opportunity and funding were available. It is hardly a path that can be followed any longer, as technology sophistication requires specific and systematic formal research training, and when the arc of opportunity and of available sustained research support are progressively narrowing. The new generation of clinical researchers, psychotherapy and otherwise, is no doubt tougher and incomparably better trained for the complexities and uncertainties of the clinical research task. I think, however, that it is more than wistful nostalgia to feel that something has also been lost by the process of change in the nature of the enterprise, and in the way that one comes into it.

REFERENCES

Appelbaum, S. A. (1977). *The anatomy of change: A Menninger Foundation report on testing the effects of psychotherapy*. New York: Plenum Press.

Group for the Advancement of Psychiatry. (1966). Psychiatric research and the assessment of change (Report No. 63, pp. 357–479). Formulated by the Committee on Research; Robert Wallerstein, chairman. New York: Author.

Horwitz, L. (1974). *Clinical prediction in psychotherapy*. New York: Jason Aronson.

Kernberg, O. F., Burstein, E. D., Coyne, L., Appelbaum, A., Horwitz, L., & Voth, H. (1972). Psychotherapy and psychoanalysis: Final report of The Menninger Foundation's Psychotherapy Research Project. *Bulletin Menninger Clinic, 36*; i–275.

Malan, D. H. (1963). A study of brief psychotherapy. London & New York: Tavistock Publications & Charles C Thomas.

Pfeffer, A. Z. (1959). A procedure for evaluating the results of psychoanalysis: A preliminary report. *Journal of the American Psychoanalytic Association, 7,* 418–444.

Pfeffer, A. Z. (1961). Follow-up study of a satisfactory analysis. *Journal of the American Psychoanalytic Association, 9,* 698–718.

Pfeffer, A. Z. (1963). The meaning of the analyst after analysis: A contribution to the theory of therapeutic results. *Journal of the American Psychoanalytic Association, 11,* 229–244.

The Psychotherapy Research Project of The Menninger Foundation: Second report [Special issue]. (1958). *Bulletin Menniger Clinic, 22,* 115–166.

The Psychotherapy Research Project of The Menninger Foundation: Third report [Special issue]. (1960). *Bulletin Menninger Clinic, 24,* 157–216.

Rubinstein, E. A., & Parloff, M. B. (Eds.). (1959). *Research in psychotherapy.* Washington, DC: American Psychological Association.

Sargent, H. D. (1961). Intrapsychic change: Methodological problems in psychotherapy research. *Psychiatry, 24,* 93–108.

Sargent, H. D., Coyne, L., Wallerstein, R. S., & Holtzman, W. H. (1967). An approach to quantitative problems of psychoanalytic research. *Journal of Clinical Psychology, 23,* 243–291.

Sargent, H. D., Horwitz, L., Wallerstein, R. S., & Appelbaum, A. (1968). Prediction in psychotherapy research: A method for the transformation of clinical judgments into testable hypotheses [Monograph 21]. *Psychological Issues, 6,* 1–146.

Shlien, J. M. (Ed.). (1968). *Research in psychotherapy* (Vol. III). Washington, DC: American Psychological Association.

Strupp, H., & Luborsky, L. (Eds.). (1962). *Research in psychotherapy* (Vol. II). Washington, DC: American Psychological Association.

Voth, H. M., & Orth, M. H. (1973). *Psychotherapy and the role of the environment.* New York: Behavioral Publications.

Wallerstein, R. S. (Ed.). (1957). Hospital treatment of alcoholism: A comparative experimental study. *Menninger Monograph Series* (No. 11). New York: Basic Books.

Wallerstein, R. S. (1964). The role of prediction in theory building in psychoanalysis. *Journal of the American Psychoanalytic Association, 12,* 675–691.

Wallerstein, R. S. (1986). *Forty-Two Lives in Treatment: A Study of Psychoanalysis and Psychotherapy.* New York: Guilford Press.

Wallerstein, R. S., Robbins, L. L., Sargent, H. D., & Luborsky, L. (1956). The Psychotherapy Research Project of The Menninger Foundation. *Bulletin Menninger Clinic, 20,* 221–278.

THE CHICAGO NORTHWESTERN STUDIES

Kenneth I. Howard and David E. Orlinsky

We are two remarkably dissimilar individuals who have been with one another in friendship and research for more than 30 years. We met in the fall of 1956 at the University of Chicago, through the accident of simultaneously starting graduate study in psychology. One of us, Kenneth Howard, was returning from 2 years as an officer in the U.S. Army in Germany, after undergraduate years as a chemist, poet, and psychologist at University of California at Berkeley. The other, David Orlinsky, was an early graduate of the Hutchins College at the University of Chicago, a lapsed pre-med turned philosophical poet. Beginning a new phase of life together and mutually attracted as opposites can be, not understanding very well how the other's mind worked but complementing each other's strengths and compensating for weaknesses, through common plight, elective affinity, reciprocal rescues, and shared laughter, we grew deeply determined to be comrades.

In graduate school, Howard studied psychometrics, factor analysis, and methodology with Lyle Jones, Jack Butler, and Donald Fiske. Orlinsky studied psychoanalysis and personality theory with Morris Stein and Sheldon Korchin and did dream research under Joe Kamiya in Nathaniel Kleitman's laboratory. We learned behaviorism from Howard Hunt, biopsychology from Austin Riesen and Eckert Hess, developmental psychology from Helen Koch and Sheldon White, and cognitive neuropsychology from Ward Halstead and Joseph Wepman. We were clinical students, too, and trained together at the Veterans Administration—where, peripherally at least, we came in contact with another major locus of psychotherapy research in the 1950s, operating under the general direction of Maurice Lorr. We took classes with Carl Rogers and Jack Butler but, evidently lacking sufficient empathy, warmth, and genuineness, were not recruited to be part of the Rogerian inner circle.

When we turned to psychotherapy research in 1964, it was because we had become used to doing research in other fields, because we were at the time working evenings as therapists at the same local clinic, and because we were friends. Our collaboration provided a way for us to synthesize practice and research. In the 1960s and early 1970s, we pursued our studies through the support of the Illinois Institute for Juvenile Research. During the 1980s, our main research base was the Psychotherapy Program at Northwestern University's Institute of Psychiatry.

Our involvement in psychotherapy research has always been infused with a playful spirit, and it is possible that we have been outlaws of a sort. We could not or would not bring ourselves to do psychotherapy research in the conventionally accepted way, to make tape recordings of therapy sessions, take brief randomly selected excerpts, and rate those excerpts with scales or coding schemes. Given the naive realism of the time, it was believed that researchers could by this means hear for themselves what was "actually happening" in therapy, bypassing the traditional clinical reliance on the (presumably biased) subjective experience, memory, and reflection of the psychotherapist.

The conventional way to do outcome research was to assess the patients' psychopathology (typically by giving a battery of psychological tests) before therapy, at termination, and after a reasonable interval of time past termination. Researchers were preoccupied by their need to respond to Eysenck's challenge concerning the efficacy of psychotherapy: to demonstrate whether or not therapy "worked." If it "worked," then patients should have improved by the end of treatment—never mind how. Moreover, if it "really worked," then patients should have maintained their gains intact against the passage of time—never mind what their lives were like.

We, on the other hand, insisted on studying therapeutic processes through the experiences of patients and therapists. We held fast to the notion that psychotherapy *is* what patients and therapists experience, consciously and unconsciously, when they do what they do with each other. They can tell us about the former aspect of their experiences directly, and about the latter indirectly, when asked to do so. Our effort to ask patients and therapists about their experiences in therapy resulted in the formulation, in the mid-1960s, of the *Therapy Session Report* (TSR) questionnaires.

The TSR provides a good example of systematically searching for the obvious. We conceived of it as an interview and imagined ourselves meeting with patients as they finished their therapy sessions. What did we want to ask them? What was there in the experience of a therapy session that patients could be asked about? It seemed to us that the therapy session as experienced could be described in five complementary ways. Most obviously, it is a conversation or dialogue between patient and therapist. Thus, our questions for the patient were: "What did you talk about during the session?" and "What were you concerned about during the session?"

Almost as obvious, a therapy session is experienced as a process of exchange, a transaction in which patients hope to get something, in which therapists intend to give something, and which may or may not result in patients getting what they sought and paid for. Hence our questions for the patient were, "What did you want or hope to get out of this session?" and "What do you feel that you got out of this session?" Of the therapist, in a parallel questionnaire, we asked, "What did your patient seem to want out of this session?" and "In what direction were you working with your patient during this session?"

Furthermore, it seemed clear that the dialogue and exchange experienced by the patient in therapy occurred in the context of a relationship. We wanted to know how the patient experienced this relationship, and accordingly asked, "How did you act toward your therapist during this session?" and "How did your therapist act toward you during this session?" Moreover, it seemed to us that the dialogue and exchange experienced in the therapeutic relationship always has a great deal to do with feelings—that when therapy happens, it involves a change of heart as much or more than it does a change of mind. Consequently we asked: "How did you feel during this session?" and (because feelings are contextualized in a relationship) "How did your therapist seem to feel during this session?"

Finally, a therapy session develops over the course of an hour. Having a beginning, middle, and end, the session has the natural structure of an enacted narrative, or drama. How eager were the patient and therapist for the play to begin? How well did they each play their parts? How far did the play progress toward a satisfactory end? And because the participants are audiences and critics, we asked for their overall evaluation of the session.

Our accumulated pool of TSR data includes approximately 5,000 reports from over 600 patients, as well as reports from approximately 250 therapists. These data came from outpatient visits at the Katherine Wright Mental Health Clinic in Chicago in the late 1960s, the Michael Reese Hospital Medical Center in the 1970s, and Northwestern University's Institute of Psychiatry in the 1980s. Versions of the TSR have also been designed for use by patients in group therapy and couples therapy (Orlinsky & Howard, 1987a). Our book, *Varieties of Psychotherapeutic Experience* (Orlinsky & Howard, 1975) covers only the original pilot sample.

More recently, we have developed other instruments for a major new project at the Institute of Psychiatry to assess different aspects of therapeutic experience. One of these, the *Intersession Therapeutic Experience Questionnaire* (designed with M. Tarragona), focuses on patients' subjective representations of therapy and their therapists in the times between sessions and, in this way, complements the TSR. Another, the *Therapeutic Procedures Inventory* (designed with M. Luncy, C. Davidson, and M. O'Mahoney) provides therapists and patients with a systematic checklist of technical interventions and offers researchers an alternative to manualization as a method of documenting the treatment delivered to patients.

A second area of study has been our attempt to help resolve some of the conceptual complexities that have limited outcome research to such ultimately frustrating questions as "Which type of therapy works best?" For example, what does it mean to say that patients get better or worse, that the conditions of their personalities improve or deteriorate, or that therapy caused or contributed significantly to these changes? Assessment of change has typically been confounded with value judgments. The specific effects of therapy and of other life circumstances, and especially of the relations between them, have rarely been systematically studied. Instead of treating outcome as a black box problem by assessing patients at intake and termination, we have tried to focus attention on the process of outcome. In other words, we have sought to ask about the ways in which gains realized by patients in sessions are brought into problematic life situations as micro-outcomes, and how the latter accumulate over the course of time into macro-outcomes.

As a third area of interest, we have tried to offer a conceptually coherent synthesis of research findings, especially in the literature relating process to outcome (Orlinsky & Howard, 1978, 1986), culminated in the formulation of a research-based theoretical model of therapy. Our Generic Model (Orlinsky & Howard, 1987b) offers testable explanations of certain salient findings in the field, such as the ubiquity of the therapeutic relationship (e.g., bond, alliance) as an apparent determinant of outcome, the rather inconsistent effects of certain technical interventions (e.g., interpretation, confrontation) on outcome, and the tendency of healthier patients to benefit more from treatment.

Fourth, we have tried to show that psychotherapy must be understood as practiced in the real world, not as a context-free, laboratory-controlled phenomenon. This has been done by linking therapy research to epidemiological research on service utilization (Howard, Davidson, O'Mahoney, Orlinsky, & Brown, 1989) and social context. A major impetus was our work on the dose-response effect, which used probit-analysis to demonstrate quantitatively the relationship between treatment duration (dose) and outcome (response) (Howard, Kopta, Krause, & Orlinsky, 1986).

Fifth, we have had a major role in organizing the Society for Psychotherapy Research (SPR), which has grown from about 70 U.S. members in 1968 to over 1,000 members now in more than two dozen countries. Over the past 20 years, SPR has become the principal meeting place for the international community of psychotherapy researchers, a place for regulars to have fun doing business, and for students and scholars entering the field.

REFERENCES

Howard, K. I., Davidson, C. V., O'Mahoney, M. T., Orlinsky, D. E., & Brown, K. P. (1989). Patterns of psychotherapy utilization. *American Journal of Psychiatry, 146,* 775–778.

Howard, K. I., Kopta, S. M., Krause, M. S., & Orlinsky, D. E. (1986). The dose-response relationship in psychotherapy. *American Psychologist, 41,* 159–164.

Orlinsky, D. E., & Howard, K. I. (1975). *Varieties of psychotherapeutic experience.* New York: Columbia Teachers College Press.

Orlinsky, D. E., & Howard, K. I. (1978). The relation of process to outcome in psychotherapy. In A. Bergin & S. Garfield (Eds.), *The handbook of research in psychotherapy and behavior change* (2nd ed.; pp. 283–329). New York: Wiley.

Orlinsky, D. E., & Howard, K. I. (1986). Process and outcome in psychotherapy. In S. Garfield & A. Bergin (Eds.), *Handbook of psychotherapy and behavior change* (3rd ed.; pp. 311–381). New York: Wiley.

Orlinsky, D. E., & Howard, K. I. (1987a). The psychological interior of psychotherapy: Explorations with the Therapy Session Reports. In L. S. Greenberg & W. M. Pinsof (Eds.), *The psychotherapeutic process: A research handbook.* New York: Guilford Press.

Orlinsky, D. E., & Howard, K. I. (1987b). A generic model of psychotherapy. *Journal of Integrative and Eclectic Psychotherapy, 6,* 6–27.

OUTCOME RESEARCH

Allen E. Bergin

My interest in psychotherapy research derives from a conviction that human beings are by nature oriented toward personal growth and development, and from my bent toward the objective, experimental, and mathematical. I can still recall the warm spring day in 1959 when I discovered the report of the first American Psychological Association (APA) conference on psychotherapy research (Rubinstein & Parloff, 1959). I spent my lunch hour on the grounds of the Fort Miley VA Hospital in San Francisco, where I was an intern, reading the first chapter of the book, in which Jerome Frank discussed the problem of controls in psychotherapy research. In the succeeding days, I read the book from cover to cover and digested the issues, findings, and implications of the work reported there. Somehow, there was a perfect fit between my dispositions and what these people were doing. It was then and there that I determined to become a therapy researcher.

My new focus helped shape my career. Working with Albert Bandura (as chair) and Leon Festinger, I did a dissonance theory experimental analog of personality change for my dissertation in 1959–1960. Bandura, with his warm sense of humor and his intellectual brilliance, helped me anchor the conviction that rigorous empirical methods could be applied to the psychotherapy situation.

After finishing at Stanford, I obtained an NIMH postdoctoral research fellowship to work with Carl Rogers at the University of Wisconsin. Rogers was an intensive mentor who had a profound effect on my self-image and style as a psychologist, as a therapist, and as a person. I shared an office with Charles Truax during that year and helped him develop various scales for measuring the Rogerian therapeutic conditions.

One of the more significant events of that year took place at a weekly research meeting in which Truax suggested that some of the patients in the schizophrenia psychotherapy research project might be getting worse while others might be getting better. It struck me during the seminar that Truax's preliminary statement might have in it a possible solution to the Eysenck 1952 report of the apparent null effect of therapy. Perhaps the benefits of good therapy were diluted by the negative effects of bad therapy when average group change scores were computed. I later noticed that some previous studies had reported similar findings, including greater variance in the outcome estimates for the treated groups. This event occurred sometime early in 1961, and Truax and I reported on the phenomenon in an APA symposium in 1962 (Bergin, 1963; Truax, 1963). I reviewed it more broadly again in a 1964 APA symposium and finally published what became a seminal article on positive versus negative effects in 1966 (Bergin, 1966).

Although I did a number of empirical studies of psychotherapy over the years, none had as large an impact as my attempts to synthesize, reinterpret, or conceptualize the research evidence on psychotherapy (Bergin, 1971; Bergin & Lambert, 1978; Lambert, Shapiro, & Bergin, 1986). My reinterpretations of the Eysenck data, along with many other outcome reports, confirmed that I was able to make sense out of disparate data and move the field forward better than with my own carefully designed studies.

In moving from the University of Wisconsin to Teachers College at Columbia University in 1961, I found a stimulating context for my scholarly work. It was particularly significant to have Sol Garfield move to Columbia in 1964. In the following years, we collaborated on an important outcome research project that resulted in a number of studies and doctoral dissertations by students. In addition, we edited the first edition of *The Handbook of Psychotherapy and Behavior Change* (Bergin & Garfield, 1971), which was later acknowledged as a historic synthesis of the extant literature on the evaluation of therapy. Those were exciting times.

During those same years, I had the opportunity to collaborate with Hans Strupp (who was at Vanderbilt University) on several projects, some of which were supported by NIMH grants (Bergin & Strupp, 1972; Strupp & Bergin, 1969). These were synthesizing, summarizing efforts that attempted to set directions for the field.

The work with Garfield and with Strupp continued for a brief period after I moved to Brigham Young University (BYU) in 1972. There were a few articles and some books that flowed from the energy and investment of the earlier work (Bergin & Strupp, 1972; Bergin & Suinn, 1975; Garfield & Bergin, 1978, 1986). In about 1975, my interest in psychotherapy research became less intense and I became preoccupied with a broader spectrum of human change than occurs in pathology and psychotherapy situations. Fortunately, I was able to develop a very fruitful collaboration with Michael J. Lambert, a BYU therapy researcher, who has since carried much of the load of our joint work in the therapy area and who has made distinguished contributions of his own as well (see chapter 11 in this volume).

My focus during the 1980s was more precisely in the area of values and religion (Bergin, 1980a, 1980b). It took me several years to get a sense of that field, to gather some of my own data, and to publish on the relationship of values to personality, psychopathology, and therapeutic change (Bergin, 1991).

I was surprised to discover, in this context, some of the same issues and problems that exist in psychotherapy research. One of the most important observations was of the dual effect of religiosity. Religion seems to have ingredients that are healthy while it also embodies influences that are not; the same has been found in psychotherapy, where some therapies and some therapists create casualties, whereas others obtain positive effects.

My intention in the 1990s is to bring these two areas together more fully. There is a surprising and growing openness of therapists and researchers to the spiritual and value-related dimensions of human growth (Bradford & Spero, 1990; Graham, 1980). I also have a renewed interest in the social, developmental, and cognitive–learning models and the ways in which they might be harmonized with spiritual ones in developing more powerful models of change in the clinical setting.

In concluding, I reiterate that I have gained somewhat more satisfaction from synthesizing than from data collection. My influence has come more from summarizing, editing, interpreting, and educating than it has from programmatic research projects. I am happy to be a quiet facilitator in this way, regardless of how my other work may fare on the academic scene. Perhaps synthesizing and facilitating have a place in the ecology of scholarship, and, indeed, it seems that these are also the functions of therapy itself. So in a sense, for me, education and therapy are overlapping modes with similar goals.

REFERENCES

Bergin, A. E. (1963). The effects of psychotherapy: negative results revisited. *Journal of Counseling Psychology, 10*, 244–250.

Bergin, A. E. (1966). Some implications of psychotherapy research for therapeutic practice. *Journal of Abnormal Psychology, 71,* 235–246.

Bergin, A. E. (1971). The evaluation of therapeutic outcomes. In A. E. Bergin & S. L. Garfield (Eds.), *Handbook of psychotherapy and behavior change* (pp. 217–270). New York: Wiley.

Bergin, A. E. (1980a). Psychotherapy and religious values. *Journal of Consulting and Clinical Psychology, 48,* 95–105.

Bergin, A. E. (1980b). Religious and humanistic values: A reply to Ellis and Walls. *Journal of Consulting and Clinical Psychology, 48,* 642–645.

Bergin, A. E. (1991). Values and religious issues in psychotherapy and mental health. *American Psychologist, 46,* 394–403.

Bergin, A. E., & Garfield, S. L. (Eds.). (1971). *Handbook of psychotherapy and behavior change.* New York: Wiley.

Bergin, A. E., & Lambert, M. J. (1978). The evaluation of therapeutic outcomes. In S. L. Garfield & A. E. Bergin (Eds.), *Handbook of psychotherapy and behavior change* (2nd ed.; pp. 139–189). New York: Wiley.

Bergin, A. E., & Strupp, H. H. (1972). *Changing frontiers in the science of psychotherapy.* Chicago: Aldine-Atherton.

Bergin, A. E., & Suinn, R. M. (1975). Individual psychotherapy and behavior therapy. In M. R. Rosenzweig & L. W. Porter (Eds.), *Annual review of psychology* (Vol. 26; pp. 509–556). Palo Alto, CA: Annual Reviews Inc.

Bradford, D. T., & Spero, M. H. (Eds.). (1990). Psychotherapy and religion [Special issue]. *Psychotherapy, 27*(1).

Garfield, S. L., & Bergin, A. E. (Eds.). (1978). *Handbook of psychotherapy and behavior change* (2nd ed.). New York: Wiley.

Garfield, S. L., & Bergin, A. E. (Eds.). (1986). *Handbook of psychotherapy and behavior change* (3rd ed.). New York: Wiley.

Graham, S. R. (Ed.) (1980). Values in psychotherapy [Special issue]. *Psychotherapy, 17*(4).

Lambert, M. J., Shapiro, D. A., & Bergin, A. E. (1986). The effectiveness of psychotherapy. In S. L. Garfield & A. E. Bergin (Eds.), *Handbook of psychotherapy and behavior change* (3rd ed.; pp. 157–211). New York: Wiley.

Rubinstein, E. A., & Parloff, M. B. (Eds.). (1959). *Research in psychotherapy.* Washington, DC: American Psychological Association.

Strupp, H. H., & Bergin, A. E. (1969). Some empirical and conceptual bases for coordinated research in psychotherapy. *International Journal of Psychiatry, 7,* 18–90.

Truax, C. B. (1963). Effective ingredients in psychotherapy: An approach to unraveling the patient–therapist interaction. *Journal of Counseling Psychology, 10,* 256–263.

A PROGRAM OF CLINICAL RESEARCH ON DEPRESSION

Peter M. Lewinsohn

I received my PhD from The Johns Hopkins University in 1955. Although I wanted to become a clinical psychologist, I did not understand that not all programs offered clinical training. Hopkins did not, and I may be the only clinical PhD to come out of that program. I made my own arrangements with David Rosenthal to get some clinical training at the Phipps Clinic. I also got to know Morris Parloff, Stanley Imber, and Jerome Frank. They were just starting some of their ground-breaking research on psychotherapy, and the Powdermaker and Frank (1953) book on group psychotherapy had just come out. I was excited by the research they were doing, and they invited me to attend clinical conferences.

Because I did not have much clinical training when I received my degree, I took positions in clinical settings, first at a state hospital in Kansas and then in Philadelphia. In terms of promoting my interest in doing clinical research, the most influential experience was the year I spent at the Philadelphia Child Guidance Clinic, where John Rose and Sol Gordon were important role models and teachers.

My initial research activities were focused on psychosomatic issues (Lewinsohn, 1956), assessment (Lewinsohn & May, 1963), the measurement of improvement (Lewinsohn & Nichols, 1964), and hallucinations and delusions (Lewinsohn, 1968). Starting in 1964, my research interests began to focus on the topic of depression, which has been central to all of my research since then.

Depression is probably unrivaled in the breadth of issues that it raises. It can easily raise all or almost all of the clinical, theoretical, and methodological issues that are of importance in psychotherapy research. Its study and treatment involves interactions among cognitions, emotions, and overt behavior; among psychophysiology, brain chemistry, and environmental influences; and among developmental issues. Depression is the most common mental disorder, especially if one considers that it occurs by itself and also in conjunction with many other mental and physical disorders. Thus, depression is an extremely broad-band condition that can be used to focus on many theoretically and clinically challenging questions.

My focus on depression was strongly influenced by Charles Ferster. We were colleagues at the Indiana University Medical Center from 1959 through 1963. He was on the staff of the Research Institute, and I was the chief psychologist at the La Rue D. Carter Memorial Hospital. Focusing on the passivity (i.e., low behavior rate) of depressed individuals, it was a relatively small step to postulate that they must be on an extinction schedule, that is, that a lack of, or a reduction in, response-contingent positive reinforcement might be an important antecedent for the occurrence of depression. This idea was not inconsistent with other observations and theorizes postulating losses of various kinds that would remove important reinforcers as antecedents for the occurrence of depression-like phenomena (e.g., Spitz, 1954). All of this inquiry led me to formulate what later became a behavioral model of depression and to develop specific interventions (Lewinsohn, Weinstein, & Shaw, 1969). If people become depressed because their behavior no longer leads to reinforcement, then one needs to help them change their behavior and their environment.

My move to the University of Oregon in 1965 was important. Being a member of the clinical faculty and participating in the clinical supervision of graduate students gave me the necessary control over a clinical setting where we could combine good clinical training with research. We accomplished this by focusing our practicum teaching on a specific clinical phenomenon like depression. The department supported our efforts by agreeing that practicum supervision would constitute half of our teaching load.

The point of origin for my clinical research team was a conceptual framework that a reduced rate of contingent positive reinforcement is a necessary and sufficient cause of depressive phenomena. From this formulation we derived treatment (e.g., Lewinsohn, 1974, 1976) and assessment strategies (Lewinsohn & Shaffer, 1971; MacPhillamy & Lewinsohn, 1982; Lewinsohn, Antonuccio, Steinmetz, & Teri, 1984). These strategies were designed at first for use with individual patients on whom we published reports on single cases (Lewinsohn & Atwood, 1969; Lewinsohn & Shaw, 1969; Robinson & Lewinsohn, 1973) and later for use with groups (Lewinsohn, Weinstein, & Alper, 1970). We also conducted laboratory studies to test hypotheses derived from the conceptual framework (e.g., Flippo & Lewinsohn, 1971; Lewinsohn, Lobitz, & Wilson, 1973) and eventually were able to conduct treatment outcome studies as part of the practicum (Brown & Lewinsohn, 1984; Zeiss, Lewinsohn, & Muñoz, 1979).

Over a period of many years, I became involved in the treatment of depressed patients while supervising students. The existence of advanced clinical research practica was also attractive to the graduate students because it allowed them to combine clinical work with research.

A turning point in my career began with a phone call from Arthur Ulene, who was interested in using the strategies described in a self-help book in his television program (Feeling Fine). Specifically, he asked us to assist him in the treatment of depressed individuals as the basis for a miniseries on depression, which, it was hoped, would prove useful for depressed people. With some trepidation, four of us (Toni Zeiss, Mary Ann Youngren, Ricardo Muñoz, and I) treated these individuals (in a hall in San Francisco rented by NBC) using our book, *Control Your Depression* (Lewinsohn, Muñoz, Youngren, & Zeiss, 1986), as the basis for the "course." At the end of the treatment, the patients appeared improved, and the resulting 10 4-minute segments were aired during a 2-week period in late 1978 (Muñoz, Glish, Soo-Hoo, & Robertson, 1982).

When I returned to Oregon, I discussed with Rick Brown, a graduate student who was then a member of the Depression Practicum and who needed a dissertation topic, the idea of developing a Coping with Depression course. Rick and I created the syllabi for each treatment session and ran the first groups. I was awarded a NIMH grant to evaluate the efficacy of the course, and we completed a systematic treatment outcome study (Brown & Lewinsohn, 1984). In the next few years, the Advanced Clinical Practicum became the vehicle for the dissertations of Julia Steinmetz-Breckenridge and David Antonuccio, resulting in the publication of the treatment protocol for the Coping with Depression course (Lewinsohn et al., 1984).

As a function of my exposure to colleagues from the University of Oregon's Gerontology Center, to Larry Thompson and Dolores Gallagher of the Andrus Center at the University of Southern California (USC), and my participation in the APA "Older Boulder" Conference on Training Psychologists for Work in Aging (Santos & VandenBos, 1982), I had become keenly aware of the fact that we needed to do more to train our students for work with the elderly. Consequently, we modified the training program in clinical psychology at the University of Oregon in 1981 to provide students with didactic and experiential training in the delivery of clinical services to older adults. The key component of the program was the Aging Practicum (Lewinsohn, Teri, & Hautzinger, 1984; Lewinsohn & Tilson, 1988). Our own efforts to modify the treatment approach we had developed for use with elders (Lewinsohn & Teri, 1983; Teri & Lewinsohn, 1985a; Teri & Lewinsohn, 1985b; Zeiss & Lewinsohn, 1986) were complemented by the efforts of Gallagher and Thompson, who adapted, modified, and evaluated behavioral approaches to depression for use with elders (Gallagher et al., 1981; Thompson & Gallagher, 1983).

My involvement with children and adolescents was stimulated by two graduate students, Harry Hoberman and Greg Clarke. Harry was an active participant in the Depression Practicum (Hoberman & Lewinsohn, 1985; Hoberman, Lewinsohn, & Tilson, 1988) and did his dissertation on depression in young children (Hoberman, 1984). Greg had worked with Ivar Lovaas as an undergraduate at the University of California, Los Angeles (UCLA) and thus was familiar with behavioral approaches to the treatment of young people. For his dissertation, he adapted the Coping course for use with adolescents, and we are now in the fourth year of a 7-year treatment–outcome study (Clarke & Lewinsohn, 1989; Lewinsohn, Clarke, & Hoberman, 1989; Lewinsohn, Clarke, Hops, Andrews, & Williams, 1989).

In the future, we will probably move even more into psychoeducational and community modes. We would like to see the efficacy of the Coping course evaluated as a preventive measure in schools and in health maintenance organizations in order to determine whether the approach can be adapted to prevent episodes of depression in the many who are at elevated risk.

REFERENCES

Brown, R. A., & Lewinsohn, P. M. (1984). A psychoeducational approach to the treatment of depression: Comparison of group, individual, and minimal contact procedures. *Journal of Consulting and Clinical Psychology, 52,* 774–783.

Clarke, G. N., & Lewinsohn, P. M. (1989). The Coping with Depression course: A group psychoeducational intervention for unipolar depression. *Behavior Change, 6,* 54–69.

Flippo, J., & Lewinsohn, P. M. (1971). Effects of failure on the self-esteem of depressed and nondepressed subjects. *Journal of Consulting and Clinical Psychology, 36,* 151.

Gallagher, D., Thompson, L., Baffa, G., Piatt, C., Ringering, L., & Stone, V. (1981). *Depression in the elderly: A behavioral treatment manual.* Los Angeles: University of Southern California Press (currently distributed by H. C. Health & Co., Lexington, MA).

Hoberman, H. M. (1984). *Distinguishing psychosocial characteristics of a community sample of depressed children.* Unpublished doctoral dissertation, University of Oregon, Eugene.

Hoberman, H. M., & Lewinsohn, P. M. (1985). The behavioral treatment of depression. In E. E. Beckham & W. R. Leber (Eds.), *Handbook of depression: Treatment, assessment and research* (pp. 39–81). Homewood, IL: Dorsey Press.

Hoberman, H. M., Lewinsohn, P. M., & Tilson, M. (1988). Group treatment of depression: Individual predictors of outcome. *Journal of Consulting and Clinical Psychology, 56,* 393–398.

Lewinsohn, P. M. (1956). Some individual differences in physiological reactivity to stress. *Journal of Comparative Physiological Psychology, 49,* 271–277.

Lewinsohn, P. M. (1968). Characteristics of patients with hallucinations. *Journal of Clinical Psychology, 24,* 423.

Lewinsohn, P. M. (1974). A behavioral approach to depression. In R. J. Friedman & M. M. Katz (Eds.), *The psychology of depression: Contemporary theory and research* (pp. 157–185). New York: John Wiley & Sons.

Lewinsohn, P. M. (1976). Activity schedules in the treatment of depression. In C. E. Thoresen & J. D. Krumboltz (Eds.), *Counseling methods* (pp. 74–83). New York: Holt, Rinehart and Winston.

Lewinsohn, P. M., Antonuccio, D., Steinmetz, J., & Teri, L. (1984). *The Coping with Depression course: A psychoeducational intervention for unipolar depression.* Eugene, OR: Castalia Publishing.

Lewinsohn, P. M., & Atwood, G. (1969). Depression: A clinical research approach. The case of Mrs. G. *Psychotherapy: Theory, research and practice, 6,* 166–171.

Lewinsohn, P. M., Clarke, G. N., & Hoberman, H. M. (1989). The Coping with Depression course: Review and future directions. *Canadian Journal of Behavioral Science, 21,* 470–493.

Lewinsohn, P. M., Clarke, G. N., Hops, H., Andrews, J. A., & Williams, J. A. (1989). *Cognitive–behavioral treatment for depressed adolescents.* Unpublished manuscript.

Lewinsohn, P. M., Lobitz, W. C., & Wilson, S. (1973). Sensitivity of depressed individuals to average stimuli. *Journal of Abnormal Psychology, 81,* 259–263.

Lewinsohn, P. M., & May, J. (1963). A technique for the judgment of emotion from figure drawings. *Journal of Projective Techniques in Personality Assessment, 27,* 79–85.

Lewinsohn, P. M., Muñoz, R., Youngren, M. A., & Zeiss, A. (1986). *Control your depression* (rev. ed.). Englewood Cliffs, NJ: Prentice-Hall.

Lewinsohn, P. M., & Nichols, R. C. (1964). The evaluation of changes in psychiatric patients during and after hospitalization. *Journal of Clinical Psychology, 20,* 272–279.

Lewinsohn, P. M., & Shaffer, M. (1971). Use of home observations as an integral part of the treatment of depression: Preliminary report and case studies. *Journal of Consulting and Clinical Psychology, 37,* 87–94.

Lewinsohn, P. M., & Shaw, D. (1969). Feedback about interpersonal behavior as an agent of behavior change: A case study in the treatment of depression. *Psychotherapy and Psychomatics, 17,* 82–88.

Lewinsohn, P. M., & Teri, L. (Eds.) (1983). *Clinical geropsychology.* New York: Pergamon Press.

Lewinsohn, P. M., Teri, L., & Hautzinger, M. (1984). Training clinical psychologists for work with older adults: A working model. *Professional Psychology: Research and Practice, 15,* 187–202.

Lewinsohn, P. M., & Tilson, M. D. (1988). Psychotherapy services for older adults: Innovative roles for clinical geropsychologists. *Gerontology & Geriatrics Education, 7,* 111–123.

Lewinsohn, P. M., Weinstein, M., & Alper, T. (1970). A behavioral approach to the group treatment of depressed persons: A methodological contribution. *Journal of Clinical Psychology, 4,* 525–532.

Lewinsohn, P. M., Weinstein, M., & Shaw, D. (1969). Depression: A clinical research approach. In R. D. Rubin & C. M. Frank (Eds.), *Advances in behavior therapy* (pp. 231–240). New York: Academic Press.

MacPhillamy, D. J., & Lewinsohn, P. M. (1982). The Pleasant Events Schedule: Studies on reliability, validity, and scale intercorrelations. *Journal of Consulting and Clinical Psychology, 50,* 433–435.

Muñoz, R. F., Glish, M., Soo-Hoo, T., & Robertson, J. (1982). The San Francisco mood survey project: Preliminary work toward the prevention of depression. *American Journal of Community Psychology, 10,* 317–329.

Powdermaker, F., & Frank, J. D. (1953). *Group psychotherapy.* Cambridge, MA: Harvard University Press.

Robinson, J., & Lewinsohn, P. M. (1973). Experimental analysis of a technique based on the Premack Principle changing verbal behavior of depressed individuals. *Psychological Reports, 32,* 199–210.

Santos, J. F., & VandenBos, G. R. (Eds.). (1982). *Psychology and the older adult: Challenges for training in the 1980s.* Washington, DC: American Psychological Association.

Spitz, R. A. (1954). Infantile depression and the general adaptation syndrome. In P. H. Hoch & J. Zubin (Eds.), *Proceedings of the 42nd Annual Meeting of the American Psychopathological Association* (pp. 93–108). New York: Grune and Stratton.

Teri, L., & Lewinsohn, P. M. (1985a). Group intervention for unipolar depression. *The Behavior Therapist, 8,* 109–111.

Teri, L., & Lewinsohn, P. M. (Eds.). (1985b). *Geropsychological assessment and treatment: Selected topics.* New York: Springer.

Thompson, L. W., & Gallagher, D. (1983). A psychoeducational approach for treatment of depression in elders. *Psychotherapy in Private Practice, 1,* 25–27.

Zeiss, A. M., & Lewinsohn, P. M. (1986). Adapting behavioral treatment for depression to meet the needs of the elderly. *The Clinical Psychologist, 39,* 98–100.

Zeiss, A. M., Lewinsohn, P. M., & Muñoz, R. (1979). Nonspecific improvement effects in depression using interpersonal skills training, pleasant activity schedules, or cognitive training. *Journal of Counseling and Clinical Psychology, 47,* 427–439.

THE LANGLEY PORTER PROJECTS

Mardi J. Horowitz

The major themes of my career in psychotherapy research involved choices of psychopathological phenomena, research methods, and arenas of theory. Training as a psychiatrist, psychoanalyst, and research scientist allowed me to take both qualitative and quantitative perspectives. I selected the phenomena of stress response syndromes (what later became known as

Post Traumatic Stress Disorder, or PTSD) because I came to psychotherapy research from clinical, field, and experimental work on the effects of stressful perceptions, especially in producing intrusive phenomena such as recurrent unbidden images (Horowitz, 1976, 1986). The research methods I chose were video recordings and nested research plans in which one could simultaneously plan a series of investigations of a clinical population using descriptive, correlative, and contrast group designs (Horowitz, 1982). The arenas of theory were (a) conscious representations as reflected in communicative structures, (b) unconscious processes that led to what was and was not expressed, and (c) processes of control over the emergence of ideas and emotions of importance to the self. Fortunately, these particular selections of phenomena, method, and theory area were well aligned, and a pathway of work emerged.

Where issues of consciousness and unconscious formative processes were concerned, I had an early disbelief in the importance of Occam's razor: The mind synthesizes many factors in producing its higher forms, so searching for single causes is misleading. I had selected to study every patient I could who experienced the phenomenon of recurrent unbidden images. I attempted to explain the repetition in content, the intrusive quality, and changes in the images over time by a multifactor theory. I found that one of the explanations manifest repeatedly in patient after patient was the previous occurrence of a traumatic event, its memory transformed in the unbidden images, so that the original perceptions were in sometimes more disguised and sometimes more direct form. There were, in the course of psychotherapy, periods of more intrusiveness and also more avoidance of recollections of such traumas as I worked with some of these patients.

I changed my focus from the symptom of recurrent unbidden images to the topic of how stressful life events were processed. I could see that this would be an exciting route into research on improved treatment; one could know with high validity the situation the person was in now because one knew what had recently happened. Out of the fantastic array of complex factors I found in my psychoanalytic patients, I could select in more focal psychotherapies the fact of an injury, death, loss, or frightening situation, and trace its association to other information structures and the set of ideas, emotions, memories, and fantasies processed over time.

With the encouragement of Robert Wallerstein, who became my department chairman, Nancy Kaltreider, and Nancy Wilner, I founded the Psychotherapy Evaluation and Study Center at the University of California at San Francisco. Our original goal was to integrate a research effort with a clinic. We also had a teaching mission, combining research with service skills in brief therapy. When we received two successive NIMH Clinical

Research Center Grants, we renamed the center, The Center for the Study of Neuroses. Many colleagues and trainees worked as a group in this context: Janice Krupnick, Charles Marmar, Daniel Weiss, Katheryn DeWitt, Alan Skolnikoff, Michael Windholz, Michael Hoyt, and Robert Rosenbaum.

The patients were persons with stress response syndromes. A battery of tests for dispositions, specific and general symptoms, functional capacities, psychotherapy process, and outcome evaluation was developed from the scales already formed. The strategy was to have few patients, study them carefully, and aim at long-range planning that would develop an archive of video-recorded and faculty-treated cases that could be used for descriptive, correlational, and standard contrast group or comparison designs.

We were able to define stress response syndromes in ways that helped lead to a new diagnosis of PTSD in *DSM-III*, provided useful measures to the field, explained the formation of intrusive and avoidant phases of response, and gave a rationale that yielded well-defined treatment approaches.

In exploring the descriptive paradigm for research on the psychotherapy of stress response syndromes, my colleagues and I went through many efforts to be systematic while accepting many points of view on how to explain even a singular phenomenon such as intrusive images of a long-past traumatic event. The war between brand names within psychoanalysis, within psychotherapies, and within the emerging field of cognitive psychology seemed hard to win because everyone—to oversimplify it—had a good point. Integration of psychotherapies seemed the way to go, and a synthetic, harmonizing effort to integrate cognitive and dynamic theory was made. This led to a systematic method for describing change called configurational analysis (Horowitz, 1979, 1987).

A key aspect of configurational analysis as a descriptive scientific technique was to group phenomena according to varied states of mind. A brief psychotherapy of a bereavement reaction was used as the means for presenting states of mind theory; we concretely linked states of mind to both transcribed text of psychotherapy sessions and nonverbal communications as observed in videotapes of those sessions.

As we demonstrated the efficacy of a brief therapy for stress response syndromes, it was encouraging to find that it could, as hoped, be used for other syndromes (Horowitz, Marmar, Weiss, Kaltreider, & Wilner, 1986), such as depressive ones. And our therapy had an advantage: The theory—and, so the technique—involved addressing issues of how the current life changes and stressful events were or were not integrated with the information structures that were inferred as part of the individual's preexisting personality configuration. Repertoires of self and other and of role–rela-

/tionship models, as well as habitual schemas for coping and defense, were aspects of theory developed and used in the context of this group's psychotherapy research. Use of such evolving person schemas theory culminated in the application of configurational analysis, by two independent teams, to cases with the same life event (e.g., death of a parent) but diverse personality styles (Horowitz, Marmar, Krupnick, et al., 1984).

Using a disposition-to-process-to-outcome correlational design and stepwise multiple regression statistics, we were then able to combine successive cohorts of patients in the Center archives in a major study using standard and new measures of each of three main sets of variables. The results suggested that process-to-outcome measures, even with new techniques, such as Therapist and Patient Action Scales and the evolution of existing ones, such as the California Therapeutic Alliance Scales (Marmar, Marziali, Horowitz, & Weiss, 1986), would lead to washed-out results if dispositions and cross-over effects were not taken into account (Horowitz, Marmar, Weiss et al., 1984). Important among the dispositional variables were self-organization and habitual control process issues.

Observation of phases of intrusive emotional outcry, denial, recurrent intrusion, working through and completion, and the techniques that facilitated phasic progression in stress response syndromes clarified how to characterize the states of mind in a person. Explaining each state in terms of basic schema of self and others, and state changes in terms of shifts in schema, led to a revised theory of defense and coping as applied to basic but high-level cognitive processes.

In order to get better theory and better variables to tackle psychotherapy research at a new level, we confronted the gap between psychodynamics and cognitive science. Work so far in intensive single-case studies of persons with pathological grief and social phobia, seen in recorded psychotherapy and concomitant research studies, has led to a new book, *Introduction to Psychodynamics: A New Synthesis* (Horowitz, 1988a), as well as edited volumes, *Psychodynamics and Cognition* (Horowitz, 1988b), and *Person Schemas and Maladaptive Behavioral Patterns* (Horowitz, 1991). These works emphasize repertoires in each person so that regulatory processes may affect the multiple self schema that may be a dominant organizer of a state of mind and those role relationship models might be inhibited or facilitated in activation as an organizer of interpersonal emotion and action.

REFERENCES

Horowitz, M. J. (1976) *Stress response syndromes*. New York: Aronson.
Horowitz, M. J. (1979). *States of mind: Configurational analysis of individual psychology*. New York: Plenum.

Horowitz, M. J. 1982. Presidential Address, Society for Psychotherapy Research: Strategic dilemmas and the socialization of psychotherapy researchers. *British Journal of Clinical Psychology, 21,* 119–127.

Horowitz, M. J. (1986). *Stress response syndromes* (2nd ed.). New York: Aronson.

Horowitz, M. J. (1987). *States of mind: Configurational analysis of individual psychology* (2nd ed.). New York: Plenum Press.

Horowitz, M. J. (1988a). *Introduction to psychodynamics: A new synthesis.* New York: Basic Books.

Horowitz, M. J. (Ed.). (1988b). *Psychodynamics and cognition.* Chicago: University of Chicago Press.

Horowitz, M. J. (Ed.). (1991). *Person schemas and maladaptive interpersonal patterns.* Chicago: University of Chicago Press.

Horowitz, M. J., Marmar, C., Krupnick, J., Wilner, N., Kaltreider, N., & Wallerstein, R. (1984). *Personality styles and brief psychotherapy.* New York: Basic Books.

Horowitz, M. J., Marmar, C., Weiss, D. S., DeWitt, K., & Rosenbaum, R. (1984). Brief psychotherapy of bereavement reactions: The relationship of process to outcome. *Archives of General Psychiatry, 41,* 438–448.

Horowitz, M. J., Marmar, C., Weiss, D., Kaltreider, N., & Wilner, N. (1986). Comprehensive analysis of change after brief dynamic psychotherapy. *American Journal of Psychiatry, 143,* 582–589.

Marmar, C. R., Marziali, E., Horowitz, M. J., & Weiss, D. S. (1986). The development of the therapeutic alliance rating system. In L. Greenberg & W. Pinsof (Eds.), *The psychotherapeutic process: A research handbook.* New York: Guilford Press.

THE TEMPLE PSYCHOTHERAPY PROJECT

R. Bruce Sloane and Fred R. Staples

In the middle 1960s, Temple University Medical School's psychiatry department was psychoanalytically oriented. Spurgeon English had been a most distinguished chairman for more than 30 years, and the majority of senior staff were analysts.

One of us, R. Bruce Sloane, had been trained at London's Maudsley Hospital, which had an eclectic view with a heavy biological orientation, probably much greater than the majority of American departments at that time. It also had Jungian, Kleinian, and Freudian senior staff members and a good number of eclectic psychotherapists. Experimental behavior therapies were carried out at the Maudsley by students of Eysenck. We had worked together in Canada on operant reinforcement in patients to test some of the introversion–extroversion theories of Eysenck; they did not work, at least in our hands.

Clinical behavior therapy was beginning to make its presence felt in the middle 1960s, and Joe Wolpe, who was then at the University of Virginia, joined the department at Temple. He in turn recruited Arnold Lazarus, and a behavioral therapy division of the department was set up at the Eastern Pennsylvania Psychiatric Institute (EPPI). There was an uneasy truce between the two camps, maintained in part by the few miles of separation between EPPI and the university hospital.

Some time later, Neil Yorkston arrived, fresh from the Maudsley as an extreme disciple of behavior therapy. Allan Cristol, a member of the faculty who had done his residency at Temple, constituted the fourth member of the research team, and Kay Whipple, from Stanford, who had an abiding interest in psychotherapy, completed our group as a research assistant. After obtaining a doctorate in clinical psychology, Kay trained as a Jungian analyst, perhaps rounding out our diverse views.

We decided to find out how the two therapies worked with the sort of patients who came to our outpatient clinic and were considered "suitable for psychotherapy." Immediately, we encountered the vanishing patients whom Koegler and Brill (1967) had described in their study. The outpatient department, of which Allan Cristol was a longtime member, was very cooperative. However, the faculty feared that we would steal the best patients for residency training and, moreover, plug up the clinic with our rejects when we had finished the study. We survived on both counts and without too many bruised feelings, except for a few remarks such as "psychotherapy cannot be studied" or "psychotherapy cannot be studied in this way" (Sloane, Staples, Cristol, Yorkston, & Whipple, 1975).

Some psychotherapists, as many have found, do not like being studied, and one in particular was forever forgetting to switch on the tape recorder for his sessions. However, they cooperated manfully—indeed, they were all men because we had no female behavior therapists, possibly due to the sexism of the 1960s. Although our therapists may have been buoyed by their expectation that their own modality would prove the better, they were wonderful and we remain eternally grateful to them.

As the study progressed, the department was awash with the ferments of the time, community psychiatry, the razing of the mental hospitals, and so on. Biological psychiatry arrived in the presence of Charlie Shagass. However, the residents retained a keen interest in psychotherapy.

Allan Cristol, Neil Yorkston, and one of the writers (Sloane) acted as the assessors. Cristol, by virtue of his residency at Temple, believed that the psychoanalytic approach would do better; Yorkston, although a disciple of behavior therapy, was sufficiently imbued by the nihilism of the Maudsley to be skeptical that either treatment would be very effective. In fact, he viewed neurosis as a spontaneously remitting condition. Sloane cannot really remember what he expected, but possibly gave the edge to behavior therapy as better adapted to brief therapy. Probably all therapists and as-sessors alike were surprised that the treatments seemed to work equally well and better than minimal therapy.

The most important outcome at that time was that behavior therapy was useful for a typical outpatient population of mixed neurotics rather than for those exhibiting specific syndromes such as phobias. It was possibly more flexible in dealing with a broader range of disorders, including acting-out patients, than was psychotherapy. Probably the most important finding was that *brief* treatment worked well and that its benefits were continued. However, economic issues have influenced the movement to shorter therapy far more than this or a multitude of better studies could have done.

Another important finding was the emphasis that successful patients in both therapies regarded the personal interaction with the therapist as the single most important part of their treatment. Although this was not unexpected in the psychotherapeutic treatment, it helped to remove the myth of the mechanical nature of behavior therapy.

It has indeed proven difficult over the years to tease out the individual properties of the therapist from the modality used. The psychotherapies have always been taught within an apprenticeship system. Most good ther-apists are good teachers, and the success of some methods has depended more on the ability of their mentors to proselytize them than the underlying theories or methods. Therapists are believers in therapy, and much of their efficacy depends on the transmittal of their belief systems. They usually do not believe in research and its results; and those who do believe in it, namely researchers, are not necessarily very good therapists.

REFERENCES

Koegler, R. R., & Brill, N. T. (1967). *Treatment of psychiatric outpatients.* New York: Appleton-Century-Crofts.

Sloane, R. B., Staples, F. R., Cristol, A. H., Yorkston, N. J., & Whipple, K. (1975). *Psychotherapy versus behavior therapy.* Cambridge, MA: Harvard Uni-versity Press.

THE DEVELOPMENT OF AN ANXIETY RESEARCH CLINIC

David H. Barlow

My career in psychotherapy research began at Boston College in 1964, where I obtained a master's degree in clinical psychology with Joseph Cautela. He introduced me to a radical new approach called behavior therapy. I became fascinated with the idea that people with seemingly intractable problems could be treated successfully in a relatively brief period of time. Cautela arranged for me to spend the summer of 1966 working with Joseph Wolpe, who was quickly becoming a focus of international attention.

In the doctoral program at the University of Vermont in the late 1960s, I came under the influence of two very different mentors—Stewart Agras, with a rich knowledge of psychopathology, and Harold Leitenberg, with his creative ideas on applying the methods of operant psychology to issues in psychotherapy. Over the next 3 years, we examined the process and outcome of behavior therapy procedures. Most of our strategies involved intensive experimental analyses of single cases (e.g., Agras, Leitenberg, & Barlow, 1968; Barlow, Leitenberg, & Agras, 1969). Our clinical research team would meet for nearly 2 hours every day to go over new data collected in our various projects. The flexibility of this single-case approach dictated that each day we consider whether it were an appropriate time to change therapeutic conditions. Usually this involved either withdrawing or introducing a new therapeutic component. It was this fine-grained examination of the process of behavior change and the influence of operationally defined therapeutic components that shaped my career in psychotherapy research and continues to influence me to this day.

After moving to Mississippi with Stewart Agras, we recruited a creative and energetic group of people including Ed Blanchard, Michel Hersen, Peter Miller, and Richard Eisler. (Barlow & Hersen, 1984; Hersen & Barlow, 1976). It was particularly exciting to focus on processes of individual change, manipulating such variables as expectancy, instructional set, and active therapeutic components in any given psychotherapeutic approach. It was gratifying to see these research procedures adopted in the context of a wide range of approaches to psychotherapy research in the ensuing years.

During a 5-year stay at Brown University, it became clear that clinical research, in particular psychotherapy research, was my first love. Realizing this, I took advantage of an excellent offer from the State University of New York at Albany to set up a research center devoted to this endeavor. In 1979, Ed Blanchard, one of my former colleagues from Mississippi, and I teamed up to create the Center for Stress and Anxiety Disorders.

The National Institute of Mental Health (NIMH) supports separate projects at the Center that investigate the nature and treatment of agoraphobia, the treatment of panic disorder, the cause of sexual dysfunction, and the classification of anxiety disorders. Another project is a new, large, multicenter collaborative study carried out in conjunction with the departments of psychiatry at Yale, Cornell, and Columbia. In this project we are investigating the separate and interactive effects of drugs with our newly developed psychological treatment for panic disorder.

The remaining projects in our clinic include a substantial project from a pharmaceutical company evaluating drugs and cognitive behavioral treatments for cases of mixed anxiety and depression; a grant from NIMH through the American Psychiatric Association to determine the feasibility of creating a new diagnostic category of mixed anxiety depression for *DSM-IV*; and a small grant from the National Alliance for Research in Schizophrenia and Depressive Disorders (NARSAD) to investigate certain aspects of the relationship between anxiety and depression.

We are able to see a wide range of patients in our Albany clinic and take responsibility for their care from admission to discharge. Physical exams are provided when necessary by staff physicians, and pharmacological agents are administered when this serves our more fundamental purpose of developing or testing new psychological treatments.

Perhaps the most visible contribution over the past several years has been the development of a new treatment for panic disorder (Barlow, Craske, Cerny, & Klosko, 1989; Klosko, Barlow, Tassinari, & Cerny, 1990). Coming on the heels of a well-publicized set of results suggesting the efficacy of pharmacological approaches for panic disorder (Ballenger et al., 1988), the development of an effective psychological treatment proved to be important. The timing was propitious because most mental health professionals, including many psychologists, were ready to accept the conclusion that panic disorder responded only to pharmacological approaches and should, without exception, be treated in that manner. The discovery that close to 90% of patients treated with our procedures were panic-free at the end of treatment provided the kind of sufficiently dramatic results that one seldom sees in psychotherapy research. Similar reports from other centers strengthened these conclusions (e.g., Beck, 1988; Clark, 1988). The further demonstration that these results were as good—or better— than the most popular pharmacological approach, alprazolam (Klosko et al., 1990), reinforced our efforts.

We have gone beyond the stage of simply testing techniques, and for several years now, we have been examining the role of the interpersonal context in treatment. This has occurred primarily in our project on treating agoraphobia. We include members of the family (particularly the spouse) directly in treatment and look at changes in the interpersonal system of the client in addition to changes in the specific symptoms of agoraphobia. Our finding that integrating the interpersonal system of the client into treatment in this way provides a superior outcome, particularly at follow-up (Cerny, Barlow, Craske, & Himadi, 1987), seems to portend further important developments.

Having realized a long-held hope of making some small contributions to the advancement of psychotherapy, I am looking forward to the next decade. As the importance of schools of psychotherapy diminishes and empiricism and science advance, greater knowledge should be gained more rapidly in the years ahead than in years past.

REFERENCES

Agras, W. S., Leitenberg, H., & Barlow, D. H. (1968). Social reinforcement in the modification of agoraphobia. *Archives of General Psychiatry, 19,* 423–427.

Ballenger, J. C., Burrows, G. D., DuPont, R. L., Lesser, I. M., Noyes, R., Pecknold, J. C., Rifkin, A., & Swinson, R. P. (1988). Alprazolam in panic disorder and agoraphobia: Results from a multicenter trial. I. Efficacy in short term treatment. *Archives of General Psychiatry, 45,* 423–428.

Barlow, D. H., Craske, M. G., Cerny, J. A., & Klosko, J. S. (1989). Behavioral treatment of panic disorder. *Behavior Therapy, 20,* 261–282.

Barlow, D. H., & Hersen, M. (1984). *Single case experimental designs: Strategies for studying behavior change* (2nd ed.). New York: Pergamon Press.

Barlow, D. H., Leitenberg, H., & Agras, W. S. (1969). Experimental control of sexual deviation through manipulation of the noxious scene in covert sensitization. *Journal of Abnormal Psychology, 74,* 596–601.

Beck, A. T. (1988). Cognitive approaches to panic disorder: Theory and therapy. In S. Rachman & J. D. Maser (Eds.), *Panic: Psychological perspectives.* Hillsdale, NJ: Erlbaum.

Cerny, J. A., Barlow, D. H., Craske, M. G., & Himadi, W. G. (1987). Couples treatment of agoraphobia: A two-year follow-up. *Behavior Therapy, 18,* 401–416.

Clark, D. M. (1988). A cognitive model of panic attacks. In S. Rachman & J. D. Maser (Eds.), *Panic: Psychological perspectives.* Hillsdale, NJ: Erlbaum.

Hersen, M., & Barlow, D. H. (1976). *Single case experimental designs: Strategies for studying behavior change.* New York: Pergamon Press.

Klosko, J. S., Barlow, D. H., Tassinari, R. B., & Cerny, J. A. (1990). A comparison of alprazolam and behavior therapy in the treatment of panic disorder. *Journal of Consulting and Clinical Psychology, 58,* 77–84.

THE MT. ZION PSYCHOTHERAPY RESEARCH GROUP

Harold Sampson and Joseph Weiss

The authors' research collaboration began in 1965, although in 1958, Weiss had begun to investigate, through close review of process notes of psychoanalyses, how patients make progress in treatment. He had observed that important changes may take place spontaneously, that is, without interpretations by the analyst. Patients may, without interpretation, change their behavior in significant ways, change their view of themselves and their world, acquire new insights, or recall significant but long-forgotten events. As the changes could not be explained by existing hypotheses, Weiss gradually developed new ones, based upon his observations. Because they had greater explanatory power, we decided to subject them, along with competing hypotheses, to rigorous empirical scrutiny.

According to Weiss, the infant and child are powerfully motivated to understand their world in order to adapt to it (Stern, 1985; Weiss, 1990). As part of their efforts at adaptation, children form beliefs about themselves and their world. Patients' problems stem, not from repressed wishes seeking gratification without regard to reality, as in Freud's early theory, but rather from certain painful (and usually unconscious) beliefs. These beliefs may be called pathogenic because they impair functioning. They do so by warning the person that if he or she pursues certain reasonable goals, the person will be endangered and will suffer from fear, anxiety, guilt, or shame. For example, a young woman may unconsciously believe that if she becomes independent of her parents, she will harm them by making them feel unneeded and excluded, and therefore will herself suffer from intolerable guilt if she moves toward independence.

Pathogenic beliefs are acquired by inference from experience, usually, but not necessarily, from childhood experience with family members. In a pathogenic belief, almost any goal or desirable psychic state (e.g., to feel happy or confident) may become linked to a dangerous consequence. Hence, pathogenic beliefs are highly individual and varied.

Psychotherapy patients are motivated unconsciously to disconfirm their pathogenic beliefs in an effort to overcome their problems. They devise plans, with the help of the therapist, to change these beliefs. For example, the woman mentioned earlier might test her pathogenic belief by behaving independently and observing whether the therapist appeared to be hurt by not being needed. If the therapist did not seem hurt by her independence, her belief would begin to be disconfirmed. Patients also work by using interpretations to gain greater understanding of their pathogenic beliefs, and to change them.

The authors shared an interest in both psychoanalysis and the conviction that empirical research was essential. Because we were under no external pressure to produce immediate results, we were able to proceed at our own pace in developing our research approach. We met for at least one regularly scheduled hour each work day beginning in 1966. Our discussions were initially freewheeling, concerned with philosophy of science, theory, clinical observations, and the state of the field. We concluded that significant advances could be made by testing broad hypotheses that purported to account for significant phenomena in our domain.

Testing Weiss's hypotheses against alternatives required several preliminary steps: clarifying the hypotheses, figuring out precisely what they asserted about nature, deducing specific empirical consequences of each, identifying situations in which alternative hypotheses predicted different clinical observations, selecting or developing reliable and valid measures, and finally, devising research designs with appropriate controls for sources of error (Sampson & Weiss, 1986; Weiss & Sampson, 1986b). Our extended discussion of these problems produced the intellectual "capital" to undertake formal research.

We began pilot studies in 1967, and 5 years later published our first research paper (Sampson, Weiss, Mlodnosky, & Hause, 1972). Having conceptualized a broad research program, we felt able to respond to the interest of some members of our local professional community and invited them to join with us in the proposed work. In this manner, the Mt. Zion Psychotherapy Research Group (MZPRG) was formed in 1972.

The group meets for 1 hour weekly. Members participate out of interest in the work. Because they support themselves by practice or other employment, they often have limited time for research. Nonetheless, a volunteer group has some compensating advantages: We are not entirely dependent on the vicissitudes of external support, there is no rivalry for funded positions, and we do not have the distractions of hirings, promotions, dismissals, and salary disputes. Our members are self-selected and they are free to determine the extent of their participation.

MZPRG members are heterogeneous in professional background, training, experience, and credentials. Diversity has proven intellectually stimulating, and it counteracts the limited perspective of each discipline. Participants generally earn their standing with fellow members through their actual contributions rather than on the basis of discipline, prior educational level, or amount of clinical or research training and experience.

The MZPRG initially carried out a series of closely related studies on a single case (Weiss, Sampson, & The Mt. Zion Psychotherapy Research Group, 1986). The case was an audio-recorded psychoanalysis of more than

5 years' duration, carried out in another city by an analyst unfamiliar with our work. Studies on this case took many years. Our unique commitment to long-term, intensive research on one case has been invaluable. It enabled us to develop and test new methods that have been applied successfully in later research to numerous other cases treated for varying lengths of time (including brief, time-limited psychotherapies) by many different therapists trained in varying theoretical orientations. Patients in these later studies have differed in presenting problems, in childhood histories, in age (including many elderly patients), and in social and cultural backgrounds. Our original findings from the intensive study of a single psychoanalysis have been strongly supported in these later studies.

In response to increased interest in our work, we have formed a second volunteer research group. The second group has enabled us to begin new research on the acquisition of insight and its relation to outcome. It has also provided us with an additional pool of readily available raters for studies.

Our findings support the idea that patients' behavior in therapy can be predicted more accurately from inferences about their conscious and unconscious goals, plans, beliefs, and anticipations than from inferences about their wishes and defenses (Broitman, 1985; Bush & Gassner, 1986; Silberschatz, 1986; Silberschatz, Fretter, & Curtis, 1986). These findings support Weiss's theory of mental functioning, psychopathology, and therapy (Weiss & Sampson, 1986a).

Our findings also support the idea that patients make progress in therapy when it is safe to do so (Gassner, Sampson, Weiss, & Brumer, 1982). These results support Weiss's hypotheses about unconscious control and his concept of pathogenic belief.

Furthermore, the results from our study demonstrate that patients react differently to interpretations that are compatible with their plans for disconfirming pathogenic beliefs (plan-compatible interpretations) than to interpretations that are incompatible with their plans. Plan-compatible interpretations tend to lead to immediate patient progress; plan-incompatible interpretations do not (Broitman, 1985; Bush & Gassner, 1985; Fretter, 1984; Silberschatz, Fretter, & Curtis, 1986). In addition, studies suggest that the degree to which a therapist's interpretations are plan-compatible over the course of therapy is positively associated with favorable treatment outcome (Fretter, 1984; Norville, 1989; Silberschatz, Fretter, & Curtis, 1986).

Thus, our findings indicate that what the therapist says—the *content* of interpretations—is related to immediate patient progress and may determine outcome. This further supports Weiss's concept of pathogenic beliefs, as well as the hypothesis that patients' plans guide their behavior in treatment. These results also indicate that interpretations do not work primarily by providing patients any coherent framework or narrative for understanding themselves, for only interpretive frameworks compatible with patients' plans are helpful. Moreover, progress cannot be explained only in terms of generic features of the therapist–patient relationship, for the specific content of interpretations is critical to whether or not the patient makes progress.

Although our findings show the importance of a certain kind of interpretation for patient progress, they also demonstrate that patients sometimes make significant progress *without any interpretation*. Patients may do so by testing pathogenic beliefs with the therapist and monitoring their responses. If the therapist's response (which may include silence, or verbal interventions other than interpretations) disconfirms the pathogenic belief, patients make immediate progress. They becomes less anxious, more productive, and more favorably disposed towards the therapy and the therapist (Silberschatz, 1986; Silberschatz, Curtis, Sampson, & Weiss, 1991).

REFERENCES

Broitman, J. (1985). Insight, the mind's eye: An exploration of three patients' processes of becoming insightful (Doctoral dissertation, Wright Institute, 1985) *Dissertation Abstracts International, 46*, 2797-B. (University Microfilms No. 85-20425)

Bush, M., & Gassner, S. (1986). The immediate effect of the analyst's termination interventions on the patient's resistance to termination. In *The psychoanalytic process: Theory, clinical observations, and empirical research* (pp. 299–320). New York: Guilford Press.

Fretter, P. (1984). The immediate effects of transference interpretations on patients' progress in brief, psychodynamic psychotherapy. (Doctoral dissertation, University of San Francisco, 1985) *Dissertation Abstracts International, 46*, 1519-A. (University Microfilms No. 85–12112)

Gassner, S., Sampson, H., Weiss, J., & Brumer, S. (1982). The emergence of warded-off contents. *Psychoanalysis and Contemporary Thought, 5*, 55–75.

Norville, R. (1989). *Plan compatibility of interpretations and brief psychotherapy outcome*. Unpublished doctoral dissertation, Pacific Graduate School of Psychology, Palo Alto, CA.

Sampson, H., & Weiss, J. (1986). Testing hypotheses: The approach of the Mt. Zion Psychotherapy Research Group. In L. Greenberg & W. Pinsof (Eds.), *The psychotherapeutic process: A research handbook* (pp. 591–613). New York: Guilford Press.

Sampson, H., Weiss, J., Mlodnosky, L., & Hause, E. (1972). Defense analysis and the emergence of warded-off mental contents: An empirical study. *Archives of General Psychiatry, 26,* 524–532.

Silberschatz, G. (1986). Testing pathogenic beliefs. In *The psychoanalytic process: Theory, clinical observations, and empirical research* (pp. 256–266). New York: Guilford Press.

Silberschatz, G., Curtis, J. T., Sampson, H., & Weiss, J. (1991). Research on the process of change in psychotherapy: The approach of the Mount Zion Psychotherapy Research Group. In L. Beutler & M. Crago (Eds.), *International psychotherapy research programs.* Washington, DC: American Psychological Association.

Silberschatz, G., Fretter, P., & Curtis, J. (1986). How do interpretations influence the process of psychotherapy? *Journal of Consulting and Clinical Psychology, 54,* 646–652.

Stern, D. N. (1985). *The interpersonal world of the infant.* New York: Basic Books.

Weiss, J. (1990). The centrality of adaptation. *Contemporary Psychoanalysis, 26,* 660–676.

Weiss, J., & Sampson, H. (1986a). *The psychoanalytic process: Theory, clinical observations, and empirical research.* New York: Guilford Press.

Weiss, J., & Sampson, H. (1986b). Testing alternative psychoanalytic explanations of the therapeutic process. In J. M. Masling (Ed.), *Empirical studies of psychoanalytic theories* (Vol. II; pp. 1–26). Hillsdale, NJ: Lawrence Erlbaum Associates.

Weiss, J., Sampson, H., & The Mount Zion Psychotherapy Research Group. (1986). *The psychoanalytic process: Theory, clinical observations, and empirical research.* New York: Guilford Press.

THE VANDERBILT CENTER FOR PSYCHOTHERAPY RESEARCH

William P. Henry and Hans H. Strupp

In 1953, when I, Hans Strupp, began to do psychotherapy research, that area of investigation was in its infancy. Furthermore, psychotherapy was considered largely a medical specialty, its practice being the proper province of psychiatrists and medically trained psychoanalysts. Psychologists who showed an interest in research and practice (notably the latter) were eyed with suspicion by medical colleagues and viewed as potential disturbers of the "peace." Counseling was seen as a more appropriate field for psychologists. Following Freud, whose work has had a profound influence in my life, I have always believed that the psychological forces in psychoanalysis, psychotherapy, and counseling are on a continuum and not categorically different from each other.

I had come to the United States as a refugee from Nazi Germany in

1939 and advanced my education through part-time study at the College of the City of New York and later at George Washington University, while earning a living as a bookkeeper and accountant (Strupp, 1990). Since formal psychoanalytic training was not available to psychologists at the "official" institutes, I entered the training program of the Washington School of Psychiatry, the creation of Harry Stack Sullivan, whose work had also begun to fascinate me (I graduated in 1952). From the beginning—and for personal reasons—I wanted to learn more about the person and the activities of the psychotherapist. I also sensed early that therapeutic techniques and the person of the psychotherapist are throroughly intertwined. With the support of my mentors at George Washington University (Curtis Tuthill, Thelma Hunt, and E. Lakin Phillips), I completed a dissertation (in 1954) involving an experimental study of the relationships between therapists' techniques, their theoretical orientation, professional affiliation, and other biographical variables. In this and subsequent studies (Strupp, 1960, p. 352) I adduced evidence that negative attitudes toward a patient tended to be associated with unempathic therapist communications and unfavorable clinical judgments, whereas the opposite was true of respondents who felt more positively toward the patient. I considered this a serendipitous finding whose implications for research, training, and practice I have been trying to explore ever since.

My academic career was launched with the award of an NIMH grant in 1955. I had reason to believe I owed the grant to Jerome D. Frank, whom I came to admire greatly as a person and as a scientist. I emerged from professional isolation in 1957, when I accepted a faculty position at the Medical School of the University of North Carolina in Chapel Hill. I soon acquired some outstanding graduate students who became valuable collaborators. In 1966, I moved to the Department of Psychology at Vanderbilt University, where I was again blessed with a number of superb graduate students and postdoctoral fellows whose contributions are reflected in jointly authored articles and books. William P. Henry, in particular, has become a valuable collaborator.

The emphasis on analyzing salient aspects of the therapist's behavior and its consequences on the development of the therapeutic relationship as well as its outcome led to a project dealing with patients' retrospective accounts of their therapy experience (Strupp, Fox, & Lessler, 1969, p. 220). Results showed that patients' positive attitudes toward the therapist were closely associated with success in therapy, irrespective of how success was measured. Successful patients described their therapists as warm, attentive, interested, understanding, and respectful. They also perceived the therapist as experienced and active in the therapeutic situation. In short, the composite picture of the "good" therapist drawn by our respondents was more "human" in contrast to the stereotype of the impersonal, detached analyst.

The Vanderbilt Center for Psychology Research came into being in the early 1970s. The overall aim of our program has been to investigate the therapeutic process in dynamic/interpersonal psychotherapy as it relates to differential therapeutic outcome.

A number of interrelated subareas of investigation have followed from this basic emphasis on therapeutic process:

1. *Process–outcome links.* Our chief thrust has been to focus on the quality and determinants of the therapeutic relationship and the manner in which this relationship relates to other aspects of process, techniques, and outcome. In attempting to measure the nature of the alliance, we have moved progressively from scales designed to tap the general affective and attitudinal climate of the participants to a more highly structured examination of moment-by-moment interpersonal dyadic process using Benjamin's (1974) Structural Analysis of Social Behavior (SASB).

2. *Therapist variables.* On the basis of our central belief in the importance of the person of the therapist, we have been carrying out studies attempting to relate therapist personal characteristics to therapeutic process and outcome. In particular, we have focused on the interpersonal patterns in the therapists' own families of origin as reflected in the structure of the therapists' introject and in instances of problematic interpersonal process engaged in by these therapists.

3. *Outcome measurement.* In order to render process research more intelligible, we have come to believe that the principle of Problem–Treatment–Outcome (PTO) congruence should be followed where possible (Strupp, Schacht, & Henry, 1988). In other words, the conceptualization and measurement of a patient's presenting problem, the therapeutic interventions, and resultant change should all be placed in a common metric. Thus, we have begun to develop intrapsychic and interpersonal outcome measures based on the same measurement system (SASB) that is used to chart the patient's initial interpersonal patterns and the interpersonal process occurring in therapy.

4. *Effects of training.* A recurrent observation made in our research has been that even well-trained, experienced therapists often have difficulty managing the therapeutic relationship with difficult patients. We thus initiated a major

study designed to explore the extent to which this problem might be ameliorated by specialized training. Our analyses of the complex effects (both positive and negative) of this training have led us to the development of measures designed to operationalize therapist competence in a manner that transcends simple technical adherence to a manualized treatment protocol. We are also exploring the effects of training procedures on the manner in which novices to a given approach acquire and initially implement complex skills.

5. *Research ecology.* An area of particular concern in psychotherapy research is the potential extent to which the phenomena studied are altered by, and interact with, the research procedures designed to study them. In our most recent project, we conducted extensive post-therapy interviews with patients in an attempt to better understand such variables as the extent to which patients felt obligated to stay in therapy or report favorable outcomes because they were involved in a research project, the effect of videotaped sessions on therapeutic process, and the potential positive or negative effects of extensive assessment batteries.

6. *Training technology.* We have come to believe that the development of improved training methods based on empirical process research and on our previous experience in training therapists in Time-Limited Dynamic Psychotherapy (TLDP) is the logical next step in bridging the gap between clinical research and clinical practice. We are attempting to extract relevant principles from cognitive and educational research that address the acquisition of complex skills.

Two main process-rating instruments designed for use by independent raters have been developed. The Vanderbilt Psychotherapy Process Scale (VPPS) was developed as a general-purpose instrument for assessing patient and therapist attitudes and behaviors that capture the salient features of their interaction. Second, The Vanderbilt Negative Therapist Indicator Scale (VNIS), a scale structurally and procedurally similar to the VPPS, was developed on the assumption that the presence of an appreciable number of negative indicators in early therapy sessions will be predictive of poor therapeutic outcome (Suh, O'Malley, & Strupp, 1986). One VNIS subscale, Errors in Technique (failure to focus the sessions, failure to address resistance, failure to examine the patient–therapist interaction, etc.), has proven particularly useful. More recently, we have developed instruments to measure therapist adherence to specific TLDP technical dictates.

Collaboration with Allen E. Bergin over a period of several years was designed to explore the feasibility of large-scale studies in psychotherapy (Bergin & Strupp, 1972). This work eventually led to the design of the Vanderbilt I study, which investigated the incremental effectiveness of professional training on process and outcome by attempting to separate specific and nonspecific factors. We contrasted a group of neurotic patients (MMPI peaks on Scales 2–7–0) treated by college professors who were selected for their understanding and warmth (thought to represent the nonspecific factors common to all psychotherapies), with a comparable group of patients treated by experienced professional therapists (who were thought to contribute additional or specific technical factors). Both treated groups had outcomes superior to untreated controls, but our original group analyses did not demonstrate statistical superiority in outcomes for the professional therapists.

The absence of the predicted group difference was a highly provocative finding that required further explanation. Intensive process studies were conducted to shed light on the factors differentiating successful from unsuccessful outcomes (Gomes-Schwartz, 1978; Hartley & Strupp, 1983; Sachs, 1983; Strupp 1980a, 1980b, 1980c, 1980d).

Another topic addressed by members of the Vanderbilt research team in the 1970s was the problem of negative effects in psychotherapy (Strupp, Hadley, & Gomes-Schwartz, 1977).

Following completion of the Vanderbilt I study, we developed and tested a manual for time-limited dynamic psychotherapy (Strupp & Binder, 1984), which was used in our next study. The Vanderbilt II investigation was designed to focus on the manner in which specialized training might improve the quality of the patient–therapist relationship and the therapeutic process. The research plan required 16 experienced therapists (clinical psychologists and psychiatrists) to treat two patients before and two patients after training in TLDP (during which time they saw an additional training case).

It became clear that manualized training involves potentially positive and negative effects and that it does not lead to a straight-line function between technical adherence and outcome. The training program was successful in teaching our manualized form of therapy (TLDP) to independently judged technical adherence criteria. Although a number of positive benefits seem to have accrued as the result of specific training, we continue to confront an observation of major importance that may be described as the central theme of the Vanderbilt group, namely, the pronounced inability of therapists to avoid countertherapeutic processes with difficult patients.

Our recent experience in training therapists has driven home the discrepancy between therapists' conceptual knowledge of therapeutic principles and procedures on the one hand, and their ability to translate that knowledge into consistently skillful performance (that transcends technical adherence per se). We consider it essential to develop training programs that are aimed at imparting fundamental interpersonal skills as a point of departure for other forms of training. At the heart of this training will be efforts to increase trainees' abilities to perceive and act upon the nuances of interpersonal in-session transactions as they occur. By developing new instructional approaches, we hope to narrow the gap between basic psychotherapy research and its application to clinical practice and training.

REFERENCES

Benjamin, L. S. (1974). Structural analysis of social behavior. *Psychological Review*, *81*, 392–425.

Bergin, A. E., & Strupp, H. H. (1972). *Changing frontiers in the science of psychotherapy*. Chicago: Aldine-Atherton.

Gomes-Schwartz, B. (1978). Effective ingredients in psychotherapies: Prediction of outcome from process variables. *Journal of Consulting and Clinical Psychology*, *46*, 1023–1035.

Hartley, D. E., & Strupp, H. H. (1983). The therapeutic alliance: Its relationship to outcome in brief psychotherapy. In. J. Masling (Ed.), *Empirical studies of psychoanalytical theories* (Vol. 1; pp. 1–38). Hillsdale, NJ: The Analytic Press.

Sachs, J. S. (1983). Negative factors in brief psychotherapy: An empirical assessment. *Journal of Consulting and Clinical Psychology*, *51*, 557–564.

Strupp, H. H. (1960). *Psychotherapists in action: Explorations of the therapist's contribution to the treatment process*. New York: Grune & Stratton.

Strupp, H. H. (1980a). Success and failure in time-limited psychotherapy: A systematic comparison of two cases. *Archives of General Psychiatry*, *37*, 395–603.

Strupp, H. H. (1980b). Success and failure in time-limited psychotherapy: A systematic comparison of two cases. *Archives of General Psychiatry*, *37*, 708–716.

Strupp, H. H. (1980c). Success and failure in time-limited psychotherapy: With special reference to the performance of a lay counselor. *Archives of General Psychiatry*, *37*, 831–841.

Strupp, H. H. (1980d). Success and failure in time-limited psychotherapy: Further evidence. *Archives of General Psychiatry*, *37*, 947–954.

Strupp, H. H. (1990). Reflections on my career in clinical psychology. In C. E. Walker (Ed.), *The history of clinical psychology in autobiography* (pp. 293–329). Pacific Grove, CA: Brooks/Cole.

Strupp, H. H., & Binder, J. L. (1984). *Psychotherapy in a new key: A guide to time-limited dynamic psychotherapy*. New York: Basic Books.

Strupp, H. H., Fox, R. E., & Lessler, K. (1969). *Patients view their psychotherapy*. Baltimore, MD: Johns Hopkins Press.

Strupp, H. H., Hadley, S. W., & Gomes-Schwartz, B. (1977). *Psychotherapy for better or worse: An analysis of the problem of negative effects*. New York: Jason Aronson.

Strupp, H. H., Schacht, T. E., & Henry, W. P. (1988). Problem–Treatment–Outcome Congruence: A principle whose time has come. In H. Dahl, H. Kachele, & H. Thoma (Eds.), *Psychoanalytic process research strategies* (pp. 1–14). New York: Springer-Verlag.

Suh, C. S., O'Malley, S. S., & Strupp, H. H. (1986). The Vanderbilt Process Measures: The Vanderbilt Psychotherapy Process Scale (VPPS) and the Negative Indicators Scale (VNIS). In L. S. Greenberg & W. M. Pinsof (Eds.), *The psychotherapeutic process: A research handbook* (pp. 285–324). New York: Guilford Press.

THE NIMH TREATMENT OF DEPRESSION COLLABORATIVE RESEARCH PROGRAM

Morris B. Parloff and Irene Elkin

Over the life span (1977–1990) of the NIMH Treatment of Depression Collaborative Research Program (TDCRP) (Elkin, Parloff, Hadley, & Autry, 1985), we developed many devices for coping with the inevitable but nonetheless distressing moments when collaboration went temporarily askew. One of our favorite mechanisms was to fantasize that someday we would reveal that despite sullen mutterings to the contrary, our administrative and technical decisions had been unerringly correct and inspired exclusively by our selfless dedication to the truth. In addition we would finally divulge the unmitigated truth about the origins and purposes of the project. We were, therefore, enormously pleased to receive the editors' invitation to reveal "the kinds of things not usually included in research reports, for example, difficulties you had to overcome. . . ."

In the preparation of these notes, we rediscovered why such reports are rarely published. Once the small difficulties and contretemps have been resolved, they tend to fade not only in importance but from memory. There is much to be said for the smoothed curve. However, with regard to identifying the important secrets of this project, we were startled to learn from the imaginative reporting by the media and the creative discussions at professional meetings that perhaps the biggest secret remains the precise and limited purposes of the NIMH TDCRP.

We wish now to clarify the study's goals not only by indicating what we intended but by correcting some misconstruals of our aims. We are aware that such a retrospective account may inadvertently be the beneficiary of our increasingly user-friendly memories. However, the reader may be comforted by the knowledge that the reaches of our fancy have been constrained by the public record.

During the course of the study, it became apparent that the authors gave different emphases to the various scientific, economic, cultural, and administrative influences that affected the development of the NIMH TDCRP. However, we are in full agreement that the project may best be viewed as the result of two sets of forces acting upon us: (a) institutional pressures to answer pragmatic Treatment/Assessment/Research questions posed by Congress, health care agencies, third-party payers, practitioners, the public, and so forth and (b) the repeated expression by psychotherapy researchers of the need for developing a cumulative base of knowledge regarding the effectiveness of different forms of therapy, in order to enhance the usefulness of psychotherapy in the treatment of specified problems and of patients. In addition, the researchers showed an increased interest in studying change processes in order to better understand how therapeutic changes are effected.

The authors' joint interest in furthering the scientific development of the field of psychotherapy dates back to 1959, when they met in the NIMH Intramural Psychology Laboratory. Irene Elkin was then a postdoctoral research fellow (sponsored by David Shakow, Laboratory chief), and Morris Parloff was chief of the Laboratory's Section on Personality. Over the intervening years, while maintaining a primary interest in psychotherapy, we each took excursions into other fields of study. Elkin investigated the psychological effects of "mind-altering" drugs, while Parloff studied the personality characteristics of creative individuals.

We were reunited in 1972 when Parloff became chief of a section of which Elkin was already a member: the Psychotherapy and Behavioral Intervention Section, Division of Extramural Research Programs, NIMH. Among the publications produced by our collaboration were a volume on psychotherapy change measures (Waskow & Parloff, 1975) and a review of therapist variables (Parloff, Waskow, & Wolfe, 1978). Over the course of our long association, we shared various notions and fantasies of what might constitute an ideal psychotherapy research study. Certainly this may have influenced our subsequent willingness to undertake a somewhat less grandiose version of some of our earlier visions.

In attempting to reconstruct the origins of this study, we realized that Parloff had always given more weight to the overt institutional demands, and Elkin had attended more to the inferred needs of investigators. These differences we now attribute in large part to the fact that we each played quite different administrative roles prior to and during the life of the NIMH TDCRP. Parloff, for example, had a more direct role in negotiating with the Alcohol, Drug Abuse, and Mental Health Administration (ADAMHA) and NIMH the scope and limits of the proposed large-scale clinical trials study. Elkin had more direct communication with leaders in the psychotherapy research field in regard to the value and feasibility of conducting such a study.

As NIMH psychotherapy research administrators (Extramural Research Programs), our primary responsibilities were to the investigators in that field and to the NIMH director and administrator, ADAMHA. With regard to researchers, our shared task included identifying the current needs and the most promising directions for the field of psychotherapy research and supporting investigations that gave promise of working toward those goals. Thus, we were called upon to serve both the pragmatic interests of the federal establishment, which included consumers, and the basic research interests of the academic community.

We differed, however, in the nature and degree of our direct responsibility to the agency leadership. Parloff, initially as chief of the Psychotherapy and Behavioral Intervention Section, Clinical Research Branch, and later as chief of the Psychosocial Treatments Research Branch, was responsible for responding to and (if possible) anticipating queries regarding psychotherapy addressed to the NIMH Director and the ADAMHA administrator by Congress, other federal and state agencies, and third-party payers.

Prior to Elkin's appointment in March 1978 to the position of coordinator, NIMH Treatment of Depression Collaborative Research Program, she had been spared the brunt of such responsibilities. From June 1969 to September 1977 she had been on part-time status as a member of the Psychotherapy and Behavioral Intervention Section and was involved mainly in administering research grant programs and facilitating the conduct of research in the field.

Until the mid-1970s, our different responsibilities to the agency and to the field investigators were easily reconciled because the concerns of NIMH appeared to be isomorphic with those of the academician-researcher.

Turning to the roles that each of us played with regard to TDCRP, Parloff was directly associated with the project from 1977 to 1983. In 1983, he retired from NIMH but continued a relationship as a special consultant to the TDCRP staff and as a member of the advisory group. In short, his hands-on involvement was limited to the planning stage, the pilot study, and the initial phases of the main study. Elkin held the post of coordinator, NIMH Treatment of Depression Collaborative Research Program, through 1990—that is, throughout its life.

We wish now to review the goals of the TDCRP. Within the overarching aim of advancing the scientific study of psychotherapy, our two major purposes were (a) to test the feasibility and applicability of the collaborative clinical trials method to psychotherapy outcome research and (b) to study the effectiveness of two specific forms of psychotherapy (thereby also testing the specificity–nonspecificity hypothesis).

The study was also designed to permit a subsequent third investigation: to study the processes of therapeutic change. This goal was deferred pending completion of the basic study.

The possibility of conducting collaborative psychotherapy outcome studies, similar to those carried out in the field of psychopharmacology, had been raised repeatedly over the years by psychotherapy researchers themselves. It was hoped that such research might accelerate the accumulation of definitive findings regarding the effectiveness of various forms of psychotherapy. The need for the NIMH to demonstrate that large collaborative studies were possible in this field was evident by virtue of the fact that independent investigators had previously been hesitant to initiate such extensive and expensive studies.

Earlier, Bergin and Strupp had been invited to explore this issue on behalf of the NIMH. During the late 1960s, they surveyed the literature and interviewed a sample of 35 eminent researchers in the field. They concluded that the feasibility and necessary enthusiasm for such a collaborative venture did not exist (Bergin & Strupp, 1972). By 1977, on the basis of our informal reconnaissance of the attitudes of prominent psychotherapy researchers, we concluded that the time of mounting a well-designed and well-funded collaborative study was now more propitious. Our judgment was further buttressed by our awareness that the steady reduction of NIMH research support funds had had a chilling impact upon independent investigators. Even high-quality psychotherapy research, small in scale and usually unreplicated, could not provide the answers to the kinds of questions that were now of primary interest to some investigators, many federal agencies, and all of Congress. The initiation and funding of the NIMH TDCRP was strongly prodded by Congressional and administrative interests.

We intended that the NIMH-initiated collaborative study would provide a model of a research effort directed at answering some high-priority applied psychotherapy research questions. The study would also test the application of the collaborative clinical trials approach.

One of the primary, although perhaps not explicitly stated, aims of the TDCRP was to encourage independent investigators to undertake similar cooperative programmatic studies by demonstrating their feasibility and appropriateness. We recognized that demonstrating that the NIMH staff, with its vast institutional resources, had found the model feasible, might not automatically assure independent investigators that they too would find this model workable. Such reassurance could best be given by the relevant collaborating investigators.

When ADAMHA and NIMH assumed a more prominent role as third-party mediators between mental health care suppliers and consumers, they also assumed a greater responsibility for responding to congressional concerns regarding the mounting expenditures for mental health care, especially via Medicare and Medicaid. Congress became intensely preoccupied with the fear that the costs for such care might become prohibitive. This dread remains.

Reflecting part of this concern the ADAMHA was expected to take on greater responsibilities for assuring the quality of the mental health care being offered to the public. It was proposed that psychotherapy document its efficacy, safety, and cost-effectiveness with experimental research evidence that met rigorous scientific standards.

A clear example of an effort of congressional staff to exert pressure on the ADAMHA and NIMH to undertake scientific tests of the psychotherapies is found in the exchange of correspondence between Jay Constantine, chief, Health Professional Staff Committee on Finance, U.S. Senate, and Gerald Klerman, the ADAMHA administrator. Constantine wrote:

> Based upon evaluations of the literature and testimony it appears clear to us that there are virtually no controlled clinical studies, conducted and evaluated in accordance with generally accepted scientific principles, which confirm the efficacy, safety and appropriateness of psychotherapy as it is conducted today.
>
> Our concern is that, without validation of psychotherapy and its manifest forms and methods, and in view of the almost infinite demand (self-induced and practitioner-induced) which might result, we could be confronted with tremendous costs, confusion and inappropriate care. (Nov. 15, 1979)

Klerman's response, in part, was:

> On the whole I agree with your general approach which is to affirm the basic principle that federal funds be used to reimburse those treatments which are demonstrated safe and effective by scientific methods. (Feb. 27, 1980)

The fact that the TDCRP used a clinical trials design was frankly upsetting to many dynamically oriented psychotherapy clinicians. Since that design was more commonly associated with drug efficacy investigations, such clinicians feared that its application to a psychotherapy study might be quite inappropriate: For example, treatment would focus on symptoms rather than causes and would be delivered in standardized fashion rather than flexibly adapted to meet the individual needs of the patient.

Although we believe that the study has demonstrated that these concerns were exaggerated, we must acknowledge one unintended and possibly untoward consequence. NIMH review committees have tended to adopt elements of the TDCRP's meticulous design as a standard for assessment studies, to the discomfiture of some grant applicants. This is particularly true with regard to requiring the replicability of treatment conditions, the manualization of treatment, the training of therapists to predetermined standards of mastery, and the monitoring of the application of the treatment.

The question of the relative efficacy of the particular therapies selected—Interpersonal Therapy (IPT) and Cognitive Behavior Therapy (CBT)—with the particular clinical problem treated, Major Depressive Disorder, although potentially of great clinical importance, was viewed by us as secondary to the more fundamental research questions raised here.

In selecting the particular therapies, we sought the advice of experts regarding psychotherapies that were ready for clinical trials study—that is, were sufficiently standardized (manualized) and had demonstrated in prior small-scale studies an encouraging degree of efficacy in the treatment of outpatient depression. The focus on the area of depression was influenced both by the work then being carried out in the Psychobiology of Depression Collaborative Research Program and by the development of promising new brief psychotherapies for treating outpatient depression.

The therapy nominees that best approximated our criteria were CBT and IPT. Although the two therapies reflected major conceptual differences in the field, they could not be equated with the more established forms of psychotherapy. Thus, generalizations could not easily be made to the more usual psychotherapies provided to depressed patients. At the time that this investigation was planned (1977), IPT and CBT were little known and represented only a small fraction of clinical practice.

One of the reasons we were particularly pleased to accept IPT and CBT into study was a clear opportunity to test the specificity–nonspecificity hypothesis, which had been of intense interest to the field.

We are well aware of the many criticisms that have subsequently been leveled against the hypothesis and those who would explore it. We shall deny ourselves the opportunity to explicate our current enlightened position, which reflects not only our own further musings but the subtle and sophisticated contributions of our colleagues over the intervening years.

Our original interest in the specificity–nonspecificity controversy was stimulated by the failure of a considerable body of research to detect statistically significant differences between the changes found in comparable patients who were treated by quite different forms of psychotherapy. The specificity hypothesis would lead one to expect that specific benefits are associated with the application of specific strategies, procedures, techniques, and experiences.

The failure to find empirical support for such expectations provoked the formulation of the nonspecificity or common factors hypothesis (Frank, 1973). It proposes that all therapies are effective, and comparably effective, because they all wittingly or unwittingly share the same therapeutic elements. These elements are particularly useful in the treatment of a universal problem associated with all psychological problems or disorders, namely, demoralization.

Abandoning the specificity hypothesis and accepting the nonspecificity hypothesis on the basis of no difference findings would carry serious implications for the field. In addition to casting doubt on the value of current psychotherapy training, the findings regarding the nonspecificity hypothesis—as interpreted by many laymen—cast doubt on the credibility of the entire field. The concept of nonspecificity has been broadly interpreted as including everything that is not encompassed in the construct of specificity. It has been used to refer to placebo and to common elements such as the therapeutic alliance, suggestion, attention, and hope.

The reported no-difference findings may, of course, be correct, but they may also be due to limitations of the research that preclude the detection of any real differences. Thus, we sought in the TDCRP to test the specificity hypothesis more rigorously than had ever been attempted previously.

We did not, however, seek to establish an FDA-type of mechanism for psychotherapy assessment, nor was it ever part of anyone's plan for the extramural NIMH to serve as an in-house psychotherapy assessment program to determine which therapies were efficacious and therefore worthy of third-party reimbursement (Parloff, 1980, 1982).

We also did not seek to conduct a competition between psychotherapy and antidepressant drug therapy. Our intent was to compare the relative efficacy of two quite different forms of psychotherapy in the treatment of comparable patients. We wished in particular to assess their mode-specific functioning and the differential role of various patient and therapist factors in bringing about improvement.

In the absence of a suitable psychotherapy standard reference condition, it became necessary to include in the study a standard reference treatment condition drawn from pharmacotherapy. The particular drug condition for which the most definitive efficacy data existed at the time the study was designed was imipramine hydrochloride.

That the emphasis of this study was on psychotherapy is implicit in the original title of the program, Psychotherapy of Depression Collaborative Research Program. It became necessary to remove the word psychotherapy from the title of the study because it confused study patients receiving only medication to learn from the labels on their pill bottles that they were in a psychotherapy study.

Finally, we conclude that the TDCRP has effectively accomplished its stated aims. This will be documented by its publications and by its continuing contributions to the resolution of methodological, technical, and even some political issues that inhere in the conduct of collaborative studies.

REFERENCES

Bergin, A. E., & Strupp, H. H. (1972). *Changing frontiers in the science of psychotherapy.* Chicago: Aldine-Atherton.

Elkin, I. E., Parloff, M. B., Hadley, S. W., & Autry, J. H. (1985). NIMH Treatment of depression collaborative research program: Background and research plan. *Archives of General Psychiatry, 42,* 305–316.

Frank, J. (1973). *Persuasion and healing* (rev. ed.). Baltimore: John Hopkins University Press.

Parloff, M. B. (1980). Psychotherapy and research: An anaclytic depression. *Psychiatry, 43,* 279–293.

Parloff, M. B. (1982). Psychotherapy evidence and reimbursement decisions: Bambi meets Godzilla. *American Journal of Psychiatry, 139,* 718–729.

Parloff, M. B., Waskow, I. E., & Wolfe, B. E. (1978). Research on therapist variables in relation to process and outcome. In S. L. Garfield & A. E. Bergin (Eds.), *Handbook of psychotherapy and behavior change: An empirical analysis* (2nd ed.; pp. 233–282). New York: John Wiley.

Waskow, I. E., & Parloff, M. B. (Eds.). (1975) *Psychotherapy change measures: Report of the Clinical Research Branch Outcome Measures Project.* Washington, DC: U.S. Government Printing Office.

IV

THE PRACTICE OF PSYCHOTHERAPY

OVERVIEW

THE PRACTICE OF PSYCHOTHERAPY

HERBERT J. FREUDENBERGER AND DONALD K. FREEDHEIM

The practice of psychotherapy has expanded exponentially over the last 100 years. How to capture the meaning and thrust of that movement has been a difficult and challenging task. The guiding principle for this section of the *History of Psychotherapy* was to focus on who, what, and where. That is, who are the recipients of psychotherapy, what psychotherapy techniques are used, and where are these techniques practiced? The latter issue has been covered earlier (see chapter 2). Because the context of therapy seemed so important in considering the general overview of the field, we placed that particular area in the introductory portion of this volume. However, it should be read in conjunction with this section, as the site of practice is often intimately connected to the types of clients seen and, at times, even to the techniques used.

The "who is treated" raises the further question of "by whom," which became themes for two chapters in this section. The same cultural influences and prejudices that influence our client population also impinge upon the providers of service. The chapters on women and on ethnic minorities trace a sometimes harsh picture of suppression, if not outright distortion. But, we believe that any truthful history of our field must recognize the realities of our behavior. In singling out children and the elderly as distinct populations, we recognize the special significance they have with regard to origins of the field of psychotherapy as well as emerging trends and directions for the future.

One of the most difficult decisions was selecting the methods to be covered in this section. We knew that we could provide only a small sampling of the many practices current in the field, now estimated to be over 400 in number. We also realized that any writings on technique would inevitably overlap with other portions of the volume, particularly the one devoted to theories (Section II). We hope the reader will understand the necessity for some omissions from the text. For example, we are unable to fully cover the role of hypnosis in psychotherapy with its initial prominence, later demise, and now increasing importance in the spectrum of self-regulating therapies, as well as within the emerging field of psychoneuroimmunology. Hypnosis is alluded to in a number of contexts in the volume, and it continues to play an important role in the technical armamentarium of psychotherapists.

Family therapy is presented in a chapter in the theory section (chapter 7) and includes many references to techniques that will be helpful to the practitioner. We recognize that we have not given sufficient attention to the self-help therapies which have developed into a major force in the mental health field and which we believe will continue to grow in the future.

Unfortunately, space did not permit a chapter on assessment as related to psychotherapy, as we believe that assessment techniques—perhaps the only manifest unique skill or technique of the psychologist as opposed to other professionals engaged in psychotherapy—must not be neglected in the understanding of our clients. We recognize that assessment not only guides our thinking and work with clients, but also serves as an important criterion for measuring progress in our work. Assessment has always been and will continue to be a cornerstone in the treatment process and certainly will not be neglected as an important skill of the psychologist. Also, we recognize that we did not give adequate attention to the emergence of psychological treatments of the addictions, which will make an increasing impact on our field, as well as on the training required for psychologists to function in the field of addictionology.

Authors of additional chapters in this section represent both well-known writers and those gaining a place in the field. Unfortunately, it is too late to have Carl Rogers comment on his own techniques, but we have two former students who worked closely with him describing the evolving course of his important contributions.

We are fortunate to have one of the pioneers of the group psychotherapy movement coauthor a chapter with two leading historians of the
group psychotherapy field. It is interesting to note that the American
Psychological Association has just approved a new division devoted to the
interests of group psychotherapy.

The coeditors of this section sought to give both an overview and an
in-depth picture of psychotherapy practice. We hope the following sample
of historical topics, as selective as they may be, will provide a useful guide
for those who wish to understand the developing highlights of the field and
will provide further insights into the history of psychotherapy as well as
emerging trends for the future.

13

EVOLUTION OF PRACTICE IN CHILD PSYCHOTHERAPY

GERALD P. KOOCHER AND EUGENE J. D'ANGELO

Perhaps the earliest account of child psychotherapy recorded in the scholarly literature was Jean-Marc Itard's attempts to "civilize" the "wild boy of Aveyron" (1799/1932). The child, found living in the wild, was estimated to be between 10 and 12 years old and to have been on his own since the age of 2 or 3. Itard was only 25 years old at the time, but he disagreed with the diagnosis of congenital idiocy assigned by Pinel, Itard's teacher. The intensive efforts Itard invested in working with the boy he named Victor over the next 5½ years laid the foundation for early work with severely disturbed children.

Itard used an intensive approach (i.e., bringing the child into his home and devoting many hours to working with him daily) while trying to establish interpersonal contact and teach basic communication skills to the child, whose behavior fit the description of what might today be called autism. Victor made promising progress during his first year with Itard, learning to speak some words and to write some with chalk. Although Victor lived to the age of 40, he showed little progress beyond the gains of his initial year.

Freud's classic case of "Little Hans" (S. Freud, 1909/1955) is the earliest account of a psychodynamic approach to child treatment. As our discussion will show, however, this case represents a broader approach to the treatment of children's emotional and behavior problems. This was probably the beginning of what is considered the mainstream of child psychotherapy.

The forerunner of modern behavioral therapies was almost certainly the work of Watson and Raynor (1920) with "little Albert." In an experiment that would be deemed unethical by today's standards, they subjected an 11-month-old boy who was fond of animals to a loud noise (made by striking a steel bar with a hammer) whenever he reached for a white rat placed nearby. Albert developed a conditioned fear of a white rat that soon generalized to other furry animals.

A few years later Mary Cover Jones (1924) demonstrated the ability to eliminate such fears using what might today be called a desensitization approach. By pairing gradual approach with the positively reinforcing activity of eating, she rid the child of his conditioned anxiety to a white rabbit. Although couched as a laboratory study of fear, this was probably one of the first records of empirical outcome research in child behavior therapy.

The evolution of practice in child psychotherapy has been shaped by many factors. The role of the children in their families, changes in Western society, theoretical developments, and economic forces have each exerted powerful influences on child treatment. In the pages that follow, we shall try to adopt a historical and evolutionary focus on child treatment. That is to say, we do not attempt to address all theories and techniques that have been used to treat children with emotional or behavioral problems. Rather, we trace the blooming of the field of child psychotherapy in historical perspective and speculate about future developments in such work. We begin with a discussion of early techniques and move on to explore the organizing constructs of therapeutic alliance, use of interpretation, integration of developmental issues, evolution of the child guidance movement, and influences of institutional and social policy.

EVOLUTION OF PLAY-ORIENTED PSYCHOTHERAPY

Play-oriented psychotherapy, which is largely, but not exclusively, based in psychodynamic theory, remains the dominant and most enduring approach to child treatment practiced by clinicians (Kazdin, 1988, 1990; Koocher & Pedulla, 1977; Tuma & Pratt, 1982).

Influence of Sigmund Freud

Although often underappreciated, Sigmund Freud had an early and significant influence on the development of child psychotherapy. As Novick (1989) observed, Freud had considerable involvement with children during the initial phase of his career. He studied at the Adolf Baginsky Clinic in Berlin before accepting the directorship of the neurological department in Vienna at a public institute for children's diseases, where he worked three days a week from 1886 until 1893. Subsequently, he published a book on aphasia and several papers on paralysis in children. Between 1887 and 1895, he fathered six children and spent much time working at home and interacting with his children. Letters written to his colleague, Wilhelm Fleiss, are replete with references to the various statements and activities of his children (Novick, 1989). Despite assertions by Jones (1955) to the contrary, Freud was both interested in and sensitive to the lives of children.

As Glenn (1978a) noted, Freud did not fully appreciate the differences between the cognitive abilities of a young child and an adult. Still, he did emphasize that children should be permitted to communicate with adults in age-appropriate ways, including with play. He was convinced that children's environments could have a significant influence in their development, although this observation was not made until well after his initial efforts to look directly at the lives of children, and hence, does not figure prominently in his formulations. It is clear, however, that the origins of psychodynamic child technique emanated from the early works of Sigmund Freud, who utilized observations of his own children, the limited treatment of a friend's child, and the recollections of his adult psychoanalytic patients to generate the basis for his theories on sexuality.

Freud's case study of "Little Hans" (S. Freud, 1909/1955) is probably the classic example of early psychodynamic treatment of children. Although Freud considered this child to be "normal," Hans developed a phobia of horses which was interpreted as the result of displaced aggression toward his beloved father and castration anxiety, feelings stimulated by his taboo desire to snuggle in bed with his mother. Although this case study was unique from a theoretical perspective, the therapeutic strategies employed to reach what Freud definitively considered a positive therapeutic outcome actually represented an amalgam of treatment strategies used today in a variety of clinical paradigms. Because the relevance of these strategies to subsequent clinical techniques is important, we shall recount the different techniques used in the treatment of Hans.

First, Freud did not personally conduct a classical psychoanalysis of the child. Instead, he offered direct guidance to the boy's father, who observed his son's behavior and responded to him according to the inferences that Freud derived from the clinical material reported by the father. Second, interpretations were provided directly to Hans by his father in the form of "enlightenments" as to the meanings underlying his behaviors, fantasies, feelings, and verbalizations. Freud instructed the father to tell Hans that his fear of horses was "a piece of nonsense and nothing more" (S. Freud, 1909/1955; p. 46). Moreover, because the preoccupation with horses was considered to be associated with the boy's intense interest in their "Wi-wimachers" (penises), representing displaced concerns about the genital differences between the sexes, Freud proposed that the father further enlighten his son about these matters with direct information regarding sex differences at an opportune time. (However, Freud did comment that even though the father had provided clear information about general sex differences, his explanations were not elaborated sufficiently so that the boy's subsequent questioning could have been curtailed.) Third, the metaphorical features of the boy's fantasies and associations were clarified by his father's statements about their true representations. Hence, when Hans observed that one should not place one's finger near a white horse or it might bite, his father responded, ". . . it strikes me that it isn't a horse you mean, but a Wiwimacher, that one mustn't put one's hand to" (S. Freud, 1907/1963; p. 70). Fourth, elements of the boy's fantasies were elaborated by the father and associated with previous images which the boy had articulated. In this way, Hans would elaborate the metaphor further and in the service of promoting further associations. For example, in the father's effort to embellish his inference that his son's concerns about white horses were also related to the son's apprehensions about the father, the following exchange was reported to have taken place while the boy watched his father washing himself,

Hans: Daddy, you *are* so lovely! You're so white.
I: Yes, like a white horse.
Hans: The only black thing's your mustache. . . . Or perhaps it's a black muzzle? (S. Freud, 1907/1963; p. 93).

Finally, Freud clarified that whenever the father asked too many questions and more forcefully directed the lines of inquiry, Hans would resist, producing clinically meaningful material. Freud cautioned that the analyst/father had to be patient with his child so that Hans might generate his own thoughts and elaborations upon his fantasies.

This case report established the initial guidelines for psychoanalytic treatment of children. The analysis (a) was undertaken within the context of the affectionate relationship between the son and analyst/father; and (b)

the analysis encouraged the child's production of fantasy material, metaphorical themes, and their associations. (c) Informative answers were given in response to the child's questions about his confused thoughts regarding sexuality, in this case, sex differences; (d) "enlightenments," through direct interpretive statements, were provided by the analyst/father to his son regarding the inappropriate and unnecessary reactions to the metaphorical objects in his world which represented forbidden desires; (e) the father/analyst "joined" his son in contributing to the metaphors in an effort to facilitate the boy's greater appreciation of the multiple facets of his fantasies and established the basis for more direct interpretation; and (f) this case underscored the importance of permitting the child to develop fantasy themes and metaphors as a way to facilitate communication, instead of barraging the child with numerous questions or lines of inquiry which were not comfortably pursued at that point in time.

Consistent with adult analysis, the essential feature of child analysis became the interpretation of the child's conflicting drives and defenses (Glenn, 1978b). It was assumed that the interpretation of defenses leads to both the discovery and recognition of drive derivatives, and with insight one might learn how to struggle more successfully with forbidden urges. As a result, the ego would begin to function more adaptively, alterations in defenses would occur, the superego would be modified, and more appropriate means for drive gratification would be discovered. Consequently, a child would experience the diminution of regressive tendencies, inhibitions would be overcome so that developmental arrests would dissipate, and the released or neutralized energies would be available for sublimated activities (Glenn, 1978b). Even before World War I, Freud had recognized several of the technical problems which separated adult from child psychoanalytic technique, specifically, the lack of verbal free associations, the need to obtain extra-analytic support and information to sustain the treatment, and the manifestation of rapid transference reactions by the children (Young-Bruehl, 1988).

A significant contribution to child analytic technique during the pre-war years was the work of Hermine von Hug-Hellmuth, a retired elementary-school teacher who had a doctoral degree in Philosophy. She advocated use of educational methods based on psychoanalytic principles in order to facilitate the development of both moral and aesthetic values (Hug-Hellmuth, 1920). In contrast to Freud, she utilized play experiences within children's own homes to better understand their distress. From these home-based observations, Hug-Hellmuth recognized that a child's own toys and games could be used productively to generate analytic material. In fact, she often joined in the play and intimated that such activities could be considered an important process by which an entire analysis might take place. Hence, the play experience could become, along with free association and dream analysis, a technique by which the analyst might explore "secrets" which the child withheld from educators and other adults in positions of authority (Dyer, 1983). These techniques were subsequently revised and described at the Psychoanalytic Congress of 1920 held in The Hague (Hug-Hellmuth, 1921). Despite these significant contributions, Hug-Hellmuth considered Freud's approach to Little Hans to be the more "correct" basis for the psychoanalytic treatment of children and felt that her play techniques were merely preliminary strategies to be used in the initial phase of treatment (Dyer, 1983).

Elaboration of Technique by Anna Freud and Melanie Klein

In the postwar period, particularly the 1920s, child analytic practice and technique formally emerged, stimulated by the training of lay analysts. Moreover, these individuals came from more heterogeneous academic backgrounds than did their primarily adult-focused counterparts, and they were predominantly women. Two groups of analysts dominated this subspecialty. The first group was trained by Sandor Ferenczi, included both Melanie Klein and Ada Schott, and established Berlin as the initial center for child analysis. The second group emerged from Vienna and was presided over by Anna Freud.

Apparently influenced by the techniques described by Hug-Hellmuth (1921), Klein began her analytic work with children by playing with them in their homes. She had originally attempted to use the "Little Hans" technique with a 5-year-old boy; however, when it was apparent that his difficulties were not sufficiently alleviated, she had direct contact with him in his home (Klein, 1955). In a subsequent case, she made the transition from providing treatment in the child's home to her consultation room when she realized that the girl's mother felt very ambivalent toward her (Klein), which created a hostile environment in which to undertake the analysis. Because she did not have access to the child's toys in her consultation room, she borrowed toys from her own children, assembling her own group of toys that she felt would facilitate the child's generation of play themes and permit a more standardized basis for inferring meaning from these metaphors. She also introduced play that was kinesthetically-stimulating and commonly used in kindergarten settings (e.g., sand and water tables).

Conceptually, Klein believed that children experienced more acute anxiety than adults, therefore, it was essential to establish the analytic relationship as rapidly as possible (Klein, 1932/1975). She observed that the child's fantasies expanded and inhibitions to play lessened through continual interpretation of the play material. She proposed that the interpretation had to be of sufficient depth to reach the "mental layer which is being activated" during the play sequence. These interpretations took the form of direct verbal statements about the representations of the metaphors generated during the course of the child's play. Both primitive defenses and transference to the analyst were focused on early in the course of treatment. Because the impact of a child's environment was considered by Klein and her followers to have minimal impact on the development of neurosis, little contact was made with parents.

The basis for such intense and rapid interventions was the theoretical speculation that the infant possessed an intricate psychic system which was elaborated soon after birth. Hence, the infant was assumed to be capable of highly sophisticated fantasies and prone to experience complicated psychological conflicts (e.g., the oedipal complex) within the first year of life. Although not particularly germane to the present discussion, she also proposed a number of other conceptions of mental functioning which proved to be highly controversial as well (Klein, 1964). In response to an invitation from Ernest Jones, Klein moved to London in 1926 and consolidated her theories into what became known as the "British school of psychoanalysis." This group originated the increased attention to object relations theory, the most prominent analysts from that era being D. W. Winnicott and W. R. D. Fairbairn.

Contemporaneously with Klein, Anna Freud was creating a different line of practice in Vienna. As the secretary to the training committee of the local Psychoanalytic Society, she developed a series of seminars attended by a number of analysts who ultimately contributed to what was subsequently referred to as the Vienna School of Child Analysis. These included Birnbaum, Aichorn, Buxbaum, A. Reich, Sterba, and M. Kris. The initial series of child analyses undertaken by Anna Freud used the "Little Hans technique" of consultation with the parents to effect clinical change (A. Freud, 1923).

Anna Freud gave a series of lectures for the Vienna Psychoanalytic Society in 1926 in which she articulated her technical and theoretical differences with Melanie Klein (A. Freud, 1927). Although clearly impressed by and willing to use the play technique espoused by Klein, Anna Freud objected to the assumption that infants possessed a highly complex and intact mental functioning such that sophisticated emotional conflicts could emerge prior to one year of age (A. Freud, 1976). Moreover, she questioned the Kleinian assertion that play sequences were the child's equivalent to the adult's free associations in the psychoanalytic setting. In contrast to the adult analysand, she asserted, the child does not participate in treatment with the same awareness of its purpose. Because of this lack of recognition of purpose, not all of the productions during the analytic session are imbued with symbolic meaning, hence, do not lend themselves to interpretation. Anna Freud also questioned the Kleinian understanding of transference within child analysis. She maintained that a positive trans-ference was an important prerequisite to a successful treatment relationship. In fact, she asserted that child analysis required a greater attachment than did adult treatment. In contrast, negative transference had to be worked through rapidly, lest it totally disrupt the analytic process.

The Kleinian viewpoint held that negative transference could be dealt with in the manner similar to adult analysis, that is, through interpretation over a longer period of time. Consistent with her belief in the importance of a positive attachment being essential to successful treatment, Anna Freud encouraged this process by pre-analytic activities within the initial phase of treatment. These activities, contrasted with more traditional psychoan-alytic practice with adults, included direct statements about the prospect for positive outcome, joining children in conflicts with their parents, and the analyst becoming indispensable to the child in times of distress (Dyer, 1983).

In essence, a transference neurosis was not developed and the analyst was to become an important person to the child, not restricting one's responsiveness as was more characteristic of adult analysis (A. Freud, 1966). However, Klein did underscore the importance of other orthodox inter-ventions such as dream interpretation, which she felt was easier to undertake with children than for adults. She also emphasized the meaningfulness of drawing to the child analytic process. Finally, Anna Freud stressed the necessity for extra-analytic contact, particularly with parents. In this way, important information about the child's functioning was obtained, guidance for the parents regarding aspects of childrearing were provided, and aspects of the home environment were modified. These clinical theories espoused by Anna Freud resulted in the establishment of several centers devoted to both treatment and observation of children, as well as the influence of psychoanalytic practice on education (Young-Bruehl, 1988).

The theoretical differences between Anna Freud and Melanie Klein contributed significantly to the divergences in their techniques for child analysis. It is clear that many aspects of their respective styles have been incorporated, to varying degrees and according to individual clinician pref-erences, into current child psychotherapeutic practice (Coppolillo, 1987). Dyer (1983) has suggested that the greatness of Klein lay in her ability to "see more of the child's psyche than almost anyone else could" (p. 79). Unfortunately, her efforts to establish the validity of her theoretical observations and technical interventions remained weak. Klein relied more on inference than on systematic demonstration of effectiveness. Anna Freud sought to balance her creativity with some personal skepticism about her own observations.

Despite their personal and theoretical differences, it is from the collective work of Anna Freud and Melanie Klein that the basis for much of child psychotherapy emerged. One can easily see the influences of these techniques in present-day, psychoanalytic child psychotherapy practice. In essence, Klein contributed significantly to practice by moving treatment from the child's home to the consultation room; by introducing toys that did not belong to the child but could serve to stimulate important play themes revealing the conflicts and concerns that needed expression; by expanding the appreciation of the symbolic function of play within the psychotherapy session; by elaborating upon the utility of interpretation as an important intervention within the therapeutic relationship; and by recognizing the role of transference and its manifestations during the course of analytic treatment.

Anna Freud emphasized the role of a positive treatment alliance as an essential element in the therapeutic process; the role of a pre-analytic phase of treatment to establish this positive alliance; the use of specific techniques such as drawings and dream interpretations to facilitate the evolution of clinical material; and the importance of parent guidance and extra-analytic contacts with the caregivers as essential to the education and psychosocial development of the child. Variants of both traditions pervade current clinical practice and became the basis for social efforts such as the child guidance movement.

From Psychoanalytic Treatment to Eclectic Play Therapy

The debate between Anna Freud and Melanie Klein was never adequately resolved by either party or their followers. Instead, it resulted in an early phase (i.e., throughout the late 1920s and the 1930s) of rigid adherence to either the heavily interpretive techniques of Melanie Klein or the more supportive strategies espoused by Anna Freud. As Woltmann (1950) noted, increased theoretical confusion occurred during the 1930s because of varying adherence to traditional psychoanalytic technique, the ideological shifts as to how emotional disturbances in children originated and emerged, and the often indistinct emphases on "play" and "therapy," terms which were no longer considered to be synonymous by practitioners of child treatment.

As a result, the literature on play therapy grew rapidly during the 1930s and subsequent years (Allen, 1942). For example, Phillips (1985) noted that between 1930 and 1985, over 300 articles were published on play therapy. However, most of these papers were case studies or anecdotal reports with little formal embellishment on technique. Very few of them were systematic investigations of the efficacy of such treatment strategies.

TREATMENT STRATEGY CONSTRUCTS

The elaboration of play-oriented treatment strategies can be understood by examining the maturation of four interrelated, organizing constructs which, for the purposes of elaboration, are described independently of each other. From this discussion it will become apparent that these constructs do not represent theoretically orthodox forms of technique. Rather, they are ideological hybrids from which intervention strategies emerged. These organizing constructs include (1) the changing conceptualizations of the therapeutic alliance; (2) the use of interpretive statements; (3) appreciation of developmental issues and their impact on child treatment; and (4) the influences of institutional and social policy demands.

Evolution of the Therapeutic Alliance

During the 1930s, clinicians became increasingly focused on the therapist as a curative force within treatment and expanded the understanding of play and its influence on the child. Within the individual therapy tradition, the assumption remained that serious problems caused an arrest in a child's emotional growth, with therapy seeking to recreate this process in a more condensed manner (Allen, 1942). However, it was emphasized that such a process could only occur within the context of the child's basic needs, physical and emotional, being adequately met. This required extending the concept of curative factors in treatment beyond the influence of the therapist on the child to include some reorganization of the environment in which that child lived (Hellersberg, 1955). Corresponding to the metapsychological shift away from drive theory, greater emphasis was focused on ego functions, which appeared to more accurately represent the evolving psychosocial needs of the child.

Initial modifications of child analytic technique came from within the traditional psychoanalytic movement. For example, August Aichorn was a nonmedical psychoanalyst who sought to apply child psychoanalytic theory and technique to intervention with problems of major social concern. A dominant focus of his work was related to the problems of delinquency; however, his thinking and development of clinical strategies significantly influenced the further refinement of child psychoanalytic techniques.

In his classic book, *Wayward Youth* (1925/1935), Aichorn proposed that all individual development, whether along social or dissocial lines, was the result of the interaction between both innate and environmental factors. To that end, he moved away from the metapsychological debate between Anna Freud and Melanie Klein and focused more on the interactive experiences between parents and young children as having considerable influence over subsequent emotional growth. Accordingly, he presaged the interest in early object relations (A. Freud, 1951), whereby disturbances and disruptions in these earliest parental relationships were considered to lead to both significant distress as well as to set forth a basis from which social deviance, particularly delinquency, can subsequently emerge. In 1932, he developed a child guidance service for the Vienna Psychoanalytic Society which focused on the development of child guidance strategies. Aichorn perceived this work as both a branch of education and of child psychoanalytic technique.

Aichorn's major contribution to therapeutic technique was the further elaboration of the role of transference in the therapeutic relationship. As he observed, in adult psychoanalysis, transference is used to both repeat and reveal past experiences (Aichorn, 1925/1935). In contrast, when working with children and adolescents, the transference relationship provides an opportunity to have an intense, interpersonal experience that can both undo the deviations of past experience and make up for these deficiencies in early libidinal experience. This was subsequently described as "a corrective emotional experience" (A. Freud, 1951). Accordingly, he sought to identify what was considered to be the narcissistic transference of difficult delinquent children whom he referred to as "delinquent impostors." In his view, the delinquent's attachment to the therapist was through an "overflow of narcissistic libido" and not associated with the true feelings for the therapist as a real person (Hoffer, 1949). In this and other initial constructions of narcissistically-based psychopathology, Rosenfeld (1964) pointed out that such individuals were considered to be quite refractory to effort at providing insight through interpretation. The therapeutic alliance became the primary medium by which corrective efforts could be experienced. Consequently, Aichorn helped to establish greater interest in children who narcissistically acted out in the larger community (particularly delinquents), and he emphasized the importance of the therapeutic relationship as the primary basis of intervention.

Langs (1976) provided a comprehensive history of the origin of the term *therapeutic alliance*. He observed that, with the increased interest in reality factors within the treatment process, efforts were made to artificially dichotomize the overall therapeutic relationship into a *transference* and *real* relationship. In particular, an increased emphasis in the 1930s and 1940s was concentrated on the conscious perceptions of the therapist and unconscious aspects of the treatment process and the role of intrapsychic changes. In contrast, countertransference issues and errors of technique were only minimally considered.

As the shift toward increased emphasis on the therapeutic alliance occurred, Allen (1934) provided a significant conceptual move regarding play-oriented treatment of children and the relationship necessary for this to succeed. From his point of view, one of the common features of all psychotherapies was that a relationship exists between the child and therapist. Differences in therapeutic philosophy arise as to how this relationship is used by the therapist in the treatment setting. In Allen's (1934) framework, children are given the opportunity to experience themselves in a "new and present relation, and in terms of the present and not in the past" (p. 197). Comments were provided to the child by the therapist only as they related to their present relationship. The child was given relative freedom to determine what type of play was undertaken and the various means for personal expression during the session. The content of the play was also of secondary importance other than the way children made use of it to relate with the therapist. The emphasis for the therapist was on trying to make the relationship feel as "natural" as possible for the child. In essence, the goal was to provide a balance between quiet attentiveness and active participation in a play sequence. In contrast to Anna Freud (1927), Allen believed the positive relationship between child and therapist was not considered to be a precursor to effective treatment but was primarily therapeutic in nature.

Hellersberg (1955) further articulated this redefinition of the therapist's role in child treatment. Greater emphasis was placed on developmental observations, comments about the current relationship, and fostering a nurturant attitude which would facilitate the children's discovery of their needs. Through the use of the toys in the therapist's office, children are able to be enriched by the relationship with the therapist. Reality issues were cautiously introduced by the therapist who used warnings and cautions about the pursuit of activities which could have negative consequences for the relationship. In essence, the therapist assumed a role as intermediary between the child and the environment of the playroom. Through the relationship, the child became better able to merge self-expression with self-control, with a corresponding improvement in self-respect.

A focus on the present features of the relationship also had an impact on more insight-oriented therapies as well. Lord (1985) described features of the corrective emotional experience he considered ". . . that part of the therapeutic process which provides an interaction between the patient and therapist *affectively different* from those past and/or present experiences which induced or are inducing the bases for the symptomatology" (p. 55; italics in original). While not de-emphasizing the importance of interpretive interventions, realistic responses to a child's needs, particularly if they were central to his or her sense of distress, were considered to be helpful both to attaining symptom change and to deepening the positive therapeutic relationship.

Anna Freud also consistently emphasized the importance of maintaining a positive transference or treatment alliance for a child's treatment. The therapeutic alliance has conceptually evolved from being merely instrumental in forming the basis for insight-oriented work to its having a definitive, beneficial effect in its own right on a child's functioning (Greenspan & Wieder, 1984).

Use of Therapeutic Interpretation

As described earlier, Sigmund Freud facilitated the direct interpretation of Little Hans' symbolic concerns with horses into explanations regarding confusions about sexuality. This model of direct interpretation of symbolic material into its clinical meaning was the hallmark of early child analytic practice. Supportive activities and a focus on building a therapeutic alliance were considered subordinate and preliminary efforts to the direct interpretative stance. This approach was extended to the therapeutic play session used by Klein (1955) and modified to the extent that play themes were explained within the context of the child's underlying apprehensions, conflicts, or apperceptions. These "metaphorical interpretations" (Ekstein, 1983) were to reduce the level of anxiety the child experienced. A variety of therapeutic media, including storytelling (Brandell, 1984; Brooks, 1981; Gardner, 1971; Kritzberg, 1975), puppetry (Bender & Woltmann, 1936; Gondor, 1957), drawing and painting (Rambert, 1949), and use of clay (Woltmann, 1950) were used to generate play themes. Interpretations were considered to be one important element in the sequence of "uncovering" processes in child psychotherapy (i.e., confrontation, clarification, interpretation, working through; Langs, 1973) which were similar in nature to the work of adult psychoanalytic psychotherapy.

As the child psychotherapy practices of the 1930s moved away from the more traditional psychoanalytic model, a shift occurred in both the understanding of and methods used for uncovering the child's emotional difficulties. In addition, societal demands that child psychotherapy address social problems involving children (e.g., delinquency) led to treatment opportunities for a wider range of emotional problems that did not lend themselves to more traditional interpretative processes. For example, Chethik (1989) observed that the use of more direct interpretations was expanded beyond their focus on conflict and transference manifestations, to facilitate the "rebuilding of ego functions." The therapist was now able to make use of "mutative interpretations," the primary purpose of which was to promote symptom changes, not merely to promote conflict resolution.

These newer interpretative strategies were necessitated by the changing population of child psychotherapy patients, whose levels of emotional distress and clinical disorganization did not lend themselves to direct interpretative efforts. Instead, "binding interpretations" (Chethik, 1989, p. 170) were provided to these children. Such interpretations offered insights whose purposes were not to stimulate more clinical material during the session but to facilitate the organization of the existing information in an understandable way so that the child could use it to better regulate the sense of distress.

In addition to differences in clinical population, theoretical changes brought child psychotherapy out of the realm of psychoanalytic treatment and into a variety of other philosophies of treatment and clinical etiology. This resulted in a significant shift in focus for the psychotherapist, from an open-ended interpretive treatment to a more focal, goal-directed approach (Sours, 1976). As Gardner (1975) observed, these philosophical changes produced therapeutic strategies that sought to capitalize on the child's enjoyment in play. In his analysis, it was play that provided the primary motivation for the child to return to the treatment setting on a weekly basis.

Within psychoanalytic traditions, child therapists also incorporated a number of therapeutic strategies to facilitate the production of clinical material in the treatment session (Sours, 1976). In particular, the treatment of borderline and psychotic children proved to be a source of stimulation for further advances in interpretative method. Because of their tendency toward rapid clinical regression, these children required more active involvement by the therapist with their fantasy productions (Winnicott, 1971). Therapists working with such children also consciously used the children's regressed language to convey understanding of their inner world and feelings. Ekstein (1983) termed this active joining in the play and making interpretative statements based on the child's fantasy themes "interpretations within the regression" or "interpretation within the metaphor." Instead of formulating interpretations regarding the metapsychological basis for a play sequence during a child psychotherapy session, fantasy characters from the child's play sequences were used to convey understanding. Ekstein distinguished between interpretation within the regression and the metaphoric interpretation used with more neurotic patients.

> In metaphoric interpretations, in which the therapist's immediate responses uses the metaphor of the patient's communication, there follows rapidly an explication which elaborates meaning and intent in mature secondary-process language. Interpretation within the regression, however, is predicated on the assumption that the patient's ego state directly reflects the extent of his ability to come to terms with the conflict. Therefore, communication remains within the confines of the patient's expression until some future time in the treatment when the patient himself indicates his capacity for fuller understanding. (Ekstein, 1983, p. 121)

Interpretation within the regression was designed, in large part, to maintain the therapeutic relationship.

In summary, the process of interpretation evolved from the "enlightenments" provided from Sigmund Freud to the father of Little Hans for his carefully timed use; to the metaphorical interpretations of Klein (1955) and variations on her technique; and ultimately to the interpretations within the metaphor developed by Ekstein (1983) for use with more clinically disturbed children.

Appreciation of Developmental Issues

Sigmund Freud had a variable appreciation as to the complexities and capacities of a child's cognitive and emotional life. He left this line of inquiry to his followers to elaborate in greater detail. Accordingly, Klein (1955) posited a highly developed, and almost adult-like, psychic life in children as young as one year of age. While her hypotheses subsequently met with much skepticism (Dyer, 1983), the emergence of ego psychology brought a more accurate focus on the nature of developmental issues in child treatment. First, there was an increased recognition that child therapeutic techniques would have to be modified according to the developmental level of the child. Kramer and Byerly (1978) noted that the majority of child therapeutic techniques were derived from work with latency-age children. Modifications were made for pre-latency children (Glenn, 1978a), based on the concepts of various developmental investigators (Erikson, 1963; Mahler, Pine, & Bergman, 1975; Piaget & Inhelder, 1969). Similarly, therapeutic work with adolescents was influenced by variations in adult psychotherapeutic technique.

As the academic discipline of developmental psychology became more prominent and revealed increased knowledge about the cognitive, emotional, and interpersonal aspects of childhood, therapists learned new information about these interactive processes in shaping developmental variations in children's lives (Greenspan, 1981). Concepts of regression changed (Ekstein, 1983), and the child's ability to accurately process increasingly complex information was better understood. Related observations formed the basis of more nondirective approaches to therapy, as well.

Working in an era when free association and the rule of the unconscious were powerful conceptual forces, Axline was a strong proponent of the nondirective approach to child treatment. She based her work on the assumption that individuals have both a positive "growth impulse" and the ability to solve their own problems within themselves (1964). She was a strong proponent of nondirective play, focusing on play as the child's natural medium for self-expression (1947). She seemed to be the therapist of infinite patience who would wait indefinitely, offering warmth, acceptance, permissiveness, reflection, and only those limitations necessary to anchor the therapy in reality. From her perspective, the therapist would never attempt to lead or hurry the child in treatment (1964).

As psychoanalytically based developmental hypotheses shifted away from drive theory, an increased emphasis became focused on the emergence of ego functions, areas of adaptation which progressed along developmental lines (A. Freud, 1965). Childhood disorders were considered to be products of both developmental deviations and neurotic conflicts. With this conceptual shift, there was a corresponding reappraisal of the role of play, particularly within the therapeutic relationship. Changes in ego functioning, particularly as movement was made toward greater signs of emotional health and maturity, suggested evolving ways in which play could be manifested within the treatment relationship.

Hellersberg (1955) contended that children could make contact with the world through play, which would yield opportunities to experience the extent of their ego strength and boundaries. In such an analysis, play was no longer considered by the clinician as primarily a metaphorical expression of need states and intrapsychic conflicts, but also an avenue for personal growth. This perspective emphasized continued use of the psychoanalytic literature to create optimal environments for emotional growth, while simultaneously suggesting a more limited role for verbal interpretations as a medium of intervention (Allen, 1942; Hellersberg, 1955).

It was assumed that the types of conflict that the child was experiencing would be manifested by and worked through within the particular play activities that he or she elected to pursue within the session. Regardless of the conflicts arising for the children, the play activities they utilized within the treatment setting were considered "the only possible way for them to solve their problems" (Hellersberg, 1955, p. 487). Hence, the role of the therapist in the treatment was to foster a nurturing environment where the child felt encouraged to identify needs and seek appropriate gratifications. Play within the therapy became a vehicle for the child to concretely experience the world within the confines of an accepting and positive environment.

Within the spectrum of child psychotherapy, selected treatment strategies have been developed to focus on specific aspects of overall functioning. More recently, Santostefano (1978, 1984) has developed a therapeutic strategy that integrates both psychodynamic psychotherapy and the use of cognitive restructuring techniques. Known as "cognitive control therapy," this approach focuses on those cognitive structures needed to facilitate learning and to regulate activities and affects, particularly those associated with aggression. The goal is to develop sufficient cognitive controls so as to maintain sufficient "cognitive–affective balance" such that learning, flexibility in adapting to new information, and overall development can occur. While Santostefano's own writings (1985) provide the best description of the procedures underlying the cognitive control techniques, it is important to recognize that this treatment is focused directly on the developmental level of functioning for each cognitive control.

Finally, work with particular clinical populations, ranging from chronically ill to learning disordered or developmentally delayed children have prompted a number of modifications in clinical strategies based on developmental functioning (Roberts, 1986). Therapeutic interventions are carefully organized so that they clearly acknowledge the developmental functioning of the child before particular clinical material is broached or selected strategies are introduced. As more information has accumulated about the nature of child development, the concepts underlying theories of dysfunction as well as personality growth have undergone revision. Particular therapeutic strategies (e.g., Roberts, 1986; Santostefano, 1984) also focus on developmental difficulties as targets for intervention because they can exacerbate socioemotional dysfunction.

Evolution of the Child Guidance Movement

Child psychotherapeutic practice was influenced by social movements, the way societal problems were conceptualized, and how institutions were developed to address these difficulties. One of the earliest forms of mental health service was developed by a psychologist, Lightner Witmer, in 1896. He originated the first psychological clinic in the United States at the University of Pennsylvania. This clinic was grounded in the more experimentally based psychological traditions and attempted to systematically utilize a series of standard tests to measure memory, attention, association abilities, and the capacity to learn new tasks. He referred to his method as "diagnostic education," which asserted that clinicians could not make any diagnoses of children without first attempting to teach something to them. In his analysis, diagnostic teaching was an experimental method whereby particular educational techniques were introduced to the child to evaluate those skills or deficits that were thought to underlie the problem (Witmer, 1908–1909).

The psychotherapeutic strategy utilized in the psychological clinic had a reality-based, problem-solving focus. In a school-based setting, if the child began to manifest some form of emotional distress or difficulty (e.g., inappropriately lose his or her temper), an "assistant trainer" would interpret this behavior as self-defeating, discuss the nature of the distress immediately, and evaluate with the child the situation in which it occurred. The assistant trainer would then label the affective state and relate it for the child to its consequences, suggesting that when those feelings occurred, they should be immediately identified so that greater self-control could be exercised (Witmer, 1917–1918).

The rise of urban industrial society after the Civil War was also accompanied by a corresponding number of social ills. Successive waves of immigrants arrived, the labor movement arose, and widespread riots and strikes of the 1870s and 1880s called attention to the problems of the working class (Levine & Levine, 1970). Settlement houses developed, and "visiting teachers" became active in problem solving for families in the court system, social agencies, and welfare services, particularly on behalf of children. As Levine and Levine (1970) noted, psychotherapeutic methods were not highly developed at the time. However, the visiting teachers would often provide an opportunity for family members to openly express themselves about personal issues or concerns. The teachers collaborated with other agency personnel, particularly those in the early child guidance clinics, where the orientation was to improve the social situation for families, thereby helping to relieve their children's distress. By the 1920s, efforts toward significant social reform had diminished, and the visiting teachers were absorbed as a profession into the field of social work. At the time social work was heavily influenced by psychiatric and psychoanalytic thinking. Casework became formalized and "social service," the hallmark of this earlier era, became less important to professionally trained workers. Professional practice focused on the internal conflicts of the child and only minimally on the social context in which it occurred.

William Healy, a psychiatrist, became increasingly interested in the causes of delinquency and attempted both to develop a project that would investigate these origins as well as to create a clinic that would treat children with behavior difficulties. As described by Levine and Levine (1970), Healy traveled the United States prior to embarking on this project and found that, with the exception of Witmer's psychological clinic and another experimental laboratory, no programs existed to provide clinical services to children. In 1909, he established the Juvenile Psychopathic Institute in Chicago. Although influenced by social scientists of the day as well as by the psychoanalytic movement, Healy conceptualized juvenile delinquency as a product of serious psychopathology.

He applied both psychotherapeutic method and psychoanalytic concepts to the treatment of delinquency. His therapeutic methods were quite broadly conceived. For example, Healy's psychotherapeutic focus with delinquents was on what he called "reeducation of families." Unfortunately, he provided an inadequate description of the specific strategies utilized in this clinical process. It was apparent, however, that he preferred to work with the children and parents by himself rather than separate their treatment using two therapists, which was the hallmark of later child guidance practice (Levine & Levine, 1970). It is also evident that he had appreciation for the positive effects of brief psychotherapeutic efforts (Healy & Bronner, 1948). He emphasized the role of psychoanalytic thinking as the dominant method to comprehensively understand the difficulties of behaviorally disordered children.

In 1921, the Commonwealth Fund launched a program for the prevention of juvenile delinquency. As part of the program, child guidance centers were established as demonstration clinics to work closely with schools and other agencies. Such programs were carefully designed to maximize their effect on different community resources. As initially conceived, the Commonwealth Fund programs resembled community mental health centers whose purpose was to modify aspects of the community and to provide preventive services. However, the centers rapidly became treatment agencies, dealing with individuals who were seeking help. Therapy was originally carried out by other personnel in the community sites under the supervision of the staff members of the child guidance centers. However, by the 1930s, emphasis was placed on direct clinical services at the centers as opposed to consultation at community sites.

Stevenson and Smith (1934) reported that the clinic population and service delivery model changed during this transition. Initially, the child guidance clinics worked with individuals exhibiting significant mental retardation and the most recalcitrant delinquents. Subsequently, the centers were referred aggressive and disruptive children who were followed by an assortment of youngsters with anxiety and habit disorders. Levine and Levine (1970) also note that the direct service model and the change in clinical populations seen at the child guidance centers corresponded with their increased importance as training sites for mental health professionals. They noted that case selection at these institutions was increasingly based on the case's perceived teaching potential. Case conferences became a primary teaching method in these clinics and the forum by which the latest in psychoanalytic theory and technique could be elaborated (Blanton, 1925).

The new training mandate was a critical development in the history of psychotherapeutic practice because the child guidance clinic became the primary training institution for teaching child psychotherapy and served to legitimize particular ways of undertaking practice without any particular systematic evaluation (as was characteristic of Witmer's psychological clinic). Although the leadership of the child guidance clinics was predominantly psychiatric, the training concentrated on social work. Stevenson and Smith (1934) identified the embrace of psychoanalytic technique with children by social work and psychiatry as influential in the child guidance centers' subsequent shift in clinical populations. The presenting problems of children coming to the child guidance centers shifted dramatically from the more overwhelming to less severe. By the mid-1930s, it was estimated that between 25 and 33 percent of the children seen in child guidance centers were referred from sources more likely serving middle- and upper-class families.

By 1948, the same pattern held true for the Judge Baker Guidance Center in Boston, where 60 percent of the cases were family referrals, not agency referred, for child and parent psychotherapies (Levine & Levine, 1970). Psychoanalytic theory tended to increase the focus of treatment on parent-child relationship difficulties and the presumed need for formal treatment services to parents (Allen, 1948). Ultimately, involvement of parents (chiefly the mothers) became a basic requirement before a child would be accepted for treatment in these centers (Stevenson & Smith, 1934). This model of the child receiving psychoanalytic, play-oriented psychotherapy while the mother engaged in separate individual treatment became the hallmark of child guidance services. This format continues to exert considerable influence over the child psychotherapy field, although economic and other forces discussed next provide pressure for change.

After World War II, a number of theoretical and social changes occurred which initiated modifications in therapeutic interventions. First among these was the development of family therapy and the increased recognition that family members other than the mother and the identified patient-child (e.g., most notably, the father) could significantly affect the type of problems being presented and the course of treatment (Ackerman, 1972). Second, behavior therapy emerged as a significant contribution from psychology to the mental health field. Apart from its dramatically different theoretical basis, this model of treatment emphasized increased specificity in the therapeutic plan and made systematic efforts to measure outcome and the efficacy of the intervention strategies. A third factor was the rapid growth of the community mental health center movement in the 1960s which stimulated the interest once again of socially based treatment strategies.

Finally, during the 1970s and 1980s health maintenance organizations and managed health care programs evolved rapidly in response to increasing health care costs. These plans tended to shift therapeutic goals away from personality reconstruction and intrapsychic conflict resolution to a more limited focus, symptom alleviation (Budman, 1981). As a result, the role of the child guidance clinic as a major innovator for psychological services to children diminished considerably during this period. The more traditional intervention strategies increasingly failed to adequately assist multi-problem and low income families. At first, working class families abandoned them as health insurance carriers redirected them to other providers and agencies. One interesting result has been a recent resurgence of work with more seriously disturbed children (e.g., those with multiple social problems as their primary type of referral), a group of children these centers were initially established to serve in the 1920s.

RECENT INSTITUTIONAL, SOCIAL, AND ECONOMIC FORCES

In the past three decades we have seen other dramatic changes in the practice of child psychotherapy which parallel changes in society as a whole and in the health care system in particular. The intact family with a male head-of-household is no longer the cultural norm in the United States. Homelessness and unemployment are major societal problems. Many children have two working parents and spend their early years first in substitute child care and then as so-called "latchkey children." Divorce is a common event, and increasingly, children are growing up in single-parent or blended families. Child custody disputes reach the courts in greater numbers. At the same time, mental health professionals have shown an increasing awareness of the need for sensitivity to racial, ethnic, and cultural differences in undertaking therapeutic work with children.

Time-Limited, Intermittent Therapy

Recent economic influences have significantly reduced the length of inpatient stays for children and, in an increasing number of situations, have changed the manner in which individuals can gain access to mental health providers. With the advent of preferred provider and health maintenance organizations, primary care physicians (chiefly pediatricians and family physicians) have assumed increasing responsibility for identifying extant mental health needs, selecting providers, and even authorizing the duration of psychotherapeutic treatment in some cases.

"Time-limited, intermittent therapy for children" has emerged as a model for clinical service delivery (Kreilkamp, 1989). Adhering to the health care philosophy espoused by health maintenance organizations (HMOs: e.g., the Harvard Community Health Plan based in Massachusetts), "child treatment" is distinguished from traditional "child psychotherapy" by the use of intervention strategies that cross several theoretical traditions. This therapeutic model relies on the "institutional transference" of the health maintenance organization under which the agency is identified as an extended "helping system," where a variety of health-related concerns are addressed, not merely providing for just one area of medical specialization (Kreilkamp, 1989). The underlying assumption of this helping system is that it establishes a framework whereby rapid, decisive assistance can be obtained from the agency, not only from a physician or psychotherapist. Hence, the HMO becomes considered part of the benevolent treatment relationship. Still, although clearly identified as a helping agency, the HMO is also a "resource-limited system," hence, the therapists need to deliver services considered effective within a time-limited framework rather than provide the more open-ended treatment which has been the hallmark of more traditional child psychotherapy. The degree to which any given managed-care system realistically fits the benevolent treatment agency model is open to question.

In this model, child treatment is not pursued with the goal of complete personality reconstruction or insight into one's emotional responses. Rather, such treatment seeks to resolve the presenting problem in a rapid, practical manner, relying not on one mode of approaching the problem but utilizing several treatment strategies simultaneously. As an eclectic model, it has not generated new treatment techniques but uses existing forms of family and couples therapies, behavioral interventions, parent guidance, and various types of child psychotherapy to address child-focused problems.

Kreilkamp (1989) has identified several aspects of the time-limited, intermittent model: First, it is a philosophy of treatment that identifies the developmental processes of both the child's growth and the family's evolution as a critical component of healthy problem resolution. Accordingly, children, parents, or other relevant family members may need to have contacts with psychotherapists at selected points in their life to resolve specific problems being confronted. For example, a preschooler's family may be seen to help treat the child's sleep disorder; that child at age 7 might be treated for peer relationship problems; and, again, to resolve struggles around dating at age 14. In essence, different developmental phases both for the child and in family life result in time-limited interventions.

Second, the therapist assumes an active approach to treatment. Evaluation of problems is undertaken rapidly; advice and suggestions are utilized as interventions where considered appropriate; feedback to the children and families is behaviorally specific and nontechnical in nature; and all participants in treatment are expected to be responsible for their active involvement in the therapeutic effort. All interventions are based on a pragmatic philosophy, whereby "doing leads to self-knowledge (Kreilkamp, 1989, p. 34)." Third, each identified problem may be the focus of a different type of intervention. Hence, a child's problems with staying in bed at night might be addressed through a behavioral plan; anxieties about school, in a focused, individual psychotherapy; and parental disagreements, in couples therapy. Finally, although feelings are not ignored, the focus of treatment is not on expression of affect, but rather its containment. Interpretations are used educatively and with the purpose of instigating action, and only secondarily to promote self-understanding.

Institutionalization and the Reluctant Volunteer

In some circumstances economic forces have led to an increase in the utilization of inpatient hospitalization for children with emotional problems (Weithorn, 1988). For example, at the time this chapter is being written, some states have mandated benefit laws which provide all family members with a fixed annual amount of outpatient mental health benefits and an additional fixed interval of inpatient psychiatric hospital coverage. The middle-class family with a troubled child may reach the conclusion that inpatient care is a "better" choice than outpatient therapy, which would cost more out of pocket. Vigorous advertising by proprietary (i.e., for-profit) psychiatric hospitals and court rulings declining to interfere with parental powers to admit their children for such treatment without judicial review (*Parham v. J. R.*, 1979) have also tended to boost hospital admissions for children.

If one concedes that outpatient psychotherapy for children has some coercive potential, then institutionalization or residential treatment certainly represents an extreme end of that continuum. Adults cannot be involuntarily hospitalized for more than a brief emergency interval, unless a formal court proceeding finds them dangerous to themselves or to others. Children have no such constitutional protections. Beyer and Wilson (1976) described this situation as the case of the "reluctant volunteer," referring to the legal authority of a parent or guardian to commit a minor child to a psychiatric facility "voluntarily" (i.e., without a formal court hearing).

In *Bartley v. Kremmens* (1975) a three-judge federal district court ruled that a Pennsylvania statute permitting parents to commit their children "voluntarily" to a state mental hospital violated the due process clause of the Constitution. A similar ruling by a federal tribunal in Georgia (*J. L. v. Parham*, 1976) was subsequently overturned by the U.S. Supreme Court (*Parham v. J. R.*, 1979). In writing the majority opinion, Chief Justice Warren Burger noted: "Although we acknowledge the fallibility of medical and psychiatric diagnosis, we do not accept the notion that the shortcomings of specialists can always be avoided by shifting the decision . . . to an untrained judge." The Burger court assumed, somewhat idealistically, that the parent will inevitably act to promote the child's welfare. In addition, the court suggested that the medical officer at the hospital who authorizes the admission is actually providing the child with a kind of due process hearing obviating the need for or even the wisdom of additional formal court proceedings.

Although there is general agreement that the "least restrictive alternative" is the most desirable, the questions "How restrictive is necessary?" and "Who is best able to provide it?" remain difficult to answer. This type of situation has three problematic parts. First is the issue of the circumstances under which parents ought to be able to commit their child to a psychiatric hospital without extra-familial legal review. Another part involves interpreting the meaning of the phrase "least restrictive alternative" and who ought to decide on such issues. The third part of the problem involves potential conflicts of interest when the for-profit sector of the mental health industry is involved.

Tarasoff Obligations

Society has increasingly demanded that mental health professionals support the role of the state in exercise of the *parens patriae* doctrine (Koocher

& Keith-Spiegel, 1990), that is to say, the concept that the state must care for those who cannot care for or protect themselves. This has led to case law creating a duty to protect third parties in the face of threats made by clients, or so-called *Tarasoff* obligations.

Although most mental health professionals are aware of the *Tarasoff* case (*Tarasoff v. Regents of the University of California*, 1976), many are unaware of important "duty to protect" case law involving child clients. Such cases do occur, and clinicians would be wise to be sensitive to the possibility and to formulate plans for dealing with them should they arise. Consider these three examples:

- **Case 1:** Lee Morgenstern, a teenaged client, told his therapist (a psychiatrist named Milano) of sexual adventures, acting-out behavior, and jealousy related to Kimberly McIntosh, the young woman next door. The therapist did not particularly believe him. Later the teen shot the woman to death, and the psychiatrist was sued. He sought summary judgment, but it was not granted, and the case went on to a trial. The jury ultimately found no negligence on Dr. Milano's part (*McIntosh v. Milano*, 1979).

- **Case 2:** A teenaged juvenile offender named James who was in county custody threatened to "off" someone when released from incarceration. Sent home on a leave in his mother's custody, he tortured a 5-year-old neighborhood boy to death. The parents sued the county and advanced the *Tarasoff* doctrine as part of their case. The court disallowed application of that doctrine because there was no specific identifiable victim of the teenager's nonspecific threats. In addition, the court ruled that the official decision to grant leave and similar correctional release decisions were immune from liability (*Thompson v. County of Alameda*, 1980).

- **Case 3:** The mother of a mentally retarded juvenile, who was also known to be a fire-setter, sued state and county authorities for failure to warn, after they sent him home on a pass and he set a fire that killed one person and severely burned another. The case was dismissed in part because the plaintiff knew of the danger, and there were no specific identified victims (*Cairl v. Minnesota*, 1982)

No liability was assessed against mental health professionals in any of these cases; however, that does not eliminate potential risk in future cases. In addition, no one wants to have one of their child clients perpetrate a homicide or face the significant stresses and costs of defending a wrongful death lawsuit. Thoughtful assessment and sensitivity to risk and responsibility are the key issues to be evaluated, considering such factors as past behavior, impulse control, access to weapons, formulation of specific plans to harm someone, and delusional content related to threats of harm (Blau, 1987; Botkin & Nietzel, 1987).

Mandated Child Abuse Reporting Laws

All 50 states have statutes mandating the reporting of suspected child abuse. Such laws are based on two important concepts: first, that parents' interests and rights are not always congruent with those of their children (Racusin & Felsman, 1986), and second, that the state has a compelling interest in protecting vulnerable children. Effective child abuse protection laws in the United States are a relatively recent development. In a 1962 conference on the battered child syndrome, C. Henry Kempe and his colleagues brought the topic of child abuse into the public and political limelight (Radbill, 1980).

To encourage compliance with mandated reporting laws, all states provide mandated reporters with immunity from liability for reports made in good faith. Forty-five states have a criminal penalty for willful failure to report suspected cases of child abuse (Saulsbury & Campbell, 1985). Prosecution of mandated reporters for failure to report suspected child abuse is a new and real concern (see, for example, Denton, 1987; Diesenhouse, 1988).

In a case which stirred much professional controversy, a "limited license psychologist" in Michigan was prosecuted for failure to report suspected child abuse. Part of the psychologist's defense included the argument that the Michigan reporting threshold ("reasonable cause to suspect") was vague and not objective. The psychologist was ultimately acquitted at a jury trial (Kavanaugh, 1989).

The Michigan case helped to surface complaints by professionals that reporting thresholds, as defined by statute, are completely subjective and difficult to implement. Other concerns focus on a lack of specificity in the statutes about what behaviors constitute neglect or abuse (Faller, 1985; Kavanaugh, 1988; Misener, 1986). Faller (1985) notes that clinicians worry about the impact of reporting on the client-therapist relationship. She suggests that when the professional is obligated to report abuse, the formation of a trusting relationship with the family may be difficult and the family may not "open up" in therapy. Kavanaugh (1988) and Faller both believe that reporting laws involve an invasion of privacy. Kavanaugh suggests that most people would not enter therapy if they believed their therapists would report them to a state agency.

Other professionals believe that mandated reporting laws are protective of both children and professionals. Koocher (1989) points out that psychotherapists do not have the legal authority to investigate or intervene in cases of child abuse and cannot control the behavior of family members outside the office. He acknowledges that reporting suspected abuse may anger a family but that disruption of the client-therapist relationship is not inevitable. Koocher points out that protection of the child is of utmost importance and that this duty is assigned to the state. Harper and Irvin (1985) concur that filing a child abuse report does not inevitably disrupt the therapeutic relationship or interfere with therapeutic goals.

Denton (1987) states that mental health professionals commonly fail to report suspected child abuse. Anecdotal evidence exists to support these claims, however, there is little research on professional compliance with mandated reporting laws. A 1981 national incidence study cited by Faller (1985) reportedly found that mandated professionals only report one-fifth of the cases in which they suspect child abuse. Lest the reader also dismiss the possibility of sexual abuse of children by mental health professionals, we suggest reviewing the results of a survey by Bajt and Pope (1989). Ninety of 100 senior clinical psychologists responded to their request to anonymously report on any instances of sexual intimacy between a psychotherapist and a minor client that they had personally discovered during the course of their professional work. A total of 81 instances were reported by 22 different respondents. An additional five psychologists reported hearsay accounts of cases for which they lacked first-hand knowledge. Age ranges were reported for 20 female patients (range = 3 to 17 years, M = 13.75, SD = 4.12) and 18 male patients (range = 7 to 16 years, M = 12.5, SD = 3.01). These findings suggest that mental health professionals treating children must also be sensitive to the possibility of sexual abuse by prior therapists.

Psychotherapy for Children in the Court System

The juvenile court system and other so-called "diversion" programs were historically intended to keep children out of the courts and prisons. In the criminal arena, however, there is an increasing tendency to treat juveniles charged with major crimes (especially homicides) as adults, rather than in the juvenile or family court system. The legal procedure for accomplishing this shift is often referred to as a transfer or waiver hearing to move the case from juvenile to adult jurisdiction. This is not an issue of "competency to stand trial," which involves the ability to comprehend the roles of court officers, cooperate in one's own defense, and appreciate the potential consequences of the proceedings. Rather, the trend reflects a growing public sentiment that dangerous children (i.e., violent juvenile offenders, especially in highly publicized cases) should not to be "let off the hook" simply by virtue of their age. Some states have lowered the age of jurisdiction for criminal court, either for all juvenile offenders or for selected types of offenses. Other states have expanded the basis for transfer of cases from juvenile court to adult criminal jurisdictions by either expanding the criteria for transfer or by shifting the burden of proof from the state to the defendant. Still other states have established concurrent jurisdictions for selected offenses or offenders, giving prosecutors great latitude in selecting the judicial forum in which to adjudicate adolescent crimes (Fagan & Deschenes, 1988). Traditionally, transfer decisions have been based on criteria such as the adjustment of the juvenile in the community (i.e., at home and at school), the juvenile's supposed amenability to treatment, and the nature of the offense.

Psychotherapists will increasingly be asked to address issues such as amenability to treatment in such cases. Other cases will almost certainly involve the question of whether or not a death sentence should be imposed (where legally authorized) on children who commit homicide.

Another arena of increasing involvement for psychologists is that of court-ordered therapies. Often such circumstances as custody disputes, reunification in abusive families, or the return of children removed from the home on court orders lead to judicial mandates for therapy. At times this can be appropriate, but in many circumstances professionals must strive to educate judges who seek to use psychotherapy as a means of social control. For example, it is inappropriate to order psychotherapy for a 12-year-old child who does not wish to visit a noncustodial parent following a divorce with the sole purpose of the therapy being to facilitate the visitation. Similarly, ordering abusive parents to enter psychotherapy as a means of monitoring the safety of a child returned to their care provides neither good therapy nor adequate monitoring.

Other Treatment Settings

Public Law 94–142 and other similar legislation is increasingly mandating the involvement of public schools in providing psychotherapeutic services. Similarly, prevention and early intervention programs have become new contact points for child psychotherapists and their families. Medical settings ranging from tertiary-care hospitals, to clinics, to pediatricians' private offices have also evolved into sites where psychotherapeutic consultations and services can be found on a routine basis (see Roberts,

1986). Patterns of care are clearly changing, and each new type of setting will obviously impose a unique set of contingencies on the conduct of psychotherapy in that environment.

Psychotherapy practitioners are increasingly competing with each other for clients and in so doing are not always sensitive to the question of their own competence to work with child clients. The *Ethical Principles of Psychologists* (American Psychological Association [APA], 1981), for example, enjoin all psychologists to maintain high standards of competence and to recognize both the boundaries of their competence and the limitations of their techniques. For many of our colleagues in the mental health professions, however, enthusiasm (or arrogance) too often clouds or exceeds competence. In addition, there is no clear consensus within the field as to whether work with children and families is a specialty, subspecialty, or simply a special proficiency. When it comes to child and family work, there are no written guidelines to follow with respect to establishing a basic threshold of competence. It is possible to complete a doctoral degree program which is "fully approved" by the American Psychological Association, from course work through internship in clinical or counseling psychology at many universities, without ever assessing or treating a child and without any formal training in family therapy.

CONCLUSIONS

The evolution of child psychotherapy has been shaped by diverse theoretical views and social circumstances (Johnson, Rasbury, & Siegel, 1986). The field remains an ill-understood arena of practice in which clinical technique evolved as a function of case reports, theoretical refinements, and the changing sociopolitical mandate of the mental health professions. This evolution has been driven chiefly by demands for service to different clinical populations whose needs required the development of new interventions. More recently, economic demands have influenced the scope, style, and duration of intervention efforts.

Kazdin (1990) has concluded that, despite many of the methodological difficulties in outcome studies, major advances have been made regarding the efficacy of selected treatment techniques in child and adolescent psychotherapy, many of these being behavioral in nature. Nonetheless, as several reviews suggest, the dominant practice in child psychotherapy is based on psychoanalytic principles, despite the fact that there is little systematic evaluation research to support the effectiveness of these strategies (Koocher & Pedulla, 1977; Tuma & Pratt, 1982). Speculating about the future of child psychotherapy, it is reasonable to anticipate that increased attention will focus on outcome, with an eye toward both *effectiveness* and *efficiency*. Third-party payors will demand well-controlled, empirically based outcome studies. Selected case reports will no longer be acceptable. It is particularly incumbent upon practitioners of more expressive and insight-oriented psychotherapies to address the issues of effectiveness and efficiency in this manner, lest they run the risk of being considered too costly or idiosyncratic by health insurers and government regulators who will increasingly define the nature and scope of health service delivery.

These demands on psychotherapeutic practice will undoubtedly affect the nature of training in clinical child psychology. Increasingly, such training will incorporate an emphasis on developing broad clinical problem-solving approaches and a diverse array of intervention strategies (Elbert, Abidin, Finch, Sigman, & Walker, 1988). Such approaches place less emphasis on training in narrow theoretical traditions, but utilize the importance of comprehensive treatment planning as the key to both effective and efficient service delivery. To that end, more eclectic training is necessary, with "eclecticism" reflecting the atheoretical combination of clinical methods based on their demonstrated efficacy (Norcross, 1990). Efforts at *theoretical integration*, "the conceptual synthesis of diverse theoretical systems" (Norcross, 1990, p. 297), will most likely contribute to this emergent basis for training. Similarly, efforts to improve access to mental health services for culturally diverse families and to explore the theoretical assumptions underlying these practices is needed to improve the way psychotherapy is offered and utilized (Smirnow & Bruhn, 1984; Tyler, Sussewell, & Williams-McCoy, 1985).

Despite diverse theoretical and philosophical underpinnings, the cornerstones of child psychotherapy remain the thoughts, emotions, and actions of individuals guided by "assumptions about reality" (Frank, 1987). One can conclude that the continued evolution of child psychotherapy will focus on the meanings which children attach to these phenomena, regardless of the techniques used in the process.

REFERENCES

Ackerman, N. (1972). The growing edge of family therapy. In C. Sager & H. Kaplan (Eds.), *Progress in group and family therapy* (pp. 440–456). New York: Brunner/Mazel.

Aichorn, A. (1925/1935). *Wayward youth.* New York: Viking.

Allen, F. (1934). Therapeutic work with children. *American Journal of Orthopsychiatry, 4*, 193–202.

Allen, F. (1942). *Psychotherapy with children.* New York: W. W. Norton.

Allen, F. (1948). The Philadelphia Child Guidance Clinic. In L. Lowrey & V. Sloane (Eds.), *Orthopsychiatry, 1923–48: Retrospect and prospect* (pp. 134–145). New York: American Orthopsychiatric Association.

American Psychological Association. (1981). *Ethical principles of psychologists.* Washington, DC: Author.

Axline, V. (1947). *Play therapy.* Boston: Houghton Mifflin.

Axline, V. (1964). The eight basic principles. In M. R. Haworth (Ed.), *Child psychotherapy* (pp. 93–94). New York: Basic Books.

Bajt, T. R., & Pope, K. S. (1989). Therapist–patient sexual intimacy involving children and adolescents. *American Psychologist, 44*, 455.

Bartley v. Kremmens, 402 F. Supp. 1039 (E.D. Pa. 1975).

Bender, L., & Woltmann, A. (1936). The use of puppet shows as a psychotherapeutic method for behavior problems in children. *American Journal of Orthopsychiatry, 6*, 341–354.

Beyer, H. A., & Wilson, J. P. (1976). The reluctant volunteer: A child's right to resist commitment. In G. P. Koocher (Ed.), *Children's rights and the mental health professions* (pp. 133–148). New York: Wiley-Interscience.

Blanton, S. (1925). The function of the mental hygiene clinic in the schools and colleges. In J. Addams (Ed.), *The child, the clinic and the court.* New York: New Republic.

Blau, T. H. (1987). *Psychotherapy tradecraft.* New York: Brunner/Mazel.

Botkin, D., & Nietzel, M. (1987). How therapists manage potentially dangerous clients. *Professional Psychology: Research and Practice, 18(1)*, 84–86.

Brandell, J. A. (1984). Stories and story-telling in child psychotherapy. *Psychotherapy, 21*, 54–62.

Brooks, R. (1981). Creative characters: A technique in child therapy. *Psychotherapy, 18*, 131–139.

Budman, S. (1981). *Forms of brief therapy.* New York: Guilford.

Cairl v. Minnesota, 323 N.W. 2d 20 (Minn., 1982).

Chethik, M. (1989). *Techniques of child therapy: Psychodynamic strategies.* New York: Guilford.

Coppolillo, H. P. (1987). *Psychodynamic psychotherapy of children.* Madison, CT: International Universities Press.

Denton, L. (1987). Child abuse reporting laws. Are they a barrier to helping troubled families? *APA Monitor, 18*, p. 1.

Diesenhouse, S. (1988, January 31). Child sex abuse cases rising in Massachusetts. *New York Times.*

Dyer, R. (1983). *Her father's daughter: The work of Anna Freud.* New York: Jason Aronson.

Ekstein, R. (1983). *Children of time and space, of action and impulse* (2nd ed.). New York: Jason Aronson.

Elbert, J., Abidin, R., Finch, A., Sigman, M., & Walker, C. E. (1988). Guidelines for clinical child psychology internship training. *Journal of Clinical Psychology, 17*, 280–287.

Erikson, E. (1963). *Childhood and society.* New York: W. W. Norton.

Fagan, J., & Deschenes, E. P. (1988). *The juvenile court and violent youths: Determinants of the judicial transfer decision.* Unpublished manuscript, John Jay College of Criminal Justice.

Faller, K. C. (1985). Unanticipated problems in the United States child protection system. *Child Abuse and Neglect, 9*, 63–69.

Frank, J. (1987). Psychotherapy, rhetoric, and hermeneutics: Implications for practice and research. *Psychotherapy, 24*, 293–302.

Freud, A. (1923). Ein hysterisches Symptom bei einen zweieinvierteljahrigen Knaben [A hysterical symptom in a child of two years and three months]. *The writings of Anna Freud* (Vol. I; pp. 158–161). New York: International Universities Press.

Freud. A. (1927). Einfuhrung in die Kinderanalyse [Four lectures on child analysis]. *The writings of Anna Freud* (Vol. I; pp. 3–69). New York: International Universities Press.

Freud, A. (1951). August Aichorn: July 27, 1878–October 17, 1949. *International Journal of Psychoanalysis, 32*, 51–56.

Freud, A. (1965). Normality and pathology in childhood: Assessment of development. *The writings of Anna Freud* (Vol. VI). New York: International Universities Press.

Freud, A. (1966). A short history of child analysis. *The Psychoanalytic Study of the Child* (Vol. 21; pp. 7–14). New York: International Universities Press.

Freud, A. (1976). Psychopathology seen against a background of normal development. *The writings of Anna Freud* (Vol. VIII; pp. 82–95). New York: International Universities Press.

Freud, S. (1955). Analysis of a phobia in a five-year-old boy. In J. Strachey (Ed. and Trans.), *The standard edition of the complete psychological works of Sigmund Freud* (Vol. 10; pp. 1–152). London: Hogarth Press. (Original work published 1909).

Freud, S. (1963). *The sexual enlightenment of children.* New York: Collier Books. (Original work published 1907)

Gardner, R. (1971). *Therapeutic communication with children.* New York: Jason Aronson.

Gardner, R. (1975). *Psychotherapeutic approaches to the resistant child.* New York: Jason Aronson.

Glenn, J. (1978a). The psychoanalysis of prelatency children. In J. Glenn (Ed.), *Child analysis and therapy* (pp. 164–203). New York: Jason Aronson.

Glenn, J. (1978b). An overview of child analytic technique. In J. Glenn (Ed.), *Child analysis and therapy* (pp. 3–26). New York: Jason Aronson.

Gondor, L. (1957). Use of fantasy communications in child psychotherapy. *American Journal of Psychotherapy, 5,* 323–335.

Greenspan, S. (1981). *Psychopathology and adaptation in infancy and early childhood: Principles of clinical diagnosis and preventive intervention.* New York: International Universities Press.

Greenspan, S., & Wieder, S. (1984). Dimensions and levels of the therapeutic process. *Psychotherapy, 21,* 5–23.

Harper, G. P., & Irvin, E. (1985). Alliance formation with parents: Limit-setting and the effect of mandated reporting. *American Journal of Orthopsychiatry, 55,* 550–560.

Healy, W., & Bronner, A. (1948). The child guidance clinic: Birth and growth of an idea. In L. Lowrey & V. Sloane (Eds.), *Orthopsychiatry, 1923–48. Retrospect and prospect* (pp. 14–49). New York: American Orthopsychiatric Association.

Hellersberg, E. F. (1955). Child's growth in play therapy. *American Journal of Psychotherapy, 9,* 484–502.

Hoffer, W. (1949). Deceiving the deceiver. In K. R. Eissler (Ed.), *Searchlights on delinquency* (pp. 150–155). New York: International Universities Press.

Hug-Hellmuth, H. (1920). Collective review: Child psychology and education. *International Journal of Psychoanalysis, 1,* 316–323.

Hug-Hellmuth, H. (1921). On the technique of child analysis. *International Journal of Psychoanalysis, 2,* 287–305.

Itard, J. (1932). *The wild boy of Aveyron, Paris.* G. Humphrey & M. Humphrey (Trans.). New York: Century. (Original work published in 1799)

J. L. v. Parham, 412 F. Supp. 112 (M.D. Ga. 1976).

Johnson, J. H., Rasbury, W. C., & Siegel, L. J. (1986). *Approaches to child treatment: Introduction to theory, research, and practice.* New York: Pergamon Press.

Jones, E. (1955). *Sigmund Freud* (Vol. 1). London: Hogarth.

Jones, M. C. (1924). A laboratory study of fear: The case of Peter. *Pedagogical Seminary, 31,* 308–315.

Kavanaugh, P. B. (1988). Reporting cases of suspected child abuse. *The Independent Practitioner, 8,* 22.

Kavanaugh, P. B. (1989, March–April). People v. Cavaiani: Cavaiani wins. *Michigan Psychologist,* p. 8.

Kazdin, A. E. (1988). *Child psychotherapy: Developing and identifying effective treatments.* New York: Pergamon Press.

Kazdin, A. E. (1990). Psychotherapy for children and adolescents. *Annual Review of Psychology, 41,* 21–54.

Klein, M. (1955). The psychoanalytic play technique. *American Journal of Orthopsychiatry, 25,* 223–237.

Klein, M. (1964). *Contributions to psychoanalysis: 1921–1945*. New York: McGraw-Hill.

Klein, M. (1975). *The psychoanalysis of children*. New York: Delacorte Press. Trans. 1949 by Alix Strachey. (Original work published 1932)

Koocher, G. P. (1989). Ethical issues in legally mandated child abuse reporting. *The Independent Practitioner, 9*, 43–44.

Koocher, G. P., & Keith-Spiegel, P. C. (1990). *Children, ethics, and the law*. Lincoln, NE: University of Nebraska Press.

Koocher, G. P., & Pedulla, B. M. (1977). Current practices in child psychotherapy. *Professional Psychology, 8*, 275–287.

Kramer, S., & Byerly, L. (1978). Technique of psychoanalysis of the latency child. In J. Glenn (Ed.), *Child analysis and therapy* (pp. 205–236). New York: Jason Aronson.

Kreilkamp, T. (1989). *Time-limited, intermittent therapy with children and families*. New York: Brunner/Mazel.

Kritzberg, N. (1975). *The structured therapeutic game method of child analytic psychotherapy*. Hicksville, New York: Exposition Press.

Langs, R. (1973). *The technique of psychoanalytic psychotherapy* (Vol. I). New York: Jason Aronson.

Langs, R. (1976). *The therapeutic interaction: Volume II. A critical overview and synthesis*. New York: Jason Aronson.

Levine, M., & Levine, A. (1970). *A social history of helping services*. New York: Appleton-Century-Crofts.

Lord, J. P. (1985). *A guide to individual psychotherapy with school-age children and adolescents*. Springfield, IL: Charles C. Thomas.

Mahler, M., Pine, F., & Bergman, A. (1975). *On symbiosis and the vicissitudes of individuation*. New York: International Universities Press.

McIntosh v. Milano, 403 A. 2d 500 (N.J. Super. Ct. 1979).

Misener, T. R. (1986). Toward a nursing definition of child maltreatment using seriousness vignettes. *Advances in Nursing Science, 8*, 1–14.

Norcross, J. (1990). Commentary: Eclecticism misrepresented and integration misunderstood. *Psychotherapy, 27*, 297–300.

Novick, J. (1989). How does infant work affect our clinical work with adolescents? A clinical report. In S. Dowling & A. Rothstein (Eds.), *The significance of infant observational research for clinical work with children, adolescents, and adults* (pp. 27–37). Madison, CT: International Universities Press.

Parham v. J. R. 442 U.S. 584 (1979).

Phillips, R. (1985). Whistling in the dark? A review of play therapy research. *Psychotherapy, 21*, 752–760.

Piaget, J., & Inhelder, B. (1969). *The psychology of the child*. New York: Basic Books.

Racusin, R. J., & Felsman, J. K. (1986). Reporting child abuse: The ethical obligation to inform parents. *Journal of the American Academy of Child Psychiatry, 25*, 485–489.

Radbill, S. X. (1980). Children in a world of violence: A history of child abuse. In C. H. Kempe & R. E. Helfer (Eds.), *The battered child.* Chicago, IL: University of Chicago Press.

Rambert, M. (1949). *Children in conflict.* New York: International Universities Press.

Roberts, M. C. (1986). *Pediatric psychology: Psychological intervention and strategies for pediatric problems.* New York: Pergamon Press.

Rosenfeld, H. (1964). On the psychopathology of narcissism: A clinical approach. *International Journal of Psychoanalysis, 45*, 332–337.

Santostefano, S. (1978). *A biodevelopmental approach to clinical child psychology: Cognitive controls and cognitive control therapy.* New York: John Wiley.

Santostefano, S. (1984). Cognitive control therapy with children: Rationale and technique. *Psychotherapy, 21*, 76–91.

Santostefano, S. (1985). *Cognitive control therapy with children and adolescents.* New York: Pergamon Press.

Saulsbury, F. T., & Campbell, R. E. (1985). Evaluation of child abuse reporting by physicians. *American Journal of Diseases of Children, 139*, 393–395.

Smirnow, B. W., & Bruhn, A. R. (1984). Encopresis in a hispanic boy: Distinguishing pathology from cultural differences. *Psychotherapy, 21*, 24–30.

Sours, J. (1976). The application of child analytic principles to forms of child psychotherapy. In J. Glenn (Ed.), *Child analysis and therapy* (pp. 615–646). New York: Jason Aronson.

Stevenson, G., & Smith, G. (1934). *Child guidance clinics: A quarter century of development.* New York: Commonwealth Fund.

Tarasoff v. Regents of the University of California, 17 Cal. 3d 425, 551 P. 2d 334, 131 Cal. Rptr. 14. (1976).

Thompson v. County of Alameda, 614 P. 2d 728 (Cal. Super. Ct. 1980).

Tuma, J. M. & Pratt, J. M. (1982). Clinical child psychology practice and training: A survey. *Journal of Clinical Child Psychology, 11*, 27–34.

Tyler, F. B., Sussewell, D. R., & Williams-McCoy, J. (1985). Ethnic validity in psychotherapy. *Psychotherapy, 22*, 311–320.

Watson, J. B., & Raynor, R. (1920). Conditioned emotional reactions. *Journal of Experimental Psychology , 3*, 1–14.

Weithorn, L. A. (1988). Mental hospitalization of troublesome youth: An analysis of skyrocketing admission rates. *Stanford Law Review, 40*, 773–838.

Winnicott, D. W. (1971). *Therapeutic consultations in child psychiatry.* New York: Basic Books.

Witmer, L. (1908–1909). Retrospect and prospect: An editorial. *Psychological Clinic, 2*, 1–4.

Witmer, L. (1917–1918). Diagnostic education: An education for the fortunate few. *Psychological Clinic, 11,* 69–78.

Woltmann, A. (1950). Mud and clay: Their functions as developmental aids and as media of projection. In N. Wolff (Ed.), *Personality: Symposia on topical issues* (pp. 35–50). New York: Grune & Stratton.

Young-Bruehl, E. (1988). *Anna Freud: A biography.* New York: Summit Books.

14

WOMEN IN PSYCHOTHERAPY: SELECTED CONTRIBUTIONS

NANCY FELIPE RUSSO AND AGNES N. O'CONNELL

Since the very beginning of psychology, women have been active in all of the discipline's subfields. In particular, they have contributed to clinical, counseling, and school psychology and have been more likely to work in applied settings. By 1940, women were 30% of all psychologists, but they held 51% of the positions in guidance centers, clinics, schools, educational systems, hospitals, and custodial centers. By 1944, although the proportion of women overall in psychology was unchanged, the latter figure rose to 60% (Bryan & Boring, 1946). In 1985, women comprised 32% of employed psychologists but held 40% of the positions in schools and educational systems and 34% of the positions in hospitals and clinics (Kohut, 1990).

We would like to express our deep appreciation to Laura Urbanski, who served as research assistant on the project. Ria Hermann, Julie Jones, Jan Lamoreaux and Carolyn Powers provided invaluable assistance. We would also like to thank Allen Meyer and Thomas O'Connell for their support. Judith Alpert, Laura Brown, Donald Freedheim, Stephanie Stolz, and Ursula Delworth generously provided feedback on the manuscript. Marie Crissey provided helpful information, and Gwen Puryear Keita, information about the history of APA's Committee on Women in Psychology. This work was supported by a minigrant from the College of Liberal Arts and Sciences, Arizona State University.

Although women have been leaders and major contributors in applied psychology, the historical neglect of applied fields by academic psychology has led to a lack of full appreciation for the number, quality, and diversity of women's contributions. It is impossible to mention all deserving women here. However, we hope that these highlights of selected women contributors will engender an appreciation for women's contributions to psychotherapy. In addition to contributions as psychologists, psychiatrists, or psychoanalysts, women have shaped the development of psychotherapy through the roles of client, benefactor, advocate, and policy maker.

THE INITIAL CONTEXT: A WOMAN'S ILLNESS

Before Josef Breuer and Sigmund Freud published their book *Studies in Hysteria* (1893–1895/1955b) and before Freud and his followers began to develop the tenets of psychoanalysis, mental problems were considered to have roots in a physical condition. In the tradition of Hippocrates, who viewed hysteria as caused by a wandering uterus, neuroses were viewed as "woman's illness" (Veith, 1965). Ovary removal was used as a treatment for hysteria; cauterization or removal of the clitoris were also used to treat women's complaints (Reisman, 1976).[1]

Soon, a dynamic psychotherapy developed as an alternative to such treatments, initially relying on hypnotism and suggestion (Ellenberger, 1970). A debate began between the "somatic" side and the "mental" side of psychiatry, the latter becoming represented by psychoanalysis. "The somatic approach won the day" and "as a result, psychiatry and psychoanalysis developed independently of one another until World War II" (Fine, 1979, p. 10). (Ilze Veith, 1965, has provided a more detailed summary of this debate, which continues today.)

Freud's Women Patients

In 1880, Josef Breuer began to treat an articulate and intelligent hysteric, Bertha Pappenheim (1859–1936), better known as "Anna O." Her case was critical in the discovery of the healing power of the psychoanalytic "talking cure." She and Breuer engaged in a trial-and-error process not guided by application of established technique (Monte, 1987). The joint discovery of the cathartic method by Breuer and Anna O. was

---

[1]Even through the first half of the twentieth century in the United States, surgery or cauterization of the clitoris or blistering the inside of thighs, vulva or clitoral area was recommended in pediatric textbooks as a treatment for masturbation (Spitz, 1952).

later recognized as establishing that repressed emotions would affect mental functioning (Breuer & Freud, 1893–1895/1955b).

Breuer related the case to Freud, who became extremely interested and repeatedly asked Breuer to tell him the story (Breuer & Freud, 1893/1955a; Breuer & Freud, 1893–1895/1955b; Jones, 1953; Monte, 1987). Thus, in one sense, psychoanalysis began with a woman. Later, Pappenheim relocated to Germany, where she became a prominent figure in social work.[2] Among her contributions was the translation of Mary Wollstonecraft's *A Vindication of the Rights of Women* into German (Freeman & Strean, 1987).

Anna O. was not the only patient to contribute to the discovery of therapeutic technique. In the beginning, the majority of Freud's patients were women (Lerman, 1986). Frau Emmy von N. was the first case in which Freud himself employed "the cathartic procedure" (Freeman & Strean, 1987, p. 145). Freud's analysis of Cecelia M. documented the effectiveness of catharsis in relieving emotional effects of a forgotten trauma (Freeman & Strean, 1987). There was also the case of Miss Lucy R. which illustrated that repression was the foundation of psychoanalysis (Freeman & Strean, 1987, p. 154). To treat Fraulein Elisabeth von R., Freud experimented with the technique that was to become free association, another example of the many contributions of women patients to Freud's development of the psychoanalytic method (Freud, in Breuer & Freud, 1893–1895/1955b, p. 63; p. 268).[3]

EXPANDING THE HORIZONS OF PSYCHOANALYSIS: SOME PIONEER WOMEN

The participation of women in psychoanalysis reflected and shaped the larger social context. Psychoanalysis was focused on childhood during a time when children were viewed as women's province. At first this both increased the value of the "women's sphere" in society and legitimized women's participation in psychoanalysis (later it also helped "blame" women, particularly mothers, for society's ills). Further, Freud considered women less competitive and threatening than men. He accepted them as students, relied on them to screen and further his ideas, and used them as a support system. Although his views were not enlightened by today's standards, the fact that he recognized women as part of his circle meant that women would always have a legitimate and visible presence in psychoanalysis.

---

[2]In 1954 the West German government issued a postage stamp with her picture (Ellenberger, 1970).
[3]Of course Freud did not always listen and learn from his women patients, however, the case of Dora being a notable example.

Although women were among the leaders in the extension of analytic concepts and techniques to children, their contributions are not limited to this domain. Early in the evolution of psychoanalysis, alternatives to Freudian conceptions of women were offered, women's psychology becoming the main point of contention in psychoanalysis in the years between 1925 and 1935 (Zilboorg, 1944/1973).

Some women, such as Ruth Mack Brunswick, Marie Bonaparte, Helene Deutsch, Edith Jacobson, and Therese Benedek, did not pose essential contradictions to the Freudian tradition (Moulton, 1974). However others, including Karen Horney and Clara Thompson, challenged the givens of the Freudian psychoanalytic scheme that contributed to the myths about women. They developed new understandings of the psychology of women that went beyond the early psychoanalytic focus on sexuality. Their work became an integral part of psychoanalytic thinking and was essential in the creation of a psychoanalytic understanding of the *human* psyche.

Women in other disciplines also extended psychoanalytic concepts as well as influenced psychoanalytic debates. For example, Mary Chadwick (1925) introduced psychoanalytic concepts into nursing care. Psychoanalysis had a substantial influence on anthropology (Roheim, 1950), and the Rorschach and Thematic Apperception Tests became part of the field-worker's armamentarium (Fine, 1979, p. 467). Women anthropologists such as Margaret Mead, Ruth Benedict, Florence Kluckhohn, and Cora du Bois both reflected and influenced psychoanalysis. Sociologist Nancy Chodorow, who had undergraduate training in culture and personality with Beatrice and John Whiting, melded psychoanalytic concepts with a feminist analysis. She came to describe herself as intellectually "hooked" on analysis (Chodorow, 1989). Jane Goodall contributed to the incest taboo debate with her report that she had never observed mother–son sexual intercourse among chimpanzees in their natural habitat (Fine, 1979). Richard Feldstein and Judith Roof (1989) provide an overview of feminist applications of psychoanalysis to literary texts. This illustrative sampling is but the tip of a very large iceberg.

Early Women Analysts

Freud bestowed a copy of his ring on loyal disciples whom he felt could disseminate psychoanalysis to the world. Women who received the cherished ring included Lou Andreas-Salome, Marie Bonaparte, Ruth Mack Brunswick, Anna Freud, Dorothy Burlingham, Katharine Jones, Gisela Ferenczi, Jeanne Lampl-de Groot, Edith Jackson, and Henny Freud. Other women involved in the development of psychoanalysis were Helene Deutsch,

Margarete Hilferding, Hermine von Hug-Hellmuth, Anny Katan, Marianne Kris, Mira Oberholzer, Eugenia Sokolnicka, Joan Riviere, Eva Rosenfeld, and Beata (Tola) Rank (Freeman & Strean, 1987; Lerman, 1986; Roazen, 1975).

Lou Andreas-Salome

Freud had a close relationship with Lou Andreas-Salome (1861–1937), feminist novelist and biographer. At 50 years of age, she met Freud and began to study with him. She was the first woman invited to attend the weekly Wednesday night sessions held at Freud's home. He described her as "a perceptive and understanding sounding board" for his ideas. He also labeled her "the poet of psychoanalysis" (Freeman & Strean, 1987, p. 102). For many years this colorful, unorthodox figure served as an important "maternal correspondent-confessor" for Anna Freud (Young-Bruehl, 1988), who wrote "I cannot tell you how often I think of a sentence you spoke to me once . . . that it does not matter what fate one has if one only really lives it" (Young-Bruehl, 1988, p. 230).

Although Freud was almost a cult-like figure to many of his followers, Andreas-Salome recognized the link between his achievements and weaknesses. She asked, "confronted by a human being who impresses us as great, should we not be moved rather than chilled by the knowledge that he might have attained his greatness only through his frailties?" (quoted in Roazen, 1975, p. 322).

Marie Bonaparte

Princess Marie Bonaparte (1882–1962), a great-grandniece of Napoleon, was described as "the most important" of Freud's female students (Roazen, 1975, p. 448). She met Freud in 1925 and became a loyal friend, colleague, and benefactor. Bonaparte conducted one of the first psychoanalytic studies of a murderer, "The Case of Madame Lefebvre," involving the crime of a woman who killed her pregnant daughter-in-law (Freeman & Strean, 1987, p. 88). She founded the *Société Psychoanalytique de Paris* in 1926 and was a vice-president of the Council of the International Psychoanalytical Association (Stein-Monod, 1966).

Marie Bonaparte was interested in female sexuality (Bonaparte, 1953) and contributed to early psychoanalytic conceptions of women's sexual development as well as women's character traits. She and Helene Deutsch have been described as "chief architects" of the theory of feminine masochism (Person, 1974, p. 252). Like Freud, Bonaparte believed that gender development diverged with the discovery that boys had penises and girls lacked them. She also believed in bisexuality because "neither 'pure mas-culinity' nor 'pure femininity' was found in anyone" (Freeman & Strean, 1987, p. 89). It was to her that Freud addressed his famous remark, "The great question that has never been answered despite my thirty years of research into the feminine soul is, 'What does a woman want?'" (Freeman & Strean, 1987, p. 200).

Bonaparte also contributed to psychoanalysis in the role of benefactor. In 1927, her financial support founded the *Revue Française de Psychanalyse*; she edited its nonmedical section (Stein-Monod, 1966). In 1929, she rescued Verlag, Freud's publishing house, from bankruptcy (Strouse, 1974). She helped the Freud family escape to England, paying the ransom the Nazis demanded for his departure. She served as a "European way station for refugee analysts" emigrating to the United States and helped "hundreds of Jews escape Nazi persecution" (Strouse, 1974, p. 368). Through courageous action under the eyes of the Gestapo, she saved an important piece of psychoanalytic history by preserving Freud's letters to Wilhelm Fliess. She also defied Freud's instructions that she destroy them (Fine, 1979; Freeman & Strean, 1987).

Ruth Mack Brunswick

Ruth Mack Brunswick (1897–1946), Freud's "favorite" in Vienna (Roazen, 1975, p. 421), was a graduate of Tufts Medical School. She arrived in Vienna in 1922, at age 25. Freud used her to screen his ideas, and she influenced his thinking about the importance of the mother in child development. He also took seriously her contention that psychoses could be treated by psychoanalysis. Freud referred the Wolf Man, his former patient, to Brunswick—a high compliment (Brunswick, 1928). He wrote that Brunswick was the first person to describe a case of neurosis that could be traced to a fixation of the pre-oedipal stage that never reached the oedipal situation at all (Freeman & Strean, 1987, p. 125). By developing theoretical formulations within the framework of the psychology of women while retaining the importance of the Oedipus constellation, she tactfully incorporated ignored phenomena within Freud's libido theory (Roazen, 1975). Brunswick came to be an important mediator and referral point between the American analysts and the Viennese psychoanalytic circle. Karl Menninger was her most famous American student (Roazan, 1975).

Helene Deutsch

Helene Deutsch (1884–1982), described as one of Freud's "Dutiful Daughters" (Chesler, 1972, p. 72), trained as a physician at the University of Vienna. She spent a year in analysis with Freud in 1918, and that year she became the second woman to be admitted to the Vienna Psychoanalytic Society (Roazen, 1985). In 1925 she became Director of the Vienna Psychoanalytic Institute, a position she held until she emigrated to the United States in 1934.

Although Deutsch's work is within the classical Freudian framework, nonetheless she expanded some concepts as they applied to women. Deutsch described herself, Ruth Mack-Brunswick, and Jeanne Lampl-de Groot, as "pioneers in feminine psychology" (Freeman & Strean, 1987, p. 113). Deutsch believed that penis envy played a secondary, not primary, role in a girl's personality development. She also differed with Freud regarding the resolution of the oedipal conflict in girls. She believed that the girl's bond with her mother is crucial to her personality development—the major detachment from the mother and the strong attachment to the father that Freud described in female resolution of the oedipal conflict was inaccurate. Deutsch saw the mother as more powerful in female personality development than Freud did, and she made important contributions to understanding mother–daughter relationships (Freeman & Strean, 1987).

Deutsch nonetheless viewed narcissism, passivity, and masochism as an integral triad in feminine personality. Deutsch shared with Freud certain basic assumptions regarding women's anatomy, physiology, role, and function in society. Inherent in these assumptions was a dual view of women's and men's roles. A woman's biological destiny was motherhood. Women who deviated from traditional roles were perceived as neither normal nor feminine (Deutsch, 1944, 1945).

Both Freud and Deutsch assumed a biologically determined relationship between femininity and masochism, whereas Karen Horney (1933) disagreed with this position. It is ironic, perhaps, that Freud was far less influential in disseminating the idea of feminine masochism than Helene Deutsch (1930/1969, 1944, 1945) and Marie Bonaparte (1953; see Benjamin, 1986). Deutsch, in particular, elaborated on this theme in lengthy publications on female sexuality. Although she initially argued that vaginal orgasm was a mark of a woman's psychological maturity (Deutsch, 1945), she later revised that position to view the clitoris as the sexual organ and the vagina as the organ of reproduction (Deutsch, 1961).

Extensions and Applications: Child Psychoanalysis, Ego Psychology, and Object Relations

Hermine von Hug-Hellmuth

From the case of Little Hans until 1919, only Hermine von Hug-Hellmuth (1871–1924) attempted to analyze children (Segal, 1979, p. 36).

Hug-Hellmuth obtained a doctoral degree from the University of Vienna in 1909. She was a pioneer in using play in child analysis, setting therapeutic goals for child psychoanalysis, and advocating psychoanalytic child observation. She preceded Anna Freud and Melanie Klein in her work on the play technique and psychoanalysis of children, publishing her first article on play therapy in 1913 (Young-Bruehl, 1988, p. 64). Sigmund Freud viewed pedagogical applications of psychoanalysis as an important innovation (Young-Bruehl, 1988). In contrast to Melanie Klein, Hug-Hellmuth believed that analysis was not possible before the child was 7 or 8 years of age.

Melanie Klein

Melanie Klein (1882–1960) was the first person to practice actual analysis, rather than use educative techniques, with younger children. Although Anna Freud and Hug-Hellmuth agreed with Sigmund Freud that children could not form transferences in the same manner as adults, Klein disagreed. She believed that children expressed their unconscious fantasy life when engaged in free, undirected play, and she developed the technique of play therapy, which could be used to treat a child as young as 2 years of age (Klein, 1926/1975, 1932/1984a; Segal, 1980). Klein (1926/1975) described the fantasy life of children almost a decade before Alice and Michael Balint's work (cf. M. Balint, 1953) on the concept of object relations (Cohler, 1989). She made significant contributions to the understanding of pre-oedipal psychological processes (Klein, 1928; Segal, 1980).

Klein (1928), Lampl-de Groot (1927), and Horney (1924) saw the importance of the child's pre-oedipal dependency on the mother's unconditional love and acceptance (Moulton, 1986). Klein's discovery that projective identification is the dominant type of relationship to one's objects in the early months of life placed the mother, not the father, at the center of the formative developmental process (Caper, 1988). Although the influence of both parents was important, the critical relationship was with the mother (Klein, 1963/1984b; Litwin, 1986). While Sigmund Freud viewed the superego as resulting from the internalization of the father's authority, Klein held the revolutionary view that it resulted from the child's guilt at its own greed and aggression toward its mother (Alford, 1989).

Interpretation of transference as well as of play, art, and free associations is essential to the Kleinian psychoanalytic method (Cohler, 1989). Klein viewed transference as "underlying baby feelings, fantasies and mechanisms" (Segal, 1979, p. 170). She believed that transference was based on projection and introjection. This position emphasizes the interaction between psychoanalyst and patient.

Klein pioneered in research on artistic expression and the application of classical analytic techniques with psychotics (Rosenfeld, 1965). She was also the first to recognize the significance of hostile fantasies and postulated an earlier appearance of the superego than had Freud (Fine, 1979, p. 217). Klein considered the fundamental developmental task to be the same for males and females, that is, to integrate love and hate. Some feminists, dissatisfied with Freud's account of sexual differentiation, have adopted Klein's perspective (Alford, 1989, p. 165).

Klein articulated what she called the "depressive position," in which children come to terms with the recognition that the mother who frustrates them and the mother who meets their needs are one and the same. Out of the resolution come efforts at reparation—the basis for a morality that is based on love and that potentially "flies higher than Freud's" (Alford, 1989, p. 38).

Melanie Klein's work in child analysis and object relations has been controversial (Segal, 1980). At the same time, she "opened up areas of investigation into what Freud called 'the dim and shadowy era' of early childhood, which is also the dim and shadowy area of the more primitive layers of the unconscious, and she has provided both a conceptual framework for understanding them and a technical tool for their investigation" (Segal, 1979, p. 177).

Klein's approach is currently used throughout the world. There is general agreement in child psychoanalytic circles with her position that children can experience a transference neurosis similar to that of adults. Cohler (1989) suggested that, after Sigmund Freud, of course, Melanie Klein could be considered the single most influential psychoanalyst in the world, based on the number and professional stature of psychoanalysts who identify themselves with her. Although she did not develop the social implications of her work, later psychoanalysts, including Dorothy Dinnerstein (1976), "have drawn upon Klein to explain 'sexual arrangements and the human malaise'" (Alford, 1989, p. 1).

Interestingly, Klein remains relatively unknown in the United States (Cohler, 1989). Nonetheless, studies of children based on the influential psychoanalytic perceptions of Klein, Anna Freud, and British psychoanalyst Susan Isaacs are recognized as having stimulated child development researchers in the United States to ask "why" instead of "how" (Senn, 1975, p. 41). Today the interest in object relations in feminist psychoanalysis can be considered a legacy of Melanie Klein (Alford, 1989).

According to Reuben Fine, Melanie Klein and Anna Freud "may fairly be said to have initiated the psychoanalytic treatment of children" (1979, p. 100). He describes the distinctive feature of British psychoanalysis as the harmonious existence of three schools, under the leadership of Melanie Klein, Anna Freud, and an uncommitted middle group, respectively (p. 145).

Anna Freud

Anna Freud (1895–1982) broke boundaries both in child psychoanalysis and ego psychology (A. Freud, 1965–1974). She was the youngest child of Sigmund Freud (Fine, 1990; Young-Bruehl, 1988). Anna Freud was among her father's most devoted colleagues and sought to work within his theoretical framework (Liebert & Spiegler, 1987). But her work expanded and shifted the emphasis of psychoanalysis to the ego and its mechanisms of defense (A. Freud, 1946). She extended Freudian theory in systematizing and legitimizing ego psychology (Monte, 1987).

Anna Freud distinguished six developmental lines with the common theme of gradual mastery of oneself and one's reality. Development began with dependency, progressed to emotional self-reliance, and concluded with egocentricity and companionship. She considered these the basis for a normal life. She strongly influenced other theorists, including ego psychologist Erik Erikson who studied with her and who, in lifelong collaboration with Joan Erikson, developed their life-cycle theory of human development (Goleman, 1988).

Anna Freud and her coworkers developed a formalized system of diagnosis that emphasized the sequence of personality development. She developed an assessment instrument, the Metapsychological Profile (A. Freud, 1965, pp. 138–146) to systematize data for psychoanalysis, which integrated theoretical propositions and observable clinical phenomena. Anna Freud is also known for her innovations in the uses of play in child analysis. She believed that child therapy requires the child's educational dependency and a positive, affectionate quality toward the analyst. In contrast to Klein, she believed that the child does not form a transference neurosis, and thus she focused on educative techniques. She was an admirer of Italian physician and educator, Marie Montessori (Rambusch, 1990).

In 1940, during World War II, Anna Freud established the Hampstead Wartime Nursery for Homeless Children to serve displaced children (Fine, 1990). In response to the urging of Kate Friedlander (Lantos, 1966), Anna Freud and her longtime friend and colleague Dorothy Burlingham established the Hampstead Child Therapy Clinic that developed from her wartime nurseries. The clinic was established to study children, provide treatment, and train therapists in child psychoanalysis. Freud and Burlingham described their experiences and observations in their co-authored works, *War and Children* (1943) and *Infants Without Families* (1944).

Dorothy Burlingham (1891–1979), daughter of glass designer Louis C. Tiffany, became "almost one of the Freud family" (Freeman & Strean, 1987, p. 74). She lived and worked closely with Anna Freud in the development of child psychoanalysis. Burlingham financed the Hampstead Clinic, which she co-directed with Anna Freud, and headed the group that piloted the classification of case material that eventually became the Hampstead Index (Fine, 1979). She conducted research on identical twins for many years under the auspices of the clinic (Pumpian-Mindlin, 1966).

Margaret S. Mahler

Margaret S. Mahler (1897–1985) also changed ego psychology and object relations. She made landmark contributions to understanding the process by which the infant assumes its own physical and psychological identity (Mahler, 1968; Mahler, Pine, & Bergmann, 1975). For Mahler, the psychological birth of the infant is a process of separation and individuation (Monte, 1987). Her theory, like those of Anna Freud, Melanie Klein, and others, is based on clinical and naturalistic observations of children at play (Liebert & Spiegler, 1987).

Mahler's paradigm is now applied to relationships throughout the life-span (Fine, 1979), and the theme of separation-individuation has became a central focus of psychoanalytic theory. Her work on normal development is summarized in *The Psychological Birth of the Human Infant* (Mahler et al., 1975) and has been influential in the development of Kohut's (1977) self psychology. Mahler also explored infantile psychosis, postulating faulty individuation based on organic causes as the core of that condition (Mahler, 1968). She made a major contribution in her articulation of the concept of *rapprochement crisis*, which expresses the child's ambivalence about separating from the mother (Mahler, et al., 1975). Mahler's theory would predict that the closer the infant–mother attachment, the more independence and exploration the child will display (Eagle, 1984). This prediction has been supported by Mary Ainsworth (1983, 1984; Ainsworth, Bell, & Stayton, 1971).

The careful studies of infant development by Mahler and her colleagues challenged Freud's idea that gender differentiation occurred in the phallic stage. It has subsequently been accepted that the development of gender and its elaborations depend upon the larger familial and social context. The importance of the role of biological factors varies. As the work of John

Money and Anke Ehrhardt (1972) has shown, this is true even when the child's anatomical sex is unclear.

Individuation requires the ability to synthesize aggressive and libidinal strivings toward the mother and the capacity to draw sustenance from an internalized representation of her. Thus, both Klein and Mahler have shown that the roots of identity lie much earlier in development than the oedipal complex and are more influenced by the mother than Sigmund Freud's viewpoint suggests (Monte, 1987).

Frieda Fromm-Reichmann

Influenced by Harry Stack Sullivan, Frieda Fromm-Reichmann (1889–1957) recommended bold modifications in psychoanalytic techniques that forced revisions in psychoanalytic theory (Wallerstein, 1975). She and Anna Freud were instrumental in developing psychoanalytic psychotherapy, the former with schizophrenics, the latter with children (Chessick, 1977). Whereas Mahler (1968) viewed psychosis as resulting from a child's inability to use maternal care, Fromm-Reichmann viewed psychosis as resulting from damaging behavior in early infancy by the mother. In fact, she coined the unfortunate term "schizophrenogenic mother" (Fine, 1979, p. 152).

Fromm-Reichmann was the therapist of Hannah Green (aka Joanne Greenberg), who wrote *I Never Promised You a Rose Garden* (1964). She conceptualized the Oedipus complex as a wish for closeness and tenderness with one parent while feeling envious resentment toward the other. She also urged that therapists consider the adult client as a person of his or her present age, and that therapists should not insist there has been regression and fixation to an infantile stage of development (Reisman, 1976). Fromm-Reichmann, along with Edith Weigert and others, was a founding Fellow of the Academy of Psychoanalysis (Millette, 1966). Margaret Rioch, the only psychologist allowed to conduct psychotherapy at the Chestnut Lodge Sanitarium where Fromm-Reichmann was located, described Fromm-Reichmann as an approachable, positive, and powerful person: "I used to say that her many cures . . . were in part . . . a matter of her will power. She made it very clear that the patient *would* get well. . . ." (Rioch, 1983, p. 177).

Fromm-Reichmann also extended thinking about cultural influences in women's psychology, including (a) the lack of value in the culture put upon female procreation, (b) men's fear and envy of women's procreative ability, and (c) the need for women to conceal the pleasurable sexual experiences associated with women's reproductive experiences, including those associated with breast feeding. Her position is summarized in a presentation by Fromm-Reichmann and Virginia K. Gunst (1950/1973) that appears in Jean Baker Miller's classic collection of historic works related to the psychology of women (Miller, 1973).

The Evolving Place of Motherhood

In id psychology, analytic theory was critical of the family, viewing it as a source of repression and, therefore, psychopathology. In ego psychology, the family was transformed into a source of love and support (especially from the mother). Separation anxiety became more important than castration anxiety in the 1940s (Fine, 1979). Research on child development and emphasis on the role of the mother reflected an appreciation of the fact that children exist in relationship to their environments. The family began to receive attention, and there began a quest to identify the characteristics of healthy parents (e.g., S. Brody, 1956).

Women psychoanalysts such as Klein, Mahler, and Fromm-Reichmann were crucial in articulating the importance of the maternal role in child development, whether for good or ill. Regrettably, all too often mothers became portrayed as transmitters of pathology despite the failure of research to establish factors that clearly differentiated families of schizophrenics, neurotics, or individuals with behavior disorders (Osmond, Franks, & Burtle, 1974).

As mothering became recognized as critical to infant development, psychoanalysts took up the call for better mothering. In 1943, New York analyst Margaret Ribble published *The Rights of Infants* (Ribble, 1943) in which she coined the term "tender loving care" (TLC) and emphasized the importance of a warm interpersonal relationship between mother and child (Fine, 1979, p. 152). Sylvia Brody (1956; S. Brody & Axelrad, 1978) also identified a warm, empathic mother as the single most important element in healthy child development. Nancy Chodorow (1989) provides an interesting summary of the evolution of views on motherhood, including those of feminist psychoanalysts.

There can be no doubt that psychoanalysis changed the American approach to child care. For example, Martha Wolfenstein (1953) studied government advice on infant care, documenting a permissive change in official attitudes toward childhood sexuality in response to the influence of psychoanalysis.

Dreams and Emotions

Erika Fromm

As more women trained and participated in the field of psychoanalysis, they both refined and challenged Freud's beliefs in other ways. Erika Fromm

(b. 1910) established the first psychological laboratory in a Dutch mental hospital. In her book with Thomas French on dream interpretation (1964/1986), is cited as a "modern classic of psychoanalysis" by International Universities Press. In contrast to Freud, Fromm viewed the dream as a product of ego functioning and as an attempt to find a solution for a current conflict. Although Freud came to reject hypnotism, Fromm conducted pioneering research in the field of hypnoanalysis (Fromm, 1988).

Many women have studied dreams, including Mary Calkins, the first woman president of the American Psychological Association (1905) and inventor of the paired associate technique. Calkins viewed her research, which demonstrated the link between dream content and daily life, as contradicting the Freudian conception of dreams (Furumoto, 1990). However, Freud himself (1900/1953) cited Calkins' research as providing statistical evidence in support of his impressions. Rosalind Dymond Cartwright, who worked with Carl Rogers (Rogers & Dymond, 1954), has also made substantial contributions to understanding dreams (Cartwright, 1977, 1978).

Helen Flanders Dunbar

During the 1930s, the development of emotions became a focus of research. Helen Flanders Dunbar (1902–1959), who helped found the American Psychosomatic Society, published the first compendium of research on psychosomatic relationships, *Emotions and Bodily Changes* (1935). Described as a "major theoretician" of the time, she held that there was a correlation between personality type and illness. She was also the first editor of *Psychosomatic Medicine*.

Catherine Bacon's work with Alexander Bacon on peptic ulcer laid the groundwork for theories about the relation between emotions and disease (Millette, 1966). Women who contributed to understanding of emotions include Magda Arnold and Katherine Banham (Banham, 1983). Helen Block Lewis (1971) linked shame and guilt with cognitive style and viewed shame and guilt as having distinctive operations in the self.

Women's Challenges to Classical Psychoanalysis: The Importance of Interpersonal and Cultural Processes

Work that emphasized the importance of childhood helped to promote a legitimate role for women in psychoanalysis and drew attention to the importance of the role of mothers in child development. However, it also helped to support stereotypes about women and "blame" them for the origin of mental illness. Freud's early pronouncements about women, particularly with regard to anatomy being destiny, supported stereotypes about women and served as a quasi-scientific rationale for perpetuating them.

Psychoanalysis evolved from "an oversimplified identification of the cognitive functions with instinctual drives in the id period, to early clarification of ego mechanisms, particularly cognitive controls, to the current sophisticated image of an interplay of ego and id in all cognitive functioning" (Fine, 1979, p. 350). Women played important roles in the elaborations and challenges that resulted in that evolution as well as the challenges that forced increased recognition of the importance of interpersonal and cultural processes to human functioning.[4]

As psychoanalysis evolved, splinter groups formed that focused on interpersonal relationships and cultural influences and challenged the idea that women's lot could not change. At the New York Psychoanalytic Institute, Karen Horney and Clara Thompson promoted attention to issues of culture (O'Connell, 1990). Thompson served as the first president of the Baltimore–Washington Psychoanalytic Society, where she worked with Frieda Fromm-Reichmann, Mabel Blake Cohen, and Lucille Dooley before joining the Institute in 1933 (Moulton, 1974). The New York Psychoanalytic Institute offered "the most formidable alternatives to classical Freudian psychoanalysis" (Fine, 1979, p. 113). Other women who played important roles in its organization and teaching included Helen Flanders Dunbar, Phyllis Greenacre, Marion Kenworthy, Edith Jacobson, and Margaret Mahler (Millette, 1966).

In 1939, Karen Horney's *New Ways in Psychoanalysis* was published, and in 1941, Karen Horney, Clara Thompson, William Silverberg, and others established the Association for the Advancement of Psycho-analysis because they felt a lack of academic freedom in the New York Psychoanalytic Institute. In 1942, citing similar grounds, Clara Thompson, Erich Fromm, and Harry Stack Sullivan withdrew from this new association to form what became the William Alanson White Institute of Psychiatry, Psychoanalysis, and Psychology (Millette, 1966). Among the students of Clara Thompson and Frieda Fromm-Reichmann was Ruth Moulton, who also contributed to writings on the psychology of women (Moulton, 1966, 1970, 1974). Thus, women were leaders of post–World War II splinter groups that emphasized the critical role of culture in the development of personality and neurosis.

Karen Horney

Karen Horney (1885–1952) desexualized the oedipal complex, interpreting the process as symptomatic of disturbed interpersonal relationships

---

[4]For an expanded discussion of the historical roots of psychotherapy, its evolution in type of patient, and its treatment of women, see Osmond, Franks, and Burtle (1974).

(O'Connell, 1990). She theorized that the "passionate clinging to one parent and jealousy toward the other" (1939, p. 83) is the result of basic anxiety produced by a disturbed parent–child relationship and not a result of the oedipal complex. Neuroses were brought about by cultural factors "which more specifically meant that neuroses were generated by disturbances in human relationships" (1945, p. 12). Horney identified and defined the causes of neurosis and "the character structure which recurs in nearly all neurotic persons of our time in one or another form" (1937, p. vii). She found that a childhood marked by lack of warmth and security and a feeling of isolation and helplessness in a potentially hostile world can lead to neurosis. The underlying cause was the same for women and men: basic anxiety produced by a disturbed parent–child relationship and the repression of basic hostility in the interest of survival and security. Anxiety and hostility were interlocking components of neurotic character structure. Horney thus illuminated the influence of cultural and social influences on human growth and the achievement of self-realization (O'Connell, 1990).

Horney theorized that unhealthy functioning resulted in alienation from the real self (the true person, including potentialities and the urge for self-realization) and "a devil's pact," that is, the adoption of an unrealistic idealized self (1950, pp. 17, 87). In an attempt to regain security, the neurotic person attempts to mold the self into something valued by the culture. Her work has provided "a major reframing of how we comprehend personality and its disorders . . . [many of her] contributions have been assimilated into American psychology and psychoanalysis" (Ingram, 1985, p. 308). Horney also identified a variety of defense mechanisms, including some that reflected problems associated with behaviors considered a normal part of male roles: neurotic competitiveness and quest for power, prestige, and possession (Horney, 1937), neurotic pride, appeal of mastery, and search for glory (Horney, 1950). These insights and concepts have influenced theorists and practitioners of diverse perspectives including humanists, self psychologists, cognitive therapists, psychoanalysts, feminists, and existentialists (O'Connell, 1990).

Karen Horney pioneered and developed a feminine psychology that provided a new way of thinking about women (O'Connell, 1990). She was the first woman to present a paper on feminine psychology at an international meeting, the Seventh International Psychoanalytic Congress held in Berlin in 1922. Her interest in feminine psychology came from her feeling that psychology was androcentric and that, as a woman, it was her task to "work out a fuller understanding for specifically female trends and attitudes in life" (Kelman, 1971). She objected to the development of a psychology of women based on the psychology of men. She wrote fourteen papers that were compiled posthumously into a volume titled *Feminine Psychology* (Kelman, 1967), in which she emphasized the importance of cultural and societal factors on women's "inferior position" and stated her belief that what women envy is not the penis but the superior position of men in society (O'Connell, 1980). She refuted previous theories about female masochism and challenged the belief in the pervasiveness of this phenomenon (Horney, 1935). She effectively demonstrated that cultural and societal factors encourage women to be dependent upon men for love, prestige, wealth, care, and protection (1934).

Horney was a member of the Berlin Psychoanalytic Society and the New York Psychoanalytic Society. She was a founder of the Association for the Advancement of Psychoanalysis; a founder and dean of the American Institute for Psychoanalysis, a training institute; and a founder and the editor of the *American Journal of Psychoanalysis*. In 1955 a clinic named for her was opened in New York City, slightly more than two years after her death on December 4, 1952 (Rubins, 1978).

Clara Thompson

Clara Thompson (1893–1958) belonged to the school of psychoanalysis that viewed interpersonal relationships as central to adjustment and well-being (Williams, 1983). In her work she articulated the personal, social, and cultural conflicts of women that are basic to modern feminist consciousness (Moulton, 1974). She viewed personality development as a process of acculturation rather than a process of transforming sexual energy and repression. Like Horney, Thompson disagreed with Freud's biological views on female personality. She supported the position that culture, not biology, explained the phenomenon of penis envy and women's "inferiority" (Thompson, 1942/1964).

Thompson proclaimed that women envied male status and felt inferior because of their social disadvantages, asking if the warfare between the sexes is indeed "different in kind from other types of struggle which go on between humans . . ." (Thompson, 1943/1973, p. 44). She drew parallels between race and sex, noting that the penis or lack of a penis was a distinguishable mark of difference used to justify sex discrimination in a manner similar to the way that black skin was used to justify racial discrimination (Thompson, 1943/1973, p. 45).

Later in her career, in the 1950s, Thompson focused on issues of transference and countertransference. Her book *Psychoanalysis: Evolution and Development* (1950) was "the first to integrate the various theories of Freud and the early deviants—Adler, Jung, Rank, Ferenczi, Reich—and to compare them with latter dissidents such as Sullivan, Fromm, and Horney" (Moulton, 1974, p. 285).

THE EMERGENCE OF APPLIED PSYCHOLOGY: SOME PIONEER WOMEN

Psychoanalysis and American psychology evolved along fairly independent lines until World War II. Understanding the evolution of applied fields in American psychology and the opportunities for psychotherapy in them requires appreciation of events in the larger social context.

Social and economic factors that shaped American culture during the formative years of psychology included the women's suffrage, progressive education, and child welfare movements; the rise of professionalism; World War I; the Great Depression; World War II and its social and economic aftermath;[5] the civil rights movement; and the second wave of the women's movement in the 1960s and 1970s (see Russo, 1983; Russo & Denmark, 1987; Russo & O'Connell, 1980 for overviews). Women were involved in all fields of psychology. However, the progressive education and child welfare movements provided opportunities for women to contribute to research and applications in child development, mental retardation, and mental testing. These movements stimulated the development of child guidance clinics and child welfare institutes where women could find supportive work environments. From such positions they contributed to theory and research on human development and behavior that illuminated all psychology.

Education and Child Guidance

Although university-based psychological clinics did not have a dynamic perspective, pioneering applications of psychoanalytic techniques were used in education and in the treatment of juvenile delinquents. One of the most effective advocates for psychology in "progressive education" was Caroline Zachry (1894–1945). Zachry, who founded what became the Caroline B. Zachry Institute of Human Development, has been described as "one of the first people really well-trained in analytic theory who become active in education in the United States (Senn, 1975). Benjamin Spock credited Zachry with influencing him to think in terms of parent–child

---

[5]Laura Fermi (1971) reported that psychoanalysis was one of "two areas in which the impact of the Europeans was most felt" (p. 17) (the other was atomic science). She observed that about 30 percent of immigrant psychoanalysts were women; by 1958, however, women were only 9 percent of students in the American Psychoanalytic Association's approved training institutions.

relationships and to challenge pediatricians to help parents rear their children.

Expansion of psychotherapeutic techniques occurred when Jane Addams founded Hull House, the first settlement house in the United States, in effect beginning the field of social work (Crovitz & Buford, 1978). In 1908, social worker Julia Lathrop, Allen Burns, and psychiatrist William Healy met at Hull House to plan a program of research to determine the causes of juvenile delinquency. As a result, the Juvenile Psychopathic Institute, the first child guidance clinic, opened in 1909 with its three-person staff, psychiatrist William Healy as Director, psychologist Grace M. Fernald, and a secretary (Reisman, 1976). The dynamic orientation of the Institute contrasted with that of the first university-based, education-oriented psychological clinic founded by Lightner Witmer. Its work provided important intellectual roots for child guidance and counseling and child psychiatry (Smirnoff, 1971).

Augusta Fox Bronner

In 1913, Augusta Fox Bronner (1881–1966) joined the Institute staff. She and William Healy organized the Judge Baker Foundation, which made diagnostic evaluations for the courts. When the Illinois legislature enacted a law in 1917 that allowed a psychologist to serve on the commission to certify persons for commitment to institutions for the retarded, Augusta Bronner was the first to serve in that position. Child guidance clinics multiplied, and in 1924, child guidance clinicians founded the American Orthopsychiatric Association. In 1931, Augusta Bronner was elected to its presidency (Reisman, 1976).

"With the development of the child guidance movement, under the leadership of William Healy and Augusta Bronner, the close partnership of psychoanalysis and clinical psychology was recognized as desirable in the study and treatment of children's disorders" (Millette, 1966, p. 581). Subsequently, Marion Kenworthy, a student of Healy, helped inaugurate a two-year guidance curriculum at the New York School of Social Work. "The . . . interdisciplinary team, psychiatrist, psychologist, and social worker, was the natural product of these early collaborative enterprises" (Millette, 1966, p. 591).

FEMINIST PSYCHOLOGY: THE "FIRST WAVE"

Stephanie Shields (1975) summarized the prejudices and stereotypes about women that pervaded psychology at the turn of the century. Among the most outspoken was APA founder G. Stanley Hall, who asserted that a woman who chose a career over marriage violated her biological ethic—and risked her mammary function (Ehrenreich & English, 1978). As early as 1918, psychoanalytic concepts were used to denigrate feminist efforts as "very largely a compensation for a strong but imperfectly repressed masochistic tendency" (Ryan, 1983).

Feminist psychologists, such as Helen Thompson Woolley (1874–1947) and Leta Stetter Hollingworth (1886–1939) used their scientific skills to advance understanding of the psychology of women in order to rebut gender stereotypes about women's nature and abilities. Their work challenged beliefs in female inferiority and the idea that biology was destiny. Such women represent the "first wave" of feminist psychology in the United States. In particular, Leta Hollingworth demanded that psychology apply scientific rigor in research on women (Benjamin & Shields, 1990). She proceeded to refute the myths of the time through empirical research on mental and physical performance during the menstrual cycle, on the variability hypothesis (which erroneously attributed men's higher status to greater male variability), and on women's marriage and motherhood roles (Shields, 1975).

Fliegal (1986) discussed the debate about women's nature and development that was occurring in psychoanalytic circles during this period. Karen Horney, strongly supported by Ernest Jones, played a central role in the controversy. Helene Deutsch and Jeanne Lampl-de Groot supported aspects of the Freudian scheme, and Otto Fenichel attempted to moderate the differences. Fliegel observed that nuances in contemporary formulations become more clear when considered in the context of these early dissensions. She pointed out that the controversy was "more extensive than is quite apparent from the printed record" (1986, p. 4).

During the 1930s, several significant events affected the participation of women in applied psychology in the United States (Russo, 1983). The economic crash of 1929 and the subsequent Great Depression resulted in societal attempts to restrict married women's employment. The New Deal institutionalized sex discrimination, particularly against married women. Constructions of knowledge that could be used to justify legal sanctions against employed women became in vogue. As backlash against women's employment gained momentum, both "scientific" evidence and psychoanalysis were used to urge women to confine themselves to domestic activities in order to avoid guilt and psychic conflicts (Deutsch, 1944). Women such as Georgene Seward, however, continued to use their scientific expertise to challenge stereotypes and promote a fuller understanding of women's lives (Stevens & Gardner, 1982).

Minority Women

During the years 1920–1950, 32 doctorates in psychology (PhD) and education (EdD) went to Black Americans; eight of them were earned by Black women. Of the 13,800 women holding psychology doctorates in 1984, 7.2% were members of minority groups—3.6% Black, 2.2% Asian, and 1.2% Hispanic. The percentage of Native American women holding doctorates is less than 1%. Ethnic groups are not equally distributed across subfields. Overall, 61% of doctoral psychologists are found in clinical, counseling, or school psychology. Hispanics are more likely (69% of all Hispanic psychologists) and Asians less likely (54% of all Asian psychologists) to work in those fields.

Information on the contributions of ethnic minority women to psychotherapy is meager. The first Black woman to earn a PhD in psychology in 1934, Ruth Howard (Beckham), interned at the dynamically-oriented Illinois Institute for Juvenile Research and became a practicing psychologist (Howard, 1983). She and her husband, psychologist Albert S. Beckham, codirected the Center for Psychological Services in Chicago (Guthrie, 1976).

Similarly, Alberta Banner Turner, the second Black woman to earn a PhD in psychology pursued a clinical career. A clinician at the Ohio Bureau of Juvenile Research, her name was "synonymous with mention of the field of juvenile rehabilitation and treatment in Ohio for 27 years" (Guthrie, 1976, p. 148).

Mamie Phipps Clark (1917–1983) was another famous Black woman psychologist who expanded the bounds of psychological services. In 1946, in response to the lack of psychological and psychiatric services for minority children in New York City, she and her husband Kenneth Clark opened the Northside Testing and Consultation Center, which became the Northside Center for Child Development. It "was the first full-time child guidance center offering psychiatric, psychological, and casework services to children and families in the Harlem area" (Clark, 1983, p. 273). The Clarks jointly conducted the research on racial identification in children that came to be used in the *Brown v. the Board of Education* Supreme Court decision to desegregate the nation's schools.

Carolyn Robertson Payton (b. 1925) also improved psychological services for minorities. She advocated special training in psychotherapy for those who work with ethnic minority clients. At Howard University, she trained hundreds of counselors and psychotherapists to work with ethnic minority populations. She also served on the American Psychological Association's Task Force on Sex Bias and Sex Role Stereotyping in Psychotherapeutic Practice, the first formal APA body to undertake a feminist critique of psychotherapeutic practice. In 1981, when she chaired the APA Committee on Women in Psychology (CWP), sexism in training was a priority area for the committee. She contributed to an important consumer handbook for women in psychotherapy that was widely circulated under the CWP auspices during her tenure (Liss-Levinson et al., 1985). In 1982 she received the APA Award for Distinguished Contributions to Public Service. Among her other accomplishments, she was the first woman and first Black psychologist to serve as Director of the U. S. Peace Corps (Keita & Muldrow, 1990; Payton, 1988).

After World War II: Conflicts and Contradictions in Women's Lives

In the 1950s, a cult of femininity arose, which led to increasing contradictions between women's idealized roles and their realities. Freudianism, as constructed in the United States, achieved the status of an ideology and was used to support beliefs in male supremacy and female subordination (Donovan, 1990). Women were urged to return to the home, and the literature on the need for mother love proliferated. Ironically, while public ideology extolled motherhood and domesticity, in 1950, one in three married women was employed (Ryan, 1983). Women pursuing professional careers in clinical, counseling, and school psychology were not immune to conflicts and the negative attitudes expressed toward professional women during this period (Mednick, 1988).

The 1960s was a period of renewed social reform and the civil rights movement. Betty Friedan (1963) published the *Feminine Mystique*, and the second wave of the feminist movement began to emerge. The idea that the goal of therapy for women was adjustment to their prescribed roles was challenged, and elimination of sex bias in psychology became a part of the national agenda. Classical psychoanalytic assumptions about women continued to be challenged by new research and theoretical developments. Drawing attention to the work of William Masters and Virginia Johnson (1966) on human sexual response, Mary Jane Sherfey (1966) elaborated its implications for psychoanalytic theory. In particular, this work challenged the psychoanalytic tenet that vaginal orgasm was an index of psychosexual maturity.

FEMINIST PSYCHOLOGY: THE SECOND WAVE

As the feminist movement took form, so too did a feminist psychology of women that produced major critiques of Freudian psychology and psychotherapy and organized efforts to change the concepts and conduct of psychotherapeutic theory, research, and practice (Chesler, 1972; Fields, 1975; Firestone, 1970; Millett, 1970; Tennov, 1975; Weisstein, 1970). In 1971, two textbooks appeared, *On the Psychology of Women* (Sherman, 1971) and *Psychology of Women* (Bardwick, 1971), which summarized feminist criticisms of Freudian theory of feminine development. These authors and other feminists challenged the psychoanalytic idea of male development as the norm and the goal of therapy as adjustment to sex roles of marriage and motherhood. Biological determinism was rejected and the importance of going beyond intrapsychic approaches and examining effects of the social context was emphasized. Problems that had been ignored or trivialized, including incest and violence against women, were named, and new approaches to them based on feminist analyses were developed (Franks & Burtle, 1974; Mander & Rush, 1974; Rawlings & Carter, 1977; Williams, 1976).

Feminists worked through their professional associations to promote empowerment of women in all aspects of psychology, including psychotherapy. The American Psychological Association established a Committee on Women in Psychology that provided an important organizing base for feminist psychologists (American Psychological Association, 1973). CWP worked to establish the APA Task Force on Sex Bias and Sex Role Stereotyping in Psychotherapeutic Practice (American Psychological Association, 1975). The Task Force report identified four areas of treatment that were of particular concern: (1) fostering traditional sex roles, (2) bias in expectations and devaluation of women, (3) sexist use of psychoanalytic concepts, and (4) responding to women as objects, including seduction of female clients. It also developed "Guidelines for Therapy with Women" (1978) which identified thirteen general principles for ethical and effective psychotherapy with women. Similarly, the APA Division of Counseling Psychology's Committee on Women published *Principles Concerning the Counseling/Therapy of Women* that became widely endorsed (American Psychological Association, 1979; Fitzgerald & Nutt, 1986).

Policy makers were responsive to a focus on women's issues. At the request of the Women's Council of the Alcohol, Drug Abuse, and Mental Health Administration, the National Institute of Mental Health (NIMH) commissioned at least three annotated bibliographies related to women's mental health in the 1970s. The first two had little information about psychotherapy (Astin, Parelman, & Fisher, 1975; Cromwell, 1972). In 1979, however, NIMH published an annotated bibliography titled *Changing Directions in the Treatment of Women* (Zuckerman, 1979), covering the years 1960–1977 and specifically focused on studies of clinical judgment, the process and outcome of treatment, and studies having implications for treatment.[6] The burgeoning interest in women's mental health issues in the 1970s is evidenced in the fact that of 407 summaries, only 33 were published before 1970. While women were leaders and major contributors in this research, men participated as well: Of the 381 contributors listed, 66% could be identified by name as women, 30% as men.

Feminists have become increasingly sophisticated in their critique of psychotherapy, documenting subtle and pervasive sex bias in psychotherapeutic theories, research, and applications (Alpert, 1986; Brodsky & Hare-Mustin, 1980; Dutton-Douglas & Walker, 1988; Rieker & Carmen, 1984). In developing new theories, methods, and techniques, feminists also offer innovative perspectives on women's development. Women's mental health is viewed in political and social context, and consumer issues are emphasized (American Psychological Association, 1987; Liss-Levinson et al., 1985). Feminists have integrated feminist principles into therapy theories and have developed a variety of feminist approaches to therapies. They have developed alternatives to therapy, including consciousness-raising, assertiveness training, and self-help groups (C. M. Brody, 1984; Dutton-Douglas & Walker, 1988; Rosewater & Walker, 1985).

Effective psychotherapy rests on an understanding of women's development and experiences. Feminist psychotherapists have strongly advocated for research in the psychology of women and assumed leadership positions in APA's research-oriented Division of the Psychology of Women (Division 35). Feminist researchers have explored neglected areas in women's lives such as menstruation and menopause, breast cancer, body image and eating disorders, anger, reproductive events, motherhood, job stress, stereotyping, discrimination, homelessness, sexual harassment, lesbian issues, ethnic minority women's issues, elderly women's issues, and poverty. They have taken new looks at relationships including dependency, violence in intimate relationships, incest, and marital disruption.

These women and men have emphasized the importance of examining inequities of power in the therapy context. They have pointed to the devastating effects of dependency and devaluation for women and promoted a shift of emphasis in therapy from adjustment to agency. They have also sought to identify and celebrate women's strengths and relationships and to empower women (Alpert, 1986; Brodsky & Hare-Mustin, 1980; C. M. Brody, 1984, 1987; Cantor & Bernay, 1986; Dutton-Douglas & Walker, 1988; Eichenbaum & Orbach, 1983; Franks & Rothblum, 1983; Lerman,

---

[6]Irene Elkin Waskow was the NIMH project officer and Ellen Jaffe searched the literature and developed the abstracts. A cursory review of the name indexes suggests there was little overlap with the two earlier bibliographies.

1986; Lerner, 1988; Notman & Nadelson, 1990; Rieker & Carmen, 1984; Robbins & Siegel, 1985; Rosewater & Walker, 1985; Russo, 1985; Sobel & Russo, 1981).

CONCLUSION

What does one learn from learning about women's participation in psychotherapy? How can one construct meaning from accounts of women's history? Increased understanding of women's contributions generates appreciation of the importance of social relations and networks in the building of careers and reputations and defining what is a contribution and what is not. There is a new awareness of difficulties in attributing "credit" for achievement, as conceptions of historical figures begin to include human frailties. Greatness is clearly partially a function of whether or not others perceive one as great and are willing to spread the word (Russo & O'Connell, 1980).

A broader lesson is found in the awareness of the role of the broader social context in the evolution of psychology and its subfields. Women's participation in psychology has both reflected and shaped that larger social context. The study of women's history in psychotherapy documents the power of society's norms and institutions to affect the development of the field as well as the career paths of individuals. Society's needs dictated priorities in psychology, and societal conceptions of "women's sphere" and "women's work" clearly influenced choices open to women who wished to become researchers and practitioners.[7] If ever there were evidence that psychotherapists must play active roles in shaping public policy, women's history in psychotherapy provides it, if only because the opportunities for women in psychotherapy continue to be tied to those for women in the larger society.

The history of women in psychotherapy also reveals how myths perpetuated by psychology (and by psychoanalytic theory in particular) have been used to justify a disadvantaged status for women. Psychotherapists have an ethical responsibility to promote a societal context that will promote the health and well-being of all persons. Without understanding women's development, roles, and circumstances, that responsibility cannot be fulfilled.

Although their opportunities were shaped by the social context, women

---

[7]However, it must be pointed out that until 1974, men were the majority of psychology doctoral recipients in all subfields, including developmental.

in psychology nonetheless have clearly been and still are active agents, seizing available opportunities and creating new ones. They have participated in every subfield of psychology and affected the entire discipline. By their cross-cutting involvement in science, practice, and public interest, they demonstrate a model of the scientist-practitioner who uses her or his expertise on behalf of larger concerns.

In this chapter, which sacrifices depth for breadth and still cannot cover enough, we put women at the center of our analysis. This perspective provides a sharp contrast to the usual accounts in history books. In the celebratory spirit of psychology's centennial, we have focused on contributions and accomplishments rather than barriers and devaluation. A full account would include the anger, frustrations, and tragedies of women psychotherapists. These, too, are a part of psychology's history. We hope that these brushstrokes will stimulate an interest in learning more about the broader picture. We look forward to a synthesis of the new scholarship on women and a reconstruction of psychology's history so that we have an enriched understanding of psychotherapy and psychotherapists, past, present, and future.

REFERENCES

Ainsworth, M. D. (1983). [Autobiography]. In A. N. O'Connell & N. F. Russo (Eds.), *Models of achievement: Reflections of eminent women in psychology* (pp. 200–219). New York: Columbia University Press.

Ainsworth, M. D. (1984). Attachment. In N. S. Endler & J. McV. Hunt (Eds.), *Personality and the behavior disorders* (rev. ed.). New York: Wiley.

Ainsworth, M. D., Bell, S. M., & Stayton, D. C. (1971). Individual differences in a strange-situation behavior in one-year-olds. In H. R. Schaeffer (Ed.), *The origins of human social relations*. New York: Academic Press.

Alford, C. F. (1989). *Melanie Klein and critical social theory: An account of politics, art, and reason based on her psychoanalytic theory*. New Haven, CT: Yale University Press.

Alpert, J. (Ed.). (1986). *Psychoanalysis and women*. Hillsdale, NJ: Analytic Press.

American Psychological Association, Task Force on the Status of Women in Psychology. (1973). Report of the Task Force on the Status of Women in Psychology. *American Psychologist, 28*, 611–616.

American Psychological Association. (1975). Report of the Task Force on Sex Bias and Sex Role Stereotyping in Psychotherapeutic Practice. *American Psychologist, 30*, 1169–1175.

American Psychological Association. (1978). Report of the Task Force on Sex

Bias and Sex Role Stereotyping in Psychotherapeutic Practice. Guidelines for therapy with women. *American Psychologist, 33,* 1122–1123.

American Psychological Association, Division 17, Counseling Psychology. (1979). Principles concerning the counseling and therapy of women. *Counseling Psychologist, 8*(1), 21.

American Psychological Association, Committee on Women in Psychology. (1987). *If sex enters into the psychotherapy relationship.* Washington, DC: American Psychological Association.

Astin, H., Parelman, A., & Fisher, A. (1975). *Sex roles: A research bibliography.* Rockville, MD: National Institute of Mental Health.

Balint, M. (Ed.). (1953). *Primary love and psycho-analytic technique.* New York: Liveright Publishing Corporation.

Banham, K. M. (1983). [Autobiography]. In A. N. O'Connell & N. F. Russo (Eds.), *Models of achievement: Reflections of eminent women in psychology* (pp. 27–41). New York: Columbia University Press.

Bardwick, J. M. (1971). *Psychology of women.* New York: Harper & Row.

Benjamin, J. (1986). The alienation of desire: Women's masochism and ideal love. In J. L. Alpert (Ed.), *Psychoanalysis and women: Contemporary reappraisals* (pp. 113–138). Hillsdale, NJ: Analytic Press.

Benjamin, L., Jr., & Shields, S. (1990). Leta Stetter Hollingworth. In A. N. O'Connell & N. F. Russo (Eds.), *Women in psychology: A bio-bibliographic sourcebook* (pp. 173–183). Westport, CT: Greenwood.

Bonaparte, M. (1953). *Female sexuality.* New York: International Universities Press.

Breuer, J., & Freud, S. (1955a). On the psychic mechanism of hysterical phenomena: A preliminary communication. In J. Strachey (Ed. and Trans.), *The standard edition of the complete psychological works of Sigmund Freud* (Vol. II). London: Hogarth Press. (Original published in 1893)

Breuer, J., & Freud, S. (1955b). Studies in hysteria. In J. Strachey (Ed. and Trans.), *The standard edition of the complete psychological works of Sigmund Freud* (Vol. II). London: Hogarth Press. (Original published 1893–1895)

Brodsky, A., & Hare-Mustin, R. (Eds.). (1980). *Women and psychotherapy.* New York: Guilford Press.

Brody, C. M. (Ed.). (1984). *Women therapists working with women: New theory and process of feminist therapy.* New York: Springer.

Brody, C. M. (Ed.). (1987). *Women's therapy groups: Paradigms for feminist treatment.* New York: Springer.

Brody, S. (1956). *Patterns of mothering.* New York: International Universities Press.

Brody, S., & Axelrad, S. (1978). *Mothers, fathers, and children.* New York: International Universities Press.

Brunswick, R. M. (1928). A supplement to Freud's "History of an infantile neurosis." *International Journal of Psychoanalysis, 9,* 439–476.

Bryan, A. I., & Boring, E. G. (1946). Women in American psychology: Prolegomenon. *American Psychologist, 1,* 71–79.

Cantor, D., & Bernay, T. (1986). *The psychology of today's woman: New psychoanalytic visions.* Hillsdale, NJ: Analytic Press.

Caper, R. (1988). *Immaterial facts: Freud's discovery of psychic reality and Klein's development of his work.* Northvale, NJ: Jason Aronson.

Cartwright, R. D. (1977). *Night life: Explorations in dreaming.* Englewood Cliffs, NJ: Prentice-Hall.

Cartwright, R. D. (1978). *A primer on sleep and dreaming.* Reading, MA: Addison-Wesley.

Chadwick, M. (1925). *Psychology for nurses.* London: William Weinemann.

Chesler, P. (1972). *Women and madness.* Garden City, NY: Doubleday.

Chessick, R. D. (1977). *Great ideas in psychotherapy.* New York: Jason Aronson.

Chodorow, N. J. (1989). *Feminism and psychoanalytic theory.* New Haven, CT: Yale University Press.

Clark, M. P. (1983). Mamie Phipps Clark. In A. N. O'Connell & N. F. Russo (Eds.), *Eminent women in psychology* (pp. 266–277). New York: Human Sciences Press.

Cohler, B. J. (1989). Stirring within psychoanalysis: The English school legacy. [Review of J. M. Hughes, *Reshaping the psychoanalytic domain: The work of Melanie Klein, W. R. D. Fairbairn, and D. W. Winnicott.*] *Reading: A Journal of Reviews and Commentary in Mental Health,* 4–9.

Cromwell, P. E. (1972). *Women and mental health—A bibliography.* Rockville, MD: Division of Scientific and Technical Information, National Institute of Mental Health.

Crovitz, E., & Buford, E. (1978). *Courage knows no sex.* North Quincy, MA: Christopher Publishing House.

Deutsch, H. (1944). *The psychology of women: A psychoanalytic interpretation* (Vol. 1). New York: Grune & Stratton.

Deutsch, H. (1945). *The psychology of women: A psychoanalytic interpretation* (Vol. 2). New York: Grune & Stratton.

Deutsch, H. (1961). Frigidity in women. *Journal of the American Psychoanalytic Association, 9,* 571–584.

Deutsch, H. (1969). The significance of masochism in the mental life of women. In R. Fleiss (Ed.), *The psychoanalytic reader.* New York: International Universities Press. (Original published in 1930)

Dinnerstein, D. (1976). *The mermaid and the minotaur: Sexual arrangements and human malaise.* New York: Harper Colophon Books.

Donovan, J. (1990). *Feminist theory: The intellectual traditions of American feminism.* New York: F. Ungar Publishing Co.

Dunbar, F. (1935). *Emotions and bodily changes.* New York: Columbia University Press.

Dutton-Douglas, M. A., & Walker, L. E. (Eds.). (1988). *Feminist psychotherapies: Integration of therapeutic and feminist systems.* Norwood, NJ: Ablex.

Eagle, M. N. (1984). *Recent developments in psychoanalysis: A critical evaluation.* New York: McGraw-Hill.

Ehrenreich, B., & English, D. (1978). *For her own good.* New York: Anchor Press.

Eichenbaum, L., & Orbach, S. (1983). *Understanding women: A feminist psychoanalytic approach.* New York: Basic Books.

Ellenberger, H. (1970). *The discovery of the unconscious.* New York: Basic Books.

Feldstein, R., & Roof, J. (Eds.). (1989). *Feminism and psychoanalysis.* Ithaca, NY: Cornell University Press.

Fermi, L. (1971). *Illustrious immigrants: The intellectual migration from Europe, 1930– 1941* (2nd ed.). Chicago: University of Chicago Press.

Fields, R. M. (1975). *Psychotherapy: The sexist machine.* Pittsburgh, PA: Know.

Fine, R. (1979). *A history of psychoanalysis.* New York: Columbia University Press.

Fine, R. (1990). Anna Freud (1895–1982). In A. N. O'Connell & N. F. Russo (Eds.), *Women in psychology: A bio-bibliographic sourcebook* (pp. 96–103). Westport, CT: Greenwood.

Firestone, S. (1970). *The dialectic of sex: The case for feminist revolution.* New York: William Morrow.

Fitzgerald, L., & Nutt, R. (1986). The Division 17 principles concerning the counseling/psychotherapy of women: Rationale and implementation. *The Counseling Psychologist, 14,* 180–216.

Fliegel, Z. (1986). Women's development in analytic theory: Six decades of controversy. In J. Alpert (Ed.), *Psychoanalysis and women.* Hillsdale, NJ: Analytic Press.

Franks, V., & Burtle, V. (Eds.). (1974). *Women in therapy: New psychotherapies for a changing society.* New York: Brunner/Mazel.

Franks, V., & Rothblum, E. D. (Eds.). (1983). *The stereotyping of women: Its effects on mental health.* New York: Springer.

Freeman, L., & Strean, H. S. (1987). *Freud & Women.* New York: Continuum.

French, T. M., & Fromm, E. (1986). *Dream interpretation: A new approach* (2nd ed.). New York: International Universities Press. (Original work published 1964)

Freud, A. (1946). *The ego and the mechanisms of defense.* New York: International Universities Press.

Freud, A. (1965–1974). *The writings of Anna Freud* (Vol. 1–7). New York: International Universities Press.

Freud, A. (1965). Normality and pathology in childhood. In *The writings of Anna Freud* (Vol. 6). New York: International Universities Press.

Freud, A., & Burlingham, D. (1943). *War and children.* New York: Medical War Books.

Freud, A., & Burlingham, D. (1944). *Infants without families: The case for and against residential nurseries.* London: Allen & Unwin.

Freud, S. (1953). The interpretation of dreams. In J. Strachey (Ed. & Trans.),

The standard edition of the complete psychological works of Sigmund Freud (Vols. 4 & 5). London: Hogarth. (Original work published 1900)

Friedan, B. (1963). *The feminine mystique.* New York: Dell.

Fromm, E. (1988). [Autobiography]. In A. N. O'Connell & N. F. Russo (Eds.), *Models of achievement: Reflections of eminent women in psychology* (Vol. 2; pp. 88–101). Hillsdale, NJ: Erlbaum.

Fromm-Reichmann, F., & Gunst, V. K. (1973). On the denial of women's sexual pleasure. In J. B. Miller (Ed.), *Psychoanalysis and women: Contributions to new theory and therapy* (pp. 75–82). New York: Brunner/Mazel. (Original published 1950)

Furumoto, L. (1990). Mary Whiton Calkins (1863–1930). In A. N. O'Connell & N. F. Russo (Eds.), *Women in psychology: A bio-bibliographic sourcebook* (pp. 57–65). Westport, CT: Greenwood Press.

Goleman, D. (1988, June 14). Erickson, in his old age, expands his view of life. *New York Times,* p. C14.

Green, H. (1964). *I never promised you a rose garden.* New York: Holt.

Guthrie, R. (1976). *Even the rat was white.* New York: Harper & Row.

Horney, K. (1924). The genesis of the castration complex in women. *International Journal of Psycho-Analysis, 5,* 50–75.

Horney, K. (1933). Maternal conflicts. *American Journal of Orthopsychiatry, 3,* 455–463. [Also in H. Kelman (Ed.) (1967), *Feminine psychology.* New York: Norton.]

Horney, K. (1934). The overvaluation of love: A study of common present-day feminine type. *Psychoanalytic Quarterly, 3,* 605–638.

Horney, K. (1935). The problem of feminine masochism. *Psychoanalytic Review, 22,* 241–257.

Horney, K. (1937). *The neurotic personality of our time.* New York: Norton.

Horney, K. (1939). *New ways in psychoanalysis.* New York: Norton.

Horney, K. (1945). *Our inner conflicts.* New York: Norton.

Horney, K. (1950). *Neurosis and human growth.* New York: Norton.

Howard, R. W. (1983). [Autobiography]. In A. N. O'Connell & N. F. Russo (Eds.), *Models of achievement: Reflections of eminent women in psychology* (pp. 55–67). New York: Columbia University Press.

Ingram, D. H. (1985). Karen Horney at 100: Beyond the frontier. *American Journal of Psychoanalysis, 45,* 305–309.

Jones, E. (1953). *The life and work of Sigmund Freud: The formative years and the great discoveries* (Vol. 1). New York: Basic Books.

Keita, G. P., & Muldrow, T. (1990). Carolyn Robertson Payton (1925–   ). In A. N. O'Connell & N. F. Russo (Eds.), *Women in psychology: A bio-bibliographic sourcebook* (pp. 266–274). Westport, CT: Greenwood.

Kelman, H. (1967). *Feminine psychology.* New York: Norton.

Kelman, H. (1971). *Helping people: Karen Horney's psychoanalytic approach*. New York: Science House.

Klein, M. (1928). Early stages of Oedipal conflict. *International Journal of Psycho-Analysis, 9*, 332–345.

Klein, M. (1975). The psychological principles of early analysis. In *Love, Guilt and reparation and other works, 1921–1945* (pp. 128–138). New York: Macmillan. (Original work published 1926)

Klein, M. (1984a). *The psychoanalysis of children*. New York: Macmillan. (Original work published 1932)

Klein, M. (1984b). Some reflection on the Oresteia. In *Envy and gratitude and other works, 1946–1963* (pp. 275–299). New York: Macmillan. (Original work published 1963)

Kohut, H. (1977). *The restoration of the self*. New York: International Universities Press.

Kohut, J. (1990, May). [Unpublished tables from the APA Employment Survey.]

Lampl-de Groot, J. (1927). The evaluation of the oedipal complex in women. *International Journal of Psycho-Analysis, 9*, 332–345.

Lantos, B. (1966). Kate Friedlander: 1903–1949. In F. Alexander, S. Eisenstein, & M. Grotjahn (Eds.), *Psychoanalytic pioneers* (pp. 508–518). New York: Basic Books.

Lerman, H. (1986). *A mote in Freud's eye: From psychoanalysis to the psychology of women*. New York: Springer.

Lerner, H. G. (1988). *Women in therapy*. Northdale, NJ: Jason Aronson.

Lewis, H. (1971). *Shame and guilt in neurosis*. New York: International Universities Press.

Liebert, R. M., & Spiegler, M. D. (1987). *Personality: Strategies and issues*. Homewood, IL: Dorsey Press

Liss-Levinson, N., Clanar, A., Ehrenberg, O., Fidell, L., Maffel, P., Redstone, J., Russo, N. F., Solomons, D., & Tennov, D. (1985). *Women in psychotherapy: A consumer handbook*. Washington, DC: National Coalition for Women's Mental Health.

Litwin, D. (1986). Autonomy: A conflict for women. In J. L. Alpert (Ed.), *Psychoanalysis and women: Contemporary reappraisals* (pp. 183–213). Hillsdale, NJ: Analytic Press.

Mahler, M. (1968). *On human symbiosis and the vicissitudes of individuation*. New York: International Universities Press.

Mahler, M., Pine, F., & Bergman, A. (1975). *The psychological birth of the human infant: Symbiosis and individuation*. New York: Basic Books.

Mander, A. V., & Rush, A. K. (1974). *Feminism as therapy*. New York: Random House.

Masters, W. H., & Johnson, V. E. (1966). *Human sexual response*. Boston: Little, Brown & Co.

Mednick, M. T. (1988). [Autobiography]. In A. N. O'Connell & N. F. Russo

(Eds.), *Models of achievement: Reflections of eminent women in psychology* (Vol. 2; pp. 246–259). Hillsdale, NJ: Erlbaum.

Miller, J. B. (Ed.). (1973). *Psychoanalysis and women: Contributions to new theory and therapy.* New York: Brunner/Mazel.

Millett, K. (1970). *Sexual politics.* New York: Doubleday.

Millette, J. (1966). Psychoanalysis in the United States. In F. Alexander, S. Eisenstein, & M. Grotjahn (Eds.), *Psychoanalytic pioneers* (pp. 546–596). New York: Basic Books.

Money, J., & Ehrhardt, A. A. (1972). *Man and woman, boy and girl.* Baltimore, MD: Johns Hopkins University Press.

Monte, C. F. (1987). *Beneath the mask: An introduction to theories of personality* (3rd ed.). New York: Holt, Rinehart, & Winston.

Moulton, R. (1966). Multiple factors in frigidity. In J. Masserman (Ed.), *Science in psychoanalysis* (Vol. X; pp. 75–93). New York: Grune & Stratton.

Moulton, R. (1970). A survey and reevaluation of the concept of penis envy. *Contemporary Psychoanalysis, 7*(1), 84–104.

Moulton, R. (1974). The role of Clara Thompson in the psychoanalytic study of women. In J. Strouse (Ed.), *Women in analysis: Dialogues on psychoanalytic view of femininity* (pp. 278–287). New York: Grossman Publishers.

Moulton, R. (1986). Professional success: A conflict for women. In J. Alpert (Ed.), *Psychoanalysis and women: Contemporary reappraisals* (pp. 161–181). Hillsdale, NJ: Analytic Press.

Notman, M., & Nadelson, C. (Eds.). (1990). *Women and men: New perspectives on gender differences.* Washington, DC: American Psychiatric Press, Inc.

O'Connell, A. N. (1980). Karen Horney: Theorist in psychoanalysis and feminine psychology. In A. N. O'Connell & N. F. Russo (Eds.), *Eminent women in psychology* (pp. 81–93). New York: Human Sciences Press. (Special issue of the *Psychology of Women Quarterly,* 5).

O'Connell, A. N. (1990). Karen Horney (1885–1952). In A. N. O'Connell & N. F. Russo (Eds.), *Women in psychology: A bio-bibliographic sourcebook* (pp. 184–196). Westport, CT: Greenwood.

O'Connell, A. N., & Russo, N. F. (Eds.). (1983). *Models of achievement: Reflections of eminent women in psychology.* New York: Columbia University Press.

Osmond, H., Franks, V., & Burtle, V. (1974). Changing views of women and therapeutic approaches: Some historical considerations. In V. Franks & V. Burtle (Eds.), *Women in therapy: New psychotherapies for a changing society* (pp. 3–24). New York: Brunner/Mazel.

Payton, C. R. (1988). [Autobiography]. In A. N. O'Connell & N. F. Russo (Eds.), *Models of achievement: Reflections of eminent women in psychology* (Vol. 2; pp. 228–242). Hillsdale, NJ: Erlbaum.

Person, E. (1974). Some new observations on the origins of femininity. In J. Strouse (Ed.), *Women in psychoanalysis: Dialogues on psychoanalytic views of femininity* (pp. 250–261). New York: Grossman Publishers.

Pumpian-Mindlin, E. (1966). Anna Freud and Erik H. Erikson. In F. Alexander, S. Eisenstein, & M. Grotjahn (Eds.), *Psychoanalytic pioneers* (pp. 519–533). New York: Basic Books.

Rambusch, N. M. (1990). Maria Montessori (1870–1952). In A. N. O'Connell & N. F. Russo (Eds.), *Women in psychology: A bio-bibliographic sourcebook* (pp. 246–255). Westport, CT: Greenwood Press.

Rawlings, E. I., & Carter, D. K. (Eds.). (1977). *Psychotherapy for women: Treatment toward equality.* Springfield, IL: Charles C Thomas.

Reisman, J. M. (1976). *A history of clinical psychology.* New York: Irvington.

Ribble, M. A. (1943). *The rights of infants: Early psychological needs and their satisfactions.* New York: Columbia University Press.

Rieker, P. P., & Carmen, E. H. (1984). *The gender gap in psychotherapy: Social realities and psychological processes.* New York: Plenum Press.

Rioch, M. J. (1983). In A. N. O'Connell & N. F. Russo (Eds.), *Models of achievement: Reflections of eminent women in psychology* (pp. 172–186). New York: Columbia University Press.

Roazen, P. (1975). *Freud and his followers.* New York: Alfred A. Knopf.

Roazen, P. (1985). *Helen Deutsch: A psychoanalyst's life.* Garden City, NY: Anchor Press.

Robbins, J. H., & Siegel, R. J. (1985). *Women changing therapy: New assessments, values, and strategies in feminist therapy.* New York: Harrington Park Press.

Rogers, C., & Dymond, R. (Eds.). (1954). *Psychotherapy and personality change: Coordinated research studies in the client-centered approach.* Chicago: University of Chicago Press.

Roheim, G. (1950). *Psychoanalysis and anthropology.* New York: International Universities Press.

Rosenfeld, H. (1965). *Psychotic states.* London: Hogarth Press.

Rosewater, L., & Walker, L. (Eds.). (1985). *The handbook of feminist therapy: Women's issues in psychotherapy.* New York: Springer.

Rubins, J. L. (1978). *Karen Horney: Gentle rebel of psychoanalysis.* New York: Dial Press.

Russo, N. F. (1983). Psychology's foremothers: Their achievements in context. In A. N. O'Connell & N. F. Russo (Eds.), *Models of achievement: Reflections of eminent women in psychology* (pp. 9–24). New York: Columbia University Press.

Russo, N. F. (Ed.). (1985). *A Women's Mental Health Agenda.* Washington, DC: American Psychological Association.

Russo, N. F., & Denmark, F. L. (1987). Contributions of women to psychology. *Annual Review of Psychology, 38,* 279–298.

Russo, N. F., & O'Connell, A. (1980, Fall). Models from our past: Psychology's foremothers. *Psychology of Women Quarterly,* 11–54.

Ryan, M. P. (1983). *Womanhood in America from colonial times to the present.* New York: Franklin Watts.

Segal, H. (1979). *Melanie Klein*. New York: Viking Press.

Segal, H. (1980). *Introduction to the works of Melanie Klein* (2nd ed.). New York: Basic Books.

Senn, M. L. (1975). Insights on the child development movement in the United States. *Monographs of the Society for Research in Child Development, 40*, (3–4, serial no. 16), 1–106.

Sherfey, M. J. (1966). The evolution and nature of female sexuality in relation to psychoanalytic theory. *Journal of the American Psychoanalytic Association, 14*(1), 28–128.

Sherman, J. A. (1971). *On the psychology of women: A survey of empirical studies.* Springfield, IL: Charles C Thomas.

Shields, S. A. (1975). Functionalism, Darwinism, and the psychology of women. *American Psychologist, 30*, 739–754.

Smirnoff, V. (1971). *The scope of child analysis.* New York: International Universities Press.

Sobel, S. B. & Russo, N. F. (1981). Equality, public policy, and professional psychology. *Professional Psychology, 12*, 180–189.

Spitz, R. (1952). Authority and masturbation: Some remarks on a bibliographic investigation. *Psychoanalytic Quarterly, 21*, 490–527.

Stein-Monod, C. (1966). Marie Bonaparte: 1882–1962. In F. Alexander, S. Eisenstein, & M. Grotjahn (Eds.), *Psychoanalytic pioneers* (pp. 399–414). New York: Basic Books.

Stevens, G. & Gardner, S. (1982). *The women of psychology: Expansion and refinement* (Vol. II). Cambridge, MA: Schenkman.

Strouse, J. (Ed.). (1974). *Women in psychoanalysis: Dialogues on psychoanalytic views of femininity.* New York: Grossman Publishers.

Tennov, D. (1975). *Psychotherapy: The hazardous cure.* New York: Ablard Schumen.

Thompson, C. (1950). *Psychoanalysis: Evolution and development* (with Patrick Mullahy). New York: Hermitage House.

Thompson, C. (1964). Cultural pressures in the psychology of women. In M. R. Green (Ed.), *Interpersonal psychoanalysis: The selected papers of Clara Thompson.* New York: Basic Books. (Original work published 1942)

Thompson, C. (1973). Penis envy in women. Reprinted in J. B. Miller (Ed.), *Psychoanalysis and women: Contributions to new theory and therapy* (pp. 43–48). New York: Brunner/Mazel. (Original work published in 1943, *Psychiatry, 6*, 123–125.)

Veith, I. (1965). *Hysteria: The history of a disease.* Chicago: University of Chicago Press.

Wallerstein, R. S. (1975). *Psychotherapy and psychoanalysis: Theory, practice, research.* New York: International Universities Press.

Weisstein, N. (1970). *Kinder Kirche* as scientific law: Psychology constructs the female. In R. Morgan (Ed.), *Sisterhood is powerful.* New York: Vintage Books.

Williams, E. (1976). *Notes of a feminist therapist.* New York: Dell.

Williams, J. H. (1983). *Psychology of women* (2nd ed.). New York: Norton.

Wolfenstein, M. (1953). Transient infant care. *American Journal of Orthopsychiatry, 23,* 120–130.

Young-Bruehl, E. (1988). *Anna Freud: A biography.* New York: Summit.

Zilboorg, G. (1973). Masculine and feminine: Some biological and cultural aspects. Reprinted in J. B. Miller (Ed.), *Psychoanalysis and women: Contributions to new theory and therapy* (pp. 83–111). New York: Brunner/Mazel. (Original published in 1944, in *Psychiatry, 7,* 257–296.)

Zuckerman, E. (1979). *Changing directions in the treatment of women.* (DHEW Publication no. ADM 79-749). Rockville, MD: NIMH.

15

PSYCHOTHERAPY AND THE OLDER ADULT

BOB G. KNIGHT, MIRIAM KELLY, AND MARGARET GATZ

This chapter is a review of the first century of psychotherapy with older adults. The first 60 years are covered in one section, followed by sections tracking developments in each decade. Within each decade, one or more themes are singled out as particularly salient during those years. Reflecting the debates explicitly and implicitly embedded in the literature, we use the question of the distinctiveness of working with older adults as the primary organizing theme. Thus, each section emphasizes the evolution of thinking about the feasibility of therapy with this population and the therapeutic rationale underlying modifications in technique. More specifically, is psychotherapy with older adults different from psychotherapy with younger adults or is it simply the application of existing therapies to the older population? Are the differences between younger adults and older adults in psychotherapy related to issues brought into therapy by the two populations or are there characteristics of the two groups that demand different therapeutic techniques?

The dominant answers to these debates have shifted over time. There have clearly been increases in both clinical experience and empirical knowledge about the elderly across the nearly nine decades covered in this review. New theoretical approaches to general adult therapy and new conceptual approaches to understanding the psychology of adult development and aging have combined to provide a solid basis for psychotherapeutic work with the elderly.

THE EARLY YEARS (1904–1959): PSYCHOANALYSIS

The first mention of age as a factor in psychotherapy was in a speech by Freud to the faculty of the Medical College in Vienna in 1904 (Freud, 1905/1953). In this early phase of the development of his thinking, and speaking to what he seemed to regard as a hostile audience, Freud addressed the indications and contraindications for psychotherapy. He first stated that they can ". . . scarcely be definitely laid down as yet, because of the many practical limitations to which my activities have been subjected" (p. 263). He went on to state several limitations, including seeing therapy as unsuitable for persons with "neuropathic degeneracy" and persons with psychoses, confusional states and "deeply rooted" depression. "A reasonable degree of education and a fairly reliable character" are required for successful therapy. In this context, he said the following about age:

> The age of patients has this much importance in determining their fitness for psycho-analytic treatment, that, on the one hand, near or above the age of fifty the elasticity of the mental processes, on which the treatment depends, is as a rule lacking—old people are no longer educable—and, on the other hand, the mass of material to be dealt with would prolong the duration of the treatment indefinitely. (p. 264)

Freud was 48 at the time of this address.

An early response to Freud came from Abraham (1919/1953) as he cautioned against preconceived notions of treatment with older adults. He stated that it was the task of psychoanalysis to ask whether and under what conditions it could be effective with older patients. Abraham wrote about successful treatment with some older neurotic patients (referring to patients who were about 50 years of age), stating that the prognosis was good if the neurosis became severe long after puberty, if the individual had several years of normal sexual functioning, and a period of social productivity. In short, "the age of the neurosis is more important than the age of the patient" (p. 317).

Freud's early dictum is often cited as a basis of therapeutic pessimism about working with the older adult, although few modern therapists would seriously consider persons of around 50 years of age to be no longer educable.

Other psychoanalytic writers (Jelliffee, 1925; Kaufman, 1937) were in agreement with Abraham on the possibility of psychoanalysis with older adults. However, the concern of all these psychoanalytic writers was with the appropriateness of the older adult for treatment rather than with adjusting the treatment to accommodate the patient's increased age.

Alexander (1944) introduced the consideration of modified analytic techniques with older patients. He suggested that the older adult's ego strength be assessed before choosing insight-oriented psychotherapy or supportive therapy. Meerloo (1955) also recommended modifications, suggesting that the therapist be more active, educational, and tolerant of resistance and play an ongoing supportive role in the patient's life. Meerloo observed the approach of death leads the older adult to life review, the evaluation of accomplishments, and decreased defensiveness, allowing *easier* access to the patient's unconscious.

Goldfarb (1953) went the furthest, developing a brief psychotherapy model for use with older adults based on psychoanalytic theory. It is important to emphasize that Goldfarb was working with institutionalized elderly patients who had multiple psychological and organic problems, a distinction that was sometimes lost in early reviews. Goldfarb's brief therapy is historically significant because it was developed from a working knowledge of the problems, resources, and limitations of this population. The brief therapy, averaging five to nine weekly sessions of about 15 minutes' duration, worked via the transference relationship so that the diminished resources of the older adult were not an impediment. Goldfarb used the increased dependency of older adult patients to foster the illusion of the therapist as a powerful parent who provides gratification of the patient's emotional needs. The patient's self-esteem was increased by the positive feeling of having won over or mastered the therapist.

The early years were largely but not entirely psychoanalytic. Cutner (1950) reported on a successful Jungian analysis. The Jungian approach was argued to be more appropriate to the older adult because Jung (1933) saw the second half of life as having its own tasks and as involving the development of previously neglected aspects of the personality.

Another early pioneer was Lillien Martin, a psychologist who founded a counseling center for the elderly after her retirement in 1929. The "Martin Method" anticipated many later developments, such as systematic life review, searching for dysfunctional thoughts and behavior patterns, and teaching of new cognitions to correct emotional distress in late life.

In the first integrative review of psychotherapy with older adults, Rechtschaffen (1959) presented a generally optimistic portrayal, although he left open the question as to whether psychotherapy with older adults requires modification. His case summaries encompassed subgroups that have become more salient and distinctive in the years since 1959. For example, he did not separate institutionalized residents with organic brain disorders from other elderly when surveying types of interventions. In particular, it is commonly accepted now that the subgroup of older adults with serious cognitive impairment (described as "senile dementia" in the review) would not be suitable for unmodified psychoanalytic therapy.

In summary, although Freud's pessimistic remarks about the appropriateness of psychoanalysis with persons over the age of 45 were a poor start for the field, these remarks were refuted 15 years later by Abraham. In this early period, there were many positive reports of therapy with older adults, including older adults with dementing illness. While the question of the need for adaptation of technique was raised in these early articles, the writers did not make it entirely clear whether the modifications were needed because of developmental changes or because of cognitive impairment. Today the latter would be seen as resulting from disease rather than age.

THE 1960s: LIFE REVIEW AND BEHAVIOR THERAPY

The principal developments of the 1960s in psychotherapy with older adults were (1) the emergence of life review therapy as a conceptually age-specific form of psychotherapeutic work with the elderly, and (2) the essentially unmodified application of behavioral interventions and concepts to older populations. Until this time, interest in the elderly on the part of psychoanalytic writers would seem to have been prompted by contact with older clients who presented for therapy or by the therapist's personal experience of growing older. Within the psychoanalytic tradition, this is largely true even now (cf. Myers, 1984; Nemiroff & Colorusso, 1985).

Life review is the first product of specific interest in aging as a developmental process. Life review arose chiefly out of the study of adult development and aging, although it is somewhat reflective of psychoanalytic concepts. Robert Butler, who developed the life review technique, was a part of a research group studying healthy aging men at the National Institute of Mental Health. This project was one of the first longitudinal studies of adult development in the United States. The other main conceptual influence on life review comes from Erik Erikson's theory of psychosocial stages of development. Erikson was part of the ego psychology tradition which was then working on extending psychoanalytic concepts of development into adolescence and adulthood.

In contrast, behavior therapy developed as a reaction to psycho-dynamic approaches to helping people. There was no particular focus on any age group, although there tended to be an emphasis on problems that were amenable to behavioral intervention. Behavior therapists were committed theoretically to the universality of learning principles across organisms of all kinds. Practically, they were often limited in those days to applying their ideas in institutional settings. It is not surprising that behaviorists applied their approach to older adults early on and that their heuristic assumption was that their techniques would not need to be modified.

These two developments can be seen as opposing answers to the question of the need for adaptation of theories to work with the aged. Life review is, in principle, the therapeutic use of late life developmental stages. It is presented as uniquely applicable to older adults. Behavioral therapies, in contrast, assume that change is mediated by environmental contingencies rather than attributes of the organism. Behavior therapy simply applies the same methods to older individuals as to any other population.

Life Review

Butler (1963) observed that older adults have a propensity for life review, the spontaneous progressive remembering of past experiences "brought about by the realization of approaching dissolution and death" (Lewis & Butler, 1974). The life review process serves a therapeutic function as the older adult reflects on his or her life in an attempt to resolve, reorganize, and reintegrate unresolved conflicts. The therapist taps into this ongoing self-analysis in an effort "to enhance it, make it more conscious, deliberate, and efficient" (Lewis & Butler, 1974, p. 166).

Erikson (1968), like Butler, described later life as a time for review and the achievement of a sense of integrity. Erikson's conceptualization of a life long series of developmental stages also became a major influence in the 1960s. As noted by Kastenbaum (1978), the hunger for theory among psychotherapists working with the elderly was so strong that Erikson's views on old age, expressed in two pages each in *Identity, Youth, and Crisis* (1968) and in *Childhood and Society* (1950/1963) became one of the major theoretical influences in understanding the elderly. Erikson's life stage theory does introduce the notion that development continues beyond adolescence and that the failure to complete developmental tasks in younger adulthood or in middle age will have psychological consequences in late life similar to the consequences of unresolved conflicts in childhood (Erikson, 1978). Erikson described the eighth stage of development as a conflict between ego integrity versus despair and noted that a spontaneous review of one's life is part of resolving the conflict. Lewis and Butler (1974) suggested that the greatest introspection seems to occur between age 60 and 70 and then appears to lessen in the next two decades of life.

Life review therapy employs various methods to evoke reminiscence in older adults, such as asking the older adult to write an autobiography, make a pilgrimage to his or her childhood home, attend reunions, research genealogy and ethnic heritage, or bring in scrapbooks and photographs. Life review has been used in psychotherapy with older adults and in age-integrated therapy groups. The concept has at times been used to justify less structured reminiscence on the premise that reminiscence always leads to positive outcomes. In a caution not widely attended to, Butler (1963) argued, however, that life review can also lead to depression, perhaps comparable to Erikson's notion of both more and less successful resolutions of developmental crises. Considering the long history of the life review concept and its influence on the field, there are surprisingly few published reports evaluating its effectiveness. Those few controlled studies provide a mixed picture of the effectiveness of life review with both positive results (Fry, 1983; Haight, 1988) and reports of no difference from current events discussion groups (Rattenbury & Stones, 1989) or control groups (Sherman, 1987).

Behavior Therapy

Several of the first writers to apply behavioral ideas to older adults were known for their pioneering work in behavior therapy, not as gerontologists. For example, Lindsley (1964) proposed a model of a "prosthetic environment" where a functional analysis of the behavioral deficits of the older patient are used to design prosthetics such as calendars and signs for the cognitively disoriented, bars and rails for the physically impaired, and personal memorabilia for the memory-impaired older adult patients. Cautela (1966, 1969) emerged as a proponent of classical conditioning theory in explaining problems in late life, arguing for the use of a wide range of behavioral interventions with the elderly including relaxation, assertion training, systematic desensitization, and covert sensitization. These approaches met with early success, mainly in institutions (Gottesman, Quarterman, & Cohn, 1973) but also in outpatient settings (Flannery, 1974).

The application of behavioral analysis and behavior therapy to the problems of older adults is of interest for three reasons: (1) Behaviorists are committed to a high level of optimism about the potential for change in older adults. Whereas psychodynamic theories make plausible the assumption that change will be impossible or at least difficult in late life, behavior analysis emphasizes environmental contingencies and potential for change, even in the institutionalized elderly. Indeed, Kastenbaum (1968) argued that the behavioral emphasis on environmental contingencies served as an alternative to the assumption that the problems of the aged are biological in origin and presumably resistent to psychosocial change strategies. (2) There is virtually no time lag between the origination of behavior therapy (dating from Wolpe, 1958) and its application to older adults. Behaviorists were quick to embrace the elderly along with other populations considered by psychodynamic theory as untreatable or very difficult to treat. (3) The change of theoretical focus to include environmental variables opened the way to considering explanations for the behavior of the older person that were outside of the person, that is, to cease blaming the old for their problems. As noted by Cautela and Mansfield (1977), because the emphasis of behavioral treatment was on the target behavior rather than on the patient's lengthy history, behaviorism did not entail the use of negative labels such as senility.

Few modifications were recommended in applying behavioral techniques to the problems of older adults. For example, Cautela and Mansfield (1977) suggested that older adults may take longer to learn to relax than other age groups, that older adults may need more detail and more time in proceeding through the steps of systematic desensitization, and that the overall health of the older adult had to be considered when presenting aversive stimuli. On the other hand, they also observed that spontaneous recovery occurred more frequently with older clients.

As will be discussed further, the "cognitive revolution" in behavior therapy during the 1970s also affected work with older adults immediately. Eisdorfer and Stotsky (1977) observed that the cognitive approach could be modified to accommodate the status of the patient and the situation. Kastenbaum (1978) singled out two models of cognitive therapy that were especially well-suited to working with the elderly: Kelly's (1955) theory of personality would explain the way the older adult construed the world, while Seligman's (1975) model of learned helplessness could be applied to understanding the effects of long-term institutionalization on older adults.

The 1960s brought two developments of importance to the evolution of psychotherapy with the elderly. Life review therapy and the associated Eriksonian theory of adult life stages furthered the understanding of the adult life cycle and provided a step toward an age-specific therapy. Possible continuities between life review processes in older adults and introspection as part of any psychodynamic treatment were not highlighted. In sharp contrast, behavior therapy showed a willingness to apply principles and techniques developed for other ages (younger adults, school children, and mentally retarded people) to the elderly without a priori modification. Grounded in separate theoretical systems, these two approaches provided contradictory answers to the the question: Does psychotherapy with older adults need to be different from work with younger adults?

THE 1970s: GERONTOLOGY AS AN INFLUENCE ON PSYCHOTHERAPY

The primary theme in the 1970s was life span developmental psychology, which provided a major impetus for the growth of psychotherapy with older adults. The attractiveness of life span developmental theory for the psychologist interested in psychotherapy with older adults is that life span theory holds out the promise of a conceptual framework for understanding and hence settling the question of the distinctiveness of therapy with the elderly. Gerontology began to develop as an interdisciplinary area after World War II. In the 1960s, developmentally oriented research psychologists began to study the processes of development in adulthood, primarily intellectual or cognitive change, and to develop methodologies that incorporated features of both cross-sectional and longitudinal studies. These methods made it possible to separate developmental effects from cohort differences and other sources of difference between younger and older adults (e.g., Schaie, 1965), and stimulated the growth of life span developmental theory (Baltes & Danish, 1980; Baltes & Schaie, 1973).

Cohort, an important concept from life span developmental psychology, refers to a group of people born at about the same time who grow up and who age together in historical time. To illustrate cohort differences, educational levels have increased in each successive cohort in the twentieth century; thus, today's older adults are less educated than today's younger adults. Such differences are sometimes incorrectly interpreted to be effects of the process of aging. While none of us would say that people become less educated as they grow older, other cohort differences such as personality differences and political values are often mistakenly attributed to the aging process rather than to the historical context in which a particular generation matured.

The new methodologies and the publication of data from early longitudinal studies on adult development led to increasing recognition of life span development as a specific area of empirical research. The findings suggested stability of functioning over time rather than decline, as had been traditionally expected. The life span approach was also finding individual variability in patterns of aging and a clear potential for modifiability of cognitive functioning among the nondemented elderly (cf. Baltes & Schaie, 1976), including indications of greater cognitive and emotional complexity with increasing life experience (Labouvie-Vief, DeVoe, & Bulka, 1989; Rybash, Hoyer, & Roodin, 1986). Summarizing this approach, Schaie (1973) argued that psychological and physiological functions underlying socially significant behaviors are not subject to decrement in normal aging and that a major share of perceived age decrements are due to age-graded expectations of society.

These ideas hold obvious relevance for psychotherapy with older adults. Different cohorts have experienced quite different understandings of mental illness and its treatment, especially the role of the mental institution. This experience is brought with the older client to treatment, if the individual does seek help at all. Recent research has tended to indicate that older adults are more likely to go to a general medical provider for help with a mental health problem than to a mental health professional, although it is true in all age groups that the majority of mental health problems go untreated (George, Blazer, Winfield-Laird, Leaf, & Fischbach, 1988). It is easy to assume that expectations of what will happen when a professional is consulted are influenced by societal images of psychiatric illness and its treatment, and these images have changed markedly over the past 40 years.

Life span developmental psychology has further served to replace folklore with empirical data on very basic questions. Freud based one of his major objections to work with the older adult on the folk belief that the old are not educable; this assertion is now known to be false for healthy older adults. The life span approach has led to a conceptual framework that distinguishes normal aging not only from cohort differences, but also from the influence of disease processes, including dementing illnesses.

A secondary theme in the 1970s was application of community psychology to older adults. Community psychology emerged in the 1960s, with a distinctive set of values. Prevention was urged as an alternative to treating problems after they have already occurred; social factors were targeted as part of prevention and as an alternative to blaming individuals for their own problems. Community mental health centers were opened and deinstitutionalization mandated. Initially, older adults were mostly overlooked in this major reorientation of the mental health system.

In 1974, a conference on the clinical psychology of aging, entitled "Geropsychology: A Model of Training and Clinical Service," was convened at Duke University. It appears to have been the earliest organized effort in the United States at integrating the academic study of the psychology of aging with clinical psychology in order to treat older adults. The conference brought together both life span theory and ideas from community psychology. At the time, graduate training programs and internships either excluded older adults or only exposed the psychologist to institutionalized elderly, and human behavior was not presented from the newly emerging life span developmental perspective.

In the area of clinical service, psychology had not been particularly concerned with the problems of aging and the elderly (Lawton, 1979). At the Duke conference, Gottesman (1977) laid out roles that psychologists could play in clinical service delivery to older adults: the role of test constructor and test administrator; the role of therapist or listener with individuals or groups of older adults; the role of developer in institutional settings of behavioral modification and milieu treatment programs; the role of care manager in the community; and the role of government policy maker. Kahn (1975, 1977) made the then innovative case that elderly who had grown old in institutions had problems related to their chronic mental disorders and to institutional living, problems which should not be confused with genuine geriatric disorders. Consequently, he urged, the best treatment for geriatric patients in the community was "minimum intervention" that would not undermine independence and induce the sorts of problems seen in institutionalized patients (Kahn, 1975). The idea of prevention offered a framework that was an alternative to old institutional ways of treatment and that linked the life span developmental perspective and community psychology (Gatz, Hurley, & Nagel, 1977; Smyer & Gatz, 1979).

In summary, the seventies brought an awareness of the neglect of older adults by clinical psychology and an attempt to place clinical training for this population in the theoretical framework of life span developmental psychology, compelling attention to both normative aging and to common psychological problems in late life. There began to be a systematic knowledge base (e.g., Storandt, Siegler, & Elias, 1978; Zarit, 1980). With regard to the distinctiveness of working with older adults, the question could be refined: what is different and what is the same about psychological intervention with older adults?

THE 1980s: MATURATION OF THERAPY WITH OLDER CLIENTS

Growing out of the activities in the 1970s, the 1980s saw a considerable increase in clinical writing about the elderly. Several books and chapters were published that presented a unified viewpoint about work with the aged on the basis of experience, theory, and empirical knowledge about aging. Even though there is a diversity of theoretical viewpoint and of interpretation of gerontological literature, these books share six general themes: the need for careful assessment of the older client, the need for the psychotherapist to be able to act as a caseworker, appreciation of the common stressors of later life, some focus on diversity within the population of older adults, a consideration of the interaction of younger therapists with older clients, and the emergence of an empirical literature.

Assessment

The chief assessment task is distinguishing among dementia, delirium, and depression (Zarit, 1980), although the assessment questions have become more refined with the surge of research interest in Alzheimer's disease and the new popularity of clinical neuropsychology. Beyond reiterating the need for differential assessment within the domain of the psychological disorders, Knight (1986) discussed the need for distinguishing among physical, psychological, and social domains of problems. Applying developmental concepts to assessment also leads to highlighting the difference between lifelong characteristics and distress that can be traced to events in later life. Taking all of these dimensions into account, it is useful to make a practice of specifying for whom an intervention applies. For instance, Sherman (1981) stipulated that his approach to counseling the elderly was aimed at those aged who were neither physically nor cognitively impaired. In general, there has been a consensus through the 1980s that assessment of the elderly requires specific skills, including some knowledge of neuropsychology and health psychology (Knight, 1986), whether or not the subsequent psychotherapy requires any special adaptation due to the client's age.

The Therapist as Caseworker

The need for psychotherapists to be able to take on nontraditional roles has been a common theme, with most writers agreeing that therapists need to be able to function as a caseworker for older adults. The older adult is seen as frequently having urgent social service needs as well as psychological and medical problems. Zarit (1980), Sherman (1981), and Knight (1986, 1989) have all argued that it is sometimes appropriate and necessary for the therapist to actively address these problems by making referrals and even providing direct assistance when needed. For instance, older adults are quite likely to have pressing needs for transportation, assistance with housework, legal advice, and sensible referrals for social activity. There is a logical sequence in which urgent direct needs take precedence initially but then a shift is made away from casework toward psychotherapy. All of these writers emphasize that the longer term goal of therapy is the client's independence and the resolution of psychological problems.

Common Stressors of Later Life

Although the tasks are understood differently, another common dimension has been a perception of the problems of the elderly as a series of stressors that are associated with late life rather than viewing old age as a unitary, unvarying phase of the life cycle. This focus has drawn noticeably on the general literature about stress and coping (Lazarus & Folkman, 1984). Zarit, for example, turned naturally from a concern for the accurate assessment of dementia to a focus on interventions to assist the family caregivers of demented older adults with the task of caregiving (cf. Zarit, Orr, & Zarit, 1985). Storandt (1983), coming from a cognitive behavioral perspective, saw a major focus of work with the elderly as coping with two life transitions typical of the older years: widowhood and retirement. Knight (1986) argued that the topics of therapy with older adults commonly concerned chronic illness, grieving for loved ones who die, coping with the aging process and facing one's own death, and the marital and family issues of the older family. These topics provide a distinctive tone for the content of therapy, but do not imply changes in technique and process. In fact, this problem-centered approach encourages attention to commonalities with younger adults facing similar problems.

Diversity of the Elderly

A common theme among writers in the 1980s is the need to recognize diversity among older adults. Diversity encompasses age or cohort differences, gender differences, ethnic differences, and individual differences in functioning that have persisted since young adulthood. For instance, Sherman (1981) used Neugarten's (1975) categories of young-old (ages 55–75) and old-old (from 75 on) to suggest that the old-old are more apt to require social services to deal with chronic illnesses and poor circumstances while the young-old would be better educated and more likely to view psychotherapy positively and to seek it out. Of course, such an observation probably mixes age and cohort differences, both of which must be kept in mind to explain many of the differences that might exist at any one time between younger and older clients (Knight, 1986). Storandt (1983), in discussing the relevance of mean differences in learning between young and old adults, also noted that there is considerable individual variation, and the therapist will have to adapt accordingly. Gender differences and ethnic differences remain important in late life and more attention needs to be given to how gender and ethnicity affect the experience of aging and the response to the common stressors of late life. In particular, the kinds of considerations suggested for younger women and ethnic minority clients (see chapters 14 and 16 in this volume) do not diminish in relevance simply because the individuals have turned age 65.

The Younger Therapist's Reaction to Older Clients

Many of these writers consider a major issue in psychotherapy with the aged to be the reaction of younger therapists to the older person or to the common problems of later life. This theme has a long history. Kastenbaum (1964) described "the reluctant therapist," attributing the reluctance to the therapist's own problems in dealing with aging and death, unresolved conflicts with older family members, and the feeling that the investment of time and energy is not worth it because the old will die soon anyway. Butler (1975) called the phenomenon "therapeutic nihilism" and accused psychotherapists of sharing in societal ageism. The theme reemerged in the eighties, less as a barrier to initiating treatment but more as a distinctive quality of the therapist's experience. The therapist must confront illness, disability, death—losses that are not replaceable. It is easy for the therapist to become overwhelmed by the enormity of the problems and to wonder what one possibly has to offer (Knight, 1989). There is also a need to monitor oneself for the tendency to be protective—to take care of older people rather than to help older adults care for themselves—or to be supportive and not actively seek change (Thompson, Gallagher, & Breckenridge, 1987; Zarit, 1980). Not only are different countertransference issues elicited by older clients, but also these are typically issues that are in the therapist's future and so are more anxiety-arousing than issues raised by younger clients (Knight, 1989). In general, the perception that therapy is different with older adults is now thought to be due more to the emotional impact on the therapist of working with the elderly than to actual differences in technique, process, or likelihood of success.

Recent Evaluation Research

In 1985, the empirical literature on psychological treatment of older adults emphasized nontraditional psychological interventions and institutional programs at the expense of psychotherapy, with a handful of controlled research on effectiveness of therapy with older adults just beginning to be carried out (Gatz, Popkin, Pino, & VandenBos, 1985). Three large projects have addressed the treatment of depression, all entailing cognitive-behavioral approaches. Steuer et al. (1984) conducted a study to determine whether depressed outpatient older adults would respond positively to group psychotherapy and whether they would respond differently to cognitive-behavioral group therapy and psychodynamic group therapy. Older adults in both treatment conditions showed significant decreases on multiple measures of depression.

Beutler, Scogin et al. (1987) compared the relative effectiveness of an antidepressant drug and group-administered cognitive therapy with depressed older adults. The effects of cognitive group therapy—both with and without associated drug treatment—were positive for relieving the symptoms of depression, while the medication alone appeared relatively ineffective as a treatment for depression among the older adults.

Thompson, Gallagher, and Breckenridge (1987) compared the effectiveness of individual short-term behavioral, cognitive, and psychodynamic psychotherapies with depressed older adults. The results of the study replicated their previous work (Gallagher & Thompson, 1982), demonstrating that short-term psychotherapy is effective in treating depression in older adults. However, the three treatment approaches did not affect the patients differently, showing instead a nonspecific improvement effect on the symptoms of depression among older adults. Subsequently, more enduring effects have been shown for behavioral and cognitive interventions than supportive approaches, and treatment has been described as less effective for some forms of depression (endogenous or with concurrent features of personality disorder) than for others.

Knight (1983, 1988) compared older and younger clients in a community mental health center on therapist ratings of change and found that older adults showed more improvement than the younger adults on both occasions. In the second study, within the group of clients over 60, age was found to be negatively related to outcome. Even this effect seemed to be counteracted if the oldest old (over 80) received more sessions of therapy. Taken together, these studies all support the therapeutic optimism suggested by the scanty pre-1980 literature, although clearly more research is needed to analyze the processes of therapy with older adults.

The six themes that comprised the maturation of clinical writing about psychotherapy with the elderly can be viewed as a portrait of how psychotherapy with older adults differs from work with younger adults. First, assessment of presenting problems is universally seen as different and crucial, especially the need for competence in recognizing dementing illnesses and in recognizing the effects of medical problems and of medications on psychological disorders. Second, there is a general consensus that psychotherapists working with older adults must be prepared to acknowledge and assist with practical social problems that are often seen as out of the therapist's domain in work with younger adults. Third, there is a trend toward seeing the specificity of working with the elderly in psychotherapy as due to certain stressors being more common in late life but not uniquely associated with the older years (e.g., widowhood, chronic illness, preparation for dying). Fourth, like younger adults, older adults are seen as differing from one another in ability, health, gender, ethnicity, and age. Fifth, psychotherapists often experience working with the elderly as being different, although the perception may stem from the therapists' response to the problems of later life or to older people rather than as characteristic of any special nature of psychotherapy with the aged. Sixth, as with younger adults, controlled evaluation studies support the efficacy of psychotherapeutic interventions. Is psychotherapy different with the elderly? The set of answers to this question presented in the 1980's moves beyond the generalization of affirming similarity or distinctiveness to describe a specific set of differences and similarities.

EMERGING AND REEMERGING THEMES IN THE 1990s

Although projecting the past into the future is always a chancy enterprise, there are three themes that have begun to surface in the late 1980s to early 1990s that show promise for becoming important emphases in the future development of therapy with older adults. These three themes are family therapy with older families, interventions for caregivers of the elderly, and therapy with the chronically mentally ill elderly.

Family Therapy

Whereas many of the other approaches to psychotherapy have been fairly quickly and generally applied to work with older adults, family systems theories seem to be crossing over into later life quite recently. Herr and Weakland (1979) provided an early example of using family concepts in working with the elderly. The theme seemed to be dropped until the late 1980s when publications like Carter and McGoldrick's *The Changing Family Life Cycle* (1988) and Bumagin and Hirn's *Helping the Aging Family* (1990) helped to bridge theory and practice. Qualls (1988) used these viewpoints to provide guidelines for integrating cognitive-behavioral and family systems approaches in working with older families.

The general family therapy literature almost exclusively concerns families with minor children, without taking other generations into account. At the same time, gerontologists have tended to limit their thinking about family issues to caregiving for impaired elders and making nursing home placement decisions. It can only be speculated that these divergent tendencies have delayed the integration of family systems and gerontology. The bringing together of these two perspectives has promising implications for both sides. The family systems approach applied to work with the elderly also serves as a reminder that the older adult is an integral member of the family and of society: Families are inherently intergenerational networks.

Intervention With Caregivers

Considerable effort throughout the 1980s was directed toward psychological interventions with caregivers of older adults, especially caregivers of demented elderly. A distinctive caregiving literature swelled within gerontology. At the end of the decade, Zarit (1989) judged the results to date to have been unimpressive both conceptually and in terms of the empirical results of published outcome studies. Zarit called for both greater clarity of thinking about "caregiver burden" and for better designed interventions and evaluations of them.

The close of the decade brought signs that caregiver burden was drawing on a wider set of psychological concepts and interventions. Caregiver distress has been conceptualized as a reactive depression (Lovett & Gallagher, 1988) and as a type of chronic stressor (Pearlin, Mullan, Semple, & Skaff, 1990). Reports of evaluations of intervention strategies based on these conceptualizations, depression coping classes and stress reduction training, have been more positive (Lovett & Gallagher, 1988; Toseland & Smith, 1990). Consistent with the emerging interest in family systems approaches to understanding older families, Niederehe and Fruge (1984) as well as Gatz, Bengtson, and Blum (1990) have argued for understanding caregiving families within the context of family systems theories. After a decade of caregiver-specific theory and intervention, caregivers are being construed as persons reacting in individualized ways to one of the stresses of later life. The return of thinking about caregivers to the mainstream of psychotherapy and aging has promise for improving the understanding of caregiver burden and for extending the analysis of other types of stressors in late life.

Chronic Mental Illness Among the Elderly

The mental health community in the United States has been slow to recognize the existence of either late-life onset psychosis or of the aging of psychotic adults (Miller & Cohen, 1987). The emergence of coexisting medical problems and cognitive decline in the older psychotic patient and the eligibility of that patient for aging services in addition to mental health services complicates their care in the mental health system (Knight & Carter, 1990). Cohen (1987) suggested that the treatment of schizophrenia in late life should consider intrapsychic, behavioral, and psychosocial dynamics. He described home visits to schizophrenic older adults living independently in a senior housing complex and reported several successful case examples of ongoing, supportive psychotherapy with older schizophrenics with an emphasis on facilitation of drug treatment, relief of anxiety, and stabilization of the older patient's social situation. This latter goal often involved educating others in the environment (e.g., the housing manager) about the nature of schizophrenia in late life.

Patterson and associates (1982) described a behavioral program for returning long-term state hospital residents to the community and for helping to reduce recidivism. With an emphasis on teaching, transferring and maintaining behavioral competence in activities of daily living, social skills, and psychological support, the program was used successfully and cost effectively in both institutional and day treatment modes. Gatz and Smyer (in press) predicted that an emphasis on the chronically mentally ill aged will be a major trend of the 1990s, due to extending the late 1980s concern with the homeless to include the aged and due to nursing home reform that emphasizes screening out of psychiatric patients from the settings where they now live. Both psychotherapy and behavioral interventions are important techniques in the successful support of aging psychotic patients in the community.

These three themes for the 1990s provide examples of a broader tendency. We suggest that the present decade will see greater integration of the aged into regular clinical literature, reflecting recognition of the aged as a significant part of the population. One further example of this evolution is seen in the shift over the decades from the language of "professional ageism" to analysis of systemic impediments to greater service provision to older adults. A common topic addressed in virtually all early literature is the underservice of older adults by psychotherapists. The typical piece of writing on psychotherapy and aging prior to 1980 begins with a polemic on the neglect of older adults by psychotherapists. In the 1980s, a section about barriers to treatment remained mandatory in any chapter or book. By the end of the eighties, the section had been moved to the end of the chapter (e.g., Smyer, Zarit, & Qualls, 1990), and it had shifted its emphasis from rhetoric about psychologists' neglect of the elderly to an analysis of policy influences on availability and use of mental health services by older adults.

CONCLUSION

The question traced throughout this chapter is whether psychotherapy with older adults is different enough from psychotherapy with younger adults to warrant special treatment models. Over the decades, theorists have sometimes emphasized differences and other times, similarities. Gatz, Popkin et al. (1985) proposed that overemphasis on differences between treatment of older and younger adults may actually have limited progress because knowledge about psychotherapy with other age groups may not have been tapped to inform work with older adults. They posit "that the particular individual and the problem presented, not age per se, should be regarded as the primary determinant in establishing intervention goals and selecting therapeutic approaches" (p. 765). An emphasis on age over the presenting problem and the individual's personality is the essence of stereotyping in any group. In general, current practitioners would caution against age as the criterion, instead suggesting that the therapeutic issues and the individual should determine the treatment approach.

On the other hand, older adults have certain qualities that make the experience of working with the population special. One major source of such difference is the probabilistic association of certain diseases with chronological age. A significant minority of older adults have an acquired cognitive impairment, a type of disorder that requires special consideration at any age. Chronic health problems are more commonly found in older adults, causing distress associated with illness and disability at any age.

A second source of distinctiveness for older adults is cohort: The era in which individuals grow up, become adults, and establish careers and families exerts a shaping influence that interacts with other personal characteristics to affect the perception of psychological distress and of mental health treatment. Moreover, bringing older adults and younger therapists together may be best understood as involving the need for the therapist to understand the worldview, the values, and the language of earlier born cohorts. While challenging, the result is also maturing for the therapist. In the words of George Norlin (President of the University of Colorado, 1919–1939), "He who knows only his own generation remains always a child."

A third source of specificity is the result of the accumulation of a lifetime of experience over the adult life span. With this longer life history comes the dilemma for the therapist of the need to decide how much of this history to explore. Because it is not possible to explore in detail the older person's entire life, decisions will have to be made regarding what will be explored and what can safely be ignored in the successful resolution of a specific problem. With increasing life experience, older people may become more mature and more complex both cognitively and emotionally. This maturity provides many older adults with well-practiced coping skills and a greater resiliency in the face of new stresses in late life.

In this view, psychotherapy with the older client becomes a matter of working with more mature adults, who are members of earlier-born cohorts and who face the rigorous challenges of late life. Understood in this way, psychotherapy with older adults is neither fundamentally altered nor is it a weaker version of work with younger adults. To the contrary, the changes that are necessary will challenge therapists intellectually and emotionally to reach a maturity beyond their years.

REFERENCES

Abraham, K. (1919/1953). The applicability of psychoanalytic treatment to patients at an advanced age. In S. Steury & M. L. Blank (Eds.), *Readings in psychotherapy with older people* (pp. 18–20). Washington, DC: U.S. Department of Health, Education, and Welfare.

Alexander, F. G. (1944). The indications for psychoanalytic therapy. *Bulletin of New York Academy of Medicine, 20*, 319–334.

Baltes, P. B., & Danish, S. J. (1980). Intervention in lifespan development and aging: Issues and concepts. In R. R. Turner & H. W. Reese (Eds.), *Lifespan developmental psychology: Intervention* (pp. 49–78). New York: Academic Press.

Baltes, P. B., & Schaie, K. W. (1973). On lifespan developmental research paradigm: Retrospects and prospects. In P. Baltes & K. W. Schaie (Eds.), *Lifespan developmental psychology: Personality and socialization* (pp. 366–432). New York: Academic Press.

Baltes, P. B., & Schaie, K. W. (1976). On the plasticity of intelligence in adulthood and old age. *American Psychologist, 31*, 720–725.

Beutler, L. E., Scogin, L., Kirkish, P., Schretlen, D., Corbishley, A., Hamblin, D., Meredith, K., Potter, R., Bamford, C. R., & Levenson, A. I. (1987). Group cognitive therapy and Alprazolam in the treatment of depression in older adults. *Journal of Consulting and Clinical Psychology, 55*, 550–556.

Bumagin, V. E., & Hirn, K. F. (1990). *Helping the aging family.* Glenview, IL: Scott, Foresman.

Butler, R. N. (1963). The life review: An interpretation of reminiscence in the aged. *Psychiatry, 119*, 721–728.

Butler, R. N. (1975). Psychiatry and the elderly: An overview. *American Journal of Psychiatry, 132*, 893–900.

Carter, B., & McGoldrick, M. (Eds.). (1988). *The changing family life cycle.* New York: Gardner Press, Inc.

Cautela, J. R. (1966). Behavior therapy and geriatrics. *Journal of Genetic Psychology, 108*, 9–17.

Cautela, J. R. (1969). A classical conditioning approach to the development and modification of behavior in the aged. *The Gerontologist, 9*, 109–113.

Cautela, J. R., & Mansfield, L. (1977). A behavioral approach to geriatrics. In W. D. Gentry (Ed.), *Geropsychology: A model of training and clinical service.* Cambridge, MA: Ballinger.

Cohen, G. D. (1987). Psychotherapeutic approaches to schizophrenia in later life. In N. E. Miller & G. D. Cohen (Eds.), *Schizophrenia and aging* (pp. 287–298). New York: Guilford Press.

Cutner, M. (1950). Analysis in later life. *British Journal of Medical Psychology, 23*, 75–86.

Eisdorfer, C., & Stotsky, B. A. (1977). Intervention, treatment, and rehabilitation of psychiatric disorders. In J. E. Birren & K. W. Schaie (Eds.), *Handbook of the psychology of aging* (pp. 724–750). New York: Van Nostrand Reinhold.

Erikson, E. (1950/1963). *Childhood and society* (2nd ed.). New York: W. W. Norton.

Erikson, E. (1968). *Identity: Youth and crisis.* New York: W. W. Norton.

Erikson, E. H. (1978). Reflections on Dr. Borg's life cycle. In E. H. Erikson (Ed.), *Adulthood: Essays.* New York: W. W. Norton.

Flannery, R. B. (1974). Behavior modification of geriatric grief: A transactional perspective. *International Journal of Aging and Human Development, 5*, 197–203.

Freud, S. (1905/1953). On psychotherapy. In J. Strachey (Ed. and Trans.), *The standard edition of the complete psychological works of Sigmund Freud* (Vol. 6; pp. 249–263). London: Hogarth.

Fry, P. S. (1983). Structured and unstructured reminiscence training and depression among the elderly. *Clinical Gerontologist, 1*(3), 15–17.

Gallagher, D. E., & Thompson, L. W. (1982). Treatment of major depressive disorder in older adult outpatients with brief psychotherapy. *Psychotherapy: Theory, Research and Practice, 19*, 482–490.

Gatz, M., Bengtson, V. L., & Blum, M. J. (1990). Caregiving families. In J. E. Birren and K. W. Schaie (Eds.), *Handbook of the psychology of aging* (3rd ed.; pp. 405–426). San Diego: Academic Press.

Gatz, M., Hurley, D., & Nagel, G. S. (1977). Community geropsychology: Issues of training and service. In W. D. Gentry (Ed.), *Geropsychology: A model of training and clinical service* (pp. 111–126). Cambridge, MA: Ballinger.

Gatz, M., Popkin, S. J., Pino, C. D., & VandenBos, G. R. (1985). Psychological interventions with older adults. In J. E. Birren and K. W. Schaie (Eds.),

Handbook of the psychology of aging (2nd ed.; pp. 755–788). New York: Van Nostrand Reinhold.

Gatz, M., & Smyer, M. A. (in press). The mental health system and older adults in the 1990s. *American Psychologist.*

George, L. K., Blazer, D. F., Winfield-Laird, I., Leaf, P. J., & Fischbach, R. L. (1988). Psychiatric disorders and mental health service use in later life: Evidence from the Epidemiologic Catchment Area program. In J. Brody & G. Maddox (Eds.), *Epidemiology and aging* (pp. 189–219). New York: Springer.

Goldfarb, A. I. (1953). Psychotherapy of aged persons. *Psychoanalytic Review, 42,* 180–187.

Gottesman, L. E. (1977). Clinical psychology and aging: A role model. In W. D. Gentry (Ed.), *Geropsychology: A model of training and clinical service* (pp. 1–8). Cambridge, MA: Ballinger.

Gottesman, L. E., Quarterman, C. E., & Cohn, G. M. (1973). Psychosocial treatment of the aged. In C. Eisdorfer & M. P. Lawton (Eds.), *The psychology of adult development and aging* (pp. 378–427). Washington, DC: American Psychological Association.

Haight, B. (1988). The therapeutic role of a structured life review process in homebound elderly subjects. *Journal of Gerontology, 43,* 40–44.

Herr, J. J., & Weakland, J. H. (1979). *Counseling elders and their families: Practical techniques for applied gerontology.* New York: Springer.

Jelliffe, S. E. (1925). The old age factor in psycho-analytic therapy. *Medical Journal of Records, 121,* 7–12.

Jung, C. G. (1933). *Modern man in search of a soul.* New York: Harcourt Brace Jovanovich.

Kahn, R. L. (1975). The mental health system and the future aged. *The Gerontologist, 15,* 24–31.

Kahn, R. L. (1977). Perspectives in the evaluation of psychological mental health problems for the aged. In W. D. Gentry (Ed.), *Geropsychology: A model of training and clinical services.* Cambridge, MA: Ballinger.

Kastenbaum, R. (1964). The reluctant therapist. In R. Kastenbaum (Ed.), *New thoughts on old age* (pp. 137–145). New York: Springer.

Kastenbaum, R. (1968). Development and modification of behavior in the aged. *The Gerontologist, 8,* 280–283.

Kastenbaum, R. (1978). Personality theory, therapeutic approaches, and the elderly client. In M. Storandt, I. C. Siegler, & M. F. Elias (Eds.), *The clinical psychology of aging* (pp. 199–224). New York: Plenum.

Kaufman, M. R. (1937). Psychoanalysis in late-life depressions. *Psychoanalytic Quarterly, 6,* 308–335.

Kelly, G. A. (1955). *The psychology of personal constructs.* New York: W. W. Norton.

Knight, B. (1983). Assessing a mobile outreach team. In M. A. Smyer & M. Gatz

(Eds.), *Mental health and aging: Programs and evaluations* (pp. 23–40). Beverly Hills, CA: Sage.

Knight, B. (1986). *Psychotherapy with older adults.* Beverly Hills, CA: Sage.

Knight, B. (1988). Factors influencing therapist-rated change in older adults. *Journal of Gerontology, 43,* 111–112.

Knight, B. (1989). *Outreach with the elderly: Community education, assessment, and therapy.* New York: New York University Press.

Knight, B., & Carter, P. M. (1990). Reduction of psychiatric inpatient stay for older adults by intensive case management. *The Gerontologist, 30,* 510–515.

Labouvie-Vief, G., DeVoe, M., & Bulka, D. (1989). Speaking about feelings: Conceptions of emotion across the life span. *Psychology and Aging, 4,* 425–437.

Lawton, M. P. (1979). Clinical geropsychology: Problems and prospects. In *Master lectures on the psychology of aging.* Washington, DC: American Psychological Association. (Originally presented at the annual convention of the American Psychological Association, Toronto, August, 1978).

Lazarus, R. S., & Folkman, S. (1984). *Stress, appraisal, and coping.* New York: Springer.

Lewis, M. I., & Butler, R. N. (1974). Life review therapy: Putting memories to work in individual and group psychotherapy. *Geriatrics, 29,* 165–172.

Lindsley, O. R. (1964). Geriatric behavioral prosthetics. In R. Kastenbaum (Ed.), *New thoughts on old age* (pp. 41–60). New York: Springer.

Lovett, S., & Gallagher, D. (1988). Psychoeducational interventions for family caregivers: Preliminary efficacy data. *Behavior Therapy, 19,* 321–330.

Miller, N. E., & Cohen, G. D. (Eds.). (1987). *Schizophrenia and aging.* New York: The Guilford Press.

Meerloo, J. A. M. (1955). Psychotherapy with elderly people. *Geriatrics, 10,* 583–587.

Myers, W. A. (1984). *Dynamic therapy of the older patient.* New York: Aronson.

Nemiroff, R. A., & Colarusso, C. A. (1985). *The race against time: Psychoanalysis and psychotherapy in the second half of life.* New York: Plenum.

Neugarten, B. L. (1975). The future and the young-old. *The Gerontologist, 15,* 4–9.

Niederehe, G., & Fruge, E. (1984). Dementia and family dynamics: Clinical research issues. *Journal of Geriatric Psychiatry, 17,* 21–56.

Patterson, R. L., Dupree, L. W., Eberly, D. A., Jackson, G. M., O'Sullivan, M. J., Penner, L. A., & Kelly, C. D. (1982). *Overcoming deficits of aging.* New York: Plenum Press.

Pearlin, L. I., Mullan, J. T., Semple, S. J., & Skaff, M. M. (1990). Caregiving and the stress process: An overview of concepts and their measures. *The Gerontologist, 30,* 583–594.

Qualls, S. H. (1988). Problems in families of older adults. In N. Epstein, S. E.

Schlesinger, & W. Dryden (Eds.), *Cognitive–behavioral therapy with families* (pp. 215–253). New York: Brunner/Mazel.

Rattenbury, C., & Stones, M. J. (1989). A controlled evaluation of reminiscence and current topics discussion groups in a nursing home context. *The Gerontologist, 29,* 768–771.

Rechtschaffen, A. (1959). Psychotherapy with geriatric patients: A review of the literature. *Journal of Gerontology, 14,* 73–84.

Rybash, J. M., Hoyer, W. J., & Roodin, P. A. (1986). *Adult cognition and aging.* New York: Pergamon Press.

Schaie, K. W. (1965). A general model for the study of developmental problems. *Psychological Bulletin, 64,* 92–107.

Schaie, K. W. (1973). Intervention toward an ageless society? *The Gerontologist, 13,* 31–35.

Seligman, M. E. P. (1975). *Helplessness: On depression, development, and death.* San Francisco: W. H. Freeman.

Sherman, E. (1981). *Counseling the aging.* New York: Free Press.

Sherman, E. (1987). Reminiscence groups for community elderly. *The Gerontologist, 29,* 307–313.

Smyer, M. A., & Gatz, M. (1979). Aging and mental health: Business as usual? *American Psychologist, 34,* 240–246.

Smyer, M. A., Zarit, S. H., & Qualls, S. H. (1990). Psychological intervention with the aging individual. In J. E. Birren & K. W. Schaie (Eds.), *Handbook of the psychology of aging* (3rd ed.; pp. 375–404). San Diego, CA: Academic Press.

Steuer, J. L., Mintz, J., Hammen, C. L., Hill, M. A., Jarvick, L. F., McCarley, T., Motoike, P., & Rosen, R. (1984). Cognitive–behavioral and psychodynamic group psychotherapy in treatment of geriatric depression. *Journal of Consulting and Clinical Psychology, 52,* 180–189.

Storandt, M. (1983). *Counseling and therapy with older adults.* Boston, MA: Little, Brown.

Storandt, M., Siegler, I. C., & Elias, M. F. (1978). *The clinical psychology of aging.* New York: Plenum.

Thompson, L. W., Gallagher, D. E., & Breckenridge, J. S. (1987). Comparative effectiveness of psychotherapies for depressed elders. *Journal of Consulting and Clinical Psychology, 55,* 385–390.

Toseland, R. W., & Smith, G. C. (1990). Effectiveness of individual counseling by professional and peer helpers for family caregivers of the elderly. *Psychology of Aging, 5,* 256–263.

Wolpe, J. (1958). *Psychotherapy by reciprocal inhibition.* Stanford, CA: Stanford University Press.

Zarit, S. H. (1980). *Aging and mental disorders.* New York: Free Press.

Zarit, S. H. (1989). Issues and directions in family intervention research. In E.

Light & B. Lebowitz (Eds.), *Alzheimer's disease treatment and family stress* (pp. 458–486; DHHS Publication No. ADM 89-1569). Washington, DC: U.S. Government Printing Office.

Zarit, S. H., Orr, N., & Zarit, J. (1985). *Hidden victims of Alzheimer's disease: Families under stress.* New York: New York University Press.

16

PSYCHOTHERAPY AND ETHNIC MINORITIES

VICKIE M. MAYS AND GEORGE W. ALBEE

Let us begin with a demographic fact: Members of ethnic minority groups are neither major users of traditional psychotherapy nor purveyors of psychotherapy in anything like their proportion in the population. Indeed, it is relatively rare, statistically speaking, for African-Americans, Hispanics, and Native American Indians to use psychotherapy in the formal sense in which the term is ordinarily used. The same statement can be made for most forms of private or third-party supported services in the field of mental health including treatment for alcohol addiction, drug addiction, serious mental disorders, and mental retardation (Albee, 1977, 1979; Marmor, 1975; National Mental Health Association, 1986; President's Commission on Mental Health, 1978; Sue, 1988).

This pattern of usage should not be confused with levels of need or help-seeking for emotional problems. In general, ethnic minorities experience a higher proportion of poverty and social stressors typically regarded as antecedents of psychiatric and psychological disorders than Whites. Measured by numerous social indicators of economic stability and benefit, ethnic minorities as a group are seriously disadvantaged relative to Whites

(Health Resources Administration, 1980; Heckler, 1986; *Healthy People 2000*, 1990). While studies of race differences in psychological distress find African-Americans are no greater than Whites in *average* stress levels, non-Whites are twice as likely to report *extreme* levels of stress as a function of *greater exposure* to stress (Kessler, 1979; Kessler & Neighbors, 1986; Neighbors, 1984). Poverty, substandard housing, educational disadvantages, and problems of discrimination are all stressful events that are often associated with emotional problems and are increasing in the lives of ethnic minorities.

The potential impact of the conditions of poverty has been documented in studies relating stressful economic life events to changes in health and mental health status (Catalano & Dooley, 1983; Dohrenwend, 1990; Haan, Kaplan & Camacho, 1987). For example, it was found that environmental stress resulted in greater psychological distress for lower socioeconomic status (SES) African-Americans as compared with middle SES and lower SES Whites (Ulbrich, Warheit, & Zimmerman, 1989). The study illustrated that lower socioeconomic status African-Americans were more vulnerable to discrete events of stress as opposed to chronic strain. Although the poorer African-Americans in this study were able to cope better with the chronic stress of their economic deprivation, it was the daily hassles that accompany that poverty that most affected their emotional status.

Yet, in spite of the preponderance of these events in their lives, ethnic minorities are often underserved by high quality mental health resources (Wu & Windle, 1980). Studies of mental health utilization patterns of African-Americans indicate a higher usage of public rather than private mental health facilities (Mays, Caldwell & Jackson, 1991; Smith, 1981). Reliance on public facilities, marked by the instability of programs caused by financial constraints, federal budget reductions, sporadic state funding, and categorical rather than discretionary funding mechanisms, often results in second-rate care when compared with private facility services (Edwards & Mitchell, 1987). Services in private mental health facilities, in contrast to public facilities, are distinguished by choice of provider, stability of treatment regimes, choice in types of treatment approaches, specialists, long-term treatment programs, and better trained service providers.

For a variety of reasons some members of ethnic minority groups will choose to use informal rather than formal sources of help for emotional problems (see Flaskerud, 1986; Mays, Caldwell, & Jackson, 1991; Neighbors & Jackson, 1984). Help is often sought from family physicians, herbalists, acupuncturists, *curanderos*, root doctors, clergy, the church and other family members (Flaskerud, 1986). Family, friends, and traditional healers are sought not only because they share a world view of the person, but also because inaccessibility, costs, waiting time, distance, stigma, or cultural insensitivity in traditional psychotherapy services have rendered those services unappealing.

Whereas the disparity between the mental health service needs and usage patterns of formal traditional services of ethnic minorities is explained by some as a function of culture and differences in expectations on the part of this population, the disparity is also due to neglect and a failure of the profession of psychology to develop and promote relevant and adequate mental health services for this population. Several studies have found that use of community mental health center services by ethnic minorities is significantly enhanced when the centers are placed near the population (Flaskerud, 1986; Sue & Morishima, 1982); when language and ethnic/racial matches in staff personnel are offered (Flaskerud, 1986; Sue & Morishima, 1982; Zane, Sue, Castro & George, 1982); when therapy that is active, supportive, immediate, and directive is available (Sue & Morishima, 1982; Lin, 1983; Flaskerud, 1986); and when provision of referral to services for social, economic, legal and medical problems are incorporated (Dworkin & Adams, 1987; Flaskerud, 1986). Undoubtedly, ethnic minorities will use mental health services when the services are accessible, culturally relevant, and comprehensive.

The real problem is that the overwhelming majority of ethnic minorities do not have high quality psychotherapeutic services for the treatment of their mental health problems. Moreover, given the continuing increase in the population of ethnic group members in the United States and rising costs of health care, it is apparent that the bulk of these people will not enjoy such services in the foreseeable future if our profession does not change. While a segment of this population will always choose an informal source of help for its problems, the vast majority, if adequate and appropriate services were available, would take advantage of such formal services. It is to this group that the profession must respond.

These facts have been documented often enough so they need not delay us very long from considering some of the reasons for this lack of use or coverage. The most detailed examination of these issues was contained in the report of the President's (Carter) Commission on Mental Health (1978).

WHO?

Who are the underserved? They are identified repeatedly in several different places in the Carter report: children, adolescents, and the elderly.

Together, these three groups represent "more than half" of the nation's population—and a disproportionately large number of these underserved groups are ethnic minorities. Elsewhere there is discussion of underserved minority groups as a whole—including 22 million Black Americans, 12 million Hispanic Americans, 3 million Asian and Pacific Island Americans, and 1 million American Indians and Alaska natives. All of these groups are underserved or, in many instances, inappropriately served, by persons insensitive to cultural differences or incompetent in appropriate languages.

While these identified groups (totaling 38 million persons) clearly overlap somewhat with the three specific age groups identified as underserved, we are not yet at the end of the statistical complexities. Five million seasonal and migrant farm workers are largely excluded from mental health care. Elsewhere in the report of the Commission (1978) we discover that women also often do not receive appropriate care in the mental health system. Neither do persons who live in rural America, or in small towns, or in the poor sections of American cities. Neither do 10 million persons with alcohol-related problems, nor an unspecified number of persons who misuse psychoactive drugs, nor the very large number of children and parents affected by child abuse, nor 2 million children with severe learning disabilities, nor 40 million physically handicapped Americans, nor 6 million persons who are mentally retarded. While the Carter Commission made some very brave statements about "recent improvements" in the availability of mental health care in this society, it seems clear that this improved care must have been available largely to those groups not identified as being underserved—who could only be well educated, White, and living in the affluent sections and suburbs of major American cities!

The Commission (1978) also heard that migrant farm workers, largely drawn from minority groups, had the most abysmal care in both the areas of physical health and mental health. Similarly, Marmor's (1975) study, *America's Psychiatrists*, found that psychiatrists practicing psychotherapy in private offices saw very few persons from ethnic minority groups. Ethnic minority males were least frequently seen. All these statements apply even more profoundly to ethnic minority children.

In 1986 and two presidents later, the U.S. Secretary of Health (Heckler) Task Force on Black and Minority Health reiterated many of the same findings, although some indicators of health and mental health were worse. The task force found that among African-Americans, approximately 40–47% of total annual deaths were calculated to be excess deaths. Homicides and accidental deaths accounted for 35% of these excess deaths in African-Americans under the age of 45 years and 19% in the under-70 age group. While not quite as high, the same pattern was true for Hispanics and, in particular, Native Americans. No other cause of mortality so greatly differentiated African-Americans from other Americans as did homicide. Although technically, homicide is often viewed as a matter for the health arena, the prevention and cessation of violence and altering the nature of violence are clearly within the realm of psychological interventions.

Thirteen years after the President's Commission and five after the Heckler report, the conditions of health and mental health for ethnic minorities have improved for a few but worsened for many. *Healthy People 2000* (1990) cites a whole range of data supporting this conclusion. African-Americans have significantly higher rates of coronary deaths; African-American women, Hispanic women, Native American women, and men with high blood pressure (most likely African-American) are found to have a high prevalence of obesity (from poor diets). Growth retardation among low-income children is more common among African-American children, Hispanic children, Asian and Pacific Islander children. Baby bottle tooth decay is often associated with the failure to breast feed or the short duration of breast feeding, and these are more common among ethnic minority groups. Ethnic minority groups are more likely to smoke cigarettes (Southeast Asian men are highest) and youth of low socioeconomic status more commonly start smoking early. Smoking during pregnancy is more common, as is the use of smokeless tobacco, among ethnic minorities. Motor vehicle crash deaths are startlingly high among Native American men, and cirrhosis is high among this group, as well as among African-American males. The heavy use of alcohol and the use of other drugs is more common among ethnic minorities. Premature pregnancy, mostly unintended, is high among African-American and Hispanic adolescent girls. Young Black men and young Hispanic men are the most common targets for homicide. Deaths by motor vehicular accidents and by drowning are more common among minority males. The prevalence of dental caries, untreated caries, and gingivitis is especially common among ethnic minorities. Infant mortality, fetal deaths, maternal mortality, low birth weight infants, and failure to receive prenatal care all affect ethnic minority groups disproportionately. African-American and Hispanic women are less likely to receive breast exams, mammograms, or Pap tests. Chronic disabling conditions and reduced life expectancy are problems associated with ethnic minority group status in the United States.

As health psychology grows in importance as a new subfield within psychology, mounting evidence supports the critical role of lifestyle and behavioral components in health and mental health status. Central to almost every problem that psychology can treat is the reduction of stress. In spite of the overwhelming evidence that damaging environmental stressors are experienced by many ethnic group members, the presence of violence, and the impact of the conditions of poverty on their psyches, traditional psychotherapy looks inside the sufferer for an answer. As Albee (1990) stated in an address at a substance abuse prevention meeting:

> Problems are not inside the person. Problems are inside an unjust society. . . . We should ask ourselves what are the causes of poverty, low self-esteem, boredom and hopelessness. If we focus only on counseling to change self-esteem, we may fail to identify the causes.

The "who" so in need of services are often the socially marginal people in our society—victims of poverty, prejudice, homelessness, involuntary unemployment, exploitation and other damages brought on by our society.

Brown et al. (1990–1991) present an excellent analysis of how society contributes to the condition of ethnic minorities. In the past 20 years, there has been a restructuring of the labor market. In the United States, our economic base has shifted from one of a labor-intensive goods production to a highly technical information-processing market. One result, according to Brown et al. (1990–1991), has been the closing or relocation of manufacturing plants. America's urban centers were most affected because large numbers of inner-city ethnic minorities were employed in the low-skill, goods-producing occupations. While the American economy has benefitted from its change to less labor-intensive jobs by switching to high technologic, automated outputs, it has left large numbers of inner-city ethnic minorities unable to move into this employment sector. The sectors experiencing growth in the current economy are high-technology manufacturing, administrative support, and advanced services. All require high levels of education and skills. Yet the federal government, particularly during the Reagan administration, cut and eventually ended job training programs and reduced educational loan and scholarship programs. Clearly, "a look inside" will not be the sole remedy for many of the mental health problems faced by ethnic minorities, who were left "marginal" because of the switch to a high technologically oriented society.

WHY?

Bias

What are some of the reasons for the lack of availability of high quality mental health services or the patterns of psychotherapy utilization by ethnic minority group members? Clearly it is not because of the lack of mental health problems, because we know from epidemiological studies that significantly high rates of emotional distress are found among African-Americans and Hispanics (Myers et al., 1984). Such epidemiologic findings reflect, of course, a diagnostic system based on criteria developed largely by Western, White, middle-class, male psychiatrists.

As Mays (1985) pointed out, the descriptive criteria used to diagnose emotional disorders have a strong bias influenced by Euro-American values emphasizing the importance of individualism, competition, and separateness. A number of ethnic minority cultures hold different values and stress different behaviors, and therefore their members are more likely to get diagnosed as different or disturbed. In many Native American cultures, for example, cooperation is far more important than competition; Hawaiian children do poorly in competitive intellectual pursuits. Indeed, the average IQ of Hawaiian children is lower than that of the children of any other minority group, not because Hawaiian children are unintelligent, but because the measures used are inappropriate.

The Larry P. case (Lambert, 1981) in California established the inappropriateness of individual intelligence tests, like the Binet, for classifying minority children, a disproportionate number of whom are placed in classes for the "mildly retarded." Their performance on other measures of social adaptability often exceeded White norms. Jane Mercer (1973) has reported a careful study of the social role performance of children with IQs below 69 in the schools of Riverside, California. She compared Anglo (White middle-class) children with Black and Mexican-American children. Basically she found that the Anglo children called *educable mentally retarded* (EMR) were failing in their social roles. Children from the two other ethnic groups classified as EMR were less likely to be failing socially. Most important, she found a low correlation between behavior described as adaptive or competent and measured intelligence. Sixty percent of the Chicano (Mexican-American) children who had "failed" their intelligence test were able to pass a measure of good adaptive behavior. They were competent. Ninety percent of the African-American children in this same EMR group were also able to pass a measure of adaptive behavior.

Mercer suggests that the educable mentally retarded should be divided into three groups. The first group would include those children damaged by identifiable organic factors (a relatively small group); the second would be those retarded because of the operation of polygenic inheritance; the third would be those who were culturally different from the norm. It is in this third group that objective measures of intelligence and objective measures of adaptive competent behavior do not agree. She found that at least half of the Mexican-American adults who might have been classed as mentally retarded in school were leading effective competent lives: They had married, were gainfully employed, and were adapting successfully to their environment. Few had psychotherapy.

In regard to Asian Americans, considerable debate has taken place concerning assertiveness (Sue & Morishima, 1982). Studies have identified, in particular, Chinese and Japanese as "quiet, verbally inhibited and non-assertive" (Zane, Sue, Hu, & Kwon, 1991). Researchers have concluded that this behavior is the culprit in problems ranging from limited occupational mobility to dating patterns with lower preference for Asian males by Asian women (see Zane, Sue et al., 1991). Although the studies were indeed able to document that the Asians were less assertive than Whites, they missed what is probably a fairer question of whether they are less likely to perform such behaviors if necessitated in certain social roles. As Zane and his group established, Asians report being able to behave as assertively as Whites, although they may experience greater anxiety and guilt over such behavior.

The psychotherapist who attempts to use anxiety management to assist such individuals without a full appreciation of the cultural undertones may miss the mark. As Zane, Sue et al. (1991) point out, the assumption of most anxiety management programs is that the anxiety has an *irrational* or *maladaptive* learning base. Once the therapist is able to extinguish or expose this faulty premise, anxiety reduction will occur. When the basis for such anxiety is the result of cultural conflict, the question raised is whether an assumption of irrationality is a meaningful one. Building on the work of Sue (1983), in which he describes cultural conflicts that involve two equally valid sets of values clashing with each other, attempting to expose one as irrational is futile. Rather the experience of anxiety and guilt is one that would be indicative of a bicultural functioning, which is a positive attitude!

Access

Psychotherapy as traditionally practiced is largely a middle-class phenomenon, and psychotherapists tend to congregate in middle-class communities and neighborhoods. Even though there are more psychotherapists per capita in Washington, DC than anywhere else in the world, nearly all of them can be found in the White areas of Northwest Washington and in suburbia. More than 20 years ago, William Ryan (1969), in a major study of mental health care in Boston, demonstrated clearly the unavailability of mental health services, including psychotherapy, to the poor and disadvantaged. He found that five groups: multi-problem families, the elderly, persons discharged from state hospitals, children in need of residential care, and adolescents—mostly ethnic minorities—had almost no access to mental health facilities in a city that had more mental health resources than any other in the nation. He reported that the typical psychotherapy recipient was a White, non-Catholic, college-educated woman between the ages of 30 and 40 who was likely to live in one of three contiguous census districts in upper-middle-class Boston.

Services available to persons who are poor and/or members of minority groups are most likely to be in tax-supported agencies where less adequately trained therapists are available or are from underfunded tax-supported social agencies or probation departments where staff are in short supply.

Shortage of Minority Professionals

A factor influencing the use of psychotherapy by ethnic minority group members is the limited availability of bilingual and bicultural professionals, particularly minority therapists (Casas, 1985). It is not hard to empathize with those beset with both the ordinary stresses of life as well as with the extra stresses of being victims of prejudice and discrimination. That they may hesitate or refuse to talk about their troubles with Anglo therapists is understandable when some may view these therapists as representatives of the culture that has caused many of their problems.

The numbers of African-American and Hispanic psychotherapists is extremely small because of the long existing barriers to education for ethnic minority group members. This bias was particularly acute in the field of psychology. Graduate programs in psychology were long closed to members of ethnic minority groups (and also to women). Between 1879 and 1920, of ten thousand doctorates awarded in psychology, only eleven were earned by Black scholars. Between 1920 and 1966, the ten most prestigious departments of psychology awarded a grand total of eight doctorates to African-American candidates while granting a total of 3,767 PhDs during this period (see Albee, 1969).

The first Black PhD, Francis Cecil Sumner, was awarded the degree from Clark University in 1920. While a graduate student at Clark, he wrote letters to local newspapers pointing out that Americans should not be represented by the press as "self-appointed paragons of virtue" in contrast to the papers' portrayal of Germany's barbaric and immoral culture. He argued that Americans were not aware of nor concerned about the social injustices and widespread discrimination toward Blacks. For this, he was required by his University to apologize in a letter to the newspaper for his "disloyalty to his native country." Sumner, like many later Black PhDs, had to teach in Black colleges because of the reluctance of White colleges and universities to employ members of minority groups.

Similar problems have been faced by Hispanic young people seeking graduate studies in psychology. Carlos Albizu-Miranda, a giant in Puerto Rican psychology, returned to his native island to open his own school to train Puerto Rican psychologists-therapists, and a large majority of Puerto Rican psychotherapists have done their work at the school he founded there.

The early history of the American Psychological Association is replete with examples of racism and racist and sexist discrimination. The most convincing evidence of race differences in ability came from the psychological testing of soldiers during World War I. APA President Robert Yerkes and his consultant, Edward Lee Thorndike (another President of APA), were largely responsible, although it was a book by Carl Brigham (1923) of Princeton University that brought the "evidence" to the educated public. Brigham's book, (based on the Army's tests of soldiers), found a clear-cut relationship between the proportion of Nordic, Alpine, and Mediterranean blood and performance on intelligence tests. The book was praised by the chairman of the U.S. Senate Committee considering immigration law change. Brigham says, near the end of his "scientific" review:

> We must face a possibility of racial admixture here that is infinitely worse than that faced by any European country today, for we are incorporating the negro [sic] into our racial stock, while all of Europe is comparatively free from this taint. . . . The decline of American intelligence will be more rapid . . . owing to the presence here of the negro. (pp. 209–210)

A laudatory foreword to the book was written by APA President Yerkes. (It may be of some historical interest to note that Brigham designed the Scholastic Aptitude Test and served as Secretary of the College Entrance Examining Board. Later he was elected Secretary of APA.)

Because the Army IQ tests had shown that Jews, Negroes, Spanish-Mexicans, Poles, Italians, French Canadians, and other "brunette nationalities" performed at the feebleminded level in at least 80 percent of the cases, the immigration laws were changed to defend (rather late in the day) the purity of the native-born White Protestants. As Kamin (1974) points out, "There is nowhere in the records of the Congressional hearings—nowhere—a single remark by a single representative of the psychological profession to the effect that the results of the Army testing program were in any way being abused or misinterpreted" (p. 24). (For a fuller account of the racist beliefs of early American and British psychologists like Galton, Spearman, Pearson, Burt, G. S. Hall, Yerkes, Terman, see Albee, 1982; Fernando, 1988; Mays, 1985.)

Lest we forget, Fernando (1988) reminds us that, while overt scientific racism is clearly not in vogue, there was a resurgence of a "scientific racism" evidenced in the theories of race in the 1970s. One such example is Jensen's (1969) genetic explanation for IQ differences between Blacks and Whites. Considering his idea far from dead, Jensen (1984) defended his position in a commentary to a 1984 book titled, *Race, Social Class and Individual Differences in IQ* by Sandra Scarr.

It was not until the Civil Rights movement of the 1960s and the establishment of the Association of Black Psychologists (as well as the Hispanic Psychological Association, the American Indian Psychological Association, and the Asian-American Psychological Association) that American mainstream psychology was forced to confront its racism in issues involving admissions to graduate training and governance activities by the American Psychological Association. Finally in 1980, the American Psychological Association incorporated into its governance structure a Board of Ethnic Minority Affairs (BEMA) and in 1986 a Division-Society for the Psychological Study of Ethnic Minority Issues.

The supply of ethnic minority psychologists increased moderately in the 1970s and 1980s but is still far below the proportion in this population. With the U.S. population approximately 12 percent African-American and 7 percent Hispanic, only 2 percent of psychologists earning the PhD in recent years are African-American and fewer than 1-1/2 percent are Hispanic. The status of available psychological providers who are American Indians is worse and the future looks equally bleak. La Fromboise (1988) calculated that in 1976 there was 1 psychologist of any ethnic background for every 43,000 American Indians. By 1985, with 180 master's- and doctorate-level self-identified American Indian psychologists, the rate was increased to 1 American Indian professional for every 8,333 Indian persons. She contrasts this to a 1 in 2,213 rate of available psychologists for the general population. Due to the small number of American Indian psychologists to serve as role models, few students consider psychology as a career. This lack of career choice is exacerbated by tribal priorities that stress medical and legal careers (La Fromboise, 1988).

In Table 1, we show the percentage of practicing minority mental health professionals across the four disciplines of psychiatry, psychology, social work, and nursing as compiled by the Heckler report (1986) from 1980 data. Table 2 specifically presents the pool of clinical psychologists available that is equally as unrepresentative. Later data (see Table 3) compiled by the American Psychological Association show race of 1989 PhDs by subfields. Out of a total of 1,491 PhDs awarded in Clinical and Counseling psychology, ethnic minorities received only 161 degrees. One step taken by the Board of Ethnic Minority Affairs of the American Psychological

TABLE 1
Percentages of Practicing Professionals by Race/Ethnicity

Profession	Non-Minority	Black	American Indian	Asian/Pacific Islander	Hispanic	Unknown
Psychologists	95.6	1.4	0.2	1.1	0.7	0.9
Psychiatrists	69.4	1.5	0.4	5.6	2.5	20.7
Social Workers	88.5	5.8	NA	1.6	1.8	2.2
Nurses	91.5	3.7	0.3	2.0	1.2	1.3

Note: Primary data sources are membership surveys of the American Psychological Association (1982), American Psychiatric Association (1977), National Association of Social Workers (1982), a Health Resources and Services Administration survey of registered nurses (1980), and a National League for Nursing survey of 1980–1981 graduations of minority students from basic baccalaureate nursing programs. From *Report of the Secretary's Task Force on Black and Minority Health* by M. M. Heckler, 1986, U.S. Department of Health and Human Services, Washington, DC: U.S. Government Printing Office.

Association to assist ethnic minorities to receive ethnically sensitive and culturally appropriate treatment has been the drafting of the Guidelines for Providers of Psychological Services to Ethnic, Linguistic, and Culturally Diverse Populations (Myers, Wohlford, Guzman, & Echemendia, 1991).

In addition to the unavailability of minority psychotherapists, there are further problems affecting the availability of help for members of minority groups. Thirty years ago, the American Medical Association was often quoted as saying that the country did not need more physicians because no American lived more than a few miles from the nearest doctor. This was a small comfort to the residents of Harlem who, though they lived only five miles from Park Avenue, might as well have lived five light years away for all the help they might receive.

Clearly psychotherapy can be considered an intervention used by societies that are industrialized and subgroups who are relatively affluent.

TABLE 2
Numbers and Percentages of Clinical Psychologists in the United States by Race/Ethnicity and by Graduate Degree

Racial/Ethnic Group	PhD		Master's	
	Number	Percent	Number	Percent
Nonminority	15,885	96.2	2,360	94.9
African-American	159	1.0	38	1.5
Hispanic	164	1.0	19	0.8
American Indian	182	1.1	29	1.2
Asian/Pacific Islander	6	0.4	8	0.3
Unknown	123	0.7	32	1.3
Total	16,519	100	2,486	100

Note: Data from *Report of the Secretary's Task Force on Black and Minority Health* by M. M. Heckler, 1986, U.S. Department of Health and Human Services, Washington, DC: U.S. Government Printing Office.

TABLE 3
Number of 1989 PhDs Awarded in Psychology by Subfield and Race/Ethnicity

Racial/ Ethnic Group	Subfields		School
	Clinical	Counseling	
Total, all races[a]	1,021	470	98
American Indian	2	4	0
Asian	23	6	0
Black	44	15	4
Hispanic	47	10	6
Other ethnic	10	4	2
Total ethnic minorities	126	39	12

Note: Data from National Research Council, 1990, *1990 Summary Report: Doctorate Recipients from United States Universities*. Table compiled by Office of Demographic, Employment, and Education Research, American Psychological Association, June, 1990.
[a]Excludes degrees awarded to students who are foreign citizens.

Recent papers at the 1990 Vermont Conference on the Primary Prevention of Psychopathology (Albee, Bond, & Monsey, 1992) by Sefa-Dedeh of Ghana and by El-Mouelly from Egypt as well as reports by psychologists and psychiatrists from Pakistan (Arshad), India (Sonty), and Eastern Europe (Sek) present a picture of massive human social problems untouched by psychotherapy. In spite of the impossibility of reaching more than a handful of the billions of people who live in Third World countries in Africa, Asia, and elsewhere, many university psychology departments in countries of the Third World are embarking on the training of psychotherapists.

WHAT IS NEEDED?

While the history of psychotherapy derives from many sources, it is safe to say that a major tap root leading to the growth of modern traditional psychotherapy was the work of Freud. Freud treated middle-class White women in Vienna who, as a consequence of the repressive patriarchal culture of the time, had symptoms rooted in repressed sexuality. Freud's "discovery" of the unconscious, of unconscious motivation, repression, and the ego mechanisms opened many compartments of the human mind that led to excited explorations by his followers and by subsequent therapists. Other chapters in this volume provide rich background in the history of various therapies. Let it suffice for us to assert that therapy is largely available to the middle class, especially women, and not to ethnic minorities and to other disadvantaged groups for economic, cultural, and social reasons. In this respect it is no different from many other forms of human services and health care.

Most of the 40 million Americans who are not covered by any kind of health insurance are drawn from the ranks of the poor ethnic minorities. Concomitant with inescapable poverty and powerlessness is a higher-than-average incidence of a great range of physical and mental disorders. If minority groups suffer so disproportionately from untreated physical illnesses and have little or no protection, we should not be surprised that they suffer too from untreated mental disorders as psychotherapy has come to be part of the health care system, and persons without coverage through health insurance or other group protection cannot afford its high cost.

The view that social, economic and political conditions are primary factors in the psychological problems of ethnic minorities calls for a reorienting of mental health services to create less stressful environments (Cannon & Locke, 1977). This approach advocates a public health prevention model in which psychological problems will be reduced through the prevention and eradication of factors that contribute to poverty, substandard and nonexistent housing, low self-esteem, and lack of personal competence and power.

Albee (1981; 1990) designed a model supporting the basic principles of a public health model—involving the host, the agent, and the environment.

$$\text{Reducing incidence} = \frac{\text{organic factors} + \text{stress} + \text{exploitation}}{\text{coping skills} + \text{self-esteem} + \text{support system}}$$

The factors above the line in the diagram represent noxious agents that contribute to psychopathology. The factors below the line are ways we can strengthen the resistance of the host and thus prevent or ameliorate the behavior. In Albee's model, the equation can be applied to either a population or an individual. Within the context of primary prevention, the focus would be the population. The goal would be either to decrease the components in the numerator or to increase the components in the denominator.

Nobles (1986; 1990) advocates an "Afrocentric prevention model" of psychotherapy for African-Americans that emphasizes empowerment and Black identity. Nobles believes the primary function of culture is to give individuals patterns for interpreting reality. Then, culture has the responsibility for determining what should be prevented or promoted as normal and abnormal human behavior. According to Nobles, culture gives to individuals and communities several critical elements—self-worth, legitimacy, spiritual rejuvenation, power, self-determination, and bonding that effective prevention programs must replicate.

Several other culture-specific psychotherapy models have been developed since the mid 1970s with the emergence of more ethnic minority professionals into the field (Mays & Comas-Diaz, 1988; see Jackson, 1990). Yet the effectiveness of many of these models is limited by their relationships to our current payor system. For those ethnic minorities able to afford mental health services through private insurance, they can choose either an ethnic provider and or a model of psychotherapy that is culturally specific. But for the vast majority of ethnic minorities in need of mental health services, without changes in who provides the services, the structure of financing of those services, the orientation of the interventions, and a focus on the underlying social conditions producing the mental health problems, these models will be unattainable.

Bataille (1989) advocates a multifaceted and adaptable psychotherapy of the future. She envisions a practice of psychotherapy in which exclusivity of practice in an office or hospital will be the exception rather than the rule. Instead, therapy will expand to become environmental, interventions will be woven more intricately into the client's life. This could include home, school or worksite visits, or interacting with informal sources of emotional support.

Public psychotherapy in the 1990s and in psychology's next 100 years will require some tough decision making on the part of our profession. Psychology as a profession—if it is to remain a credible and ethical body—must develop adequate, relevant, and effective models of public psychotherapy that meet the needs of all consumers. Psychotherapy as delivered in our current health and mental health care system must become a relic encased in our traveling exhibits. We need a payor system that will sustain and champion diverse methods such as community support systems rather than focusing only on outpatient psychotherapy (Anthony & Blanch, 1989; Kupers, 1981; Parrish & Lieberman, 1977). The system will need to include a flexibility that allows for the reimbursement of supportive activities. This can only be accommodated through a transformation of our current system of mental health care. The possibility of such a transformation will be a direct function of psychology's ability and commitment to work to create a public mental health system that will be responsive to all in need of mental health services.

REFERENCES

Albee, G. W. (1969). A conference on the recruitment of Black and other minority students and faculty. *American Psychologist, 24,* 720–723.

Albee, G. W. (1977). Does including psychotherapy in health insurance represent a subsidy to the rich from the poor? *American Psychologist, 32*, 719–721.

Albee, G. W. (1979). Psychiatry's human resources: 20 years later. *Hospital and Community Psychiatry, 30*(11), 783–786.

Albee, G. W. (1981). Preventing prevention in the community mental health centers. In H. Resnick, C. Ashton, & C. Palley (Eds.), *The health care system and drug abuse prevention: Toward cooperation and health promotion.* Washington, DC: National Institute on Drug Abuse.

Albee, G. W. (1982). Preventing psychopathology and promoting human potential. *American Psychologist, 37*, 1043–1050.

Albee, G. W. (1990, February). *Looking for external causes.* Invited presentation at the Third National Learning Community Conference: Substance Abuse Prevention Among High-Risk Youth and Pregnant and Postpartum Women and Their Infants, Washington, DC.

Albee, G. W., Bond, L. A., & Monsey, T. (Eds.). (1992). *Improving children's lives: Global perspectives on prevention.* Newbury Park, CA: Sage.

Anthony, W. A., & Blanch, A. (1989). Research on community support services: What have we learned? *Psychosocial Rehabilitation Journal, 12*(3), 55–82.

Bataille, G. G. (1990). Psychotherapy and community support: Community mental health systems in transition. *New Directions for Mental Health Services, 46*, 9–18.

Brigham, C. C. (1923). *A study of American intelligence.* Princeton, NJ: Princeton University Press.

Brown, L., Clark, C., Cobb, J., Dare, R., Delpiccolo, Fass, M., Martinez, M., Monseratt, L., Nemko, A., Parker, M., & Russo, V. (1990–1991). Poverty in California: A theoretical and empirical analysis. *UCLA Center for the Study of Urban Poverty Occasional Working Paper Series,* Vol. 1, 2. Los Angeles: UCLA.

Casas, J. M. (1985). The status of racial- and ethnic-minority counseling: A training perspective. In P. Pedersen (Ed.), *Handbook of cross-cultural counseling and therapy* (pp. 267–274). Westport, CT: Greenwood.

Catalano, R., & Dooley, D. (1983). Health effects of economic instability: A test of economic stress hypothesis. *Journal of Health and Social Behavior, 24*, 46–60.

Dohrenwend, B. P. (1990). Socioeconomic status (SES) and psychiatric disorders. *Social Psychiatry and Psychiatric Epidemiology, 25*, 41–47.

Dworkin, R. J., & Adams, G. L. (1987). Retention of Hispanics in public sector mental health services. *Community Mental Health Journal, 23*(3), 204–216.

Edwards, L. S., & Mitchell, C. C. (1987). Strategies for cutback management in community mental health centers. *Community Mental Health Journal, 23*(2), 140–151.

Fernando, S. (1988). *Race and culture in psychiatry.* London: Croom Helm.

Flaskerud, J. H. (1986). The effects of culture-compatible intervention on the utilization of mental health services by minority clients. *Community Mental Health Journal, 22*(2), 127–141.

Haan, M., Kaplan, G., & Camacho, T. (1987). Poverty and health. Prospective evidence from the Alameda County study. *American Journal of Epidemiology, 125*(6), 989–998.

Health Resources Administration. (1980). *Health of the disadvantaged* (DHHS Pub. No. HRA 80-633. Public Health Service). Washington, DC: U.S. Government Printing Office.

Healthy People 2000. (1990). (Report of the Public Health Service, U.S. Department of Health and Human Services). Washington, DC: U.S. Government Printing Office.

Heckler, M. M. (1986). *Report of the Secretary's Task Force on Black and minority health.* (Publication of U.S. Department of Health and Human Services). Washington, DC: U.S. Government Printing Office.

Jackson, A. (1990). Evolution of ethnocultural psychotherapy. *Psychotherapy: Theory, Research, Training, and Practice, 27*(3), 428–435.

Jensen, A. R. (1969). How much can we boost IQ and scholastic achievement? *Harvard Educational Review, 39,* 1–123.

Jensen, A. R. (1984). Obstacles, problems, and pitfalls in differential psychology. In S. Scarr (Ed.), *Race, social class, and individual differences in IQ.* Hillsdale, NJ: Erlbaum.

Kamin, L. (1974). *The Science and politics of IQ.* Potomac, MD: Erlbaum.

Kessler, R. (1979). Stress, social status, and psychological distress. *Journal of Health and Social Behavior, 20,* 259–272.

Kessler, R., & Neighbors, H. W. (1986). A new perspective on the relationships among race, social class, and psychological distress. *Journal of Health and Social Behavior, 27,* 107–115.

Kupers, T. A. (1981). *Public therapy: The practice of psychotherapy in the public mental health clinic.* New York: Free Press.

La Fromboise, T. (1988). American Indian mental health policy. *American Psychologist, 43*(5), 388–397.

Lambert, N. M. (1981). Psychological evidence in Larry P. vs. Wilson Riles: An evaluation by a witness for the defense. *American Psychologist, 36*(9), 937–952.

Lin, T. (1983). Psychiatry and Chinese culture. *Western Journal of Medicine, 139,* 829–834.

Marmor, J. (1975). *Psychiatrists and their patients: A national study of private office practice.* Washington DC: Joint Information Service of the American Psychiatric Association and the National Association for Mental Health.

Mays, V. M. (1985). The Black American and psychotherapy: The dilemma. *Psychotherapy: Theory, Research, and Practice, 22,* 379–388.

Mays, V. M., Caldwell, C. H., & Jackson, J. S. (1991). *Factors associated with Black women's utilization of community mental health centers for mental health services.* Manuscript under review.

Mays, V. M., & Comas-Diaz, L. (1988). Feminist therapy with ethnic minority populations: A closer look at Blacks and Hispanics. In M. A. Walker & L. Walker (Eds.), *Feminist psychotherapies: Integration of therapeutic and feminist systems.* New York: Ablex.

Mercer, J. (1973). Pluralistic assessment project: Sociocultural effects in clinical assessment. *School Psychology Digest, 2*(4), 10–18.

Myers, H. F., Wohlford, P., Guzman, L. P., & Echemendia, R. J. (Eds.). (1991). *Ethnic minority perspectives on clinical training and services in psychology.* Washington, DC: American Psychological Association.

Myers, J., Weissman, M., Tischler, G., Holzer, C., Leaf, P., Orvaschal, H., Anthony, J., Boyd, J., Burke, J., Kramer, M., & Stoltzman, R. (1984). Six-month prevalence of psychiatric disorders in three communities. *Archives of General Psychiatry, 41,* 959–967.

National Mental Health Association (1986). *The prevention of mental–emotional disabilities. Report of the Commission on Prevention.* Alexandria, VA: Author.

Neighbors, H.W. (1984). The distribution of psychiatric morbidity in Black Americans: A review and suggestions for research. *Community Mental Health Journal, 20*(3), 169–181.

Neighbors, H. W., & Jackson, J. S. (1984). The use of formal and informal help: Four patterns of illness behavior in the Black community. *American Journal of Community Psychology, 12*(6), 629–644.

Nobles, W. (1986). *African psychology: Toward its reclamation, reascension, and revitalization.* Oakland, CA: Black Family Institute Publications.

Nobles, W. (1990, July–August). The afrocentric prevention model. (Office for Substance Abuse Prevention). *ADAMHA News, 16*(4; Suppl.), 9.

Nobles, W. (1989). Psychological nigrescence: An Afrocentric view. *Counseling Psychologist, 17,* 253–257.

Parrish, J., & Lieberman, M. (1977). *Toward a model plan for a comprehensive, community-based mental health system.* Rockville, MD: National Institute of Mental Health.

President's Commission on Mental Health. (1978). *Report to the President.* Washington, DC: U.S. Government Printing Office.

Ryan, W. (Ed.). (1969). *Distress in the city: Essays on the design and administration of urban mental health services.* Cleveland, OH: The Press of Case Western Reserve University.

Scarr, S. (Ed.) (1984). *Race, social class, and individual differences in IQ.* Hillsdale, NJ: Erlbaum.

Smith, E. J. (1981). Mental health and delivery systems for Black women. *Journal of Black Studies, 12*(2), 126–141.

Sue, S. (1983). Ethnic minority issues in psychology: A reexamination. *American Psychologist, 38,* 583–592.

Sue, S. (1988). Psychotherapeutic services for ethnic minorities. *American Psychologist, 43*(4), 301–308.

Sue, S., & Morishima, J. K. (1982). *The mental health of Asian Americans*. San Francisco: Jossey-Bass.

Ulbrich, P., Warheit, G., & Zimmerman, R. (1989). Race, socioeconomic status, and psychological distress: An examination of differential vulnerability. *Journal of Health and Social Behavior*, 30, 131–146.

Wu, I-H., & Windle, C. (1980). Ethnic specificity in the relative minority use and staffing of community mental health centers. *Community Mental Health Journal*, 16(2), 156–168.

Zane, N. W. S., Sue, S., Castro, E. G., & George, W. (1982). Service system models for ethnic minorities. In L.R. Snowden (Ed.), *Reaching the underserved: Mental health needs of neglected populations*. Beverly Hills, CA: Sage.

Zane, N. W. S., Sue, S., Hu, L., & Kwon, J-H. (1991). Asian-American assertion: A social learning analysis of cultural differences. *Journal of Counseling Psychology*, 38(1), 63–70.

17

PSYCHOANALYSIS AND DYNAMIC TECHNIQUES

ZANVEL A. LIFF

One hundred years since the birth of psychoanalysis, the core of Freudian technique—quiet listening in a state of "evenly suspended attention," a stance of objectivity and abstinence, interpretation-based interventions, and the working through of resistance and transference—remains the cornerstone of psychoanalytic practice (Pine, 1990). The attainment of insight has traditionally been the therapeutic goal and the catalytic ingredient of psychoanalysis. More recently, there has been a widening of perspective, in which the sphere of interest has extended from the patient's intrapsychic processes to the actual interrelationship in the treatment.

Clinicians, particularly those with an object relations orientation, have begun to use the realities of the therapeutic relationship, the dynamic, here-and-now interchange between analyst and analysand, to facilitate therapeutic change. This shift in focus has had a direct impact on how clinicians conceptualize and work with important aspects of the treatment process, such as transference and countertransference, interpretations and resistance. They have focused on a greater awareness of the personal role of the analyst in contributing to or impeding therapy (Strupp & Binder, 1984) and a differentiation of techniques for various pathological conditions.

It is not the purpose of this chapter to encompass a comprehensive chronology of all the technical contributions to treatment methodology. Rather, the focus will be on the technical advances that have developed historically in four major analytic conceptualizations—id or drive, ego, object relations, and self. The two predominant curative agents, transference interpretation and the therapeutic or working alliance, will be examined as well.

FREUD AND THE BEGINNING OF PSYCHOTHERAPY IN THE UNITED STATES

Psychoanalysis was imported into the United States in 1909 when Freud was invited by G. Stanley Hall to deliver the Clark lectures. It wasn't until after World War II, however, that the full force of American psychoanalytic practice took hold. Over the past century, theory and practice have evolved in response to the clinical demands of diverse populations ranging from Freud's psychoneurotics to young children, and to severely disturbed adults suffering from disorders of self. In America, new methods focusing on how the conscious ego can control unconscious conflict evolved from id or drive psychology. In England, object relations theorists formulated a new relational paradigm, based on pre-oedipal pathology and influenced by early interactions between mother and infant. More recently, in Chicago, Heinz Kohut (1971, 1977) introduced self psychology theory, reconceptualizing the disorders of the self experience in terms of cohesion, continuity, and fragmentation.

Psychoanalysis has continued to evolve as a psychological theory of the individual's relation to self and to others. Throughout its history, theoretical differences arose, which led to further reformulations and methodological refinements, so that contemporary practice may differ in its primary focus on either the intrapsychic or the interpersonal.

The founding of American psychology actually coincided with the birth of psychoanalysis. In the fall of 1892, G. Stanley Hall gathered a small group of colleagues in Philadelphia and formed the American Psychological Association. It was the first institutional body to represent the new science of the mind. That same year, in Vienna, Freud had embarked on his first full-length "analysis" of a hysterical patient, without the use of hypnotic suggestion.

Initially, Freud hoped to establish his psychology as a neurologically-based science. In his own clinical work, Freud had been applying the methods in use at the time—electrical stimulation, hydrotherapy, physical pressure. Gradually he began to conceive of mental phenomena as psychically determined. The often bizarre, medically inexplicable neurotic symptomatology that Freud observed spurred the creation of a new mentalistic language of memories, intentions, dreams, and desires. It was this language which enabled Freud to name the primitive, irrational, nonlinguistic part of the self, the dynamic unconscious, and to provide a new method of free association for its expression.

Freud's new free association technique continued to evolve in his clinical work with Frau Elisabeth von R., described in the volumes *Studies in Hysteria* (Breuer & Freud, 1893–1895/1955), written in collaboration with Josef Breuer. Frau Elisabeth, 24 years old, was referred because of crippling pains in her leg. Freud initially hoped hypnosis would uncover her repressed memories concerning the origin and fluctuations of her symptoms, but her lack of responsivity to this procedure forced him to abandon direct hypnotic suggestion and further pursue the free association method. Freud already believed that the symptoms of hysteria were caused by active, emotionally-charged ideas dissociated into the unconscious mind; that patients, when repressing certain of these charged memories from consciousness, converted affect into somatic sensations of pain; and that with the recall and discharge of feelings (abreactions), the symptoms would disappear. Freud also realized that to remember without strong emotions would be useless.

In this detailed case study, Frau Elisabeth's leg pains, which specifically radiated to her right thigh, were traced to the exact place upon which her father's swollen leg rested every morning while she changed his bandages. In free associating, Frau Elisabeth revealed how her happy feelings of her first love commingled with her sadness about her father's illness.

After further free association, Freud helped her recognize that a secondary experience leading to her painful symptoms related to the death of her nearest older sister. Frau Elisabeth had always been fond of her brother-in-law, and after her sister's death, she was greatly troubled by her wish to benefit from his new freedom by becoming his wife. Once her memories had been liberated by Freud's interpretation of her love for her brother-in-law, her symptoms were "spoken away" through abreaction and catharsis. It was Freud's goal to lead the patient directly to the traumatic event and release the suppressed affect. Through association, Freud stated that what was formerly unconscious in mental life may be made accessible to consciousness even without hypnosis. Once the amnesias had been removed, continuation of the morbid condition was prevented.

This critical case made clear to Freud that hypnosis was not necessarily a useful technique for all patients and that the encouragement to associate would bring about similar symptomatic cures. From his work with Frau Elisabeth, he discovered the phenomenon of "willful forgetting." He learned also that a single recital of the traumatic event was not sufficient to overcome the tenacity of resistance; traumas had to be worked through. His efforts, he reported, were like "excavating a buried city."

By 1892, Freud had established the broad outlines of psychoanalytic technique. Although no formally codified technique was set forth, it was generally acknowledged that the main technical innovation Freud offered was to listen intently to the patient and to encourage the free flow of uncensored material. The analyst would interpret to the patient the connections between the symptoms and events in his or her life that seemed to fit the paradigm of trauma. This systematic approach to resolving neurosis led to the changes that would ultimately free the patient to arrive at adaptive life solutions.

Freud's probing curiosity extended to "the most important patient for himself, his own person." From 1895 to 1902, a period of intense introspection, he systematically explored his own thoughts, dreams, memories, and free associations and penetrated his unconscious mind. This momentous self-analytic process (Anzieu, 1986) meshed with many of the discoveries he had made with his patients, especially those regarding the lingering infantile sexuality and "early child" within himself.

It was also during this period that Freud reformulated his thinking about memories as being recollections of actual events. Instead he conceptualized the primacy of fantasy productions. Actually, his initial conceptions of neurosis, which postulated that all neurosis is a consequence of early childhood trauma, foreshadowed the later object relations approach.

The magnum opus of Freud's self-analysis was the landmark volume, *The Interpretation of Dreams* (1900/1955). In this semi-autobiographical book, he universalized his own unconscious oedipal strivings, both sexual and parricidal, and acknowledged his infantile sexual levels. Although the unconscious had long been recognized as a phenomenon, it was his investigative approach through the medium of dreams and free associations that uncovered the powerful dynamic forces hidden from awareness.

With the beginning of the new century, Freud produced a burst of clinical writings, including several papers on technique (S. Freud, 1912/1949a, 1912/1949b, 1912/1949c, 1913/1949, 1914/1939, 1915/1939). He continued to refine his recommendations to the growing number of practitioners interested in the psychoanalytic method. He advised that patients be carefully selected to insure that they had sufficient stability and intelligence to endure the treatment situation and that their reality situation should not be too oppressive or demanding.

By 1904, he described the beginning of his work as asking patients to "let themselves go" as in a conversation leading from "cabbages to kings." He instructed them to relate everything that passed through their minds, even if they thought it was unimportant, irrelevant, or nonsensical and he stressed that they should not omit anything because it might be embarrassing or painful to them.

Freud looked for the gaps or amnesias in the flow of material which were the result of repression. The unintentional thoughts provided the linkage to the repressed psychological material to be liberated by the interpretation technique.

Basically, Freud conceived the treatment method as *partly* a collaborating together, "a regular rapport" (thus anticipating the working or therapeutic alliance components so emphasized at present), and partly a battle to overcome the inevitable resistance which opposed this work. Freud used tactical military metaphors as well as references to chess playing to yield free associations and combat the neurosis.

He recommended a trial period of work to assess the analyzability of the patient. He worked with patients on the couch 6 days a week and acknowledged that the treatment was time-consuming, taking from 6 months to several years. The working through process was viewed as an "arduous task for the patient and a trial of patience for the analyst" (Freud 1914/1939, p. 376).

Freud asserted that the therapist needed to listen carefully without selecting or distorting the material. He advised against any note-taking which would distract or divert the analyst's attention. He called on colleagues to "model themselves during the psychoanalytic treatment on the surgeon, who puts aside all his feelings, even his sympathy, and concentrates his mental forces on the single act of performing the operation as skillfully as possible" (1912/1949c, p. 327). The doctor should be opaque to his patients and, like a mirror, should show them nothing but what is shown to him.

By 1914, he wrote the classic paper, "Recollection, Repetition, and Working Through" (Freud, 1914/1939) which already stressed that the heart of treatment is in the working through of the resistance to becoming cognizant of the experience of the past in the present transference. He stressed that the doctor should only interpret, not gratify or reject the transference.

He cautioned against "wild" psychoanalysis, or the repetitive acting out of memories rather than their recall. By 1919 it was very clear to Freud that analytic treatment should be carried out as far as possible in a state of abstinence by the analyst so that external interferences would be minimized.

EGO PSYCHOLOGY

In the first years of the 20th century, control or autonomy were not central issues for Freud, who conceptualized the individual as governed primarily by instinctual urges and reactive defenses. But during the 1920s and 1930s, the theme shifted to the capacity for control over the unconscious, summarized by Freud's statement, "Where id was, there ego shall be."

In 1926, he further differentiated his ideas in *The Ego and the Id*. In the germinal work, he developed his structural or tripartite theory of the mind, which articulated the dynamic conflictual interaction of id, ego, and superego. Resistance in the superego was introduced as an equally formidable obstacle, particularly the internalized unconscious guilt which works against enjoyment of life. The ego was like a "beleagured garrison" always warding off assaults from the id, the superego, and the outside world. The structural notion added a new dimension to his evolving metapsychology. Freud's earlier view of the topographic theory of conscious, preconscious, and unconscious layers of mind, a mechanistic view that emphasized the automatic mental operations of instincts and defenses and neglected higher cognitive functions, such as the capacity to think, reflect, and regulate.

By 1926, in his paper "Inhibitions, Symptoms, and Anxiety," Freud elaborated on the role of anxiety and its avoidance in neurosis (1926/1959). He described unconscious warnings of danger, in relation to unacceptable impulses and wishes that trigger anxiety signals, which are alleviated by defensive inhibitions and symptoms. He originally postulated that repression caused anxiety; he now theorized that anxiety was the cause of repression.

Thus the decades of ego psychology became preoccupied with the structures and strategies of the ego as the executive agency of the personality. From the perspective of technique, it sharpened clinicians' perceptions of the multiple defensive and resistive patterns to alleviate anxieties. Anna Freud's volume *The Ego and Mechanisms of Defense* (1936) instructed analysts to give equal weight to each of the structural components. This book also shifted the focus to the operational functions of the ego and not just on the actions of the id.

Anna Freud summarized ten defenses and added her discovery of an important new defense, that is, identification with the aggressor. So that clinicians could analyze defenses with more sophistication and sensitivity, she described how the ego utilized the following defenses: repression, reaction formation, projection, introjection, regression, sublimation, isolation, undoing, reversal, and turning against the self. These defensive behaviors were employed by patients to allay anxiety and resist the awareness and working through of the transferential reenactments in the analytic treatment.

Nevertheless, the pervasive focus still continued to be the analysis through interpretation of neurotic symptoms as ineffectual compromises against unconscious wishes and anxiety. With the increased recognition of how defenses alleviated anxiety over unacceptable impulses, the implications for clinical technique became clear.

Effective interpretations acknowledged the necessity of defenses, however inappropriate, and based on early childhood assumptions. Defenses were treated with respect and sensitivity. The interpretations were aimed to shift the dynamic unconscious by accepting and understanding (a) the lingering wish or impulses, (b) the endangering anxiety, and (c) the required defensive strategy.

Timing was also an important factor. When the analyst observed that the free associative process or the overall flow of material was blocked or inhibited, it was evident that the defenses, in the form of resistances, were being reenacted. Transferential expectations of punishment, rejection, humiliation were at play. Thus, an effective interpretation conveyed the historical within the immediate, vivid moment. The patient was able to experience the inappropriateness of the wishes, fears, and defenses.

Three years after Anna Freud's book, Heinz Hartmann (1939) expanded ego psychology into an overall theory of adaptation, especially in its conflict-free spheres. This exploration led to additional functions of the ego beyond specific defensive operations. Among the other attributes of the ego were the functions of regulating, integrating, reality testing and judgment, as well as the overall memory, perception, and thought processes. Also included in the ego functions were both object relations and the sense of self and others, which anticipated later and more contemporary developments in the field.

OBJECT RELATIONS

While America became the hub of psychoanalytic movement, the British School of object relations was contributing considerably to new understandings of the unconscious mind, particularly pre-oedipal pathology and the significance of the mother–infant bond. Freud regarded biological urges as man's primary motivating and developmental force, a view that presupposed the self as essentially a closed system struggling with intrapsychic conflicts predetermined at an early age. One's earliest relationships were governed by these instinctual libidinal drives and seemed relatively impervious to external influence.

Object relations, though really a spectrum of theoretical positions, shifted the emphasis from the primacy of the instinctual drive to the actual relational bond between the self and its objects (which are its mental representations of significant others). Object relations stressed the motivational force of relationship-seeking and, specifically, the patient's own relationship to and interaction with the therapist as an active determinant of therapeutic change.

Melanie Klein was one of the earliest architects of object relational theory. While Freud developed his structural tripartite model and focused on the ego processes in the 1920s, Melanie Klein, in London, established herself as one of the first (along with Anna Freud) to apply classical psychoanalytic techniques in the treatment of young children. Klein acknowledged, as all child analysts do, that one gains access to the child's inner life through symbolic play, in which fantasy, identification, and shifting role assignments are expressed. She preserved the earlier notion of trauma as she probed the deeper derivative levels of pre-oedipal phenomena. Her book on the psychoanalysis of children was published in 1932, but not until after World War II did her work and that of her followers, including D.W. Winnicott, become fully recognized.

Klein's focus on the self–other configuration, or good and bad objects, evolved naturally out of her analytic treatment of children. Her pioneering work challenged the Freudian orthodoxy in Britain which promoted the drive–defense–discharge model. Yet her understanding of the environmental forces that impinge on and become internalized in the young child during the establishment of his or her first relational bonds is basically rooted in instinct theory. She vividly depicted the powerful emotional forces at work in the relationships of early life and developed the interactional patterns with predicted later schizoid, depressed, and paranoid behavior.

It is important to note that the Kleinian position and its clinical applications are dominant in much of the world. Even in the United States and western Europe, where her influence has been less strong, the combined object relations and self psychology approach has gained prominence in both theory and practice.

Winnicott (1958) expanded Klein's (1952) work with his notion of the self as struggling between twin desires for individuation and intimacy. He perceived that, for the infant, this struggle took place between the "object mother," who satisfied id longings and the "environmental mother," who provided emotional security. Failures in maternal care lead to a fragmentation of the early child experience and result in a split between "true" and "false" selves. The latter complied with maternal expectations rather than the child's own needs and desires.

Winnicott (1956) also observed the importance of the child's interpersonal surroundings, and developed the concepts of the holding and facilitating environment. He stressed defects in early caretaker relationships rather than conflicted fantasy scenarios and sought transference resolution by creating a "holding environment" in which the patient could safely relive early states of disturbed object relations.

Winnicott's work led to a deeper understanding of how the therapist can utilize countertransference to help treatment; recognizing that countertransference can be induced by patients and then used as a diagnostic and therapeutic tool required an open-system mentality, also referred to as intersubjectivity. The treatment implication was that the therapist could be deeply affected by the patient without acting out his or her role assignment. Rather, the therapist must understand, accept, and interpret these induced feelings as reflecting either restitution or revengeful transference feelings from past traumas.

In addition, analysts working within the object relations mode often experience a role reversal phenomenon, that is, the patient relates to the analyst in the manner in which the patient was related to by the original "bad" objects. This is similar to Anna Freud's defensive notion of identification with the aggressor.

Behaviorally, when patients "treat" the analyst with devaluation, indifference, and neglect, object relations analysts need to permit a relevant disclosure of their own feelings of being devalued. This experience is then utilized as a vital clue to feeling what the patient actually went through as a child. This technical procedure tends to enhance the emotional relationship with the patient through the communication of truly being understood.

SELF PSYCHOLOGY

During the 1970s the concept of self emerged as an alternative to the Freudian notion of ego. One impetus for this theoretical shift was the extension of analytic treatment to new clinical populations. The emerging patient groups were more severely disturbed, lower functioning, and less "analyzable" than the traditional psychoneurotic. For this new population, the ego came to be seen as a remote construct, whereas the self was more sympathetically viewed as closer to actual experience.

The work of Heinz Kohut (1971, 1977, 1984) of Chicago focused on narcissistic or self disorders, specifically on the ebb and flow of tension states revolving around the cohesion or fragmentation of the self. It was a new paradigm—to conceptualize psychopathology without primary reference to sexual and aggressive drives or oedipal conflict. Kohut's theory did, however, acknowledge that drive and oedipal phenomena existed, but only on the firm foundation of a cohesive sense of self.

In Kohut's self psychology model, the child experienced a failure in self and object differentiations. The early parental environment was felt as unresponsive or abusive, and it led to a sense of premature disappointment and arrested development. The self emerged as enfeebled, craving selfobject mirroring and merger experiences as well as enhancement and validation. By stressing the pre-oedipal universe, Kohut also extended the psychoanalytic domain to encompass earlier level problems and refocused attention on preverbal trauma.

The reformulation of narcissistic phenomena as central to preneurotic pathology, including the borderline and schizoid personalities, aroused great interest among practitioners working within the classical frame with patients not diagnosed as neurotic. As a consequence of these extended diagnostic formulations, a new treatment methodology arose which stressed the working through in treatment of the inevitable disappointments and empathic failures. For Kohut, it was the actual interpersonal experience with the analyst that determined the treatment's therapeutic action.

Unlike the Freudian approach which relied on interpretations of drive–defense conflicts to help patients on higher developmental levels, Kohut recognized that developmentally arrested patients with powerful affiliative and selfobject needs required an alignment with the fragile self, rather than reliance on interpretations of content-symbolic material.

His approach, similar to Winnicott's "holding environment," emphasized empathic attunement as a means by which the therapist can rehabilitate or restore the cohesion and continuity of the self. Kohut's recognition of the importance of therapeutic empathy, of the quality of the therapist–patient interaction, and of the emotional milieu in which the therapy was conducted reflected a growing awareness in psychoanalytic circles that external or objective reality, in addition to the patient's intrapsychic life, was a critical factor in treatment.

Within the evolving self psychology treatment model, a patient's anger or withdrawal in the session was connected to the analyst's failure to convey an accurate sense of empathy. The Kohutian analyst acknowledges his or her own limitations or lapses in being truly understanding and that the patient's disappointment is directly related to the analyst's imperfections.

Narcissistic and borderline patients often expect idealized responses from others for the continuation of their self experience. In the treatment, they learn that they can survive the frustration and experience the analyst as a separate, differentiated person.

TRANSFERENCE

Of all of Freud's clinical contributions, few have proved more valuable than his discovery of transference, that is, the realization that, in the analytic situation, patients inevitably relive and displace onto the analyst the conflictual feelings they experienced in relationships in the past. Use of the transference response, for the psychoanalytic practitioner, has continued to be the most powerful therapeutic tool. Its technical significance is threefold: It provides a means whereby the analyst can better understand the patient's fantasies, wishes, fears, and defenses; it enables the patient to experience these fantasies and fears as they arise in relation to the therapist; and it gives the patient the critical opportunity for working through in the analytic situation (Cooper, 1987). How psychodynamic clinicians view and use transference is a barometer of their evolving conceptualizations of the therapeutic relationship and its use in achieving the greatest therapeutic gain.

Freud's (1912/1949a) conception of transference as an intrapsychic phenomenon, in which the patient displaces fantasies onto the therapist, rendered the analyst's behavior and communications immaterial. The transference, according to Freud, emerged spontaneously; it was not imposed by the analyst. He considered transference to be fundamentally a problem of resistance, a "false connexion" which impeded therapeutic progress. Ultimately, Freud came to view the unfolding of the transference neurosis as a replay of the original neurosis in the treatment situation itself and as a vital necessity for completing a successful analysis.

Increasingly, clinicians appreciated the positive or facilitating aspects of transference and recognized the therapist's active participation in the transference process. Sullivan (1953) viewed the analyst as a "participant-observer" functioning within an interpersonal field. Thus, he contributed to an evolving interpersonal psychology emphasizing more active and interactional approaches by the therapist.

Recently, there has been a resurgence of interest in the transference phenomenon. Much of this has centered on a controversy as to whether transference can be split into two distinct processes, that is, a basic transference (or what is also known as a therapeutic alliance) and the analytic transference (the transference neurosis). Some authors (e.g., Brenner, 1982) take issue with such a distinction and maintain there is only one unitary transference. At the other end of the spectrum, Schafer (1983), for example, has asserted that transference is the "emotional experiencing of the past as it is now remembered, not as it 'really' happened." This view presupposes that transference is constantly an act of creation and, as such, a product of a living therapeutic interaction.

Similarly, Gill (1976) maintained that the actuality of the analyst's person and behavior is a powerful determinant of the patient's transference reactions. By emphasizing the importance of working through and interpreting transference reactions in the here-and-now of the analytic situation, he also reconceptualized transference as an interactional phenomenon of interdependence between analyst and patient.

The general consensus is that interpretation of the transference fixated on the past can become a biographic exercise. It should neither be fixated on reconstructing past material nor on the self-contained present. Instead, both perspectives should be integrated so as to respect past and present determinants. In this way, transference content can become more immediate and vivid and allow for the analyst to be experienced "not only as a listener but as an implicit participant in the relived event and an intrinsic part of the new meaning and experience of it" (Schimek, 1983).

THE THERAPEUTIC OR WORKING ALLIANCE

One outgrowth of clinical work on transference, and in particular the transference neurosis, is the concept of the therapeutic alliance (Zetzel, 1956) or working alliance (Greenson, 1965). It deepens the emotional bond or collaborative partnership established between therapist and patient that recognizes reciprocal role investments and that many psychoanalytic psychotherapists regard as a prime building block for therapeutic change.

Zetzel indicated that some analysts, misreading Freud's emphasis on abstinence, convey an attitude that is "austere, aloof, and even authoritarian," thus impeding positive therapeutic results. Greenson maintained that to resolve transference responses, the analyst must acknowledge, clarify, and nurture nontransference reactions. Increasingly, clinicians have looked upon psychoanalytic therapy as a two-person interactional process. Strupp & Binder (1984) indicated that critical predictors of good outcome are the therapists' positive or "affiliative" attitudes toward the patient and how effectively these attitudes are communicated to or processed by the patient. Not all clinicians have agreed that such a distinction is useful because the collaboration between analysand and analyst is implicit in the notion of transference (Brenner, 1982).

To some extent, Freud neglected this relational aspect of treatment, conceptualizing the analyst as a "blank screen" upon which the analysand could project feelings and fantasies. During the mid-1920s, Ferenczi and Rank attempted to shorten analysis by increasing the activity of the therapist and promoting planned, future-oriented action, but they received little formal consideration from their peers. With the advent of object relations, the positive aspects of transference, namely, the establishment of a powerful here-and-now bond between patient and therapist, attained greater recognition.

SHORT-TERM DYNAMIC PSYCHOTHERAPY

From the application of analytic practice to wider population groups, there also emerged a trend toward short-term treatment. Since the First International Symposium on Short-Term Dynamic Psychotherapy was held in Montreal in 1975, dynamic brief therapy has been used with patients with different pathologies, from those with mild dysfunction to those who suffer from chronic psychoneurotic and characterological conditions. Proponents of this new technique in the therapeutic repertoire (Davanloo, 1980; Sifneos, 1987) dispute that the depth which can be achieved in psychotherapy is directly related to the length of its duration and frequency of its visits. They claim that personality changes of an impressive and lasting nature can occur in a relatively short number of clinical interviews, on the average, between 10 and 25.

Without utilizing the couch, short-term dynamic psychotherapy adheres to traditional psychoanalytic principles by relying on interpretation as a key therapeutic tool and by actively using the transference reaction (Davanloo, 1980). After an initial trial interview, the therapist works to release the patient's hidden feelings by interpreting the resistances and revealing the links between the patient's transference and important individuals in his or her current and past life. The therapist assumes a more actively confrontational role, challenging the defenses forcefully so that the conflicts emerge in a more overt form.

Sifneos' Short-Term Anxiety Provoking Therapy (STAPP) maintains an "oedipal focus" and relies on a program of anxiety-provoking questions, clarifications, and interpretations. Criteria for patient selection include a circumscribed, chief complaint; psychological mindedness; capacity for flexible interaction with the therapist and for emotional expression; and, perhaps most importantly, a conscious motivation for change rather than simple symptom relief. These conditions are all set forth and mutually agreed upon in an initial "therapeutic contract" (Sifneos, 1987). STAPP therapy also stresses the value of educational components of treatment and endeavors to help patients build new learning and problem-solving skills which they can continue to develop and apply after treatment completion. Unlike Davanloo's method, which has worked effectively with phobias and obsessive-compulsive symptomatology, STAPP is recommended for higher functioning individuals who do not suffer from severe psychopathology.

Whereas the classical analyst tends to deal with defenses first, short-term therapists immediately try to establish a therapeutic alliance and positive transference to help the patient focus on the core problem and refuse to allow the patient to use pregenital characterological issues defensively (Sifneos, 1987). By confronting the patient's passivity and dependence (Davanloo, 1980), they actively avoid the development of a symbiotic transference relationship. Such an approach has led to a greater willingness on the part of the patient to participate in his or her own treatment.

SUMMARY

Dynamic techniques have been modified during the past 100 years as the scope of psychoanalytic practice embraced more varied patient populations. Freud's hysterical and obsessional neurotics were treated by interpretive insight into their unconscious conflict, which was transferentially reenacted with the analyst. This was based on the theory of biological oedipal drive and defenses against anxiety.

From clinical work with children as well as with borderline and narcissistic patients, a new focus shifted to issues of pre-oedipal developmental arrest and structural deficits in the self experience. Treatment procedures with these populations emphasized the actual relationship bond or the therapeutic or working alliance as equally important to the transferential projection. The utilization of empathic attunement to heal and promote self-deficit became widespread with the advent of self psychology theory.

REFERENCES

Anzieu, D. (1986). *Freud's self-analysis.* London: Hogarth Press.

Brenner, C. (1982). *The mind in conflict.* New York: International Universities Press.

Breuer, J., & Freud, S. (1955). Studies on Hysteria. In J. Strackey (Ed. & Trans.), *Standard edition, of the complete psychological works of Sigmund Freud* (Vol. 2). London: Hogarth Press. (Original work published 1893–1895)

Cooper, A. M. (1987). Changes in psychoanalytic ideas: Transference interpretation. *Journal of the American Psychoanalytic Association, 35*, 77–98.

Davanloo, H. (1980). *Short-Term dynamic psychotherapy* (Vol. I). New York: Jason Aronson.

Freud, A. (1936). *The ego and the mechanisms of defense*. New York: International Universities Press.

Freud, S. (1939). Further recommendations in the technique of psycho-analysis: Recollection, repetition, and working through. In *Collected papers*, (Vol. 2, pp. 366–376). London: Hogarth Press. (Original work published 1914)

Freud, S. (1939). Further recommendations in the technique of psycho-analysis: Observations on transference love. In *Collected papers*, (Vol. 2, pp. 377–391). London: Hogarth Press. (Original work published 1915)

Freud, S. (1949). Further recommendations in the technique of psycho-analysis. On beginning the treatment. The question of the first communication. The dynamics of the cure. In *The collected papers*, (Vol. 2, pp. 342–365). London: Hogarth Press. (Original work published 1913)

Freud, S. (1949a). The dynamics of transference. *Collected papers: Vol. II*. London: Hogarth Press. (Original work published 1912)

Freud, S. (1949b). The employment of dream-interpretation in psychoanalysis. *Collected papers: Vol. II* (pp. 305–311). London: Hogarth Press. (Original work published 1912)

Freud, S. (1949c). Recommendations for physicians on the psychoanalytic method of treatment. *Collected papers: Vol. II*. London: Hogarth Press. (Original work published 1912)

Freud, S. (1955). *The interpretation of dreams*. New York: Basic Books. (Original work published 1900)

Freud, S. (1959). Inhibitions, symptoms, and anxiety. *Standard edition* (Vol. 20). London: Hogarth. (Original published 1926)

Freud, S. (1961). The ego and the id. *Standard edition* (Vol. 19). London: Hogarth. (Original published 1926)

Gill, M. M. (1976). *Analysis of transference*. New York: International Universities Press.

Greenson, R. R. (1965). *The technique and practice of psychoanalysis* (Vol. 1). New York: International Universities Press.

Hartmann, H. (1939). *Ego Psychology and Problems of Adaptation*. New York: International Universities Press.

Klein, M. (1932). *The psychoanalysis of children*. London: Hogarth Press.

Klein, M. (1952). *Developments in psychoanalysis*. London: Hogarth Press.

Kohut, H. (1971). *The analysis of the self*. New York: International Universities Press.

Kohut, H. (1977). *The restoration of the self.* New York: International Universities Press.

Kohut, H. (1984). *How does analysis cure?* Chicago: University of Chicago Press.

Pine, F. (1990). *Drive, ego, object, and self.* New York: Basic Books.

Schafer, R. (1983). *The analytic attitude.* New York: Basic Books.

Schimek, J. G. (1983). The construction of the transference: The relativity of the "here and now" and the "there and then." *Psychoanalysis and Contemporary Thought, 6,* 435–456.

Sifneos, P. (1987). *Short-term dynamic psychotherapy.* New York: Plenum.

Strupp, H. H., & Binder, J. L. (1984). *Psychotherapy in a new key.* New York: Basic Books.

Sullivan, H. S. (1953). *The interpersonal theory of psychiatry.* New York: Norton.

Winnicott, D. W. (1956). On transference. *International Journal of Psycho-Analysis, 37,* 386–388.

Winnicott, D. W. (1958). *Through pediatrics to psychoanalysis.* London: Tavistock Publications.

Zetzel, E. R. (1956). Current concepts of transference. *International Journal of Psycho-Analysis, 37,* 367–376.

18

BEHAVIOR THERAPY

CAROL R. GLASS AND DIANE B. ARNKOFF

Behavior change strategies have most likely been employed throughout history. For centuries, parents have attempted to socialize their children by using praise and punishment and by encouraging them to confront feared situations directly. Franks (1969) cites the efforts of Pliny the Elder, who treated alcoholism by means of punishment and by placing putrid spiders in the bottom of a glass, and Kazdin and Pulaski (1977) have detailed the work of Joseph Lancaster in the early 1800s and his "monitorial system" for providing rewards and prizes to students who completed academic tasks and paid attention. In fact, historical precedents can be found for most current behavior therapy techniques, such as exposure, contingency management, aversion therapy, relaxation training, and systematic desensitization.

In preparing this chapter, we decided to conduct 1-hour interviews with a number of the major figures in the development of behavior therapy. Most of these interviews (8) were conducted face-to-face, with an additional four conducted by phone, during November and December 1989. The experts we interviewed, in alphabetical order, are: Teodoro Ayllon, Gerald Davison, Cyril Franks, Marvin Goldfried, Leonard Krasner, Arnold Lazarus, Michael Mahoney, Rosemery Nelson-Gray, Stanley Rachman, Andrew Salter, G. Terence Wilson, and Joseph Wolpe. We are grateful for their time and contributions to this chapter. When the name of one of these individuals is mentioned in this chapter, along with a citation to "personal communication, 1989," we will be referring to the interviews we conducted.

Despite such important precursors, behavior therapy has been described as a field with a "long past but a short history" (O'Leary & Wilson, 1987, p. 1). The beginnings of modern behavior therapy date back only to the 1950s and early 1960s, although solid theoretical foundations were established earlier in this century. The work of Pavlov and Bechterev in Russia and Watson in the United States, in particular, stand out as crucial for the development of the current behavior therapy movement.

In this chapter, we will begin with these learning theory foundations and describe some of the earliest applications of these principles. The origins of current behavior therapy approaches will be presented, highlighting the work of Wolpe, Eysenck, and Skinner and their students and colleagues. We will then trace the development of new behavioral techniques and focus on their clinical applications. Value issues and the broadening of behavior therapy will also be considered, along with information concerning the theoretical orientation that clinical psychologists and other professionals endorsed in large surveys conducted between 1953 and the present.[1] Finally, we will offer some speculations on the future of behavior therapy.

LEARNING THEORY FOUNDATIONS AND EARLY CLINICAL APPLICATIONS

Pavlov and Bechterev

The theoretical foundations of modern behavior therapy were laid in the late 19th and early 20th centuries. Ivan Pavlov's work on conditioned reflexes represented the beginnings of classical conditioning (Pavlov, 1927, 1928). His famous experiments demonstrated that, after pairing a neutral event like a bell with the presentation of food (the "unconditioned stimulus"), dogs would begin salivating (the previously "unconditioned response") in the mere presence of the tone, which had acquired the properties of a conditioned stimulus.

Although Pavlov's work is better known, at least in this country, Vladimir Bechterev's "reflexology" and focus on conditioning of motoric reflexes is applicable to the clinical problems of human behavior (Bechterev, 1932). In summarizing the most important features of the Russian experimental research for behavior therapy, Kazdin (1978, 1982) highlighted Pavlov's use of objective research methods, a focus on learning and envi-

---

[1] Additional material on the history of behavior therapy can be found in books, chapters, and articles by Craighead (1982), Kazdin (1978, 1982), Krasner (1982, 1990), Schorr (1984), and Yates (1970).

ronmental explanations of behavior, and the emphasis on the development of conditioning. Franks (1969) also provided a useful discussion of the Pavlovian origins of behavior therapy.

Watson

It has been argued that there were other "behaviorists" prior to John Watson, but J. C. Burnham (1968) and most others date the start of behaviorism to the presentation and publication of Watson's 1913 manifesto, "Psychology as the Behaviorist Views It." Influenced by the work of both Pavlov and Bechterev, Watson's behaviorism insisted on objectivity and rejected mentalism and the study of consciousness. His famous study of "Little Albert" (Watson & Rayner, 1920) represented the first laboratory attempt to produce a conditioned negative emotion, using an 11-month-old boy as the subject of an applied Pavlovian conditioning paradigm. Albert, who initially was not fearful of white rats, eventually began to cry and withdraw from the animal after several presentations of the rat paired with the striking of a steel bar. This fear response later generalized to other furry objects, such as a white rabbit and a Santa Claus mask with a white fuzzy beard.

In spite of his pivotal contributions to a science of behavior, Watson is also remembered for his extreme environmentalism, along with his cold and detached recommendations for child rearing (Skinner, 1959). Nevertheless, his approach appealed to young psychologists and to those outside the field, who hoped that behaviorism would be an answer to some of humanity's problems (Willis & Giles, 1978).

Learning Theories

The period between 1920 and 1950 was marked by increasing attention to the psychology of learning, which, in addition to Pavlov and Watson, provided additional theoretical grounding for what would later be called behavior therapy. One of the most important of these later theorists was Thorndike, whose formulation of the laws of learning and emphasis on the role of positive consequences set the stage for work in instrumental or operant conditioning (Thorndike, 1931). Guthrie's (1935) work on eliminating responses, Hull's (1943) principles of behavior, and Mowrer's (1947) two-factor learning theory represent other major contributions. Although Skinner's initial work also occurred during this period (Skinner, 1938), we will focus on the impact of his later writings and research in the next section of this chapter. The theoretical origins of behavior therapy are addressed in greater detail in Fishman and Franks' chapter in this volume.

Clinical Applications

The 1920s and 1930s also brought the appearance of a number of early clinical applications of learning theory. We can highlight only a half dozen of the most important; a more complete review of this period can be found in the references on the history of behavior therapy cited earlier. The first major clinical demonstration was conducted by one of Watson's students, Mary Cover Jones (1924b). Jones speculated that if fears could be established by conditioning, perhaps they could be eliminated by use of the same principles. Her famous study was conducted with 3-year-old Peter, who was afraid of a variety of furry objects like rabbits, fur coats, and cotton. As Peter sat eating his favorite foods, a caged rabbit was brought into the room at sufficient distance not to interfere with his eating. Over time, the rabbit was brought progressively closer until it was close enough for him to touch.

Jones (1924a) also published a report of treatments with other institutionalized children who had a variety of fears, using direct conditioning and social imitation of nonfearful child models. This report compared the outcomes of behavioral treatment strategies in a scientific manner; thus, from the very beginning, behavior therapy valued empirically based interventions. Nevertheless, Jones, who was once introduced by Wolpe as the "mother of behavior modification" (Krasner, 1988a), never identified herself as a "behaviorist" and believed more in the importance of integrating behavioral techniques with other approaches to psychotherapy.

In that same year, William Burnham published his book *The Normal Mind*, describing applications of conditioning to inhibit fears and to provide positive consequences for desired behavior in the classroom. This book was described by Yates as a "classic and a landmark" (1970, p. 14). Dunlap's (1930, 1932) use of negative practice (extreme repetition of the unwanted behavior) represented one of the first systematic attempts to treat undesirable habits such as stuttering, tics, nailbiting, and thumb sucking. Franks (personal communication, 1989) commented that the ideas in Dunlap's *Habits: Their Making and Unmaking* (1932) are the precursors of many of the behavior therapy techniques used today.

Examples of early clinical practice still in use today must include Mowrer and Mowrer's (1938) landmark "bell and pad" treatment of enuresis. The Mowrers, while serving as house parents for a childrens' home, found that about half of the children had problems with bedwetting. Consistent with principles of Pavlovian conditioning, a pad was placed in each child's bed and attached to a doorbell, which would ring at the first sign of urination. Just as the sound of the bell first elicited waking and sphincter control, after repeated pairings the children were able to respond to their bladder distention (the "conditioned stimulus") and sleep through the night or anticipate urination in time to use the bathroom. Despite protests from psychoanalytic clinicians, Hobart Mowrer reports that this technique was received so enthusiastically that his supply of 500 reprints was gone in just 2–3 weeks (Redd, Porterfield, & Andersen, 1979)!

Our final two examples both influenced Wolpe's later development of reciprocal inhibition procedures. In 1929, Jacobson's book on progressive relaxation was published, which was introduced as a treatment for a variety of clinical problems such as hypertension, anxiety, phobias, colitis, insomnia, and tics. A later classic by Salter (1949), *Conditioned Reflex Therapy*, drew on Pavlovian notions of neurosis as the result of excessive inhibition of thoughts, feelings, and behavior. Salter focused on direct practice in expressing oneself in actual situations, which he viewed as going in the direction of greater excitation. His work is thus an important forerunner of modern assertion training, behavior rehearsal, and self-control techniques. Salter (personal communication, 1989) recalls that a client of his talked about being "assertive" back in 1941.

Lack of Impact

In general, although conditioning principles were applied to a large number of disorders in the 1920s and 1930s, these and other early applications of behavioral principles remained isolated from each other and failed to have much impact on the development of a behavior therapy "movement." As Willis and Giles (1978) pointed out, references to behaviorism in the *Reader's Guide to Periodical Literature* (perhaps indicative of the public's interest and attention) peaked in 1928, but by 1936 only one article was cited.

In considering why this was so, we must realize that this period was marked by the rise of psychoanalysis. Until the period immediately following World War II, the practice of psychotherapy tended to be restricted to psychiatrists, who were (and still are) primarily psychoanalytically trained and lacked exposure to learning theory and research in experimental psychology. School counselors who broke away from psychoanalytic influences tended to turn instead to Rogers' client-centered model (Craighead, 1982).

M. C. Jones (1975) also speculates that the field declined in the 1930s and 1940s because of the loss of Watson's leadership, but Willis and Giles (1978) argue that his extreme positions and dogmatic presentation may have worked against continued systematic development of behavioral applications. These authors also suggest that the terminology of behaviorism employed words and phrases that had negative associations or were difficult to understand. Additionally, they point out that early behaviorists relied on a narrow set of explanations for human behavior, rejecting internal events, feelings, and consciousness, and thus alienated many colleagues and the lay public who saw behaviorism as shallow and inapplicable to human beings. On the other hand, Boring (1950) argued that a school of behaviorism might never have been established without the presence of someone with such strong faith who could forcefully present this alternative position.

BEGINNINGS OF MODERN BEHAVIOR THERAPY

An equally interesting question is why the behavior therapy movement finally did develop an identity in the late 1950s and early 1960s. In addition to highlighting fifteen "streams" of development that came together at this time, Krasner (1971, 1982, 1988b) has argued that behavior therapy in American psychology was influenced by the broader society and should be viewed in the context of the social, political, and cultural climate that existed after World War II. Specifically, there was a sense of social responsibility and of idealism, optimism, and utopian hopes, with an emphasis on planning the social environment to bring out the best in human behavior.

Another direct impact of the war was a tremendous need for therapeutic services, so that clinical psychologists were allowed to practice psychotherapy and not remain primarily in the assessment and diagnosis field (Franks, 1969). Federal support was available through the GI Bill and Veterans Administration (VA) traineeships for doctoral training in psychology. The growth of the field of clinical psychology in the postwar years was also directly linked to the scientist-practitioner model, which emphasized training in experimental psychology and research methods as well as clinical applications. Students who would become the behavior therapists of the future thus received training with a strong scientific foundation (Krasner, 1988b).

By this time, concerns were growing about the dominant medical model of psychopathology, as well as doubts about the efficacy and theoretical basis of psychoanalysis. In the child-clinical area, Craighead (1982) cited the "milestone critiques" of Levitt (1957, 1963), who concluded that there was little empirical support for the effectiveness of psychodynamic psychotherapy. Thus behavior therapy was seen as an exciting alternative to the status quo and represented what Krasner (1971) saw as a paradigm shift.

Finally, Kazdin (1982) suggested that the field finally developed a true identity as a visible movement when Eysenck published his (1960) book of clinical applications (the first book to use "behaviour therapy" in the title). Three years later, in 1963, came the founding (by Eysenck and Rachman) of the first behavior therapy journal, *Behaviour Research and Therapy*, which served as an outlet for work from both England and North America and which was very influential in stimulating further research and clinical applications (Rachman, personal communication, 1989). The most important influences on the field in the 1950s were Joseph Wolpe and Arnold Lazarus in South Africa, Hans Eysenck and his colleagues at the Maudsley Hospital in London, and B. F. Skinner and Ogden Lindsley in the United States.

Wolpe and Lazarus

Although his initial work was psychoanalytically focused, by 1944, Wolpe was moving away from this approach in search of something more effective. At this time he began reading the work of Pavlov and Masserman, which together stimulated Wolpe's early research in the production of experimental neurosis (Wolpe, personal communication, 1989). Just as pairing shock with cats' approach toward food produced inhibition of eating, he speculated that this avoidance could be eliminated by providing opportunities and physical guidance to produce eating. Initially, this reconditioning took place in rooms most dissimilar to the room the cats had been shocked in, gradually becoming increasingly closer to that setting. By the late 1940s, Wolpe had also been exposed to the writings of Hull, Salter, and Mary Cover Jones.

These learning principles became the basis for Wolpe's landmark work, *Psychotherapy by Reciprocal Inhibition* (1958), which he feels was his most influential publication (personal communication, 1989). Wolpe not only developed specific therapy techniques but provided numerous case histories with outcome data in support of the efficacy of this "systematic desensitization" approach. With clients, he drew on the work of Jacobson (1929) and used relaxation as the incompatible response to be paired with anxiety-arousing imagined situations. In a creative extension of his animal work, Wolpe had clients visualize a hierarchy of scenes while they were totally relaxed, beginning with the least threatening and working up to situations eliciting maximum anxiety.

At the University of Witwatersrand in South Africa, Wolpe met frequently with several colleagues and students who were excited about this new and effective way to treat anxiety and phobias. Arnold Lazarus and Stanley Rachman were among those in this group, and they mention Wolpe as an important influence (personal communications, 1989). They later helped to spread Wolpe's systematic desensitization technique to England and the United States, where Wolpe himself moved in 1963. In fact, Lazarus is one of those credited with the earliest use of the term *behaviour therapy*, referring to the addition of Wolpe's objective techniques to traditional methods of support and insight in the treatment of neurosis (Lazarus, 1958).

Early applications of systematic desensitization focused on the treatment of a variety of disorders, including phobias (of small animals, dark places, heights, cars, injections, public speaking, agoraphobia), guilt, general anxiety reactions, impotence and "frigidity," voyeurism and exhibitionism, obsessive thoughts, and stuttering. Gordon Paul's well-known outcome study (Paul, 1966) compared systematic desensitization to insight-oriented therapy and to both an attention-placebo and no-treatment control, and helped to establish the use of therapy manuals in behavior therapy.

Eysenck and Shapiro

In 1952, Eysenck published his now-famous article, in which he argued that roughly two-thirds of all patients recover or improve significantly within 2 years whether or not they receive (nonbehavioral) psychotherapy. Eysenck's subsequent writings and theoretical work at the Institute of Psychiatry in London influenced his colleagues and students, who met weekly at his house to discuss dissatisfactions with traditional psychotherapy and to develop and provide empirical support for an alternative model for treatment based on theoretical foundations provided by Hull and Pavlov (Franks, personal communication, 1989). Certainly the direction and support of M. B. Shapiro, who was head of the clinical section at the Maudsley Hospital, also helped the origination of the behavior therapy movement in England (Gibson, 1981; Yates, 1970).

Early studies applying learning theory to individual clients were conducted by H. G. Jones (1956), Meyer (1957), and Yates (1958). Although Eysenck himself did not see clients, his previously mentioned edited book of clinical applications (Eysenck, 1960) and his 1965 book coauthored with Rachman, *The Causes and Cures of Neurosis*, were important for publicizing and advancing this approach (Gibson, 1981). Wolpe had visited London several times during the 1950s, and Eysenck described Wolpe's systematic desensitization approach to the European community. Eysenck (1959) is also credited with being one of the first to use the term *behaviour therapy* to refer to the application of learning theory (based broadly on the work of Hull, Pavlov, Guthrie, and to a lesser degree Skinner) to the treatment of psychological disorders. Krasner (1982) says that this term probably originated at one of the meetings of the Maudsley group, as they searched for a term to describe this treatment.

Cyril Franks (personal communication, 1989) recalls that early clinical applications at the Maudsley Hospital included procedures that were given their commonly used names much later: the use of reinforcement and aversive conditioning with alcoholics, Wolpe's desensitization, the elements of assertion training and behavior rehearsal, and conditioning techniques with children suffering from enuresis. Rachman describes this period as a tremendously exciting time. Because psychoanalysts in England were not as influential as in the United States, behavior therapy techniques were developed and introduced into clinical training and were met with less opposition (Rachman, personal communication, 1989).

Skinner, Lindsley, and Operant Conditioning

The origins of the behavior therapy movement in the United States were largely in Skinner's theoretical work on operant conditioning. In his 1953 book, *Science and Human Behavior*, Skinner suggested a role for contingency management in the areas of psychotherapy and education. Lindsley and Skinner demonstrated at Metropolitan State Hospital that chronic schizophrenics' behavior on a plunger-pulling task could be controlled by delivering various reinforcements like candy or cigarettes (Lindsley, 1956, 1960). In an early status report of this research, Lindsley, Skinner, and Solomon (1953) first used the term *behavior therapy* to refer to the application of conditioning principles to psychological problems. Later, "applied behavior analysis" and "behavior modification" were much more frequently used to refer to the application of operant contingency management techniques, terms popularized by Ullmann and Krasner's (1965) *Case Studies in Behavior Modification* and the initial publication of the *Journal of Applied Behavior Analysis* in 1968.

Perhaps the first application of Skinnerian conditioning in a clinical setting was conducted by Paul Fuller (1949), who conditioned and extinguished an arm-raising response in an 18-year-old "vegetative idiot" at a state institution by using a sugar-milk solution as reinforcement. Fuller (1973) says he did not encounter many objections to applying such techniques with such a mentally handicapped individual, but that when he planned a similar approach with clinical and hospital patients, he was met with "tirades" from psychiatrists and analytically oriented psychologists. One such plan involved nonreinforcement of undesired behavior and reinforcement of desirable behavior with a rebellious boy, to which the clinic director remarked, "You can't treat a child like you do your rats and pigeons!" Fuller (1973) comments that "I could and I did," and he credits J. R. Kantor with supporting the extension of operant studies from the animal laboratory to the clinic.

The work of Teodoro Ayllon is also important because it included creative applications of operant techniques in mental hospital settings. Ayllon and his colleagues did creative work in training psychiatric nurses as "behavioral engineers" and using operant conditioning and satiation to deal with patients' disruptive behaviors such as towel hoarding and pestering visits to the nurses' station (Ayllon, 1963; Ayllon & Haughton, 1964; Ayllon & Michael, 1959). Ayllon recalls (personal communication, 1989) that these applications were appreciated by and not threatening to the psychiatrists, who saw them as management issues and not therapy. These applications were important precursors to Ayllon and Azrin's later work on token economies (1968).

Token economies use operant conditioning in a systemwide approach to modify the behavior of a group. Conditioned reinforcers (usually tokens or points earned for useful or necessary behavior such as participating in work, therapy, social activities, and self-care) are exchangeable for primary and backup reinforcers such as items from the commissary or opportunities for recreation and social interaction. Ayllon and Azrin's (1965) report on the effectiveness of their token economy program at Anna State Hospital, which took a full 18 months to plan, stimulated a great deal of interest. As Ayllon stressed (personal communication, 1989), it was not just the tokens but the *contingencies* that were critical, so that the program stopped working if tokens were given to patients noncontingently prior to task participation. By the end of 1969 there were no fewer than 27 ongoing token economy programs within VA hospitals alone (Kazdin & Bootzin, 1972), including Atthowe and Krasner's (1968) work at the Palo Alto VA Hospital.

The token economy approach was soon extended to use with severely retarded institutionalized children, in classrooms and sheltered workshops for retarded children and adults, for behavior problems in the classroom, with delinquents, and with autistic children (Kazdin & Bootzin, 1972). One particularly important token economy and teaching program was Achievement Place, a community-based treatment home for delinquent boys (Phillips, 1968; Phillips, Phillips, Fixsen, & Wolf, 1971). The points that boys earned for activities such as doing chores and good school behavior could be exchanged for privileges, although as soon as possible each boy was put on a merit system in which points were phased out and privileges were free. This program had a significant effect on recidivism, school attendance, and grades.

Many applications of operant principles in the 1960s were conducted with children in educational settings, especially those who were diagnosed as mentally retarded or autistic. For example, Bijou and his colleagues used operant programs to decrease excessive crawling, crying, and social isolation and to increase skills and academic performance (e.g., Bijou, Birnbrauer, Kidder, & Tague, 1966). Ferster and DeMyer's (1962) laboratory studies demonstrating the feasibility of operant control over the behavior of autistic children led others, such as Lovaas (1968), to develop programs to decrease the self-injurious behavior of these children while teaching skills for language and social interaction. One especially well-known study conducted with Dicky, an autistic boy who had frequent episodes of tantrums and self-destructive behavior, demonstrated how a combination of reinforcement and punishment contingencies could be employed effectively to eliminate this behavior (Wolf, Risley, & Mees, 1964).

EXPANSION AND GROWTH OF BEHAVIOR THERAPY

By the mid-1960s, more and more mental health professionals were becoming interested in and beginning to employ behavioral approaches in clinical practice.

Organizations and Training

One important influence on the practice of behavior therapy, especially in North America, was the birth in 1966 of the Association for Advancement of Behavior Therapy (AABT), a multidisciplinary interest group. Beginning as a small group of about 10 colleagues meeting in the New York City apartment of Dorothy Susskind (Franks, personal communication, 1989), AABT has grown to encompass nearly 4,000 members (Suinn, 1990). Cyril Franks, who was a member of Eysenck's behavior therapy group in England, played a key role in focusing the new organization on inquiry rather than ideology and on the advancement of empirical knowledge and understanding (Franks, 1987). Other influential associations include the Behavior Therapy and Research Society, the Society for the Experimental Analysis of Behavior, and the Association of Behavior Analysis. Organizations with members interested in behavior therapy have also appeared in England, France, Germany, The Netherlands, Sweden, Israel, Japan, Mexico, and South America, and the European Association of Behavior Therapy was founded in 1971 (Kazdin, 1978).

Although the first behavior therapy conference was most likely that sponsored by Wolpe, Salter, and Reyna in 1962 (which focused on the "conditioning therapies"), AABT's annual convention quickly became the most important source of information on the practice of and research in behavior therapy. The first such conference, which was held concurrently with the American Psychological Association annual convention in 1967 and consisted of six papers, attracted an audience of 12 (Franks, personal communication, 1989). In contrast, more than 2,200 people attended AABT's 25th convention in 1991 (M. J. Eimer, personal communication, January 6, 1992).

In the mid-1950s, Leonard Krasner set up a training program with a behaviorist orientation at the Palo Alto VA Hospital. When he moved to the State University of New York at Stony Brook in 1965, Krasner began one of the first behaviorally oriented doctoral programs in clinical psychology (personal communication, 1989). The role of a number of other universities in producing the leading "behavior shapers" of the 1960s and 1970s is described in Goodall (1972).

Journals and Newsletters

As mentioned in the previous section, Eysenck and Rachman's *Behaviour Research and Therapy* (BRAT) was the first published journal in the field. This journal was begun, in part, because of a lack of interest in and receptivity to behavior therapy on the part of the (psychodynamic) editors and reviewers of existing journals (Rachman, personal communication, 1989). In North America, the first publication was the AABT newsletter edited by Cyril Franks, which, from its first issue in 1966, discussed and presented current research, issues, and practice in behavior therapy. The first outlet for articles on applications of Skinnerian operant principles, many applying to work with children, appeared in 1968—the *Journal of Applied Behavior Analysis* (JABA), edited by Montrose Wolf.

By 1970, AABT decided to launch its official journal for the publication of scholarly research, *Behavior Therapy* (with Cyril Franks as its first editor). The official journal of the Behavior Therapy and Research Society, *Journal of Behavior Therapy and Experimental Psychiatry*, also began the same year and was edited by Joseph Wolpe. During the 1970s, at least a dozen other journals were started in the field, reflecting a growing worldwide interest in behavior therapy.

New Techniques and Applications

As behavior therapy expanded, early techniques continued to be used and expanded, such as successful interventions for schizophrenics (Paul & Lentz, 1977) and programs for autistic children (Lovaas, 1987). Procedures involving aversive stimuli decreased in popularity, in part because of objections that were raised to these methods, although aversive control therapy for physically self-destructive behavior remains the treatment of choice (Masters, Burish, Hollon, & Rimm, 1987). As behavior therapy expanded, new or revised methods were created that came to be standard in the behavior therapist's repertoire.

Behavioral Assessment

Behavior therapy employs a wide variety of therapeutic methods, and, thus, assessment conducted to choose the primary target behavior and the best method to change it is of vital importance. Behavioral assessment, which developed because of the initial interest in behavioral treatment methods, is different from traditional assessment in emphasizing what the client *does* rather than traits the client *has* (cf. Mischel, 1968). Observation of behavior in the natural setting, such as the classroom or home, is probably the most innovative assessment method contributed by behavior therapists.

Other behavioral assessment methods used in clinical practice include observation of behavior in the office during role playing, behaviorally oriented interviews with clients, client self-monitoring of behavior, interviews with clients' significant others, structured questionnaires, and physiological measures of anxiety and sexual arousal (Nelson-Gray, personal communication, 1989). The emphasis in behavioral assessment is on providing a highly specific picture of the presenting problem and the immediate determinants and consequences of the problem (Bellack & Hersen, 1988). Assessment continues throughout therapy, so that the effectiveness of procedures can be evaluated and modifications made as needed. As Nelson-Gray described in our interview, publications that provided descriptions of behavioral assessment for the practicing clinician (e.g., Nelson, 1981) have had an important impact on the field.

Exposure and Flooding

Among newer behavior therapy techniques, in vivo exposure and flooding are alternatives to systematic desensitization that have an important place in reducing avoidance behavior in the treatment of anxiety disorders. Wolpe (1982) reports that he initially used in vivo, or real-life, exposure to feared situations and then turned to imaginal exposure because of its greater flexibility. In the 1970s, in vivo exposure became an important treatment for both agoraphobia and obsessive-compulsive disorder.

In agoraphobia, the client is exposed to the feared situation (e.g., going to a busy shopping mall) accompanied by the therapist/model. The exposure can either be graduated, which is typically referred to as "in vivo exposure" (Chambless, 1985), or be flooded. Flooding (Marks, 1972, 1975) is the exposure of the client to the anxiety-producing situation with the intent of increasing anxiety, and the client is required to stay in the situation until the anxiety extinguishes. Both flooding and graduated, in vivo exposure have been demonstrated to be effective, even more effective than systematic desensitization (Marks, 1987). Clinically, the choice depends upon the preferences of the client, for many will not agree to flooding for obvious reasons even though it might be effective.

In obsessive-compulsive disorder, flooded exposure to the feared situation (such as dirt) is paired with response prevention, in which the therapist does not allow the client to perform the compulsive behavior (such as washing). Exposure plus response prevention is an effective treatment for the compulsions of obsessive-compulsive disorder, though this difficult disorder often requires supplementary interventions as well (Grayson, Foa, & Steketee, 1985).

Modeling

Modeling, or the display of desired behavior so the client can learn to imitate it, was first used clinically in the 1950s. Bandura's (1969) extensive research on modeling popularized it, so that by the 1970s modeling was considered a major component of behavior therapy, along with operant conditioning and exposure methods. Modeling is often paired with behavior rehearsal, in which the client attempts to imitate or practice the modeled behavior and then receives feedback.

These procedures have been used for a variety of problems including phobias and depression (Masters et al., 1987). A particularly effective variant of modeling is participant modeling, in which there is modeling followed by the therapist guiding the client through the behavior that has been modeled (e.g., Bandura, Jeffery, & Gajdos, 1975). Modeling was interpreted by Bandura (1969) as involving symbolic representation rather than automatic reinforcement, and this argument helped pave the way for the cognitive influence in behavior therapy.

Social Skills Training

Assertiveness training and social skills training are treatment packages that combine modeling and behavior rehearsal with coaching, instruction, and feedback to help clients meet interpersonal goals. These methods are often used with groups of clients in order to take advantage of the opportunities available in the group for models and for feedback. Assertiveness training was very popular in the 1970s and 1980s and was often used for fairly functional clients. A more assertive person is able to stand up for his or her personal rights and express "thoughts, feelings, and beliefs in *direct*, *honest*, and *appropriate* ways which do not violate another person's rights" (Lange & Jakubowski, 1976, p. 7).

Social skills training is a broader training package that has been applied successfully to a wider variety of problems, including social anxiety (Twentyman & McFall, 1975), schizophrenia (Heinssen & Glass, 1990; Liberman, DeRisi, & Mueser, 1989), and depression (Becker, Heimberg, & Bellack, 1987), as well as to children's social behavior (Matson & Ollendick, 1988). It may include a focus on appropriate communication skills, nonverbal behavior, and the norms and cues present in social interaction.

Self-control

Behaviorists have discussed self-control, or the use of methods to change one's own behavior, since Skinner (1953), but self-control became an important part of behavior therapy only in the late 1960s and early 1970s. Initially behavior therapists were reluctant to endorse self-control because of its popular connotation of a mysterious willpower, but eventually self-change came to be seen as operating on the same principles as other types of change (Masters et al., 1987). Mahoney (personal communication, 1989) recalls that he became interested in self-control while in graduate school. In response to his inquiry, Bandura (his adviser) suggested that the only way to convince more operant behaviorists that this new direction was worthwhile was to "get a rat or a pigeon to do it." Mahoney subsequently demonstrated that pigeons would peck noncontingently in the presence of free food, which was described as self-reward (Mahoney & Bandura, 1972).

Ferster, Nurnberger, and Levitt (1962) and Goldiamond (1965) contributed some of the first clinical applications of behavioral self-control. Homme's (1965) influential paper on "coverants, the operants of the mind" provided a strong impetus to the development of behavioral self-control methods by discussing internal processes as subject to behavioral control (and, like modeling, setting the stage for the cognitive revolution in behavior therapy). Further, Kanfer (1970, 1971; Kanfer & Karoly, 1972) helped organize the field by dividing self-control into self-monitoring (self-observation both for assessment and as a method to change behavior), self-evaluation, and self-reinforcement.

By the early 1970s, sufficient research had been undertaken to stimulate two summary books on behavioral self-control (Goldfried & Merbaum, 1973; Thoresen & Mahoney, 1974). Although this area does not seem to be the source of as much research recently, behavioral self-control methods have been absorbed into the armamentarium of the behavior therapist, so that teaching the client methods to change his or her own behavior has become a standard goal of behavior therapy.

Self-help

Consistent with the goal of giving the client the tools to change his or her own behavior are self-help behavioral methods as delineated in books and tapes, as well as self-improvement courses and self-help groups and organizations. Several popular books have assisted an untold number of individuals, such as *Don't Say Yes When You Want To Say No* (Fensterheim & Baer, 1975), *Toilet Training in Less Than a Day* (Azrin & Foxx, 1974), and *Stopping Baby's Colic* (Ayllon, 1989).

In our cursory review of this literature, we found other books with applications for parenting and child behavior, as well as adult problems such as insomnia, smoking, obesity, phobias, sexual dysfunctions, study skills, depression, marital communication, and deficits in social skills. In fact, an earlier review of self-help materials found over 75 behaviorally oriented self-help manuals and books, many of them unfortunately supported by weak or nonexistent evidence of effectiveness (Glasgow & Rosen, 1978). Influenced by commercial considerations, "rather than 'giving psychology away,' as suggested by George Miller, many psychologists are simply finding 'new ways to sell it'" (Rosen, 1987, p. 46).

Covert Conditioning

In the 1960s the move to interpret thoughts as covert behavior led to the development of covert conditioning techniques. Cautela (1967) developed covert sensitization, which he described as a blend of respondent and operant conditioning (Cautela, 1990). This approach aims to decrease undesired behavior, such as drinking, by imaginal pairing of the undesired behavior with aversive consequences. For example, the individual imagines being in a bar, ordering a drink, and drinking it, and then imagines in great, nauseating detail becoming violently ill. Additional covert methods developed include imaginal variants on other behavioral methods, such as covert positive and negative reinforcement, covert punishment and extinction, and covert modeling.

Although there was a great deal of interest in the covert methods in the late 1960s and early 1970s, the development and spread of cognitive methods, along with a lack of evidence of the effectiveness of the most of the covert methods (Mahoney & Arnkoff, 1978), seem to have decreased their popularity both clinically and in research. Nevertheless, the covert conditioning techniques were crucial in opening the field to combinations of cognitive and behavioral interventions.

Behavioral Medicine

With the publication of his 1973 book, *Biofeedback: Behavioral Medicine*, Lee Birk can be credited with originating the concept of "behavioral medicine" (Krasner, 1990). By 1979, there was a journal called *Behavioral Medicine*, a Society of Behavioral Medicine, and a major review article in the *American Psychologist* (Pomerleau, 1979). Behavioral applications for the evaluation, management, prevention, and treatment of physiological problems and physical disease had indeed become a "hot" topic, and behavior therapy journals broadened their focus to reflect the expansion within the field from psychiatric to medical and health problems (Rachman, 1987).

Biofeedback became a popular approach in the 1970s (Schwartz & Beatty, 1977) and was applied to the treatment of a wide variety of disorders such as tension headaches, migraines, hypertension, and Raynaud's disease. Unfortunately, evidence for the efficacy of biofeedback above and beyond simple relaxation for stress-related problems has not been consistently found (O'Leary & Wilson, 1987).

Clinical applications in behavioral medicine and cognitive–behavioral approaches in health psychology have focused not only on changing problematic behavior, but on interventions to increase adherence to treatment (Meichenbaum & Turk, 1987) and to modify unhealthy habits seen as risk factors for disease (Matarazzo, Weiss, Herd, Miller, & Weiss, 1984). For example, applications of relaxation, biofeedback, stress-management, and self-control techniques for smoking, obesity, and Type A behavior have implications for the prevention of heart attacks, hypertension, and coronary artery disease (Pomerleau, 1979).

Taylor (1990), in a recent review of the health psychology field, also points to potential applications for the following areas: the prevention of relapse and reversion to previous poor health habits, the development of approaches for pain and stress management, and the use of cognitive and behavioral coping strategies to assist in recovery from illness, in coping with chronic disease and its treatment, and in preparing for noxious medical procedures such as surgery. Finally, DeLeon (1979) highlighted a trend toward increased government commitment to involving consumers in their own health care management, in which psychologists and behavioral medicine may play a role in reducing patients' reliance on the orders of the physician.

Child Behavior Disorders

Broadening of applications to child disorders represents another development in behavior therapy, as reflected by recent handbooks and textbooks on behavior therapy with children (Bornstein & Kazdin, 1985; Ross, 1981). In addition to work with severely disturbed, retarded, and autistic children, interventions have been focused on delinquent children and adolescents, children with hyperactivity and other behavior problems, and broad applications in parent training and child rearing. As the behavioral field expanded, child behavior therapy was increasingly used to treat less severely disturbed children, demonstrating a greater concern with modeling and cognitive and thinking skills and a decreased emphasis on modifying disruptive behavior (Craighead, 1982).

Patterson's work over the past 20 years on behavioral treatment of aggressive children is especially noteworthy (Patterson, 1982), and it stresses the importance of understanding such problems from the viewpoint of *family* interaction and parental behavior and adjustment. Parent training, in which parents learn to produce change in the home, has become an important intervention in dealing with child behavior problems. Because most child behavior therapists assume that parents are better able to implement treatment programs if they understand the concepts involved (Ross, 1981), educating the parents by using programmed texts on child behavior management, such as Patterson's *Living with children* (1976), has been successful.

Behavior Therapy Outside the Office

Behavior therapy started to be used much more frequently outside the therapist's office, especially with problems of a nonpsychiatric nature, and therapy was conducted by a wider range of individuals (such as parents, teachers, peers, and paraprofessionals). Behavioral assessment was also extended to naturalistic settings, using, for example, participant-observers such as parents and teachers to record data on children (Nelson-Gray, personal communication, 1989). Just as behavior therapy initially progressed from the laboratory to applications in clinics and mental hospitals, by the early 1970s, it had spread to the "natural" social environment—perhaps influenced by the social issues and movements of the 1960s that sought to develop a better environment (Krasner, 1990). As behavior therapy grew into the society at large, it began to emphasize systems, ecology, community, sociological, ethical, and professional issues to a greater extent (Franks, 1987).

This new movement included work in what came to be called *behavioral community psychology* (Nietzel, Winett, MacDonald, & Davidson, 1977) and *environmental design* (Krasner, 1980), which included large-scale applications in schools, neighborhoods, and communities. For example, behavioral applications listed by Krasner (1982) include social and environmental problems and objectives such as pollution control, energy conservation, waste recycling, community self-government, racial integration, and military training. The notion of "behavior therapy in the natural environment" (Tharp & Wetzel, 1969) extended behavioral approaches into the home, business and industry, educational settings, parenting, prisons, nursing homes, halfway houses, day-care centers, sports, the fine arts, and medicine. Kazdin's (1989) *Behavior Modification in Applied Settings* is an especially important resource that contains information on development and evaluation of programs.

Values, Misconceptions, and Ethical Issues

Although behavior therapy became accepted as a school of psychology in the 1960s and 1970s, a number of misconceptions in the minds of other psychotherapists and the public continued to plague the field, and these misconceptions may have hindered its growth. Behavior therapy was often seen as inhumane, particularly when practiced in institutions such as mental hospitals and prisons (Kazdin, 1978). The 1971 film, *A Clockwork Orange*, which depicted cruel, enforced behavioral control, was the image many had of behavior therapy. An examination of articles appearing in the *New York Times* in the 1970s revealed that behavior therapy was also often confused with methods outside its area, such as psychosurgery, and equated with brainwashing and torture (Turkat & Feuerstein, 1978).

In 1974, the U.S. Law Enforcement Assistance Administration announced that anti-crime funds would no longer be used for behavior modification programs in prisons. This event led the American Psychological Association to form a commission to study ethics in behavior modification and to recommend whether special ethical guidelines were needed for the practice of behavior therapy. The conclusion (Stolz, 1977) was that special rules were unnecessary because behavior therapy posed the same ethical dilemmas as any psychotherapy. The report did include guidelines for ensuring client rights in settings such as prisons in which there is inherently an extreme imbalance in power between therapist and client, but the guidelines are useful for any program involving persuasion.

In fact, behavior therapists argue that behavior therapy is inherently humane, in that the role of the therapist is to teach clients the means to reach their goals (Mahoney, Kazdin, & Lesswing, 1974; Wolpe, 1981). Mahoney has described a conversation he had with B. F. Skinner in the early 1970s (personal communication, 1989). Skinner was basically supportive of his work on self-control and felt this emphasis could counterbalance some of the negative propaganda about behaviorism as a system encouraging totalitarian control of behavior.

The misunderstandings of behavior therapy may be partly attributable to protection of professional turf on the part of traditional forms of therapy. However, it seems likely that behavior therapists also contributed to misconceptions about their work in their zeal to demonstrate that their methods were new and different. The early behavior therapists claimed that they differed from traditional therapy by emphasizing techniques and technology over warmth and relationships.

Clinical writings on behavior therapy have always stated the need for a good relationship (e.g., Goldfried & Davison, 1976; Wolpe, 1958). Part of the motivation for Goldfried and Davison's book *Clinical Behavior Therapy* was, in fact, their awareness that there were things going on clinically in the practice of behavior therapy that were not written down (Goldfried, personal communication, 1989). Research articles and theoretical work did not, however, emphasize the therapeutic relationship; the aim was to show how behavior therapy differed from traditional therapy. Between professional competition and the narrow way in which behavior therapy was initially promoted, it is not surprising that misconceptions abounded. Interestingly, the image of behavior therapy seems to have changed as it matured; a subsequent analysis of *New York Times* articles found primarily a positive and accurate depiction of behavior therapy (Carey, Carey, & Turkat, 1983).

Thus the *Clockwork Orange* image of behavior therapy is not as prevalent as it was initially. Nevertheless, there are still major misconceptions, or at least misinformation, about behavior therapy, so that it does not receive the interest that is warranted given its demonstrated effectiveness. Carey et al. (1983) noted that while references to behavior therapy in the *New York Times* were more positive than previously, there were also fewer references in recent years.

Franks (1987) lamented the striking gap between research findings in behavior therapy and their impact on public policy and clinical practice. For example, the Paul and Lentz (1977) study cited earlier that involved a social learning program for chronic schizophrenics produced impressive and unprecedented results: 97% were able to function in the community after treatment. Yet the government of the state of Illinois (following a change of administration) responded by cutting the funding for the program. This is not an isolated case; behavior therapy continues to fight an uphill battle for implementation of its successful treatments. An exception may be child behavior therapy, which has had wide impact on treatment, education, and parenting (Franks, 1987).

As noted earlier, ethical issues were raised about behavior therapy from the beginning, particularly when it was practiced in institutional settings (Kazdin, 1978). Though behavior therapists firmly argued that behavior therapy is not unethical in principle (Krasner, 1976; Mahoney, Kazdin et al., 1974) and that token economies give greater control and choices to patients (Ayllon, personal communication, 1989), the issues raised did lead to some debates in behavioral circles. For example, in many cases in institutional settings, the target behaviors in early programs were of benefit mainly to the institution and not the individual (e.g., performance of routine hospital tasks in mental hospital programs or docile classroom behavior in school programs). Debates on the ethical issues involved led to a greater emphasis on changing behavior relevant to the individual client, such as improving academic performance or learning skills to be used outside the hospital (Kazdin, 1978). Litigation also led to some changes in operant programs in psychiatric hospitals; for example, *Wyatt v. Stickney* (1972) set forth patient rights to noncontingent receipt of many items that had been reinforcers in some behavioral programs, such as time off the ward.

Behavior therapists have faced value clashes in other aspects of practice as well. For example, in the early 1970s a prominent method for attempting to change the sexual preference of homosexuals was orgasmic reconditioning, which involved gradually shifting the fantasies used in masturbation from same-sex to opposite-sex images. Davison was one of the major figures involved in research on orgasmic reconditioning, having demonstrated the effectiveness of this approach in changing sadistic fantasies (1968). Through a number of influences, including individuals in the gay community, discussion with students and colleagues, and books and articles on the ethics of therapy, Davison (personal communication, 1989) became convinced that it is ethically wrong for therapists to try to change sexual preference, both because it is ineffective and because it enforces a repressive social status quo that says that homosexuality is wrong. He announced this initially controversial conclusion in his presidential address to AABT (Davison, 1976) and was instrumental in convincing AABT to publish a report arguing against this practice. Davison's stand was one of several that were instrumental in the deletion of homosexuality as a psychiatric disorder from the Diagnostic and Statistical Manual of Mental Disorders. Today there is very little in the literature on methods to change homosexual preference; the most comprehensive textbook on behavior therapy (Masters et al., 1987) does not advocate such treatment.

Broadening

Behavior therapy has resulted in important treatment successes in a number of disorders, including phobic and obsessive-compulsive disorders, sexual disorders, and some childhood disorders. But even early behavior therapy was more complex than many professionals outside the field expected. Klein, Dittmann, Parloff, and Gill (1969) spent several days observing Wolpe and Lazarus doing therapy and found, for example, that the presenting problem was often not the problem dealt with once a full assessment was done. Lazarus (1971) titled his influential book *Behavior Therapy and Beyond* to indicate his belief that the most effective therapy would involve a broad spectrum of methods. He believes it played an important role in widening people's perceptions of what behavior therapy could and should entail. However, he was met with a strong negative reaction from Wolpe, among others, who accused him of watering down and destroying the purity of behavior therapy. For this reason, Eysenck removed Lazarus from the editorial board of *Behaviour Research and Therapy* (Lazarus, personal communication, 1989).

The complexity of behavior therapy in practice increased in the 1970s and beyond, to the point where behavior therapy is now much broader than its original conception. By the 1980s, much of the present practice of behavior therapy fell outside the original narrow-band definitions (Franks, 1987). There are several reasons for the broadening of behavior therapy, particularly behavioral practice. These include the cognitive movement, the need to deal with complex disorders and problems, and clinical failures using behavioral techniques. Behavior therapy has become extremely diverse with regard to theory, techniques used, and behaviorists' views on what the field should encompass (Kazdin & Hersen, 1980). As Hersen said, treatment now is "lengthier, more comprehensive in scope, and considerably more sophisticated as to the elements necessary for ensuring maintenance of gains" (1983, p. 5).

Fishman and Lubetkin (1983) report that their current approach to behavioral therapy is conducted for a mean of 50 sessions, compared to 22 sessions 10 years earlier. They highlight the fact that the private practice of behavior therapy has shifted from a focus on techniques that modify specific problems to an attempt to impart to clients more general coping skills and strategies for dealing with problems.

Some of the factors leading to a broadening of behavior therapy may be called political, in the broad sense of the term. Once behavior therapy was established, the narrow allegiance of its proponents, which is required of a specialization trying to prove itself, was no longer necessary. Further, behavior therapists, who are overwhelmingly psychologists, have had to be sensitive to the need to collaborate with psychiatrists and nurses in initiating and implementing behavior therapy programs in hospitals (Hersen & Bellack, 1978). As the role of psychopharmacology in the treatment of mental disorders has increased, behavior therapists have become more amenable to the combination of medication and behavioral interventions; such combinations may be particularly effective (Hersen, 1979). The title of Hersen's presidential address to AABT (1981) was particularly apt: "Complex problems require complex solutions." Davison (personal communication, 1989) also notes that, as behavior therapy has broadened, there is less of a gap between what is written and what is practiced.

It has been argued that "there is no clearly agreed upon or commonly accepted definition of behavior therapy" (Kazdin & Wilson, 1978, p. 1), and recent textbooks in the field instead list what are considered to be a number of core characteristics or major postulates of behavior therapy (see Masters et al., 1987; O'Leary & Wilson, 1987). Recent definitions of behavior therapy have focused upon the application of principles broadly derived from psychological research (across experimental, social, cognitive, and developmental psychology), rejecting a traditional intrapsychic or disease model of disordered behavior, and with an emphasis on the empirical evaluation of treatment effectiveness.

As might be expected, this new, broader field is less tied to conditioning models of change. The field of behavior therapy today is far from a single monolithic model (Mahoney, Kazdin et al., 1974), and it now includes applications based upon applied behavior analysis, the learning-conditioning (mediational stimulus–response) model, social learning theory, and cognitive behavior therapy (Agras, Kazdin, & Wilson, 1979). (Cognitive approaches to psychotherapy are discussed in detail in chapter 20 of this volume.) Redd et al. (1979) also include eclectic behaviorism as a fifth approach. Although some of the early pioneers feel it is a step backward to abandon learning theory (Krasner and Wolpe, personal communications, 1989; Wolpe, 1989), others (Franks, personal communication, 1989; Russo, 1990) believe that behavior therapy has retained its intellectual vigor. Currently, conceptual models of clinical practice rely to a great extent on cognitive and social learning theory explanations (Fishman & Franks, chapter 5 in this volume; Fishman & Lubetkin, 1983).

In fact, the role of learning theory in conceptualizing practice has always been controversial (Wilson, 1982). London (1972) notes that clinical practice was always "seat-of-the-pants" (p. 914). Clinical behavior therapy has, to a great extent, developed from clinical practice (which may be the case for all therapies). The early behavioral literature thus underplayed the "attention to detail and the nuances of the specific case" needed in practice (Hersen, 1983, p. 5).

The Therapeutic Relationship

As noted earlier, behavior therapists have always emphasized the therapeutic relationship in practice to a greater degree than either the early behavioral literature claimed or those outside behavior therapy believed. Initially the relationship was minimized in behavioral writing (with some exceptions such as Wolpe, 1958) in order to differentiate behavior therapy from psychodynamic therapy and because the relationship had not been defined operationally (Kazdin & Hersen, 1980). Wilson (personal communication, 1989) recalls that a paper he wrote in the late 1960s (Wilson, Hannon, & Evans, 1968) on the therapist–patient relationship, arguing that behavior therapy "didn't ignore it, shouldn't ignore it, couldn't ignore it", unfortunately had relatively little impact. However, in their observations of Wolpe and Lazarus, Klein et al. (1969) noted that the relationship seemed instrumental in these prominent therapists' treatment, for the relationship helped to raise clients' expectations, provide a rationale for treatment methods, and reassure clients.

The therapeutic relationship in behavior therapy has come to be seen as a necessary, though not sufficient, aspect of treatment. For example, Swan and MacDonald (1978) found that AABT members responded in a survey that they used relationship enhancement methods with 58% of clients; this was the most frequently cited type of procedure.

The relationship in behavior therapy does tend to be different from that in other therapies (such as psychodynamic or client-centered). In behavior therapy, the relationship is a collaborative one; usually the therapist is a consultant, teaching the client self-change skills (Sweet, 1984). A positive relationship is necessary to raise expectations and to motivate the client to follow the change procedures, and this activity can be understood within social learning theory (Wilson, 1980). In fact, Fishman and Lubetkin (1983) state that in clinical practice, only a small percentage of time is spent on techniques; "the greater portion of each hour is spent providing understanding to clients, lending support and encouragement for their intentional therapeutic steps, and helping them to generate alternatives to the way they may interpret life situation(s)" (p. 24). Linehan's dialectical behavior therapy for borderline personality disorder clients is a good example of an approach incorporating specific relationship enhancement strategies, therapist self-disclosure, and relationship problem-solving along with more typical behavioral methods (Linehan, 1987).

Apparently, this understanding and collaboration are seen as positive by clients. A number of studies have found that clients of behavior therapists report a good therapeutic relationship (e.g., O'Leary, Turkewitz, & Taffel, 1973; Turkewitz & O'Leary, 1981). In fact, in Sloane, Staples, Cristol, Yorkston, and Whipple's (1975) often-cited comparison of behavior therapy and psychodynamic therapy, clients of behavior therapists found their therapists to be more genuine than did clients of insight-oriented therapists; there were no differences between groups on therapist warmth and empathy.

Influence on Other Forms of Therapy

Although behavior therapists have never constituted a large percentage of therapists in North America, their influence on research and practice has been profound. As Nelson-Gray (personal communication, 1989) pointed out, the trend toward eclecticism led people who were never trained behaviorally to use some behavioral techniques and assessment in their practice (although without their theoretical underpinnings). In research this influence has been felt in numerous ways, including the move to greater specificity with regard to target population, assessment, and techniques. O'Leary (1984) noted that the impact of behavior therapy on psychology has become enormous: in 1983, 44 percent of the editorial board members of the major clinical psychology journal, the *Journal of Consulting and Clinical Psychology*, belonged to AABT (and our calculation in 1990 also totaled 44 percent). The trend to "manualize" therapies, including psychodynamic treatments (e.g., Luborsky, 1984), has been influenced by behavior therapy's insistence on specificity.

The empirical evaluation of treatment that has been an inherent aspect of behavior therapy also is in keeping with the need for accountability to third-party payers, who naturally attempt to control the cost of psychotherapy (Berman et al., 1987). It is clear that the brevity of behavior therapy was partly instrumental in the general movement toward shorter therapies. It is difficult to justify a long-term therapy when a short, or perhaps a moderate-length, therapy is at least equally effective. Interestingly, the clinical impact, to a great extent, has been the incorporation of behavioral approaches into traditional therapies rather than a wholesale adoption of behavior therapy by practitioners, as the following section on surveys shows.

TABLE 1
Percentage of Survey Respondents Who Endorsed Behavior Therapy

Surveys of APA Division 12 Members and Other General Samples of Psychologists

Kelly (1961) Fellows	10[a]
Members	8[a]
Lubin (1962)	5(7)[a,b]
Goldschmid et al. (1969)	12
Garfield & Kurtz (1976)	10
Wade & Baker (1977)	13
Kelly et al. (1978)	5
Norcross & Prochaska (1982)	14
Smith (1982)	7
Prochaska & Norcross (1983)	6
Watkins et al. (1986)	6
Norcross, Prochaska, & Gallagher (1989)	16

Surveys of Academic Psychologists

Shemberg & Leventhal (1978)	34
Sayette & Mayne (1990)	56[c]

Surveys of Psychologists in Full or Part-time Practice

Tryon (1983)	8
Norcross & Prochaska (1983)	6
Norcross, Nash, & Prochaska (1985)	8

Comparisons of Several Professions

Norcross, Strausser-Kirtland, & Missar (1989)	
Psychologists	8
Psychiatrists	1
Social Workers	4
Jensen et al. (1990)	
Psychologists	8
Marital and Family Therapists	0
Social Workers	3
Psychiatrists	0
Total	3

[a]"Learning theory" was actual category in survey.
[b]Total adds to 70%; figure in parentheses is prorated for 100%.
[c]Sum of two separate categories reflecting behavioral orientation: applied behavioral/behavior analytic/radical behavioral (14%), and cognitive behavioral/social learning (42%).

SURVEYS ON THE PRACTICE OF BEHAVIOR THERAPY

Surveys of members of Divisions of the American Psychological Association (APA) and other organizations have frequently been used to discover the views and practices of psychologists and other mental health professionals in the United States. Table 1 shows the percentage of subjects in a variety of surveys who endorsed behavior therapy; most of these surveys have been taken of members of APA Division 12, the Division of Clinical Psychology.

Theoretical Orientations

As can be seen in the table, the three earliest surveys of Division 12 showed a substantial endorsement of behavior therapy (then called learning theory) in the early 1960s, nearly as large as the endorsement in later surveys. By this early date, then, a substantial minority of psychologists saw themselves as behavioral in theory and practice.

As behavior therapy developed in the 1960s and 1970s, the surveys taken then showed a small gain in the percentage of psychologists who endorsed it as their primary theoretical orientation. By 1989, Norcross, Prochaska, and Gallagher found that 16% of their sample of members of APA Division 12 called themselves behavioral or learning oriented. This figure is as high as has ever been found in such a survey. The percentage of psychologists who claim a primary behavioral orientation has never been large in the United States, as opposed to Britain (Rachman, personal communication, 1989). Nevertheless, the development of behavior therapy exerted considerable influence on the practice of clinical psychology in North America. This influence can be seen in the widespread reliance on behavior therapy by eclectic therapists. Garfield and Kurtz (1977), for example, asked psychologists who called themselves eclectic in their 1976 survey to name the two orientations most characteristic of them. Learning theory was named most frequently by those surveyed.

One source of influence of behavior therapy comes from the prevalence of behavior therapists in the faculties of psychology doctoral programs. As Table 1 shows, Shemberg and Leventhal (1978) found that 34% of academic clinical psychologists called themselves behavioral. Sayette and Mayne (1990), in their analysis of the orientations of faculty in APA-accredited PhD and PsyD programs, found that 14% were described as having an applied behavioral, behavior analytic, or radical behavioral approach, with an additional 42% described as cognitive behavioral or social learning.

Similarly, Norcross and Prochaska (1982) found that a significantly greater percentage of academic and research psychologists in their sample of psychologists in Division 12 endorsed behavior therapy as a primary or secondary orientation (38.1%) than did practitioners (22.3%). Further, Nevid, Lavi, and Primavera (1986) analyzed ratings of the orientation of scientist-practitioner training programs in the United States. An operant-conditioning behavioral orientation was endorsed as most emphasized or tied for most emphasized in 41% of the programs, and a classical conditioning behavioral orientation was endorsed in this fashion by 26% of the programs. A cluster analysis of the ratings of the programs found that the second-largest cluster of programs (14% of the programs) could be described as broad-spectrum behavioral (the largest being eclectic–cognitive–behavioral).

The prevalence of behavior therapy in the United States has clearly been greater among psychologists than among other mental health professionals, however, as shown by the surveys of different professions by Norcross, Strausser-Kirtland, and Missar (1989) and Jensen, Bergin, and Greaves (1990; see Table 1). This is the case even in work with children, where behavior therapy has had many successes; Koocher and Pedulla (1977) found in a survey of child psychologists and psychiatrists that 55% of the psychologists found behavior modification often or always useful, while only 28% of the psychiatrists did. Dickerson (1989) surveyed private psychiatric hospitals and found that 60% had no behavior therapists, inpatient behavior therapy programs, nor behavioral consultations, again reflecting the widespread disinterest by the psychiatric community in behavioral interventions. This discrepancy between psychologists and psychiatrists is, no doubt, part of the reason that behavioral programs, as noted earlier, have not been adopted as widely as the evidence would warrant.

Problems and Interventions

A number of surveys of behavior therapists have been undertaken to assess their views and practice. For the most part, practice is in keeping with the published literature on behavior therapy, but in some areas actual practice as revealed in these surveys has been found to diverge from behavior therapy as it is presented in theory and research.

Table 2 shows the responses of AABT members in four surveys to questions on types of client problems most typically seen and interventions used most frequently. Each study used a different set of terms for problems treated, but the lists do correspond with problems dealt with in the theoretical and research literature on behavior therapy. The only possible surprise is that "thinking" is listed as the second most frequent client problem in the Swan and MacDonald (1978) study. Either the subjects in this study had already been influenced by the early cognitive movement within behavior therapy, or their responses show why many behavior therapists so eagerly embraced cognitive procedures when those methods were developed.

Most of the interventions reportedly used frequently are behavioral or cognitive–behavioral. It is noteworthy that by 1982, cognitive restructuring edged out systematic desensitization as the method used by the highest percentage of therapists (Gochman, Allgood, & Geer, 1982), although reinforcement was mentioned as often as cognitive restructuring in Guevremont and Spiegler's (1990) survey. Again the "surprise," if it may be

TABLE 2
Most Frequently Reported Problems Treated and Interventions Used in
Surveys of Behavior Therapists

Problems Treated	Interventions Used
Swan & MacDonald (1978)	
Emotional behavior	Therapeutic relationship
Thinking	enhancement methods
Fears	Operant methods
Inappropriate habits	Modeling methods
	Self-management methods
Wade, Baker, & Hartmann (1979)	
Anxiety	Operant conditioning
Child management	Systematic desensitization
Marital relationships	Modeling
Depression	RET
Gochman, Allgood, & Geer (1982)	
Neuroses	Cognitive restructuring
Adjustment disorders	Systematic desensitization
Phobias	Contingency contracts
Psychosomatic disorders	Modeling
Guevremont & Spiegler (1990)	
Anxiety disorders	Reinforcement
Depression	Cognitive restructuring
Interpersonal relations	Behavioral rehearsal
Adjustment disorders	Relaxation training

Note: Columns regarding "problems treated" and "interventions used" should be considered independently; items in the same row are *not* paired with each other. Responses from Swan and MacDonald and Wade et al. are ordered in terms of percent of clients seen; Gochman et al. and Guevremont and Spiegler are ordered in terms of percent of subjects reporting the item. All four surveys were of AABT members.

called that, was in the Swan and MacDonald (1978) survey, in which subjects reported that they used therapeutic relationship enhancement methods most frequently (with 58% of clients). As we have previously emphasized, clearly the *practice* of behavior therapy involves the establishment of a positive therapeutic relationship, even though research articles on behavior therapy and some behavioral theorizing may not emphasize it.

Morrow-Bradley and Elliott (1986) surveyed members of APA's Division 29 (Psychotherapy) and divided them by theoretical orientation. The behavior therapist subsample (which also included those identifying themselves as cognitive) reported that they found research to be more useful in making clinical decisions than did the sample as a whole, whereas those in the psychodynamic subsample found it less useful than the group as a whole. Mahoney, Norcross, Prochaska, and Missar (1989) found that in their sample from APA's Division 12, behavior therapists agreed less than did those with other orientations with questionnaire items on inviting emotional expression in therapy, interpreting, and reflecting rather than answering client questions. They were more likely to say they would offer explicit behavioral assignments than other orientations, and they were less likely than other orientations (though still very likely) to help the client clarify personal thoughts and feelings.

Assessment, Populations, and Treatment Duration

Assessment has also been investigated in surveys of behavior therapists. The subjects in Swan and MacDonald's (1978) survey reported that their most frequent assessment procedure was the interview (for 89% of clients); client self-monitoring (51%), interview with a significant other (49%), and direct observation *in situ* (40%) were also used frequently. The authors note that interviews are used almost routinely, but have not been extensively researched, while behavioral self-report measures, which have received much research attention, are used less frequently (30% of clients). Ford and Kendall (1979) also found that assessment did not rely on "empirical clinical guidelines" as frequently as might be expected; subjects reported that their assessment procedures were limited because of constraints of time and expense.

Another area in which survey findings diverge from the behavioral literature is in the affluence of the clientele seen. In spite of the desire of behavior therapists to reach disadvantaged populations, the subjects in Swan and MacDonald's (1978) survey reported that fully 70% of their clients were middle-class or above in socioeconomic status.

Other findings in surveys of behavior therapists have been more in keeping with the public face of behavior therapy. Norcross and Wogan (1983) surveyed members of AABT, Division 32 of APA (Humanistic Psychology), and Division 29 (Psychotherapy). AABT subjects saw clients less frequently and for a shorter duration than did members of the two APA divisions, even though there were no differences between the AABT subjects and others in the settings in which they practiced.

THE FUTURE OF BEHAVIOR THERAPY

As we have shown, behavior therapy has broadened considerably since the 1950s. In the future, even greater expansion is likely. As the costs of health care continue to rise and psychologists become increasingly involved in health issues, there will be a need for even greater integration of behavioral self-help, relaxation, and self-management programs into medical practice (Taylor, 1990). We should also see more emphasis on the identification and treatment of those at risk for medical problems due to poor health habits, where psychologists become the teachers and trainers of health care providers (Pomerleau, 1979). Rachman (personal communication, 1989) sees a continuing movement beyond the treatment of psychiatric problems into all branches of health care, including pediatrics, pain, and cardiovascular disease.

Also in the medical realm, Bellack and Hersen (1985) have argued that a combination of cognitive–behavioral therapy and pharmacotherapy is the "wave of the future" with adult psychiatric clients (p. 15). Drugs can help to control acute symptoms, allowing clients to benefit more from behavior therapy. Conversely, behavioral interventions can help to enhance drug compliance, reduce the risk of relapse and drop-out, and interact with biologic treatments to produce more extensive change (Agras, 1987).

In the future we should continue to see increasing emphasis on changing behavior in the real world, where the criterion for success is the extent to which therapy change generalizes from the office to the client's natural environment. Agras (1987) suggested that computer technology in the client's home could be used to provide cues to initiate specific interventions, give feedback and praise contingent upon goal attainment, and allow for the recording of behavior. He has also highlighted the need for the development of models of family interaction in the natural environment, so that techniques for behavioral family therapy can be developed. We would add that a focus on risk factors and prevention of childhood emotional disorders should also be increasingly emphasized in the years to come.

As the field of behavior therapy continues to grow, it will need to focus more on the training of future therapists, by identifying necessary behavioral and conceptual competencies and the most efficient and effective ways to teach them (Collins, Foster, & Berler, 1986). Many of those we interviewed were committed to the notion that training should remain based in the scientist-practitioner model. Students should thus learn scientific methodology and learning theory in addition to behavioral techniques, so that as practitioners they are committed to assessing and employing interventions that have been supported by the empirical literature. Our interviewees stressed the need for the fruits of research to affect what therapists do and the need to continue collecting evidence that what we do works (e.g., Wolpe, Wilson, Goldfried). Barlow (1980) suggests that future practitioners contribute to the data base for behavior therapy by using practical measures to assess change in individual clients.

Cautela has commented on the shift in conceptual models within the behavior therapy field and sees "an even more drastic divison in the future between the learning-based approach and the so-called cognitive approach" (Cautela, 1990, p. 212). Several other important behavior therapy figures (e.g., Wolpe, Krasner) argued in interviews with us that continuing to broaden behavior therapy, especially through the introduction of cognitive techniques, is undesirable and merely dilutes and weakens the field. However, others approved of these more cognitive directions and felt that behavior therapy should *continue* to broaden as the field of psychology learns more about cognition, motivation, affect, and behavior (Wilson, personal communication, 1989). The behavior therapy of the future, thus, should remain a field resting on empirically based interventions (Davison, personal communication, 1989). Franks additionally pointed out that behavior therapy will avoid becoming too broad if it retains an emphasis on philosophical and conceptual issues and a strong theoretical and methodological base.

REFERENCES

Agras, W. S. (1987). So where do we go from here? *Behavior Therapy, 18,* 203–217.

Agras, W. S., Kazdin, A. E., & Wilson, G. T. (1979). *Behavior therapy: Toward an applied clinical science.* San Francisco: W. H. Freeman.

Atthowe, J. M., Jr., & Krasner, L. (1968). Preliminary report on the application of contingent reinforcement procedures (token economy) on a "chronic" psychiatric ward. *Journal of Abnormal Psychology, 73,* 37–43.

Ayllon, T. (1963). Intensive treatment of psychotic behavior by stimulus satiation and food reinforcement. *Behaviour Research and Therapy, 1,* 53–61.

Ayllon, T. (1989). *Stopping baby's colic.* New York: Perigee Books.

Ayllon, T., & Azrin, N. H. (1965). The measurement and reinforcement of behavior in psychotics. *Journal of the Experimental Analysis of Behavior, 8,* 357–383.

Ayllon, T., & Azrin, N. H. (1968). *The token economy: A motivational system for therapy and rehabilitation.* New York: Appleton-Century-Crofts.

Ayllon, T., & Haughton, E. (1964). Modification of symptomatic verbal behavior of mental patients. *Behaviour Research and Therapy, 2,* 87–97.

Ayllon, T., & Michael, J. (1959). The psychiatric nurse as a behavioral engineer. *Journal of the Experimental Analysis of Behavior, 2,* 323–334.

Azrin, N. H., & Foxx, R. M. (1974). *Toilet training in less than a day.* New York: Simon & Schuster.

Bandura, A. (1969). *Principles of behavior modification.* New York: Holt, Rinehart & Winston.

Bandura, A., Jeffery, R. W., & Gajdos, E. (1975). Generalizing change through participant modeling with self-directed mastery. *Behaviour Research and Therapy, 13,* 141–152.

Barlow, D. H. (1980). Behavior therapy: The next decade. *Behavior Therapy, 11,* 315–328.

Bechterev, V. M. (1932). *General principles of human reflexology: An introduction to the objective study of personality* (E. Murphy & W. Murphy, trans.). New York: International Publishers.

Becker, R. E., Heimberg, R. G., & Bellack, A. S. (1987). *Social skills training treatment for depression.* New York: Pergamon.

Bellack, A. S., & Hersen, M. (1985). General considerations. In M. Hersen & A. S. Bellack (Eds.), *Handbook of clinical behavior therapy with adults* (pp. 3–19). New York: Plenum.

Bellack, A. S., & Hersen, M. (1988). *Behavioral assessment: A practical handbook* (3rd ed.). New York: Pergamon.

Berman, W. H., Kisch, J., DeLeon, P. H., Cummings, N. C., Binder, J. L., & Hefele, T. J. (1987). The future of psychotherapy in the age of diminishing resources. *Psychotherapy in Private Practice, 5*(4), 105–118.

Bijou, S. W., Birnbrauer, J. S., Kidder, J. D., & Tague, C. (1966). Programmed instruction as an approach to the teaching of reading, writing, and arithmetic to retarded children. *Psychological Record, 16,* 505–522.

Birk, L. (Ed.). (1973). *Biofeedback: Behavioral medicine.* New York: Grune & Stratton.

Boring, E. G. (1950). *A history of experimental psychology* (2nd ed.). New York: Appleton-Century-Crofts.

Bornstein, P., & Kazdin, A. E. (Eds.). (1985). *Handbook of clinical behavior therapy with children.* Monterey, CA: Brooks/Cole.

Burnham, J. C. (1968). On the origins of behaviorism. *Journal of the History of the Behavioral Sciences, 4,* 143–151.

Burnham, W. H. (1924). *The normal mind.* New York: Appleton-Century-Crofts.

Carey, K. B., Carey, M. P., & Turkat, I. D. (1983). Behavior modification in the media: A five-year follow-up. *American Psychologist, 38,* 498–500.

Cautela, J. R. (1967). Covert sensitization. *Psychological Reports, 20,* 459–468.

Cautela, J. (1990). The shaping of behavior therapy: An historical perspective. *the Behavior Therapist, 13,* 211–212.

Chambless, D. L. (1985). Agoraphobia. In M. Hersen & A. S. Bellack (Eds.), *Handbook of clinical behavior therapy with adults* (pp. 49–87). New York: Plenum.

Collins, F. L., Jr., Foster, S. L., & Berler, E. S. (1986). Clinical training issues for behavioral psychology. *Professional Psychology: Research and Practice, 17,* 301–307.

Craighead, W. E. (1982). A brief clinical history of cognitive-behavior therapy with children. *School Psychology Review, 11,* 5–13.

Davison, G. C. (1968). Elimination of a sadistic fantasy by a client-controlled counterconditioning technique: A case study. *Journal of Abnormal Psychology,* *73*, 84–90.

Davison, G. C. (1976). Homosexuality: The ethical challenge. *Journal of Consulting and Clinical Psychology, 44,* 157–162.

DeLeon, P. H. (1979). The legislative outlook for psychology: A health care profession. *Academic Psychology Bulletin, 1,* 187–192.

Dickerson, F. (1989). Behavior therapy in private hospitals: A national survey. *the Behavior Therapist, 12,* 158.

Dunlap, K. (1930). Repetition in the breaking of habits. *Scientific Monthly, 30,* 66–70.

Dunlap, K. (1932). *Habits: Their making and unmaking.* New York: Liveright.

Eysenck, H. J. (1952). The effects of psychotherapy: An evaluation. *Journal of Consulting Psychology, 16,* 319–324.

Eysenck, H. J. (1959). Learning theory and behaviour therapy. *Journal of Mental Science, 105,* 61–75.

Eysenck, H. J. (Ed.). (1960). *Behaviour therapy and the neuroses.* London: Pergamon.

Eysenck, H. J., & Rachman, S. (1965). *The causes and cures of neurosis.* London: Routledge & Kegan Paul.

Fensterheim, H., & Baer, J. (1975). *Don't say yes when you want to say no.* New York: Dell.

Ferster, C. B., & DeMyer, M. K. (1962). A method for the experimental analysis of the behavior of autistic children. *American Journal of Orthopsychiatry, 32,* 89–98.

Ferster, C. B., Nurnberger, J. I., & Levitt, E. B. (1962). The control of eating. *Journal of Mathetics, 1,* 87–109.

Fishman, S. T., & Lubetkin, B. S. (1983). Office practice of behavior therapy. In M. Hersen (Ed.), *Outpatient behavior therapy: A clinical guide* (pp. 21–41). New York: Grune & Stratton.

Ford, J. D., & Kendall, P. C. (1979). Behavior therapists' professional behaviors: A survey study. *Professional Psychology, 10,* 772–773.

Franks, C. M. (1969). Behavior therapy and its Pavlovian origins: Review and perspectives. In C. M. Franks (Ed.), *Behavior therapy: Appraisal and status* (pp. 1–26). New York: McGraw-Hill.

Franks, C. M. (1987). Behavior therapy and AABT: Personal recollections, conceptions, and misconceptions. *the Behavior Therapist, 10,* 171–174.

Fuller, P. R. (1949). Operant conditioning of a vegetative human organism. *American Journal of Psychology, 62,* 587–590.

Fuller, P. R. (1973). Professors Kantor and Skinner—the "grand alliance" of the 40s. *Psychological Record, 23,* 318–324.

Garfield, S. L., & Kurtz, R. (1976). Clinical psychologists in the 1970s. *American Psychologist, 31,* 1–9.

Garfield, S. L., & Kurtz, R. (1977). A study of eclectic views. *Journal of Consulting and Clinical Psychology, 45,* 78–83.

Gibson, H. B. (1981). *Hans Eysenck: The man and his work*. London: Peter Owen.

Glasgow, R. E., & Rosen, G. M. (1978). Behavioral bibliotherapy: A review of self-help behavior therapy manuals. *Psychological Bulletin, 85*, 1–23.

Gochman, S. I., Allgood, B. A., & Geer, C. R. (1982). A look at today's behavior therapists. *Professional Psychology, 13*, 605–609.

Goldfried, M. R., & Davison, G. C. (1976). *Clinical behavior therapy*. New York: Holt, Rinehart & Winston.

Goldfried, M. R., & Merbaum, M. (Eds.). (1973). *Behavior change through self-control*. New York: Holt, Rinehart & Winston.

Goldiamond, I. (1965). Self-control procedures in personal behavior problems. *Psychological Reports, 17*, 851–868.

Goldschmid, M. L., Stein, D. D., Weissman, H. N., & Sorrells, J. (1969). A survey of the training and practices of clinical psychologists. *The Clinical Psychologist, 22*(Winter), 89–94, 107.

Goodall, K. (1972, November). Shapers at work. *Psychology Today*, pp. 53–63, 132–134, 136–138.

Grayson, J. B., Foa, E. B., & Steketee, G. (1985). Obsessive-compulsive disorder. In M. Hersen & A. S. Bellack (Eds.), *Handbook of clinical behavior therapy with adults* (pp. 133–165). New York: Plenum.

Guevremont, D. C., & Spiegler, M. D. (1990, November). *What do behavior therapists really do?: A survey of the clinical practice of AABT members*. Paper presented at the meeting of the Association for Advancement of Behavior Therapy, San Francisco, CA.

Guthrie, E. R. (1935). *The psychology of learning*. New York: Harper.

Heinssen, R. K., & Glass, C. R. (1990). Social skills, social anxiety, and cognitive factors in schizophrenia. In H. Leitenberg (Ed.), *Handbook of social and evaluative anxiety* (pp. 325–355). New York: Plenum.

Hersen, M. (1979). Limitations and problems in the clinical application of behavioral techniques in psychiatric settings. *Behavior Therapy, 10*, 65–80.

Hersen, M. (1981). Complex problems require complex solutions. *Behavior Therapy, 12*, 15–29.

Hersen, M. (1983). Perspectives on the practice of outpatient behavior therapy. In M. Hersen (Ed.), *Outpatient behavior therapy: A clinical guide* (pp. 3–20). New York: Grune & Stratton.

Hersen, M., & Bellack, A. S. (1978). Staff training and consultation. In M. Hersen & A. S. Bellack (Eds.), *Behavior therapy in the psychiatric setting* (pp. 58–87). Baltimore: Williams & Wilkins.

Homme, L. E. (1965). Perspectives in psychology: XXIV. Control of coverants, the operants of the mind. *Psychological Record, 15*, 501–511.

Hull, C. L. (1943). *Principles of behavior*. New York: Appleton-Century-Crofts.

Jacobson, E. (1929). *Progressive relaxation*. Chicago: University of Chicago Press.

Jensen, J. P., Bergin, A. E., & Greaves, D. W. (1990). The meaning of eclecticism:

New survey and analysis of components. *Professional Psychology: Research and Practice, 21*, 124–130.

Jones, H. G. (1956). The application of conditioning and learning techniques to the treatment of a psychiatric patient. *Journal of Abnormal and Social Psychology, 52*, 414–419.

Jones, M. C. (1924a). The elimination of children's fears. *Journal of Experimental Psychology, 7*, 383–390.

Jones, M. C. (1924b). A laboratory study of fear: The case of Peter. *Pedagogical Seminary, 31*, 308–315.

Jones, M. C. (1975). A 1924 pioneer looks at behavior therapy. *Journal of Behavior Therapy and Experimental Psychiatry, 6*, 181–187.

Kanfer, F. H. (1970). Self-regulation: Research, issues and speculations. In C. Neuringer & J. L. Michael (Eds.), *Behavior modification in clinical psychology* (pp. 178–220). New York: Appleton-Century-Crofts.

Kanfer, F. H. (1971). The maintenance of behavior by self-generated stimuli and reinforcement. In A. Jacobs & L. B. Sachs (Eds.), *The psychology of private events* (pp. 39–57). New York: Academic Press.

Kanfer, F. H., & Karoly, P. (1972). Self-control: A behavioristic excursion into the lion's den. *Behavior Therapy, 3*, 389–416.

Kazdin, A. E. (1978). *History of behavior modification.* Baltimore, MD: University Park Press.

Kazdin, A. E. (1982). History of behavior modification. In A. S. Bellack, M. Hersen, & A. E. Kazdin (Eds.), *International handbook of behavior modification and therapy* (pp. 3–32). New York: Plenum.

Kazdin, A. E. (1989). *Behavior modification in applied settings* (4th ed.). Pacific Grove, CA: Brooks/Cole.

Kazdin, A. E., & Bootzin, R. R. (1972). The token economy: An evaluative review. *Journal of Applied Behavior Analysis, 5*, 343–372.

Kazdin, A. E., & Hersen, M. (1980). The current status of behavior therapy. *Behavior Modification, 4*, 283–302.

Kazdin, A. E., & Pulaski, J. L. (1977). Joseph Lancaster and behavior modification in education. *Journal of the History of the Behavioral Sciences, 13*, 261–266.

Kazdin, A. E., & Wilson, G. T. (1978). *Evaluation of behavior therapy: Issues, evidence, and research strategies.* Cambridge, MA: Ballinger.

Kelly, E. L. (1961). Clinical psychology—1960: Report of survey findings. *Newsletter: Division of Clinical Psychology of the American Psychological Association, 14*(1), 1–11.

Kelly, E. L., Goldberg, L. R., Fiske, D. W., & Kilkowski, J. M. (1978). Twenty-five years later: A follow-up study of the graduate students in clinical psychology assessed in the VA selection research project. *American Psychologist, 33*, 746–755.

Klein, M. H., Dittmann, A. T., Parloff, M. B., & Gill, M. M. (1969). Behavior therapy: Observations and reflections. *Journal of Consulting and Clinical Psychology, 33,* 259–266.

Koocher, G. P., & Pedulla, B. M. (1977). Current practices in child psychotherapy. *Professional Psychology, 8,* 275–287.

Krasner, L. (1971). Behavior therapy. *Annual Review of Psychology, 22,* 483–532.

Krasner, L. (1976). Behavioral modification: Ethical issues and future trends. In H. Leitenberg (Ed.), *Handbook of behavior modification and behavior therapy* (pp. 627–649). Englewood Cliffs, NJ: Prentice-Hall.

Krasner, L. (Ed.). (1980). *Environmental design and human behavior: A psychology of the individual in society.* Elmsford, NY: Pergamon Press.

Krasner, L. (1982). Behavior therapy: On roots, contexts, and growth. In G. T. Wilson & C. M. Franks (Eds.), *Contemporary behavior therapy: Conceptual and empirical foundations* (pp. 11–62). New York: Guilford.

Krasner, L. (1988a). Mary Cover Jones: A legend in her own time. *the Behavior Therapist, 11,* 101–102.

Krasner, L. (1988b). Paradigm lost: On a historical/sociological/economic perspective. In D. B. Fishman, F. Rotgers, & C. M. Franks (Eds.), *Paradigms in behavior therapy: Present and promise* (pp. 23–44). New York: Springer.

Krasner, L. (1990). History of behavior modification. In A. S. Bellack, M. Hersen, & A. E. Kazdin (Eds.), *International handbook of behavior modification and therapy* (2nd ed., pp. 3–26). New York: Plenum.

Lange, A. J., & Jakubowski, P. (1976). *Responsible assertive behavior.* Champaign, IL: Research Press.

Lazarus, A. A. (1958). New methods in psychotherapy: A case study. *South African Medical Journal, 32,* 660–664.

Lazarus, A. A. (1971). *Behavior therapy and beyond.* New York: McGraw-Hill.

Levitt, E. E. (1957). The results of psychotherapy with children: An evaluation. *Journal of Consulting Psychology, 21,* 189–196.

Levitt, E. E. (1963). Psychotherapy with children: A further evaluation. *Behaviour Research and Therapy, 1,* 45–51.

Liberman, R. P., DeRisi, W. J., & Mueser, K. T. (1989). *Social skills training for psychiatric patients.* New York: Pergamon.

Lindsley, O. R. (1956). Operant conditioning methods applied to research in chronic schizophrenia. *Psychiatric Research Reports, 5,* 118–139.

Lindsley, O. R. (1960). Characteristics of the behavior of chronic psychotics as revealed by free-operant conditioning methods [Monograph]. *Diseases of the Nervous System, 21,* 66–78.

Lindsley, O. R., Skinner, B. F., & Solomon, H. C. (1953). *Studies in behavior therapy* (Status Report 1). Waltham, MA: Metropolitan State Hospital.

Linehan, M. M. (1987). Dialectical behavioral therapy: A cognitive behavioral approach to parasuicide. *Journal of Personality Disorders, 1,* 328–333.

London, P. (1972). The end of ideology in behavior modification. *American Psychologist, 27,* 913–920.

Lovaas, O. I. (1968). Some studies on the treatment of childhood schizophrenia. In J. M. Shlien (Ed.), *Research in psychotherapy* (Vol. 3, pp. 103–121). Washington, DC: American Psychological Association.

Lovaas, O. I. (1987). Behavioral treatment and normal educational and intellectual functioning in young autistic children. *Journal of Consulting and Clinical Psychology, 55,* 3–9.

Lubin, B. (1962). Survey of psychotherapy training and activities of psychologists. *Journal of Clinical Psychology, 18,* 252–256.

Luborsky, L. (1984). *Principles of psychoanalytic psychotherapy.* New York: Basic.

Mahoney, M. J., & Arnkoff, D. B. (1978). Cognitive and self-control therapies. In S. L. Garfield & A. E. Bergin (Eds.), *Handbook of psychotherapy and behavior change* (2nd ed., pp. 689–722). New York: Wiley.

Mahoney, M. J., & Bandura, A. (1972). Self-reinforcement in pigeons. *Learning and Motivation, 3,* 293–303.

Mahoney, M. J., Kazdin, A. E., & Lesswing, N. J. (1974). Behavior modification: Delusion or deliverance? In C. M. Franks & G. T. Wilson (Eds.), *Annual review of behavior therapy* (Vol. 2, pp. 11–40). New York: Brunner/Mazel.

Mahoney, M. J., Norcross, J. C., Prochaska, J. O., & Missar, C. D. (1989). Psychological development and optimal psychotherapy: Converging perspectives among clinical psychologists. *Journal of Integrative and Eclectic Psychotherapy, 8,* 251–263.

Marks, I. M. (1972). Flooding (implosion) and allied treatments. In W. S. Agras (Ed.), *Behavior modification: Principles and clinical applications* (pp. 151–214). Boston: Little, Brown.

Marks, I. M. (1975). Behavioral treatments of phobic and obsessive-compulsive disorders: A critical appraisal. In M. Hersen, R. M. Eisler, & P. M. Miller (Eds.), *Progress in behavior modification* (Vol. 1, pp. 65–158). New York: Academic.

Marks, I. M. (1987). *Fears, phobias, and rituals: Panic, anxiety, and their disorders.* New York: Oxford University Press.

Masters, J. C., Burish, T. G., Hollon, S. D., & Rimm, D. C. (1987). *Behavior therapy* (3rd ed.). San Diego: Harcourt Brace Jovanovich.

Matarazzo, J. D., Weiss, S. M., Herd, J. A., Miller, N. E., & Weiss, S. M. (Eds.) (1984). *Behavioral health: A handbook of health enhancement and disease prevention.* New York: Wiley.

Matson, J. L., & Ollendick, T. H. (1988). *Enhancing children's social skills: Assessment and training.* New York: Pergamon.

Meichenbaum, D., & Turk, D. C. (1987). *Facilitating treatment adherence.* New York: Plenum.

Meyer, V. (1957). The treatment of two phobic patients on the basis of learning principles. *Journal of Abnormal and Social Psychology, 55,* 261–266.

Mischel, W. (1968). *Personality and assessment.* New York: John Wiley & Sons.

Morrow-Bradley, C., & Elliott, R. (1986). Utilization of psychotherapy research by practicing psychotherapists. *American Psychologist, 41*, 188–197.

Mowrer, O. H. (1947). On the dual nature of learning—a reinterpretation of "conditioning" and "problem-solving." *Harvard Educational Review, 17*, 102–148.

Mowrer, O. H., & Mowrer, W. M. (1938). Enuresis: A method for its study and treatment. *American Journal of Orthopsychiatry, 8*, 436–459.

Nelson, R. O. (1981). Realistic dependent measures for clinical use. *Journal of Consulting and Clinical Psychology, 49*, 168–182.

Nevid, J. S., Lavi, B., & Primavera, L. H. (1986). Cluster analysis of training orientations in clinical psychology. *Professional Psychology: Research and Practice, 17*, 367–370.

Nietzel, M. T., Winett, R. A., MacDonald, M. L., & Davidson, W. S. (1977). *Behavioral approaches to community psychology.* New York: Pergamon.

Norcross, J. C., Nash, J. M., & Prochaska, J. O. (1985). Psychologists in part-time independent practice: Description and comparison. *Professional Psychology: Research and Practice, 16*, 565–575.

Norcross, J. C., & Prochaska, J. O. (1982). A national survey of clinical psychologists: Affiliations and orientations. *The Clinical Psychologist, 35*(3), 1–2, 4–6.

Norcross, J. C., & Prochaska, J. O. (1983). Psychotherapists in independent practice: Some findings and issues. *Professional Psychology: Research and Practice, 14*, 869–881.

Norcross, J. C., Prochaska, J. O., & Gallagher, K. M. (1989). Clinical psychologists in the 1980s: II. Theory, research, and practice. *The Clinical Psychologist, 42*(3), 45–53.

Norcross, J. C., Strausser-Kirtland, D., & Missar, C. D. (1989). The processes and outcomes of psychotherapists' personal treatment experiences. *Psychotherapy, 25*, 36–43.

Norcross, J. C., & Wogan, M. (1983). American psychotherapists of diverse persuasions: Characteristics, theories, practices, and clients. *Professional Psychology: Research and Practice, 14*, 529–539.

O'Leary, K. D. (1984). The image of behavior therapy: It is time to take a stand. *Behavior Therapy, 15*, 219–233.

O'Leary, K. D., Turkewitz, H., & Taffel, S. J. (1973). Parent and therapist evaluation of behavior therapy in a child psychological clinic. *Journal of Consulting and Clinical Psychology, 41*, 279–283.

O'Leary, K. D., & Wilson, G. T. (1987). *Behavior therapy: Application and outcome* (2nd ed.). Englewood Cliffs, NJ: Prentice-Hall.

Patterson, G. R. (1976). *Living with children: New methods for parents and teachers* (rev. ed.). Champaign, IL: Research Press.

Patterson, G. R. (1982). *Social learning approach to family intervention: Vol. 3. Coercive family process.* Eugene, OR: Castalia.

Paul, G. L. (1966). *Insight vs. desensitization in psychotherapy.* Stanford, CA: Stanford University Press.

Paul, G. L., & Lentz, R. J. (1977). *Psychosocial treatment of chronic mental patients.* Cambridge, MA: Harvard University Press.

Pavlov, I. P. (1927). *Conditioned reflexes: An investigation of the physiological activity of the cerebral cortex* (G. V. Anrep, trans.). London: Oxford University Press.

Pavlov, I. P. (1928). *Lectures on conditioned reflexes* (W. H. Gantt, trans.). London: Lawrence & Wishart.

Phillips, E. L. (1968). Achievement Place: Token reinforcement procedures in a home-style rehabilitation setting for "predelinquent" boys. *Journal of Applied Behavior Analysis, 1,* 213–223.

Phillips, E. L., Phillips, E. A., Fixsen, D. L., & Wolf, M. M. (1971). Achievement Place: Modification of the behaviors of predelinquent boys within a token economy. *Journal of Applied Behavior Analysis, 4,* 45–59.

Pomerleau, O. F. (1979). Behavioral medicine: The contribution of the experimental analysis of behavior to medical care. *American Psychologist, 34,* 654–663.

Prochaska, J. O., & Norcross, J. C. (1983). Contemporary psychotherapists: A national survey of characteristics, practices, orientations, and attitudes. *Psychotherapy: Theory, Research and Practice, 20,* 161–173.

Rachman, S. (1987). Editorial. *Behaviour Research and Therapy, 25,* i.

Redd, W. H., Porterfield, A. L., & Andersen, B. L. (1979). *Behavior modification: Behavioral approaches to human problems.* New York: Random House.

Rosen, G. M. (1987). Self-help treatment books and the commercialization of psychotherapy. *American Psychologist, 42,* 46–51.

Ross, A. O. (1981). *Child behavior therapy.* New York: Wiley.

Russo, D. C. (1990). A requiem for the passing of the three-term contingency. *Behavior Therapy, 21,* 153–165.

Salter, A. (1949). *Conditioned reflex therapy.* New York: Farrar, Straus.

Sayette, M. A., & Mayne, T. J. (1990). Survey of current clinical and research trends in clinical psychology. *American Psychologist, 45,* 1263–1266.

Schorr, A. (1984). *Die verhaltenstherapie: Ihre geschichte von den anfangen bis zur gegenwart* [Behavior therapy: Its history from the beginning to the present]. Weinheim, Germany: Beltz Verlag.

Schwartz, G. E., & Beatty, J. (Eds.). (1977). *Biofeedback: Theory and research.* New York: Academic Press.

Shemberg, K. M., & Leventhal, D. B. (1978). A survey of activities of academic clinicians. *Professional Psychology, 9,* 580–586.

Skinner, B. F. (1938). *The behavior of organisms: An experimental analysis.* New York: Appleton-Century-Crofts.

Skinner, B. F. (1953). *Science and human behavior.* New York: Macmillan.

Skinner, B. F. (1959). John Broadus Watson, Behaviorist. *Science, 129,* 197–198.

Sloane, R. B., Staples, F. R., Cristol, A. H., Yorkston, N. J., & Whipple, K. (1975). *Psychotherapy versus behavior therapy*. Cambridge, MA: Harvard University Press.

Smith, D. (1982). Trends in counseling and psychotherapy. *American Psychologist, 37*, 802–809.

Stolz, S. B. (Ed.). (1977). *Report of the American Psychological Association Commission on Behavior Modification*. Washington, DC: American Psychological Association.

Suinn, R. M. (1990). Association for Advancement of Behavior Therapy minutes of the annual meeting of members, November 4, 1989. *the Behavior Therapist, 13*, 35–37.

Swan, G. E., & MacDonald, M. L. (1978). Behavior therapy in practice: A national survey of behavior therapists. *Behavior Therapy, 9*, 799–807.

Sweet, A. A. (1984). The therapeutic relationship in behavior therapy. *Clinical Psychology Review, 4*, 253–272.

Taylor, S. E. (1990). Health psychology: The science and the field. *American Psychologist, 45*, 40–50.

Tharp, R. G., & Wetzel, R. J. (1969). *Behavior modification in the natural environment*. New York: Academic Press.

Thoresen, C. E., & Mahoney, M. J. (1974). *Behavioral self-control*. New York: Holt, Rinehart & Winston.

Thorndike, E. L. (1931). *Human learning*. New York: Century.

Tryon, G. S. (1983). Full-time private practice in the United States: Results of a national survey. *Professional Psychology: Research and Practice, 14*, 685–696.

Turkat, I. D. & Feuerstein, M. (1978). Behavior modification and the public misconception. *American Psychologist, 33*, 194.

Turkewitz, H., & O'Leary, K. D. (1981). A comparative outcome study of behavioral marital therapy and community therapy. *Journal of Marital and Family Therapy, 7*, 159–169.

Twentyman, C. T., & McFall, R. M. (1975). Behavioral training of social skills in shy males. *Journal of Consulting and Clinical Psychology, 43*, 384–395.

Ullmann, L. P., & Krasner, L. (Eds.). (1965). *Case studies in behavior modification*. New York: Holt, Rinehart & Winston.

Wade, T. C. & Baker, T. B. (1977). Opinions and use of psychological tests: A survey of clinical psychologists. *American Psychologist, 32*, 874–882.

Wade, T. C., Baker, T. B., & Hartmann, D. P. (1979). Behavior therapists' self-reported views and practices. *the Behavior Therapist, 2*(1), 3–6.

Watkins, C. E., Jr., Lopez, F. G., Campbell, V. L., & Himmell, C. D. (1986). Contemporary counseling psychology: Results of a national survey. *Journal of Counseling Psychology, 33*, 301–309.

Watson, J. B. (1913). Psychology as the behaviorist views it. *Psychological Review, 20*, 158–177.

Watson, J. B., & Rayner, R. (1920). Conditioned emotional reactions. *Journal of Experimental Psychology, 3,* 1–14.

Willis, J., & Giles, D. (1978). Behaviorism in the twentieth century: What we have here is a failure to communicate. *Behavior Therapy, 9,* 15–27.

Wilson, G. T. (1980). Toward specifying the "nonspecific" factors in behavior therapy: A social-learning analysis. In M. J. Mahoney (Ed.), *Psychotherapy process* (pp. 283–307). New York: Plenum.

Wilson, G. T. (1982). Psychotherapy process and procedure: The behavioral mandate. *Behavior Therapy, 13,* 291–312.

Wilson, G. T., Hannon, A. E., & Evans, W. I. M. (1968). Behavior therapy and the therapist-patient relationship. *Journal of Consulting and Clinical Psychology, 32,* 103–109.

Wolf, M. M., Risley, T. R., & Mees, H. L. (1964). Application of operant conditioning procedures to the behavior problems of an autistic child. *Behaviour Research and Therapy, 1,* 305–312.

Wolpe, J. (1958). *Psychotherapy by reciprocal inhibition.* Stanford, CA: Stanford University Press.

Wolpe, J. (1981). Behavior therapy versus psychoanalysis: Therapeutic and social implications. *American Psychologist, 36,* 159–164.

Wolpe, J. (1982). *The practice of behavior therapy* (3rd ed.). New York: Pergamon.

Wolpe, J. (1989). The derailment of behavior therapy: A tale of conceptual misdirection. *Journal of Behavior Therapy and Experimental Psychiatry, 20,* 3–15.

Wyatt v. Stickney, 344 F. Supp. 373, 344 F. Supp. 387 (M.D. Ala. 1972) affirmed sub nom. Wyatt v. Aberholt, 503 F. 2d. 1305 (5th Cir. 1974).

Yates, A. J. (1958). The application of learning theory to the treatment of tics. *Journal of Abnormal and Social Psychology, 56,* 175–182.

Yates, A. J. (1970). *Behavior therapy.* New York: Wiley.

19

CARL ROGERS AND CLIENT/PERSON-CENTERED THERAPY

FRED M. ZIMRING AND NATHANIEL J. RASKIN

The 50 years that have elapsed since the beginning of client-centered therapy are divisible into four periods, each of which starts with the publication of a work by Carl Rogers. In the first two periods, the main focus of Rogers' work was on individual psychotherapy. In the latter periods, the focus changed to new contexts in which the basic client-centered attitudes were applied: groups, education, and conflict resolution. These changes in context necessarily resulted in changes in the operations used to implement Rogers' basic principles.

FIRST PERIOD

The first period of the client-centered approach was initiated when Rogers addressed the Psi Chi chapter (an undergraduate psychology honor society) at the University of Minnesota in December 1940 on "Some Newer Concepts of Psychotherapy." Rogers had begun a professorship at Ohio State University in that year and was in the process of delineating emerging trends in the child guidance field. He had described these trends in the book, *The Clinical Treatment of the Problem Child*, published in 1939. Rogers was already expert in the use of tests and interviews with children and parents, and he communicated these skills in a practicum course he taught at Ohio State.

Even as he was practicing and teaching, however, Rogers was refocusing his professional interest from working with children and their parents to therapy with adults. One outcome of the diagnostic process in which child guidance clinics engaged was the decision to offer treatment. In the late 1930s, at institutions such as the Judge Baker Guidance Center in Boston and the Rochester (New York) Guidance Center which Rogers administered, treatment resulted for approximately one third of the cases assessed. For Rogers, there was an abrupt shift from being a clinician who employed some diagnostic methods to being a therapist who eschewed diagnosis. As he was moving rapidly toward centering his efforts on therapy with adults, he made no significant distinction between "counseling" and "psychotherapy."

One expression of the change being described here is that approximately one third of Rogers' book, *Counseling and Psychotherapy* (Rogers, 1942), is devoted to the verbatim account of an eight-interview treatment course with an adult, "Herbert Bryan."

Beginning with this volume, Rogers employed a hypothetical format which persisted throughout his career: "If we do this, then such and such will follow." In *Counseling and Psychotherapy*, the hypothesis took the following form: If the therapist accepts, recognizes, and clarifies the feelings expressed by the client, there will be movement from negative feelings to positive ones, followed by insight and positive actions which are initiated by the client.

Rogers placed particular stress on two aspects of the therapist's role. One was the importance of responding to feelings rather than content. The other was the acceptance by the therapist of the feelings expressed, whether they were positive, negative, or ambivalent.

In *Counseling and Psychotherapy* (1942), Rogers illustrated the difference between responding to feeling and content. A student (S.), in his first contact with the counselor (C.), states his problem as follows (phonographic recording):

> S. I've always realized that my methods of study, my study habits, are wrong. I don't feel as though I am a very brilliant person, but I don't think I am as stupid as my brains indicate. (p. 133)

Rogers states that it is plain that the student "is feeling disappointed at the discrepancy between his ability and his grades and concerned lest his grades be taken to represent the true measure of his ability." To make some response to this feeling would have been a move toward deeper revelation of the problem, but the counselor responds:

> C. Well, how bad are your grades? I thought they were pretty good.
> S. My cumulative average is about 2.3 or 2.4. I had a 3.1 last quarter. (pp. 133–34).

This response to content by the counselor clearly has the effect of keeping the student on a content level and makes it difficult for him to go further with the feeling that he was developing.

Rogers gave a comparable instance where there "is more adequate response to the feeling expressed." The student in this case is describing the difficulty of writing his parents to inform them that his grades have worsened:

> S. I don't know if they're going to condemn me. I think so, because that's what they've done in the past. They've said, "It's your fault. You don't have enough will power, you're not interested." That's the experience I've had in the past. I've been sort of telling them that I improved in this respect. I was alright [sic] the first quarter. Well, I wasn't entirely all right, but I just got worse. (Pause.)
> C. You feel that they'll be unsympathetic and they'll condemn you for your failures.
> S. Well, my—I'm pretty sure my father will. My mother might not. He hasn't been—he doesn't experience these things; he just doesn't know what it's like. "Lack of ambition," is what he'd say. (Pause.)
> C. You feel that he could never understand you?
> S. No, I don't think he is—is capable of that, because I don't get along with him, don't at all![1]

It is clear that this counselor's response to the student's feelings has facilitated a process of exploration and expansion of feeling, of sharing, and perhaps of awareness.

The Counselor's Acceptance of the Client's Feelings

Rogers believed that at the same time that the counselor attended to feeling rather than content, the counselor's *acceptance* of whatever feelings were expressed was crucial. He emphasized both the difficulty and the importance of accepting negative feelings, the kind of feelings which often

---

[1]From *Counseling and Psychotherapy* (pp. 135–136) by C. R. Rogers, 1942, Boston: Houghton Mifflin. Copyright 1942 by Houghton Mifflin. Reprinted by permission.

dominate the early phases of therapy (Rogers, 1942). Here is a particularly cogent passage:

> When the client is thoroughly discouraged, when he feels that he is "no good," when his fears are overwhelming, when he hints that he has thought of suicide, when he pictures himself as completely unstable, completely dependent, entirely inadequate, unworthy of love—in short, when he is expressing any type of negative feeling toward himself, the natural tendency on the part of the inexperienced counselor is to try to convince him that he is exaggerating the situation. This is probably true, and the counselor's argument is intellectually logical, but it is not therapeutic. The client feels worthless, no matter how many good qualities may be objectively pointed out to him. He knows that he has contemplated suicide, no matter how many reasons may be pointed out for not doing so. He knows that he has worried about going insane, no matter how unlikely that possibility may be made to appear. The counselor is giving more genuine help if he assists the client to face these feelings openly, recognize them for what they are, and admit that he has them. Then, if he no longer has to prove that he is worthless or abnormal, he can, and does, consider himself more comfortably and find in himself more positive qualities.[2]

Rogers then gave an example of this principle of acceptance from an interview with a student (S.) by a counselor (C.):

> S. I—uh—have the opinion that I'm inferior. That's the—that's the opinion I have.
> C. You just know darn well that you don't measure up, is that it?
> S. That's right. (Pause)
> C. Want to tell me some more about that?
> S. Well, I'll tell you. I've been interested in anthropology to some extent, and especially criminal anthropology. (Pause) Well, I continually compare physiques of people, and I feel that mine is inferior, and I don't stop—I don't—I also believe that the behavior of an individual is an approximation of his physique, you might say. That's what my belief is. I've read too much of Hooton (laugh). Did you ever hear of him? (C. nods.) I expected you did.
> C. And—uh—as you look about on other physical types, you just feel that yours is inferior, the lowest of the low.
> S. No, not exactly, I wouldn't say that.
> C. But you're far down in the scale?
> S. Yes, (laugh) that's the way I feel. And I'd have to have some real basis to change my mind about it.

The counselor continues his consistent acceptance of the student's

---

[2]From *Counseling and Psychotherapy* (p. 144) by C. R. Rogers, 1942, Boston: Houghton Mifflin. Copyright 1942 by Houghton Mifflin. Reprinted by permission.

negative feelings, and toward the end of the interview, there is this exchange:

> S. I do have abilities and I realize some—among them I have a certain knack for mathematics. I think I do. And I've always been more advanced than my fellow students in that, I think I can safely say.
> C. Then there's one thing at least in which you really excel most of the students that you work with.[3]

This excerpt exemplifies the expression of positive attitudes following the counselor's consistent acceptance of negative feelings. Rogers points out that "when the counselor overstates" the student's attitude, suggesting that he feels he is "the lowest of the low," the student objects, "already giving a hint of the fact that his evaluation of himself is not all negative" (1942, pp. 146).

Accepting Ambivalent Feelings

Rogers (1942) also emphasized the importance of accepting ambivalent feelings:

> Where the client is conflicted in his feelings, where both love and hostility, attraction and repulsion, or both sides of a difficult choice, are being expressed it is particularly important to recognize this clearly as an ambivalent attitude. Some of the sorts of recognition which may be given are exemplified in such statements as, "You feel you should go into commerce, but music is the thing you really like"; "in spite of your bitterness toward your father, you do like him"; "You want to come for help, yet still at times you feel it is too difficult". . . . A forward step in therapy is made when such ambivalences are definitely clarified. The client is well along toward solution when the client feels it to be a conflict with clear-cut choices. On the other hand, to recognize only one aspect of such muddled feelings may retard therapy. . . . To recognize only an attitude of hostility toward a parent, when elements of affection are also being expressed, may make it difficult for the client to bring out more fully these positive feelings. Consequently, ambivalent attitudes need to be brought into the discussion as openly as positive or negative feelings, since it is through their clarification that the client is enabled to find a solution to them.[4]

---

[3]From *Counseling and Psychotherapy* (pp. 144–146) by C. R. Rogers, 1942, Boston: Houghton Mifflin. Copyright 1942 by Houghton Mifflin. Reprinted by permission.
[4]From *Counseling and Psychotherapy* (pp. 147–148) by C. R. Rogers, 1942, Boston: Houghton Mifflin. Copyright 1942 by Houghton Mifflin. Reprinted by permission.

The Clarification of Feelings

Rogers, in 1940 and 1942, talked of "accepting, recognizing, and *clarifying* feelings." In view of the nondirective nature of this orientation, it seems important to clarify the concept of clarifying. A good example occurs in the third interview of the case of "Herbert Bryan" (Rogers, 1942) a young man in his late twenties (S. in following):

> S. Well, I feel that sex is very fundamental in life and that the least a man can do is be a good copulater; that should be one of the fundamentals. Of course, he should be a lot more, of course, if he does have the potentialities, but at least any animal can do that.
>
> C. That's one of the reasons why it strikes you so hard if there is— if you have some doubt or some uncertainty as to your own abilities along those lines.
>
> S. Yes, I feel that there's something fundamentally wrong there— something wrong with the very foundation, as it were—that any other achievement I might have would not be adequate compensation for a blocking in that fundamental field. I used to think that perhaps I would become an ascetic—go in entirely for intellectual life, and so forth, but I couldn't bring myself to value that wholeheartedly. I had the definite conviction that no intellectual achievement could make up for that fundamental blocking there. (Pause.) I want to be a healthy animal first of all, then I feel that the super-elements there will grow out of that healthy foundation. I feel that any achievement that was the result of overcompensations would be pretty unsatisfying, no matter how great the achievement, no matter how great the world's applause. My private knowledge of that fundamental blocking would bring me down so much that the world's applause wouldn't make up for it.
>
> C. In other words, you've got to have some respect for yourself on a pretty fundamental basis, in order to have any achievements in any line.
>
> S. M-hm. Of course, I overvalue sex now as a direct result of my inhibition. That is I think more about it than I would if I didn't have the inhibition, but I want to put it somewhere between food and music. It has—well, you could make the analogy that it is somewhat like food; it's sort of a physical gusto, and on the other hand, it also has the artistry of music about it. And I feel that it can have an important place without being dwelt on, as it were.[5]

Rogers saw his last response in the preceding excerpt as a particularly good clarification of a complex conversation which brings the client to a very significant insight. In his last statement he "realizes quite frankly that he overvalues sex and places too much stress upon his thinking about sex.

---

[5]From *Counseling and Psychotherapy* (pp. 329–330) by C. R. Rogers, 1942, Boston: Houghton Mifflin. Copyright 1942 by Houghton Mifflin. Reprinted by permission.

This is a result which would not have been obtained if the counselor had been in any way judgmental" (1942, p. 330).

It is clear that Rogers wished to clarify the client's responses in a manner which did not go beyond the client's own meanings and feelings. There were, in fact, many instances in the case study of "Herbert Bryan" where Rogers went further, but he was critical of those instances. His practice was catching up with his theory, and even his theory still had elements of directiveness. He wrote that "the cautious and intelligent use of interpretive techniques can increase the scope and the clarity of . . . self understanding (1942, p. 216)". This may surprise many therapists. More surprising is the fact that the term *empathy* is not to be found in *Counseling and Psychotherapy* (1942). Rogers' "acceptance, recognition and clarification of feelings" phrase does, however, contain the roots of the client-centered empathic attitude and technique.

The basic hypothesis formulated by Rogers (1942) at the time was: Effective counseling consists of a definitely structured, permissive relationship which allows the client to gain an understanding of himself to a degree which enables him to take positive steps in the light of his new orientation. In the course of the book, Rogers makes clear that the increase in self-understanding which comes from successful therapy involves the "recognition and acceptance of the self."

In this first period of client-centered therapy, then, the main therapeutic technique was the clarification of feelings with the emphasis on the client obtaining insight into those feelings. The goal was for the client to be able to cope and to act more positively.

SECOND PERIOD

The second period lasted from the beginning of the 1950s, when *Client-Centered Therapy* was published (Rogers, 1951), to the early 1960s, when *On Becoming a Person* (Rogers, 1961) was published. At the beginning of this period Rogers made explicit his basic hypothesis for therapy. He also specified the necessary conditions and sufficient conditions for therapeutic change (Rogers, 1957).

In *Client-Centered Therapy* (1951) Rogers emphasized that, rather than any particular technique, the attitude and orientation of the therapist was central. The basic attitude of the client-centered therapist was, for Rogers, the belief in the capacity of the individual to deal with his or her psychological situation and to deal constructively with whatever comes into consciousness.

Central Importance Given to the World of the Client

Early in the second period there was increased emphasis on the importance of the client's world as the client sees it. In *Client-Centered Therapy* (Rogers, 1951), some propositions were set out. Rogers' first proposition was that "The individual exists in a continually changing world of experience of which he is the center"(p. 483). Proposition II was that "The organism reacts to the field as it is experienced and perceived" (p. 484). The perceptual field is, for the individual, "reality." For Rogers, it was this world to which the therapist attends. It is not the true reality which is important, but rather the world as the client sees it. These propositions meant that Rogers did not try to understand the causes of the person's problem. Instead, Rogers attended only to the client's perspective. In Proposition VII he says, "The best vantage point for understanding behavior is from the internal frame of reference of the individual himself" (p. 494). The internal frame of reference was later defined as "all of the realm of experience which is available to the awareness of the individual at a given moment. It includes the full range of sensations, perceptions, meanings and memories which are available to consciousness" (Rogers, 1959, p. 210).

Self-Actualization: The Basic Motivation for Change

If the therapist only attends to the world of the client, why does change occur? For Rogers, there is a fundamental, basic motivating force for change. The function of the therapist is to facilitate the action of this basic motivating force. Rogers was convinced that when the individual clearly perceived all elements "the balance seems invariably in the direction of the painful but ultimately rewarding path of self-actualization or growth" (from *Journal of Consulting Psychology*, 4, as quoted in Rogers, 1951, p. 490). How does the therapist facilitate this basic motivation for change? He or she must unconditionally prize and attend to the client's internal frame of reference.

The emphasis on the world of the client and on understanding the client's internal frame of reference shifts the emphasis from clarification of feelings to understanding the way the client sees his or her world. The following excerpt in which Rogers finds the client's meanings more important than her feelings is an example. It is from "Mrs. Ett," a series of therapy interviews recorded and transcribed in the late 1940s. (S represents the client, C, Carl Rogers.)

S244[6]: Yes, they are very strong, they're there. I'm getting so emo-

---

[6]Number tags identify individual statements by each party according to sequence.

tional I can't talk. What I meant to say is that they are there and I feel them very strongly and, ah, oh, I don't know, it's like little demons inside of me at work all the time, it doesn't give me a chance to sit and rest quietly to read, there's always conflict, it's either that or this. Such a great indecision; I can't tell you the—if I were to tell anybody the amount of indecision, it's almost pathological. I have a maid, a new maid now, and I'm very much upset about this. She's the epitome of efficiency and yet I hate her. I can't stand her, I think I'll have to let her go just because she's too efficient. She is, ah, taking away Bonnie from me. If I hold Bonnie in my arms, whoops, she's right out of my arms and she is re-diapering the baby, feeding her, and many times I would tell her that these are her duties and those are mine, but she has entered as the matriarch of the house—a colored woman—very nice, the type of a person, we hired her because of her appearance, very efficient and intelligent, but I find—oh my God! It didn't occur to me until just now that she's beginning to represent a mother figure to me. Isn't that—I never thought of it until right now, that I resent her because she's domineering, she's oh, she's very much like my mother.

C244: So that you resent her not only for her efficiency and her struggle to take over Bonnie but perhaps even more deeply because she is a mother.

S245: Oh, yes. Well, not so much a mother person as perhaps the type of person my mother is, because I notice that if I tell her something she won't listen to me, but she will continue to do it her way, which is what I have as the problem with mother all the time. And yesterday, Mr. L, . . . towards the end of the evening I was in such a fog, I was so undecided and so unhappy without knowing why, and now, darn it, I see why it is, it's that. I think I'll have to get rid of her for that reason, or what do you think I should do? Should I hang onto her and fight it out myself and use this as a good opportunity to vent out a lot of my feelings? It might be the ideal opportunity to struggle within myself against mother and then ultimately win, or should I dismiss her because she is rubbing me the wrong way at a time when I shouldn't be rubbed the wrong way. I mean what would your opinion be, I'm sure you won't give me an opinion, because you always turn everything back to a question, but from a clinical—

C245: It's not a question, you mean, but it's to know how to go at it—because you see yourself all that I would see there—ah, you might get rid of her because she represents your mother and you dislike her, or conceivably you might be able to adjust to her, which would certainly be a step toward adjusting to your mother, but, ah—

S246: I might have an awful lot of struggle, a lot of tension. I think there would be. Because for the past two or three days there's been an awful lot of tension in—I didn't know it until just now that she represents the mother figure to me, which is sometimes acceptable, very acceptable, and desirable, but at the other time, which is so upsetting for me.

C246: You feel pulled two ways by it, as you do with your own mother.

Looking first at the beginning of S244, Mrs. Ett says that she is getting very emotional at the moment and almost can't talk. Rogers could have responded to her feeling in the moment, her experience of getting very emotional. Rogers did not choose to emphasize this. She then goes to her experience of indecision which is like having little demons inside. Again, Rogers did not choose to respond to the feeling. She then talks about her new maid and comes to the present realization, which seems important to her, that she resents the maid as a mother figure. Note that if she had been involved in following the experience of the "little demons," she might not have come to the realization of her resentment of the maid as a mother figure.

In C244, Rogers responds to her resentment. Notice that it is not the "feel" or sensation of the resentment to which he responded. Instead, he chose to couple her present reaction, her resentment of her maid, with her present perception of her maid as mother. Rogers could have emphasized the feelings, the anger and loathing that Mrs. Ett seemed to feel for the maid. Instead, Rogers was interested in the connection between the relationship that Mrs. Ett saw between her present reaction and elements of her world (maid's efficiency and being a mother).

In S245, Mrs. Ett is trying to decide what to do about the maid and is weighing the various alternative courses of action and the feelings to which each is connected. Rogers simply reflects these alternatives without trying to heighten their feeling aspects.

In S246 Mrs. Ett repeats the connection between the tension of the past few days and the realization of the maid as a mother figure. In addition, she describes her ambivalence about the mother figure. It is this ambivalence which is responded to by Rogers, not her feeling of tension. Again, it is her present experience ("You feel pulled two ways") to the content of her perception ("as you do with your mother") that is of primary importance, not the qualitative or emotional aspects of her tension and struggle.

The Therapist's Congruence

As this period proceeded there was increased specification of what the therapist should do. In 1959, in an important chapter, Rogers (Rogers, 1959) discussed a theory of therapy, personality, and interpersonal relations. Here, among other conditions required for therapy to occur, he specified "that the therapist is congruent in the relationship" (p. 213). This condition, which he also called genuineness, was one of the growing edges of the theory and meant that the therapist should accurately symbolize his or her experience of himself or herself in the relationship. This might include the therapist's limits in the relationship as it did in this brief excerpt from the case of Miss Tir (Rogers, 1951).

> C (*client*): I think emotionally I'm dying for sexual intercourse, but I don't do anything about it. The thing I want is to have sexual intercourse with you. I don't ask you 'cause I'm afraid you would have to be non-directive.
>
> T (*therapist*): You have this awful tension, and want so much to have relations with me.
>
> C: (Goes on in this vein. Finally asks the therapist.) Can't we do something about it? This tension is awful! Will you relieve this tension? Can you give me a direct answer? I think it might help both of us.
>
> T: The answer would be no. I can understand how *desperately* you feel, but I would not be willing to do that.[7]

Note that the therapist does not say that he is doing this for the good of the client. Instead, he takes responsibility for his own behavior after indicating his understanding of the client's experience.

Unconditional Positive Regard

In an article on the necessary and sufficient conditions of therapeutic change, Rogers (1957) set out as one of the conditions of the therapy process that the therapist must experience unconditional positive regard toward the client. The therapist should not approve, or disapprove, of some things that the client talks about more than others, even if what the client is talking about could, in another framework, be seen as destructive. Take, as an example, the following excerpt (Rogers, 1951) from the case of Miss Gill who has for a number of interviews been sounding quite hopeless about herself.

> C(*client*): I've never said this to anyone before—but I've thought for such a long time—This is a terrible thing to say, but if I could just—well (short bitter laugh; pause), if I could find some glorious cause that I could give my life for I would be happy. I cannot be the kind of person I want to be. I guess maybe I haven't the guts—or the strength—to kill myself—and if someone would relieve me of the responsibility—or I would be in an accident—I—I just don't want to live.
>
> T(*therapist*): At the present time things look so black to you that you really can't see much point in living.

---

[7]From *Client-Centered Therapy: Its Current Practice, Implications, and Theory* (p. 211) by C. R. Rogers, 1951, Boston: Houghton Mifflin. Copyright 1951 by Houghton Mifflin. Reprinted by permission. (Emphasis in original.)

C: Yes—I wish I had never started this therapy. I was happy when I was living in my dream world. There I could be the kind of person I wanted to be—But now—There is such a wide, wide gap—between my ideal—and what I am. I wish people hated me. I try to make them hate. Because then I could turn away from them and blame them—but no—It's all in my hands—here is my life—and I either accept the fact that I am totally worthless—or I fight whatever it is that holds me in this terrible conflict. And I suppose if I accepted the fact that I am worthless, then I could go away someplace—and retreat back to the security of my dream world where I could do things, have clever friends, be a pretty wonderful sort of person.

T: It's a really tough struggle—digging into this like you are—and at times the shelter of your dream world looks more attractive and comfortable.

C: My dream world or suicide.

T: Your dream world or something more permanent than dreams.

C: Yes. (A long pause. Complete change of voice.) So I don't see why I should waste your time—coming in twice a week—I'm not worth it—What do you think?

T: It's up to you, Gill—It isn't wasting my time—I'd be glad to see you—whenever you come—but it's how you feel about it—it's up to you.

C: You are not going to suggest I come in oftener? You're not alarmed and think I ought to come in every day—until I get out of this?

T: I believe you are able to make your own decision. I'll see you whenever you want to come.

C: (Note of awe in her voice.) I don't believe you are alarmed about—I see—I may be afraid of myself—but you aren't afraid of me.

T: You say you may be afraid of yourself—and are wondering why I don't seem afraid for you?[8]

There were two aspects of this situation that the therapist accepted unconditionally. One was the client's discussion of, and positive feelings about, suicide. Even though the therapist occasionally hedged his response to the client, for example, by referring to her attitudes as existing "at the present time," in the main he accepted her negative feelings. Even more impressive was his acceptance of her discussion about having less therapy and his belief that she could make her own decision.

In summary, this period started with a strong emphasis on the centrality of the world of the client. Rogers defined his basic hypothesis, his faith in the individual's capability. Rogers then became more explicit about the actualizing tendency as being the motivating force in the change of the

---

[8]From *Client-Centered Therapy: Its Current Practice, Implications and Theory* (pp. 46–47) by C. R. Rogers, 1951, Boston: Houghton Mifflin. Copyright 1951 by Houghton Mifflin. Reprinted by permission.

client. This was followed by his becoming more specific about what the therapist should do to aid this tendency.

THIRD PERIOD

The third period started with the publication of *On Becoming a Person* in 1961. The book, a collection of papers by Rogers, has a theme, stated in the title, that conveys the direction in which Rogers moved from that time on. In the earlier periods the aim was that the person become congruent with his or her experience, that the self become based on this experience. In the latter period, the goal was to become a person, to become one's experiential organism. It is no longer sufficient to know your experience. Now you *become* your experience. "To be that self that one truly is," one of Rogers' statements of the goal, involves the absence of a self-monitoring experience. Thus, Rogers says, "Consciousness, instead of being the watch-man over a dangerous and unpredictable lot of impulses, of which few can be permitted to see the light of day, becomes the comfortable inhabitant of a society of impulses and feelings and thoughts, which are discovered to be very satisfactorily self-governing when not fearfully guarded" (Rogers, 1961 p. 119).

In the following example a graduate student has been puzzling over a vague feeling which he gradually identifies as a frightened feeling, a fear of failing, of not getting his PhD. The interview continues:

> C: I was kind of letting it seep through. But I also tied it in with you and my relationship with you. And one thing I feel about it is a kind of fear of going away; or that's another thing—it's so hard to get hold of—there's kind of two pulling feelings about it. Or two "me's" somehow. One is the scared me that wants to hold on to things, and that one I guess I can feel clearly right now. You know, I kinda need things to hold on to—and I feel kind of scared.
>
> T: M-hm. That's something you can feel right this minute, and have been feeling and perhaps are feeling in regard to our relationship too.
>
> C: Won't you let me *have* this, because, you know, I kinda *need* it. I can be so lonely and scared without it.
>
> T: M-hm, M-hm. Let me hang on to this because I'd be terribly scared if I didn't. Let me *hold* on to it. (Pause)
>
> C: It's kinda the same thing—*Won't* you let me have my thesis or my Ph.D. so then . . . Cause I kinda *need* that little world. I mean . . .
>
> T: In both instances it's kind of a pleading thing isn't it? Let me *have* this because I need it so *badly*. I'd be awfully frightened without it. (long pause.)

C: I get a sense of—I somehow can't get much further—It's the kind of *pleading* little boy, somehow even—What's this gesture of begging? (Putting hands together as if in prayer) Isn't it funny? Cause that—

T: You put your hands in sort of supplication.

C: Ya, that's right! Won't you do for me, kinda—Oh, that's *terrible*! Who, me, *beg*?[9]

In this excerpt, the client *becomes* his feeling of begging. There is no separation between the self and the experience. In the therapy hour he became his process of experiencing. For Rogers, successful therapy resulted in movement away from the rigid structure of the self. The person becomes the process of experiencing. At first, this happens only for a short while and then the structural self reappears. This can be seen in the excerpt where after the client becomes his experiencing, his old self reappears and passes judgment.

The person who emerges from this process of becoming one's experience has several characteristics. He or she is *open to experience*. That is, the person is able to take in reality without distortion. A self structure does not interpose itself between reality and the person. Late in therapy a man (C.) is reporting on the changes he feels has occurred as a result of therapy

C: It doesn't seem to me it would be possible for anyone to report all the changes you feel. But I have certainly felt recently that I have more respect for, more objectivity for my physical makeup. I mean I don't expect too much of myself. This is how it works out: It feels to me that in the past I used to fight a certain tiredness I felt after supper. Well, now I am pretty sure I really *am* tired—that I am not making myself tired—that I am just physiologically lower. It seems to me I was constantly criticizing my tiredness.[10]

A second characteristic of the person who emerges from therapy is that the person comes to *place trust in one's organism*. That is, the person is able to make decisions by weighing and balancing the data from all levels of his or herself, without being afraid of the mistakes that might result from his or her emotions.

A third characteristic is a change in the *locus of evaluation*. The person looks less and less to others for approval and disapproval and for standards to live by. Instead, the person increasingly feels that the locus of evaluation is within the self, that he or she is the locus of choice and evaluation.

Another characteristic of the emerging person is the *willingness to be*

---

[9]From *On Becoming a Person* (pp. 112–113) by C. R. Rogers, 1961, Boston: Houghton Mifflin. Copyright 1961 by Houghton Mifflin. Reprinted by permission. (Emphasis in original.)
[10]From *On Becoming a Person* (p. 116) by C. R. Rogers, 1961, Boston: Houghton Mifflin. Copyright 1961 by Houghton Mifflin. Reprinted by permission. (Emphasis in original.)

a process. The individual changes from wanting to be a product, such as something or someone "successful," to being a person in process, that is, to be a stream of becoming rather than a finished product. Thus, a client at the end of therapy says

> I haven't finished the process of integrating and reorganizing myself, but that's only confusing and not discouraging, now that I realize this is a continuing process . . . . It's exciting, sometimes upsetting, but deeply encouraging to feel yourself in action, apparently knowing where you are going even though you don't always consciously know where that is."[11]

The therapist also became one's experience. This is what is meant by *congruence*, a concept that became increasingly important. Here the therapist is in the relationship without facade. The therapist is openly being the feelings that are flowing in himself at the moment.

For Rogers, the person's experiencing was occurring continually and automatically. The goal was to become this experiencing. The emphasis on the primacy of the process of experiencing led, in some quarters, to techniques such as focusing (Gendlin, 1981), which are thought to aid the person to get in touch with his or her experiencing and which has led some therapists to practice experiential, rather than the more orthodox client-centered therapy.

FOURTH PERIOD

The fourth phase covers the 1970–1980 period. It is the period in which the basic hypotheses and attitudes about psychotherapy were used in other contexts. It emphasizes the application of the principles of *client-centered therapy* to education, to groups, and to peace and conflict resolution. Carl Rogers wrote two editions of *Freedom to Learn*, (1969, 1983), *Carl Rogers on Encounter Groups* (1970), and a number of articles on peace and conflict resolution. The phrase, *person-centered approach*, becomes meaningful and appropriate in this phase of the development of the client-centered movement, as client-centered principles are applied to education, industry, and other human relations contexts.

---

[11]From *On Becoming a Person* (p. 122) by C. R. Rogers, 1961, Boston: Houghton Mifflin. Copyright 1961 by Houghton Mifflin. Reprinted by permission.

Clear examples of the applicability of the client-centered philosophy and methodology to other interpersonal contexts were the changes Rogers made to the practice of teaching. One of this chapter's authors, Nathaniel Raskin, had been a student in many of Rogers' courses at Ohio State University in 1940–41. Rogers was very respectful of students, but he clearly directed the course and assumed responsibility for the evaluation of the student. Later, at the University of Chicago, "Dr. Rogers" offered himself as just one learning resource, and even though he came across as an extremely competent and self-confident psychologist, he had clearly shifted the responsibility for learning and grading to the student. The initial reaction of most students was doubt and even resentment, but most came to believe that students were responsible for their own education.

Rogers' twelve years at Chicago (1945–1957) and six at the University of Wisconsin (1957–1963) deepened his convictions about student-centered learning. Moving to La Jolla, California, in 1964 to the Western Behavioral Sciences Institute accelerated his interest in going beyond the psychotherapy office and even the classroom to further develop and apply his ideas.

In his foreword to the first edition of *Freedom to Learn* (1969), Rogers wrote, "The conceptions that I wanted to present broadened into the theoretical and philosophical realms" (p. v). This was a complete contrast to the Rogers at Ohio State who disdained theory in favor of what worked. He makes clear later in the Foreword the extent and the depth of his trepidation.

> . . . Let me state briefly some of the questions which concern me. . . . Can education fulfill its central role in dealing effectively with the explosive racial tensions which are steadily increasing? . . . Can education prepare us to live responsibly, communicatively, in a world of increasing international tensions, increasingly irrational nationalism? . . . Can the educational system as a whole, the most traditional, conservative, rigid, bureaucratic institution of our time . . . come to grips with the real problems of modern life?[12]

So profound was Rogers' feeling about traditional education that he characterized the adjectives in the preceding sentence as descriptive rather than critical. In the Prologue to the same book, he amplifies his views,

> . . . in the vast majority of our schools, at all educational levels,

---

[12]From *Freedom to Learn* (pp. vi–vii) by C. R. Rogers, 1969, New York: Macmillan. Copyright 1969 by Bell & Howell Company. Reprinted by permission of Merrill, an imprint of Macmillan Publishing Company.

we are locked into a traditional and conventional approach which makes significant learning improbable if not impossible. When we put together in one scheme such elements as a *prescribed curriculum, similar assignments for all students, lecturing* as almost the only mode of instruction, *standard tests* by which all students are externally evaluated, and *instructor-chosen grades* as the measure of learning, then we can almost guarantee that meaningful learning will be at an absolute minimum. [13]

Rogers described the way he changed his way of operating in the class at the University of Chicago and how he introduced a class (Rogers, 1983):

> I ceased to be a teacher. It wasn't easy. It happened rather gradually, but as I began to trust students, I found they did incredible things in their communication with each other, in their learning of content material in the course, in blossoming out as growing human beings. Most of all they gave me courage to be myself more freely, and this led to profound interaction. They told me their feelings, they raised questions I had never thought about. I began to sparkle with emerging ideas that were new and exciting to me, but also, I found, to them. I believe I passed some sort of crucial divide when I was able to begin a course with a statement something like this: This course has the title *Personality Theory* (or whatever), but what we do with this course is up to us. We can build it around the goals we want to achieve, within that very general area. We can decide mutually how we want to handle these bugaboos of exams and grades. I have many resources on tap, and I can help you find others. I believe I am one of the resources, and I am available to the extent that you wish. But this is our class. So what do we want to make of it? This kind of statement said in effect, we are free to learn what we wish, as we wish. It made the whole climate of the classroom completely different. Though at the time I had never thought of phrasing it this way, I changed at that point from being a teacher and evaluator, to being a facilitator of learning—[a] very different occupation. [14]

In his two editions of *Freedom to Learn*, (1969, 1983) Rogers illustrated the implementation of person-centered education by a number of individuals in a variety of settings: a 6th-grade class, a course on the fundamentals of psychology, a secondary school French class, and a special project in one school which allowed pupils ranging from slow learners in the 7th grade to gifted 11th-graders to spend about one quarter of their school time learning what they wanted individually to learn, in their own way, to supplement and synthesize their regular schedule of required subjects.

---

[13]From *Freedom to Learn* (p. 5) by C. R. Rogers, 1969, New York: Macmillan. Copyright 1969 by Bell & Howell Company. Reprinted by permission of Merrill, an imprint of Macmillan Publishing Company. (Emphasis in original.)

[14]From *Freedom to Learn for the 80's* (p. 26) by C. R. Rogers, 1983, Columbus, OH: Charles E. Merrill. Copyright 1983 by Charles E. Merrill. Reprinted by permission.

In these diverse settings, a host of methods for implementing student-centered education are described. As in the field of psychotherapy, Rogers believed in the importance of backing up a theory or philosophy or belief system with specific practices. At the same time, the diversity of methods which are presented indicate the primacy of principles for Rogers.

Rogers believed strongly that the power relationship which exists in traditional education must be reversed in order for learning and personal growth to occur optimally. He also believed that the most fruitful education involves an integration of cognition and emotions. Therefore, he advocated both self-directed learning of external subject matter and the use of intensive groups in which individuals exchange feelings in the process of interacting as persons.

Such groups for administrators and teachers were key elements in two systemwide educational experiments in which Rogers was involved. He described (Rogers, 1983) how Superintendent Newman Walker employed groups in his attempt to revive the public schools of Louisville, Kentucky.

> During a six-month period in the spring and summer, he enrolled 1600 members of the system in week-long human relations workshops—intensive group experiences held in a residential retreat setting. Included were Walker himself, the whole board of education, principals, teachers, central office staff and clerical workers. In these labs people came to know each other as persons and to confront differences. They communicated informally and learned about themselves and how they were perceived by others. They were more open in expressing their feelings. The cognitive was not ignored. They learned new ways of working with students, new ways of promoting learning.[15]

Encounter groups were also used extensively by Rogers and associates from the Center for Studies of the Person in the Immaculate Heart system in Los Angeles.

Person-Centered Groups

It did not take long for the principles of client-centered therapy to be applied to group situations. Before the end of the 1940s there were client-centered therapy groups and client-centered play groups for children.

In the 1950s and 1960s, the client-centered approach was used in therapy groups for blind and other physically handicapped children, parents of handicapped children, and staff development groups for mental health professionals, to name some of the populations.

---

[15]From *Freedom to Learn for the 80's* (p. 228) by C. R. Rogers, 1983, Columbus, OH: Charles E. Merrill. Copyright 1983 by Charles E. Merrill. Reprinted by permission.

Typically, such groups would meet once a week for an hour and a half. *The basic contribution of the leader was an attitude of respect for the participants, implemented by disciplined empathic listening and communication.* This often resulted in an atmosphere characterized by the necessary and sufficient conditions formulated by Rogers in 1957. (Raskin, 1986, p. 278. Emphasis in original)

With the advent of the intensive group, a new chapter was begun in the history of client-centered therapy and the person-centered approach. Intensive groups helped Rogers to learn increasingly to *operate in terms of his feelings.* He responded empathically, particularly to feelings of hurt. He thought it important to express persistent feelings toward an individual or group. He valued his *awareness* of different feelings and the choice of expressing them or not, if it felt inappropriate. He wished to express positive or loving feelings as well as negative ones; it was difficult personally for him to express affection or anger in a group, but he grew in his ability to do this and believed it was helpful to the group process.

When Rogers confronted individuals in a group, he did so on the specifics of their behavior, and with feelings he was able to claim as his own: "I don't like the way you chatter on. Seems to me you give each message three or four times. I wish you would stop when you've completed your message" (Rogers, 1970 p. 58).

Although he had to overcome a feeling of professional conscience in doing so, Rogers favored *expressing a current personal problem* or feeling of distress in a group. He believed that if he held back, he would not listen as well and that, in addition, the group would pick up his disturbance and might feel they were somehow to blame.

Being sensitive to artificiality, Rogers *eschewed planned procedures, exercises,* or *gimmicks* in a group. He distinguished this kind of planned operation by the leader from something that might arise spontaneously in the group, like a participant's suggesting that role-playing might be helpful at a particular point. Rogers wrote that *spontaneity* was the most precious, and at the same time elusive, element that he knew.

Rogers also *avoided interpretive or process comments.* He did not wish to make group members self-conscious or to interfere with the spontaneous experience of the group. He viewed interpretations as high-level guesses that would also place him in an unwanted authoritative role. Similarly, he believed in making use of the therapeutic power of the whole group if a serious situation arose, such as a bizarre behavior on the part of a group member. He felt there was therapeutic advantage in a participant's relating to the problem member as a person over a leader's tendency to relate to the member as an object.

Finally, Rogers wrote of his increased ability to be *physically expressive* in a group and to provide *physical contact* (Rogers, 1970) "when this seems real and spontaneous and appropriate . . . When a person is suffering and I feel like going over and putting my arm around him, I do just that. . . . I do not try consciously to promote this kind of behavior. I admire the younger people who are looser and freer in this respect" (p. 63).

Peace and Conflict Resolution

As early as 1948, Rogers proposed the application of client-centered principles to dealing with social tensions (Rogers, 1948). In 1960, he suggested that a person-centered approach to the conduct of foreign policy might result in a much more fruitful kind of dialogue than is customary between nations. It would include a frank expression of selfish interests as well as idealistic purposes, of mistakes as well as achievements. His hypothesis was that a more honest initiative of this nature would result in a more honest response and a much more satisfying way of relating to other nations.

Sanford led conflict resolution groups with Rogers in South Africa and the Soviet Union. Rogers' peace and conflict resolution efforts were built on a foundation of years of experience of learning to build community in large intensive groups, work he shared with Bowen, Henderson, McGaw, Miller (later O'Hara), Rice, N. Rogers, Solomon, Swenson, and J. K. Wood, and in cross-cultural meetings in Europe, Asia, and Latin America with Devonshire, Zucconi, Tausch, Thorne, Lietaer, Segrera, and Tsuge.

Rogers' Collaborators

Rogers' students also made vital contributions to theory and practice at Ohio State, Chicago, and the University of Wisconsin. During the Ohio State years, Covner (1942, 1944a, 1944b), a student of Rogers at both the University of Rochester and Ohio State, supplied the technical expertise for making phonographic recordings of interviews and then did research which showed their superiority over notes from memory. Porter (1943) completed a doctoral dissertation at Ohio State in 1941 by demonstrating that a system of classifying counselor responses in electronically recorded interviews could be used reliably and could bring out differences between counseling methods. Snyder (1945) developed categories for classifying both counselor and client responses in nondirective therapy and obtained findings which supported nondirective hypotheses (e.g., the acceptance by the counselor of client attitudes and feelings was followed, regularly, by client insights). Raimy (1948) was the author of another Ohio State dissertation in which he developed a theory of the self and applied it to self-references in recorded interviews. Virginia Axline, Arthur Combs, Charles Curran, Thomas Gordon, Donald Grummon, Nicholas Hobbs, Nathaniel Raskin, and Bernard Steinzor were some of the other Ohio State students who made important research contributions, many of which were published as books. Seeman and Raskin (1953) have summarized much of this research.

At the University of Chicago in the late 1940s, Raskin, Seeman, Haigh, Hoffman, Sheerer, and Stock analyzed the data from ten fully recorded cases and published the results in an entire issue of the *Journal of Consulting Psychology* (Rogers, Raskin et al., 1949). In the same period, Aidman (1951) and Bowman (1951) carried out studies which showed an increasing congruence between the client's present and ideal self as expressed in the course of nondirective therapy. Seeman was the coordinator of research at the University of Chicago Counseling Center during the time of an even more sophisticated cooperative effort backed by the Rockefeller Foundation and reported in a book edited by Rogers and Dymond (1954). This project was regarded as state-of-the-art in the field of psychotherapy research and included a Q-technique investigation by Butler and Haigh (1954) hypothesizing that client-centered therapy would reduce the difference between the perceived self and ideal self.

Dymond (1954), using self-sorts, measured adjustment changes over therapy. Rudikoff (1954) compared changes in the concepts of the self, of the ordinary person, and of the self-ideal. Seeman (1954) studied counselor judgments of process and outcome. Gordon and Cartwright (1954) researched the effect of psychotherapy upon certain attitudes toward others. Tougas (1954) showed ethnocentrism to be a limiting factor in verbal therapy. Grummon (1954) studied personality changes as a function of time.

Other students and collaborators at Chicago were Barrett-Lennard, who devised the Relationship Inventory still widely used in research on psychotherapy of diverse orientations (1986), Bown, Gendlin, Shlien, Standal, Streich, and Zimring. Bown (1951) and Streich (1951) helped develop the concept of a freely functioning therapist. Gendlin and Zimring (1955) examined the dimensions of experiencing and their change. Shlien (1964) compared time-limited, client-centered, and Adlerian therapy. Standal (1954) contributed a doctoral dissertation on positive regard, which helped conceptualize unconditional positive regard as one of the three "necessary and sufficient" therapist-offered conditions.

During Rogers' tenure at the University of Wisconsin from 1957 to 1963, the client-centered hypothesis was tested within a population of hospitalized patients diagnosed as schizophrenic; it was believed that "the greater the degree to which the conditions of therapy exist in the relationship, the greater will be the evidence of therapeutic process or movement in the client" (Kiesler, Klein, & Mathieu, 1967, p. 187). Rogers (1958) and Rablen had developed a Process Scale, and Gendlin and Tomlinson a scale of experiencing (Gendlin & Tomlinson, 1967, p. 509), regarded as a central component of process change. This large-scale project with schizophrenic subjects was reported in a volume edited by Rogers, Gendlin, Kiesler, and Truax (1967). Others who contributed to the development of the research design and the scales of measuring therapist conditions and patient process and who analyzed the data collected by these scales, included Ginzberg, Moursand, Schoeninger, Stoler, van der Veen, and Waskow.

Rogers' theory of therapy and of personality are important elements of basic texts in psychology, psychotherapy, and personality theory. The concepts of self and empathy and the client-centered conceptualization of the psychotherapeutic relationship have had an impact on the theory and practice of orientations as diverse as psychoanalytic and behavior modification. Self-esteem has become a concept with which the general population is conversant. Activities such as parent effectiveness training, peer counseling, and hot lines are based on empathic listening in the Rogerian tradition.

Several books published recently include summaries of theory and research. In *Client-Centered Therapy and the Person-Centered Approach* (Levant & Shlien, 1984), many aspects of Rogers' therapy were examined. Lietaer (1984) was concerned with unconditional regard and Bozarth (1984) with the reflection of feelings. Seeman (1984) was concerned with the fully functioning person and Rice (1984) with client tasks. In addition, Barrett-Lennard, Levant, and Guerney each wrote chapters (1984) about family therapy. Hackney and Goodyear were concerned about the client-centered approach to supervision (1984).

There have been some recent discussions of the technique of client or person-centered therapy. Mearns and Thorne's (1988) *Person-Centered Counselling in Action* is the first systematic text since *Client-Centered Therapy* and is proving very valuable for teaching. Raskin and Zimring's 1991 chapter describes the progress of a client over a number of interviews.

Prior to 1980, Rogers had discouraged the institutionalization of client-centered therapy. He hoped to turn people on to their own self-directed patterns, rather than to develop followers or "little Rogerians." This attitude delayed for decades the initiation of an organization or journal promulgating his theories.

In the late 1970s, there was strong pressure both nationally and internationally for organization. Rogers, heeding this pressure, explained his support for the launching of the *Person-Centered Review* in 1986 by David Cain: "There has . . . developed a large number of people in many nations—therapists, teachers, business people, doctors, social workers, researchers, lay people, pastors—who have a strong interest in the continuing development of a client-centered/person-centered approach" (Rogers, 1986 p. 4).

The *Review* has published articles about many aspects of client-centered therapy. In addition, *Client-Centered and Experiential Psychotherapy in the Nineties* (Lietaer, Rombauts, & Van Balen, 1990) contains many papers about clinical problems of various populations. These sources have included papers about the client-centered response (Patterson, 1990; Zimring, 1990) as well as papers about Carl Rogers and his development (Bozarth, 1990; Cain, 1987; Raskin, 1990; Seeman, 1990). Also included are papers about the use of the client-centered or person-centered approach with various populations. These are concerned with working with children and child therapy (Boukydis, 1990; Ellinwood, 1989; Gordon, 1988; Santen, 1990); family and couple therapy (Anderson, 1989a, 1989b; Bozarth & Shanks, 1989; Esser & Schneider, 1990; Gaylin, 1990; Rombauts & Devriendt, 1990); working with disturbed clients (Elliot *et al.*, 1990; Hamelinck, 1990; Prouty, 1990; Prouty & Pietrzak, 1988; Teusch, 1990), and working with clients who are working with fears of death and dying (Tausch, 1988).

Carl Rogers died in February 1987, at the age of 85. The first International Conference on Client-Centered and Experimental Psychotherapy convened September 12–16, 1988, in Leuven, Belgium (Lietaer, Rombauts, & Van Balen, 1990). Yearly international meetings have continued, following the first successful conferences.

REFERENCES

Aidman, T. (1951). *An objective study of the changing relationship between the present self and the ideal self pictures as expressed by the client in nondirective psychotherapy.* Unpublished PhD dissertation, University of Chicago.

Anderson, W. J. (1989a). Client/person-centered approaches to couple and family therapy: Expanding theory and practice. *Person-Centered Review, 4,* 245–247.

Anderson, W. J. (1989b). Family therapy in the client-centered tradition: A legacy in the narrative mode. *Person-Centered Review, 4,* 295–307.

Barrett-Lennard, G. T. (1984). The world of family relationships: Theory and research. In R. F. Levant & J. M. Shlien (Eds.), *Client-centered therapy and the person-centered approach* (pp. 222–242). New York: Praeger.

Barrett-Lennard, G. T. (1986). The relationship inventory now: Issues and advances in theory, method, and use. In L. S. Greenberg & W. M. Pinsof (Eds.), *The psychotherapeutic process: A research handbook* (pp. 439–476). New York: Guilford.

Boukydis, C. F. Z. (1990). Client-centered/experiential practice with parents and infant. In G. Lietaer, J. Rombauts, R. Van Balen (Eds.), *Client-centered and experiential psychotherapy in the nineties* (pp. 797–811). Leuven, Belgium: Leuven University Press.

Bowman, P. H. (1951). *A measure of discrepancy between different areas of the self-concept.* Unpublished PhD dissertation, University of Chicago.

Bown, O. H. (1951). *An investigation of therapeutic relationship in client-centered psychotherapy.* Unpublished PhD dissertation, University of Chicago.

Bozarth, J. D. (1984). Beyond reflection: Emergent modes of empathy. In R. F. Levant & J. M. Shlien (Eds.), *Client-centered therapy and the person-centered approach* (pp. 59–75). New York: Praeger.

Bozarth, J. D., & Shanks, A. (1989). Person-centered group therapy. *Person-Centered Review, 4,* 280–294.

Bozarth, J. D. (1990). The evolution of Carl Rogers as a therapist. *Person-Centered Review, 5,* 387–393.

Butler, J. M., & Haigh, G. V. (1954). Changes in the relation between self-concepts and ideal concepts consequent upon client-centered counseling. In C. R. Rogers & R. F. Dymond (Eds.), *Psychotherapy and personality change* (pp. 55–75). Chicago: University of Chicago Press.

Cain, D. J. (1987). Carl Rogers's life in review. *Person-Centered Review, 2,* 476–506.

Covner, B. J. (1942). Studies in phonographic recordings of verbal material: I and II. *Journal of Consulting Psychology, 6,* 105–113, 149–153.

Covner, B. J. (1944a). Studies in phonographic recordings of verbal material: III. The completeness and accuracy of counseling interview reports. *Journal of General Psychology, 30,* 181–203.

Covner, B. J. (1944b). Studies in phonographic recordings of verbal material: IV. Written reports of interviews. *Journal of Applied Psychology, 28,* 181–203.

Dymond, R. F. (1954). Adjustment changes over therapy from self-sorts. In C. R. Rogers & R. F. Dymond (Eds.), *Psychotherapy and personality change* (pp.167–195). Chicago: University of Chicago Press.

Ellinwood, C. (1989). The young child in person-centered family therapy. *Person-Centered Review, 4,* 256–262.

Elliot, R., Clark, C., Kemeny, V., Wexler, M. M., Mack, C., & Brinkerhoff, J. (1990). The impact of experiential therapy on depression: The first ten cases. In G. Lietaer, J. Rombauts, R. Van Balen (Eds.), *Client-centered and experiential psychotherapy in the nineties* (pp. 549–578). Leuven/Louvain, Belgium: Leuven University Press.

Esser, U., & Schneider, I. (1990). Client-centered partnership therapy as relationship therapy. In G. Lietaer, J. Rombauts, & R. Van Balen (Eds.), *Client-*

centered and experiential psychotherapy in the nineties (pp. 829–846). Leuven, Belgium: Leuven University Press.

Gaylin, N. L. (1990). Family-centered therapy. In G. Lietaer, J. Rombauts, & R. Van Balen (Eds.), *Client-centered and experiential psychotherapy in the nineties* (pp. 813–828). Leuven, Belgium: Leuven University Press.

Gendlin, E. (1981). *Focusing.* New York: Everest House.

Gendlin, E., & Tomlinson, T. M. (1967). A scale for the rating of experiencing. In C. Rogers, E. Gendlin, D. Kiesler, & C. Truax (Eds.), *The therapeutic relationship and its impact: A study of psychotherapy with schizophrenics* (pp. 589–592). Madison: University of Wisconsin Press.

Gendlin, E., & Zimring, F. (1955). The qualities or dimensions of experiencing and their change. *Counseling Center Discussion Papers 1, #3.* Chicago: University of Chicago Counseling Center.

Gordon, T. (1988). The case against disciplining children at home or in school. *Person-Centered Review, 3,* 59–85.

Gordon, T., & Cartwright, D. S. (1954). The effect of psychotherapy upon certain attitudes toward others. In C. R. Rogers & R. F. Dymond (Eds.), *Psychotherapy and personality change* (pp. 167–195). Chicago: University of Chicago Press.

Grummon, D. L. (1954). Personality changes as a function of time in persons motivated for therapy. In C. R. Rogers & R. F. Dymond (Eds.), *Psychotherapy and personality change* (pp. 238–258). Chicago: University of Chicago Press.

Guerney, B. G., Jr. (1984). Contributions of client-centered therapy to filial, marital, and family relationship enhancement. In R. F. Levant & J. M. Shlien (Eds.), *Client-centered therapy and the person-centered approach* (pp. 261–277). New York: Praeger.

Hackney, H., & Goodyear, R. K. (1984). Carl Rogers's client-centered approach to supervision. In R. F. Levant & J. M. Shlien (Eds.), *Client-centered therapy and the person-centered approach* (pp. 278–296). New York: Praeger.

Hamelinck, L. (1990). Client-centered therapy and psychiatric crisis intervention following suicide attempts. In G. Lietaer, J. Rombauts, & R. Van Balen (Eds.), *Client-centered and experiential psychotherapy in the nineties* (pp. 579–597). Leuven, Belgium: Leuven University Press.

Kiesler, D. J., Klein, M. H., & Mathieu, P. L. (1967). Therapist conditions and patient process. In C. R. Rogers, E. T. Gendlin, D. J. Kiesler, & C. B. Truax (Eds.), *The therapeutic relationship and its impact: A study of psychotherapy with schizophrenics* (pp. 187–220). Madison: University of Wisconsin Press.

Levant, R. F., & Shlien, J. M. (1984). *Client-centered therapy and the person-centered approach.* New York: Praeger.

Levant, R. F. (1984). From persons to system: Two perspectives. In R. F. Levant & J. M. Shlien (Eds.), *Client-centered therapy and the person-centered approach* (pp. 243–260). New York: Praeger.

Lietaer, G. (1984). Unconditional positive regard: A controversial basic attitude in client-centered therapy. In R. F. Levant & J. M. Shlien (Eds.), *Client-*

centered therapy and the person-centered approach (pp. 41–58). New York: Praeger.

Lietaer, G., Rombauts, J., & Van Balen, R. (1990). *Client-centered and experiential psychotherapy in the nineties.* Leuven, Belgium: Leuven University Press.

Mearns, D., & Thorne, B. (1988). *Person-centred counselling in action.* London: Sage.

Patterson, C. H. (1990). Involuntary clients: A person-centered view. *Person-Centered Review, 5,* 316–320.

Porter, E. H., Jr. (1943). The development and evaluation of a measure of counseling interview procedures. *Educational and Psychological Measurement, 3,* 105–126, 215–238.

Prouty, G. F. (1990). Pre-therapy: A theoretical evolution in the person-centered/ experiential psychotherapy of schizophrenia and retardation. In G. Lietaer, J. Rombauts, & R. Van Balen (Eds.), *Client-centered and experiential psychotherapy in the nineties* (pp. 645–658). Leuven, Belgium: Leuven University Press.

Prouty, G. F., & Pietrzak, S. (1988). The pre-therapy method applied to persons experiencing hallucinatory images. *Person-Centered Review, 3,* 426–441.

Raimy, V. C. (1948). Self reference in counseling interviews. *Journal of Consulting Psychology, 12,* 153–163.

Raskin, N. J. (1986). Client-centered group psychotherapy, part I. *Person-Centered Review, 1,* 272–290.

Raskin, N. J. (1990). The first 50 years and the next 10. *Person-Centered Review, 5,* 364–372.

Raskin, N. J., & Zimring, F. (1991). Person-centered therapy. In R. J. Corsini (Ed.), *Five therapists and one client* (pp. 59–102). Itasca, IL: Peacock.

Rice, L. N. (1984). Client tasks in client-centered therapy. In R. F. Levant & J. M. Shlien (Eds.), *Client-centered therapy and the person-centered approach* (pp. 182–202). New York: Praeger.

Rogers, C. R. (1939). *The clinical treatment of the problem child.* Boston: Houghton Mifflin.

Rogers, C. R. (1942). *Counseling and psychotherapy.* Boston: Houghton Mifflin.

Rogers, C. R. (1948). *Dealing with social tensions: A presentation of client-centered counseling as a means of handling interpersonal conflict.* New York: Hinds, Hayden, & Eldredge.

Rogers, C. R. (1951). *Client-centered therapy: Its current practice, implications, and theory.* Boston: Houghton Mifflin.

Rogers, C. R. (1958). A process conception of psychotherapy. *American Psychologist, 13,* 142–149.

Rogers, C. R. (1959). A theory of therapy, personality, and interpersonal relationships, as developed in the client-centered framework. In S. Koch (Ed.), *Psychology: A study of science: Vol. 3. Formulations of the person and the social context.* New York: McGraw-Hill.

Rogers, C. R. (1961). *On becoming a person.* Boston: Houghton Mifflin.

Rogers, C. R. (1969). *Freedom to learn: A view of what education might become.* Columbus, OH: Charles E. Merrill.

Rogers, C. R. (1970). *Carl Rogers on encounter groups.* New York: Harper & Row.

Rogers, C. R. (1983). *Freedom to learn for the 80's.* Columbus, OH: Charles E. Merrill.

Rogers, C. R. (1986). A commentary from Carl Rogers. *Person-Centered Review, 1,* 3–5.

Rogers, C. R., & Dymond, R. F. (Eds.) (1954). *Psychotherapy and personality change.* Chicago: University of Chicago Press.

Rogers, C. R., Gendlin, E. T., Kiesler, D. V., & Truax, C. (Eds.) (1967). *The therapeutic relationship and its impact: A study of psychotherapy with schizophrenics.* Madison: University of Wisconsin Press.

Rogers, C. R., Raskin, N. J., Seeman, J., Sheerer, E., Stock, D., Haigh, G., Hoffman, A., & Carr, A. (1949). A coordinated research in psychotherapy. *Journal of Consulting Psychology, 13,* 149–220.

Rombauts, J., & Devriendt, M. (1990). Conjoint couple therapy in client-centered practice. In G. Lietaer, J. Rombauts, & R. Van Balen (Eds.), *Client-centered and experiential psychotherapy in the nineties* (pp. 847–863). Leuven, Belgium: Leuven University Press.

Rudikoff, E. C. (1954). A comparative study of the changes in the concepts of the self, the ordinary person, and the ideal in eight cases. In C. R. Rogers & R. F. Dymond (Eds.), *Psychotherapy and personality change* (pp. 85–98). Chicago: University of Chicago Press.

Santen, B. (1990). Beyond good and evil: Focusing with early traumatized children and adolescents. In G. Lietaer, J. Rombauts, & R. Van Balen (Eds.), *Client-centered and experiential psychotherapy in the nineties* (pp. 779–796). Leuven, Belgium: Leuven University Press.

Seeman, J. (1954). Counselor judgments of therapeutic process and outcome. In C. R. Rogers & R. F. Dymond (Eds.), *Psychotherapy and personality change* (pp. 99–108). Chicago: University of Chicago Press.

Seeman, J. (1984). The fully functioning person: Theory and research. In R. F. Levant & J. M. Shlien (Eds.), *Client-centered therapy and the person-centered approach* (pp. 131–152). New York: Praeger.

Seeman, J. (1990). Theory as autobiography: The development of Carl Rogers. *Person-Centered Review, 5,* 373–386.

Seeman, J., & Raskin, N. J. (1953). Research perspectives in client-centered therapy. In O. H. Mowrer (Ed.), *Psychotherapy: Theory and research* (pp. 205–234). New York: Ronald Press.

Shlien, J. M. (1964). Comparison of results with different forms of psychotherapy. *American Journal of Psychotherapy, 18,* 15–22.

Snyder, W. U. (1945). An investigation of the nature of nondirective psychotherapy. *Journal of General Psychology, 33,* 193–223.

Standal, S. (1954). *The need for positive regard: A contribution to client-centered theory.* Unpublished PhD thesis, University of Chicago.

Streich, E. R. (1951). *The self-experience of the client-centered therapist.* Unpublished paper, The Counseling Center, University of Chicago.

Tausch, R. (1988). Reappraisal of death and dying after a person-centered behavioral workshop. *Person-Centered Review, 3,* 213–216.

Teusch, L. (1990). Positive effects and limitations of client-centered therapy with schizophrenic patients. In G. Lietaer, J. Rombauts, & R. Van Balen (Eds.), *Client-centered and experiential psychotherapy in the nineties* (pp. 637–644). Leuven, Belgium: Leuven University Press.

Tougas, R. R. (1954). Ethnocentrism as a limiting factor in verbal therapy. In C. R. Rogers & R. F. Dymond (Eds.), *Psychotherapy and personality change* (pp. 196–214). Chicago: University of Chicago Press.

Zimring, F. (1990). A characteristic of Rogers's response to clients. *Person-Centered Review, 5,* 433–448.

20

COGNITIVE THERAPY AND PSYCHOTHERAPY INTEGRATION

DIANE B. ARNKOFF AND CAROL R. GLASS

This chapter will consider the practice of both cognitive therapy and psychotherapy integration. It is fitting to unite these two topics because cognitive therapy itself can be considered an integrative therapy (Alford & Norcross, 1991), combining the behavioral and intrapsychic branches of psychotherapy into a new form of treatment. In fact, the development of cognitive therapy spurred interest in eclectic and integrative approaches to psychotherapy.

We will first present a brief overview of the nature of and early development of cognitive therapies and trace the history of cognitive therapy from rational–emotive therapy (RET) up to more recent constructivist

---

Like our chapter on the practice of behavior therapy in this volume (chapter 18), in preparing this chapter we conducted interviews with a number of the major figures in the development and practice of cognitive therapy and psychotherapy integration. Six of these 1-hour interviews were conducted face-to-face, and 5 were conducted by phone, during November and December, 1989. The experts we interviewed, in alphabetical order, are: Gerald Davison, Albert Ellis, Sol Garfield, Marvin Goldfried, Philip Kendall, Arnold Lazarus, Michael Mahoney, Donald Meichenbaum, Paul Wachtel, G. Terence Wilson, and Barry Wolfe. We wish to thank them for their invaluable assistance. When the name of one of these individuals is mentioned in this chapter, along with a citation to "personal communication, 1989," we are referring to the interviews we conducted.

conceptualizations. The current practice, prevalence, and future of cognitive interventions will also be addressed.

Our second topic is eclectic psychotherapy and psychotherapy integration. We will consider the forces at work behind this most recent movement and trace the development of psychotherapy approaches that have attempted to deviate from those of "pure-form" schools. Surveys on eclectic practice will be a special focus, leading up to a consideration of current and future directions for integrative psychotherapy.

COGNITIVE THERAPY

Opinions differ as to whether cognitive therapy should be considered as an evolution within modern behavior therapy or as a revolution leading to a new point of view. In chapter 18 we discussed the expansion and growth of behavior therapy over the past 25 years. One result of that growth was that *cognitive behavior therapy* or CBT became accepted by many clinicians as part of the behavior therapist's repertoire. Wilson (1978), for example, sees CBT as the result of a gradual shift in behavior therapy away from more simplistic stimulus–response models, but consistent with a core commitment to measurement and procedures derived from experimental psychology and with a focus on the modification of behavior. Mahoney (1977), however, used the term "cognitive revolution" in describing cognitive therapy as part of a paradigm shift in the field of psychology. This new perspective, integrating behavioral and traditional approaches to psychotherapy, recognizes private events and intrapersonal factors along with the importance of environmental variables. In fact, as we will see, the backgrounds of the first leaders in the cognitive therapy field are split between those whose first training was behavioral and those whose first training was psychodynamic.

The historical origins of cognitive therapy can be traced to philosophy, psychological theory, and writings on self-change. The Phrygian stoic philosopher Epictetus (ca. A.D. 55–ca. 135) once maintained that "people are disturbed not by things, but by the view which they take of them." This way of looking at events, along with the writings of Popper, Reichenbach, Kant, and Russell, provided early philosophical underpinnings for Albert Ellis' development of rational–emotive therapy (RET). Ellis also cites Karen Horney's (1950) work on the "tyranny of the shoulds" and that of Alfred Adler (1927) as important influences on RET (Dryden & Ellis, 1988), and has written recently on the history of cognition in psychotherapy (Ellis, 1989). For example, G. A. Kelly's (1955) personal construct theory and Rotter's (1954) expectancy learning theory emphasized cognitive factors as part of larger theories of personality and abnormal behavior. Finally, early "thought management" programs (Carnegie, 1948; Coué, 1922; Dubois 1904/1905; Peale, 1960) dealt with the importance of what people say to themselves.

Beginnings of Modern Cognitive Therapy

Modern cognitive therapy emerged in the mid-1950s when Ellis developed rational–emotive therapy. His *Guide to Rational Living* (Ellis & Harper, 1961) had an important influence on practice. Still, cognitive therapy did not become a strong movement within psychotherapy until the mid-1970s. At that time Beck's *Cognitive Therapy and the Emotional Disorders* (1976), Mahoney's *Cognition and Behavior Modification* (1974), and Meichenbaum's *Cognitive-Behavior Modification* (1977) appeared when clinicians were increasingly looking for a way of conceptualizing and changing inner experience.

Why was there a rapid growth in the 1970s in the number of clinicians interested in cognitive interventions? The clinical motivation for behavior therapists was that they were becoming dissatisfied with techniques that did not target the internal dialogue that they saw their clients engaging in and that seemed to maintain maladaptive behavior. Goldfried (personal communication, 1989) has thus stated that cognitive techniques initially grew more out of clinical need than from experimental findings.

Another important factor was that a "cognitive revolution" was also taking place in experimental psychology (Dember, 1974) as mediational concepts were being developed and investigated. Private events had actually been a part of behavior therapy from the beginning, such as Wolpe's use of imaginal procedures, but an adequate theoretical base to justify cognitive interventions became available only in the 1970s.

The nonmediational behavioral model, which had long ignored covert phenomena and private events, was increasingly seen as having limited practical use and as inadequate for explaining all of human behavior (Mahoney, 1974). In 1965, Breger and McGaugh argued that learning theory could not account for research evidence and offered a reformulation emphasizing the role of central cognitive processes. This stimulated a symposium at the 1968 convention of the American Psychological Association on "cognitive processes in behavior modification" that emphasized the influence of expectation, attribution, reasoning, and planning on behavior change and which encouraged the development of new cognitive procedures (Goldfried, 1968).

Bandura's 1969 book was also pivotal, emphasizing the importance of cognitive mediational processes in the regulation of behavior and helping to initiate a focus within behavior therapy on social learning theory and self-control. In fact, in the very first volume of the journal *Behavior Therapy* (1970) is an article by Beck on cognitive therapy (albeit with a negative reply by Ullmann, saying that private events could be handled just like public ones).

Finally, many therapists who had been trained psychoanalytically were dissatisfied with the prime role given to the unconscious, the emphasis on history over current behavior, and the insistence on long-term therapy (Dobson & Block, 1988). The sparse outcome literature on traditional psychotherapies also pushed some therapists toward adoption of cognitive therapy, as an approach emphasizing both internal factors and an empirical evaluation of the efficacy of therapy.

Interventions and Assessment

In this section we will describe the types of interventions that are grouped within the broad heading of cognitive therapy. (We are using the term "cognitive therapy" to refer to the entire range of cognitive and cognitive–behavioral interventions, not only to the approach originated by Beck.) Hollon and Beck (1986) define cognitive therapies as "those approaches that attempt to modify existing or anticipated disorders by virtue of altering cognitions or cognitive processes" (p. 443).

In comparing the varying forms of cognitive therapy, which often share similar treatment strategies, a number of common features and propositions become apparent (Dobson & Block, 1988; Kendall & Bemis, 1983): (a) a collaborative relationship between client and therapist, (b) the assumption that emotional disorders and behavior are at least in part a function of disturbances in cognitive processes, (c) a focus on changing cognitions in order to produce desired changes in affect and behavior, and (d) a generally time-limited and educative treatment focusing on specific target problems.

In 1978, Mahoney and Arnkoff divided the field into three groups of interventions. Cognitive restructuring approaches, including RET, cognitive therapy (Beck), and self-instructional training, are therapies that attempt to change maladaptive thought patterns. Second, problem-solving programs involve methods that teach a systematic approach to personal problems. Finally, coping skills approaches, including anxiety management and stress inoculation, use a variety of interventions to help clients deal with stressful events. In both research and practice, the cognitive restructuring approaches have clearly been most important since the late 1970s.

Rational–Emotive Therapy (RET)

In explaining the origins of RET, Ellis (personal communication, 1989) observed that when he practiced analysis, his clients started to feel better, but did not *get* better in terms of changing their behavior. So he surveyed the literature for alternative methods and began to experiment with various behavioral, cognitive, and affective interventions. He united what he saw as the most effective of these into a new form of therapy, which he eventually called rational–emotive therapy. RET also was influenced by Ellis' own experiences of (successfully) attempting to self-modify his fears of public speaking and of approaching women.

The basic tenet of RET is that people's irrational beliefs about how things *must* and *should* be lead to their making themselves miserable. The acronym "ABC" summarizes this position: People start out thinking that the unfortunate activating events (A) in their lives, like social rejection, are the cause of disturbing behavioral and emotional consequences (C), such as depression and anxiety. Ellis argues that such consequences are actually caused by people's irrational beliefs (B). The practice of RET (Ellis, 1962) involves the discovery and exploration of the individual's "musturbatory" irrational beliefs, such as a client's belief that everyone *must* love her. In RET, the therapist would work to show this client that an event (A) like rejection by a new acquaintance is unfortunate, but not in and of itself a disaster; rather, she feels terrible (C) only because she believes she is worthless if anyone rejects her (B).

Direct teaching of RET principles is very important to the practice of RET, which attempts to persuade the client to adopt a new, more rational philosophy of life. RET also uses other interventions to persuade, such as role playing and modeling. Homework to be done between sessions intended to discover and refute irrational beliefs, as well as to try out new behavior, is a very important part of the therapy. Ellis has written many books for the general public, such as the *New Guide to Rational Living* (Ellis & Harper, 1975), that serve as adjuncts to therapy.

Many therapists in training reject RET as an option for their work after seeing Ellis on film or videotape. Ellis is unusually, even extremely, didactic and argumentative with clients. It should be noted that the methods of RET can be separated to a certain extent from Ellis' therapeutic style. Although RET by its nature uses teaching and explanations, many RET therapists do not emulate his manner. The therapeutic style presented, for example, in Walen, DiGiuseppe, and Wessler's (1980) *Practitioner's Guide to RET* is less challenging while still forthright, and thus is more acceptable to many practitioners.

RET, unfortunately, has not been evaluated in many controlled studies, although there have been a few investigations of RET applied to certain disorders. These studies have generally found RET superior to no treatment, but not different in outcome from other cognitive or behavioral interventions (Hollon & Beck, 1986). A structured variant of RET called systematic rational restructuring (Goldfried, Decenteceo, & Weinberg, 1974) has been the topic of a number of studies and has shown success with anxiety problems, but controlled evaluations with clinical populations have not been done (Hollon & Beck, 1986).

In spite of its sparse empirical base, RET remains popular in clinical practice. Mahoney, Lyddon, and Alford (1989) suggest that features of the therapy make it attractive to both clinicians and clients. Their evaluation of its appeal is that it is straightforward, involves relatively simple explanations for problems, and uses a wide variety of interventions for alleviating distress.

Cognitive Therapy

Cognitive therapy, originated by Aaron T. Beck, is the second major cognitive restructuring therapy. Like Ellis, Beck was trained psychoanalytically but became dissatisfied with analytic theory and therapy. Beck's development of cognitive therapy originated from his research on depression (Beck, 1967). In the 1950s, Beck began to test the psychodynamic theory of depression that assumed depressed individuals have a "need to suffer." His initial research seemed to support this theory, but as evidence accumulated, he concluded that far from having a need to suffer and be rejected by others, depressed individuals worked to gain the approval of others (Beck, Rush, Shaw, & Emery, 1979). He hypothesized instead that depressed persons make a fundamental cognitive error in seeing the world as more negative than is warranted. This depressive "schema," or cognitive structure that organizes information, contains a negative cognitive triad consisting of a negative view of oneself, one's world, and one's future. From this base in research on psychopathology, Beck devised a therapy to change maladaptive thought patterns, which he called *cognitive therapy* (Beck, Rush et al., 1979).

Cognitive therapy, like RET, helps the client to identify maladaptive thinking and persuades him or her to develop a more adaptive view. However, cognitive therapy tends to deal more with whether beliefs and thoughts are realistic than whether they are rational. For example, a depressed client may feel that he has nothing to offer others and thus that he is bound to be rejected. In cognitive therapy, a real-life experiment would be devised to test his hypothesis that everyone will reject him.

The therapeutic relationship in cognitive therapy is a collaborative one, as in behavior therapy. The therapist's goals and methods are generally clear to the client; they are working together against the client's unfortunate and unrealistic negative perceptions. Beck tends to employ a Socratic dialogue, in other words, asking questions in such a way that the clients' answers persuade *themselves* away from maladaptive thinking. Like RET, cognitive therapy also uses behavioral methods. Early in therapy with severely depressed clients, for example, daily activities are agreed on by the therapist and the client. This type of homework is designed both to bolster the client's confidence that he or she can accomplish tasks, thereby countering the client's negative self-view, and to increase the opportunities for pleasure in the client's life. Bibliotherapy may be used as well; for example, Burns' *Feeling Good* (1980) is often assigned for clients to read (and is available to the public in most bookstores).

The success of cognitive therapy for treating depression has been investigated extensively in controlled research with clinically severe populations. It has been shown to be at least as effective as tricyclic pharmacotherapy and sometimes more effective (Dobson, 1989; Hollon & Beck, 1986). However, in the National Institute of Mental Health Treatment of Depression Collaborative Research Program, with the subgroup of more severely depressed subjects, both imipramine and interpersonal therapy were more effective than the placebo plus clinical management condition, while cognitive therapy was not (Elkin et al., 1989).

The Mahoney et al. (1989) analysis of the attractive features of RET, mentioned previously, holds for cognitive therapy as well. The basic premise is straightforward (though it is more difficult to learn to do well than it may appear). Because of its appeal, plus its impressive record of effectiveness, cognitive therapy has become a widely practiced treatment for depression.

Beck (1976) has extended his premise of maladaptive schemas in psychopathology to disorders other than depression, particularly anxiety disorders (Beck & Emery, 1985) and relationship problems (Beck, 1988). However, cognitive therapy for disorders other than depression has not been evaluated sufficiently to warrant firm conclusions (Hollon & Beck, 1986).

Self-Instructional Training

The third type of cognitive restructuring therapy is self-instructional training, developed by Donald Meichenbaum. This approach grew out of his graduate school clinical training, which was behavioral, and some of his most stimulating scholarly training, which was from cognitively oriented psychologists (personal communication, 1989). In studies using operant conditioning with schizophrenics to get them to emit "healthy talk," Meichenbaum (1977) noticed that when they were tested, they often spontaneously instructed themselves to follow the experimental directions. Drawing on developmental literature on the establishment of self-regulation, he created an intervention called "self-instructional training" (SIT), in which the therapist teaches the individual to use self-talk or self-statements to change and guide behavior.

SIT has been used successfully on a variety of problems with adults, including test, speech, and social anxiety (Hollon & Beck, 1986). However, the most extensive use of SIT has been with impulsive and conduct-disordered children. For example, Kendall and his colleagues (Kendall & Braswell, 1982, 1985; Kendall, Reber, McLeer, Epps, & Ronan, 1990) have used SIT plus modeling and response cost procedures with impulsive and conduct-disordered children and found improvement in various areas, including teacher ratings of the children's behavior. Although this approach is promising, questions remain about generalization and maintenance of change (Hollon & Beck, 1986; Ollendick, 1986).

Problem Solving

The approach used by Kendall and his colleagues unites SIT with aspects of problem-solving training. Problem solving is a cognitive strategy borrowed from experimental psychology that teaches people to cope with problems systematically. Whereas the cognitive restructuring therapies deal to a great extent with clients' problematic internal events, the problem solving and coping skills therapies are focused more on dealing with stressful external events (Dobson & Block, 1988).

D'Zurilla and Goldfried (1971) outlined the steps of personal problem solving: general orientation or set, problem definition, generation of alternative solutions, decision making, and evaluation of the success of the solution. A problem is defined as a life situation that requires a response, but for which no response is immediately available; thus problem solving is a general skill that is helpful in a multitude of situations.

Problem-solving training, or as it has been called recently, social problem solving, has been applied successfully to several child and adult problems, including depression and antisocial behavior (D'Zurilla, 1986; Kazdin, Esveldt-Dawson, French, & Unis, 1987; Nezu, 1986). Spivack, Platt, and Shure (1976) used a related approach focusing on perspective taking (i.e., being able to see the situation from the point of view of the other person), the generation of alternatives, and means-ends thinking (learning to choose alternatives that will meet the desired goal). This approach has been used successfully with children and adolescents, among other populations (Spivack et al., 1976).

Coping Skills

The coping skills approaches to therapy combine cognitive and behavioral procedures, again to help clients deal with a variety of problems and stressful situations. Suinn and Richardson (1971) developed anxiety management training, which includes a combination of relaxation and imaginal coping (also see Suinn, 1990).

A widely used coping skill therapy is Meichenbaum's stress inoculation training (Meichenbaum, 1977, 1985; Meichenbaum & Cameron, 1973). Stress inoculation consists of (a) a conceptualization phase, in which clients are taught to recognize and understand stress; (b) a skills acquisition and rehearsal phase, in which clients are taught a wide variety of cognitive and behavioral methods, including self-instructions, relaxation, and problem solving; and (c) an application and follow-through phase, in which clients rehearse and gradually apply the skills they have learned. Stress inoculation training thus includes deliberate exposure to difficult situations so that the person can learn how to cope in real life; it aims to "inoculate" the individual against stress. Stress inoculation has had several applications, including teaching people to cope with medical problems like chronic pain (Turk, Meichenbaum, & Genest, 1983) and teaching people (such as military drill instructors and recruits) to cope with their stressful occupations (Novaco, Cook, & Sarason, 1983).

Cognitive Assessment

Just as in behavior therapy, when new interventions were developed, a new form of assessment was needed. In the cognitive area, measures of cognitive processes were needed to assess the new theories of psychopathology and to measure cognitive change in therapy (Kendall & Hollon, 1981; Merluzzi, Glass, & Genest, 1981). One taxonomy of cognition (Kendall & Ingram, 1987) consists of cognitive structure or organization, cognitive propositions or content, cognitive operations or process, and cognitive products or conscious experience. Most of the work to date has been on the assessment of products such as self-statements and content such as self-efficacy (Bandura, 1977) and schemata, although structure and process assessment is beginning (Arnkoff & Glass, 1989; D. A. Clark, 1988; Segal & Shaw, 1988).

How Cognitive Therapy Became Established

As noted earlier, the new cognitive treatment approaches were initiated during the prime days of behavior therapy. RET began in the 1950s, cognitive therapy in the 1960s, and self-instructional training in the 1970s. Mahoney's (1974) book *Cognition and Behavior Modification* was a landmark for the field, both because it was entirely devoted to these new cognitive procedures and because it provided scholarly arguments for including mediational factors in models of behavior. Beginning in 1975, Meichenbaum edited the "Cognitive–Behavior Modification Newsletter," which allowed researchers and clinicians to communicate and feel a sense of community. The original mailing list for the newsletters was about 100, but it grew to nearly 3,000 people in 20 countries (Meichenbaum, personal communication, 1989).

The feeling of belonging to a cohesive group provided by the newsletters was important, because the founders of cognitive therapy who originally were trained psychoanalytically (Beck and Ellis), as well as those who had been behavioral (Goldfried, Mahoney, and Meichenbaum) were being challenged by their colleagues for their "heretical" views. After he wrote his 1974 book, Mahoney (personal communication, 1989) was warned by some behavioral colleagues to "cease and desist" if he wished to remain in good standing. In the mid-1970s, some members of the Association for Advancement of Behavior Therapy (AABT) unsuccessfully pushed to exclude cognitive presentations from the conference (Mahoney, 1984; Meichenbaum, personal communication, 1989). Cognitively oriented books were banned from some clinical psychology doctoral programs that were strictly behavioral (Mahoney & Gabriel, 1990).

In this climate, cognitive proponents considered leaving AABT and forming their own organization. They decided not to split off because of their conviction that cognitive therapy should have an empirical basis (Meichenbaum, personal communication, 1989). This choice has been vindicated in later years; in 1990, Craighead found in a survey of AABT members that 69% identified themselves as cognitive–behavioral, while only 27% called themselves behavioral.

In spite of the resistance from their colleagues, and in some ways because of it, the cognitive proponents persevered, confidently believing that this new direction was both theoretically and clinically needed. As in the early days of modern behavior therapy, they were excited at being at the forefront of an important new movement. They decided to create a journal, *Cognitive Therapy and Research*, whose first editor was Mahoney. The establishment of a successful journal gave the field credibility, as well as a means to disseminate information. The premier issue in 1977 contained an article by Rush, Beck, Kovacs, and Hollon, who compared cognitive therapy and imipramine in the treatment of depression. This was the first article to find any psychotherapy superior to pharmacotherapy in the treatment of depression. This study gave further legitimacy to the movement.

Surveys on the Practice of Cognitive Therapy

Surveys of psychologists did not, of course, include questions about cognitive therapy until its influence began to be felt in the mid-1970s. 'As can be seen from Table 1, the Garfield and Kurtz (1976), E. L. Kelly, Goldberg, Fiske, and Kilkowski (1978), and Shemberg and Leventhal (1978) surveys all included rational–emotive therapy, and 2% of the respondents in each of these surveys answered that RET was their primary orientation. As the various cognitive therapies became better developed and studied, the percentage of psychologists using cognitive therapy grew, so that from the early 1980s, 8 to 15% of psychologists in most surveys reported that it was their primary orientation. (In the Jensen, Bergin, and Greaves (1990) survey, those calling themselves both cognitive and behavioral were classified as eclectic.)

The influence of cognitive therapy in psychology is even greater than these surveys would indicate, in that a broadly cognitive–behavioral orientation is prevalent in many scientist-practitioner training programs (Nevid, Lavi, & Primavera, 1986). Sayette and Mayne (1990) found that 42% of clinical psychology faculty in APA-accredited PhD and PsyD programs were identified as having a cognitive behavioral/social learning orientation. Further, D. Smith (1982) found that Ellis was rated by clinical and counseling psychologists as the psychotherapist who was the second most-influential on current practice (Rogers was first, Freud third); Lazarus was fifth, Beck seventh, and Meichenbaum tenth. However, as is the case with behavior therapy, the influence of cognitive therapy is much greater with psychologists than with psychiatrists or social workers, as Table 1 shows.

The line distinguishing behavior therapy from cognitive therapy has become blurred, to the point that *cognitive–behavioral* is a widely accepted term. In fact, virtually all of the behavioral research on treatment of anxiety disorders currently funded by the National Institute of Mental Health includes cognitive methods (Wolfe, personal communication, 1989). As noted earlier, Craighead (1990) found that a majority of AABT members surveyed

TABLE 1
Percentage of Survey Respondents Who Endorsed Cognitive and Eclectic Therapy Orientations

	Orientation	
	Cognitive	Eclectic
Surveys of Division 12 Members and Other General Samples of Psychologists		
Shaffer (1953)	—	35[a]
E. L. Kelly (1961) Fellows	—	48
Members	—	36
Lubin (1962)	—	19 (27)[b]
Goldschmid et al. (1969)	—	24
Garfield & Kurtz (1976)	2[c]	55
E. L. Kelly et al. (1978)	2[c]	58
Norcross & Prochaska (1982)	6	31
D. Smith (1982)	12[d]	41
Prochaska & Norcross (1983)	8	30
Watkins et al. (1986)	11	40
Norcross, Prochaska, & Gallagher (1989)	13	29
Survey of Academic Psychologists		
Shemberg & Leventhal (1978)	2[c]	33
Sayette & Mayne (1990)	42[e]	—
Surveys of Psychologists in Full or Part-time Practice		
Tryon (1983)	—	56
Norcross & Prochaska (1983)	8	31
Norcross, Nash et al. (1985)	15	26
Comparisons of Several Professions		
Norcross, Strausser-Kirtland, & Missar (1989)		
Psychologists	8	34
Psychiatrists	1	53
Social Workers	4	34
Jensen et al. (1990)		
Psychologists	5	70[f]
Marital and Family Therapists	2	72[f]
Social Workers	0	68[f]
Psychiatrists	1	59[f]
Total	2	68[f]

[a]Percentage of those who do therapy; 20% of sample did not do therapy.
[b]Total across all orientations sums to 70%; figure in parentheses is prorated for 100%.
[c]*Rational–emotive therapy* was actual category in survey.
[d]*Cognitive–behavioral* (10.36%) plus *RET* (1.69%) responses.
[e]Cognitive behavioral/social learning were actual categories in survey.
[f]Includes both those who checked *eclectic* and also those who checked two or more categories (such as *cognitive* and *behavioral*).

called themselves cognitive–behavioral, and the cognitive methods we have discussed generally include behavioral techniques. These behavioral components have been found to be crucial, for example, in interventions with children (Kendall, 1987). Cognitive (and cognitive–behavioral) therapists also share with behavior therapists an interest in empirical research to evaluate therapy and theory. Wilson (personal communication, 1989) believes that the cognitive influence in behavior therapy has been a positive one, leading to new treatment methods, new explanations for old methods, and the capability to describe and explain the therapeutic relationship.

Current and Future Developments

For clinical, theoretical, and empirical reasons, then, cognitive approaches to therapy became important in a brief span of time. A recent development in this area of psychotherapy is the emergence of constructivist cognitive therapies. Examples of constructivist theories are Guidano and Liotti's structural cognitive therapy (Guidano, 1987; Guidano & Liotti, 1983; Liotti, 1986), recent applications of personal construct theory (G. A. Kelly, 1955; Neimeyer, 1986), and Mahoney's (1990) cognitive developmental therapy.

Constructivist theories differ from rationalist cognitive theories such as RET in philosophy of science, in theories of psychopathology and change, and in some important clinical aspects (Mahoney & Gabriel, 1987). Whereas rationalist cognitive theories assume that the therapist can know the true state of affairs through logic or sensory observation, constructivist theories posit that each person creates his or her reality. Therefore, a constructivist therapist cannot presume to know "the" truth and simply pass it on to the client. Constructivist theories emphasize developmental processes, limiting themselves in therapy to the current state or presenting problem less than do the rationalist therapies.

Emotion is also viewed quite differently, with extreme negative emotion considered a problem to be controlled in rationalist therapies, but seen in the constructivist therapies as an important aspect of knowing and self-reorganization. The constructivists view the relationship as a safe context for client self-exploration (Mahoney, 1990) and as a central focus for new learning about concepts of the self and attachment to others (Guidano & Liotti, 1983). Interestingly, the constructivist cognitive therapies have more points of contact with current psychodynamic theories than do the rationalist therapies (Belliveau et al., 1990). Though the constructivist therapies have not developed clear clinical procedural guidelines and have not been subjected to extensive empirical validation, they are an intriguing new development.

There is a great deal of variation in theory and practice in cognitive therapy, so that a "uniformity myth" should not be imposed, and in fact, no one knows what cognitive therapists "really do in their offices" (Golden & Dryden, 1986). Nevertheless, there are some common patterns. Like behavior therapy, the cognitive therapies emphasize empirical evaluation of theory and treatment, incorporate behavioral methods, and are relatively brief in length. In fact, Kendall and Bemis (1983) have argued that behavioral influences predominate in the current practice of cognitive therapy. Like psychodynamic therapies, though, cognitive therapies focus on intrapsychic determinants of behavior. The therapeutic relationship is recognized as very important, at least as a prerequisite for change, and in some views as an important means to change. Thus, it is not surprising that cognitive therapy has fostered the movement to the integration of psychotherapies.

Interest in affect in cognitive therapy has grown (Greenberg & Safran, 1987, 1989), and this development, which is a turn away from the direction of traditional behavior therapy, will most likely continue. Similarly, the role of interpersonal relationships in theory and therapy is a new and exciting development (Safran, 1990a, 1990b; Safran & Segal, 1990). Models of the development of psychopathology will also be a direction for cognitive therapy (Dobson, 1988). In fact, Ellis, Kendall, and Meichenbaum (personal communications, 1989) see an important role for cognitive principles to be incorporated into education, to teach children to self-regulate and treat themselves humanely.

Applications of cognitive therapy in the 1970s were primarily focused on depression. One strong area of interest in the 1980s was anxiety disorders (e.g., D. M. Clark, 1986). Currently, as in other schools of therapy, interest in personality disorders and their treatment is growing (Beck, Freeman, & Associates, 1990; Young, 1990).

In recent years, cognitive–behavioral treatment programs designed specifically for certain disorders have been developed, for example, for bulimia (e.g., Fairburn, 1985) and panic disorder (e.g., Barlow & Cerny, 1988). Garfield (personal communication, 1989) notes that in the past, therapists were trained to be generalists, and forms of therapy were intended to be useful for every problem, whereas now there seems to be a trend to specialization. In fact, Wilson (personal communication, 1989) predicts that the knowledge required to treat particular disorders will soon become so vast that therapists will need to specialize even more.

In cognitive therapy, the current emphasis on the therapeutic relationship is likely to grow (Goldén & Dryden, 1986). Similarly, theories about the process of cognitive therapy and research into process and mechanisms of change should play a greater role than they have (Hollon & Beck, 1986). As the interest in the integration of therapies continues to develop, such research will allow a better understanding of the relationship between cognitive therapy and other forms of therapy.

PSYCHOTHERAPY INTEGRATION

Early History

Attempts at integrating streams of psychotherapy began very early in the history of psychotherapy (Arkowitz, 1984; Goldfried & Newman, 1986), although the integrative "movement" got underway only in the 1970s. In one of the first publications on integration, French (1933) compared psychoanalysis and respondent conditioning. As might be expected, this paper was heavily criticized, but Kubie (1934) continued this line of reasoning in explaining certain aspects of psychoanalysis in conditioning terms. A landmark early publication, often cited in behavior therapy, was Dollard and Miller's (1950) book that included learning theory explanations of psychoanalytic methods. Alexander (1963) also saw learning principles operating in psychoanalytic therapy. Marks and Gelder (1966) noted similarities between behavior therapy and psychoanalysis, but also differences, and argued that the two forms of therapy had contributions to make to each other.

Stampfl and Levis (1967) created a treatment for avoidance behavior called implosive therapy, which has similarities to systematic desensitization and flooding in technique, but is based on an integration of psychodynamic and learning theory. In implosive therapy, the client imagines scenes related to the feared object or situation so that the anxiety thus aroused can extinguish. In contrast to behavioral methods, however, the scenes are devised to touch on hypothesized themes of psychodynamic conflict such as aggression and rejection.

Rosenzweig (1936) was probably the first to discuss a *common factors* approach to psychotherapy, arguing that the effectiveness of therapies is due to similarity in their processes, such as providing an alternative view of the client's problems. Garfield's (1957) text on clinical psychology contained a discussion of the common factors across psychotherapies, a point of view carried on in his later work (e.g., 1980, 1989). A few years later, Frank (1961) published the landmark work *Persuasion and Healing*, in which he argued that all healing procedures, including all psychotherapies, operate through common processes.

Lazarus (1967) introduced the term *technical eclecticism*, the idea that methods originating in different schools of therapy may be combined for maximal therapeutic effectiveness. In early eclectic contributions, Weitzman (1967) discussed the use of systematic desensitization within an analytic therapy, and Kraft (1969) demonstrated the unconscious material brought out through desensitization.

These writings, plus the therapeutic "underground" among practitioners (Goldfried & Davison, 1976) that has always existed, influenced a large number of therapists to adopt an eclectic point of view long before it became a "movement." As can be seen from Table 1, the percentage of clinical psychologists who called themselves eclectic in surveys before 1970 ranged from 27 to 48%, which is certainly high. Thus the question of why integrative and eclectic therapy became a movement in the 1970s is not a matter of why people became interested at this time, because practitioners were always interested, but rather why it began to be *perceived* as an important new direction, a school of therapy in and of itself.

Why Interest Grew in the 1970s

Three general trends have contributed to the focused interest in eclectic and integrative psychotherapy (Beitman, Goldfried, & Norcross, 1989). Two were internal to the field of therapy, namely, dissatisfaction clinically with any single school and research evidence of similar outcomes and common factors across psychotherapies. The third was external to the field: the move to third-party payments and resulting accountability required of psychotherapy providers, who had to present a united front to assure reimbursement for psychotherapeutic services.

In chapter 18 of this volume, we discussed the trend in behavior therapy toward broader treatments to deal with more complex clinical problems. In psychodynamic and humanistic therapies as well, failures and complexities in clinical practice led to dissatisfaction with narrow explanations and methods, a trend that Goldfried and Padawer (1982) described as "paradigm strain." This dissatisfaction with existing therapies may have contributed to the proliferation of new types of therapy, to the point that hundreds of therapies have been developed (Beitman et al., 1989; Garfield, 1982). None of these new therapies has proven to be fully satisfactory either, which is leading to a crisis and ultimate search for unity among therapies (Goldfried & Padawer, 1982). Clinically, then, practitioners acknowledge the need for broad theories as well as therapeutic flexibility in order to be successful with complex clinical problems.

The research literature also contributed to the movement to integrate therapies. A number of frequently cited studies and reviews found few differences between therapies (e.g., Luborsky, Singer, & Luborsky, 1975; Sloane, Staples, Cristol, Yorkston, & Whipple, 1975; M. L. Smith, Glass, & Miller, 1980). A careful analysis of the outcome literature does not, however, lead to the simple conclusion that all therapies are equal. In their review of the outcome of psychotherapy, Lambert, Shapiro, and Bergin (1986) concluded that although there is little evidence of clinically meaningful superiority of one form of psychotherapy over another with respect to moderate out-patient disorders, behavioral and cognitive methods appear to add a significant increment of efficacy with respect to a number of difficult problems (e.g., phobias and compulsions) and to provide useful methods with a number of nonneurotic problems with which traditional therapies have shown little effectiveness (e.g., childhood aggression, psychotic behavior, stuttering). (p. 201)

Nevertheless, for many disorders, few differences in outcome have been found across therapies. Even for clinicians socialized strongly into one school of therapy, the failure of any one school to dominate research findings for all disorders has been striking; as Davison said (1990), "The data don't scream, but they do whine." Furthermore, carefully designed studies have generally not found changes with treatment that are specific to the issues focused on in the therapy. For example, cognitive changes have been found in psychopharmacological and interpersonal forms of therapy at a rate no different from that in cognitive therapy, even though the methods used in the different treatments can be reliably discriminated (Garfield, 1987; Imber et al., 1990; Simons, Garfield, & Murphy, 1984).

These outcome and process data, plus clinical needs for flexible therapies, led to the interest in going beyond a narrow school-based approach to practice. Three main paths can be identified in current writings on therapy integration (Arkowitz, 1989): technical eclecticism, theoretical integration, and the search for common factors across therapies. All three can be seen as resulting from perceptions of the clinical and empirical status of existing therapies.

A third factor that has led to the integrative movement at this time, one that is external to the field, is the change from payment for psychotherapy by individuals to payments predominantly by third-party providers, such as health insurance and Medicare. One result has been pressure toward "accountability," that is, the need to prove the effectiveness and cost-effectiveness of psychotherapy. The potential threat to the profession of psychotherapy has led many therapists toward greater cooperation in order to develop therapies with demonstrated effectiveness (Beitman et al., 1989).

Integrative and Eclectic Work in the 1970s

In this section, we are emphasizing integrative and eclectic approaches to clinical practice. In chapter 8 in this volume, Arkowitz provides a more complete description of theories of psychotherapy integration.

Arnold Lazarus and Technical Eclecticism

Lazarus' multimodal therapy is perhaps the best example of eclectic psychotherapy. While working as a behavior therapist, Lazarus began to think about the decision rules that guided his choice of clinical interventions (Lazarus, 1987) and about why observers could not agree on why clients had improved (Lazarus, 1989). This led him to write his 1967 article in support of technical eclecticism and to the notion that one can accept empirically valid techniques without having to accept their underlying theories.

In addition, Lazarus began to question the stability of change in behavior therapy clients. Further, he found that many clients, in addition to changing behavior, also talked of changes in their outlook on life and greater self-esteem (Lazarus, 1987). These clinical experiences influenced him to write *Behavior Therapy and Beyond* (1971), which helped to introduce cognitive factors and a broad-spectrum approach to behavior therapy. This extremely influential book was a precursor to later work on multimodal behavior therapy (Lazarus, 1976) and eventually to what he calls "multimodal therapy" (Lazarus, 1981, 1985).

In the multimodal therapy approach, the therapist tailors the therapy to the clients' problem areas and favored modalities on the basis of an analysis of seven factors: behavior, affect, sensation, imagery, cognition, interpersonal relationships, and biological functioning (the "BASIC I.D."). Although the interventions used are primarily cognitive and behavioral because of their demonstrated effectiveness (personal communication, 1989), Lazarus employs a total of perhaps four dozen actual techniques, including medication, imagery and fantasy, Rogerian reflection, and Gestalt empty chair exercises (Lazarus, 1986).

Psychoanalysis and Behavior Therapy

In addition to multimodal therapy, the integration of psychodynamic and behavior therapy has also received a good deal of attention and clinical interest. In the early 1970s, Feather and Rhoads (1972a, 1972b) described an approach to psychodynamic behavior therapy in which they reviewed differences and areas of convergence in order to provide a rationale for a more integrative approach. For example, more psychodynamic techniques of directed fantasy can be used to discover the nature of the unacceptable impulses and conflicts that are the basis for the phobic symptoms, yet a hierarchy of imagined scenes can also be used to help clients confront the situation in real life (see also Rhoads & Feather, 1974). Silverman (1974) wrote that nonanalytic treatment failures may be due to the inadvertent support of transference expectations and that nonanalytic techniques may lead to benefits not available solely through psychoanalytic treatment.

It is interesting that in an article published in the first volume of *Behavior Therapy*, Birk (1970) advocated this sort of integration of the "breadth and depth" of insight-seeking psychodynamic approaches with the "power and efficiency" of more change-producing behavioral techniques. Twelve years later, this journal also published a series of papers presenting four different positions on integration (Garfield, 1982; Goldfried, 1982; Kendall, 1982; Wachtel, 1982).

An additional demonstration of interest on the part of behavior therapists in the integration of psychodynamic and behavior therapy took place in 1978, when Hal Arkowitz chaired a symposium at the annual convention of the Association for Advancement of Behavior Therapy on this topic, featuring papers by Paul Wachtel and Cyril Franks and discussions by Merton Gill and Hans Strupp. In 1980, there was a dialogue at the AABT conference between Marvin Goldfried and Hans Strupp on the topic of rapprochement.

From the psychodynamic perspective, an interest in behavior therapy among psychiatrists resulted in formation of a task force on behavior therapy within the American Psychiatric Association (Birk et al., 1974). They suggested that psychiatry would "benefit further from incorporating concepts and techniques derived from the behavioral tradition" (p. 83) and hoped that points of contact would continue to be explored.

Other Influential Figures

Perhaps the most influential book on the integration of psychodynamic and behavioral approaches was Wachtel's *Psychoanalysis and Behavior Therapy* (1977), described by Arkowitz as a "major factor" in the growing interest in integration and the "single most important work in the 1970s on the issue of integration" (Arkowitz, 1984, p. 13). Wachtel was initially trained in a psychodynamic perspective and completed postdoctoral analytic training. To prepare for a symposium that was actually intended to *bury* behavior therapy, he began to read the behavior therapy literature and was surprised to discover a convergence between behavioral approaches and his own interpersonal approach to psychoanalytic psychotherapy (Wachtel, personal communication, 1989). He later took part in an intensive one-month training program run by Joseph Wolpe in Philadelphia, and also observed Gerald Davison's clinical behavior therapy demonstrations at the State University of New York at Stony Brook.

With this exposure to behavior therapy, Wachtel began to incorporate some of the ideas into his practice. He discovered that the imaginal exposure to feared or conflictual situations that he was now trying with clients actually facilitated psychodynamic exploration of important themes. Further, behavioral tasks, such as homework to practice acting assertively, not only altered the client's behavior, but also, because of the resulting change in how others reacted to the client, led to a change in the client's internal structure (personal communication, 1989).

Wachtel's observation of and comments on Davison's behavior therapy cases in the early 1970s also affected Davison's clinical supervision and the content of Goldfried and Davison's book (1976) *Clinical Behavior Therapy* (Davison, personal communication, 1989).

As Goldfried described in our interview, although initially trained clinically in a psychodynamic perspective, he was frustrated by the lack of concrete guidance in analytic writings on how to do' therapy. He took a position at SUNY—Stony Brook, where Krasner was hired to direct a doctoral clinical psychology training program based on learning principles. There Goldfried became committed to a behavioral and later a cognitive–behavioral approach through the influence of colleagues, clinical experiences, and readings of authors such as Ellis.

By the late 1970s, while reading additional literature in order to expand his behavior therapy course for first-year clinical students, Goldfried was struck by the similarities between behavioral and more traditional approaches to psychotherapy and by the fact that his clinical demonstrations to students often were not straight behavior therapy. In the late 1970s, while on sabbatical, he wrote about this move toward integration in an often-cited article on therapeutic change principles (Goldfried, 1980). Although he was worried that he was "sticking [his] neck out," he thought it was important for the field to develop in this way (personal communication, 1989).

Another influential individual, Sol Garfield, who received his degree in 1942, was inclined to be eclectic from the start of his career (Garfield, personal communication, 1989). In his clinical work, he found that different clients needed and responded to very different approaches. Garfield also places great importance on research in psychotherapy, as shown by the empirical emphasis in the *Handbook of Psychotherapy and Behavior Change* (3rd ed., 1986), which he edited with Allen Bergin. In the early stage of Garfield's career, only Rogers and his colleagues were doing extensive research on psychotherapy, which is one reason Garfield became interested in client-centered therapy even though he felt it was too superficial to be satisfactory on its own. Behavior therapy also struck him as superficial in its early years, but later he began using behavioral and cognitive–behavioral methods, both because behavior therapy had become more broad and especially because of its strong research findings (personal communication, 1989).

Another continuing interest of Garfield's has been the common factors underlying different therapies, and again, this interest grew because of both his clinical experience and research findings (e.g., Heine, 1953). Garfield's common factors perspective is reflected extensively in *Psychotherapy: An Eclectic Approach* (1980), which he feels is his most influential clinical book to date (personal communication, 1989), and in *The Practice of Brief Psychotherapy* (1989).

Establishment of and Reactions to Psychotherapy Integration

Growth of the Movement

One of the major forces for psychotherapy integration today is the Society for the Exploration of Psychotherapy Integration (SEPI), founded in 1983 through the initial efforts of Marvin Goldfried and Paul Wachtel. Their conversations and a small conference held in 1981 established a dialogue with others with different perspectives. Goldfried and Wachtel, with consultation from Hans Strupp, thus evolved the idea for a group and sent out a questionnaire to recruit members (Goldfried, personal communication, 1989).

Most of those who responded favored a formal organization. The name chosen for this group implied not a commitment to integration but a willingness to explore ideas (Wachtel, personal communication, 1989). National conferences have been held since 1985 and members continue to support open-mindedness and rapprochement. The SEPI journal, the *Journal of Psychotherapy Integration*, began publication in 1991, with Hal Arkowitz as its first editor.

Reactions

Approaches emphasizing integrative and eclectic themes have not always been met with enthusiasm from the psychotherapy establishment. For example, Goldfried and Davison, who urged behavior therapists to enter into discussion with nonbehavioral clinicians (1976), were met with opposition from some behavioral colleagues, who felt they were selling out. "One conversion is enough," Goldfried was told (Goldfried, personal communication, 1989). Wachtel's psychoanalytic colleagues asked him, in an ironic sense, why he did not just become a behaviorist, whereas to his surprise, behavior therapists were more receptive to his integrative ideas (personal communication, 1989).

Another kind of reaction to psychotherapy integration is based more on a concern that the field should continue to emphasize the empirical evaluation of the effectiveness of therapies. Wilson (1982, personal communication, 1989) advocates integration of only those methods that have already been shown to be effective. He is concerned that many therapists have (erroneously, in his view) concluded that all therapies are effective and that therefore no one needs to be concerned with efficacy any longer. Although we agree with Wilson that the field should continue to emphasize the evaluation of effectiveness, we believe it is possible that some methods may be more effective in combination than by themselves. Thus some approaches that have not shown unequivocal empirical support may turn out to be highly effective when combined with other methods that complement their strengths and weaknesses.

Barriers to Integration

The future of psychotherapy integration will depend on its ability to deal with a number of other issues. There are those who feel that there is little hope for conceptual integration and that behavioral and psychodynamic approaches are "totally different, irreconcilable, and incompatible" (Franks, 1984, p. 245). Messer and Winokur (1984) described how therapists from each of these orientations have different perspectives on reality, different world views, and different views of client functioning. Messer (1986) has also illustrated how behavioral and psychoanalytic therapy would proceed differently at therapeutic choice points, but has made suggestions for therapists who are interested in incorporating different perspectives. Beitman et al. (1989) and Goldfried and Newman (1986) also highlighted differences in views of the role of the unconscious, importance of transference, and goals of therapy across varying orientations.

In addition, different perspectives are steeped in jargon and a particular language system, which results in a lack of understanding or active avoidance of concepts used by different orientations (Goldfried, 1987). "Transference" and "reinforcement" are but two examples of such "X-rated" terms. Goldfried argues that integration is unlikely to be attained unless a common language is found to facilitate communication among colleagues trained in different perspectives, and he suggests the use of the vernacular. His research group has developed a coding system for therapeutic feedback that does use language not tied to any theory and that can therefore be used to investigate any form of therapy (e.g., Kerr, Goldfried, Hayes, & Goldsamt, 1989).

From a political point of view, most clinicians have been trained within a single orientation, and professional associations, group memberships, and even friendships help to keep approaches isolated from each other and foster an "us versus them" attitude (Goldfried, 1980). Arkowitz (1984) also pointed out that therapists and writers from both behavioral and psychodynamic orientations are not very aware of recent developments in the other field. For example, behavior therapists may be uninformed as to recent developments in ego psychology, interpersonal psychoanalysis, and object relations theory, while analysts continue to view behavior therapy as a narrow set of techniques based on the work of Wolpe and Skinner. If it is to survive, the movement toward integration must overcome these misconceptions and expose clinicians to multiple approaches and integrative perspectives, as well give practicing clinicians information to improve their treatment choices.

Surveys of the Practice of Eclectic and Integrative Therapy

In spite of these potential difficulties, the power of the push toward psychotherapy integration can be seen in the surveys of practice carried out in recent years. As shown in Table 1, Garfield and Kurtz (1976) found that 55% of the clinical psychologists surveyed called themselves eclectic. This figure was stunning and an important landmark in the movement toward psychotherapy integration. The increase in this percentage over previous surveys was largely at the expense of psychodynamic points of view.

Later surveys of psychologists have continued to find a high number who endorse eclectic therapy (Table 1), though not always as high as in Garfield and Kurtz (1976). The most firm conclusion is that a sizable portion, from one third to one half in most surveys, call themselves eclectic. Surveys of psychologists in academia and in full or part-time practice also show a variable, but sizable, proportion of psychologists who call themselves eclectic. Similarly, Table 1 shows that surveys that have included psychiatrists, social workers, and marital and family therapists also found a large proportion calling themselves eclectic.

Because eclectic or integrative therapy is not an organized school of therapy, it is impossible to discern what the respondents actually *do* in therapy from these figures alone. Garfield and Kurtz (1977) did a follow-up survey of those who called themselves eclectic in their 1976 survey. Nearly half of these individuals reported that they previously had adhered to one school of therapy, primarily psychoanalytic. When asked to select the two orientations that were most characteristic of their views, psychoanalytic plus learning theory was selected most often (21% of respondents), followed by neo-Freudian plus learning (16%). Subjects' most frequent definition of eclecticism was to select whatever approach seems best for the client (called the pragmatic approach by Garfield and Kurtz), followed by integration of various orientations, and finally by the adherence to two or three orientations. Garfield and Kurtz (1977) concluded that "the designation eclectic covers a wide range of views, some of which are apparently quite the opposite of others" (p. 79).

In a short span of time, psychologists' interest in eclecticism and integration has shifted somewhat from the pragmatic approach found in Garfield and Kurtz (1977) toward an interest in integrating theories. Norcross and Prochaska (1982) asked subjects who called themselves eclectic to choose a type of eclecticism that characterized their approach. By far the most frequent answer was synthetic (the integration of theories), followed by technical eclecticism (choose procedures from different schools), and then atheoretical (no preferred theory).

Other recent surveys have found a similar emphasis on theoretical integration (Norcross & Prochaska, 1988; Watkins, Lopez, Campbell, & Himmell, 1986). Half of the subjects in the former survey said they saw a difference between eclectic and integrative, with eclectic being seen as technical, unsystematic, and passive, and integrative as theoretical, systematic, and active. Thus Norcross and Prochaska (1988) concluded that the trend to eclecticism has moved from a dissatisfaction with schools of therapy to a positive attempt at integration—from eclecticism "by default" to integration "by design" (p. 173).

As in Garfield and Kurtz's 1977 study, Norcross and Prochaska (1988) found that of the eclectic clinical psychologists surveyed, the most frequent previous orientation among those psychologists who had had a previous orientation was psychodynamic or psychoanalytic. However, when asked which orientations they combined, the top three combinations involved cognitive therapy: cognitive–behavioral, humanistic–cognitive, and psychoanalytic–cognitive. Overall, half of the subjects chose a combination that included cognitive and/or behavior therapy.

As might be expected, the emphasis on cognitive and behavior therapy found in eclectic psychologists' views does not hold as strongly in other professions. In Jensen et al.'s (1990) survey of four professions, eclectic subjects were asked which schools they used in practice. For psychologists, the orientations used by more than half the respondents were cognitive (63%), dynamic (62%), and behavioral (56%). More than half of the marriage and family therapists endorsed dynamic (67%), systems (65%), and cognitive (52%). For psychiatrists, the orientations used by more than half the respondents were dynamic (88%) and cognitive (53%), with behavioral endorsed by close to half the subjects (49%). The social workers were perhaps the most eclectic of the four professions, reporting that they used dynamic (78%), systems (60%), humanistic (56%), behavioral (51%), and cognitive therapy (49%).

Current and Future Developments

Current Status

At present, the field of psychotherapy integration is best characterized as diverse. A handbook and casebook of eclectic therapy (Norcross, 1986, 1987) and the recommendations from a National Institute of Mental Health conference on integration (Wolfe & Goldfried, 1988) show the range of areas being developed.

One of the most active areas is that of the search for common factors and general overviews of psychotherapy. Goldfried (1980) has suggested that the common factors in psychotherapy can best be found at a level of abstraction dealing with clinical strategies and principles, between the level of theory and that of observable clinical techniques. Examples of clinical strategies are therapeutic feedback and corrective emotional experience. Garfield (1980, 1989) discusses the therapeutic variables that are common across psychotherapies and that form the foundation of his proposal for brief therapy. Beitman's (1987) overview of the structure of therapy focuses on four stages: engagement, pattern search, change, and termination.

Based on a program of research, Prochaska and DiClemente (1984) have proposed a "transtheoretical model" of therapy that consists of 10 processes, 4 stages, and 5 levels of change. In another empirically driven overview of therapy, Orlinsky and Howard's (1987) review of psychotherapy research led to a "generic model" of psychotherapy focusing on five components of therapeutic process: the therapeutic contract, therapeutic interventions, the therapeutic bond, the client and therapist's states of "self-relatedness" or experience of the self, and the attainment of immediate in-session goals.

Lazarus' multimodal therapy (1981) remains one of the most important systems of technically eclectic psychotherapy. Additionally, other models of the choice of interventions have appeared. For example, Beutler's (1983) proposal, based on empirical research, focuses on client or problem dimensions. Frances, Clarkin, and Perry (1984) presented a system of treatment planning based on five aspects of client characteristics and treatment options. Beutler and Clarkin (1990) have combined and extended Beutler (1983) and Frances et al. (1984), proposing a decision model based on client predisposing variables, the treatment context, relationship variables, and strategies and techniques.

With regard to the integration of existing therapeutic schools, Gold-fried (1987) argues that one facet of psychotherapy integration is a search for *complementary* methods; the focus in different therapies on different aspects of human functioning and change means that schools of therapy may "each have something unique to offer" (p. 810). Recent discussions of integration continue to center around behavioral and psychodynamic approaches (Arkowitz & Messer, 1984; Marmor & Woods, 1980; Wolfe, 1989), although integration of behavioral and humanistic approaches has been considered (Wandersman, Poppen, & Ricks, 1976), as well as the integration of approaches to marital and family therapy (Feldman & Pinsof, 1982; Lebow, 1984; Segraves, 1982).

Future of Psychotherapy Integration

The movement toward psychotherapy integration continues to grow. As Beitman et al. (1989) state, it may represent the "*Zeitgeist* of the next several decades of psychotherapy research and practice" (p. 145).

With this increased interest, questions have arisen concerning how best to train future clinicians in an integrative approach (Beutler et al., 1987; Norcross, Beutler et al., 1986). Many have argued against socializing students into one or another school of thought and urge that trainees be provided with various options without labeling them correct or incorrect so that they learn to recognize the value of each approach (Beitman et al., 1989; Lazarus, 1990). Achieving this goal may be easier said than done, however. Students would have to be taught multiple types of interventions and taught how to choose when to do each intervention. "Both are un-precedented training objectives in the history of psychotherapy" (Beutler & Clarkin, 1990, p. 290). It may be an empirical question whether the best approach is to train therapists thoroughly in one perspective before encouraging exploration of alternative directions or whether to train for competence in a number of different orientations from the beginning.

Even if a training program chooses to emphasize only one approach, it is important to teach students to work cooperatively with clinicians of different orientations, with exposure to their concepts, assumptions, and methods (Collins, Foster, & Berler, 1986). These authors, in writing about training in behavior therapy, emphasize the need for behavioral clinicians to be able to rephrase their techniques in nonbehavioral language and to demonstrate the effectiveness of their approach to their nonbehavioral colleagues. Rather than one therapist being all things to every client, Wachtel (personal communication, 1989) anticipates continuing diversity in therapeutic "styles," but each therapist will have more respect for the ability of those with different styles and thus be more willing to refer clients when appropriate.

In the coming years, the practice of psychotherapy (including integrative and eclectic approaches) will be influenced by a number of issues. For example, we have previously mentioned the recent trend toward a climate of accountability and a demand on the part of public and government agencies for evidence in support of the efficacy of psychotherapy (Garfield, 1987). Beitman et al. (1989) feel that ideally, clients would be given clear information about just what they are receiving so that they will be able to make better judgments about what therapy or therapist to choose.

The above issue highlights the need for more empirical support for psychotherapeutic effectiveness, including integrative approaches. Garfield (1987) has spoken of the need for an "empirically based and scientifically oriented eclectic psychotherapy" (p. 99). He believes that there is still much to accomplish in evaluating the efficacy of psychotherapy, especially in comparing different approaches systematically and in looking for common therapeutic variables and factors accounting for change. This will be a costly proposition and a potential barrier to psychotherapy integration (Goldfried & Newman, 1986).

Ideally, responsible therapists should use interventions that the research literature has shown to be the most effective with a specific disorder (Goldfried & Hayes, 1989), based also on an understanding of the process of change. As noted earlier, Goldfried's recent research has attempted to provide an empirical demonstration of what actually occurs in therapy across different orientations, with the goal of understanding what therapists are doing. In developing an integrative perspective, Goldfried and Safran (1986) have written that both "top down" and "bottom up" directions should be pursued, working from both the level of theory and that of clinical practice. Thus we need research to know more about what eclectic therapists actually do that is effective (Wolfe & Goldfried, 1988) as well as to use outcome research to suggest what they should do.

The current swing of the research pendulum toward process research, or process-outcome research, also is in keeping with the integration movement. The search for common processes, such as the therapeutic alliance, and their role in influencing outcome is important for the future of therapy integration (Wolfe interview). It is not yet known whether the conclusion from this research will be that all effective therapies make use of common factors equally or that some approaches make better use of some of these factors. Similarly, it is an open question as to whether some therapies (such as packages designed for a given disorder) have specific factors that lead to a better outcome than do other treatments that do not contain these elements.

Finally, an important question for the future of psychotherapy integration is whether there will be competition among specific schools of integrative therapy, just as there has been intense competition among "pure-form" schools. In their survey of SEPI members about obstacles to therapy integration, Norcross and Thomas (1988) found that the most frequently mentioned obstacle was "partisan zealotry" (p. 76), but the second most-frequent obstacle was the lack of developed integrative frameworks, that is, no well-defined schools.

We do seem to be headed in the direction of the development of such frameworks, as we discussed in the previous section. This is an important step for the field. However, Wachtel (personal communication, 1989) cautions that partisanship and competition between these developing integrative models, which would simply be repeating history in psychotherapy, would be a mistake. Rather, therapists writing a history of psychotherapy in the year 2092 will be most likely to conclude that psychotherapy integration led to progress in the field only if present-day therapists begin to explore multiple points of view and attend to the findings of empirical research.

REFERENCES

Adler, A. (1927). *Understanding human nature.* New York: Greenberg.

Alexander, F. (1963). The dynamics of psychotherapy in light of learning theory. *American Journal of Psychiatry, 120,* 440–448.

Alford, B. A., & Norcross, J. C. (1991). Cognitive therapy as integrative therapy. *Journal of Psychotherapy Integration, 1,* 175–190.

Arkowitz, H. (Chair). (1978, November). *Behavior therapy and psychoanalysis: Compatible or incompatible?* Symposium presented at the meeting of the Association for Advancement of Behavior Therapy, Chicago, IL.

Arkowitz, H. (1984). Historical perspective on the integration of psychoanalytic therapy and behavior therapy. In H. Arkowitz & S. B. Messer (Eds.), *Psychoanalytic therapy and behavior therapy: Is integration possible?* (pp. 1–30). New York: Plenum.

Arkowitz, H. (1989). The role of theory in psychotherapy integration. *Journal of Integrative and Eclectic Psychotherapy, 8,* 8–16.

Arkowitz, H., & Messer, S. B. (Eds.). (1984). *Psychoanalytic therapy and behavior therapy: Is integration possible?* New York: Plenum.

Arnkoff, D. B., & Glass, C. R. (1989). Cognitive assessment in social anxiety and social phobia. *Clinical Psychology Review, 9,* 61–74.

Bandura, A. (1969). *Principles of behavior modification.* New York: Holt, Rinehart & Winston.

Bandura, A. (1977). Self-efficacy: Toward a unifying theory of behavioral change. *Psychological Review, 84,* 191–215.

Barlow, D. H., & Cerny, J. A. (1988). *Psychological treatment of panic.* New York: Guilford.

Beck, A. T. (1967). *Depression: Clinical, experimental, and theoretical aspects.* New York: Hoeber. (Republished as *Depression: Causes and treatment.* Philadelphia: University of Pennsylvania Press, 1972.)

Beck, A. T. (1970). Cognitive therapy: Nature and relation to behavior therapy. *Behavior Therapy, 1,* 184–200.

Beck, A. T. (1976). *Cognitive therapy and the emotional disorders.* New York: International Universities Press.

Beck, A. T. (1988). *Love is never enough.* New York: Harper & Row.

Beck, A. T., & Emery, G. (1985). *Anxiety disorders and phobias: A cognitive perspective.* New York: Basic Books.

Beck, A. T., Freeman, A., & Associates. (1990). *Cognitive therapy of personality disorders.* New York: Guilford.

Beck, A. T., Rush, A. J., Shaw, B. F., & Emery, G. (1979). *Cognitive therapy of depression.* New York: Guilford.

Beitman, B. D. (1987). *The structure of individual psychotherapy.* New York: Guilford.

Beitman, B. D., Goldfried, M. R., & Norcross, J. C. (1989). The movement toward integrating the psychotherapies: An overview. *American Journal of Psychiatry, 146,* 138–147.

Belliveau, T. J., Jobes, D. A., Arnkoff, D. B., Dolan, R. T., Gershefski, J. J., Glass, C. R., & Victor, B. J. (1990, April). *The process of change in psychotherapy from object-relations and cognitive–constructivist perspectives.* Paper presented at the meeting of the Society for the Exploration of Psychotherapy Integration, Philadelphia.

Beutler, L. E. (1983). *Eclectic psychotherapy: A systematic approach.* New York: Pergamon.

Beutler, L. E., & Clarkin, J. F. (1990). *Systematic treatment selection: Toward targeted therapeutic interventions.* New York: Brunner/Mazel.

Beutler, L. E., Mahoney, M. J., Norcross, J. C., Prochaska, J. O., Robertson, M. H., & Sollod, R. N. (1987). Training integrative/eclectic psychotherapists II. *Journal of Integrative and Eclectic Psychotherapy, 6,* 296–332.

Birk, L. (1970). Behavior therapy: Integration with dynamic psychiatry. *Behavior Therapy, 1,* 522–526.

Birk, L., Stolz, S. B., Brady, J. P., Brady, J. V., Lazarus, A. A., Lynch, J. J., Rosenthal, A. J., Skelton, W. D., Stevens, J. B., & Thomas, E. J. (1974). *Behavior therapy in psychiatry: A report of the American Psychiatric Association Task Force on Behavior Therapy.* New York: Aronson.

Breger, L., & McGaugh, J. L. (1965). Critique and reformulation of "learning-theory" approaches to psychotherapy and neurosis. *Psychological Bulletin, 63,* 338–358.

Burns, D. M. (1980). *Feeling good.* New York: Morrow.

Carnegie, D. (1948). *How to stop worrying and start living.* New York: Simon & Schuster.

Clark, D. A. (1988). The validity of measures of cognition: A review of the literature. *Cognitive Therapy and Research, 12,* 1–20.

Clark, D. M. (1986). A cognitive approach to panic. *Behaviour Research and Therapy, 24,* 461–470.

Collins, F. L., Jr., Foster, S. L., & Berler, E. S. (1986). Clinical training issues for behavioral psychology. *Professional Psychology: Research and Practice, 17,* 301–307.

Coué, E. (1922). *The practice of autosuggestion.* New York: Doubleday.

Craighead, W. E. (1990). There's a place for us: All of us. *Behavior Therapy, 21,* 3–23.

Davison, G. C. (1990, April). Commentary. In E. Shostrom (Chair), *Integrative psychotherapy: A six-part videotape series and panel discussion.* Symposium presented at the meeting of the Society for the Exploration of Psychotherapy Integration, Philadelphia.

Dember, W. N. (1974). Motivation and the cognitive revolution. *American Psychologist, 29,* 161–168.

Dobson, K. S. (1988). The present and future of the cognitive-behavioral therapies. In K. S. Dobson (Ed.), *Handbook of cognitive–behavioral therapies* (pp. 387–414). New York: Guilford.

Dobson, K. S. (1989). A meta-analysis of the efficacy of cognitive therapy for depression. *Journal of Consulting and Clinical Psychology, 57,* 414–419.

Dobson, K. S., & Block, L. (1988). Historical and philosophical bases of the cognitive–behavioral therapies. In K. S. Dobson (Ed.), *Handbook of cognitive–behavioral therapies* (pp. 3–38). New York: Guilford.

Dollard, J., & Miller, N. E. (1950). *Personality and psychotherapy.* New York: McGraw-Hill.

Dryden, W., & Ellis, A. (1988). Rational-emotive therapy. In K. S. Dobson (Ed.), *Handbook of cognitive–behavioral therapies* (pp. 214–272). New York: Guilford.

Dubois, P. (1905). *The psychic treatment of nervous disorders (The psychoneuroses and their moral treatment)* (S. E. Jelliffe & W. A. White, Ed. and Trans.). New York: Funk & Wagnalls. (Original work published 1904)

D'Zurilla, T. J. (1986). *Problem-solving therapy.* New York: Springer.

D'Zurilla, T. J., & Goldfried, M. R. (1971). Problem solving and behavior modification. *Journal of Abnormal Psychology, 78,* 107–126.

Elkin, I., Shea, M. T., Watkins, J. T., Imber, S. D., Sotsky, S. M., Collins, J. F., Glass, D. R., Pilkonis, P. A., Leber, W. R., Docherty, J. P., Fiester, S. J., & Parloff, M. B. (1989). National Institute of Mental Health Treatment of Depression Collaborative Research Program. *Archives of General Psychiatry*, 46, 971–982.

Ellis, A. (1962). *Reason and emotion in psychotherapy*. New York: Lyle Stuart.

Ellis, A. (1989). History of cognition in psychotherapy. In A. Freeman, K. M. Simon, L. E. Beutler, & H. Arkowitz (Eds.), *Comprehensive handbook of cognitive therapy* (pp. 5–19). New York: Plenum.

Ellis, A., & Harper, R. A. (1961). *A guide to rational living*. Englewood Cliffs, NJ: Prentice-Hall.

Ellis, A., & Harper, R. A. (1975). *A new guide to rational living*. North Hollywood, CA: Wilshire.

Fairburn, C. G. (1985). Cognitive–behavioral treatment for bulimia. In D. M. Garner & P. E. Garfinkel (Eds.), *Handbook of psychotherapy for anorexia nervosa and bulimia* (pp. 160–192). New York: Guilford.

Feather, B. W., & Rhoads, J. M. (1972a). Psychodynamic behavior therapy: I. Theory and rationale. *Archives of General Psychiatry*, 26, 496–502.

Feather, B. W., & Rhoads, J. M. (1972b). Psychodynamic behavior therapy: II. Clinical aspects. *Archives of General Psychiatry*, 26, 503–511.

Feldman, L. B., & Pinsof, W. M. (1982). Problem maintenance in family systems: An integrative model. *Journal of Marriage and Family Therapy*, 8, 295–308.

Frances, A., Clarkin, J., & Perry, S. (1984). *Differential therapeutics in psychiatry: The art and science of treatment selection*. New York: Brunner/Mazel.

Frank, J. D. (1961). *Persuasion and healing*. Baltimore: Johns Hopkins University Press.

Franks, C. M. (1984). On conceptual and technical integrity in psychoanalysis and behavior therapy: Two fundamentally incompatible systems. In H. Arkowitz & S. B. Messer (Eds.), *Psychoanalytic therapy and behavior therapy: Is integration possible?* (pp. 223–247). New York: Plenum.

French, T. M. (1933). Interrelations between psychoanalysis and the experimental work of Pavlov. *American Journal of Psychiatry*, 89, 1165–1203.

Garfield, S. L. (1957). *Introductory clinical psychology*. New York: Macmillan.

Garfield, S. L. (1980). *Psychotherapy: An eclectic approach*. New York: Wiley.

Garfield, S. L. (1982). Eclecticism and integration in psychotherapy. *Behavior Therapy*, 13, 610–623.

Garfield, S. L. (1987). Towards a scientifically oriented eclecticism. *Scandinavian Journal of Behaviour Therapy*, 16, 95–109.

Garfield, S. L. (1989). *The practice of brief psychotherapy*. New York: Pergamon.

Garfield, S. L., & Bergin, A. E. (Eds.). (1986). *Handbook of psychotherapy and behavior change* (3rd ed.). New York: Wiley.

Garfield, S. L., & Kurtz, R. (1976). Clinical psychologists in the 1970s. *American Psychologist*, 31, 1–9.

Garfield, S. L., & Kurtz, R. (1977). A study of eclectic views. *Journal of Consulting and Clinical Psychology*, 45, 78–83.

Golden, W. L., & Dryden, W. (1986). Cognitive-behavioural therapies: Commonalities, divergences and future developments. In W. Dryden & W. L. Golden (Eds.), Cognitive–behavioural approaches to psychotherapy (pp. 356–378). London: Harper & Row.

Goldfried, M. R. (1968, August). Cognitive processes in behavior modification. Symposium presented at the 76th annual convention of American Psychological Association, San Francisco, CA.

Goldfried, M. R. (1980). Toward the delineation of therapeutic change principles. American Psychologist, 35, 991–999.

Goldfried, M. R. (1982). On the history of therapeutic integration. Behavior Therapy, 13, 572–593.

Goldfried, M. R. (1987). The challenge of psychotherapy integration. In W. Huber (Ed.), Progress in psychotherapy research (pp. 801–823). Louvain-la-Neuve, Belgium: Presses Universitaires de Louvain.

Goldfried, M. R., & Davison, G. C. (1976). Clinical behavior therapy. New York: Holt, Rinehart & Winston.

Goldfried, M. R., Decenteceo, E. T., & Weinberg, L. (1974). Systematic rational restructuring as a self-control technique. Behavior Therapy, 5, 247–254.

Goldfried, M. R., & Hayes, A. M. (1989). Can contributions from other orientations complement behavior therapy? the Behavior Therapist, 12, 57–60.

Goldfried, M. R., & Newman, C. (1986). Psychotherapy integration: An historical perspective. In J. C. Norcross (Ed.), Handbook of eclectic psychotherapy (pp. 25–61). New York: Brunner/Mazel.

Goldfried, M. R., & Padawer, W. (1982). Current status and future directions in psychotherapy. In M. R. Goldfried (Ed.), Converging themes in psychotherapy (pp. 3–49). New York: Springer.

Goldfried, M. R., & Safran, J. D. (1986). Future directions in psychotherapy integration. In J. C. Norcross (Ed.), Handbook of eclectic psychotherapy (pp. 463–483). New York: Brunner/Mazel.

Goldfried, M. R., & Strupp, H. H. (1980, November). Empirical clinical practice: A dialogue on rapprochement. Symposium presented at the meeting of the Association for Advancement of Behavior Therapy, New York, NY.

Goldschmid, M. L., Stein, D. D., Weissman, H. N., & Sorrells, J. (1969). A survey of the training and practices of clinical psychologists. The Clinical Psychologist, 22(Winter), 89–94, 107.

Greenberg, L. S., & Safran, J. D. (1987). Emotion in psychotherapy: Affect, cognition and the process of change. New York: Guilford.

Greenberg, L. S., & Safran, J. D. (1989). Emotion in psychotherapy. American Psychologist, 44, 19–29.

Guidano, V. F. (1987). Complexity of the self: A developmental approach to psychopathology and therapy. New York: Guilford.

Guidano, V. F., & Liotti, G. (1983). Cognitive processes and emotional disorders: A structural approach to psychotherapy. New York: Guilford.

Heine, R. W. (1953). A comparison of patients' reports on psychotherapeutic experience with psychoanalytic, nondirective and Adlerian therapists. *American Journal of Psychotherapy*, *7*, 16–23.

Hollon, S. D., & Beck, A. T. (1986). Research on cognitive therapies. In S. L. Garfield & A. E. Bergin (Eds.), *Handbook of psychotherapy and behavior change* (3rd ed., pp. 443–482). New York: Wiley.

Horney, K. (1950). *Neurosis and human growth.* New York: Norton.

Imber, S. D., Pilkonis, P. A., Sotsky, S. M., Elkin, I., Watkins, J. T., Collins, J. F., Shea, M. T., Heber, W. R., & Glass, D. R. (1990). Mode-specific effects among three treatments for depression. *Journal of Consulting and Clinical Psychology*, *58*, 352–359.

Jensen, J. P., Bergin, A. E., & Greaves, D. W. (1990). The meaning of eclecticism: New survey and analysis of components. *Professional Psychology: Research and Practice*, *21*, 124–130.

Kazdin, A. E., Esveldt-Dawson, K., French, N. H., & Unis, A. S. (1987). Problem-solving skills training and relationship therapy in the treatment of antisocial child behavior. *Journal of Consulting and Clinical Psychology*, *55*, 76–85.

Kelly, E. L. (1961). Clinical psychology—1960: Report of survey findings. *Newsletter: Division of Clinical Psychology of the American Psychological Association*, *14*(1), 1–11.

Kelly, E. L., Goldberg, L. R., Fiske, D. W., & Kilkowski, J. M. (1978). Twenty-five years later: A follow-up study of the graduate students in clinical psychology assessed in the VA selection research project. *American Psychologist*, *33*, 746–755.

Kelly, G. A. (1955). *The psychology of personal constructs.* New York: Norton.

Kendall, P. C. (1982). Integration: Behavior therapy and other schools of thought. *Behavior Therapy*, *13*, 559–571.

Kendall, P. C. (1987). Cognitive processes and procedures in behavior therapy. In G. T. Wilson, C. M. Franks, P. C. Kendall, & J. P. Foreyt, *Review of behavior therapy: Theory and practice* (Vol. 11, pp. 114–153). New York: Guilford.

Kendall, P. C., & Bemis, K. M. (1983). Thought and action in psychotherapy: The cognitive–behavioral approaches. In M. Hersen, A. E. Kazdin, & A. S. Bellack (Eds.), *The clinical psychology handbook* (pp. 565–592). New York: Pergamon.

Kendall, P. C., & Braswell, L. (1982). Cognitive-behavioral self-control therapy for children: A components analysis. *Journal of Consulting and Clinical Psychology*, *50*, 672–689.

Kendall, P. C., & Braswell, L. (1985). *Cognitive–behavioral therapy for impulsive children.* New York: Guilford.

Kendall, P. C., & Hollon, S. D. (Eds.). (1981). *Assessment strategies for cognitive–behavioral interventions.* New York: Academic Press.

Kendall, P. C., & Ingram, R. (1987). The future for cognitive assessment of anxiety: Let's get specific. In L. Michelson & L. M. Ascher (Eds.), *Anxiety and stress disorders: Cognitive–behavioral assessment and treatment* (pp. 89–104). New York: Guilford.

Kendall, P. C., Reber, J., McLeer, S., Epps, J., & Ronan, K. R. (1990). Cognitive–behavioral treatment of conduct-disordered children. *Cognitive Therapy and Research, 14,* 279–297.

Kerr, S., Goldfried, M. R., Hayes, A. M., & Goldsamt, L. A. (1989, June). *Differences in therapeutic focus in an interpersonal–psychodynamic and cognitive–behavioral therapy.* Paper presented at the meeting of the Society for Psychotherapy Research, Toronto, Canada.

Kraft, T. (1969). Psychoanalysis and behaviorism: A false antithesis. *American Journal of Psychotherapy, 23,* 482–487.

Kubie, L. S. (1934). Relation of the conditioned reflex to psychoanalytic technique. *Archives of Neurology and Psychiatry, 32,* 1137–1142.

Lambert, M. J., Shapiro, D. A., & Bergin, A. E. (1986). The effectiveness of psychotherapy. In S. L. Garfield & A. E. Bergin (Eds.), *Handbook of psychotherapy and behavior change* (3rd ed., pp. 157–212). New York: Wiley.

Lazarus, A. A. (1967). In support of technical eclecticism. *Psychological Reports, 21,* 415–416.

Lazarus, A. A. (1971). *Behavior therapy and beyond.* New York: McGraw-Hill.

Lazarus, A. A. (1976). *Multimodal behavior therapy.* New York: Springer.

Lazarus, A. A. (1981). *The practice of multimodal therapy.* New York: McGraw-Hill.

Lazarus, A. A. (Ed.). (1985). *Casebook of multimodal therapy.* New York: Guilford.

Lazarus, A. A. (1986). Multimodal therapy. In J. C. Norcross (Ed.), *Handbook of eclectic psychotherapy* (pp. 65–93). New York: Brunner/Mazel.

Lazarus, A. A. (1987). The multimodal approach with adult outpatients. In N. S. Jacobson (Ed.), *Psychotherapists in clinical practice: Cognitive and behavioral perspectives* (pp. 286–326). New York: Guilford.

Lazarus, A. A. (1989). Why I am an eclectic (not an integrationist). *British Journal of Guidance and Counselling, 17,* 248–258.

Lazarus, A. A. (1990). Can psychotherapists transcend the shackles of their training and superstitions? *Journal of Clinical Psychology, 46,* 351–358.

Lebow, J. L. (1984). On the value of integrating approaches to family therapy. *Journal of Marital and Family Therapy, 10,* 127–138.

Liotti, G. (1986). Structural cognitive therapy. In W. Dryden & W. L. Golden (Eds.), *Cognitive-behavioural approaches to psychotherapy* (pp. 92–128). London: Harper & Row.

Lubin, B. (1962). Survey of psychotherapy training and activities of psychologists. *Journal of Clinical Psychology, 18,* 252–256.

Luborsky, L., Singer, B., & Luborsky, L. (1975). Comparative studies of psychotherapies: Is it true that "Everybody has won and all must have prizes"? *Archives of General Psychiatry, 32,* 995–1008.

Mahoney, M. J. (1974). *Cognition and behavior modification.* Cambridge, MA: Ballinger.

Mahoney, M. J. (1977). Reflections on the cognitive–learning trend in psychotherapy. *American Psychologist, 32,* 5–13.

Mahoney, M. J. (1984). Behaviorism, cognitivism, and human change processes. In M. A. Reda & M. J. Mahoney (Eds.), *Cognitive psychotherapies: Recent developments in theory, research, and practice* (pp. 3–30). Cambridge, MA: Ballinger.

Mahoney, M. J. (1990). *Human change processes: Theoretical bases for psychotherapy.* New York: Basic.

Mahoney, M. J., & Arnkoff, D. B. (1978). Cognitive and self-control therapies. In S. L. Garfield & A. E. Bergin (Eds.), *Handbook of psychotherapy and behavior change* (2nd ed., pp. 689–722). New York: Wiley.

Mahoney, M. J., & Gabriel, T. J. (1987). Psychotherapy and the cognitive sciences: An evolving alliance. *Journal of Cognitive Psychotherapy, 1,* 39–59.

Mahoney, M. J., & Gabriel, T. J. (1990). Essential tensions in psychology: Longitudinal data on cognitive and behavioral ideologies. *Journal of Cognitive Psychotherapy, 4,* 5–21.

Mahoney, M. J., Lyddon, W. J., & Alford, D. J. (1989). An evaluation of the rational-emotive theory of psychotherapy. In M. E. Bernard & R. DiGiuseppe (Eds.), *Inside rational–emotive therapy* (pp. 69–94). New York: Academic.

Marks, I. M., & Gelder, M. G. (1966). Common ground between behavior therapy and psychodynamic methods. *British Journal of Medical Psychology, 39,* 11–23.

Marmor, J., & Woods, S. M. (Eds.). (1980). *The interface between the psychodynamic and behavioral therapies.* New York: Plenum.

Meichenbaum, D. H. (1977). *Cognitive–behavior modification.* New York: Plenum.

Meichenbaum, D. (1985). *Stress inoculation training.* New York: Pergamon.

Meichenbaum, D. H., & Cameron, R. (1973). Training schizophrenics to talk to themselves: A means of developing attentional controls. *Behavior Therapy, 4,* 515–534.

Merluzzi, T. V., Glass, C. R., & Genest, M. (1981). *Cognitive assessment.* New York: Guilford.

Messer, S. B. (1986). Behavioral and psychoanalytic perspectives at therapeutic choice points. *American Psychologist, 41,* 1261–1272.

Messer, S. B., & Winokur, M. (1984). Ways of knowing and visions of reality in psychoanalytic therapy and behavior therapy. In H. Arkowitz & S. B. Messer (Eds.), *Psychoanalytic therapy and behavior therapy: Is integration possible?* (pp. 63–100). New York: Plenum.

Neimeyer, R. A. (1986). Personal construct therapy. In W. Dryden & W. L. Golden (Eds.), *Cognitive–behavioural approaches to psychotherapy* (pp. 224–260). London: Harper & Row.

Nevid, J. S., Lavi, B., & Primavera, L. H. (1986). Cluster analysis of training orientations in clinical psychology. *Professional Psychology: Research and Practice, 17,* 367–370.

Nezu, A. M. (1986). Efficacy of a social problem-solving therapy approach for unipolar depression. *Journal of Consulting and Clinical Psychology, 54,* 196–202.

Norcross, J. C. (Ed.). (1986). *Handbook of eclectic psychotherapy.* New York: Brunner/Mazel.

Norcross, J. C. (Ed.). (1987). *Casebook of eclectic psychotherapy.* New York: Brunner/Mazel.

Norcross, J. C., Beutler, L. E., Clarkin, J. F., DiClemente, C. C., Halgin, R. P., Frances, A., Prochaska, J. O., Robertson, M., & Suedfeld, P. (1986). Training integrative/eclectic psychotherapists. *International Journal of Eclectic Psychotherapy, 5,* 71–94.

Norcross, J. C., Nash, J. M., & Prochaska, J. O. (1985). Psychologists in part-time independent practice: Description and comparison. *Professional Psychology: Research and Practice, 16,* 565–575.

Norcross, J. C., & Prochaska, J. O. (1982). A national survey of clinical psychologists: Affiliations and orientations. *The Clinical Psychologist, 35*(3), 1–2, 4–6.

Norcross, J. C., & Prochaska, J. O. (1983). Psychotherapists in independent practice: Some findings and issues. *Professional Psychology: Research and Practice, 14,* 869–881.

Norcross, J. C., & Prochaska, J. O. (1988). A study of eclectic (and integrative) views revisited. *Professional Psychology: Research and Practice, 19,* 170–174.

Norcross, J. C., Prochaska, J. O., & Gallagher, K. M. (1989). Clinical psychologists in the 1980s: II. Theory, research, and practice. *The Clinical Psychologist, 42*(3), 45–53.

Norcross, J. C., Strausser-Kirtland, D., & Missar, C. D. (1989). The processes and outcomes of psychotherapists' personal treatment experiences. *Psychotherapy, 25,* 36–43.

Norcross, J. C., & Thomas, B. L. (1988). What's stopping us now? Obstacles to psychotherapy integration. *Journal of Integrative and Eclectic Psychotherapy, 7,* 74–80.

Novaco, R. W., Cook, T. M., & Sarason, I. G. (1983). Military recruit training: An arena for stress-coping skills. In D. Meichenbaum & M. E. Jaremko (Eds.), *Stress reduction and prevention* (pp. 377–418). New York: Plenum.

Ollendick, T. H. (1986). Child and adolescent behavior therapy. In S. L. Garfield & A. E. Bergin (Eds.), *Handbook of psychotherapy and behavior change* (3rd ed., pp. 525–564). New York: Wiley.

Orlinsky, D. E., & Howard, K. I. (1987). A generic model of psychotherapy. *Journal of Integrative and Eclectic Psychotherapy, 6,* 6–27.

Peale, N. V. (1960). *The power of positive thinking.* Englewood Cliffs, NJ: Prentice-Hall.

Prochaska, J. O., & DiClemente, C. C. (1984). *The transtheoretical approach: Crossing the traditional boundaries of therapy.* Homewood, IL: Dow Jones-Irwin.

Prochaska, J. O., & Norcross, J. C. (1983). Contemporary psychotherapists: A national survey of characteristics, practices, orientations, and attitudes. *Psychotherapy: Theory, Research and Practice, 20,* 161–173.

Rhoads, J. M., & Feather, B. W. (1974). The application of psychodynamics to behavior therapy. *American Journal of Psychiatry, 131,* 17–20.

Rosenzweig, S. (1936). Some implicit common factors in diverse methods in psychotherapy. *American Journal of Orthopsychiatry, 6,* 412–415.

Rotter, J. B. (1954). *Social learning and clinical psychology.* Englewood Cliffs, NJ: Prentice-Hall.

Rush, A. J., Beck, A. T., Kovacs, M., & Hollon, S. D. (1977). Comparative efficacy of cognitive therapy and pharmacotherapy in the treatment of depressed outpatients. *Cognitive Therapy and Research, 1,* 17–37.

Safran, J. D. (1990a). Towards a refinement of cognitive therapy in light of interpersonal theory: I. Theory. *Clinical Psychology Review, 10,* 87–105.

Safran, J. D. (1990b). Towards a refinement of cognitive therapy in light of interpersonal theory: II. Practice. *Clinical Psychology Review, 10,* 107–121.

Safran, J. D., & Segal, Z. V. (1990). *Interpersonal process in cognitive therapy.* New York: Basic.

Sayette, M. A., & Mayne, T. J. (1990). Survey of current clinical and research trends in clinical psychology. *American Psychologist, 45,* 1263–1266.

Segal, Z. V., & Shaw, B. F. (1988). Cognitive assessment: Issues and methods. In K. S. Dobson (Ed.), *Handbook of cognitive–behavioral therapies* (pp. 39–81). New York: Guilford.

Segraves, R. T. (1982). *Marital therapy: A combined psychodynamic–behavioral approach.* New York: Plenum.

Shaffer, L. F. (1953). Of whose reality I cannot doubt. *American Psychologist, 8,* 608–623.

Shemberg, K. M., & Leventhal, D. B. (1978). A survey of activities of academic clinicians. *Professional Psychology, 9,* 580–586.

Silverman, L. H. (1974). Some psychoanalytic considerations of non-psychoanalytic therapies: On the possibility of integrating treatment approaches and related issues. *Psychotherapy: Theory, Research, and Practice, 11,* 298–305.

Simons, A. D., Garfield, S. L., & Murphy, G. E. (1984). The process of change in cognitive therapy and pharmacotherapy for depression: Change in mood and cognition. *Archives of General Psychiatry, 41,* 45–51.

Sloane, R. B., Staples, F. R., Cristol, A. H., Yorkston, N. J., & Whipple, K. (1975). *Psychotherapy versus behavior therapy.* Cambridge, MA: Harvard University Press.

Smith, D. (1982). Trends in counseling and psychotherapy. *American Psychologist, 37,* 802–809.

Smith, M. L., Glass, G. V., & Miller, T. I. (1980). *The benefits of psychotherapy*. Baltimore: Johns Hopkins University Press.

Spivack, G., Platt, J. J., & Shure, M. B. (1976). *The problem-solving approach to adjustment*. San Francisco: Jossey-Bass.

Stampfl, T. G., & Levis, D. J. (1967). Essentials of implosive therapy: A learning-theory-based psychodynamic behavioral therapy. *Journal of Abnormal Psychology, 72,* 496–503.

Suinn, R. M. (1990). *Anxiety management training: A behavior therapy*. New York: Plenum.

Suinn, R. M., & Richardson, F. (1971). Anxiety management training: A non-specific behavior therapy program for anxiety control. *Behavior Therapy, 2,* 498–510.

Tryon, G. S. (1983). Full-time private practice in the United States: Results of a national survey. *Professional Psychology: Research and Practice, 14,* 685–696.

Turk, D., Meichenbaum, D., & Genest, M. (1983). *Pain and behavioral medicine*. New York: Guilford.

Ullmann, L. P. (1970). On cognitions and behavior therapy. *Behavior Therapy, 1,* 201–204.

Wachtel, P. L. (1977). *Psychoanalysis and behavior therapy: Toward an integration*. New York: Basic Books.

Wachtel, P. L. (1982). What can dynamic therapies contribute to behavior therapy? *Behavior Therapy, 13,* 594–609.

Walen, S. R., DiGiuseppe, R., & Wessler, R. L. (1980). *A practitioner's guide to rational–emotive therapy*. New York: Oxford University Press.

Wandersman, A., Poppen, P. J., & Ricks, D. F. (Eds.). (1976). *Humanism and behaviorism: Dialogue and growth*. Oxford: Pergamon.

Watkins, C. E., Jr., Lopez, F. G., Campbell, V. L., & Himmell, C. D. (1986). Contemporary counseling psychology: Results of a national survey. *Journal of Counseling Psychology, 33,* 301–309.

Weitzman, B. (1967). Behavior therapy and psychotherapy. *Psychological Review, 74,* 300–317.

Wilson, G. T. (1978). Cognitive behavior therapy: Paradigm shift or passing phase? In J. P. Foreyt & D. P. Rathjen (Eds.), *Cognitive behavior therapy: Research and application* (pp. 7–32). New York: Plenum.

Wilson, G. T. (1982). Psychotherapy process and procedure: The behavioral mandate. *Behavior Therapy, 13,* 291–312.

Wolfe, B. E. (1989). Phobias, panic, and psychotherapy integration. *Journal of Integrative and Eclectic Psychotherapy, 8,* 264–276.

Wolfe, B. E., & Goldfried, M. R. (1988). Research on psychotherapy integration: Recommendations and conclusions from an NIMH workshop. *Journal of Consulting and Clinical Psychology, 56,* 448–451.

Young, J. E. (1990). *Cognitive therapy for personality disorders: A schema-focused approach*. Sarasota, FL: Professional Resource Exchange.

21

PSYCHOTHERAPY IN GROUPS

MAX ROSENBAUM, MARTIN LAKIN, AND HOWARD B. ROBACK

While therapy in groups is as ancient as history itself—in healing rites, collective confessionals, and mutual support as well as mutual criticism—the spectacle of secular groups specifically organized for the purpose of enabling the participants to cope with psychological distress or dysfunction would scarcely be comprehensible to our ancestors. And yet, the spectacular proliferation of all kinds of group therapies in our own times is not only responsive to the idea of more treatment for more people; it also meets longings among people for deeper interpersonal contact that remain unsatisfied owing to many alienative features of our own culture. For example, Shapiro and Shapiro (1985) pointed out that the replacement of regular social contact with fellow workers by the video display terminal is but another example of the increasing loss of human connectedness in daily living.

Group forms of psychotherapy, as well as group "quasi-therapies," are growing at such a rapid rate that it is becoming increasingly important to assess their purposes as well as their processes and effects. For the individual help-seeker, a group form of therapy might or might not be the therapy of choice; we therapists know that our "consumers" can have little prior understanding of the dynamics of the specific treatment to which we might direct them. As difficult as it is to explain the procedures of individual psychotherapy, explaining group therapy is even harder. Later in the chapter we will identify the attempts of various clinicians to ameliorate this problem. But no solution can be expected to fundamentally resolve issues about which we therapists are also on occasion confused.

Being referred for group therapy is one possible channel to a multi-person treatment context. Others include family groups, couples groups, and self-help or support groups. The question comes naturally, "Why this form of treatment rather than that one?" However, the processes and the probable consequences of one form of psychotherapy rather than another are infrequently considered by therapists and seldom explored in introductory sessions with patients/clients. Fulfilling their professional responsibilities requires that psychotherapists, in general, and group therapists in particular, make sincere efforts to render intelligible and comprehensible what they propose.

Psychotherapy systems have been characterized as technologies for personal change. But each is more than merely a collection of techniques for altering mood or behavior. Each orientation in therapy, and, to a lesser extent, each modality, conveys certain ways of looking at the world, a "world view" in the ways that problems are interpreted and dealt with. Each of the theories of psychotherapy has a developmental history of its own, shaped by the experiences and perspectives of its pioneer practitioners. This is no less true of the history of group psychotherapy than of other modes of treatment. The individuals who influenced its early years, as well as those who shape its present forms, expressed—and are still implicitly expressing—"philosophic" points of view about what participants suffer psychologically and about what must be done in order to ameliorate their distress. Group therapists conceive their treatments in terms of implicit notions about pathology and health that relate to the context of treatment and that have concrete implications for the clients who participate in their groups. These therapists may not even be fully conscious of these implications when they refer the help seeker to their groups.

In the light of these considerations, we will consider the following issues in this chapter:

- The background of the origins and of the present expressions of group psychotherapies;

- Comparing individual and group forms of psychotherapy, particularly the part played by group dynamics;

- Current trends in group therapy practice;

- The dynamics of self-help, support, encounter, and other groups;

- Intergroup conflict resolution groups; and

- Ethical issues of therapeutic group experience.

THE DISPUTES IN GROUP PSYCHOTHERAPY

Although the group confessional originated in ancient religious practice, it persists in contemporary group therapies. Its persistence derives from the power of ritualistic disclosure of personal misdeeds to one's peers and signifies the determination to modify one's previously injurious or socially maladaptive behavior. As such, confessionals came to be regarded as a legitimate way of coping with anxiety and guilt. Group confessions and individual confessions in groups apparently also had the effect of diminishing in-group rivalries and uniting the group (Kiev, 1964). In present day groups, self-disclosure—the modern form of confession—is still a major criterion for judging the sincerity of the client's therapeutic wish and purpose.

Patterns of behavior in "therapeutic groups" in western societies frequently involved not only personal and collective confession, they also included relaxed standards and norms of behavior. Thus, Wolf and Kiev, Mischel and Mischel, and Leiris (in Kiev, 1964) reported phenomena of "role exchange" among male and female participants. For instance, the females, nominally passive and relatively obsequious to the males, would become bold and defiant, even acting out sexually aggressive roles. The males, for their parts, would take on the passive ways traditionally assigned by the culture to the females. The group, through the authority of those who conducted it, would give sanctions for such temporary relaxation of the cultural norms for the purpose of "emotionally corrective experience." Such latitude for behavioral expressions is not typical for contemporary group therapies, to be sure. However, some relaxation of conventional expectations for member behavior is not only routine; it is essential for reducing participants' feelings of negative uniqueness. It is such feelings that contribute to the estrangement of those who feel mentally distressed from their families and friends.

It seems that cultures have always employed group forms of treatment as corrective emotional experiences and as a means of mutual support. The use of groups for these purposes in "communitarian" societies is an expression of their emphasis on social behaviors. However, even in our own so-called individualistic society, the various group psychotherapies appear to be responsive to our persistent needs for inclusion and belongingness.

Another common feature of all therapeutic group experiences is the feeling that "We are all in the same boat." Achieving a level of cohesion and recognizing that the progress of individual participants depends on the other members' help reduce even further the feelings of estrangement and isolation that characterize many people who seek help. Thus, it is natural to emphasize ideas of togetherness and common fate. Equally important, because religious and moralistic prescriptions for mental health traditionally regarded psychological suffering as the consequence of moral missteps (in thought and intent, if not in action), participation in modern psychotherapy groups often reduces fears of personal moral culpability. Anxieties about personal moral responsibility for one's psychological distress are common even among non-religious persons in our relatively secular society.

In most Western societies the "adjusted" person was communally involved, while those who held themselves apart from others could only be viewed as pathologically deviant. Even privacy is a modern idea (see Simmel, in Wolff, 1950). Knowing about others and having them know about you was inescapable in the village life of a bygone era, in contrast to our modern age. In our time, as Jourard (1964) asserted, we fear being known— if we were, we could/would be harmed. Thus, there is a residual ambivalence about self-disclosure. Hope for acceptance is countered by fear of rejection. It may be for this reason that in today's group therapies, unburdening oneself to the group and receiving feedback from the other participants has such emotional significance.

Self-disclosure and emotional dependence on a group in which one's inner feelings are revealed leads to ambivalence about participation. Participants are inescapably anxious about what the group might do *to* them, even as they excitedly hope for the good that the group might do *for* them. There are significant reasons for ambivalence that have nothing to do with personal mental pathology or health. For instance, Horkheimer and Adorno (1973) phrased the issue in terms of our interconnections to, but also our resistance to, others. Koch (1971) argued, "However inefficient the ordinary conditions of character formation, it is diabolical to make these contingent on group engineering [sic] . . . authenticity can only be achieved by allowing *intrapersonal* [our emphasis] factors the fullest possible play. . . ." The differentiation of reality and distortion of group participation is played out in each therapy group, most often benignly, but sometimes aversively.

Therapeutic group experience inevitably involves expressing one's need to belong, but fearing suffocation by the collective; being responsive to group norms, but possibly becoming enmeshed in conforming; becoming more independent, but requiring reiterated affirmation and confirmation from other participants.

For the pioneers of group therapy the social element was the essential missing link in psychotherapeutic approaches. Individualism and emphasis on personal achievement had eroded the sense of belongingness that is necessary to mental health according to Durkheim (1953). For Burrow (1927) and Moreno (1953, 1957), group therapy was *social* treatment for what they considered *social* pathology. Like Bakan (1966), they regarded the split between communitarian and "agentic" impulses as dangerous to mental health. According to Bakan, integrating our agentic with our communitarian needs is the challenge for maintaining mental health; that is, being part of, yet separate from; trying to master, yet yielding to others' mastery; protecting ourselves from others, yet remaining open to their benign influence on ourselves; maintaining personal independence, but wanting to use the support and encouragement of others; standing ready to help others, but resisting exploitation by them.

Understanding how these contending needs and the group processes interact is important for responsible conduct of therapeutic groups. But it is not clear that most group therapists do, in fact, fully understand the processes that occur in their groups. To do so, it is necessary to review the separate strands of group experiences that have patterned the group therapy movement in our society. Then we will be in a better position to consider present practices and the issues emanating from them.

DEVELOPMENT OF GROUP THERAPY

In the early 1900s J. H. Pratt, a medical practitioner, combined classroom instruction and mutual support among his patients (1953). The inspiration for using these elements came partly from his reading of the French psychiatrist, Dejerine (1913) and partly from his conviction that a group context could be supportive to the medically ill individual in one's struggles to regain or maintain health. What we usually think of as psychological understanding or self insight played virtually no role in his groups. Nevertheless, the elements of mutual comradeship and support as well as explicit or implicit mutual criticism are still major aspects of all group therapies, even self-help organizations and quasi-therapy experiential groups.

Lazell (1921), a psychiatrist, lectured to his groups about psychopathology and mentally healthy behavior. Even though his patients were reportedly schizophrenic, he used virtually the same techniques as Pratt. Noting that when his patients were grouped, they seemed to be encouraged and less apprehensive, he explained this to be the result of the newfound companionship offered in the group (Lazell, 1921). Later, Marsh (1935), another innovator, developed an almost revivalistic atmosphere in his "classes," based on his beliefs that groups have inherent curative influences. He created the catch phrase, "By the crowds they have been broken; by the crowds they shall be healed!"

Similar to Marsh, a psychiatrist named Wender (1936) also began his group sessions by lecturing to his patients about issues of development, the reasons for psychopathology, and ways of maintaining mental health. After these lectures the patients would discuss their personal problems in the light of the points made by their doctor. However, because he was psychoanalytically oriented—one of the first group leaders who were—his groups were characterized by attempts to develop self-insight, that is, deeper understanding of personal drives and needs, as well as by exchanging information and mutual support. He and Schilder (1939) were first in relating their group work to their psychoanalytic ideas of psychological pathology. Schilder made extensive use of detailed personal histories—shared by group members—in his groups. He recommended groups as the treatment of choice for those he termed "social neurotics" (i.e., his patients who were distinguished by their discomfort and anxiety in interpersonal situations). Probably the first widely read publication about group therapy techniques was Wender's. He described the group treatment of psychiatric cases in 1936, and the article was then adopted by the military as a manual and was, consequently, widely used during World War II.

"Psychodrama" has persisted as a significant influence on the practice of group psychotherapy from early in the century. Moreno, its undisputed creator (1924, 1953, 1957), was an "outsider" to the mental health establishment who initiated his psychodrama by having actors and audiences play out unrehearsed events that had been reported in daily newspapers. He called this the "Theatre of Spontaneity." In the prewar days of Vienna the public regarded the activity as partly entertainment, although Moreno thought of it as therapeutic. According to Moreno, a person's disturbed or conflicted feelings are about parents, siblings, spouses, children, and friends. The disturbed relationships with such closely tied people underlie many instances of emotional distress that eventuate in real dysfunction. Amelioration—even remediation—of these conditions can be achieved through "dramatizations and reenactments" with those actual persons or with persons who could symbolize or "stand in" for them. His "theatre" provided a setting in which the tensions of those relationships could be role-played and bring about catharsis, relief, and insight. Members of the audience were recruited to various roles in the dramatization after which all active participants and members of the audience would compare their in-role reactions and further analyze the problem for the presumed benefit of the central person.

Distinct traces of psychodrama are powerfully reflected in the emotionalized interactions between members when disclosures and shared anxieties lead to similar reenactments, particularly when the characteristics of other members remind one of key figures in one's personal past. In fact, the processes of some psychoanalytically oriented groups are held to be working through precisely such "horizontal transference" reactions, once they are clearly elicited and demonstrated.

Some therapists insisted that social factors represented in group therapies were so important that groups should completely replace dyads as treatment contexts. One of those was Burrow (1927, 1958), who went so far as to assert that the individual treatments had been developed in error and that the sources as well as the cures of psychological disorder lay in social factors, that is, failures to relate and to establish mutually satisfying relationships. Coincidentally, Burrow, a psychoanalyst, came to believe in a more social and egalitarian view of therapy and of human relations in general. In his own groups he shunned the role of expert in favor of curing by means of mutual understanding, candor, and supportiveness among helpers and help seekers.

Foulkes (1966) voiced similar objections—though not as stridently—to the preeminence of individual psychotherapies. He also stressed the importance of communitarian feelings and outlets for their expression, the lack of which was a major factor in psychonoxious stresses. But pioneers of the group therapy movement did not all speak with one voice in such matters. For instance, Slavson (1964) actually warned against engendering too much mutual support or cohesion in therapeutic groups, lest they become resistive to the personal change that they, in fact, were organized to facilitate!

For the most part, psychotherapists regarded groups as ancillary or supplementary rather than primary treatment vehicles. As Schilder (1939) asserted, his individual analyses were "enriched" by the analysands' meeting in groups. Similarly, other dynamically oriented therapists thought of their group work as ancillary or "secondary," persisting in viewing the goals of the groups in ways that depended primarily on the person's individual psychotherapy experience. Groups could certainly extend the patient's understandings into social and interpersonal areas, but these therapists did not consider group procedures special; they were simply extensions of individual therapy.

To illustrate, we can recall psychoanalysts' reasons for devaluing group therapy. They stated that individual psychotherapy and psychoanalysis were naturally preferable to groups because one could not possibly develop or resolve "real transference" reactions in the multiperson context. In response, proponents of psychoanalytic group psychotherapy actually evolved the idea of what they termed the "horizontal transference," consisting of elicitation of the symbolized sibling and authority-centered problems that could develop or surface over the course of a group experience. To what extent this conception became popular and how widely it was employed cannot now be ascertained. In any event, the argument about whether or not such characteristically psychoanalytic phenomena fully or only partially developed in groups has largely subsided.

Efforts to connect group procedures with various schools of therapy have persisted. Early on, Slavson tried to merge educational goals, psychodynamics, and group processes based on the ideals of "experiential learning" propounded by the philosopher John Dewey (1948). Powdermaker and Frank (1953) documented group therapy procedures. Foulkes and Anthony (1965) integrated their perspective on psychoanalytic therapy with the group dynamic conceptions of Kurt Lewin, as did George Bach (1954). Among other early books describing group therapies were Corsini's *Methods of Group Psychotherapy* (1957), Mullan and Rosenbaum's *Group Psychotherapy* (1962), and Rosenbaum and Berger's *Group Psychotherapy and Group Function* (1963). Clinical reports and novel conceptions of group work began to be published in 1950 in the *International Journal of Group Psychotherapy* and in other professional journals.

British interdisciplinary teams had also begun to use groups with discharged veterans, former prisoners of war, and delinquents (Bion, 1961; Jones, 1953) in treatment and rehabilitation programs. In England, too, there was debate about the wisdom of substituting group for individual work. Most therapists outside Britain, even those convinced of the value of group therapies, were persuaded that individual treatments could probe more deeply and could be more comprehensive; groups were deemed to be more "present-oriented" and, therefore, probably more superficial. Some group therapists vigorously disagreed, particularly Wolf and Schwartz (1962), who asserted that the group could, in fact, be even more facilitative for analytic work than a traditional one-to-one relationship. It seems clear, in retrospect, that proponents and adversaries in these debates failed to recognize that group therapies are not necessarily more, or less deep; more, or less comprehensive; more, or less dynamic; or more, or less anything! They are simply different in experiential ways that could have significant influences on outcomes. We will return to this issue later in the chapter.

CO-OPTING GROUP METHODS TO INDIVIDUAL THERAPY SYSTEMS

A therapy that is conceived in social terms would naturally find group methods congenial. Thus, the "individual psychology" of Alfred Adler, with emphasis on "social interest" and on coping with feelings of inferiority, related to group methods that made such issues salient. The conviction that self-absorption could lead to dysfunction was natural to groups as well as one of the main ideas of the therapy system. The group would provide a needed corrective social experience in which one could learn how better to cope with the excessive power drives and excessively rivalrous feelings that the therapy would bring to the fore. Social commitments of the successfully treated would replace previously asocial or antisocial ways of adaptation.

Neo-Freudian therapists found group procedures almost as congenial for similar reasons. Moreover, they could more readily interpret the here-and-now behaviors of participants from their interactions in the groups and not have to rely on the "archeologies" of personal histories. The "psychodramatization" of problems was, in the therapists' view, a sufficiently corrective emotional experience. At the same time, however, there were continuing efforts to combine the "group analytic" ideas of Bion (1961) with analytic ideas gleaned from studying individual therapy hours. For instance, Whitaker and Lieberman (1964) integrated Bion's ideas of primitive group patterns of response (dependent, aggressive, and sexual responses) with Thomas French's idea that every single session held an identifiable specific theme. They then proceeded to demonstrate how almost every group session could be shown to contain a struggle between one or another of these primitive impulses and reactive fears of retaliation for expressing it. From this perspective, the role of group therapists was to point out uses of "restrictive" (neurotic) as opposed to "enabling" (healthier) strategies.

Gestalt[1] therapy and transactional analysis (TA) quickly adapted group methods. The former modeled on Perls's (1969) strategies of demonstrating "role-playing phoniness," that is, eliciting dissembling feelings and reactions, which could be discarded in favor of more genuine self-representation. The group would become the stage for session-targeted individuals who would be encouraged (coaxed, persuaded, goaded) into expressing their feelings (resentments, longings, etc.). For TA, the group modality was especially congenial to the playing out of emotions and other reactions in the roles of the schema laid down by the therapy system's creator, Eric Berne (viz., as "child," "parent," or "adult"). The "games patients play" would be dramatically illustrated in terms of their enduring "scripts" that had to be challenged and confronted in order for change to take place. By encouraging such "scripted" interactions to take place, the therapist uses the group to remediate conflicts that underlie disordered relationships.

---

[1] A term Perls adopted but which has no relationship to Gestalt theory.

With less "dynamic" ballast—because they deliberately avoid it—behavioral and cognitive behavioral therapies have also co-opted group methods for pragmatic reasons: (a) reinforcement for "desirable" behavior change can be relatively easily mobilized among peers in groups; (b) discussion and clarification of problems, a necessary step in behavior change, takes place more naturally in group contexts; and (c) group treatment obviously allows not only for simultaneous treatment of a number of persons; it also amplifies the "therapeutic message."

Carl Rogers and some of his followers also turned to group methods as extensions of their client-centered approach. At first their group treatment was consistent with the basically accepting and reflecting strategies of his individual therapy. However, in the mid-1960s, Rogers' group therapy emerged as a preoccupation with emotionally charged interactions in "encounter groups." Toward the end of his life, Rogers increasingly emphasized their significance in overcoming not only personal inhibitions and stress as well as interpersonal alienation, but even in coping with interethnic and international conflicts (1968, 1973, 1980; also see chapter 19 in this volume).

Only one mainstream system of therapy remained ideologically resistant—although not all of its practitioners have always rejected group methods. When C. G. Jung (Illing, 1963) was asked to give his views about the spread of group methods, he responded,

> In our time which puts so much weight on the socialization of the individual, because a special capacity for adjustment is needed, the psychologically oriented group formation is of great importance. However, in view of the notorious inclinations of people to lean on others and on "isms" rather than on inner security and independence, which should have first place, there is the danger that the individual will equate the group with father and mother, and will, thereby, remain as dependent, insecure, and infantile as ever. (p. 184)

Jung would probably have agreed with Schoeck (1966) who wrote, "It may be that man experiences his (group) membership not as fulfillment, but actually as diminution . . . as compromise with his true being . . ." (p. 89).

It is worthwhile to classify theoretical approaches to therapy that have adapted or co-opted group methods by the aspect of group experience that is emphasized in their group techniques. For the most part, psychodynamically oriented group therapies are likely to encourage somewhat more "regressive–reconstructive" or personal history as well as present-time exchanges, whereas the behaviorally oriented groups are more likely to be in tailoring programs oriented toward planned change and developing in-group schemes for rewarding (reinforcing) changes in desired directions.

However, it is important to emphasize that all of the groups—regardless of their therapist's positions on intrapsychic or interpersonal conceptions of psychological distress and dysfunction—are bound to try to mobilize the group forces for purposes of personal change. The forces are basically the same in all therapeutic change induction groups. The longing for belonging, the power of mutual support, mutual criticism, and social comparison are used to bring about wanted changes. Whether the group is *more* or *less* here-and-now, *more* or *less* psychodynamic, or *more* or *less* cognitive-behavioral, these elements are used first to try to integrate the individual as an active member of the group itself, then to become "changed" within it, and ultimately to work on re-entering one's own life community and dealing with life problems in that context.

Despite the commonality—perhaps because of it—theories underlying these group approaches have remained at a relatively primitive level. Indeed, what group therapists say they do in terms of group techniques and what they actually do are not necessarily always concordant. Moreover, the overlap in rationales between one type of group and another virtually blot out what might be meaningful distinctions. Many rely on relatively "dynamic" interpretations of personal and group behaviors, but others do not. Some are carefully here-and-now oriented, while others regularly delve into personal histories. Some therapists appear to routinely "pull for" emotional self-disclosure from the group's beginnings, but others are more conservative in their demand for self-revelations. One gets the impression that the more charismatic leaders of groups are sometimes "hazardous" to their clients/patients' health. A "long-tenured" therapy group can even become a kind of Greek chorus, echoing and amplifying the interrogations and the prescriptions of its leaders, to the detriment of its ostensible therapy purpose.

Critics of group therapy would agree with its practitioners that its proliferation is one of the most remarkable developments in mental health services in this century. However, these critics would certainly argue about whether the supportive and corrective interpersonal experiences offered in groups is therapy that is hard to find elsewhere. In particular, the critics might say that therapy groups and quasi-therapy groups are often less therapy than a kind of psychological searching. Marin (1975) bitterly characterized the "fringe" encounter group movement as a middle-class preoccupation. The psychologist Boring (1972) complained about the ambiguity of many therapy group experiences; "While some complain that a group is passed off as entertainment when in truth it is (a) therapy, others complain (that) it is being passed off as therapy when in truth it is entertainment" (p. 3).

Whereas most therapeutic group experiences will exploit the group's tendency to elicit and reinforce the reenactments or psychodramatizations of personal problems, all of them will mobilize participants in support of the group's change induction program. Although therapists in some groups share their intervention initiatives with their members, others act in more authoritarian ways. Self-expression is more valued in some, while greater self-control is sought in others. Therapists, therefore, differ also in terms of the degree of their deliberate stimulation of emotionalized responses and their elicitation of personal disclosures.

The differences seem to stem less from knowledge and understanding of group processes as such, than from some point of view or therapy "ideology" that has little relation to the processes that are intrinsic to the interactional flow of group experience. In fact they seem more to be products of conceptions nurtured in training for individual roles and functions as individual psychotherapists that are "carried over" into group practice of the therapist. That is one reason the actual procedures of group therapies are so difficult to analyze. The fact that there is as yet no generally accepted theory of group therapy is in no small part due to this plethora of undifferentiated group and individual concepts that characterize the "cognitive maps" of many group therapists.

GROUP DYNAMICS: ABORTIVE STEPS TOWARD A THEORY OF THERAPEUTIC GROUP PROCESSES

The influence of the small face-to-face group on its members' productivity began to be studied only in the mid-1930s when Mayo (1933) and Roethlisberger and Dickson (1939) became impressed by the importance of informal relationships in small workers' groups for determining personal as well as collective output. Group attitudes—in the final analysis, interpersonal attitudes—influenced productivity more than technological improvements that were specifically designed to boost it. In reviewing group dynamics studies, Back (1974) and Greenbaum (1979) pointed out how significant relationships were for combat units and air crews in wartime when effective intragroup cooperation was literally a matter of life or death.

The years following World War II were a fertile period in the study of group interactions, a time of experimentation in academic settings as well as field trials of ideas. Group techniques were applied to problems as varied as labor-management conflict, ethnic and racial tensions, psychotherapy, rehabilitation, and other social problems. In Britain, as in the United States, there was considerable optimism about using such techniques to resolve problems in industrial settings, to ameliorate social integration, to correct delinquency, and to effect psychotherapeutic change. The Tavistock Clinic's Institute for Human Relations began to incorporate many group techniques into its own psychotherapy training program as well as in its ancillary programs for general physicians and for human relations specialists.

In such an intellectual atmosphere the conceptions of Sherif's "frames of reference" (1948), Homans' ideas of "reference groups" (1950), Asch's studies in the processes and consequences of conformist pressures (1956), and especially, Lewin's (1947, 1948) group standards, "force-field analysis," and his other group dynamic innovations appeared to have an almost instantaneous relevance for many societal as well as personal problems.

In the United States "human relation labs" and workshops developed from the fortuitously serendipitous discovery that group experiences become most powerfully instructive when the personal and interpersonal experiences of the participants themselves emerge as topics of discussion and on-the-spot analysis. The National Training Laboratories (NTL) engendered enthusiasm for this kind of group and personal learning without, at first, relating it directly to psychotherapeutic purposes. However, rival conceptions that emphasized more psychotherapy-like concerns soon spread around the country. Even the NTL shifted its original institutional change focus in favor of the more popular personal experiential model. Derivative group experiences, including the "encounter group" idea at Esalen and subsequently co-opted by Rogers, organizations like Erhard's "est" and the currently popular "Lifespring," have, in their emphasis on emotional "highs," turned the original learning group process-focused experience into something quite different from what Kurt Lewin, its founder, had in mind.

Lewin had conceived of the minimally structured learning group as similar to a personality subject to reciprocal influences of the collective and the individual. Any topic, any emotional reaction or response, or any breach of the group's norms could become the basis of group discussion and evolve through clarification and understanding as a basis for change. The way to induce change in the group was to "unfreeze" the stance of the group or of individual members and to overcome the forces resistant to change that anchor the group or its members in unwanted or dysfunctional patterns of behavior. Lewin's conception of "force field" was an effort to conceptualize—eventually to quantify—obstacles to change as well as the forces impelling it.

Group dynamics did not produce a comprehensive perspective on therapy group processes. However, important studies of involvement (Bavelas, 1950; Leavitt, 1951), social comparison (Festinger, 1954), and cohesiveness (Back, 1951; Schacter, 1951) contributed to our understanding of the dynamics of therapy groups in terms of not only their benign influences, but also the potentially distortive processes that can produce negative effects on individual participants. Although its legacy is not a comprehensive theory, it has left us enduring, significant questions, such as: What are optimal group processes? How can group procedures be most efficaciously employed for the benefit of the individual participant? Can we specify those group processes that facilitate positive, as contrasted with negative, changes? To what extent may a group's therapist rely on spontaneously evolving group dynamics; to what extent must the therapist direct them? How can one best facilitate the useful carryover of group gains to the daily lives and close relationships of participants? The answers to these vital questions still elude us.

THE PHENOMENON OF SELF-HELP IN GROUPS

Group therapies would seem to be natural vehicles for mutual aid by and for people facing difficult life circumstances, whether psychological in origin or not. But a somewhat specialized species of helping group, the "self-help" group, has arisen. Its historic origins were consumer cooperatives, utopian communes, some extraordinary trade unions, the "Friendly Societies" of Britain, and other institutional associations with commitments to ideas of mutual aid and mutual responsibility. These ideas were, as in some therapy groups, often blended with religiously derived notions of collective confession and corrective criticism. According to Reissman and Gartner (1979), their effectiveness lay in their self-reliant responsiveness to shared afflictions. In most self-help organizations, group procedures are either directly under participants' control or are codified in governance guidelines. Even where health specialists or other professionals have initiated the groups, they are supposed to adhere to principles of self-guidance, mutual reliance, and mutual aid. (However, it must be noted that currently, they are increasingly being organized and conducted by professional leaders.)

Self-help groups are organized for so many different purposes and populations that Lieberman (1976, p. 253) characterized the self-help movement as ". . . (groups) for almost every conceivable end with almost every conceivable (group) arrangement for almost every conceivable type of person." For instance, there are groups for easing personal bereavement, groups for the terminally ill, groups for easing psychological adjustments to the various "ostomies" that may follow surgery for cancer, groups for alcohol abusers as well as for the relatives of such abusers, groups for battered and abused wives as well as groups for the abusers themselves, groups for addicts—the list goes on and on, as endless as the range and variety of human afflictions and human indulgences. The groups vary enormously in their constituencies, appealing as they do to such a broad band of people.

They also vary greatly in terms of their intended therapeutic focus. Some emphasize "inner" aspects of experience, attitudes, feelings, and impulses, but others emphasize "outer" aspects (either social/adaptational or activity designed to reduce isolation or to become involved in community action). Some, at the fringes of conventional therapy practices, seem to have adopted what may be termed sociopolitical goals and ideologies that appear to call for societal, not personal, change. Much of the emotional ambience of these groups depends on whether they are organized along one or another of these lines.

Many appear to be religiously inspired even if they do not espouse particular theologies, but few proselytize in conventionally religious terms. As noted, some see themselves concerned as much, or even more, with social and political changes as with personal changes. The former characterization fits Alcoholics Anonymous (AA) and many other abuse-focused groups, while the latter emphasis is seen in gender therapies and ethnotherapy groups. Again, despite this difference, both types of groups achieve their goals through the same types of group dynamics, such as, cohesion, mutual support, and varying degrees of criticism, individual and/or collective disclosure, and interpersonal feedback. Whether the ideological principles of the group are secular or spiritual, whether they aim at only in-group change or personal change beyond it, they are fitted to some conceptual framework—no matter how loosely—that is adapted to a concordant interpretation of member problems.

Frank (1974) and Antze (1979) have explained how therapy processes alter links in the cognitive chains developed by the help seekers that have prevented them from beneficially changing. These processes are also effective in challenging and modifying the participant's "assumptive world." As in all therapies, the intention is to modify personal interpretations of reality and personal expectations and meanings attributed to the actions of others. To take examples from the self-help movement, AA counters the presumed assertiveness of the alcoholic by demonstrating one's undeniable vulnerability. Recovery, Inc., which includes chronic patients who have repeatedly been hospitalized, promotes a view of self as stronger, more resilient, and more capable of being self-responsible than the individual has been led to believe. By contrast Synanon, at one time the most effective group treatment for drug abusers (now defunct), tried to alter the abuser's characteristic detachment through graduated group confrontations—angry criticisms alternating with tearful reconciliations—in the course of which many of those so treated became so strongly bonded to their groups that they also became committed to its program of abstinence (Antze, 1979).

Even though the focus of these groups differs from traditional therapeutic groups, their processes are not so different in kind. They also present certain ethical problems of their own, among them, (a) few controls over excessive influence from stronger or more influential members; (b) overly ideological interpretations of problems and prescriptive solutions that tend to be collective rather than related to individual concerns; (c) the possibility of an authoritarian solution to the participants' problems.

On the other hand, at least two of these ethical risks hold true for other psychotherapeutic experiences in groups. At the same time, it seems clear that many people have been profoundly helped by similar mechanisms of experiencing solidarity, mutual support, and opportunities to repair their damaged sense of personal identity. Overall, the success of self-help groups is such that group therapists should seriously study them in order to learn how, even without professional leadership, these groups bring about personal "remoralization." At the very least, they confirm the ameliorative power of certain group forces.

Especially noteworthy is the resurgence of group activity with medical and surgical patients. Spitz (1984) noted with satisfaction a renewed interest in the kind of activity Joseph Pratt initiated over 80 years ago. Groups are conducted to help patients follow treatment plans and deal, preventively, with psychological conditions that contribute to, or are by-products of, serious physical illnesses. Roback (1984) edited a volume describing such group methods for helping people to cope with medical problems. The programs described included groups for patients and for their families who were dealing with such afflictions as chronic pain, spinal cord injuries, renal disease, multiple sclerosis, or sickle cell anemia. Spiegel, Bloom, Kraemer, and Gottheil (1989) found that those cancer patients who joined support groups lived longer than those who did not. Meanwhile, the professional organizations of group therapists increased their involvement in the treatment of chronically mentally ill and deinstitutionalized persons.

In a related development, Keith and Matthews (1982) found that groups could increase the social competence of formerly hospitalized schizophrenics as well as decrease their negative symptomatology (as was demonstrated by Recovery, Inc. years ago). It seems that there are also steadily increasing applications of combined treatment plans that include group psychosocial interventions and pharmacotherapy.

ENDURING CONCEPTUAL ISSUES: THE SIGNIFICANCE OF DIFFERENCE

Certain ethical pitfalls are characteristic of the "group therapy scene." They include such areas as the need for appropriate training in group procedures and failures to sensitize therapists to potential vulnerabilities imposed on those who participate in groups. But first we will discuss the concept that groups are conducted simply as extensions of their leaders' individual-practice habits of thought and techniques. This is an ethical, as well as a technical, concern.

Virtually all therapeutic group experience is based on sharing and comparing, in contrast to the emphasis on individual experience in dyadic therapy. Consequently, patients are "acculturated" in the different modes of treatment. The modes may be thought of as "meta-therapeutic" (that is, as distinctions in how one is taught to approach one's problems). Existential issues (such as the meaning of one's existence or one's innerself assessment) are sometimes best approached in the autobiographical ambience of the one-to-one setting. Confronting reactions of others to one's self—seeing how one reacts to others—is better done in the group. The group highlights different aspects of human experience—the interpersonal, social self—and the individual therapy relationship is usually better suited to reflecting on the inner, impulse and feeling self. The point is that problems are, to some degree at least, redefined in the course of their treatment.

The differences between the modalities will inevitably influence that redefinition. Among the reasons for this are the following:

- If the group *qua* group is really employed as a therapeutic medium, peer influence will play a major role in personal change. The dyadic relationship, by contrast, is structured by the patient's individual therapist.

- Group/communal feelings are inevitably involved in the therapy for better or worse; individual therapy exclusively involves the feelings and reactions of the individual patient (countertransference reactions excepted).

- Moods are "contagious" among group participants. In dyadic therapy the therapist's judgment should not be affected by the patient's emotional state.

- "Reality" is collectively defined in the group, unlike in the dyad, where its characterization is ordinarily the therapist's responsibility.

- Privacy or secrecy is normative for individual psychotherapy. Groups are relatively public and permeable by their natures. Hence, responsibility for establishing or maintaining confidentiality is of greater concern.

- The forces of the group are intrinsically blind; they may be directed by participants who neither have professional training nor bear professional accountability toward their peers.

Obviously, much depends on the wisdom and skill of the group therapist in mediating the dynamics and the power factors that are intrinsic to a functioning group. The potency of such factors (referred to as "curative" by Corsini and Rosenberg, 1955, and by Yalom, 1975) has been described by workers in the field. But how these same factors could have destructive effects has not yet received much attention. Three major dynamics in group therapy—cohesion, conformity, and commitment—are examples of potentially positive or negative effects:

- Cohesion—feelings of togetherness and belonging—is vital to the group's success, is basic for members to attain the confidence to make disclosures and to accept feedback from other members, and is essential to their attempting to carry-over insights or changes "back home." Two sources of negative effects are (a) one becomes vulnerable to damaging evaluations, social comparisons, and reckless feedback; and (b) as Slavson (1964) warned, long-enduring groups sometimes congeal into attitudes of defense of the status quo to preserve the comfort of their achieved relations. He also was concerned about groups meeting on their own without a leader, what have been called "alternate groups."

- Abiding by the group's norms (e.g., attending faithfully, maintaining the group's confidences, trying to be honest with other members, trying to be helpful, etc.) is essential to its success. But other norms may include demands for specific types or levels of disclosures, for specific types or levels of emotional expression, or even a commitment to certain psychopolitical stances or actions. In short, the group could demand behaviors, or the expression of attitudes, unrelated to the individual's concerns, but that would redefine those concerns in group-sanctioned terms. Because of the threat of the group's disapproval, this could lead to dissembling emotions or attitudes in order to retain group approval (i.e., pretending to remain in conformity with it).

- The participants' commitment to change is reflected in their willingness to disclose and in their support for the disclosures of others. The evidence of emotional expressiveness accompanying such disclosures is regarded as a kind of "ticket of admission." While there is no doubt that emotional expressiveness in therapy groups aids in disinhibiting those who would otherwise remain frozen in fear of other members' reactions, the expression of emotionality sometimes comes to be valued as a group token. While some members come to feel they are failures in not living up to the group's standard for emotionality, others "get a charge" from doing so. Group therapists have an ethical as well as a technical responsibility to help participants distinguish helpful emotionality from the kind that is consequent on group pressures and to prevent countertherapeutic expressions of the latter.

We know the presence of other members—an audience of a kind—is a powerful influence on the therapy process. Needs in a multiperson context vary. States of the group cannot be as "regularized" as might those of an individual therapy, and groups are always changing simply because of the multiplicity of issues represented by different members. Fresh claims on group support are made with every disclosure, with every new interaction. One's personal standing—one's acceptance—may be repeatedly renegotiated even in longstanding groups. The group also requires "fresh" disclosures from those present, veterans as well as new members, so as to have the material of new psychodramas. Therefore, such evocative elements as self-disclosure and confrontation need to be skillfully guided by the group therapist. The ethical question is: Is the member thus pressured being helpfully or exploitatively dealt with?

Mays and Franks (1985) edited a volume about harmful treatment effects among major psychotherapy approaches. In the chapter on negative effects in group psychotherapies, Dies and Teleska (1985) also acknowledged that misapplication of group "curative" factors—the group forces—can lead to deleterious outcomes. They discussed particular leader intervention styles that have been implicated in these negative effects. For example, manipulative and excessively charismatic leaders may fail to recognize crumbling defenses or to take account of individual differences. Of course, attrition from therapy may be similarly due to inappropriate interventions. Roback and Smith (1987) suggested that attrition could be traced back to interacting therapist–patient and patient–group factors. The appropriate referral question to be asked at the time of diagnostic consultation is: "Is this particular individual suitable for a particular group conducted by its particular therapist?" In order to reduce attrition and, at the same time, develop at least minimal familiarity with the group context, Spitz suggests that pretraining should be employed (1984). Piper and colleagues (Piper, Debbane, Bienvenu, & Garant, 1982; Piper, Debbane, Garant, & Bienvenu, 1979) reported favorable results with such pretraining orientation.

RESEARCH AND TRAINING

Research Issues

Historically, the fields of group psychotherapy practice and research have been distant and cool neighbors. The researcher has viewed the practitioner as inefficient and mercenary, while the clinician has viewed the scholar's efforts as unrealistic, if not irrelevant (Roback, Abramowitz, & Strassberg, 1979). However, in the 1980s we witnessed an emerging detente as it became clear that the two endeavors could benefit from closer association. Pressures on the practitioner emanated from a shrinking health care dollar and associated demands on service providers to demonstrate the efficacy of their therapeutic procedures. Strupp (1979) warned that society is taking an increasingly close and critical look at the kinds of services provided by the mental health professions. "Legislators, insurance companies, and the patient-consumer demand to know what the providers of psychosocial treatments can do to stem the tide of emotional disturbances, behavior disorders, and human suffering. . . . What is demanded is empirical evidence, hard data" (p. ix). Similarly, there has been increasing pressure on the researcher seeking external funding to demonstrate the benefits to society of their proposed research.

Thus, it is apparent that group psychotherapists have much to gain from, and contribute to, a coalition with science. Roback, Abramowitz, and Strassberg (1979) encouraged the rapprochement between group therapy and research by emphasizing that almost all treatment methods have either been reconceptualized and refined by scientific advances or they have succumbed to the ravages of time. There is no doubt that large-scale multivariate studies would offer promise in evaluating relations between persons and processes, given the undeniable complexities of group interventions and interactions among its members.

Perhaps Hartman's (1979) suggestion of small, well-designed, replicable studies involving multiple measures of outcome will have to suffice for the present, given the shortage of funding for larger scale research. Such smaller studies might permit comparisons across participant characteristics, styles of leadership, and associated intervention techniques. On many occasions in the past, calls for the cooperation of practitioners and researchers have been issued, in order to facilitate obtaining answers to the critically important question of how to develop and emphasize benign processes in groups. However, no one should anticipate dramatic breakthroughs in this difficult quest. Accumulation of knowledge about how groups work will probably continue to lag behind the uses of group methods for all kinds of therapeutic as well as quasi-therapeutic purposes.

Training Issues

Lakin (1985, 1988, 1991) has cautioned that increased attention to how we train group therapists in professional schools and in graduate training programs should be a priority of training, accreditation, and ethics committees. Understanding how a group works and how its procedures may affect its participants adversely should be the first order of concern in training programs rather than whether its group orientation is dynamic or cognitive–behavioral. For instance, many group therapists have acted as if extensive self-disclosure is always helpful; now we have learned that it can be quite damaging for schizophrenic patients, and we cannot assume that it is otherwise for other severely disturbed persons (Strassberg, Roback, Anchor, & Abramowitz, 1975).

Most group therapists today, like their colleagues who engage in mainly individual psychotherapy, identify themselves as "eclectic," presumably using techniques from the best of the orientations to which they have been exposed. If this self-picture is questionable for individual therapists, it is even more so for group therapists, many of whom operate with very little formal training in group processes or in techniques of conducting a therapeutic group.

GROUPS AS THERAPEUTIC CONTEXTS FOR RESOLVING SOCIAL PROBLEMS

A contemporary phenomenon is the use of group therapy processes for the purpose of changing an aspect of the society. Looking back at some of the philosophical and ideological sources of group therapies, it should not be altogether surprising that group change-induction techniques are sometimes brought to bear on problems ordinarily thought of as social or even political. For example, group procedures are currently being employed in order to change attitudes, mobilize and channel resentments, or build self-esteem on the basis of group identity. Some of the pioneers of group therapy would not have been surprised at this development. On the contrary, they seemingly had confidence, or perhaps faith, in the wisdom and positive aspects of spontaneous group processes, but they overlooked questions of how the group members could be misled or be channeled toward political rather than personal goals. For instance, there are currently a number of different kinds of groups organized for purposes of "ethnotherapy," gender therapy, for fighting societal oppression (gay and lesbian groups), and for intergroup conflict resolution.

It should be immediately evident that the traditional "value-neutral" stance that is supposed to characterize most conceptions of psychological treatment is deliberately disavowed in favor of acknowledged ideological positions, flavoring the interventions that the therapist in such groups makes and influencing participants' behavior. As one example of the procedures of such a group, we can consider all-women therapeutic groups. Once primarily conducted as "consciousness-raising" groups outside the therapy mainstream, they are now usually conducted by credentialed therapists as gender-exclusive, regular therapy groups. What differentiates these groups from traditional therapy groups is not, as is the usual obligation, keeping one's psychopolitical beliefs out of the treatment situation, but precisely the opposite conviction (i.e., that the political aspects of therapy values are an inevitable and welcome aspect of therapy, that they should influence techniques and goals).

As in the ethnotherapies, the interpretation of group purpose is that group identity (in this case, gender identity) needs to be strengthened. Personal psychological ills are invariably traceable to in-group oppression and mistreatment at the hands of more powerful or more influential groups in the society. The group therapeutic procedures are a means of building a stronger sense of cohesion and of identity. In these groups, the most significant emotional experiences are consequently those of mutual support, the sharing of resentments against those who had mistreated participants, and the venting of feelings about them. Beyond cathartic release and bonding, the goals may involve some kind of commitment to social action during and after the group.

Procedures and interventions naturally vary from group to group according to leader style. However, the outlines of the general approach are discernible from reports by Johnson (1976, 1987), Schubert-Walker (1987), and Burden and Gottlieb (1987). These descriptions of feminist therapy groups parallel similar identification processes in ethnotherapy groups that have been reported. We will use the former to illustrate the general issues. These groups may be said to engage in the following discussions—referred to as "stages of development" by the therapists: (a) expressions of discontent with personal and collective power relative to men; (b) sharing and comparing personally frustrating and defeating experiences; (c) resolving that personal and collective social actions will be redemptive and mentally healthy. Themes of having been "duped, sold out, raped and betrayed by the sexist society dominated by males" animate the discussion (Avery, 1977).

There are other group-centered therapies that appear to address group, rather than individual, differences and associated concerns. In fact, what therapists would usually consider as personal problems are reinterpreted in line with such slogans as "Personal is political!" or "We live in a racist society!" Regardless of the justice of the political sentiments, the fact that these therapies interpret group differences as the source of the person's

Pakistanis, French- and English-speaking Canadians, and between Arabs and Jews in Israel.

The idea that supports the strategy of such intergroup meetings is that change induction efforts in them requires challenging mutually held stereotypes by developing better understanding of "the other." The group is at once the arena of *exchange*, the arena of *challenge* and *confrontation*, and the arena of *personal change*. It is "safer" to discuss intergroup problems in a context that is designed to sanction greater latitude for interpersonal communication about conflictful issues and to allow relatively benign social comparison about cultures as well as persons. (Of course, it also risks developing in precisely opposite ways!) If positive changes *do* occur that are group-sanctioned, the group may continue to serve as a supportive referent for its participants in the "real world" of the group hostilities and conflict from which they come and to which they return.

A pioneer and innovator in this high-risk area of intergroup conflict was Kurt Lewin, whose works, "Frontiers in Group Dynamics" (1947) and *Resolving Social Conflicts* (1948), set forth the dimensions of groups as powerful change inductive experiences that could be used to reduce intergroup tensions. One of this chapter's authors, Martin Lakin, had conducted such intergroup workshops (Lakin, Lomranz, & Lieberman, 1969). Since then a number of others have been reported. Like gender-exclusive and ethnotherapy groups, these groups are conducted with ideological purpose. However, unlike the former, they do not purport to be therapies for the individual problems of participants.

It would be useful to examine the rationale for applying specific group techniques. How do they relate to and how do they differ from more traditional therapeutic group interventions? Are they universally relevant or are they culture bound and therefore likely to be misapplied in foreign lands? Above all, we need evaluations of their likely consequences; what contributions to peace and intergroup mental health might realistically be anticipated from these well-intentioned efforts? Beyond their epistemological significance, answers to such questions have obvious societal and moral relevance in a world that is characterized by near-murderous intergroup hostilities.

CONCLUSIONS

We conclude by asserting that group therapies are firmly established as treatment modalities in their own right, but, as with all the mainstream therapy systems and modalities, the relation between their processes and their outcomes have not yet been satisfactorily articulated. There is, as yet, no generally accepted comprehensive theory of group therapy processes anchored in individual experience, on the one hand, and traceable through group experience, on the other.

Group therapies work, but how, and why, and with whom is still less clear than therapists (and their patients) would wish. The challenge to develop this kind of knowledge grows greater with the rapid increase in the bewildering variety of helping experiences that use group approaches.

Throughout this chapter, we have stressed the importance of group practitioners becoming more aware of the potential for misuses of groups as therapy and for cognate purposes. Concretely, this means that group therapists should try to be more self-conscious about why and how they employ certain group techniques rather than others; it means vigilance with respect to the constant question: "For whose benefit and in whose interest?" It certainly requires that we ask ourselves whether the group we propose is appropriate to the particular individual's problems and needs. The development of group therapies for the amelioration and resolution of social problems should have our sympathetic, but also our vigilant, interest. The century of developments in group psychotherapy has given us a powerful vehicle and its intrinsic forces for influencing behavior change. We must channel them for good and not for ill.

REFERENCES

Antze, P. (1979). Role of ideologies in peer psychotherapy groups. In M. A. Lieberman & L. D. Borman (Ed.), *Self-help groups for coping with crisis*. San Francisco: Jossey-Bass.

Asch, S. E. (1956). Studies of independence and conformity: A minority of one against a unanimous majority. *Psychological Monographs, 70* (Whole No. 416).

Avery, D. M. (1977). The psychosocial stages of liberation. *Illinois Guidance and Personnel Association Quarterly, 63*, 36–42.

Bach, G. R. (1954). *Intensive group therapy*. New York: Ronald Press.

Back, K. W. (1951). Influence through social communication. *Journal of Abnormal and Social Psychology, 46*, 9–23.

Back, K. W. (1974). Intervention techniques: Small groups. *Annual Review of Psychology* (pp. 367–388). Palo Alto, CA: Annual Reviews, Inc.

Bakan, D. (1966). *The duality of human existence*. Chicago: Rand McNally.

Bavelas, A. (1950). Communication patterns in task-oriented groups. *Journal of Acoustical Society of America, 22*, 725–730.

Bion, W. R. (1961). *Experiences in groups*. New York: Basic Books.

Boring, F. (1972). American Psychological Association. *APA Monitor*, p. 3.

Burden, D. S., & Gottlieb, N. (1987). Women's socialization and feminist groups. In C. M. Brody (Ed.), *Women's therapy groups* (pp. 24–42). New York: Springer.

Burrow, T. (1927). The group method of analysis. *Psychoanalytic Review, 19*, 268–280.

Burrow, T. (1958). *A search for man's sanity: The selected letters of Trigant Burrow.* New York: Oxford University Press.

Corsini, R. J. (1957). *Methods of group psychotherapy.* New York: McGraw-Hill.

Corsini, R., & Rosenberg, B. (1955). Mechanisms of group psychotherapy. *Journal of Abnormal and Social Psychology, 51*, 406–411.

Dejerine, J. J. (1913). *Psychoneuroses and their treatment by psychotherapy.* Philadelphia: J. B. Lippincott.

Dewey, J. (1948). *Experience and education.* New York: Macmillan.

Dies, R. R., & Teleska, P. A. (1985). Negative outcome in group psychotherapy. In D. T. Mays & C. M. Franks (Eds.), *Negative outcome in psychotherapy and what to do about it.* New York: Springer.

Durkheim, J. (1953). *Sociology and philosophy.* London: Cohen and West.

Festinger, L. (1954). A theory of social comparison processes. *Human Relations, 7*, 117–140.

Foulkes, S. H. (1966). Some basic concepts in group psychotherapy. In J. L. Moreno (Ed.), *The international handbook of group psychotherapy.* New York: Philosophical Library.

Foulkes, S. F., & Anthony, E. J. (1965). *Group psychotherapy* (2nd ed.). Baltimore: Penguin Books.

Frank, J. D. (1974). *Persuasion and healing.* Baltimore: Johns Hopkins University Press.

Freud, S. (1934). *Why war: Open letters between Einstein and Freud.* London: New Commonwealth Publications.

Greenbaum, C. W. (1979). The small group under the gun: Uses of small groups in battle conditions. In M. Lakin (Ed.), *What's happened to small group research?* [Special edition]. *Journal of Applied Behavioral Science, 15*(3), 392–406.

Hartman, J. (1979). Small group methods of personal change. *Annual Review of Psychology, 37*, 453–476.

Homans, G. C. (1950). *The human group.* New York: Harcourt, Brace & World.

Horkheimer, M., & Adorno, T. (1973). *Aspects of sociology.* London: Heinemann Educational Books.

Illing, H. A. C. G. (1963). Jung on the present trends in-group psychotherapy. In M. Rosenbaum & M. Berger (Eds.), *Group psychotherapy and group function* (p. 184). New York: Basic Books.

Jones, M. (1953). *The therapeutic community: A new treatment method in psychiatry.* New York: Basic Books.

Johnson, M. (1976). An approach to feminist therapy. *Psychotherapy: Theory, research and practice, 13*(1), 72–76.

Johnson, M. (1987). Feminist therapy in groups: A decade of change. In C. M. Brody (Ed.), *Women's therapy groups* (pp. 13–23). New York: Springer.

Jourard, S. (1964). *The transparent self.* Princeton, NJ: D. Van Nostrand.

Keith, S., & Matthew, R. (1982). Group, family, and milieu therapists and psychosocial rehabilitation in the treatment of the schizophrenic disorders. In L. Grinspoon (Ed.), *Annual Review of Psychiatry* (pp. 10–41). Washington, DC: American Psychiatric Press.

Kelman, H. C., & Cohen, S. P. (1986). Resolution of international conflict: An interactional approach. In S. Worchel & W. G. Austin (Eds.), *Psychology of intergroup relations* (2nd ed.). Chicago: Nelson-Hall.

Kiev, A. (1964). *Magic, faith and healing.* New York: Free Press.

Kimble, C. E., Yoshikawa, J. C., & Zehr, H. D. (1981). Vocal and verbal assertiveness in same sex and mixed sex groups. *Journal of Personality and Social Psychology, 40*, 1047–1054.

Koch, S. (1971, January). *The image of man in encounter group theory.* Address at the annual meeting of the American Association for the Advancement of Science, Philadelphia, PA.

Lakin, M. (1985). *The helping group.* Reading, MA: Addison-Wesley.

Lakin, M. (1988). *Ethical issues in the psychotherapies.* New York: Oxford University Press.

Lakin, M. (1991). *Coping with ethical dilemmas in psychotherapy.* New York: Pergamon Press.

Lakin, M., Lomranz, J., & Lieberman, M. A. (1969). *Arab and Jew in Israel: A case study in a human relations approach to conflict.* Washington, DC: National Training Laboratories, Institute for Applied Behavioral Science.

Lazell, E. W. (1921). The group treatment of dementia praecox. *Psychoanalytic Review, 8*, 168–179.

Leavitt, H. J. (1951). Some effects of certain communication patterns on group performance. *Journal of Abnormal and Social Psychology, 46*, 38–50.

Lewin, K. (1947). Frontiers in group dynamics: Concept, method, and theory in social science: Social equilibrium. *Human Relations, 1*, 5–40.

Lewin, K. (1948). *Resolving social conflicts.* New York: Harper.

Lieberman, M. A. (1976). Change induction in small groups. *Annual Review of Psychology, 27*, 217–250. Palo Alto, CA: Annual Reviews, Inc.

Marin, P. (1975, October). The new narcissism. *Harpers*, p. 45.

Marsh, L. C. (1935). Group therapy and the psychiatric clinic. *Journal of Nervous and Mental Disease, 82*, 381–392.

Mayo, E. (1933). *The human problems of an industrial civilization*. New York: Macmillan.

Mays, D., & Franks, C. (1985). *Negative outcome in psychotherapy and what to do about it*. New York: Springer.

Moreno, J. L. (1924). *Das stegreiftheater* [The theater of improvisation]. Potsdam, Germany: Gustav Kropenheuer.

Moreno, J. L. (1953). *Who shall survive?* New York: Beacon House.

Moreno, J. L. (1957). *The first book on group psychotherapy*. New York: Beacon House.

Mullan, H., & Rosenbaum, M. (1962). *Group psychotherapy*. New York: Free Press.

Osgood, C. E. (1962). *An alternative to war or surrender*. Urbana, IL: University of Illinois Press.

Perls, F. S. (1969). *Gestalt therapy verbatim*. Lafayette, CA: Real People Press.

Piper, W. E., Debbane, E. G., Bienvenu, J. P., & Garant, J. (1982). A study of group pre-training for group psychotherapy. *International Journal of Group Psychotherapy, 32*, 309–325.

Piper, W. E., Debbane, E. G., Garant, J., & Bienvenu, J. P. (1979). Pre-training for group psychotherapy: A cognitive-experiential approach. *Archives of General Psychiatry, 36*, 1250–1256.

Powdermaker, F. L., & Frank, J. D. (1953). *Group psychotherapy*. Cambridge, MA: Harvard University Press.

Pratt, J. H. (1953). The use of Dejerine's methods in the treatment of the common neuroses by group psychotherapy. *Bulletin of the New England Medical Center, 15*, 1–9.

Reissman, F., & Gartner, A. (1979, December). *Made for each other*. Paper presented at the meeting of the Canadian Psychological Association, Manitoba, Canada.

Roback, H. (1984). *Helping patients and their families cope with medical problems*. San Francisco: Jossey-Bass.

Roback, H., Abramowitz, S., & Strassberg, D. (1979). *Group psychotherapy research*. New York: Robert E. Krieger.

Roback, H., & Smith, M. (1987). Patient attrition in dynamically-oriented treatment groups. *American Journal of Psychiatry, 144*, 426–431.

Roethlisberger, F., & Dickson, W. (1939). *Management and the worker*. Cambridge, MA: Harvard University Press.

Rogers, C. R. (1968). Interpersonal relationships: USA 2000. *Journal of Applied Behavioral Science, 4*, 265–280.

Rogers, C. R. (1973). *On encounter groups*. New York: Harper & Row.

Rogers, C. R. (1980). *A way of being*. Boston: Houghton Mifflin.

Rosenbaum, M., & Berger, M. (1963). *Group psychotherapy and group function*. New York: Basic Books.

Schachter, S. (1951). Deviation, rejection and communication. *Journal of Abnormal and Social Psychology, 46*, 190–207.

Schilder, P. (1939). Results and problems of group psychotherapy in severe neurosis. *Mental Hygiene, 23*, 87–98.

Schoeck, H. (1966). *Envy* (p. 89). New York: Harcourt, Brace & World.

Schubert-Walker, L. J. (1987). Women's groups are different. In C. M. Brody (Ed.), *Women's therapy groups*. New York: Springer.

Shapiro, J., & Shapiro, S. (1985). Group work to 2001. *Journal for Specialists in Group Work, May*, 83–87.

Sherif, M. (1948). *An outline of social psychology*. New York: Harper.

Sherif, M., & Sherif, C. W. (1953). *Groups in harmony and tension*. New York: Harper Brothers.

Slavson, S. R. (1964). *A textbook in analytic group psychotherapy*. New York: International Universities Press.

Spiegel, D., Bloom, J., Kraemer, H., & Gottheil, E. (1989). Effect of psychosocial treatment on survival patients with metastatic breast cancer. *The Lancet*, October 14, 888–891.

Spitz, H. (1984). Contemporary trends in group psychotherapy. *Hospital and Community Psychiatry, 35*, 132–142.

Strassberg, D., Roback, H., Anchor, K., & Abramowitz, S. (1975). Self-disclosure in group therapy with schizophrenics. *Archives of General Psychiatry, 32*, 1259–1261.

Strupp, H. (1979). Foreword in H. Roback, S. Abramowitz, & D. Strassberg (Eds.), *Group psychotherapy research*. New York: Robert E. Krieger.

Tolman, E. C. (1942). *Drives toward war*. New York: D. Appleton-Century.

Wender, L. (1936). The dynamics of group psychotherapy and its applications. *Journal of Nervous and Mental Disease, 84*(1), 54–60.

Whitaker, D. S., & Lieberman, M. A. (1964). *Psychotherapy through the group process*. New York: Atherton Press.

White, R. K. (1988). Specifics in a positive approach to peace. *Journal of Social Issues, 44*(2), 191–202.

Wolf, A., & Schwartz, E. K. (1962). *Psychoanalysis in groups*. New York: Grune & Stratton.

Wolff, K. (Ed.). (1950). *The sociology of Georg Simmel*. New York: Collier-Macmillan.

Yalom, I. (1975). *The theory and practice of group psychotherapy* (2nd ed.). New York: Basic Books.

V

EDUCATION AND TRAINING IN PSYCHOTHERAPY

OVERVIEW

EDUCATION AND TRAINING IN PSYCHOTHERAPY

DONALD R. PETERSON

Many early American psychologists saw as much promise in a profession of psychology as in a science of psychology. Applications were quick to come, although the earliest ventures were restricted mainly to assessment and applied research, with large-scale involvement in the practice of psychotherapy delayed for many years. Despite the emphasis on professional application in American psychology, however, education for the practice of psychology has developed slowly, has been accepted reluctantly by the academic community, and is still resisted by many educators who believe that psychology must preserve its identity as a science at any cost. The history of education for psychotherapy is a tale of conflict, resolved at first by avoidance, engaged primarily by force of external circumstance, and only recently evolving into an uneasy pluralism, in which education for research, education combining research and practice in the scientist-professional tradition, and direct education for practice are all accorded some measure of academic legitimacy.

Cohen begins the story by describing the academic department, the first setting in which psychologists were educated and still the organization in which most psychologists are trained. The history he traces is a general history of academic psychology, which formed the cultural background from which training for psychotherapy in clinical and counseling psychology eventually emerged. Cohen describes the importation to America of European models of graduate education, especially the apprentice system that prevailed in Germany, where most of the pioneers in American psychology went to learn the new science. He shows how the academic establishment in America came to accept psychology, and later clinical psychology, how psychology responded to two world wars and the changing demands of the 20th century, and how the discipline reacted to the growing professional emphasis in psychology. Cohen introduces us to the conferences, from Boulder through Miami, Chicago, and Vail, to Utah, which have been organized to consider issues related to the education of psychologists, particularly in regard to professional training. He concludes with a plea that the best intent of these conferences be expressed in the psychology of the future.

Riess continues with a description of some of the earliest settings in which outright training of psychologists for the practice of psychotherapy took place: the multidisciplinary psychoanalytic institutes that were established shortly after World War II. His account focuses particularly on the Postgraduate Center for Mental Health, the largest and arguably the best psychoanalytic institute that invited psychologists to learn the skills of psychotherapy in those times. Riess was one of the first psychologists to enter training at the Center. His story is rich in anecdotes about the efforts of organized psychiatry to exclude "lay" practitioners, such as psychologists, from the training required to practice psychoanalysis. The emphasis on research and community service as well as thorough training for psychoanalytic practice that permeated the Center was unique at the time, created a model after which other institutes were patterned, and has influenced the education of psychotherapists far beyond the province of the Center.

Some historians have claimed that modern clinical psychology was invented by the Veterans Administration (VA) in 1946. Financial support for training and jobs for graduates were suddenly available on a large scale. Graduate students flowed into the field in high numbers. The American Psychological Association (APA) Division of Clinical Psychology soon became the largest in the discipline. In her chapter on the VA program, Moore shows how it all came about, beginning with the tradition of care for American war veterans that goes back to the Plymouth colony, continuing through the frequently faltering efforts of the U.S. government to accommodate masses of veterans returning from major wars, and moving through establishment of VA programs in the mental health fields after

World War II. Psychology's place in this development was scarcely assured at the time. Moore shows how it might never have happened except for the enterprise of one psychologist/psychiatrist, whose name you will find in her account.

In the early 1950s, only one clinical psychology program in the country declared a readiness to train psychologists expressly for practice. That was the program at Adelphi University, directed by Gordon Derner. The Adelphi story is told in the chapter by Stricker and Cummings on the professional school movement in psychology. Cummings, an Adelphi graduate, went on to found the California School of Professional Psychology. He tells that story, too, how appeals to expand university clinical programs were rebuffed and how the demands of students and practitioners for professional training led to the creation of professional schools, first in California and then throughout the country until, by now, at least one third of students receiving doctorates in psychology are graduated from professional schools. Reminiscences by other activists show the unique histories of the various schools but reveal common themes in the initial resistance to their establishment, the persistence of the founders, and the recent shift in the attitudes of professional school personnel from defense and survival to an emphasis on quality.

Shortly before establishment of the California School, the first Doctor of Psychology (PsyD) program was inaugurated at the University of Illinois, with Lloyd Humphreys as head of the department and Donald Peterson as director of clinical training. This followed the deliberations of a "blue ribbon" committee on the scientific and professional aims of psychology that found the prevailing scientist-practitioner programs insufficient, and recommended establishment of outright professional programs. Peterson describes the process through which the Illinois program was formed and the slow growth of comparable programs until the Vail Conference, where the professional doctorate and professional schools both received positive sanction. The stories of PsyD programs developed since that time, as well as discontinuation of the original Illinois program, furnish substance for some reflections on the conditions that foster or discourage direct education for the practice of psychology.

The best practitioner programs, as well as the best scientist-practitioner programs, are allegedly based on a foundation of scientific knowledge. In the last chapter of the section, Matarazzo and Garner review research on the training of psychotherapists. In the early days, when psychotherapy and psychoanalysis were nearly synonymous terms, training consisted of didactic analyses of trainees and supervision within an authoritarian master–apprentice relationship. No research on training was seen in those times.

Empirical studies of process and outcome in training began with the client-centered therapy of Carl Rogers. Paradoxically, client-centered therapy cast more responsibility on the therapist to provide a constructive therapeutic environment than was required by prevailing psychodynamic views. From studies of ways in which the "necessary and sufficient conditions" of client-centered therapy might be taught, through planned modification of the operant behavior of behavior therapists, to training in a wide range of insight-oriented therapies and complex forms of broad spectrum behavior therapy, a substantial amount of research has been done on the training of psychotherapists. Much of the work done so far, however, is less informative than critical scholars would like it to be, and many questions remain unanswered. The authors show not only the directions future research seems likely to take but also the urgent need to move forward with inquiries of these kinds if psychology is to remain true to its claim as a science-based profession.

22

THE ACADEMIC DEPARTMENT

LOUIS D. COHEN

Up to the second half of the 19th century, the American higher education establishment was largely nonexistent. Available institutions were limited to church-related colleges and universities that emphasized a liberal arts education. Professional education and scientific research were not stressed. As the century progressed, an emerging concern for academic freedom resulted in the creation of a number of secular colleges, and the growing importance of science encouraged an emphasis on scientific research. In 1861, Yale University awarded the first PhD in the United States to three students, and in 1872, Harvard University followed. The Johns Hopkins University was established as a graduate school in 1876. Within a few years, scientific and professional education became widely available in the United States.

American graduate education in psychology has been especially influenced by European graduate education in general and German graduate education in particular. American leaders in academia in the last half of

I am indebted to Dr. John Reisman's (1976) volume, A History of Clinical Psychology, for its scholarship, detailed annotation, and appreciation of the extensive history of clinical psychology, which made it possible for me to report various events in a much rounder style than would have been possible otherwise.

the 19th century, such as G. Stanley Hall at The Johns Hopkins University and Clark University, James McKeen Cattell at the University of Pennsylvania and Columbia University, and Lightner Witmer at the University of Pennsylvania all studied directly with Wilhelm Wundt at the University of Leipzig. Wundt was the developer of the first psychology laboratory in 1879. These American scholars and William James at Harvard University, Mark Baldwin at Princeton University and the University of Toronto, and E. W. Scripture at Yale University, among others, studied in various British, French, and German psychology laboratories as part of their psychological training and personal growth. The American academic scene also included a few Europeans who were invited to permanent posts in American universities: Hugo Münsterberg from the University of Leipzig at Harvard, Edward B. Tichener from Oxford University and Leipzig at Cornell University, and William McDougall from Cambridge University, Oxford, and Göttingen at Harvard and Duke Universities. These were the key figures of early American psychology whose personalities and erudition attracted graduate students and set up schools of thought. Through their scholarly excellence and ideological leadership, they set the tone for American psychology and the graduate education establishment from then on.

THE MODEL

The German graduate research institute, with its senior independent professor and series of satellite docents, graduate students, research laboratories, and lecture activities, was located in universities but had independent status, the professor's position being almost fully autonomous. American universities varied somewhat from this model in that the professors were not as independent of the university, and there could be a number of professors in closely related fields who functioned under the direction of a department head. Yet the guiding spirit was similar in both countries.

A typical scenario might read as follows: The graduate student selected an area within which he (nearly all were men) wanted to study, and arranged to be admitted into lectures offered by the professor. The student attended lectures, read extensively, and learned as much as he could about the professor's research. When he felt prepared and quite knowledgeable about the area of the professor's competence, he offered himself for examination, and if found meritorious, was matriculated into study for the doctoral degree. Frequently this involved apprenticeship to the professor's research program and work as a research assistant. As the student progressed, he might be able to identify a next step in the professor's research program, and if all was congenial, the student might be authorized to proceed in the research under the professor's guidance. Upon completion of the research and report of the study, the student would defend this work and his unique contribution. If this was done to the satisfaction of the faculty of the university, he would be awarded the doctoral degree. Not in every case, nor in many cases, did everything go smoothly as described here. Indeed, there were many points where students were bogged down, for years or even forever.

What emerges from this model is the student's personal responsibility for learning about his field and doing independent work to gain a mastery of it. No curriculum was laid out! The focus was on research and conceptual innovation, plus an ability to convince faculty of the unique and significant contribution he was making. The student was expected to move from apprentice to master by exhibiting the appropriate erudition and leadership expected of a senior scholar. The final product of scholarship and defense was the measure of competence. The professor was the center of this process, and students showed great loyalty and dependence on the professor's goodwill and influence. This relationship has appeared in many settings in America and has been described as the apprentice model.

GETTING STARTED

The major concerns of the aforementioned American professors were to separate psychology from philosophy, to describe and elaborate on the domain of psychology, its subject matter, and its scientific methods, especially the latter.

In his summary of the major activities of experimental psychology in this early period in America, Edwin Boring (1950) identified sensation, reflexes, nerve excitation, and brain function as continuation of research activities begun with and by physiologists. The personal equation, reaction time, and the beginnings of motivational and attitude research came from starts by astronomers. Moreover, much of the European psychology needed to be absorbed by the new American psychology: from France, the work on neuroses and hypnosis; from Germany, the work on vision, hearing, and Gestalt psychology; and from England, Charles Darwin's work on animal psychology and Galton's work on mental testing and statistical measurement of human capacities.

With the 20th century, a new psychology emerged, more in the direction of motivation, to questions of the unconscious and the application of psychology to education, mental health, and industry. The developing

American industrial and agricultural enterprises required technical education. Already successful entrepreneurs responded warmly to the opportunity to create research centers and new universities by endowing universities usually carrying their names: Johns Hopkins, George Peabody, George Vanderbilt, James B. (Buck) Duke, and Leland Stanford. The major emphasis was on "investigation"; the work of giving instruction was secondary (Rudolph, 1962).

With the turn of the century, a new optimism emerged in America. By this time, America boasted a two-ocean navy, world power status, burgeoning economic development, and a thrust to proactive confrontation with significant problems. This assertiveness was reflected in the new uses to which psychology was put. Rather than be confined to the academic pattern of laboratory science, psychologists reached out and asserted themselves in dealing with problems of individual growth, development, adaptation, or failure to adapt. A leading proponent of outreach was Lightner Witmer, who had all the correct credentials: a PhD with Wundt, a professorship at the University of Pennsylvania, a psychological clinic devoted to problems of child development, the first of its kind in the world, and a journal, *The Psychological Clinic*, which was published from 1907 to 1935. From his predecessor at the University of Pennsylvania, James McKeen Cattell (the first in America to hold the title Professor of Psychology), Witmer inherited a culture of innovation and a focus on individual differences.

It is interesting to reflect that despite the authenticity of Witmer's background and preparation, he had a very limited impact on American university life during the time of his active professorship (Garfield, 1964). Yet he contributed the name of the major professional specialty in psychology, "clinical psychology," conducted an independent psychologically directed clinic, and addressed a range of problems that are still on the agenda for the profession. He developed psychological tests of children's performance, especially of sensory functions and intelligence, and he worked at helping children overcome their handicaps and disabilities.

In 1892, G. Stanley Hall, president of Clark University, called together seven men who there and then founded the American Psychological Association (APA). These seven, all professors, formed the Council, the governing body of APA. They were Hall, G. S. Fullerton of the University of Pennsylvania, Joseph Jastrow of the University of Wisconsin, William James of Harvard, G. T. Ladd of Yale, J. McKeen Cattell of Columbia, and J. M. Baldwin of the University of Toronto. The Council elected 24 others to membership. Hall became the first president of the APA, followed by Ladd, who was well known for his text on physiological psychology.

After Ladd, in sequence, the presidents were James, Cattell, Fullerton, Baldwin, Hugo Münsterberg, and John Dewey.

At the APA meeting in 1896, Lightner Witmer presented a description of the psychological clinic he had set up at the University of Pennsylvania. Witmer is reported to have felt that he was presenting something new and important. In the clinical and diagnostic methods of teaching and by the creation of the psychology clinic, he believed that he had established an institution for social and public service, for original research, and for instruction of students in areas of vocational, educational, correctional, hygienic, industrial, and social guidance. His APA talk is reported to have made very little impact, however (Reisman, 1976, p. 46).

In reflecting on the responses of the early psychologists, almost all of them academics, Reisman (1976) suggests that the limited approval of Witmer was probably due to four conditions: (a) The majority of psychologists thought of themselves as scientists and did not regard the roles proposed by Witmer as appropriate for them; (b) even if they regarded the suggestions as admirable, few psychologists were prepared by training or experience to perform the functions proposed by Witmer; (c) the academics were not about to jeopardize their tenuous status as scientists by premature application of what they had learned; and (d) Witmer was described as having an aptitude for antagonizing his colleagues.

However accurate the latter observation may be, it hardly seems to account for the distance between academics and clinicians that has continued over the decades, even to the recent establishment in 1988 of the American Psychological Society (APS) by psychologists concerned primarily with research and teaching who saw APA as excessively preoccupied with professional concerns and politically dominated by practitioners. It seems likely that the first three considerations noted by Reisman represent more fundamental reasons for the chilly response of American academic psychologists to Witmer's proposals. Either Witmer was before his time, or the psychology of the time, struggling to define itself as a science, was not yet ready to become a profession.

However unenthusiastically his ideas were received, Witmer was in an ideal position to pioneer training in clinical psychology, which he began in a modest way in 1903–1904 at the University of Pennsylvania. His clinic provided space for examining people and for demonstrating the behavior of the person in front of a group of students, investigators, and other skilled staff personnel. In addition to Witmer as director, the staff included an assistant director, five trained PhD examiners, one social worker, three assistant social workers, and a recorder. When needed, medical consultation was provided by the distinguished Dr. S. Weir Mitchell, the medical school neurologist. The clinic had to be of substantial size to house all these people.

Formal courses were taught at the graduate and undergraduate levels. The undergraduate offerings consisted mainly of abnormal psychology, but for the graduate students, there were three courses in developmental psychology, one in abnormal psychology, and one in physical and mental defects of schoolchildren. One course was concerned with the operation and culture of the clinic. The 1904–1905 medical school catalogue listed two courses, in psychiatry and neuropathology, that were available to psychology students for credit (Reisman, 1976, p. 87).

In addition to Witmer's clinic and patterned after it, the Iowa Psychological Clinic was founded at the University of Iowa in 1908 by Carl Seashore and R. L. Sylvester. Seashore was very much interested in singing, and his clinic was especially concerned with remedying speech and reading disabilities as well as mental defects. In 1909, Clark University also established a psychological clinic. Courses in clinical psychology were introduced at the University of Minnesota and at the University of Washington, followed later by psychological clinics. Reisman (1976), in reporting on the establishment of these clinics, notes that an underlying assumption was that they would not deal with people who were mentally ill. Rather, they were dealing with persons who had learning difficulties. Both in academic and in nonacademic settings, psychologists were employed to do research, mental testing, and pedagogy. They were not employed to treat the mentally ill.

Only a few psychologists worked outside of universities. In 1906, Henry Goddard, a student of G. Stanley Hall, was appointed director of research at the Institute for Backward Children in Vineland, New Jersey. Edmund Huey was appointed to the State Institution for the Feebleminded in Lincoln, Illinois, and F. Lyman Wells succeeded Shepherd Ivory Franz as psychologist at the McLean Hospital in Boston.

EXPANDING OUT OF THE ACADEMIC WORLD

Shortly after the turn of the century, in keeping with Lightner Witmer's focus on children, the child guidance movement came into being. Psychiatrist William Healy and psychologist Grace Fernald founded the Chicago Juvenile Psychopathic Institute (later called the Institute for Juvenile Research) and, in a series of steps, created the child guidance center movement. Later, beginning in 1917, they founded and directed the Judge Baker Guidance Center in Boston. Child guidance clinics offered a new service delivery model. With the addition of social work to psychiatry and psychology, the clinic created a multidisciplinary clinical task force that was imitated widely throughout the country. The concept of the three-profession team had great influence on the subsequent roles of all three professions.

William Healy, psychiatrist, would conduct the therapy with the children. Grace Fernald, psychologist, would evaluate the child's abilities, intelligence, fantasies, and the like. The social worker would help the family deal with problems of living, such as income, housing, health, and faulty communication. As time went by and as clinic teams gained skill and experience, psychologists began to conduct individual therapy with parents and children. Soon therapy groups were started, one of the early ones by psychologist Helen Durkin (1939).

MENTAL TESTS

The development of intelligence tests and other tests of mental function and the sequelae of that effort proved to be an outstanding accomplishment for psychology in the first few decades of the 20th century. Alfred Binet was undoubtedly among the most significant figures in the measurement field. He had been a student of great range, having earned a law degree and studied medicine, psychology, and philosophy; having given attention to thinking, hypnosis, and hysteria; and having helped set up the first physiological psychology laboratory in France. He had earned a doctoral degree in natural sciences with a thesis on the nervous system of the insect.

Binet and his colleague, Théodore Simon, struggled hard to define the concept of intelligence and develop an appropriate set of tasks with which to exhibit the attributes. The technical problem was to scale the various tasks to chronological age (CA). The more sophisticated question was that of mental age (MA).

Binet and Simon presented their original tentative scale in 1905, and introduced the mental age concept in the revision presented in 1908 (Matarazzo, 1972). The final version, a thorough revision, was published in 1911. Binet died prematurely in 1912, but interest in Binet's work was so intense that a number of translations from the French appeared almost immediately. Henry Goddard is credited with introducing the Binet-Simon Scale to the American public. Modifications were offered by Kuhlman, Wallin, Whipple, and Huey. For a while, Goddard's test was among the best received. Then in 1916, Lewis Terman of Stanford University presented his translated revision and new normative data based on an American population. The Stanford Binet, as this revision was called, became the standard American intelligence test for many years.

Wilhelm Stern, University of Breslau, introduced the concept of intelligence ratio by dividing MA by CA. Terman multiplied the ratio by 100 to derive the intelligence quotient (IQ), a single number that became the symbol of intellectual status. The individually administered Binet-Simon test required sensitive understanding of the client's emotional state when taking the test and imposed responsibility on the clinician to facilitate maximum performance on the part of the client.

The advent of World War I and the opportunity for using intelligence testing as an aid to the military for classifying the abilities of military recruits encouraged the development of group tests. The verbal group test based on Arthur Otis' self-administered mental abilities test was called the Army Alpha. Since a test for nonliterate persons was also needed, the Pintner-Paterson performance test became the prototype for the Army Beta, a nonverbal test. The tests were administered to millions of military recruits, and assignments in and out of the military as well as assignments to special duties were based in part on the scores obtained. Under the leadership of Robert Yerkes of Yale and Robert Woodworth of Columbia, these and other tests were developed for the military, and psychology became a significant contributor to the management of personnel.

SIGMUND FREUD

Among the most significant events for psychology at century's turn was Sigmund Freud's presentation of his startling observations about the meaning of dreams and such concepts as repression and the unconscious. These descriptions and ideas offered a coherent conceptual scheme for understanding mental illness. Much of the strange and occult now appeared reasonable and understandable. Only a century earlier, the mentally ill had been chained and confined for fear of the demons that possessed them, demons that might break loose and harm the innocent bystander.

Freud had studied with Jean Martin Charcot and Pierre Janet in Paris and had learned to use hypnosis (Mesmerism) as a means of treating hysteria. But he soon found that dreams and free association were more useful methods for him, giving him access to underlying conflicts and repressed taboo ideas. Most of the latter he believed were sexual in nature. His emerging and developing method of psychoanalysis provided a path for studying the underlying processes of mental disorders and also created a method of treating the analysand's conflicts and resultant symptoms.

The ability to confront the heretofore secret problems of the individual and to find solutions for them shifted the attitude toward mental illness from hopeless to difficult-but-possible! Freud had attracted a group of student-colleagues from around the world that met regularly with him, and soon his ideas began to circulate around the world.

The American Academy was most intrigued by Freud. When G. Stanley Hall, then president of Clark University, decided to arrange a convocation in 1909 to celebrate the 20th anniversary of the opening of Clark University, he invited Dr. Sigmund Freud of the University of Vienna, Professor Carl G. Jung of the University of Zurich, Professor Wilhelm Stern of the University of Breslau, Professor E. B. Tichener of Cornell, Professor Franz Boaz of Columbia, and Professor Adolph Meyer of Johns Hopkins, among others, to speak and to receive honorary degrees. Many of the elite of American psychology attended, among them Professor William James of Harvard, Professor James Jastrow of Wisconsin, Professor Guy Whipple of the University of Michigan, and Professor R. R. Porter of Clark University. The convocation welcomed the eminent university professors of psychology of the day. Freud was impressive, we are told. He was modest and sincere in presenting stimulating, intellectually revolutionary ideas. William James is reported to have said to Freud, "The future of psychology belongs to your work" (Reisman, 1976, p. 61).

Despite Freud's endorsement of lay analysis and his urging of separation of psychoanalysis from medicine, medically trained psychoanalysts were unwilling to relinquish control of the practice of psychoanalysis to any other profession. Freud's relationship to psychology was sharpened when a prominent nonmedical member of the Vienna psychoanalytic group, Theodore Reik, was sued for breach of an old Austrian law against "quackery" by a person he had been treating psychoanalytically. This law made it illegal for anyone without a medical degree to treat patients. Freud launched a vigorous defense with the legal authorities, stating his position forcefully in a monograph titled *The Problem of Lay Analysis* (1927). The monograph was published within 3 months, and the suit was dropped "for lack of satisfactory evidence."

The monograph presented a cogent, clear, and lively statement of Freud's theory. His statement is one psychologists are fond of quoting in relation to psychoanalysis, psychology, and medicine: "Psychoanalysis is not a specialized branch of medicine. I cannot see how it is possible to refute this. Psychoanalysis is a part of psychology" (Freud, 1927, as quoted in Freud, 1959, p. 232). This was an elaboration of a position Freud had begun to formulate in 1913.

Nonetheless, A. A. Brill, a medical psychoanalyst and the major

American translator of Freud, in 1925 wrote in a New York newspaper that no one except a physician should practice psychoanalysis! Shortly thereafter, the New York state legislature passed a bill making it illegal for anyone to practice "lay" analysis. It should be noted that practitioners of psychoanalysis first took a personal analysis and then were supervised in a training analysis until they had gained sufficient skill to function on their own. Thus, under New York state law, psychologists were ineligible for a training analysis. With psychology's current maturity in worldly and legislative matters, no such law could easily be passed today. The restraint of access to psychoanalysis created unnecessary conflict and interfered with the smooth exploitation of the methods and insights of Freud. For years it stood in the way of the fullest test of Freudian ideas.

Many psychologists, either in emotional distress or out of curiosity, had entered analytic treatment. Some foreign-born scholars who promised to take their training back to their home countries and not practice in the United States were allowed to take full analytic therapy. At one point, in 1929, the American Psychoanalytic Association agreed to allow laypersons working with children to be analyzed. Through these exceptions, a considerable number of psychologists experienced the role of analysand as patient or subject, and had a chance to develop the skills for offering psychoanalysis to others.

MEDICAL EDUCATION IN THE UNITED STATES

At this juncture, it is instructive to consider another profession, medicine, concerned with the delivery of a healing service based in part on knowledge gained in a number of sciences such as biology and chemistry. Like psychology, these sciences are constantly growing, and scientist-physicians are needed who appreciate the problems involved in applying their research findings to medical practice. In order to produce the cadre of scientists required in medicine, both practitioners and scientists have worked together in laboratories and clinics and have shared their knowledge and skills. Some persons have been trained in both areas and are able to take advantage of this dual training to facilitate the production and use of new information. In medicine, the physician interested in scientific research usually earns a second degree, the PhD. The scientist who wishes to apply his research to the human condition often earns a medical degree, the MD.

It is interesting to note that while psychology in America was at an infantile stage of development in its professional service role early in the 20th century, medicine in the United States was in deep trouble at that time with regard to professional training, education, standards, and professional organization. Problems in medicine were so widespread and serious that the Carnegie Foundation for the Advancement of Teaching undertook a national study on the training of physicians and surgeons. The Foundation selected Abraham Flexner, a Johns Hopkins holder of the bachelor's degree with a major in sociology, to conduct the study. As it turned out, Flexner was a loyal and worshipful alumnus of Johns Hopkins, and it was clear over the years of implementing the recommendations for the organization of medical education that the Hopkins medical program was the model that Flexner followed. It was not a bad model. It was designed to incorporate both science and clinical practice in both the structure of the curriculum and the operation of the medical school and teaching hospital.

The visits of Flexner (1910) to each medical school were described in his book, and his report included his opinions, something no review committee would dare to do in this day of litigation and supersensitive thresholds for slander or bias. Indeed, Flexner made bitter enemies as he imposed the model program he endorsed on the medical education of the time.

The essence of his proposal was that the medical school curriculum be divided into two parts. The first would be a 2-year intensive exposure to the basic sciences in biology and chemistry, which were the foundations upon which medicine was to be based. Anatomy, biochemistry, physiology, microbiology, pathology, and other basic sciences were the core courses. The early emphasis was on the normal body and normal development, slowly shifting to concern with pathology. The second 2-year period provided a series of clerkship rotations in the teaching hospital as a 3rd-year and then a 4th-year student moved through internal medicine, to surgery, to obstetrics/gynecology, to pediatrics. If the medical school included other specialties, students could apply for affiliation as electives.

The teaching hospitals were usually "charity hospitals." In a sense, patients paid for their treatment by being subjects for the students. The professors, often distinguished members of the community medical fraternity, would make scheduled rounds to review each patient's condition and recommend treatment. Residents and medical interns provided the basic care, and medical students in the early stages of training learned by caring for patients under the general guidance of the professor and the residents and interns.

What Flexner had found in his visits to the existing medical schools was a lack of laboratories, or even space and simple equipment for them, a lack of cadavers for basic instruction in anatomy and related sciences, and a lack of supervised teaching activities involving patients. His recommendations for reform were along the lines of the Hopkins model.

In time, the press for conformity resulted in a common medical school curriculum throughout the United States, especially in the preclinical 2 years. The quality of programs varied with the quality of the clinical faculty the school was able to recruit. Over time, some schools began to recruit clinical teachers who were employed full-time and practiced in the teaching hospital, using medical students at various stages of training to help care for patients, some of whom would be in the public wards, and others in private sections of the teaching hospital.

In the early 1950s, Western Reserve Medical School pioneered a new curriculum combining preclinical and clinical teaching around the patient as focus. It was a most difficult program to conduct, but the attempt stimulated similar and diverse experiments with the standard curriculum all over the United States.

Not all medical schools had departments of psychiatry in the period from 1910 to 1935, and toward the end of this time, the Commonwealth Fund encouraged and supported such training by grants for faculty. Later grants were provided to support specialization training for psychiatric residents. However, the major development of psychiatry departments took place after World War II, when the Veterans Administration (VA) and the National Institute of Mental Health (NIMH) both undertook to increase the numbers of psychiatric and mental health specialists needed to provide services for the mentally ill veterans as well as other civilian casualties throughout the country. The training grant programs that were supporting medical school psychiatry departments produced a considerable growth, and at one point, as many as 8% of medical school graduates accepted appointments for residency training in psychiatry. Today, in the 1990s, that percentage is far lower.

Both the Commonwealth Fund and NIMH fostered the development of behavioral science departments and administrative units associated with departments of psychiatry in the years just after World War II. Sociologists, anthropologists, and psychologists joined in the research and teaching activities of psychiatry departments, which then formally organized as joint departments of psychiatry and behavioral sciences. In some medical schools, as at the University of Oklahoma, the behavioral science unit also offered a PhD in biological psychology.

THE 1930s: INTERNAL STRUGGLES IN PSYCHOLOGY

By the late 1930s, applied psychologists were highly visible, in demand, and in relatively short supply. Academic psychologists were very much in the majority of the discipline, but the applied psychologists were moving into many institutional settings and exploring ways to use their skills wherever they went. The world of primary and secondary education, K–12, had become very much involved with psychology. Tests of intelligence gave a perspective on the achieving and underachieving child. Standardized tests of ability and school achievement provided a national yardstick for school functioning. The emerging tests of personality, which were easy to administer, offered some guidance on how remediation might be accomplished. With these tools at hand, guidance clinics and services could be set up in the schools, and a host of technically sophisticated methods could be made available for intervening with and modifying behavior.

High on the list of therapists was Carl Rogers, who was developing nondirective, client-centered therapy, which he demonstrated in clinical settings in the city of Rochester, New York, and later at Ohio State University (see chapter 19 in this volume). Another, less well-known leader in the field was John Levy (1938), a psychiatrist who was director of the Brooklyn Child Guidance Clinic in New York. In the latter part of the 1930s, he was teaching relationship therapy at Columbia University and conducting a clinical placement at the Child Guidance Clinic as part of the training program for psychology students at Columbia.

Other therapists at the time, such as Harry Stack Sullivan and Frederick Thorne, encouraged a "directive" approach, asserting that many patients lacked the ability to regulate themselves and needed the structure of therapeutic guidance. There was sufficient ferment and activity to encourage the Executive Committee of the Association for Consulting Psychologists to establish a subcommittee on psychotherapy in 1932, thus asserting a claim on that activity.

Psychology was a growing field of study and practice, particularly the practice portion. In 1910, there had been 222 members of APA. When S. W. Fernberger (1932) reported on the history of APA up to 1928, he noted that 616 members of APA had PhD degrees. Of these, 324 had earned degrees in just four universities: Columbia with 135 PhDs, Chicago with 80, Harvard with 56, and Clark with 50. At that time, 77% of APA members held academic positions, and 104 were engaged in clinical work. In 1930, there were 1100, and in 1939, approximately 2200 members of APA. In 1931, 800 psychologists were engaged in clinical work.

The lack of progress by APA in taking responsibility for professional psychology caused the formation in 1930 of the Association of Consulting Psychologists. This was actually an expansion of the New York Association of Consulting Psychologists, formed in 1921. The applied psychologists were asking for initiatives from APA. They were asking for a training outline for clinical psychology and other applied specialties in consulting, educational, and industrial psychology. They wanted an explicit method of recognizing qualified professional psychologists in order to differentiate them from the unqualified, as well as to help in legal certification.

In 1931 an effort was made to establish a prescribed training program in clinical psychology by the Clinical Section of APA. The committee that was set up, the Committee on Standards of Training in Clinical Psychology, reported back in 1935. It defined clinical psychology as that art and technology that deals with the adjustment problems of human beings. The committee called for a PhD or equivalent degree in psychology and a year of supervised experience as requirements for the title of clinical psychologist. It also defined a psychologist holding an MA degree and with a year's experience as an "assistant psychologist."

During the mid-1930s, despite the economic depression, the number of clinics and clinical positions continued to increase. In 1930, there were about 500 clinics in the United States offering psychiatric services, of which 125 were child guidance centers staffed by psychiatrists, psychologists, and social workers. By 1936, there were approximately 676 psychiatric clinics and some 87 psychoeducational clinics, compared with 20 in 1914. The psychoeducational clinics were mainly affiliated with universities and colleges and directed by psychologists.

In 1936, the Department of Psychology at Columbia University proposed a tentative curriculum for clinical psychologists that included 2 years of graduate work and a 1-year internship. On circulating the proposal for reactions from colleagues in other universities, Professor Poffenberger received a host of demurrers and exceptions. Strong objections were raised to the proposed award of a certificate rather than a PhD degree in psychology. There was strong endorsement to include a wide range of studies to ensure not only comprehensive knowledge of psychological science but requests for solid training in the social and biological sciences as well. Furthermore, there was a recognized need for practical experience but little recognition of what needed to be done to implement it. It seemed from these reactions that no hint of second-class preparation of the clinical psychologist was to be tolerated, notwithstanding the improbability of fitting comprehensive research training and comprehensive clinical training experience into a 3-to-4-year program. Even if more years might be needed, less preparation would not be acceptable.

As the positive gains to be secured by going in its own direction became more evident, the applied psychologists, the consulting, the clinical, the educational, and the industrial and business groups decided to create a new national organization, the American Association of Applied

Psychologists (AAAP), to represent the applied interests of American psychologists more effectively. Their organizing meeting, held in Minneapolis in September 1937, was reported in their own *Journal of Consulting Psychology* in January 1938.

WORLD WAR II

The success of psychologists during World War I had been so impressive in developing tests for the classification of recruits and draftees, in working with psychiatrically troubled military personnel, and in other helpful activities that the military called on psychology to anticipate the threatening hostilities of World War II. In 1940, a committee of psychologists was asked to develop group tests for the evaluation of military personnel. They produced the Army General Classification Test as well as a number of other tests to help deal with illiterates and with handicapped personnel.

Psychologists were called to duty to serve the Office of Strategic Services (OSS) in its responsibility for carrying out intelligence missions behind the enemy lines. Psychologists selected and trained persons, and late in the war, under the direction of Professor Henry Murray of Harvard, a study of selection methods was conducted and reported in a book titled *The Assessment of Men* (Office of Strategic Services, 1948).

The shortage of professionally qualified psychologists and psychiatrists to work with military casualties caused the army to experiment with the training and utilization of qualified and almost qualified psychologists, bringing them to a level of professional competence for diagnosis and treatment of psychiatric casualties in the military hospitals. Psychologists were found to be as efficient as psychiatrists in carrying out these functions. The military prisons employed many psychologists in rehabilitation centers and disciplinary barracks. Psychologists conducted the classification activities at both types of institutions and diagnosed and treated the disturbed prisoners.

By 1941, the AAAP had 615 members for whom it provided leadership. However, the war effort encouraged national cooperation, and William Malamud, a distinguished psychiatrist, and Walter S. Hunter, chairman of the Psychology Department at Brown University, serving together on a National Research Council committee, sponsored a report urging cooperation between psychiatry and psychology in the interests of national defense. This report probably helped pave the way for the recognition of military clinical psychology (Reisman, 1976). In 1942, under the leadership of Robert M. Yerkes, a subcommittee of the National Research Council began work on bringing APA and the AAAP together. In 1944, after considerable negotiation and reorganization, the AAAP disbanded and joined APA.

More than 1700 psychologists had served in the armed forces during World War II. In addition to the more clinically oriented tasks, psychologists were used to solve human engineering and human factor problems, to develop mass communications and propaganda activities, to work in leadership selection and training, to help solve visual problems associated with night combat, to manage job classification and assignment, and to provide many other services (Altman, 1987).

Before the war was over, it became clear that much needed to be done in the postwar period, and that psychologists could help do it. The problem of dealing with the psychiatric casualties in the veterans hospitals created an obvious target, and the war experience had demonstrated that psychologists could help alleviate the problem. Beyond clinical work with individuals, some psychologists were interested in the larger picture, in assisting with modifying international tensions and preserving the peace. Gardner Murphy wrote on the psychological requisites for a sound foreign policy (1946) and over the next few years described how psychology could help improve society (1948) and with colleagues described the place of emotions in world problems (1948).

CREATION OF PROFESSIONAL CLINICAL PSYCHOLOGY IN THE ACADEMIC ESTABLISHMENT

In taking a hard look at the help it would need, the VA noted a population pool of 16 million veterans of World War II, plus 4 million from previous wars. As it anticipated the aging of this group and the increasing demand for treatment of emotional problems from those veterans with service-related disabilities, it seemed clear that more psychiatrists, psychologists, and related personnel would be needed. VA estimates called for 4,700 clinical psychologists to help treat the 44,000 neuropsychiatric casualties already in hospitals. The vocational counselors that would be needed to help readjust the millions of discharged military men and women to civilian life would come to more than 1,500 psychologically sophisticated counselors, more than one and one half times the total United States supply. A new source of professional psychologists was needed.

APA and the AAAP set up a joint committee headed by David Shakow to consider a training program that would produce new clinical psychologists. Rather than plan a new group of training sites, the committee in 1944 recommended that training take place in existing graduate programs, and that these programs be enhanced with public funds to accommodate the necessary proposed expansion.

Funds were made available by the U.S. government through both the VA and NIMH to promote the training effort. A grant structure was devised for NIMH and a collaborative apprentice system for the VA. In order to create a system for awarding federal funds, APA was asked to set up the criteria for a training/education program and a mechanism for identifying qualified university programs for awards.

The Shakow Committee suggested a model program that called for 4 years postbaccalaureate education: the 1st year to the study of general psychology, scientific foundations, research methods, and theory; the 2nd year, practicums; the 3rd year, internship; and the 4th year, dissertation.

In 1946, the VA and NIMH undertook the encouragement and support of training of psychiatrists. In the same year, NIMH established a program of training grants for clinical psychology, and the VA implemented its collaborative psychology training program, which provided for a specific number of work/training assignments to be allocated to qualified universities. Collaboration between psychiatry and psychology was close at many universities. At Duke University, for example, both the psychology and psychiatry departments were on campus, with the medical school and hospital abutting on the central university quadrangle. Each department took responsibility for training its own professionals, but cooperation prevailed. To solve the problem of supplying psychiatric and psychological services to veterans in the central North Carolina area, the Duke University Medical School built a psychiatric clinic near the hospital in which the veteran patients could be treated. Psychiatry and psychology students could get experience working with VA patients as well as nonveterans, and students in both disciplines could learn to work with each other in helping the people they intended to serve.

This collaboration had many benefits. Instruction in the diagnosis and treatment of mental illness was at the leading edge of knowledge. Students in both professions grew up together and learned to respect each other. Patients got excellent care, which pleased the VA and the veterans themselves. The university was able to undertake the various programs by the infusion of government funds, and the federal government was pleased to see its support of graduate training awarded to its war veterans, who were thus solving their own career problems, as well as those of their patients.

The training programs for the psychiatry residents and psychology interns differed in many ways, but there were many overlapping activities. The psychologists were actively involved in research, the psychiatric residents, rarely. The residents used drugs in a number of ways, for example, sodium amytal or sodium pentothal for abreaction treatments. Psychologists only assisted in the interviews in such cases. The psychology students were intensely concerned with assessment and in understanding the internal dynamics for the patient. The residents were concerned with diagnosis, disposition, and treatment.

Formal training in psychotherapy for psychologists in 1946–1947 had a lower priority than research and diagnosis. One great plus at Duke was the presence of Bingham Dai, a Chinese psychoanalyst who had earned his PhD at the University of Chicago in sociology in the early 1930s and had completed a full psychoanalysis with Leon Salzman of the Washington School of Psychiatry, with the understanding that Dai would be going back to China to practice there. This he did. But shortly after World War II, Richard Lyman, who was to become the first professor of psychiatry at Duke, traveling on a Rockefeller Foundation grant, visited the Peking Medical College. There he met Dai working in the Psychiatry Department. Lyman invited Dai to join the Duke Medical School faculty, where Dai provided short-term personal analyses for the psychiatric residents, some selected medical residents, and some psychology interns. The program of self-study that he developed and wrote up (1956), which required some 30–40 hours of analysis, was a most exciting and productive experience for the students who were able to participate.

The students in the early post–World War II period were a mature group. Most were recently married veterans, older than the usual prewar student, very serious, and in many cases eager to devote their lives to a career of helping make a better world. These students provided a pleasant and even exhilarating teaching experience for the university professors who taught them. To students, a career in clinical psychology seemed to have popular appeal, so that as soon as university programs in clinical psychology were prepared and announced, large numbers of potential students applied for admission. This provided the faculty with the opportunity to select very bright and personable candidates for the scholarships that became available.

NIMH training grants provided funds for both clinical and non-clinical faculty, if such faculty were needed to meet APA criteria for an accredited clinical program. NIMH grants also provided scholarships for clinical students. Thus, a department of psychology not well equipped to offer a graduate clinical program could use a clinical grant to add faculty strength in the department's nonclinical scientific programs, and, because outside money would help support clinical graduate students, it could use its university-budgeted money for the support of graduate students in general psychology. In this way, training grants for clinical programs also offered benefits for general programs in psychology. Indeed, the stronger and more varied the general program, the more directions clinical students could take in pursuing their doctoral dissertation problems.

This symbiosis nurtured the development of a multifaceted department of psychology that encouraged individual initiative but did not necessarily lead to collaboration among the many possible groups that could work together in research. One major problem for many programs was in conducting authentic service delivery operations within which both practicum and internship training could be conducted under the direction of fully qualified mental health professionals, including clinical psychologists serving as role models. The Duke model noted previously was able to meet the requirements. The hospital had a psychiatric treatment floor staffed by psychiatrists, clinical psychologists, social workers, and all the usual medical specialists. Pediatric and general medical services were offered to populations of all ages, both sexes, and varied sociocultural characteristics. Furthermore, the hospital was in operation 24 hours a day, 7 days a week, and responsive to all crises in the community, such as epidemics and major accidents. In all its branches, the research orientation of the program was very strong.

In contrast, some university clinical psychology programs located in universities far from large cities or medical school hospitals, with limited mental health personnel in the community, had to develop their own resources. The University of Tennessee in Knoxville, for example, was at the other end of the state from the state medical school at Memphis. The University of Tennessee clinical program developed its own clinic center, securing a building and providing service to both the community of Knoxville and to the campus. Its major focus was on the treatment of the "worried well," the rather pejorative characterization given to the major group of patients and clients who currently occupy much of the time of psychiatric and psychological practitioners. A local state mental hospital made access to the mentally ill possible for students and staff.

In the University of Tennessee example, there was a strong emphasis on therapy, the objectives being to put the client at ease, to reduce tensions, and to help clients move to self-fulfillment. There was little emphasis on some of the diagnostic work required in the Duke example. The model also demonstrated a psychologist role model in the director of the clinic, who was concerned with such activities as professional direction and supervision, budgets, and legal testimony, as well as direct service to clients.

A third pattern developed in the clinical program at Columbia University, which was originally located at Teachers College, just across the street from the graduate school campus. It was miles away from the medical school and Columbia's teaching hospitals but was ideally placed to develop a very strong child focus and to be concerned with the role of psychology in elementary and high school education. Columbia's graduate program under Robert Woodworth and A. Poffenberger in the 1930s was very sympathetic to the applied aspects of psychology. In World War I, Woodworth had developed one of the earliest incomplete sentence personality questionnaires for use in the army. The clinical program at Columbia had a strong focus on the facilities that were readily available to students at Teachers College and its affiliated model experimental schools. Most Columbia graduates were especially experienced in child and school problems, although the program was flexible and the training of some students took idiosyncratic directions.

Where university colleges of education had set up teaching clinics for elementary and high school students with learning problems and had established liaison with experimental teaching settings, natural laboratories existed and good clinical/counseling teaching opportunities flourished. Some universities also established guidance clinics or counseling centers to serve their own troubled students and used such agencies for the training of their own clinical/counseling graduate students.

Happenstances of location and relationship affected the focus of research as well as practice among psychologists. In a medical school environment, where high emphasis would be placed on the treatment of referred and selected patients, the psychologists would be expected to do diagnostic studies to help the treating psychiatrists responsible for hospitalizing patients, prescribing drugs, and managing courses of treatment. The medical school setting encouraged diagnostic neuropsychological studies to aid in the localization of brain lesions and the assessment of early intellectual deterioration. A whole range of consultation relationships to medical school faculty became possible, and service activities in evaluation and treatment developed with departments of pediatrics, internal medicine, neurosurgery, neurology, endocrinology, and others.

The VA was eager to start producing clinical psychologists. In late 1945, they asked the APA to provide a list of institutions that possessed adequate facilities for providing training at the doctoral level in clinical psychology. By September 1946, some 22 universities were identified as adequate by the APA Committee on Graduate and Professional Training. After appropriate negotiations with recommended universities, the VA began to introduce students from these universities into their hospitals and clinics—about 200 during that first year. By 1947, APA's Committee on Graduate and Professional training was able to enlarge the list to 29 out of the 40 universities that had applied (see Table 1). As the remaining 11 universities met the criteria, they too were approved. The universities were located all over the United States, both private and state-supported, both large and small, both prestigious and modest (Sears, 1947).

In order to qualify as an "adequate" or approved institution, the interested universities were asked to fill out questionnaires describing clinical and nonclinical faculty, to outline the curriculum in clinical psychology offered by the university, and to describe the practicum facilities to be used in a variety of specified areas of experience. In general, broad practical training experience was requested, including (a) work with psychotic and neurotic patients and team work with a psychiatrist, especially for students training in veterans hospitals and clinics; (b) experience with children with emotional problems in a typical children's guidance clinic; and (c) an additional practicum setting to be chosen by the university. The criteria, while fairly specific, were offered with the recognition that individual innovations and additions were to be expected. Despite these allowances, the guidelines were almost slavishly followed by most universities.

By 1949, enough experience with the problems of conducting a graduate training program in clinical psychology had been gained in the various adequate universities to consider bringing representatives from all the training sites together to consolidate their suggestions for improvements and changes. This was done in Boulder, Colorado at the University of Colorado, under the sponsorship of NIMH. This 2-week long retreat into the mountains became the definitive conference for the education of clinical psychologists (Raimy, 1950), establishing the goals, qualities, and specifics of education and training in clinical psychology that extend into the present time.

The basic agenda for the Boulder meeting in 1949 had been set out in the 1947 report of APA's Committee on Graduate Training in Clinical Psychology, better known as the Shakow Report (APA Committee on Training in Clinical Psychology, 1947). This committee could look to no prior model for its recommended program and had regretted not having the time to test out their proposals before they were promulgated. Under the press of the federal agencies' needs, programs had been proposed and implemented within a very short period of time and insufficient opportunity for careful planning. Now it seemed appropriate to bring together all the universities for their feedback on the programs they had adopted, the problems that had emerged, and the sense of progress they had attained.

True to its tradition of involvement with science and the reality of limited knowledge of mental illness and the ways in which to treat it, early consensus was reached on the priority of research training as a basic ingredient of the clinical program. Although a number of very able nondoctoral persons were known to have served the public well, the conference took a

TABLE 1
Institutions That Applied in 1947 to the APA Committee on Graduate and Professional Training for Recognition of Their "Adequate Facility" for Conducting Doctoral Training in Clinical Psychology

Institution	Administrative officer	Address	Criteria
California: Berkeley[a]	E. C. Tolman	Berkeley	A. Basic Staff
California: Los Angeles[a]	Roy M. Dorcus	Los Angeles	1. Seven Class A persons on staff[b]
Catholic Univ. of Am.[a]	Thomas V. Moore	Washington, DC	2. Graduate nonclinical teaching = 2 full-time
Cincinnati[a]	Arthur G. Bills	Cincinnati, OH	graduate teachers[c]
Clark[a]	Vernon Jones	Worcester, MA	B. Curriculum requirements
Colorado	K. F. Muenzinger	Boulder	1. Statistical or quantitative methods
Columbia Univ.[a]	H. E. Garrett	New York, NY	2. Experimental methods
Columbia: TC[a]	L. F. Shaffer	New York, NY	3. Systems or theory
Denver	L. W. Miller	Denver, CO	4. Personality and psychodynamics
Duke[a]	Donald K. Adams	Durham, NC	5. Projective techniques
Florida	E. D. Hinckley	Gainesville	C. Graduate clinical staff
George Washington	Thelma Hunt	Washington, DC	1. One class A clinical teacher[d]; not less than half-
Georgia	A. S. Edwards	Athens	time on department budget
Harvard[a]	Robert W. White	Cambridge, MA	2. Three persons for regular teaching of graduate
Illinois[a]	Herbert Woodrow	Urbana	students in clinical psychology
Indiana[a]	B. F. Skinner	Bloomington	3. Their combined graduate teaching load = not
Iowa[a]	K. W. Spence	Iowa City	less than 1 full-time graduate teacher
Kentucky[a]	M. M. White	Lexington	D. Practicum facilities[e]
Michigan State Coll.	H. H. Anderson	East Lansing	1. Psychiatric facility; students have opportunity
Michigan, Univ. of[a]	D. G. Marquis	Ann Arbor	to work in team with psychiatrist
Minnesota, Univ. of[a]	R. M. Elliott	Minneapolis	2. A child clinic
Nebraska	D. W. Dysinger	Lincoln	3. One additional practicum of any kind
	D. A. Worcester		
Northwestern[a]	R. H. Seashore	Evanston, IL	
Ohio State[a]	H. E. Burtt	Columbus	

Institution		Location
Pennsylvania State Coll.[a]	B. V. Moore	State College
Pennsylvania, Univ. of[a]	R. A. Brotemarkle	Philadelphia
Pittsburgh[a]	Wayne Dennis	Pittsburgh, PA
Purdue[a]	F. B. Knight	Lafayette, IN
Rochester[a]	G. R. Wendt	Rochester, NY
Univ. Southern Calif.[a]	Neil Warren	Los Angeles
Stanford[a]	E. R. Hilgard	Stanford Univ., CA
Syracuse[a]	Roland McKee	Syracuse, NY
	R. G. Kuhlen	
Texas	L. A. Jeffress	Austin
Tulane	Cecil W. Mann	New Orleans, LA
Washington U.: St. Louis[a]	John P. Nafe	St. Louis, MO
U. of Wash.: Seattle	Roger Loucks	Seattle
Wayne Univ.	Gertha Williams	Detroit, MI
Western Reserve[a]	Calvin S. Hall	Cleveland, OH
Wisconsin[a]	Norman Cameron	Madison
Yale[a]	C. I. Hovland	New Haven, CT

Note: Adapted from "Clinical Training Facilities: Report of the Committee on Graduate and Professional Training, APA" by R. R. Sears, 1947, *American Psychologist, 2,* 202–203.

[a]Those institutions that met the criteria in that year and were recommended to the Veterans Administration (VA).

[b]Class A nonclinical teacher = PhD previous to 1944; evidence of research orientation (e.g., published papers, directed theses, teaching research methods).

[c]Full-time graduate teacher = a sum of 1.0 obtained by adding together the fractional amounts of time contributed to graduate teaching by the various staff members.

[d]Class A clinical teacher = PhD previous to 1944, or MA (or later PhD) with 3 years of clinical experience, or qualifies as Fellow in Clinical Division, APA; shows evidence of research orientation.

[e]Class A practicum supervisor = PhD, or MA with 3 years of clinical experience. Must be a psychologist, *not* psychiatrist, etc.

stand favoring the conservation of energy at that time by emphasizing education of the doctoral level clinical psychologists to lead the way. They voted to reserve the title of clinical psychologist exclusively for holders of the doctoral degree. Participants recognized that the time would come for the consideration of ways in which persons with less than doctoral training could be used in the mental health field, but decided that this was not the time to deal with the issue. The clinical psychologist was seen to have creative responsibilities, and it was anticipated that many functions about to be created would require high technical skill that could be delegated eventually to specially trained assistants.

The internship, which had been declared a sine qua non of the program, needed great elaboration as to its sequence in the curriculum, its content, and the center of its control and supervision. In a number of articles by Woodworth, Poffenberger, and Shakow in 1937 and 1938, there had been strong endorsement of the need for an internship in training. But more specific issues, like whether to hold the internship on or off the campus of the university, whether to have an internship or an externship, the place of the internship in relation to the dissertation, whether there should be pre- or postgraduation timing of the internship, and how to integrate theory and practice, were not easily resolved and have persisted for a number of years. The Shakow Report asserted that the internship was to be predoctoral and was the responsibility of the university. It was to be considered a part of the university program, and if it was not handled appropriately in management and function, the university accreditation could be threatened. More to the point, it was felt that the internship represented a rare opportunity for learning the craft and the aspirations of clinical psychology and as such needed to be used in the most constructive possible fashion.

Shakow, who had directed the internship program for many years at Worcester State Hospital, had the Worcester model in mind in his description of the ideal internship. For him, the long-standing high level of function of the research wing of the Worcester State Hospital, with eminent persons teaching and interning there (Adolph Meyer, David Shakow, Eliot Rodnick, Saul Rosenzweig, Leslie Philips, Charles Spielberger, and Raymond Fowler, to mention a few) provided a rare learning opportunity. Not many internships have reached the eminence of the Worcester program; its image has been a guide to all other programs.

The requirement of an internship and of practicum facilities put heavy pressure on the universities to affiliate with or to create authentic service delivery installations: The clinics, counseling centers, mental health units, and child guidance centers within which services were offered and training for service could be provided. If appropriate facilities could not be found on the campus or in the city in which the university was located, medical schools and their psychiatry departments or community mental health centers could be used.

THE TRAINING CONFERENCES

Nine major training conferences and almost as many more with special training foci have been devoted to the training of psychologists in the 40 years since Boulder. Perhaps Table 2 will help visualize the events.

The 1949 Boulder Conference focused on clinical psychology and did a profoundly significant job of asserting a pattern and system of training that is still the dominant guide as we write. The 1951 Northwestern and 1954 Thayer meetings were intended to do the same for counseling and school psychology. The 1955 Stanford meeting was a consciousness-raising meeting designed to alert the participants to the research possibilities in public mental health but at the same time to consider some questions that had arisen since Boulder. The scientist-practitioner model was reaffirmed, and in view of the diversity in training emphases, in clinical as in counseling and school psychology, a core training program was considered to permit basic preparation over a wide range of professional psychology fields. Also at the Stanford meeting, the newly developed community mental health centers were acknowledged as a possible practicum resource. It was noted that relationships between universities and practicum internship centers had not worked well and that more effort needed to be directed toward facilitating communication. Training in psychotherapy was identified as an area for special nurturance in light of its importance in the future competence of the professional clinical psychologist.

TABLE 2
Major Training Conferences

Date	Location	Topic
1949	Boulder, CO	Training for clinical psychology
1951	Northwestern University	Training for counseling psychology
1954	Thayer, NY	Training for school psychology
1955	Stanford University	Psychology in mental health
1958	Estes Park, CO	Training in research in mental health
1958	Miami Beach, FL	Graduate training in psychology
1965	Chicago, IL	Diversification in clinical training
1973	Vail, CO	Diversity of training models: people trained, people served, people serving
1987	Salt Lake City, UT	Graduate training in psychology

The 1958 Estes Park Conference on Research Training seemed satisfied with the essentials of the apprenticeship model for research training then firmly in place in the academic culture.

The 1958 Miami Beach Conference, in session for 8 days, was focused on all fields of psychology, and some of the questions raised at Boulder were raised again for their relevance to the training of psychologists in all fields. There was agreement on a common core of knowledge, but there was no interest in prescribing such a core. Decisions about sampling and selection of psychological knowledge were to be left to each university department. The major characteristic of the psychologist was his or her research training, and here the conference felt the training should be comprehensive. No definite stand was taken on the timing of the internship if the specialty should require one. The conference noted wide variation in this timing and preferred to allow experimentation to identify the best sequence. Considerable dissatisfaction was noted in the coordination of the work of internship facilities and universities. In view of the massive need for trained personnel, there was decided interest in clarifying ways of using nondoctoral personnel to offer psychological service.

The 1965 Chicago Conference (Hoch, Ross, & Winder, 1966) was a stormy one, especially in regard to determining alternate patterns of training and alternate degrees. A major proposal was that the conference endorse an alternate model for training in clinical psychology: a practitioner model and a new degree, the Doctor of Psychology (PsyD) degree. This would require enhanced field training and supervision and special concentration on clinical training. If the Boulder model had anticipated a 50/50 concentration on research/clinical, the Chicago conferees were asked to realize that the balance had shifted in many departments to a 75/25 emphasis on research and were asked to consider an additional model along the lines of a research/clinical allocation of 25/75. Although Boulder had encouraged experimentation on models, the Chicago meeting spent hours struggling with the problem and then refused to endorse or encourage consideration of such an alternate course. By a narrow margin, it agreed to "recognize" that such an alternate course existed.

Nevertheless, Donald Peterson and Lloyd Humphreys of the University of Illinois had cleared the way at their university to award a PsyD degree as an alternate to the PhD for clinical psychology students. After 3 years of planning, the PsyD program was initiated in 1968. The PhD program for students with dominant interests in research was retained. Although the original plan for the PsyD (Peterson, 1966) (see chapter 26 in this volume) did not call for a dissertation, the University of Illinois Graduate College would not approve the proposal without a thesis requirement.

Henceforth, all Illinois PsyDs completed dissertations, and nearly all the PsyD programs that followed include a dissertation requirement.

The Chicago Conference did not resolve the basic issues underlying direct education for the practice of psychology. Neither did it clarify the issues, anticipated at Boulder, surrounding the training of nondoctoral psychologists. The professional MA was still in limbo. The Conference did allow for expression of deep-seated feelings about discrimination against the clinical psychology professors, some of whom felt their clinical work was not as keenly appreciated as was work on research, nor was it rewarded. This complaint had been very much in the air since Boulder, and it reflected many perceived inequities in promotion and salary.

The possibility of a freestanding professional school (unaffiliated with a university) offering a graduate training program was discussed in Chicago, and in keeping with the spirit of experimentation, some recognition was gained. But, typical of the meeting, there was also great dissension. Nonetheless, in 1969, the California School of Professional Psychology (CSPP) was founded, offering a 6-year PhD program for the education of practitioners. The rationale for this action was the societal need for more psychologists, the long period of time university programs took to graduate their doctoral students, and the tiny number of students universities were admitting to their research programs in the face of large numbers of well-qualified applicants interested in professional careers. The press for independence from university affiliation was a measure of the dissatisfaction with the existing state of affairs.

The 1973 Vail Conference was a "happening," and made the heated and controversial Chicago Conference seem like a tea party. American society during the 1965–1975 period was undergoing an enormous struggle. Among its major issues were questions of human rights, especially equal rights for women and minority groups. The place of minorities in the competition for access to education and training in clinical psychology came under close scrutiny at Vail. The PhD programs, with their elitist selection, could exclude competent, well-motivated, and dedicated potential practitioners from serious consideration for admission. Also, the PhD programs did not promise training for a practitioner role. The academic establishment was sharply criticized for its unresponsiveness to the need for competent practitioners and the demand by students for access to the necessary education. Applications for admission to university programs were soaring, but limited admissions caused a consistent low in production. The existing nonuniversity program, the California School of Professional Psychology, promised a solution, since it could admit and undertake to train a great many more professional psychologists than the existing university programs were producing.

The Vail Conference called for more flexibility in both the locus of the training programs and the degree offered. The levels of training needed to serve people in trouble, bachelor's, master's, or doctoral level, had been discussed at previous conferences, but very little had been done to create qualified helpers in a world full of credential requirements. Discussion also centered on who was to be helped. There was strong endorsement for helping the poor in crisis rather than expending most of our resources in providing personal growth or self-enhancing programs for the middle- or upper-class people in our society.

The winds of change encouraged the development of professional schools, the adoption of the Doctor of Psychology degree, and the creation of master's level programs on professional psychology. Although the consensus of the conference encouraged master's professional programs, the traditional academic establishment showed little if any interest in implementing such programs. However, over 25 master's level professional programs were developed after Vail, with the Vail resolution as their sanction. They now produce as many graduates as the doctoral programs (Peterson, personal communication, 1990). A movement to provide graduate education outside of the established academic world was encouraged and implemented, and the emphasis on serving the public by skilled practitioners was endorsed.

Within the academic community, however, much of the intense fervor of the meeting seems to have had a negative result. Many of the participants could agree with the validity of the ideas proposed but could not see how to address the issues or produce a satisfactory result. One sign of the difficulty of implementing solutions was that the report of the conference came out 3 years later (Korman, 1976). For the most part, the academic establishment ignored the Vail resolutions and continued to educate research-oriented psychologists in the traditional way.

In a striking and provocative article, Irwin Altman (1987) provided an introduction to a major theme at the Utah Conference held at Salt Lake City in June 1987 on the subject of graduate education in psychology. Altman developed the theme of centripetal and centrifugal trends in psychology as he looked at the history of psychology in the 20th century. He identified the period from 1892 (the establishment of APA) to 1960 as a centripetal period, in which unifying trends in psychology gained strength and the field of psychology consolidated on many fronts: theoretical, substantive, methodological, philosophical, and institutional. He described the many ways in which APA held together the diverse membership it contained, and maintained the consolidation and unification of the discipline during the years from 1900 to 1960.

Altman described the period of 1960 to 1987 as centrifugal, reflecting violent upheavals on several fronts. He noted the rise of Black Power and other minority movements, the challenge to discrimination, the riots, burnings, and conflict in the cities. On the national scene, he pointed to the deepening tarnish and loss of prestige of the United States presidency and to the deep societal division created by opposition to the Vietnam War. For balance, he noted some centripetal trends in the patriotism and conservatism of Americans, reflecting a force toward a more unified social system. Forces were working in both directions, yet the dominant force appeared to be centrifugal.

From this perspective, Altman looked at the scene in higher education, and at psychology in particular. He noted the boom years of the 1960s and 1970s, the increase in the numbers of mature students, products of the postwar "baby boom," the popularity of psychology enrollment in undergraduate and graduate programs, the financial support for professional training and for research by the federal government, and the burgeoning demand for entrance into the growing psychological service delivery profession. Although the earlier years of this period were times of plenty, the later years witnessed rapidly declining, unstable support. Within American psychology, Altman saw considerable disorganization, very little willingness to support the parent organization, and an emphasis on individualism— very much the same pattern for which our larger society is often criticized.

The period after Vail saw the growth of freestanding graduate programs, but graduate programs also went into other than arts and sciences colleges in the university. Health psychology and clinical psychology programs are now found in medical schools and allied health professions colleges. Organizational psychology programs are sometimes housed in schools of business. Colleges of education are housing counseling psychology or educational psychology departments. Psychology as a discipline has spread into liaison with a wide range of university programs. Professors of psychology engaged in forensics are often affiliated with colleges of law. Those concerned with management and systems design may be affiliated with schools of business and engineering, those in environmental design with schools of architecture, those with knowledge of animal behavior with colleges of agriculture.

The organization and preparation for the Utah Conference were unusually thorough. As described in Bickman's (1987) report, there was wide exchange of opinion, careful synthesis of issues, and extensive interaction prior to the formal initiation of the conference. The major concern was the explosive development of new and different activities in graduate education that the university structure of the period before Vail had not been designed to handle.

Four themes were articulated. The first was *unity*. Was there a central corpus to psychology? Could a core curriculum be defined? Was there a core for service providers? Was that core separate from the core for the rest of psychology? A solution was found in a two-phased answer: an APA-specified core curriculum for students preparing for service roles requiring licenses, and freedom for departments to identify their own values and goals in setting up their own core program for students who were not preparing to enter legally certifiable professional specialties.

The second theme was *diversity*. Was there acceptance of multiple and diverse views on a wide range of variables—ethnic, religious, age, gender, and sexual preference? Departments were encouraged to take responsibility for providing experiences in cultural diversity in formal courses and in actual field work. Alternate models of training, in addition to the scientist-practitioner model, were to be accepted, but sharper delineation and more specific quality standards for the various models were urgently recommended.

The third theme was *quality*. There was great concern over the quality of graduate education and of the students involved, especially in regard to freestanding professional schools. Strong liaison between freestanding schools and universities was recommended, with the expectation that both universities and professional schools would gain from each other and that the freestanding schools would ultimately affiliate with universities. It was also recommended that study of evaluation methods and procedures be undertaken and that the study attempt to deal as well with levels of quality.

The fourth theme was *humanity*. It called for a recognition that not courses but people were involved. The quality of academic life for faculty and students needed careful review. Recruitment of students and their retention in the program warranted study and review, and faculty responsibility for monitoring and supporting students' professional life was stressed (Bickman, 1987).

In effect, the recommendations of the Utah Conference called for an integration of various divisive growth activities of the post-Vail period, and suggested some mechanisms that might bring it about. By confronting some of these muttered dissensions, it was possible to loosen irritating postures and allow the underlying problems to be explored and for some of them to be solved.

CONCLUSION

Beginning in 1879, the university faced the problem first of identifying the boundaries and content of psychology, which over this century have tended to defy restraint and confinement. Among psychology's many attributes was its potential for improving the welfare of human beings. From the very beginning, practical application to the service of humans became a driving force in the growth of the field. The academic world, however, has never been entirely comfortable in moving toward professional application. The academy felt uncertain about the state of knowledge in those areas and did not feel competent to apply untested findings to the amelioration of human distress. Throughout much of our history the academy has maintained arms distance from involvement.

Society's ills, however, have overwhelmed this reluctance. In times of deep emergency, as in World War I and particularly in World War II and the years following, psychology put its shoulder to the wheel and found that much of its learning could be useful in the national effort. Indeed, psychology as science could be applied to almost any endeavor that involved people.

Of the therapeutic knowledge and skills developed early, the techniques of psychoanalysis and client-centered counseling took hold first and spread rapidly. Among a host of others that followed came Gestalt therapy, behavioral therapy, and cognitive therapy, methods that made it possible to help people in trouble move toward relief of distress, and in some cases, achieve full mastery of their lives. As the various therapies seemed to be increasingly successful, ever greater numbers of students sought training at the universities best equipped to offer it.

At first, the universities were eager to help, as the federal government had expressed tangibly its strong support for preparing professionals to meet the acute need. However, as external financial supports diminished, and the demands of professional involvement and the number of persons requiring and capable of professional training started to stretch university resources, stresses became apparent. Departments of psychology accustomed to leisurely and thoughtful probing of problems found themselves facing demands for practical and applied experiences in areas about which they knew little and for which they possessed limited resources. Some universities could create joint facilities on and off campus and were stimulated to develop and experiment with new utilizations of knowledge, including community service. The challenges of public service are severe, however, and many an academician retained the belief that the best thing psychologists could do was develop their basic science, or at most a proven technology, before leaping into the treacherous seas of professional application.

As psychologists became independent deliverers of service to the public, questions of professional competence arose. Training and experience had to be verified, and the curricula and other characteristics of the program were pressed toward standardization. To many, this constituted an unacceptable threat to academic freedom. Furthermore, it devolved upon universities to provide students with supervised experience that would ensure a professional level of performance for the public. That required a heavy investment of resources, and if conforming to professional demands over-extended the wherewithal so that other specialties could not grow, then admissions to the clinical program had to be limited to those students most likely to emerge as future leaders of the profession.

The slow rate of production of service providers and the especially high demand for admission to the university-based professional programs pushed administrators of these programs and of professional psychology organizations to urge change in both the locus and the type of degree. The long process, initiated around 1965, produced at first a large number of freestanding programs, of which some succeeded and others failed. New programs were introduced into some universities with and without prior experience in conducting professional courses. Like the freestanding schools, some of these succeeded while others failed.

The Utah Conference confronted the task of bringing universities together with the freestanding professional schools for some type of consolidation, recognizing the existing university-based traditional PhD scientist-practitioner model as well as the newer practitioner model and the PsyD degree. It is to be hoped that the missions, models, and loci of training programs will move in the directions proposed by the Utah Conference and that the constructive efforts proposed there will be the order of the future. We also look forward to a system wherein clinical psychologists attend at least as energetically to the prevention of mental illness and social maladaptation as to its amelioration. The passionately inspired but poorly financed prevention programs for children show great promise (Goldston, 1990). Treatment of psychotic patients in community-based deinstitutionalization programs offers positive results when projects are properly administered (Kiesler & Morton, 1988). More needs to be done in exploring social rehabilitation routes to adaptive behavior (Fairweather, 1969). Finally, there is some special significance in the newly created division in APA to study peace on earth. We must develop and add to the science and application necessary to see that peace becomes a steady state of the world.

REFERENCES

Altman, I. (1987). Centripetal and centrifugal trends in psychology. *American Psychologist, 42,* 1058–1069.

APA Committee on Training in Clinical Psychology. (1947). Recommended graduate training program in clinical psychology. *American Psychologist, 2,* 539–558.

Bickman, L. (1987). Graduate education in psychology. *American Psychologist, 42,* 1041–1047.

Boring, E. G. (1950). *A history of experimental psychology.* New York: Appleton-Century.

Dai, B. (1956). Intensive personality study as a method of training in psychotherapy. *Psychological Newsletter, NYU, 7,* 59–63.

Durkin, H. (1939). Dr. John Levy's relationship therapy as applied to a play group. *American Journal of Orthopsychiatry, 9,* 583–597.

Fairweather, G. W. (Ed.). (1969). *Community life for the mentally ill: An alternative to institutional care.* Chicago: Aldine.

Fernberger, S. W. (1932). The American Psychological Association: A historical summary, 1892–1930. *Psychological Bulletin, 29,* 1–89.

Flexner, A. (1910). *Medical education in the United States and Canada: A report to the Carnegie Foundation for the Advancement of Teaching.* New York: Carnegie Foundation.

Freud, S. (1927). *The problem of lay analysis.* New York: Brentano's.

Freud, S. (1959). The question of lay analysis. In J. Strachey (Ed.), *Standard edition of complete psychological works of Sigmund Freud* (Vol. 20). London: Hogarth.

Garfield, S. (1964). *Clinical psychology.* Chicago: Aldine.

Goldston, S. (Ed.). (1990). *Preventing mental health disturbances in childhood.* Washington, DC: American Psychiatric Press.

Hoch, E. L., Ross, A. O., & Winder, C. L. (1966). Conference on the professional preparation of clinical psychologists: A summary. *American Psychologist, 21,* 42–51.

Kiesler, C. A., & Morton, T. L. (1988). Psychology and public policy in the health care revolution. *American Psychologist, 43,* 993–1003.

Korman, M. (Ed.). (1976). *Levels and patterns of professional training in psychology: Conference proceedings, Vail, Colorado, 1973.* Washington, DC: American Psychological Association.

Levy, J. (1938). Relationship therapy. *American Journal of Orthopsychiatry, 8,* 64–69.

Matarazzo, J. (1972). *Wechsler's measurement and appraisal of adult intelligence* (5th ed.). Baltimore, MD: Williams and Wilkins.

Murphy, G. (1946). Psychological requisites for a sound foreign policy. *Journal of Social Issues, 2,* 15–26.

Murphy, G. (1948). Psychology serving society. *Survey Graphic, 37,* 12–15.

Office of Strategic Services. (1948). *Assessment of men.* New York: Rinehart.

Peterson, D. R. (1966). Professional program in an academic psychology department. In E. L. Hoch, A. O. Ross, & C. L. Winder (Eds.), *Professional preparation of clinical psychologists*. Washington, DC: American Psychological Association.

Poffenberger, A. T. (1938). The training of a clinical psychologist. *Journal of Consulting Psychology, 2*, 1–6.

Raimy, V. (1950). *Training in clinical psychology*. Englewood Cliffs, NJ: Prentice-Hall.

Reisman, J. M. (1976). *A history of clinical psychology*. New York: Irvington.

Rudolph, F. (1962). *The American college and university*. New York: Knopf.

Sears, R. R. (1947). Clinical training facilities: Report of the Committee on Graduate and Professional Training, APA. *American Psychologist, 2*, 199–206.

Shakow, D. (1938). An internship year for psychologists (with special reference to psychiatric hospital). *Journal of Consulting Psychology, 2*, 73–76.

Woodworth, R. S. (1937). The future of clinical psychology. *Journal of Consulting Psychology, 1*, 4–5.

23

POSTDOCTORAL TRAINING: TOWARD PROFESSIONALISM

BERNARD F. RIESS

In 1929, when I began doctoral studies in the psychology department at Columbia University, the only clinical course was given by a psychologist from the Neurological Institute, Carney Landis. This situation was not unusual. Shakow (1969) writes,

> If we were to characterize the situation at the beginning of this decade (1930–40), one might say that, although a considerable amount of clinical work was being done by psychologists in community clinics and hospitals, as well as in university clinics (which, however, had taken on a decidedly secondary role), their training for this work was, with few exceptions, unsystematically acquired. Though there was wide concern with problems of training, little that was systematic had been achieved. Whatever background the clinical psychologist had was largely self-organized. It was surprisingly little determined by programs emanating from universities or any other official psychological institution. (p. 6)

In the development of training, there was no mention of psychotherapy as a field of clinical practice. The psychologist-clinician was still a combination of an activist social psychologist and psychometrician. Assessing or measuring a behavioral problem, and then labeling it, was the modal practice. Although preparation for clinical work was limited in amount and unsystematic as to organization, psychologists did not hesitate to seek governmental recognition as a certifiable, legally recognized independent profession. The pressure for legal status required psychologists to attend to issues of training for practice, but the intrusion of professional concerns into the psychological domain was, from the beginning, a subject of vigorous debate (Fretz & Mills, 1980). The word *profession* was included in the charter of the American Psychological Association in 1892 only after long and heated discussion. To make psychology professional, according to scientific purists, was to change its goal from the pursuit of knowledge to the offering of services.

Once the professional orientation was included as part of the "science and profession" of psychology, however, legal recognition was required. Attempts to secure state recognition started around 1945 with a division between those who wanted a generic title *psychologist* to cover anyone with a PhD in psychology, and those who wanted a specific clinical certificate or license recognizing training in a professional speciality. The leading state associations in this division of legislative sanctions were Virginia, arguing for specific limitations, and Connecticut, arguing for the overall, generic type. The debate was settled in favor of the more general title, with legalization of a license rather than a certificate in a specific practice area. Connecticut became the first state to recognize psychology in its definitions of certified or licensed professions. But despite legal recognition of the title, practice was loosely and variably defined by the statutes of those states that established licensure laws, and educational requirements for licensure were written with comparable vagueness.

STRUGGLES WITH PSYCHIATRY

The controversies within psychology, however, were mild compared to the battles with other disciplines, mainly medicine and psychiatry. From the middle of the 1940s to the end of the 1950s, organized medicine, particularly psychiatry, intervened in state legislatures and even in local organizations to preserve the monopoly of psychotherapy as a medical specialty. For example, in Westchester County, New York, the Mental Health Association put psychologists on its referral panel; then the Nassau County Psychiatric Association sent a representative to pressure the Westchester Mental Health Association to reject psychologists, not only as members of the referral group but also as members of the association. State legislators were bombarded with literature claiming that the hospital training of psychiatrists was essential in dealing with emotionally disturbed people, the so-called mentally ill. The struggle in the legislature in New York state centered around psychiatry's assertion of the necessity of medical knowledge and hospital training against psychology's claim that training in human relationships, psychopathology, and research, along with grounding in the general scientific discipline, were sufficient for professionals who dealt with the psychological problems of human beings.

Psychology's opportunities for involvement in psychotherapy arose in part from the social neglect of a disadvantaged population—children. In England during this period, the legal right to engage in psychotherapy was limited to medically trained professionals, except for practitioners who had child patients. Here the treatment bans were inoperative. Almost anyone could treat children. So, too, in the United States, no special mention was made in legislation about therapy or even diagnosis of childhood problems. For years, psychologists and social workers had been working with children in child guidance clinics. As long as they avoided use of the word *therapy* in describing what they did, and as long as they stayed away from the adult who controlled the family finances, they could escape the scrutiny of legislative committees. It is interesting to ponder the basis on which legal distinctions of this kind are made. In 1990, psychologists in the Indian Service can prescribe medication for their Native American patients, although they are forbidden to do so in treating non-Indian people.

In all the agitation about the role of psychology in mental health, no specific mention was made of psychotherapy or psychodynamic psychotherapy. The medical antagonists of organized psychology were almost exclusively hospital-oriented and hospital-affiliated psychiatrists. Training in psychoanalysis was not seen as an important area for the professional practicing psychologist. In those years, state licensure or certification was seen as the essential permit to practice whatever the public legislation sanctioned. It was the narrow gate that separated the untrained from the trained practitioner. In nearly all jurisdictions, the basic criterion for state recognition was possession of a PhD in psychology. One of the major debates in New York state was whether to license psychologists to do therapy or to use such terms as *reeducation* or *emotional retraining*. There was even debate over whether *diagnosis* was an exclusively medical term. So much of the energy and money of state psychological organizations was spent in legislative activity that little remained for substantive training issues.

Success of legislation in New York state was allegedly due in part to the serendipitous intervention of the governor's physician, whose child was in treatment with a psychologist. During a visit to Governor Dewey, who was ill, the physician is said to have put in a good word for a licensing bill, which had passed both legislative houses several times, but had previously been vetoed by the governor.

No arguments about psychoanalysis as a practice for psychologists were heard in those times because formal analytic training was completely controlled by the American Psychoanalytic Association. Where psychologists were allowed to participate in the institutes governed by the American Psychoanalytic Association and the International Psychoanalytical Association, they were limited by a "yellow dog" contract that prohibited them from practicing psychoanalysis, although they were allowed to conduct or direct research on psychoanalysis as practiced by members of the psychoanalytic associations.

In the United States and elsewhere, strange peculiarities of right and responsibility could be seen. In Mexico, for instance, two groups of psychoanalysts emerged. One, led by Erich Fromm, himself a nonmedically trained analyst, called itself the Mexican Society of Psychoanalysis. Despite Fromm's background, formal rules of organization restricted membership to medical doctors. The other, the Mexican Group for Psychoanalytic Studies, admitted psychologists and as a group was part of the International Psychoanalytical Association. It was therefore possible for PhD psychologists to gain membership in the International Psychoanalytical Association through acceptance in Mexico (Schwartz, 1957).

Meanwhile, the American Psychological Association and, early in the 1940s, the American Association for Applied Psychology worked in several ways to define the roles and educational requirements of clinical psychologists. Joint meetings were arranged with parallel groups from the American Psychiatric Association. The discussions were permeated with the concept of the mental health team, of which the psychiatrist was clearly assumed to be captain. In a paper on the mental health team, Schwartz (1958) makes the following comment:

> As to the dynamics of the three professions, the occupational hazard of being a psychotherapist is the God complex. The psychiatrist knows he is God; the psychologist wants to be God. The psychiatrist and the psychologist are in titanic conflict as to who will be God on the mental health Olympus. Only the social worker abstains from overt engagement in the battle before the totem feast. She [sic] does not enter into the struggle as to who will be God-the-Father. She is content to be the Mother of God. (pp. 439–450)

STANDARDS FOR TRAINING

As noted elsewhere in this volume (See chapters 22, 25, and 26), standards for the degree and other issues related to education for the practice of psychology were discussed and debated in several national conferences, most conspicuously at Boulder in 1949, Miami in 1958, and Chicago in 1965. Specific mention of psychoanalytic training was sparse throughout, although a recommendation was made to the Chicago conference that Freudian and post-Freudian psychoanalytic theories be mandated in the third year of graduate training in clinical psychology. No specific means for implementation were suggested. Through all these conferences, the preferred model of training was that of the scientist-professional, with some recognition of an outright professional model finally emerging at Chicago. Postdoctoral training was seen as "organized preparation for one of the specialties in clinical psychology, such as clinical research, psychotherapy, community psychology or clinical child psychology" (Hoch, Ross, & Winder, 1966, p. 46).

There was little distinction made between journeyman competence and higher levels of professional expertise. State licensure examinations guarded legal rights to practice, but could never do more than set lower bounds on acceptable levels of competence. The example medicine offered, in according diplomate status to persons demonstrating outstanding professional qualifications, led to the creation of the American Board of Examiners in Professional Psychology (ABEPP) in 1947. One of the goals of the ABEPP (American Board of Professional Psychology, 1990) was "to award diplomas of advanced competency in the field of professional psychology to qualified applicants . . . and to maintain a registry for holders of such diplomas" (p. iii). A related goal was "to arrange and conduct investigations and examinations to determine the qualifications of individuals who apply for the diplomas issued by the Corporation" (p. iii). Shortly after its inception, ABPP (as it is now abbreviated) divided its process of review into four specialities: clinical, school, industrial–organizational, and counseling. Unlike diplomas in medicine, ABPP diplomas do not confer any privileges upon the holders, but serve only to document that the possessor of a diploma has passed an examination designed to select the top practitioners in a given field. At the present time, ABPP is organized as the central diplomating body in professional psychology, with organizational jurisdiction over boards of clinical neuropsychology, forensic psychology, and family psychology, as well as the original four fields. Psychoanalysis is a candidate for inclusion under ABPP, but its admission has been delayed because of division within its own field between the "orthodox Freudians" and the more loosely defined "psychologist psychoanalysts."

THE PSYCHOANALYTIC INSTITUTE

Having set the stage for the emergence of independent, free-based postdoctoral training centers, let us now describe the origin and subsequent development of the largest and arguably the first such institution, the Postgraduate Center for Mental Health (PGC). To understand the philosophy of the Center, one must understand the character and other personal qualities of its founders. Lewis Wolberg was, until his death in 1988, the central figure in the Center, and its ever-present director. He shared the load with his wife, Arlene, who was trained as a social worker.

It has been frequently said that Wolberg was a Renaissance man. He was an innovator and expert in many diverse fields within the broad area of psychiatry and community mental health. Born in 1905 in Russia, his family came to the United States in 1906 and eventually settled in Rochester. After he received his MD from Tufts Medical School and completed internships in Poughkeepsie, New York and Los Angeles, he became a resident in psychiatry at Boston's Psychopathic Hospital and then for 13 years served as senior medical supervisor at Kings Point Hospital in New York City. While at Kings Point, he commuted to the New York Psychoanalytic Institute as an analysand of Clara Thompson and a student of Karen Horney. Both of these eminent analysts helped Wolberg to stress society's influence on mental illness. Horney and Thompson left the New York Psychoanalytic Institute because it rejected Horney's social orientation in favor of a more orthodox Freudian ideology. Invited to affiliate with the Flower-Fifth Avenue Hospital's Psychiatric Department, the dissidents founded the Association for the Advancement of Psychoanalysis, of which the American Institute for Psychoanalysis was the training branch.

Between 1941 and 1943, another split developed, this time around the faculty appointment for Erich Fromm, who held a PhD rather than an MD degree. Thompson, Horney, Fromm, Harry Stack Sullivan, David and Margaret Rioch, and Frieda Fromm-Reichmann left the American Association and started the William Alanson White group, a satellite of the Washington School. Through all the divisiveness, Wolberg became the leading agitator for the recognition by organized social work of the right of MSWs to practice therapy.

In 1946, the New York Consultation Center, as the Wolbergs had called their creation, accepted a contract with the Veterans Administration to treat ex-servicemen. The caseload extended to 600 servicemen and women, and required a staff of 75 part-time psychiatrists, 5 social workers, and 5 clinical psychologists. When the contract ended, the caseload was referred to private practitioners, and the Wolbergs faced a demand for low-cost treatment and short-term therapy. They decided to train multidisciplinary, experienced practitioners in this novel approach. The New York Board of Regents granted a provisional charter to them as an educational organization, and so the Postgraduate Center for Psychotherapy became a viable unit.

From 1945 to the early 1960s, the relation of the Center's MD graduates to organized psychiatry was a problem. Hospitals and psychoanalytic training institutes threatened to expel medical professionals working with the Wolbergs because of the Center's multidisciplinary approach to training. In 1966, Wolberg wrote,

> In attempting to function as a true community service agency, we soon recognized that progress in our work would come only from pooling the knowledge of many schools and various disciplines for the common good. Out of this realization grew our pioneering concept of the four-fold program which has become the unique mark of the Postgraduate Center: (1) interdisciplinary professional training in comprehensive mental health practices; (2) low-cost psychotherapy; (3) research; and (4) community service and education. (Riess, 1968, p. xi)

These principles were not merely asserted in words, they were translated into practical terms. Professional training was defined as intensive commitment to work with patients, at least 20 hours per week of didactic, supervisory, and treatment work. Each trainee had to become part of a research team, had to participate in the child and adolescent program, had to present a case history, and had to be involved in a community project— all before certification. In addition to the formal requirements, personal psychoanalysis was mandated on a traditional schedule of three or more sessions per week for a minimum of 1,000 hours. Training analysts had to be approved by the Executive Committee, and the approval initially required certification of graduation from a recognized analytic institute plus 10 years of postcertification practice. Throughout the 4 to 6 years of training, the basic conceptual orientation was exclusively psychoanalytic. Although the views of such theorists as Adler, Jung, and Sullivan were recognized, the major ideology for many years was Freudian. Even today, cognitive and behavioral approaches to psychotherapy are not taught.

What was unique about the Center, and strongly resisted by the then recognized psychoanalytic training institutes, included (a) participation by the three core mental health disciplines, psychiatry, psychology, and clinical social work; (b) the requirement that each trainee engage in and report on the application of psychoanalytic skills to a community enterprise; (c) intensive and extended psychoanalytic treatment of adults, children, and adolescents; and (d) conduct of a research project involving the application of psychoanalytic concepts.

The principles were not always easy to put into practice. As long as NIMH financed training grants, psychologists and social workers flocked to the Center, but the Center has had difficulty in recruiting medical practitioners throughout its existence. The research projects that trainees undertook were ambitious and complex. The projects included a long-range study of the life history and interpersonal relationships of two carefully matched groups of female homosexuals and female heterosexuals (Gundlach & Riess, 1968). A study of former patients after the termination of therapy showed that those who had received treatment earned a weekly average of $28 more than people in comparable occupations who had just begun treatment (Riess, 1967).

As the Center evolved and its principles became more acceptable, the Wolbergs developed other programs. A group therapy department was established under the direction of Asya Kadis. The department still trains people of all three disciplines in group therapy. Supervision was seen as a special area requiring special training. The certificate in supervision was based on a prerequisite of completion of training in individual psychoanalytic therapy, plus 2 years of didactic course work and supervised experience in the supervision of therapy. Community services were extended to training programs for clergy and counselors, and a special grant-funded analytic experience was provided for selected artists, actors, and musicians who suffered from blocks to creativity.

To what extent has the pioneering structure of the Center affected analytic training institutes and facilities? On the organizational side, many training centers have been founded by alumni and alumnae of the PGC not only in the city and state of New York but in California and as far away as Sweden. In Greece, George and Vasso Vassiliou modeled their Institute of Anthropos on the Postgraduate Center in New York, although neither was directly trained by the Wolbergs. Close cooperation with other training groups brought about the migration from the Center. Earl Witenberg moved from his position as medical director of the PGC to become director of the William Alanson White Institute. Emanuel K. Schwartz helped develop the postdoctoral programs at Adelphi and New York University. Clifford Sager left the PGC to develop sex therapy at several psychiatric hospitals. Theodora Abel left the Center to become active in family therapy at the University of New Mexico as well as teaching in Japan and Mexico.

The relevance of the psychoanalytic approach to a wide range of community issues appears to be sustained by the varied activities of PGC graduates whose careers have not been primarily devoted to the practice of individual or group therapy. Among these are Morton Deutsch, the eminent social psychologist, Milton Schwebel, for years dean of the Graduate School of Education at Rutgers, and Morton Bard, who has worked extensively with police and fire departments and now is with the American Cancer Society. My interest in gerontology stemmed from a research program on the application of psychoanalytic modalities of treatment for the "old-old," as well as a group therapeutic approach for the age bracket. Although the basic orientation of the Center was psychoanalytic, the education of trainees was extended broadly to include many areas besides psychodynamics. The intellectual scope of the Center was broad and multifaceted, but its leaders never abandoned the psychoanalytic belief in the primacy of unconscious motivation and the preeminent influence of resistance, transference, and countertransference in psychotherapy.

CURRENT DEVELOPMENTS

Free-standing analytic training institutes in operation today vary widely on the definition of training. Some exist in facilities chartered or recognized by state regulating agencies and others issue certificates of program completion. To complicate matters still more, a third type of organizational structure has emerged. This is the psychoanalytic training given by departments of psychiatry in psychiatric hospitals, not all of which are university-affiliated.

Types and levels of training are also dependent on the ideological, theoretic bias of the faculties. The turbulent history of psychoanalysis (see chapter 4 in this volume), with its competing theories and the idiosyncratic personalities of its spokespeople, continues into the present. From Freud versus Adler, Jung, and Reich, through Horney, Thompson, and Sullivan, to Kohut, Guntrip, and Klein, each group defines its training needs differently, and in part, uniquely.

A recent successful lawsuit (DeAngelis, 1989) establishing the right of psychologists to be trained in psychoanalytic centers controlled by the American Psychoanalytic Institute has not diminished the claims of psychiatry that medical training and hospital experience are essential for psychoanalytic practice. The ever-extending reach of psychologists toward total psychological care of their patients manifests itself in the recent push for full hospital privileges and the right to prescribe psychoactive drugs. If psychologists succeed in these moves, training in psychopharmacology will obviously be required, and for a time at least, it is likely that some of the training will be provided by postdoctoral institutes, including those of psychoanalytic orientation.

ORGANIZATION

Within the field of psychology, progressive segmentation continues to affect the organization and development of training agencies. For a postdoctoral practitioner who seeks specialized formal education and experience in practicing some variant of psychoanalysis, several avenues are open. One is through application to an institute operated by a member or group of the American Psychoanalytic Association. Becoming a member-trainee of one of the multidisciplinary, state chartered agencies is another route, although few such choices are available. In many geographical areas, there are centers developed by psychologists that include psychoanalysis as a certifiable speciality. Finally, there is a growing supply of local psychoanalytic groups, many belonging to the Division of Psychoanalysis (39) and calling themselves study groups. These smaller interest associations generally give advanced practitioners the opportunity to establish new analytic skills and hone skills that they have developed previously.

Postdoctoral training has been enhanced by the increase in the numbers of independent graduate schools of professional psychology (as described in chapter 25 in this volume). The American Psychological Association (APA) publication on Graduate Study in Psychology and Associated Fields lists several hospitals and clinics providing graduate or postdoctoral training as preparatory to the practice of psychotherapy.

In 1990, a coalition of practice divisions of the American Psychological Association and other interested groups completed a report (Stigall et al., 1990) on professional education in psychology that included a listing of 150 postdoctoral training programs. In their report, the Joint Council urged APA "to approve accreditation criteria for postdoctoral residency training . . ." (p. 25).

The movement toward accredited postdoctoral training for psychologists is clearly under way.

REFERENCES

American Board of Professional Psychology. (1990). *ABPP directory*. Columbia, MO: Author.

DeAngelis, T. (1989). Suit opens doors to analysis training. *The APA Monitor*, 20, 16.

Fretz, B., & Mills, D. (1980). *Licensing and certification of psychologists and counselors*. San Francisco: Jossey-Bass.

Gundlach, R., & Riess, B. F. (1968). Self and sexual identity in the female: A study of female homosexuals. In B. F. Riess (Ed.), *New Directions in Mental Health, 1,* 205–232.

Hoch, E. L., Ross, A. E., & Winder, C. L. (1966). Conference on preparation of clinical psychologists: A summary. *American Psychologist, 21,* 42–51.

Riess, B. F. (1967). Changes in patient income concomitant with psychotherapy. *Journal of Consulting Psychology, 31.*

Riess, B. F. (Ed.). (1968). *New directions in mental health* (Vol. 1). New York: Grune & Stratton.

Schwartz, E. K. (1957). Psychotherapy in Mexico. In B. F. Riess (Ed.), *Progress in psychotherapy.* New York: Grune & Stratton.

Schwartz, E. K. (Ed.). (1958). A psychoanalytic approach to the mental health team. *American Imago, 15,* 437–451.

Shakow, D. (1969). *Clinical psychology as a science and profession: A forty year odyssey.* Chicago: Aldine.

Stigall, T. T., Bourg, E. F., Bricklin, P. M., Kovacs, A. L., Larsen, K. G., Lorion, R. P., Nelson, P. D., Nurse, A. R., Pugh, R. W., & Wiens, A. N. (1990). *Report of the Joint Council on Professional Education in Psychology.* Baton Rouge, LA: The Joint Council on Professional Education in Psychology.

24

THE VETERANS ADMINISTRATION AND THE TRAINING PROGRAM IN PSYCHOLOGY

DANA L. MOORE

It is not entirely inconceivable that the development of a considerable group of soundly prepared clinical psychologists would have an appreciable effect on the future of psychology as a whole. (American Psychological Association [APA] & American Association for Applied Psychology [AAAP], 1945, p. 244)

The Veterans Administration (VA) Psychology Training Program began in 1946. It is difficult, in the 1990s, to look back with real understanding even 50 years — within living memory — at the role that psychology played in the 1940s. Yet we need to look back even further in order to understand the tremendous impact that the VA had on the profession of psychology.

THE ROLE OF PSYCHOLOGISTS AND NEUROPSYCHIATRISTS

Before World War II, psychology was still largely an academic discipline, founded in the laboratories of Fechner and Wundt and transplanted to America with the aim of creating a serious science. Psychologists did research and taught, and even in applied settings, psychology had an educational focus. Psychologists who worked with patients did intellectual and psychological testing and wrote diagnostic reports. Some did psychotherapy, but in medical settings, it was clearly understood that this was done only under the supervision of psychiatrists.

The practice of psychiatry was different, too. Neurology had not yet become a separate medical specialty, and psychiatrists were called neuropsychiatrists. In essence, they were responsible for treating anything that went wrong with the brain. To treat patients, neuropsychiatrists used psychoanalytic psychotherapy, electroconvulsive therapy, insulin therapy, and psychosurgery such as lobotomies; there were as yet no psychotropic drugs. Chronic patients tended to stay in the hospital.

RESPONSIBILITY FOR VETERANS

The Department of Veterans Affairs was created as a Cabinet-level agency on March 15, 1989. Prior to that time, it had been an independent agency called the Veterans Administration, founded in 1930. Both the Department of Veterans Affairs and the Veterans Administration are referred to as the "VA." The VA's motto and mission statement literally comes from Abraham Lincoln's second inaugural address, given March 4, 1865: "to care for him who shall have borne the battle and for his widow and his orphan."

Even before the establishment of the VA in 1930, the care of veterans with psychiatric diagnoses was a major issue for the organizations responsible for the care of veterans. In one form or another, American governments have provided veterans benefits since even before the Revolutionary War — extending as far back as the Plymouth colony in 1636. During the Pilgrims' war with the Pequot Indians, a law was passed assuring that "if any man shalbee sent forth as a souldier and shall return maimed, hee shalbee maintained competently by the collonie during his life" (VA, 1977). After all wars, veterans have pressed the government for the expansion of those benefits and their centralized administration.

THE VETERANS' BUREAU

There were 4.7 million veterans following World War I, and it seemed that all of them were confused about where to go for specific benefits.

Various veterans' service groups had organized after World War I — the American Legion, the Veterans of Foreign Wars, and other, smaller groups. Because of their dissatisfaction with piecemeal services and concern about duplication of effort, they lobbied for a single agency for veterans' services.

The Veterans' Bureau, a predecessor organization to the VA, was established in 1921 to consolidate three organizations: the Bureau of War Risk Insurance, those U.S. Public Health Service hospitals that focused on veterans, and the Rehabilitation Division of the Federal Board for Vocational Education.

Under the Veterans' Bureau, medical care and treatment was available to veterans with disabilities that were service-connected. In other words, medical treatment was provided only to veterans who were disabled during or as a result of their service in the military. The two major diagnostic categories of patients treated then were those with tuberculosis and neuropsychiatric disorders. There were no effective drugs for either kind of disease.

The earliest mention of a shortage of doctors to care for veterans with psychiatric problems is in the Annual Report to Congress of the director of the U.S. Veterans' Bureau for the fiscal year ending on June 30, 1922:

> Plans were also instituted to arrange details of a course of training for neuropsychiatrists, so that the bureau would be able to train qualified physicians in general medicine for special work in neuropsychiatry in order to have at its disposal a sufficient number of trained neuropsychiatrists, inasmuch as such personnel was unobtainable from other sources owing to the fact that it did not exist in this country. (p. 32)
>
> Even with those plans, the Veterans' Bureau still had a problem. In 1922, Congress had authorized the hospitalization of elderly Spanish-American war veterans whether or not their illnesses were connected with their time in service. General Frank T. Hines, then Director of the Veterans' Bureau and Administrator of the VA until 1945, recommended that any honorably discharged veteran be eligible for hospital care if space was available. President Calvin Coolidge agreed and Congress passed the necessary legislation in 1924. In one of the world's great miscalculations, General Hines did not think that too many veterans would take advantage of it. (VA, 1967, pp. 131–132)

Consequently, the Veterans' Bureau was again in 1929 talking about their problems in obtaining trained psychiatrists (United States Veterans' Bureau, 1929):

> One of the immediate problems confronting the bureau is the securing of sufficient trained medical personnel to meet its growing needs. There has always existed a shortage of competent physicians trained in neuropsychiatry, which condition will become more pronounced upon

completion of the current extensive program of hospital construction. In an attempt to meet this situation a reservoir of young physicians has been created by selections from the civil-service registers. These appointees, consisting of recent graduates of accredited medical schools will be assigned to selected veterans' hospitals for special training before being given definite duties and responsibilities. In addition to this constructive step, postgraduate schools for special training of physicians already in the service of the bureau were inaugurated in October, 1928, at the diagnostic centers at Washington, D.C., and Palo Alto, Calif. Courses of four months are provided each class, and the curriculum is of a character which will materially broaden the professional equipment and administrative effectiveness of the physicians selected to take the training. (p. 2)

However, the report goes on to add a growing concern:

In the matter of hospitalization, the bureau now controls sufficient Government beds to care for all veterans requiring hospitalization because of service-connected disabilities and whose hospitalization has been authorized. However, since the passage of the law authorizing the hospitalization of veterans of all wars, regardless of the origin or nature of their disabilities, an increased pressure for hospitalization has been continuously experienced so that for neuropsychiatric cases the demand for beds has exceeded the available supply. . . On June 30, 1929, 11,800 patients, or 43 per cent of the entire load of the bureau, were nonservice-connected cases. (p. 3)

THE VETERANS' ADMINISTRATION

Even though the establishment of the Veterans' Bureau had combined many services for veterans, not all of them had been brought together. A desire to give veterans a single point of contact, reduce conflicting administrative requirements, and generally make for a more effective organization led to another consolidation. On July 21, 1930, President Herbert Hoover signed an Executive Order establishing the Veterans' Administration as the single agency responsible for veterans issues. (The apostrophe in "Veterans' Administration" did not generally disappear until 1948.) This order consolidated the United States Veterans' Bureau with the National Home for Disabled Volunteer Soldiers and the Bureau of Pensions.

There was, in 1931, the usual cry that although there were sufficient beds available for service-connected veterans, the new Veterans' Administration "experienced difficulty in fulfilling all of the demand for Government hospital facilities, due to the constantly increasing pressure for hospitalization that is being exerted by veterans with disabilities not attributable to military service" (VA, 1931, p. 6). The report went on to predict that "For the neuropsychiatric type there has been a marked and consistent growth in the hospital load which should continue for the next 20 years . . ." (p. 6).

THE BONUS MARCHERS

Sometimes, the most important lesson we can learn is how not to do things — we learn to avoid our past failures. To some extent, the United States has learned to deal with veterans in this manner.

In 1919, 4 million men were demobilized, released from service, at the conclusion of World War I. They all received $60 mustering-out pay and a ticket home, but many had no jobs to return to, no homes. There was tremendous unemployment and unrest. During this era, veterans were frequently viewed as vagrants, hobos, bums.

Veterans groups finally succeeded in 1924 in getting Congress to pass a bonus authorizing approximately $1,500 for each World War I veteran; however, it was not to be paid out for 20 years — not until 1944. By 1932, the country was in the midst of the Great Depression. Veterans without jobs needed their bonuses paid immediately.

A group of veterans from Oregon decided to march to Washington to demand payment of their bonus, hence the name "bonus marchers." By the time they arrived, in June of 1932, approximately 12,000 men had joined the protest. They built a shantytown on the Anacostia mud flats, across the Anacostia River from the Capital, and spent almost 2 months lobbying, demonstrating, and picketing. These techniques did not work, however; President Hoover refused to act on their demands. Many people even feared that these former soldiers would be a focal point for real rebellion.

Although about half of the veterans had already left Washington by late July, there were escalating conflicts with local police. President Hoover ordered the Army Chief of Staff, General Douglas MacArthur, to remove the squatters from their camp. MacArthur was assisted by his aide, Col. Dwight D. Eisenhower. A cavalry charge was led by Col. George Patton. The shantytown was burned. The veterans, exhausted and disheartened, were pushed back into Virginia.

The VA had no role in clearing the bonus marchers from the Anacostia flats, but Congress authorized the agency to pay veterans for their return transportation costs home, along with 75¢ a day in living expenses. Most of the bonus marchers accepted the VA offer of free train tickets home, and nearly $77,000 was authorized to pay expenses for 5,200 veterans. The Red Cross spent a similar amount to pay family members' travel expenses (VA, 1967, pp. 150–153).

The efforts of the bonus marchers to get immediate payment had come to nothing, at great cost to themselves and resulting in animosity toward the government. However, it did serve as an indictor of what could happen when veterans were demobilized en masse, without resources, jobs, or homes to which they could return.

PSYCHOLOGY IN THE VA THROUGH WORLD WAR II

Prior to 1946, none of the "psychologists" in the VA were at the doctoral level; they were psychology technicians — psychometricians — at the baccalaureate or master's level (J. G. Miller, personal communication, June 1990). Furthermore, the treatment of psychiatric patients left little room for psychology. In those days, patients with paralytic dementia resulting from syphilis were treated with malaria inoculations, although "fever therapy" induced by short-wave diathermy was coming into vogue. Schizophrenia, or dementia praecox, as it was then more commonly called, was treated by insulin shock or electroconvulsion. Any psychotherapy that might be attempted was administered entirely by neuropsychiatrists.

Psychology in the Military in World Wars I and II

The VA had not made any use of doctorally trained psychologists, but the military had. Psychology found its first military role in personnel selection and placement for the United States Army in World War I (Seidenfeld, 1966). Military psychologists had begun to work on rehabilitating disabled soldiers in collaboration with the Division of Physical Reconstruction, but this role was not expanded until World War II.

In 1942, six psychologists were commissioned as first lieutenants in the Sanitary Corps and assigned to duty with the neuropsychiatric sections of six permanent general hospitals. By 1943, the chief of the Neuropsychiatry Branch of the Surgeon General's Office in the U.S. Army was a Col. William C. Menninger. Col. (later Brigadier General) Menninger was an enthusiastic supporter of having more psychologists available in his neuropsychiatric facilities and an ardent advocate of the neuropsychiatric team that included psychiatrists, psychologists, and social workers (J. G. Miller, personal communication, June 1990).

The justification for assigning psychologists to neuropsychiatric treatment facilities was that "where these officers have been employed, they have been invaluable assistants to the hard pressed neuropsychiatrists. . . . The services of these clinical psychologists are needed more than ever before because of the increasing scarcity of neuropsychiatrists" (Letter from Lt. Col. Robert J. Carpenter, Medical Corps, Executive Officer, Surgeon General's Office, to the Commanding General, Army Service Forces, Washington, DC, May 23, 1944; subject: clinical psychologists. Cited in Seidenfeld, 1966, p. 571).

Once psychologists were assigned to hospitals, their work varied. A War Department Personnel Audit Team report of May 5, 1945, cited in Seidenfeld (1966, pp. 587–590), studied 33 different medical installations — general hospitals, convalescent hospitals, and regional hospitals, with 79 officers, 236 enlisted personnel, and 4 civilians on duty in clinical psychology. Psychologists did testing, case histories, and individual as well as group psychotherapy, along with administrative work and educational training. In general hospitals, psychologists worked directly under the administrative and professional authority of neuropsychiatrists. Staffing ratios ended up with one officer (and 64 enlisted men) for each 255 neuropsychiatric patients. If they had delivered services to all patients, as psychologists in Army Air Forces hospitals did, the ratio of officer psychologists to total patients would have been 1 to 1,025 (Seidenfeld, 1966, p. 589).

Preparing for World War II Demobilization

In 1943, it seemed evident that the Allies, including the United States, would win the war within a few years. President Roosevelt had formed a council to consider postwar problems. Only World War II had managed to propel the United States out of the economic depression that it had been in since 1930. But with the end of the war, 16 million Americans would be returning to an economy that was not ready for them. No one wanted a repeat of the bonus march of 1932.

Beyond concerns for what would happen after the war, service organizations such as the American Legion and the Veterans of Foreign Wars were concerned about the care being provided currently to those newly disabled veterans for whom the war was already over. There was a great deal of dissatisfaction about the length of time that it took for these veterans to file for and to receive disability compensation and to get rehabilitation, a period during which they received no mustering-out pay. If the Veterans' Administration had trouble dealing with veterans in 1943, before the war was over, how could it possibly handle the demobilization of 16 million or more in 2 to 3 years?

THE GI BILL

One of the answers to the problem of the oncoming massive demobilization was the passage of the Servicemen's Readjustment Act of 1944, better known as the GI Bill of Rights. A survey by Consumer Reports in 1986 identified the GI Bill as one of the most significant pieces of legislation in the 20th century. On December 15, 1943, the first draft of the bill was written in longhand by Harry Colmery of the American Legion on hotel stationary in a room at the Mayflower Hotel in Washington, DC. After 6 busy months of lobbying, it passed through Congress and was signed by President Roosevelt on June 22, 1944 (Thompson, 1990). The GI Bill had three main features:

1. *Readjustment benefits.* Unemployed veterans could draw up to 52 weeks of unemployment compensation at $20 a week.

2. *Guaranteed loans.* The government would cover loans for a home, farm, or business for any amount up to a limit, initially $2,000 with a maximum interest rate of 4 percent.

3. *Education benefits.* Veterans could go to school for up to 3 years and receive $500 a year for tuition plus up to $75 a month subsistence initially. The program was flexible and could be used for college or technical schools. When the legislation was first passed, Congress put an age limit of 25 on this program, assuming that older veterans already had their education or job skills.

ORGANIZING SERVICES FOR VETERANS

In May of 1945, Harry Truman had become President following President Franklin D. Roosevelt's death in office. Stories of newly returning wounded veterans receiving inadequate care were being highlighted by the press. Veterans organizations were complaining about slow and bureaucratic procedures within the VA. President Truman knew that he needed someone of lofty stature and tremendous organizational ability to get the Veterans' Administration ready for millions of returning veterans. General Omar Bradley was his man.

Omar N. Bradley graduated from West Point in 1915 in the same class as Dwight D. Eisenhower. He was appointed Commander in Chief of

American ground forces preparing for the invasion of Western Europe in 1944 under the Supreme Allied Commander, General Eisenhower. In August of 1944, he took command of the 1.3 million men of the U.S. Twelfth Army Group of Western Europe, the largest American field command ever. Bradley was stunned to learn that President Truman wanted him to head up the Veterans' Administration in Washington, where his organizational talents were desperately needed.

When General Bradley took office, there were 5 million veterans. By the end of his first 8 months in office, demobilization more rapid than originally planned had more than tripled the veteran population to 17 million. Bradley became Administrator of an agency that had 65,000 employees and was already the largest independent agency in government. It had 97 hospitals caring for 71,000 patients with most being treated for non-service-connected illnesses. Eight hospitalized men were veterans of the Civil War and 2,793 had served in the Spanish-American War. The agency was paying pensions to 1.5 million veterans, their widows, and dependents, including one 88-year-old dependent of the War of 1812 and 229 Civil War veterans whose average age was 98. It had 18 million policy holders in its GI insurance program (VA, 1945).

General Bradley thought that the age limitation of 25 that Congress had put on the GI Bill educational benefits was discriminatory and that for many veterans, their experiences in the war had taught them the value of college or specialized training. He persuaded Congress to repeal the age ceiling and open the educational benefits to all World War II veterans. It was this repeal of the age ceiling that allowed many veterans who had already attended college to use the GI bill for graduate study in psychology.

ORGANIZING HEALTH CARE

One of the most difficult issues that Bradley faced was that of the quality of medical care provided to veterans, and one of the most difficult aspects of that situation was the supply of trained medical personnel. Many physicians, nurses, and orderlies had left the VA in order to join the service during the war or to go into higher paying wartime industrial production. Late in the war, the VA had to ask the army to detail enlisted personnel with limited time left in the military and conscientious objectors to VA medical centers as attendants. There was some evidence that some of these personnel, contrary to regulations, had handled some psychiatric patients "ineptly or inhumanely" (VA, 1967, p. 174). However, the major problems were recognized as those of the poor salaries offered physicians under civil service, tremendous delays getting lists of available physicians from Civil Service Commission registers, and the general quality of medicine practiced in the VA.

Bradley's determination to staff VA medical centers with the best doctors, despite some opposition that led him to threaten to resign, brought about the creation of the Title 38 employment program for physicians. This program had been urged on the VA and Congress by various consultant groups prior to Bradley's appointment, but the agency had never been able to get it passed over objections by the Civil Service Commission. Under Title 38, physicians were not hired through the Civil Service Commission, nor was the VA limited to civil service pay schedules. The new program worked, and within 6 months, 4,000 physicians were hired.

Medicine had made great strides during World War II. In the Civil War, death from infected wounds killed more soldiers than were killed outright in battle. In both the Mexican War and the Spanish-American War, there was more death from disease than battle. During World War II, selection of inductees was better, as were training for physical fitness, nutrition during service, appropriate clothing, inoculations, and sanitary facilities in the field. Medical science had only recently made plasma for blood transfusions and sulfa drugs available. Penicillin was a new drug. Treatment techniques had improved as well, especially those for burns and for neuroses. Two thirds of all wounded were returned to active duty during World War II. The death rate from wounds was less than half what it had been in World War I, and less than 1% of the military died from noncombat causes (VA, 1967). Wars always improve medical treatment. But many of the improved techniques were not yet in place in VA facilities because VA staff had not been trained in them.

To help turn this situation around, Bradley asked General Paul R. Hawley to help him plan an improved health care system. Dr. Hawley was the son and grandson of physicians. After he completed medical school and tried practice with his father, he decided to practice military medicine and joined the army shortly before World War I. He had done well in the army, rising to the rank of major general. At the close of World War II, he served in Europe under General Eisenhower as chief surgeon of the European Theatre of Operation (senior medical officer for the war in Europe), with 16,000 physicians under his command. Bradley had met him and knew that Hawley was the effective medical administrator he needed.

Under General Hawley, as chief surgeon in the European Theatre of Operation, the army's medical units had been affiliated with medical schools in the United States for instruction, supervision, and consultation, as they had been in World War I. It seemed readily apparent to Hawley that affiliations with medical schools would benefit the Veterans' Administration as well. There was, however, no legal authority for such affiliations. Things can happen quickly in Washington when they have to. The necessary bill passed the House of Representatives on December 7, 1945 and passed the Senate on December 20. It was signed into law by President Truman on January 3, 1946 as Public Law 293, creating the Department of Medicine and Surgery (DM&S) with a chief medical director (CMD) as its head.

Hawley and his assistants had been desperate for the bill to pass. On January 30, 1946, the VA's Policy Memorandum Number 2 was issued by the chief medical director. Its subject is "Policy in association of veterans' hospitals with medical schools," and it is still in effect. It lays out the groundwork for the relationship between a local VA facility and its affiliated medical school. The VA is responsible for care of patients and the school is responsible for graduate education and training. This training, and the operation of the affiliation in general, are overseen by a deans' committee of senior faculty members organized by the medical school.

The relationship established by the policy was beneficial to both parties. Medical schools needed to provide residency training and refresher courses for thousands of physicians whose training had been interrupted by the war. In addition, there was an increased demand for admission to medical training by those who only held baccalaureate degrees. The Veterans' Administration had to provide physicians for all the veterans returning from the war who needed medical care, and it needed to upgrade the skills of the medical staff it already had. Even with the new bill, which placed the hiring and employment of VA DM&S physicians under the direct control of the administrator of Veterans' Affairs rather than the Civil Service Commission, the VA could not hire a sufficient number of physicians. With faculty members from medical schools as attending staff, however, along with consultants and residents, there were enough resources to do the job. The Department of Medicine and Surgery began its medical school affiliations with 63 of the nation's 77 medical schools. Seventy new hospitals were built, most of them in proximity to those medical schools.

VA staff benefited from the consultation and supervision provided by the medical school faculty as well as by the vastly increased research operation put into place. Residents in the medical schools (and therefore the schools themselves) benefited from the clinical training and the financial support that they received from the VA. Most important, veteran patients got care "second to none."

THE VA TRAINING PROGRAM IN PSYCHOLOGY: ORIGIN AND EARLY DEVELOPMENTS

For years, the VA had struggled to overcome a shortage of psychiatrists. Would it fare any better in seeking psychologists? In an article about graduate internship training in psychology (APA & AAAP, 1945), the Sub-committee on Graduate Internship Training reported that 17% of the doctoral level members of APA and 31% of the master's level members were doing full-time professional work, that is, functioning as clinical psychologists. The directory of AAAP listed 650 members. When the committee discussed employment possibilities, they pointed out that 174 state psychiatric hospitals surveyed in 1941 reported having 64 full-time psychologists and psychometricians. This made for a staff patient ratio of 1 to 6,000. The job market for applied (clinical) psychologists was obviously large. Although the article was nominally about graduate internship training, committee members believed that they could not discuss internships without considering the undergraduate and graduate academic preparation of clinical psychologists.

The APA/AAAP article argued that clinical psychology might be considered to be the "ground work for *all* professional psychology, whether educational, industrial, or consulting" (italics in original). With great boldness, they went on to assert, parenthetically, "(It might even be held, with some cogency, that a background in clinical psychology is an essential part of the preparation of all but a few academic psychologists)" (p. 244). Tucked into a footnote is the prescient comment: It is not entirely inconceivable that the development of a considerable group of soundly prepared clinical psychologists would have an appreciable effect on the future of psychology as a whole. (APA & AAAP, 1945, p. 244).

An article in *American Psychologist* by Sears (1946) gave detailed information about schools that offered graduate study in psychology in various specialized areas, especially those with a focus on clinical psychology. The article provided prospective graduate students, who were acknowledged to be primarily men and women getting out of the military, information on where they might go, what admission requirements and tuition were, what sorts of financial support were available, and some information about what kinds of academic and clinical work were required. The information was also intended to help APA's Committee on Graduate and Professional Training see what would be involved in recommending quality standards to APA and even eventually evaluating departments against them. It is clear from the article that training in clinical psychology was far from standardized:

> . . . there are wide variations among universities as to methods of teaching, use of practicum facilities, content of curriculum, and level of staff experience. This represents, in part, genuine differences of opinion as to what constitutes training for this field, but in consequence, the statement that a given institution provides "reasonably

complete training" is not as revealing as it might seem. (Sears, 1946, p. 139)

Thus, there was no corps of solidly trained clinical psychologists available for the VA to hire at a time when there was no doubt that psychologists could be of real service in both treatment and research with neuropsychiatric patients. The recent experience of World War II had demonstrated that. Nor was there any doubt that the VA health care system would be deluged by patients. It had already begun to happen. General Bradley and the chief medical director, Dr. Hawley, had acted quickly to make changes. It was a "can do" era, which focused, as during the war, on accomplishing a mission and cleaning up the details later.

Public Law 293, signed by President Truman on January 3, 1946, authorized the Department of Medicine and Surgery as a significant organizational element within the Veterans' Administration. Dr. Hawley issued Policy Memorandum Number 2 on January 30, giving broad outlines about how the VA's new physician residency programs, in affiliation with the country's medical schools, would be carried out. Technically speaking, however, the only training authority the agency had was for the conduct of medical residency programs and for the assignment of regular full-time staff to outside courses.

MILLER'S MANEUVER

Enter James Grier Miller. Miller received his baccalaureate and master's degrees in psychology from Harvard in 1937 and 1938, at a time when psychology and philosophy were the same academic department. He then enrolled in the Harvard Medical School and also continued graduate work in psychology. Miller did his doctoral work in experimental psychology under Edwin G. Boring, but he did not get the degree in psychology right away. In those times, Harvard had a rule that no student could get two doctoral degrees in the same year, so Miller received his MD from Harvard Medical School in 1942 and his PhD in 1943.

Following service with the military in 1944–1946, he became chief of the Division of Clinical Psychology in the Neuropsychiatric Service of the Veterans Administration Central Office in Washington, DC. He served in this position from 1946 through 1947. (In January 1946, the Veterans' Administration employed three psychologists.)

Despite technical limitation of the new VA residency program to physicians, Miller saw room for psychology in interpretation of law. Since Public Law 293 provided authority for the employment of part-time and temporary full-time staff, Miller decided that psychology students could be employed as part-time staff. Their assignment would be being trained in providing service. He was supported in this interpretation by the VA's first consultant in psychology, George A. Kelly, and by General Bradley. Thus, the VA was going to have a training program in psychology, too.

In June of 1946, Miller published an article in *American Psychologist* that gave operational details of the new program. He began with a simple statement of the VA's need: "When the positions which psychologists can hold in the Vocational Advisement and Guidance Division and the Division of Clinical Psychology [of the Veterans Administration] are added together, they number well above the total of all qualified clinical psychologists in the country" (Miller, 1946, p. 181).

Like many other educators, Miller believed that before the war, it had been almost impossible to find an adequate educational program for the profession of clinical psychology. He argued that existing programs either were in the traditional experimental, academic model aimed at research and teaching, or they amounted merely to individually designed on-the-job training programs with little supervision by qualified psychologists.

Miller spelled out the role that psychologists had played in the war effort, beginning with personnel selection and expanding to recognition of their diagnostic skills and "their superior understanding of the principles of normal behavior and how these can be applied to problems of personal adjustment" (Miller, 1946, p. 181). He argued as follows:

> Clinical psychology did much during the war to improve the practice of psychiatry by making available to the psychiatrists old and new procedures for diagnosing personality and mental disease. Furthermore, it is probable that a majority of military clinical psychologists carried on psychotherapy in certain types of cases. Almost always this was under the direction of, or in collaboration with, psychiatrists or medical officers who attended to the somatic problems involved, but nevertheless in the military situation, working together as a team, both professions did nearly similar tasks for patients without somatic involvement or serious mental abnormality. This was therapy and it was called "therapy"; recourse was rarely had to the euphemism "counseling." (Miller, 1946, p. 182)

Miller buttressed his arguments about the growing recognition of the profession of clinical psychology by pointing out that some states were beginning to pass licensing laws permitting psychological practice. Then he came back to the need. Given both the VA's preexisting patient load of chronic psychiatric patients and the influx of returning soldiers from World War II with psychiatric problems, at the end of fiscal year 1946,

57.6% of hospitalized veterans were being treated for neuropsychiatric conditions, whereas only 33% were being treated for general medical and surgical conditions (VA, 1946, p. 4).

Miller planned to place psychologists in five different types of settings: mental hygiene clinics, neuropsychiatric convalescent centers, neuropsychiatric (NP) hospitals, paraplegia centers in general hospitals, and aphasia centers in general hospitals.

The role of qualified clinical psychologists in psychotherapy was described by the VA as follows:

> The clinical psychologist will carry out individual or group therapy under direction of the responsible neuropsychiatrist. This means that the neuropsychiatrist will first review the case and decide whether it is the type of problem which may reasonably be handled by a clinical psychologist. If the case involves such fields as readjustment of habits; personality problems within the normal range; educational disabilities such as reading defects, speech impairments, or similar difficulties requiring re-education; or relatively minor psychoneurotic conditions without important somatic components, the patient may be referred to a clinical psychologist for individual or group treatment. The Chief Neuropsychiatrist will delegate such therapeutic duties only when he believes the individual clinical psychologist to be fully competent to carry them out. The clinical psychologist periodically at staff meetings or other times will report to the responsible neuropsychiatrist on the progress of the therapy and consult with him as to further measures to be taken. (Miller, 1946, p. 184)

Miller had no doubt that psychologists would continue to do psychotherapy. But he seemed to be more excited about the research possibilities. Psychologists had research training that most psychiatrists did not have. It was evident to him that "Studies can be so devised as to advance basic science at the same time as they make a direct contribution to the welfare of the individual patients" (Miller, 1946, p. 184). The VA's chief medical director, Dr. Hawley, had already assumed that making research a part of basic medical care in all VA facilities would be one way to get VA medicine up to the best of modern standards and keep it there. No one in the new group feared that veterans would be made into "guinea pigs." Miller described research that today we would call "program evaluation research"; he anticipated large-scale cooperative studies done jointly by many different VA hospitals.

It is clear that the role that clinical psychologists were expected to fill was what came to be called the *scientist-practitioner* model after the Boulder Conference was held in 1949 (Raimy, 1950). Miller attended the conference in his role at that time as chair of the Department of Psychology at the University of Chicago. The Conference affirmed that clinical psychology was neither science alone nor practice alone, but both together, so that both science and practice would benefit.

What standards would the VA set for the clinical psychologists it planned to hire? Miller envisioned requirements in three areas: appropriate personality traits for the work, actual clinical experience, and sufficient education. Knowing that they could not find sufficient numbers of doctorally prepared psychologists, they planned initially to hire individuals with either all the coursework for the doctorate or at least 10 courses in specific areas. These individuals would qualify only for a grade of P-3 with an annual salary of $3,640. To qualify for grade P-4 (salary of $4,300), one had to have a doctoral degree in psychology from a college or university of "recognized standing." Chiefs of large stations could be P-5s, with a salary of $5,180, and the chiefs at the VA's thirteen branch offices, who needed to be "mature and experienced men"[1] (Miller, 1946, p. 185) would be P-6s with a salary of $6,230.

Although Miller announced in his 1946 article that a large number of appointments were still open at the P-3, predoctoral, level, he hastened to add that they would only be eligible for promotion when they completed their doctorate. He argued as follows:

> Clinical psychologists are receiving comparable responsibilities with psychiatrists, and if they are to retain the respect of their professional colleagues, they must maintain comparable high standards. Just as no one would expect a physician to practice without a medical degree, so clinical psychologists should not be expected to assume their full responsibilities without a doctor's degree in psychology. Moreover, it is essential that this training be not wholly academic, but that real experience be obtained in the clinical techniques which can be learned only in the doing. So a doctor's degree in psychology alone is by no means qualifying for these positions. (Miller, 1946, p. 185)

Staff hired below the doctoral level held only temporary appointments and could not be promoted without receiving the doctoral degree. After the first 3 years, no more appointments of psychologists at the predoctoral level were made. By 1951, all of the predoctoral employees had either completed their doctorates, entered the training program, or left the VA (Ash, 1968).

---

[1]In reading such phrases as "mature and experienced men," we see language that would be called sexist today. At that time, it was considered merely descriptive. Society was sexist, and that included the profession of psychology. Today's graduate students may not realize how recently psychology was a dominantly male profession, and with what seriousness of intent the American Psychological Association set about changing that in the early 1970s, largely by force of its accreditation standards.

DETAILS OF PROGRAM OPERATION

As Sears (1946) had done, Miller bemoaned the lack of standardized curricula in clinical psychology. He applauded the proposal laid out by the Subcommittee on Graduate Internship Training (APA & AAAP, 1945). Because there was general recognition that universities could supply the academic, theoretical preparation for clinical psychologists, it seemed evident that the VA could offer an arena for the applied work. It had most of the same advantages that the medical affiliation program had. Students would be paid for part-time clinical work under appropriate supervision, universities would have clinical placements for students, university faculty would be paid for supervising or doing in-service education in the VA, and veterans would receive treatment.

Although nonveterans were eligible for training, veterans were by law given preference. Because of the educational benefits paid by the GI Bill or benefits paid to service-connected disabled veterans getting VA vocational rehabilitation, veterans' take-home pay was also much better. Consequently, most of the trainees in the early days were veterans. Even though the program was designed as a predoctoral one, individuals who already had a doctoral degree in psychology but wanted to respecialize, to change their specialty to clinical psychology, were also eligible.

The program was planned to begin in the fall of 1946 with 200 authorized positions. At the VA's request, APA identified 22 universities that could give complete doctoral training in clinical psychology; the schools had stated how many students and at what level of advancement they could accept. The 200 VA positions were allocated among the schools proportionally, based on how many students their facilities allowed them to accept. Once a school had selected a candidate for the VA program, the candidate's application was sent to the chief of the Division of Clinical Psychology in VA Central Office for final approval. They were routinely approved, and the trainee was hired by the VA and detailed to the VA facility nearest his or her university.

Trainees were expected to work half-time in the VA but were allowed to train briefly in other clinic settings in order to receive well-rounded experience. Their supervised duties at the VA were detailed for each of the four levels of training. First-year trainees would receive $1,160 (half of a regularly employed P-1's $2,320), and 2nd-year trainees, $1,490 (half of a P-2's $2,980. Both 3rd- and 4th-year students were paid $1,820, which was half of the P-3's $3,640. Trainees were paid by the hour at the rate listed and could receive overtime pay; in addition, they could work additional hours during the summer when they were not in school. As in the plan detailed by the Subcommittee on Graduate Internship Training (APA & AAAP, 1945), it was intended that a full-time internship would be done generally in the 3rd year. This could be done at a VA facility away from the student's university.

Faculty members from the schools could be appointed as consultants to the VA, to conduct research, to do in-service training with staff or to supervise students, or to advise on clinical practice. Full professors were to be paid $50 for visits of 3 to 4 hours, with lower ranking individuals receiving proportionally less; no more than $6,000 could be paid to any one person in a year's time.

At the end of 1946, the VA had 146 staff psychologists (not all of them yet doctoral level) and 200 trainees. Because students stayed for several years, the program grew rapidly. By 1951, 700 students and 300 staff psychologists were employed.

EARLY POLICY DECISIONS

Many policy questions had already been settled. It had been determined that the VA psychology training program would be academically based but require applied training as well — a program to produce the scientist-practitioner. The VA had determined what kind of psychologists it would hire, what the qualification standards were, what qualifications it would "settle for" until it could find enough doctorally prepared applicants, and what kind of training program it would support. The VA would look to the professional association, APA, to determine what schools should be accredited and therefore receive funding for their students. Perhaps most important, although it was always stated up front that it was expected that VA psychology trainees would continue to work in the VA (Miller, 1946), the program was not set up as an indentured one. In other words, there was no requirement that people "repay" the agency with a certain number of years of service. The thinking was that the VA would get the psychologists who were most dedicated to the agency's mission by making employment following training a voluntary action and by making the jobs sufficiently attractive to recruit and retain well-qualified professionals. The policy was also justified on grounds that those who took jobs in other agencies would be knowledgeable about veterans and veterans' issues and that this was advantageous to the VA.

In July 1952, the Department of Medicine and Surgery instituted a vocational counseling program in its hospitals. They had concluded that the sort of program they wanted could only be carried out by doctorally prepared counseling psychologists. Because of the problem of finding employees with appropriate credentials and because of the experience with the clinical psychology training program, a counseling psychology training program was begun in the fall semester of 1953 with 55 training positions. It grew to an average of 150 positions a year. By 1958, the VA employed 130 doctoral level counseling psychologists, in addition to 612 clinical psychologists.

LATER DEVELOPMENTS

Following establishment by James G. Miller in 1946, the training program in psychology was run for a time jointly, consensually, by those psychologists who worked in VA Central Office. Eventually, however, it came to be the primary responsibility of psychologist Elton Ash. When the VA psychology training program celebrated its 20th anniversary, Dr. Ash was the chief of Psychology Education and Training, in the VA Central Office. He published a two-part article (Ash, 1968) that summarized the program up to that time.

> The period from 1946–1950 was one of rapid growth, increasing from 200 trainees in 1946 to 650 by 1950. Since that time there have been approximately 700 graduate psychology trainees participating each year . . . in collaboration with 71 Graduate Schools and Departments of Psychology accredited by APA in Clinical Psychology and 23 Universities approved in Counseling Psychology. . . . (p. 68)

Of the approximately 800 clinical and counseling psychologists in the VA at that time, 72% had been VA trainees. Ash reported that "over a 20-year period 1174 individual psychologists who completed the training program accepted VA staff positions as their first professional position" (p. 68), whereas others came to the VA after having had other positions. Furthermore, he reported that "in 1966 of those completing the Psychology Training Program, 30% accepted staff positions" (p. 68).

In the mid-1960s, there was growing recognition that the country was facing a projected shortage of human resources in the area of health. Not only would the demand for care go up because over time the population would be older, but also there was legislation calling for the provision of new health care benefits, such as the establishment of Medicare. Community mental health centers were being established to make deinstitutionalization of psychiatric patients possible.

It was already clear that the VA could no longer measure its success merely by how many of these trainees came to work for the VA. Legislation approved on November 7, 1966, Public Law 89-785, entitled the "Veterans Hospitalization and Medical Services Modernization Amendments of 1966" and popularly called the "Medical Omnibus" law, made education a part of the VA's mission as well as patient care and research. That meant that the VA had a mandate not only to train for its own staffing needs but also for the nation.

Like most organizations, the VA has tended to increase the structure of programs the longer they continue in existence. Since 1946, training of health professionals had been an important part of the VA. Programs in specific disciplines had initially been designed and run by professionals in those disciplines working under the assistant chief medical director (ACMD) for Professional Affairs. In October 1973, the Office of Academic Affairs (O/AA) was created under a new ACMD for Academic Affairs. O/AA's student training programs consisted of the Medical/Dental Service, which trained medical and dental residents and students, and the Associated Health Professions and Occupations Service, which trained everybody else. In all, students in approximately 40 different health disciplines were being trained. It was at this time that Elton Ash moved from a purely psychology role in Mental Health and Behavioral Sciences Service in the Office of Professional Affairs to Associated Health Professions and Occupations Division within the Office of Academic Affairs. Because not all of the health care disciplines could be represented among the staff, the position of "education specialist" was established. Professionals in this position would be responsible for training in several disciplines. The program assignment for each specialist depended not only on their individual professional background, but also on the workload in the office as a whole and the background of the other specialists.

After Dr. Ash's retirement at the end of 1974, the education specialist position for psychology was filled in September 1975 by Jule D. Moravec, a counseling psychologist. Moravec left in August 1977; his replacement, Dana L. Moore, a clinical psychologist, arrived in October 1977. Staying until March 1985, she oversaw the transition of VA training to a focus on APA-approved internships. Subsequently, the education specialists who handled the psychology program have been nonpsychologists: Dorothy Stringfellow, a dietitian with a PhD in nutrition science (June 1985– January 1988) and Gloria Holland, a medical librarian with a PhD in administration of health services (September 1988 to present).

IMPACT OF THE VA PROGRAM ON PSYCHOLOGY

Beyond the obvious importance of the VA psychology training program in creating a large body of professionally trained clinical psychologists, it was the VA that led APA to begin its accreditation program.

Since August 1946, the VA and APA's accreditation have continued to have recurring impact upon one another. APA's Policy and Planning Board noted that "the Association has received a request for appraisal of graduate departments of psychology from the Veterans Administration in connection with the VA program for training of clinical psychologists" (APA, 1946, p. 334). Because this would greatly involve the graduate departments of psychology, the Policy and Planning Board recommended that the Council of Representatives establish a Committee of University Departmental Chairmen and that this group complete plans for an independent Association of Graduate Departments of Psychology. It was further recommended that "the several professional Divisions give consideration to the need and desirability for an inter-divisional committee to set standards for internship training and to give formal status and designation to the internships meeting these standards" (p. 335).

All of APA's accreditation activities began in the flurry of activity after World War II with APA's attempt to respond to the request by the VA to designate those schools that could provide complete training in clinical psychology. Schools that identified themselves as providing doctoral work in clinical psychology were identified (Sears, 1946), and following that, standards were drawn up and initial site visits made (APA, 1948). In 1949, the Committee on Training in Clinical Psychology paused to assess what had happened and issued a report about the status of doctoral training in clinical psychology (APA, 1949). The procedures used in accreditation were described, with a discussion of the problems identified by the schools and the site visitors. It is clear that boundary lines were already being drawn; after stating that "programs in the forty-one schools that have wished to take VA trainees or have applied for assistance from the Mental Hygiene Division of the USPHS [United States Public Health Service]" had been evaluated, a footnote added that

> Although in theory at least the VA and USPHS use the recommendations of this Committee in determining their degree of collaboration with the schools, the Committee has not deemed it wise either to seek guidance from the federal agencies with regard to action or policy nor specifically to recommend any action or policy to these agencies in their relationship with the schools. (p. 337)

The report concluded that "on the whole an excellent job is being done" (p. 339) but also offered some cautionary generalizations about the state of training in clinical psychology. It was already of some concern to the Committee that the scope and nature of clinical psychology were too narrowly conceived. The view that it was "more or less limited to psychiatric hospitals and clinics dealing with psychotic, neurotic and seriously disturbed patients — a result in part due to the emphasis on VA training — needs modification" (p. 340). Although they agreed that "perfection of skills" (p. 340) in psychotherapy was something that would happen in postdoctoral training, the committee urged that "training and supervised practice in psychotherapy . . . be included in the doctoral program" (p. 340).

Having moved so rapidly on the accreditation of doctoral programs, no one was ready to move as quickly with regard to accrediting internship level programs. The first listing was published in December 1956 (APA, 1956); it explained that "only independent agencies, that is, those agencies accepting interns from more than one university" were included. They explained further:

> Captive agencies, that is, those agencies in which practicum training is available only to students of a particular university, are not listed. The agencies affiliated with an approved university training program are evaluated at the time of the visit to the university and consequently they are not listed here. The practicum training facilities of the Veterans Administration are yet to be evaluated, and therefore are not included. (p. 710)

It was not until 1974 that the first individual VA facility was approved by APA for internship training — the VA hospital in Topeka, Kansas. In 1975, the VA Hospital-Highland Drive in Pittsburgh, Pennsylvania was added. Two more followed in 1976, the hospitals in Houston, Texas and Seattle, Washington, for a total of four approved. In addition, there were VA facilities in Wichita, Kansas and Memphis, Tennessee, which were involved in formal internship consortia. In a consortium, a number of typically smaller agencies grouped their resources in order to be able to offer well-rounded internship training. Other VA facilities were so closely linked to their affiliated medical schools, that they had interns, but the program was accredited only in the name of the university medical school.

By the fall of 1977, 13 VA medical centers had independent APA approval of their internships (11 had full approval and 2 were provisional), and 2 others were recognized members of approved consortia. It seemed evident to those psychologists in the VA Central Office that beyond broadly based, quality training programs, the best thing the VA psychology training program could do for graduate students was to give them recognized credentials. Therefore, the VA Central Office required medical centers to seek accreditation for their internships. By 1985, 84 VA medical centers had APA-approved internship programs. Most were independent VA internships; a few were members of consortia.

CONCLUSION

It had been a tenet since James G. Miller that the VA psychology training program needed to prepare students for continued learning throughout their careers. The psychologists in the VA Central Office who had been VA trainees after World War II knew that psychologists filled vastly different roles in 1976 than the ones they had trained for 30 years earlier. Treatment techniques change. New problems present themselves. Funding agencies pay for different sorts of work. Credentials become more structured. Even people who are not doing research or developing new treatment techniques need to be able to evaluate the efficacy of the ones they use.

The 1949 Committee on Training in Clinical Psychology report contained a thoughtful comment that deserves close attention now and in the years ahead:

> There is an over-emphasis upon training in clinical techniques at the expense of education in psychological theory and research methodology. It would seem that this emphasis is due, on the one hand, to pressure from students and field agencies, and on the other, to the residue of our own history of fifteen to thirty years of clinical psychology which developed as a practice almost entirely limited to the use of tests. Perhaps this is not unexpected. As a profession we are still somewhat gropingly exploring and finding our way. Perhaps because there is still considerable and reasonable doubt concerning the validity of much of our knowledge and theory in the field of personality and clinical problems, we are inclined to devote much attention to tangibles such as techniques which can be acquired rather easily and give immediate evidence of specialized knowledge. Unfortunately, we may be on no firmer ground on questions of the validity and use of testing techniques than we are in aspects of psychological theory. Major effort must be exerted at this stage of our development to analyze and test many of our basic assumptions in clinical theory, practice and teaching. It is fortunate that there is so much agreement that the PhD shall be maintained as the training level of the clinical psychologist, representing as it does training primarily in the ability to develop, test, and use ideas. (APA, 1949, pp. 339–340)

REFERENCES

American Psychological Association & American Association for Applied Psychology, Subcommittee on Graduate Internship Training. (1945). Graduate internship training in psychology. *Journal of Consulting Psychology, 9,* 243–266.

American Psychological Association. (1956). Internships for doctoral training in clinical psychology approved by the American Psychological Association. *American Psychologist, 11,* 710–711.

American Psychological Association, Committee on Training in Clinical Psychology. (1948). Clinical training facilities: 1948. *American Psychologist, 3,* 317–318.

American Psychological Association, Committee on Training in Clinical Psychology. (1949). Doctoral training programs in clinical psychology: 1949. *American Psychologist, 4,* 331–341.

American Psychological Association, Policy and Planning Board. (1946). Annual report. *American Psychologist, 1,* 330–335.

Ash, E. (1968). The Veterans Administration psychology training program. *Clinical Psychologist, 21,* 67–69, 121–123.

Miller, J. G. (1946). Clinical psychology in the Veterans Administration. *American Psychologist, 1,* 181–189.

Raimy, V. C. (Ed.). (1950). *Training in clinical psychology.* New York: Prentice-Hall.

Sears, R. R. (1947). Clinical training facilities: 1947. *American Psychologist, 2,* 199–205.

Sears, R. R. (1946). Graduate training facilities: I. General information II. Clinical psychology, *American Psychologist, 1,* 135–150.

Seidenfeld, M. A. (1966). Clinical psychology. In R. S. Anderson (Ed.), *Neuropsychiatry in World War II: Vol. I. Zone of interior.* Washington, DC: Office of the Surgeon General, Department of the Army.

Thompson, J. (1990, May). *Veterans benefits: Their history and administration.* Paper presented at a meeting of Leadership VA, Philadelphia, PA.

*United States Veterans' Bureau. (1922). *Annual report of the Director United States Veterans' Bureau for the fiscal year ended June 30, 1922.* Washington, DC: U.S. Government Printing Office.

*United States Veterans' Bureau. (1929). *Annual report of the Director United States Veterans' Bureau for the fiscal year ended June 30, 1929.* Washington, DC: U.S. Government Printing Office.

*Veterans' Administration. (1931). *Annual report of the Administrator of Veterans' Affairs for the fiscal year ended June 30, 1931.* Washington, DC: U.S. Government Printing Office.

Veterans' Administration. (1940). *Annual report of the Administrator of Veterans' Affairs for the fiscal year ended June 30, 1940.* Washington, DC: U.S. Government Printing Office.

Veterans' Administration. (1941). *Annual report of the Administrator of Veterans' Affairs for the fiscal year ended June 30, 1941.* Washington, DC: U.S. Government Printing Office.

*Veterans' Administration. (1945). *Annual report of the Administrator of Veterans' Affairs for the fiscal year ended June 30, 1945.* Washington, DC: U.S. Government Printing Office.

Veterans' Administration. (1946, January 30). *Department of Medicine and Surgery Policy Memorandum Number 2*. Washington, DC: Author.

Veterans Administration. (1954). *Annual report of the Administrator of Veterans' Affairs for the fiscal year ended June 30, 1954*. Washington, DC: U.S. Government Printing Office.

Veterans Administration. (1967). *Medical care of veterans*. Washington, DC: U.S. Government Printing Office.

Veterans Administration. (1977). *VA history in brief*. Washington, DC: Author.

---

*These documents are not readily available but may be seen at the Veterans Health Administration Library at the Department of Veterans Affairs, 810 Vermont Avenue NW, Washington, DC.

25

THE PROFESSIONAL SCHOOL MOVEMENT

GEORGE STRICKER AND NICHOLAS A. CUMMINGS

Until 1957, no accredited program in clinical psychology proclaimed a goal as radical as training for the practice of clinical psychology. In that year, Adelphi University received accreditation. In 1991, at least one third of the students receiving doctorates in clinical psychology graduated from professional programs. The movement is still expanding, it is increasingly influential, and it deserves careful scrutiny concerning its origins. In this chapter, we examine the roots of the professional school movement, tracing its development from decade to decade and highlighting the important contextual elements that influenced it.

THE EARLY YEARS

Prior to World War II, there were a number of abortive attempts to establish psychology as a profession, but the primary setting for professional

We would like to thank Elizabeth Davis-Russell, Ronald Fox, Leonard Goodstein, Ronald Kurz, James McHolland, David Pilon, Neill Watson, Bruce Weiss, and Robert Weitz, each of whom contributed material to be used in this chapter. In some cases the material could not be used and in almost every case it was edited, but this was because of a shortage of space rather than any deficiency in the submission, which was provided generously and promptly by each of them.

training occurred in surroundings akin to current internships, apart from traditional academic institutions. The burden of training fell on the student who, in the absence of formal training programs, constructed learning experiences through a succession of supervised experiences. Prewar precedents can be found for the Doctor of Psychology (PsyD) degree, a professional curriculum, an association devoted to psychology as an applied science, and the professional practice of psychology. As several other authors in this book have noted, however, training in clinical psychology as it is known today did not emerge until after World War II. Under pressure from the Veterans Administration and the United States Public Health Services, the American Psychological Association (APA) established a committee chaired by David Shakow to develop an academic model for training in clinical psychology (APA, Committee on Training in Clinical Psychology, 1947). The model proposed by the Shakow committee has come to be known as the *scientist-practitioner model*. The conclusions of the Shakow committee were endorsed almost entirely at the 1949 Boulder Conference, which established the basis of current training in clinical psychology and provided the point against which the professional school movement was the counterpoint. For this reason, it deserves careful attention.

The Boulder Conference

The Boulder Conference launched an experiment that was unprecedented in professional education for any discipline. An attempt would be made to train clinical psychologists as scientists and as practitioners, not in professional schools but in traditional academic institutions. The scientist-practitioner model proposed to combine training that typically was separated and to offer a dual career choice rather than separating the choice by separating the curricula and training experiences. Although doubt was expressed at the conference as to whether students could be trained in both areas, the recommendation was to make research and practice equal.

As we will show in reporting the recommendations of this and succeeding conferences, the conclusions often may be predicted from a knowledge of the affiliation of the participants. The Boulder Conference brought together psychologists predominantly from traditional academic departments, and these participants recommended that training take place in those departments and that it emphasize functions that those departments valued. Although the Boulder Conference has been seen as a conservative statement of traditional values, it actually was a radical statement of an experimental format, and the inability of the model to produce a large number of true scientist-practitioners may be due to the failure of the departments to implement the model as it was recommended. Rather than train students evenly in science and practice, the departments valued and emphasized research more strongly than practice. This situation produced generations of students who entered practice feeling that they had not been properly trained and that their activities were not valued by their mentors. It is instructive to review what the Boulder Conference actually recommended because those recommendations foreshadowed some developments in the professional schools. In fact, it is ironic that some of the professional schools may be among the first institutions to approach the implementation of the true scientist-practitioner model.

The Boulder Conference endorsed a diversity of training patterns in clinical psychology, a diversity intended to take advantage of the unique resources of each institution and to ensure "the continued possibility of experimentation with new methods of education to the end that quality and vitality are not sacrificed for uniformity" (Raimy, 1950, p. 30). There was a clear rejection of the early crystallization of training methods that resulted immediately after the Boulder Conference. Accreditation was endorsed, but there was a recognition that the legitimate interest in maintaining standards through accreditation carried the danger of stultification through the discouragement of experimentation. This fear was prescient, and it took almost three decades before the professional school experiment was legitimized widely through accreditation.

Although diversity and experimentation were endorsed, so was the concept of a core curriculum. The core, however, specifically was designed to include areas of required study rather than a simple list of required courses. Implementation seems to have followed the "laundry list" model, and recent recommendations from a conference of the National Council of Schools of Professional Psychology (NCSPP; Peterson et al., 1991) return to the earlier recommendation. In order to implement the scientist-practitioner model, it was recommended that early clinical experience be integrated closely with academic course work. Again, this was not implemented widely until the development of the professional school movement.

Three recommendations of the Boulder Conference deserve special attention because of the neglect that they suffered, leading to the necessity for professional schools. First, "each department should establish the standards of clinical competence expected at each stage of training, and should maintain a continuous evaluation of students in regard to these standards" (Rainy, 1950, p. 127). The neglect of clinical competence that followed the emphasis on research training led to the dissatisfaction of many graduate students. Second, "teachers of clinical psychology should maintain their clinical skills by continuing some clinical practice" (p. 130). The press to "publish or perish" did not support the continuation of clinical practice among many university faculty members, who found themselves preaching what they did not practice. Third, "the internship is not a 'repair shop' in which the failures of the academic center are taken care of. The university must adequately carry out its function of providing the necessary training in tool subjects so that the student may take the fullest advantage of what the internship is set up primarily to provide, namely, material on which to use these tools" (pp. 230–231). The failure of the university to emphasize this necessary training led to dissatisfaction among psychologists working in the internship sites as well as among graduate students. It was left up to the professional schools to take these recommendations seriously.

THE 1950s

The 1950s was a decade of development within the boundaries developed by the Boulder Conference. In 1950, there were 35 accredited programs, and none could be described as professional in nature. During the decade, the clinical psychology program in the Department of Psychology at Adelphi University was accredited, and it can be seen as the forerunner of the professional school movement.

Adelphi University

The early, pre-APA approval days at Adelphi University were a time of excitement and energy. The students were risk-takers, and the faculty dared to challenge many traditional approaches to training clinical psychologists. The preparation for the first APA accreditation team that visited Adelphi was characterized by problem-solving meetings underscored by the zealous belief that only one thing was important: The program *had* to be successful. Everyone—faculty and students alike—felt like a pioneer. Student complaints, faculty contentiousness, and every other form of conflict was suspended in order to make the program look good to the APA visiting team. There was an esprit de corps we have personally seen only twice in the history of psychology. The first was during those early days when Adelphi was seeking APA approval. The second was years later when the California School of Professional Psychology (CSPP) was facing the same accreditation evaluation by APA.

Gordon Derner was particularly effective in the process. He was a maverick and a rebel who enjoyed a good fight, regardless of whether it was with the atavists in the APA or the psychiatrist who most recently had attacked psychology. He loved psychology and had a vision for the profession that he shared generously.

The history of clinical psychology at Adelphi University began in 1957 with this initial accreditation. It is interesting that although the site team recommended favorably, the Accreditation Committee denied approval, and accreditation ultimately was granted on appeal. Derner was fond of recalling being told that the objection to granting accreditation was that the program was 20 years ahead of its time: To accredit it would open the door to the development of professional programs. How true!

There have been a number of other milestones in the developments at Adelphi University. In 1966, the clinical psychology training program separated from the Department of Psychology and was reconstituted as the Institute of Advanced Psychological Studies, a professional program within the College of Arts and Sciences, and with its director, Gordon Derner, the equivalent of a department chairperson. In 1971, the institute left the college and became an autonomous professional school within Adelphi University, and Derner became its founding dean. In 1984, shortly after Derner's death, the institute fittingly was renamed the Gordon F. Derner Institute of Advanced Psychological Studies. That formal title has been shortened in common parlance, so that current students refer to their program as "Derner," a rightful tribute to the man who can be viewed as the father of the professional school movement.

The Miami Conference

The 1950s also was the occasion of a seminal conference: the Miami Conference on graduate education in psychology (Roe, Gustad, Moore, Ross, & Skodak, 1959). This conference was concerned with the spectrum of issues in graduate education, but there were a number of important conclusions that concerned training in clinical psychology. The conference grew out of the difficulties created by a dual attempt to develop as a science and as a profession. In his opening remarks, Bobbitt (1959) expressed the tension well by stating that

> the employers want competence, skill, and ability to perform. The trainees want a degree that stands for occupational opportunity and an income that will at least keep pace with inflationary trends. The educators still want to produce something identifiable as scientists and scholars (or in other words, psychologists). (pp. 21–22)

This is an early and clear presentation of the differences between the needs of the students and the consumers on the one hand and the wishes of the academy on the other. These differences inevitably led to the formation of professional schools, a setting in which the curriculum was consistent with the needs of students and employers.

Nonetheless, the time had not yet come for outright professional training, and the Miami Conference reinforced the conclusions of the Boulder Conference as they had been implemented by the programs of that time. Conference participants endorsed the continued emphasis on research training, the "defining characteristic of the PhD psychologist" (Roe et al., 1959, p. 44). One dissatisfaction with the Boulder model was the poor integration between the university and the internship, so that the internship had come to be viewed as an interruption to academic work rather than as an integral part of it. This, of course, was not implied by the Boulder model but was an example of the implementation that departed from that model, to the detriment of clinical training.

Fleeting reference was made both to a professional degree and to professional schools. The reaction to the professional degree was "one of indifference with some negative overtones" (Roe et al., 1959, p. 63). The PhD was viewed as a research degree and no alternative was seriously considered. Some positive feeling toward professional schools was expressed, but this was viewed as the training of psychologists in settings such as medical schools, not in autonomous schools of psychology.

THE 1960s

The 1960s, in psychology as everywhere else, was a decade of ferment. In 1960, there were 83 accredited training programs, and only one of these, Adelphi University, could be seen as a professional program. During the 1960s, the Chicago Conference was held, CSPP developed, and the PsyD degree was offered at the University of Illinois. The PsyD degree was a critical development in the history of professional schools because it opened the door to the development of a large number of professional programs (see chapter 26).

The Chicago Conference

Prior to the Chicago Conference, a committee was convened by APA to study the state of training in clinical psychology and then to report back to the governance structure. The committee was composed evenly of practicing clinicians (e.g., Bernard Riess, Robert A. Harper), scientist-practitioners (e.g., Paul Meehl, Carl Rogers), and researchers in experimental and social psychology (e.g., Lloyd Humphreys, Kenneth Spence, Jerome

Bruner). The committee was highly critical of the training that was taking place and was particularly concerned about the lack of commitment to and, sometimes, respect for clinical psychology in many of the departments that housed the training programs. They recommended radical shifts in the approach to training, including variations in administrative structure, inclusion on the faculty of clinically experienced practitioners, the use of part-time faculty in order to be able to engage active practitioners, and the awarding of a professional degree. There was a clear place for research in the curriculum of such a program, but it emphasized research consumption rather than research production. The preliminary report of the committee was widely circulated in 1964 (APA, Committee on the Scientific and Professional Aims of Psychology, 1965). It captured the feelings of many of the clinicians of that time and provided a backdrop for the Chicago Conference.

The Chicago Conference (Hoch, Ross, & Winder, 1966) was concerned specifically with the professional preparation of clinical psychologists and was convened, in part, because of the undercurrent of dissatisfaction expressed in the report summarized in the previous paragraph. In their overview of then-current clinical training practices, Alexander and Basowitz (1966) noted that

> the clinical student frequently comes away from his graduate days with a whetted appetite, a limited exposure to various therapeutic techniques, and a lack of competency feelings about his ability to perform as a therapist. In our attempts to prepare a "generalist" we have consistently discouraged those students with committed interest in psychotherapy from preparing themselves thoroughly while in predoctoral status. (p. 18)

Alexander and Basowitz (1966) attributed this to the inclination of universities to select faculty on the basis of research promise rather than clinical interest or skill and to the academic reward system that discouraged clinical activities. This left the student without a role model of an effective scientist-practitioner, let alone of an active and successful practitioner. They concluded by echoing all previous conferences and recommending multiple models of training, a recommendation that was not followed until the development of professional schools.

Rodnick (1966) was asked to provide some comments on the Boulder model and he noted, quite accurately, that some of the conditions of the model had not been met. These included the absence of experienced clinical psychologists on the faculty, the separation of fieldwork and practicum experiences from the academic program, and the irrelevance of the research experience to clinical psychology. Thus, as noted previously, the development of the professional school movement was not entirely a response against the Boulder model but against the distorted interpretation of the model that was prevalent in training programs of the time.

The Chicago Conference report supported the Boulder model and the scientist-professional image of clinical psychology, but it also noted that the ideal scientist-professional was rarely encountered and remained an ideal rather than a reality. The report was critical of the model of research that characterized clinical training. It rejected the model of research as laboratory experiment and the model of research as scholarly inquiry in favor of a model of research that incorporated imaginative modifications of scientific methodology so that clinical problems could be studied in a meaningful way. The position concerning research was summarized with a reminder "that the basis of the PhD degree was independent scholarly work representing a contribution to knowledge, and that research was but one form of scholarship and empirical experiments but one form of research" (Rodnick, 1966, p. 56). This sentiment has been incorporated in the curricula of many of the professional programs in psychology.

The matter of suitable faculty was also considered, and the necessity for role models and the inclusion of practitioners on the faculty was noted. Because of the deeply entrenched reward system in the university, it was stated clearly that a radically different structure was needed; there was also a recognition that a professional school and a professional degree could provide such a structure. Aside from the obvious absence of practitioners on most faculties, the conferees also noted the scarcity of good clinical researchers.

The conference supported an integrated pattern of training for research and practice, but it recognized that very few people would have interest and competence in both areas, so that building all training programs around this model was not warranted. The professional model was considered but not endorsed, perhaps because it represented too radical a departure from current practice. Nonetheless, there was a commitment to openness to evidence about the efficacy of alternative models. The conferees noted that the endorsement of diversity was a reaffirmation of a similar statement at the Boulder Conference and recognized that the Boulder model had often been misinterpreted and frequently had not been implemented with enthusiasm.

In many ways, the Chicago Conference conferees were keenly aware of the shortcomings of contemporary clinical training practices, and they contemplated experimentation with departures from that practice before returning to the Boulder model that was thought to underlie those programs. They even recognized that most clinical programs then in effect represented distortions of the Boulder model, but they did not take the necessary final step toward recommending that some programs focus on the training of practitioners, developing curricula that incorporated research in a manner suitable for the needs of the practitioner. It remained for the professional school movement to undertake this step.

Leonard Goodstein was a participant in the Chicago Conference and graciously prepared the following reminiscence of his experience at the conference:

> The Chicago Conference presaged a number of important changes in graduate education in psychology, but it also presaged a number of important changes in people's personal lives as well, including my own. In September, 1965 I had just completed my first year as Director of Professional Training at the University of Cincinnati's Department of Psychology. The post was an unusual one, especially at that time, as it combined the overall management and coordination of the graduate programs in Clinical, Counseling, and School psychology. Having spent the preceding 13 years as a faculty member at the rather traditional, more academically focused department at the University of Iowa, I very much was aware of the limitations of that type of education and, having found my sea legs at Cincinnati, was searching for some new models of professional training, or at least some variants of the old model.
>
> One of my strong recollections is of my roommate at the Conference, Donald Peterson, who was just beginning to formulate his ideas about direct education for the practice of psychology. Because those ideas were still nascent, he was happy to use the vehicle of late night roommate chats to work on these ideas; chats that occurred while we both were still too wound up with the day's activities conveniently to fall off to sleep, but too tired to keep the lights on.
>
> As the Conference went on—and the nights, and the chats, became later and later—Don's ideas became more and more clear. Looking back at those exchanges, it seems difficult to believe that those ideas have been as important as they are. Don and his ideas helped to catalyze a movement that has profoundly affected American psychology—the professional doctorate, and ultimately the independent graduate school of professional psychology.
>
> Another important evolutionary change that emerged from the Chicago Conference was that of the Psychological Service Center, one based upon the university hospital model. These centers would be department-based facilities that simultaneously could offer the community the highest level of a broad-range of psychological services and could provide an opportunity for student training, just as the university hospital offered cutting-edge medical treatment and training for medical students and residents.
>
> In the Fall of 1966, the University of Cincinnati's Community Psychology Institute opened its doors. Some 14 years later, the Institute is still functioning, although the NIMH [National Institute of Mental

Health] funding is long since gone. The Chicago Conference thus was critical not only to the development of the professional school movement, but also served to develop another innovative trend in the graduate education of professional psychologists: the Psychological Service Center. (L. Goodstein, personal communication, 1990)

The California School of Professional Psychology

In 1967, the University of California graduated only six doctoral clinical psychologists. One of the authors (Cummings) sought and obtained the cooperation of California's governor, who appointed a blue-ribbon commission headed by Sheldon Korchin to study the issue. One year later, this commission issued its conclusion: The number of doctorates graduating annually in clinical psychology would not be increased from 6 to 18 as requested but would be cut to 4. The emphasis on training scientists that followed Sputnik, the successful Russian space probe, was cited as the reason. Several leading American universities, led by Harvard and Stanford on opposite coasts, closed down their clinical psychology programs entirely.

Cummings then decided the only way professional psychology could control its own destiny was to have professional schools. His colleagues were highly skeptical, but Cummings first obtained a commitment from the governor and then barnstormed the state and the nation, giving 86 speeches in 1 year to clinical audiences and publishing 14 papers on the subject in that same year. Within a short time, the concept captured the imagination of professional psychologists from coast to coast. In 1970, classes opened on two CSPP campuses, San Francisco and Los Angeles, just 1 year after the report of California's blue-ribbon commission had stated that nothing could be done through the university system. The first classes enrolled 68 students, all with master's degrees and chosen from over 400 applicants, who were willing to risk very high tuition on the vision of a successful professional school. Cummings also was able to persuade more than 250 psychologists, psychiatrists, and physicians to teach one to two courses each, without compensation, over the first 18 months. This was CSPP's initial endowment, enabling the school to create a working capital and to open two additional campuses, in San Diego and in Fresno, in each of the next 2 years.

The governor kept his promise to Cummings and, within 1 year, expedited a degree-granting state charter, but there were still two formidable tasks ahead: (a) regional accreditation by an accrediting organization that had never before approved a free-standing school of any kind and (b) APA approval by the Education and Training Board, which was openly hostile from the outset. Furthermore, although several ranking psychologists at the

National Institute of Mental Health (NIMH) were very intrigued by the concept, there was open opposition to CSPP being considered for financial support prior to its receiving APA approval. Without funding and with no university affiliation, CSPP had little chance of surviving as a tuition-based, free-standing school.

Cummings was able to persuade Norton Simon, the head of a vast business empire, to join the CSPP Board of Directors for 2 years. During that time, Simon did two things: First, he started the school's endowment fund by making a very generous contribution of his own. Second, he called the secretary of Health, Education, and Welfare monthly to inquire about the progress of the grant applications to NIMH from CSPP-San Francisco and CSPP-Los Angeles. Through channels, the secretary then directed NIMH to render a full report. After several months of this procedure, CSPP received notice that its first 2 training grants had been awarded. In addition, NIMH brought about the convening of a conference at Vail in 1973 on patterns and training in professional psychology.

In philosophy, curriculum faculty, and interface with the professional community, as well as in all other matters, Cummings implemented what he had seen and learned 20 years earlier in Derner's original professional program. The innovation that Cummings introduced was that of freeing professional psychology from the graduate schools of letters and sciences. The large-scale replication of this innovation, which had the potential of placing the destiny of the profession with the profession, is what clearly captured the minds of professional psychologists everywhere. A grassroots movement to create professional schools began.

The Fuller Theological Seminary

During the years that CSPP was in development, the Fuller Theological Seminary, which had been sponsoring programs in pastoral counseling, made the decision in 1965 to found a school of professional psychology. This began a movement within theological academic circles toward schools of professional psychology, of which Fuller and Rosemead (now located in Biola University) are the most prominent and which continue successfully to this day.

THE 1970s

In 1970, there were 104 accredited doctoral programs, of which two (Adelphi and Illinois) were professional programs. The 1970s were a decade of explosion. The Vail Conference took place, the National Council of Schools of Professional Psychology was formed, and a large number of professional schools, many of them free-standing, were formed. The model provided by CSPP, coupled with the possibility of a professional degree and the spirit of the times, led to the remarkable growth of professional schools. Some of the schools did not survive the decade, but many of them have developed to gain accreditation and now occupy a central role in the training of clinical psychologists.

The Vail Conference

The Vail Conference (Korman, 1976) was different from any conference that preceded or followed it. It grew out of a continued dissatisfaction with the allegiance of most graduate programs toward a distorted version of the scientist-practitioner model. However, by design, it included a great many people who had not been involved in previous conferences or even in matters of professional training, and many of those who were experienced were systematically excluded from the list of delegates. As a natural consequence of the selection of delegates, many important topics, such as minority issues, student rights, and feminist issues, were considered, and training in professional practice was viewed differently than it ever had been before. Perhaps because of the lack of positions of influence of many of the delegates, the Vail Conference has become a symbol for many worthy causes, but it did not exert much immediate influence on the academic establishment or on APA agencies concerned with training decisions in clinical psychology. Some doggerel that circulated was that "after all the travail, Vail would be of no avail." This was only partially true. Much has been made of the importance of the Vail model, but APA legislation to promote that model has been slow, ambivalent, and of limited effect.

The first resolution from the conference held that "the development of psychological science has sufficiently matured to justify creation of explicit professional programs, in addition to programs for training scientists and scientist-professionals" (Korman, 1976, p. 99). This represented a significant advance from Boulder, where the opinion was that an independent profession was not justified by the state of psychological science. Professional schools were considered to be a setting for training and implicitly were endorsed, as criteria were established for programs with the implication that any setting that could meet these criteria was satisfactory for establishing a training program. The PsyD degree was explicitly endorsed and recommended as the degree of choice for professional programs, in contrast to the PhD, which was to be reserved for graduates of scientist-practitioner programs. NCSPP wrestled with this question of appropriate degree for many fruitless years and finally decided to leave the choice of degree to the program, with no specific guidelines for appropriateness.

Ronald Kurz, who was associate administrative officer of APA's Office of Educational Affairs at the time of the Vail Conference, prepared the following remembrance.

> In 1969 I was unprepared for the storm brewing over professional education in psychology. I had been a professor and director of clinical training in a traditional scientist-professional program. I was aware of the recent development of the professional school in California and the PsyD degree in Illinois, but I never anticipated the passionate dissatisfaction with the status quo I heard in the early meetings of the Ad Hoc Committee. Jack Darley (Chair) cogently communicated to the parent boards the concerns expressed by many groups over the direction of professional training in psychology. The 1965 Chicago Conference had reaffirmed the scientist-professional model, which many believed was no longer appropriate as the exclusively sanctioned model of training. The ad hoc committee expressed the urgency felt by many trainers and practitioners over the lack of relevance of traditional doctoral programs, their lack of responsiveness to social issues, the exclusive emphasis on doctoral training, and the uncritical endorsement of the scientist-professional training model. A new conference was needed that would be more representative of developments in professional practice and training, and more responsive to the social activism that had engulfed American society in the late 1960s. In the fall of 1969 the Council of Representatives charged the ad hoc committee to "seek funds for a national conference on new patterns and levels of professional training with greater relevance to contemporary social problems. (R. Kurz, personal communication, 1990)

The conference had an important impact on the field. The endorsement of the "professional model" and alternative degrees (e.g., PsyD), and the legitimizing of the professional schools, directly stimulated the growth of new programs and the broadening of traditional university-based scientist-practitioner programs. The conference wisely ensured its own impact by providing for a follow-up procedure to bring its message to other APA boards and committees, particularly the accreditation committee, which broadened its criteria to give credence to the professional training model.

The National Council of Schools of Professional Psychology

The several years following the Vail Conference were characterized by a flurry of activity in which a score of professional schools were founded or in the process of being founded. In the APA, however, there was almost no movement. In large measure, the Education and Training Board continued to apply Boulder model accreditation criteria to the professional schools. With the exception of Adelphi University's Derner Institute (then still called the Institute of Advanced Psychological Studies), which made the transition to a professional school with its long-standing APA approval, the emerging professional schools were not likely to become accredited by the APA for several years. The absence of clear-cut criteria and standards that were consistent with the excellence of training provided by some of the professional schools created a vacuum into which many marginal schools fell, some of which were outright "diploma mills." One such school consisted of one room and gave credit toward a doctorate (at substantial tuition cost) for life experiences. It even obtained the services of some prominent psychologists to read dissertations at $1,000 each. A crisis of confidence was brewing that threatened the professional school movement.

After agreeing to resign from CSPP, Cummings remained in office for 6 more months. He used that time to form the NCSPP. He contacted all of the serious professional schools and scheduled an all-day meeting the day before the APA convention in August 1976. Acting as president pro tempore, he convened the meeting, established a membership of the 19 professional schools that had been invited and were present, and charged the group with its first task: defining a professional school of psychology.

The NCSPP had originated in a climate of protest and rebellion. The pioneers who built the organization struggled with the existing bureaucracy for legitimacy, and did so with great success. Gordon Derner provided early leadership, followed by Donald Peterson, Joanne Callan, Russel Bent, Edward Bourg, George Stricker, James McHolland, David Singer, and Elizabeth Davis-Russell. The mission of the organization has changed from fighting with the establishment to becoming an equal partner in an attempt to shape the nature of clinical training in psychology, with clear recognition granted to the professional model as one of a number of valuable approaches to training.

Program Development

The 1970s saw the establishment of a large number of professional programs, some of which were of very high quality and have gone on toward accreditation, whereas others varied from exploitative diploma mills to programs with more idealism than resources. For a number of years, and for motives that can be questioned, the existence of the less desirable programs was used as an argument to resist the legitimacy of the quality programs. There still is some prejudice in some quarters, but much of that has faded and programs are more likely to be evaluated on their merit rather than on their model.

In order to capture the spirit of the times, we invited a few of the organizers of those early programs to describe their innovative efforts. The sites that are described in the following pages include a major research university, a large state university, a proprietary free-standing school, and a consortium. Each is now accredited, and the breadth reflects the vitality of the professional school movement.

Rutgers University[1]

The plan for the development of a professional school dates back to April 1969, when a group of practicing psychologists met to discuss the feasibility of establishing low-cost psychological service centers. The initial concept was to set up centers in poverty-stricken areas staffed by neophyte psychologists and upper graduate students to be supervised by experienced psychological practitioners. Milton Theaman, director of the New York State Psychological Association Service Center, was a guest at the initial meeting so that he could describe the operation of that center.

Despite the enthusiasm of the group to establish the service centers, it soon became apparent that the plan was not feasible because of the lack of available psychological personnel to staff the centers. It was learned that the two universities in New Jersey that offered graduate psychology programs—Rutgers and Princeton—actually graduated very few psychologists who could qualify as practitioners. Furthermore, it was learned that there were currently 45 vacancies for psychologists in the state institutions, as well as numerous additional vacancies in a variety of settings throughout New Jersey. This situation was further complicated by the production, nationwide, of less than 1,000 PhDs in all areas of psychology, only a small fraction of whom specialized in clinical psychology. Finally, a study by Gerald Gelber determined that psychologists were a "vanishing species" in New Jersey because there were more leaving practice in the state by moving or death than were entering.

The group's reaction to this situation resulted in a unanimous decision to work toward the development of a professional school of psychology in New Jersey. After weeks of discussion, the council voted to plan for the establishment of the New Jersey College of Professional Psychology. Robert Weitz was appointed executive vice-president and acting dean. The school would be free-standing and offer a professional-scientist model of practi-

---

[1]This section was prepared by Robert Weitz, who was involved in the formation of the program.

tioner preparation leading to the PsyD degree. Later, the idea of a free-standing school had to be abandoned when it was learned from the Department of Higher Education that, to open the school, the council would need to show assets of approximately $4 million, the estimated amount required to guarantee sufficient financial security to graduate the first class. At this juncture, the council moved to seek affiliation with one of the state's universities.

The efforts to affiliate with an established university resulted in frustrations until November 1973, when the council was invited by Stanley S. Bergen, Jr., president of the New Jersey College of Medicine and Dentistry, to affiliate with that institution. The invitation was gladly accepted by the council and, within a few weeks, an official proposal to establish the School of Psychology was presented to the New Jersey State Board of Higher Education.

Until that time, the psychology faculties at Rutgers University were opposed to the concept of a professional school; however, on learning of the proposal submitted by the College of Medicine and Dentistry, the Rutgers faculties, led by Peter Nathan, Virginia Bennett, and Jack Bardon (and with the blessings of the Rutgers academic hierarchy), submitted a proposal of their own to the State Board.

After weeks of debate, on February 15, 1974, the State Board voted that the professional school be established at Rutgers University with the input of the Organizing Council and that joint programs be developed with the College of Medicine and Dentistry. The Graduate School of Applied and Professional Psychology of Rutgers University was born.

Wright State University[2]

The move to establish a school of professional psychology in Ohio began in 1974 when Ronald E. Fox received permission from the Ohio Psychological Association to establish a committee of 12 prominent psychologists in the state to study the feasibility of such an enterprise for Ohio. After extensive study of the relevant literature, visits to several of the schools then in existence, conversations with consultants, and a review of legislation covering degree granting authority, the committee recommended the establishment of a school of professional psychology to be located in an existing university, and it pledged itself to work toward that end.

Several universities expressed interest in the proposal, but they were reluctant to say so out of fear of displeasing the Ohio Board of Regents,

---

[2]This section was prepared by Ronald Fox, the founding dean of the program.

which oversees higher education in the state and which was opposed to any additional doctoral programs in psychology at that time. Without a mandate to do so, most presidents were unwilling to make any commitments. Several universities were unwilling to cooperate because of the strong opposition of their psychology departments. Wright State University, a new state university ambitious to build doctoral programs and excited about the possibility of having the only PsyD program in the state, was willing to make a commitment, provided that it did not have to say so publicly.

A highly influential representative from Wright State's region was recruited to introduce legislation establishing the school of professional psychology at the university, authorizing it to grant the PsyD degree, and providing $900,000 for start-up costs. With the help of the Ohio Psychological Association, the senate majority leader was convinced to be the advocate in the senate for the new school. All of the other state universities opposed the bill on the grounds that the new school was not needed.

The legislation establishing the new school was signed into law in the fall of 1977. The charter class was admitted on schedule and then graduated in 1982. By the time the first class graduated, the school was fully accredited by APA. Seven years later, the school dedicated a new 20,000-square-foot clinical, teaching, and research center to complement its existing facilities. Twenty-five to 30 people graduate each year, and they are establishing themselves as practitioners, as program directors, and as officers in professional associations.

Born in controversy and established by political fiat, the school now has assumed its place as a legitimate component of the public higher education system in Ohio.

The Illinois School of Professional Psychology[3]

The Illinois School of Professional Psychology (ISPP) was established in 1976, after 2 or 3 years of planning and discussions by several Illinois psychologists and an attorney interested in mental health. The need for a practitioner-oriented training program was seen as important because existing doctoral programs in Illinois trained primarily in research skills, except for the tiny, increasingly academic, and apparently moribund PsyD program at the University of Illinois.

Early struggles at ISPP revolved about two issues: The credibility of the PsyD degree and the proprietary nature of the school. Early in the

---

[3]This section was prepared by James McHolland, the president of the Illinois School of Professional Psychology.

school's history, a philosophical difference developed in the faculty over whether it was appropriate to operate a graduate school as a business. The issue really concerned whether the profit motive would allow for the development of a high-quality training program. Some people believed the latter was impossible and split off and established another nonprofit school.

With the hiring of a full-time core faculty in 1979, ISPP began its ascent toward quality, as indicated by the achieving of provisional and then full approval of its doctoral program in clinical psychology by APA. The central stabilizing force throughout all of ISPP's history has been its dean, Marc Lubin. Faculty have reported that his commitment to excellence and justice permeates the school.

In 1986, ISPP began the process of establishing a branch of its program in Minneapolis/St. Paul, Minnesota. Although practicing psychologists in the state were receptive to both the PsyD degree and to the ISPP, certain clinical faculty of the University of Minnesota psychology department were not. They sought to prevent the state from issuing degree-granting authority. Prior to establishment of the Minnesota School of Professional Psychology (MSPP), the University of Minnesota in Minneapolis was the only graduate program in the state approved to offer a doctoral degree in clinical psychology. Clearly, a need existed that was recognized by the state. Those who opposed the establishment of ISPP's branch resorted to the promotion of false information about professional schools. The "scientists" had abandoned the principle of basing claims on facts, apparently in favor of supporting biases that were not supported by facts. Arguments and data provided by ISPP were not ignored by state educational authorities, however. Approval was granted, and MSPP accepted its first class of students in 1987.

The Virginia Consortium[4]

The Doctor of Psychology Program of the Virginia Consortium for Professional Psychology began operation in 1978 as the brainchild of the State Council of Higher Education for Virginia. A consortium of three state universities and a private medical school, the State Council considered the arrangement to be an efficient use of existing resources to do what none of the individual institutions could do alone without great increases in faculty and funding. Although there were consortial internship programs already in existence, the Virginia Consortium was the first consortial doctoral program in the nation.

---

[4]This section was prepared by Neill Watson, the chairperson of the Virginia Consortium for Professional Psychology.

As the first consortial doctoral program, the Virginia Consortium pushed the limits of the APA accreditation criteria. The criterion at issue was none other than Criterion 1A, the fundamental requirement that a program be located in a regionally accredited institution.

The Doctor of Psychology Program of the Virginia Consortium is a single, unified program comprised of four academic departments: the psychology departments of the College of William & Mary, Norfolk State University, and Old Dominion University, and the Department of Psychiatry and Behavioral Science of Eastern Virginia Medical School. The three universities have regional accreditation. At the time that the program applied for APA accreditation, the medical school, a free-standing institution, had accreditation only from the Liaison Committee for Medical Education. The APA Accreditation Committee ruled that the program was ineligible for accreditation by the APA because one of the institutions in the consortium did not have regional accreditation.

The consortium appealed the ruling, pointing out that all aspects of the program met the academic standards of three regionally accredited universities. Ultimately, this point was acknowledged, and the consortium was declared eligible for review of accreditation by the APA. The outcome of the review was full accreditation for 5 years for a "formidable program," to quote the site visit team. Moreover, the APA adopted a guideline for the interpretation of accreditation Criterion 1A for consortial doctoral programs that was based on the organizational structure of the Virginia Consortium.

THE 1980s

The 1980s was a decade of consolidation for professional schools. At the beginning of the decade, in 1980, there were 164 accredited programs and, of these, 11 were located in professional schools, including the one at the University of Illinois that no longer was accepting students. At the close of the decade, in 1989, there were 252 accredited programs and, of these, at least 26 were located in professional schools or programs. Because of the influence of the professional school movement, it is becoming increasingly difficult to do the tally, as many programs with a professional model are now located in departments of psychology. Not only are at least 10% of the accredited programs located in professional schools, but these schools, because they enroll many more students than departmental research programs, graduate approximately 33% of the students. With the achievement of respectability, the leadership of the professional schools could turn its attention away from battles for acceptance and toward the consideration of crucial issues in clinical training. A number of important conferences held in the latter half of the 1980s and in 1990 began to define the essentials of clinical training with greater clarity and detail than the field had ever known before.

Mission Bay

The Mission Bay Conference (Bourg, Bent, McHolland, & Stricker, 1989) was sponsored by NCSPP and held in December 1986; its preconference materials and proceedings are presented in Bourg et al. (1987). The conference followed an earlier report that summarized a conference held in La Jolla and presented a self-study of the member organizations of NCSPP (Callan, Peterson, & Stricker, 1986). The Mission Bay Conference can be considered a watershed in the history of NCSPP in that it focused on issues of quality assurance in graduate education, presented a set of resolutions that continue to guide program development, and set the stage for a series of conferences that amplified the themes introduced at Mission Bay.

The general resolutions of the conference represent the superordinate goals and philosophy of the professional school movement. They state (a) a commitment to practitioner training, (b) the reliance of professional training on a knowledge base rooted in but not limited to psychology, and (c) a recognition of the obligation of professional training to be responsive to issues of ethnic diversity. The specific resolutions that followed from this general position expressed a commitment to the development of knowledge, skills, and competency, with a recognition of the importance of attitudes and values for practitioners.

Finally, the Mission Bay Conference was the first occasion on which the generic core of professional training was fully defined. The core was seen as consisting of six basic competency areas: relationship, assessment, intervention, research/evaluation, consultation/teaching, and management. These competencies reflect areas of study, not a list of courses, and display an approach to curriculum construction first stated at the Boulder Conference but rarely actualized in the course-conscious curricula that followed.

Utah

In 1987, APA sponsored a conference intended to deal with the range of issues confronting all of graduate education (APA, 1987). In part, the motivation for the Mission Bay Conference was to prepare a statement articulating the views of professional schools before this larger conference. The resolutions of the Utah Conference concerned many issues other than professional education but also addressed some issues of vital concern to professional schools.

There was agreement between the two conferences on the matter of degree designation. Both endorsed a range of degrees, recognizing the appropriateness of the PhD and the PsyD (as well as the EdD), and understanding that programs fall on a continuum with varying emphases on research and on practice. Furthermore, the degree awarded often is related more closely to political circumstances and contextual factors than it is to program philosophy, one factor that led the NCSPP to forego the interesting but fruitless debate about appropriate degrees. There also was agreement on issues such as the importance of student socialization, the central value of diversity, and the need for the integration of a large and interdisciplinary body of knowledge.

In the important matter of the core curriculum, the Utah conferees endorsed the basic knowledge areas specified in the accreditation criteria but left the responsibility for specifying the core to the individual departments of psychology. Mission Bay specified a much more elaborate outline of a core, in keeping with the difference between the professional training that is the focus for the NCSPP and the academic training that was the concern of the conferees at Utah. This difference, and the inevitable tension between the values of professional education and academic freedom, is one of the key sources of the difficulty in implementing programs that train students for the dual roles of scientist and practitioner.

The most serious disagreement between the Mission Bay and the Utah Conferences concerned the setting in which education was to take place. Utah conferees resolved that "the critical issue in education and training is the substance and quality of the doctoral program and not the university unit in which it is housed" (APA, 1987, p. 1074). If not for the insertion of the mischievous word *university*, professional schools would be in support of the focus on substance and quality. However, the unnecessary specification that the venue, and not the quality, of the program is of central importance led professional schools to disagree with this resolution. Utah conferees called for an end to free-standing schools. The NCSPP agreed that the university setting was conducive to the development of quality but did not believe the university venue was either necessary or sufficient.

It is more interesting to note the vast areas of agreement than to dwell on the residual, politically inspired attempt to discredit one setting for professional education. The groups seemed to be moving closer together in spirit and substance even while proclaiming the residual differences that the aims of practice and research require.

San Juan

An appreciation of the contributions of ethnic diversity to clinical training has been incorporated into the standards for accreditation of APA (APA, 1986) and is endorsed by training programs of all varieties. Unfortunately, the endorsement is not always followed by action, and a substantial number of programs can be identified with low ethnic minority enrollments (Jones, 1990). Ethnic minorities remain underrepresented in psychology (Kohout & Pion, 1990) despite efforts to correct that problem by a number of training programs. In response to this need, which is felt as both a social responsibility and an important component of training in clinical psychology, the NCSPP devoted its 1989 conference, held in San Juan, Puerto Rico, to the issue of ethnic diversification in psychology.

The San Juan Conference (Stricker et al., 1990) considered the issues of institutional change, faculty–administration recruitment and retention, student recruitment and retention, curriculum, and service to underserved populations. The book that resulted from that conference contains a series of chapters in these areas and can be used effectively by programs that wish to be informed about the issues of relevance to the promotion of affirmative diversity. The conference concluded with a series of resolutions through which the NCSPP committed itself to promoting recruitment and curricular efforts toward the goal of ethnic diversification and made subscribing to those resolutions a condition of membership in the organization. The conference "was a landmark event because it marked the first time that a national, professional organization made a clear and accountable commitment to pursue a policy of affirmative diversity within the association itself and within each of its member schools" (Stricker et al., 1990, p. 232).

Elizabeth Davis-Russell, the chairwoman of the NCSPP's Committee on Minority Participation and Service to Underserved Populations at the time of the San Juan Conference, provided the following comments:

> In February 1989, in Puerto Rico, the National Council of Schools of Professional Psychology convened its midwinter conference. The theme of the Conference was ethnic minority issues in clinical training, and the conference heralded a milestone in the development of psychology. Although it may never acquire the stature of the Boulder or Vail conferences, it certainly deserves recognition for its historic precedence. For years, ethnic minority psychological associations such as the Association of Black Psychologists had called attention to psychology's inadequate or distorted treatment of ethnic minorities, but this was the

first time that a nonethnic minority organization, in its entirety, not just as a caucus, focused its attention and resources on the inclusion of ethnic minorities and ethnic minority issues.

Tension permeated the conference; it was evident in the planning and execution. During the planning, ethnic minorities saw the opportunity to shape the conference to reflect their issues, whereas the leadership sought to retain control. Failure to recognize the impact of decades of exclusion on the perceptions and attitudes of ethnic minorities exacerbated the tension. Some of this was dissipated by some discussion, but a long history of distrust is not easily erased. The ethnic minorities caucused to arrive at some consensus regarding minimal acceptable outcomes of the conference. The tension did not escape the caucus. Here it was embodied in the split between those who were more progressive and wanted to push for more and the more reticent who felt that pushing too hard would cause a backlash. A compromise as reflected in the resolutions emanating from the small groups was more than the Conference participants were ready to accept. The resolutions would result in a structural change of the organization. That uncertainty regarding what the new organization would look like, coupled with the realization that White males would now have to share power with people of color, might even have to be replaced by some of them, was too radical a move for most participants to embrace. The task then became to arrive at some compromise that would be minimally acceptable to most. The turning point came when the steering committee of the conference could work out the issues among themselves. This was significant because the composition of the steering committee was fifty percent ethnic minority.

The conference was significant in a number of ways. First, an organized body in psychology, whose members educate 33% of clinical psychologists, sought to forge a new direction in training, a direction that was long overdue. Second, that body made a commitment to the expansion of psychology to include groups that have been underrepresented. Third, the conference highlighted an important fact: Any attempt to include ethnic minorities in psychology must be a comprehensive one that integrates a number of facets: aggressive recruitment and retention of faculty, students, and administrators; integration of ethnic minority issues into the curriculum; and service to underserved populations. (E. Davis-Russell, personal communication, 1990)

Gainesville

In January 1990, the National Conference on Scientist-Practitioner Education and Training for the Professional Practice of Psychology (Department of Clinical and Health Psychology, 1990) was held in Gainesville, Florida, under the initiative of the scientist-practitioner caucus, with the joint sponsorship of a wide variety of groups, including the NCSPP. The purpose of the conference was to define the essential characteristics of the scientist-practitioner model. In many ways, the conference can be seen as an attempt to resurrect the Boulder model, the influence of which had been curtailed both by the professional model and the model that favored more pure research training.

The conference resolutions clearly favored the retention of an academic core consistent with current accreditation requirements and the specification of a practice core that focused on assessment and intervention. In addition to didactic cores, experiential cores both in science and in practice were recommended. The key concept was the integration of the basic scientific core with the didactic and experiential components of the curriculum, so that the training of scientist-practitioners, consistent with the meaning if not the actualization of the Boulder model, would be accomplished. Although the conference focused on the scientist-practitioner model and did not consider other models, the university was specified as the ideal location for training programs.

San Antonio

One week after the Gainesville Conference ended, the NCSPP sponsored a conference in San Antonio, Texas, on the core curriculum in professional psychology (Peterson et al., 1991). The conference addressed the curriculum that had been articulated at the Mission Bay Conference, amplifying the curricular requirements for each of the six competency areas (relationship, assessment, intervention, research/evaluation, consultation/teaching, and management) developed earlier. One of the authors (Stricker) attended both the Gainesville and the San Antonio conferences and found the overlap and occasional contrast to be striking.

The content of the Gainesville resolutions emphasized an integrative approach to science and practice. Genuine concern was expressed for the adequacy of training for practice, a concern that was noticeably absent in many of the earlier programs that referred to themselves as following a Boulder model. In fact, the professional schools developed largely in response to this deficiency in earlier programs. If concern for practice had been present earlier, the professional schools might never have developed. The San Antonio resolutions also favored an emphasis on the integration of science and practice, but viewed science in a manner that emphasized local practice (Trierweiler & Stricker, 1991), an issue that was not considered at Gainesville.

As might be expected, the Gainesville Conference addressed the integration of science and practice, whereas the San Antonio Conference addressed training for practice. Nonetheless, the curriculum recommendations of the two conferences did not differ broadly in content. Both groups supported early and varied clinical practice, the presence of a clinically active faculty, and a diversity of scientific methods. Gainesville conferees endorsed the accreditation requirements for a core curriculum, but San Antonio conferees amplified the required core by calling for specific coverage of developmental psychology, psychopathology, individual and systems functioning and change, and cultural bases of behavior.

Perhaps the greatest difference between the two conferences was in the tone. Despite substantive agreements, deeply held prejudice against a stereotyped image of the professional school was apparent at the Gainesville Conference, and the hostility and suspicion held toward professional schools was disconcerting. This was most clear in the endorsement of the university as the ideal venue, but it also provided a backdrop for much of the discussion. Nonetheless, it is possible that the two models can be seen as occupying different places on a continuum of appropriate training alternatives rather than factions at war over the proper definition of clinical training.

THE 1990s AND BEYOND

The pattern of growth noted within the professional school movement is striking. Adelphi University was the forerunner of the movement, establishing a program and earning accreditation by 1957, but the statement that it was 20 years ahead of its time was prophetic. The establishment of the California School of Professional Psychology ushered in the explosive decade of the 1970s. Many of the programs that were established in this period matured and became accredited, usually in the 1980s, but others withered during this time, so that the 1980s can be seen as a decade of consolidation. It is always difficult to foretell the future, but it is possible to hazard some guesses. It seems unlikely that there will be much growth in free-standing settings, largely because of the cost and the political problems, and partially because of the prejudice against the venue that was expressed most clearly at the Utah Conference. The major research universities will probably not be receptive to establishing professional schools. To date, only two (Rutgers and Yeshiva) have done so, and a number of others (Harvard, Stanford, and Chicago) have closed their scientist-practitioner programs in clinical psychology.

Nonetheless, the professional model has seen increasing acceptance and influence. Where, then, are the programs of the future likely to develop? There are two likely directions in which this expansion may occur. First, the smaller colleges and universities have shown an inclination to welcome professional programs and are likely to continue to do so. Second, and perhaps most important, it is likely that a number of existing programs will begin to convert to the professional model in response to the expressed needs of the students and the community of consumers.

The Boulder model was the major source of influence for over a quarter of century of training in clinical psychology. The professional model has been an increasingly influential force over the past decade. However, the Boulder model has seen a recent resurgence, with a greater influence on practice than was the case in the early years. At the same time, the maturation of the professional model has placed more emphasis on scholarship and an expanded definition of research than had been the case in its early years. The bifurcation of these two models led to the battles of the 1960s and 1970s. There is a recognition that the models fit on a continuum, ranging from some research-oriented programs that have little use for clinical training or practice to some professional programs that continue to devalue the potential contribution of research. However, the great majority of programs fall between these poles and are more closely alike than different. In the 1990s, the ways that the models are similar may be more compelling than the ways that have separated them. If we can tolerate shades of difference and then develop by recognizing and valuing our diversity, rather than exaggerating our differences and defensively attacking those who choose other paths, the training of future generations of clinical psychologists will profit from the development.

REFERENCES

Alexander, I. G., & Basowitz, H. (1966). Current clinical training practices: An overview. In E. L. Hoch, A. O. Ross, & C. L. Winder (Eds.), *Professional preparation of clinical psychologists* (pp. 15–20). Washington, DC: American Psychological Association.

American Psychological Association. (1986). *Accreditation handbook.* Washington, DC: Author.

American Psychological Association. (1987). Resolutions approved by the National Conference on Graduate Education in Psychology. *American Psychologist, 42,* 1070–1084.

American Psychological Association, Committee on Training in Clinical Psychology. (1947). Recommended graduate training program in clinical psychology. *American Psychologist, 2,* 539–558.

American Psychological Association, Committee on the Scientific and Professional

Aims of Psychology. (1965). Preliminary report. *American Psychologist, 20,* 95–100.

Bobbitt, J. M. (1959). Opening remarks. In A. Roe, J. W. Gustad, B. V. Moore, S. Ross, & M. Skodak (Eds.), *Graduate education in psychology* (pp. 19–23). Washington, DC: American Psychological Association.

Bourg, E. F., Bent, R. J., Callan, J. E., Jones, N. F., McHolland, J., & Stricker, G. (1987). *Standards and evaluation in the education and training of professional psychologists: Knowledge, attitudes, and skills.* Norman, OK: Transcript Press.

Bourg, E. F., Bent, R. J., McHolland, J., & Stricker, G. (1989). Standards and evaluation in the education and training of professional psychologists: The National Council of Schools of Professional Psychology Mission Bay Conference. *American Psychologist, 44,* 66–72.

Callan, J. E., Peterson, D. R., & Stricker, G. (1986). *Quality in professional psychology training: A national conference and self-study.* Norman, OK: Transcript Press.

Department of Clinical and Health Psychology. (1990). *National Conference on Scientist-Practitioner Education and Training for the Professional Practice of Psychology: Policy recommendations.* (Available from Department of Clinical and Health Psychology, University of Florida, Gainesville, FL 32611.)

Hoch, E. L., Ross, A. O., & Winder, C. L. (Eds.). (1966). *Professional preparation of clinical psychologists.* Washington, DC: American Psychological Association.

Jones, J. M. (1990). Invitational Address: Who is training our ethnic minority psychologists, and are they doing it right? In G. Stricker, E. Davis-Russell, E. Bourg, E. Duran, W. R. Hammond, J. McHolland, K. Polite, & B. E. Vaughn (Eds.), *Toward ethnic diversification in psychology education and training* (pp. 17–34). Washington, DC: American Psychological Association.

Kohout, J., & Pion, G. (1990). Participation of ethnic minorities in psychology: Where do we stand today? In G. Stricker, E. Davis-Russell, E. Bourg, E. Duran, W. R. Hammond, J. McHolland, K. Polite, & B. E. Vaughn (Eds.), *Toward ethnic diversification in psychology education and training* (pp. 153–165). Washington, DC: American Psychological Association.

Korman, M. (Ed.). (1976). *Levels and patterns of professional training in psychology.* Washington, DC: American Psychological Association.

Peterson, R. L., McHolland, J., Bent, R. J., Davis-Russell, E., Edwall, G. E., Magidson, E., Polite, K., Singer, D. L., & Stricker, G. (1991). *The core curriculum in professional psychology.* Washington, DC: American Psychological Association.

Raimy, V. (Ed.). (1950). *Training in clinical psychology.* Englewood Cliffs, NJ: Prentice-Hall.

Rodnick, E. H. (1966). Comments on the "Boulder" model. In E. L. Hoch, A. O. Ross, & C. L. Winder (Eds.), *Professional preparation of clinical psychologists* (pp. 21–23). Washington, DC: American Psychological Association.

Roe, A., Gustad, J. W., Moore, B. V., Ross, S., & Skodak, M. (Eds.). (1959).

Graduate education in psychology. Washington, DC: American Psychological Association.

Stricker, G., Davis-Russell, E., Bourg, E., Duran, E., Hammond, W. R., McHolland, J., Polite, K., & Vaughn, B. E. (1990). *Toward ethnic diversification in psychology education and training.* Washington, DC: American Psychological Association.

Trierweiler, S. J., & Stricker, G. (1991). Training the local clinical scientist. In R. L. Peterson, J. McHolland, R. J. Bent, E. Davis-Russell, G. E. Edwall, E. Magidson, K. Polite, D. L. Singer, & G. Stricker (Eds.), *The core curriculum in professional psychology* (pp. 103–113). Washington, DC: American Psychological Association.

26

THE DOCTOR OF PSYCHOLOGY DEGREE

DONALD R. PETERSON

The first formal proposal for a professional program leading to the Doctor of Psychology degree was made by Loyal Crane in 1925.[1] In an article titled "A Plea for the Training of Psychologists" (Crane, 1925) Crane expressed his concern about confusions in the training of clinical psychologists. Scientific education and the PhD credential were inappropriate for practicing clinicians. People receiving professional services were not clear about the differences between psychiatrists and psychologists. They were either unsure or incorrect in guessing what psychologists were supposed to do. Relations with the medical profession were ill-defined, and when definitions became established, they were usually detrimental to psychologists.

Some of the material in this chapter appeared originally under the title "Origins and Development of the Doctor of Psychology Concept" in *Educating professional psychologists* (pp. 19–38) edited by G. R. Caddy, D. C. Rimm, N. Watson, & J. H. Johnson, 1982, New Brunswick, NJ: Transaction Books. Copyright 1982 by Transaction Publishers. Used by permission.

By letter or conversation, article or brochure, the following people have contributed background information or material substance to this chapter: Jules Abrams of Widener University, Leonard Bart of Pace University, Alan Boneau of George Mason University, Edward Bourg of the California School of Professional Psychology, Kenneth E. Clark, formerly of Rochester University,

According to Crane however, the main problems arose not from public misperception but from the profession of psychology itself. The designation *psychologist* lacked social and legal specificity. Anyone who chose to use the title could do so. The PhD was no guarantee of professional competence "for the simple reason that the degree may be obtained as well by the student of chemistry, mathematics or history as by the student of psychology" (Crane, 1925, p. 228). Because psychology had failed to come to grips with the responsibilities of professional training, the limited prestige psychologists gained from members of related professions and the general public was sadly justified.

Why not, said Dr. Crane, put truly "relevant" substance into the training of professional psychologists and use a professional degree to certify completion of that training? He proposed a 4-year graduate curriculum with heavy emphasis on psychology and those aspects of medicine most clearly pertinent to the study and treatment of psychological problems. He suggested that the Doctor of Psychology degree be awarded upon completion of the program. Would not this help bring professional psychology the recognition it deserved? Would not this help clarify the relationship between professional psychology and medicine? Would not the public, ill-used by psychology in the past, but now treated by fully competent professional psychologists, benefit gratefully from the improved services Doctors of Psychology would bring them?

Crane's plea scarcely brought a ripple to the stream of professional activity as it was flowing at the time. Soon after Crane made his statement, A. E. Davies (1926) published a comment on the uncertain state of knowledge in early 20th-century psychology and stressed the difficulties such limitations entailed for professional applications of psychology. Inevitably,

---

Ronald Fox of Wright State University, Jeffrey Grip of the Chicago School of Professional Psychology, Jim Hedstrom of Pepperdine University, Lloyd Humphreys and Julian Rappaport of the University of Illinois, Nelson Jones of Denver University, James McHolland of the American Schools of Professional Psychology, Paul Meehl and William Schofield of the University of Minnesota, Barbara Melamed and Lillian Zack of Yeshiva University, Bruce Narramore of Biola University, David Singer of the Antioch New England Graduate School, Gilbert Trachtman and Bernard Kalinkowitz of New York University, and Leon VandeCreek of Indiana University of Pennsylvania. I apologize to those who wrote statements that could not be included for lack of space, and I thank gratefully all those who contributed information of any kind, whether or not I could work it into print.

[1]Despite my own efforts and those of the historians and archivists whose help I have sought, I have been unable to find out where Crane was working when he wrote the article, where he received his doctoral education, or anything else about him. He is identified in the heading of the article only as "Loyal Crane, PhD." Authors affiliated with universities who submitted manuscripts to the *Journal of Abnormal and Social Psychology* in those days seemed always to identify the institutions that employed them, and in his article, Crane discusses requirements in the New York Mental Deficiency Law for recognition as a "qualified examiner of mental defect." It seems safe to assume that he was working in one of the "insane asylums" or institutions for the "feeble-minded" in New York state at the time.

he suggested that a committee be formed to study the various issues involved, and in due time a committee was appointed. The group was made up of Andrew Brown, Robert Brotemarkle, Clara Town, and Maud Merrill, with Brown as chairman. Their efforts constituted the first systematic consideration of the issues involved in education for the practice of psychology by an officially designated organization (Reisman, 1966).

A survey of self-defined "clinical psychologists" working in various professional settings at the time showed that there was little agreement either about the nature of the field or the kinds of preparation that psychologists should have for professional work. In their recommendations, the Brown Committee suggested that clinical psychology be conceived as "that art and technology which deals with the adjustment problems of human beings" and that training be based on a comprehensive knowledge of psychological science extending on the one side to the biophysical bases of human disorder and on the other to the knowledge of sociology and social psychology required for a grasp of family and community life. At least 1 year of supervised practical experience was to be required, and completion of formal training was to be certified by award of the PhD "or equivalent degree in psychology from an accredited university" (APA, 1935).

However contemporary and reasonable these recommendations may seem today, nothing much came of them at the time they were made. Clinical psychology had not yet established the knowledge or developed the technology to qualify as an independent profession. In most of its applications, it was functionally ancillary and administratively subordinate to medicine. In the politics of professional power, clinical psychology did not have the force to be regarded even as a significant upstart by well established medical professionals. Fernberger's analysis of American Psychological Association (APA) composition in 1928 showed that only 104 doctorally accredited members were engaged in primarily clinical work. The medical authorities in control of mental health services were careful to see that the professional activities of psychologists were restricted to diagnostic testing, under medical supervision. "With occasional noteworthy exceptions," Crane had written, "the attitude of the medical profession toward the practicing psychologist is one of tolerant condescension, courteous withal yet ever watchful lest, during an unguarded moment, some remunerative executive post, which should 'properly be filled by an M.D.', pass into the control of a psychologist" (Crane, 1925, p. 228).

Even at that early time, a few ideological leaders recognized that medicine was not a suitable base for a profession dealing with human psychological problems. Sigmund Freud (1927) had argued at length that psychology, not medicine, was the basic discipline on which the practice of psychoanalysis should rest. Even earlier, in 1923, Karl Menninger had expressed his belief that medicine was an insufficiently comprehensive foundation for dealing with the full range of human problems. He realized that preventive efforts as well as remedies were needed, and that the intellectual discipline at the base of professional work would have to include psychological and social substance as well as biological content. He proposed the term *orthopsychics* to designate the field (cf. Reisman, 1966).

Neither Freud's argument nor Menninger's was heeded by the politically dominant medical practitioners of the day. Most psychoanalysts came into the profession by way of medicine and managed to define all practitioners who did not possess medical credentials as "laymen." Even Freud failed to grasp the significance of this semantic condition. He presented his arguments concerning the psychological basis for psychoanalytic practice under the self-defeating title, "The Problem of Lay Analysis." Medical men in charge of the rapidly forming psychoanalytic societies were firmly opposed to Freud's views, and medical training soon became established as a requirement for the fully qualified practice of psychoanalysis. Karl Menninger's proposals were molded to fit medical definitions by the society he organized to deal with human problems. The first group became known as the American Orthopsychiatric Association, rather than an orthopsychic or orthopsychological association. Active membership was required to hold office, and although members of all human service disciplines were invited to participate in the organization, active membership was restricted to Doctors of Medicine.

At the time Crane, Freud, and Menninger presented their proposals, professional psychology was small in size, indefinite in function, uncertain as to usefulness, and unclear about its own identity. Then and for the two decades to follow, the discipline was too weak to be taken seriously as a profession.

THE BOULDER CONFERENCE: SCIENCE ABOVE ALL

The first strong definition of clinical psychology came with statement of the scientist-practitioner concept by the Shakow committee (APA, 1947). Clinical psychologists were to be trained for research *and* practice. They were to be psychologists (read "scientists") first, and practitioners second. The concept was ratified and elaborated in the Boulder Conference (Raimy, 1950), whose impact is considered thoroughly in previous histories (e.g., Reisman, 1966; Watson, 1953) and does not need a detailed discussion here. For this account, it is enough to note that the Boulder Conference accomplished most of the aims it was designed to meet. The profession of clinical psychology was more securely established than it had been before, and the research needed for improving professional service was encouraged. During a period when the technical stock of clinical psychology consisted almost entirely of test-based diagnoses and evocative psychotherapies whose weaknesses were even then beginning to show, emphasis on research and development was sorely needed. Even more clearly, identification with science carried an important political advantage. In moments of candor, both psychiatrist and psychologist might admit their doubts about the benefits they could offer their clients. But now, when the psychiatrist said, "At least I know medicine," the psychologist could reply, "Well, I know science" and feel as secure as the physician. Psychologists might lose power skirmishes now and then, but their identity was established, and assurance as scientists, if not as professionals, could not easily be shaken.

The Boulder model served its purpose, but it also had its limitations as the only pattern for training clinical psychologists. Within a decade, flaws in the concept of a science-profession began to show. One problem with the scientist-practitioner programs was that they offered a poor match with student interests. Contrary to the assumptions of the Shakow Committee and the Boulder Conference, few students entered clinical training with strong interests in both research and service. As Thorndike (1955) suggested and later research (Peterson & Knudson, 1979) confirmed, clinical psychologists tended to be interested *either* in research *or* in practice (more commonly in the latter). A single hybrid program, requiring devotion to productive scholarship as well as human service, was ill-suited to their needs. Students interested in practice had to conceal their intentions to gain admission to research-oriented graduate programs. Once admitted, they either had to maintain the pretense, reveal their aims and incur the disfavor of their professors, or withdraw from training altogether.

An even more fundamental problem was that clinical programs in academic psychology departments came to emphasize research much more strongly than practice and offered poor preparation for the careers of professional service toward which many graduates were headed. In 1962, a turning point was reached in American psychology. For the first time, psychologists in academia were outnumbered by those in nonacademic positions (Tryon, 1963). At the APA convention in Los Angeles in 1964, impassioned practitioners seized microphones to shout that they had been betrayed by their professors. They had not been given the training they needed to meet the demands of professional life. For all the praise of science students heard in graduate school, relatively few did any research once they became immersed in practice. In two surveys (Kelly & Goldberg, 1959; Levy, 1962), the modal number of publications of clinical psychologists was shown to be zero. The scientist-practitioner model was designed to meet the dual purposes of scientific inquiry and professional service. In trying to reach both aims, it evidently accomplished neither. As scientists, the Boulder-style PhDs were unproductive. As professionals, they were incompetent.

THE CHICAGO CONFERENCE: TIMID EXPERIMENTATION

These conditions did not go unnoticed in organized psychology. In 1963, APA formed a committee on the scientific and professional aims of psychology with Kenneth E. Clark as chair and a distinguished membership that included Jerome Bruner, Lloyd Humphreys, Paul Meehl, Carl Rogers, and Kenneth Spence, among others. The committee met every 6 weeks over the academic year 1963–1964 and examined the issues of scientific and professional education in a searching way. With near unanimity, the committee concluded that the PhD programs then in effect for educating scientist-practitioners were neither preparing scientists for contributory research nor professionals for effective practice. They recommended creation of a two-track educational system. Students interested predominantly in research would be prepared to do research and receive the PhD degree. Students interested predominantly in practice would be prepared for professional service and receive the PsyD degree. Students interested in combining careers of research and practice would complete both courses of study and receive both degrees (APA, 1967).

The Clark Committee report was widely discussed in psychology departments and at state-level training conferences around the country, but the recommendation to develop professional doctoral programs was not generally well received. Psychologists in the state of Washington considered the issues of professional training at some length, but all they finally proposed were some master's level programs in applied psychology, and even these failed to materialize in the years to follow. A training conference in Ann Arbor, Michigan denounced the Doctor of Psychology concept and reaffirmed the scientist-professional model. Only two departments appeared to give the Clark Committee proposal the kind of consideration that might lead to the actual formation of professional doctoral programs. In Stillwater, Minnesota, Paul Meehl presented the main arguments for explicit professional training before a conference of psychologists working in academic and professional positions in that state. Meehl later said the conference participants seemed to agree with most of his proposals, but when a vote was called on the actual development of a Doctor of Psychology program in Minnesota, the proposal failed.

At the University of Illinois, Lloyd Humphreys brought the preliminary report of the Clark Committee before the psychology department faculty and proposed that Illinois undertake the formation of a Doctor of Psychology program. A formal debate was conducted on the issue, and at the end of the debate, a standing vote was taken among the 40 faculty members who attended the meeting. A more precise split of opinion could not have occurred. Ten people voted for the proposal, 10 voted against it, and 20 were undecided. This took place in June, 1965, a summer away from the Chicago Conference, where the issues of direct professional training were to receive more thorough examination than they had in previous national conferences.

The general outcomes of the Chicago Conference (Hoch, Ross, & Winder, 1966) are considered in previous chapters of this book. On the issue of outright professional training, ambivalence prevailed. As a majority opinion, the concept of the PhD-bearing scientist-professional stood supreme. A need to experiment with other patterns of training, however, was also generally appreciated, and the members of the conference were willing to wait and see what experimental efforts like the proposed Doctor of Psychology program at Illinois would come to. At the final vote, 12% gave "full endorsement" to the training alternative offered by a professional degree program. A larger group, 31%, offered "active encouragement" to such a development. The majority, however, 57%, were merely willing to extend "recognition" to the idea that explicit professional training programs might be attempted in some university departments, and that the results of those efforts should provide a basis for evaluating the programs at a later time.

I was seated next to Israel Goldiamond at the final plenary session. As the debate wore on into the early morning hours, Goldiamond became more and more amused at the blend of presumption and timidity our colleagues were showing, and he began to write his own resolutions. On the proposal for separate schools of psychology, rather than mere departments, he wrote, "We urge APA to consider a series of universities of psychology, within which the various specialties will be separate colleges, the subspecialties divisions, and the faculty members departments. Thus we would have a Department of Matarazzo in the Division of Interview Analysis in the College of Clinical Psychology in the University of Psychology." On the issue of levels of training, Goldiamond wrote, "We firmly resolve to look at a Bachelor of Psychology program. We observe a Master of Psychology program, provided it is not called a Master of Clinical Psychology program. We note a Doctor of Psychology program."

However pusillanimous the resolutions of the Chicago Conference seemed to some of us at the time, they at least allowed experimentation with the educational process and offered a willingness to let the results of responsibly conducted training experiments speak for themselves. After further debate in the autumn of 1965, another vote was taken at the University of Illinois to determine whether or not to establish a practitioner program there. This time, results were decisive. Full-time faculty voted 3.5 to 1 to go ahead with the program. Three more years were required to plan the curriculum, develop the admission procedures, gain the approvals, secure the supports, and recruit the faculty needed to operate the program. In September, 1968, the first class of students began graduate study (Peterson, 1968). Although other doctoral practitioner programs had been attempted before—at the University of Ottawa in the 1940s and at McGill University in the 1950s—and although the PsyD program at the University of Illinois has since been discontinued, the Illinois program carried the force of a respected faculty in a prestigious university, a rigorous curriculum, and an appearance of solidity that paved the way for other programs to follow.

In efforts to gain APA accreditation, early classes were disadvantaged by the policy that denies eligibility to programs that have not yet produced graduates. On grounds of institutional strength and stability, we proposed that a new category, "provisional approval," be created to accommodate programs that met the structural conditions for accreditation but were too new to offer performance records of graduates. The category was established in 1971. In 1972, the Illinois program became the first to be approved under the new designation we had helped create. Related problems were encountered with the U.S. Civil Service Commission, where requirements for clinical psychologists in the highest grades specified attainment of the PhD degree. With support from top-level administrators in the Veterans Administration (VA), the Civil Service requirements were rewritten in ways that accommodated our graduates. Since most state licensure and certification laws already allowed acceptance of other doctoral degrees than the PhD, such as the EdD, they did not appear to present problems of discriminatory exclusion, though they clearly presented problems of permissive overinclusion. Most of the laws permitted people with very questionable training in professional psychology to obtain the legal credentials needed to keep their jobs. For the time being, few changes were needed to assure the employability of our graduates, but we earnestly hoped that the movement we were starting would encourage more stringent licensure legislation in the future.

During the next few years, discussions about practitioner programs took place in many universities. Serious proposals were advanced in several, including New York University, the University of Minnesota, and Harvard, where the EdD rather than the PsyD degree would have certified completion of a program in clinical psychology and public practice, had the program ever gone into effect. For various local reasons, proposals for practitioner programs failed in all of the major research universities. During the 5 years following establishment of the Illinois program, only the Hahnemann Medical School and Baylor University developed PsyD programs.

THE VAIL CONFERENCE: OPENING THE DOOR

Dissatisfaction with professional training as conducted in traditional PhD programs continued to deepen, however, and insistence on change was expressed in many ways. At the time, the PsyD program at Illinois appeared vigorous and successful. The California School of Professional Psychology (CSPP; see chapter 25 in this volume) had grown in size and significance. Actions to develop professional schools in other states were well advanced. Important changes had occurred within and beyond psychology. Clinical psychology was a different discipline from that conceived at the Boulder Conference. School psychology was assuming a more definite form and higher stature than before. Early methods of assessment, treatment, and reeducation had been found wanting, and the assumptions underlying those methods had been questioned. A more mature professional psychology, yielding a few demonstrably effective methods and promising others, had taken shape. In the world beyond graduate school, the job market had changed. Psychologists with PhDs could no longer be sure of university positions and research opportunities upon graduation. At the same time, the public need for psychological services continued to grow. Mental hospitals were still being staffed by psychiatrically unschooled physicians and inadequately trained psychologists. The need for competent professional psychologists was as great as ever, and forecasts of our social future acknowledged a continuing need for effective applications of psychology. Programs that offered clear and obvious public benefits received more support than at any time since the early days of the land grant agricultural and technical schools. Psychology, higher education, and the general public all seemed ready for the development of expressly professional training programs.

These conditions culminated in another national training conference, at Vail, Colorado in 1973. Again, the complete report of the conference is on record (Korman, 1976), and some of its effects are described elsewhere in this volume (see chapter 25). For professional training in general and the Doctor of Psychology concept in particular, two resolutions were particularly important. First, "The development of psychological science has sufficiently matured to justify creation of explicit professional programs, in addition to programs for training scientists and scientist-professionals." Second, "We recommend that completion of doctoral level training in explicitly professional programs be designated by award of the Doctor of Psychology degree and that completion of doctoral level training in programs designed to train scientists or scientist-professionals be designated by award of the Doctor of Philosophy degree . . . Where primary emphasis in training and function is upon direct delivery of professional services and the evaluation and improvement of those services, the Doctor of Psychology degree is appropriate. Where primary emphasis is upon the development of new knowledge in psychology, the PhD degree is appropriate" (Korman, 1974, p. 443).

In the year following the Vail Conference, activities leading to establishment of the Graduate School of Applied and Professional Psychology at Rutgers University took place in rapid order. For years, an organizing council had been working to develop a school of professional psychology in New Jersey. The group consisted mainly of private practitioners in the state, with help from private citizens who possessed both personal interests in the education of professional psychologists and financial means to help the school get under way. Supportive relationships with legislators in the state were also formed. The original hope of the organizing council was to establish a freestanding school in the California pattern. The New Jersey Commission of Higher Education, however, had different rules from those in California. The leaders of the council were told that a degree-granting charter would be awarded only if enough capital were amassed to qualify the school as a private college, an amount far in excess of any sum the council seemed able to realize. From the council's side, the search began for a receptive university host. From the side of higher education, proposals to develop a school of professional psychology were put forward by the College of Medicine and Dentistry and by Rutgers, the State University of New Jersey. After a round of reviews and hearings, responsibility for establishing the school was assigned to Rutgers.

When the Graduate School of Applied and Professional Psychology admitted its first class of students in September 1974, it became the first university-based school of professional psychology to grant the Doctor of

Psychology degree. Two PsyD programs were created, one in school psychology and the other in clinical psychology. The PhD program in clinical psychology already in operation at Rutgers was continued. However, its purpose, to educate people for research in applied psychology, was more clearly defined than before.

The Vail Conference also recognized "the variety of new organizational settings within which professional training programs have begun to develop: e.g., medical schools; departments, schools and colleges of education; freestanding schools of professional psychology; autonomous professional schools in academic settings—in addition to departments of psychology in universities" (Korman, 1974, p. 443). This endorsement encouraged the establishment of professional schools, both inside and outside of universities, as well as Doctor of Psychology programs. The two developments were closely related, but not isomorphic. The founders of the CSPP thought they had enough resistance to overcome in establishing the first freestanding professional school of psychology without taking on the additional challenge of a new, controversial degree. They invoked the precedent and rationale of the Adelphi program (see chapter 25 in this volume) in persuading educational authorities in California that the PhD degree was the appropriate credential for "scholar-professionals" in psychology. Other professional schools in California followed suit. In states other than California, however, and especially in university-based programs wherever they were located, the joint policy of the Association of American Universities and the Council of Graduate Schools in the United States held sway. This policy is firm in stipulating that the professional doctor's degree be awarded in recognition of academic preparation for professional practice, whereas the Doctor of Philosophy degree be awarded in recognition of preparation for research, whether pure or applied. The MD, DDS, DVM, EdD, and DBA are cited as examples of professional degrees in the policy document.

The years following the Vail Conference saw rapid development of Doctor of Psychology programs, as shown in Table 1. The growth curve based on data in the table accelerates around 1974–1976 and shows an approximately linear increase from then on. Most of the recent additions, however, are not entirely new programs or professional schools. Rather, they are satellite campuses of previously established freestanding schools (e.g., the Minnesota School and the Missouri campus of the Forest Institute) or conversions to the PsyD of practitioner programs that had previously awarded the PhD degree. Partly because of growing acceptance of the PsyD and partly in response to pressure from their regional accrediting associations, several professional schools in California revised their programs in a two-track form, preserving relatively small PhD programs devoted primarily

TABLE 1
Establishment of Doctor of Psychology Programs From 1968 to 1991

Year	Institution
1968	University of Illinois (discontinued in 1980)
1970	Hahnemann Medical School (program now located at Widener University)
1971	Baylor University
1974	Fielding Institute
	Rutgers University
1975	Rosemead Graduate School (now affiliated with Biola University)
1976	Denver University
	Illinois School of Professional Psychology
	United States International University
1977	Central Michigan University
	Massachusetts School of Professional Psychology
	Wright State University
1978	Nova Unversity
	Virginia Consortium in Professional Psychology
1979	Chicago School of Professional Psychology
	Forest Institute
	Pace University
	Oregon School of Professional Psychology
1980	American Institute of Psychotherapy (now affiliated with Forest Institute)
	Florida Institute of Technology
	New York University
	Wisconsin School of Professional Psychology
	Yeshiva University
1981	Hawaii School of Professional Psychology (now affiliated with Forest Institute)
	Indiana State University
1982	Antioch New England Graduate School
	George Mason University (converted to PhD in 1990)
	Spalding University
1984	Indiana University of Pennsylvania
	Hartford University
1985	Forest Institute, Missouri campus
1986	Pepperdine University
1987	Alfred Adler Institute
	Minnesota School of Professional Psychology (affiliated with the Illinois School in the American Schools of Professional Psychology)
1988	California School of Professional Psychology (CSPP) at Los Angeles (conversion of PhD practitioner program to PsyD)
1991	Georgia School of Professional Psychology (affiliated with the American Schools of Professional Psychology)
	CSPP at Berkeley-Alameda (conversion from PhD to PsyD)
	CSPP at Fresno (conversion from PhD to PsyD)
	CSPP at San Diego (conversion from PhD to PsyD)

to education for applied research, and awarding the PsyD degree to the larger numbers of students enrolled in programs designed unambiguously as preparation for practice. This is the model originally proposed by the Clark Committee, implemented in the Illinois PsyD program, and kept in force in the Rutgers school, as well as the schools at Nova, Yeshiva, and Denver Universities. The Rosemead Graduate School, now affiliated with Biola University, was the first school in California to adopt the two-track pattern. More recently, the Fuller Graduate School, followed by the Los Angeles campus of the California School, and in 1991, the other three campuses of CSPP, at Berkeley-Alameda, Fresno, and San Diego, began to offer the PsyD to students preparing for professional careers, while maintaining PhD programs for students intending to pursue research careers.

SUCCESSES AND FAILURES: REFLECTIONS ON THE FIRST 25 YEARS

Each of the programs listed in Table 1 has a history of its own. The particular confluences of time, place, and person that led each effort on its course cannot be described fully in the space remaining. Attempted here is brief comment about some of the more conspicuous developments in the PsyD story, and a few tentative generalizations that the experiences of the first quarter century appear to justify.

The PsyD program at the University of Illinois was terminated in 1980. The most important conditions that led to this outcome were that the values of direct professional service, especially individual psychotherapy, were never deeply held nor widely shared by the faculty and administrators of the Illinois Psychology Department, and the administrative location of the program, in an academic department of a graduate college of a major research university, did not offer the autonomy and clarity of mission that a thoroughgoing professional program requires. A dissertation requirement was imposed by the Graduate College, and in time the requirement got out of hand. As the experimentalists, mathematical statisticians, biopsychologists, and clinical behaviorists who brought renown to the Illinois Psychology Department scrutinized PsyD dissertations, they seemed unable or unwilling to modify criteria to suit the projects that students in the practitioner program undertook. These were frequently ambitious field experiments of high complexity. The combination of problem difficulty and demand for scientific rigor led students into projects that took 2 and 3 years to complete. By the time the program was ended, the median time required to obtain the PsyD was 7.4 years.

After all this investment by faculty and students alike, substantial numbers of graduates went into private practice, devoting much of their time and energy to individual psychotherapy, an activity that few if any of the Illinois faculty approved. I paraphrase comments by the director of clinical training in charge when the PsyD program was discontinued: "No matter what we told applicants, no matter how carefully we described the preventive, community-oriented, behavioral emphasis in our program, students came in dreaming about professional lives as private practitioners of psychotherapy. Then they graduated and went out and did it. That was never what our program was designed to do."

The demise of the Illinois PsyD program is sometimes taken to mean that practitioner programs cannot survive in major research universities. The inaccuracy of this projection is shown by the evident prosperity of the programs at Rutgers and Yeshiva, both Class I research universities. The success of the Rutgers and Yeshiva programs seems due in large part to their location in relatively autonomous professional schools rather than academic departments. The PsyD program in school psychology at New York University (NYU), another major research university, also appears to be vigorous and durable, although many years of effort were required and many obstacles had to be overcome before Gilbert Trachtman and his colleagues managed to establish it. Attempts to develop a PsyD program in clinical psychology at NYU offer a demonstration on the other side, that is of the opposition to practitioner programs that is typical of research-oriented departments and typically defeats them.

Ideological conflict over the PsyD degree was intense in New York state. In a movement parallel with that of the council working to establish a school of professional psychology in New Jersey, a task force made up largely of practitioners from the New York State Psychological Association labored for nearly 5 years to create a freestanding professional school that would award the PsyD degree in New York. Their efforts were opposed by another faction, with objection to the practitioner degree led most conspicuously by Gordon Derner. Derner was an aggressive advocate of the scholar-practitioner model of education but a bitter opponent of the PsyD degree. Use of the degree, he believed, would damage the prestige of the profession.

The same division of opinion was represented among members of the New York Board of Regents, whose approval would be required for any new degree programs. A formal proposal for a PsyD program at Pace University, however, along with the activity at NYU and movement toward a graduate school of psychology that would grant the PsyD degree at Yeshiva University finally broke the deadlock. With support from the Secretary of the Board, the Regents approved the degree in March 1979. The program at Pace University was the first to be approved under the new ruling, followed shortly by the school psychology program at NYU and the Ferkauf Graduate School of Psychology at Yeshiva University.

Controversy over the degree has also been heated in other university settings. In New Hampshire, administrators and faculty seeking to establish the Antioch New England Graduate School of Psychology initially proposed award of the PhD degree, with strong encouragement from Gordon Derner, who was a member of their advisory board. Site visitors reporting to the New Hampshire Commission on Higher Education, however, made clear that the facilities, faculty, and intent of the Antioch program did not justify award of the PhD, although the necessary requirements for a professional program leading to the PsyD degree appeared to be met. Under these conditions, the Antioch team decided to "keep the ship and change the flag." Favorable recommendation by the New Hampshire Commission followed shortly thereafter.

A proposed program at George Mason University in Virginia bore most of the earmarks of a PhD scientist-practitioner program. Approval as a PhD program was denied, however, ostensibly on grounds that enough PhD programs were already operating in Virginia. In the face of apparently unbeatable opposition from educators at other Virginia universities, Alan Boneau and the George Mason faculty settled for approval of a program with clinical, industrial/organizational, and applied experimental components leading to the PsyD degree. After nearly 10 years of operation under that title, permission to award the PhD degree was granted by the State Council on Higher Education in Virginia.

The most successful university-based PsyD programs appear to be those that are organized within relatively autonomous academic units with a clear professional mission, as in the professional schools of Rutgers, Yeshiva, Wright State, and Denver Universities, or as departmental programs in regional or private universities where the emphasis on public service is strong and the demand for research production is not as consuming as it is in many of the major research universities. The program at Baylor has functioned quietly and effectively ever since its inauguration in 1971. The Virginia Consortium, Pace University, and Indiana State University, among others, all appear to be maintaining healthy PsyD programs.

In gauging prospects for success of a practitioner program, the importance of the institutional setting in which the program is located and of the value attributed to the practice of psychology in the surrounding community cannot be overemphasized. The histories of the program at Wright State University and of the program that was developed and maintained for years at the Hahnemann Medical School but was recently moved to Widener University offer vivid illustrations.

Part of the Wright State story is told in the preceding chapter, but a written account by its founder, Ronald Fox (1986), reveals even more sharply the importance of cultivating political and community support in ventures of this kind. At the time Fox returned from the Vail Conference, resolved to establish a professional school that would award the PsyD degree in Ohio, he was on the faculty of the Psychology Department at Ohio State University, and his first efforts were directed toward developing a professional school in his own institution. The actions that he took, however, were not confined to academia. His first step was to suggest to the President of the Ohio Psychological Association (OPA) the establishment of a committee, with Fox as chair, to study the desirability and feasibility of establishing a school in Ohio.

The OPA committee was duly established, incorporated as a separate nonprofit academy for education and research in professional psychology, in affiliative partnership with the OPA but not subject to supervision by the OPA Board of Trustees. They met with leaders of the Ohio General Assembly to secure advice on the cultivation of legislative support for the establishment of a professional school and secured the allegiance of the legislators as participants in creation of the school. The Academy found a welcome at Wright State University, the newest state university and one which did not have any other doctoral programs in operation. Not only persuaded by the soundness of the proposal, but almost surely motivated to attain the status of "doctoral degree-granting institution" within the higher education community, the Wright State administration offered the academy a home. Representatives from several universities and a number of psychology departments opposed creation of the program, but their efforts, according to Fox, were "poorly conceived and naively implemented." By ignoring state association affairs, leaders of existing university programs had lost touch with practitioners. By remaining aloof from the political arena, they had failed to earn the support of legislators.

When the University of Illinois closed its doors to PsyD applicants in 1980, the program at the Hahnemann Medical School became the oldest PsyD program in the country. It was organized as a Division of Psychology in the Department of Psychiatry. Relationships with the dean of the Medical School were cordial, and relationships with the chairman of the Department of Psychiatry were unusually close. The chairman of Psychiatry had worked with Jules Abrams, director of the Division of Psychology, to create the PsyD program, and held a sense of involvement and pride in it. He was later replaced by another chairman, Israel Zwerling, who had not only trained in psychiatry but had a doctoral degree in psychology. Zwerling and Abrams were instrumental in proposing a change in the name of the department from Psychiatry to Mental Health Sciences. The respect and support accorded to the administration, faculty, and students in the PsyD program in those years encouraged the development of a strong program that attracted several hundred applicants per year and became the second PsyD program to gain accreditation by APA.

These conditions began to change dramatically when the program was about 17 years old. At that time, a new dean of the Medical School was appointed and was at the same time appointed Senior Vice President for Academic Affairs of Hahnemann University (no longer Medical School). Shortly thereafter, a new chairman of the Department of Psychiatry (as he consistently referred to the Department of Mental Health Sciences) was hired. In keeping with general trends in medicine and psychiatry, the mission of the University had changed. Education of nonmedical professionals was clearly subordinated to research, especially in the neurosciences and biological substrates of "psychiatric diseases." The autonomy that the PsyD program once enjoyed eroded quickly. On more than one occasion, the chairman of the psychiatry department attempted to change the PsyD curriculum. He made clear to the director of the Division of Psychology that he regarded clinical psychology as subordinate to psychiatry. These conditions struck a mortal blow to the morale of Abrams, his faculty colleagues, and students. They also threatened APA accreditation and the future of the program.

An effort was made to reorganize the division as an autonomous department in the Graduate School of Hahnemann University. The dean of the Graduate School supported the move, but the chairman of the psychiatry department would not hear of it. The psychiatry chair was supported in this decision by the Senior Vice President for Academic Affairs, and the issue was closed.

Quietly, the search began for another aegis. Over the years, other universities in the Philadelphia area had approached the faculty and administration of the PsyD program, and contact was soon established with Widener University through the president of a third institution. Widener University, accredited by the Middle State Association of Schools and Colleges, was and is a rapidly growing institution whose major graduate educational mission is the training of practitioners in a variety of fields including law, education, nursing, health care management, and engineering. The general mission of the university was and is clearly consonant with that of the PsyD program. Negotiations to provide faculty appointments, physical space, additional library facilities, curriculum approvals, and other requirements were concluded rapidly but carefully, and in June 1989, the Hahnemann program moved en masse to Widener University as the Institute for Graduate Clinical Psychology, with its director an associate dean reporting directly to the dean of the Graduate School of Arts and Sciences.

Medical schools elsewhere have also offered fickle support for the education of professional psychologists. For years, clinical psychology and psychiatry worked together harmoniously at the University of Minnesota. A separate division of clinical psychology, within the psychiatry department but with all the autonomy psychologists required, was established there by Starke Hathaway. Hathaway and J. Charnley McKinley, chairman of the Department of Psychiatry, were co-authors of the original Minnesota Multiphasic Personality Inventory (MMPI). For a time, Hathaway was acting chairman of the psychiatry department. Over the years, however, equity in the relationship between psychiatry and psychology was seen to depend on the attitudes of medical administrators. In the 1970s, a proposal to develop a PsyD program in health psychology in the University of Minnesota medical school was squelched by a medical administration that some Minnesota psychologists have described as hostile, although ambivalent support from the academic psychology faculty also played a part in shelving the plan.

Besides academic departments and university-based professional schools, the main institutional settings for PsyD programs are freestanding professional schools. In every case, establishing these has been a demanding enterprise. As founders of independent professional schools, the organizers have faced formidable challenges in providing required resources. The physical plant, the library, the computer facilities, the faculty, and staff that are financed mainly by tax and endowment funds in universities are funded largely, in some cases almost entirely, by student tuition. This has meant either that tuition rates have been set at very high levels, or the quality of education has been so limited that regional and professional accreditation were difficult to attain.

Freestanding professional schools that award the PsyD degree are in double jeopardy, not only from economic constraints but also from the uncertainties that many still perceive in the PsyD degree. Despite these obstacles, 17 independent professional schools now award the PsyD degree in 10 different states. In many of the program plans, the PsyD was deliberately chosen as the preferred degree. In others, the practitioner degree was forced upon the schools by state authorities who would only approve degree-granting privilege on condition that the PsyD rather than the PhD be awarded. The recent shift to the PsyD among professional schools in California appears to have been motivated at least as strongly by pressure from their regional accrediting agency, the Western Association of Schools and Colleges, as by conviction that a coherent professional program and a professional degree are appropriate for practitioners.

Practitioners in state psychological associations have usually provided the moving force for creation of the schools. Formation of new schools, as in Massachusetts and Oregon, as well as incursions from one state to another, as in extension of the Illinois School to Minnesota and of the Forest Institute to Missouri, have typically followed invitations from practicing psychologists in states whose universities have previously restricted doctoral education in psychology to their own small research-oriented programs. In nearly every case, the proposals to develop PsyD programs in independent schools have been opposed by university psychologists, usually on grounds that the university programs are already meeting the need for professional psychologists, and often on grounds that preparation for the Doctor of Psychology degree is "unscholarly." Unlike academic psychologists, however, legislators and members of the general public on the executive boards of sanctioning agencies have found no difficulty in distinguishing between research production and scholarly education. They have recognized needs for competent practitioners in their communities, they have seen how poorly academic research programs meet those needs, and they have appreciated the public honesty of awarding a professional degree to practitioners of psychology.

Most of the programs they have approved, both inside and outside of universities, appear to be firmly established. Concerns about quality continue (Peterson, 1985, 1991) but are receiving more systematic and sustained attention through the conferences and related activities of the National Council of Schools of Professional Psychology (cf. chapter 25 in this volume) than ever before in the history of our field. The assumption that location of a program in a prestigious university guarantees quality but at the same time prohibits close external evaluation lest the sanctity of academic freedom be violated is no longer accepted as readily as it once was. Neither is the assumption that all practitioner programs are bad. Over the past 25 years, direct education for the practice of psychology and for the Doctor of Psychology degree, which is the strongest symbol of professional education in psychology, have been woven securely into the fabric of our institutions.

REFERENCES

American Psychological Association. (1935). (Section on Clinical Psychology, Committee on the Training of Clinical Psychologists.) The definition of clinical psychology and standards of training for clinical psychologists. *Psychological Clinic, 23*, 1–8.

American Psychological Association. (1947). Committee on Training in Clinical Psychology. Recommended graduate training program in clinical psychology. *American Psychologist, 2*, 539–558.

American Psychological Association. (1967). (Committee on Scientific and Professional Aims of Psychology.) The scientific and professional aims of psychology. *American Psychologist, 22*, 49–76.

Crane, L. (1925). A plea for the training of professional psychologists. *Journal of Abnormal and Social Psychology, 20*, 228–233.

Davies, A. E. (1926). An interpretation of mental symptoms of dementia praecox. *Journal of Abnormal and Social Psychology, 21*, 284–295.

Fox, R. E. (1986). Building a profession that is safe for practitioners: A personal perspective. *Psychotherapy in Private Practice, 4*, 3–12.

Freud, S. (1927). *The problem of lay analysis.* New York: Brentano's.

Hoch, E. L., Ross, A. E., & Winder, C. L. (Eds.). (1966). *Professional preparation of clinical psychologists.* Washington, DC: American Psychological Association.

Kelly, E. L., & Goldberg, L. R. (1959). Correlates of later performance and specialization in psychology: A follow-up study of the trainees assessed in the VA Selection Research Project. *Psychological Monographs, 73* (No. 12; Whole No. 482).

Korman, M. (1974). National conference on levels and patterns of professional training in psychology: The major themes. *American Psychologist, 29*, 441–449.

Korman, M. (Ed.). (1976). *Levels and patterns of professional training in psychology.* Washington, DC: American Psychological Association.

Levy, L. H. (1962). The skew in clinical psychology. *American Psychologist, 17*, 244–249.

Peterson, D. R. (1968). The Doctor of Psychology program at the University of Illinois. *American Psychologist, 23*, 511–516.

Peterson, D. R. (1985). Twenty years of practitioner training in psychology. *American Psychologist, 40*, 441–551.

Peterson, D. R. (1991). Connection and disconnection of research and practice in the education of professional psychologists. *American Psychologist, 46*, 422–429.

Peterson, D. R., & Knudson, R. M. (1979). Work preferences of clinical psychologists. *Professional Psychology, 10*, 175–182.

Raimy, V. C. (Ed.). (1950). *Training in clinical psychology.* Englewood Cliffs, NJ: Prentice-Hall.

Reisman, J. M. (1966). *The development of clinical psychology.* New York: Appleton-Century-Crofts.

Thorndike, R. L. (1955). The structure of preferences for psychological activities among psychologists. *American Psychologist, 10,* 205–207.

Tryon, R. C. (1963). Psychology in flux: The academic-professional bipolarity. *American Psychologist, 18,* 134–143.

Watson, R. J. (1953). A brief history of clinical psychology. *Psychological Bulletin, 50,* 321–346.

27

RESEARCH ON TRAINING FOR PSYCHOTHERAPY

RUTH G. MATARAZZO AND ANN M. GARNER

Explicit training for psychotherapy has a relatively brief history. Research on training for psychotherapy has a briefer history still. Nineteenth-century psychiatry, like other fields of study, followed the pattern of "master" and students. Charcot, for example, had as his students Janet, Binet, Freud, and many other younger learners who were to contribute to the field. As is well known, Freud himself had his circle of followers (Jung, Adler, and others) to whom he imparted the results of his own work with patients. Often a case conference was employed, as in Freud's Wednesday evening meetings in 1905 (Strupp, Butler, & Rosser, 1988). In a famous case, one of Freud's first "students" was the father of a 5-year-old phobic boy; the father was instructed by Freud in ways of collecting information from his son and responding in a therapeutic manner. Detailed consideration of developments in this early period may be found in chapters 3, 4, 13, and 17 of this volume and in Strupp et al. (1988). Like Sigmund Freud before them, Anna Freud of the "Vienna School," Melanie Klein of the "English School," and Adolf Meyer of the "Boston group" taught their students in the manner of master to apprentice.

The influence of Freud and his early students permeated psychotherapy during the 1920s and 1930s. Direct lines of connection become blurred with time, however, and it is doubtful that one can speak of the professionals of those years as having been trained in a formal way. To learn psychoanalysis, one had to be analyzed. In current terminology, this could be described as modeling and experiential learning. Supervision techniques also were similar to those of treatment. The supervisor listened to a recounting of what the therapist remembered to be important and interpreted the dynamics of both trainee and patient. In this, as in forms of training that have developed subsequently, it was hoped that the student would develop increased self-awareness and personal effectiveness, as well as increased psychotherapeutic skill.

From the earliest years of the 20th century, two major lines of training in psychotherapy have prevailed. One is the *didactic* approach, which depends upon the imparting of knowledge and skills by a teacher to a student. The other is the *supervisory* approach, which depends upon a dyadic interaction between teacher and student in which, typically, the details of a particular ongoing case are discussed. Each approach may be used in either an individual or group setting. Historically, however, the didactic approach has more often been a group enterprise, such as lectures or modeling for a graduate class, whereas the supervisory approach has more commonly been an individual, face-to-face interaction between supervisor and supervisee.

In the learning experience itself, students ordinarily go through the didactic phase first, in the context of a graduate psychology department or professional school. Later, during internship or residency, they develop a supervisee role in a relationship with one or more supervisors. The latter role may persist for many years, even throughout their professional careers, as they seek guidance from peers when difficult therapeutic issues arise.

Neither in its didactic aspect nor in supervision, however, was formal research on training for psychotherapy as we know it today to be seen in the first three decades of the 20th century. Statements of desirable or necessary qualities in students wishing to become psychotherapists were numerous, but no objective definitions of these qualities or their correlations with effective psychotherapy were developed.

The dominance of a broadly defined psychoanalytic/dynamic orientation within a predominantly medical model served as a rationale for psychiatrists to screen patients before referring them when anyone other than a psychiatrist was allowed to conduct therapy, and to supervise psychotherapy. The zeitgeist favored a nonempirical, theoretical persuasion taught in a relatively authoritarian manner, by what its members believed was the most prestigious (medical) profession, to junior members of their own profession or those of lesser rank (psychologists, social workers, and psychiatric nurses, in that order).

DIDACTICS OF TRAINING

Beginnings of Research in Training for Psychotherapy

As early as the 1930s, however, in a university counseling center free of medical domination, Carl Rogers began to develop an empirical approach to establishing what he postulated to be the measurable, effective ingredients of psychotherapy, and a specified series of graded experiences to teach them most effectively to graduate students in psychology (Rogers, 1942, 1957; also, see chapter 19 in this volume).

Some of the ingredients were behaviorally defined skills of the therapist in contrast to the earlier, almost exclusive emphasis on the therapist's understanding and interpretation of patient dynamics. Therapist behavior itself had tended not to be observed, nor were its effects considered. Therapists were not to intrude upon the psychological processes of their patients. To maintain objectivity and to avoid reactive effects, they were relatively passive listeners, allowing their patients to structure therapy, and allowing dynamics to unfold for later interpretation.

By turning primary attention from the understanding of patient dynamics to provision of a *therapeutic atmosphere*, Rogers' client-centered, or *nondirective* therapy paradoxically empowered the therapist and made him or her more responsible for patient improvement. No longer could patient resistance be considered the primary factor in therapeutic failure. The therapist's behavior needed to be considered as well, along newly defined dimensions. Despite the nondirective appellation, Rogers' theory dictated a more responsible role for the therapist in which his or her behavior and attitude were important in determining patient progress. At the same time, the client's dignity, importance, and responsibility were elevated by the more egalitarian nature of the relationship and recognition of the client's own drive toward psychological growth, which the therapist was to release.

The client-centered school was thus in tune with a newly emerging zeitgeist; increased empiricism, emphasis upon behavior rather than cognitive understanding, and egalitarianism characterized by increased openness to observation, the use of peer teaching, and a nonauthoritarian relationship between trainer and trainee, in which the trainer could be fallible. Beyond the private preserve of medical psychiatrists and their *patients*, psychologists now were free to treat their *clients*, and to engage in empirical research, the hallmark of their profession, not only on process and outcome in psychotherapy, but also on the preparation of trainees for the psychotherapeutic task.

Rogers (1942, 1957) was the first psychologist to describe a theory and technique of psychotherapy that gave psychology a "home of its own." He and his students provided the strongest influence toward making psychotherapy observable, its practice and training techniques specifiable, and its results measurable. The 1950s through the 1970s were an era of enthusiastic research in the teaching of client-centered therapy. Rogers (1957) developed a series of graded training experiences. These were examined and elaborated further by Truax and Carkhuff (1967), who developed a didactic–experiential training program, primarily designed to teach Rogers' "necessary and sufficient" basic therapeutic skills, which were largely attitudinal. This program was broadly based on psychological theories and psychologists' research. It combined Rogers' theoretical ideas and graded steps in learning with ideas from programmed learning, behavior modification, social learning theory, and group therapy. It employed didactic material; recorded role-playing with feedback; recorded actual interviews with self-observation, peer, and supervisor feedback; and used quasigroup therapy. Research instruments (scales) were developed for supervisors and others to rate student therapists' behavior on such therapist "conditions" as empathy and patients' behavior on such variables as depth of self-exploration. Dozens of research articles were stimulated by this general approach.

Later Developments in Teaching Experiential Psychotherapy

Criticisms of the research on client-centered therapy grew through the late 1960s and into the 1970s. Criticisms, however, were directed toward research methodology and therapeutic concepts rather than toward teaching method per se. Difficulty in developing instruments of measurement became apparent. Researchers' ratings of empathy, for example, often did not agree with patient ratings of the same interview (Burstein & Carkhuff, 1968; Caracena & Vicory, 1969; Hansen, Moore & Carkhuff, 1968). Judges' ratings on some scales apparently were not measuring what they were presumed to measure; for example, "accurate empathy" seemed to be a general "good–bad" dimension (Chinsky & Rappaport, 1970; Rappaport & Chinsky, 1972). Empathy ratings apparently were related to therapist reflection of emotion, whether accurate or not (Wenegrat, 1974). Single, subjective ratings of brief taped segments of therapist behavior were found to be inadequate, with validity and reliability problems indicating that a change of approach was necessary for further progress (see Matarazzo, 1978; Matarazzo & Patterson, 1986).

This was a stage of research that clearly revealed the necessity for increased sophistication and objectivity in specification of behaviors to be measured and the means of measurement. The teaching of techniques themselves essentially could not be evaluated because of the complexity or vagueness of variables to be measured and the inadequacies of the means of measurement.

Some Beginnings in Using More Objectively Defined Variables

Some objectively measurable interview variables have been recorded by means of the Interaction Recorder (Wiens, Matarazzo, & Saslow, 1965). With this instrument, the therapist's and patient's number and length of utterances (talk-time), latency of responses (silence), and number of interruptions can be recorded. Matarazzo, Phillips, Wiens, & Saslow (1965) and Matarazzo, Wiens, & Saslow (1966) correlated the chronograph measurements with therapist "errors" as rated on a check list. With training, therapists decreased their errors and their talk-time while patients increased their average length of utterance. Students showed the greatest progress when supervisors observed their interviews regularly and followed up with combined supervisor and peer discussion. Matarazzo and Wiens (1977) subsequently found a relationship between length of therapist reaction time, length of utterance, and judges' ratings of empathy.

Microtraining

Ivey and Authier (1978); and Ivey (1980, 1983) developed a training program to teach basic interviewing skills (*microtraining*, later developed into Modern Rogerian Encounter Skill Pattern [MRESP]). The skills are similar to those described by the client-centered group but are more specifically and behaviorally defined. One behaviorally defined skill was to be taught at a time. For example, *attending* behavior is described in written material given to the student. It is defined as including eye contact, specific body language, verbal encouragement for the client to continue speaking, and intermittent paraphrasing to indicate that close attention is being paid to content and feeling.

In addition to giving more behavioral definition to therapeutic skills, Ivey's training program is more exactly specified, and stages of learning are evaluated by videotape rather than audiotape. Training proceeds through five specific steps: (a) conducting a 5-minute interview; (b) reading didactic material describing one of the skills, such as attending behavior; (c) viewing videotaped models who display both good and poor examples of attending; (d) viewing one's own initial interview and identifying good and poor examples of attending; and (e) re-interviewing the same client in a second, videotaped interview. The other skills are reflection of feeling, summarization, and self-disclosure. Ivey has described these as skills of listening and of influencing without directing (Weinrach, 1990). The brevity and simplicity of these training steps made it possible to repeat the procedure as needed to criterion level for any single skill before proceeding to the next.

The results of research by Ivey and others indicate that this training procedure is effective, and apparently more effective than the Truax and Carkhuff model (Moreland, Ivey, & Phillips, 1973; Toukmanian & Rennie, 1975) in teaching the intended therapist behaviors. Unfortunately, the problem of measuring resulting patient improvement has not been studied as well, although some attempts have been made and positive results have been reported (e.g., Haase & DiMattia, 1970). The importance of additional input from a supportive supervisor has been noted (e.g., Ivey, 1983; Kelley, 1971). This will receive more detailed discussion in the section on supervision to follow.

Considerable further research has been conducted on the relative effectiveness of various subparts of the training program. The variables that have been examined most frequently include didactic material, modeling, videotaping with subsequent self-confrontation, supervision, peer feedback, and both simulated and in vivo practice, studied as individual variables or in varying combinations.

Not surprisingly, a combination of several training components seems to be more effective than only one or a few components. For example, students did not learn as effectively to decrease their duration of speech and number of interruptions by viewing their own videotaped interviews alone as they did by viewing the tapes in the company of a supervisor (Kelley, 1971). Specificity and immediacy of supervisor input also appeared to be important (Doyle, Foreman & Wales, 1977; Payne, Winter & Perry, 1975). Modeling of both high and low levels of skill was more effective than modeling of high skills alone (Eskedal, 1975; Saltmarsh, 1973). It appears that each component of training is helpful, and, in general, the more components, the better. In this program, as in the Didactic–Experiential program of Truax and Carkhuff, it is clear that some important new components have been provided.

However, the ultimate measurement of training adequacy, that of patient improvement, for the most part has continued to be relatively crudely measured, if at all. Historic problems in measurement of patient benefit have been described by Korchin and Sands (1980). In the 1950s, researchers made crude global comparisons of one group's level of improvement with that of another, mixing those who had improved a little with those who had improved a great deal, and dimensions of change were not considered. Also, it has been difficult to gain access to individuals who would constitute appropriate no-treatment controls. It is necessary to group patients by problem type, as well as by other characteristics that are likely to affect outcome.

Manual-Guided Training

Over the past decade, manual-guided training has become an important tool in research on the efficacy of psychotherapy. Manuals are intended for use by the journeyman psychotherapist and give explicit directions for conducting psychotherapy with a given patient population by means of a specific, theoretically based program. For the purpose of studying treatment outcome, manuals have been found to reduce variability in therapist adherence to the program and thus to reduce one important source of error variance. In one such study, Rounsaville, O'Malley, Foley, and Weissman (1988) trained therapists to provide interpersonal psychotherapy for depression. Therapeutic goals were stated to be alleviation of depression and improved interpersonal functioning. The training process included a review of the training manual (Klerman, Weissman, Rounsaville, & Chevron, 1984), a seminar, and the supervised conduct of psychotherapy.

The manual provided descriptions of specific techniques and strategies, and the seminar further explicated this material and provided videotaped illustrations of therapeutic techniques. Individual supervision included discussion of videotaped sessions. Later assessment of therapist competence was accomplished via four rating forms developed especially to evaluate therapist competence in regard to technique and strategy. This study demonstrated the potential usefulness of manual-guided instruction, employing the additional training techniques of seminars and supervision with videotaping. Experienced psychotherapists were able to achieve a high rate of competence after relatively brief training, and their competence was maintained over time. Furthermore, those who showed greatest adherence to the program were shown to have higher ratings of efficacy.

This and related studies suggest that manuals may be another step in the development of new methods of teaching some basic aspects of psychotherapeutic skill. The importance of adjunctive supervision and observation, however, is noted. Several additional manuals stem from different theoretical orientations. Gendlin has written a description of focusing (1981); Rennie (1987) has produced a manual to teach client-centered skills; and

Rice and Saperia (1984) have described the steps to problem resolution with clients. These and other manuals (Luborsky, 1984; Strupp & Binder, 1983) describing "second-generation" experiential therapy are described by Greenberg and Goldman (1988). The manuals attempt to specify what experiential therapists do, when a specific intervention should be used, and what therapist intentions lie behind the behaviors. Preliminary research suggests that the skills can be learned at least to a moderate degree of expertise through manuals so that, for example, experiential therapists' therapeutic behaviors are discriminable from the behaviors of therapists who follow other orientations.

It should be noted that manuals have been used primarily for the journeyman to upgrade skills or to ensure, in research studies, that an experienced therapist is following the particular theoretical model of treatment for a given diagnostic group under study. This is a large step forward from early studies in which psychotherapy was conceptualized as a generic form of treatment for a variety of emotional and behavioral problems.

Evolution of Behavioral Approaches to Psychotherapy: Training Behavior Therapists

There is some overlap between research on the training process and research on the process and outcome of psychotherapy itself. Both involve administering those conditions thought to be most efficacious in producing behavioral change in the direction of growth. Presumably the factors that enable patients to develop more effective behavior in living also will be instrumental in enabling the therapist-in-training to increase his or her skill. Theories of psychotherapy are based upon theories of how behavior can be altered. In the psychodynamic view, it involves recall of traumatic memories, abreaction, relating to the therapist as one did to parental figures, and coming to understand through therapist interpretation the child's view of what was happening at an earlier, problematic time. Thus, the training analysis for would-be psychoanalysts follows the pattern of psychoanalysis with clinical patients. In the client-centered, experiential view discussed previously, one of the therapists' dominant responsibilities is to provide a therapeutic, egalitarian, open atmosphere in which the natural growth tendencies of clients are nurtured toward their fullest level of development. This atmosphere is likewise to be provided to student therapists. In behavioral approaches to treatment, by contrast, the therapist is cast as a psychological educator whose job is to identify patterns of dysfunctional behavior displayed by clients and to engineer changes in the conditions, both external and internal, that have given rise to or are maintaining maladaptive behavior. This "educational" attitude is seen especially clearly in the training of parent-therapists.

Operant and Respondent Conditioning

Behavior therapy started with Pavlov's *conditioning*, and was probably first used with humans by Watson in the 1920s. However, behavior therapy did not become an important form of treatment until the 1960s, as it was first applied with relative success to groups that were considered poor therapeutic risks, including chronic psychotic populations, individuals with impulse control problems, some phobias, and young children.

An important class of behavioral techniques, namely operant methods, had their origin in the work of B. F. Skinner, who, with Ogden Lindsley, first applied operant principles to change the behavior of chronic psychotics who were not capable of participating in goal-directed verbal interactions with a therapist (Lindsley, 1960; Skinner & Lindsley, 1954). The patients were reinforced, often with candy, for lever-pressing behavior, as an attempt to motivate them to perform simple problem solving. The techniques were received enthusiastically by other professionals and used in many settings in which lay therapists were employed. Training and supervision of the lay therapists was largely unspecified, however, and its inadequacy appears to have been an important factor in possible misuse of the techniques with incarcerated populations. This resulted in public criticism and abandonment or retrenchment of many of the programs.

Lovaas and his collaborators (Lovaas, 1978; Lovaas & Newsom, 1976; Lovaas & Simmons, 1969; Lovaas & Smith, 1989) were among the first to apply operant conditioning techniques to the individual behavioral excesses and deficiencies of autistic, retarded, and schizophrenic children, rewarding them for appropriate verbal interactions and conformity to verbal requests from their therapists. Nonprofessional therapists were used, but their specific training procedures were not emphasized. Another well-developed program for children is that of Patterson and his colleagues (Patterson, 1982; Patterson, Cobb, & Ray, 1973). They, as well as numerous others, have taught operant techniques to parents whose children were noncompliant. In these programs, major interest has focused on behavior improvement of the children rather than techniques of training the parent-therapists. However, some publications of this group have described lay therapist training programs in detail. A didactic component has been used, along with modeling, group discussion, homework and record keeping, and reinforcement. Eyberg and Matarazzo (1980) found individual parent training with observation and coaching to be more effective than group instruction with homework and discussion. Fortunately, in these operant conditioning programs, it is relatively easy to measure patient in-session behavior change (e.g., child's compliance, number of tantrums) and thus to monitor both treatment efficacy and parent-therapist acquisition of therapeutic skills.

Classical Pavlovian conditioning, extended to incorporate the principle of reciprocal inhibition, was first applied to clinical populations by Wolpe (1958), who has used it primarily in the treatment of anxiety and phobias. At the outset, it was thought that application of operant or classical conditioning principles would in itself effect the desired changes. However, most behavior therapists now believe that the therapist must be trained more broadly to provide a therapeutic climate and to employ a variety of therapeutic strategies.

Behavior therapy, being concerned with overt symptoms, is positioned to define specific aspects of the patient's problem and treatment goals (i.e., an increase or decrease in observable, targeted behaviors). The process of therapy has been described simply as *re-education*. In the past decade, most behavior therapists have come to believe that this re-education involves cognitive processes that mediate between the stimulus and response (e.g., cognitive *expectancies*), thus removing behavior therapy from its earlier, simpler format, but at the same time introducing somewhat less defined clinical skills and procedures.

Fairly precise initial assessment is the sine qua non of behavior therapy and probably the characteristic that most distinguishes it from other therapies. Thus, one of the trainee's first tasks is to develop assessment skills. The latter include the ubiquitous interview of the patient and perhaps of significant others, but also additional observations and ratings. Often the patient must engage in record keeping of self, and ratings of patient behavior by others may be requested. The therapist also observes the patient, perhaps using ratings or data recording. After the diagnostic formulation has been completed, the actual therapeutic procedures are often administered by lay therapists.

One of the most ambitious and demonstrably successful programs of this kind has been developed over a 20-year period by Gordon Paul (1987). Paul has described the importance of thorough behavioral assessment of both patients and staff in inpatient treatment settings. He refers to the underutilization and inefficient use of resources that make inpatient treatment cost-ineffective and contribute to the well-known "revolving door" phenomenon in mental hospitals. He noted that less than 15% of staff time is spent in client contact in state and Veterans Administration (VA) hospitals, and less than 25% in private hospitals.

By creating a well-defined system of activities, attitudes, and locations, it was possible to develop a reliable rating system that could be carried out by nonprofessional staff on an hourly basis. As Paul (1987) points out, the specific behaviors, their frequency of occurrence, and other situation-specific information are of primary importance in pinpointing the individual patient's mental health problems, in documenting the occurrence of therapeutic intervention and improvement in patient behavior, and in documentation of staff development. Specific activity (e.g., playing cards), the social orientation of the individual during this occurrence (e.g., patient is alone), his or her facial expression and physical position, and location on the service are all highly meaningful when documented hourly over a period of days or weeks. The data are computerized and available for training purposes, research, quality assurance studies, and so forth. It is a relatively sophisticated program that provides hope for further improvement in the efficacy of behavioral treatment, staff training, and research.

As with other theoretical orientations to psychotherapy, didactic presentation of behavioral principles by itself has not been found to be a fully effective teaching technique. Gardner (1972) found that, in teaching the principles of behavior therapy to lay therapists, role playing was more effective than didactic presentation. Salzinger, Feldman, and Portnoy (1970) taught the mothers of brain-injured children to carry out behavior modification programs. They employed both presentation of didactic material and implementation of follow-up procedures such as checking parent record keeping. They found that effectiveness of the therapy depended upon *maintaining* parental conformity to the program. Among lay therapists—including parents—socioeconomic status, education, and motivation have been found to be important factors in both the learning and maintenance of treatment skill.

Both group and individual training have been attempted, with greater effect sometimes for one and sometimes for the other. However, from the literature, it is not clear what specific aspects of individual or group training are most effective, whether group process has been effectively used, or how subjects have been selected. As with the teaching of professionals, it appears that didactic presentation is a necessary starting point, but modeling, role-playing, videotaping, and feedback/reinforcement have been found in some studies to be especially important in the training of lay therapists.

Cognitive–Behavioral Therapy

New developments in behavior therapy over the past decade involve both cognitive and behavioral components. In these treatments, more subtle and less objectively defined variables have replaced the simpler variables that were considered appropriate to treatment and to teaching operant techniques solely. Lipsey (1987) has pointed out that current behavior therapies are dependent upon a number of "small theories" about the cause of a problem behavior and how it can be ameliorated. Definition of the problem and selection of treatment method may vary according to the particular theory.

Bootzin and Ruggill (1988) have described the necessary aspects of a training program for broad spectrum behavior therapists. These include operational definition of therapeutic behavioral skills, specification of training objectives, an accurate description of the training processes, the use of quantitative measures of student change, pretraining assessments, the use of control groups, equivalent training time across treatment groups, and multiple criterion measures. These are recognized as reasonable and necessary criteria, but seldom have they been fulfilled.

The aforementioned authors recommended broad, scientific training as a core element and see the primary goal of professional training as "to prepare students to be active learners over the course of their professional lifetime" (Bootzin & Ruggill, 1988). They note the need for valid, useful instruments for measuring competence in skills which are then related to client improvement. Sechrest and Chatel (1987) indicate that self-assessment programs should be developed so that practitioners can monitor their own competence years after licensure and specialty board examinations.

In rational–emotive therapy, which falls under the broad umbrella of cognitive–behavioral orientation, training programs are described, but little actual research has been done on training outcome (Ellis, 1989; Wessler & Ellis, 1980). It is interesting to note that the varied training techniques initiated by Rogers are now followed, with some variations, by most theoretical persuasions, including that of the rational–emotive group. The training is described as starting with a master–apprentice relationship, in which teaching takes place primarily in small groups. Tape recordings are used, with playback in the group, and selective listening for behaviors identified as significant in this theoretical orientation (e.g., "irrational beliefs"). Training involves role playing among group members, modeling of new interventions by the supervisor, follow-up and feedback on case progress, videotaping of the supervisory group for replay, and exchange of tape recordings among students, who give each other written feedback comments. To check on supervisee learning and follow-through, he or she may be asked to tape-record a session in which the ideas given in the supervisory group are being practiced.

Self-supervision, with a checklist of things to listen for (e.g., Was the session actively structured? What irrational beliefs were identified?) is suggested during training and as a later means for therapists to give themselves regular supervisory check-ups.

Convergence of Theoretical Viewpoints

Dating from the early 1970s, the tenor of both theorizing and research in psychotherapy has been changing. An increasingly ecumenical and eclectic climate has followed the discovery of interrelationships among variables from differing theoretical viewpoints. An acceptance of some basic, common variables is supported by research showing that different forms of psychotherapy are equally effective, although probably for different kinds of problems. Over several decades of research, no theoretical orientation has been demonstrated to be consistently more effective than others, suggesting that we should look for their common ingredients (e.g., Korchin & Sands, 1980). All seem to include, for example, "the communication of person-related understanding, respect, and a wish to be of help" (Reisman, 1971, p. 66). It is important to measure what therapists actually do, as opposed to what they say they do or intend for others to do.

Korchin and Sands have discussed therapeutic competence as consisting of two factors: (a) therapeutic climate, and (b) therapeutic process and strategies. The importance of a therapeutic climate appears to be an area of agreement among schools and is essentially what the client-centered group first defined. It was primarily this less intellectual, more affective and interpersonal aspect of therapy that the client-centered group struggled, with mixed success, to measure.

Therapeutic process and strategies, the second factor identified by Korchin and Sands, continues to be more subject to theoretical dispute, although here also, areas of agreement can be found, as in the importance of self-exploration, the placebo effect, and the need for emotional relearning in a therapeutic context. Some of these differences are beginning to be addressed by the earlier described studies that are using manual-based training. The latter research seems to suggest that more than one form of therapy may be about equally effective for a given psychological condition.

It is clear that much further research remains to be done on training efficacy. We have learned that multiple measures of both therapist behavior and patient improvement are necessary to study the complex, interrelated aspects of the therapeutic process and to compensate for the fact that many of our concepts remain poorly defined and most measuring instruments crude.

SUPERVISION

The majority of the training methods we have described are most suitable for a didactic teaching situation, broadly defined. A second group of training approaches is more likely to involve the supervisory aspect of training, which requires a different form of conceptualization.

Once the basic therapeutic philosophies and skills have been mastered through didactic learning in classroom and practicum, students begin to do psychotherapy full-scale, and entrance into a supervisory relationship follows. As indicated earlier, efforts to define the supervisory relationship can be traced back many decades. Changes over time depend upon the traditions of the profession, the nature of the therapy being taught, technical advance in treatment methods, prevailing philosophies of the teacher, and doubtless many other factors. The elemental composition and basic nature of the supervision model, however, remain the same: a one-on-one, face-to-face discussion between teacher and learner.

Supervision, viewed in this context, has been defined as ". . . a quintessential interpersonal interaction with the general goal that one person, the supervisor, meets with another, the supervisee, in an effort to make the latter more effective in helping people in psychotherapy" (Hess, 1980, p. 25). To most educators, "Supervision is still the cornerstone of clinical training" (e.g., Moldawsky, 1980, p. 134).

The unique characteristics of the supervisory relationship make it a triangular one, involving all the complexities and perils of such a relationship. In this configuration, each apex of an equilateral triangle represents one of the three participants in this relationship; supervisor, supervisee, and client. Each side then represents a two-way interpersonal relationship: supervisor–supervisee, supervisee–client, and supervisor–client. Supervisor and supervisee develop a mutual interaction, in which the principal focus is upon the client. Inevitably, however, relationship issues arise between supervisor and supervisee stemming from possible differences in experience, theoretical stance, gender, cultural background, and teaching method. Concomitantly, supervisee and client are also developing a mutual interaction, the explicit purpose of which, broadly stated, is a change in the client's behavior in the direction of greater effectiveness or maturity. The many variables present in these two interactions form the basis for a large part of the research on supervision.

The supervisor and the client, on the other hand, develop no explicit interaction. The client may be informed that there is a supervisor, but to the client, this person remains a shadowy figure about whom no identifying information is known. For the supervisor's part, the client may be known only second-hand, through verbal reports from the supervisee, although ideally also through intermittent observation or videotaping of therapy sessions.

Although any social situation as complex, important, and regularly enacted as this would seem to lend itself to a variety of analyses and studies, in reality there is a paucity of acceptable psychological research on supervision. A cursory survey suggests that even in the number of publications on supervision, regardless of quality, psychology lags behind such fields as counseling and social work.

Research on supervision as a separate phenomenon, apart from the broad field of learning psychotherapy, began in the 1920s (Leddick & Bernard, 1980). This was the period of the development of supervisory models, most notably the model based on dynamic psychoanalytic theory. This decade yielded little formal research; interest centered rather upon the characteristics and needs of the supervisee. Relationships between trainee and supervisor were authoritarian, following the earlier psychoanalytic pattern. It remained for Rogers, in the 1950s, to use notions of empathy and unconditional positive regard as a component of supervision (Rogers, 1957). His program of graded experiences provided opportunities for modeling and practice. However, the precise variables involved in this procedure, and the means by which trainees were to identify and use them, were not explicitly defined. As has been seen earlier in this chapter, it remained for Truax and Carkhuff (1967) to define the terms operationally.

Once some definitions were available, investigators studied such variables as supervisor roles, nature of supervisor–supervisee relationships, effects of supervisory experience upon the trainee, and similarities between supervisory and therapeutic relationships. Results of these early investigations were contradictory and for the most part, uninformative (see Leddick & Bernard, 1980).

The methodological problems that characterize the published studies are many. Subjects of investigation are often beginning students, or even paraprofessionals, with little experience in the therapeutic situation. Numbers are too small for decisive statistical analysis. Situations studied are often analogues, contrived for research purposes, but providing a shaky base for generalization. When samples of behavior taken from actual therapeutic interchange are used, they are necessarily brief and difficult to comprehend out of context. Although numerous measuring devices are available for assessing change in supervisee or client, they do not always meet commonly accepted standards of reliability and validity. The designs of many studies are questionable. Attempts to study changes over time, for example, may employ different measures in pre- and posttreatment appraisal.

Effects of Supervisor and Supervisee Characteristics Upon the Supervisory Situation

The goal of any training situation is to alter the behavior of the trainee in certain defined directions. In the supervisory model, presumably, supervisors seek to promote the development of supervisees along lines that increase their effectiveness in treating troubled clients. To this task, the supervisors bring an array of interrelated personal and professional characteristics, experience, theoretical orientations, preferred teaching methods, cultural backgrounds, and—equally important—such inherent qualities as gender and race. However, the effect of any one characteristic cannot be easily isolated and varied for research purposes. Although all these variables have been investigated, their relationship to the effective practice of psychotherapy remains obscure. Let us now consider them briefly.

Effects of Experience

In a review of research on the effects of experience upon supervision, Worthington (1984, 1987) concludes that the supervisor does not necessarily increase in effectiveness with increasing supervisory experience. Studies of supervisors varying in degree level, in student-faculty rank, or in licensure revealed no differences attributable to these variables for supervisors who were beyond the master's level. Nor have studies revealed differences in ratings of effectiveness, quality of relationship, specification of trainee needs, or identification of clients' problems that could be attributed to degree of supervisory experience. Worthington points out that if indeed supervisors do not improve with experience, they may at least *change* through identification with student status, energy, commitment, mastery of technique, and a host of other qualities. These changes may then affect supervisee behavior. Less speculative, however, are the undoubted facts that few supervisors undergo training in supervision and that opportunities for continuing education in supervisory skills are severely limited.

A related study (Marikis, Russell, & Dell 1985), suggests that there may be little or no correlation between level of supervisory experience and selected elements of supervisor behavior. Using an analog procedure, Marikis et al. isolated two supervisory behaviors: presession planning and in-session verbalization with a trainee. Supervisors with low and high experience levels differed from no-experience supervisors, and were rated more positively by trainees than the no-experience group. However, the fact that the presession planning statements were unrelated to those occurring during the actual supervisory session calls into question both the appropriateness of the analog procedure and the complexity of the supervisory situation as limiting factors in research on supervision.

Effects of Theoretical Orientation

The supervisor comes to the supervisory session with a particular theoretical orientation that inevitably influences the behavior and attitudes of the trainee. As we have seen earlier, certain theoretical slants in psychotherapy have been predominant at various times in the past: psychoanalytic–dynamic theory, self-theory, learning theory, and behavior theory. Presumably, the theoretical orientation of the supervision should determine, or at least influence, methods of teaching. In the area of teaching psychotherapy, however, little formal research has emerged on the relationship of these earlier theories to differences in supervisory practice.

Currently, the theoretical orientation which is most strongly influencing research in the teaching of counseling and psychotherapy is one loosely termed *developmental*. The basic assumption of this approach is that in learning psychotherapy, the trainee passes through certain definable stages. These stages should define his or her own appropriate teaching orientation. Varieties of developmental theories have proliferated. In one attempt to summarize the field, Worthington (1987) identified 16 different models, each with its own appropriate supervisor behavior.

The developmental approach has stimulated considerable investigation. For example, Stoltenberg's (1981) *counselor complexity* model led to research by McNeill, Stoltenberg, & Pierce (1985) that indicated that supervisees with greater experience, as compared with those of less experience, reported self-perceptions of behavior that were congruent with predictions from the model. By contrast, Heppner and Roehlke (1984), studying graduate students at three levels, found an orderly progression with different levels of training, but no single developmental model could account for all of the obtained results.

In addition to Stoltenberg's development model, at least two other models have stimulated recent research: those of Bernard (1979) and Littrell, Lee-Borden, and Lorenz (1979). Ellis and Dell (1986), and Ellis, Dell & Good, (1988) employed these models in three studies testing the dimensionality of supervisory roles: one model based on supervisee perception of experience, the other upon supervisor perceptions. Three dimensions emerged in these studies: process versus conceptual-focused supervision; directive versus nondirective supervision; and challenging, cognitive–behavioral versus supportive, emotional supervision. Although Bernard's model received some support and Littrell's minimal support in these studies, neither model accounted for all three dimensions.

Recurring problems of research on the developmental model are addressed by Holloway (1987), who points out that the methodology employed is simply not appropriate to answering developmental questions. Cross-sectional rather than longitudinal designs have been used. He indicates that there is undue reliance upon self-reports, a technique that he recommends be supplemented by open-ended questions, structured interviews, or, ideally, direct observation.

Effects of Gender, Race, and Cultural Background

It has generally been assumed that matching supervisor and supervisee on a number of variables, including gender, race, and cultural background, should enhance the positive effects of supervision. Supervisory pairs matched for gender have been presumed to form closer relationships than unmatched pairs. One study, however (Worthington & Stern, 1985), investigating supervisor–supervisee relationships over a semester's time, yielded results somewhat different from these presumptions. With supervisor–supervisee pairs unmatched in gender and based upon the supervisors' perceived knowledge of the supervisees' feelings and actions, male supervisors reported their relationship to their supervisees as stronger than did female supervisors, saw themselves as contributing more to the supervisees' learning and as having greater closeness of relationship. Similarly, male supervisees rated their relationship with supervisors of both genders as better than female supervisees did.

However, when supervisor and supervisee were matched for gender and compared with unmatched pairs, supervisors' perceptions of the relationship showed no significant differences. Supervisees in matched pairs, on the other hand perceived their relationship with the supervisor as closer than did supervisees in unmatched pairs. They also rated their improvement resulting from supervision as greater than did those in unmatched pairs. Worthington and Stern suggest, among other hypotheses, that the supervisors' ratings would support the notion that supervision was seen by them as a task rather than as a relationship.

In a comparable vein, Cook and Helms (1988) sought to examine the influence of cultural factors upon the supervisory relationship. Using a mailed questionnaire method, these authors obtained from a group of "non-Caucasian" graduate students information on the supervisory relationship and on satisfaction with supervision, as well as their evaluation of the supervisor's competence. Factor analysis indicated that the supervisor's liking and interest correlated with supervisee satisfaction. The authors suggest that supervisors consult books and training models dealing with culturally sensitive issues.

It should be emphasized again that studies such as the foregoing depend almost exclusively upon self-report questionnaires and that results must be interpreted cautiously in the light of this constraint.

Characteristics of Supervisor–Supervisee Interaction

As we have seen, the personal characteristics of participants in the supervisory dyad, as well as such variables as experience and theoretical stance, may alter the behavior and attitudes of each member. Also, a unique interpersonal relationship develops between the two and may further limit or facilitate the progress of the client.

Supervisor Roles

Hess (1980) has identified six training models: lecturer, teacher, case conference, collegial peer, monitor, and therapist. Of these, the roles of lecturer and therapist were developed earliest in the history of supervisory interaction. Both are outgrowths of the psychiatric–psychoanalytic tradition and both survive today, the lecturer as the main participant in the earlier didactic process and the therapist in those schools that recommend psychotherapy for students in clinical training. A number of writers have noted the essential similarity between the ideal supervisor and the ideal therapist and have pointed out that supervisors and therapists share such personal qualities as empathy, understanding, unconditional positive regard, and genuineness (Carifio & Hess, 1987; Rogers, 1957; Storm & Heath, 1985). However, psychotherapy for the trainee during supervision is generally decried, and supervisors are advised to respect the boundaries between behaviors that are directly germane to supervisory issues and those of a more personal nature. Nonetheless, individual trainee need may occasionally dictate whether a lecturer or therapist role is assumed by the supervisor and may lead to trainee–supervisor conflict.

Power Struggles Between Supervisor and Supervisee

Differences in characteristics of supervisor and trainee occasionally eventuate in power struggles. Supervisory styles vary widely, even within a given model. Historically, as we have seen, the early psychoanalytic style was essentially authoritarian. The advent of self-psychology and nondirective counseling (Rogers, 1957) to a large extent replaced authoritative supervisory attitudes with an essentially egalitarian approach. An analysis of sex roles and power relationships in supervision is provided by Munson (1987), who details helpful information for the supervisor who deals with the increasing number of female supervisees.

The "Ideal Supervisor"

A review of the research on psychotherapy supervision published in the past 10 years (Carifio & Hess, 1987) yields information that makes possible a description of the hypothetical "ideal" supervisor. The qualities that describe this ideal, presumably derived at least in part from empirical studies, are strikingly similar to those described in much earlier publications and based upon the intuition and clinical experiences of the writers. These qualities are the now-familiar ones: empathy, understanding, respect, self-disclosure. In their relationship with trainees, ideal supervisors apparently display such additional qualities as openness, trust, two-way communication, and collaboration.

What the ideal supervisor does, as identified by Carifio & Hess (1987), is to set clear and explicit goals for the supervision. An additional task is to determine what actually went on in a therapy session, not only from the supervisee's report but also from observation, either direct or by audiotape or videotape. The ideal supervisor uses a variety of teaching methods but avoids the role of therapist. Furthermore, the style in which the supervisor provides feedback (didactic, experiential) may vary among ideal supervisors and still prove helpful to the trainee.

It should be emphasized that the means by which information regarding the ideal supervisor is obtained range from casual, intuitive, descriptive remarks to a few studies that endeavor to control, vary, and quantify variables. Most often, data upon which the studies are based are ratings, judgments, or preferences of supervisees with whom the supervisor interacts. It is rare that investigators proceed to the next step, that of studying effect upon trainee behavior. It is even rarer that relationships are sought between the supervisee's training in the supervisory relationship and his or her actual performance with a client. Most unfortunately, it is unusual indeed to find investigations of the final step: the effect, for better or worse, upon the behavior of the client. To this crucial problem we now turn.

Effect of Supervisor–Supervisee Relationship Upon Client Behavior

Interesting though the questions examined in the preceding paragraphs may be, they are preliminary to the basic question of client behavior change. To what extent and in what ways do the characteristics of supervisor, supervisee, and the relationship between them contribute to the personal growth of the client and the alleviation of his or her distress? There is practically no well-designed and executed research on this question, and as yet there are no definitive answers.

Studies of psychotherapy outcome indicate that one factor of importance in behavior change or skill acquisition is the relationship between therapist and client. Although components of that relationship can be specified in terms of interpersonal skills, and those skills may be addressed in supervision, their effect upon a particular client, or upon a group of similarly diagnosed clients, has not been established. In the enormously complex matrix of client behavior, measurement of behavior change and the systematic specification of that change pose a challenging research problem.

Group Supervision

Although the classical model of supervision is a dyadic one, with trainee and supervisor in a one-to-one relationship, other forms of supervision are also possible (Forsyth & Ivey, 1980). A group approach is probably most effective in instructional situations in which relatively inexperienced trainees are learning skills. Such an approach to microcounseling, for example, has been found to be as effective as individual instruction, as shown in studies by Gluckstern, Hearn, and Scroggins, and Forsyth and Ivey (Forsyth & Ivey, 1980, p. 249). Here, the creation of a learning environment in the group of trainees precedes the conventional steps in skill acquisition. Such a learning environment requires that the supervisor assess the particular needs of the trainee, establish an atmosphere of trust, and model group facilitator behavior.

RETROSPECT AND PROSPECT: WHAT HAVE WE LEARNED AND WHAT DO WE NEED TO LEARN?

During the past 100 years, psychotherapy and training in psychotherapy have changed from a primarily theoretical–philosophical base to a more empirical one and from a master–student relationship between therapist, patient, and trainee to more egalitarian, empathic problem-solving partnerships. Psychology has played a pivotal role in these changes because of its dedication to empirical science and unwillingness to accept traditions.

At this time in our history, knowledge about what we need to teach neophyte psychotherapists is limited and infirm, but considerable credit for progress should also be taken. Psychology's contributions have come not only from clinical psychologists but also from basic scientists (e.g., learning theorists, test designers, and personality/social psychologists). Psychology's many researchers, starting from different viewpoints, have made varied contributions that have led to a number of minitheories that may more effectively approach the varied problems and backgrounds of clients.

Teaching methods also have benefited from such knowledge generated by psychological research as: (a) specification and definition of behaviors to be learned (rather than more vaguely defined insights or personality changes); (b) the importance of graded experiences during the learning process; (c) multiple sources of feedback; and (d) the importance of learning climate. The refinement of feedback to the learner has been of great importance in teaching psychotherapy skill. We have moved away from case reporting by the trainee, with feedback based primarily upon that information source, to the use of audiotape, co-counseling, observation through one-way mirrors, and finally to videotaped self-confrontation. This change is of vital importance because of the increased accuracy and completeness of information about what has taken place. Videotaped self-confrontation, of course, is an ultimate source of feedback to the trainee, who has been shown to benefit more from it, however, when viewing it with a supervisor.

Evaluation of teaching depends upon our ability to specify necessary and sufficient ingredients of effective psychotherapy and the skills, strategies, and knowledge that are important in producing client improvement. There is now much agreement across "schools" regarding basic therapeutic climate and basic, facilitative interviewing skills. Manual-based training shows some promise of effectiveness by specifying, within a given theoretical orientation, the therapist's methods and tasks.

Methods of teaching and the important ingredients of therapy are inextricably intertwined. Both involve helping the individual to change some kinds of interpersonal behavior. Among students, as among patients, certain teaching methods are likely to be more effective than others on an idiosyncratic basis. Students, like patients, start from different baselines in various areas of effectiveness, and have different rates of learning. However, it is clear that some didactic presentations regarding therapeutic variables and principles need to be followed by practice that is objectively observed or recorded and by feedback given to the learner through as many channels as possible. Increasingly, there is concern that it may be important to have continued, lifetime monitoring of therapist competence, possibly including self-monitoring by means of recorded sessions that can be reviewed.

The matter of measuring therapist competence has not been resolved because both therapist and patient variables are not sufficiently well defined or agreed upon and also because our measuring instruments—partly in consequence—are of questionable validity and reliability. Scofield and Yoxtheimer (1983) call for increased psychometric rigor in evaluating therapist performance. They point out that many rating scales possess face validity only, and they recommend using multiple measures of therapist competency in order to increase credibility.

Psychotherapy, dealing primarily with interpersonal relationships, personal goals and attitudes, and their relationship to societal values, demands, and strictures, is heavily influenced by the culture in which it is practiced. Cultural changes have made possible greater openness and egalitarianism in the therapeutic relationship and in teaching methods, including patient feedback to therapist, trainee feedback to trainer, and peer observations and feedback. Cultural/professional/economic changes also have made psychotherapists more accountable for demonstration of patient benefit.

Only a few years back, psychologists were fighting in the legislatures of every state for the privilege of licensure. Now licensure is ubiquitous, is dictating the need for "proof" of competence, and also is requiring legally defensible, publicly credible documentation of the effectiveness of training for the practice of psychology. There is increasing societal pressure for more information regarding the cost-effectiveness of psychotherapy as practiced by individual psychologists who have achieved specific credentials. Acquisition of this information will require systematic study. For all the reasons we have shown, the issue is exceedingly complex. Criterion problems, questions of skill definition and measurement, theoretical differences regarding therapeutic approach, and other complexities impede research in this as in other "soft" areas of psychology. Nonetheless, among all the mental health professions, psychology is probably the best equipped to provide answers on a continuing basis to the questions that confront us. We have questioned traditions and prior convictions established in a relatively pre-empirical era and are clearly on the path to asking increasingly specific questions and thereby obtaining more meaningful answers. If psychologists are to be true to our most fundamental traditions and our strongest convictions, we need to continue to focus in upon our skills in evaluation research, to examine our own performances as educators and lifelong learners, and to use the knowledge we acquire in continually improving the services we offer.

REFERENCES

Bernard, J. M. (1979). Supervisory training: A discrimination model. *Counselor Education and Supervision, 19*, 60–68.

Bootzin, R. R., & Ruggill, J. S. (1988). Training issues in behavior therapy. *Journal of Consulting and Clinical Psychology, 56*(5), 703–709.

Burstein, J., & Carkhuff, R. (1968). Objective therapist and client ratings of therapist-offered facilitative conditions of moderate- to low-functioning therapists. *Journal of Clinical Psychology, 24,* 240–249.

Caracena, P., & Vicory, J. (1969). Correlates of phenomenological and judged empathy. *Journal of Consulting Psychology, 16,* 510–515.

Carifio, M. S., & Hess, A. K. (1987). Who is the ideal supervisor? *Professional Psychology: Research and Practice, 18,* 244–250.

Chinsky, J. M., & Rappaport, J. (1970). Brief critique of the meaning and reliability of "accurate empathy" ratings. *Psychological Bulletin, 73,* 379–382.

Cook, D. A., & Helms, J. E. (1988). Visible racial/ethnic group supervisees' satisfaction with cross-cultural supervision as predicted by relationship characteristics. *Journal of Counseling Psychology, 15*(3), 268–274.

Doyle, W. E., Foreman, M. E. & Wales, E. (1977). Efforts of supervision in the training of nonprofessional crisis-intervention counselors. *Journal of Counseling Psychology, 24,* 72–78.

Ellis, A. (1989). Thoughts on supervising counselors and therapists. *Psychology: A Journal of Human Behavior, 26,* 3–5.

Ellis, M. V., & Dell, D. M. (1986). Dimensionality of supervisory roles: Supervisors' perceptions of supervision. *Journal of Counseling Psychology, 33,* 282–291.

Ellis, M. V., Dell, D. M., & Good, G. E. (1988). Counselor trainees' perceptions of supervisor roles: Two studies testing the dimensionality of supervision. *Journal of Counseling Psychology, 35,* 315–324.

Eskedal, G. A. (1975). Symbolic role modeling and cognitive learning in the training of counselors. *Journal of Counseling Psychology, 22,* 152–155.

Eyberg, S., & Matarazzo, R. G. (1980). Comparison of individual and group instruction in mother–child interaction training. *Journal of Clinical Psychology, 36,* 492–499.

Forsyth, D. R., & Ivey, A. E. (1980). Microtraining: An approach to differential supervision. In A. K. Hess, (Ed.), *Psychotherapy supervision: Theory, research and practice* (pp. 242–261). New York: Wiley.

Gardner, J. M. (1972). Teaching behavior modification to nonprofessionals. *Journal of Applied Behavior Analysis, 10,* 75–84.

Gendlin, E. (1981). *Focusing.* New York: Bantam.

Gluckstern, N. L. (1973). Training parents as drug counselors in the community. *Personnel & Guidance Journal, 51,* 676–680.

Greenberg, L. S., & Goldman, R. L. (1988). Training in experiential therapy. *Journal of Consulting and Clinical Psychology, 56,* 696–702.

Haase, R., & DiMattia, D. (1970). The application of the microcounseling paradigm to the training of support personnel in counseling. *Counseling Education and Supervision, 10,* 16–22.

Hansen, J., Moore, G., & Carkhuff, R. (1968). The differential relationship of objective and client perceptions of counseling. *Journal of Clinical Psychology, 24*, 244–246.

Hearn, M. (1976). *Three models of training counsellors: A comparative study.* Unpublished doctoral dissertation, University of Western Ontario.

Heppner, P. P., & Roehlke, H. J. (1984). Differences among supervisees at different levels of training: Implications for a developmental model of supervision. *Journal of Counseling Psychology, 31*(1), 76–90.

Hess, A. K. (1980). Training models and the nature of psychotherapy supervision. In A. K. Hess, (Ed.), *Psychotherapy supervision: Theory, research and practice* (pp. 15–25). New York: Wiley.

Holloway, E. L. (1987). Developmental models of supervision: Is it development? *Professional Psychology: Research and Practice, 18*(3), 209–216.

Ivey, A. E. (1980). *Counseling and psychotherapy: Skills, theories and practice.* Englewood Cliffs, NJ: Prentice-Hall.

Ivey, A. E. (1983). *Intentional interviewing and counseling.* Monterey, CA: Brooks/ Cole.

Ivey, A. E., & Authier, J. (1978). *Microcounseling: Innovations in interviewing, counseling, psychotherapy and psychoeducation* (2nd ed.). Springfield, IL: Charles C. Thomas.

Kelley, M. D. (1971). Reinforcement in microcounseling. *Journal of Counseling Psychology, 13*, 268–272.

Klerman, G., Weissman, M., Rounsaville, B., & Chevron, E. (1984). *Interpersonal psychotherapy of depression.* New York: Basic Books.

Korchin, S. J., & Sands, S. (1980). Principles common to all psychotherapies. In A. K. Hess (Ed.), *Psychotherapy supervision: Theory, research and practice* (pp. 270–299). New York: Wiley.

Leddick, G. R., & Bernard, J. M. (1980). The history of supervision: A critical review. *Counselor Education and Supervision*, 186–196.

Lindsley, O. (1960). Characteristics of the behavior of chronic psychotics as revealed by free operant conditioning methods. *Monograph Supplement, 21*, 66–78.

Lipsey, M. W. (1987, April). *Theory as method: Small theories of treatments.* Paper presented at the Health Services Research Methodology Conference, Strengthening Causal Interpretations of Nonexperimental Data, Tucson, AZ.

Littrell, J. M., Lee-Borden, N., & Lorenz, J. (1979). A developmental framework for counseling supervision. *Counselor Education and Supervision, 19*, 129–136.

Lovaas, O. (1978). Parents as therapists. In E. Schpolee & M. Rutter (Eds.), *Autism: A reappraisal of concepts and treatment.* New York: Plenum.

Lovaas, O. I., & Newsom, C. D. (1976). Behavior modification with psychotic children. In H. Leitenberg (Ed.), *Handbook of behavior modification and behavior therapy.* Englewood Cliffs, NJ: Prentice-Hall.

Lovaas, O., & Simmons, J. Q. (1969). Manipulation of self-destruction in three retarded children. *Journal of Applied Behavior Analysis, 2,* 143–152.

Lovaas, O. I., & Smith, T. (1989). A comprehensive behavioral theory of autistic children: Paradigm for research and treatment. *Journal of Behavior Therapy and Experimental Psychiatry, 20,* 17–29.

Luborsky, L. (1984). *Principles of psychoanalytic psychotherapy: A manual for supportive–expressive treatment (SE).* New York: Basic Books.

Marikis, D. A., Russell, R. K., & Dell, D. M. (1985). Effects of supervisory experience level on planning and in-session supervisor verbal behavior. *Journal of Counseling Psychology, 32*(3), 410–416.

Matarazzo, J. D., & Wiens, A. N. (1977). Speech behavior as an objective correlate of empathy and outcome in interview and psychotherapy research: A review with implications for behavior modification. *Behavior Modification, 1,* 453–480.

Matarazzo, R. G. (1978). Research on the teaching and learning of psychotherapeutic skills. In S. L. Garfield & A. E. Bergin (Eds.), *Handbook of psychotherapy and behavior change* (pp. 941–966). New York: Wiley.

Matarazzo, R. G., & Patterson, D. R. (1986). Methods of teaching therapeutic skill. In S. L. Garfield & A. E. Bergin (Eds.), *Handbook of psychotherapy and behavior change* (pp. 821–843). New York: Wiley.

Matarazzo, R. G., Phillips, J. S., Wiens, A. N., & Saslow, G. (1965). Learning the art of interviewing: A study of what beginning students do and their pattern of change. *Psychotherapy: Theory, Research & Practice, 2,* 49–60.

Matarazzo, R. G., Wiens, A. N., & Saslow, G. (1966). Experimentation in the teaching and learning of psychotherapy skills. In L. A. Gottschalk & A. Auerbach (Eds.), *Methods of research in psychotherapy* (pp. 297–635). New York: Appleton-Century-Crofts.

McNeill, B. W., Stoltenberg, C. D., & Pierce, R. A. (1985). Supervisees' perception of their development: A test of the counselor complexity model. *Journal of Counseling Psychology, 32*(4), 630–633.

Moldawsky, S. (1980). Psychoanalytic psychotherapy supervision. In A. K. Hess. (Ed.), *Psychotherapy supervision: Theory, research and practice,* (p. 134). New York: Wiley.

Moreland, J. R., Ivey, A. E., & Phillips, J. S. (1973). An evaluation of microcounseling as an interviewer training tool. *Journal of Consulting and Clinical Psychology, 41,* 294–300.

Munson, C. E. (1987). Sex roles and power relationships in supervision. *Journal of Professional Psychology, 18*(3), 236–243.

Patterson, G. R. (1982). *Coercive family process.* Eugene, OR: Castalia Publishing.

Patterson, G. R., Cobb, J. A., & Ray, R. S. (1973). A social engineering technology for retraining the families of aggressive boys. In H. E. Adams & I. P. Unikel (Eds.), *Issues and trends in behavior therapy* (pp. 193–210). Springfield, IL: Charles C. Thomas.

Paul, G. L. (1987). Rational operations in residential treatment settings through ongoing assessment of client and staff functioning. In D. R. Peterson & D. B. Fishman (Eds.), *Assessment for decision* (pp. 145–203). Brunswick, NJ: Rutgers University Press.

Payne, P., Winter, D., & Perry, M. A. (1975). Modeling and instructions in training for counselor empathy. *Journal of Counseling Psychology, 22,* 173–179.

Rappaport, J., & Chinsky, J. M. (1972). Accurate empathy: Confusion of a construct. *Psychological Bulletin, 77,* 400–404.

Reisman, J. M. (1971). *Toward the integration of psychotherapy.* New York: Wiley Interscience.

Rennie, D. (1987). *Psychotherapy inside out: A training guide to second generation person-centered therapy.* Unpublished manual, York University, Toronto.

Rice, L., & Saperia, E. (1984). A task analysis of the resolution of problematic reactions. In L. Rice & L. Greenberg (Eds.), *Patterns of change: Intensive analysis of psychotherapeutic process* (pp. 29–66). New York: Guilford Press.

Rogers, C. R. (1942). *Counseling and psychotherapy.* Boston: Houghton Mifflin.

Rogers, C. R. (1957). Training individuals to engage in the therapeutic process. In C. R. Strother (Ed.), *Psychology and mental health* (pp. 76–92). Washington, DC: American Psychological Association.

Rounsaville, B. J., O'Malley, S., Foley, S., & Weissman, M. (1988). Role of manual-guided training in the conduct and efficacy of interpersonal psychotherapy for depression. *Journal of Consulting and Clinical Psychology, 56,* 681–688.

Saltmarsh, R. E. (1973). Development of empathic interview skills through programmed instruction. *Journal of Counseling Psychology, 20,* 375–377.

Salzinger, K., Feldman, R. S. & Portnoy, S. (1970). Training parents of brain-injured children in the use of operant conditioning procedures. *Behavior Therapy, 1,* 4–32.

Scofield, M. E. & Yoxtheimer, L. L. (1983). Psychometric issues in the assessment of clinical competencies. *Journal of Counseling Psychology, 30,* 413–420.

Scroggins, W. (1973). *An evaluation of microcounseling as a model to train resident staff.* Unpublished doctoral dissertation, University of Massachusetts.

Sechrest, L., & Chatel, D. (1987). Evaluation and accountability in training for professional psychology: An overview. In B. A. Edelstein & E. S. Berier (Eds.), *Evaluation and accountability in clinical training* (pp. 1–37). New York: Plenum Press.

Skinner, B. F., & Lindsley, O. (1954). A method for the experimental analysis of the behavior of psychotic patients. *American Psychologist, 9,* 419–420.

Stoltenberg, C. (1981). Approaching supervision from a developmental perspective: The counselor complexity model. *Journal of Counseling Psychology, 28,* 59–65.

Storm, C., & Heath, A. (1985). Models of supervision: Using therapy theory as a guide. *The Clinical Supervisor, 3,* 87–92.

Strupp, H., & Binder, J. L. (1983). *Time-limited dynamic psychotherapy: A treatment manual*. Unpublished manuscript. (Available from H. H. Strupp, PhD, Department of Psychology, Vanderbilt University, 134 Wesley Hall, Nashville, TN 37240.)

Strupp, H. H., Butler, S. F., & Rosser, C. L. (1988). Training in psychodynamic therapy. *Journal of Consulting and Clinical Psychology, 56,* 689–695.

Toukmanian, S. G., & Rennie, D. L. (1975). Microcounseling versus human relations training: Relative effectiveness with undergraduate trainees. *Journal of Counseling Psychology, 22,* 345–352.

Truax, C. B., & Carkhuff, R. (1967). *Toward effective counseling and psychotherapy: Training and practice*. Chicago: Aldine.

Weinrach, S. G. (1990). Rogers and Gloria: The controversial film and the enduring relationship. *Psychotherapy: Theory, research and practice, 27,* 282–290.

Wenegrat, A. (1974). A factor analytic study of the Truax accurate empathy scale. *Psychotherapy: Theory, research and practice, 11,* 48–51.

Wessler, R. L., & Ellis, A. (1980). Supervision in rational–emotive therapy. In A. K. Hess (Ed.), *Psychotherapy supervision: Theory, research and practice* (pp. 181–205). New York: Wiley.

Wiens, A. N., Matarazzo, J. D., & Saslow, G. (1965). The interaction recorder: An electronic punched paper tape unit for recording speech behavior during interviews. *Journal of Clinical Psychology, 21,* 142–145.

Wolpe, J. (1958). *Psychotherapy by reciprocal inhibition*. Stanford, CA: Stanford University Press.

Worthington, E. L. (1984). Empirical investigation of supervision of counselors as they gain experience. *Journal of Counseling Psychology, 31*(1), 63–75.

Worthington, E. L. (1987). Changes in supervision as counselors and supervisors gain experience: A review. *Professional Psychology: Research and Practice, 18*(3), 189–209.

Worthington, E. L., & Stern, A. (1985). Effects of supervisee degree level and gender on the supervisory relationship. *Journal of Counseling Psychology, 32*(2), 252–262.

VI

CONCLUSION

28

INTO THE FUTURE: RETROSPECT AND PROSPECT IN PSYCHOTHERAPY

JOHN C. NORCROSS AND DONALD K. FREEDHEIM

History, according to G. K. Chesterton, is a hill or high point of vantage, from which people can see the place in which they live or the age in which they are living. We would advance Chesterton's line of reasoning to suggest that the history of psychotherapy is also an indispensable vantage point from which to view—and perhaps to guide—the future of psychotherapy.

In this concluding chapter, the temporal focus is reversed from the past to the future. Our objective is not to predict events in a soothsayer's manner but to extract and to amplify salient trends that may occupy us in the next decade. We will draw on three principal sources in addressing the future of psychotherapy: (a) the preceding chapters in this volume; (b) the extant literature on the future of psychotherapy; and (c) a survey of the book's contributors. We begin by reviewing the results of our poll in which 40 contributors to this volume served as a panel of experts. Next, by integrating converging developments articulated in this and previous literature, we sketch six emerging themes for psychotherapy practitioners, researchers, and trainers. Finally, we offer some comments on the events and issues that will shape psychotherapy into the 21st century.

A POLL ON THE FUTURE OF PSYCHOTHERAPY

Innovations appear and vanish with bewildering rapidity on the diffuse, heterodox psychotherapeutic scene. Yalom (1975, p. 204) cautioned that only a truly intrepid observer would attempt to differentiate evanescent from potentially important and durable trends in the field. Furthermore, as Ekstein (1972) warned, many predictions in the uncertain world of psychotherapy tend to be self-fulfilling prophecies or magical wish-fulfillments.

For these reasons, we polled this volume's authors, who represent commitments to diverse orientations and specializations, and elicited their prediction of what *will* happen, not what they personally would *like* to happen (tempting as that might be). The following results are the composite forecasts on the future of psychotherapy by 40 contributors to this book.

Questionnaire and Method

A seven-page survey was developed, drawing heavily on the items of Prochaska and Norcross (1982) and, to a lesser extent, the scenarios of Anderson, Parente, and Gordon (1981). The survey form was divided into five sections: therapeutic interventions (33 items); psychotherapy providers (13 items); therapy modalities (9 items); theoretical orientations (14 items); and forecast scenarios (26 items). For the first four sections, participants predicted the relative growth or decline on a seven-point, Likert-type scale (1 = great decrease, 2 = moderate decrease, 3 = slight decrease, 4 = remain same, 5 = slight increase, 6 = moderate increase, 7 = great increase). For the fifth section, they predicted the probability of a situation occurring within the next decade. Participants were reminded to predict the future as they perceived it, not as they desired it.

Forty-seven contributors to this volume, excluding the present chapter authors, were contacted by mail in June 1990. Forty-three returned the questionnaire; however, three questionnaires were incomplete. Thus, 40 usable questionnaires, an 85% response rate, were employed as the basis of the results.

All 40 respondents held a doctorate (37 PhDs, 2 MDs, 1 both) and had an average of 27 years of postdoctoral experience. Thirty-three were men and seven were women. They devoted an average of 32% of their time to research, 24% to clinical work, 17% to teaching, 16% to administration, and 8% to supervision. Primary employment sites were university departments (58%), medical schools (15%), community clinics (8%), and private practices (8%). Predominant theoretical orientations, in descending frequency, were psychodynamic (28%), eclectic (25%), behavioral (12.5%), cognitive (8%), client-centered (8%), and psychoanalytic (8%).

Compared to American psychologists practicing psychotherapy as a whole (Norcross, Prochaska, & Gallagher, 1989a; Prochaska & Norcross, 1983), this select sample was definitely older, more experienced, over-represented by men, more academically and research inclined, and more psychodynamically oriented. To the extent that one's age, gender, theoretical orientation, and professional affiliation may influence forecasts of future trends, these proportional disparities should be borne in mind.

Results

Regarding therapeutic interventions of the future, our respondents predicted that present-centered, structured, and directive techniques would increase markedly in the forthcoming decade. As shown in Table 1, audio/video feedback, problem-solving techniques, cognitive restructuring, self-change techniques, in vivo exposure, and communication skills all received mean ratings greater than 5.0 on the 7-point scale. Additional procedures predicted to accelerate, with average scores between 4.5 and 5.0, were homework assignments, self-control training, expressing support/warmth, imagery and fantasy, social skills training, accurate empathy, behavioral contracting, teaching/advising, relaxation, and computerized therapies. These composite results also portend that clinical work will increasingly blend client's work between sessions (e.g., exposure, homework) with therapist's interpersonal skills within sessions (e.g., empathy, warmth).

By contrast, aversive, unstructured, and relatively passive procedures are expected to decline. Aversive conditioning, free association, encounter exercises, and dream interpretation all received ratings in the moderate to slight decrease range.

Regarding psychotherapy providers of the future, our intrepid observers forecast that self-help groups, psychiatric nurses, master's-level social workers, and clinical psychologists will provide an increasing proportion of mental health services. Modest increments, as displayed in Table 2, were also predicted for the services of pastoral counselors, counseling psychologists, paraprofessionals, master's-level psychologists, master's-level counselors, mass media "therapy shows," and peer counselors. By contrast, psychiatrists and baccalaureate-level therapists were expected to experience moderate declines in the proportion of psychotherapeutic services rendered.

Regarding therapy modalities or formats, the panel expressed strong positive expectations for short-term therapy (M = 5.95, SD = .72) but stronger negative expectations for long-term work (M = 2.74, SD = 1.19)

TABLE 1
Composite Predictions of Therapeutic Interventions of the Future in
Ranked Order

Intervention	Mean	Median	SD
Audio/Video Feedback	5.23	5.00	1.06
Problem-Solving Techniques	5.18	5.00	1.00
Cognitive Restructuring	5.18	5.00	1.14
Self-Change Techniques	5.10	5.00	1.00
In Vivo Exposure	5.05	5.00	1.14
Communication Skills	5.02	5.00	1.00
Homework Assignments	5.00	5.00	1.01
Self-Control Procedures	4.90	5.00	1.00
Expressing Support/Warmth	4.87	5.00	0.86
Imagery and Fantasy	4.85	5.00	1.04
Assertion/Social Skills Training	4.77	5.00	0.96
Accurate Empathy	4.74	5.00	0.95
Behavioral Contracting	4.65	5.00	0.75
Teaching/Advising	4.60	4.00	1.03
Relaxation Techniques	4.56	5.00	0.91
Computerized Therapies	4.53	5.00	1.52
Behavior Modification	4.44	4.00	1.31
Bibliotherapy	4.42	4.00	1.15
Therapist Self-Disclosure	4.41	4.00	1.16
Biofeedback	4.39	4.00	1.01
Reassurance	4.28	4.00	1.08
Confrontation	4.18	4.00	0.97
Paradoxical Interventions	4.10	4.00	1.27
Cathartic Methods	4.05	4.00	0.94
Hypnosis	4.02	4.00	0.93
Systematic Desensitization	3.92	4.00	1.11
Analysis of Resistance	3.90	4.00	1.12
Transference Interpretation	3.74	4.00	1.29
Emotional Flooding/Implosion	3.53	3.00	1.20
Dream Interpretation	3.31	4.00	0.92
Encounter Exercises	3.18	3.00	1.11
Free Association	3.10	3.00	0.95
Aversive Conditioning	2.46	2.00	1.23

Note: 1 = great decrease, 4 = remain the same, 7 = great increase.

in the next decade. Individual therapy and network therapy were predicted to remain about the same in professional utilization; however, slight to moderate increases were foreseen for psychoeducational groups (M = 5.13, SD = 1.10), marital/couples therapy (M =5.05, SD = .69), conjoint family therapy (M = 5.03, SD = .78), crisis intervention (M = 4.85, SD = .99), and group therapy (M = 4.63, SD = .94).

Regarding theoretical orientations of the future, composite predictions are presented in Table 3 in ranked order. As seen there, theoretical integration and technical eclecticism were presaged to lead the way, with the former attempting to meld disparate theories and the latter synthesizing diverse techniques. Cognitive therapy and systems theory were expected to

TABLE 2
Composite Predictions of Psychotherapy Providers of the Future in Ranked Order

Psychotherapist	Mean	Median	SD
Self-Help Groups	5.38	5.50	1.17
Psychiatric Nurses	5.02	5.00	1.19
Master's-Level Social Workers	4.95	5.00	1.28
Clinical Psychologists	4.82	5.00	1.22
Peer Counselors	4.47	5.00	1.18
Mass Media "Therapy" Shows	4.42	5.00	1.29
Master's-Level Counselors	4.32	5.00	1.33
Paraprofessionals	4.32	4.00	1.25
Master's-Level Psychologists	4.30	5.00	1.22
Counseling Psychologists	4.10	4.00	1.17
Pastoral Counselors	4.07	4.00	0.97
BA-Level Therapists	3.50	4.00	1.48
Psychiatrists	2.85	3.00	0.86

Note: 1 = great decrease, 4 = remain same, 7 = great increase.

expand moderately, while psychobiological, behavioral, and feminist orientations expand only slightly between the years 1990 and 2000. Marked declines in transactional analysis and (classical) psychoanalysis were anticipated; however, psychodynamic (neo-Freudian) approaches were expected to decrease only slightly. In general, paralleling the predictions in clinical interventions and therapy modalities, the trend is encouraging for active, present-oriented systems and discouraging for comparatively passive, historically oriented systems of psychotherapy.

Regarding mental health forecast scenarios, the panel was reasonably

TABLE 3
Predictions of Theoretical Orientations of the Future in Ranked Order

Orientation	Mean	Median	SD
Theoretical Integration	5.28	5.00	0.93
Technical Eclecticism	5.26	5.00	1.10
Cognitive	5.20	5.00	1.00
Systems/Family Systems	5.13	5.00	0.89
Psychobiological	4.77	5.00	1.09
Behavioral/Social-Learning	4.61	5.00	0.93
Feminist	4.48	5.00	1.14
Humanistic	3.82	4.00	1.09
Psychodynamic/Neo-Freudian	3.75	4.00	1.21
Client/Person-Centered	3.37	3.00	1.05
Existential	3.26	3.00	0.91
Neuro-Linguistic Programming	3.18	3.00	1.37
Psychoanalytic	2.97	3.00	1.18
Transactional Analysis	2.74	3.00	0.97

Note: 1 = great decrease, 4 = remain same, 7 = great increase.

confident that mental health specialists will be included in a national health insurance plan (M = 5.21, SD = 1.24), that psychotherapists will become specialists rather than general practitioners (M = 4.91, SD = 1.42), that program accreditation will become a major issue (M = 4.90, SD = 1.80), and that peer review will become a standard part of therapy practice (M = 4.77, SD = 1.45) by the end of this century. All these changes, should they actualize, are hallmarks of a mature discipline and, at the same time, manifestations of a tightening mental health reimbursement system. Economic pressures as well as biochemical advances may also explain the fact that the panel foresees pharmacotherapy expanding at the expense of psychotherapy (M = 4.82, SD = 1.38). Concomitantly, it seems quite unlikely that funding for psychotherapy research (M = 3.63, SD = 1.54) and training (M = 2.74, SD = 1.36) will increase relative to inflation in the foreseeable future.

Finally, the respondents were asked to indicate the probability of a group of experienced psychotherapists accurately predicting the future of the field. The average response of 3.30 (SD = 1.72) fell between "slightly unlikely" and "uncertain." This response provides a sage warning that psychotherapists are neither confident in predicting nor powerful in directing the future of our discipline. As a profession, we have historically been reactive and passive in responding to "the noisy yammerings of the secular world," as Parloff (1979) put it. Without concerted efforts to guide our own evolution, we fear that governmental and insurance regulations rather than client needs will increasingly dictate treatment decisions in the forthcoming decade.

SIX EMERGING THEMES

The preceding chapters suggest several nascent directions for the near future of psychotherapy. These themes run deeply and ofttimes subtly, but their ramifications are invariably audible. Some themes represent a continuation of contemporary trends, while others portend a future divergent from the past. There is little need here to amplify directions that are widely recognized as having "come of age," such as health psychology and psychotherapy integration. Instead, we choose to give voice and presence to six newer and recurring themes that emerge throughout the text: pluralism; contextualism; prescriptionism; therapeutic alliance; economic pressures; and process-outcome linkages.

Pluralism

One of the remarkable events of modern society is how quickly professions change and diversify. Only 100 years ago, a veritable wink of the eye in an historical sense, psychotherapy was practiced almost exclusively in an individual format by medically trained men in independent practice from a psychoanalytic perspective with middle-class women (and a few men) in Vienna. The chapters in this volume underscore the escalating pluralism of the psychotherapeutic scene.

VandenBos, Cummings, and DeLeon (chapter 3, this volume) explicate the expanding host of settings for the practice of psychotherapy—private practice, universities, psychiatric hospitals, child and family guidance centers, schools, HMOs, community mental health centers, prisons, the military, and so forth. Each setting involves differing patient populations, and thus each one influences views on the best means for facilitating psychological and behavior change. Broader availability of psychotherapeutic services also begets pluralism of another sort, creation of psychotherapeutic interventions and theories for a fuller range of behavioral dysfunctions.

In tracing the evolution of psychoanalytic theory, Eagle and Wolitzky (chapter 4) note that the present time is characterized by a theoretical diversity and pluralism within what might be called the mainstream of psychoanalytic thought. They point out, as do many of the contributors, that it is inaccurate to speak of a single theory or uniform practice of any particular theoretical orientation. To do so falls prey to the uniformity myth (Kiesler, 1966).

Current conceptualizations of the nature of therapeutic change are more complex and multifaceted than ever, both within and between theoretical camps. What seems to be distinctive, observe both Arkowitz (chapter 8) and Liff (chapter 17), is the tolerance for and assimilation of formulations that were once viewed as deviant and heretical. The multiplicity, if not proliferation, of purportedly distinct psychotherapies is one prime motivator for the establishment of integrative and eclectic therapies, which now represent the most popular theoretical orientation (see Arnkoff & Glass, chapter 20; Norcross & Grencavage, 1989). But even those who believe that the call for rapprochement is unlikely to herald either an era of scientific progress or patient benefit do generally advocate a spirit of tolerance of vigorously promulgated positions. That is, mutual acceptance and openness are preferable alternatives to destructive antagonism (Frank, 1984).

Additionally, pluralism is evident in the range of therapy providers, clients, formats, and training opportunities. The chapters on the history of women (Russo & O'Connell, chapter 14) and ethnic minorities (Mays & Albee, chapter 16) in psychological practice reflect historical male-centered and Caucasian biases. Going beyond the critique of psychotherapy as androcentric and culturally insensitive, the authors document new approaches and methods predicated upon a pluralistic perspective. Similarly, ethnic minorities (Mays & Albee, chapter 16), children (Koocher & D'Angelo, chapter 13), and elderly (Knight, Kelly, & Gatz, chapter 15)—three historically underserved client populations—are receiving increased (though still insufficient) services and research attention from the psychotherapy community.

Although initially dominated by psychiatrists and psychoanalysts, psychotherapy is now primarily conducted by nonmedical and nonpsychoanalytic clinicians. Psychologists outnumber psychiatrists as mental health service providers, and the number of clinical social workers outnumber both combined (see VandenBos et al., chapter 3). Where individual therapy once dominated, recent research (e.g., Norcross, Prochaska, & Gallagher, 1989b) and the foregoing chapters (7 by Guerin & Chabot, and 21 by Rosenbaum, Lakin, & Roback, in particular) note that clinical psychologists routinely conduct marital/couples and conjoint family therapy. And where a scant 50 years ago virtually all clinical psychologists were educated in the Boulder model, scientist-practitioner PhD tradition, the "holy wars of the 1960s and 1970s" (see Stricker & Cummings, chapter 25) have produced a number of training models and virtual parity in the number of graduates between the professional model and the Boulder model. Furthermore, there is an escalating recognition that the two models fall on a continuum, ranging from research-oriented programs that provide little experience in clinical practice to professional programs that minimize the potential contribution of research.

Pluralism must be reconciled, of course, with client benefit and empirical validation. While applauding theoretical innovation and creative applications of a variety of research designs, Strupp and Howard (chapter 9) remind us of the "scientific requirement to demonstrate the relative efficacy of these new approaches." Uncritical acceptance is not prized. This view is embodied in the distinction between informed pluralism and uninformed faith. As a Maharasi was once reported to have said: "Keep an open mind; an open mind is a very good thing, but don't keep your mind so open that your brains fall out."

Contextualism

Cushman's (chapter 2) historically situated interpretation of psychotherapy invoked the writings of F. Scott Fitzgerald to emphasize the idea that personal change does not last unless it is grounded in an ongoing, shared tradition of history and culture. His chapter highlights psychotherapy trends within the larger body politic, with Cushman repeatedly warning against the peculiarly American notion of "decontextualized" personal transformation and psychotherapy history. The cultural history—and future—of psychotherapy requires consideration of historical antecedents, economic constituents, and political consequences.

The lesson of contextualism is being learned, or relearned, in psychotherapy practice, research, and advocacy. "A broader lesson," in the words of Russo and O'Connell (chapter 14), "is found in the awareness of the role of broader social context in the evolution of psychology." Societal norms and institutions shape both individual lives and professions' trajectories. Harshly put, "contextless is meaningless," without a full appreciation of the surrounding sociopolitical environment.

In practice, there is a reluctant recognition that psychotherapy can no longer be conducted in a vacuum. The therapist and patient are not alone; the "third-party" is frequently involved with its own demands and agendas. As the economic, social, and political forces shaping the parameters of psychotherapy are acknowledged, we will create and apply more responsive models of mental health delivery that fit into, not fight against, the rapidly changing conditions of American culture (Austad & Hoyt, 1992).

Various treatment orientations are renewing their acquaintance with contextualism. For example, behavior therapy historically has paid attention to environmental contingencies but has more recently moved outside the consultant's office to broader social and community concerns (see Glass & Arnkoff, chapter 18). Also, psychoanalysis has widely reconceptualized change in an individual "as context-dependent, a process subject to the situational, interpersonal, as well as intrapsychic influences" (see Liff, chapter 17). More radical contextual emphasis is evident in the expanding popularity of systemic approaches (see Guerin & Chabot, chapter 7) and community interventions. An extreme etiologically-tinged form of contextualism can be witnessed in Mays and Albee's (chapter 16) conviction that, "Problems are not inside the person. Problems are inside an unjust society. . . ."

Psychotherapy researchers, too, are realizing that the meaning of any therapist's or client's behavior is informed by context (Heatherington, 1989). In chapter 10, Garfield laments that in most research studies "very little attention" is paid to the impact of events outside of therapy. Process and outcome studies on environmental factors in the life of the patient remain a significant lacunae in the literature. Concurrently, the twin myths of "disembodied technique" and "therapist-less treatment" are giving way to the dawning recognition (really a reawakening) that the therapist is the focal process of change (Norcross & Guy, 1989).

Prescriptionism

Abraham Maslow was fond of repeating the adage, "If you only have a hammer you treat everything like a nail." The history of psychotherapy has repeatedly confirmed this observation. It is not uncommon for our inveterate colleagues to recommend the identical treatment (e.g., their treasured proficiency) to virtually every patient who crosses their paths (Norcross, 1985). Psychotherapists of the future, we predict, will develop and employ an expanded toolbox instead of senselessly "hammering away" at anything remotely similar to a nail.

Prescriptionism is concerned with that elusive, empirically driven match among patient, disorder, and treatment (Norcross, 1991a). With increasing refinement in the categorization of disorders and more precise delineation of change strategies, further advantages of prescriptive treatments may be found. At that point, effective therapy will be "defined not by its brand name, but by how well it meets the need of the patient" (Weiner, 1975, p. 44). The question will no longer be, "Does it work?" but rather, "Does it work *best* for this client?"

The need to match patient and treatment has been recognized from the beginning of psychotherapy (Frances, 1988). As early as 1919, according to Liff (chapter 17), Freud introduced psychoanalytic psychotherapy as an alternative to classical analysis on the recognition that the more rarified approach lacked universal applicability and that many patients did not possess the requisite psychological-mindedness.

Common wisdom and empirical results related to treatment matching are seldom codified (see Beutler & Clarkin, 1990, for a recent exception). Additional examples of prescriptive matching culled from the preceding chapters include:

1. The type of group therapy is frequently contingent on the client's diagnosis and needs. Directive–didactic approaches are more likely in public psychiatric institutions with hospitalized patients, and group psychoanalysis for higher-functioning psychoneurotic patients in independent practice (see Rosenbaum et al., chapter 21).

2. The form of psychotherapy for addictive disorders may be predicated on clients' characterological traits. Wallerstein's (see chapter 12c) early comparative treatment study of

hospitalized alcoholics found that "conditioned-reflex therapy," widely experienced as "punishing," did in fact work better than antabuse or group hypnotherapy with more masochistic patients.

3. Different rates of response to different psychotherapy procedures are predicted by patients' coping style and reactance levels. Ongoing research (Beutler, Mohr, Grawe, Engle, & MacDonald, 1991) found, among diagnostically homogeneous groups, that directive treatments are more effective than nondirective ones with low reactant patients. Treatments focusing most explicitly on overt behavior were differentially effective over internally focused approaches with clients with externalizing coping styles.

Among the more important achievements of psychotherapy research is the "demonstration of the unique effectiveness of a few therapies with specific disorders" (Lambert & Bergin, chapter 11). These include behavior therapy for specific symptoms and cognitive therapy for depression. Furthermore, what Strupp and Howard (see chapter 9) label "the desideratum of specificity" has enormous potential implications for the future.

The emerging theme of prescriptionism—also known as differential therapeutics, treatment matching, and the specificity factor—will complement, rather than replace, the "common factors" approach. The fact that disparate technical procedures appear to secure comparable outcomes, the "equivalence paradox" (Stiles, Shapiro, & Elliott, 1986), supports the immense power of therapeutic commonalities, but is "still not a popularly accepted explanation" (Garfield, chapter 10). The failure of the recent NIMH Collaborative Study of the Treatment of Depression (Parloff & Elkin, chapter 12l) to discern differential efficacy of specific treatments also supports the role of "nonspecific" treatment, client, and therapist characteristics in determining outcome. But the nascent consensus on the specific versus common factors controversy is that it is not either/or, not a dualism. Lambert, Shapiro, and Bergin (1986), in their comprehensive review, uncovered little evidence of clinically meaningful superiority of one form of (systematically evaluated) psychotherapy with respect to moderately severe outpatient disorders, but there are recurring exceptions. These exceptions, such as behavioral treatments for childhood aggression, can be accentuated by employing matching strategies. In sum, as Garfield (chapter 10) concludes, "The proper use of common *and* specific factors in therapy will probably be the most efficacious approach to psychotherapy."

Therapeutic Alliance

The two previous themes, we predict, will converge to produce a renewed but modified emphasis on the therapeutic alliance in the future.

Contextualism will contribute a heightened sensitivity to the interpersonal relationship and remind us that the value of a clinical intervention is inextricably bound to the relational context in which it is applied; prescriptionism will remind us that a unitary therapeutic relationship will not suffice for diverse clients and will mandate that therapists tailor interpersonal stances and styles to fit the unique needs of individual clients.

Specific delineations among therapeutic technique, strategy, and relationship are nearly impossible in practice, as they are interwoven in the contextual fabric of psychotherapy. Hans Strupp (1986) has offered an analogy to illustrate the inseparability of the constituent elements of psychotherapy: Suppose you want a teenage son to clean his room. One technique for achieving this is to establish clear standards. Fine, but the effectiveness of this technique will vary depending on whether the relationship between you and the boy is characterized by warmth and mutual respect or by anger and distrust. This is not to say that the technique is useless; merely, how well it works depends upon the context in which it is used.

There is virtual unanimity among the contributors and among reviewers of the outcome research (Lambert & Bergin, chapter 11) that the therapist–patient relationship is central to positive change. Moreover, strong consensus is arising that a facilitative therapeutic alliance is a common, transtheoretical feature (Grencavage & Norcross, 1990). For example, a unique and early article published by a number of psychoanalytically oriented psychotherapists (Klein et al., 1969), reported their intensive observations of two leading behavior therapists (Arnold Lazarus, Joseph Wolpe) for a week. They found that the therapeutic relationship exerted far more power in behavior therapy than had been recognized previously. Likewise, in chapter 18, Glass and Arnkoff argue that behavior therapists have emphasized the relationship in practice to a greater degree than the early behavioral literature claimed. They reviewed mail surveys and observational studies which attest to the high frequency—and probable strong impact—of relationship enhancement methods among behavior therapists. They also note (see Arnkoff & Glass, chapter 20) that the current emphasis in cognitive therapy and psychotherapy integration on the therapeutic relationship is likely to grow.

A similar trend is evident in psychoanalytic practice and research as well. A decisive shift involving a relative deemphasis on interpretation and insight (see Eagle & Wolitzky, chapter 4) and increasing emphasis on the therapist–patient interaction and the emotional milieu (see Liff, chapter 17) reflects the growing awareness of contextual and relational influences. Concomitant shifts are also visible in the reconceptualization of transference and countertransference to reflect a more interactional, two-person view of the treatment. Henry and Strupp's (chapter 12k) conclusion of the Vanderbilt I study is that the patient–therapist working alliance is formed rather quickly and is an important predictor of outcome. Working from another time-limited psychodynamic perspective, Luborsky (chapter 12b) reviewed eight studies and discerned significant positive correlations between the alliance measured in the early sessions and the outcome of treatment, an impressively consistent pattern in a field fraught with nonsignificant and contradictory findings.

What will distinctly characterize the 1990s emphasis on the therapeutic alliance is the prescriptive use of therapists' interpersonal stance in short-term treatment. One way to conceptualize the issue, parallelling the notion of "treatment of choice" in terms of techniques, is how clinicians determine the "relationship of choice" in terms of their interpersonal stances and stimulus value for individual clients (Norcross, 1991b). The challenge will be to articulate and operationalize the grounds on which the alliance is fitted to various client presentations (Beutler & Clarkin, 1990).

In this sense, the meaning of prescriptive matching will be broadened to denote not only specific clinical procedures but also therapist relationship stances (Lazarus, Beutler, & Norcross, 1992). Systematic studies on relational "match-making in psychotherapy" (Talley, Strupp, & Morey, 1990) will examine the commonly shared perception among therapists of feeling oneself to be better suited to deal interpersonally with some patients rather than others. The accumulating empirical literature will then be able to generate prescriptive matching decisions for use of technical as well as interpersonal interventions in specific circumstances.

Economic Pressures

According to Koocher and D'Angelo (see chapter 13), the emphasis on the therapeutic alliance has historically increased with an emphasis on reality factors within the treatment process. Whether correlational or causal, this covariance will undoubtedly extend into the next century as "reality factors" in the form of economic pressures on psychotherapy continue unabated. In fact, several futurists (e.g., Adams, 1992; Cummings, 1986; Zimet, 1991) have persuasively argued that the health care dollar will determine, in large measure, the type, focus, and availability of psychotherapeutic services. Theoretical developments and clinical innovations will be influenced by the dictates of third parties in the therapeutic relationship.

In the past there was little demand on the part of public or federal agencies for evidence demonstrating the efficacy of psychotherapy. However, the situation has changed (see Garfield, chapter 10), and the demands have grown dramatically. No longer is it sufficient to demonstrate efficacy; cost-efficiency and pragmatic resolution of the presenting problem are becoming necessary. What takes place in the consulting room is not only a matter of empirical interest to researchers but also of economic concern to the health-care industry. Restrictions in psychotherapy coverage, including number of visits and cost per session, illustrate harsh economic realities in a competitive health-care marketplace.

These economic pressures will lead, *inter alia*, to a reduction in long-term psychotherapy and acceleration of self-change and minimal treatment. "In such a climate," write Koocher and D'Angelo (chapter 13), "long-term, open-ended psychotherapy will soon be an option limited to the wealthy." Also in the service of cost-containment will be a rising number of referrals to self-help organizations, self-change materials, and psychoeducational groups for specific disorders, such as Lewinsohn's (chapter 12f) "Coping with Depression" course. As was evident in our experts' forecast on the future of various formats, mental health agencies will provide clients with information to change on their own and recommend "do-it-yourself" therapies. We are entering a period, like it or not, of the enactment of cost-containment measures that will result in limitations of private fee-for-service practice, restrictions on patients' freedom of provider choice, intrusion into the formerly private world of therapist and client, and insistence on short-term, problem-specific treatments (Kiesler & Morton, 1988; Lowman, 1991).

Process—Outcome Linkages

Historically there has been a segregation of process and outcome researchers into discrete camps. Members of the outcome camp were taught to distrust process enthusiasts as entrapped by fuzzy concepts, adhering to insupportable theories, and using largely nonempirical methods. Members of the process camp, in turn, criticized outcome enthusiasts for favoring sterile number crunching over clinical utility, operating under academic ideals rather than theory-driven treatment, and being generally unresponsive to the issues and methods that could benefit practicing clinicians (Beutler, 1990). This division is embodied in the two distinct questions of the Psychotherapy Research Project of the Menninger Foundation (see Wallerstein, chapter 12c): "What changes will take place?" (the traditional outcome question) and "How are these changes brought about through therapeutic interaction?" (the traditional process question).

Gradually, however, the distinction between process and outcome research is fading, and explicit linkages between the two are being forged. From the 1970s onward, increasing energy has been devoted to analysis of process, sustained by the belief that psychotherapy outcomes "could be illuminated, perhaps even explained, by intensive study of the transactions between patients and therapists" (see Strupp & Howard, chapter 9). In fact, Howard and Orlinsky's (chapter 12d) principal objective has been to produce a "conceptually coherent synthesis of research findings, especially in the literature relating process to outcome." The current swing of the research pendulum toward process-outcome research is also in keeping with the integration zeitgeist (see Arnkoff & Glass, chapter 20).

This dual thrust has become the hallmark of psychotherapy research, together with the realization that the two must necessarily complement each other. The continuous and productive feedback loop between process and outcome, as Strupp and Howard (chapter 9) and Sampson and Weiss (chapter 12j) see it, represents the ideal relationship between research and practice. Outcome research should inspire process research, and process research should inform our understanding of outcome research. Systematic examination of the causal linkages between process and outcome will increasingly characterize sophisticated psychotherapy research.

In clinical training, too, the "genuine concern" and "growing consensus" for the adequacy of training for practice (see Riess, chapter 23) will yield systematic examination of the connections between training components (process) and clinical competence (outcome) (see Matarazzo & Garner, chapter 27). Two achievements from process research—therapy manuals and process rating scales (Lambert & Bergin, chapter 11)—will be successfully employed to train novice therapists. Also, more attention will be given to evaluations of training programs and to certification of competence (Norcross, Beutler, & Clarkin, 1990). The wide hiatus between therapist's conceptual knowledge on the one hand, and their ability to translate that knowledge into consistently skillful performance, on the other (Henry & Strupp, chapter 12k), will be gradually bridged as we link training processes to educational outcomes in the preparation of psychotherapists for the 21st century.

INTO THE NEXT CENTURY

There are powerful movements in contemporary society that exert and will continue to exert an impact on the practice of psychotherapy well into the 21st century.

One is the changing composition of the nuclear family. After years of relative stability, families are experiencing high mobility and increasing divorce. Children are being raised by one parent, by same-sex parents, or by two parents who work outside the home. The implications of these transformations on stability of relationships and childrearing are enormous. We are already experiencing pressures on mental health and social service agencies throughout the country as parents seek counseling to deal with the escalating struggles encountered with their children. One of the minor, yet practical, consequences is the difficulty in even finding time for children to attend regular appointments. Communities are just beginning to develop programs, easily accessed through the school system, that will provide behavioral/learning and family counseling programs for children or parents who need such assistance (Milliken, 1987).

A second emergent reality is the pressure on young single adults as the conflicts usually associated with adolescence are extending into the twenties and beyond. Contributing factors are economic dependency on parents (mainly due to educational requirements for career entry), threats of sexually transmitted diseases in the face of relaxed mores on sexual behavior, and expectations for women to enter professional and career fields.

Another phenomenon of importance to the therapist is the change in domain of persons with severe mental disorder and retardation from distant institutions to the community. Thus far this process has left many individuals homeless and without daily occupation (Bingham, Green, & White, 1987). The mental health community must share in the habilitation of this growing population. This will necessitate a shift in orientation in our training programs. Students will be trained to work in the community and to help educate citizens to understand behaviors which may appear aberrant. In addition, clinical training programs will include study on the uses of psychotropic drugs, with prescription privileges for specially licensed professionals.

A great influence on our society during the current generation is the development of the microchip. The ramifications of the computer age are still to be encountered. One consequence appears to be an increase in individual isolation within society. The computer allows, if not demands, that workers communicate via machines, often at long distances from one another. A person can spend the entire work day at a computer, conducting business, ordering meals, banking, and shopping. Even entertainment can be confined to a television set. The necessity for verbal communication diminishes with computers. Telephone conversation is at risk: We are getting so accustomed to the ubiquitous answering machine that it can be an inconvenience to reach someone in person and converse!

In the future we may find more psychotherapeutic efforts directed toward helping individuals to interact, if not to communicate. Avoiding boredom and enriching interpersonal relationships may assume a high priority in the 21st century. Some 20 years ago, Levine and Levine (1970) wrote, "The reduced need to commit human energies to making a living creates a situation in which it becomes imperative to encourage and to value a great variety of ways of being" (p. 288). Psychotherapists should have an important role in shaping the institutions which will develop new "ways of being" in response to our changing society.

Further, the coming impact of enormous population increases, expansion of minorities in America, aging of the general population, and the rise of leisure time—all will eventually come to the door of the psychotherapist. And, the therapist will reach out more to the community, as seen today in such diverse areas as disaster relief (Jacobs, Quevillon, & Stricherz, 1990) and sports teams (Feldman, 1991).

CONCLUDING REMARKS

From the vantage point of history we have tried to extract and amplify salient trends in the future of psychotherapy. In the Janusian tradition (Rothenberg, 1988), we have examined the dialectical interplay of retrospect and prospect, simultaneously looking backwards and forward. Despite the rapid transformations in the field, members of the profession themselves are rarely registering and considering these changes (Phillips, 1982). We have attempted to conceptualize them in ways that counter a defensive propensity and that assist the reader in actively considering the evolution of the field.

During the latter half of this century the surest prediction one could make was that there would be changes. In fact, we have become so accustomed to change that it is difficult to think of life that is static. The fact that there was a period of over 3,000 years in Egypt when even clothing styles remained the same is difficult to comprehend today. We are now in a period when the wildest fantasies of the future (e.g., remember Dick Tracy's wrist phone?) are becoming realities. Perhaps our safest prediction would be simply that psychotherapy will continue to change.

At the beginning of this century Münsterberg (1909) wrote that, "the aim of the last generation was to explain the world; the aim of the next generation will be to interpret the world. . . ." (p. 3). Although it appears that we have progressed little toward understanding, much less interpreting, the major conflicts that confront humanity today, psychotherapy has begun to address the tasks set forth a century ago. In its short history, psychotherapy has played an important role in acquiring insight into and providing relief from the complexity of our lives. But the mind is as mysterious as the universe, and the complete understanding of human behavior—and of the future of psychotherapy—will never be an undisputed certainty.

REFERENCES

Adams, D. B. (1992). The future roles of psychotherapy in the medical–surgical arena. *Psychotherapy, 29.*

Anderson, J. K., Parente, F. J., & Gordon, C. (1981). A forecast of the future of the mental health profession. *American Psychologist, 36,* 848–855.

Austad, C. S., & Hoyt, M. F. (1992). The managed care movement and the future of psychotherapy. *Psychotherapy, 29,* 109–118.

Beutler, L. E. (1990). Introduction to the special series on advances in psychotherapy process research. *Journal of Consulting and Clinical Psychology, 58,* 263–264.

Beutler, L. E., & Clarkin, J. (1990). *Systematic treatment selection: Toward targeted therapeutic interventions.* New York: Brunner/Mazel.

Beutler, L. E., Mohr, D. C., Grawe, K., Engle, D., & MacDonald, R. (1991). Looking for differential treatment effects: Cross-cultural predictors of differential psychotherapy efficacy. *Journal of Psychotherapy Integration, 1,* 121–141.

Bingham, R., Green, R., & White, S. (Eds.). (1987). *The homeless in contemporary society.* San Francisco: Sage.

Cummings, N. A. (1986). The dismantling of our health system: Strategies for the survival of psychological practice. *American Psychologist, 41,* 426–431.

Ekstein, R. (1972). In quest of the professional self. In A. Burton (Ed.), *Twelve therapists: How they live and actualize themselves.* San Francisco: Jossey-Bass.

Feldman, L. (1991, July 7). Strikeouts and psych-outs. *The New York Times Magazine, 140,* 10–13, 27, 30, 33.

Frances, A. (1988, May). *Sigmund Freud: The first integrative therapist.* Invited address to the 4th Annual Convention of the Society for the Exploration of Psychotherapy Integration, Boston, MA.

Frank, G. (1984). The Boulder model: History, rationale, and critique. *Professional Psychology: Research and Practice, 15,* 417–435.

Grencavage, L. M., & Norcross, J. C. (1990). Where are the commonalities among the therapeutic common factors? *Professional Psychology: Research and Practice, 21,* 372–378.

Heatherington, L. (1989). Toward more meaningful clinical research: Taking context into account in coding psychotherapy interaction. *Psychotherapy, 26,* 436–447.

Jacobs, G. A., Quevillon, R. P., & Stricherz, M. (1990). Letters from the aftermath of Flight 232. *American Psychologist, 45,* 1329–1335.

Kiesler, C., & Morton, T. (1988). Psychology and public policy in the "health care revolution." *American Psychologist, 43,* 993–1003.

Kiesler, D. J. (1966). Some myths of psychotherapy research and the search for a paradigm. *Psychological Bulletin, 65,* 110–136.

Klein, M., Dittmann, A. T., Parloff, M. B., & Gill, M. M. (1969). Behavior therapy: Observations and reflections. *Journal of Consulting and Clinical Psychology, 33,* 259–266.

Lambert, M. J., Shapiro, D. A., & Bergin, A. E. (1986). The effectiveness of psychotherapy. In S.L. Garfield & A.E. Bergin (Eds.), *Handbook of psychotherapy and behavior change* (3rd ed.). New York: Wiley.

Lazarus, A. A., Beutler, L. E., & Norcross, J. C. (1992). The future of technical eclecticism. *Psychotherapy, 29,* 11–20.

Levine, M., & Levine, A. (1970). *A social history of helping services.* New York: Appleton-Century-Crofts.

Lowman, R. L. (Ed.). (1991). Special section: Managed mental health care. *Professional Psychology: Research and Practice, 22,* 5–59.

Milliken, W. E. (1987). *Cities in Schools, Inc.* Annual Report (Available from 1023 18th St. N.W., Suite 600, Washington, D.C. 20005).

Münsterberg, H. (1909). *Psychotherapy.* New York: Moffat, Yard and Company.

Norcross, J. C. (1985). For discriminating clinicians only. *Contemporary Psychology, 30,* 757–758.

Norcross, J. C. (1991a). Prescriptive matching in psychotherapy: Psychoanalysis for simple phobias? *Psychotherapy, 28,* 439–443.

Norcross, J. C. (1991b, August). (Chair). *Tailoring the therapist's interpersonal stance to client needs: Four perspectives.* Symposium presented at the 99th annual convention of the American Psychological Association, San Francisco, CA.

Norcross, J. C., Beutler, L. E., & Clarkin, J. F. (1990). Training in differential treatment selection. In *Systematic treatment selection: Toward targeted therapeutic interventions* (pp. 289–307). New York: Brunner/Mazel.

Norcross, J. C., & Grencavage, L. M. (1989). Eclecticism and integration in psychotherapy: Major themes and obstacles. *British Journal of Guidance and Counseling, 17,* 227–247.

Norcross, J. C., & Guy, J. D. (1989). Ten therapists: The process of becoming and being. In W. Dryden & L. Spurling (Eds.), *On becoming a psychotherapist* (pp. 215–239). London: Routledge.

Norcross, J. C., Prochaska, J. O., & Gallagher, K. M. (1989a). Clinical psychologists in the 1980s: I. Demographics, affiliations, and satisfactions. *The Clinical Psychologist, 42,* 138–147.

Norcross, J. C., Prochaska, J. O., & Gallagher, K. M. (1989b). Clinical psychologists in the 1980s: II. Theory, research, and practice. *The Clinical Psychologist, 42*(3), 45–53.

Parloff, M. B. (1979). Can psychotherapy research guide the policymaker? A little knowledge may be a dangerous thing. *American Psychologist, 34,* 296–306.

Phillips, E. L. (1982). *Stress, health, and psychological problems in the major professions.* Lanham, MD: University Press of America.

Prochaska, J. O., & Norcross, J. C. (1982). The future of psychotherapy: A Delphi poll. *Professional Psychology, 13,* 620–627.

Prochaska, J. O., & Norcross, J. C. (1983). Contemporary psychotherapists: A national survey of characteristics, practices, orientations, and attitudes. *Psychotherapy: Theory, Research and Practice, 20,* 161–173.

Rothenberg, A. (1988). *The creative process of psychotherapy.* New York: Norton.

Stiles, W. B., Shapiro, D. A., & Elliott, R. (1986). "Are all psychotherapies equivalent?" *American Psychologist, 41,* 165–180.

Strupp, H. H. (1986). The nonspecific hypothesis of therapeutic effectiveness: A current assessment. *American Journal of Orthopsychiatry, 56,* 513–520.

Talley, P. F., Strupp, H. H., & Morey, L. C. (1990). Matchmaking in psychotherapy: Patient–therapist dimensions and their impact on outcome. *Journal of Consulting and Clinical Psychology, 58,* 182–188.

Weiner, I. B. (1975). *Principles of psychotherapy.* New York: Wiley.

Yalom, I. D. (1975). *The theory and practice of group psychotherapy* (2nd ed.). New York: Basic Books.

Zimet, C. N. (1991). Managed care is here and is not going away. *The Psychotherapy Bulletin, 25*(4), 21–22.

INDEX

assessment in, 599, 616, 859–860

for autism, 188, 597

behavioral medicine in, 603–604

change rating scales, 381

with children, 604

clinical practices surveyed, 614–616

cognitive techniques in, 183, 267

contemporary developments in, 188–191

covert conditioning in, 602–603

defining, 172–174

for depression, 417–418

desensitization techniques, 593–594

development of, 40–42, 161–169, 592–595

dismantling procedure in, 340

with elderly, 531–535, 544

ethical issues in, 605–608

exposure techniques, 599–600, 883

with families, 256–257

future of, 616–617, 885

with groups, 704

integrated with psychodynamic therapy, 674–677, 678

interactional perspective in, 181–187

lack of conceptual development in, 189

learning theory in, 588–592, 609–610

modeling techniques, 600

for obsessive-compulsive disorders, 600

operant conditioning techniques in, 595–597

outcome study, 321

paradigm shift in, 179–181

for phobic disorders, 366–368

positivist epistemology in, 178–179

professional acceptance, 612–614

professional societies/publications, 597–598

public perception of, 605–606

related to cognitive therapy, 160, 658

relations with cognitive therapists, 666

research in, 366–368

role of therapist in, 857

self-control techniques in, 601–602

social skills training in, 600–601

sociocultural context of, 160, 161, 889

in Soviet Union, 168–169

and technical eclecticism, 286

theoretical basis, 160, 187–188, 608–610, 617

  metatheory, 174–175

in theoretical integration, 264–272

theoretical submovements, 169–171

therapeutic relationship in, 610–611, 892

token economies, 596–597

training, 617, 857–860

treatment settings, 604–605

in university counseling settings, 71

Behavioral Avoidance Test, 382

Behavioral contracting, 883

Bell, J., 239–240

Bentham, Jeremy, 26

Bergin, A. E., 312, 364

  on research career, 413–415

Berlin Psychoanalytic Institute, 361–362

Bernays, E., 41

Bernfeldt, S., 74

Beutler, L. E., 286–288, 541

Bijou, S. W., 597

Binder, J. L., 582

Binet, A., 737

Binswanger, L., 203

Biofeedback, 603–604

Birk, L., 267

Birth trauma, 42

Bonaparte, M., 497–498

Bonus marchers, 780–781

Borderline personality disorder, 49, 115

  behavior therapy for, 611

  in children, 470

  Kernberg on, 146–148

Horowitz, M. J., 321–322
    on research career, 422–425
Hospitals, psychoanalytic training in, 773
Howard, K. I., 321
    on research career, 407–412
Howard (Beckham), R., 513
Hug-Hellmuth, H. von, 461–462, 499–500
Hull, C. L., 55, 589
Hull House, 511
Human Figure Drawings test, 381
Humanistic psychology, 55. *See also* Existential therapy; Gestalt therapy
    core beliefs in, 197–199
    development of
        client-centered approach, 199–202
        existential approach, 203–204
        Gestalt approach, 202–203
    experiential search in, 211–212, 250
    future of, 217–219
    phenomenological basis, 198, 204–207
    recent developments in, 216–217
    research in, 214–216
    self-actualizing tendency in, 198, 208–211
    therapeutic relationship in, 212–214
Humphreys, L., 834
Hutt, M., 76
Hypnotherapy, 232, 454, 738. *See also* Mesmerism
Hysteria, 28, 29, 112–113

Illinois School of Professional Psychology, 816–817
Imaginal therapy, 676, 883
Imipramine, 340, 449
Implosive therapy, 671
Individualism
    concepts, in mesmerism, 32
    and social belonging, 699
    and social structure, 25–28
Infant–mother relationship, 50

Bowen on differentiation in, 241, 242
    in ego psychology, 505
    Mahler on, 143–144
    in object relations theory, 500–501, 578–579
    and oedipal conflict theory, 499, 508
    rapprochement crisis theory, 503–504
    Sullivan on, 133
Informed consent, and research, 395
Insight
    in humanistic psychotherapy, 205
    relation to outcome, 434
Instinct and instinctual drives
    in psychoanalytic theory, 111–113
    in self psychology, 138, 580
Institutionalization
    of children, 479–480
Insurance. *See* Third-party payments
Integration of therapies, 350–351. *See also* Common factors, in psychotherapy; Society for the Exploration of Psychotherapy Integration; Technical eclecticism; Theoretical integration
    barriers to, 678–679, 684
    behavior therapy in, 172–173, 608–611
    in child psychotherapy, 473
    defining, 261–263
    development of, 289–290, 671–672, 679–682
    future of, 884
    humanistic therapies in, 217–218
    impact of, 292
    Kernberg on, 146–148
    models for, 271
    objections to, 677–678
    psychodynamic behavior therapy in, 674–677
    research needs of, 292, 683–684
    role in training, 682
    role of research in, 375
    standardized language in, 678

Menninger, C., 69. *See also* Menninger Clinic

Menninger, K., 316–317, 498, 832

Menninger, W., 76

Menninger Clinic, 67, 69, 77

Menninger Foundation, 312, 316–317, 344, 397, 401–407, 894

Mental health teams, 72–73, 768

Mental Hygiene movement, 22, 39–40, 42

Mental Research Institute, 230, 234

Mental retardation, 558–559, 858, 896

Mercer, J., 558–559

Mesmer, Anton. *See* Mesmerism

Mesmerism, 22, 30–32, 34

Messer, S. B., 270–271

Metapsychological Profile, 502

Metatheory, 174–175

Mexican Group for Psychoanalytic Studies, 768

Mexican Society of Psychoanalysis, 768

Miami Conference, 756, 805–806

Microtraining, 854–856

Milan Associates, 233–234

Military mental health care. *See also* Veterans Administration
    development of, 778–779
    intelligence testing in, 738
    and mental hygiene movement, 40
    and psychologist prescription privileges, 95
    in World Wars, 75–77, 745–746, 781–783

Miller, J. B., 505

Miller, J. G., 78, 180–181, 788–791

Miller, N. E., 166, 264–265, 671

Miller, T. I., 312–313, 364

Minnesota Multiphasic Personality Inventory, 347, 381

Minnesota School of Professional Psychology, 818

Minorities. *See* Ethnic/racial minorities

Minuchin, S., 247–248, 252–255

Mischel, W., 184

Mission Bay Conference, 820, 821, 824

Mitchell, S. W., 33

Modeling, behavior, 367, 600

Modeling, therapeutic, 265

Modern Rogerian Encounter Skill Pattern, 854

Moreno, J. L., 700

Moulton, R., 507

Mowrer, O. H., 165, 589, 590–591

Mowrer, W. M., 590–591

Mt. Zion Psychotherapy Research Group, 433–435

Muller, G. E., 4

Multidimensional Scalogram Analysis, 404, 405

Multimodal therapy. *See* Technical eclecticism

Munoz, R. F., 374

Nagy, I., 238–239

Narcissism
    in children, 467–468
    in Freudian theory, 136
    in self psychology, 136–139, 580

National Committee on Mental Hygiene, 72

National Conference on Scientist-Practitioner Education and Training for the Professional Practice of Psychology, 823–824

National Council of Schools of Professional Psychology, 803, 812, 813–814, 821, 822, 823, 824, 847

National Institute of Mental Health
    Clinical Research Branch, 324–325
    in development of psychology training, 742, 747–748
    in funding Postgraduate Center for Mental Health, 771–772
    Psychotherapy and Behavioral Intervention Section, 325
    psychotherapy training programs, 78–81

goals of, 861, 865

graded assessments in, 853–854

of group therapists, 714–715

growth of, 74–75

integrative therapies, 682

internships, 754

in interpersonal techniques, 440–441

key figures in, 731–732

major conferences on, 751–760

manual-guided, 856–857

and medical education, 740–742

Miami Conference on, 756, 805–806

microtraining, 854–856

Mission Bay Conference on (1986), 820, 821

models, 866–867, 868

National Conference on Scientist-Practitioner Education and Training for the Professional Practice of Psychology, 823–824

National Institute of Mental Health programs, 78–81

postdoctoral psychology, 774

at Postgraduate Center for Mental Health, 770–773

and prescription privileges, 95

process–outcome linkage in, 895

psychoanalytic, for psychologists, 768, 773

psychoanalytic, in hospitals, 773

psychology, in medical schools, 846

rating scales in, 380–381

in rational–emotive therapy, 861

of rational–emotive therapy, 661–662

related to therapeutic process, 871

research in, 438–439

role of psychology in, 870–871

San Antonio Conference on (1990), 824–825

San Juan Conference on (1989), 822–823

settings, 750, 759, 821, 825, 839, 846

sociocultural factors in, 867–868

specialist vs. generalist, 886

standardizing, early efforts at, 743–744

standards, in psychology, 768–769

theoretical orientation of faculties, 613

trends in, 888

Utah Conference on (1987), 820–822

Utah conference on (1987), 758–760

Vail Conference on (1973), 757–758, 812–813, 837–841

Veterans Administration programs, 77–78, 746–747, 750, 776, 786–795

World War II military efforts, 745

Transactional analysis, 885

and group therapy, 703

Transference

and analyst neutrality, 119–120

analytic vs. basic, 581–583

in child therapy, 464, 467–468, 500–502

in children, 502

conceptual trends, 892–893

defining, 121–123

within families, 238

in group therapy, 701–702

mirroring in self psychology, 140–141

in object relations theory, 583

and outcome, 398

in psychodynamic–behavioral integration, 270

role of, 581

Treatment dose, 377–378, 412, 894. *See also* Brief therapies

in child therapy, 478–479

in dynamic psychotherapy, 583–584

research in, 319, 340, 377–378

in systemic family therapy, 233

and third-party payment, 611

trends in, 883–884

Treatment manuals, 290, 856–857

Treatment matching. *See* Prescriptionism

Treatment models, 681

ABOUT THE EDITORS

Donald K. Freedheim, PhD, has been an editor for most of his professional life. He founded the journals *The Clinical Psychologist* and *Professional Psychology*. He is currently completing his second term as editor of *Psychotherapy* and is coauthor of a chapter on psychotherapy research in the *Handbook of Clinical Child Psychology* (Wiley, 1983). He has been on the psychology faculty at Case Western Reserve University since 1960 and is also in part-time clinical practice. In addition, he is past president of the Division of Psychotherapy of the American Psychological Association (APA).

Herbert J. Freudenberger, PhD, is an independent practitioner in New York City. He is the author of *Burnout: The High Cost of High Achievement* (Anchor, 1980).

Jane W. Kessler, PhD, is Distinguished Professor of Psychology Emeriti at Case Western Reserve University and the author of *Psychopathology of Childhood* (Prentice-Hall, 1988), which is in its second edition.

Stanley B. Messer, PhD, is professor of clinical psychology at Rutgers University. He is coeditor and contributor to *Psychoanalytic Therapy and Behavior Therapy: Is Integration Possible?* (Plenum Press, 1984) and to *Hermeneutics and Psychological Theory* (Rutgers University Press, 1988). He was formerly associate editor of *American Psychologist*.

Donald R. Peterson, PhD, professor emeritus at Rutgers University, was the founder of the Doctor of Psychology program at the University of Illinois and first dean of the Graduate School of Applied and Professional

Psychology at Rutgers University. He has published widely in the area of professional education in psychology.

Hans H. Strupp, PhD, is Distinguished Professor of Psychology at Vanderbilt University. He is past president of the Society for Psychotherapy Research and coauthor of *Psychotherapy in a New Key: A Guide to Time-Limited Dynamic Psychotherapy* (Basic Books, 1984).

Paul L. Wachtel, PhD, is Distinguished Professor of Psychology at City University of New York. He is author of *Psychoanalysis and Behavior Therapy* (Basic Books, 1977) and *Action and Insight* (Guilford Press, 1987).